Also by Robert M. Parker, Jr.

BORDEAUX: The Definitive Guide for the Wines
Produced Since 1961

THE WINES OF THE RHÔNE VALLEY AND PROVENCE

PARKER'S WINE BUYER'S GUIDE 1987–1988

PARKER'S WINE BUYER'S GUIDE 1989–1990

BURGUNDY: A Comprehensive Guide to the Producers,
Appellations, and Wines

BORDEAUX: A Comprehensive Guide to the Wines
Produced From 1961–1990

PARKER'S WINE BUYER'S GUIDE 1993–1994

PARKER'S WINE BUYER'S GUIDE 1994–1995

THE WINES OF THE RHÔNE VALLEY,
Revised and Expanded Edition

BORDEAUX

REVISED THIRD EDITION

A COMPREHENSIVE GUIDE TO THE WINES PRODUCED FROM 1961 TO 1997

ROBERT M. PARKER, JR.

Drawings by
CHRISTOPHER WORMELL

Maps by
JEANYEE WONG

SIMON & SCHUSTER

SIMON & SCHUSTER
Rockefeller Center
1230 Avenue of the Americas
New York, NY 10020

Designed by Meryl Sussman Levavi/digitext, inc.

Manufactured in the United States of America

1   3   5   7   9   10   8   6   4   2

Library of Congress Cataloging-in-Publication Data

Parker, Robert M.
Bordeaux: a comprehensive guide to the wines produced from 1961–1997 /
Robert M. Parker, Jr. ; drawings by Christopher Wormell; maps
by Jeanyee Wong. — Rev. 3rd ed.
p.   cm.
Includes bibliographical references and index.
1. Wine and wine making—France—Bordelais.   I. Title.
TP553.P36   1998
641.2′.2′094471—dc21   98-28778
                                                         CIP

ISBN 0-684-80015-2

To my father,
who always embodied the joy of living

ACKNOWLEDGMENTS

To the following people, thanks for your support: Hanna, Johanna and Eric Agostini, Jean-Michel Arcaute, Jim Arseneault, Ruth and the late Bruce Bassin, Jean-Claude Berrouet, Bill Blatch, Jean-Marc Blum, Thomas B. Böhrer, Monique and Jean-Eugène Borie, Christopher Cannan, Dick Carretta, Corinne Cesano, Bob Cline, Jean Delmas, Dr. Albert H. Dudley III, Barbara Edelman, Michael Etzel, Paul Evans, Terry Faughey, Joel Fleischman, Han Cheng Fong, Maryse Fragnaud, Laurence and Bernard Godec, Dan Green, Philippe Guyonnet-Duperat, Josué Harari, Alexandra Harding, Ken-ichi Hori, Dr. David Hutcheon, Brenda Keller, Barbara G. and Steve R. R. Jacoby, Jean-Paul Jauffret, Nathaniel, Archie and Denis Johnston, Ed Jonna, Allen Krasner, Françoise Laboute, Susan and Bob Lescher, Christian, Jean-Françoise and Jean-Pierre Moueix, Jerry Murphy, Bernard Nicolas, Jill Norman, Les Oenarchs (Bordeaux), Les Oenarchs (Baltimore), Daniel Oliveros, Bob Orenstein, Frank Polk, Bruno Prats, Martha Reddington, Dominique Renard, Dr. Alain Raynaud, Huey Robertson, Helga and Hardy Rodenstock, Dany and Michel Rolland, Carlo Russo, Tom Ryder, Ed Sands, Erik Samazeuilh, Bob Schindler, Ernie Singer, Park B. Smith, Jeff Sokolin, Elliott Staren, Daniel Tastet-Lawton, Steven Verlin, Peter Vezan, Robert Vifian, Sona Vogel, Karen and Joseph Weinstock, Jeanyee Wong, Dominique and Gérard Yvernault, Murray Zeligman.

A very special thanks is in order to those people who have done a splendid job in bringing this mass of information to book form: Janice Easton, my editor at Simon & Schuster, Hanna Agostini, my assistant and translator in France, Joan Passman, my assistant stateside, and my former *Wine Advocate* proofreader, editor, and life-long drinking, eating, and tasting friend, Dr. Jay Miller. In addition, Florence Falkow, Pierre-Antoine Rovani, and his father, Yves Rovani, were immensely helpful, and I am indebted to them.

CONTENTS

1: USING THIS BOOK

There can be no question that the romance, if not downright mysticism, of opening a bottle of Bordeaux from a famous château has a grip and allure that are hard to resist. For years writers have written glowing accounts of Bordeaux wines, sometimes giving them more respect and exalted status than they have deserved. How often has that fine bottle of Bordeaux from what was allegedly an excellent vintage turned out to be diluted, barely palatable, or even repugnant? How often has a wine from a famous château let you and your friends down when tasted? On the other hand, how often has a vintage written off by the critics provided some of your most enjoyable bottles of Bordeaux? And how often have you tasted a great Bordeaux wine, only to learn that the name of the château is uncelebrated?

This book is about just such matters. It is a wine consumer's guide to

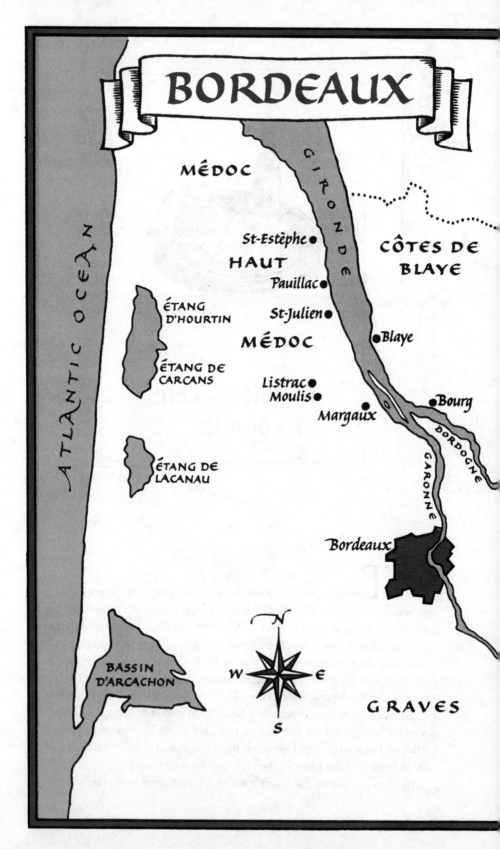

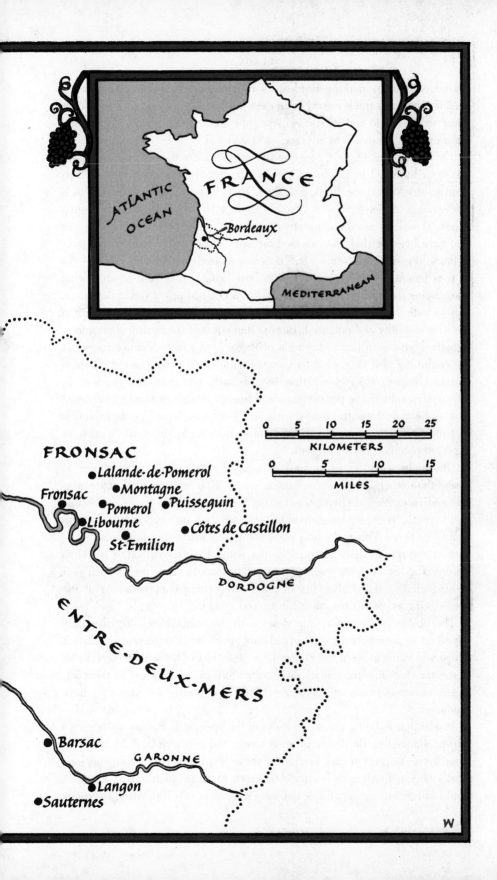

Bordeaux. Who is making Bordeaux's best and worst wines? What has a specific château's track record been over the last 20–30 years? Which châteaux are overrated and overpriced, and, of course, which are underrated and underpriced? These issues are discussed in detail.

The evaluations that are contained in this work are the result of extensive tastings conducted in Bordeaux and in America. I have been visiting Bordeaux every year since 1970, and since 1978 I have gone to Bordeaux as a professional at least twice a year to conduct barrel tastings of the young wines, as well as to do comparative tastings of different wines and vintages that have been bottled and released for sale. Since 1970 I have tasted most of the wines in the top years a half dozen or more times.

It is patently unfair to an estate to issue a final judgment about a wine after tasting it only once. Consequently, when I do tastings of young Bordeaux, I try to taste them as many times as possible to get a clear, concise picture of the wine's quality and potential. I have often equated the tasting of an infant, unbottled wine with that of taking a photograph of a long-distance runner at the beginning of a race. One look or tasting of such a wine is only a split-second glimpse of an object that is constantly changing and moving. To effectively evaluate the performance and quality in a given vintage, one must look at the wine time after time during its 16–24-month prebottling evolution and then evaluate it numerous times after bottling to see if the quality or expected potential is still present.

Obviously, some wines as well as general vintages are much easier to assess than others. For certain, tasting young wine requires total concentration and an extreme dedication to tasting the wine as many times as possible in its youth, both at the individual château and in comparative tastings against its peers. This is the only valid method by which to obtain an accurate look at the quality and potential of the wine. For this reason, I travel to Bordeaux at least twice a year, spending over a month in the region each year visiting all the major châteaux in all of the principal appellations of the Médoc, Graves, Sauternes, St.-Emilion, and Pomerol.

The châteaux visits and interviews with the winemakers are extremely important in accumulating the critical data about the growing season, harvest dates, and vinification of the château's wines. Most of the winemakers at the Bordeaux châteaux are remarkably straightforward and honest in their answers, whereas owners will go to great lengths to glorify the wine they have produced.

In addition to doing extensive visits to the specific Bordeaux châteaux in all appellations of Bordeaux in good, poor, and great vintages, I insist on comparative tastings of cask samples of these new vintages. For these tastings I call many of Bordeaux's leading *négociants* to set up what most consumers would call massive comparative day-long tastings of 60–100 wines. In groups of 10–15 wines at a time, an entire vintage, from major classified growths to minor Crus Bourgeois, can be reviewed several times over a course of 2 weeks of extensive tastings. Such tastings corroborate or refute the quality I have found to exist when I have visited the specific château. Because I do these types of broad, all-inclusive tastings at least three times before the young Bordeaux wine is bottled, I am able to obtain numerous looks at the infant wine at 6, 9, and 18 months of age, which usually give a very clear picture of the wines' quality.

Despite the fact that young Bordeaux wines are constantly changing during their evolution and aging process in the barrel, the great wines of a given vintage are usually apparent. It has also been my experience that some wines that ultimately turn out to be good or very good may be unimpressive or just dumb when tasted in their youth from the cask. But the true superstars of a great vintage are sensational, whether they are 6 months or 20 months old.

When I taste young Bordeaux from the cask, I prefer to judge the wine after the final blend or assemblage has been completed. At this stage, the new wine has had only negligible aging in oak casks. For me, it is essential to look at a wine at this infant stage (normally in late March and early April following the vintage) because most wines can be judged without the influence of oak, which can mask fruit and impart additional tannin and aromas to the wine. What one sees at this stage is a naked wine that can be evaluated on the basis of its richness and ripeness of fruit, depth, concentration, body, acidity, and natural tannin content, unobscured by evidence of oak aging.

The most important component I look for in a young Bordeaux is fruit. Great vintages, characterized by ample amounts of sunshine and warmth, result in grapes that are fully mature and produce rich, ripe, deeply fruity wines. If the fruit is missing, or unripe and green, the wine can never be great. In contrast, grapes that are allowed to stay on the vine too long in hot, humid weather become over-ripe and taste pruny and sometimes raisiny and are also deficient in acidity. They too have little future. Recent vintages that, in their youth, throughout all appellations of Bordeaux, have been marked by the greatest ripeness, richness, and purity of fruit are 1982, 1985, 1986, 1989, 1990, 1995, and 1996, all high-quality vintages for Bordeaux. Vintages that exhibited the least fruit and an annoying vegetal character have been 1974, 1977, and 1984, poor to mediocre vintages.

In early summer or fall following the vintage, I return to Bordeaux to get another extensive look at the wines. At this time the wines have settled down completely but are also marked by the scent of new oak barrels. The intense grapy character of their youth has begun to peel away, as the wines have now had at least 3–4 months of cask aging. If extensive tastings in March or April give a clear overall view of the vintage's level of quality, comprehensive tastings in June and again the second March following the vintage are almost always conclusive evidence of where the vintage stands in relation to other Bordeaux vintages and how specific wines relate in quality to each other.

With regard to vintages of Bordeaux in the bottle, I prefer to taste these wines in what is called a "blind tasting." A blind tasting can be either "single blind" or "double blind." This does not mean one is actually blindfolded and served the wines, but rather that in a single-blind tasting, the taster knows the wines are from Bordeaux but does not know the identities of the châteaux or the vintages. In a double-blind tasting, the taster knows nothing other than that several wines from anywhere in the world, in any order, from any vintage, are about to be served.

For bottled Bordeaux, I usually conduct all my Bordeaux tastings under single-blind conditions. I do not know the identity of the wine, but since I prefer to taste in peer groups, I always taste wines from the same vintage. Additionally, I never mix Bordeaux with non-Bordeaux wines, simply because whether it be California or Australia Cabernet Sauvignons, the wines are distinctly different, and while comparative tastings of Bordeaux versus California may be fun and make interesting reading, the results are never very reliable or especially meaningful to the wine consumer who desires the most accurate information. Remember that whether one employs a 100-point rating system or a 20-point rating system, the objectives and aims of professional wine evaluations are the same—to assess the quality of the wine vis-à-vis its peers and to determine its relative value and importance in the international commercial world of wine.

When evaluating wines professionally, it goes without saying that proper glasses and the correct serving temperature of the wine must be prerequisites to any objective and meaningful tasting. The best generally available glass for critical tasting is that approved by the International Standards Organization. Called the ISO glass, it is tulip shaped and has been designed specifically for tasting. As for the temperature, 60–65 degrees Fahrenheit is best for evaluating both red and white wines. Too warm a temperature and the bouquet becomes diffuse and the taste flat. Too cold a temperature and there is no discernible bouquet and the flavors are completely locked in by the overly chilling effect on the wine.

When I examine a wine critically, there is both a visual and physical examination. Against a white background, the wine is first given a visual exam for brilliance, richness, and intensity of color. A young Bordeaux wine that is light in color, hazy, or cloudy has serious problems. For Bordeaux red wines, color is extremely important. Virtually all the great Bordeaux vintages have shared a very deep, rich, dark ruby color when young, whereas the poorer vintages often have weaker, less rich-looking colors because of poor weather and rain. Certainly, in 1982, 1983, 1985, 1986, 1989, 1990, 1995, and 1996 the general color of the red wines of Bordeaux has been very dark. In 1978 and 1975 it was dark but generally not so deep in color as the aforementioned vintages. In 1973, 1974, 1980, and 1984 the color was rather light.

In looking at an older wine, examine the rim of the wine next to the glass for amber, orange, rust, and brown colors. These are signs of maturity and are normal. When they appear in a good vintage of a wine under 6 or 7 years old, something is awry. For example, young wines that have been sloppily made and exposed to unclean barrels or air will mature at an accelerated rate and take on the look of old wines when in fact they are still relatively young by Bordeaux standards.

In addition to looking at the color of the wines, I examine the "legs" of the wine. The legs are the tears or residue of the wine that run down the inside of the glass. Rich Bordeaux vintages tend to have "good legs" because the grapes are rich in glycerol and alcohol, giving the wine a viscosity that causes this "tearing" effect. Examples of Bordeaux vintages that produced wines with good to excellent legs would be 1996, 1995, 1990, 1989, 1986, 1985, 1983, 1982, 1970, and 1961.

After the visual examination is completed, the actual physical examination of the wine takes place. The physical exam is composed of two parts: the wine's smell, which depends on the olfactory sense; and the wine's taste, the gustatory sense, which is tested on the palate. After swirling a wine, the nose must be placed into the glass (not the wine) to smell the aromas that issue from the wine. This is an extremely critical step because the aroma and odor of the wine will tell the examiner the ripeness and richness of the underlying fruit, the state of maturity, and whether there is anything unclean or suspicious about the wine. The smell of a wine, young or old, will tell a great deal about the wine's quality, and no responsible professional taster understates the significance of a wine's odors and aromas, often called the nose or bouquet. Emile Peynaud, in his classic book on wine tasting, *Le Goût du Vin* (Bordas, 1983), states that there are nine principal categories of wine aromas:

1. animal odors: smells of game, beef, venison
2. balsamic odors: smells of pine trees, resin, vanilla
3. woody odors: smells of new wood of oak barrels
4. chemical odors: smells of acetone, mercaptan, yeasts, hydrogen sulfide, acidity, and fermentation
5. spicy odors: smells of pepper, cloves, cinnamon, nutmeg, ginger, truffles, anise, mint
6. empyreumatic odors: smells of crème brûlée, smoke, toast, leather, coffee
7. floral odors: smells of violets, roses, lilacs, jasmine
8. fruity odors: smells of black currants, raspberries, cherries, plums, apricots, peaches, figs
9. vegetal odors: smells of herbs, tea, mushrooms, vegetables

The presence or absence of some or all of these aromas, their intensity, their complexity, their persistence, all serve to create the bouquet or nose of a wine that can be said to be distinguished, complete, and interesting or flawed and simple.

Once the wine's aroma or bouquet has been examined thoroughly, the wine is tasted, sloshed, or chewed around on the palate while also inhaled to release the wine's aromas. The weight, richness, depth, balance, and length of a wine are apparent from the tactile impression the wine leaves on the palate. Sweetness is experienced on the tip of the tongue, saltiness just behind the tongue's tip, acidity on the sides, and bitterness at the back. Most professional tasters will spit out the wine, although some wine is swallowed in the process.

The finish or length of a wine, its ability to give off aromas and flavors even though it is no longer on the palate, is the major difference between a good young wine and a great young wine. When the flavor and the aroma of the wine seem to last and last on the palate, it is usually a great, rich wine that has just been tasted. The great wines and great vintages are always characterized by a purity, opulence, richness, depth, and ripeness of the fruit from which the wines are made. When the wines have both sufficient tannin and acidity, the balance is struck. It is these qualities that separate many a great Bordeaux from a good one.

TASTING NOTES AND RATINGS

All of my tastings were done in peer group, single-blind conditions when possible (meaning that the same types of wines were tasted against each other and the producers' names were not known), in my tasting room, in the cellars of the producers, or in the offices of major Bordeaux *négociants*. The ratings reflect an independent, critical look at the wines. Neither price nor the reputation of the producer/grower affects the rating in any manner. I spend 3 months of every year tasting in vineyards. During the other 9 months of the year, 6- and sometimes 7-day work weeks are devoted solely to tasting and writing. I do not participate in wine judgings or trade tastings for many reasons, but principal among these are the following: 1) I prefer to taste from an entire bottle of wine; 2) I find it essential to have properly sized and cleaned professional tasting glasses; 3) the temperature of the wine must be correct; and 4) I alone will determine the time allocated to the number of wines to be critiqued.

THE RATING SYSTEM

96–100   Extraordinary
90–95   Outstanding
80–89   Above average to very good
70–79   Average
50–69   Below average to poor

The numerical rating given is a guide to what I think of the wine vis-à-vis its peer group. Certainly wines rated above 85 are very good to excellent, and any wine rated 90 or above will be outstanding for its particular type. While some have suggested that scoring is not well suited to a beverage that has been romantically extolled for centuries, wine is similar to other consumer products. There are specific standards of quality that full-time wine professionals recognize, and there are benchmark wines against which all others can be judged. I know of no one with three or four different glasses of wine in front of him or her, regardless of how good or bad the wines might be, who cannot say, "I prefer this one to that one." Scoring wines is simply taking a professional's opinion and applying some sort of numerical system to it on a consistent basis. Scoring permits rapid communication of information to expert and novice alike.

The rating system I employ in my wine journal, *The Wine Advocate,* is the one I have utilized in this book. It is a 50–100-point scale, the most repugnant of all wines meriting 50 since that is the starting point of the scale and the most glorious gustatory experience commanding 100. I prefer my system to the once widely quoted 20-point scale called the Davis scale—of the University of California at Davis—because it permits much more flexibility in scoring. It is also easier to understand because the numbers correspond to the American grading system and avoid the compression of scores from which the Davis scale suffers. It is not without problems, however, because readers will often wonder what the difference is between an 86 and 87, both very good wines. The only answer I can give is a simple one: When tasted side by side, I thought the 87-point wine slightly better than the 86-point wine.

The score given for a specific wine reflects the quality of the wine at its best. As I mentioned earlier, I often tell people that evaluating a wine and assigning a score to a beverage that will change and evolve in many cases for up to 10 or more years is analogous to taking a photograph of a marathon runner. Much can be ascertained, but like the moving object that has been photographed, the wine will also evolve and change. I retry wines from obviously badly corked or defective bottles, since a wine from such a single bad bottle does not indicate an entirely spoiled batch. Many of the wines reviewed here I have tasted many times, and the score represents a cumulative average of the wine's performance in tastings to date. Scores do not tell the entire story about a wine. The written commentary that accompanies the ratings is often a better source of information regarding the wine's style and personality, the relative quality level vis-à-vis its peers, the relative value, and its aging potential than any score could ever indicate.

Here, then, is a general guide to interpreting the numerical ratings:

A score of 90–100 is equivalent to an A and is given only for an outstanding or special effort. Wines in this category are the very best produced for their type and, like a three-star Michelin restaurant, merit the trouble to find and try. There is a big difference between a 90 and a 99, but both are top marks. As you will note throughout the text, few wines actually make it into this top category simply because there just are not many truly great wines.

A score of 80–89 is equivalent to a B in school, and such a wine, particularly in the 85–89 range, is very, very good; many of the wines that fall into this range often are great values as well. I would not hesitate to have any of these wines in my own collection.

A score of 70–79 represents a C, or an average mark, but obviously 79 is a much more desirable score than 70. Wines that receive scores between 75 and 79 are generally pleasant and straightforward, but lacking in complexity, character, or depth. If inexpensive, they may be ideal for uncritical quaffing. Below 70 is a D or an F, depending on where you went to school; here, too, it is a sign of an imbalanced, flawed, or terribly dull or diluted wine that will be of little interest to the knowledgeable wine consumer.

In terms of awarding points, my scoring system gives every wine a base of 50 points. The wine's general color and appearance merit up to 5 points. Since most wines today are well made, thanks to modern technology and the increased use of professional oenologists, they tend to receive at least 4, often 5, points. The aroma and bouquet merit up to 15 points, depending on the intensity level and extract of the aroma and bouquet as well as the cleanliness of the wine. The flavor and finish merit up to 20 points, and again, intensity of flavor, balance, cleanliness, and depth and length on the palate are all important considerations when giving out points. Finally, the overall quality level or potential for further evolution and improvement—aging—merits up to 10 points.

Scores are important to let the reader gauge a professional critic's overall qualitative placement of a wine vis-à-vis its peers. However, it is also vital to consider the description of the wine's style, personality, and potential. No scoring system is perfectly objective, but a system that provides for flexibility in scores, if applied without prejudice, can quantify different levels of wine quality and provide the reader with a professional's judgment. However, there can never be any substitute for your own palate or any better education than tasting the wine yourself.

ANTICIPATED MATURITY— WHAT IS IT?

Because of the number of inquiries I receive regarding when a given Bordeaux wine has reached a point in its evolution that it is said to be ready to drink, I have provided an estimated range of years over which the châteaux's wines should be consumed for the specific vintage. I call this time frame the "anticipated maturity." Before one takes my suggestions too literally, let me share with you the following points:

1. If you like the way a wine tastes when young, do not hesitate to enjoy it in spite of what the guidelines may say. There can never be any substitute for your own palate.
2. I have had to make several assumptions, the primary ones being that the wine was purchased in a healthy state and that you are cellaring the wine in a cool, humid, odor- and vibration-free environment that does not exceed 65 degrees Fahrenheit in the summer.
3. The estimates are an educated guess based on how the wine normally ages, its quality, balance, and the general depth of the vintage in question.
4. The estimates are conservative. I have assumed a maturity based on my own palate, which tends to prefer a wine more fresh and exuberant over one that has begun to fade, but one that may still be quite delicious and complex.

Consequently, if you have cool, ideal cellars, the beginning year in the estimated range of maturity may err in favor of drinking the wine on the young side. I presume most readers would prefer, given a choice, to open a bottle too early rather than too late. This philosophy has governed my projected maturity period for each wine.

EXAMPLES

Now. Totally mature; immediate drinking is suggested within several years of the "last tasted" date.

Now–may be in decline. Based on the age of the wine and knowledge of the château and the specific vintage, this designation is utilized where a fully mature wine discussed in the 1985 edition of *Bordeaux* has not been recently retasted and is believed to have passed its apogee and begun its decline.

Now–probably in serious decline. Based on the age of the wine and knowledge of the château and the specific vintage, this designation is utilized when a wine in the 1985 edition of *Bordeaux* was at the end of its plateau of maturity and, while not recently retasted, is believed to be well past its plateau of maturity.

Now–2001. The wine has entered its plateau of maturity, where it should be expected to remain until 2001, at which time it may begin slowly to decline. The "now" dates from the time of the last tasted note.

1999–2010. This is the estimated range of years during which I believe the wine will be in its plateau period—the years over which it will be at its best for drinking. Please keep in mind that Bordeaux wines from top vintages tend to decline slowly (just the opposite of Burgundy) and that a wine from an excellent vintage may take another 10–15 years to lose its fruit and freshness after the last year in the stated plateau period.

ABOUT THE BOOK'S ORGANIZATION

This book has been divided into the major geographical regions of Bordeaux. Within each region, the famous châteaux and many minor châteaux deserving recognition are reviewed. The emphasis, for obvious reasons, is on the major Bordeaux estates that are widely available and well-known in this country. The quality of these wines over the period 1961–1989 is examined closely. For lesser-known châteaux, the selection process has been based on two factors, quality and recognition. High-quality, lesser-known estates are reviewed, as are those estates that have gotten distribution into the export markets, regardless of their quality. I have made every effort over the last 25 years to discover and learn about the underpublicized châteaux in Bordeaux. Because older vintages of these wines are virtually impossible to find, and the majority of the Crus Bourgeois wines must be drunk within 5–7 years of the vintage, the focus for most of these lesser-known Crus Bourgeois wines is on what they have accomplished in the period 1982–1996. I feel the châteaux that are reviewed are the best of these lesser-known estates, but to err is human, and it would be foolish for both you and me to believe that there is not some little estate making exquisite wine that I have omitted altogether.

At the beginning of each chapter on the Bordeaux appellations is my classification of the wines from that appellation. This analysis is based on their overall quality vis-à-vis each other. This is not a book that will shroud quality differences behind skillfully worded euphemisms. Within each appellation the châteaux are reviewed in alphabetical order. For those who love lists, my overall classification of the top 160 wine-producing estates of Bordeaux may be found beginning on page 1349.

With respect to the specific vintages covered, tasting emphasis has generally been given only to the good vintages. Vintages such as 1991, 1977, 1972, 1968, 1965, and 1963 are generally not reviewed because they were very poor years, and few Bordeaux châteaux made acceptable-quality wine in those years. Furthermore, such vintages are not commercially available. As for the actual tasting notes, the "anticipated maturity" refers to the time period at which I believe the wine will be at its apogee. This is the time period during which the wine will be fully mature and should ideally be drunk. These estimates as to anticipated maturity are conservative and are based upon the assumption that the wine has been purchased in a sound, healthy condition and has been kept in a vibration-free, dark, odor-free, relatively cool (below 65 degrees Fahrenheit) storage area. For the wine-tasting terms I employ, and for the proper methods of cellaring Bordeaux wines, see Chapter 6, "A User's Guide to Bordeaux," and Chapter 8, "A Glossary of Wine Terms."

ONE FURTHER CAVEAT

When a book such as this is revised, difficult decisions must be made regarding the retention of tasting notes on wines that have not been reevaluated in the 13 years that have lapsed since I wrote the first edition. As readers will discover, many of the finest wines in top vintages have been retasted since the last edition and the changes in text and ratings, where warranted, have been made. Because a serious tasting note is the professional's photograph of a wine during its life and, moreover, since all the tasting notes in this book are dated, I have opted to leave those original tasting critiques in the book as part of the history of that property's record of wine quality.

2: A SUMMARY OF BORDEAUX VINTAGES: 1945–1997

This chapter is a general assessment and profile of the Bordeaux vintages 1945 through 1997. While the top wines for each acceptable vintage are itemized, the perception of a vintage is a general view of that particular viticultural region. In mediocre and poor vintages, good wines can often be made by skillful vintners willing to make a careful selection of only the best grapes and cuvées of finished wine. In good, even great, years, thin, diluted, characterless wines can be made by incompetent and greedy producers. For wine consumers, a vintage summary is important as a general guide to the level of potential excellence that could have been attained in a particular year by a conscientious grower or producer of wine.

1997—A Quick Study
(9-5-97)

St.-Estèphe ***   Graves Red ***

Pauillac ***   Graves White **

St.-Julien ***   Pomerol ****

Margaux ***   St.-Emilion ****

Médoc/Haut-Médoc Crus Bourgeois **   Barsac/Sauternes ***

Size: An exceptionally abundant vintage, but slightly less than in 1996 and
1995

Important information: A seductive, user-friendly, soft (low acidity/high pHs)
vintage that will have exceptionally broad appeal because of the wines'
precociousness and evolved personalities. Most wines will have to be
drunk during their first decade of life.

Maturity status: A quickly evolving vintage that, except for the most concentrated wines, will be over the hill in 10–12 years.

Price: At the time of writing, prices for 1997 Bordeaux wine futures had not
been established. However, in March 1998, despite talk of dropping
prices in view of the fact that the vintage was less successful than the
very high priced vintages of 1996 and 1995, most producers told me
they intended to increase prices, largely because of the unprecedented
ruthless selections they made in order to put good wine in the bottle.

After 2 weeks spent intensively tasting all of the major, and many of the
minor, wines of Bordeaux (often four separate times), there can be no doubt
that this is a good vintage. Stylistically, the wines, whether Merlot or Cabernet
Sauvignon based, are characterized by very good ripeness (often an element
of over-ripeness is present), extremely low acidity, high PHs, and juicy,
succulent personalities with sweet tannin and an easily appreciated, friendly
style. While exceptions exist, and some profoundly concentrated, long-lived
wines were produced, this is a vintage that will require consumption at a
relatively early age. Almost all the best petits châteaux, Cru Bourgeois, and
lesser cru classé wines already offer delicious drinking, even though they are
only 6 months old. Since they will not be bottled for another year, I fully
expect these wines to be delicious upon release and best drunk within their
first 2–6 years of life. The top classified growths, particularly those estates
that produced bigger, more dense wines, will be capable of lasting 10–15
years, but all of them will have appeal and charm when released.

In contrast with 1996, where the Cabernet Sauvignon–dominated wines
were clearly superior to the Merlot-based wines, no appellation stands out in
1997 as being superior to any other. The Pomerols are superior to their 1996
counterparts, and there is a bevy of exciting 1997 St.-Emilions, but soft,
open-knit, supple-textured, somewhat diffuse wines are commonplace in

every appellation. After considerable reflection over which vintage 1997 could be compared with, I found it impossible to find a similar vintage in my 20 years of tasting Bordeaux. Other vintages (1985) were easy to taste from barrel and possessed a similar smoothness and tenderness, but 1997 differs considerably from 1985. Most 1997s are not "big," muscular wines; rather, they are graceful and seductive, full of charm and elegance, yet somewhat fragile. I believe this vintage will be ideal for restaurants and consumers looking for immediate gratification. Because of that, there is no intelligent reason for speculators to "invest" in this vintage and drive up the prices. However, the market has become increasingly complicated, and the demand for top-quality Bordeaux remains insatiable.

I think everyone who enjoys a good glass of wine will find the 1997s attractive. Consumers are unlikely to be knocked out by their depth or flavor intensity, but they are well-made, soft, user-friendly wines that are highly complementary to such vintages as 1996, 1995, and 1994, all tannic years that require significant bottle age.

The 1997 vintage began auspiciously. For the last 18 years I have spent the final 2 weeks of March in Bordeaux, and March 1997 was the hottest I have ever experienced. Temperatures were in the mid-80s, and even hit 90 degrees on occasion, making me think it was late June rather than March. This hot weather jump-started the vineyards, causing a roaring vegetative cycle. The flowering occurred at the earliest dates on record, leading many châteaux to conclude that the harvest would be well under way by mid-August.

The flowering hit a few glitches and tended to drag on for nearly a month. The irregular flowering, which led to uneven ripening of the grapes, was exacerbated by the unusual pattern of summer weather. The weather was hot at the beginning of June, but it cooled off and became very wet later in the month. July was abnormal. Usually a torridly hot month in Bordeaux, in 1997 it was cool yet humid. By the end of July high pressure had settled in and the weather became sultry. July was followed by unusual tropical-like weather in August, with record-breaking levels of humidity as well as high temperatures. Despite extensive crop-thinning and leaf-pulling efforts by well-run châteaux the prolonged flowering, unusual end of June, and tropical August (growers said it felt more like Bangkok than Bordeaux) created severe uneven ripening within each grape bunch. The most heard complaint was that within each bunch of grapes there were red grapes, green grapes, and rosé-colored grapes —a nightmare scenario for growers.

The incredibly early spring, bud break, and flowering did prompt some Pessac-Léognan properties to harvest (in full view of the nation's television cameras) their white wine grapes as early as August 18. This made 1997 an "earlier" vintage than the legendary 1893. Just after the beginning harvest for the whites, the hot tropical weather deteriorated, and a succession of weather depressions buffeted Bordeaux. From August 25 through September 1, sizable quantities of rain fell throughout the region. The fact that so many 1997s are soft, with low acidity but without the great concentration and density found in the finest 1996s and 1995s, is no doubt attributable to these heavy rains. One need not be a nuclear physicist to understand the taste of wines made from bloated grapes. Producers who panicked and began picking in early September, fearing the onset of rot and further weather deterioration, made the vintage's least successful wines. However, those who had the intestinal fortitude and discipline to wait were rewarded with a fabulous month of September. Aside from a few scattered rain showers on September 12 and 13, it was one of the driest, sunniest Septembers this century. The later a producer was able to wait, the more the vines, and subsequently the wine, benefited.

Virtually all of the Merlot was picked between September 2 and 23. The Cabernet Franc was harvested between mid-September and early October. The Cabernet Sauvignon harvest began slowly in mid-September but lasted even longer, with some producers waiting until mid-October to harvest their last Cabernet Sauvignon parcels.

One of the more intriguing statistics about this unusual weather pattern is the extraordinary "hang time" the grapes enjoyed between the date of flowering and the harvest date. In Bordeaux the general rule is that if the producer can get 110 days between flowering and harvest, they will harvest mature grapes. In 1997 it was not bizarre for the Merlot vineyards to be harvested 115–125 days after flowering. For the Cabernet Sauvignon, a whopping 140 days was not an unusual hang time. Normally this would be a sign of extraordinary flavor concentration, but the weather at the end of August destroyed all hopes for a great vintage.

Yields were relatively modest, and when the overall production for Bordeaux was tabulated, the region's harvest was slightly smaller than either 1996 or 1995. More important, and the obvious explanation for the quality at the classified growth level, is the unprecedented selection that took place. It was not unusual to learn that anywhere from 50% to 30% of a château's total crop was all that was deemed acceptable for the estate's grand vin.

The Bordeaux marketplace has become almost impossible to predict. Last year I was positive that prices would come out at the same level as the 1995s, and although I anticipated active futures buying for many of the great Médocs, I was not prepared for the buying hysteria that would ensue or the high prices demanded by the châteaux. It seems to me that the 1997s should be priced below the 1996s and 1995s, but I can fully understand the predicament of top producers who made rigorous selections and thus produced far less wine under the grand vin label than usual. Since all the top wines sell out so quickly, why shouldn't they take advantage of what is obviously an overheated marketplace? Nevertheless, are the 1997s worth buying as futures? Certainly for some of the limited-production wines, as well as the first-growths and super-seconds (always the most difficult wines to procure), purchasing futures may continue to make sense, if only to guarantee getting such wines. However, this is a vintage not for speculators, but for true wine drinkers. I do not see prices for 1997s escalating significantly, as have the top 1995s and 1996s. However, since I totally underestimated the worldwide demand for Bordeaux over the last few years, who knows what will happen? In November the feeling in Bordeaux was that prices would drop, but by March the hotels were full of buyers from around the world, all clamoring (despite complaints about the prices) to buy as much as they could, desperate to ensure they will be guaranteed their allocations when the 1998s and 1999s—and, God forbid, the 2000s!—become available. At the time of publication nobody knows what prices will emerge for the 1997s.

There is one thing I do know. No one has ever gone wrong buying the finest Bordeaux from a profoundly great vintage, or even superb Bordeaux wines from an excellent vintage. As the tasting notes that follow indicate, 1997 is not a great vintage, nor are there that many great wines, but there are many consumer-friendly, satisfying efforts that will, hopefully, be reasonably priced.

THE BEST WINES

St.-Estèphe:	Cos d'Estournel, Montrose
Pauillac:	Lafite-Rothschild, Latour, Lynch-Bages, Mouton-Rothschild, Pichon-Longueville Baron
St.-Julien:	Branaire, Gloria, Gruaud-Larose, Lagrange, Léoville-Barton, Léoville-Las Cases, Léoville-Poyferré, Talbot
Margaux:	Angludet, Château Margaux
Médoc/Haut-Médoc Crus Bourgeois:	Sociando-Mallet
Graves Red:	Les Carmes-Haut-Brion, Domaine de Chevalier, Haut-Brion, Pape-Clément, Smith-Haut-Lafitte
Graves White:	Domaine de Chevalier, de Fieuzal, Haut-Brion, Laville-Haut-Brion, Smith-Haut-Lafitte
Pomerol:	Clinet, Clos L'Eglise, L'Eglise-Clinet, L'Evangile, La Fleur-Pétrus, Lafleur, Pétrus, Le Pin, Trotanoy
St.-Emilion:	Angélus, Ausone, Cheval Blanc, Clos de l'Oratoire, Faugères, Gracia, Grandes Murailles, l'Hermitage, Monbousquet, La Mondotte, Moulin-St.-Georges, Pavie-Decesse, Pavie-Macquin, Troplong-Mondot, Valandraud

Barsac/Sauternes: I do not believe in commenting on these sweet wines
until they are at least a year old, so judgment is
reserved. It should be at least a 3-star vintage based
on the wines tasted.

1996—A Quick Study
(9-16-96)

St.-Estèphe *****

Pauillac *****

St.-Julien *****

Margaux ****

Médoc/Haut-Médoc Crus Bourgeois ***

Graves Red ****

Graves White ***

Pomerol ***

St.-Emilion ****

Barsac/Sauternes ****

Size: An exceptionally large crop, just behind the superabundant 1995 and
1986 vintages.

Important information: In addition to being the most expensive young Bordeaux vintage in history, with opening prices 50%–100% above the
opening future prices of the 1995s, this is a great vintage for the Médoc
and Cabernet Sauvignon–based wines.

Maturity status: The powerful Cabernet Sauvignon–based wines of the Médoc
will be more accessible than the vintage 1996 most closely resembles,
1986, but in general the wines will require 10–15 years of cellaring
following bottling. The wines from Graves and the right bank will be
more accessible at a younger age and should be drinkable by 7–10
years of age.

Price: As indicated, this is a very expensive vintage with record-breaking
prices.

For over 20 years I have followed (in considerable detail) the weather
patterns during Bordeaux's spring, summer, and early fall. I have also studied
available information on the weather patterns for virtually every significant
Bordeaux vintage this century. Several conclusions can be readily gleaned
from such weather statistics. Most of Bordeaux's greatest years have been the
product of exceptionally hot, dry summers, with below average rainfall and
above average temperatures. While a number of this century's celebrated
vintages have had moderate amounts of rain in September, unless a significant
quantity falls, the effect on quality has usually been minor. In every viticultural region of France, vignerons sing the same tune: "June makes the quantity and September makes the quality." Some go even further, saying, "August
makes the style."

Given the number of high-quality wines produced in 1996, Bordeaux's
weather from March through mid-October was decidedly unusual. The winter
of 1996 was wet and mild. When I arrived in Bordeaux on March 19, 1996, I

thought it was mid-June rather than March, thanks to the blast of heat the region was experiencing. This heat wave lasted the entire 12 days I was there. Many growers predicted an early flowering and, consequently, an early harvest. The heat wave broke in early April, with a cold period followed by another burst of surprisingly high temperatures in mid-April. Atypically, the month of May was relatively cool.

When I returned to France for 17 days in mid-June, the country was experiencing blazingly torrid temperatures in the 90+ degree range. This made for a quick and generally uniform flowering. In Bordeaux most estates were thrilled with the flowering, which took only 3–4 days rather than the usual 7–10. The cold spell that hit during the end of May and beginning of June caused severe *millerandage* (the failure of a vine to fully set its entire bunch, thus reducing yields) for the warmer *terroirs* on the plateau of Pomerol. By the end of June a large, precocious crop was anticipated. Except for the reduced crop size in Pomerol, viticulturally speaking, things could not have looked better. Then the weather turned unusually bizarre.

While the period between July 11 and August 19 was relatively normal (statistically it was slightly cooler and wetter than usual), the first 11 days of July and the period between August 25 and 30 received abnormally huge quantities of rainfall, in addition to below normal temperatures. Statistics can be misleading, as evidenced by the fact that while the normal amount of rainfall for Bordeaux during the month of August is just over 2 inches (53 millimeters), in 1996 the quantity of rainfall was a whopping 6 inches (144 millimeters). Yet the heaviest rainfall was localized, with over 4 inches falling on Entre-deux-Mers and St.-Emilion, 2 inches on Margaux, 1.75 inches on St.-Julien, 1.5 inches on Pauillac, and under 1 inch in St.-Estèphe and the northern Médoc. I remember telephoning several friends in Bordeaux around America's Labor Day weekend and receiving conflicting viewpoints about the prospects for the 1996 vintage. Those in the southern Graves and on the right bank were obviously distressed, expressing concern that the vintage was going to be a disaster along the lines of 1974. They hoped that a miraculous September would turn it into a 1988 or 1978. In contrast, those in the Médoc, especially from St.-Julien north, were optimistic, sensing that a good September would result in a terrific vintage. The large quantities of rain that had bloated the grapes to the south and east had largely missed the Médoc. The below average quantity of rain the Médoc did receive kept the vines flourishing, as opposed to shutting down photosynthesis as a result of excessive heat and drought, which had occurred in 1995 and 1989.

Large quantities of early September rain had been a pernicious problem in 1991, 1992, 1993, 1994, and to a lesser extent 1995, but this climatic pattern would not repeat itself in 1996. Between August 31 and September 18 there was a remarkable string of 18 sunny days, followed by light showers throughout the region on September 18 and 19. There were several days of clear weather, then drizzle on September 21, and, finally, the arrival of heavy rains the evening of September 24 that lasted through September 25.

Another important characteristic of this period between August 31 and September 24 was the omnipresent gusty, dry, easterly and northeasterly winds that played a paramount role in drying the vineyards after the late August rains. Moreover, these winds were consistently cited by producers as the reason sugar accumulated at rates that seemed impossible at the end of August. Another beneficial aspect to this windy period was that any potential for rot was minimized by Mother Nature's antibiotic.

The Merlot harvest took place during the last 2 weeks of September. The Cabernet Franc was harvested during late September and the first 4–5 days of October. The later-ripening, thicker-skinned Cabernet Sauvignon grapes were harvested between the end of September and October 12. Except for a good-size rainfall throughout the region on October 4, the weather in October was sunny and dry, offering textbook conditions for harvesting Cabernet Sauvignon. In fact, most Médoc producers saw a distinct parallel between the Cabernet Sauvignon harvest in 1996 and that of 1986. While rain had marred the 1986 harvest for the early-ripening varietals (such as Merlot and Cabernet Franc), it stopped, to be followed by a nearly perfect 4 weeks of dry, windy, sunny weather, during which the Cabernet Sauvignon harvest took place under ideal conditions.

Given this weather pattern, it is not surprising that most of 1996's finest wines emerged from the Médoc, which harvested Cabernet 10–18 days later than vineyards having high proportions of Merlot.

As was expected from the highly successful flowering during the torrid month of June, the 1996 Bordeaux harvest produced an abundant crop (6.5 million hectoliters), which is marginally below the 1995 crop size (which produced a crop of 6.89 million hectoliters). However, readers should recognize that the production of some of the top Pomerol estates, especially those on the plateau, was off by 30%–50%. In St.-Emilion many estates produced 10%–15% less wine than normal. Most of the top Médoc estates produced between 45 and 55 hectoliters per hectare, about 20%–30% less than their 1986 yields.

In conclusion, there are eight things to know about the 1996 vintage:

1. This is the most expensive young Bordeaux vintage in the history of the region, with opening prices 50%–100% above the opening prices for the 1995s.

2. In contrast with 1995, which had a fabulous summer marred by a rainy September, 1996's weather pattern was most unusual. The 1996 started off as one of the earliest vintages of the century, with blazingly hot weather in

early spring, followed by a cold period, and then torrid temperatures in June. The summer was relatively normal, except for several abnormally cold periods. Late August, usually hot and dry, witnessed freakish quantities of rain, in addition to below normal temperatures. September was a relatively dry and, most important, windy month. The gusty northern winds played a paramount role in drying out the vineyards after the late August rains. In addition, these winds (along with the dry, sunny days) were the primary reason for the extraordinary accumulation of sugar in the grapes, particularly the Cabernet Sauvignon, which was harvested very late.

3. A giant crop was produced with quantities slightly below the 1995 crop.

4. This is an irregular vintage without the quality consistency of 1995. The great strength of 1996 is the Cabernet Sauvignon–dominated wines of the Médoc.

5. I spent several weeks in November 1997 tasting through all the wines again, and in the 20 years I have been visiting the area and tasting young Bordeaux vintages, I have never tasted Cabernet Sauvignon as rich, ripe, pure, and intense as the finest 1996 Médocs exhibit. I believe some Cabernet Sauvignon–based wines of the Médoc may turn out to be among the greatest red wines Bordeaux has produced in the last 50 years.

6. The 1996 vintage is most comparable to the 1986 because of the weather pattern and the fact that the late-picked Cabernet Sauvignon was so successful for both vintages. When I first tasted the 1996s it was easy to see the comparison, as it was in November 1997. However, the finest 1996 Cabernet-based wines of the Médoc have a sweetness, completeness, and aromatic and flavor dimensions that exceed the greatest 1986s.

7. The lofty prices fetched by the 1996s in the overheated Bordeaux marketplace of 1997 ensured that many 1996s, particularly wines below the first-growth and super-second levels, have not sold through to the consumer. There have been reports of canceled orders, in addition to merchants unable to make their payments on the 1996s. Much of this has been verified with colleagues in Bordeaux, but other markets have stepped in to absorb any returned stock that was unsold by the American wine trade. Undoubtedly there are 1996s that remain overpriced vis-à-vis their quality. Yet once consumers have a chance to taste the 1996 Cabernet Sauvignon–dominated wines, it will become evident that many Médoc estates have produced a profoundly great vintage of classic, long-lived wines that will rival such heralded vintages as 1990, 1989, 1982, 1961, and 1959. That being said, readers should not make the mistake of thinking that the finest 1996s will be flamboyant, delicious, and opulently textured in their youth. The vintage's most compelling wines will require patience.

8. It is no secret that Pomerol, St.-Emilion, and Graves (including the north-

ern tier with the appellation of Pessac-Léognan) were less successful, but there were still some extraordinary wines produced in these appellations. However, readers should be aware that none of these appellations is as consistent in quality as 1995.

THE BEST WINES

St.-Estèphe:	Calon-Ségur, Cos d'Estournel, Haut-Marbuzet, Lafon-Rochet, Montrose
Pauillac:	D'Armailhac, Batailley, Clerc-Milon, Duhart-Milon, Grand-Puy-Lacoste, Haut-Batailley, Lafite-Rothschild, Latour, Lynch-Bages, Lynch-Moussas, Mouton-Rothschild, Pichon-Longueville Baron, Pichon-Longueville–Comtesse de Lalande, Pontet-Canet
St.-Julien:	Branaire (Duluc Ducru), Ducru-Beaucaillou, Gloria, Gruaud-Larose, Hortevie, Lagrange, Léoville-Barton, Léoville-Las Cases, Léoville-Poyferré, Talbot
Margaux:	Angludet, d'Issan, Kirwan, Malescot St.-Exupéry, Château Margaux, Palmer, Rauzan-Ségla, du Tertre
Médoc/Haut-Médoc Crus Bourgeois:	Cantemerle, Charmail, Domaine de Chiroulet Réserve, Les Grandes Chênes Cuvée Prestige, La Lagune, Lanessan, Reignac Cuvée Spéciale, Roc des Cambes, Sociando-Mallet
Graves Red:	Les Carmes Haut-Brion, Haut-Bailly, Haut-Brion, La Mission-Haut-Brion, Pape-Clément, Smith-Haut-Lafitte, La Tour-Haut-Brion
Graves White:	De Fieuzal, Haut-Brion, Laville-Haut-Brion, Pape-Clément, Smith-Haut-Lafitte
Pomerol:	Beau-Soleil, Bon Pasteur, Clinet, La Conseillante, La Croix du Casse, l'Eglise-Clinet, l'Evangile, La Fleur de Gay, La Fleur Pétrus, Gazin, Lafleur, Latour à Pomerol, Pétrus, Le Pin, Trotanoy, Vieux-Château-Certan
St.-Emilion:	Angélus, L'Arrosée, Ausone, Beau-Séjour Bécot, Beauséjour-Duffau, Canon-La-Gaffelière, Cheval Blanc, Clos Fourtet, Clos de l'Oratoire, La Couspaude, La Dominique, Ferrand-Lartigue, La Gaffelière, La Gomerie, Grand-Mayne, Grand-Pontet, Larmande, Monbousquet, La Mondotte, Moulin-St.-Georges, Pavie-Macquin, Rol Valentin, Le Tertre-Roteboeuf, Troplong-Mondot, Trotte Vieille, Valandraud

Barsac/Sauternes: This is a promising, potentially four-star, vintage, but at the time of writing it was too early to effectively evaluate the wines.

1995—A Quick Study
(9-20-95)

St.-Estèphe ****

Pauillac ****/*****

St.-Julien ****/*****

Margaux ****

Médoc/Haut-Médoc Crus Bourgeois ***

Graves Red ****/*****

Graves White ***

Pomerol *****

St.-Emilion ****

Barsac/Sauternes **

Size: Another huge harvest, just short of the record-setting crop of 1986. However, most major châteaux crop-thinned, and yields were more modest. In addition to crop thinning, the selection process of the top first-growths, super-seconds, and quality-oriented châteaux was severe, resulting in far less wine being produced under their grand vin label than in such abundant vintages as 1989 and 1990.

Important information: The most consistently top-notch vintage since 1990. Almost all the major appellations turned in exceptional wines of uniform quality.

Maturity status: While it has been reported that the highly successful 1995 Merlot crop resulted in precocious wines meant to be consumed immediately, all of my tastings have revealed that while the Merlot is undoubtedly successful, the Merlot, Cabernet Sauvignon, and Cabernet Franc produced wines with considerable weight, tannin, and structure. Although there are obvious exceptions, most of the finest 1995 Bordeaux are classic *vin de garde* wines with considerable tannin and, while accessible, require bottle age. I do not see the big wines being close to full maturity before 2003–2005.

Price: The second most expensive young Bordeaux vintage, both as futures and in the bottle . . . ever.

June, July, and August made the 1995 vintage, as they were among the driest and hottest months in the last 40 years. However, like most vintages since 1991, the Bordelais could not get past the first week of September without the deterioration of weather conditions. The showery weather lasted only between September 7 and 19, rather than the entire month, as it had in 1992, 1993, and 1994, and, to a lesser extent, 1991. Unlike the record rainfall of 275 millimeters in September 1992, and 175 millimeters in September 1994, the rainfall in September 1995 was only 145 millimeters. In the northern Médoc communes of St.-Julien, Pauillac, and Pomerol, the amount of rain ranged from 91 millimeters to 134 millimeters.

While it was a huge harvest, the key to the most successful 1995s appears to have been a severe selection once the wines had finished alcoholic and malolactic fermentations. The Merlot was certainly ripe, but this was the first vintage since 1990 where the Cabernet Sauvignon (at least the late-harvested Cabernet) was extremely ripe. Most châteaux that delayed their harvest until late September were rewarded with physiologically mature Cabernet Sauvignon.

In short, there are seven things to remember about the 1995 vintage, a year that should be considered both exceptional and uniform:

1. This was the second most expensive young Bordeaux vintage this century.
2. In spite of a rainy September, the outstanding success enjoyed by many châteaux in the 1995 vintage was the result of splendid weather in June, July, and August, a period that was among the driest and hottest in the last 40 years.
3. A huge crop of wine was produced, but the ruthless selection process employed by many top châteaux has resulted in more modest quantities of top classified-growths than in such abundant vintages as 1989 and 1990.
4. This vintage has turned out to be consistently uniform throughout all appellations. From cask, the vintage looked particularly strong in St.-Julien, Pauillac, and Pomerol, but since bottling, it does not appear to have any regional weaknesses except for the dry whites of Graves and the sweet whites of Barsac/Sauternes, which are pleasant but generally of average quality.
5. Readers who purchased the 1995s early, before prices began to soar, will be thrilled to know that after bottling, the 1995s, for the most part, are exhibiting more promise than they did from cask. At the minimum, 1995 is an excellent vintage, yet given the high percentage of outstanding wines, a strong argument can be made that 1995 comes close to rivaling such great vintages as 1990 and 1982.
6. It is hard to generalize about the overall style of a vintage, but readers should not assume that the highly successful 1995 Merlot crop resulted in precocious wines meant to be consumed immediately. My tastings revealed that while the Merlot and Cabernet Sauvignon had taken on flesh, weight, and fat during their time in barrel (*élevage*), they had also taken on more delineation and tannin. While there are obviously exceptions, most of the finest 1995 Bordeaux are classic *vin de garde* wines with considerable tannin and, while accessible, require bottle age.
7. In summary, 1995 is an excellent to outstanding vintage of consistently top-notch red wines across all appellations. As I have stated from the beginning, the 1995 vintage may represent a modern-day clone of 1970. However, given today's winemaking, selection process,

and the fact that the overall commitment to quality is far higher, there are undoubtedly more outstanding wines in 1995 than in 1970. Prices of the bottled 1995s are extremely high, but from an overall perspective, 1995 has produced the most consistently high-quality wines since 1990.

THE BEST WINES

St.-Estèphe: Calon-Ségur, Cos d'Estournel, Cos Labory, Lafon-Rochet, Montrose

Pauillac: D'Armailhac, Clerc-Milon, Grand-Puy-Lacoste, Haut-Batailley, Lafite-Rothschild, Latour, Lynch-Bages, Mouton-Rothschild, Pichon-Longueville Baron, Pichon-Longueville–Comtesse de Lalande, Pontet-Canet

St.-Julien: Branaire (Duluc Ducru), Ducru-Beaucaillou, Gloria, Gruaud-Larose, Lagrange, Léoville-Barton, Léoville-Las Cases, Léoville-Poyferré, Talbot

Margaux: Angludet, Malescot St.-Exupéry, Château Margaux, Palmer, Rauzan-Ségla

Médoc/Haut-Médoc
Crus Bourgeois: Charmail, La Lagune, Roc des Cambes, Sociando-Mallet

Graves Red: De Fieuzal, Haut-Bailly, Haut-Brion, La Mission-Haut-Brion, Pape-Clément, Smith-Haut-Lafitte, La Tour-Haut-Brion

Graves White: De Fieuzal, Haut-Brion, Laville-Haut-Brion, Pape-Clément, Smith-Haut-Lafitte

Pomerol: Bon Pasteur, Bourgneuf, Certan de May, Clinet, La Conseillante, La Croix du Casse, l'Eglise-Clinet, l'Evangile, La Fleur de Gay, La Fleur Pétrus, Gazin, Grand-Puy-Lacoste, La Grave à Pomerol, Lafleur, Latour à Pomerol, Pétrus, Le Pin, Trotanoy, Vieux-Château-Certan

St.-Emilion: Angélus, L'Arrosée, Ausone, Beau-Séjour Bécot, Canon-La-Gaffelière, Cheval Blanc, Clos Fourtet, Clos de l'Oratoire, Corbin-Michotte, La Couspaude, La Dominique, Ferrand-Lartigue, Figeac, La Fleur-de-Jaugue, La Gomerie, Grand-Mayne, Grand-Pontet, Larmande, Magdelaine, Monbousquet, Moulin-St.-Georges, Pavie-Macquin, Le Tertre-Roteboeuf, Troplong-Mondot, Valandraud

Barsac/Sauternes: Rieussec, La Tour Blanche, Climens, Coutet

1994—A Quick Study
(9-24-94)

St.-Estèphe ***

Pauillac ***/****

St.-Julien ***/****

Margaux ***

Médoc/Haut-Médoc Crus Bourgeois **

Graves Red ****

Graves White *****

Pomerol ****

St.-Emilion ***

Barsac/Sauternes *

Size: Another exceptionally large Bordeaux crop; however, the top properties had to be exceptionally severe in their selection process in order to bottle under the grand vin label only the finest cuvées. Consequently production of the top estates is relatively modest.

Important information: A hot, dry summer provided the potential for a great vintage, but the weather deteriorated in September, and a whopping 175 millimeters of rain fell between September 7 and September 29. Producers who were unwilling to declassify 30%–50% of their harvest were incapable of making top-quality wines. Those who did enjoyed considerable success in this vintage, the finest year after 1990 and before 1995. Merlot was the most successful grape in this inconsistent vintage. Even the most successful Médocs employed a higher percentage of Merlot than Cabernet Sauvignon, which had a tendency to be austere and herbaceous, with very high tannin. Another key to understanding 1994 is that the best drained vineyards (those lying next to the Gironde in the Médoc and Graves) tended to produce very good wines, assuming they made a strict selection.

Maturity status: Most 1994s will be slow to evolve given their relatively high tannin levels. This is a classic, *vin de garde* vintage, with the top wines being well colored and quite structured and powerful. They require additional bottle age.

Price: Initially reasonably priced, the 1994s have benefited from the international interest and, at times, speculation in all good-quality Bordeaux vintages. Prices appear to be high for the vintage's potential.

At the top level, 1994 has produced some excellent, even outstanding, wines, with far higher peaks of quality than 1993. However, too many wines have not fared well since bottling, with the fragile fruit stripped out by excessive fining and filtration. As a result, the wines' more negative characteristics, a hollowness and high levels of harsh tannin, are well displayed. The 1994 could have been an exceptional vintage had it not rained, at times heavily, for 13 days between September 7 and September 29. As is so often the case with a vintage that enjoyed 3 months of superb weather during the summer, only to be negatively impacted by excessive rain before and during the harvest, the willingness of the producer to declassify 30%–50% of the harvest was often the difference between producing a high-quality wine and one that is out of balance.

The overall characteristic of the 1994s is a backwardness, caused in large part by the high tannin levels. Yet the vintage's great successes possess the fruit and extract necessary to balance out the tannin. Those who failed to make a strict selection, or had too little Merlot to flesh out and counterbalance the more austere Cabernet Sauvignon, have turned out dry, hard, lean, and attenuated wines. The 1994 is unquestionably an irregular vintage and is more frustrating to taste through than 1993, but some outstanding wines were produced. Shrewd buyers will find a number of smashing wines, but this is a vintage where cautious selection is mandatory.

In 1994, much as in 1993, the most favored appellations were those that either had a high percentage of Merlot planted or had exceptionally well-drained soils. As in 1993, Pomerol appears once again to have been the most favored region. However, that is not a blanket endorsement of all Pomerols, as there are disappointments. The Graves and Médoc estates close to the Gironde, with gravelly, deep, stony, exceptionally well-drained soils, also had the potential to produce rich, well-balanced wines. However, it was essential in 1994, particularly in the Médoc, to eliminate a considerable quantity of the crop (the top estates eliminated 30%–50% or more) and to utilize a higher percentage of Merlot in the final blend. Moreover, the wines had to be bottled "softly," without excessive fining and filtering, which will eviscerate flavors and body.

THE BEST WINES

St.-Estèphe:	Cos d'Estournel, Lafon-Rochet, Montrose
Pauillac:	Clerc-Milon, Grand-Puy-Lacoste, Lafite-Rothschild, Latour, Lynch-Bages, Mouton-Rothschild, Pichon-Longueville Baron, Pichon-Longueville–Comtesse de Lalande, Pontet-Canet
St.-Julien:	Branaire-Ducru, Clos du Marquis, Ducru-Beaucaillou, Hortevie, Lagrange, Léoville-Barton, Léoville-Las Cases, Léoville-Poyferré
Margaux:	Malescot St.-Exupéry, Château Margaux
Médoc/Haut-Médoc Crus Bourgeois:	Roc des Cambes, Sociando-Mallet
Graves Red:	Bahans-Haut-Brion, Haut-Bailly, Haut-Brion, La Mission-Haut-Brion, Pape-Clément, Smith-Haut-Lafitte
Graves White:	Domaine de Chevalier, de Fieuzal, Haut-Brion,

Laville-Haut-Brion, Pape-Clément,
Smith-Haut-Lafitte, La Tour-Martillac

Pomerol: Beauregard, Bon Pasteur, Certan de May, Clinet, La
Conseillante, La Croix du Casse, La Croix de Gay,
l'Eglise-Clinet, l'Evangile, La Fleur de Gay, La Fleur
Pétrus, Gazin, Lafleur, Latour à Pomerol, Pétrus, Le
Pin

St.-Emilion: Angélus, L'Arrosée, Beau-Séjour Bécot,
Beauséjour-Duffau, Canon-La-Gaffelière, Cheval
Blanc, Clos Fourtet, La Dominique, Ferrand-Lartigue,
Forts de Latour, Grand-Pontet, Larcis-Ducasse,
Magdelaine, Monbousquet, Pavie-Macquin, Le
Tertre-Roteboeuf, Troplong-Mondot, Valandraud

Barsac/Sauternes: None

1993—A Quick Study
(9-26-93)

St.-Estèphe **   Graves Red ***
Pauillac **   Graves White ***
St.-Julien **   Pomerol ***
Margaux *   St.-Emilion **
Médoc/Haut-Médoc Crus Bourgeois *   Barsac/Sauternes *

Size: A very large crop.

Important information: Another vintage conceived under deplorable weather
conditions. However, this one offers a number of pleasant surprises. It
has produced more attractive clarets than either 1992 or 1991.

Maturity status: The finest wines should continue to drink well through the
first 5–6 years of the next century.

Price: The last reasonably priced vintage of the nineties still available in the
marketplace, the 1993s came out at low prices and have remained
essentially reasonably priced.

In some quarters 1993 has been written off as a terrible vintage due to the
enormous amount of rainfall in September. The amount of rainfall in 1991
and 1992 was frightfully high, but what fell in and around Bordeaux in
September 1993 broke a 30-year average rainfall record by an astonishing
303%! For this reason it was easy to conclude that no one could have possibly
made good wine. Moreover, the spring weather was equally atrocious, with
significant rainfall in both April and June.

However, July was warmer than normal, and August was exceptionally hot
and sunny. In fact, before the weather deteriorated on September 6, the
proprietors were beginning to think that an exceptional vintage was attain-

able. The September rain destroyed this optimism, but because of exceptionally cold, dry weather between the deluges, the rot that growers feared the most did not occur. Most châteaux harvested when they could, finishing around mid-October.

The better wines of 1993 suggest it is a deeply colored, richer, potentially better vintage than either 1991 or 1992. The wines can be characterized as deeply colored, with an unripe Cabernet Sauvignon character, good structure, more depth and length than expected, and some evidence of dilution.

THE BEST WINES

St.-Estèphe: Cos d'Estournel, Montrose
Pauillac: Clerc-Milon, Grand-Puy-Ducasse, Grand-Puy-Lacoste, Latour, Mouton-Rothschild
St.-Julien: Clos du Marquis, Hortevie, Lagrange, Léoville-Barton, Léoville-Las Cases, Léoville-Poyferré
Margaux: Château Margaux
Médoc/Haut-Médoc
Crus Bourgeois: Sociando-Mallet
Graves Red: Bahans-Haut-Brion, de Fieuzal, Haut-Bailly, Haut-Brion, La Mission-Haut-Brion, Smith-Haut-Lafitte, La Tour-Haut-Brion
Graves White: Haut-Brion, Laville-Haut-Brion, Smith-Haut-Lafitte
Pomerol: Beauregard, Bon Pasteur, Clinet, La Conseillante, La Croix de Gay, l'Eglise-Clinet, l'Evangile, La Fleur de Gay, Gazin, Lafleur, Latour à Pomerol, Pétrus, Le Pin, Trotanoy
St.-Emilion: Angélus, L'Arrosée, Beau-Séjour Bécot, Beauséjour-Duffau, Canon-La-Gaffelière, Cheval Blanc, La Dominique, Ferrand-Lartigue, Grand-Pontet, Magdelaine, Monbousquet, Pavie-Macquin, Le Tertre-Roteboeuf, Troplong-Mondot, Valandraud
Barsac/Sauternes: None

1992—A Quick Study
(9-29-92)

St.-Estèphe**   Graves Red**
Pauillac**   Graves White***
St.-Julien**   Pomerol***
Margaux*   St.-Emilion**
Médoc/Haut-Médoc Crus Bourgeois*   Barsac/Sauternes*

Size: A large crop was harvested, but the top properties implemented a ruthless selection. Consequently, quantities of the top wines were modest.

Important information: At the top level, the 1992s are pleasantly soft, yet even the finest wines had trouble avoiding the taste of dilution and herbaceousness from the excessive amounts of rain that fell before and during the harvest.

Maturity status: Most 1992s should be drunk during their first 10–12 years of life.

Price: Because of the vintage's poor to mediocre reputation, prices are very low. The real value of this vintage is that many of the first-growths could be purchased for $35–$40 and the second- through fifth-growths for $15–$25 . . . remarkably low prices in the overheated Bordeaux wine market.

The 1992 vintage was marked not by a tragic frost, as in 1991, but, rather, by excessive rainfall at the worst possible time. Following a precocious spring, with an abundance of humidity and warm weather, the flowering of the vines occurred 8 days earlier than the 30-year average, raising hopes of an early harvest. The summer was exceptionally hot, with June wet and warm, July slightly above normal in temperature, and August well above normal. However, unlike such classic hot, dry years as 1982, 1989, and 1990, there was significant rainfall (more than three times the normal amount) in August. For example, 193 millimeters of rain were reported in the Bordeaux area in August 1992 (most of it falling during several violent storms the last 2 days of the month), compared with 22 millimeters in 1990 and 63 millimeters in 1989.

By mid-August it was evident that the harvest would be enormous. For the serious estates, it was imperative that crop thinning be employed to reduce the crop size. Properties that crop-thinned produced wines with more richness than the light, diluted offerings of those that did not.

The first 2 weeks of September were dry, although abnormally cool. During this period the Sauvignon and Semillon were harvested under ideal conditions, which explains the excellent and sometimes outstanding success (despite high yields) of the 1992 white Graves.

From September 20 through most of October the weather was unfavorable, with considerable rain interspersed with short periods of clear weather. The harvest for the majority of estates took place over a long period of time, although most of the Merlot crop from both sides of the Gironde was harvested during 3 days of clear, dry weather on September 29, 30, and October 1. Between October 2 and October 6, more violent rainstorms lashed the region, and the châteaux, realizing nothing could be gained from waiting, harvested under miserable weather conditions. To make good wine it was essential to hand-pick the grapes, leaving the damaged, diseased fruit on the vine. An even stricter selection was necessary in the cellars.

Overall, 1992 is a more successful vintage than 1991 because no appellation produced a high percentage of poor wines, such as happened in Pomerol and St.-Emilion in 1991. The 1992s are the modern-day equivalents of the 1973s. But with better vinification techniques, stricter selection, better equipment, and more attention to yields, the top properties produced 1992s that are more concentrated, richer, and overall better wines than the best 1973s or, for that matter, the 1987s. All the 1992s tend to be soft, fruity, and low in acidity, with light to moderate tannin levels and moderate to good concentration.

The appellation that appears to have fared best is Pomerol. Certainly the top properties of the firm of Jean-Pierre Moueix crop-thinned severely. In the case of their two flagship estates, Trotanoy and Pétrus, Christian Moueix boldly employed an innovative technique, covering these two vineyards with black plastic at the beginning of September. The heavy rains that subsequently fell accumulated on the plastic and ran off instead of saturating the soil. I have seen photographs of this elaborate, costly endeavor, and after tasting the wines I can say that Moueix's daring and brilliance paid off. Trotanoy and Pétrus are two of the three most concentrated wines of the vintage, confirming that the incredible amount of labor required to cover the 21-acre Trotanoy vineyard and 28-acre Pétrus vineyard with black plastic was well worth the effort.

Elsewhere there are successes and failures in every appellation, with no real consistency to be found. Those properties that were attentive to the enormous crop size and crop-thinned, who were lucky enough to complete part of their harvest before the deluge of October 2–6, and discarded any questionable grapes have turned out fruity, soft, charming wines that, like the 1991s, will have to be drunk in their first 10–12 years of life.

THE BEST WINES

St.-Estèphe:	Haut-Marbuzet, Montrose
Pauillac:	Lafite-Rothschild, Latour, Pichon-Longueville Baron
St.-Julien:	Ducru-Beaucaillou, Gruaud-Larose, Léoville-Barton, Léoville-Las Cases
Margaux:	Giscours, Château Margaux, Palmer, Rauzan-Ségla
Médoc/Haut-Médoc Crus Bourgeois:	None
Graves Red:	Carbonnieux, Haut-Bailly, Haut-Brion, La Louvière, La Mission-Haut-Brion, Smith-Haut-Lafitte
Graves White:	Domaine de Chevalier, de Fieuzal, Haut-Brion, Laville-Haut-Brion, Smith-Haut-Lafitte
Pomerol:	Bon Pasteur, Certan de May, Clinet, La Conseillante,

l'Eglise-Clinet, l'Evangile, La Fleur de Gay, La Fleur
Pétrus, Gazin, Lafleur, Pétrus

St.-Emilion: Angélus, L'Arrosée, Beauséjour-Duffau, Canon,
Fonroque, Magdelaine, Troplong-Mondot, Valandraud

Barsac/Sauternes: None

1991—A Quick Study
(9-30-91)

St.-Estèphe**

Pauillac**

St.-Julien**

Margaux*

Médoc/Haut-Médoc Crus Bourgeois 0

Graves Red**

Graves White 0

Pomerol 0

St.-Emilion 0

Barsac/Sauternes**

Size: A very small crop, largely because the killer freeze during the weekend
of April 20–21 destroyed most of the crop in Pomerol and St.-Emilion.

Important information: A disaster in the right bank appellations of Pomerol
and St.-Emilion, but as one proceeds north in the Médoc, the quality
improves. Some surprisingly pleasant, even good, wines were produced
in Pauillac and St.-Estèphe.

Maturity status: The wines are maturing quickly and should be drunk within
their first 10–12 years of life.

Price: Because of the vintage's terrible reputation, this has always been an
easily affordable, low-priced vintage.

The year 1991 is remembered for the big freeze. During the weekend of
April 20–21 temperatures dropped as low as -9 degrees centigrade, destroying most vineyards' first-generation buds. The worst destruction occurred in
Pomerol and St.-Emilion, east of the Gironde. Less damage occurred in the
northern Médoc, especially in the northeastern sector of Pauillac and the
southern half of St.-Estèphe. The spring that followed the devastating freeze
did see the development of new buds, called "second-generation fruit" by
viticulturists.

Because the crop size was expected to be small, optimists began to suggest
that 1991 could resemble 1961 (a great year shaped by a spring killer frost
that reduced the crop size). Of course, this hope was based on the assumption that the weather would remain sunny and dry during the growing season.
By the time September arrived, most estates realized that the Merlot harvest
could not begin until late September and the Cabernet Sauvignon harvest in
mid-October. The second-generation fruit had retarded most vineyards' harvest schedules, yet sunny skies in late September gave hope for another
1978-ish "miracle year." Then, on September 25, an Atlantic storm dumped

116 millimeters of rain, precisely twice the average rainfall for the entire month!

Between September 30 and October 12 the weather was generally dry. Most of the Merlot vineyards on the right bank (Pomerol and St.-Emilion) were harvested during this period as quickly as possible. In Pomerol and St.-Emilion there was significant dilution, some rot, and unripe grapes. In the Médoc much of the Cabernet Sauvignon was not yet fully ripe, but many estates recognized that it was too risky to wait any longer. Those estates that harvested between October 13 and 19, before the outbreak of 6 consecutive days of heavy rain (another 120 millimeters), picked unripe but surprisingly healthy and low-acid Cabernet Sauvignon. Those properties that had not harvested by the time the second deluge arrived were unable to make quality wine.

The 1991 vintage is a poor, frequently disastrous one for most estates in Pomerol and St.-Emilion. I find it inferior to 1984, making it the worst vintage for these two appellations since the appalling 1969s. Many well-known estates in Pomerol and St.-Emilion completely declassified their wines, including such renowned St.-Emilion estates as L'Arrosée, Ausone, Canon, Cheval Blanc, La Dominique, and Magdelaine. In Pomerol several good wines were somehow made, but overall it was a catastrophe for this tiny appellation. Among the better-known Pomerol châteaux that declassified their entire crop are Beauregard, Bon Pasteur, L'Evangile, Le Gay, La Grave à Pomerol, Lafleur, Latour à Pomerol, Pétrus, Trotanoy, and Vieux-Château-Certan.

Despite all this bad news, some soft, pleasant, light- to medium-bodied wines did emerge from Graves and those Médoc vineyards adjacent to the Gironde. Consumers will be surprised by the quality of many of these wines, particularly from St.-Julien, Pauillac, and St.-Estèphe. In these northern Médoc appellations, much of the first-generation fruit was not destroyed by the frost, resulting in diluted but physiologically riper fruit than second-generation fruit produced. However, the good wines must be priced low or no consumer interest will be justified.

The appellations that stand out for consistently good wines in 1991 are St.-Julien, Pauillac, and St.-Estèphe. These areas suffered less frost damage to the first-generation grapes. Virtually all of the better-run estates in these appellations made above average, sometimes excellent, wine.

Because the intelligent properties in the Médoc utilized more Merlot in the blend rather than the unripe Cabernet Sauvignon, the 1991s are soft, forward wines that will need to be drunk in their first decade of life.

THE BEST WINES

St.-Estèphe:	Cos d'Estournel, Lafon-Rochet, Montrose
Pauillac:	Forts de Latour, Grand-Puy-Lacoste,
	Lafite-Rothschild, Latour, Lynch-Bages,

	Mouton-Rothschild, Pichon-Longueville Baron, Pichon-Longueville–Comtesse de Lalande, Réserve de la Comtesse
St.-Julien:	Beychevelle, Branaire-Ducru, Clos du Marquis, Ducru-Beaucaillou, Langoa-Barton, Léoville-Barton, Léoville-Las Cases
Margaux:	Giscours, Château Margaux, Palmer, Rauzan-Ségla
Médoc/Haut-Médoc Crus Bourgeois:	Citran
Graves Red:	Carbonnieux, Domaine de Chevalier, Haut-Brion, La Mission-Haut-Brion, Pape-Clément, Smith-Haut-Lafitte, La Tour-Haut-Brion
Graves White:	None
Pomerol:	Clinet
St.-Emilion:	Angélus, Troplong-Mondot
Barsac/Sauternes:	None

1990—A Quick Study
(9-12-90)

St.-Estèphe *****　　　　　　　　　　　Graves Red ****
Pauillac *****　　　　　　　　　　　　Graves White ***
St.-Julien *****　　　　　　　　　　　Pomerol *****
Margaux ****　　　　　　　　　　　　St.-Emilion *****
Médoc/Haut-Médoc Crus Bourgeois ****　　Barsac/Sauternes *****

Size: Enormous; one of the largest crops ever harvested in Bordeaux.

Important information: The hottest year since 1947 and the sunniest year since 1949 caused extraordinary stress in some of the best vineyards in the Graves and Médoc. Consequently, the heavier soils from such appellations as St.-Estèphe, the limestone hillsides and plateau areas of St.-Emilion, and the Fronsacs excelled, as did those top châteaux that made a severe selection.

Maturity status: Exceptionally low-acid wines, but high tannins have consistently suggested early accessibility. The most complete wines have another 20–25 years of longevity, but there is not a wine from this vintage that cannot be drunk with a great deal of pleasure in the late nineties.

Price: Opening future prices were down 15%–20% below 1989, but no modern-day Bordeaux vintage, with the exception of 1982, has appreciated more in price than 1990.

Most of the great Bordeaux vintages of this century are the result of relatively hot, dry years. For that reason alone, 1990 should elicit considerable attention. The most revealing fact about the 1990 vintage is that it is the second-hottest vintage of the century, barely surpassed by 1947. It is also the second-sunniest vintage, eclipsed only by 1949 in the post–World War II era. The amount of sunshine and the extraordinarily hot summers Bordeaux has enjoyed during the eighties are frequently attributed to the so-called greenhouse effect and consequent global warming about which such ominous warnings have been issued by the scientific community. Yet consider the Bordeaux weather for the period between 1945 and 1949. Amazingly, that era was even more torrid than 1989–1990. (One wonders if there was concern then about the glaciers of the North and South Poles melting.)

The weather of 1990 was auspicious because of its potential to produce great wines, but weather is only one part of the equation. The summer months of July and August were the driest since 1961, and August was the hottest since 1928, the year records were first kept. September (the month that most producers claim "makes the quality") was not, weather-wise, a particularly exceptional month, and 1990 was the second wettest among the great hot-year vintages, surpassed only by 1989. As in 1989, the rain fell at periods that were cause for concern. For example, on September 15 a particularly violent series of thunderstorms swept across Bordeaux, inundating much of the Graves region. On September 22–23 there was modest rainfall over the entire region. On October 7 and October 15 light showers were reported throughout the region. Most producers have been quick to state that the rain in September was beneficial. They argue that the Cabernet Sauvignon grapes were still too small and their skins too thick. Many Cabernet vines had shut down, and the grapes refused to mature because of the excessive heat and drought. The rain, the producers suggest, promoted further ripening and alleviated the blocked state of maturity. This is an appealing argument that has merit. While some panicked and harvested too soon after these rainstorms, the majority of the top estates got the harvest dates covered.

When tasting the wines from 1990, the most striking characteristic is their roasted quality, no doubt the result of the extremely hot summer. The September rains may have partially alleviated the stress from which those vineyards planted with Cabernet in the lighter, better-drained soils were suffering, but they also swelled many of the grape bunches and certainly contributed to another prolifically abundant crop size.

There is no doubt that the great vintages have all been relatively hot, dry years. But was 1990 too torrid? Were the yields so high that in spite of the exceptional weather there were just too many grapes to make profound wines? The weather in 1990 put even more stress on the Bordeaux vineyards than the heat and drought of 1989. One of the keys to understanding this vintage is that the finest wines of 1990 have emerged from 1) those vineyards planted on the heavier, less well-drained, less desirable vineyard soil, and 2) those top châteaux that employed a particularly ruthless selection process. For example, in my tasting notes, heavier soils from such appellations as St.-Estèphe, Fronsac, and the hillside and plateau vineyards of St.-Emilion produced richer, more concentrated, and more complete wines than many of the top vineyards planted on the fine, well-drained, gravel-based soils of Margaux and the Graves.

The crop size was enormous in 1990, approximately equivalent to the quantity of wine produced in 1989. In reality, more wine was actually made, but because the French authorities intervened and required significant declassifications, the actual declared limit matches 1989, which means that for both vintages the production is 30% more than in 1982. Officially, however, many châteaux (especially the first-growths and super-seconds) made even stricter selections in 1990 than in 1989, and the actual quantity of wine declared by many producers under the grand vin label is less than in 1989.

Across almost every appellation, the overall impression one gets of the dry red wines is that of extremely low acidity (as low as and in some cases even lower than in 1989), high tannins (in most cases higher than in 1989), but an overall impression of softness and forward, precocious, extremely ripe, sometimes roasted flavors. Because the tannins are so soft (as in 1982, 1985, and 1989), these wines will provide considerable enjoyment when they are young, yet they possess decades or more of longevity.

The second consecutive year of great heat, sunshine, and drought apparently caused even more stress for those vineyards planted in light, gravelly soil than in 1989. Many proprietors in the Graves and Margaux regions suggested that they were almost forced to harvest their Cabernet too soon because it was drying up on the vine. This, combined with extremely high yields, no doubt explains why the Graves and Margaux appellations, much as in 1989 and 1982 (two other hot, dry years), were less successful. Yet each appellation produced some brilliant wines.

Some surprising strengths in this vintage include most of the Médoc first-growths (Mouton-Rothschild being the exception). It can be said that they have made richer, fuller, more complete wines in 1990 than in 1989. Elsewhere in the Médoc, particularly in St.-Julien and Pauillac, a bevy of relatively soft, round, forward, fruity wines with high alcohol, high, soft tannin, and extremely low acidity have been made. For me, the most intriguing aspect of the 1990 vintage is that as the wines aged in cask and continued their evolution in bottle, the vintage took on additional weight and structure, much like 1982 (but not 1989). I clearly underestimated some of the St.-Juliens and Pauillacs early on, as it was apparent at the time of bottling that these appellations had generally produced many profoundly rich, concentrated wines that were to be the greatest young Bordeaux since 1982. The fly in the ointment when attempting to comprehend this vintage early on was that two of Bordeaux's superstars, Mouton-Rothschild and Pichon-Lalande, produced wines that were far less complete than their 1989s. Their wines were somewhat disappointing for the vintage and well below the quality of their peers. The puzzling performances of these two châteaux continues to be confirmed by my tastings in the late nineties. However, the other top wines in the Médoc have gained considerable stature and richness. They are the most exciting wines produced in Bordeaux between 1982 and 1995/1996.

On the right bank, it first appeared that Pomerol enjoyed a less successful vintage than 1989, with the exception of those estates situated on the St.-Emilion border—L'Evangile, La Conseillante, and Bon Pasteur—which from the beginning had obviously produced wines that were richer than their 1989 counterparts. However, as the Pomerols evolved in cask, the vintage, while never quite approaching 1989 in terms of greatness, did seem to strengthen from an overall perspective, with the wines gaining weight, definition, and complexity. As the end of the century approaches, 1990 is a vintage that produced some profoundly great Pomerols, but overall, the vintage is less harmonious than 1989.

St.-Emilion, never a consistent appellation, has produced perhaps its most homogeneous and greatest vintage of the last 50 years for all three sectors of the appellation—the plateau, the vineyards at the foot of the hillsides, and the vineyards on sandy, gravelly soil. It is interesting to note that Cheval Blanc, Figeac, Pavie, L'Arrosée, Ausone, and Beauséjour-Duffau produced far greater 1990s than 1989s. In particular, both Cheval Blanc and Beauséjour-Duffau look to be wines of legendary quality. Figeac is not far behind, with the 1990 being the finest wine made at this estate since its 1982 and 1964.

The dry white wines of Graves, as well as generic white Bordeaux, have enjoyed a very good vintage that is largely superior to 1989, with two principal exceptions, Haut-Brion-Blanc and Laville-Haut-Brion. There is no doubt that the 1989 Haut-Brion-Blanc and 1989 Laville-Haut-Brion are two of the greatest white Graves ever produced. Both are far richer and more complete than their 1990s. Poor judgment in picking the 1989s too soon was not repeated with the 1990s, which have more richness and depth than most 1989s.

As for the sweet white wines of the Barsac/Sauternes region, this vintage was historic in the sense that most of the sweet white wine producers finished their harvest before the red wine producers, something that had not happened since 1949. While powerful, sweet, and sugary in cask and early in bottling, the wines have slowly begun to take on more complexity and focus. It really comes down to personal preference as to whether readers prefer 1990, 1989, or 1988 Barsacs and Sauternes, but there is no question this is the third and last vintage of a glorious trilogy, with the most powerful and concentrated Barsacs and Sauternes produced in many years. The wines, which boast some of the most impressive statistical credentials I have ever seen, are monster sized in their richness and intensity. They possess 30–40 years of longevity. Will they turn out to be more complex and elegant than the 1988s? My instincts suggest they will not, but they are immensely impressive, blockbuster wines.

In summary, readers should consider the following four points with respect to the 1990 vintage:

1. I have consistently written that 1990 is a greater vintage overall than 1989. I have also stated that, in my opinion, 1990 is an even greater vintage than 1982—particularly in view of the fact that a number of estates making superb wine today were not especially well managed or motivated in 1982. For examples of this, readers need look no further than such châteaux as Angélus, Beauséjour-Duffau, Canon-La-Gaffelière, Clinet, Clos Fourtet, l'Eglise-Clinet, La Fleur de Gay, Gazin, Lafon-Rochet, Lagrange (St.-Julien), Monbousquet, Pape-Clément, Phélan-Ségur, Pichon-Longueville Baron, Smith-Haut-Lafitte, Le Tertre-Roteboeuf, Troplong-Mondot, and Valandraud, all estates trying to produce superlative wine in the nineties that were indifferently administered (or nonexistent, in the case of Valandraud) in 1982. It is undoubtedly one of the greatest young Bordeaux vintages of modern times, with a style not dissimilar from 1982, but with more consistency from top to bottom than 1982. Yet the extraordinary concentration and opulence of the most profound 1982s still exceed that of the best 1990s.

2. With the exception of Pomerol and the two splendid performances by La Mission-Haut-Brion and Haut-Brion in 1989, 1990 usually triumphs in side-by-side tastings of the two vintages. There are several other exceptions, but in general the 1990s are more concentrated, complex, and richer than their 1989 counterparts, excepting, of course, the Pomerols and 1989 La Mission-Haut-Brion and Haut-Brion, which are undoubtedly legendary wines.

3. Prices for the 1990s are even higher than the 1982s. Sadly, I do not see any direction but upward for the prices of the 1990s or, for that matter, the 1982s. There are too many wealthy people in the world who insist on having the best of the best at any cost. The wine market today is considerably more diversified and broader than it was 5 or 10 years ago. Furthermore, a depressed economy in one country is not likely to cause a decline in prices for the greatest wines from the greatest vintages . . . a sad but inescapable conclusion based on today's international wine market.

4. In looking at the finest Bordeaux vintages this century, it seems apparent that there are two types of great vintages. There are torridly hot, dry years that produce low-acid wines with explosive levels of fruit and what the

French call *sur-maturité* (over-ripeness). Wines from these type of vintages tend to be delicious young because of their ripe tannin and low acidity. It is easy to think such vintages will not keep, but based on some ancient vintages that possessed these characteristics, the wines have proved age-worthy for a remarkably long time. Great vintages that fall in this category include 1900, 1921, 1929, 1947, 1949, 1959, 1961, 1982, 1989, 1990, and possibly 1995.

The other type of great Bordeaux vintage produces extremely concentrated but formidably tannic wines that taste more dominated by Cabernet Sauvignon. These wines are almost impenetrable when young and, as a result, test their purchasers' patience for decades. This type of great vintage is often a more questionable purchase, since 10–20 years of cellaring is often required for the wine to shed sufficient tannin to be enjoyable. The twentieth century's greatest vintages for wines of this style include 1926, 1928, 1945, 1948, 1955 (for the Médoc and Graves), 1975 (for the Pomerols and a selected handful of other estates), and 1986 as well as 1996 (but only for the Médoc).

THE BEST WINES

St.-Estèphe:	Calon-Ségur, Cos d'Estournel, Cos Labory, Haut-Marbuzet, Montrose, Phélan-Ségur
Pauillac:	Les Forts de Latour, Grand-Puy-Lacoste, Lafite-Rothschild, Latour, Lynch-Bages, Pichon-Longueville Baron
St.-Julien:	Branaire-Ducru, Gloria, Gruaud-Larose, Lagrange, Léoville-Barton, Léoville-Las Cases, Léoville-Poyferré
Margaux:	Malescot St.-Exupéry, Margaux, Palmer, Rausan-Ségla
Médoc/Haut-Médoc/ Moulis/Listrac/Crus Bourgeois:	Lanessan, La Tour St.-Bonnet, Moulin-Rouge, Sociando-Mallet, Tour Haut-Caussan, Tour du Haut-Moulin
Graves Red:	Haut-Bailly, Haut-Brion, La Louvière, La Mission-Haut-Brion, Pape-Clément
Graves White:	Domaine de Chevalier, Clos Floridène, de Fieuzal, La Tour-Martillac
Pomerol:	Bon Pasteur, Certan de May, Clinet, La Conseillante, l'Eglise-Clinet, l'Evangile, La Fleur de Gay, Gazin, Lafleur, Petit-Village, Pétrus, Le Pin, Trotanoy, Vieux-Château-Certan

Fronsac/Canon

Fronsac:	Canon-de-Brem, de Carles, Cassagne-Haut-Canon-La-Truffière, Fontenil, Pez-Labrie, La Vieille-Cure
St.-Emilion:	Angélus, L'Arrosée, Ausone, Beauséjour-Duffau, Canon, Canon-La-Gaffelière, Cheval Blanc, La Dominique, Figeac, Grand-Mayne, Pavie, Pavie-Macquin, Le Tertre-Roteboeuf, Troplong-Mondot
Barsac/Sauternes:	Climens, Coutet, Coutet Cuvée Madame, Doisy-Daëne, Lafaurie-Peyraguey, Rabaud-Promis, Raymond-Lafon, Rieussec, Sigalas-Rabaud, Suduiraut, La Tour Blanche, Yquem

1989—A Quick Study
(8-31-89)

St.-Estèphe****	Graves Red***
Pauillac*****	Graves White**
St.-Julien****	Pomerol*****
Margaux***	St.-Emilion****
Médoc/Haut-Médoc Crus Bourgeois****	Barsac/Sauternes****

Size: Mammoth; along with 1990 and 1986, the largest declared crop in the history of Bordeaux.

Important information: Excessively hyped vintage by virtually everyone but the Bordeaux proprietors. American, French, even English writers were all set to declare it the vintage of the century until serious tasters began to question the extract levels, phenomenally low acid levels, and puzzling quality of some wines. However, plenty of rich, dramatic, fleshy wines have been produced that should age reasonably well.

Maturity status: High tannins and extremely low acidity, much like 1990, suggest early drinkability, with only the most concentrated wines capable of lasting 20–30 or more years.

Price: The most expensive opening prices of any vintage, until 1995 and 1996.

The general news media, primarily ABC television and *The New York Times,* first carried the news that several châteaux began their harvest during the last days of August, making 1989 the earliest vintage since 1893. An early harvest generally signifies a torrid growing season and below average rainfall—almost always evidence that a top-notch vintage is achievable. In his annual *Vintage and Market Report,* Peter Sichel reported that between

1893 and 1989 only 1947, 1949, 1970, and 1982 were years with a similar weather pattern, but none of these years were as hot as 1989.

Perhaps the most revealing and critical decision (at least from a qualitative perspective) was the choice of picking dates. Never has Bordeaux enjoyed such a vast span of time (August 28–October 15) over which to complete the harvest. Some châteaux, most notably Haut-Brion and the Christian Moueix —managed properties in Pomerol and St.-Emilion, harvested during the first week of September. Other estates waited and did not finish their harvesting until mid-October. During the second week of September, one major problem developed. Much of the Cabernet Sauvignon, while analytically mature and having enough sugar to potentially produce wines with 13% alcohol, was actually not ripe physiologically. Many châteaux, never having experienced such growing conditions, became indecisive. Far too many deferred to their oenologists, who saw technically mature grapes that were quickly losing acidity. The oenologists, never ones to take risks, advised immediate picking. As more than one proprietor and *négociant* said, by harvesting the Cabernet too early, a number of châteaux lost their chance to produce one of the greatest wines of a lifetime. This, plus the enormously large crop size, proba- bly explains the good yet uninspired performance of so many wines from the Graves and Margaux appellations.

There was clearly no problem with the early-picked Merlot, as much of it came in between 13.5% and a whopping 15% alcohol level—unprecedented in Bordeaux. Those properties that crop-thinned—Pétrus and Haut-Brion— had yields of 45–55 hectoliters per hectare and superconcentration. Those that did not crop-thin had yields as preposterously high as 80 hectoliters per hectare.

Contrary to the reports of a totally "dry harvest," there were rain showers on September 10, 13, 18, and 22 that did little damage unless the property panicked and harvested the day after the rain. Some of the lighter-style wines may very well be the result of jittery châteaux owners who unwisely picked after the showers.

The overall production was, once again, staggeringly high.

In general, the wines are the most alcoholic Bordeaux I have ever tasted, ranging from 12.8% to over 14.5% for some Pomerols. Acidities are extremely low and tannin levels surprisingly high. Consequently, in looking at the structural profile of the 1989s, one sees wines 1%–2% higher in alcohol than the 1982s or 1961s, with much lower acidity levels than the 1982s, 1961s, and 1959s, yet high tannin levels. Fortunately the tannins are generally ripe and soft, à la 1982, rather than dry and astringent as in 1988. This gives the wines a big, rich, fleshy feel in the mouth, similar to the 1982s. The top 1989s have very high glycerin levels, but are they as concentrated as the finest 1982s, 1990s, 1995s, and 1996s? In Margaux the answer is a resounding "No," as this is clearly the least-favored appellation, much as it was in 1982. In Graves, except for Haut-Brion, La Mission-Haut-Brion, Haut-Bailly, and de Fieuzal, the wines are relatively light and undistinguished. In St.-Emilion, the 1982s and 1990s are more consistent as well as more deeply concentrated. Some marvelously rich, enormously fruity, fat wines were made in St.-Emilion in 1989, but there is wide irregularity in quality. However, in the northern Médoc, primarily St.-Julien, Pauillac, and St.-Estèphe, as well as in Pomerol, many exciting, full-bodied, very alcoholic, and tannic wines have been made. The best of these seem to combine the splendidly rich, opulent, fleshy texture of the finest 1982s with the power and tannin of the 1990s yet curiously taste less concentrated than these two vintages.

As with the 1982s, this is a vintage that will probably be enjoyable to drink over a broad span of years. Despite the high tannin levels, the low acidities combined with the high glycerin and alcohol levels give the wines a fascinatingly fleshy, full-bodied texture. While there is considerable variation in quality, the finest 1989s from Pomerol, St.-Julien, Pauillac, and St.-Estèphe will, in specific cases, rival some of the greatest wines of the last twenty years.

THE BEST WINES

St.-Estèphe:	Cos d'Estournel, Haut-Marbuzet, Meyney, Montrose, Phélan-Ségur
Pauillac:	Clerc-Milon, Grand-Puy-Lacoste, Lafite-Rothschild, Lynch-Bages, Mouton-Rothschild, Pichon-Longueville Baron, Pichon-Longueville–Comtesse de Lalande
St.-Julien:	Beychevelle, Branaire-Ducru, Ducru-Beaucaillou, Gruaud-Larose, Lagrange, Léoville-Barton, Léoville-Las Cases, Talbot
Margaux:	Cantemerle, Margaux, Palmer, Rausan-Ségla
Médoc/Haut-Médoc/Moulis/Listrac/Crus Bourgeois:	Beaumont, Le Boscq, Chasse-Spleen, Gressier Grand-Poujeaux, Lanessan, Maucaillou, Moulin-Rouge, Potensac, Poujeaux, Sociando-Mallet, La Tour de By, Tour Haut-Caussan, Tour du Haut-Moulin, La Tour St.-Bonnet, Vieux-Robin
Graves Red:	Bahans-Haut-Brion, Haut-Bailly, Haut-Brion, La Louvière, La Mission-Haut-Brion
Graves White:	Clos Floridène, Haut-Brion, Laville-Haut-Brion
Pomerol:	Bon Pasteur, Clinet, La Conseillante, Domaine de l'Eglise, l'Eglise-Clinet, l'Evangile, Lafleur, La Fleur

de Gay, La Fleur Pétrus, Le Gay, Les Pensées de
Lafleur, Pétrus, Le Pin, Trotanoy,
Vieux-Château-Certan

Fronsac/Canon
    Fronsac: Canon, Canon-de-Brem, Canon-Moueix,
Cassagne-Haut-Canon-La-Truffière, Dalem, La
Dauphine, Fontenil, Mazeris, Moulin-Haut-Laroque,
Moulin-Pey-Labrie

    St.-Emilion: Angélus, Ausone, Cheval Blanc, La Dominique, La
Gaffelière, Grand-Mayne, Magdelaine, Pavie,
Pavie-Macquin, Soutard, Le Tertre-Roteboeuf,
Troplong-Mondot, Trotte Vieille

Barsac/Sauternes: Climens, Coutet, Coutet-Cuvée Madame,
Doisy-Védrines, Guiraud, Lafaurie-Peyraguey,
Rabaud-Promis, Raymond-Lafon, Rieussec,
Suduiraut, Suduiraut-Cuvée Madame, La Tour
Blanche, Yquem

1988—A Quick Study
(9-20-88)

St.-Estèphe***   Graves Red*****
Pauillac****   Graves White***
St.-Julien****   Pomerol****
Margaux***   St.-Emilion***
Médoc/Haut-Médoc Crus Bourgeois**   Barsac/Sauternes*****

Size: A large crop equivalent in size to 1982, meaning 30% less wine than
was produced in 1989 and 1990.

Important information: Fearing a repeat of the rains that destroyed the potential for a great year in 1987, many producers once again pulled the
trigger on their harvesting teams too soon. Unfortunately, copious quantities of Médoc Cabernet Sauvignon were picked too early.

Maturity status: Because of good acid levels and relatively high, more astringent tannins, there is no denying the potential of the 1988s to last for
20 or 30 years. How many of these wines will retain enough fruit to
stand up to the tannin remains to be seen.

Price: Range 20%–50% below more glamorous vintages, so the best wines
offer considerable value.

The year 1988 is a good but rarely thrilling vintage of red wines and one
of the greatest vintages of this century for the sweet wines of Barsac and
Sauternes.

The problem with the red wines is that there is a lack of superstar performances on the part of the top châteaux. This will no doubt ensure that 1988 will always be regarded as a very good rather than an excellent year. While the 1988 crop size was large, it was exceeded in size by the two vintages that followed it, 1989 and 1990. The average yield in 1988 was between 45 and 50 hectoliters per hectare, which was approximately equivalent to the quantity of wine produced in 1982. The wines tend to be well colored, tannic, and firmly structured. The less successful wines exhibit a slight lack of depth and finish short, with noticeably green, astringent tannins. Yet Graves and the northern Médoc enjoyed a fine, rather deliciously styled vintage.

These characteristics are especially evident in the Médoc, where it was all too apparent that many châteaux, apprehensive about the onset of rot and further rain (as in 1987), panicked and harvested their Cabernet Sauvignon too early. Consequently they brought in Cabernet that often achieved only 8%–9% sugar readings. Those properties that waited, or made a severe selection, produced the best wines.

In Pomerol and St.-Emilion the Merlot was harvested under ripe conditions, but because of the severe drought in 1988 the skins of the grapes were thicker and the resulting wines were surprisingly tannic and hard.

In St.-Emilion many properties reported bringing in Cabernet Franc at full maturity and obtaining sugar levels that were reportedly higher than ever before. However, despite such optimistic reports much of the Cabernet Franc tasted fluid and diluted in quality. Therefore St.-Emilion, despite reports of a very successful harvest, exhibits great irregularity in quality.

The appellation of Graves probably produced the best red wines of Bordeaux in 1988.

While there is no doubt that the richer, more dramatic, fleshier 1989s have taken much of the public's attention away from the 1988s, an objective look at the 1988 vintage will reveal some surprisingly strong performances in appellations such as Margaux, Pomerol, and Graves and in properties in the northern Médoc that eliminated their early-picked Cabernet Sauvignon or harvested much later. The year 1988 is not particularly good for the Crus Bourgeois because many harvested too soon. The lower prices they receive for their wines do not permit the Crus Bourgeois producers to make the strict selection that is necessary in years such as 1988.

The appellations that did have a superstar vintage were Barsac and Sauternes. With a harvest that lasted until the end of November and textbook weather conditions for the formation of the noble rot, *Botrytis cinerea,* 1988 is considered by some authorities to be one of the finest vintages since 1937. Almost across the board, including the smaller estates, the wines have an intense smell of honey, coconut, oranges, and other tropical fruits. It is a remarkably rich vintage, with wines of extraordinary levels of botrytis, great concentration of flavor; yet the rich, unctuous, opulent textures are balanced beautifully by zesty, crisp acidity. It is this latter component that makes these wines so special.

THE BEST WINES

St.-Estèphe:	Calon-Ségur, Haut-Marbuzet, Meyney, Phélan-Ségur
Pauillac:	Clerc-Milon, Lafite-Rothschild, Latour, Lynch-Bages, Mouton-Rothschild, Pichon-Longueville Baron, Pichon-Longueville–Comtesse de Lalande
St.-Julien:	Gruaud-Larose, Léoville-Barton, Léoville-Las Cases, Talbot
Margaux:	Monbrison, Rausan-Ségla
Médoc/Haut-Médoc/ Moulis/Listrac/Crus Bourgeois:	Fourcas-Loubaney, Gressier Grand-Poujeaux, Poujeaux, Sociando-Mallet, Tour du Haut-Moulin
Graves Red:	Les Carmes Haut-Brion, Domaine de Chevalier, Haut-Bailly, Haut-Brion, La Louvière, La Mission-Haut-Brion, Pape-Clément
Graves White:	Domaine de Chevalier, Clos Floridène, Couhins-Lurton, de Fieuzal, Laville-Haut-Brion, La Louvière, La Tour-Martillac
Pomerol:	Bon Pasteur, Certan de May, Clinet, l'Eglise-Clinet, La Fleur de Gay, Gombaude-Guillot-Cuvée Speciale, Lafleur, Petit-Village, Pétrus, Le Pin, Vieux-Château-Certan
St.-Emilion:	Angélus, Ausone, Canon-La-Gaffelière, Clos des Jacobins, Larmande, Le Tertre-Roteboeuf, Troplong-Mondot
Barsac/Sauternes:	D'Arche, Broustet, Climens, Coutet, Coutet-Cuvée Madame, Doisy-Daëne, Doisy-Dubroca, Guiraud, Lafaurie-Peyraguey, Lamothe-Guignard, Rabaud-Promis, Rayne-Vigneau, Rieussec, Sigalas Rabaud, Suduiraut, La Tour Blanche, Yquem

1987—A Quick Study
(10-3-87)

St.-Estèphe **
Pauillac **
St.-Julien **
Margaux **
Médoc/Haut-Médoc Crus Bourgeois *

Graves Red ***
Graves White ****
Pomerol ***
St.-Emilion **
Barsac/Sauternes *

Size: A moderately sized crop that looks almost tiny in the scheme of the gigantic yields during the decade of the eighties.

Important information: The most underrated vintage of the 1980s, producing a surprising number of ripe, round, tasty wines, particularly from Pomerol, Graves, and the most seriously run estates in the northern Médoc.

Maturity status: The best examples are deliciously drinkable and should be consumed before 2000.

Price: Low prices are the rule rather than the exception for this sometimes attractive, low-priced vintage.

More than one Bordelais has said that if the rain had not arrived during the first 2 weeks of October 1987, ravaging the quality of the unharvested Cabernet Sauvignon and Petit Verdot, then 1987—not 1989 or 1982—would be the most extraordinary vintage of the 1980s. Wasn't it true that August and September had been the hottest 2 months in Bordeaux since 1976? But the rain did fall, plenty of it, and it dashed the hopes for a top vintage. Yet much of the Merlot was primarily harvested before the rain. The early-picked Cabernet Sauvignon was adequate, but that picked after the rains began was in very poor condition. Thanks in part to the two gigantic-size crops of 1985 and 1986, both record years at the time, most Bordeaux châteaux had full cellars and were mentally prepared to eliminate the vats of watery Cabernet Sauvignon harvested in the rains that fell for 14 straight days in October. The results for the top estates are wines that are light to medium bodied, ripe, fruity, round, even fat, with low tannins, low acidity, and lush, captivating, charming personalities.

While there is a tendency to look at 1987 as a poor year and to compare it with such other recent uninspiring vintages as 1977, 1980, and 1984, the truth is that the wines could not be more different. In the 1977, 1980, and 1984 vintages the problem was immaturity because of cold, wet weather leading up to the harvest. In 1987 the problem was not a lack of maturity, as the Merlot and Cabernet were ripe. In 1987 the rains diluted fully mature, ripe grapes.

The year 1987 is the most underrated vintage of the decade for those estates where a strict selection was made and/or the Merlot was harvested in sound condition. The wines are deliciously fruity, forward, clean, fat, and soft, without any degree of rot. Prices remain a bargain, even though the quantities produced were relatively small. This is a vintage that I search out on restaurant wine lists. I have bought a number of the wines for my cellar because I regard 1987, much like 1976, as a very soft, forward vintage that produced wines for drinking in their first decade of life.

THE BEST WINES

St.-Estèphe: Cos d'Estournel

Pauillac: Lafite-Rothschild, Latour, Mouton-Rothschild, Pichon-Longueville Baron, Pichon-Longueville–Comtesse de Lalande

St.-Julien: Gruaud-Larose, Léoville-Barton, Léoville-Las Cases, Talbot

Margaux: Angludet, Margaux, Palmer

Médoc/Haut-Médoc/Moulis/Listrac/Crus Bourgeois: None

Graves Red: Bahans-Haut-Brion, Domaine de Chevalier, Haut-Brion, La Mission-Haut-Brion, Pape-Clément

Graves White: Domaine de Chevalier, Couhins-Lurton, de Fieuzal, Laville-Haut-Brion, La Tour-Martillac

Pomerol: Certan de May, Clinet, La Conseillante, l'Evangile, La Fleur de Gay, Petit-Village, Pétrus, Le Pin

St.-Emilion: Ausone, Cheval Blanc, Clos des Jacobins, Clos Saint-Martin, Grand-Mayne, Magdelaine, Le Tertre-Roteboeuf, Trotte Vieille

Barsac/Sauternes: Coutet, Lafaurie-Peyraguey

1986—A Quick Study
(9-23-86)

St.-Estèphe ****   Graves Red ***

Pauillac *****   Graves White **

St.-Julien *****   Pomerol ***

Margaux ****   St.-Emilion ***

Médoc/Haut-Médoc/Crus Bourgeois ***   Barsac/Sauternes *****

Size: Colossal; one of the largest crops ever produced in Bordeaux.

Important information: An irrefutably great year for the Cabernet Sauvignon grape in the northern Médoc, St.-Julien, Pauillac, and St.-Estèphe. The top 1986s beg for more cellaring, and one wonders how many purchasers of these wines will lose their patience before the wines have reached full maturity.

Maturity status: The wines from the Crus Bourgeois, Graves, and the right bank can be drunk now, but the impeccably structured Médocs will not become accessible until 2005.

Price: Still realistic except for a handful of the superstar wines.

The year 1986 is without doubt a great vintage for the northern Médoc, particularly for St.-Julien, Pauillac, and St.-Estèphe, where many châteaux produced wines that are their deepest and most concentrated since 1982, and with 20–30-plus years of longevity. Yet it should be made very clear to readers that unlike the great vintage of 1982, or very good vintages of 1983 and 1985, the 1986s are not flattering wines to drink young. Most of the top wines of the Médoc will require a minimum of a decade of cellaring to shed their tannins, which are the highest ever measured for a Bordeaux vintage. If you are not prepared to wait for the 1986s to mature, this is not a vintage that makes sense to buy. If you can defer your gratification, then many of these will prove to be the most exhilarating Bordeaux wines produced since 1982.

Why did 1986 turn out to be such an exceptional year for many Médocs as well as Graves wines and produce Cabernet Sauvignon grapes of uncommon richness and power? The weather during the summer of 1986 was very dry and hot. In fact, by the beginning of September Bordeaux was in the midst of a severe drought that began to threaten the final maturity process of the grapes. Rain did come, first on September 14 and 15, which enhanced the maturity process and mitigated the drought conditions. This rain was welcome, but on September 23 a ferocious, quick-moving storm thrashed the city of Bordeaux, the Graves region, and the major right bank appellations of Pomerol and St.-Emilion.

The curious aspect of this major storm, which caused widespread flooding in Bordeaux, was that it barely sideswiped the northern Médoc appellations of St.-Julien, Pauillac, and St.-Estèphe. Those pickers who started their harvest around the end of September found bloated Merlot grapes and unripe Cabernets. Consequently, the top wines of 1986 came from those châteaux that 1) did most of their harvesting after October 5, or 2) eliminated from their final blend the early picked Merlot, as well as the Cabernet Franc and Cabernet Sauvignon harvested between September 23 and October 4. After September 23 there were an extraordinary 23 days of hot, windy, sunny weather that turned the vintage into an exceptional one for those who delayed picking. It is, therefore, no surprise that the late harvested Cabernet Sauvignon in the northern Médoc that was picked after October 6, but primarily between October 9 and 16, produced wines of extraordinary intensity and depth. Château Margaux and Château Mouton-Rothschild, which produced the vintage's two greatest wines, took in the great majority of their Cabernet Sauvignon between October 11 and 16.

In Pomerol and St.-Emilion, those châteaux that harvested soon after the September 23 deluge got predictably much less intense wines. Those that waited (such as Vieux-Château-Certan, Lafleur, Le Pin) made much more concentrated, complete wines. As in most vintages, the harvest date in 1986 was critical, and without question the late pickers made the finest wines. Perhaps the most perplexing paradox to emerge from the 1986 vintage is the generally high quality of the Graves wines, particularly in spite of the fact that this area was ravaged by the September 23 rainstorm. The answer in part may be that the top Graves châteaux eliminated more Merlot from the final blend than usual, thereby producing wines with a much higher percentage of Cabernet Sauvignon.

Last, the size of the 1986 crop established another record, as the harvest exceeded the bumper crop of 1985 by 15% and was 30% larger than the 1982 harvest. This overall production figure, equaled in both 1989 and 1990, is somewhat deceiving, as most of the classified Médoc châteaux made significantly less wine in 1986 than in 1985. It is for that reason, as well as the super maturity and tannin levels of the Cabernet Sauvignon grape, that most Médocs are noticeably more concentrated, more powerful, and more tannic in 1986 than they were in 1985. All things considered, 1986 offers numerous exciting as well as exhilarating wines of profound depth and exceptional potential for longevity. Yet I continue to ask myself, How many readers are willing to defer their gratification until the turn of the century, when these wines will be ready to drink?

THE BEST WINES

St.-Estèphe:	Cos d'Estournel, Montrose
Pauillac:	Clerc-Milon, Grand-Puy-Lacoste, Haut-Bages-Libéral, Lafite-Rothschild, Latour, Lynch-Bages, Mouton-Rothschild, Pichon-Longueville Baron, Pichon-Longueville–Comtesse de Lalande
St.-Julien:	Beychevelle, Ducru-Beaucaillou, Gruaud-Larose, Lagrange, Léoville-Barton, Léoville-Las Cases, Talbot
Margaux:	Margaux, Palmer, Rausan-Ségla
Médoc/Haut Médoc/ Moulis/Listrac/Crus Bourgeois:	Chasse-Spleen, Fourcas-Loubaney, Gressier Grand-Poujeaux, Lanessan, Maucaillou, Poujeaux, Sociando-Mallet
Graves Red:	Domaine de Chevalier, Haut-Brion, La Mission-Haut-Brion, Pape-Clément
Graves White:	None
Pomerol:	Certan de May, Clinet, l'Eglise-Clinet, La Fleur de Gay, Lafleur, Pétrus, Le Pin, Vieux-Château-Certan
St.-Emilion:	L'Arrosée, Canon, Cheval Blanc, Figeac, Pavie, Le Tertre-Roteboeuf
Barsac/Sauternes:	Climens, Coutet-Cuvée Madame, de Fargues, Guiraud, Lafaurie-Peyraguey, Raymond-Lafon, Rieussec, Yquem

1985—A Quick Study
(9-29-85)

St.-Estèphe***　　　　　　　　　　　　Graves Red****
Pauillac****　　　　　　　　　　　　　Graves White****
St.-Julien****　　　　　　　　　　　　Pomerol****
Margaux***　　　　　　　　　　　　　St.-Emilion***
Médoc/Haut-Médoc Crus Bourgeois***　　Barsac/Sauternes**

Size: A very large crop (a record at the time) that was subsequently surpassed by harvest sizes in 1986, 1989, and 1990.

Important information: The top Médocs may turn out to represent clones of the gorgeously seductive, charming 1953 vintage. Most of the top wines are surprisingly well developed, displaying fine richness, a round, feminine character, and exceptional aromatic purity and complexity. It is one of the most delicious vintages to drink in 1998.

Maturity status: Seemingly drinkable from their release, the 1985s continue to develop quickly yet should last in the top cases for another 10–15 years. The top Crus Bourgeois are delicious and should be consumed before the end of the nineties.

Price: Released at outrageously high prices, the 1985s have not appreciated in value to the extent of other top vintages.

Any vintage, whether in Bordeaux or elsewhere, is shaped by the weather pattern. The 1985 Bordeaux vintage was conceived in a period of apprehension. January 1985 was the coldest since 1956. (I was there on January 16 when the temperature hit a record low minus 14.5 degrees centigrade.) However, fear of damage to the vineyard was greatly exaggerated by the Bordelais. One wonders about the sincerity of such fears and whether they were designed to push up prices for the 1983s and create some demand for the overpriced 1984s. In any event, the spring and early summer were normal, if somewhat more rainy and cooler than usual in April, May, and June. July was slightly hotter and wetter than normal, August was colder than normal but extremely dry. The September weather set a meteorological record—it was the sunniest, hottest, and driest September ever measured. The three most recent top vintages—1961, 1982, and 1989—could not claim such phenomenal weather conditions in September.

The harvest commenced at the end of September, and three things became apparent in that period between September 23 and September 30. First, the Merlot was fully mature and excellent in quality. Second, the Cabernet Sauvignon grapes were not as ripe as expected and barely reached 11% natural alcohol. Third, the enormous size of the crop caught everyone off guard. The drought of August and September had overly stressed the many Cabernet vineyards planted in gravelly soil and actually retarded the ripening process. The smart growers stopped picking Cabernet, risking foul weather but hoping for higher sugar levels. The less adventurous settled for good rather than very good Cabernet Sauvignon. The pickers who waited and picked their Cabernet Sauvignon in mid-October clearly made the best wines, as the weather held up throughout the month of October. Because of the drought, there was little botrytis in the Barsac and Sauternes regions. Those wines have turned out to be monolithic, straightforward, and fruity but lacking complexity and depth.

In general, 1985 is an immensely seductive and attractive vintage that has produced numerous well-balanced, rich, very perfumed yet tender wines. The 1985s are destined to be consumed over the next 15 years while waiting for the tannins of the 1986s to melt away and for richer, fuller, more massive wines from vintages such as 1982, 1989, 1990, and 1996 to reach full maturity. The year 1985 was one of great sunshine, heat, and drought, so much so that many of the vineyards planted on lighter, more gravelly soil were stressed.

In the Médoc, 1985 produced an enormous crop. Where the châteaux made a strict selection, the results are undeniably charming, round, precocious, opulent wines with low acidity and an overall elegant, almost feminine quality. The tannins are soft and mellow. Interestingly, in the Médoc it is one of those years, much like 1989, where the so-called super-seconds, such as Cos d'Estournel, Lynch-Bages, Léoville-Las Cases, Ducru-Beaucaillou, Pichon-Longueville–Comtesse de Lalande, and Léoville-Barton, made wines that rival and in some cases even surpass the more illustrious first-growths. In many vintages (1986, for example) the first-growths soar qualitatively above the rest. That is not the case in 1985.

In the best-case scenario, the top 1985s may well evolve along the lines of the beautiful, charming 1953 vintage.

Most of the Médoc growers, who were glowing in their opinion of the 1985s, called the vintage a blend in style between 1982 and 1983. Others compared the 1985s to the 1976s. Both of these positions seem far off the mark. The 1985s are certainly lighter, without nearly the texture, weight, or concentration of the finest 1982s or 1986s, but at the same time most 1985s are far richer and fuller than the 1976s.

On Bordeaux's right bank, in Pomerol and St.-Emilion, the Merlot was brought in at excellent maturity levels, although many châteaux had a tendency to pick too soon (such as Pétrus and Trotanoy). While the vintage is not another 1982 or 1989, it certainly is a fine year in Pomerol. It is less consistent in St.-Emilion because too many producers harvested their Cabernet before it was physiologically fully mature. Interestingly, many of the Libournais producers compared 1985 stylistically to 1971.

The vintage, which is one of seductive appeal, was priced almost too high when first released. The wines have not appreciated to the extent that many deserve and now look more reasonably priced than at any time in the past.

THE BEST WINES

St.-Estèphe:	Cos d'Estournel, Haut-Marbuzet
Pauillac:	Lafite-Rothschild, Lynch-Bages, Mouton-Rothschild, Pichon-Longueville–Comtesse de Lalande
St.-Julien:	Ducru-Beaucaillou, Gruaud-Larose, Léoville-Barton, Léoville-Las Cases, Talbot
Margaux:	Angludet, Lascombes, Margaux, Palmer, Rausan-Ségla
Graves Red:	Haut-Brion, La Mission-Haut-Brion
Graves White:	Domaine de Chevalier, Haut-Brion, Laville-Haut-Brion
Pomerol:	Certan de May, La Conseillante, l'Eglise-Clinet, l'Evangile, Lafleur, Le Pin, Pétrus
St.-Emilion:	Canon, Cheval Blanc, de Ferrand, Soutard, Le Tertre-Roteboeuf
Barsac/Sauternes:	Yquem

1984—A Quick Study
(10-5-84)

St.-Estèphe *
Pauillac *
St.-Julien *
Margaux *
Médoc/Haut-Médoc Crus Bourgeois *

Graves Red **
Graves White *
Pomerol *
St.-Emilion **
Barsac/Sauternes *

Size: A small- to medium-size crop of primarily Cabernet-based wine.

Important information: The least attractive current vintage for drinking today, the 1984s, because of the failure of the Merlot crop, are essentially Cabernet-based wines that remain well colored, but compact, stern, and forbiddingly backward and tannic.

Maturity status: These wines need to be consumed.

Price: Virtually any 1984 can be had for a song, as most retailers who bought this vintage are still stuck with the wines, even in 1998.

After three abundant vintages, 1981, 1982, and 1983, the climatic conditions during the summer and autumn of 1984 hardly caused euphoria among the Bordelais. First, the vegetative cycle began rapidly, thanks to a magnificently hot, sunny April. However, that was followed by a relatively cool and wet May, which created havoc in the flowering of the quick-to-bud Merlot grape. The result was that much of the 1984 Merlot crop was destroyed long before the summer weather actually arrived. The terrible late spring and early summer conditions made headlines in much of the world's press, which began to paint the vintage as an impending disaster. However, July was dry and hot, and by the end of August some overly enthusiastic producers were talking about the potential for superripe, tiny quantities of Cabernet Sauvignon. There were even several reporters who were calling 1984 similar to the 1961 vintage. Their intentions could only be considered sinister, as 1984 could never be compared to 1961.

Following the relatively decent beginning in September, the period between September 21 and October 4 was one of unexpected weather difficulties climaxed by the first cyclone (named Hortense) ever to hit the area, tearing roofs off buildings and giving the jitters to winemakers. However, after October 4 the weather cleared up and producers began to harvest their Cabernet Sauvignon. Those who waited picked relatively ripe Cabernet, although the Cabernet's skin was somewhat thick and the acid levels were extremely high, particularly by the standards of more recent vintages.

The problem that existed early on with the 1984s and that continues to present difficulties today is that the wines lack an important percentage of Merlot to counterbalance their narrow, compact, high-acid, austere, and tannic character. Consequently there is a lack of fat and charm, but these herbaceous wines are deep in color, as they were made from Cabernet Sauvignon.

Unquestionably the late pickers made the best wines, and most of the more interesting wines have emerged from the Médoc and Graves. They will be longer lived but probably less enjoyable than the wines from the other two difficult vintages of that decade, 1980 and 1987.

In St.-Emilion and Pomerol, the vintage, if not quite an unqualified disaster, is disappointing. Many top properties—Ausone, Canon, Magdelaine, Belair, La Dominique, Couvent-des-Jacobins, and Tertre-Daugay—declassified their entire crop. It was the first vintage since 1968 or 1972 where many of these estates made no wine under their label. Even at Pétrus only 800 cases were made, as opposed to the 4,500 cases produced in both 1985 and 1986.

In 1998 the better 1984s remain relatively narrowly constructed, tightly knit wines still displaying a healthy color but lacking fat, ampleness, and charm. It is unlikely they will ever develop any charm, but there is no doubt that the better-endowed examples will keep for another decade.

THE BEST WINES

St.-Estèphe:	Cos d'Estournel
Pauillac:	Latour, Lynch-Bages, Mouton-Rothschild, Pichon-Longueville–Comtesse de Lalande
St.-Julien:	Gruaud-Larose, Léoville-Las Cases
Margaux:	Margaux

Graves Red:	Domaine de Chevalier, Haut-Brion, La Mission-Haut-Brion
Graves White:	None
Pomerol:	Pétrus, Trotanoy
St.-Emilion:	Figeac
Barsac/Sauternes:	Yquem

1983—A Quick Study
(9-26-83)

St.-Estèphe **	Graves Red ****
Pauillac ***	Graves White ****
St.-Julien ***	Pomerol ***
Margaux *****	St.-Emilion ****
Médoc/Haut-Médoc Crus Bourgeois **	Barsac/Sauternes ****

Size: A large crop, with overall production slightly inferior to 1982, but in the Médoc most properties produced more wine than they did in 1982.

Important information: Bordeaux, as well as all of France, suffered from an atypically tropical heat and humidity attack during the month of August. This caused considerable overripening as well as the advent of rot in certain *terroirs,* particularly in St.-Estèphe, Pauillac, Pomerol, and the sandier plateau sections of St.-Emilion.

Maturity status: At first the vintage was called more classic (or typical) than 1982, with greater aging potential. Fifteen years later the 1983s are far more evolved and, in most cases, fully mature—unlike the 1982s. In fact, this is a vintage that attained full maturity at an accelerated pace.

Price: Prices for the best 1983s remain fair.

The year 1983 was one of the most bizarre growing seasons in recent history. The flowering in June went well for the third straight year, ensuring a large crop. The weather in July was so torrid that it turned out to be the hottest July on record. August was extremely hot, rainy, and humid, and as a result, many vineyards began to have significant problems with mildew and rot. It was essential to spray almost weekly in August 1983 to protect the vineyards. Those properties that did not spray diligently had serious problems with mildew-infected grapes. By the end of August, a dreadful month climatically, many pessimistic producers were apprehensively talking about a disastrous vintage like 1968 or 1965. September brought dry weather, plenty of heat, and no excessive rain. October provided exceptional weather as well, so the grapes harvested late were able to attain maximum ripeness under sunny, dry skies. Not since 1961 had the entire Bordeaux crop, white grapes and red grapes, been harvested in completely dry, fair weather.

The successes that have emerged from 1983 are first and foremost from the appellation of Margaux, which enjoyed its greatest vintage of the decade. In fact, this perennial underachieving appellation produced many top wines, with magnificent efforts from Margaux, Palmer, and Rausan-Ségla (the vintage of resurrection for this famous name), as well as d'Issan and Brane-Cantenac. These wines remain some of the best-kept secrets of the decade.

The other appellations had numerous difficulties, and the wines have not matured as evenly or as gracefully as some prognosticators had suggested. The northern Médocs, particularly the St.-Estèphes, are disappointing. The Pauillacs range from relatively light, overly oaky, roasted wines that are hollow in the middle to some exceptional successes, most notably from Pichon-Longueville–Comtesse de Lalande, Mouton-Rothschild, and Lafite-Rothschild.

The St.-Juliens will not be remembered for their greatness, with the exception of a superb Léoville-Poyferré. In 1983 Léoville-Poyferré is amazingly as good as the other two Léovilles, Léoville-Las Cases and Léoville-Barton. During the eighties there is not another vintage where such a statement could be made. The Cordier siblings, Gruaud-Larose and Talbot, made good wines, but overall 1983 is not a memorable year for St.-Julien.

In Graves, the irregularity continues, with wonderful wines from those Graves châteaux in the Pessac-Léognan area (Haut-Brion, La Mission-Haut-Brion, Haut-Bailly, Domaine de Chevalier, and de Fieuzal) but with disappointments elsewhere.

On the right bank, in Pomerol and St.-Emilion, inconsistency is again the rule of thumb. Most of the hillside vineyards in St.-Emilion performed well, but the vintage was mixed on the plateau and in the sandier soils, although Cheval Blanc made one of its greatest wines of the decade. In Pomerol, it is hard to say who made the best wine, but the house of Jean-Pierre Moueix did not fare well in this vintage. Other top properties, such as La Conseillante, L'Evangile, Lafleur, Certan de May, and Le Pin, all made wines that are not far off the quality of their great 1982s.

THE BEST WINES

St.-Estèphe:	None
Pauillac:	Lafite-Rothschild, Mouton-Rothschild, Pichon-Longueville–Comtesse de Lalande
St.-Julien:	Gruaud-Larose, Léoville-Las Cases, Léoville-Poyferré, Talbot
Margaux:	Angludet, Brane-Cantenac, Cantemerle (southern Médoc), d'Issan, Margaux, Palmer, Prieuré-Lichine, Rausan-Ségla

Médoc/Haut Médoc/
Moulis/Listrac/Crus
       Bourgeois: None
     Graves Red: Domaine de Chevalier, Haut-Bailly, Haut-Brion, La
                           Louvière, La Mission-Haut-Brion
    Graves White: Domaine de Chevalier, Laville-Haut-Brion
        Pomerol: Certan de May, l'Evangile, Lafleur, Pétrus, Le Pin
     St.-Emilion: L'Arrosée, Ausone, Belair, Canon, Cheval Blanc,
                           Figeac, Larmande
 Barsac/Sauternes: Climens, Doisy-Daëne, de Fargues, Guiraud,
                           Lafaurie-Peyraguey, Raymond-Lafon, Rieussec,
                           Yquem

1982—A Quick Study
(9-13-82)

St.-Estèphe *****   Graves Red ***
Pauillac *****   Graves White **
St.-Julien *****   Pomerol *****
Margaux ***   St.-Emilion *****
Médoc/Haut-Médoc Crus Bourgeois ****   Barsac/Sauternes ***

Size: An extremely abundant crop, which at the time was a record year but
    has since been equaled in size by 1988 and surpassed in volume by
    1985, 1986, 1989, and 1990.

Important information: The most concentrated and potentially complex and
    profound wines between 1961 and 1990 were produced in virtually
    every appellation except for Graves and Margaux.

Maturity status: Most Crus Bourgeois should have been drunk by 1995, and
    the lesser wines in St.-Emilion, Pomerol, Graves, and Margaux are fully
    mature. For the bigger-styled Pomerols, St.-Emilions, and the northern
    Médocs—St.-Julien, Pauillac, and St.-Estèphe—the wines are evolving
    at a glacial pace. They have lost much of their baby fat and have gone
    into a more tightly knit, massive, yet much more structured, tannic
    state.

Price: With the exception of 1990, no modern-day Bordeaux vintage since
    1961 has accelerated as much in price and yet continues to appreciate
    in value. Prices are now so frightfully high, consumers who did not
    purchase these wines as futures can only look back with envy at those
    who did buy the 1982s when they were first offered at what now appear
    to be bargain basement prices. Who can remember a great vintage
    being sold at such enticing opening case prices for châteaux like Pichon
    Lalande ($110), Léoville-Las Cases ($160), Ducru-Beaucaillou ($150),
    Pétrus ($600), Cheval Blanc ($550), Margaux ($550), Certan de May

($180), La Lagune ($75), Grand-Puy-Lacoste ($85), Cos d'Estournel ($145), and Canon ($105)? These were the average prices for which the 1982s were sold during the spring, summer, and fall of 1983! Yet potential buyers should be careful, as many fraudulent 1982s have shown up in the marketplace, particularly Pétrus, Lafleur, Le Pin, Cheval Blanc, and the Médoc first-growths.

When I issued my report on the 1982 vintage in the April 1983 *Wine Advocate,* I remember feeling that I had never tasted richer, more concentrated, more promising wines than the 1982s. Fifteen years later, despite some wonderfully successful years such as 1985, 1986, 1989, 1990, 1995, and 1996, 1982 remains the modern-day point of reference for the greatness Bordeaux can achieve.

The finest wines of the vintage have emerged from the northern Médoc appellations of St.-Julien, Pauillac, and St.-Estèphe, as well as from Pomerol and St.-Emilion. They have hardly changed since their early days in barrel, and while displaying a degree of richness, opulence, and intensity I have rarely seen, as they approach their sixteenth birthdays, the vintage's top wines remain relatively unevolved and backward.

The wines from other appellations have matured much more quickly, particularly those from Graves and Margaux and the lighter, lesser wines from Pomerol, St.-Emilion, and the Crus Bourgeois.

Today, no one could intelligently deny the greatness of the 1982 vintage. However, in 1983 this vintage was received among America's wine press with a great deal of skepticism. There was no shortage of outcries about these wines' lack of acidity and "California" style after the vintage's conception. It was suggested by some writers that 1981 and 1979 were "finer vintages" and that the 1982s, "fully mature," should have been "consumed by 1990." Curiously, these writers fail to include specific tasting notes. Of course, wine tasting is subjective, but such statements are nonsense, and it is impossible to justify such criticism of this vintage, particularly in view of how well the top 1982s taste in 1998 and how rich as well as slowly the first-growths, super-seconds, and great wines of the northern Médoc, Pomerol, and St.-Emilion are evolving. Even in Bordeaux the 1982s are now placed on a pedestal and spoken of in the same terms as 1961, 1949, 1945, and 1929. Moreover, the marketplace and auction rooms, perhaps the only true measure of a vintage's value, continue to push prices for the top 1982s to stratospheric levels.

The reason so many 1982s were remarkable was the outstanding weather conditions. The flowering occurred in hot, sunny, dry, ideal June weather that served to ensure a large crop. July was extremely hot and August slightly cooler than normal. By the beginning of September the Bordeaux producers were expecting a large crop of excellent quality. However, a September burst of intense heat that lasted for nearly 3 weeks sent the grape sugars soaring, and what was considered originally to be a very good to excellent vintage was transformed into a great vintage for every appellation except Margaux and the Graves, whose very thin, light, gravelly soils suffered during the torrid September heat. For the first time many producers had to vinify their wines under unusually hot conditions. Many lessons were learned that were employed again in subsequent hot vinification years such as 1985, 1989, and 1990. Rumors of disasters from overheated or stuck fermentations proved to be without validity, as were reports that rain showers near the end of the harvest caught some properties with Cabernet Sauvignon still on the vine.

When analyzed, the 1982s are the most concentrated, high-extract wines since 1961, with acid levels that, while low, are no lower than in years of exceptional ripeness such as 1949, 1953, 1959, 1961, and, surprisingly, 1975. Though some skeptics pointed to the low acidity, many of those same skeptics fell in love with the 1985s, 1989s, and 1990s, all Bordeaux vintages that produced wines with significantly lower acids and higher pH's than the 1982s. Tannin levels were extremely high, but subsequent vintages, particularly 1986, 1988, 1989, and 1990, produced wines with even higher tannin levels than the 1982s.

Recent tastings of the 1982s continue to suggest that the top wines of the northern Médoc need another 5–10 years of cellaring. Most of the best wines seem largely unevolved since their early days in cask. They have fully recovered from the bottling and display the extraordinary expansive, rich, glycerin- and extract-laden palates that should serve these wines well over the next 10–20 years. If the 1982 vintage remains sensational for the majority of St.-Emilions, Pomerols, St.-Juliens, Pauillacs, and St.-Estèphes, the weakness of the vintage becomes increasingly more apparent with the Margaux and Graves wines. Only Château Margaux seems to have survived the problems of overproduction, loosely knit, flabby Cabernet Sauvignon wines from which so many other Margaux properties suffered. The same can be said for the Graves, which are light and disjointed when compared with the lovely 1983s Graves produced. Only La Mission-Haut-Brion and Haut-Brion produced better 1982s than 1983s.

On the negative side are the prices one must now pay for a top wine from the 1982 vintage. Is this a reason why the vintage still receives cheap shots from a handful of American writers? Those who bought them as futures made the wine buys of the century. For today's generation of wine enthusiasts, 1982 is what 1945, 1947, and 1949 were for an earlier generation of wine lovers.

Last, the sweet wines of Barsac and Sauternes in 1982, while maligned originally for their lack of botrytis and richness, are not that bad. In fact, Yquem and the Cuvée Madame of Château Suduiraut are two remarkably powerful, rich wines that can stand up to the best of the 1983s, 1986s, and 1988s.

THE BEST WINES

St.-Estèphe:	Calon-Ségur, Cos d'Estournel, Haut-Marbuzet, Montrose
Pauillac:	Les Forts de Latour, Grand-Puy-Lacoste, Haut-Batailley, Lafite-Rothschild, Latour, Lynch-Bages, Mouton-Rothschild, Pichon-Longueville Baron, Pichon-Longeville–Comtesse de Lalande
St.-Julien:	Beychevelle, Branaire-Ducru, Ducru-Beaucaillou, Gruaud-Larose, Léoville-Barton, Léoville-Las Cases, Léoville-Poyferré, Talbot
Margaux:	Margaux, La Lagune (southern Médoc)
Médoc/Haut Médoc/ Moulis/Listrac/Crus Bourgeois:	Tour Haut-Caussan, Maucaillou, Potensac, Poujeaux, Sociando-Mallet, La Tour St.-Bonnet
Graves Red:	Haut-Brion, La Mission-Haut-Brion, La Tour-Haut-Brion
Graves White:	None
Pomerol:	Bon Pasteur, Certan de May, La Conseillante, l'Enclos, l'Evangile, Le Gay, Lafleur, Latour à Pomerol, Petit-Village, Pétrus, Le Pin, Trotanoy, Vieux-Château-Certan
St.-Emilion:	L'Arrosée, Ausone, Canon, Cheval Blanc, La Dominique, Figeac, Pavie
Barsac/Sauternes:	Raymond-Lafon, Suduiraut-Cuvée Madame, Yquem

1981—A Quick Study
(9-28-81)

St.-Estèphe **	Graves Red **
Pauillac ***	Graves White **
St.-Julien ***	Pomerol ***
Margaux **	St.-Emilion **
Médoc/Haut-Médoc Crus Bourgeois *	Barsac/Sauternes *

Size: A moderately large crop that in retrospect now looks modest.

Important information: The first vintage in a succession of hot, dry years that would continue nearly uninterrupted through 1990. The year 1981 would have been a top vintage had the rain not fallen immediately prior to the harvest.

Maturity status: Most 1981s are close to full maturity, yet the best examples are capable of lasting for another 5–10 years.

Price: A largely ignored and overlooked vintage, 1981 remains a reasonably good value.

This vintage has been labeled more "classic" than either 1983 or 1982. What classic means to those who call 1981 a classic vintage is that this year is a typically good Bordeaux vintage of medium-weight, well-balanced, graceful wines. Despite a dozen or so excellent wines, 1981 is in reality only a good vintage, surpassed in quality by both 1982 and 1983 and also by 1978 and 1979.

The year 1981 could have been an outstanding vintage had it not been for the heavy rains that fell just as the harvest was about to start. There was a dilution of the intensity of flavor in the grapes as heavy rains drenched the vineyards between October 1 and 5 and again between October 9 and 15. Until then the summer had been perfect. The flowering occurred under excellent conditions; July was cool, but August and September were hot and dry. One can only speculate that had it not rained, 1981 might well have also turned out to be one of the greatest vintages in the post–World War II era.

The year 1981 did produce a large crop of generally well-colored wines of medium weight and moderate tannin. The dry white wines have turned out well but should have been consumed by now. Both Barsacs and Sauternes suffered as a result of the rains, and no truly compelling wines have emerged from these appellations.

There are a number of successful wines in 1981, particularly from such appellations as Pomerol, St.-Julien, and Pauillac. Seventeen years after the vintage, the 1981s have reached their plateau of maturity, and only the best will keep for another 5–7 years. The wines' shortcomings are their lack of the richness, flesh, and intensity, qualities more recent vintages have possessed. Most red wine producers had to chaptalize significantly because the Cabernets were harvested under 11% natural alcohol and the Merlot under 12%, no doubt because of the rain.

THE BEST WINES

St.-Estèphe:	None
Pauillac:	Lafite-Rothschild, Latour, Pichon-Longueville–Comtesse de Lalande
St.-Julien:	Ducru-Beaucaillou, Gruaud-Larose, Léoville-Las Cases, St.-Pierre
Margaux:	Giscours, Margaux
Médoc/Haut-Médoc	
Crus Bourgeois:	None

Graves Red: La Mission-Haut-Brion
Graves White: None
Pomerol: Certan de May, La Conseillante, Pétrus, Le Pin,
                Vieux-Château-Certan
St.-Emilion: Cheval Blanc
Barsac/Sauternes: Climens, de Fargues, Yquem

1980—A Quick Study
(10-14-80)

St.-Estèphe*   Graves Red**
Pauillac**   Graves White*
St.-Julien**   Pomerol**
Margaux**   St.-Emilion*
Médoc/Haut-Médoc Crus Bourgeois*   Barsac/Sauternes****

Size: A moderately sized crop was harvested.

Important information: Nothing very noteworthy can be said about this mediocre vintage.

Maturity status: With the exception of Château Margaux and Pétrus, virtually
every 1980 should have been consumed.

Price: Low.

For a decade that became known as the golden age of Bordeaux, or the decade of the century, the eighties certainly did not begin in an auspicious fashion. The summer of 1980 was cool and wet, the flowering was unexciting because of a disappointing June, and by early September the producers were looking at a return of the two most dreadful vintages of the last 30 years, 1963 and 1968. However, modern-day antirot sprays did a great deal to protect the grapes from the dreaded *pourriture.* For that reason, the growers were able to delay their harvest until the weather began to improve at the end of September. The weather in early October was favorable until rains began in the middle of the month, just as many producers began to harvest. The results have been light, diluted, frequently disappointing wines that have an unmistakable vegetal and herbaceous taste and are often marred by excessive acidity as well as tannin. Those producers who made a strict selection and picked exceptionally late, such as the Mentzelopoulos family at Château Margaux (the wine of the vintage), made softer, rounder, more interesting wines that began to drink well in the late eighties and should continue to drink well until the turn of the century. However, the number of properties that could be said to have made wines of good quality are few.

As always in wet, cool years, those vineyards planted on lighter, gravelly, well-drained soils, such as some of the Margaux and Graves properties, tend to get better maturity and ripeness. Not surprisingly, the top successes generally come from these areas, although several Pauillacs, because of a very strict selection, also have turned out well.

As disappointing as the 1980 vintage was for the red wine producers, it was an excellent year for the producers of Barsac and Sauternes. The ripening and harvesting continued into late November, generally under ideal conditions. This permitted some rich, intense, high-class Barsac and Sauternes to be produced. Unfortunately, their commercial viability suffered from the reputation of the red wine vintage. Anyone who comes across a bottle of 1980 Climens, Yquem, or Raymond-Lafon will immediately realize that this is an astonishingly good year.

THE BEST WINES

St.-Estèphe:	None
Pauillac:	Latour, Pichon-Longueville–Comtesse de Lalande
St.-Julien:	Talbot
Margaux:	Margaux
Médoc/Haut-Médoc/ Moulis/Listrac/Crus Bourgeois:	None
Graves Red:	Domaine de Chevalier, La Mission-Haut-Brion
Graves White:	None
Pomerol:	Certan de May, Pétrus
St.-Emilion:	Cheval Blanc
Barsac/Sauternes:	Climens, de Fargues, Raymond-Lafon, Yquem

1979—A Quick Study
(10-3-79)

St.-Estèphe **   Graves Red ****
Pauillac ***   Graves White **
St.-Julien ***   Pomerol ***
Margaux ****   St.-Emilion **
Médoc/Haut-Médoc Crus Bourgeois **   Barsac/Sauternes *

Size: A huge crop that established a record at that time.

Important information: In the last 2 decades this is one of the only cool years that turned out to be a reasonably good vintage.

Maturity status: Contrary to earlier reports, the 1979s have matured very slowly, largely because the wines have relatively hard tannins and good acidity, two characteristics that most of the top vintages during the decade of the eighties have not possessed.

Price: Because of the lack of demand, and the vintage's average to good reputation, prices remain low except for a handful of the limited-production, glamour wines of Pomerol.

The year 1979 has become the forgotten vintage in Bordeaux. A record-setting crop that produced relatively healthy, medium-bodied wines that displayed firm tannins and good acidity closed out the decade of the seventies. Over the next decade this vintage was rarely mentioned in the wine press. No doubt most of the wines were consumed long before they reached their respective apogees. Considered inferior to 1978 when conceived, the 1979 vintage will prove superior—at least in terms of aging potential. Yet aging potential alone is hardly sufficient to evaluate a vintage, and many 1979s remain relatively skinny, malnourished, lean, compact wines that naive commentators have called classic rather than thin.

Despite the inconsistency from appellation to appellation, a number of strikingly good, surprisingly flavorful, rich wines have emerged from appellations such as Margaux, Graves, and Pomerol.

With few exceptions, there is no hurry to drink the top 1979s, since their relatively high acid levels (compared with more recent hot year vintages), good tannin levels, and sturdy framework should ensure that the top 1979s age well for at least another 10–15 years.

This was not a good vintage for the dry white wines of Graves or sweet white wines of Barsac and Sauternes. The dry whites did not achieve full maturity, and there was never enough botrytis for the Barsac and Sauternes to give the wines the honeyed complexity that is fundamental to their success.

Prices for 1979s, where they can still be found, are the lowest of any good recent Bordeaux vintage, reflecting the general lack of excitement for most 1979s.

THE BEST WINES

St.-Estèphe:	Cos d'Estournel
Pauillac:	Lafite-Rothschild, Latour, Pichon-Longueville–Comtesse de Lalande
St.-Julien:	Gruaud-Larose, Léoville-Las Cases
Margaux:	Giscours, Margaux, Palmer, du Tertre
Graves Red:	Les Carmes Haut-Brion, Domaine de Chevalier, Haut-Bailly, Haut-Brion, La Mission-Haut-Brion
Pomerol:	Certan de May, l'Enclos, l'Evangile, Lafleur, Pétrus
St.-Emilion:	Ausone
Barsac/Sauternes:	None

1978—A Quick Study
(10-7-78)

St.-Estèphe**
Pauillac***
St.-Julien***

Graves Red****
Graves White****
Pomerol**

Margaux *** 　　　　　　　　　　　　　　　St.-Emilion ***

Médoc/Haut-Médoc Crus Bourgeois ** 　　　　Barsac/Sauternes **

Size: A moderately sized crop was harvested.

Important information: The year Harry Waugh, England's gentlemanly wine commentator, dubbed "the miracle year."

Maturity status: Most wines are fully mature.

Price: Overpriced for years, the 1978s are fairly priced 20 years after the vintage.

The year 1978 turned out to be an outstanding vintage for the red wines of Graves and a good vintage for the red wines from the Médoc, Pomerol, and St.-Emilion. There was a lack of botrytis for the sweet white wines of Barsac and Sauternes, and the results were monolithic, straightforward wines of no great character. The dry white Graves, much like the red wines of that appellation, turned out exceedingly well.

The weather profile for 1978 was hardly encouraging. The spring was cold and wet, and poor weather continued to plague the region through June, July, and early August, causing many growers to begin thinking of such dreadful years as 1963, 1965, 1968, and 1977. However, in mid-August a huge anticyclone, high-pressure system settled over southwestern France and northern Spain, and for the next 9 weeks the weather was sunny, hot, and dry, except for an occasional light rain shower that had negligible effects.

Because the grapes were so behind in their maturation (contrast that scenario with the more recent advanced maturity years such as 1989 and 1990), the harvest began extremely late, on October 7. It continued under excellent weather conditions, which seemed, as Harry Waugh put it, miraculous in view of the miserable weather throughout much of the spring and summer.

The general view of this vintage is that it is a very good to excellent year. The two best appellations are Graves and Margaux, which have the lighter, better-drained soils that support cooler weather years. In fact, Graves (except for the disappointing Pape-Clément) probably enjoyed its greatest vintage after 1961. The wines, which at first appeared intensely fruity, deeply colored, moderately tannic, and medium bodied, have aged much faster than the higher-acid, more firmly tannic 1979s, which were the product of an even cooler, drier year. Most 1978s had reached full maturity 12 years after the vintage, and some commentators were expressing their disappointment that the wines were not better than they had believed.

The problem is that, much like in 1979, 1981, and 1988, there is a shortage of truly superstar wines. There are a number of good wines, but the lack of excitement in the majority of wines has tempered the postvintage enthusiasm. Moreover, the lesser wines in 1978 have an annoyingly vegetal, herbaceous taste because those vineyards not planted on the best soils never fully ripened despite the impressively hot, dry *fin de saison*. Another important consideration is that the selection process, so much a fundamental principle in the decade of the eighties, was employed less during the seventies, as many properties simply bottled everything under the grand vin label. Many proprietors today feel that 1978 could have lived up to its early promise had a stricter selection been in effect when the wines were made.

This was a very difficult vintage for properties in the Barsac/Sauternes region because very little botrytis formed owing to the hot, dry autumn. The wines, much like the 1979s, are chunky and full of glycerin and sugar, but they lack grip, focus, and complexity.

THE BEST WINES

St.-Estèphe:	None
Pauillac:	Les Forts de Latour, Grand-Puy-Lacoste, Latour, Pichon-Longueville–Comtesse de Lalande
St.-Julien:	Ducru-Beaucaillou, Gruaud-Larose, Léoville-Las Cases, Talbot
Margaux:	Giscours, La Lagune (southern Médoc), Margaux, Palmer, Prieuré-Lichine, du Tertre
Médoc/Haut-Médoc/ Moulis/Listrac/Crus Bourgeois:	None
Graves Red:	Les Carmes Haut-Brion, Domaine de Chevalier, Haut-Bailly, Haut-Brion, La Mission-Haut-Brion, La Tour-Haut-Brion
Graves White:	Domaine de Chevalier, Haut-Brion, Laville-Haut-Brion
Pomerol:	Lafleur
St.-Emilion:	L'Arrosée, Cheval Blanc
Barsac/Sauternes:	None

1977—A Quick Study
(10-3-77)

St.-Estèphe 0	Graves Red*
Pauillac 0	Graves White*
St.-Julien 0	Pomerol 0
Margaux 0	St.-Emilion 0
Médoc/Haut-Médoc Crus Bourgeois 0	Barsac/Sauternes*

Size: A small crop was produced.

Important information: A dreadful vintage, clearly the worst since 1972; it remains, in a pejorative sense, unequaled since.

Maturity status: The wines, even the handful that were drinkable, should have
        been consumed by the mid-eighties.
Price: Despite distress sale prices, there are no values to be found.

    This is the worst vintage for Bordeaux during the decade of the seventies.
Even the 2 mediocre years of the eighties, 1980 and 1984, are far superior to
1977. Much of the Merlot crop was devastated by a late spring frost. The
summer was cold and wet. When warm, dry weather finally arrived just prior
to the harvest, there was just too little time left to save the vintage. The
harvest resulted in grapes that were both analytically and physiologically
immature and far from ripe.

    The wines, which were relatively acidic and overtly herbaceous to the
point of being vegetal, should have been consumed years ago. Some of the
more successful wines included a decent Figeac, Giscours, Gruaud-Larose,
Pichon Lalande, Latour, and the three Graves estates of Haut-Brion, La
Mission-Haut-Brion, and Domaine de Chevalier. However, I have never been
able to recommend any of these wines. They have no value from either a
monetary or a pleasure standpoint.

1976—A Quick Study
(9-13-76)

St.-Estèphe ***	Graves Red *
Pauillac ***	Graves White ***
St.-Julien ***	Pomerol ***
Margaux **	St.-Emilion ***
Médoc/Haut-Médoc Crus Bourgeois *	Barsac/Sauternes ****

Size: A huge crop, the second largest of the decade, was harvested.
Important information: This hot, drought-like vintage could have proved to
        be the vintage of the decade had it not been for pre-harvest rains.
Maturity status: The 1976s tasted fully mature and delicious when released
        in 1979. Yet the best examples continue to offer delightful, sometimes
        delicious, drinking. It is one of a handful of vintages where the wines
        have never closed up and been unappealing. Yet virtually every 1976
        (with the exception of Ausone and Lafite Rothschild) should be con-
        sumed prior to 2000.
Price: The 1976s have always been reasonably priced because they have
        never received accolades from the wine pundits.

    A very highly publicized vintage, 1976 has never quite lived up to its
reputation. All the ingredients were present for a superb vintage. The harvest
date of September 13 was the earliest since 1945. The weather during
the summer had been torridly hot, with the average temperatures for the
months of June through September exceeded only by the hot summers of

1949 and 1947. However, with many vignerons predicting a "vintage of the century," very heavy rains fell between September 11 and 15, bloating the grapes.

The crop that was harvested was large, the grapes were ripe, and while the wines had good tannin levels, the acidity levels were low and their pH's dangerously high. The top wines of 1976 have offered wonderfully soft, supple, deliciously fruity drinking since they were released in 1979. I had fully expected that these wines would have to be consumed before the end of the eighties. However, the top 1976s appear to have stayed at their peak of maturity without fading or losing their fruit. I wish I had bought more of this vintage given how delicious the best wines have been over such an extended period of time. They will not make "old bones," and one must be very careful with the weaker 1976s, which have lacked intensity and depth from the beginning. These wines were extremely fragile and have increasingly taken on a brown cast to their color as well as losing their fruit. Nevertheless, the top wines continue to offer delicious drinking and persuasive evidence that even in a relatively diluted, extremely soft-styled vintage, with dangerously low acid levels, Bordeaux wines, where well stored, can last 15 or more years.

The 1976 vintage was at its strongest in the northern Médoc appellations of St.-Julien, Pauillac, and St.-Estèphe, weakest in Graves and Margaux, and mixed in the Libournais appellations of Pomerol and St.-Emilion. The wine of the vintage is Ausone.

For those who admire decadently rich, honeyed, sweet wines, this is one of the two best vintages of the seventies, given the abundant quantities of botrytis that formed in the vineyards and the lavish richness and opulent style of the wines of Barsac/Sauternes.

THE BEST WINES

St.-Estèphe:	Cos d'Estournel, Montrose
Pauillac:	Haut-Bages-Libéral, Lafite-Rothschild, Pichon-Longueville–Comtesse de Lalande
St.-Julien:	Beychevelle, Branaire-Ducru, Ducru-Beaucaillou, Léoville-Las Cases, Talbot
Margaux:	Giscours, La Lagune (southern Médoc)
Médoc/Haut Médoc/ Moulis/Listrac/Crus Bourgeois:	Sociando-Mallet
Graves Red:	Haut-Brion
Graves White:	Domaine de Chevalier, Laville-Haut-Brion
Pomerol:	Pétrus
St.-Emilion:	Ausone, Cheval Blanc, Figeac
Barsac/Sauternes:	Climens, Coutet, de Fargues, Guiraud, Rieussec, Suduiraut, Yquem

1975—A Quick Study
(9-22-75)

St.-Estèphe **	Graves Red **
Pauillac ***	Graves White ***
St.-Julien ***	Pomerol *****
Margaux **	St.-Emilion ***
Médoc/Haut-Médoc Crus Bourgeois ***	Barsac/Sauternes ****

Size: After the abundant vintages of 1973 and 1974, 1975 was a moderately sized crop.

Important information: After 3 consecutive poor to mediocre years, the Bordelais were ready to praise to the heavens the 1975 vintage.

Maturity status: The slowest-evolving vintage in the last 30 years.

Price: Trade and consumer uneasiness concerning the falling reputation of this vintage, as well as the style of even the top wines (which remain hard, closed, and nearly impenetrable), make this an attractively priced year for those with the knowledge to select the gems and the patience to wait for them to mature.

Is this the year of the great deception or the year where some irrefutably classic wines were produced? Along with 1964 and 1983, this is perhaps the most tricky vintage with which to come to grips. There are some undeniably great wines in the 1975 vintage, but the overall quality level is distressingly uneven, and the number of failures is too numerous to ignore.

Because of the three previous large crops and the international financial crisis brought on by high oil prices, the producers, knowing that their 1972, 1973, and 1974 vintages were already backed up in the marketplace, pruned their vineyards to guard against a large crop. The weather cooperated; July, August, and September were all hot months. However, in August and September several large thunderstorms dumped enormous quantities of rain on the area. It was localized, and most of it did little damage except to frazzle the nerves of winemakers. However, several hailstorms did ravage the central Médoc communes, particularly Moulis, Lamarque, and some isolated hailstorms damaged the southern Léognan-Pessac-Arcins region.

The harvest began during the third week of September and continued under generally good weather conditions through mid-October. Immediately after the harvest, the producers were talking of a top-notch vintage, perhaps the best since 1961. So what happened?

Looking back after having had numerous opportunities to taste and discuss the style of this vintage with many proprietors and winemakers, I am convinced that the majority of growers should have harvested their Cabernet

Sauvignon later. Many feel it was picked too soon, and the fact that at that time many were not totally destemming only exacerbated the relatively hard, astringent tannins in the 1975s.

This is one of the first vintages I tasted (although on a much more limited basis) from cask, visiting Bordeaux as a tourist rather than a professional. In 1975 many of the young wines exhibited great color, intensely ripe, fragrant noses, and immense potential. Other wines appeared to have an excess of tannin. The wines immediately closed up 2–3 years after bottling and in most cases still remain stubbornly hard and backward. There are a number of badly made, excessively tannic wines where the fruit has already dried out and the color has become brown. Many of them were aged in old oak barrels (new oak was not nearly as prevalent as it is now), and the sanitary conditions in many cellars were less than ideal. However, even allowing for these variations, I have always been struck by the tremendous difference in the quality of wines in this vintage. To this day the wide swings in quality remain far greater than in any other recent year. For example, how could La Mission-Haut-Brion, Pétrus, L'Evangile, and Lafleur produce such profoundly great wines yet many of their neighbors fail completely? This remains one of the vintage's mysteries.

This is a vintage for true Bordeaux connoisseurs who have the patience to wait the wines out. The top examples, which usually come from Pomerol, St.-Julien, and Pauillac (the extraordinary success of La Mission-Haut-Brion and La Tour-Haut-Brion and, to a lesser extent, Haut-Brion is an exception to the sad level of quality in Graves), are wines that have still not reached their apogees. Could the great 1975s turn out to resemble wines from a vintage such as 1928, which took 30-plus years to reach full maturity? The great successes of this vintage are capable of lasting and lasting because they have the richness and concentration of ripe fruit to balance out their tannins. However, many wines are too dry, too astringent, or too tannic to develop gracefully.

I purchased this vintage as futures, and I remember thinking I secured great deals on the first-growths at $350 a case. But I have invested in 23 years of patience, and the wait for the top wines will be at least another 10 years. This is the vintage of delayed gratification.

THE BEST WINES

St.-Estèphe:	Haut-Marbuzet, Meyney, Montrose
Pauillac:	Lafite-Rothschild, Latour, Mouton-Rothschild, Pichon-Longueville–Comtesse de Lalande
St.-Julien:	Branaire-Ducru, Gloria, Gruaud-Larose, Léoville-Barton, Léoville-Las Cases
Margaux:	Giscours, Palmer

Médoc/Haut-Médoc/	
Moulis/Listrac/Crus	
Bourgeois:	Greysac, Sociando-Mallet, La Tour St.-Bonnet
Graves Red:	Haut-Brion, La Mission-Haut-Brion, Pape-Clément, La Tour-Haut-Brion
Pomerol:	l'Eglise-Clinet, l'Enclos, l'Evangile, La Fleur Pétrus, Le Gay, Lafleur, Nenin, Pétrus, Trotanoy, Vieux-Château-Certan
St.-Emilion:	Cheval Blanc, Figeac, Magdelaine, Soutard
Barsac/Sauternes:	Climens, Coutet, de Fargues, Raymond-Lafon, Rieussec, Yquem

1974—A Quick Study
(9-20-74)

St.-Estèphe *   Graves Red **
Pauillac *   Graves White *
St.-Julien *   Pomerol *
Margaux *   St.-Emilion *
Médoc/Haut-Médoc Crus Bourgeois *   Barsac/Sauternes *

Size: An enormous crop was harvested.

Important information: Should you still have stocks of the 1974s, it is best to consume them over the next several years or donate them.

Maturity status: A handful of the top wines of the vintage are still alive and well, but aging them any further will prove fruitless.

Price: These wines were always inexpensive, and I can never imagine them fetching a decent price unless you find someone in need of this year to celebrate a birthday.

As a result of a good flowering and a dry, sunny May and June, the crop size was large in 1974. The weather from mid-August through October was cold, windy, and rainy. Despite the persistent soggy conditions, the appellation of choice in 1974 turned out to be Graves. While most 1974s remain hard, tannic, hollow wines lacking ripeness, flesh, and character, a number of the Graves estates did produce surprisingly spicy, interesting wines. Though somewhat compact and attenuated, they are still enjoyable to drink 24 years after the vintage. The two stars are La Mission-Haut-Brion and Domaine de Chevalier, followed by Latour in Pauillac and Trotanoy in Pomerol. Should you have remaining stocks of these wines in your cellar, it would be foolish to push your luck. In spite of their well-preserved status, my instincts suggest drinking them soon.

The vintage was equally bad in the Barsac/Sauternes region. I have never seen a bottle to taste.

It is debatable as to which was the worst vintage during the decade of the seventies—1972, 1974, or 1977.

1973—A Quick Study
(9-20-73)

St.-Estèphe**	Graves Red*
Pauillac*	Graves White**
St.-Julien**	Pomerol**
Margaux*	St.-Emilion*
Médoc/Haut-Médoc Crus Bourgeois*	Barsac/Sauternes*

Size: Enormous; one of the largest crops of the seventies.

Important information: A sadly rain-bloated, swollen crop of grapes in poor to mediocre condition was harvested.

Maturity status: The odds are stacked against finding a 1973 that is still in good condition, at least from a regular-size bottle.

Price: Distress sale prices, even for those born in this year.

In the mid-seventies the best 1973s had some value as agreeably light, round, soft, somewhat diluted yet pleasant Bordeaux wines. With the exception of Domaine de Chevalier, Pétrus, and the great sweet classic, Yquem, all of the 1973s have faded into oblivion.

So often the Bordelais are on the verge of a top-notch vintage when the rains arrive. The rains that came during the harvest bloated what would have been a healthy, enormous grape crop. Modern-day sprays and techniques such as *saigner* were inadequately utilized in the early seventies, and the result in 1973 was a group of wines that lacked color, extract, acidity, and backbone. The wines were totally drinkable when released in 1976. By the beginning of the eighties, they were in complete decline, save for Pétrus.

THE BEST WINES

St.-Estèphe:	De Pez
Pauillac:	Latour
St.-Julien:	Ducru-Beaucaillou
Margaux:	None
Médoc/Haut-Médoc/ Moulis/Listrac/Crus Bourgeois:	None
Graves Red:	Domaine de Chevalier, La Tour-Haut-Brion
Graves White:	None
Pomerol:	Pétrus
St.-Emilion:	None
Barsac/Sauternes:	Yquem

1972—A Quick Study
(10-7-72)

St.-Estèphe 0

Pauillac 0

St.-Julien 0

Margaux *

Médoc/Haut-Médoc Crus Bourgeois 0

Graves Red *

Graves White 0

Pomerol 0

St.-Emilion *

Barsac/Sauternes 0

Size: A moderately sized crop was harvested.

Important information: Rivals 1977 as the worst vintage of the decade.

Maturity status: Most wines have long been over the hill.

Price: Extremely low.

The weather pattern of 1972 was one of unusually cool, cloudy summer months with an abnormally rainy month of August. While September brought dry, warm weather, it was too late to save the crop. The 1972 wines turned out to be the worst of the decade—acidic, green, raw, and vegetal tasting. The high acidity did manage to keep many of them alive for 10–15 years, but their deficiencies in fruit, charm, and flavor concentration were far too great even for age to overcome.

As in any poor vintage, some châteaux managed to produce decent wines, with the well-drained soils of Margaux and Graves turning out slightly better wines than elsewhere.

There are no longer any wines from 1972 that would be of any interest to consumers.

THE BEST WINES *

St.-Estèphe:	None
Pauillac:	Latour
St.-Julien:	Branaire-Ducru, Léoville-Las Cases
Margaux:	Giscours, Rausan-Ségla
Médoc/Haut-Médoc/ Moulis/Listrac/Crus Bourgeois:	None
Graves Red:	La Mission-Haut-Brion, La Tour-Haut-Brion
Graves White:	None
Pomerol:	Trotanoy
St.-Emilion:	Cheval Blanc, Figeac
Barsac/Sauternes:	Climens

* This list is for informational purposes only, as I suspect all of the above wines, with the possible exception of Pétrus, are in serious decline unless found in larger-format bottlings that have been perfectly stored.

1971—A Quick Study
(9-25-71)

St.-Estèphe **   Graves Red ***
Pauillac ***   Graves White **
St.-Julien ***   Pomerol ****
Margaux ***   St.-Emilion ***
Médoc/Haut-Médoc Crus Bourgeois **   Barsac/Sauternes ****

Size: Small to moderate crop size.

Important information: A good to very good, stylish vintage, with the strongest efforts emerging from Pomerol and the sweet wines of Barsac/Sauternes.

Maturity status: Every 1971 has been fully mature for nearly a decade, with only the best cuvées capable of lasting another decade.

Price: The small crop size kept prices high, but most 1971s, compared with other good vintages of the last 30 years, are slightly undervalued.

Unlike 1970, 1971 was a small vintage because of a poor flowering in June that caused a significant reduction in the Merlot crop. By the end of the harvest the crop size was a good 40% less than the huge crop of 1970.

Early reports of the vintage have proven to be overly enthusiastic. Some experts (particularly Bordeaux's Peter Sichel), relying on the small production yields when compared with those of 1970, even claimed that the vintage was better than 1970. This has proven to be totally false. Certainly the 1971s were forward and delicious, as were the 1970s when first released, but unlike the 1970s, the 1971s lacked the great depth of color, concentration, and tannic backbone. The vintage was mixed in the Médoc, but it was a fine year for Pomerol, St.-Emilion, and Graves.

Buying 1971s now could prove dangerous unless the wines have been exceptionally well stored. Twenty-five years after the vintage there are a handful of wines that have just reached full maturity—Pétrus, Latour, Trotanoy, La Mission-Haut-Brion. Well-stored examples of these wines will continue to drink well for at least another 10–15 years. Elsewhere, storage is everything. This could be a vintage at which to take a serious look provided one can find reasonably priced, well-preserved bottles.

The sweet wines of Barsac and Sauternes were successful and are in full maturity. The best of them have at least 1–2 decades of aging potential and will certainly outlive all of the red wines produced in 1971.

THE BEST WINES

St.-Estèphe: Montrose
Pauillac: Latour, Mouton-Rothschild
St.-Julien: Beychevelle, Gloria, Gruaud-Larose, Talbot

Margaux: Palmer
Médoc/Haut-Médoc/
Moulis/Listrac/Crus
Bourgeois: None
Graves Red: Haut-Brion, La Mission-Haut-Brion, La
Tour-Haut-Brion
Graves White: None
Pomerol: Petit-Village, Pétrus, Trotanoy
St.-Emilion: Cheval Blanc, La Dominique, Magdelaine
Barsac/Sauternes: Climens, Coutet, de Fargues, Yquem

1970—A Quick Study
(9-27-70)

St.-Estèphe ***
Pauillac ***
St.-Julien ***
Margaux ***
Médoc/Haut-Médoc Crus Bourgeois ***

Graves Red ****
Graves White ***
Pomerol ****
St.-Emilion ***
Barsac/Sauternes ***

Size: An enormous crop that was a record setter at the time.

Important information: The first modern-day abundant crop that combined high quality with large quantity.

Maturity status: Initially, the 1970s were called precocious and early maturing. Most of the big 1970s have aged very slowly and are now in full maturity, with only a handful of exceptions. The smaller wines, Crus Bourgeois, and lighter-weight Pomerols and St.-Emilions should have been drunk by 1980.

Price: Expensive, no doubt because this is the most popular vintage between 1961 and 1982.

Between the two great vintages 1961 and 1982, 1970 has proved to be the best year, producing wines that were attractively rich and full of charm and complexity. They have aged more gracefully than many of the austere 1966s and seem fuller, richer, more evenly balanced, and more consistent than the hard, tannic, large-framed but often hollow and tough 1975s. The 1970 proved to be the first modern-day vintage that combined high production with good quality. Moreover, it was a uniform and consistent vintage throughout Bordeaux, with every appellation able to claim its share of top-quality wines.

The weather conditions during the summer and early fall were perfect. There was no hail, no weeks of drenching downpours, no frost, and no spirit-crushing inundation at harvest-time. It was one of those rare vintages where everything went well, and the Bordelais harvested one of the largest and healthiest crops they had ever seen.

The 1970 was the first vintage that I tasted out of cask, visiting a number of châteaux with my wife as tourists on my way to the cheap beaches of Spain and north Africa during summer vacations in 1971 and 1972. Even from their early days I remember the wines exhibiting dark color, an intense richness of fruit, fragrant, ripe perfume, full body, and high tannin. Yet when compared with the finest vintages of the eighties and nineties, 1970 seems to suffer. Undoubtedly the number of top wines from vintages such as 1982, 1985, 1986, 1988, 1989, 1990, 1994, 1995, and 1996 exceed those produced in 1970.

As for the sweet wines, they have had to take a backseat to the 1971s because there was less botrytis. Although the wines are impressively big and full, they lack the complexity, delicacy, and finesse of the best 1971s.

In conclusion, 1970 will no doubt continue to sell at high prices for decades to come, because this is the most consistent, and in some cases outstanding, vintage between 1961 and 1982.

THE BEST WINES

St.-Estèphe:	Cos d'Estournel, Haut-Marbuzet, Lafon-Rochet, Montrose, Les-Ormes-de-Pez, de Pez
Pauillac:	Grand-Puy-Lacoste, Haut-Batailley, Latour, Lynch-Bages, Mouton-Rothschild, Pichon-Longueville-Comtesse de Lalande
St.-Julien:	Ducru-Beaucaillou, Gloria, Gruaud-Larose, Léoville-Barton, St.-Pierre
Margaux:	Giscours, Lascombes, Palmer
Médoc/Haut-Médoc/ Moulis/Listrac/Crus Bourgeois:	Sociando-Mallet
Graves Red:	Domaine de Chevalier, de Fieuzal, Haut-Bailly, La Mission-Haut-Brion, La Tour-Haut-Brion
Graves White:	Domaine de Chevalier, Laville-Haut-Brion
Pomerol:	La Conseillante, La Fleur Pétrus, Lafleur, Latour à Pomerol, Pétrus, Trotanoy
St.-Emilion:	L'Arrosée, Cheval Blanc, La Dominique, Figeac, Magdelaine
Barsac/Sauternes:	Yquem

1969—A Quick Study
(10-6-69)

St.-Estèphe 0	Graves Red*
Pauillac 0	Graves White 0
St.-Julien 0	Pomerol*
Margaux 0	St.-Emilion 0
Médoc/Haut-Médoc Crus Bourgeois 0	Barsac/Sauternes*

Size: Small.

Important information: My candidate for the most undesirable wines produced in Bordeaux in the last 30 years.

Maturity status: I never tasted a 1969, except for Pétrus, that could have been said to have any richness or fruit. I have not seen any of these wines except for Pétrus for a number of years, but they must be unpalatable.

Price: Amazingly, the vintage was offered at a relatively high price, but almost all the wines except for a handful of the big names are totally worthless.

Whenever Bordeaux has suffered through a disastrous vintage (like that of 1968), there has always been a tendency to lavish false praise on the following year. No doubt Bordeaux, after their horrible experience in 1968, badly wanted a fine vintage in 1969, but despite overly optimistic proclamations by some leading Bordeaux experts at the time, 1969 has turned out to be one of the least attractive vintages for Bordeaux wines in the last 3 decades.

The crop was small, and while the summer was sufficiently hot and dry to ensure a decent maturity, torrential September rains dashed everyone's hopes for a good vintage, except some investors who irrationally moved in to buy these insipid, nasty, acidic, sharp wines. Consequently, the 1969s, along with being extremely unattractive wines, were quite expensive when they first appeared on the market.

I can honestly say I have never tasted a red wine in 1969 I did not dislike. The only exception would be a relatively decent bottle of Pétrus (rated in the upper 70s) that I had 20 years after the vintage. Most wines are harsh and hollow, with no flesh, fruit, or charm, and it is hard to imagine that any of these wines are today any more palatable than they were during the seventies.

In the Barsac and Sauternes region, a few proprietors managed to produce acceptable wines, particularly d'Arche.

1968—A Quick Study
(9-20-68)

St.-Estèphe 0	Graves Red *
Pauillac 0	Graves White 0
St.-Julien 0	Pomerol 0
Margaux 0	St.-Emilion 0
Médoc/Haut-Médoc Crus Bourgeois 0	Barsac/Sauternes 0

Size: A small, disastrous crop in terms of both quality and quantity.

Important information: A great year for California Cabernet Sauvignon, but not for Bordeaux.

Maturity status: All of these wines must be passé.

Price: Another worthless vintage.

The 1968 was another of the very poor vintages the Bordelais had to suffer through in the sixties. The culprit, as usual, was heavy rain (it was the wettest year since 1951) that bloated the grapes. However, there have been some 1968s that I found much better than anything produced in 1969, a vintage with a "better" (I am not sure that is the right word to use) reputation.

At one time wines such as Figeac, Gruaud-Larose, Cantemerle, La Mission-Haut-Brion, Haut-Brion, and Latour were palatable. Should anyone run across these wines today, the rule of caveat emptor would seemingly be applicable, as I doubt that any of them would have much left to enjoy.

1967—A Quick Study
(9-25-67)

St.-Estèphe**   Graves Red***
Pauillac**   Graves White**
St.-Julien**   Pomerol***
Margaux**   St.-Emilion***
Médoc/Haut-Médoc Crus Bourgeois*   Barsac/Sauternes****

Size: An abundant crop was harvested.

Important information: A Graves, Pomerol, St.-Emilion year that favored the early harvested Merlot.

Maturity status: Most 1967s were drinkable when released in 1970 and should have been consumed by 1980. A handful of wines (Pétrus and Latour, for example), where well stored, will keep for another few years but are unlikely to improve.

Price: Moderate.

The 1967 was a large, useful vintage in the sense that it produced an abundant quantity of round, quick-maturing wines. Most should have been drunk before 1980, but a handful of wines continue to display remarkable staying power and are still in the full bloom of their maturity. This is a vintage that clearly favored Pomerol and, to a lesser extent, Graves. Holding on to these wines any longer seems foolish, but I have no doubt that some of the biggest wines, such as Latour, Pétrus, Trotanoy, and perhaps even Palmer, will last for another 5–10 years. Should one find any of the top wines listed below in a large-format bottle (magnums, double magnums, and so forth) at a reasonable price, my advice would be to take the gamble.

As unexciting as most red wines turned out in 1967, the sweet wines of Barsac and Sauternes were rich and honeyed, with gobs of botrytis present. However, readers must remember that only a handful of estates were truly up to the challenge of making great wines during this very depressed period for the wine production of Barsac/Sauternes.

THE BEST WINES

St.-Estèphe:	Calon-Ségur, Montrose
Pauillac:	Latour
St.-Julien:	None
Margaux:	Giscours, La Lagune (southern Médoc), Palmer
Médoc/Haut-Médoc/ Moulis/Listrac/Crus Bourgeois:	None
Graves Red:	Haut-Brion, La Mission-Haut-Brion
Graves White:	None
Pomerol:	Pétrus, Trotanoy, La Violette
St.-Emilion:	Cheval Blanc, Magdelaine, Pavie
Barsac/Sauternes:	Suduiraut, Yquem

1966—A Quick Study
(9-26-66)

St.-Estèphe ***
Pauillac ***
St.-Julien ***
Margaux ***
Médoc/Haut-Médoc Crus Bourgeois **

Graves Red ****
Graves White ***
Pomerol ***
St.-Emilion **
Barsac/Sauternes **

Size: An abundant crop was harvested.

Important information: The most overrated "top" vintage of the last 25 years.

Maturity status: The best wines are in their prime, but most wines are losing their fruit before their tannins.

Price: Expensive and overpriced.

While the majority opinion is that 1966 is the best vintage of the decade after 1961, I would certainly argue that for Graves, Pomerol, and St.-Emilion, 1964 is clearly the second-best vintage of the decade. And I am beginning to think that even 1962, that grossly underrated vintage, is, on overall merit, a better year than 1966. Conceived in somewhat the same spirit as 1975 (overhyped after several unexciting years, particularly in the Médoc), 1966 never developed as well as many of its proponents would have liked. The wines, now 37 years of age, for the most part have remained austere, lean, unyielding, and tannic, losing their fruit before their tannin melts away. Some notable exceptions do exist. Who could deny the exceptional wine made at Latour (the wine of the vintage) or the great Palmer?

All the disappointments that emerged from this vintage were unexpected in view of the early reports that the wines were relatively precocious, charming, and early maturing. If the vintage is not as consistent as first believed, there are an adequate number of medium-weight, classically styled wines. However, they are all overpriced, as this vintage has always been fashionable and has had no shortage of supporters, particularly from the English wine-writing community.

The sweet wines of Barsac and Sauternes are also mediocre. Favorable conditions for the development of the noble rot, *Botrytis cinerea,* never occurred.

The climatic conditions that shaped this vintage started with a slow flowering in June, intermittently hot and cold weather in July and August, and a dry and sunny September. The crop size was large, and the vintage was harvested under sound weather conditions.

I would be skeptical about buying most 1966s except for one of the unqualified successes of the vintage.

THE BEST WINES

St.-Estèphe:	None
Pauillac:	Grand-Puy-Lacoste, Latour, Mouton-Rothschild, Pichon-Longueville-Comtesse de Lalande
St.-Julien:	Branaire-Ducru, Ducru-Beaucaillou, Gruaud-Larose, Léoville-Las Cases
Margaux:	Lascombes, Palmer
Médoc/Haut-Médoc/ Moulis/Listrac/Crus Bourgeois:	None
Graves Red:	Haut-Brion, La Mission-Haut-Brion, Pape-Clément
Pomerol:	Lafleur, Trotanoy
St.-Emilion:	Canon
Barsac/Sauternes:	None

1965—A Quick Study
(10-2-65)

St.-Estèphe 0	Graves Red 0
Pauillac 0	Graves White 0
St.-Julien 0	Pomerol 0
Margaux 0	St.-Emilion 0
Médoc/Haut-Médoc Crus Bourgeois 0	Barsac/Sauternes 0

Size: A tiny vintage.

Important information: The quintessential vintage of rot and rain.

Maturity status: The wines tasted terrible from the start and must be totally reprehensible today.

Price: Worthless.

The vintage of rot and rain. I have had little experience tasting the 1965s. It is considered by most experts to be one of the worst vintages in the post–World War II era. A wet summer was bad enough, but the undoing of this vintage was an incredibly wet and humid September that caused rot to devour the vineyards voraciously. Antirot sprays had not yet been developed. It should be obvious that these wines are to be avoided.

1964—A Quick Study
(9-22-64)

St.-Estèphe ***　　　　　　　　　　　　　Graves Red *****
Pauillac *　　　　　　　　　　　　　　　　Graves White ***
St.-Julien *　　　　　　　　　　　　　　　Pomerol *****
Margaux **　　　　　　　　　　　　　　　St.-Emilion ****
Médoc/Haut-Médoc Crus Bourgeois *　　　　Barsac/Sauternes *

Size: A large crop was harvested.

Important information: The classic example of a vintage where the early picked Merlot and Cabernet Franc produced great wine, and the late harvested Cabernet Sauvignon, particularly in the Médoc, was inundated. The results included numerous big name failures in the Médoc.

Maturity status: The Médocs are past their prime, but the larger-scaled wines of Graves, Pomerol, and St.-Emilion can last for another 5–10 years.

Price: Smart Bordeaux enthusiasts have always recognized the greatness of this vintage in Graves, Pomerol, and St.-Emilion, and consequently prices have remained high. Nevertheless, compared to such glamour years as 1959 and 1961, the top right bank and Graves 1964s are not only underrated, but in some cases underpriced as well.

One of the most intriguing vintages of Bordeaux, 1964 produced a number of splendid, generally underrated and underpriced wines in Pomerol, St.-Emilion, and Graves, where many proprietors had the good fortune to have harvested their crops before the rainy deluge began on October 8. Because of this downpour, which caught many Médoc châteaux with unharvested vineyards, 1964 has never been regarded as a top Bordeaux vintage. While the vintage can be notoriously bad for some of the properties of the Médoc and the late-harvesting Barsac and Sauternes estates, it is excellent to outstanding for the three appellations of Pomerol, St.-Emilion, and Graves.

The summer had been so hot and dry that the French minister of agriculture announced at the beginning of September that the "vintage of the century is about to commence." Since the Merlot grape ripens first, the harvest began in the areas where it is planted in abundance. St.-Emilion and Pomerol harvested at the end of September and finished their picking before the inundation began on October 8. Most of the Graves properties had also finished harvesting. When the rains came, most of the Médoc estates had just begun to harvest their Cabernet Sauvignon and were unable to successfully complete the harvest because of torrential rainfall. It was a Médoc vintage noted for some extraordinary and famous failures. Pity the buyer who purchased Lafite-Rothschild, Mouton-Rothschild, Lynch-Bages, Calon-Ségur, or Margaux! Yet not everyone made disappointing wine. Montrose in St.-Estèphe and Latour in Pauillac made the two greatest wines of the Médoc.

Because of the very damaging reports about the rainfall, many wine enthusiasts approached the 1964 vintage with a great deal of apprehension.

The top wines from Graves, St.-Emilion, and Pomerol are exceptionally rich, full bodied, opulent, and concentrated wines, with high alcohol, an opaque color, super length, and unbridled power. Amazingly, they are far richer, more interesting, and more complete wines than the 1966s and, in many cases, compete with the finest wines of the 1961 vintage. Because of low acidity, all of the wines reached full maturity by the mid-eighties. The best examples exhibit no sign of decline and can easily last for another 5–10 or more years.

THE BEST WINES

St.-Estèphe:	Montrose
Pauillac:	Latour
St.-Julien:	Gruaud-Larose
Margaux:	None
Médoc/Haut-Médoc/ Moulis/Listrac/Crus Bourgeois:	None
Graves Red:	Domaine de Chevalier, Haut-Bailly, Haut-Brion, La Mission-Haut-Brion
Pomerol:	La Conseillante, La Fleur Pétrus, Le Gay, Lafleur, Pétrus, Trotanoy, Vieux-Château-Certan
St.-Emilion:	L'Arrosée, Cheval Blanc, Figeac, Soutard
Barsac/Sauternes:	None

1963—A Quick Study
(10-7-63)

St.-Estèphe 0	Graves Red 0
Pauillac 0	Graves White 0
St.-Julien 0	Pomerol 0
Margaux 0	St.-Emilion 0
Médoc/Haut-Médoc Crus Bourgeois 0	Barsac/Sauternes 0

Size: A small- to moderate-size crop was harvested.

Important information: A dreadfully poor year that rivals 1965 for the feeble-
　　ness of its wines.
Maturity status: The wines must now be awful.
Price: Worthless.

　　The Bordelais have never been able to decide whether 1963 or 1965 was
the worst vintage of the sixties. Rain and rot, as in 1965, were the ruination
of this vintage. I have not seen a bottle of 1963 for over 20 years.

1962—A Quick Study
(10-1-62)

St.-Estèphe ****	Graves Red ***
Pauillac ****	Graves White ****
St.-Julien ****	Pomerol ***
Margaux ***	St.-Emilion ***
Médoc/Haut-Médoc Crus Bourgeois ***	Barsac/Sauternes ****

Size: An abundant crop size—in fact, one of the largest of the decade of the
　　sixties.
Important information: A terribly underrated vintage that had the misfortune
　　of following one of the greatest vintages of the century.
Maturity status: The Bordeaux old-timers claim the 1962s drank beautifully
　　by the late sixties and continued to fill out and display considerable
　　character, fruit, and charm in the seventies. As the decade of the
　　nineties ends, the top 1962s are still lovely, rich, round wines full of
　　finesse and elegance.
Price: Undervalued, particularly when one considers the prices of its prede-
　　cessor, 1961, and the overpriced 1966s.

　　Coming after the great vintage of 1961, it was not totally unexpected
that 1962 would be underestimated. This vintage appears to be the most
undervalued for Bordeaux in the post–World War II era. Elegant, supple, very
fruity, round, and charming wines that were neither too tannic nor too massive
were produced in virtually every appellation. Because of their precociousness,
many assumed the wines would not last, but they have kept longer than
anyone would have ever imagined. Most 1962s do require consumption, but
they continue to surprise me, and well-preserved examples of the vintage can
easily be kept through the turn of the century.
　　The weather was acceptable but not stunning. There was a good flowering
because of a sunny, dry May, a relatively hot summer with some impressive
thunderstorms, and a good *fin de saison,* as the French say, with a hot, sunny
September. The harvest was not rain free, but the inundations that could have
created serious problems never occurred.

Not only was the vintage very successful in most appellations, but it was a top year for the dry white wines of Graves as well as the sweet nectars from Barsac/Sauternes.

THE BEST WINES

St.-Estèphe:	Cos d'Estournel, Montrose
Pauillac:	Batailley, Lafite-Rothschild, Latour, Lynch-Bages, Mouton-Rothschild, Pichon-Longueville–Comtesse de Lalande
St.-Julien:	Ducru-Beaucaillou, Gruaud-Larose
Margaux:	Margaux, Palmer
Médoc/Haut-Médoc/ Moulis/Listrac/Crus Bourgeois:	None
Graves Red:	Haut-Brion, Pape-Clément
Graves White:	Domaine de Chevalier, Laville-Haut-Brion
Pomerol:	Lafleur, Pétrus, Trotanoy, La Violette
St.-Emilion:	Magdelaine
Barsac/Sauternes:	Yquem

1961—A Quick Study
(9-22-61)

St.-Estèphe *****
Pauillac *****
St.-Julien *****
Margaux *****
Médoc/Haut-Médoc Crus Bourgeois ***

Graves Red *****
Graves White ***
Pomerol *****
St.-Emilion ***
Barsac/Sauternes **

Size: An exceptionally tiny crop was produced; in fact, this is the last vintage where a minuscule crop resulted in high quality.

Important information: One of the legendary vintages of the century.

Maturity status: The wines, drinkable young, have, with only a handful of exceptions, reached maturity and were all at their apogee by 1990. Most of the prestige examples will keep for at least another 5–10 years, but many 1961s have begun to fade.

Price: The tiny quantities plus exceptional quality have made the 1961s the most dearly priced, mature vintage of great Bordeaux in the marketplace. Moreover, prices will only increase, given the microscopic quantities that remain—an auctioneer's dream vintage. But buyers beware—many 1961s have been poorly stored or traded frequently. Moreover, there are some fraudulent 1961s that show up in the marketplace.

The year 1961 is one of nine great vintages produced in the post–World War II era. The others—1945, 1947, 1949, 1953, 1959, 1982, 1989, 1990 —all have their proponents, but none is as revered as 1961. The wines have always been prized for their sensational concentration and magnificent penetrating bouquets of super-ripe fruit and rich, deep, sumptuous flavors. Delicious when young, these wines, which have all reached full maturity except for a handful of the most intensely concentrated examples, are marvelous to drink. However, I see no problem in holding the best-stored bottles for at least another 10 years.

The weather pattern was nearly perfect in 1961, with spring frosts reducing the crop size and then sunny, hot weather throughout the summer and the harvest, resulting in splendid maturity levels. The small harvest guaranteed high prices for these wines, and today's prices for 1961s make them the equivalent of liquid gold.

The vintage was excellent throughout all appellations of Bordeaux except for the Barsac/Sauternes. This region benefited greatly from the vintage's reputation, but a tasting of the 1961 sweet wines will reveal that even Yquem is mediocre. The incredibly dry weather conditions resulted in very little botrytis, and the results are large-scaled, but essentially monolithic sweet wines that have never merited the interest they have enjoyed. The only other appellation that did not appear to be up to the overall level of quality was St.-Emilion, where many vineyards had still not fully recovered from the killer freeze of 1956.

After tasting the 1961s, I am convinced that only two vintages are somewhat similar in richness and style; 1959 and 1982. The 1959s tend to be lower in acidity but have actually aged more slowly than the 1961s, whereas the 1982s would appear to have the same physical profile of the 1961s but less tannin.

THE BEST WINES

St.-Estèphe:	Cos d'Estournel, Haut-Marbuzet, Montrose
Pauillac:	Grand-Puy-Lacoste, Latour, Lynch-Bages, Mouton-Rothschild, Pichon-Longueville–Comtesse de Lalande, Pontet-Canet
St.-Julien:	Beychevelle, Ducru-Beaucaillou, Gruaud-Larose, Léoville-Barton
Margaux:	Malescot St.-Exupéry, Margaux, Palmer
Médoc/Haut-Médoc/ Moulis/Listrac/Crus Bourgeois:	None
Graves Red:	Haut-Bailly, Haut-Brion, La Mission-Haut-Brion, La Tour-Haut-Brion, Pape-Clément

Graves White:	Domaine de Chevalier, Laville-Haut-Brion
Pomerol:	l'Eglise-Clinet, l'Evangile, Lafleur, Latour à Pomerol, Pétrus, Trotanoy
St.-Emilion:	L'Arrosée, Canon, Cheval Blanc, Figeac, Magdelaine
Barsac/Sauternes:	None

1960—A Quick Study
(9-9-60)

St.-Estèphe **   Graves Red **
Pauillac **   Graves White *
St.-Julien **   Pomerol *
Margaux *   St.-Emilion *
Médoc/Haut-Médoc Crus Bourgeois 0   Barsac/Sauternes *

Size: A copious crop was harvested.

Important information: The two rainy months of August and September were this vintage's undoing.

Maturity status: Most 1960s should have been consumed within their first 10–15 years of life.

Price: Low.

I remember drinking several delicious magnums of 1960 Latour, as well as having found good examples of 1960 Montrose, La Mission-Haut-Brion, and Gruaud-Larose in Bordeaux. However, the last 1960 I consumed, a magnum of Latour, was drunk over 15 years ago. I would guess that even that wine, which was the most concentrated of the vintage according to the Bordeaux cognoscenti, is now in decline.

1959—A Quick Study
(9-20-59)

St.-Estèphe *****   Graves Red *****
Pauillac *****   Graves White ****
St.-Julien ****   Pomerol ***
Margaux ****   St.-Emilion **
Médoc/Haut-Médoc Crus Bourgeois ***   Barsac/Sauternes *****

Size: Average.

Important information: The first of the modern-day years to be designated "vintage of the century."

Maturity status: The wines, maligned in their early years for having low acidity and lacking backbone (reminiscent of the 1982s), have aged more slowly than the more highly touted 1961s. In fact, comparisons between the top wines of the two vintages often reveal the 1959s to be less evolved, with deeper color and more richness and aging potential.

Price: The 1959s have become increasingly more expensive as serious connoisseurs have begun to realize that this vintage not only rivals 1961,
but in specific cases surpasses it.

This is an irrefutably great vintage. The wines, which are especially strong
in the northern Médoc and Graves and less so on the right bank (Pomerol and
St.-Emilion were still recovering from the devastating deep freeze of 1956),
are among the most massive and richest wines ever made in Bordeaux. In
fact, the two modern-day vintages that are frequently compared with 1959
are the 1982 and 1989. Those comparisons may have merit.

The 1959s have evolved at a glacial pace and are often in better condition
(especially the first-growths Lafite-Rothschild and Mouton-Rothschild) than
their 1961 counterparts, which are even more highly touted. The wines do
display the effects of having been made in a classic, hot, dry year, with just
enough rain to keep the vineyards from being stressed. They are full bodied,
extremely alcoholic and opulent, with high degrees of tannin and extract.
Their colors have remained impressively opaque and dark and display less
brown and orange than the 1961s. If there is one nagging doubt about many
of the 1959s, it is whether they will ever develop the sensational perfume and
fragrance that is so much a part of the greatest Bordeaux vintages. Perhaps
the great heat during the summer of 1959 did compromise this aspect of the
wines, but it is still too soon to know.

THE BEST WINES

St.-Estèphe:	Cos d'Estournel, Montrose, Les-Ormes-de-Pez
Pauillac:	Lafite-Rothschild, Latour, Lynch-Bages, Mouton-Rothschild, Pichon-Longueville Baron
St.-Julien:	Ducru-Beaucaillou, Langoa-Barton, Léoville-Barton, Léoville-Las Cases
Margaux:	Lascombes, Malescot St.-Exupéry, Margaux, Palmer
Graves Red:	Haut-Brion, La Mission-Haut-Brion, Pape-Clément, La Tour-Haut-Brion
Pomerol:	l'Evangile, Lafleur, Latour à Pomerol, Pétrus, Trotanoy, Vieux-Château-Certan
St.-Emilion:	Cheval Blanc, Figeac
Barsac/Sauternes:	Climens, Suduiraut, Yquem

1958—A Quick Study
(10-7-58)

St.-Estèphe *	Graves Red ***
Pauillac *	Graves White **
St.-Julien *	Pomerol *

Margaux*	St.-Emilion**
Médoc/Haut-Médoc Crus Bourgeois*	Barsac/Sauternes*

Size: A small crop was harvested.

Important information: An unfairly maligned vintage.

Maturity status: The wines are now fading badly. The best examples almost
always emerge from the Graves appellation.

Price: Inexpensive.

I have fewer than two dozen tasting notes of 1958s, but several that do
stand out are all from the Graves appellation. Haut-Brion, La Mission-Haut-
Brion, and Pape-Clément made very good wines. They probably would have
provided excellent drinking if consumed during the sixties or early seventies.
I most recently had the 1958 Haut-Brion in January 1996. It was still a
relatively tasty, round, soft, fleshy, tobacco- and mineral-scented and -flavored
wine, but one could see that it would have been much better if it had been
consumed 10–15 years ago. Even richer was the 1958 La Mission-Haut-
Brion, which should still be excellent if well-preserved bottles can be found.

1957—A Quick Study
(10-4-57)

St.-Estèphe**	Graves Red***
Pauillac***	Graves White**
St.-Julien**	Pomerol*
Margaux*	St.-Emilion*
Médoc/Haut-Médoc Crus Bourgeois*	Barsac/Sauternes***

Size: A small crop.

Important information: A brutally cold, wet summer.

Maturity status: Because the summer was so cool, the red wines were extremely high in acidity, which has helped them stand the test of time.
Where well-kept examples of 1957 can be found, this could be a vintage
to purchase, provided the price is right.

Price: The wines should be realistically and inexpensively priced given the
fact that 1957 does not enjoy a good reputation.

For a vintage that has never been received very favorably, I have been
surprised by how many respectable and enjoyable wines I have tasted, particularly from Pauillac and Graves. In fact, I would be pleased to serve my most
finicky friends the 1957 La Mission-Haut-Brion or 1957 Haut-Brion. And I
would certainly be pleased to drink the 1957 Lafite-Rothschild. I had two
excellent bottles of Lafite in the early eighties but have not seen the wine
since.

It was an extremely difficult year weather-wise, with very wet periods from

April through August that delayed the harvest until early October. The wines had good acidity, and in the better-drained soils there was surprising ripeness considering the lack of sunshine and excessive moisture. The 1957 Bordeaux, much like their Burgundy counterparts, have held up relatively well given the high acid and green tannins these wines have always possessed.

1956—A Quick Study
(10-14-56)

St.-Estèphe 0	Graves Red 0
Pauillac 0	Graves White 0
St.-Julien 0	Pomerol 0
Margaux 0	St.-Emilion 0
Médoc/Haut-Médoc Crus Bourgeois 0	Barsac/Sauternes 0

Size: Minuscule quantities of pathetically weak wine were produced.

Important information: The coldest winter in Bordeaux since 1709 did unprecedented damage to the vineyards, particularly those in Pomerol and St.-Emilion.

Maturity status: I have not seen a 1956 in over 15 years and only have a total of five notes on wines from this vintage.

Price: A worthless vintage produced worthless wines.

The year 1956 stands out as the worst vintage in modern-day Bordeaux, even surpassing such unspeakably bad years as 1963, 1965, 1968, 1969, and 1972. The winter and unbelievably cold months of February and March killed many of the vines in Pomerol and St.-Emilion and retarded the budding of those in the Médoc. The harvest was late, the crop was small, and the wines were virtually undrinkable.

1955—A Quick Study
(9-21-55)

St.-Estèphe ****	Graves Red ****
Pauillac ****	Graves White ***
St.-Julien ****	Pomerol ***
Margaux ***	St.-Emilion ****
Médoc/Haut-Médoc Crus Bourgeois **	Barsac/Sauternes ****

Size: A large, healthy crop was harvested.

Important information: For a vintage that is nearly 45 years old, this tends to be an underrated, undervalued year, although it is not comparable to 1953 or 1959. Yet the wines have generally held up and are firmer and more solidly made than the once glorious 1953s.

Maturity status: After a long period of sleep, the top wines appear to finally be fully mature. They exhibit no signs of decline.

Price: Undervalued, except for La Mission-Haut-Brion, the wine of the vintage, if not the decade.

For the most part, the 1955s have always come across as relatively stern, slightly tough-textured, yet impressively deep, full wines with fine color and excellent aging potential. What they lack, as a general rule, is fat, charm, and opulence.

The weather conditions were generally ideal, with hot, sunny days in June, July, and August. Although some rain fell in September, its effect was positive rather than negative.

For whatever reason, the relatively large 1955 crop has never generated the excitement that other vintages in the fifties, such as 1953 and 1959, elicited. Perhaps it was the lack of many superstar wines that kept enthusiasm muted. Among more recent years, could 1988 be a rerun of 1955?

THE BEST WINES

St.-Estèphe:	Calon-Ségur, Cos d'Estournel, Montrose, Les-Ormes-de-Pez
Pauillac:	Latour, Lynch-Bages, Mouton-Rothschild
St.-Julien:	Léoville-Las Cases, Talbot
Margaux:	Palmer
Graves Red:	Haut-Brion, La Mission-Haut-Brion, Pape-Clément
Pomerol:	l'Evangile, Lafleur, Latour à Pomerol, Pétrus, Vieux-Château-Certan
St.-Emilion:	Cheval Blanc, La Dominique, Soutard
Barsac/Sauternes:	Yquem

1954—A Quick Study
(10-10-54)

St.-Estèphe 0	Graves Red *
Pauillac *	Graves White 0
St.-Julien *	Pomerol 0
Margaux 0	St.-Emilion 0
Médoc/Haut-Médoc Crus Bourgeois 0	Barsac/Sauternes 0

Size: A small crop was harvested.

Important information: A terrible late-harvested vintage conducted under appalling weather conditions.

Maturity status: It is hard to believe anything from this vintage would still be worth drinking.

Price: The wines have no value.

The 1954 was a miserable vintage throughout France, but especially in Bordeaux, where the producers continued to wait for full maturity after an exceptionally cool, wet August. While the weather did improve in September, the skies opened toward the end of the month and for nearly 4 weeks one low-pressure system after another passed through the area, dumping enormous quantities of water that served to destroy any chance for a moderately successful vintage.

It is highly unlikely any wine from this vintage could still be drinkable today.

1953—A Quick Study
(9-28-53)

St.-Estèphe *****	Graves Red ****
Pauillac *****	Graves White ***
St.-Julien *****	Pomerol ***
Margaux ****	St.-Emilion ***
Médoc/Haut-Médoc Crus Bourgeois ***	Barsac/Sauternes ***

Size: An average-size crop was harvested.

Important information: One of the most seductive and hedonistic Bordeaux vintages ever produced.

Maturity status: According to Bordeaux old-timers, the wines were absolutely delicious during the fifties, even more glorious in the sixties, and sublime during the seventies. Charm, roundness, fragrance, and a velvety texture were the hallmarks of this vintage, which now must be approached with some degree of caution unless the wines have been impeccably stored and/or are available in larger-format bottlings.

Price: No vintage with such appeal will ever sell at a reasonable price. Consequently, the 1953s remain luxury-priced wines.

1953 must be the only Bordeaux vintage where it is impossible to find a dissenting voice about the quality of the wines. Bordeaux old-timers and some of our senior wine commentators (particularly Edmund Penning-Rowsell and Michael Broadbent) talk of 1953 with adulation. Apparently the vintage never went through an unflattering stage. They were delicious from cask and even more so from bottle. For that reason, much of the vintage was consumed before its tenth birthday. Those who waited have seen the wines develop even greater character during the sixties and seventies. Many wines, especially on this side of the Atlantic, began displaying signs of age (brown color, dried-out fruit flavors) during the eighties. In Bordeaux, when a château pulls out a 1953 it is usually in mint condition, and these are some of the most beautifully sumptuous, rich, charming clarets anyone could ever desire. A more modern-day reference point for 1953 may be the very best 1985s, perhaps even some of the lighter 1982s, although my instincts tell me the 1982s are more alcoholic, richer, fuller, heavier wines.

If you have the discretionary income to buy this highly prized vintage, prudence should dictate that the wines be from cold cellars, and/or in larger-format bottles.

THE BEST WINES

St.-Estèphe:	Calon-Ségur, Cos d'Estournel, Montrose
Pauillac:	Grand-Puy-Lacoste, Lafite-Rothschild, Lynch-Bages, Mouton-Rothschild
St.-Julien:	Beychevelle, Ducru-Beaucaillou, Gruaud-Larose, Langoa-Barton, Léoville-Barton, Léoville-Las Cases, Talbot
Margaux:	Cantemerle (southern Médoc), Margaux, Palmer
Graves Red:	Haut-Brion, La Mission-Haut-Brion
Pomerol:	La Conseillante
St.-Emilion:	Cheval Blanc, Figeac, Magdelaine, Pavie
Barsac/Sauternes:	Climens, Yquem

1952—A Quick Study
(9-17-52)

St.-Estèphe **
Pauillac ***
St.-Julien ***
Margaux **
Médoc /Haut-Médoc Crus Bourgeois **

Graves Red ***
Graves White ***
Pomerol ****
St.-Emilion ***
Barsac/Sauternes **

Size: A small crop was harvested.

Important information: The 1952 vintage was at its best in Pomerol, which largely completed its harvest prior to the rains.

Maturity status: Most wines have always tasted hard and too astringent, lacking fat, charm, and ripeness. The best bottles could provide surprises.

Price: Expensive, but well-chosen Pomerols may represent relative values.

An excellent spring and summer of relatively hot, dry weather with just enough rain was spoiled by stormy, unstable, cold weather before and during the harvest. Much of the Merlot and some of the Cabernet Franc in Pomerol and St.-Emilion was harvested before the weather turned foul; consequently, the best wines tended to come from these appellations. The Graves can also be successful because of the superb drainage of the soil in that appellation, particularly in the Pessac/Léognan area. The Médocs have always tended to be relatively hard and disappointing, even the first-growths.

THE BEST WINES

St.-Estèphe: Calon-Ségur, Montrose
Pauillac: Latour, Lynch-Bages
St.-Julien: None
Margaux: Margaux, Palmer
Graves Red: Haut-Brion, La Mission-Haut-Brion, Pape-Clément
Pomerol: La Fleur Pétrus, Lafleur, Pétrus, Trotanoy
St.-Emilion: Cheval Blanc, Magdelaine
Barsac/Sauternes: None

1951—A Quick Study
(10-9-51)

St.-Estèphe 0

Pauillac 0

St.-Julien 0

Margaux 0

Médoc/Haut-Médoc Crus Bourgeois 0

Graves Red 0

Graves White 0

Pomerol 0

St.-Emilion 0

Barsac/Sauternes 0

Size: A tiny crop was harvested.

Important information: Even today 1951 is considered one of the all-time worst vintages for dry white, dry red, and sweet wines from Bordeaux.

Maturity status: Undrinkable young, undrinkable old.

Price: Another worthless vintage.

Frightfully bad weather in the spring, summer, and both before and during the harvest (rain and unseasonably cold temperatures) was the complete undoing of this vintage, which bears the ignominious pleasure of having one of the worst reputations of any vintage in the post–World War II era.

1950—A Quick Study
(9-17-50)

St.-Estèphe **

Pauillac ***

St.-Julien ***

Margaux ***

Médoc/Haut-Médoc Crus Bourgeois *

Graves Red ***

Graves White ***

Pomerol *****

St.-Emilion ****

Barsac/Sauternes ****

Size: An abundant crop was harvested.

Important information: Many of the Pomerols are great, yet they have been totally ignored by the chroniclers of the Bordeaux region.

Maturity status: Most Médocs and Graves are now in decline. The top heavyweight Pomerols can be splendid, with years of life still left.

Price: The quality of the Pomerols is no longer a secret.

The year 1950 is another example where the Médoc formed the general impression of the Bordeaux vintage. This relatively abundant year was the result of good flowering, a hot, dry summer, and a difficult early September complicated by large amounts of rain.

The Médocs, all of which are in decline, were soft, forward, medium-bodied wines that probably had a kinship to more recent vintages such as 1971 and 1981. The Graves were slightly better, but even they are probably passé. The two best appellations were St.-Emilion, which produced a number of rich, full, intense wines that aged quickly, and Pomerol, which had its fourth superb vintage in succession—unprecedented in the history of that area. The wines are unbelievably rich, unctuous, and concentrated and in many cases are capable of rivaling the greatest Pomerols of such more highly renowned vintages as 1947 and 1949.

The other appellation that prospered in 1950 was Barsac/Sauternes. Fanciers of these wines still claim 1950 is one of the greatest of the post–World War II vintages for sweet wines.

THE BEST WINES

St.-Estèphe:	None
Pauillac:	Latour
St.-Julien:	None
Margaux:	Margaux
Médoc/Haut-Médoc/ Moulis/Listrac/Crus Bourgeois:	None
Graves Red:	Haut-Brion, La Mission-Haut-Brion
Pomerol:	l'Eglise-Clinet, l'Evangile, La Fleur Pétrus, Le Gay, Lafleur, Latour à Pomerol, Pétrus, Vieux-Château-Certan
St.-Emilion:	Cheval Blanc, Figeac, Soutard
Barsac/Sauternes:	Climens, Coutet, Suduiraut, Yquem

1949—A Quick Study
(9-27-49)

St.-Estèphe *****	Graves Red *****
Pauillac *****	Graves White ***
St.-Julien *****	Pomerol ****
Margaux ****	St.-Emilion ****
Médoc/Haut-Médoc Crus Bourgeois ***	Barsac/Sauternes *****

Size: A small crop was harvested.

Important information: The driest and sunniest vintage since 1893 and rivaled (weather-wise, not qualitatively) in more recent years only by 1990.

Maturity status: The finest wines are still in full blossom, displaying remarkable richness and concentration, but their provenance and history of storage are critical factors when contemplating a purchase.

Price: Frightfully expensive.

Among the four extraordinary vintages of the late forties—1945, 1947, 1948, and 1949—this has always been my favorite. The wines, slightly less massive and alcoholic than the 1947s, also appear to possess greater balance, harmony, and fruit than the 1945s and more complexity than the 1948s. In short, the top wines are magnificent. 1949 is certainly one of the most exceptional vintages of this century. Only the right bank wines (except for Cheval Blanc) appear inferior to the quality of their 1947s. In the Médoc and Graves it is a terrific vintage, with nearly everyone making wines of astounding ripeness, richness, opulence, power, and length.

The vintage was marked by the extraordinary heat and sunny conditions that Bordeaux enjoyed throughout the summer. Those consumers who have been worried that 1989 and 1990 were too hot to make great wine only need to look at the weather statistics for 1949. It was one of the two hottest vintages (the other being 1947) since 1893, as well as the sunniest vintage since 1893. It was not a totally dry harvest, but the amount of rainfall was virtually identical to that in a year such as 1982. Some of the rain fell before the harvest, which, given the dry, parched condition of the soil, was actually beneficial.

Even the sweet wines of Barsac and Sauternes were exciting. Buying 1949s today will cost an arm and a leg, as these are among the most expensive and sought-after wines of the twentieth century.

THE BEST WINES

St.-Estèphe:	Calon-Ségur, Cos d'Estournel, Montrose
Pauillac:	Grand-Puy-Lacoste, Latour, Mouton-Rothschild
St.-Julien:	Gruaud-Larose, Léoville-Barton, Talbot
Margaux:	Palmer
Graves Red:	Haut-Brion, La Mission-Haut-Brion, Pape-Clément
Pomerol:	La Conseillante, l'Eglise-Clinet, l'Evangile, Lafleur, Latour à Pomerol, Pétrus, Trotanoy, Vieux-Château-Certan
St.-Emilion:	Cheval Blanc
Barsac/Sauternes:	Climens, Coutet, Yquem

1948—A Quick Study
(9-22-48)

St.-Estèphe***   Graves Red****

Pauillac****   Graves White***

St.-Julien****   Pomerol***

Margaux****   St.-Emilion***

Médoc/Haut-Médoc Crus Bourgeois***   Barsac/Sauternes**

Size: An average to below average crop size was harvested.

Important information: A largely ignored, but good to excellent vintage over-shadowed by both its predecessor and successor.

Maturity status: The hard and backward characteristics of these wines have served them well during their evolution. Most of the larger, more concentrated 1948s are still attractive wines.

Price: Undervalued given their age and quality.

When Bordeaux has three top vintages in a row it is often the case that one is totally forgotten, and that has certainly proven correct with respect to 1948. It was a very good year that had the misfortune to fall between two legendary vintages.

Because of a difficult flowering due to wet, windy, cool weather in June, the crop size was smaller than in 1947 and 1949. However, July and August were fine months weather-wise, with September exceptionally warm and dry.

Despite the high quality of the wines, they never caught on with claret enthusiasts. And who can fault the wine buyers? The 1947s were more flashy, opulent, alcoholic, and fuller bodied, and the 1949s were more precocious and richer than the harder, tougher, more tannic, and unforthcoming 1948s.

This is a vintage that in many cases has matured more gracefully than the massive 1947s. The top wines tend to still be in excellent condition. Prices remain reasonable, if only in comparison with what one has to pay for 1947 and 1949.

THE BEST WINES

St.-Estèphe: Cos d'Estournel

Pauillac: Grand-Puy-Lacoste, Latour, Lynch-Bages, Mouton-Rothschild

St.-Julien: Langoa-Barton, Léoville-Barton (the wine of the Médoc)

Margaux: Cantemerle (southern Médoc), Margaux, Palmer

Graves Red: La Mission-Haut-Brion, Pape-Clément

Pomerol: l'Eglise-Clinet, Lafleur, Latour à Pomerol,
                Petit-Village, Pétrus, Vieux-Château-Certan
St.-Emilion: Cheval Blanc
Barsac/Sauternes: None

1947-A Quick Study
(9-15-47)

St.-Estèphe ***	Graves Red ****
Pauillac ***	Graves White ***
St.-Julien ***	Pomerol *****
Margaux **	St.-Emilion *****
Médoc/Haut-Médoc Crus Bourgeois *	Barsac/Sauternes ***

Size: An abundant crop was harvested.

Important information: A year of extraordinary extremes in quality, with some
of the most port-like, concentrated wines ever produced in Bordeaux.
This is also a vintage of unexpected failures (such as the Lafite-
Rothschild).

Maturity status: Except for the most concentrated and powerful Pomerols and
St.-Emilions, this is a vintage that requires immediate consumption, as
many wines have gone over the top and are now exhibiting excessive
volatile acidity and dried-out fruit.

Price: Preposterously high given the fact that this was another "vintage of the
century."

This quintessentially hot-year vintage produced some of the most enormously concentrated, portlike, intense wines I have ever tasted. Most of the
real heavyweights in this vintage have emerged from Pomerol and St.-Emilion.
In the Médoc, it was a vintage of remarkable irregularity. Properties such as
Calon-Ségur and Mouton-Rothschild made great wines, but certain top
growths, such as Lafite-Rothschild and Latour, as well as super-seconds such
as Léoville-Barton, produced wines with excessive acidity.

The top wines are something to behold, if only because of their excessively
rich, sweet style, which comes closest in modern-day terms to 1982. Yet I
know of no 1982 that has the level of extract and intensity of the greatest
1947s.

The reasons for such intensity were the exceptionally hot months of July
and August, which were followed (much like in 1982) by a torridly hot,
almost tropical heat wave in mid-September just as the harvest began. Those
properties that were unable to control the temperatures of hot grapes had
stuck fermentations, residual sugar in the wines, and, in many cases, levels
of volatile acidity that would horrify modern-day oenologists. Those who were

able to master the tricky vinification made the richest, most opulent red wines Bordeaux has produced during the twentieth century.

THE BEST WINES

St.-Estèphe:	Calon-Ségur
Pauillac:	Grand-Puy-Lacoste, Mouton-Rothschild
St.-Julien:	Ducru-Beaucaillou, Léoville-Las Cases
Margaux:	Margaux
Graves Red:	Haut-Brion, La Mission-Haut-Brion, La Tour-Haut-Brion
Pomerol:	Clinet, La Conseillante, l'Eglise-Clinet, l'Enclos, l'Evangile, La Fleur Pétrus, Lafleur, Latour à Pomerol, Nenin, Pétrus, Rouget, Vieux-Château-Certan
St.-Emilion:	Canon, Cheval Blanc, Figeac, La Gaffelière-Naudes
Barsac/Sauternes:	Climens, Suduiraut

1946—A Quick Study
(9-30-46)

St.-Estèphe **	Graves Red *
Pauillac **	Graves White 0
St.-Julien **	Pomerol 0
Margaux *	St.-Emilion 0
Médoc/Haut-Médoc Crus Bourgeois 0	Barsac/Sauternes 0

Size: A small crop was harvested.

Important information: The only year in the post–World War II era where the Bordeaux vineyards were invaded by locusts.

Maturity status: The wines must certainly be over the hill.

Price: Except for the rare bottle of Mouton-Rothschild (needed by billionaires to complete their collections), most of these wines have little value.

A fine, hot summer, particularly in July and August, was spoiled by an unusually wet, windy, cold September that delayed the harvest and caused rampant rot in the vineyards. The 1946s are rarely seen in the marketplace. I have only eleven tasting notes for the entire vintage. I do not know of any top wines, although Edmund Penning-Rowsell claims the 1946 Latour was excellent. I have never seen a bottle.

1945—A Quick Study
(9-13-45)

St.-Estèphe ****	Graves Red *****
Pauillac *****	Graves White *****

St.-Julien *****   Pomerol *****

Margaux ****   St.-Emilion *****

Médoc/Haut-Médoc Crus Bourgeois ****   Barsac/Sauternes *****

Size: A tiny crop was harvested.

<u>*Important information:*</u> The most acclaimed vintage of the century.

<u>*Maturity status:*</u> Certain wines from this vintage (only those that have been
    stored impeccably) are still not fully mature.

<u>*Price:*</u> The most expensive clarets of the century.

No vintage in the post–World War II era, not even 1990, 1989,
1982, 1961, 1959, or 1953, enjoys the reputation of the 1945. The cele-
bration of the end of an appallingly destructive war, combined with the
fact that the weather was remarkable, produced one of the smallest, most
concentrated crops of grapes ever seen. In the late eighties I have been
fortunate to have had the first-growths on two separate occasions, and there
seems to be no doubt that this is indeed a remarkable vintage that has taken
almost 45 years to reach its peak. The great wines, and they are numerous,
could well last for another 20–30 years, making a mockery of most of the
more recent great vintages that must be consumed within 25–30 years of the
vintage.

The vintage is not without critics, some of whom have said that the
wines are excessively tannic and many are drying out. There are wines
that match these descriptions, but if one judges a vintage on the performance of the top properties, such as the first-growths, super-seconds, and
leading domaines in Pomerol and St.-Emilion, 1945 remains in a class by
itself.

The reason for the tiny crop was the notoriously frigid spell during the
month of May *(la gelée noire),* which was followed by a summer of exceptional
heat and drought. An early harvest began on September 13, the same day
that the harvest began in both 1976 and 1982.

THE BEST WINES

St.-Estèphe:	Calon-Ségur, Montrose, Les-Ormes-de-Pez
Pauillac:	Latour, Mouton-Rothschild, Pichon-Longueville–
	Comtesse de Lalande, Pontet-Canet
St.-Julien:	Gruaud-Larose, Léoville-Barton, Talbot
Margaux:	Margaux, Palmer
Graves Red:	Haut-Brion, La Mission-Haut-Brion,
	La Tour-Haut-Brion
Graves White:	Laville-Haut-Brion
Pomerol:	l'Eglise-Clinet, La Fleur Pétrus, Gazin, Lafleur, Latour

	à Pomerol, Pétrus, Rouget, Trotanoy, Vieux-Château-Certan
St.-Emilion:	Canon, Cheval Blanc, Figeac, La Gaffelière-Naudes, Larcis-Ducasse, Magdelaine
Barsac/Sauternes:	Suduiraut, Yquem

3: EVALUATING THE WINES OF BORDEAUX

ST.-ESTÈPHE

Of all the wines produced in the Haut-Médoc, those of St.-Estèphe have the reputation of being the slowest to mature, and the toughest, most tannic wines. While this generalization may have been true 20 or 30 years ago, the wines now being made in St.-Estèphe reveal an increasing reliance on the softer, fleshier Merlot grape, as well as a vinification aimed at producing more supple, earlier-maturing wines.

St.-Estèphe, which has 2,821 acres under vine, is the least prestigious of the four well-known Haut-Médoc appellations including Margaux, Pauillac, and St.-Julien. In the 1855 classification, only five wines were considered outstanding enough to be ranked. However, from a consumer's perspective, the commune of St.-Estèphe has numerous Cru Bourgeois châteaux that are currently making wine as good as several classified growths. Several of these Cru Bourgeois estates are producing better wine than at least one of the five classified growths in St.-Estèphe. In any reclassification of St.-Estèphe, Cos Labory would be hard-pressed to keep its standing, whereas top-notch, lesser-known estates making excellent wine, such as Haut-Marbuzet, Meyney, and Phélan-Ségur, would certainly merit serious consideration for elevation into the ranks of the classified growths.

Even with the growers of St.-Estèphe consciously trying to make a more supple style of wine, the wines of this region generally remain among the most backward and unyielding wines produced in Bordeaux. Of course, the soil is less gravelly in St.-Estèphe and also has a higher clay content. Consequently the drainage is slower. The resulting wines are relatively higher in acidity and lower in pH, and their textures chunkier and more burly, than, for example, wines made from vineyards planted in the light, gravelly soil of Margaux and Graves.

At present, virtually everyone agrees that Cos d'Estournel is making this commune's most popular wine, particularly since the early eighties. Coincidentally, it is also the first château one sees when crossing over the Pauillac boundary into St.-Estèphe. The eccentric pagoda-styled château sits on a ridge overlooking Pauillac's famous Lafite-Rothschild. Several recent vintages, particularly the 1996, 1995, 1990, 1986, 1985, and 1982, would even suggest that Cos d'Estournel has first-growth aspirations. Cos d'Estournel's wine represents a brilliant combination of modern technology and respect for tradition. It is a wine supple enough to drink by age 5 or 6 but made to age and improve for as many as 10–20 years.

The chief rival to Cos d'Estournel is Montrose. Montrose is hidden on one of St.-Estèphe's tiny back roads, closer to the Gironde River. Until the mid-1970s, Montrose made one of Bordeaux's biggest, deepest, and slowest-maturing wines. Many Bordelais compared it to Latour because of its weight and richness. During the mid-eighties, Montrose curiously lightened its style, but this flirtation with a more commercial style was short-lived. Vintages of Montrose still need a good 15–20 years to shed their cloak of tannin. The profound 1989 and 1990 Montrose represent a return to the style that made Montrose among the most heralded wines of the Médoc during much of this century.

Potentially as good as any St.-Estèphe, as well as just about any Médoc, is Calon-Ségur, the white-walled château just outside the village of St.-Estèphe. When Calon-Ségur does everything right, as it did in 1996, 1995, 1982, 1953, and 1947, one cannot find a better wine. But Calon-Ségur has always been unpredictable, and when one looks at its wines made in the eighties and

ST·ESTÈPHE

● CHÂTEAU ═══ ROAD

0   1   2   3
KILOMETERS

0   ½   1   1½   2
MILES

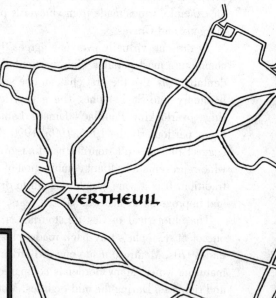

VERTHEUIL

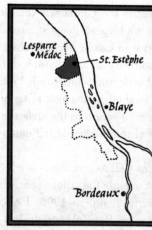

Lesparre
●Médoc   ●St. Estèphe

●Blaye

Bordeaux ●

Cissac
CISSAC-MÉDOC

nineties, Calon's propensity for inconsistency remains as troublesome as ever. Since Madame Capbern-Gasqueton assumed full control over the estate following the death of her husband, Calon-Ségur has become more consistent in quality, while also representing excellent value.

Lafon-Rochet continues to make a solid, tannic, backward style of wine that fanciers of hard, tough St.-Estèphe wines will find authentic. However, the fifth-growth Cos Labory is this commune's most overrated wine. Recent vintages have shown some improvement in quality, but this is a wine that continues to live largely off its 1855 reputation rather than modern-day quality.

One of the great attractions of St.-Estèphe is the glorious number of expertly made Cru Bourgeois wines, some of which merit elevation to classified growths.

Haut-Marbuzet, for openers, makes a splendid wine, overtly spicy and oaky and filled with the flavors and aromas of black currants. If one were to mistake it for a second-growth, I would not be surprised. The excellent Phélan-Ségur is enjoying a renaissance and is a wine that lasts nearly as long as any wine of St.-Estèphe. Shrewd collectors are now beating a path to this property's wines. Meyney is another of St.-Estèphe's outstanding Cru Bourgeois properties. Superbly located north of Montrose near the river, Meyney is a large producer, and its reliability for big, rich, deep, fine wines makes this St.-Estèphe a wine to seek out.

St.-Estèphes are not wines to look for and buy in mediocre or poor Bordeaux vintages. The best performers in off vintages are Cos d'Estournel, Montrose, and Haut-Marbuzet. However, the great vintages for this region are ones in which there are plenty of sunshine and heat, and all the grapes, particularly the Merlot, become fully mature. For these reasons, vintages such as 1959, 1961, 1970, 1982, 1986, 1989, 1990, 1994, 1995, and 1996 are superlative years for St.-Estèphe. Excessively hot and dry years, which can stress the vineyards planted on light, gravelly soil, are frequently outstanding vintages in the heavier soils of St.-Estèphe. Both 1989 and 1990, two of the hottest and driest vintages this century, are convincing case studies. Remember that the soils of this region are less porous, so drainage is not as good as in other Médoc appellations. Vintages where there was abundant rain are frequently less successful in St.-Estèphe than in nearby St.-Julien or Margaux. For example, 1987, 1983, 1980, 1977, and 1974 were more successful in other Médoc appellations. An important factor for the success of the vintage in St.-Estèphe is a healthy, very ripe Merlot crop, which will help to cut the normally higher than average acidity and tannins of St.-Estèphe's wines. The years 1995, 1990, 1989, 1982, 1976, and 1970 all favored the Merlot grape, and as a consequence, St.-Estèphe produced numerous outstanding wines.

St.-Estèphe wines, as the least glamorous of the famous Médoc, offer excellent values. This applies not only to the famous classified growths, but also to the appellation's excellent array of Cru Bourgeois wines.

ST.-ESTÈPHE
(An Insider's View)

Overall Appellation Potential: Average to Superb

The Most Potential for Aging: Calon-Ségur, Cos d'Estournel, Montrose

The Most Elegant: Cos d'Estournel

The Most Concentrated: Calon-Ségur, Cos d'Estournel, Montrose

The Best Value: Lafon-Rochet, Meyney, Phélan-Ségur, Tronquoy-Lalande

The Most Exotic: Haut-Marbuzet

The Most Difficult to Understand (when young): Calon-Ségur

The Most Underrated: Calon-Ségur, Lafon-Rochet, Phélan-Ségur

The Easiest to Appreciate Young: Haut-Marbuzet, Les-Ormes-de-Pez

Up-and-Coming Estates: Cos Labory, Lilian Ladouys, Lafon-Rochet, de Pez, Phélan-Ségur

Greatest Recent Vintages: 1996, 1995, 1990, 1989, 1986, 1982, 1961, 1959

ST.-ESTÈPHE—AN OVERVIEW

Location: The most northern of the four principal Médoc appellations, St.-Estèphe is on the left bank of the Gironde River, approximately 28 miles north of the city of Bordeaux

Acres under Vine: 3,404

Communes: St.-Estèphe

Average Annual Production: 765,000 cases

Classified Growths: Total of 5: 2 second-growths, 1 third-growth, 1 fourth-growth, and 1 fifth-growth; there are 43 Crus Bourgeois

Principal Grape Varieties: Cabernet Sauvignon and Merlot dominate, with Cabernet Franc and Petit Verdot used in small proportions

Principal Soil Type: Diverse soils; the finest vineyards are on gravel ridges, but sandy and clay soils with some limestone are commonplace.

A CONSUMER'S CLASSIFICATION
OF THE CHÂTEAUX OF ST.-ESTÈPHE

OUTSTANDING

Cos d'Estournel

Montrose

EXCELLENT
Calon-Ségur
Haut-Marbuzet

VERY GOOD
Lafon-Rochet
Meyney
Phélan-Ségur

GOOD
Chambert-Marbuzet
Cos Labory
Coutelin-Merville
Laffitte-Carcasset
Lavillotte
Lilian Ladouys
Les-Ormes-de-Pez
Petit Bocq
de Pez
Tronquoy-Lalande

OTHER NOTABLE ST.-ESTÈPHE PRODUCERS

Andron-Blanquet, Beau-Site, Bel-Air, Le Boscq, Capbern-Gasqueton, Cave
Cooperative Marquis de St.-Estèphe, La Commanderie, Le Crock,
Haut-Beauséjour, Haut-Coteau, Château La Haye, Houissant, Marbuzet,
Pomys, Les Pradines, Ségur de Cabanac, Tour-de-Marbuzet, Tour de Pez,
Tour des Termes, Valrose, Vieux Coutelin

ANDRON-BLANQUET

Classification: Cru Bourgeois
Location of vineyards: At Cos, St.-Estèphe, near those of Cos Labory and
Cos d'Estournel
Owner: Domaines Audoy
Address: 33180 St.-Estèphe
Telephone: 33 5 56 59 30 22; telefax: 33 5 56 59 73 52
Visits: By appointment only, from Monday to Friday, between 9 A.M. and
noon, and 2 P.M. and 6 P.M.
Contact: Bernard Audoy at above telephone and telefax numbers.

VINEYARDS
Surface area: 39.5 acres
Average age of vines: 25 years

Blends: 60% Cabernet Sauvignon, 25% Merlot, 15% Cabernet Franc
Density of plantation: 7,000 vines per hectare
Average yields (over the last 5 years): 55 hectoliters per hectare
Total average annual production: 100,000 bottles

GRAND VIN (red)
Brand name: Château Andron-Blanquet
Appellation: St.-Estèphe
Mean annual production: 64,000 bottles
Upbringing: Harvest is done by hand and by machine. Fermentations last
25 days in stainless-steel and cement vats (not temperature controlled),
and wines are kept in oak casks, 25% of which are new, for
approximately 12 months. Malolactics occur in vats prior to transfer of
wines in casks. Wines are fined and filtered.

SECOND WINE
Brand name: Château Saint-Roch
Average annual production: 36,000 bottles

Evaluation of present classification: Should be maintained
Plateau of maturity: 3–8 years following the vintage

Andron-Blanquet should produce better wine. The vineyard, which is
close to those of Lafite-Rothschild in neighboring Pauillac and the famous Cos d'Estournel in St.-Estèphe, is located on a plateau of gravelly
soil that is considered to be slightly warmer than other microclimates
in St.-Estèphe. However, the use of machine harvesters to pick some of
the crop is not an indication that the highest quality is sought. The wine
is vinified properly, with a relatively long maceration period, yet Andron-
Blanquet consistently lacks concentration, character, and charm. The
institution of a second wine at the request of the oenologist and proprietor, Bernard Audoy, may help explain why the 1989 is the best recent vintage.

VINTAGES

1990—The 1990 Andron-Blanquet is the most disappointing wine from St.-Estèphe
•   I tasted in the vintage. Lean, short, and hard, it possesses insufficient fruit.
74   Last tasted, 1/93.
1989—This perennial underachiever appears unable to muster the necessary motiva-
•   tion to produce high-quality wine. The 1989 is surprisingly light, but in-
82   tensely fruity in a straightforward, jammy, medium-bodied style. It should be
    drunk within its first 5–7 years of life. Anticipated maturity: Now. Last tasted,
    4/91.

1988—The 1988 is light and lacking the charming fruitiness of the 1989. It finishes
•   short and is too acidic. Anticipated maturity: Now. Last tasted, 4/91.
74

1986—Despite reports of renewed commitment to improving the quality here, this
•   estate continues to represent one of the most notorious underachievers in the
74   St.-Estèphe firmament. The 1986 is surprisingly light for the vintage, with
    medium to dark ruby color and some ripeness and length, but the overriding
    impression is one of hard tannins that are excessive for the amount of fruit.
    Anticipated maturity: Now. Last tasted, 11/89.

1985—The 1985 is a shallow, somewhat thin, and watery wine that is medium bodied
•   and has a light, innocuous fragrance of diluted fruit and a ready-to-drink
67   texture. It should be drunk over the next 3–5 years. Anticipated maturity:
    Now. Last tasted, 10/88.

BEAU-SITE

Classification: Cru Bourgeois Supérieur in 1932
Location of vineyards: St.-Estèphe
Owner: Héritiers Castéja
Address: 33180 St.-Estèphe
Mailing address: Domaines Borie-Manoux, 86, cours Balguerie
Stuttenberg, 33082 Bordeaux Cedex
Telephone: 33 5 56 00 00 70; telefax: 33 5 57 87 60 30
Visits: By appointment only
Contact: Domaines Borie-Manoux (see above)

VINEYARDS (red)
Surface area: 98.8 acres
Average age of vines: 30 years
Blend: 70% Cabernet Sauvignon, 30% Merlot
Density of plantation: 7,000 vines per hectare
Average yields (over the last 5 years): 55 hectoliters per hectare
Total average annual production: 14,000 cases

GRAND VIN (red)
Brand name: Château Beau-Site
Appellation: St.-Estèphe
Mean annual production: 14,000 cases
Upbringing: Grapes are hand-picked and totally destemmed.
Fermentations last 3 weeks in temperature-controlled stainless-steel
vats. Malolactics occur in vats, and wines are transferred to oak casks,
50% of which are new, around December. They are fined but not
filtered.

SECOND WINE
None produced.

Evaluation of present classification: The quality equivalent of a good Cru Bourgeois
Plateau of maturity: 3–10 years following the vintage

The lovely, well-situated Château Beau-Site was acquired by the well-known Bordelais family of Emile Castéja in 1955. The main part of the vineyard is situated on a plateau overlooking the Gironde River near the village of St.-Corbian. Beau-Site should be an excellent wine, but its performance in the sixties and seventies was spotty. Did the high percentage of Cabernet Sauvignon result in a wine that was too often tannic and tough? Whatever the reason, the decisions to harvest later and to utilize one-third new oak casks have all produced increasingly more supple and popular wines in the eighties. Nevertheless, this is still a fickle St.-Estèphe, with an abundance of tannin, although now the tannins are riper and smoother.

The wines of Beau-Site are distributed exclusively through the *négociant* firm of Borie-Manoux.

VINTAGES

1990—The 1990 is an easygoing, round, fruity wine that exhibits soft tannins and a
   •   velvety feel. Anticipated maturity: Now–2002. Last tasted, 1/93.
   84

1989—This is probably the best wine produced at Beau-Site since their 1982. Deep
   •   ruby/purple in color, with a moderately intense bouquet of superripe cassis
   85   fruit, minerals, and spicy oak, this medium-bodied, moderately tannic, concentrated wine has more power and opulence than most vintages of Beau-Site.
   Drinkable young, it should age gracefully for up to a decade. Anticipated
   maturity: Now–2000. Last tasted, 4/91.

1988—Medium dark ruby, with a tight but emerging bouquet of herbs, oak, and red
   •   fruits, this lean, austere, medium-bodied St.-Estèphe has abundant astringent
   77   tannins to resolve. There is some ripe fruit lurking in the wine, but the overall
   impression is one of toughness and a backward, somewhat compact style.
   Anticipated maturity: Now. Last tasted, 4/91.

1986—This Cru Bourgeois tends to produce rather firm, austere wines that are
   •   usually well made but need 2–3 years in the bottle to round out. The 1986 is
   79   medium ruby colored, with a tight yet spicy bouquet of herbaceous, curranty
   fruit. It is medium bodied, tannic, and firm. Anticipated maturity: Now. Last
   tasted, 3/89.

CALON-SÉGUR　　　EXCELLENT

Classification: Third-growth in 1855
Location of vineyards: St.-Estèphe
Owner: S.C. Château Calon-Ségur—Director: Madame Denise
Capbern-Gasqueton
Address: 33180 St.-Estèphe
Telephone: 33 5 56 59 30 08; telefax: 33 5 56 59 71 51
Visits: By appointment only
Contact: Madame Capbern-Gasqueton (see details above)

VINEYARDS (red)
Surface area: 136 acres
Average age of vines: 35 years
Blend: 45% Cabernet Sauvignon, 40% Merlot, 15% Cabernet Franc
Average yields (over the last 5 years): 40 hectoliters per hectare
Total average annual production: 280,000 bottles

GRAND VIN (red)
Brand name: Château Calon-Ségur
Appellation: St.-Estèphe
Mean annual production: 240,000 bottles
Upbringing: Grapes are hand-picked. Fermentations are rather long
(3 weeks) in temperature-controlled vats. Malolactics occur in new
oak casks for 20% of the production. The rest of the wines are
transferred to oak casks, 30% of which are new, after having completed
their malolactics in vats, for about 18–20 months. They are fined but not
filtered.

SECOND WINE
Brand name: Marquis de Calon
Average annual production: 40,000 bottles

Evaluation of present classification: Should be maintained
Plateau of maturity: 8–30 years following the vintage

Situated on a bed of sandy gravel and iron-enriched limestone in the north-ernmost reaches of the commune of St.-Estèphe is Calon-Ségur, the most northerly classified growth. Like its nearby neighbor, Château Montrose, there is a live-in owner, Madame Capbern-Gasqueton. The white château of Calon-Ségur dominates the landscape, with two towers and their unusually rounded roofs. Surrounding the château is a stone wall, or clos, which, while common in Burgundy, is unusual for Bordeaux.

The history of Calon-Ségur dates back to Roman times, when the commune of St.-Estèphe was known as "de Calones." Notoriety as a wine-producing estate is no doubt enhanced by the famous eighteenth-century quotation attributed to the Marquis de Ségur, who surprised friends with his statement, "I make my wine at Lafite and Latour, but my heart is in Calon." His emotional attachment to Calon has been immortalized with a heart on Calon's label. For much of the twentieth century, Calon-Ségur did almost everything right, often producing wines that were every bit as good as the first-growths. There were extraordinary efforts in 1926, 1928, and 1929, and in the dismal decade of the thirties a fine 1934 was produced. In the late forties and early fifties, few properties in Bordeaux could match the stunning successes that Calon-Ségur enjoyed in 1945, 1947, 1948, 1949, and 1953. Following 1953, there was not another truly profound wine produced at Calon-Ségur until 1982. They were not bad, but even the top years during the sixties and seventies tended to turn out wines that were slightly oxidized, with tired fruit and sometimes an excessive, musty, old-wood flavor, as well as excessive, astringent tannins. The feeling by knowledgeable insiders in Bordeaux was that the bringing up of the wine in the cellars—the so-called *élévage*—was suspect, and that the wines were bottled too late and the racking and cleanliness of the old barrels was often handled in a casual, if not indifferent, manner.

Since 1982 Calon-Ségur has regained its form, turning out fine wines in 1988, 1989, 1990, 1995, and 1996. This great historic estate, seemingly directionless in the seventies, has come back strongly, and while totally different in style, the wines are capable of challenging Cos d'Estournel and Montrose. Madame Gasqueton (and, before his death, her husband) would argue that of all the St.-Estèphes, Calon-Ségur remains the most faithful to the traditional style of long-lived wines that are slow to evolve and blossom. In that sense she is correct, and traditionalists would be well advised to consider the recent efforts of this beautifully situated, historically significant estate that is the last (geographically speaking) of the classified growths in the famed 1855 classification.

VINTAGES

1997—Wouldn't you know it? After naming Madame Gasqueton as one of my heroines of 1997, and having praised to the heavens Calon-Ségur's brilliant 1995
• and 1996, I was let down by the rather insubstantial, closed, tannic, and
84– evolved 1997. Tasted on three separate occasions with consistent notes, this
86 wine possesses an evolved medium ruby/garnet color and an austere, tannic personality, with astringent tannin in the finish. The wine lacks the fruit, fat, and charm offered by the finest 1997s. Not without merit, the wine possesses complex aromas of earth, black fruits, minerals, and spice, medium body, and modest length. However, the 1997 Calon-Ségur is well below the quality level achieved in both 1996 and 1995. Anticipated maturity: 2001–2012. Last tasted, 3/98.

1996 —Proprietor Madame Gasqueton (one of *The Wine Advocate*'s heroines of 1997)
• produced two unqualified back-to-back successes. The 1996 has gained
92– weight, revealing even more flesh and depth than it did in spring 1997.
94 The wine is opaque ruby/purple colored, full bodied, ferociously tannic, and
crammed with fruit and extract. Made in an uncompromising, traditional
style, this wine will require a decade of patience. There is plenty of sweet
fruit on the attack, and while the tannins are high, they are remarkably ripe,
with no evidence of astringency or vegetal characteristics. This appears to be
a profound, classic, muscular, and powerful Calon-Ségur that will age effortlessly for 30–40 years. It should be remembered that this estate possesses
one of the greatest *terroirs* of Bordeaux and produced a bevy of legendary
wines in the twenties, late forties, and early fifties. Since then it has been
something of a hit-or-miss property, but under her administration, Madame
Gasqueton has produced consistently outstanding wines. The 1996, a blend
of 60% Cabernet Sauvignon and 40% Merlot, was made from extremely low
yields of 35 hectoliters per hectare. Anticipated maturity: 2006–2035. Last
tasted, 3/98.

1995 —As I have said many times since I first tasted this wine, the 1995 Calon-
• Ségur is one of the great sleepers of the vintage (I bought the wine as a fu-
92+ ture for a mere $250 a case). The wine has closed down completely since
bottling, but it is a sensational effort that may ultimately merit an even
higher score. The wine is opaque purple colored. With coaxing, the tight
aromatics reveal some weedy cassis intertwined with truffles, chocolate, and
beef bloodlike aromas. On the palate, there is an element of *sur-maturité*
(1995 was an extremely late harvest at Calon-Ségur), fabulous density and
purity, and a boatload of tannin. This deep, broodingly backward, classic
Bordeaux will require a decade of cellaring. Anticipated maturity: 2005–
2035.

1994 —Dark ruby colored, with a closed, truffle-like aroma, this is a concentrated,
• stern, tannic wine that appears to have more weight than the 1993, but also
86+? more astringent tannin. It needs 2–3 years of cellaring. Anticipated maturity:
2000–2012. Last tasted, 1/97.

1993 —This soft, medium-bodied wine exhibits a dark ruby color, easygoing berry,
• herb, and earth flavors, low acidity, and a round, nicely textured finish.
86 Anticipated maturity: Now–2004. Last tasted, 1/97.

1991 —The deep ruby–colored 1991 exhibits a tight, old-fashioned, rustic bouquet
• of leather, cedar, tea, and ripe berry fruit, adequate body, a tight structure,
84 and fine depth. I would not be surprised to see it improve with 3–4 years of
cellaring. It should keep for 10–15 years. Last tasted, 1/94.

1990 —The dark ruby–colored 1990, which already reveals some amber, offers a
• fragrant bouquet of spicy, oaky, cherry, and herb-like fruit. This is an admira-
90 bly concentrated, surprisingly approachable, extremely well-balanced wine
with outstanding depth and purity of fruit to its medium-bodied personality.
Surprisingly, it is close to full maturity. Anticipated maturity: Now–2010.
Last tasted, 8/97.

1989 —This property has turned in a very good effort in 1989. It possesses a deep
• ruby/garnet color, a sweet, chewy, dense texture, full body, plenty of alcohol,
88 and moderately high tannin. Quite precocious, it will have a life span of at
least 15 years. It reminded me of a downsized version of the 1982, but slightly
more rustic. Anticipated maturity: Now–2010. Last tasted, 8/97.

1988 —The 1988 Calon-Ségur outshines both wines from the more heralded vintages
• of 1989 and 1990. Deeply colored, superbly balanced, rich and full bodied,
91 it appears to be a worthy candidate for another 15–20 years of longevity. It is
a classic example of this château's wine—cedary, very fragrant, with plenty
of sweet red and black currant fruit. I should also note that it is surprisingly
powerful for the vintage. It gets my nod as the finest Calon-Ségur between
1982 and 1995. Anticipated maturity: Now–2020. Last tasted, 6/97.

1987 —Light to medium ruby, with a washed-out, herbal, woody, faintly fruity bou-
• quet, this soft, medium-bodied wine should be drunk over the next 5–6 years.
75 Anticipated maturity: Now. Last tasted, 6/90.

1986 —The 1986 possesses a deep ruby/garnet color, with a tight, yet ripe, black
• currant bouquet backed up with subtle scents of herb, cedar, and sweet oak.
88 On the palate, the wine is muscular, rich, and medium to full bodied, with a
pronounced smoky, mineral, and currant character. It has fine length, with
some rustic tannin still noticeable in the finish. Curiously, in this vintage
Calon-Ségur used an inordinately high percentage of Cabernet Sauvignon
(90% Cabernet Sauvignon, 10% Merlot). Normally the percentage of Merlot
is significantly higher. Anticipated maturity: 1999–2015. Last tasted, 4/94.

1985 —The 1985 was bottled very late (January 1988), which has tended to dry out
• the wine. Medium ruby/garnet colored, with a sweet, earthy, berry, spicy,
84 somewhat herbaceous nose, this medium-bodied wine is pleasant but lacks
depth and fat. In addition, it is fully mature. Anticipated maturity: Now–
2005. Last tasted, 6/96.

1984 —The 1984 is a medium-bodied, light, relatively soft wine with some aromas of
• new oak and decent balance. The color suggests a 1973. Anticipated maturity:
75 Now. Last tasted, 9/88.

1983 —When I first tasted this wine in spring 1984, it was surprisingly soft, with
• grapey flavors, a hot, alcoholic finish, a rather fragile framework. Later in the
82 year, it was ripe and flavorful, but low in acidity and, again, alcoholic. In
style, color, and texture, it reminded me of a 1976. Revealing considerable
amber and rust to its color, this fully mature, loosely structured, rather weedy
wine should be drunk up. Anticipated maturity: Now. Last tasted, 11/94.

1982 —This wine, which was brilliant from cask, went into a frightfully backward,
• hard, austere period that now appears to be behind it. For more than a decade
94 I wondered if I was hallucinating during my cask tastings, but, finally, the
1982 Calon-Ségur is revealing its true personality. The wine had an opulent,
unctuous texture and thickness from cask that reminded me of the estate's
legendary 1947. Those characteristics are beginning to emerge again as the
wine has begun to develop more complexity and shed some of its formidable
tannin. This is a large-scale, super-concentrated wine that requires at least

sixty minutes of breathing after decanting. It exhibits a dense, plummy color with some slight amber at the edge. The intense nose of roasted coffee, sweet, jammy, fruity, leather, and spice is followed by a full-bodied, tannic wine that is beginning to display the thickness and opulence I had envisioned. Still young and backward, and made in a traditional, "no holds barred" style, this classic Calon-Ségur should reach its plateau of maturity during the first decade of the next century. Anticipated maturity: 2002–2030. Last tasted, 9/97.

1981—Rather light, but nevertheless charming, elegant, fruity, and clearly marked
•　　by wood, the 1981 Calon-Ségur reflects both the inconsistency of this famous
83　　estate and the 1981 vintage. Soft on the palate, it can be drunk now. Antici-
　　　pated maturity: Now–2000. Last tasted, 5/88.

1979—An elegant, charming, somewhat straightforward style of wine, with good, soft,
•　　supple fruit, light tannin, medium ruby color, and a pronounced ripe Merlot
80　　character. Anticipated maturity: Now. Last tasted, 10/84.

1978—A distinctly mediocre effort, with medium ruby color, a pleasing, yet one-
•　　dimensional, ripe, leafy, spicy, weedy aroma, average flavor intensity, and a
78　　short, simple finish. Some tannin is present, but this wine requires immediate
　　　consumption. Anticipated maturity: Now. Last tasted, 3/88.

1976—Once a pleasant, supple, deliciously fruity wine, the 1976 has begun to lose
•　　its fruit and commence its decline. Medium garnet in color with brown at the
78　　edge, this wine has a well-developed bouquet of hickory wood, ripe fruit, and
　　　spice. The soft flavors are marked by low acidity and an astringent dryness in
　　　the finish. Drink immediately. Anticipated maturity: Now. Last tasted, 7/87.

1975—One of the more flattering, soft, easy to understand and consume wines of the
•　　vintage, Calon-Ségur's 1975 exhibits considerable amber at the edge, a sweet
87　　nose of roasted herbs, mocha, chocolatey red and black fruits, medium body,
　　　some tannin, and spicy, gingery flavors. This wine should drink well for
　　　another decade. Anticipated maturity: Now–2006. Last tasted, 12/95.

1974—Somewhat typical of this vintage, Calon-Ségur produced a shallow, though
•　　pleasingly colored wine with just enough fruit to make it palatable. It is still
69　　holding together, no doubt because of its high acidity. Caveat emptor. Last
　　　tasted, 2/86.

1973—In its prime in 1976–1978, this was one of the more pleasant 1973 Bordeaux
•　　wines. While the wine has not been tasted recently, it would be most shocking
65　　if it had much fruit left to it. Last tasted, 9/77.

1971—Fading badly, as evidenced by the brown color, the 1971 Calon-Ségur has a
•　　decaying mushroom aroma, soft, barely alive flavors, and an acidic finish. My
65　　notes reveal I enjoyed a good bottle in 1977, but time has not been kind to
　　　this vintage of Calon-Ségur. Last tasted, 10/80.

1970—Another convincing piece of evidence that Calon-Ségur's reputation for pro-
•　　ducing long-lived wine was hardly justified by this estate's performance dur-
80　　ing much of the sixties and seventies. Fully mature in 1978, with an attractive,
　　　charming, moderately intense bouquet of ripe Merlot fruit and spicy oak, this
　　　garnet-colored, slightly brownish wine has soft, supple fruit, medium body,

and little tannin remaining. Anticipated maturity: Now—may be in decline. Last tasted, 1/81.

1967—Calon-Ségur made one of the best 1967s, which for several years outper-
•   formed its more heralded older sibling, the 1966. Rich, soft, supple, and
84   deeply fruity, the wine had a voluptuous texture. The bouquet offered ripe fruit and good cedary scents. The fruit has now begun to fade, so immediate consumption is advised. Anticipated maturity: Now—may be in decline. Last tasted, 10/80.

1966—This wine continues to hold on to life, but it is living dangerously. It has a
•   lovely, full-intensity bouquet of cedar wood and ripe fruit. Very satisfying on
87   the palate, with good concentration and length, this is arguably the best Calon-Ségur of the sixties. Anticipated maturity: Now. Last tasted, 1/87.

1964—Lacking fruit and coarsely textured, with a damp earthy, musty aroma, and
•   modest flavors and proportions, this wine is still holding together but seems
75   to hold little promise for the future. Anticipated maturity: Now—probably in serious decline. Last tasted, 6/78.

1962—My first tasting experience, early in the seventies, found the 1962 Calon-
•   Ségur to be especially light, lacking richness and fat, and browning at the
76   edge. Tasted again, in Bordeaux, in the late eighties revealed a wine that was still alive but light and uninteresting. Anticipated maturity: Now. Last tasted, 1/87.

1961—A good, solid wine, but given the vintage and overall quality of its two most
•   famous neighbors, Montrose and Cos d'Estournel, the 1961 Calon-Ségur is a
83   disappointment. The color lacks the great depth and richness of this vintage, and this wine seems much less concentrated and rich than others. In 1987 the wine was fit to drink but living dangerously, with high acidity poking its head through the moderate levels of extract. It remains a mediocre effort, particularly for a 1961. Anticipated maturity: Now. Last tasted, 6/87.

ANCIENT VINTAGES

Largely forgotten today, Calon-Ségur is one of the great Bordeaux estates. This property made extraordinary wines in the twenties, forties, and early fifties. The 1924, 1926, 1928, 1929, 1945, 1947, 1949, and 1953 are still exquisite wines. I have heard that the 1953 (96 points; last tasted 10/94) was sumptuous even before it reached 10 years of age. When drunk recently from magnum, the wine was a classic example of the glorious fragrance and velvety richness this vintage achieved. While most Calon-Ségurs possess a hefty degree of tannin, this wine offers a glorious concoction of cedar, sweet jammy fruit, full body, and remarkable intensity without the husky roughness Calon-Ségur can display. Although the color exhibits noticeable amber at the edge, this wine remains in magnificent condition.

The 1945 Calon-Ségur (90 points; last tasted 12/95) is a powerful, dense, dark garnet-colored wine with plenty of earth, mineral, and black fruits in its nose. Although tannin is still present, this is a formidably concentrated, thick, hugely extracted, amazingly youthful wine. It can be drunk now or cellared for another 25–30 years. The most opulent, generous, and decadent Calon-Ségur I have ever tasted is the 1947 (96 points; last tasted 7/97). It revealed considerable amber and rust in its color, but the sweet, jammy nose of fruitcake, cedar, and colossal quantities of unctuously textured black fruits is the stuff of legend. Thick and rich, with more glycerin, fruit, and alcohol than tannin, this is a juicy, fat wine that has been fully mature for 20+ years. It exhibited no signs of decline or fruit loss. I have experienced bottle variation with the 1949 Calon-Ségur (94 points; last tasted 12/95), ranging from bottles that were slightly austere and undernourished, to those that were superb. This bottle was an outstanding example. It did not possess the weight, unctuosity, and thickness of the 1947, or the power, youthfulness, and muscle of the 1945. It revealed considerable amber at the edge of its dark garnet color. The nose displayed a Médoc-like, cedar, spice, curranty, mineral, and damp forest scent. Medium to full bodied, with high tannin, excellent concentration, and an element of overripe fruit, this was an impressive, fully mature Calon-Ségur that can be drunk now or cellared for another 10–20 years.

The decade of the twenties was a legendary one for Calon-Ségur. The 1928 (96 points; last tasted, 12/95) revealed an opaque garnet color with a coffeelike look at the edge. Late-harvest-like in the nose, with a plummy, Asian spice, leather, and molasses-like aromas and flavors, this thick, extremely sweet, rich, full-bodied wine is astonishingly intense. It is all glycerin, richness, and intensity, with no hard edges, making one a true believer of the extraordinary longevity of Bordeaux's greatest wines. This may be the greatest ancient vintage of Calon-Ségur, although the 1926 is a close rival.

The 1926 (94 points; last tasted, 12/95) is not a wine for modern-day oenologists. The color is mainly orange/rust, with some ruby remaining. Noticeable volatile acidity blows off within several minutes. The sweet, plummy, cedary, roasted nut, and clove nose is followed by a surprisingly sweet wine, with fine ripeness and chewy glycerin. The well-balanced finish is long, authoritative, and generous. Although the feeble color suggests a degree of decrepitude, such is not the case.

CHAMBERT-MARBUZET　　　　　　　　　　　　　　　GOOD

Classification: Cru Bourgeois
Location of vineyards: St.-Estèphe
Owner: Henri Duboscq and sons
Address: 33180 St.-Estèphe
Mailing address: (same as above)
Telephone: 33 5 56 59 30 54; telefax: 33 5 56 50 70 87

Visits: From Monday to Friday, between 8 A.M. and noon, and 2 P.M. and 6 P.M.

VINEYARDS (red)
Surface area: 17.3 acres
Average age of vines: 25 years
Blend: 70% Cabernet Sauvignon, 30% Merlot
Density of plantation: 8,300 vines per hectare
Average yields (over the last 5 years): 45 hectoliters per hectare
Total average annual production: 45,000 bottles

GRAND VIN (red)
Brand name: Château Chambert-Marbuzet
Appellation: St.-Estèphe
Mean annual production: 45,000 bottles
Upbringing: Grapes are picked manually and are totally destemmed. Fermentations last 18–20 days and macerations up to 4 weeks, with frequent *saignées*. Wines are racked every 3 months and are aged half in wooden vats and half in new oak barrels. They are fined but not filtered, and bottling is done by hand and by gravity (no pumping).

SECOND WINE
None produced.

Evaluation of present classification: The quality equivalent of a fifth-growth
Plateau of maturity: 2–8 years following the vintage

The talented and flamboyant Henri Duboscq, proprietor of the better-known Château Haut-Marbuzet in St.-Estèphe, is also the owner of this small estate located near the village of Marbuzet. It was acquired by the Duboscq family in 1962. Like Haut-Marbuzet, the vinification consists of a relatively high fermentation temperature, a long *cuvaison*, the bringing up of the wine in at least 50% new oak casks, and the avoidance of any type of filtration at the time of bottling. The wines of Chambert-Marbuzet have exhibited rich fruit, married with abundant, sometimes excessive, quantities of toasty new oak. They are easy to understand and drink. If Chambert-Marbuzet is to be criticized at all, it would be because at times the wines can be entirely too obvious, and their potential to age beyond a decade is suspect. Nevertheless, the quality is reasonably high, and the wine enjoys increasing popularity.

VINTAGES

1995—The 1995 lacks depth. There is some ripeness, too much new oak, and a
 • low-acid, disjointed, clumsy style with no focus or concentration. Last tasted,
 83 3/96.

1994—It is hard to know what could have happened at Chambert-Marbuzet, but the
 • 1994 tastes like an old, musty, mediocre Spanish Rioja with too much wood
 76 and not enough fruit. The wine is thin, disjointed, and disappointing. Last
 tasted, 3/96.

1993—A minty, spicy, soft, fruity nose fades quickly, as do the wine's flavors once
 • they touch the palate. This 1993 offering is diluted, too earthy and woody,
 74 and short in the finish. Last tasted, 11/94.

1992—The 1992 has not handled its bottling too well, as this wine has lost consider-
 • able fruit. Although lighter than usual, this spicy, minty, watery wine pos-
 76 sesses medium body, decent concentration, and a short, attenuated finish.
 Drink it over the next 2–3 years. Last tasted, 11/94.

1990—Richly oaky and superspicy, the fleshy 1990 is oozing with ripe fruit. Authori-
 • tatively flavored and full bodied, this is the finest Chambert-Marbuzet
 89 yet made. It will make sensual drinking for another 5–9 years. Last tasted,
 1/93.

1989—The 1989 Chambert-Marbuzet exhibits plenty of toasty new oak and an exotic
 • bouquet of black fruits and spices, is exuberantly fruity, very soft, and me-
 86 dium bodied, and finishes with a whopping blow of alcohol and tannin. It is
 flashy but lacking some substance in the mid-palate. Drink it over the next
 7–8 years. Anticipated maturity: Now. Last tasted, 4/91.

1988—Abnormally light, fragrant, and evolved, the 1988 is surprisingly shy and
 • subdued for a wine from this estate. It should be drunk over the near term,
 83 within 2–4 years of the vintage. Anticipated maturity: Now. Last tasted,
 4/91.

1987—Green, herbal, washed-out fruit flavors are followed by a medium-bodied wine
 • with soft tannins that lacks concentration. It should be drunk up. Anticipated
 74 maturity: Now–may be in decline. Last tasted, 3/90.

1986—In all my cask tastings the 1986 was an impressive wine, with deep ruby/
 • black color, super depth, richness, full body, stunning length, and enough
 87 tannin to insure a positive evolution for 5–6 years. Muscular and brawny, it
 is marked by the toasty vanilla of 100% new oak barrels. The wine is excellent, but much lighter than I had thought it to be when tasted from cask. It is
 a sleeper of the vintage. Anticipated maturity: Now. Last tasted, 4/90.

1985—The rating of the 1985 may be conservative, as I thought it to be a slightly
 • better wine in cask prior to bottling. It is a deep, powerful wine packed with
 86 jammy fruit, an overt spicy oakiness, medium to full body, and soft texture.
 Anticipated maturity: Now. Last tasted, 3/89.

COS D'ESTOURNEL   OUTSTANDING

Classification: Second-growth in 1855
Location of vineyards: They just border Pauillac and are separated from
those of Lafite-Rothschild by a small river called La Jalle du Breuil
Owner: Domaines Prats S.A.
Address: 33180 St.-Estèphe
Telephone: 33 5 56 73 15 50; telefax: 33 5 56 59 72 59
Visits: By appointment only, from Monday to Friday, between 10 A.M. and
noon, and 2 P.M. and 5 P.M.
Contact: Catherine di Constanzo. Telephone: 33 5 56 73 15 55; telefax,
as above

VINEYARDS (red)
Surface area: 158 acres
Average age of vines: 35 years
Blend: 60% Cabernet Sauvignon, 40% Merlot
Density of plantation: 9,000 vines per hectare
Average yields (over the last 5 years): 50 hectoliters per hectare
Total average annual production: 400,000 bottles

GRAND VIN (red)
Brand name: Château Cos d'Estournel
Appellation: St.-Estèphe
Mean annual production: 300,000 bottles
Upbringing: Grapes are picked by hand, and winemaking is traditional.
Fermentations last approximately 3 weeks. Wines are transferred into oak
barrels, after having completed their malolactics in vats. In 1997, for the
first time, Prats decided to do 100% malolactic fermentation in small oak
casks. Depending upon the vintage, the percentage of new oak varies
between 60% and 100%. Wines are fined and filtered.

SECOND WINE
Brand name: Les Pagodes de Cos
Average annual production: 100,000 bottles

Evaluation of present classification: Since 1982 the quality equivalent of
a first-growth
Plateau of maturity: 8–30 years following the vintage

Under the inspired direction of Bruno Prats, Cos d'Estournel (pronounced,
surprisingly, with a sounded "oss" in *Cos*) has risen to the top of its class in
St.-Estèphe. Since 1982 the wines have gone from one strength to another,
and in most vintages Cos d'Estournel can be expected to produce one of the

Médoc's finest wines. This château, which resembles an Asian pagoda, sits on a ridge immediately north of the Pauillac border, looking down on its famous neighbor, Lafite-Rothschild. Atypically for a Médoc, Cos is distinguished by the high percentage of Merlot used in the blend—40%—and the elevated use of new oak casks—60% to 100%. This proportion of Merlot is among the highest used in the Haut-Médoc and also accounts for the fleshy, richly textured character so noticeable in recent vintages of Cos d'Estournel. Bruno Prats, the manager and owner, belongs to the avant-garde of new wine technology. This is one of the few major Bordeaux estates to be adamantly in favor of filtration of wine, before both cask aging and bottling. However, Prats may be having second thoughts, as he decided to eliminate the second filtration prior to the bottling of the 1989. The results speak for themselves—Cos d'Estournel, after having to play runner-up to Montrose in the fifties and sixties, has emerged in the eighties as one of the most popular wines in Bordeaux. Readers should also note that Cos d'Estournel has been particularly successful in difficult vintages, for example, 1993, 1992, and 1991.

VINTAGES

1997—Cos d'Estournel has again turned out one of the vintage's finest wines. Proprietor Bruno Prats and his son, Jean-Guillaume, claim that for most of the Cos d'Estournel vineyard, there was a minimum of 120 days between flowering and harvest. In normal years, 105–110 days are usual. The opaque purple–colored 1997 Cos d'Estournel offers up a gorgeously sweet nose consisting of ripe black currant fruit, Provençal olives, smoked herbs, *pain grillé*, and licorice. Rich and powerful, as well as elegant and stylish, this wine possesses plenty of fat, in addition to layers of fruit and glycerin. It is an intensely charming, graceful yet impressively endowed Cos that should, because of its low acidity and sweet tannin, be delicious when young. Anticipated maturity: 2000–2016. Last tasted, 3/98.

• 90– 91

1996—A fabulous Cos d'Estournel, along with the 1995, the 1996 is the finest wine produced at this estate since the sumptuous 1990, and it represents the essence of Cos d'Estournel. From its saturated black/ruby/purple color, to its knockout nose of Asian spices, licorice, tobacco-tinged cassis fruit, and plum-like jam, this full-bodied, extraordinarily pure wine will enjoy an immensely impressive future. Approximately 66% of the crop made it into the final blend, which includes a slightly higher percentage of Cabernet Sauvignon than usual (65% Cabernet Sauvignon and 35% Merlot). While the 1996 is similar to the 1986, the fruit and tannin in the former wine are sweeter and more abundant. It is a massive example of Cos, but neither heavy nor overbearing in view of its immense size. Anticipated maturity: 2005–2035. Last tasted, 3/98.

• 94– 96

1995—A wine of extraordinary intensity and accessibility, the 1995 Cos d'Estournel is a sexier, more hedonistic offering than the muscular, backward 1996. Opulent, with forward aromatics (gobs of black fruits intermixed with toasty

• 95

pain grillé scents and a boatload of spice), this terrific Cos possesses remarkable intensity, full body, and layers of jammy fruit nicely famed by the wine's
new oak. Because of low acidity and sweet tannin, the 1995 will be difficult
to resist young, although it will age for 2–3 decades. Anticipated maturity:
2001–2025. Last tasted, 11/97.

1994— While tasting through Cos d'Estournel's wines, it was interesting to taste the
• unfiltered 1994 against the same cuvée of wine that was put through the
91 normal filtration. The filtered cuvée was an excellent wine (I rated it 88), but
as Bruno Prats and several other people at the tasting could easily see, it had
less opacity, color, and aromatic interest and far less volume and midpalate.
Most Bordeaux châteaux continue to do too much fining and filtering, but
some of the more seriously run estates are curtailing the most abusive clarification procedures and are finally opening their minds to the negative impact
too much fining and filtration can cause. Sadly, most of my colleagues have
fallen hook, line, and sinker for the standard response from oenologists and
producers on this issue . . . "fining and filtration have no effect on a wine."

Cos d'Estournel's unfiltered 1994 is one of the top wines of the vintage. It
boasts an opaque blue/black/purple color, as well as a fabulously sweet nose
of black fruits, licorice, *pain grillé,* and Asian spices. Full bodied, with sweet,
opulent fruit that reveals none of the vintage's tough tannin, this remarkably
rich, well-balanced, classic wine will prove to be uncommonly long-lived.
Anticipated maturity: 2003–2025. Last tasted, 1/97.

1993— One of the most successful Médocs of the vintage, Cos d'Estournel's 1993
• exhibits an opaque dark purple color and a heady, sweet, pure, black currant
89 bouquet that roars from the glass. With surprising richness, fat, and glycerin,
tasters would never suspect that this medium-bodied, elegant yet authoritatively flavored wine emerged from such a difficult vintage. The wine's low
acidity and roundness guarantees 12–14 years of drinkability. This is a
splendid success in an irregular vintage. Last tasted, 1/97.

1992— One of the stars of the vintage, the 1992 Cos d'Estournel exhibits a deep
• ruby/purple color, medium to full body, scents of smoky oak, and copious
88 amounts of black currant fruit. Velvety textured and medium to full bodied,
this is an atypically ripe, concentrated, impressively endowed wine that
should drink well for 6–10 years. It is a 1992 that merits considerable
interest! Last tasted, 11/94.

1991— Cos d'Estournel's 1991 (about 50% of the harvest was declassified) is one of
• the wines to buy, given its relatively low price and fine quality. It displays a
87 dark ruby color and a big, rich nose of cassis fruit married intelligently with
spicy new oak. Offering surprising fatness and fleshiness, fine length, and a
sweet, creamy texture, it should drink well for at least a decade. Last tasted,
1/94.

1990— The 1990 will charm tasters with its flashy display of opulent Merlot (about
• 40% of the blend) mixed with ripe Cabernet Sauvignon. It was one of the
95 more forward 1990s in the tasting, which no doubt accounted for its precocious showing. This super-concentrated wine possesses a roasted herb, sweet,

jammy, black fruit–scented nose, with noteworthy opulence and succulence. Pure and full bodied, this concentrated wine conceals more tannin than it is presently revealing. The wine is open, flattering, and impossible to resist. It will continue to mature for 15–20 years. Last tasted, 11/96.

1989— The 1989, although good, does not live up to expectations given the *terroir*
•   and the vintage. Its deep ruby color is followed by a spicy vanillin, curranty
88   nose, medium body, excellent depth, but a monolithic personality. It possesses neither the concentration nor the dimension of the exceptional 1990. The 1989 possesses some hard tannin in the finish, but it is well integrated with the wine's ripe fruit. Look for this wine to drink well for the next 15+ years. Last tasted, 11/96.

1988— The 1988 has an intriguing bouquet of exotic spices and black fruits. Savagely
•   tannic in its youth, the wine has softened and developed more charm and
87   appeal. Still deep ruby/purple in color, with little signs of age, this medium-bodied, slightly austere wine possesses good cassis fruit, excellent purity, and an elegant, classic style. Anticipated maturity: 2000–2012. Last tasted, 10/96.

1987— This wine is fully ready to drink, displaying a plummy, toasty, weedy bouquet,
•   light to medium body, some soft, fleshy fruit, low acidity, and soft tannins in
83   the finish. It should be consumed over the next 7–8 years. Anticipated maturity: Now. Last tasted, 3/91.

1986— The 1986 is a highly extracted wine, with a black/ruby color and plenty of
•   toasty, smoky notes in its bouquet that suggest ripe plums and licorice.
95   Evolving at a glacial pace, it exhibits massive, huge, ripe, extremely concentrated flavors with impressive depth and richness. It possesses more power, weight, and tannin than the more opulent and currently more charming 1985. Anticipated maturity: Now–2010. Last tasted, 10/94.

1985— The 1985 from cask could have been a lighter version of the 1982 and
•   1953 vintages. Forward, with a fabulously scented bouquet of *pain grillé* and
93   concentrated red and black fruits (especially black cherries), it is rich, lush, long, and medium to full bodied. Very fragrant, with gobs of sweet black fruits, minerals, and spice in both its flavors and aromatics, this is one of the most forward wines from Cos. Anticipated maturity: Now–2010. Last tasted, 4/97.

1984— From the first time tasted, the 1984 was a success for this difficult vintage.
•   Sufficiently ruby in color with a moderately intense, spicy, tarry, oaky, cassis-
78   scented bouquet, this medium-bodied wine has decent concentration, soft yet firm tannins, and tart acidity. It may be just beginning to lose its fruit. Anticipated maturity: Now. Last tasted, 4/94.

1983— At first glimpse in March 1984, this Cos d'Estournel was raw, tannic, angular,
•   and unyielding, although it had good color and weight on the palate. Later in
81   the year the wine was showing more richness and fruit but was still decidedly tannic in a hard, lean way. Recent tastings have established that this wine is maturing quickly, taking on an advanced color. Never the picture of balance, this weedy, somewhat attenuated effort from Cos has become more com-

pressed and charmless over time. It is a disappointment for the vintage. Anticipated maturity: Now. Last tasted, 11/96.

1982—Like many 1982s, Cos d'Estournel was more flattering, opulent, and softer to
  • drink in its youth than it is today. This estate tends to make a more elegant
  96 style of Bordeaux, but the 1982 is atypically thick, super-concentrated, rich, and powerful. Although approachable and even delicious if decanted an hour or more before serving, the wine reveals no signs of age in its opaque, dark ruby/purple color. The tannin is more aggressive, but the wine still reveals that fabulous inner core of sweet, jammy, black currant and black cherry fruit. There is considerable glycerin and body in this still youthful but immensely promising example of Cos d'Estournel. It has at least 20 years of life remaining. Last tasted, 9/95.

1981—Deep ruby color, with a spicy, rich, briery, tightly knit bouquet, this wine is
  • deeper and more promising than the 1983 but is relatively light, compact,
  83 and lean. This restrained wine should be at its best if drunk over the next 5–7 years. Anticipated maturity: Now. Last tasted, 5/90.

1980—Unquestionably a success for the vintage, though obviously not a great wine,
  • the 1980 Cos d'Estournel has medium ruby color, an interesting, slightly
  83 spicy and herbaceous aroma, and well above average, fruity flavors for the vintage. Anticipated maturity: Now—may be in decline. Last tasted, 10/84.

1979—The best of the 1979 St.-Estèphes, Cos d'Estournel has a dark ruby color,
  • with a developing bouquet of ripe cherries, cassis, and some vanillin, oaky
  86 scents. Full, yet corpulent for the vintage, with surprising weight and depth, this wine has aged slowly and still needs another 2–3 years of bottle age to be fully mature. Anticipated maturity: Now–2000. Last tasted, 11/89.

1978—Very highly regarded by the château, the 1978 (I have found) is very good but
  • not as graceful or as well balanced as the 1979. It is dark ruby, with a
  85 moderately intense bouquet of herbs, black cherries, spice, oak, and leather. On the palate, the wine is medium to full bodied, with a dusty, tannic texture. Anticipated maturity: Now–2005. Last tasted, 1/88.

1976—One of the better 1976s, Cos d'Estournel somehow succeeded in avoiding the
  • feebleness and fragile character of many of the wines from this early maturing
  86 vintage. Now fully mature, but in no danger of collapse, this wine has a complex bouquet of red berry fruit, spices, and toasty oak. Supple, with good fruit, this soft, round, elegant wine should be drunk over the next 5 years. Anticipated maturity: Now. Last tasted, 2/90.

1975—This is not a pretty wine. The amber-tinged color is followed by earthy,
  • vegetal, spicy scents and little fruit. Harsh, austere, and frightfully tannic,
  76 this hollow wine will undoubtedly keep for 20–25 years, but it will never provide any pleasure. Drink it up. Last tasted, 12/95.

1974—Adequate color, but this stalky, unripe wine still tastes green and hol-
  • low. Anticipated maturity: Now–probably in serious decline. Last tasted,
  67 10/81.

1973—Eighteen years ago the fruit had already faded and the sure signs of ap-
•   proaching senility—a brownish, pale color—were apparent. It is now over
65   the hill. Last tasted, 10/80.

1971—From a vintage that was very irregular in quality, the 1971 Cos d'Estournel
•   is now fully mature. Medium to dark ruby, with an orange brownish edge,
84   this wine has a silky, rather seductive quality with good, supple fruit. It
       should be consumed immediately. Anticipated maturity: Now. Last tasted,
       1/87.

1970—The 1970 Cos d'Estournel's color remains an impressive dark garnet with
•   ruby/purple tints. The wine is medium to full bodied, tannic, rustic, and
86?   concentrated, but coarse and charmless. It will keep for another 25 years, but
       I wonder if this wine will ever blossom? Last tasted, 6/96.

1967—Now beginning to fade badly, this wine was at its prime from 1976 to 1978
•   but never had impressive depth or concentration. Anticipated maturity: Now–
73   probably in serious decline. Last tasted, 9/79.

1966—A very good 1966, yet not topflight, the Cos d'Estournel is medium to dark
•   ruby, with some browning. It has very good concentration, in the somewhat
85   lean, austere character of the vintage, and plenty of tannin in the finish.
       Although it does not yet seem to be mature, I would drink it over the near
       term before the fruit begins to fade. Anticipated maturity: Now. Last tasted,
       10/84.

1964—Because of the heavy rains in this year, wine was rather a hit-or-miss
•   proposition with most Médoc châteaux. If the grapes were picked
72   early, then the château probably made good wine, but if they were har-
       vested following the storms, the grapes were diluted by heavy rains and
       the results predictable. This wine—raw, ungenerous, yet surprisingly
       well colored—lacks fruit and complexity and is not likely to improve any
       further. Anticipated maturity: Now–probably in serious decline. Last tasted,
       10/78.

1962—This is a typical St.-Estèphe in the sense that wines from this commune
•   are generally described as being hard and unyielding. Nevertheless, all the
86   components are there, the dark ruby color, the very good concentration and
       weight, and the moderate tannin. Anticipated maturity: Now. Last tasted,
       12/83.

1961—Typically dark and densely pigmented with no sign of browning at the edge,
•   this big, intense, concentrated, still tannic wine has at least a decade of life
92   left in it. The fragrant bouquet offers up scents of cedar, Oriental spices, and
       fruitcake. It is very rich, deep, and long on the palate, with masses of ripe
       black fruits. An opulent beauty! Anticipated maturity: Now–2000. Last
       tasted, 1/91.

ANCIENT VINTAGES

The 1953 (93 points; last tasted 10/94), most recently drunk from magnums
in 1994, 1993, and 1989, is a classic example of the vintage, displaying a
huge, fragrant, flowery-, berry-scented nose. From a regular bottle I suspect

this wine could be on the downside, but from pristinely kept magnums, this fully mature wine is a terrific example of the vintage, and certainly one of the greatest wines of the century.

Another of the delicious old vintages of Cos d'Estournel that I have been privileged to taste is the 1959 (rated 92 and more youthful than the 1961 when tasted in November 1989). Other notable vintages I have tasted included three disappointing bottles of 1947 (others claim it to be fabulous) and two nasty, tannic bottles of the 1945. I drank a profound magnum of 1928 (rated 97) at the château with Monsieur Prats in March 1988, but that was followed by two hollow and dead bottles of the 1928 drunk in 1994 and 1995.

COS LABORY   GOOD

Classification: Fifth-growth
Location of vineyards: St.-Estèphe, on the plateau of Cos, in the southern part of the appellation, next to Cos d'Estournel
Owner: S.C.E. Domaines Audoy
Address: 33180 St.-Estèphe
Telephone: 33 5 56 59 30 22; telefax: 33 5 56 59 73 52
Visits: By appointment only, from Monday to Friday, between 9 A.M. and noon, and 2 P.M. and 6 P.M.
Contact: Bernard Audoy

VINEYARDS (red)
Surface area: 44.5 acres
Average age of vines: 30 years
Blend: 55% Cabernet Sauvignon, 35% Merlot, 10% Cabernet Franc
Density of plantation: 8,700 vines per hectare
Average yields (over the last 5 years): 48 hectoliters per hectare
Total average annual production: 100,000 bottles

GRAND VIN (red)
Brand name: Château Cos Labory
Appellation: St.-Estèphe
Mean annual production: 70,000 bottles
Upbringing: Picking the grapes is done by hand. Fermentations last 25 days with a maximum of 30 degrees centigrade. *Remontages* are frequent to ensure a good extraction of tannins and color. Wines spend 15 months in oak casks after having completed their malolactics in barrels. Depending upon the vintage, 30%–50% new oak is used. Racking occurs every 3 months. Wines are fined but not filtered.

SECOND WINE
Brand name: Le Charme Labory
Average annual production: 30,000 bottles

Evaluation of present classification: Should be downgraded to a Cru
Bourgeois, although the high quality of both the 1989 and the 1990
should be noted
Plateau of maturity: 5–12 years following the vintage

For decades one of the most disappointing of all the classified growths, Cos
Labory has emerged over the last 10 years as a property well worth tasting as
well as visiting. The resurrection of quality began with excellent wines in
1989 and 1990 and has continued through the 1996 vintage, although many
of the vintages of the nineties have provided raw materials that were far less
promising than those Mother Nature provided in 1989 and 1990. The wine is
now a well-made, deeply colored, rich, muscular, and tannic St.-Estèphe. A
stricter selection by proprietor Bernard Audoy, malolactic fermentation in
barrel, and bottling the wine without filtration have all helped to significantly
elevate the quality of Cos Labory.

VINTAGES

1997—Deep ruby/purple colored, with a sweet, jammy nose of cassis, prunes, and
• spicy new oak, this medium-bodied, moderately tannic wine exhibits good ripe-
86– ness, moderate concentration, and a short but tannic finish. The wine should be
87 drinkable with 2–3 years of age and last for a decade. Last tasted, 3/98.

1996—This wine offers an opaque purple color, a sweet, pure nose of black raspber-
• ries, cassis, blueberries, and minerals, good density and richness, high ex-
86– tract, and medium body, as well as a boatload of astringent tannin. Despite
87+? some positive attributes, it is questionable as to whether this wine will come
around or not. I will wait until after bottling to see how much fruit and extract
remain. At present its anticipated maturity is 2008–2020. Last tasted, 3/98.

1995—Although this dark ruby/purple–colored Cos Labory is more charming since
• bottling, aromatically it is closed, with red and black fruits just beginning to
88+? emerge. In the mouth, dusty tannin appears elevated, giving the wine a hard,
dry, rough-textured finish. However, there is medium to full body and plenty
of sweet, ripe fruit on the attack, and my instincts suggest there is good
extract behind the wall of tannin. This is not a wine for immediate gratification. Anticipated maturity: 2003–2015. Last tasted, 11/97.

1994—This wine revealed a hint of mold in the nose, which could have come from a
• defective cork. Though not bad enough to make the wine impossible to
86? evaluate, I relay the information just in case the cork was not the source of
the musty aromatics. This tannic, medium-bodied 1994 possesses a deep
ruby/purple color and plenty of ripe black currant-and-licorice-flavored fruit.

If the nose cleans up, Cos Labory's 1994 could emerge as a solid 85/86-point effort. Anticipated maturity: 2004–2012. Last tasted, 1/97.

1993—The 1993 Cos Labory exhibits a dark ruby color and a spicy, low-key, pleasant
•   but undistinguished nose of red fruits, earth, and wood. The wine is hard, but
85   there is good depth, and perhaps the fruit will ultimately balance out the wine's structure. It needs 1–2 years of cellaring and should age for 12–15 years. Last tasted, 1/97.

1992—This soft 1992 is well made, with moderate depth, medium body, fine ripe-
•   ness, and adequate length. The high tannin in the finish suggests it should be
82? cellared for at least 3–4 years, although I wonder if the modest level of fruit extraction will dry out before the tannin melts away. Last tasted, 11/94.

1991—The 1991 exhibits a surprisingly saturated color and a tight but promising
•   nose of peppery, black currant, and smoky new oak scents. Medium bodied
86   and tannic, with good depth, this wine will benefit from 4–5 years of cellaring; it should last for 15 or more years. Last tasted, 1/94.

1990—The 1990 is nearly black colored, with a reticent, spicy, licorice, mineral,
•   and cassis-scented nose. In the mouth there is great extraction, rich, full-
89   bodied, chewy texture, and a splendidly long, moderately tannic finish. Antic-ipated maturity: Now–2010. Last tasted, 1/93.

1989—The 1989 is undeniably the finest example of Cos Labory I have ever tasted
•   to date. Black/ruby in color, with a huge bouquet of cassis, this formidable
89   1989 has layers of extract, a very high tannin level, and a hefty level of alcohol. Does this vintage signal the beginning of a renaissance of Cos La-bory? Anticipated maturity: Now–2015. Last tasted, 4/91.

1988—The 1988 Cos Labory is a pleasant, well-colored, tannic, medium-bodied wine,
•   with fine overall balance and good length. It should provide decent rather than
84   inspired drinking. Anticipated maturity: Now–2000. Last tasted, 3/90.

1986—The 1986 Cos Labory is light but does exhibit a pleasant, as well as charming,
•   berry fruitiness married with an attractive subtle oakiness. It seems to reveal
79   some of the vast size of the 1986 crop, particularly the lightness of the Merlot that was apparent in some vineyards in that vintage. Anticipated maturity: Now. Last tasted, 11/89.

1985—Cos Labory performed well in 1985, producing a soft, oaky, ripe wine, with
•   medium body, good concentration, and attractive length—surprisingly com-
85   petent. Anticipated maturity: Now. Last tasted, 6/89.

1983—The 1983 is disturbingly light, innocuous, simple, and plain. A respectable
•   vin de table, but hardly a wine of classified-growth quality. Anticipated matu-
70   rity: Now–probably in serious decline. Last tasted, 6/84.

1982—In the context of the vintage, a rather mediocre wine, but in the context of
•   Cos Labory's performance record during this era, a solid, amply endowed
75   wine, with good concentration, very good color, and moderate tannins. Antici-pated maturity: Now. Last tasted, 1/88.

1979—Medium ruby, with a shallow, faint, fruity aroma, this medium-bodied wine
•   has a light intensity, dull fruitiness, simple flavors, and little tannins. Antici-
65   pated maturity: Now–probably in serious decline. Last tasted, 9/84.

1978—Fully mature, with a burnt, stemmy, leafy aroma, this light- to medium-weight
•   wine has diluted fruit flavors and light to moderate tannins. A very mediocre
67   wine. Last tasted, 5/83.

1976—Faded, damp cellar aromas offer too little ripe fruit and too much wet, earthy
•   components for a good Bordeaux wine. Light to medium ruby color now shows
55   ample evidence of age as the brown color sets in. Anticipated maturity: Now—
       probably in serious decline. Last tasted, 2/80.

1975—A tannic, angular wine, with no charm, little fruit in evidence, and a severe,
•   hard, tannic bite to it. Anticipated maturity: Now. Last tasted, 12/81.
64

1971—Poor winemaking and perhaps overcropping as well have accounted for a very
•   mediocre, thin, green, nasty wine that shows the ugliest side of Bordeaux.
52   Last tasted, 4/78.

1970—An acceptable wine that provided decent, if hardly inspired, drinking in the
•   late seventies, this medium ruby wine exhibited a simple yet straightforward
70   fruitiness, some pleasing spicy, cherry components, and light to medium
       body. Anticipated maturity: Now—probably in serious decline. Last tasted,
       2/80.

LE CROCK

Classification: Cru Bourgeois in 1932
Location of vineyards: Marbuzet, St.-Estèphe
Owner: Famille Cuvelier
Address: c/o Domaines Cuvelier, 33180 St.-Estèphe
Telephone: 33 5 56 59 30 33; telefax: 33 5 56 59 60 09
Visits: By appointment only from Monday to Friday, between 8 A.M. and
noon, and 2 P.M. and 5 P.M.
Contact: Mr. Charles Viollet (at above address and numbers)

VINEYARDS (red)
Surface area: 78.3 acres
Average age of vines: 35 years
Blend: 55% Cabernet Sauvignon, 25% Merlot, 15% Cabernet Franc, 5%
Petit Verdot
Density of plantation: 8,500 vines per hectare
Average yields (over the last 5 years): 57 hectoliters per hectare
Total average annual production: 220,000 bottles

GRAND VIN (red)
Brand name: Château Le Crock
Appellation: St.-Estèphe
Mean annual production: 180,000 bottles
Upbringing: Grapes are manually harvested. Fermentations last 3 weeks,

and wines spend 16 months in oak barrels, 20% of which are new. They are fined but not filtered.

SECOND WINE
Brand name: Château La Croix St.-Estèphe
Average annual production: 40,000 bottles

Evaluation of present classification: The quality equivalent of a Cru Bourgeois
Plateau of maturity: 5–12 years following the vintage

This attractive, two-story château, located south of the village of St.-Estèphe, has been owned by the Cuvelier family since 1903. While the superbly situated château—which sits on a hill overlooking a lake usually inhabited by numerous swans—is a site even the most jaded photographer could hardly ignore, the wines have rarely been exciting. The high percentage of Merlot used would seemingly insure plenty of flesh and suppleness, but my experience with the wines of Le Crock indicates they are entirely too tannic and tough textured and often give the impression of being severe and excessively austere.

There is nothing to criticize about the attention given by the Cuvelier family to the vineyard and the modern vinification. Nevertheless, the wines of Le Crock generally seem to lack fruit, although they are certainly full-bodied, dense wines capable of lasting 10–12 years. Perhaps the sweet, rich 1995, made under the supervision of newly hired oenologist Michel Rolland will be symbolic of a new era for this estate.

VINTAGES

1995—The 1995 exhibits a healthy dark ruby/purple color, gobs of sweet black
•   cherry and cassis fruit, good ripeness, a plush texture, low acidity, and
86   admirable length and richness in the finish. It should develop into a very
       good, possibly excellent, modestly priced wine that will drink well for a
       decade. Last tasted, 3/96.

1994—The 1994 is, frankly, a crock of . . . tannin and acidity. It is a hard, structured
•   wine without enough fruit to cover the skeletal structure. It will only dry out
74   with aging. Last tasted, 3/96.

1990—The 1990 is the finest Le Crock I have tasted. Deep ruby/purple colored, with
•   a spicy, rich nose and dense, muscular, full-bodied flavors, this big wine will
87   age impressively. Anticipated maturity: Now–2006. Last tasted, 1/93.

1989—Historically, this property turns out hard, lean, frequently charmless wines.
•   However, the 1989 has more fruit than usual, good ruby color, a blackberry
83   fruitiness, medium body, low acidity, but high tannins. It lacks complexity
       but should offer serviceable drinking over the next 5–6 years. Anticipated
       maturity: Now. Last tasted, 4/91.

1988—The 1988 Le Crock is similar in quality to the 1989 but is totally different in
• style. Leaner, smaller scaled, and neither so tannic nor so alcoholic, it should
82 be drunk over the next 5–6 years. Anticipated maturity: Now. Last tasted,
11/90.

1986—I have consistently found the 1986 Le Crock to lack richness and simply taste
• too hard and astringent for the amount of fruit that it seemingly possesses.
74 Anticipated maturity: Now. Last tasted, 4/90.

1985—The 1985 has medium body, moderately deep flavors, and some hard astrin-
• gency in the finish—too much press wine in the blend? Overall, it is an
73 uninspired winemaking effort. Anticipated maturity: Now. Last tasted, 3/89.

HAUT-MARBUZET   EXCELLENT

Classification: Cru Bourgeois
Location of vineyards: St.-Estèphe
Owner: Henri Duboscq and sons
Address: 33180 St.-Estèphe
Mailing address: Same as above
Telephone: 33 5 56 59 30 54; telefax: 33 5 56 50 70 87
Visits: From Monday to Friday, between 8 A.M. and noon, and 2 P.M. and
6 P.M.

VINEYARDS (red)
Surface area: 123.5 acres
Average age of vines: 35 years
Blend: 50% Cabernet Sauvignon, 40% Merlot, 10% Cabernet Franc
Density of plantation: 8,300 vines per hectare
Average yields (over the last 5 years): 45 hectoliters per hectare
Total average annual production: 300,000 bottles

GRAND VIN (red)
Brand name: Château Haut-Marbuzet
Appellation: St.-Estèphe
Mean average production: 250,000 bottles
Upbringing: Grapes are totally destemmed. Fermentations occur in
thermo-regulated vats and last approximately 18–20 days (macerations
last 4 weeks), with daily *remontages*. Wines are bred in new oak barrels
for 18 months. They are fined but never filtered.

SECOND WINE
Brand name: Rosé MacCarthy
Average annual production: 50,000 bottles

Evaluation of present classification: Should be upgraded to a third-growth
Plateau of maturity: 3–15 years following the vintage

Haut-Marbuzet is one of the oldest estates in St.-Estèphe, but fame can be traced only to 1952, when it was purchased by the father of the current proprietor, Henri Duboscq. The vineyard is beautifully situated facing the Gironde River, on a gradual slope of gravelly soil intermixed with calcareous clay. Duboscq, a flamboyant personality who tends to describe his wines by making analogies to the body parts of prominent female movie stars, has created one of the most immensely popular wines of Bordeaux, particularly in France, Belgium, Holland, and England, where the great majority of Haut-Marbuzet is sold. He believes in late harvesting, thereby bringing in grapes that are nearly bursting with ripeness, macerating them for at least 3 weeks, and then aging the entire crop for 18 months in 100% new oak barrels. Indeed, his methods result in an intense, opulent, and lavish fruitiness, with a rich, spicy, exotic bouquet. To the wine enthusiast, Haut-Marbuzet produces one of the most obvious yet sexiest wines of the entire Bordeaux region.

Some Duboscq critics have charged that his winemaking style borders on vulgarity, but he would argue that the new oak simply adds a charm and unctuous quality to the traditional muscular, tough texture that emerges from so many wines made in St.-Estèphe. Other critics have suggested that Haut-Marbuzet fails to age gracefully. While the wine is usually delicious when released, my tastings of old vintages back through 1961 have generally indicated that Haut-Marbuzet is best when drunk within the first 10–15 years of life.

Despite the criticisms, no one argues with the success proprietor Duboscq has enjoyed. He produces a Bordeaux that behaves more like a decadent Burgundy or Rhône.

VINTAGES

1997—I had this wine on three occasions and was surprised that it did not possess
•   more stuffing and intensity. While good, it is not up to this château's usual
84–   standards. The aggressively woody 1997 Haut-Marbuzet reveals a hollow
86   midsection, but it does offer soft, ripe, coffee, earthy, black cherry fruit
       presented in a pleasant, medium-bodied format. A bit more concentration,
       extract, and length would have been preferable. Drink this wine during its
       first 4–5 years of life. Last tasted, 3/98.

1996—Dark ruby colored, with a pronounced *pain grillé*, smoky, olive, and sweet
•   berry–scented nose, this medium-bodied, rich, attractively textured wine
86–   possesses all the telltale oak, glycerin, and heady perfume expected by long-
88   time followers of this estate. The wine displays more tannin than in such
       recent vintages as 1995 and 1994. It is a well-made, concentrated, spicy wine
       with plenty of power and length. Anticipated maturity: 1999–2010. Last
       tasted, 11/97.

1995—The dark ruby–colored 1995 reveals an over-ripe character of jammy black
•   fruits with a touch of prunes, medium to full body, and a pungent, smoky,
89   herbaceous, sweet personality. It is an ostentatious, oaky, jammy, sexpot of a

wine that does not pretend to provide any intellectual thrills. Anticipated maturity: Now–2006. Last tasted, 3/96.

1994—This is a sexy, opulent, well-endowed example of the Médoc's most exotic
•   wine. The 1994 Haut-Marbuzet is surprisingly low in acidity, with excellent
89   ripeness, sweet, smoky, grilled toast, jammy, black currant, aromatic, and flavor profiles, and long, round, luscious flavors that caress the palate with no hard edges. This is a plump, succulent wine that readers will find delicious. Drink it over the next decade. Last tasted, 3/96.

1993—I would have liked to find the 1993 more impressive, but it is austere,
•   extremely tough and tannic, and atypically hard for Haut-Marbuzet. Close
82   scrutiny does reveal some spicy, ripe cassis fruit, but there is not enough to balance out the wine's stern, hollow personality. Is my rating too generous? Last tasted, 11/94.

1992—Haut-Marbuzet's penchant for using 100% new oak works great in top years
•   such as 1990, 1989, and 1982, but in 1992 the wood dominates the wine.
82?   The excessively oaky 1992 displays a deep, concentrated ruby color, a spicy, plummy, oaky bouquet, medium-bodied, soft flavors, above average depth, low acidity, and a supple finish. Precocious and ostentatious, to an extreme in this vintage, it is best consumed in its first 6–7 years of life. Last tasted, 11/94.

1990—The 1990 is a classic, tannic, and concentrated example of Haut-Marbuzet.
•   The wine displays a dark ruby/purple color, followed by a lavishly oaked,
93   vanillin, roasted nut, herb, and sweet, jammy black currant, and olive-scented nose. Rich and opulent, with a thick, chewy texture, low acidity, and gobs of fruit, this hedonistic, decadently oaky, fruity wine will continue to drink well for 10–12 years. In my opinion, it is the finest Haut-Marbuzet since the fabulous 1982. Last tasted, 11/96.

1989—Haut-Marbuzet's 1989 revealed considerable amber to its color, as well as a
•   pronounced nose of cedar, jammy cherry fruit, seaweed, and spice. The wine
86   tasted fully mature, low in acidity, round, and sweet. Based on this bottle, which did not exhibit any evidence of exposure to heat, I would opt for drinking the 1989 Haut-Marbuzet over the next 5–6 years. Last tasted, 11/96.

1988—The 1988 is another flashy, seductive, full-bodied, amply endowed, gener-
•   ously oaked wine. The tannins are slightly more aggressive than fans of this
89   property's wines usually expect. Nevertheless, the wine exhibits plenty of extract and size. Anticipated maturity: Now–2000. Last tasted, 3/91.

1987—Surprisingly fragrant (aromas of smoky oak and herbs dominate), this soft,
•   medium-bodied, heady wine is not concentrated but is still tasty and pleasant.
82   Anticipated maturity: Now–may be in decline. Last tasted, 4/90.

1986—The 1986 has continued to improve since I first tasted it in cask. The deep
•   ruby/purple color and enormous bouquet of smoky oak, exotic spices, and
90   plummy fruit of the 1986 suggest that it can be drunk immediately, but the tannins in the finish indicate this wine will be even more stunning with several years of cellaring. An interesting, unique, and satisfying wine! Antici-pated maturity: Now–2003. Last tasted, 2/90.

1985 — The 1985 Haut-Marbuzet has the fleshpot personality that makes this wine so
* appealing. A big, toasty, plum-scented bouquet offers generous amounts of
88 fruit. On the palate, the wine is supple, spicy, rich, and immensely tasty. It is
a delight to drink now but should keep 6–9 years. Anticipated maturity: Now.
Last tasted, 5/90.

1984 — The 1984 Haut-Marbuzet has tons of oaky aromas in the bouquet, a soft,
* supple fruitiness, and decent length. However, the fruit is beginning to dry
78 out, and immediate consumption is advised. Anticipated maturity: Now—
probably in decline. Last tasted, 3/88.

1983 — Extremely dense, with an almost portlike, dark ruby color, ripe, rich, plummy
* nose, fat, intense, viscous flavor, and moderate tannin, this generous wine is
88 drinking beautifully but will keep for another 5–6 years. Anticipated maturity: Now. Last tasted, 1/85.

1982 — This wine has been decadent and seductive since it was first bottled. It
* continues to offer copious quantities of vanilla-tinged, sweet, opulent, black
94 cherry and currant fruit with intriguing aromas of coffee and cedar. Thick,
juicy, succulent, not to mention thrilling to drink, this multilayered, plush, fat
wine is almost too much of a good thing. Intense, with no hard edges, this is
a glorious example of Haut-Marbuzet that will hold at its current plateau of
full maturity for at least another 5–7 years. It has been one of the most
consistent and crowd-pleasing wines of the vintage. I have never seen this
wine perform less than brilliantly. Last tasted, 9/95.

1981 — Another intriguing wine, the 1981 Haut-Marbuzet is very deeply colored,
* with a ripe, plummy, spicy, oaky bouquet, full bodied, with plenty of concen-
85 tration and a soft, alcoholic finish. Anticipated maturity: Now. Last tasted,
10/88.

ANCIENT VINTAGES

Some positive tasting notes include the fully mature, very good vintages of 1978 (rated 87) and 1979 (rated 86), both excellent wines.
The 1975 (rated 90 in March 1989) is outstanding, as is the 1970 and
1961 (both rated 90), the latter two wines drunk with enormous pleasure
from magnum in 1988. I suspect all of these vintages would be in decline in
1998.

LAFON-ROCHET   VERY GOOD

Classification: Fourth-growth in 1855
Location of vineyards: St.-Estèphe
Owner: Guy Tesseron family
Address: 33180 St.-Estèphe
Telephone: 33 5 56 59 32 06; telefax: 33 5 56 59 72 43
Visits: By appointment only

Contact: Michel or Alfred Tesseron—telephone: 33 5 56 59 04 04;
telefax: 33 5 56 59 26 63
(Château Pontet-Canet)

VINEYARDS (red)
Surface area: 111.15 acres (only 101.3 acres are actually planted)
Average age of vines: 30 years
Blend: 55% Cabernet Sauvignon, 40% Merlot, 5% Cabernet Franc
Density of plantation: 9,800 vines per hectare
Average yields (over the last 5 years): 55 hectoliters per hectare
Total average annual production: 17,000–20,000 cases

GRAND VIN (red)
Brand name: Château Lafon-Rochet
Appellation: St.-Estèphe
Mean annual production: 13,500 cases
Upbringing: Fermentations are traditional and last 3 weeks. Wines are
kept 16–18 months in oak barrels, 40% of which are new. They are both
fined and filtered. Malolactics occur in tanks.

SECOND WINE
Brand name: N° 2 du Château Lafon-Rochet
Average annual production: 8,500 cases

Evaluation of present classification: Should be maintained
Plateau of maturity: 8–20 years following the vintage

NOTE: The harvest is always carried out manually. For those plots that
give the grand vin, eventual young vines are harvested first and
separately, and the older vines are harvested afterward, when they are
deemed fully mature. The grapes are sorted on a table that has been
specially designed for the château.

While this vineyard was ranked a fourth-growth in the 1855 classification,
most observers today argue that the superbly situated Lafon-Rochet (adjacent
to both Lafite-Rothschild and Cos d'Estournel) should routinely produce wine
with more character and flavor than it habitually does. The current owners,
the Tesserons, purchased the property in 1959 and began a gradual but
significant program to restore the vineyards and the run-down château. Today
the estate has been totally renovated, and the new cellars are housed in a
bright, cream-colored, one-story château with a two-story cave in its middle.
Over the last decade, a combination of intelligent, quality-oriented decisions,
such as 1) to destem, 2) to harvest slightly later, 3) to increase the percentage
of new oak, 4) to increase the percentage of Merlot in both the vineyard and

the blend, and 5) to make a second wine from weaker vats have resulted in more impressive first wines, culminating with a brilliant effort in 1989.

While Lafon-Rochet produced numerous disappointing wines (given the château's pedigree) during the seventies, the efforts made in the eighties clearly support its position in the 1855 classification.

VINTAGES

1997—It is no secret in Bordeaux that Alfred and Michel Tesseron are turning out
•   splendid efforts at their flagship estate in Pauillac, Pontet-Canet. They are
86–   also beginning to invest more money and effort in their St.-Estèphe property,
87+   Lafon-Rochet. In 1997, 55% of the crop made it into this well-made wine, which is still monolithic, without the accessibility of so many 1997s. The dark ruby/purple color is accompanied by straightforward aromas of black fruits, earth, and oak. While dense, this medium-bodied wine remains closed and foursquare, with noticeable tannin and structure. This is one of the few 1997s that will require cellaring. Anticipated maturity: 2003–2013. Last tasted, 3/98.

1996—Dense ruby/purple colored, this big, burly, masculine wine exhibits hard
•   tannin but also intense concentration of fruit. It tasted more monolithic and
87–   tougher textured than I expected, but there is no doubting that it is a highly
90   extracted, rich, layered wine with considerable potential. Once again, patience will be essential. Anticipated maturity: 2007–2025. Last tasted, 3/97.

1995—This wine may merit an outstanding score after several more years in the
•   bottle. Although it has closed down since bottling, it is an impressively
89+   endowed, rich, sweet cassis–smelling and –tasting Lafon-Rochet. The wine's impressively saturated deep ruby/purple color is accompanied by vanillin, earth, and spicy scents, medium to full body, excellent to outstanding richness, and moderate tannin in the powerful, well-delineated finish. Anticipated maturity: 2003–2018. Last tasted, 11/97.

1994—This should turn out to be an outstanding example of Lafon-Rochet. The 1994
•   is a breakthrough vintage for this estate, and it has been followed by an even
89+   more compelling wine in 1995. The 1994 exhibits an opaque purple color, followed by a sweet, pure nose of cassis, new oak, and beef blood. Muscular and massive, with huge body, and a boatload of tannin, this wine is crammed with extract and power. It requires 5–7 years of cellaring and will last for 20–30 years. Anticipated maturity: 2003–2025. Last tasted, 1/97.

1993—A spicy, green pepper, vegetal component detracted from this dark, opaque-
•   colored wine. While it possesses hard tannin, there is also plenty of fruit
86   (especially for a 1993). The wine is likely to dry out quickly, but those who like a rough-and-tumble style of Bordeaux with plenty of guts and muscle are advised that this wine represents a good value. It will provide a beefy mouthful of claret to consume over the next 5–10 years. Last tasted, 1/97.

1992—This 1992 appears to possess adequate rich, ripe fruit. While not a block-
•   buster wine, it is tannic and possibly ageworthy. It should drink well in 3–4
85?   years and last for 12 or more—if the fruit holds. It may be a gamble, but

Lafon-Rochet remains an obscure, underpriced, and underrated St.-Estèphe. Last tasted, 11/94.

1991 —Although compact, the 1991 is a good wine. The color is dark ruby, and
•   the nose offers ripe black cherries, herbs, and spicy scents. Despite some
85   compression, the wine offers sweet, fat fruit flavors, medium body, and fine
depth. A softening of the tannin may provide even greater richness over the
next 10–12 years. Last tasted, 1/94.

1990 —The 1990, a stunning effort for this property, offers further proof of just how
•   successful 1990 turned out to be for St.-Estèphe. Very dark ruby, with a
89   tightly knit nose of black fruits, this massively endowed wine is one of the
most powerful and concentrated Lafon-Rochets I have tasted. Patience will
be required with this offering. Anticipated maturity: Now–2022. Last tasted,
1/93.

1989 —Dark ruby, with an intense bouquet of overripe cassis, this chewy, well-
•   endowed, full-bodied wine is reminiscent of the excellent 1970. Opulent as
88   well as tannic, it may justify an outstanding rating in a decade. Anticipated
maturity: Now–2015. Last tasted, 4/91.

1988 —The 1988 has medium body, good ripe fruit, and commendable harmony.
•   Surprisingly concentrated for the vintage, this excellent dark ruby–colored
87   wine should age nicely for 5–15 years. Anticipated maturity: Now–2010.
Last tasted, 11/90.

1986 —On numerous occasions this wine seemed forbiddingly tannic from cask
•   and virtually impossible to evaluate, but it has turned out to be one of the
88   estate's best wines made during the eighties. Deep ruby/purple, with a
full-intensity, smoky, spicy, rich, curranty bouquet, this full-bodied, powerful, tannic wine will handsomely repay those who have the patience to
cellar it for at least a decade. Anticipated maturity: Now–2015. Last tasted,
2/90.

1985 —The 1985 Lafon-Rochet is fleshy, chewy, has good ruby color, firm tannins,
•   and medium body, yet lamentably, it is one-dimensional. Perhaps more char-
83   acter will emerge with additional bottle age. Anticipated maturity: Now–
1999. Last tasted, 4/89.

1983 —In early tastings against the other top St.-Estèphes, Lafon-Rochet rivaled Cos
•   d'Estournel. Rich, full bodied, deeply concentrated, and loaded with fruit,
86   this moderately tannic, dark-colored wine displays excellent potential for
extended aging. For the vintage, it is a meritorious effort. Anticipated maturity: Now–2005. Last tasted, 1/88.

1982 —This 1982 is plump, rich, and concentrated, but essentially one-dimensional
•   and simple. It offers thick, jammy fruit, but no complexity. There is some
86   tannin in the finish. My instincts suggest this wine needs to be drunk up over
the next 10–15 years. Last tasted, 9/95.

1979 —A successful wine made by Lafon-Rochet in 1979. Dark ruby, with a pro-
•   nounced aroma of new oak and black cherries, this wine has plenty of stuffing
85   and is more successful than the château's 1978. The wine has been stubborn
to shed its tannin. Will the fruit fade before enough of the tannin melts away?

It could be even more charming. Anticipated maturity: Now–1999. Last tasted, 6/89.

1978 — This is a supple, straightforward, fruity wine that could use more stuffing and
• character. Moderately dark in color, with an easygoing supple texture, pleas-
82 ant, soft, fruity flavors, and a short finish, it should be drunk over the next 5–
6 years. Anticipated maturity: Now. Last tasted, 6/89.

1976 — In this vintage, Lafon-Rochet produced a light, rather fragile wine that has
• been fully mature since 1980. Medium ruby, with some brown at the edges, it
74 offers diffuse and diluted flavors. Anticipated maturity: Now–probably in
serious decline. Last tasted, 7/81.

1975 — The 1975 Lafon-Rochet is a big, surprisingly deeply colored, chunky wine
• that continues to exhibit the harsh, tannic, angular character possessed by
82 many 1975s. Despite the color and intensity, it exhibits little complexity or
direction. While large scaled, the wine is clumsy and too one-dimensional.
Anticipated maturity: Now–2000. Last tasted, 4/88.

1973 — Now pale, with a damp, faded, musty aroma, dissipated fruit flavors, and a
• washed-out, short finish, the 1973 Lafon-Rochet is best forgotten. Last tasted,
64 10/82.

1971 — Light bodied, yet somewhat charming and fruity in 1978, this wine was fully
• mature then, and one can only imagine that 20 more years of bottle age has
76 seriously eroded any appeal it might have had. Last tasted, 6/78.

1970 — This is a chunky, muscular, big wine that has never developed a harmonious
• character. It appears the tannin will not become fully integrated. Second, the
87? wine is deficient in complexity. Nevertheless, this is a full-bodied, flavorful,
admirably concentrated, burly wine with an impressively saturated dark ruby
color and a hint of amber at the edge. This leathery, tannic 1970 reveals a
taste of concentrated, roasted meat, and beef blood. There is no rush to drink
it, but I do not anticipate much improvement in this wine. Last tasted, 6/96.

1966 — Certainly an old-style Lafon-Rochet, the 1966 remains a dusty, tannic, briery
• wine, with fading fruit, significantly browning at the edges, yet gobs of tannin
69 still in evidence. Beginning to dry out and take on a hollow, astringent
character, this wine is in serious decline. Last tasted, 6/87.

1961 — Still rich and concentrated, with plenty of astringent tannins, this spicy, ripe,
• full-bodied, and full-flavored wine has plenty of extract and a dusty, chalky
85 finish. It is a good rather than superb 1961 that can be drunk now or held for
another 5–10 years. The tannins may ultimately prove excessive for the wine's
fruit, so current drinking is recommended. Anticipated maturity: Now. Last
tasted, 11/88.

LILIAN LADOUYS   GOOD

Classification: Cru Bourgeois in 1932
Location of vineyards: St.-Estèphe (Blanquet)
Owner: Château Lilian Ladouys S.A.
Address: 33180 St.-Estèphe

Telephone: 33 5 56 59 71 96; telefax: 33 5 56 59 35 97
Visits: By appointment only
Contact: Marguerite North at the above address and telephone
number

VINEYARDS (red)
Surface area: 118.6 acres
Average age of vines: 35 years
Blend: 58% Cabernet Sauvignon, 37% Merlot, 5% Cabernet Franc
Density of plantation: 10,000 vines per hectare
Average yields (over the last 5 years): 55 hectoliters per hectare
Total average annual production: 280,000 bottles

GRAND VIN (red)
Brand name: Château Lilian Ladouys
Appellation: St.-Estèphe
Mean annual production: 224,000 bottles
Upbringing: Fermentations last 25–30 days in temperature-controlled
stainless-steel tanks, with temperatures reaching 30 degrees centigrade
maximum. Wines are then transferred into oak barrels (30%–50% of
which are new) for malolactic fermentations to occur and are bottled
after 18–20 months, depending upon the vintage. They are racked
every 3 months, and there is a slight fining, but no filtration prior to
bottling.

SECOND WINE
Brand name: La Devise de Lilian
Average annual production: 60,000 bottles

Evaluation of present classification: This resurrected property has a short
track record, but hopes are high
Plateau of maturity: 5–15 years following the vintage

This small vineyard, recently resurrected by Christian and Lilian Thiéblot
(until 1989 the wine was vinified and sold by a large cooperative), has the
advantage of both serious financial and human commitment to excellence.
The vineyard, which has vines between the ages of 25 and 45 years, is
near those of such renowned Bordeaux superstars as Cos d'Estournel and
Lafite-Rothschild. Both the 1989 and 1990 were surprisingly rich, intensely
concentrated, full-bodied, chewy wines exhibiting high class and character.
The wine will be marketed exclusively by the huge Bordeaux *négociant* firm
of Dourthe. While two vintages do not make a star, most observers feel this
up-and-coming St.-Estèphe estate will be a name to reckon with during the
nineties. In 1997, it was sold to the corporate giant Alcatel.

VINTAGES

1995—The 1995 is a clone of the 1994, with slightly denser fruit and higher tannin.
•   Reminiscent of a 1986, it will require patience, while the 1994 will have to
86   be drunk at an early age. Last tasted, 3/96.

1994—The 1994 offers good ripeness, medium body, clean, competent winemaking,
•   good concentration, and enough red and black fruit wrapped in toasty oak to
86   please most palates. Drink it over the next decade. Last tasted, 3/96.

MEYNEY   VERY GOOD

Classification: Cru Bourgeois Exceptionnel in 1932
Location of vineyards: St.-Estèphe
Owner: Domaines Cordier
Address: St.-Estèphe—33250 Pauillac
Mailing address: Domaines Cordier, 53, rue du Dehez, 33290 Blanquefort
Telephone: 33 5 56 95 53 00; telefax: 33 5 56 95 53 01
Visits: By appointment only
Contact: Domaines Cordier (see above details)

VINEYARDS (red)
Surface area: 123.5 acres
Average age of vines: 35 years
Blend: 70% Cabernet Sauvignon, 25% Merlot, 2% Petit Verdot, 3%
Cabernet Franc
Density of plantation: 7,500 vines per hectare
Average yields (over the last 5 years): 55 hectoliters per hectare
Total average annual production: 366,000 bottles

GRAND VIN (red)
Brand name: Château Meyney
Appellation: St.-Estèphe
Mean annual production: 293,000 bottles
Upbringing: Fermentations last 20–25 days in cement vats of 200
hectoliters at maximum temperatures of 30–32 degrees centigrade, with
frequent *remontages* to ensure high levels of extraction. Fifteen percent of
the yield undergoes malolactics in new oak barrels, and the rest of the wine
is transferred into casks, 15% of which are new, upon completion of
malolactics in vats. Bottling is done with fining and a slight filtration after
20 months.

SECOND WINE
Brand name: Prieuré du Château Meyney
Average annual production: 73,000 bottles
Evaluation of present classification: Should be upgraded to a fifth-growth
Plateau of maturity: 8–25 years following the vintage

Meyney, the large vineyard of 123.5 acres immediately north of Montrose, with a splendid view of the Gironde River, has made notably flavorful, robust wines that offer considerable value to the shrewd consumer looking for quality rather than prestige. The wines have been remarkably consistent and since 1975 have rivaled many of the Médoc's classified growths. The wine is fairly big styled, with good fruit and excellent aging potential of 20–25 years. Some observers have even commented that Meyney's distinctive perfume of licorice, prunes, and truffles is caused by a geological aberration; much of the Meyney vineyard sits on an outcropping of iron-enriched blue clay that has never been found elsewhere in the Médoc. Ironically, such soils also exist in Pomerol, particularly underlying the famed vineyard of Château Pétrus. For visitors to St.-Estèphe, Meyney also merits attention because this is one of the few old ecclesiastical buildings in the Médoc and has been well preserved by its owner, the Cordier firm.

Fortunately for consumers, the wines of Meyney continue to be grossly underpriced. Vinification and upbringing are controlled by one of Bordeaux's most respected oenologists, Georges Pauli. That, combined with its fabulous location in St.-Estèphe, translates into stunningly rich, individualistic wines that rival the best not only of St.-Estèphe, but of the Médoc.

VINTAGES

1996 — This reliable Cru Bourgeois estate has turned out a dense, smoky, herbal, and
• black cherry–scented, spicy wine. While not as weighty and rich as some of
(85– Meyney's best vintages, it is well made, medium bodied, and surprisingly
87) forward for the vintage. Solid tannin in the finish suggests this wine should last for another 10–15 years. Last tasted, 3/97.

1995 — The 1995 exhibits an opaque purple color and a super nose of jammy black
• cherries and cassis intertwined with scents of earth, licorice, and toasty oak.
89 Sweet, ripe, low-acid flavors cascade over the palate, creating an unctuous texture and an impressive mouthfeel. This ripe, medium- to full-bodied, concentrated Meyney should drink well young and keep for 12–15 years. Last tasted, 3/96.

1994 — This perennial overachiever has turned out an attractive 1994, with a dark
• purple color, a sweet, plummy, herb, mineral, and spice-scented nose, and
88 powerful, medium- to full-bodied, concentrated flavors with adequate acidity and moderate tannin. The wine has a certain precociousness, as well as ripe fruit and good balance. It should drink well for 12–15 years. Last tasted, 3/96.

1993 — This consumer favorite has turned in a mediocre performance in 1993. The
• color is dark ruby, but the wine is hard, with an excess of tannin for its
78 meager fruit. The result is a wine that tastes compact and attenuated and lacks charm and ripeness. Last tasted, 11/94.

1992 — In 1992 this reliable, sometimes brilliantly made wine from St.-Estèphe is
• a dark ruby-colored claret with medium body, adequate acidity, and exces-
81 sive tannin and toughness in the finish. While it is better than many

1992s, its excess of tannin will result in an ungracious evolution. Last tasted, 11/94.

1990—Though not as rich as the 1989, the 1990 is still a fine effort from Meyney. It
•　offers deep ruby/purple color, a fine nose of black fruits, herbs, and oak, ripe,
88　generous, tannin-dominated flavors, good concentration, and a moderately
　　long, tough finish. Anticipated maturity: Now–2010. Last tasted, 1/93.

1989—The 1989 Meyney is one of the finest ever produced. The opaque, black/ruby
•　color, a bouquet of minerals and damson plums, the alcoholic, massive flavors,
90　and the mouth-coating tannins all combine to create a sensory overload.
　　The 1989 will prove uncommonly long-lived as well as profoundly flavored.
　　Anticipated maturity: Now–2020. Last tasted, 1/93.

1988—If you lack patience, you will want no part of the 1988. More brutally tannic
•　than the 1989, yet packed with fruit, the 1988 will need at least a decade of
88　cellaring. It recalls the wonderful 1975 Meyney that is just now beginning to
　　drink well. Anticipated maturity: Now–2015. Last tasted, 4/91.

1987—For the vintage, this is a success. Medium deep ruby, with a fragrant, spicy,
•　herbaceous, plummy bouquet, this soft yet moderately tannic, flavorful wine
82　will make ideal drinking over the next 5–7 years. Anticipated maturity: Now.
　　Last tasted, 5/90.

1986—Having matured more quickly than many northern Médoc 1986s, Meyney is
•　a deep, dark garnet/purple–colored wine with a moderately intense fragrance
90　of minerals, licorice, smoke, roasted herbs, and sweet black currant fruit. On
　　the palate the wine still has some tannin to shed, but its expansive, savory
　　style suggests it is already accessible. With outstanding extract and layers of
　　fruit, this wine is a candidate for another 10–15 years of cellaring—at a
　　minimum. Anticipated maturity: Now–2015. Last tasted, 9/97.

1985—Totally mature, the 1985 Meyney exhibits a deep ruby color with some amber
•　at the edge. The wine possesses a seductive nose of weedy black fruits
87　intertwined with aromas of plums, tea, earth, and licorice. Sweet on the
　　attack, this medium-bodied, deliciously fruity, round, silky-textured wine
　　should continue to drink well for a decade. Anticipated maturity: Now–2006.
　　Last tasted, 9/97.

1984—The 1984 will keep for another 10–12 years; it has a deep ruby color,
•　excellent depth, medium to full body, and plenty of berry fruit. Anticipated
84　maturity: Now. Last tasted, 6/87.

1983—Meyney was successful in 1983. The wine is very dense, with a ripe, roasted,
•　black currant aroma, unctuous, thick, rich flavors, average acidity, and mod-
85　erate tannins. A fat, fleshy, concentrated, rustic wine, it is capable of evolving
　　for another 10 years. Anticipated maturity: Now–2000. Last tasted, 9/88.

1982—One of the overachievers of the vintage, Meyney's 1982 has taken on an
•　opaque garnet color and offers a flamboyant nose of licorice, Asian spices,
90　smoked meats, leather (brett?), and jammy black cherries. Full bodied, with
　　sweet, expansive fruit and a chewy texture that nearly conceals some formida-
　　ble tannin, this wine has always been delicious, but it has taken on more
　　structure over recent years. It is a juicy, well-delineated Meyney for drinking
　　now and over the next 10–15 years. Last tasted, 9/95.

1981 —Another example of Meyney's forte—chunky, densely flavored, powerful
•   wines that have plenty of color, authority, and weight. This vintage lacks
85   complexity and elegance but compensates with oodles of ripe black currant
      fruit. Anticipated maturity: Now–2000. Last tasted, 1/88.
1979 —Undoubtedly a good wine for this prolific, yet underrated vintage, the 1979
•   Meyney has dark ruby color, a rather simple grapy, spicy, stemmy aroma,
81   moderately full body, and light tannins. Anticipated maturity: Now. Last
      tasted, 3/88.
1978 —A textbook Meyney—dark colored, chunky, fruity, loaded with flavors of
•   herbs, black currants, and plums—this wine has plenty of extract, mouth-
84   gripping tannins and another 10 years of life. A good Meyney. Anticipated
      maturity: Now–2000. Last tasted, 4/87.
1976 —A mediocre effort, this wine is palatable and good for uncritical quaffing, but
•   it is now in decline and destined for senility if not consumed immediately.
74   Anticipated maturity: Now–probably in serious decline. Last tasted, 8/79.
1975 —This has consistently been an outstanding wine, revealing a dark ruby/purple/
•   garnet color with a large-scaled nose of smoked meats, cedar, spices, and
90   earthy black fruits. Full bodied, moderately tannic, fleshy, and intense, this
      wine has reached full maturity, where it should remain for another decade. It
      is one of the sleepers of the vintage. Last tasted, 12/95.
1971 —Still drinking nicely, the 1971 Meyney is dark ruby in color, chunky, "four-
•   square," as the English say, without much complexity, but offering a good
80   robust mouthful of claret. Anticipated maturity: Now. Last tasted, 9/79.
1970 —Fully mature, this dark ruby–colored wine has a trace of orange/brown at the
•   edge. It is a full-bodied, firm, austere wine with a dry, slightly astringent
83   finish. However, I would have liked to find more fruit. It should last another
      8–10 years. Anticipated maturity: Now. Last tasted, 10/89.

ANCIENT VINTAGES

In 1978, Cordier's superb oenologist, Georges Pauli, began to exercise his talents with the making of Meyney. Previously the wine had a tendency to turn out overly tannic and astringent. Vintages of the sixties, particularly 1966, 1962, and 1961, are good wines, but not comparable to the super Meyneys of the eighties. The finest old Meyney I have tasted is the 1959 (rated 86 and drunk most recently in 1987).

MONTROSE   OUTSTANDING

Classification: Second-growth in 1855
Location of vineyards: St.-Estèphe
Owner: Jean-Louis Charmolue
Address: 33180 St.-Estèphe
Telephone: 33 5 56 59 30 12; telefax: 33 5 56 59 38 48

Visits: By appointment only (visiting hours are fixed between 9 A.M. and 11 A.M., and 2 P.M. and 5 P.M., on weekdays only)
Contact: Mr. Bruno Lemoine, director, at above address and telephone and fax numbers

VINEYARDS (red)
Surface area: 168 acres
Average age of vines: 33 years
Blend: 65% Cabernet Sauvignon, 25% Merlot, 10% Cabernet Franc
Density of plantation: 9,000 vines per hectare
Average yields (over the last 5 years): 45 hectoliters per hectare
Total average annual production: 340,000 bottles

GRAND VIN (red)
Brand name: Château Montrose
Appellation: St.-Estèphe
Mean annual production: 230,000 bottles
Upbringing: Grapes are hand-picked. Vinification is traditional. Fermentations last 21–25 days in wooden and stainless-steel vats, with temperatures going up to 30–32 degrees centigrade and frequent *remontages* that ensure the best possible extraction of color and tannins. Wines then spend 19 months in oak barrels, of which 35% are new. They are fined with egg whites and racked 6 times but not filtered.

SECOND WINE
Brand name: La Dame de Montrose
Average annual production: 110,000 bottles

Evaluation of present classification: Should be maintained
Plateau of maturity: 3–25 years following the vintage for top vintages after 1970; prior to 1971, 15–35 years following the vintage

One of the Médoc's best-situated vineyards and one of the commune's most impeccably clean and well-kept cellars, Montrose was for years associated with huge, dense, powerful wines that needed several decades of cellaring to be soothing enough to drink. For example, Jean Paul Jauffret, the former head of Bordeaux's CIVB, served me the 1908 Montrose in 1982, blind, to see if I could guess its age. The wine had plenty left in it and tasted at least 30 years younger.

The owner, the affable Jean-Louis Charmolue, had obviously lightened the style of Montrose in response to his perception that dense, excruciatingly tannic wines are no longer popular with consumers. The change in style is particularly noticeable with the vintages of the late seventies and early eighties, as more Merlot has been introduced into the blend at the expense of Cabernet Sauvignon and Petit Verdot. Montrose fans were not amused by the "nouveau" style. Since 1986 Montrose has returned to a more forceful, muscular style, reminiscent of pre-1975 vintages. Certainly the 1989 and 1990 vintages for Montrose produced true blockbuster wines not seen from this property since 1961. Anyone who has had the pleasure of drinking some of Montrose's greatest vintages—1953, 1955, 1959, 1961, 1964, and 1970— can no doubt attest to the fact that Montrose produced a bevy of massive wines that deserve to be called the Latour of St.-Estèphe. The wines of Montrose were especially strong in the period 1953–1971, and 1989–present, when they were usually among the finest wines produced in the northern Médoc.

Visitors to St.-Estèphe will find the modest château of Montrose situated on the high ground with a magnificent view of the Gironde River. The property, owned by the Charmolue family since 1896, does make a worthy visit, given the splendid *cuverie,* with its old, huge, open oak vats and striking new barrel cellar. Like many of its neighbors, Château Montrose has a new state-of-the-art tasting room and reception area.

VINTAGES

1997—At Montrose, 40% of the harvest made it into the final blend (65% Cabernet
  •   Sauvignon, 29% Merlot, 5% Cabernet Franc, 1% Petit Verdot). Yields were a
87–   lowly 42 hectoliters per hectare. This wine may turn out to be outstanding
89+   after additional evolution in the barrel. It possesses a deep ruby/purple color, followed by a vibrant nose of sweet cranberry, cherry, and cassis jam, herbaceous notes, and the telltale mineral, gravelly scent often present in Montrose. On the attack, the wine, like many top-quality 1997s, is sweet, lush, and round, with no aggressiveness. Medium bodied and nicely concentrated, this vintage does reveal some dry tannin in the moderately long finish, so immediate drinkability may not be possible. However, this will be a Montrose that develops quickly, with the potential to last for 15+ years. Anticipated maturity: 2001–2015. Last tasted, 3/98.

1996—This classic Montrose's opaque purple/black color is impressive. The wine
  •   possesses exceptionally rich, over-ripe plum and cassis fruit intermingled with
90–   smoke, minerals, and spice. Only 59% of the harvest was included in this
93   blend of 72% Cabernet Sauvignon, 24% Merlot, and 4% Cabernet Franc. The wine's unctuous texture makes one think there is more Merlot in the blend, but its success is due to the superripe Cabernet Sauvignon. The 1996 is sweet (from ripeness, not sugar) and medium to full bodied, with a well-delineated personality. No doubt there is significant tannin lurking in the background, but much of it is concealed by the wine's hefty extract, glycerin, and fruit levels. Anticipated maturity: 2006–2030. Last tasted, 3/98.

1995— An explosively rich, exotic, fruity Montrose, the 1995 displays even more fat
•   and extract than the 1996. There is less Cabernet Sauvignon in the 1995 blend,
93   resulting in a fuller-bodied, more accessible, friendlier style. The wine exhibits
      an opaque black/ruby/purple color as well as a ripe nose of black fruits, vanil-
      lin, and licorice. Powerful yet surprisingly accessible (the tannin is velvety and
      the acidity low), this terrific example of Montrose should be drinkable at a young
      age. Anticipated maturity: 2003–2028. Last tasted, 11/97.

1994— An opaque purple color suggests a wine of considerable intensity. One of the
•   most successful 1994s of the northern Médoc, the wine presents closed aro-
91   matics of jammy black fruits, plums, spice, and earth. On the palate there is
      impressive extract, purity, and copious amounts of sweet black currant fruit
      balanced nicely by moderate yet ripe tannin. Medium bodied, with excellent
      to outstanding concentration, this impressive Montrose should be close to full
      maturity with another 4–5 years of cellaring. Anticipated maturity: 2002–
      2020. Last tasted, 1/97.

1993— This is a dark ruby/purple–colored wine with a grilled meat, peppery, spicy,
•   black fruit–scented nose, medium body, surprisingly sweet fruit and softness,
87   moderate tannin, and a well-balanced, firm, concentrated personality. It will
      benefit from 2–4 years of cellaring and will last for 15 years (one of the
      longer-lived wines of the vintage). Last tasted, 1/97.

1992— Dark ruby colored, with a tight but promising nose of licorice, black currants,
•   and minerals, this medium-bodied wine possesses attractively sweet, rich,
87   cassis fruit and moderate tannin. The wine reveals fine concentration and
      ripeness, but it requires 2–4 years of cellaring; it should last for 12–14 years.
      It appears to be one of the few 1992s with sufficient fruit to balance out the
      tannin. Last tasted, 11/94.

1991— The 1991 reveals a dark, saturated color (one of the most opaque wines of the
•   vintage) and a tight but promising nose of sweet, jammy, black raspberry fruit,
88   minerals, and subtle new oak. With a medium- to full-bodied personality
      boasting considerable tannin, admirable ripeness, and layers of fruit, this
      excellent wine should reach full maturity in 7–8 years and last for nearly 2
      decades. Last tasted, 1/94.

1990— The 1990 Montrose clearly revealed its incredible complexity and massive
•   character. I was especially pleased when, at a lecture I gave in London at the
100   end of March 1997, the 1990 Montrose, in very tough company (Cheval Blanc
      1989 and 1990, Pichon-Lalande 1989 and 1990, Certan de May 1989 and
      1990), proved the overwhelming choice of a crowd of nearly 400 British
      tasters. The wine is remarkably rich, with a distinctive nose of sweet, jammy
      fruit, liquefied minerals, new saddle leather, and grilled steak. In the mouth,
      the enormous concentration, extract, high glycerin, and sweet tannin slide
      across the palate with considerable ease. It is a huge, corpulent, awesomely
      endowed wine that is still relatively approachable, as it has not yet begun to
      shut down and lose its baby fat. It thoroughly embarrassed the 1989, itself an
      exceptional wine. The 1990 needs 10 more years of cellaring; it should last
      for 25–30, possibly 40–50 years. Last tasted, 3/97.

1989 — An outstanding Montrose, the 1989 is one of the vintage's stars. It possesses
•   an opaque dark ruby/purple color, a sweet nose of minerals, black fruits,
96   cedar, and wood, dense, medium- to full-bodied, highly extracted flavors, low
acidity, and moderate tannin in the long finish. While it appears to be closing
down far more quickly than the legendary 1990, it has layers of sweet fruit as
well as an elevated level of glycerin. Give it 5–7 years of cellaring, and drink
it over the subsequent 2–3 decades. Last tasted, 3/97.

1988 — Consistently unimpressive, the 1988 Montrose is light, probably too tannic,
•   and lacking in richness and depth as well as finish. High yields and too early
83   a harvest date have left their mark on the 1988. Anticipated maturity: Now–
2000. Last tasted, 11/90.

1986 — This wine has turned out to be better than I originally thought. Made during
•   a period when Montrose was flirting with a lighter style, the 1986 is one of
91   the beefier efforts from that short-lived, stylistic detour. The wine reveals a
dense ruby/purple color with only a hint of lightening at the edge. Fleshy,
muscular, and powerful, with aromas of red and black fruits, earth, and spice,
this medium- to full-bodied, still tannic, brawny Montrose is not yet close to
full maturity. It possesses a layered, chewy character, along with plenty of
unresolved tannin in the finish. Anticipated maturity: 2000–2025. Last
tasted, 10/97.

1985 — A surprisingly light, innocuous style of Montrose, the 1985 exhibits a medium
•   ruby color, followed by pleasant but washed-out aromas of sweet red currants,
85   earth, and herbs. This medium-bodied wine displays some charm and sweet
fruit on the attack, but it narrows out in the midpalate and finish. There is
also angular tannin and herbaceousness in the aftertaste. While it is an above
average, good wine, in terms of Montrose it is disappointing. Anticipated
maturity: Now–2005. Last tasted, 10/97.

1984 — Medium ruby with a light-intensity fragrance of soft, oaky, berry fruit, the
•   1984 makes a clean, adequate impression on the palate but falls off in the
77   finish. A lighter-styled, picnic Montrose. Anticipated maturity: Now. Last
tasted, 6/88.

1983 — Not nearly as big or as tannic as one might expect, the 1983 Montrose has
•   adequate tannin, a decent ruby color, a spicy, plummy nose, medium body,
83   and an astringent finish. Anticipated maturity: Now–2000. Last tasted,
11/88.

1982 — I underrated this wine when it was young, and I would now like to set the
•   record straight. Recent bottles have been stunning, although I am surprised
91   by how forward, delicious, and complex the 1982 Montrose has become. A
rapidly developing Montrose, it remains a candidate for another 20+ years of
cellaring. The wine reveals a healthy dark ruby/garnet color, followed by a
fragrant, sweet nose of black fruits intermingled with new oak and floral
scents. Full bodied and opulent, with dusty tannin in the finish, this gorgeously proportioned, rich, concentrated wine can be drunk now or held for 2
decades. It is a very impressive example of Montrose that is atypically evolved
and forward. Last tasted, 8/97.

1981—Montrose produced an elegant, understated, shy, medium-weight wine in
•   1981. This streamlined version of Montrose is fully mature but seems to lack
84   the necessary concentration and richness to last very long. I find it excessively
austere. Anticipated maturity: Now–2000. Last tasted, 12/90.

1980—Lean, tannic, with a light ruby color, this wine will likely never be more than
•   an expensive quaffing wine. It is a dubious 1980. Anticipated maturity: Now–
72   probably in decline. Last tasted, 2/84.

1979—This is a good wine, but a disappointing effort for Montrose. Medium ruby
•   colored, with a light-intensity bouquet of cherry fruit intermingled with spicy
82   oak, this austere, dry wine is astringent in the finish because of aggressive
tannins. Anticipated maturity: Now. Last tasted, 3/88.

1978—Similar to the 1979, although deeper in color, this restrained, tannic wine
•   displays good ripe fruit and a stylish, medium-weight texture, yet it lacks
84   character, complexity, and richness. This vintage marked the beginning of the
new lighter-styled Montrose. How will it age? Anticipated maturity: Now. Last
tasted, 9/88.

1976—Undoubtedly one of the successes from this vintage and destined to be one of
•   the longest-lived wines of 1976, Montrose continues to exhibit a dark ruby
86   color, a spicy, vanillin oakiness, and a generous, deep, black currant fruitiness. While many 1976s have turned brown and begun to dry out, losing
their fruit, Montrose remains young, impressive, and promising. Anticipated
maturity: Now. Last tasted, 3/89.

1975—Still backward, although the color is beginning to exhibit amber/rust at the
•   edge, this large-scaled, muscular, charmless Montrose is structured enough
87?   to be admired, but I wonder if there is enough fruit to hold for another 10
years? Full bodied, with earthy, dusty, red and black fruit aromas, this tannic
behemoth needs another 2–3 years of cellaring. The jury is still out on this
one. Last tasted, 12/95.

1974—Not a bad effort in what has turned out to be a below average quality year for
•   Bordeaux. The 1974 Montrose is lean and sinewy, but it still exhibits good
72   color, some attractive fruit, oak, and earthy scents in the bouquet, and an
acidic finish. Anticipated maturity: Now–probably in decline. Last tasted,
6/85.

1973—Between 1976 and 1979 this was a pleasant effort in a year that produced far
•   too many diluted, thin wines. Now it has lost the fruit, and only the oak,
65   alcohol, and tannin remain. The wine is only of academic interest. Last tasted,
8/86.

1971—At peak, the 1971 Montrose is attractive, with an enthralling leathery, cedary,
•   ripe, fragrant, fruity bouquet, supple, moderately rich flavors, and medium
86   body. It is still charming and surprisingly well endowed for a 1971. Owners
of this wine should make plans to drink it up. Anticipated maturity: Now.
Last tasted, 2/87.

1970—This is one 1970 that appears to possess the necessary components to develop
•   into something special. It remains youthfully hard and astringent, but there
92+   is no doubting the high levels of concentration and intensity. Moreover, the

wine exhibits a classy, complex bouquet, offering up scents of cedar, black fruits, minerals, and leather. Full bodied, powerful, and rich, with outstanding concentration, this wine requires another 7–10 years of cellaring—can you believe that? It is unquestionably a 40–50-year wine. Last tasted, 6/96.

1967—A surprisingly good wine for the vintage, Montrose was at its best between
• 1975 and 1979. Now in decline as the fruit recedes, and the dusty tannins
82 and oak become more dominant, this medium ruby–colored wine still has good body and enough interest in the bouquet to hold many people's attention. Drink up. Anticipated maturity: Now. Last tasted, 10/81.

1966—The 1966 is still dark ruby with a peppery, very spicy, yet tight, relatively
• closed bouquet. The 1966 Montrose is austere and tough on the palate, with
86 good fruit and firm, rough tannins. Comparatively, it is not as massive or as rich as the 1970, 1964, or 1961 but is still backward and austere. Will the fruit hold up to the tannins? Anticipated maturity: Now–2005. Last tasted, 1/90.

1964—The 1964 Montrose was one of only a handful of Médocs harvested prior to
• the rains, so the wine exhibits unexpected depth, richness, and vigor. Richer
92 and more intense than the 1966, with a far darker, more opaque color, this huge, old-style, ripe wine offers a substantial mouthful of rich, unctuous claret. Amazingly, it still tastes less than a decade old. It is a great success for the vintage and may prove to be the longest-lived wine of the Médoc. An extraordinary success! Anticipated maturity: 2000–2020. Last tasted, 6/97.

1962—The 1962 Montrose was likely at its peak in 1985. Dark ruby, with a complex
• bouquet of ripe, cedary, black cherry aromas, this lovely wine is surprisingly
88 rich and deep on the palate and supple and long in the finish. Delicious now. Anticipated maturity: Now. Last tasted, 5/82.

1961—A stunning wine from a superb vintage, the 1961 Montrose is still in need of
• another 10 years of cellaring. The deep, opaque dark ruby color, the huge
95 bouquet of ripe cassis fruit and mineral scents, the full-bodied, dense, compelling richness and length, and gobs of tannin all point to a monumental bottle of wine for drinking during the first 20–30 years of the next century. Anticipated maturity: 2000–2030. Last tasted, 10/94.

ANCIENT VINTAGES

The 1959 (95 points; last tasted 10/94) is a surprising clone of the 1961, with sweeter fruit, a more rustic, tannic personality, and the same enormous weight, richness, and distinctively old style found in both the 1959 and 1961. The 1959 is just reaching full maturity; it will last another 20–30 years!

The 1921 Montrose (74–90? points; tasted four times in 1995 and 1996) is variable. In one tasting, the wine started off with a promising nose of cedar, smoked meats, and a peppery, Rhône-like character, but high acidity and ferocious tannin dominated the meager flavors. Other tastings have revealed a rich, sweet, opulently textured wine that was alive and still endowed with considerable fruit. The finest bottle, from the Paris wine merchant Nicolas was drunk in 1996 at my favorite restaurant in North America, New York City's Daniel. That bottle was marvelous (meriting a 93-point score)! While the 1945 and 1947 are reputed to be superb, the bottles I have seen have been marred by high levels of volatile acidity, dry, nearly viscous levels of tannin, and a disjointedness. I have enough friends who have tasted great examples of the 1945 Montrose to make me a believer, but I sure would like to have the opportunity to taste one.

LES-ORMES-DE-PEZ   GOOD

Classification: Cru Bourgeois in 1932
Location of vineyards: Pez, St.-Estèphe
Owner: Cazes family
Address: 33180 St.-Estèphe
Mailing address: c/o Château Lynch-Bages, 33250 Pauillac
Telephone: 33 5 56 73 24 00; telefax: 33 5 56 59 26 42
Visits: By appointment only
Contact: Isabelle Faurie at above telephone and fax numbers

VINEYARDS (red)
Surface area: 81.5 acres
Average age of vines: 35 years
Blend: 70% Cabernet Sauvignon, 20% Merlot, 10% Cabernet Franc
Density of plantation: 9,500 vines per hectare
Average yields (over the last 5 years): 50 hectoliters per hectare
Total average annual production: 17,000 cases

GRAND VIN (red)
Brand name: Château Les-Ormes-de-Pez
Appellation: St.-Estèphe
Mean annual production: 17,000 cases
Upbringing: Grapes are picked manually and are totally destemmed. Fermentations last 15–17 days (except in 1996, 20 days) and take place in 18 temperature-controlled stainless-steel tanks. Malolactics occur in vats, and wines are transferred afterward into 1- or 2-year-old casks, coming from Lynch-Bages, for 15 months. They are fined (albumin) and filtered.

SECOND WINE
None produced.

Evaluation of present classification: Should be upgraded to a fifth-growth
Plateau of maturity: 5–12 years following the vintage

Les-Ormes-de-Pez is a popular wine, in large part because of the wine's gener-ously flavored, plump, sometimes sweet and fat personality. Don't discount the extensive promotional efforts of the owner, Jean-Michel Cazes, either. The wine rarely disappoints. The color of Les-Ormes-de-Pez tends to be quite dark and, since 1975, the flavors increasingly supple and designed for easy comprehen-sion by the masses. However, the wine can age for 7–12 years. Older vintages from the forties and fifties, made in a more massive, dense style, can often repre-sent outstanding values, because the wine has been impeccably made for de-cades. Les-Ormes-de-Pez is a wine to which consumers, looking for high quality at modest prices, should always give serious consideration.

VINTAGES

1996—Les Ormes-de-Pez's impressive 1996 is one of the deeper, more muscular
 • examples from this well-run Cru Bourgeois estate. The wine's deep ruby color
85– is accompanied by sweet black fruit aromas intermixed with loamy soil and
87 spicy new oak scents. In the mouth, it is medium bodied and surprisingly soft, with well-integrated tannin, acidity, and alcohol. Anticipated maturity; Now–2008. Last tasted, 3/98.

1995—I am tempted to say this wine is too obviously commercial, but it is still an
 • attractive, soft, round, medium to dark ruby–colored claret with herb, black
86 cherry, and currant fruit notes. Lush, with some elegance, medium body, soft tannin, and an easygoing finish, this wine should be drunk during its first 7–8 years of life. Last tasted, 3/98.

1993—A dark ruby color is followed by aromas of green peppers and black currants.
 • This elegant, soft, ripe, medium-bodied wine requires consumption over the
82 next 4–5 years. Last tasted, 1/97.

1992—The wine displays a dark ruby color, excellent ripe berry fruit, some tannin
 • in the finish, a lush, medium-bodied, chewy style, and fine fruit and sup-
85 pleness. It should drink well for at least 7–8 years. I may have underrated this wine. Last tasted, 11/94.

1991—The 1991 exhibits moderate tannin, spicy, herbaceous fruit, above average
 • depth for the vintage, adequate tannin, and a clean, one-dimensional finish.
81 It should drink well for 5–8 years. Last tasted, 1/94.

1990—The dark, almost opaque ruby/purple–colored 1990 exhibits excellent depth,
 • plenty of stuffing and focus, and a long, ripe, alcoholic finish. This lavishly
89 rich, full-bodied offering is supple and stunning, as well as a notable value. Drink it over the next 10–15 years. Last tasted, 1/93.

1989—An opulent and intensely fruity style of Les-Ormes-de-Pez, the dark ruby–
 • colored 1989 is full bodied and endowed with soft tannins. It should provide
86 robust drinking for at least a decade. Anticipated maturity: Now–2000. Last tasted, 11/90.

1988—The 1988 is curiously similar to the 1989, but it does not have quite the weight
 • or jammy fruit of the 1989. For the vintage, it is surprisingly forward and should
85 drink well for up to a decade. Anticipated maturity: Now. Last tasted, 11/90.

1987—Soft, weedy, diluted fruit does little to make a favorable impression. In the
•   mouth, the wine is loosely knit and overtly commercial. It requires prompt
77   drinking. Anticipated maturity: Now. Last tasted, 3/90.

1986—No doubt because of the vintage, 1986 has produced one of the more tannic and
•   intense wines from Les-Ormes-de-Pez since their exceptional 1970. This ripe,
86   deep, chewy wine has plenty of fat and fruit to balance out the aggressive tannins and should keep for several decades, although it will probably be drinkable
after another 3–4 years. Anticipated maturity: Now–2005. Last tasted, 3/89.

1985—The 1985 has turned out to be an agreeable, soft, fruity wine without a great
•   deal of depth but with a pleasant fruitiness and immediate accessibility.
83   Anticipated maturity: Now. Last tasted, 1/90.

1984—Light to medium ruby with soft, round, shallow flavors that convey the taste
•   of weeds and cassis, the 1984 should be drunk up. Anticipated maturity:
82   Now. Last tasted, 12/88.

1983—Very deeply colored, with a fat, ripe, round, richly fruity character, this
•   full-bodied, well-made wine has good, silky, but substantial tannins and low
84   acidity. Anticipated maturity: Now. Last tasted, 5/88.

1982—Although this soft, fleshy, ripe-flavored wine has been ready to drink for 5–6
•   years, it exhibits no sign of color degradation or fruit loss. Round, supple,
87   and generous, with plenty of lush, thick, earthy, black currant fruit intertwined with herbaceous scents, this chunky, husky wine should continue to
drink well for another 5–6 years. Last tasted, 9/95.

1981—This is a straightforward style of wine, which is not up to the excellent quality
•   of the 1982 or very good 1983, but it is still robust and fruity, with a generous
78   texture and a pleasing, rounded, soft finish. Anticipated maturity: Now. Last
tasted, 1/83.

1979—A mediocre effort from Les-Ormes-de-Pez, this wine is light in color, with a
•   fully mature, fruity bouquet, some damp, oaky aromas, and a soft, rather lean
75   finish. Anticipated maturity: Now–probably in decline. Last tasted, 6/84.

1978—A very good wine that exhibits deep, black currant, ripe fruit, a medium- to
•   full-bodied feel on the palate, and good solid tannins. The bouquet is begin-
85   ning to reveal complex cedary, spicy scents. The tannins are melting away. It
is a husky, fleshy wine that should age well for 10–12 years. Anticipated
maturity: Now. Last tasted, 3/88.

1976—Moderately intense jammy fruit suggests an overripe character on the palate.
•   The wine is soft, with low acidity and a diluted, thin finish. Drink up!
72   Anticipated maturity: Now–probably in serious decline. Last tasted, 5/82.

1975—Successful for the vintage, and better than several of the more expensive
•   "classified growths," the 1975 Les-Ormes-de-Pez is rich and full bodied, with
84   a leathery, ripe, fruity bouquet. Dusty, spicy, generally ripe flavors with some
astringent tannins still evident. It should be drunk over the next 4–6 years.
Anticipated maturity: Now. Last tasted, 11/88.

1971—Somewhat light and already fading when first tasted in 1977, this wine has
•   consistently exhibited a harsh, biting acidity and lack of fruit. Caveat emptor.
65   Last tasted, 6/85.

1970—The 1970 Les-Ormes-de-Pez has been a consistently strong performer. After
• having drunk nearly a case (purchased for $4.99 a bottle in 1973), I must
89 confess that not one bottle has been fully mature, and I doubt that this wine
will ever reach an ideal balance among its fruit, tannin, and acidity. The
most concentrated Les-Ormes-de-Pez I have tasted, it possesses a thick,
plum/garnet color with an amber tint at the edge. Thick, rich, and robust,
with a peppery, iron, cedary, earthy, curranty nose, this admirable, full-
throttle wine can be drunk now as well as over the next decade. Last tasted,
6/96.

ANCIENT VINTAGES

During the mid-1980s, I had the opportunity to drink the 1947, 1953, 1955,
1959, and 1961, all plucked off the wine lists of several Bordeaux restaurants.
All of them were still in fine condition, massive, robust, nearly coarse wines
that represented the old style of Bordeaux winemaking. I have no doubt that
well-stored examples of this château's wines from the forties, fifties, and
sixties could represent fine values today.

PEZ   GOOD

Classification: Cru Bourgeois in 1932
Location of vineyards: St.-Estèphe
Owner: Champagne Louis Roederer
Address: B.P. 14–33180 St.-Estèphe
Telephone: 33 5 56 59 30 26; telefax: 33 5 56 59 39 25
Visits: By appointment only
Contact: Mr. Philippe Moureau (at above address and numbers)

VINEYARDS (red)
Surface area: 59.5 acres
Average age of vines: 32 years
Blend: 46% Merlot, 43% Cabernet Sauvignon, 8% Cabernet Franc,
3% Petit Verdot
Density of plantation: 6,400 vines per hectare
Average yields (over the last 5 years): 51 hectoliters per hectare
Total average annual production: 140,000 bottles

GRAND VIN (red)
Brand name: Chatêau de Pez
Appellation: St.-Estèphe
Mean annual production: 140,000 bottles
Upbringing: Grapes are picked manually. Fermentations last
approximately 25 days in wooden vats, with temperatures going up to

29–30 degrees centigrade. Wines are transferred in December into oak casks, one-third of which are new (barrels are renewed by one-third every year), for malolactics. Wines stay in casks for 14 months when new, and 12 months when 1 or 2 years old. They are fined but not filtered.

SECOND WINE
None produced.

Evaluation of present classification: Should be upgraded to a fifth-growth
Plateau of maturity: 8–18 years following the vintage

It is difficult to miss Château de Pez and the twin towers as one passes through the one-horse village of Pez. For decades this estate has made a muscular yet excellent, sometimes tough-textured wine that is capable of lasting for up to two decades. If the wine of de Pez is to be criticized at all, it is for rarely attaining an exceptional rating. Reliable and solid as it may be, de Pez seems incapable of hitting the heights that other notable Crus Bourgeois, particularly Haut-Marbuzet, Meyney, and, since the late eighties, Phélan-Ségur, routinely achieve. I have often wondered whether an increased percentage of Merlot in the blend might not give the unduly restrained, frequently lean de Pez more flesh and character.

It will be interesting to follow de Pez given the fact that the property was acquired by the Champagne house of Louis Roederer several years ago. The former proprietor, Robert Dousson, has spent much of his life at de Pez, having been born there in 1929. A hands-on proprietor, always at the property, he believed strongly in unmanipulated wines. Additionally, the longevity of his wines and their popularity in England and northern Europe never went to his head. It is too soon to know, but changes in style and quality are likely under the new regime.

VINTAGES

1997—The owners of de Pez, the Roederer champagne firm, are intent on pushing
  •   the quality of de Pez far higher than my tasting notes suggest. The 1997 is an
84–   attractive, easygoing, somewhat commercially styled claret with low acidity,
85   straightforward berry and black currant fruit, and earthy, spicy nuances in
       the background. It should be drunk during its first 4–6 years of life. Last
       tasted, 3/98.

1996—The 1996 de Pez appears to be an astringently tannic wine that needs to flesh
  •   out to merit a higher score. There is attractive ripe, pure, black cherry fruit,
84–   medium body, and good sweetness and texture, but the tannin currently
86   dominates the wine's personality. Anticipated maturity: 2004–2012. Last
       tasted, 3/97.

1995—The 1995 possesses excellent color, a sweet, jammy, black currant aroma,
•   a monolithic but well-proportioned and concentrated feel on the palate,
86   low acidity, and mature tannin in the finish. This tasty, mouth-filling
      St.-Estèphe should drink well when released and last for a decade. Last
      tasted, 3/96.

1989—The 1989, which is opulently rich and more precocious than usual, possesses
•   layers of cassis fruit intertwined with scents of herbs and toasty oak. Surpris-
86   ingly fleshy for de Pez, with low acidity, this full-bodied effort will drink well
      young but boasts the requisite depth and balance to last for 12–15 years.
      Anticipated maturity: Now–2005. Last tasted, 1/93.

1988—The 1988 is a typical effort from de Pez, with a reserved and polite bouquet
•   of moderately ripe black currants, minerals, and wood. The wine is medium
83   bodied, slightly astringent, austere, and restrained. It lacks flesh and appears
      compact. Anticipated maturity: Now–2000. Last tasted, 1/93.

1986—I have my reservations about this vintage of de Pez only because it has been
•   so forbiddingly impenetrable and tannic. Tasted several times after bottling,
82   the wine has an impressive dark ruby color, but the nose is completely locked
      in, and on the palate the wine is abrasively coarse, revealing none of the
      flesh, charm, or concentration one expects to find even in the youngest claret.
      Nevertheless, it is hard to believe that this property has not made at least a
      good wine; but patience is most definitely required. Anticipated maturity:
      Now–2005. Last tasted, 3/90.

1985—This charming, elegant wine avoids the hard, tough tannin often found in the
•   wines of this vintage. Deep ruby, with a moderately intense, enthralling
86   bouquet of spicy oak and cassis, this medium- to full-bodied, surprisingly
      precocious-tasting de Pez drinks well yet should last for at least another 10–
      12 years. Anticipated maturity: Now–2001. Last tasted, 11/89.

1983—As well made as many of the more highly regarded 1983s, de Pez has a
•   dark color and dense, rich, ripe, fruity flavors, a significant tannin content,
85   and a spicy, moderately tannic finish. Traditionally made, it will require
      another 4–5 years of cellaring. Anticipated maturity: Now–2005. Last tasted,
      1/88.

1982—Much rounder and fruitier than the 1983, the 1982 is very dark ruby with an
•   intense cassis bouquet, round, generously endowed, luscious flavors, high but
86   velvety tannins, and a fine, heady finish. Anticipated maturity: Now–2003.
      Last tasted, 1/89.

1981—This is the least successful de Pez in the trio of fine claret vintages—1981,
•   1982, and 1983. A medium-weight wine, the 1981 is austere and unyielding
77   but has good fruit and a firm, tannic, lean structure. This wine has remained
      tight and unevolved, but I fear the fruit is beginning to dry out. Anticipated
      maturity: Now. Last tasted, 6/87.

1979—Medium to dark ruby color, with an evolved bouquet of spice and herbaceous,
•   black currant scents, this medium-bodied wine has good fruit, moderate
83   tannins, and a dry, slightly astringent, moderately long finish. Anticipated
      maturity: Now. Last tasted, 7/86.

1978—A success for de Pez, the 1978, which has more Merlot than usual because of
•　　flowering problems with the 1978 Cabernet crop, is a rich, supple, deep,
85　　fruity wine with plenty of extract and tannin. Medium to full bodied, it has
　　　developed fully but shows no signs of decline. Anticipated maturity: Now–
　　　2000. Last tasted, 11/88.

1976—From its birth, the 1976 de Pez displayed excellent winemaking and a strict
•　　selection of only the best barrels in this copious vintage. Darker colored than
84　　most 1976 Bordeaux, with a ripe, rich, fruity aroma and soft, underlying
　　　tannins, this wine has been fully mature since the early eighties. It is a
　　　top-notch effort for the vintage. Anticipated maturity: Now. Last tasted,
　　　10/87.

1975—I have consistently found this wine to be almost undrinkable because of its
•　　excruciatingly painful tannin level. At present, the tannin has melted away
84　　and there is some fruit to be found in this medium-bodied, earthy wine
　　　offering up moderate amounts of cedar, cherry fruit and dusty aromas. There
　　　is still a tannic bite, but the wine has become far more balanced than I
　　　would have ever guessed. Drink it over the next 5–7 years. Last tasted,
　　　12/95.

1973—Now faded, the 1973 was (until 1980) one of the most enjoyable wines of
•　　what turned out to be a terribly weak, diluted vintage of frail, watery wines.
76　　Not so for the de Pez, which exhibited a lovely, charming, moderately intense,
　　　berry fruitiness, and soft, supple flavor. In large formats—such as magnums
　　　—this wine may still be vibrant. Anticipated maturity: Now–probably in
　　　serious decline. Last tasted, 3/85.

1970—While the 1970 de Pez has always been a well-made, elegant, stylish
•　　wine with a distinctive mineral, curranty aroma, when tasted in December
?　　(the last bottle from my cellar) it was disappointing. Although the color was
　　　sound, the wine tasted dried out, hard, and astringent. This has been a
　　　consistently good wine, so perhaps this was an off bottle. Last tasted,
　　　12/96.

PHÉLAN-SÉGUR　　　　　　　　　　　　　　　　VERY GOOD

Classification: Cru Bourgeois in 1932
Location of vineyards: St.-Estèphe
Owner: Xavier Gardinier
Address: 33180 St.-Estèphe
Telephone: 33 5 56 59 30 09; telefax: 33 5 56 59 30 04
Visits: By appointment only
Contact: Thierry Gardinier (see details above)

VINEYARDS (red)
Surface area: 158 acres
Average age of vines: 30 years

Blend: 60% Cabernet Sauvignon, 35% Merlot, 5% Cabernet Franc
Density of plantation: 8,500 vines per hectare
Average yields (over the last 5 years): 56 hectoliters per hectare
Total average annual production: 25,000–30,000 cases

GRAND VIN (red)
Brand name: Château Phélan-Ségur
Appellation: St.-Estèphe
Mean annual production: 20,000 cases
Upbringing: Fermentations last about 20 days in temperature-controlled
stainless-steel vats, with maximum temperatures between 25 and 30
degrees centigrade. Wines are then transferred into oak barrels (40% of
which are new) for about 18 months. They are fined and filtered prior to
bottling.

SECOND WINE
Brand Name: Franck Phélan
Average annual production: 12,000 cases

Evaluation of present classification: Should be maintained, although it
should be noted that the quality since 1986 merits comparison with
Médoc's best fourth- and fifth-growths
Plateau of maturity: Since 1986, 5–14 years following the vintage

After a terribly troubled beginning in the decade of the eighties, this property
was sold by the Delon family to Xavier Gardinier in 1985. The new proprietor
was forced to recall several vintages because a foul chemical stench had
developed in many of the bottles. A lawsuit was instituted by the château
against a prominent manufacturer of herbicides, alleging that it was the use
of these chemicals that caused the off aroma. However, Phélan-Ségur is now
in firmly committed, competent hands. This beautiful estate, which has been
recently cleaned and refurbished by the new owners, has always had the
potential to produce one of the finest wines of St.-Estèphe, because the
vineyard borders both those of Montrose and Calon-Ségur. The progress made
by the new owners was especially evident with excellent wines produced
since the late eighties.

VINTAGES

1996—A return to a more typical style after their loosely knit, commercial, soft, and
flabby 1995, Phélan-Ségur's 1996 displays a deep ruby/purple color and an
86– excellent bouquet of raspberry/cassis fruit intermixed with smoke and earth.
87 Medium bodied, with admirable richness and definition, this wine possesses

moderate tannin, impressive purity, and fine texture and length. Anticipated maturity: 2001–2012. Last tasted, 3/98.

1995— Consistently open-knit, soft, and pleasant, but essentially one-dimensional
• and monochromatic, the 1995 Phélan-Ségur offers enjoyable fruit in the nose,
84 but it lacks the depth and richness of other top vintages of this well-placed St.-Estèphe Cru Bourgeois. Anticipated maturity: Now–2005. Last tasted, 11/97.

1994— The 1994 reveals red and black currants, oak, and toast in the nose. Although
• soft for a wine of this vintage, and lacking some of the midpalate intensity
86 possessed by the 1993, it is well made, dense, and medium bodied. Despite light tannin in the finish, this wine should drink well young and keep for 7–8 years. Last tasted, 1/97.

1993— In what must be one of the ironies of this vintage, Phélan-Ségur's 1993 turned
• out to be more successful, fatter, and riper than either the 1994 or the 1995
87 —surprising in view of potentially better raw materials for the two younger vintages. The 1993 exhibits a dark ruby/purple color, followed by an excellent, smoky, sweet, toasty oak, black fruit–scented nose, admirable fat and ripeness, a good midpalate with fine purity, and an attractive, medium-bodied, cedary, soft finish with no astringency. Drink this delicious, well-made 1993 over the next 5–7 years. A sleeper! Last tasted, 1/97.

1992— One of the best run Médoc properties, Phélan-Ségur is a smart choice for
• consumers looking for high quality and value. The vintages to be on the
86 lookout for (assuming readers can still find any) are the glorious 1990 and opulent 1989, but Phélan-Ségur has also turned in a fine effort in 1992. The wine exhibits dark ruby color, a sweet nose of black currants, oak, and spices, tasty, medium-bodied flavors with good ripeness, extract, and suppleness, and a chewy, smooth finish. It is a noteworthy effort for the vintage. Drink it over the next 3–4 years. Last tasted, 11/94.

1991— The 1991 is a deeply colored, soft wine with a moderately intense nose of
• black fruits, minerals, and oak. Medium bodied and soft, with fine concentra-
86 tion and a smooth, tannic finish, it should drink well for 7–10 years. Last tasted, 1/94.

1990— The 1990 is darkly colored, with a big, sweet, opulent, nearly explosive nose.
• This full-bodied wine displays excellent intensity and extract, plenty of ripe
89 tannins, and a long, rich, authoritative finish. Anticipated maturity: Now–2003. Last tasted, 1/93.

1989— A strict selection, the use of 40% new oak, and an extended maceration have
• produced a rich, full-bodied 1989 that offers both power and finesse. Deep
88 ruby/purple, with gobs of red and black fruits in its aroma, this concentrated, impressively structured wine will prove to be a crowd pleaser. It is the finest Phélan-Ségur I have ever tasted. Anticipated maturity: Now–2003. Last tasted, 4/91.

1988— The 1988 Phélan-Ségur is lighter than the 1989 but is still a textbook ex-
• ample of a St.-Estèphe. A toasty, black currant–scented bouquet is fol-
87 lowed by a medium-bodied wine with fine balance and length. It has less

aging potential than the 1989. Anticipated maturity: Now. Last tasted, 4/91.

1987—A light, weedy bouquet precedes stern, one-dimensional, tannic flavors that
• lack flesh and charm. I see no future for this wine. Anticipated maturity: Now.
71 Last tasted, 6/89.

1986—The 1986 Phélan-Ségur is the first respectable effort by the new regime.
• Medium dark ruby, with a tight-but-emerging bouquet of weedy cassis fruit,
82 this medium-bodied, tannic, yet concentrated wine lacks only flesh and complexity. Anticipated maturity: Now. Last tasted, 3/89.

OTHER ST.-ESTÈPHE ESTATES

BEL-AIR

Classification: None
Location of vineyards: St.-Estèphe
Owner: S.C. du Château Bel-Air
Address: 4, rue de Fontaugé, 33180 St.-Estèphe
Mailing address: 15, route de Castelnau, 33480 Avensan, Médoc
Telephone: 33 5 56 58 21 03; telefax: 33 5 56 58 17 20
Visits: By appointment only
Contact: Monsieur Jean-François Braquessac (at the above mailing address and indicated telephone numbers)

VINEYARDS (red)
Surface area: 10.4 acres
Average age of vines: 30 years
Blend: 65% Cabernet Sauvignon, 30% Merlot, 5% Cabernet Franc
Density of plantation: Between 8,500 and 10,000 vines per hectare
Average yields (over the last 5 years): 60 hectoliters per hectare
Total average annual production: 1,500 cases

GRAND VIN (red)
Brand name: Château Bel-Air
Appellation: St.-Estèphe
Mean annual production: 18,000 bottles
Upbringing: Fermentations and *cuvaisons* last 5 weeks in stainless-steel tanks of 90 and 110 hectoliters. Maximum temperatures reached are around 30–32 degrees centigrade. Wines are kept in 1-year-old casks for 13 months (that was the case for the 1995 vintage, which was their debut). They are fined but not filtered.

SECOND WINE

Brand name: Château Bel-Air Coutelin

Average annual production: 18,000 bottles

NOTE: Grapes are hand-picked, and there is a first sorting right in the vineyards, which are located in front of Cos d'Estournel, Marbuzet, and Montrose. Green pruning is carried out on the younger vines if necessary.

LE BOSCQ

Classification: Cru Bourgeois in 1932
Location of vineyards: St.-Estèphe
Owner: Société Civile du Château Le Boscq (estate is farmed by Dourthe since September 1995)
Address: 33180 St.-Estèphe
Mailing address: Dourthe (CVBG), B.P. 49, 45, route de Bordeaux, 33290 Parempuyre, France
Telephone: 33 5 56 35 53 00; telefax: 33 5 56 35 53 29
Visits: By appointment only
Contact: Dourthe CVBG
Telephone: 33 5 56 35 53 00; telefax: 33 5 56 35 53 29

VINEYARDS (red)
Surface area: 41 acres
Average age of vines: 25 years
Blend: 51% Merlot, 38% Cabernet Sauvignon, 6.5 % Petit Verdot, 4.5% Cabernet Franc
Density of plantation: 8,000 vines per hectare
Average yields (over the last 5 years): 55 hectoliters per hectare
Total average annual production: 120,000 bottles

GRAND VIN (red)
Brand name: Château Le Boscq
Appellation: St.-Estèphe
Mean annual production: 80,000 bottles
Upbringing: Grapes are hand-picked, fermentations (blend and parcels separate) last about 3 weeks in temperature-controlled vats. Malolactics occur in vats for part of the yield and in barrels for the rest, and wines are aged in barrels—64% new oak—(lots separate) for 15–18 months until *assemblage*. Wines are fined but not filtered.

SECOND WINE
Brand name: Not yet chosen
Average annual production: 40,000 bottles in 1995 (first year in which a second wine was produced)

Evaluation of present classification: Should be maintained
Plateau of maturity: 3–8 years following the vintage

The vineyard of Le Boscq is located at the very northern end of the appellation of St.-Estèphe, with a good view of the Gironde River. It has extremely gravelly, clay soil, and the wine is vinified in stainless-steel vats and aged in small oak casks for 18 months. Given the high percentage of Merlot, it is not surprising that the wine is soft and fruity. In years where there is a tendency toward overripeness, Le Boscq can be disjointed and flabby. Nevertheless, in good vintages, this wine provides reasonably priced, fine drinking in its first decade of life.

CAPBERN-GASQUETON

Classification: Cru Bourgeois in 1932
Location of vineyards: St.-Estèphe
Owner: Héritiers Capbern-Gasqueton
Administrator; Madame Capbern-Gasqueton
Address: 33180 St.-Estèphe
Telephone: 33 5 56 59 30 08; telefax: 33 5 56 59 71 51
Visits: By appointment only
Contact: The château (see above address and numbers)

VINEYARDS (red)
Surface area: 86.5 acres
Average age of vines: 30 years
Blend: 65% Cabernet Sauvignon, 25% Merlot, 10% Cabernet Franc
Average yields (over the last 5 years): 35 hectoliters per hectare

GRAND VIN (red)
Brand name: Château Capbern-Gasqueton
Appellation: St.-Estèphe
Mean annual production: 135,000 bottles
Upbringing: Grapes are hand-picked. Fermentations are long (about 3 weeks) in temperature-controlled stainless-steel vats. Wines are transferred to oak casks, 30% of which are new, for 18 months. They are fined but not filtered.

SECOND WINE
None produced.

Evaluation of present classification: Should be maintained
Plateau of maturity: 5–10 years following the vintage

While this is a Cru Bourgeois, it has been rumored that Capbern benefits from those vats produced at Calon-Ségur that are not deemed suitable for that estate's grand vin. The wine, which is matured entirely in small casks, has a tendency to be hard and lacking in flavor dimension and character. The best recent vintages have been the 1982, 1988, 1989, and 1990.

CAVE COOPERATIVE MARQUIS DE ST.-ESTÈPHE

Reputed to be the finest and most modernly equipped cooperative in the Médoc, this conglomerate of over two hundred producers (controlling 926 acres of vineyards) turns out an enormous quantity of wine that is sold not only under the name of the cooperative, Marquis de St.-Estèphe, but also under the name of the estate. Some of the small but reputable estates that have their wines produced and bottled at the cooperative include Les Pradines, l'Hôpital, Le Roc, and, what is probably the finest estate the cooperative can boast, Château Faget. The latter property, a tiny domain of 10 acres owned by Maurice Lagarde, consistently turns out wines that are rich, full bodied, and reasonably priced. Visitors to the cooperative should specifically request a tasting of this particular cuvée. Most of the wines of the cooperative are aged only in vats and rarely have the benefit of new oak casks; therefore they should be drunk in their first 5–6 years of life.

LA COMMANDERIE

Classification: Cru Bourgeois in 1932
Location of vineyards: St.-Estèphe
Owner: G.F.A. Château Canteloup et La Commanderie
Address: 33180 St.-Estèphe
Mailing address: J.-P. Meffre, Vignobles Meffre, 84810 Aubignan
Telephone: 33 4 90 62 61 37; telefax: 33 4 90 65 03 73
Visits: By appointment only
Contact: CVBG Dourthe, 45, rue de Bordeaux, 33290 Parempuyre.
Telephone: 33 5 56 35 53 00; telefax: 33 5 56 35 53 29

VINEYARDS (red)
Surface area: 37 acres
Average age of vines: 25 years
Blend: 55% Cabernet Sauvignon, 40% Merlot, 5% Cabernet Franc
Density of plantation: 6,000 vines per hectare
Average yields (over the last 5 years): 50 hectoliters per hectare
Total average annual production: 100,000 bottles

GRAND VIN (red)
Brand name: Château La Commanderie
Appellation: St.-Estèphe
Mean annual production: 100,000 bottles
Upbringing: Fermentations last 15–20 days depending upon the quality
of the harvest, and wines are aged, one-third in new oak barrels and the
rest in vats, for 12–15 months. They are fined and filtered.

Evaluation of present classification: Should be maintained
Plateau of maturity: 4–8 years following the vintage

This wine is made in a modern, commercial style, emphasizing supple, easy-going fruit and smooth, light tannins, and is ready to drink when bottled. It could be more complex, but it is certainly clean and understandable to the masses.

COUTELIN-MERVILLE
GOOD

Classification: Grand Cru Bourgeois in 1932
Location of vineyards: Blanquet, St.-Estèphe
Owners: Bernard and François Estager
Address: c/o G. Estager et Fils, Blanquet, 33180 St.-Estèphe
Telephone: 33 5 56 59 32 10
Visits: All day on weekdays and by appointment only during weekends
Contact: Bernard and François Estager

VINEYARDS (red)
Surface area: 52 acres
Average age of vines: 25 years
Blend: 51% Merlot, 26% Cabernet Franc, 20% Cabernet Sauvignon, 3%
Petit Verdot
Density of plantation: 8,000 vines per hectare
Average yields (over the last 5 years): 60 hectoliters per hectare
Total average annual production: 160,000 bottles

GRAND VIN (red)
Brand name: Château Coutelin-Merville
Appellation: St.-Estèphe
Mean annual production: 160,000 bottles
Upbringing: Fermentations are traditional and last 15–21 days. Wines then spend 12 months in oak casks, 20% of which are new. They are fined and undergo light filtration prior to bottling. Château Merville is another brand name used for the same wines.

Evaluation of present classification: Should be maintained
Plateau of maturity: 8–15 or more years following the vintage

NOTE: This château is situated on the highest point in St.-Estèphe.

I wish I were more familiar with the wines of this moderately sized estate. Those vintages I have tasted—1986, 1982, 1975, and 1970—all represented intensely concentrated, powerful, highly tannic, yet interesting old-style, well-made wines. The proprietors, Bernard and François Estager, from France's Corrèze region (much like the family of Jean-Pierre Moueix in Libourne), march to the beat of a different drummer in St.-Estèphe, as his blend of grapes suggests he is a great proponent of Cabernet Franc. Perhaps this explains why their wines have a compelling fragrance, but it does not explain their aging potential, power, and muscle. All things considered, this is a wine that Estager claims needs at least 15–20 years in the top vintages to reach maturity! He would appear to be right. This could well be a property to look at more seriously.

HAUT-BEAUSÉJOUR

Classification: Cru Bourgeois in 1932
Location of vineyards: St.-Estèphe
Owner: Champagne Louis Roederer
Address: Rue de la Mairie, 33180 St.-Estèphe
Telephone: 33 5 56 59 30 26; telefax: 33 5 56 59 39 25
Visits: By appointment only
Contact: Philippe Moureau (see details above)

VINEYARDS (red)
Surface area: 47 acres
Average age of vines: 24 years
Blend: 54% Merlot, 39% Cabernet Sauvignon, 4% Petit Verdot, 3% Malbec

Density of plantation: 8,300 vines per hectare
Average yields (over the last 5 years): 54 hectoliters per hectare
Total average annual production: 130,000 bottles

GRAND VIN (red)
Brand name: Château Haut-Beauséjour
Appellation: St.-Estèphe
Mean annual production: 110,000 bottles
Upbringing: Grapes are picked by hand. Fermentations last 3 weeks
in cement tanks, with temperatures up to 29–30 degrees centigrade,
and malolactics occur in vats. Wines are then transferred to oak
casks, one-third of which are new (the barrels are renewed by a
third every year), in December and stay there 14 months (new oak)
or 12 months (1- and 2-year-old barrels). They are fined but not
filtered.

SECOND WINE
None produced.

HAUT-COTEAU

Classification: Cru Bourgeois in 1932
Location of vineyards: Between St.-Estèphe and St.-Seurin de Cadourne
Owner: Brousseau family
Address: St.-Corbian, 33180 St.-Estèphe
Telephone: 33 5 56 59 39 84; telefax: 33 5 56 59 39 09
Visits: On weekdays, from 11 A.M. to 6 P.M.
Contact: B. Brousseau

VINEYARDS (red)
Surface area: 49.4 acres in all, but only 17.3 acres produce Château
Haut-Coteau
Average age of vines: 30 years
Blend: 50% Cabernet Sauvignon, 30% Merlot, 15% Cabernet Franc, 5%
Petit Verdot
Density of plantation: 8,200 vines per hectare
Average yields (over the last 5 years): 58 hectoliters per hectare
Total average annual production: 45,000 bottles

GRAND VIN (red)
Brand name: Château Haut-Coteau
Appellation: St.-Estèphe
Mean annual production: 45,000 bottles

Upbringing: Fermentations last 5–8 days, macerations 15–20 days. Wines are kept 12 months in oak barrels, 35% of which are new. They are fined but not filtered.

SECOND WINE
None produced.

LA HAYE

Classification: Cru Bourgeois in 1932
Location of vineyards: Leyssac, St.-Estèphe
Owner: Georges Lecallier
Address: Leyssac, 33180 St.-Estèphe
Mailing address: 28, rue d'Armenonville, 92200 Neuilly-sur-Seine
Telephone: 33 1 47 38 24 42; telefax: 33 1 47 38 14 41
Visits: From July 1 to September 15, from Monday to Saturday, between 10 A.M. and 7 P.M., and the rest of the year only by appointment
Contact: Sylvie Jaffre, telephone: 33 5 56 59 32 18

VINEYARDS (red)
Surface area: 25 acres
Average age of vines: 25 years
Blend: 50% Cabernet Sauvignon, 42% Merlot, 8% Cabernet Franc
Density of plantation: 8,000 vines per hectare
Average yields (over the last 5 years): 45–50 hectoliters per hectare
Total average annual production: 70,000 bottles

GRAND VIN (red)
Brand name: Château La Haye
Appellation: St.-Estèphe
Mean annual production: 50,000 bottles
Upbringing: Fermentations last 20 days in temperature-controlled vats, with maximum temperatures of 28–30 degrees centigrade. Wines then spend 15 months in oak casks, 25%–30% of which are new. They are both fined and filtered.

SECOND WINE
Brand name: Le Fleuve
Average annual production: 20,000 bottles

HOUISSANT

Classification: Cru Bourgeois Supérieur
Production: 11,000 cases
Blend: 70% Cabernet Sauvignon, 30% Merlot
Secondary label: None
Vineyard size: 50 acres
Proprietor: Jean Ardouin
Time spent in barrels: The wine is aged only in vats
Average age of vines: 15 years

Evaluation of present classification: Should be downgraded to a Cru
Bourgeois
Plateau of maturity: 3–8 years following the vintage

The half dozen or so vintages of Houissant I have tasted have never made a favorable impression. The wine tends to be disjointed, austere, and very tannic.

LAFFITTE-CARCASSET   GOOD

Classification: Cru Bourgeois
Production: 8,500 cases
Blend: 74% Cabernet Sauvignon, 25% Merlot, 1% Petit Verdot
Secondary label: Château La Vicomtesse
Vineyard size: 50 acres
Proprietor: Vicomte Philippe de Padirac
Time spent in barrels: 12–18 months
Average age of vines: 35 years

Evaluation of present classification: Should be maintained
Plateau of maturity: 5–8 years following the vintage

This is not a wine that I know well, but those vintages I have tasted—1988, 1986, 1985, and 1982—seem to belong to the elegant, finesse school of winemaking. Somewhat light, but still tasty and harmonious, with none of the tough-textured, often excessive tannin that many St.-Estèphes reveal, the wines from Laffitte-Carcasset seem to be at their best within 7–8 years of the vintage. The vineyard is well located on high ground in the very northern part of the St.-Estèphe appellation.

LAVILLOTTE

Classification: Cru Bourgeois
Production: 7,000 cases
Blend: 75% Cabernet Sauvignon, 25% Merlot
Secondary label: None
Vineyard size: 29.6 acres
Proprietor: Jacques Pedro
Time spent in barrels: 16–20 months
Average age of vines: 20 years

Evaluation of present classification: Should be upgraded to a Cru
Bourgeois Exceptionnel or fifth-growth
Plateau of maturity: 8–15 years following the vintage

At the time proprietor Jacques Pedro purchased Lavillotte in 1962, it was in deplorable condition. Pedro comes from a family of French viticulturists who had lived in Algeria until it was granted independence from France. His philosophy combines a mixture of modern technology and healthy respect for tradition. This contrast is evident: his vineyards are harvested by machine, but the *cuvaison* is at least 3 weeks long; the wine is aged in 2-year-old barrels purchased from Château Latour and fined with egg whites but is never filtered. The results, based on vintages such as 1982, 1985, 1986, and 1989 —the only vintages I have tasted—are surprisingly concentrated, full-bodied wines, with fragrance, complexity, and richness. Each of the aforementioned vintages will easily mature gracefully for over a decade. This would appear to be one of the best, yet least well-known, sources for fine wine from St.-Estèphe.

MARBUZET

Classification: Cru Bourgeois Exceptionnel in 1932
Location of vineyards: St.-Estèphe
Owner: Domaines Prats S.A.
Address: 33180 St.-Estèphe
Telephone: 33 5 56 73 15 50; telefax: 33 5 56 59 72 59
Visits: Not allowed

VINEYARDS (red)
Surface area: 17.3 acres
Average age of vines: 20 years
Blend: 60% Cabernet Sauvignon, 40% Merlot
Density of plantation: 9,000 vines per hectare

Average yields (over the last 5 years): 60 hectoliters per hectare
Total average annual production: 60,000 bottles

GRAND VIN (red)
Brand name: Château Marbuzet
Appellation: St.-Estèphe
Mean annual production: 60,000 bottles
Upbringing: Grapes are picked manually. Winemaking is traditional,
fermentations last about 3 weeks, and malolactics occur in tanks. Wines
then spend 12 months in 1-year-old barrels and are fined and filtered
prior to bottling.

SECOND WINE
None produced.

Evaluation of present classification: Until recently, this was the secondary
label of Cos d'Estournel, which blended vats not considered fine enough
for Cos d'Estournel.
Plateau of maturity: 2–8 years following the vintage

If I had to pick one of the most beautiful and romantically situated properties
in the Médoc, it would be this glorious château with its superb terrace and
wonderful gardens. In fact, the château, which faces the Gironde River, bears
a remarkable resemblance to the White House in Washington, D.C.

This tiny domain, once the second wine of Cos d'Estournel, now has its
own identity as an estate-bottled St.-Estèphe. Proprietor Bruno Prats believes
this wine should be smooth, supple, and ideal for drinking in its first 7–8
years of life. I look for this property to make better and better wines now that
it is no longer a "second" wine.

PETIT BOCQ   GOOD

Classification: Cru Bourgeois
Production: 1,000 cases
Blend: 80% Merlot, 20% Cabernet Sauvignon
Secondary label: None
Vineyard size: 5 acres
Proprietors: Francis and Modeste Souquet
Time spent in barrels: 14–16 months
Average age of vines: 25 years

Evaluation of present classification: Should be upgraded to a Grand
Bourgeois Exceptionnel or fifth-growth
Plateau of maturity: 3–12 years following the vintage

Unfortunately, this distinctive wine with the highest percentage of Merlot on any property in St.-Estèphe has never, to my knowledge, been seen in the export markets. Proprietor Souquet, who has spent his life working in a winemaking family, fashions one of St.-Estèphe's most hedonistic wines. The 1982, 1985, and 1989 were bursting with black fruits, were explosively rich and full, and possessed a juicy, thick texture, causing me to wonder why this property has not gained more recognition from Bordeaux wine enthusiasts. While the high percentage of Merlot suggests that Petit Bocq will not age well, the 1982, last tasted in 1989, was fresh and lively, possessing at least another decade of life. This is clearly a property worth representation in the world's export markets, although the quantities of wine available will no doubt be minuscule.

POMYS

Classification: Cru Bourgeois
Location of vineyards: St.-Estèphe
Owner: G.F.A. Arnaud
Address: Leyssac, 33180 St.-Estèphe
Telephone: 33 5 56 59 32 26; telefax: 33 5 56 59 35 24
Visits: Monday to Friday, between 9 A.M. and noon, and 2 P.M. and 5 P.M.
Contact: Mrs. Rechaudiat

VINEYARDS (red)
Surface area: 32.1 acres
Average age of vines: 25 years
Blend: 50% Cabernet Sauvignon, 35% Merlot, 15% Cabernet Franc
Density of plantation: 6,000 vines per hectare
Average yields (over the last 5 years): 50 hectoliters per hectare
Total average annual production: 3,500–4,000 bottles

GRAND VIN (red)
Brand name: Château Pomys
Appellation: St.-Estèphe
Mean annual production: 3,500–4,000 bottles
Upbringing: Fermentations are rather long (20 days) and occur in temperature-controlled stainless-steel vats. Wines then spend 15–18 months in oak casks, 30% of which are new. They are fined but not filtered.

The château uses a second brand name, Château St.-Estèphe.
Average production: 600 hectoliters

LES PRADINES

Unclassified
Production: 4,000 cases
Blend: 60% Cabernet Sauvignon, 35% Merlot, 5% Cabernet Franc
Secondary label: None
Vineyard size: 20 acres
Proprietor: Jean Gradit
Time spent in barrels: 12 months, primarily in vats
Average age of vines: 25 years

Evaluation of present classification: The quality equivalent of a Cru
Bourgeois
Plateau of maturity: 3–7 years following the vintage

Produced and bottled by St.-Estèphe's Cave Cooperative, these straightforward, tough-textured wines are typical of the appellation but too frequently lack charm and fruit. However, the wines are fairly priced.

SÉGUR DE CABANAC

Classification: Cru Bourgeois
Location of vineyards: St.-Estèphe
Owner: Guy Delon
Address: c/o S.C.E.A. Guy Delon et Fils, 33180 St.-Estèphe
Telephone: 33 5 56 59 70 10; telefax: 33 5 56 59 73 94
Visits: By appointment only
Contact: Guy Delon at above telephone and fax numbers

VINEYARDS (red)
Surface area: 15.4 acres
Average age of vines: 25 years
Blend: 60% Cabernet Sauvignon, 30% Merlot, 5% Cabernet Franc, 5%
Petit Verdot
Density of plantation: 8,500 vines per hectare
Average yields (over the last 5 years): 50 hectoliters per hectare
Total average annual production: 35,000 bottles

GRAND VIN (red)
Brand name: Château Ségur de Cabanac
Appellation: St.-Estèphe
Mean annual production: 35,000 bottles
Upbringing: Grapes are picked manually. Fermentations last about 3

weeks in temperature-controlled stainless-steel vats. Frequent *remontages*. Wines afterward spend 20 months in barrels, of which one-third are new (the barrels are renewed by a third each year). They are racked 7 times, fined with egg whites, but not filtered.

SECOND WINE
None produced.

TOUR-DE-MARBUZET

Classification: Cru Bourgeois
Location of vineyards: St.-Estèphe
Owner: Henri Duboscq and sons
Address: 33180 St.-Estèphe
Mailing address: Same as above
Telephone: 33 5 56 59 30 54; telefax: 33 5 56 50 70 87
Visits: From Monday to Friday, between 8 A.M. and noon, and 2 P.M. and 6 P.M.

VINEYARDS (red)
Surface area: 17.3 acres
Average age of vines: 25 years
Blend: 40% Cabernet Sauvignon, 40% Merlot, 20% Cabernet Franc
Density of plantation: 8,300 vines per hectare
Average yields (over the last 5 years): 45 hectoliters per hectare
Total average annual production: 45,000 bottles

GRAND VIN (red)
Brand name: Château Tour-de-Marbuzet
Appellation: St.-Estèphe
Mean annual production: 45,000 bottles
Upbringing: Grapes are hand-picked, totally destemmed, and fermented in temperature-controlled vats for 18–20 days with daily pumping-over. Wines are kept for a quarter of the production in new oak barrels and the rest in wooden vats. They are racked every 3 months, and bottling is done manually (by gravity). Wines are fined but not filtered.

SECOND WINE
None produced.

TOUR DE PEZ

Classification: Cru Bourgeois in 1932
Location of vineyards: St.-Estèphe
Owner: Château Tour de Pez S.A.
Director: Mr. H. Duhayot
Address: "L'Hereteyre," 33180 St.-Estèphe
Telephone: 33 5 56 59 31 60; telefax: 33 5 56 59 71 12
Visits: By appointment only (especially for groups) from Monday to
Friday, between 9 A.M. and noon, and 2 P.M. and 5:30 P.M.
Contact: Mr. F. Bellet or Mr. F. Duprat (see details above)

VINEYARDS (red)
Surface area: 72.8 acres
Average age of vines: 25 years
Blend: 45% Cabernet Sauvignon, 40% Merlot, 10% Cabernet Franc, 5%
Petit Verdot
Density of plantation: 8,000 vines per hectare
Average yields (over the last 5 years): 50 hectoliters per hectare
Total average annual production: 200,000 bottles

GRAND VIN (red)
Brand name: Château Tour de Pez
Appellation: St.-Estèphe
Mean annual production: 80,000 bottles
Upbringing: Grapes are hand-picked and sorted both in the vineyards
and in the winery. They are totally destemmed, and fermentations last 3–
4 weeks in thermo-regulated stainless-steel vats with temperatures going
up to 30–31 degrees centigrade. Wines then spend 15 months in oak
casks, 50% of which are new for the grand vin. They are fined but not
filtered.

SECOND WINE
Brand name: Château Les Hauts de Pez
Average annual production: 120,000 bottles

TOUR DES TERMES

Classification: None
Location of vineyards: Near the village of St.-Corbian (St.-Estèphe)
Owner: Jean Anney
Address: c/o Vignobles Jean Anney, 33180 St.-Estèphe
Telephone: 33 5 56 59 32 89; telefax: 33 5 56 59 73 74

Visits: From Monday to Friday, between 8 A.M. and noon, and 2 P.M. and 5 P.M.

Contact: Jean or Christophe Anney

VINEYARDS (red)
Surface area: 37 acres
Average age of vines: 30 years
Blend: 50% Merlot, 45% Cabernet Sauvignon, 5% Petit Verdot
Density of plantation: 6,665 vines per hectare
Average yields (over the last 5 years): 50 hectoliters per hectare
Total average annual production: 90,000 bottles

GRAND VIN (red)
Brand name: Château Tour des Termes
Appellation: St.-Estèphe
Mean annual production: 90,000 bottles
Upbringing: Grapes are picked manually. Fermentations last 25–28 days in temperature-controlled stainless-steel tanks, with regular pumping-over. At the end of the process, the temperature of certain vats is allowed to climb higher than that of the others. Wines are then transferred to oak barrels, one-third of which are new, for 12–15 months. They are fined but not filtered.

SECOND WINE
Brand name: Les Aubarèdes du Château Tour des Termes
Average annual production: 30,000 bottles

NOTE: This estate also produces 4,000 bottles of a special cuvée called Château Tour des Termes Collection Prestige. This wine is produced from a special plot of old vines (40 years), essentially from Merlot (70%) located on a gravelly subsoil. Vinification is traditional, but malolactics occur in barrels, and the wines spend 15 months in new oak.

TRONQUOY-LALANDE   GOOD

Classification: Cru Bourgeois in 1932
Location of vineyards: St.-Estèphe
Owner: Madame Arlette Castéja-Texier
Address: 33180 St.-Estèphe
Telephone: 33 5 56 59 30 24
Visits: By appointment only

Contact: Madame Castéja-Texier at the above address and telephone
number or Dourthe CVBG: 45, route de Bordeaux,
33290 Parempuyre, France
Telephone: 33 5 56 35 53 00; telefax: 33 5 56 35 53 29

VINEYARDS (red)
Surface area: 42 acres
Average age of vines: 25 years
Blend: 45% Cabernet Sauvignon, 45% Merlot, 10% Petit Verdot
Density of plantation: 8,500 vines per hectare
Average yields (over the last 5 years): 54 hectoliters per
hectare
Total average annual production: 115,000 bottles

GRAND VIN (red)
Brand name: Château Tronquoy-Lalande
Appellation: St.-Estèphe
Mean annual production: 85,000 bottles
Upbringing: Grapes are hand-picked. Fermentations are carried out (lots
separate) and last 20–30 days depending upon the quality of the tannins.
Wines are kept in 100% new oak barrels before bottling. They are fined
but not filtered.

SECOND WINE
Brand name: Château Tronquoy de Saint-Anne
Average annual production: 30,000 bottles

Evaluation of present classification: Should be maintained
Plateau of maturity: Since 1982, 5–10 years after the vintage; previously
the wine was very slow to evolve

Tronquoy-Lalande is a historic property with a fine twin-towered chateau on the premises. The wine was highly regarded a century ago but has
lost popularity because of the superlative quality of other St.-Estèphe
Crus Bourgeois, such as Meyney, Haut-Marbuzet, Les-Ormes-de-Pez, and,
more recently, Phélan-Ségur. I have followed every wine since the
late seventies, and they lack consistency from vintage to vintage. At best
it is a very dark, huge, clumsy sort of wine, with an earthy, distinctive
character. The wine is distributed exclusively by the Bordeaux firm of
Dourthe. The finest recent vintage is the black-colored, dense, super-ripe
1989.

VALROSE

Classification: None
Location of vineyards: St.-Estèphe
Owners: Mr. and Mrs. Jean-Louis Audoin (since 1986)
Address: 7, rue Michel Audoy, 33180 St.-Estèphe
Telephone: 33 5 56 59 72 02; telefax: 33 5 56 59 39 31
Visits: In summer, every day from 9 A.M. to noon, and 2 P.M. to 7 P.M.;
otherwise by appointment
Contact: Mr. or Mrs. Jean-Louis Audoin (see details above)

VINEYARDS (red)
Surface area: 12.4 acres
Average age of vines: 25 years
Blend: 43% Cabernet Sauvignon, 33% Merlot, 23% Cabernet Franc, 1%
Petit Verdot
Density of plantation: 7,500 vines per hectare
Average yields (over the last 5 years): 56 hectoliters per hectare
Total average annual production: 36,000 bottles

GRAND VIN (red)
Brand name: Château Valrose
Appellation: St.-Estèphe
Mean annual production: 24,000 bottles
Upbringing: Grapes are hand-picked. Fermentations last 10–20 days in
stainless-steel vats, depending upon the vintage, with pumping-over twice
a day. Wines are then transferred for 18 months into oak barrels, 40% of
which are new. They are both fined and filtered.

SECOND WINE
Brand Name: Château La Rosé Blanquet
Average annual production: 12,000 bottles

NOTE: The first estate in St.-Estèphe to start harvesting following the
méthode champenoise—that is, sorting the grapes in the vineyards first,
then at the winery.

VIEUX COUTELIN

Classification: None
Location of vineyards: St.-Estèphe
Owner: Vignobles Rocher Cap de Rive S.A.
Address: B.P. 89, 33350 Saint Magne de Castillon
Mailing address: Same

Telephone: 05 57 40 08 88; telefax: 05 57 40 19 93
Visits: By appointment only
Contact: Madame Isabel Teles Pinto at above telephone and fax numbers

VINEYARDS (red)
Surface area: 14.8 acres
Average age of vines: 20 years
Blend: 70% Cabernet, 25% Merlot, 5% Petit Verdot
Density of plantation: 7,500 hectoliters per hectare
Average yields (over the last 5 years): 59 hectoliters per hectare
Total average annual production: 1,800–2,000 cases

GRAND VIN (red)
Brand name: Château Vieux Coutelin
Appellation: St.-Estèphe
Mean annual production: 1,200 cases
Upbringing: Wines stay 18 months in oak casks (20% new) and
stainless-steel tanks. They are fined and filtered prior to bottling.

SECOND WINE
Brand name: Chevalier Coutelin
Average annual production: 600–800 cases

PAUILLAC

There is no more famous appellation of the Haut-Médoc and Bordeaux than Pauillac. While the commune of Margaux has a more lyrical and romantic name, as well as a famous first-growth château of the same title, it is Pauillac's vineyards that lay claim to three of the Médoc's four first-growths. Yes, the fabled, fabulously expensive Pauillac trio of Lafite-Rothschild, Mouton-Rothschild, and Latour all reside here, and they are formidably backed up by a bevy of wines, some brilliant, some overrated, and a few mysteriously overlooked or forgotten. Eighteen wines from Pauillac were included in the original 1855 classification, and today only two or three estates would have trouble holding on to their position should an independent study of the quality of the wines be done.

The textbook Pauillac would tend to have a rich, full-bodied texture, a distinctive bouquet of black currants and cedary scents, and excellent aging potential. Since much of the permitted vineyard acreage (2,965 acres) is controlled by the eighteen classified growths, there are fewer Cru Bourgeois wines in Pauillac than in a commune such as St.-Estèphe. However, one is likely to encounter a wide diversity in the Pauillac styles. Among the three famous first-growths, for example, the wines could not be more different. Granted, their soils all share the gravelly composition that reflects the sun's heat and affords excellent drainage. However, Lafite-Rothschild's vineyard—tucked in a northern part of Pauillac right on the St.-Estèphe border—has a limestone base, resulting in wines that are Pauillac's most aromatically complex and subtly flavored. Lafite's bouquet has of course the telltale Pauillac "cedarwood" aroma, although Lafite rarely matches Mouton-Rothschild for sheer opulence and power, or Latour for consistency. Of the other, non-first-growth Pauillacs, the lighter, aromatic Lafite style, albeit on a lower level, is best exemplified by the silky, medium-bodied Haut-Batailley.

Mouton-Rothschild sits on a gravel ridge above the Médoc's largest town, Pauillac. In addition to the gravelly soil, Mouton has more sandstone in the soil base and uses an abnormally high percentage of Cabernet Sauvignon in making the wine. When everything works out right, these factors can produce the most decadently rich, fleshy, and exotic wine of not only Pauillac, but of the entire Médoc. In many ways, the wine of Mouton was personified by the flamboyant, bold owner, the Baron Philippe de Rothschild, who died in 1988.

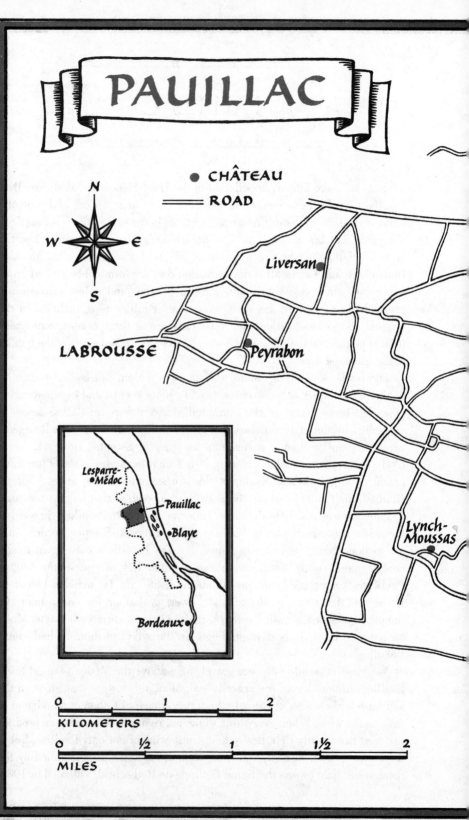

PAUILLAC

● CHÂTEAU
═══ ROAD

N
W E
S

Liversan●

LABROUSSE

●Peyrabon

Lesparre-
●Médoc

Pauillac

●Blaye

Bordeaux●

Lynch-
Moussas●

0   1   2
KILOMETERS

0   ½   1   1½   2
MILES

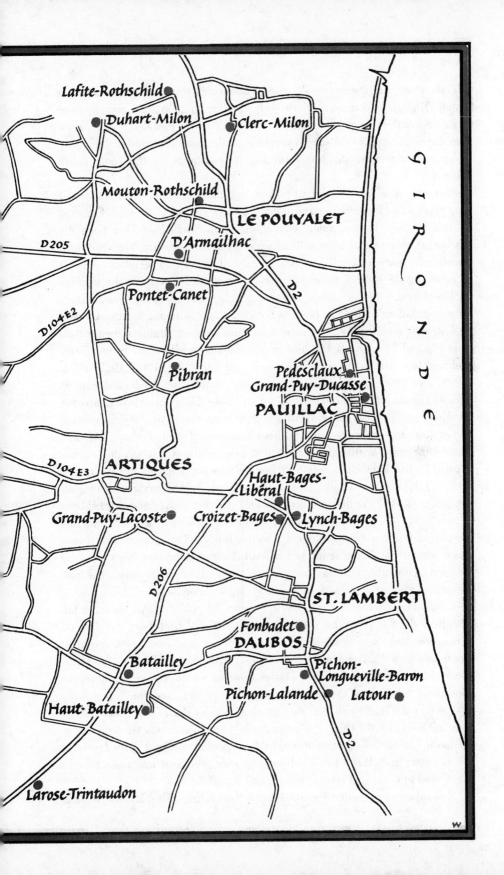

His daughter, Philippine, no shy flower, admirably continues to manage this estate. Mouton, of course, is not the only Pauillac made in a big, rich, opulent style. Several kilometers south, on another slightly elevated ridge called the Bages plateau, Lynch-Bages makes a rustic wine that can be splendidly deep and concentrated, clearly earning its reputation as the "poor man's Mouton."

Latour is Pauillac's other first-growth, and this grand old estate has few if any peers when it comes to consistency from one vintage to the next. For most of this century, Latour, along with Montrose in St.-Estèphe, has been the slowest to mature and longest-lived wine made in Bordeaux. The vineyard's location in southern Pauillac—next to St.-Julien—would seemingly suggest a more supple style of wine, but except for a brief hiccup in the eighties (1983–1989), when a softer, less formidable style of Latour surprisingly emerged, Latour's wine has been as backward and as tannic as any. The soil at Latour is almost pure fine gravel that affords superb drainage, better than that enjoyed by Lafite-Rothschild or Mouton-Rothschild. That in itself may help explain why in rainy vintages such as 1960, 1968, 1969, 1972, 1974, 1992, and 1993 Latour easily outdistanced many other Médocs. Latour is simply Latour, and in Pauillac there are no "look-alikes" in style or character.

There are several other Pauillacs that have distinctive styles, making generalizations about the wine of this commune difficult. Perhaps the most interesting wine of this group is Pichon-Longueville–Comtesse de Lalande (called Pichon Lalande by most). Pichon Lalande sits adjacent to Latour, near the St.-Julien border. Unlike Latour, Pichon does indeed produce a Pomerol/St.-Julien–styled Pauillac—silky, graceful, supple, suave, and drinkable at a relatively young age. However, it would be foolish to assume that this precocious-tasting wine does not age well—it does. The property has always made great wine, but over the last several decades theirs has been every bit as good as the other Pauillac first-growths and certainly more consistent from vintage to vintage than Lafite-Rothschild and Mouton-Rothschild.

Grand-Puy-Lacoste never seems to receive the publicity that the other top Pauillacs do. For years this property, which sits well back from the Gironde River, was the joy of Bordeaux's leading gourmet (and from some accounts, gourmand as well), Raymond Dupin. Monsieur Dupin has died, but his reputation for holding lavish dinner parties remains unchallenged by anyone in Bordeaux today. Now the property, the wine cellars, and the winemaking philosophy are in the capable, sure hands of Xavier Borie. Their first vintage was a lovely 1978. This is a property to follow, with a style somewhere between Latour and Mouton-Rothschild—powerful and rich with layers of sweet cassis fruit. It is a true Pauillac—cleaner, more consistent now than in the Dupin era, but still robust, tannic, and flavorful.

Several other classified Pauillacs merit their rating today, largely because of the exciting progress they have made since the late eighties. The most impressive rag-to-riches story is that of Pichon-Longueville Baron, the turreted château that sits across from Pichon-Longueville–Comtesse de Lalande as well as Château Latour. Pichon-Longueville Baron was Pauillac's most prominent underachiever between 1960 and 1985, but since 1986 quality has soared. The property's new owners, the huge insurance conglomerate AXA, put Jean-Michel Cazes and his brilliant team in charge of this estate, in addition to pumping millions of francs into restoring the property and building a new state-of-the-art cellar. Pichon-Longueville Baron has produced some exceptional wines under the new administration, including a fabulous 1989 and 1990.

Another château whose wines have jumped in quality, particularly since the mid-nineties, is Pontet-Canet. This property, owned by the Tesseron family, possesses a huge, relatively homogeneous vineyard situated opposite Mouton-Rothschild. Anyone who has tasted the extraordinary Pontet-Canets produced in 1929, 1945, and 1961 realizes that when well made, Pontet-Canet is far better than its fifth-growth status. The Tesserons, who made their fame and fortune in the Cognac region, have worked hard to push Pontet-Canet into the elite Pauillac châteaux. The quality in the eighties was very good, but it was apparently not sufficient for the Tesserons. In 1994 a decision was made to brutally eliminate any wine not considered perfect, and the result was one of the finest Pontet-Canets produced in over three decades. The 1994 was followed by another terrific wine in 1995 and a powerful 1996. I believe it is safe to say that this château is producing one of the classic wines of Pauillac. The antithesis of the softer, silkier style of wine, it is a true *vin de garde*. Moreover, it remains reasonably priced.

A wine I find to be the most difficult Pauillac to understand is Batailley. The estate has been well run by the Castéja family, but it produces stern, austere, broodingly tannic wines that take a decade or more to shed their tannic cloaks and exhibit charm. I consistently underrate this muscular, backward Pauillac, but I have noted that the wine appears to possess sweeter, riper fruit in recent vintages. It is another classic, old-style Pauillac that is underpriced for its ultimate potential, but patience is most certainly required.

Batailley's sister château, at least in name, Haut-Batailley, is owned by the Borie family, who also owns the famed Ducru-Beaucaillou in St.-Julien and Grand-Puy-Lacoste in Pauillac. The latter two properties tend to overshadow Haut-Batailley. The antithesis of Batailley, Haut-Batailley is a silky, soft, richly fruity, seductive style of wine that may never hit the highest level of quality but is both consistent and delicious.

Readers looking for a wine made in the style of Haut-Batailley, but more lavishly oaked, exotic, and plump, are advised to check out the two efforts of the Baroness Philippine de Rothschild—Clerc-Milon and d'Armailhac. Both are forward, richly fruity wines that critics claim are aggressively, if not excessively, oaked, but they have many admirers. The wines are, unquestionably, interesting, flavorful, and seductive.

An estate on which to keep an eye, given its extraordinary financial underpinning and its well-placed vineyards, is Duhart-Milon. Made by the winemaking staff at Lafite-Rothschild, Duhart-Milon appears poised to consistently offer a classic Pauillac made in an elegant yet ageworthy style. The Rothschilds have invested significantly in Duhart-Milon, and the wine has improved immensely.

A relatively unknown Pauillac château is Haut-Bages-Libéral. One of my more reliable buying choices in the eighties, I referred to it as "the poor person's Lynch-Bages," as it was always a fairly priced wine that offered plenty of cedar, black currant, and other jammy fruit in a chunky, fat style. However, the wine has become distressingly irregular in the nineties, and it is difficult to forecast in which direction it will move.

More than any other Médoc appellation, Pauillac, because of the dominance of the three first-growths and some prominent super seconds, tends to establish the overall reputation for a particular vintage in the Médoc. Some would even argue that how goes Pauillac, so goes the public's view of the most recent Bordeaux vintage. Although nothing so general can be viewed in black-and-white terms, there is no doubt that the quality of winemaking in Pauillac has improved significantly since the first edition of this book in 1985.

Pauillac, with its well-drained soils, still seems to excel in the relatively hot, dry years. The decade of the eighties was a golden age for all of Bordeaux, but no appellation profited more than Pauillac. After a good vintage in 1981, 1982 was spectacular—the greatest overall vintage for the appellation since 1961; 1983 was a good if uneven year, largely because of high yields; and 1984, as for most of Bordeaux, proved mediocre. The 1985 was over-rated, and 1986 was an excellent if true *vin de garde* vintage, in which many profoundly rich, tannic wines were being produced. The vintage of 1988 was very good, while 1989 was uneven and extremely overrated. The nineties have been less kind to Pauillac, as they have been to all Bordeaux, but 1990 was an extraordinary year for the first-growths, particularly Latour and Lafite-Rothschild. However, 1990 was surprisingly disappointing for Mouton-Rothschild. Among the other top estates, Pichon-Longueville–Comtesse de Lalande produced a disappointing 1990, but Pichon-Longueville Baron, Lynch-Bages, and Grand-Puy-Lacoste all produced fabulous 1990s. In Pauillac more than in any other region except for Margaux, it is essential to have a healthy crop of Cabernet Sauvignon for a top vintage. Most estates have at least two-thirds of their vineyards planted with Cabernet, so if that grape fails to ripen, the entire appellation will have problems. In the nineties, both 1995 and 1996 have turned out to be consistently excellent years. If the 1995s are more supple and charming, the 1996s are prodigious wines, undeniably powerful, immense in structure, and destined to have very long lives. In short, the 1996 Pauillacs are exceptional, on a par with 1990 and 1982!

PAUILLAC
(An Insider's View)

Overall Appellation Potential: Excellent to Superb

The Most Potential for Aging: Batailley, Grand-Puy-Lacoste, Lafite-Rothschild, Latour, Lynch-Bages, Mouton-Rothschild, Pichon-Longueville Baron, Pontet-Canet

The Most Elegant: Duhart-Milon, Grand-Puy-Ducasse, Haut-Batailley, Lafite-Rothschild, Pichon-Longueville–Comtesse de Lalande

The Most Concentrated: Grand-Puy-Lacoste, Latour, Lynch-Bages, Pichon-Longueville Baron, Pichon-Longueville–Comtesse de Lalande, Pontet-Canet (since 1994)

The Best Value: Grand-Puy-Ducasse, Grand-Puy-Lacoste, Pontet-Canet

The Most Exotic: Clerc-Milon, Mouton-Rothschild, Pichon-Longueville–Comtesse de Lalande

The Most Difficult to Understand (when young): Batailley, Lafite-Rothschild

The Most Underrated: Grand-Puy-Lacoste, Pontet-Canet (since 1994)

The Easiest to Appreciate Young: D'Armailhac, Clerc-Milon, Grand-Puy-Ducasse, Haut-Batailley, Pichon-Longueville–Comtesse de Lalande

Up-and-Coming Estates: Pontet-Canet

Greatest Recent Vintages: 1996, 1995, 1994, 1990, 1986, 1982, 1970, 1967, 1961, 1959

PAUILLAC—AN OVERVIEW

Location: On the left bank of the Gironde River, Pauillac is sandwiched between St.-Estèphe to the north and St.-Julien to the south; it is approximately 23 miles from the center of Bordeaux

Acres under Vine: 2,965

Communes: Pauillac

Average Annual Production: 640,000 cases

Classified Growths: Total of 18: 3 first-growths, 2 second-growths, 1 fourth-growth, and 12 fifth-growths; there are 16 Crus Bourgeois

Principal Grape Varieties: Cabernet Sauvignon, followed by Merlot and, to a lesser extent, Cabernet Franc and Petit Verdot

Principal Soil Type: Very deep gravel beds dominate the vineyards adjacent to the river. Farther inland, gravel mixes with sandstone and some limestone.

A CONSUMER'S CLASSIFICATION
OF THE CHÂTEAUX OF PAUILLAC

OUTSTANDING

Lafite-Rothschild
Latour
Mouton-Rothschild
Pichon-Longueville–Comtesse de Lalande

EXCELLENT

Grand-Puy-Lacoste
Lynch-Bages
Pichon-Longueville Baron
Pontet-Canet (since 1994)

VERY GOOD

Duhart-Milon
Les Forts de Latour
Haut-Batailley

GOOD

Armailhac (known as
Mouton-Baronne-Philippe between 1956 and 1989)
Batailley
Clerc-Milon
Grand-Puy-Ducasse

OTHER NOTABLE PAUILLAC PROPERTIES

La Bécasse, Bellegrave, Bernadotte, Carruades de Lafite,
Colombier-Monpelou, La Couronne, Croizet-Bages, La Fleur Milon,
Fonbadet, Gaudin, Haut-Bages-Libéral, Haut-Bages-Monpelou,
Lynch-Moussas, Pedesclaux, Pibran, Plantey, La Rose Pauillac,
Saint-Mambert

ARMAILHAC (Mouton-Baronne-Philippe)   **GOOD**

Classification: Fifth-growth in 1855
Location of vineyards: Le Pouyalet, Pauillac
Owner: Baronne Philippine de Rothschild G.F.A.
Address: 33250 Pauillac
Mailing address: Baron Philippe de Rothschild S.A., B.P. 117, 33250
Pauillac

Telephone: 33 5 56 73 20 20; telefax: 33 5 56 73 20 44
Visits: no visits

VINEYARDS (red)
Surface area: 123.5 acres
Average age of vines: 35 years
Blend: 50% Cabernet Sauvignon, 25% Merlot, 23% Cabernet Franc, 2%
Petit Verdot
Density of plantation: 8,500 vines per hectare
Average yields (over the last 5 years): 45–50 hectoliters per hectare
Total average annual production: 22,000 cases

GRAND VIN (red)
Brand name: Château D'Armailhac
Appellation: Pauillac
Mean annual production: 22,000 cases
Upbringing: Fermentations are rather long (3 weeks), and temperatures
are kept at around 25 degrees centigrade to ensure good extraction of
tannins. Wines are transferred to oak casks in December and aged in oak
casks (30% of which are new and 70% of which are 1 year old) for 15–18
months. Wines are fined, but there is no specific position on the issue of
filtration.

SECOND WINE
None Produced.

Evaluation of present classification: Should be maintained
Plateau of maturity: 5–14 years following the vintage

This remains the least well-known and, to the consuming public, the most obscure property of the late Baron Philippe de Rothschild's trio of Pauillac estates. The baron acquired Mouton-Baronne-Philippe in 1933 when it was known as Mouton d'Armailhac. In 1956 the name was changed to Mouton-Baron-Philippe and in 1975 to Mouton-Baronne-Philippe in tribute to the baron's wife, who died the following year.* The cellars are adjacent to Mouton-Rothschild, and the winemaking team of Patrick Léon and Lucien Sionneau that overlooks the renowned Mouton-Rothschild and Clerc-Milon also attends to the winemaking at d'Armailhac.

Despite the impressive age of the vineyard, the wine has tended to be relatively light, quick to mature, and easily outdistanced in complexity, character, and longevity by the two siblings. However, there has been a noticeable

---

* The name, beginning with the 1989 vintage, is once again d'Armailhac.

trend to upgrade the quality of the wines. While the quality of the 1982 is no doubt due to the vintage itself, the higher quality of d'Armailhac began in earnest with the fine 1985 and has been continued since. The 1989 may be the best wine produced at this property in modern times.

VINTAGES

1997 — The 1997 d'Armailhac (a blend of 58% Cabernet Sauvignon, 23% Merlot,
• and 19% Cabernet Franc) displays a deep ruby color, followed by an evolved,
86– plummy, currant, cedar, and spice nose, copious quantities of sweet black
87 fruit on the attack, and a soft, medium-bodied easygoing finish with little grip
or delineation. This will be a fruity, forward, low-acid wine to drink during its
first 7–10 years of life. Last tasted, 3/98.

1996 — This wine showed exceptionally well. The dense ruby/purple–colored 1996
• reveals evolved aromas of licorice, Asian spices, cassis, and subtle toasty
87– oak. A blend of 45% Cabernet Sauvignon, 25% Cabernet Franc, and 30%
88 Merlot, this medium-weight wine possesses a surprising lusciousness, atypical for this vintage. It provides a sweet midpalate, and a velvety-textured,
long, lush finish. It is a hedonistic, user-friendly Pauillac that should age
nicely. Anticipated maturity: 2001–2015. Last tasted, 3/98.

1995 — To reiterate, this may be the best d'Armailhac ever produced. The 1995 blend
• was 50% Cabernet Sauvignon, 18% Cabernet Franc, and 32% Merlot. This
89 deep ruby/purple–colored wine possesses low acidity and plenty of sweet
tannin, and in both its aromatics and flavors, gobs of ripe cassis fruit are
nicely framed by the judicious use of toasty oak. Flavorful, round, generous,
and hedonistic, this is a crowd-pleaser! Anticipated maturity: Now–2012.
Last tasted, 11/97.

1994 — Made in an attractive, more muscular style, the 1994 displays a dark ruby/
• purple color, spicy, meaty, curranty aromas with a touch of cedar and earth,
86 moderate tannin, and good flesh and structure. It may develop into an upper-
80-point wine if the tannin melts away without a loss of fruit. Anticipated
maturity: 2002–2010. Last tasted, 1/97.

1993 — This soft, peppery, herb-tinged, dark ruby–colored wine possesses excellent
• fruit, a supple texture, and round, agreeable, easy to understand and consume
86 flavors. It should be drunk over the next 6–8 years. It is a good, reasonably
priced Pauillac for restaurants and consumers looking for immediate gratification. Last tasted, 1/97.

1992 — D'Armailhac's 1992 is a charming, straightforward, richly fruity wine with
• moderate to dark ruby color and a spicy nose of roasted nuts and jammy black
86 currants. The attack offers lush, velvety-textured fruit that fades quickly.
Nevertheless, this is a pure, attractive, elegant wine for drinking over the next
5–6 years. Last tasted, 11/94.

1991 — The 1991 exhibits superficial appeal in its lavishly oaky, sweet nose, but
• once past the makeup, the wine is thin and angular, with little depth and a
74 short, tannic, tough finish. It will get more attenuated with age. Last tasted,
1/94.

1990—The 1990 d'Armailhac is dark ruby/purple, with an expressive nose of smoked
•   nuts, cassis, smoke, and chocolate. This velvety textured, round, agreeable
85   wine lacks structure and length on the palate. It is charming but less concen-
     trated than the 1989. Anticipated maturity: Now–2003. Last tasted, 1/93.

1989—The château feels the 1989 vintage of d'Armailhac is its best wine in over 3
•   decades. It exhibits a very forward, creamy richness, gobs of velvety fruit, a
87   heady alcohol content, and a fat, lush finish. Anticipated maturity: Now–
     2000. Last tasted, 1/93.

1988—When compared with the 1989, the 1988 Mouton-Baronne-Philippe is much
•   lighter, more compact, and noticeably hard and lean, and it has a short finish.
84   Anticipated maturity: Now. Last tasted, 1/93.

1987—Light to medium ruby, with a soft, round, weedy fruitiness, this is a round,
•   somewhat diluted, picnic wine. Anticipated maturity: Now. Last tasted,
77   10/89.

1986—I found the 1986 Mouton-Baronne-Philippe to be an attractively soft, rich,
•   medium-bodied wine, with a pleasing and charming suppleness, a nice dosage
86   of sweet oak, and a precocious personality, especially for a wine from this
     vintage. Anticipated maturity: Now–2002. Last tasted, 9/90.

1985—Thanks to the efforts of administrator Philippe Cottin and winemaker Patrick
•   Léon, the quality level of Mouton-Baronne-Philippe began to rise with this vin-
86   tage. The 1985 is a creamy-textured, fat, lush, lovely wine with a seductive, rich
     fruitiness, precocious personality, and low acidity. It is gorgeous for drinking
     over the next decade. Anticipated maturity: Now–2000. Last tasted, 1/89.

1983—Amply proportioned, the 1983 Mouton-Baronne-Philippe is less concentrated
•   and richly fruity than the 1982 but still impressively full, well structured,
83   and concentrated. Anticipated maturity: Now–2000. Last tasted, 3/89.

1982—While not to be confused with Mouton-Rothschild's legendary 1982, this wine
•   is commendable. Dark ruby, with a cedary, ripe black currant bouquet of
86   moderate intensity, this wine is full bodied, with very good concentration,
     plenty of dusty yet ripe tannins, and very fine length on the palate. Antici-
     pated maturity: Now–2005. Last tasted, 1/89.

1981—Dark ruby, with a rather closed, tight bouquet of currants and plums, this
•   moderately tannic wine shows good, ripe fruit, medium body, and fine length.
83   Lighter than Mouton-Rothschild, but the stylistic similarities are present.
     Anticipated maturity: Now. Last tasted, 12/84.

BATAILLEY   GOOD

Classification: Fifth-growth in 1855
Location of vineyards: Pauillac
Owner: Héritiers Castéja
Address: 33250 Pauillac
Mailing address: Domaines Borie-Manoux, 86, Cours
Balguerie-Stuttenberg, 33082 Bordeaux Cedex

Telephone: 33 5 56 00 00 70; telefax: 33 5 57 87 60 30
Visits: By appointment only, except weekends
Contact: Domaines Borie-Manoux

VINEYARDS (red)
Surface area: 135.9 acres
Average age of vines: 30 years
Blend: 70% Cabernet Sauvignon, 25% Merlot, 3% Cabernet Franc, 2% Petit Verdot
Density of plantation: 8,000 vines per hectare
Average yields (over the last 5 years): 55 hectoliters per hectare
Total average annual production: 22,000 cases

GRAND VIN (red)
Brand name: Château Batailley
Appellation: Pauillac
Mean annual production: 22,000 cases
Upbringing: Grapes are picked manually and totally destemmed. Fermentations last 3–4 weeks in temperature-controlled stainless-steel tanks. Malolactics occur in oak casks for 25% of the yield. The rest is transferred into oak casks after completion of malolactics in vats. Fifty percent new oak is used. Wines are fined with egg whites but not filtered, and bottled after 12–16 months in barrels.

SECOND WINE
None produced.

Evaluation of present classification: Should be maintained
Plateau of maturity: 10–25 years following the vintage

Batailley, an attractive château sitting in a small clearing surrounded by large trees, is located well inland from the Gironde River. The vineyards, which were all part of the 1855 classification, are situated between those of Haut-Batailley to the south and Grand-Puy-Lacoste to the north. England's David Peppercorn has frequently made the point (and I would agree completely) that because the *négociant* firm of Borie-Manoux controls the distribution of Batailley, and because the wines are not freely traded or available for tasting in the normal commercial circles of Bordeaux, there has been a tendency to ignore this estate. This has resulted in a wine that is undervalued.

The property has been run since 1961 by Emile Castéja, who continues to turn out relatively old-style, solid, well-colored, somewhat rustic Pauillac that can be difficult to assess at a young age. I have frequently commented that while the wine can handle significant cellaring, it rarely excites or inspires but is essentially reliable and fairly priced. Although I stand by those comments, I have begun to believe that I have under-rated several of the vintages. Wine enthusiasts who have patience no doubt admire Batailley's reputation for longevity, as well as its reasonable prices. Given the increased efforts to improve the quality that began in the late eighties, it is unlikely that Batailley can remain the lowest-priced classified-growth Pauillac.

VINTAGES

1997—This wine lacks depth, and the maturity of its tannin (note the scratchy edge
•   to it) is questionable. Nevertheless, it possesses a dark ruby color, as well as
80–   a sweet red and black currant, mineral, and earth nose. On the attack, the
84   wine is light to medium bodied, with the vintage's soft berry fruit and a clean, uninspiring finish. It should be drunk during its first 7–10 years of life. Last tasted, 3/98.

1996—A fine effort from Batailley, this dense ruby/purple–colored wine exhibits a
•   classic black currant and cedar nose with a touch of anise and smoky oak.
87–   Powerful and medium to full bodied, with copious quantities of sweet tannin,
89   a nicely textured mouth-feel, and no sharp edges, this is a high-class, impressively endowed Batailley. Anticipated maturity: 2003–2020. Last tasted, 3/98.

1995—The 1995 has turned out well, displaying a dark ruby/purple color and aromas
•   of minerals, black currants, and smoky new oak. In the mouth, it is a medium-
87   weight, backward, well-delineated Pauillac with plenty of tannin, and a true
        vin de garde style. Anticipated maturity: 2002–2015. Last tasted, 1/97.

1994—An attractive black/ruby/purple color is followed by aromas of sweet curranty
•   fruit and new oak. Medium bodied, with good ripeness, this sound, straightfor-
85   ward, well-made wine lacks depth and complexity, but it will provide pleasant, foursquare drinking for another 12–14 years. Last tasted, 1/97.

1993—This dark purple-colored Batailley is marred by a penetrating vegetable-like
•   nose. Furthermore, the wine is lean, hard, and tannic, lacking charm and
76   fruit. It will keep for two decades, but who cares? Last tasted, 1/97.

1992—This estate has a tendency to turn out tough-textured, hard, ageworthy wines.
•   While that may be a fine goal in many vintages, it was not a desirable agenda
77   for producing an attractive 1992. This medium-bodied wine is loaded down with an excessive amount of tannin for its fragile fruit constitution. The result is a tough, hard, sharply tannic wine that will dry out long before its tannin melts away. Last tasted, 11/94.

1990—The 1990 offers medium dark ruby color as well as an open-knit, fragrant,
•   spicy, sweet nose. In the mouth, the wine is decidedly less structured and
86   tannic when compared with the 1989, but more soft, elegant, and, at least for now, flattering. A clone of Batailley's 1962? Anticipated maturity: Now–2010. Last tasted, 1/93.

1989—The 1989 has gone into a hard, tannic, tough stage that suggests considerable
•   patience will be necessary. The ruby/purple color is sound, and the bouquet
87   of toasty, smoky oak, chocolate, and superripe cassis is followed by a medium-

bodied, rich, extracted wine with ferocious tannins and good acidity. This is a large-scale, more traditionally styled wine that will need at least a decade of bottle age. Anticipated maturity: 2000–2018. Last tasted, 1/93.

1988—Typically stern, tough, closed, and difficult to penetrate, the 1988 displays a
•   dark ruby color, a reticent bouquet of minerals, black currants, and oak,
85   medium body, and an elevated tannin level. Anticipated maturity: Now–2008.
       Last tasted, 4/90.

1986—The 1986's rating may turn out to be conservative, as this wine tends to show
•   better after 10–12 years in the bottle than it does when young. Made from
86   70% Cabernet Sauvignon, 20% Merlot, and the balance Petit Verdot and
       Cabernet Franc, the 1986 is full bodied, deep ruby/purple in color, but
       extremely hard and tannic. However, it appears to have the depth and concen-
       tration of fruit necessary to outlast the tannins. Anticipated maturity: 2000–
       2015. Last tasted, 4/90.

1985—Not surprisingly, the 1985 Batailley has the ripeness of the vintage well
•   displayed but also carries the Batailley firmness and tannic toughness as
86   personality traits. It is well made, reserved, and stylish. Anticipated maturity:
       Now–2005. Last tasted, 4/90.

1984—The 1984 Batailley is light, with moderately intense berry fruit, an underlying
•   vegetal character, low acidity, but a soft palate impression. Anticipated matu-
82   rity: Now. Last tasted, 3/88.

1982—Soft, relatively fat, fruity flavors lack the great concentration of the very best
•   1982s but nevertheless offer juicy black currants nicely mixed with a pleasing
87   vanillin oakiness. Moderate tannins have become much more noticeable in
       the late eighties, suggesting greater aging potential than I initially believed.
       Anticipated maturity: Now–2010. Last tasted, 1/90.

1980—Light, thin, and lacking fruit, this shallow, short-tasting wine is clearly not
•   one of the better efforts from this mediocre vintage. Anticipated maturity:
67   Now–may be in decline. Last tasted, 3/83.

1979—Good, dark ruby color, with a ripe but emerging bouquet of cassis fruit, oak, and
•   earthy scents. The aggressively hard tannins in the 1979 have begun to melt
83   away, revealing a spicy, compact, austere wine that will age well but never elicit
       much excitement. Anticipated maturity: Now–2000. Last tasted, 3/89.

1978—A solid, durable wine, the 1978 Batailley is quite attractive, with an exotic,
•   moderately intense bouquet of cassis, anise, and spicy components. Full
84   bodied, with surprisingly soft, supple fruit, round, ripe tannins, and good
       length, this is a very good effort from Batailley. Anticipated maturity: Now–
       2000. Last tasted, 2/84.

1976—A straightforward sort of wine, which is fully mature, this medium ruby–
•   colored wine has a spicy, plump, fruity bouquet, medium body, attractive,
81   gentle, almost polite flavors, and a rather short, yet soft finish. Anticipated
       maturity: Now. Last tasted, 4/84.

1975—An attractive, cedary, spicy, currany nose is followed by a tough-textured,
•   extremely tannic, hard, severe-tasting wine. Although this medium garnet–
82   colored wine will keep for another 10–15 years, I suspect the 1975 Batailley

will always be too tannic, and its moderate quantities of fruit will dry out even further, making the wine's balance more questionable. Last tasted, 12/95.

1971— An aroma highly suggestive of freshly brewed tea and ripe tangerines suggests
• overripeness. On the palate, the wine is diffuse, lacking direction, and some-
73 what watery and uninteresting. This is a curious and unappealing rendition of Batailley. Anticipated maturity: Now—probably in serious decline. Last tasted, 2/79.

1970— In many respects, this wine typifies Batailley and the style of wine so often
• produced there—dark ruby, with a bouquet that offers ripe fruit, some mild
82 oaky notes, but not much complexity. On the palate, the wine is chunky and fleshy, with good concentration, firm tannins, and a monolithic personality. Anticipated maturity: Now. Last tasted, 6/87.

1966— The 1966 Batailley is now entering its mature period. The bouquet offers
• modest, ripe black currant aromas. The flavors are plump and solid, but the
82 wine, which is satisfying, still leaves the taster desiring more substance, fruit, and charm. Anticipated maturity: Now. Last tasted, 3/84.

1964— Batailley turned out one of the northern Médoc's most successful wines in
• 1964. Rich, full bodied, and now fully mature, with an enthralling cedary,
87 spicy, plumlike bouquet, this large-scaled Batailley is displaying some amber at the edge but exhibits wonderful fruit and length. Anticipated maturity: Now—2000. Last tasted, 5/90.

1962— Batailley's 1962 has been disappointing when tasted stateside, yet several
• bottles opened at the château in 1988 were gloriously perfumed, supple,
87 fleshy, and totally mature. None contained the austere, sometimes rude tannins Batailley can possess. Anticipated maturity: Now. Last tasted, 3/88.

1961— In this great vintage, I have found Batailley to be a nice, compact, fruity wine,
• with good color, a robust, dusty texture on the palate, but not the best example
84 of what the 1961 vintage was all about. Anticipated maturity: Now—may be in decline. Last tasted, 3/79.

CLERC-MILON   GOOD

Classification: Fifth-growth in 1855
Location of vineyards: Pauillac
Owner: Baronne Philippine de Rothschild G.F.A.
Address: 33250 Pauillac
Mailing address: Baron Philippe de Rothschild S.A., B.P.117, 33250 Pauillac
Telephone: 33 5 56 73 20 20; telefax: 33 5 56 73 20 44
Visits: No visits

VINEYARDS (red)
Surface area: 74 acres
Average age of vines: 32 years

Blend: 70% Cabernet Sauvignon, 20% Merlot, 10% Cabernet Franc
Density of plantation: 8,500 vines per hectare
Average yields (over the last 5 years): 45–50 hectoliters per hectare
Total average annual production: 16,000 cases

GRAND VIN (red)
Brand name: Château Clerc-Milon
Appellation: Pauillac
Mean annual production: 16,000 cases
Upbringing: Fermentations are rather long (3 weeks), and temperatures
are kept at around 25 degrees centigrade to ensure good extraction of
tannins. Wines are transferred to oak casks in December and aged in oak
casks (30% of which are new and 70% of which are 1 year old) for 16–18
months. Wines are fined, but there is no information available as to
whether the wines are filtered.

Evaluation of present classification: Should be upgraded to a
fourth-growth as the quality has improved since 1985
Plateau of maturity: 5–14 years following the vintage

Another of the Baroness Philippine Rothschild estates, Clerc-Milon was acquired in 1970. While there is no château, the vineyard is brilliantly placed
next to both Mouton-Rothschild and Lafite-Rothschild, immediately adjacent
to the huge oil refinery that dominates the tranquil town of Pauillac. Until
1985, the wine produced was frequently light and undistinguished. Recent
vintages have displayed a lush fruity quality, lavish quantities of toasty new
oak, and greater depth and flavor dimension. In comparison with the baroness's other estate-bottled wines, Clerc-Milon is the most forward and easiest
to appreciate when young. Given the quality of recent vintages, the wine is
currently undervalued.

VINTAGES

1997—Clerc-Milon appears to be on a hot streak lately, turning out excellent, some-
•　　times outstanding, wines (the 1996 and 1995 were brilliant efforts) that
87–　　remain reasonably priced among Bordeaux's classified growths. The 1997
89　　(53% Cabernet Sauvignon, 33% Merlot, 9% Cabernet Franc, and 5% Petit
　　Verdot) is the product of a ruthless selection (30% of Clerc-Milon's crop was
　　declassified). The wine possesses some tannin, but its most obvious traits are
　　its dark ruby/purple color and sweet, smoky, black currant-and-cherry-
　　scented nose that jumps from the glass. Fleshy and silky textured, with more
　　noticeable tannin than its sibling, d'Armailhac, this nicely layered, pure,
　　rich, medium-bodied Pauillac will drink well young yet last for 10–12 years.
　　Last tasted, 3/98.

1996
•
89–
90
—A 51% Cabernet Sauvignon, 37% Merlot, and 12% Cabernet Franc blend, this is a fleshy, atypically succulent, voluptuously textured Pauillac that will offer delicious drinking at a young age. The wine possesses plenty of volume and punch on the palate, with gobs of fruit and a subtle dosage of new oak (about 35% new oak barrels are utilized at this estate). Low acidity and rich fruit conceal much of the wine's tannin, which is present but unobtrusive. Anticipated maturity: 2000–2012. A sleeper. Last tasted, 3/98.

1995
•
89
—The 1995 Clerc-Milon, a 56% Cabernet Sauvignon, 30% Merlot, 14% Cabernet Franc blend, reveals more tannin and grip than the 1996 (ironically, the 1995 has more of a 1996 vintage character, and vice versa for the 1996). This attractive dark ruby/purple–colored wine has impressive credentials and may merit an outstanding score with another year or 2 in the bottle. It offers a gorgeous nose of roasted herbs, meats, cedar, cassis, spice, and vanillin. This dense, medium- to full-bodied wine possesses outstanding levels of extract, plenty of glycerin, and a plush, layered, hedonistic finish. A luscious, complex wine, it reveals enough tannin and depth to warrant 15 or more years of cellaring. Anticipated maturity: 2002–2015. A sleeper. Last tasted, 11/97.

1994
•
87+?
—The qualitative equivalent of the 1993, although more backward, tannic, and weighty, this dark ruby/purple–colored, medium-bodied, spicy, rich wine is well made. It is soft for a 1994 yet capable of lasting 15–18 years. Some tannin in the finish suggests that purchasers should give it 2–3 years of cellaring. Last tasted, 1/97.

1993
•
87
—A saturated dark ruby/purple–colored, medium-bodied, well-made wine, Clerc-Milon's 1993 exhibits textbook black currant and weedy tobacco scents. Although the wine is slightly tannic, it does not reveal any of the vintage's astringency or vegetal characteristics. It should offer attractive, velvety-textured, surprisingly fine drinking for the next 10–12 years. Last tasted, 1/97.

1992
•
87
—This lush, sexy 1992 is a meritorious effort in this irregular vintage. The wine possesses a moderately dark ruby color and an up-front fragrance of *pain grillé*, roasted nuts, and cassis. Supple, with jammy black currant fruit, this silky, medium-bodied wine is ideal for drinking over the next 7–8 years. Last tasted, 11/94.

1991
•
79
—Clerc-Milon normally produces a soft, round, easy to understand and consume style of Pauillac. The 1991 is atypically hard and tough textured, with a ruby color, some intriguing spicy, cinnamon, and cassis aromas, and an angular, short finish. A little more flesh on the bones would have added to its appeal. Drink it over the next 7–8 years. Last tasted, 1/94.

1990
•
86
—Not as concentrated, opulent, and velvety as the 1989, the 1990 is still a sexy and smooth wine, with a fragrant nose of cassis, smoke, vanillin, roasted nuts, and exotic scents. This luscious wine, with a creamy texture and excellent color, falls off on the palate, much like its siblings d'Armailhac and Mouton-Rothschild. It should offer delicious drinking for another 8–10 years. Last tasted, 1/93.

1989 — The 1989 Clerc-Milon is a wonderfully hedonistic wine. Deep ruby, with an
•   intense, roasted, smoky bouquet of plums and currants, this full-bodied wine
90   is packed with fruit, chewy and opulent, and very soft and alcoholic. In spite
        of the precocious impression, the tannin levels are high—similar, in fact, to
        the 1986. For the first time in my experience, I actually prefer the Clerc-Milon
        to Mouton-Rothschild! A great value. Anticipated maturity: Now–2010. Last
        tasted, 4/91.

1988 — The 1988 is deep in color, with a moderately intense bouquet of herbs, smoke,
•   and black currants. The hardness it revealed when it was young has melted
89   away, and at present, a rich, creamy texture offers up considerable roasted
        fruit flavors complemented by lavish amounts of oak. Anticipated maturity:
        Now–2001. Last tasted, 4/91.

1987 — Soft yet ripe aromas of currants, smoky oak, and herbs can be coaxed from
•   the glass. In the mouth, the wine is ready to drink—light, but round and
76   correct. Anticipated maturity: Now. Last tasted, 12/89.

1986 — The 1986 is among the greatest Clerc-Milons in my memory and continues to
•   represent one of the better values of the 1986 vintage. Dark ruby/purple with
90   a super bouquet of sweet, toasty new oak, plums, black currants, licorice, and
        cedar, the wine is very concentrated on the palate, rich and powerful, yet
        atypically soft and fleshy for a 1986. While this wine should age well for
        another two decades, it can be drunk much earlier than many of the 1986
        Pauillacs. It is a sleeper of the vintage. Anticipated maturity: Now–2006.
        Last tasted, 1/91.

1985 — The 1985 is a gorgeous wine, deep colored with a complex bouquet of black
•   currants, minerals, and smoky oak. On the palate, this wine is rich, full
89   bodied, powerful, and surprisingly structured and long for a 1985. It is one of
        the surprises of the vintage. Anticipated maturity: Now–2000. Last tasted,
        9/89.

1984 — Beginning to exhibit some orange and amber color, this oaky, herbaceous
•   Clerc-Milon has adequate ripeness, medium body, high acidity, and a lashing
78   of tannin. It should be drunk up. Anticipated maturity: Now–may be in
        decline. Last tasted, 11/88.

1983 — This is a pleasant, lightweight wine that offers a ripe fruity, oaky bouquet yet
•   quickly falls away on the palate. A medium-bodied wine, it has matured very
79   rapidly. Anticipated maturity: Now–may be in decline. Last tasted, 1/90.

1982 — The 1982 Clerc-Milon is a charming, forward, ripe, fruity wine with an
•   open-knit, lovely bouquet of ripe berry fruit, and oaky, vanillin scents. Me-
84   dium to full bodied, with soft, light tannins, this wine is ready to drink.
        Anticipated maturity: Now. Last tasted, 1/90.

1981 — The 1981 exhibits good, dark color, medium body, a classy, complex cedary,
•   oaky, ripe black currant bouquet, some acidity in the finish, and a compact
82   personality. Anticipated maturity: Now. Last tasted, 3/87.

COLOMBIER-MONPELOU

Classification: Cru Bourgeois in 1932
Location of vineyards: On the plateau of Pauillac, next to
Mouton-Rothschild
Owner: Monsieur Bernard Jugla
Address: 33250 Pauillac
Telephone: 33 5 56 59 01 48; telefax: 33 5 56 59 12 01
Visits: By appointment only, from Monday to Friday, between 8 A.M. and
noon, and 1:30 P.M. and 5 P.M.
Contact: Patrick Ballion

VINEYARDS (red)
Surface area: 61.75 acres
Average age of vines: 34 years
Blend: 65% Cabernet Sauvignon, 25% Merlot, 5% Cabernet Franc, 5%
Petit Verdot
Density of plantation: 8,500 vines per hectare
Average yields (over the last 5 years): 52 hectoliters per hectare
Total average annual production: 170,000 bottles

GRAND VIN (red)
Brand name: Château Colombier-Monpelou
Appellation: Pauillac
Mean annual production: 100,000 bottles
Upbringing: Harvest is done both by hand and mechanically.
Fermentations last 3–4 weeks in temperature-controlled stainless-steel
tanks. Wines then spend 15–18 months in oak casks, 40% of which are
new. They are both fined and filtered prior to bottling.

SECOND WINE
Brand name: Château Grand Canyon
Average annual production: 40,000 bottles

Evaluation of present classification: Should be maintained
Plateau of maturity: 3–8 years following the vintage

This property, purchased by proprietor Bernard Jugla in 1970, consists of one
contiguous vineyard well situated on the high plateau above the village of Pauillac. Given the high percentage of Cabernet Sauvignon and the fact that the
average age of the vines is an impressive 34 years, one would expect a great
deal more concentration and intensity. Certainly the vinification and *élevage* are
completely traditional, as the wine is kept in oak casks for 15–18 months. The
problem is that most of the wines I have tasted from Colombier-Monpelou are

light, lacking concentration and distinction. Nevertheless, there is a considerable market for the wines of this château, as France's famed Savour Club remains one of their principal buyers, along with a number of European countries.

VINTAGES

1990—The 1990 is a straightforward, round, commercial, soft, fruity wine with
•   decent concentration, but no great complexity or depth, and a short finish.
81   Drink it over the next 4–6 years. Last tasted, 1/93.

1989—From cask, the 1989 Colombier-Monpelou exhibited meager flavors and a light,
•   washed-out character. While the wine now tastes better, it is clearly made in a
78   fruity, soft, forward style. Anticipated maturity: Now. Last tasted, 4/91.

1988—The 1988 possessed a very oaky nose, but not enough depth or body to
•   warrant interest. Anticipated maturity: Now. Last tasted, 4/91.
78

1986—While the 1986 Colombier-Monpelou does not compete with the classified
•   growths of Pauillac, it is an attractive, well-colored, ripe, fruity, medium- to
80   full-bodied wine that will easily repay cellaring if kept for 7–10 years. Anticipated maturity: Now. Last tasted, 11/90.

1985—I have never been particularly impressed with this wine, although, to its
•   credit, it is usually reasonably priced. The 1985 is a decent, soft, undistin-
74   guished claret. Anticipated maturity: Now. Last tasted, 3/88.

CROIZET-BAGES

Classification: Fifth-growth in 1855
Location of vineyards: Hameau de Bages, Pauillac
Owner: Jean-Michel Quié
Address: 33250 Pauillac
Telephone: 33 5 56 59 56 69 or 33 5 56 59 01 62; telefax: 33 5 56 59 23 39
Visits: By appointment only, from Monday to Friday, between 9 A.M. and noon, and 2 P.M. and 5:30 P.M.
Contact: Jean-Noël Hostein

VINEYARDS (red)
Surface area: 74 acres
Average age of vines: 20 years
Blend: 50% Cabernet Sauvignon, 40% Merlot, 10% Cabernet Franc
Density of plantation: 6,500 and 8,000 vines per hectare
Average yields (over the last 5 years): 50 hectoliters per hectare
Total average annual production: 12,000 cases

GRAND VIN (red)
Brand name: Château Croizet-Bages
Appellation: Pauillac

Mean annual production: 10,000 cases
Upbringing: Grapes are hand-picked. Fermentations last 3 weeks in
temperature-controlled stainless-steel tanks, and important *saignées*
are carried out. Malolactics occur in tanks, and wines are then
transferred into oak casks for the first 6 months, blends separate. After
assemblage, wines are returned to cask for a further 8–12 months
depending upon the vintage. Twenty percent new oak is used. Wines are
fined and filtered.

SECOND WINE
None produced.

Evaluation of present classification: Should be downgraded to a Grand
Bourgeois
Plateau of maturity: 5–12 years following the vintage

Croizet-Bages is owned and managed by the Quié family, which also owns the
well-known Margaux estate, Rauzan-Gassies and the reliable Cru Bourgeois
Bel-Orme-Tronquoy-de-Lalande. I have always found Croizet-Bages to be one
of the lightest and quickest-maturing Pauillacs. The wine has been a consistent underachiever for no valid reason. The vineyard is ideally located on the
Bages plateau, the vines are of a reasonable age (20 years), and the vinification is traditional. Crop yields and the lack of a second wine may in part
explain the disappointing results. Never terribly deep or spectacular, Croizet-
Bages is a sound, gentle, soft, fruity wine, which is generally fully mature
within 4–5 years. The positive showing of the 1995 is, I hope, an encouraging
trend.

VINTAGES

1996—A very good effort from this property, which is becoming more serious about
• quality, the 1996 Croizet-Bages possesses a moderately intense vanillin-and-
84– cassis-scented nose, medium body, excellent ripe fruit, sweet tannin, good
87 purity, and an attractively textured feel. This is a competent, moderately
weighty effort that should age nicely for 10–15 years. Anticipated maturity:
2003–2012. Last tasted, 3/98.

1995—Based on its performance from cask, I had hoped this 1995 would be slightly
• better. Nevertheless, it has turned out to be a good claret, made in a lighter
85 style. The medium ruby color is followed by straightforward, soft, berry, and
black currant aromatics. In the mouth, the wine reveals an attractive, spicy,
fleshy feel, not much weight or depth, but a superficial charm and fruitiness.
This wine can be drunk young and should last for 10–12 years. Anticipated
maturity: 2000–2009. Last tasted, 11/97.

1994—A spicy wine, without the depth of the 1993, the 1994 Croizet-Bages pos-
•   sesses light body, aggressive tannin, and a large structure, but not the fruit
78   and depth necessary to balance the wine's tannin. Anticipated maturity:
       1999–2005. Last tasted, 1/97.

1993—This charming, fruity, elegant wine lacks stuffing and intensity, but it offers
•   soft, tobacco-tinged, red currant fruit, low acid flavors, and good balance.
84   Drink it over the next 7–8 years. Last tasted, 1/97.

1989—How anyone could produce such a light, overtly herbaceous, innocuous wine
•   in 1989 escapes logic. Croizet-Bages excelled in doing just that. Anticipated
73   maturity: Now. Last tasted, 4/91.

1988—The 1988 is straightforward, pleasant, soft, but shallow. Life is too short to
•   drink Croizet-Bages. Anticipated maturity: Now. Last tasted, 4/91.
74

1987—Overtly vegetal, thin, and compact, this undistinguished wine should be
•   drunk up. Anticipated maturity: Now. Last tasted, 11/89.
69

1986—The 1986 is soft and fruity with some tannin but is essentially one-
•   dimensional and undistinguished, particularly in view of its reputation. Antic-
76   ipated maturity: Now. Last tasted, 3/89.

1985—The 1985 is soft, one-dimensional, and no better than most generic Bordeaux
•   red wines. Anticipated maturity: Now. Last tasted, 3/88.
73

DUHART-MILON   VERY GOOD

Classification: Fourth-growth
Location of vineyards: Pauillac
Owner: S.C. du Château Duhart-Milon (the Rothschilds are the principal
shareholders)
Address: 33250 Pauillac
Mailing address: 33, rue de la Baume, 75008 Paris
Telephone: 33 1 53 89 78 00; telefax: 33 1 42 56 28 79
Visits: By appointment only
Contact: Domaines Barons de Rothschild at above telephone and fax
numbers

VINEYARDS (red)
Surface area: 165.5 acres
Average age of vines: 20 years
Blend: 65% Cabernet Sauvignon, 30% Merlot, 5% Cabernet Franc
Density of plantation: 7,500 vines per hectare
Average yields (over the last 5 years): 55 hectoliters per hectare
Total average annual production: 480,000 bottles

GRAND VIN (red)
Brand name: Château Duhart-Milon
Appellation: Pauillac
Mean annual production: 200,000 bottles
Upbringing: Grapes are picked manually. Fermentations occur in temperature-controlled stainless-steel tanks for 18–25 days. Wines are transferred to oak casks when malolactics are over (around December) and stay there for 18 months. Fifty percent new oak is used, and all casks come from the *tonnellerie* of Lafite. Wines are racked every 3 months, fined with egg whites, and filtered before bottling.

SECOND WINE
Brand name: Moulin de Duhart
Average annual production: 180,000 bottles

NOTE: About 50% of the total production is selected for the grand vin and 35%–40% of the rest for the Moulin de Duhart. Surplus is sold as Pauillac.

Evaluation of present classification: Since 1982 should be upgraded to a third-growth
Plateau of maturity: 8–25 years following the vintage

The "other" Pauillac château owned by the Rothschilds of Lafite-Rothschild fame, Duhart-Milon, was purchased in 1962. The poorly maintained vineyards were totally replanted during the mid- and late sixties. Because the vineyard is still young, particularly for a classified growth, the wines of the late sixties and seventies have not lived up to the expectations of wine enthusiasts who assume the Rothschild name is synonymous with excellence. The quality began to improve in 1978, and since 1982, Duhart's wines have been generally very good and occasionally outstanding. The style veers toward the balanced elegance and finesse school of winemaking exemplified by this estate's bigger sister, Lafite-Rothschild.

This is one of the few famous Médoc properties that does not have a château. The wine is made in a large, modern, aesthetically dreadful warehouse on the back streets of Pauillac.

VINTAGES

1997—This estate's increased attention to details of quality is evident in recent
  •   offerings. The forward, seductive, low acid 1997 exhibits a dark ruby/purple
87– color, and plenty of cherry and black currant fruit nicely complemented by
88   *pain grillé* and mineral notes. This medium-bodied, soft, easy-to-understand

and drink Pauillac will be at its best during its first 10–12 years of life. Last tasted, 3/98.

1996
•
88–
90
— From a property that appears to be benefitting from increased attention to detail, the 1996 may turn out to be the finest Duhart-Milon produced since the 1982. The 1996 displays a dense ruby/purple color, followed by a pure, mineral, plum and black currant-scented nose with some spicy oak. High tannin could prove to be troublesome, but at this stage it tastes sweet and well-integrated with the wine's flesh and fruit. This is a well-made, backward, classic Pauillac that will benefit from cellaring. Anticipated maturity: 2003–2015. Last tasted, 3/98.

1995
•
87
— Made from a blend of 80% Cabernet Sauvignon, 20% Merlot, the 1995 is slightly sweeter, more supple and slender than the broader-shouldered 1996. The wine's bouquet offers aromas of ripe berry fruit intermixed with minerals, toasty oak, and spice. Medium bodied, with fine extract, it is a finesse-styled Pauillac (in the best sense of the word). Anticipated maturity: 2002–2014. Last tasted, 11/97.

1994
•
86?
— Dense color saturation is impressive, but this 1994 is astringent, austere, and severe in style. Unlike its bigger sibling, Lafite-Rothschild, the Duhart does not possess enough ripeness, weight, or sweetness in the finish, suggesting it will dry out, becoming too emaciated and attenuated with another 5–8 years of cellaring. Last tasted, 1/97.

1993
•
85
— This dark ruby/purple–colored, medium-bodied, pretty wine exhibits moderate tannin, an elegant style, and soft, pleasant fruit. Although neither substantial nor powerful, it is a well-made wine with good balance. Drink it over the next 8–9 years. Last tasted, 1/97.

1992
•
85
— This soft, currant-and-oak-scented 1992 is revealing more depth and ripeness than it did from cask. Medium bodied, spicy, ripe, and moderately rich, this supple wine should drink well for 5–7 years. Last tasted, 11/94.

1991
•
84
— Duhart's 1991 possesses more depth, ripeness, and potential complexity than the soft, light, one-dimensional 1992. Although the 1991 exhibits deep color, attractive, spicy, grilled nut, cassis, and weedy aromas, and fine depth, it reveals astringent tannin. This medium-bodied wine should be drinkable within 2–3 years and last for 10–12. Last tasted, 1/94.

1990
•
88
— The 1990, with its lead pencil– and cassis-scented nose, is firm and unevolved, but there appears to be more on the palate, and the finish is longer. There is a strong weedy, cassis, Cabernet character to the wine, as well as a sense of elegance, balance, rich extract, and tannin. Anticipated maturity: Now–2007. Last tasted, 1/96.

1989
•
88
— The 1989 has an intense bouquet of creamy black currant fruit and exotic spices. There is even a touch of the famous Pauillac lead pencil smell. Medium bodied, rich, and alcoholic, this voluptuous-styled wine has all the components necessary to seduce tasters for the next 8–12 years. Anticipated maturity: Now–2008. Last tasted, 1/93.

1988
•
88
— The 1988 Duhart-Milon exhibits a bouquet of ripe fruit, spices, cedar, and herbs. The wine is rich, full bodied, admirably concentrated, and long, with plenty of tannin. Anticipated maturity: Now–2010. Last tasted, 1/93.

1987——A surprisingly mature, attractive bouquet of herbs, cedar, and black fruits
•   suggests a richer wine than what actually exists. In the mouth, the wine is
81   round, but soft and short. Drink it over the next 4–5 years. Anticipated
        maturity: Now. Last tasted, 11/89.

1986——I have to give very good marks to the 1986, which has excellent depth, plenty
•   of richness, a lot of spicy oak, and a classy bouquet of herbaceous black
87   currants, cedar, and spicy, toasty oak. It has a good deal of tannin in the
        finish, but I just would like to see a bit more stuffing and complexity. Antici-
        pated maturity: Now–2008. Last tasted, 3/90.

1985——The 1985 Duhart is a fine, medium-bodied wine that is showing slightly less
•   intensity from the bottle than from cask. Medium deep ruby, with an open-
86   knit, spicy oak, curranty bouquet, elegant and stylish, the 1985 could use
        more depth, but for drinking over the next decade, it is a fine choice. Antici-
        pated maturity: Now–2000. Last tasted, 2/89.

1984——Moderately colored, with little bouquet, the 1984 has compact, narrow flavors,
•   a spicy, tightly knit texture, and moderate tannins in the austere, slightly
74   acidic finish. Anticipated maturity: Now. Last tasted, 10/88.

1983——The 1983 Duhart has excellent color, a solid, firm structure, yet a quickly
•   developing, expansive, ripe fruity, cassis-dominated bouquet, round, admira-
86   bly concentrated flavors, and some tannins in the finish. This is a very good,
        rich, medium- to full-bodied Duhart. Anticipated maturity: Now–2005. Last
        tasted, 6/89.

1982——This wine continues to be the finest example I have ever tasted from this
•   estate. It has surprised me in one blind tasting after another with its power,
93   complexity, and concentration. The wine's taste suggests full maturity, but
        there is plenty of grip, extract, and tannin still in evidence. Additionally,
        the color displays only slight lightening at the edge. The wine is a classic
        Pauillac, offering large quantities of cedar and black currants in a full-bodied,
        fleshy, chewy style. It should continue to drink well for another 15+ years.
        Last tasted, 9/95.

1981——All of the Lafite domains were successful in 1981. Quite backward in devel-
•   opment, this deep ruby–colored wine has an attractive bouquet that sug-
84   gests crushed black currants, fresh leather, and new oak. Relatively big,
        quite tannic, concentrated, astringent, and dry in the finish, this backward,
        somewhat dull wine begs for time. However, does the wine have enough
        fruit to outlast the tannins? Anticipated maturity: Now–2005. Last tasted,
        1/85.

1979——Quite an elegant wine, the 1979 Duhart-Milon has good, dark ruby color, with
•   a moderately intense, complex, cedary bouquet, medium body, restrained
83   power and richness, but good balance and harmony. The precocious develop-
        ment of the bouquet and amber color at the edges suggests early maturity.
        Anticipated maturity: Now. Last tasted, 7/86.

1978——A medium-bodied wine with a well-developed, ripe fruity, spicy, toasty, iron-
•   scented bouquet and soft, savory, round flavors, the 1978 Duhart-Milon is the
84   first in a succession of vintages that began to correctly reflect the style and

character of the famous sibling, Lafite-Rothschild. The 1978 Duhart-Milon is fully mature. Anticipated maturity: Now. Last tasted, 3/88.

1976— Ruby garnet, with a fully developed, moderately intense, cedary, vanillin,
•　　fragrant bouquet, this forward-styled wine has soft, round, attractive flavors,
84　　light tannins, low acidity, and a casual resemblance to Lafite, particularly in the bouquet. Its forward charms and up-front fruit have served it well, but additional cellaring would be hazardous. Drink up. Anticipated maturity: Now. Last tasted, 4/90.

1975— A disappointment given the vintage, the 1975 Duhart-Milon has a big, herbal,
•　　almost minty aroma, a spicy, vegetal fruitiness, and a sweet burnt quality that
75　　suggests overchaptalization. Fully mature, but disjointed and unique in style. Anticipated maturity: Now—may be in decline. Last tasted, 5/84.

FONBADET

Classification: Cru Bourgeois Supérieur in 1932
Location of vineyards: Pauillac
Owner: Pierre Peyronie
Address: 33250 Pauillac
Telephone: 33 5 56 59 02 11; telefax: 33 5 56 59 22 61
Visits: By appointment only
Contact: Pascale Peyronie

VINEYARDS (red)
Surface area: 39.5 acres
Average age of vines: 50–60 years
Blend: 60% Cabernet Sauvignon, 20% Merlot, 15% Cabernet Franc, 5% Petit Verdot and Malbec
Density of plantation: 9,000 vines per hectare
Average yields (over the last 5 years): 40 hectoliters per hectare
Total average annual production: 600 hectoliters

GRAND VIN (red)
Brand name: Château Fonbadet
Appellation: Pauillac
Mean annual production: 600 hectoliters
Upbringing: Grapes are picked manually and totally destemmed. Fermentations occur in cement tanks (no temperature control) and last 3–4 weeks. Malolactics occur in vats. The wines are transferred into casks in May. They are partly aged in oak casks (of which 25% are new) and partly in tanks. The *élevage* lasts 2 years. Wines are fined but not filtered. Pierre Peyronie also owns other small estates, but all wines are vinified at Fonbadet. The winemaking and *élevage* are similar to

that of Château Fonbadet. The wines are entitled to Cru Bourgeois appellation. They include the following châteaux: Château Haut-Pauillac, Château Montgrand Duron-Milon, Château Padernac, and Tour du Roc-Milon.

Evaluation of present classification: Should be a fifth-growth
Plateau of maturity: 5–15 years following the vintage

Should any reclassification of the wines of the Médoc be done, Fonbadet would have to be elevated to the rank of fifth-growth. This is an expertly vinified wine that can, in vintages such as 1990, 1986, 1982, and 1978, surpass several of the classified growths of Pauillac. In style it is always darkly colored, with a very rich, black currant bouquet, an intense concentration of flavor, and full body. I find it reminiscent of the style of the two fifth-growth Pauillacs, Lynch-Bages and Haut-Bages-Libéral. The secrets are extremely old vines (more than 50 years of age), tiny yields (usually under 40 hectoliters per hectare), and the brilliant location of the vineyard near both Pichon-Longueville Baron and Pichon-Longueville–Comtesse de Lalande.

VINTAGES

1990—The best Fonbadet since their powerful 1982, the 1990 reveals an opaque
•   dark ruby color and a pure, spicy nose of black fruits and earthy, truffle-like
87   aromas. In the mouth, there is excellent ripeness, a sweet, rich texture, plenty
      of tannin and glycerin, as well as a long, powerful finish. Anticipated maturity:
      Now–2003. Last tasted, 1/93.

1989—The 1989 is surprisingly light, soft, alcoholic and will no doubt be short-lived
•   because of its low acidity. There is plenty of fruit, but the overall effect is of
83   a flabby, unstructured wine. Anticipated maturity: Now. Last tasted, 4/91.

1988—The 1988 tastes tart, lean, and anorexic. Lack of fruit is cause for concern.
•   Anticipated maturity: Now. Last tasted, 4/91.
75

1986—The 1986 Fonbadet is certainly the best wine made at this potentially excel-
•   lent vineyard since the 1982. There is abundant chewy fruit, noticeable
86   muscle and tannin, and impressive length. The wine should come into its own
      by the early nineties but last 10–12 years thereafter. Given the extract levels
      this wine can possess, an elevated use of new oak casks at this property might
      prove beneficial. Anticipated maturity: Now–2003. Last tasted, 4/89.

1985—The 1985 has a good deep ruby color and an attractive berry perfume, but its
•   chunky flavors reveal little complexity. Anticipated maturity: Now. Last
80   tasted, 10/88.

1984—Surprisingly alcoholic, with adequate fruit, full body and an old-fashioned,
•   rustic feel to it, the 1984 is rough and disjointed. Anticipated maturity: Now–
72   may be in decline. Last tasted, 3/88.

1983—This looks to be a top-notch effort from Fonbadet. Nearly as dark as the
•   opaque 1982, but less concentrated, this rich, medium-bodied, moderately
85   tannic wine offers a generous mouthful of cedary, cassis-flavored fruit. Antici-
      pated maturity: Now. Last tasted, 3/89.
1982—The ripe, rich, blackberry aromas surge from the glass; this gorgeous wine is
•   very deep, concentrated, and well structured. On the palate, the wine is full
87   bodied, moderately tannic, opulently fruity, and long. A sleeper of the vintage.
      Anticipated maturity: Now–2000. Last tasted, 1/89.
1981—The 1981 is richly fruity, darkly colored and more precocious and will mature
•   earlier than either the 1982 or 1983. It is a wine that is charming, well
84   balanced, and satisfying. Anticipated maturity: Now–may be in decline. Last
      tasted, 2/84.
1978—A textbook Pauillac, the 1978 Fonbadet has a well-developed bouquet of
•   cedar, ripe plums, and currants and well-balanced, deeply fruity flavors.
86   Quite impressive. Anticipated maturity: Now–may be in decline. Last tasted,
      2/84.

GRAND-PUY-DUCASSE   GOOD

Classification: Fifth-growth in 1855
Location of vineyards: Grand-Puy in Pauillac
Owner: Société Civile du Château Grand-Puy-Ducasse
Administrator: J.-P. Anglivielle de la Beaumelle
Address: 33250 Pauillac
Mailing address: 17, cours de la Martinique, B.P.40, 33027 Bordeaux
Cedex
Telephone: 33 5 56 01 30 10; telefax: 33 5 56 79 23 57
Visits: By appointment for professionals of the wine trade only (Monday
to Friday, from 9 A.M. to noon, and 2 P.M. to 5 P.M.)
Contact: Brigitte Cruse

VINEYARDS (red)
Surface area: 96.3 acres
Average age of vines: 25+ years
Blend: 62% Cabernet Sauvignon, 38% Merlot
Density of plantation: 8,000–10,000 vines per hectare
Average yields (over the last 5 years): 55 hectoliters per hectare
Total average annual production: 20,000 cases

GRAND VIN (red)
Brand name: Château Grand-Puy-Ducasse
Appellation: Pauillac
Mean annual production: 18,000 cases
Upbringing: Grapes are picked manually. Fermentations last 18–21 days,

with 2 pumping-overs a day, and occur in temperature-controlled stainless-steel vats. Wines are then transferred to oak casks, of which 30% are new, for 18 months. They are racked the year prior to bottling and filtered just before bottling.

SECOND WINE
Brand name: Prelude à Grand-Puy-Ducasse
Average annual production: 2,000 cases

Evaluation of present classification: Should be maintained
Plateau of maturity: 4–14 years following the vintage

This fifth-growth Pauillac has been largely ignored by consumers and the wine press. Admittedly the wine rarely appears in tastings because the distribution is controlled exclusively by the *négociant* Mestrezat. Unquestionably, the current prices for vintages of Grand-Puy-Ducasse are below those of most other Pauillacs, making it a notable value given the fine quality that now routinely emerges from the modern cellars located not in the middle of a beautiful vineyard, but in downtown Pauillac.

Extensive renovations as well as replanting began in 1971, culminating in 1986 with the installation of a new *cuverie* equipped with computerized stainless-steel tanks. The percentage of new oak casks has been increased to 50%. As a consequence, the future looks encouraging for Grand-Puy-Ducasse. With the well-placed vineyard, one parcel adjacent to Mouton-Rothschild and Lafite-Rothschild, another on the gravelly plateau near Batailley, Grand-Puy-Ducasse is a château to which value-conscious consumers should be giving more consideration.

The style of wines here is quite fruity and supple rather than tannic, hard, and backward. Most vintages of Grand-Puy-Ducasse are drinkable within 5 years of the vintage yet exhibit the potential to last for 10–15 years.

VINTAGES

1997—A well-made wine, in a more delicate, medium-weight style, Grand-Puy-
•   Ducasse's 1997 exhibits a deep ruby color, sweet cassis fruit, low acidity, and
85–   a subtle oak-tinged character. This elegant, well-made Pauillac will be ideal
87   to drink upon its release in 2 years; it should keep for 7–8 years. Last tasted, 3/98.

1996—The 1996 is shaping up as an elegant, understated but well-made Pauillac
•   with a deep ruby/purple color, and an attractive nose of weedy tobacco, black
86–   currants, cedar, and spice. Medium bodied, with surprisingly soft tannin,
87   moderate weight, and flesh and glycerin in the supple finish, this attractive
        Pauillac will drink well young but will not be an ager. Anticipated maturity:
        Now–2009. Last tasted, 3/98.

1995—Dark ruby-colored with purple nuances, this supple, lush, fruity Pauillac
•   possesses medium body, light intensity new oak, soft tannin, and low acidity.
87   Made in a clean, medium-bodied, user-friendly, accessible style, this wine
      will have many fans. Anticipated maturity: Now–2010. Last tasted, 11/97.

1994—A seductive combination of jammy ripe black currants, smoke, toast, and new
•   oak is offered in this excellent 1994. This supple wine offers loads of fruit
87   and sweet tannin. Medium to full bodied and well balanced, this is a deli-
      cious, precocious 1994 that will drink well now and over the next 12–14
      years. Readers should also note that this wine is reasonably priced. Last
      tasted, 1/97.

1993—This dark ruby–colored 1993 reveals the herbal/green pepper character of
•   the vintage. Sweet, ripe fruit is initially attractive on the palate. The wine
81   possesses depth and body, but overall, it comes across as too herbal and
      angular. Anticipated maturity: Now–2006. Last tasted, 1/97.

1992—A saturated dark ruby color with hints of purple is impressive, particularly
•   for this vintage. Soft, ripe, cassis aromas drift from the glass. The wine's
86   attack offers plenty of sweet fruit, low tannin, and gentleness. The wine is
      medium bodied, soft, and a success for the vintage. Drink it now and over the
      next 6–7 years. Last tasted, 11/94.

1990—The 1990 is light and delicate but pleasant in a one-dimensional, fruity way.
•   Anticipated maturity: Now–1999. Last tasted, 1/93.
84

1989—The 1989 is forward, with a cedary, ripe, moderately intense bouquet. Not a
•   blockbuster, it is spicy and delicious, with abundant quantities of chocolate
87   and cassis-flavored fruit. This may be the finest wine from this property in
      decades. Anticipated maturity: Now–2002. Last tasted, 4/91.

1988—The 1988 Grand-Puy-Ducasse is a lighter-weight version of the 1989, less
•   alcoholic, but more tannic and compact. Nevertheless, it has fine fruit and
85   attractive ripeness. Anticipated maturity: Now–2000. Last tasted, 4/91.

1986—I would have liked to see a bit more depth and excitement in the 1986, but it
•   is a pretty, charming, medium-bodied, atypically lighter-styled Pauillac for
85   the vintage. Drinkable now, it will certainly last another 7–8 years. Antici-
      pated maturity: Now–2000. Last tasted, 11/90.

1985—The 1985 Grand-Puy-Ducasse is a textbook Pauillac, not a blockbuster in
•   any manner, but a cedary, spicy, fragrant wine with fine depth, a supple
86   texture, some fatness and flesh, and a smooth, graceful finish. Anticipated
      maturity: Now. Last tasted, 11/90.

1982—This wine has always been an attractive, fragrant, classic Pauillac with scents
•   of cedar, spice, and berry fruit. Although not the most concentrated wine from
86   the appellation, it is a medium-bodied, elegant example of the vintage that
      requires drinking before the turn of the century. Last tasted, 9/95.

1979—The 1979 is medium to dark ruby, with a spicy, ripe, fruity bouquet and
•   attractively silky, soft flavors that show noticeable maturity. This is a charm-
82   ing, quite fruity wine with medium body. Anticipated maturity: Now. Last
      tasted, 7/86.

1978—Good solid color, a ripe black currant, somewhat herbaceous bouquet, and
•   round, generous flavors characterize the 1978 Grand-Puy-Ducasse. Quite
82   precocious for the vintage, and showing very well at present, this is a wine to
    drink over the next 6–7 years. Anticipated maturity: Now—may be in decline.
    Last tasted, 5/84.

1975—The 1975 is dark ruby in color, with a stalky, vegetal note to an otherwise
•   attractive bouquet. Ripe, round, deep fruit has an aggressive, rustic texture
84   to it, and despite the wine's concentration and hefty proportions, the overall
    impression is one of coarseness. A good wine that just misses being excellent.
    Anticipated maturity: Now. Last tasted, 6/86.

1971—One of my favorite wines from Grand-Puy-Ducasse, this lovely, round, charm-
•   ing, effusively fruity wine was fully mature by 1978 but has continued to
85   remain at that plateau without fading or losing its fruit. A cedary, ripe fruity
    bouquet is seductive and complex. Soft, round, velvety flavors are satisfyingly
    rich and lengthy. A total success for Grand-Puy-Ducasse. Drink up. Antici-
    pated maturity: Now. Last tasted, 3/84.

GRAND-PUY-LACOSTE   EXCELLENT

Classification: Fifth-growth in 1855
Location of vineyards: Pauillac
Owner: Jean-Eugène Borie family
Address: 33250 Pauillac
Mailing address: c/o J.-E. Borie S.A., 33250 Pauillac
Telephone: 33 5 56 59 05 20; telefax: 33 5 56 59 27 37
Visits: By appointment only, from Monday to Friday, between 9 A.M. and
noon, and 2 P.M. and 5 P.M.
Contact: J.-E. Borie S.A. at above telephone and telefax numbers

VINEYARDS (red)
Surface area: 123.5 acres
Average age of vines: 35 years
Blend: 70% Cabernet Sauvignon, 25% Merlot, 5% Cabernet Franc
Density of plantation: 10,000 vines per hectare
Average yields (over the last 5 years): 45 hectoliters per hectare
Total average annual production: 15,000 cases

GRAND VIN (red)
Brand name: Château Grand-Puy-Lacoste
Appellation: Pauillac
Mean annual production: 180,000 bottles
Upbringing: Grapes are picked manually and totally destemmed.
Fermentations occur in temperature-controlled stainless-steel tanks for
17–20 days. Wines are aged for 18–20 months in oak casks, 35%–40%

of which are new. They are fined and undergo light filtration before bottling.

SECOND WINE
Brand name: Lacoste-Borie

Evaluation of present classification: Should be upgraded to a third-growth, particularly since 1978
Plateau of maturity: 7–20 years following the vintage

I never had the pleasure of meeting Raymond Dupin, the late owner of Grand-Puy-Lacoste. Dupin had a monumental reputation as one of Bordeaux's all-time great gourmets. According to some of his acquaintances he was a gourmand as well. Prior to his death in 1980, he sold Grand-Puy-Lacoste in 1978 to the highly talented and respected Jean-Eugène Borie, who then installed his son, Xavier, at the château. An extensive remodeling program for Grand-Puy's ancient and dilapidated cellars was completed by 1982, just in time to produce one of the finest wines made to date by Xavier Borie. Borie continues to live at the modernized château with his wife and family. As expected by the cognoscenti of Bordeaux, Grand-Puy-Lacoste has surged to the forefront of leading Pauillacs.

Grand-Puy-Lacoste, which sits far back from the Gironde River on the "Bages" plateau, has enjoyed a solid reputation for big, durable, full-bodied Pauillacs, not unlike its neighbor a kilometer away, Lynch-Bages. However, the wines of the sixties and seventies, like those of Lynch-Bages, showed an unevenness in quality that in retrospect may have been due to the declining health of the owner. For example, highly regarded vintages such as 1966 and 1975 were less successful at Grand-Puy than its reputation would lead one to expect. Other vintages during this period, particularly the 1976, 1971, 1969, and 1967, were close to complete failures for some unexplained reason, but probably inattentiveness to detail.

However, since 1978 Grand-Puy-Lacoste has been making excellent wines. In the case of the 1982, 1990, 1995, and 1996, great wines were produced that will be remembered as some of the finest examples in this château's long history. In comparison with the Dupin style, the Borie style of Grand-Puy-Lacoste has been to harvest later and thereby produce wines with an intense cassis fruitiness, with considerable glycerin, power, and body. Until the mid-nineties, the price of Grand-Puy-Lacoste had not kept pace with the quality, remaining modest, even somewhat under-valued.

VINTAGES

1997 —Following two phenomenally successful vintages, the 1997 Grand-Puy-
•   Lacoste is a blend of 70% Cabernet Sauvignon and 30% Merlot. No Cabernet
88–   Franc made it into the final blend. The harvest took place between September
90   11 and September 30, with approximately 35% of the production relegated to
       the estate's second wine. The 1997 is a hedonistic, dark purple-colored wine
       with sweet cassis fruit dominating all other potential nuances. In short, this
       is akin to drinking a crème de cassis cocktail. Medium bodied, with low
       acidity, admirable fat in the mid-palate, and good length, this delicious,
       approachable, classic Pauillac should drink exceptionally well young, yet last
       for 12 years. Last tasted, 3/98.

1996 —The 1996 displays an opaque purple color, as well as sweet, wonderfully
•   pure, jammy blackberry, mineral, and intriguing floral aromas. Enormously
95–   rich and full bodied, with massive intensity, this is a modern day *tour de force*
97   in winemaking. In spite of being aged in a hefty percentage of new oak, the
       wine does not reveal any evidence of new oak casks because the fruit charac-
       ter is so pronounced. Statistically, this wine possesses huge amounts of tan-
       nin, but it comes across as a seamless giant with extraordinary richness and
       intensity. This may be even greater than the exceptional 1982, but it may
       take longer to become accessible than the latter wine. Anticipated maturity:
       2007–2035. Last tasted, 3/98.

1995 —Another unbelievably rich, multidimensional, broad-shouldered wine, with
•   slightly more elegance and less weight than the powerhouse 1996, this gor-
95   geously proportioned, medium- to full-bodied, fabulously ripe, rich, cassis-
       scented and -flavored Grand-Puy-Lacoste is another beauty. It should be
       drinkable within 4–5 years, and keep for 25–30. This classic Pauillac is a
       worthy rival to the otherworldly 1996. Anticipated maturity: 2002–2025. Last
       tasted, 11/97.

1994 —The 1994 has turned out to be an outstanding effort for this estate. The wine
•   reveals even more flesh than it did prior to bottling, as well as the high
90   tannin that marks many of this vintage's wines. The color is an opaque
       ruby/purple, and the nose offers up a gorgeously pure blast of sweet cas-
       sis fruit. Medium to full bodied, with layers of extract, this classic, rich,
       powerful Pauillac will be at its best between 2003 and 2020. Last tasted,
       1/97.

1993 —This dark ruby/purple–colored wine offers a fragrant weedy, cassis-and-
•   tobacco-scented nose as well as a sexy combination of rich cassis fruit and
87   glycerin. Medium to full bodied, with low acidity, excellent ripeness, and a
       luscious mouth-feel, this is a delicious, hedonistic style of Grand-Puy-Lacoste
       for drinking over the next 7–8 years. Last tasted, 1/97.

1992 —A success for the vintage, Grand-Puy-Lacoste's ruby-colored 1992 offers
•   sweet, ripe, up-front cassis fruit, as well as some fat and softness. Although it
86   lacks the depth, focus, and concentration of the 1991 and 1993, it is a
       charming, velvety-textured wine for drinking over the next 5–6 years. Last
       tasted, 11/94.

1991—Unquestionably a star of the vintage, Grand-Puy-Lacoste's 1991 reveals a
• deep ruby color, a lovely perfumed nose of black fruits, cedar, and herbs,
87 medium body, soft, ripe, fleshy flavors, and surprising length. It should drink
well for at least 10–15 years. It is an excellent effort for the vintage. Last
tasted, 1/94.

1990—The stunning 1990 possesses an opaque ruby/purple color, as well as a stunning
• nose of jammy black currants, cedar, spice, and smoke. Full bodied, with
95 magnificent extract, excellent delineation, outstanding purity, and layers of intensity, this massive, dense, well-balanced Pauillac is the finest Grand-Puy-
Lacoste since the 1982. Anticipated maturity: Now–2015. Last tasted, 11/96.

1989—When I first tasted the 1989 Grand-Puy-Lacoste I thought it possessed a
• Graves-like tobacco/mineral character. In contrast with the blockbuster, full-
89 blown, massive wines produced by this estate in 1990 and 1982, the medium-
weight 1989 is elegant, spicy, evolved, and already revealing plenty of cedar
and cassis fruit. A delicious, generously endowed, low-acid wine, it will offer
mature drinking now and over the next 12–15 years. Last tasted, 11/96.

1988—The 1988 effort from this estate is deep ruby, has a reticent bouquet, an
• austere, firm, tannic framework, and medium body. The wine has noticeable
85 richness and depth, as well as high tannins. Anticipated maturity: Now–
2005. Last tasted, 1/93.

1987—The most pleasurable aspect of this wine is the bouquet of cassis and weedy
• scents. In the mouth, the wine is hard, tannic, and lacking charm and flesh.
76 Anticipated maturity: Now. Last tasted, 4/90.

1986—This wine is the finest Grand-Puy-Lacoste produced after 1982, 1990, and
• before 1996. The 1986 still possesses an impressive deep ruby/purple color,
91 as well as a classic nose of cedar, black currants, smoke, and vanillin. It is
full bodied, powerful, authoritatively rich, and loaded with fruit, with a solid
lashing of tannin not likely to melt away for 3–4 more years. This wine can
be drunk, although it is backward and unyielding. Certainly it is one of the
better northern Médocs of the vintage. Anticipated maturity: Now–2012. Last
tasted, 6/97.

1985—The 1985 has reached full maturity quickly. It is an excellent, nearly out-
• standing example of a juicy, succulent Pauillac oozing with sweet cedar,
89 herb-tinged, black currant fruit. Medium to full bodied, with low acidity and
a supple, nearly opulent texture, this wine is intensely charming and delicious. The only negative is its short finish, which suggests it needs to be
consumed over the next decade. Anticipated maturity: Now–2004. Last
tasted, 10/97.

1983—Open knit and ripe, with a dark ruby color and a rich, weedy, black currant
• aroma, this rapidly evolving wine exhibits good concentration, a round, gentle
86 texture, and a fine finish. It has reached full maturity. Anticipated maturity:
Now. Last tasted, 3/89.

1982—Absolutely spectacular, the 1982 Grand-Puy-Lacoste must be one of the most
• underrated wines of the vintage. The color remains an opaque ruby/purple,
95 and there is no doubting the level of quality after one sniff and sip. The wine

reveals the classic black currant, cedary profile of a great Pauillac. Still young and unevolved, this massive, sensationally concentrated, full-bodied wine offers layers of pure black currant fruit that comes across as grapy because of its intensity and youthfulness. It is a thrill to drink even though the wine is still extremely young and only hints at the possibilities that exist with another 5–10 years of cellaring. Exceptionally full bodied, with a finish that lasts for 40 seconds or more, this is the greatest Grand-Puy-Lacoste of the last 3 decades. Drink it between now and 2020. A tour de force in winemaking! P.S. Until I consumed the last bottle, this was my "house wine" at my favorite Paris bistro: L'Ami Louis. Last tasted, 9/95.

1981—Light in style for Grand-Puy, the 1981 has more in common with the 1979
•   than either the substantial 1982 or full-bodied yet elegant 1978. An elegant
80   mixture of ripe berry fruit and spicy oak overlaid with soft tannins makes this
     wine very easy to drink now. Anticipated maturity: Now. Last tasted, 4/90.

1979—Quite precocious, with a surprisingly mature bouquet of ripe berry fruit,
•   cedar, spicy oak, and flowers, medium bodied, with soft flavors, a gentle,
83   round texture, and a pleasant yet short finish, this wine is well made in a
     lighter style than usual. Anticipated maturity: Now. Last tasted, 3/88.

1978—The first vintage made under the expert management of Jean-Eugène Borie
•   and his son Xavier, the 1978 remains a classic Pauillac with fine cellaring
88   potential. Dark ruby garnet with a ripe, intense bouquet of cassis, fruit, cedar,
     and vanillin oakiness, this wine is rich, with excellent body and the tannins
     quickly melting away. It can be drunk now or cellared for another decade.
     Anticipated maturity: Now–2002. Last tasted, 4/91.

1976—An acceptable wine for certain, but this Grand-Puy-Lacoste is surprisingly
•   jammy, over-ripe, with a scent of fresh tea. Soft, flabby, and loosely knit on
72   the palate, this wine is now fully mature. Drink up! Anticipated maturity:
     Now. Last tasted, 7/80.

1975—This wine typifies the problem with many 1975s. The color is revealing
•   noticeable rust/orange. The aromatics offer plenty of cedar and spice, with an
85?   underlying vegetal, earthy, dusty character. While the flavors are full bodied
     and moderately concentrated, they are dominated by harsh tannin, making
     the wine taste compact. The wine gives the impression of being close to full
     maturity. I suspect further aging will result in more fruit loss, something this
     wine cannot afford. Drink it up. Last tasted, 12/95.

1971—Beginning to fall apart, this wine was fully mature by 1977. Quite brown in
•   color, with an oxidized, stale, faded bouquet, it has soft, dissipated, fruity
62   flavors and no tannin present. This wine possesses plenty of sharp acid-
     ity. Anticipated maturity: Now–probably in serious decline. Last tasted,
     7/77.

1970—This deep, dark ruby–colored wine exhibits good liveliness in its color. The
•   wine reveals the classic cassis, mineral, weedy tobacco, spicy nose of a top
91   Pauillac. Full bodied, concentrated, and close to full maturity, it is a flavorful,
     expansive, chewy wine. Although it has been distressingly inconsistent in
     previous tastings, I am convinced the off bottles had been cooked. In this

tasting, it was a delicious, outstanding example of the vintage that should continue to drink well for another decade. Last tasted, 6/96.

1967—Premature senility, a problem that seems to have plagued Grand-Puy-Lacoste
•　　in the sixties and early seventies, is again the culprit here. Quite brown, with
65　　a decaying, leafy aroma and shallow, feeble flavors. Last tasted, 2/83.

1966—A successful wine was produced by Grand-Puy-Lacoste in 1966. Now fully
•　　mature, with a moderately intense, smoky, cassis-dominated bouquet, soft,
84　　savory flavors, and somewhat of a short finish, this is an austere wine to
　　　enjoy over the next several years before it fades. Anticipated maturity: Now—
　　　probably in decline. Last tasted, 11/84.

1964—Quite successful in this very uneven rain-plagued vintage, the 1964 Grand-
•　　Puy-Lacoste offers robust, chunky, generous black currant flavors, a substan-
86　　tial, plump, rustic texture, good length, and sizable weight. It is now fully
　　　mature but has the requisite depth to last for another 5–7 years. Anticipated
　　　maturity: Now. Last tasted, 11/88.

1962—Just beginning to fade, this wine has a lovely bouquet of ripe fruit, caramel,
•　　and spices with a soft, savory style. It is fruity and lush on the palate but
82　　clearly tails off in the glass. Anticipated maturity: Now—probably in decline.
　　　Last tasted, 9/81.

1961—I acquired a half dozen bottles of this wine at a New York auction and have
•　　drunk 3 bottles. The wine is fully mature and probably slightly past its
88?　apogee. The color is a dark ruby/garnet with considerable orange and rust at
　　　the edge. The wine exhibits a knockout (well over 90 points) bouquet of sweet
　　　cassis and cedar. In the mouth, the attack offers plenty of glycerin, the
　　　richness of a great vintage, and a seamless, opulent texture. However, after
　　　10–15 minutes in the glass, the wine begins to fade and appears to dry out in
　　　less than 30 minutes. This is an excellent wine, if drunk immediately. More-
　　　over, I suspect well-stored magnums and larger formats could be quite bril-
　　　liant. Last tasted, 9/97.

ANCIENT VINTAGES

The 1959 Grand-Puy-Lacoste (92 points) exhibited plenty of power and muscle as well as outstanding concentration in a chunky, husky, Pauillac manner. In 1959 it truly could have been called the "non-wealthy person's Latour."

The 1949 (96 points; last tasted 10/94) exhibits a fragrant nose of cedar, black currants, and woodsy, trufflelike aromas. Gorgeously opulent and full bodied, it is a superconcentrated, velvety-textured, fully mature wine.

At a dinner party in Bordeaux in 1989, I was astonished by the superb 1947 (I rated it 94). From a private cellar in that city, it was remarkably concentrated, rich, and expansively flavored, and admirably demonstrated why Grand-Puy-Lacoste was so highly regarded in the post–World War II vintages.

HAUT-BAGES-LIBÉRAL

Classification: Fifth-growth in 1855
Location of vineyards: Pauillac, next to those of Château Latour
Owner: S.A. du Château Haut Bages Libéral
Address: 33250 Pauillac
Telephone: 33 5 56 58 02 37; telefax: 33 5 56 58 05 70
Visits: By appointment only, from Monday to Friday, 9 A.M. to 4 P.M.
Contact: Claire Villars

VINEYARDS (red)
Surface area: 69 acres
Average age of vines: 30 years
Blend: 80% Cabernet Sauvignon, 17% Merlot, and 3% Petit Verdot
Density of plantation: 10,000 vines per hectare
Average yields (over the last 5 years): 55 hectoliters per hectare
Total average annual production: 170,000 bottles

GRAND VIN (red)
Brand name: Château Haut-Bages-Libéral
Appellation: Pauillac
Upbringing: Fermentations last 3–4 weeks in temperature-controlled
stainless-steel tanks, and wines are then transferred to oak casks (40% of
which are new) for 16 months. They are fined but not filtered.

SECOND WINE
Brand name: La Chapelle de Bages

Evaluation of present classification: Should be maintained
Plateau of maturity: 5–15 years following the vintage

This modest-sized château sitting just off Bordeaux's main road of wine, D2,
has been making consistently fine undervalued wine since the mid-1970s.
The vineyard, consisting of 3 parcels, is superbly situated. The major portion (just over 50%) is adjacent to the main Latour vineyard. Another parcel
is next to Pichon Lalande, and a third is farther inland near Grand-Puy-
Lacoste.

The famous Cruse family of Bordeaux had thoroughly modernized Haut-
Bages-Libéral in the seventies but in 1983 decided to sell the property to the
syndicate run by the Villars family, which owns and manages two other
well-known châteaux, Chasse-Spleen in Moulis and La Gurgue in Margaux.
The vineyard, replanted in the early sixties, is now coming into maturity. No
doubt the young vines accounted for the mediocre quality of the wine in the
sixties and early seventies. However, in 1975 an excellent wine was produced,

and this success has been followed by several recent vintages that have also exhibited high quality, particularly 1995, 1990, 1986, and 1985.

Haut-Bages-Libéral produces a strong, ripe, rich, very black curranty wine, no doubt as a result of the high percentage of Cabernet Sauvignon.

VINTAGES

1997 — This is a yeoman-like effort from Haut-Bages-Libéral with solid, soft, plump
• berry fruit aromas intermingled with loamy soil scents. Although monolithic,
85– this mouthfilling effort will offer enjoyable, uncomplicated drinking over the
86 next 8–10 years. Last tasted, 3/98.

1996 — While many 1996 Médocs had fleshed out, with the tannin becoming sweeter,
• and the ripe Cabernet Sauvignon fruit even more impressive, this offering was
85– an exception to the rule. The tannin seemed more noticeable, and the wine
86? appeared to have a hole in the middle as well as a dry, severe finish. The
color is a healthy dark purple, and the wine reveals sweet blackberry, chocolate, and vanilla-tinged fruit on the attack, but it then falls off in the back of
the mouth. It will be interesting to retaste this 1996 after bottling. Last tasted,
3/98.

1995 — The 1995 possesses a bit more depth and intensity than its younger sibling,
• but it is also lean and austere. The attractive saturated ruby/purple color
85 suggests plenty of intensity, which is evident on the attack, but, again, the
mid-palate is deficient in fruit, glycerin, and concentration, and the finish is
dry, with a high level of tannin. This wine may soften with more bottle age
and become better than my rating suggests. Let's hope so. Anticipated maturity: 2003–2012. Last tasted, 11/97.

1994 — Showing exceptionally well, this dark ruby–colored 1994 displays no hard
• tannin or herbaceous/greenness to its aromatics or flavors. The wine is admi-
86 rably rich, with dense, black cherry, chocolatey, cassis fruit, firm but sweet
tannin, and a medium-bodied, spicy finish. Give it 2–3 years of cellaring,
and drink it over the following 15 years. Last tasted, 1/97.

1993 — This soft, round, peppery, dark ruby–colored wine reveals an attractive,
• fleshy, supple style that will give it plenty of up-front appeal over the next 5–
85 7 years. It is ideal for restaurants looking for a Pauillac that can be drunk
young. Last tasted, 1/97.

1992 — This is a light-bodied, tough-textured, tannic, insubstantial wine that is too
• astringent and hard. Drink it over the next 3–4 years before it loses any more
76 fruit. Last tasted, 11/94.

1990 — Deeply colored, with a sweet, plummy, oaky nose, the 1990 represents a
• major improvement over the indifferent 1989. Opulent and rich, this low-acid,
87 fleshy wine lacks grip, but it does offer a big, meaty mouthful of juicy
Pauillac. Anticipated maturity: Now–2005. Last tasted, 1/93.

1989 — The 1989 Haut-Bages-Libéral tastes surprisingly light. It has a brilliant ruby/
• purple color, decent acidity, and moderate tannin, but it finishes short. It is a
84 good effort but is atypically restrained and subdued for a 1989 Pauillac.
Anticipated maturity: Now–1999. Last tasted, 1/93.

1988 —The 1988 exhibits some greenness to its tannins, is medium bodied, spicy,
•   offers some curranty fruit, and finishes abruptly. Drink it over the next 4–5
81   years. Last tasted, 1/93.

1987 —Soft, diluted, weedy, and disjointed, the 1987 Haut-Bages-Libéral has a dubi-
•   ous future. Anticipated maturity: Now. Last tasted, 10/89.
72

1986 —The percentage of new oak casks used at Haut-Bages-Libéral was increased
•   and the selection process tightened, and the result in 1986 is their finest wine
90   since the 1975 and certainly one of the best wines ever made at the property.
          Dark ruby/purple, with an expansive bouquet of plums, sweet toasty oak, and
          black currants, this dense, full-bodied, chewy wine has a suppleness that
          allows it to be drunk now. But it also has the balance, richness, and tannin
          content to age well for at least another 20 years. Anticipated maturity: Now–
          2015. Last tasted, 3/90.

1985 —The black/ruby–colored 1985 is a rich, dense, full-bodied wine with great
•   color, loads of extract, and a powerful, long, ripe finish. It is one of the stars
89   of the vintage. Anticipated maturity: Now–2005. Last tasted, 9/89.

1984 —I tasted this wine many times and have terribly inconsistent tasting notes
•   covering several plump, fruity, one-dimensional examples to several that
72   tasted overripe, low in acid, and bizarre. From a bottle purchased in Bordeaux
          in 1988, the wine tasted hollow, attenuated, and charmless. Anticipated
          maturity: Now. Last tasted, 3/88.

1983 —The 1983 is a big, brash, aggressive sort of wine, with intense color, a
•   full-blown bouquet of ripe black currants, deep, full, thick, fruity flavors, and
85   a long, moderately tannic finish. This brawny wine has, like many 1983s,
          matured more quickly than expected. Anticipated maturity: Now. Last tasted,
          3/89.

1982 —Surprise, surprise! One of the least acclaimed 1982s, the Haut-Bages-Libéral
•   has developed beautifully. It is crammed with thick, juicy, licorice/olive/
91   smoky, roasted, ripe black currant fruit. Full bodied, thick, and juicy, and
          with just enough complexity to merit an outstanding rating, this mouth-filling,
          savory, super-concentrated, jammy Pauillac is already delicious, yet it reveals
          no signs of age. The color is a healthy opaque garnet/purple. This wine should
          drink well for another 15+ years. Last tasted, 4/98.

1981 —The 1981 is typical in style for Haut-Bages-Libéral: dark ruby, with a big,
•   spicy, smoky, black currant bouquet, rich, abundant flavors, medium body,
84   and a tannic, slightly astringent finish. For the vintage, it is a big, chewy
          mouthful of wine that offers broad crowd appeal. Anticipated maturity: Now–
          2000. Last tasted, 9/87.

1980 —One-dimensional, this wine has a spicy, light intensity, dull bouquet, mal-
•   nourished flavors, and a short, acidic finish. It needs to be drunk. Anticipated
69   maturity: Now–may be in decline. Last tasted, 11/86.

1979 —The 1979 is another full-flavored, robust wine from Haut-Bages-Libéral.
•   Quite dark ruby, with an appealing ripe cassis, spicy bouquet, and a full-
83   bodied, meaty texture, this wine has high acidity and enough tannin to warrant

cellaring. Neither refined nor elegant, it is robust, rustic, and straightforward. Anticipated maturity: Now. Last tasted, 2/87.

1978—A solid wine, but given the vintage, it is a bit of a disappointment. Dark
• ruby, with a stemmy, smoky, somewhat burnt bouquet, the wine is weedy
70 and herbaceous on the palate, with annoyingly high acidity in the finish. The wine's balance is suspect. Anticipated maturity: Now. Last tasted, 6/86.

1976—The 1976 is a notable success in this mixed vintage. Haut-Bages-Libéral is
• fully mature yet will hold for another 3–4 years. Dark ruby, with an amber
84 edge, this forceful, spicy, cedary, black currant–scented wine has surprising concentration for the vintage, as well as a juicy, rich, fruity texture. Anticipated maturity: Now. Last tasted, 12/88.

1975—This estate's moderate to inexpensive wines can turn out to be good surprises.
• The 1975 Haut-Bages-Libéral has always been a powerful, concentrated,
88 muscular wine. It still possesses an opaque dark ruby/garnet color, followed by a moderately intense nose of road tar, herbs, cedar, truffles, and black fruit that is somewhat dominated by the more earthy/animal side. Full bodied, coarse, and rustic, revealing exciting levels of extract, this wine will probably never come into total harmony. Nevertheless, it exhibits plenty of richness, intensity, and personality. Drink it now and over the next 15+ years. Last tasted, 12/95.

1974—Thin, hollow, and harsh on the palate, this wine lacks fruit and charm.
• Anticipated maturity: Now–probably in serious decline. Last tasted, 3/79.
55

1970—Dark ruby, with a spicy, vegetal aroma of celery and cloves, this wine tastes
• out of balance, with an emerging flavor of herbal tea. Drink up. Anticipated
70 maturity: Now–probably in serious decline. Last tasted, 4/77.

HAUT-BATAILLEY   VERY GOOD

Classification: Fifth-growth in 1855
Location of vineyards: Pauillac
Owner: Madame Brest-Borie (sister of Jean-Eugène Borie)
Administrators: J.-E. and François-Xavier Borie
Address: 33250 Pauillac
Mailing address: c/o J.-E. Borie S.A., 33250 Pauillac
Telephone: 33 5 56 59 05 20; telefax: 33 5 56 59 27 37
Visits: By appointment only
Contact: J.-E. Borie S.A. at above telephone and fax numbers

VINEYARDS (red)
Surface area: 49 acres
Average age of vines: 28 years
Blend: 65% Cabernet Sauvignon, 25% Merlot, 10% Cabernet Franc

Density of plantation: 10,000 vines per hectare
Average yields (over the last 5 years): 45 hectoliters per hectare
Total average annual production: 900 hectoliters

GRAND VIN (red)
Brand name: Château Haut-Batailley
Appellation: Pauillac
Mean annual production: 100,000 bottles
Upbringing: Grapes are picked manually and totally destemmed.
Fermentations occur in temperature-controlled stainless-steel tanks for
16–20 days. Wines are aged for 16–20 months in oak casks, 30%–40%
of which are new. They are fined and undergo a light filtration before
bottling.

SECOND WINE
Brand name: Château La Tour d'Aspic

Evaluation of present classification: Should be maintained
Plateau of maturity: 4–15 years following the vintage

Haut-Batailley is not one of the better-known estates in Pauillac. The vineyard is managed by the reputable and well-known Jean-Eugène Borie, who
lives at Ducru-Beaucaillou in St.-Julien, and also owns Grand-Puy-Lacoste.
He, along with one of his sons, Xavier, oversees this property, which is owned
by his sister. Perhaps the reasons for obscurity within the Pauillac firmament
are the modest production, the lack of a château on the estate (the wine is
made at Borie's La Couronne estate), and secluded location on the edge of a
forest, far away from the Gironde River.

Recent vintages of Haut-Batailley have demonstrated the full potential of
the property under the expert winemaking team of Borie and his son. However, the wines of this estate have not always been the model of consistency
one would expect. In general, the weakness tends toward lightness and excessive softness in style. Most wines of Haut-Batailley are fully mature long
before their first decade ends, an anomaly for a Pauillac. Nevertheless, recent
vintages, particularly the 1996 and 1995, have shown greater concentration
and grip than before. However, I tend to think of Haut-Batailley as having
more of a St.-Julien personality than that of a true Pauillac. That is ironic
given the fact that this estate was created in 1942, when it was severed from
the original vineyard of Batailley—irrefutably a classic Pauillac in both taste
and character.

VINTAGES

1997—This seductive, low-acid, soft Pauillac reveals a dark ruby color, roasted herb
•   and black currant-scented aromas, round, medium-bodied, plush flavors, no
86–   aggressiveness to its tannin, and a flat, easy finish. It should be drunk during
87   its first 7–8 years of life. Last tasted, 3/98.

1996—While this may be the most impressive Haut-Batailley I have ever tasted, I
•   am reluctant to go out on a limb and give this wine a higher rating until I can
89–   taste it a few more times from both cask and bottle. The wine exhibits a dense
91   purple color, as well as a wonderfully sweet, classic Pauillac nose of black
currants and cigar box notes. Powerful for Haut-Batailley (normally a light,
elegant, supple Pauillac), the 1996 possesses intense fruit, medium to full
body, ripe tannin, and a surprisingly long, layered finish. This appears to be
a classic and may merit an outstanding score. Anticipated maturity: 2003–
2015. Last tasted, 3/98.

1995—Silky, sexy, supple, and altogether a gorgeous effort from Haut-Batailley, the
•   1995 is a medium-bodied, seamless, beautifully pure Pauillac with gobs of
89   black currant fruit intermixed with smoke, vanilla, and lead pencil. Already
approachable, it promises to become even better over the next 10–12 years.
A very hedonistic wine. Last tasted, 11/97.

1994—Following some mediocre performances from cask, the 1994 has turned out to
•   be better in bottle. A dark ruby color is followed by a spicy, moderately tannic,
86   well-concentrated, elegant wine that reveals some tannin, yet copious quantities of fruit. It should be drunk between 2000 and 2008. Last tasted, 1/97.

1993—An herbaceous, tobacco, weedy, cassis-scented nose jumps from the glass of
•   this medium-bodied, dark ruby–colored wine. The ideal picnic wine, the soft,
85   round 1993 Haut-Batailley should be drunk over the next 5–6 years. Last
tasted, 1/97.

1992—Fortunately, Haut-Batailley's 1992 has put on weight and is now revealing
•   more fruit in its light- to medium-bodied, supple, up-front style. Low in
81   acidity with some oak apparent, this wine should be drunk over the next 3–6
years. Last tasted, 11/94.

1991—Haut-Batailley's 1991 is a far more interesting, complete wine than the light,
•   supple, diluted 1992. The 1991 exhibits attractive berry fruit aromas, good
84   ripeness, medium body, and moderate tannin in the finish. The only danger
is that the fruit may dry out before the tannin melts away. Drink it over the
next 5–7 years. Last tasted, 3/95.

1990—The 1990 offers a forward, smoky, sweet oaky nose intertwined with bold and
•   lavish aromas of black currants. Medium bodied, with low acidity, light tan-
88   nins, and layers of ripe fruit, this finesse-styled wine should provide superlative drinking for more than a decade. It is the finest Haut-Batailley since
1982. Last tasted, 1/93.

1989—The 1989 Haut-Batailley has a gorgeous amount of up-front, satiny fruit and
•   is lush and ripe as well as long. The palate impression is almost one of sweet,
87   jammy fruit because of its superrichness. Anticipated maturity: Now–2006.
Last tasted, 1/93.

1988—The 1988 Haut-Batailley is a lightweight, lean, closed, hard-edged wine that
•   lacks charm and finesse. The tannin level appears excessive for the fruit
83   component. Anticipated maturity: Now. Last tasted, 1/93.

1987—Far more flattering to taste than the 1988, Haut-Batailley has turned in a
•   respectable performance in 1987. The wine is round, agreeably fruity, spicy,
82   and charming. It should be drunk over the next 3–4 years. Anticipated
       maturity: Now. Last tasted, 4/90.

1986—After tasting this wine several times out of cask, I had believed that
•   the 1986 Haut-Batailley was one of the finest wines made at this
84   estate in more than a decade. However, three tastings from the bot-
       tle have revealed a wine that is attractive but does not have the depth
       or aging potential that I originally thought. It is atypically supple
       and silky for a 1986, with a pleasing currant fruitiness married nicely
       to toasty oak. It is medium bodied but seems to fall off on the palate,
       revealing a diffuse character. Anticipated maturity: Now. Last tasted,
       6/90.

1985—The 1985 is a soft, agreeable, elegantly wrought wine that is fruity, medium
•   bodied, and tasty but likely to be short-lived. Anticipated maturity: Now. Last
85   tasted, 3/89.

1984—Aged aromas of tea are followed by an adequately fruity wine that is light and
•   shallow. The 1984 Haut-Batailley should be drunk up. Anticipated maturity:
74   Now. Last tasted, 6/88.

1983—An indifferent vintage for Haut-Batailley, the wine exhibits youthful, dark
•   ruby color, attractive, fat, soft flavors, moderate tannins, and an unusual
82   dryness on the palate. It has never tasted harmonious. Anticipated maturity:
       Now. Last tasted, 3/89.

1982—I may be underrating this graceful, stylish, fully mature Pauillac. An attrac-
•   tive cedary, curranty nose jumps from a glass of this restrained but beautifully
89   pure, silky-textured, well-balanced wine. There is not a hard edge to be
       found, making for an even more seductive mouthful of wine. Drink it over the
       next 7–8 years. Last tasted, 9/95.

1981—This is one of my favorite Haut-Batailleys between 1971 and 1981. Silky on
•   the palate and quite perfumed, with a pronounced oaky bouquet, this velvety,
85   round, pleasant wine is quite delicious. It has matured rapidly. Anticipated
       maturity: Now. Last tasted, 2/88.

1979—Lacking depth and concentration, this light- to medium-ruby-colored wine
•   has a pleasant, round, supple texture, medium body, and a light finish. Antici-
76   pated maturity: Now. Last tasted, 3/87.

1978—A very charming, supple wine that is a delight to drink now, the 1978
•   Haut-Batailley is a straightforward, effusively fruity wine, with a nice touch
82   of spicy oak, light tannins, and a warm, round finish. Anticipated maturity:
       Now. Last tasted, 4/84.

1976—Fully mature with soft, supple, rather modest flavors, low acidity, an amber/
•   ruby color, and a short finish. Drink immediately! Anticipated maturity: Now—
74   may be in decline. Last tasted, 9/80.

1975 — The astringency of the 1975 vintage has given this wine atypical backbone
• and firmness, especially for a Haut-Batailley. A dark ruby color with just a
81 trace of amber is followed by a wine that has a ripe, plummy, open-knit
bouquet dominated by the smell of cedar and herbs. Medium bodied, with
moderate tannins and adequate depth and texture, this is a dull 1975. Anticipated maturity: Now. Last tasted, 10/88.

1973 — Shallow, watery, and now quite decrepit, this wine was at its meager best in
• 1978. It is of little interest now. Last tasted, 6/86.
64

1970 — The 1970 is a topflight effort for Haut-Batailley and a wine that behaves in
• personality and character like a true Pauillac rather than a St.-Julien. Rather
87 rich and full for Haut-Batailley, with a good, firm underpinning of tannins
still evident, this dark ruby wine has a complex bouquet and fine long finish.
Anticipated maturity: Now. Last tasted, 10/83.

1966 — Solid, firm, true in style to the 1966 vintage, Haut-Batailley has evolved
• slowly and is presently at its apogee. A modest bouquet of spices and black
84 currant fruit is quite attractive. It is medium bodied with good, rather than
excellent, concentration. The finish is solid and a bit tough. Anticipated
maturity: Now. Last tasted, 4/82.

1962 — This moderately fruity wine has soft, round, easygoing flavors, a good finish,
• and a fully developed bouquet. It has been fully mature for over a decade.
84 Drink up! Anticipated maturity: Now—may be in decline. Last tasted, 3/83.

1961 — In the context of the vintage's great reputation, this wine tastes atypical and
• comparable to the style of the 1962. Soft, ripe, spicy fruit on the nose reveals
84 full maturity. However, the intense ripeness that exists in so many 1961s is
not present in Haut-Batailley. Soft, round, plump, fruity flavors are overlaid
with oak in this medium-bodied wine. Drink up. Anticipated maturity: Now.
Last tasted, 7/83.

LAFITE-ROTHSCHILD   OUTSTANDING

Classification: First-growth in 1855
Location of vineyards: Pauillac and St.-Estèphe
Owner: Domaines Barons de Rothschild
Address: 33250 Pauillac, France
Mailing address: 33, rue de la Baume, 75008 Paris
Telephone: 33 1 53 89 78 00; telefax: 33 1 53 89 78 01
Visits: By appointment only
Contact: Domaines Barons de Rothschild at above telephone and fax
numbers

VINEYARDS (red)
Surface area: 247 acres
Average age of vines: 38 years

Blend: 70% Cabernet Sauvignon, 25% Merlot, 3% Cabernet Franc, 2% Petit Verdot
Density of plantation: 8,500 vines per hectare
Average yields (over the last 5 years): 50 hectoliters per hectare
Total average annual production: 40,000 cases

GRAND VIN (red)
Brand name: Château Lafite-Rothschild
Appellation: Pauillac
Mean annual production: 18,000–20,000 cases
Upbringing: Harvesting is done by hand. Fermentations occur in stainless-steel and wooden temperature-controlled vats, with *remontages* twice a day, and last between 18 and 25 days (temperatures go up to 30 degrees centigrade). Malolactics occur in vats, and wines are then transferred to new oak casks for 20 months. They are racked every 3 months, fined (with egg whites), and "slightly" filtered prior to bottling.

SECOND WINE
Brand name: Carruades de Lafite
Average annual production: 20,000 cases

Evaluation of present classification: Should be maintained
Plateau of maturity: 10–35 or more years following the vintage

NOTE: One-third of the total production is usually selected as Lafite, 40% as Carruades, and the rest is sold as generic Pauillac through their distribution system.

Lafite has their own *tonnellerie,* where they make their casks.

SELECTIONS: As for many other châteaux, all cuvées are tasted at the time of the assemblage, to determine those that are good enough to go into the grand vin. Since they know those *terroirs* and older vines that usually make Lafite, there is a double check after the blind tasting to verify whether the cuvées have been showing as they should. Whenever there is a doubt about a particular cuvée, it is eliminated from the grand vin. Some *vin de presse* can sometimes be included in the grand vin, up to 8%–14%.

Bordeaux's most famous property and wine, Lafite-Rothschild, with its elegant, undersized, and understated label has become a name synonymous with wealth, prestige, history, respect, and wines of remarkable longevity.

While the vintages since 1975 have witnessed the production of a succession of superlative Lafites, the record of Lafite between 1961 and 1974 was one of surprising mediocrity for a first-growth. It has always remained a mystery to me why more wine critics did not cry foul after tasting some of the Lafite wines made during this period. The official line from the château has always been that the wines were made in such a light, elegant style that they were overmatched in blind tastings by bigger, more robust wines. Certainly such things do happen, but the mediocrity of Lafite was particularly evidenced by wines from very fine vintages—1966, 1970, 1971—that were surprisingly deficient in color, excessively dry and overly oaked, and abnormally high in acidity. Several vintages—1969, 1971, 1974—were complete failures yet released for high prices under the Lafite name.

The reasons for such occurrences are not likely ever to be revealed by the Rothschild family, but given the great record of successes since 1975, the problems in the sixties and early seventies seem related to the following. The absentee owners lived in Paris and only casually supervised the goings-on at Lafite. Certainly the management of Lafite since 1975 has been diligent by a concerned and committed Eric de Rothschild. Additionally, the wine at Lafite was kept too long in oak barrels. In the past, the wine often aged a minimum of 32–36 months in oak barrels, whereas now 24–30 months is maximum. This change has undoubtedly caused Lafite to taste fruitier and fresher. Third, the current winemaking staff at Lafite consciously pick the grapes later to obtain greater ripeness and lower acidity in their wines.* Finally, Lafite-Rothschild is being bottled over a shorter period of time. There have been reports that Lafite often dragged out the bottling operation over as many as 8–12 months. If true, then more than acceptable levels of bottle variation would exist.

Regardless of the record of the immediate past, Lafite-Rothschild is now producing great wines, and the turnabout in quality clearly occurred with the magnificent 1975. One could successfully argue that since 1981, Lafite-Rothschild has produced one of the Médoc's best wines in years such as 1981, 1982, 1983, 1986, 1987, 1988, 1990, 1995, and 1996.

VINTAGES

1997—Lafite's harvest occurred between September 8 (beginning with the Merlot)
•
90–
93
and October 2. For some Cabernet Sauvignon parcels, there were an exceptional 135 days (the norm being 105–110 days) between the flowering and harvest. This estate, which made a profoundly great 1996, utilized only 28% of its harvest for the 1997 *grand vin*. Moreover, the selection for the second wine, Carruades, was also severe. The 1997 Lafite-Rothschild may turn out

---

* The selection process is undoubtedly more severe than in the past. In the abundant vintages of the late eighties, Lafite routinely eliminated half their crop. Since 1990 it has not been unusual for Lafite to eliminate at least a whopping 60% of the harvest, which is either sold off in bulk or relegated to the second wine.

to be a modern-day replay of the glorious 1976. Complex, with considerable finesse, elegance, and a sexy, approachable style, this dark ruby/purple-colored, medium-bodied wine already reveals copious quantities of the tell-tale Lafite scents of mineral, lead pencil, and cedar. This rich yet graceful Lafite displays no trace of aggressiveness or hardness. It is an approachable, lush wine that will evolve quickly, yet keep for 15–20 years. Last tasted, 3/98.

1996— This is an extraordinary Lafite-Rothschild, possibly the château's finest wine
•   since the 1986 and 1982, but it will test purchasers' patience given its
94–   backwardness. Only 38 percent of the crop was deemed good enough to use
96   in the final blend, which comprises 83% Cabernet Sauvignon, 8% Merlot, 8% Cabernet Franc, and 1% Petit Verdot. The wine boasts an opaque purple color, as well as a fabulous nose of tobacco, lead pencil, minerals, and red and black currant fruit. On the palate, this is a powerful Lafite, yet it has not lost any of its quintessential elegant personality. Medium to full bodied, with outstanding ripeness, layers of fruit, high tannin (sweet rather than astringent), and an exceptionally long, well-balanced finish, this wine will require a minimum of 10–15 years of cellaring. Anticipated maturity: 2010–2040. Last tasted, 3/98.

1995— The 1995 Lafite-Rothschild (only one-third of the harvest made it into the
•   final blend) is a blend of 75% Cabernet Sauvignon, 17% Merlot, and 8%
95   Cabernet Franc. The wine was showing spectacularly well when I tasted it in November 1997. It exhibits a dark ruby purple color, and a sweet, powdered mineral, smoky, weedy, cassis-scented nose. Beautiful sweetness of fruit is present in this medium-bodied, tightly knit, but gloriously pure, well-delineated Lafite. The 1995 is not as powerful or as massive as the 1996, but it is beautifully made with outstanding credentials, in addition to remarkable promise. Anticipated maturity: 2008–2028. Last tasted, 11/97.

1994— Made from nearly 100% Cabernet Sauvignon, this dark ruby/purple–colored
•   wine is stubbornly backward, unappealing, and severe and astringent on the
90+?   palate. There is plenty of weight, and the wine possesses admirable purity, with no suggestion of herbaceousness or underripe fruit, but the wine's personality refuses to be coaxed from the glass. The 1994 Lafite may turn out to be austere and disappointing flavor-wise, but possesses a fabulous set of aromatics (does that sound reminiscent of the 1961, another Lafite that was primarily Cabernet Sauvignon?). I am not giving up on this wine, but purchasers should be willing to wait 15–20 years before pulling a cork. Anticipated maturity: 2010–2030. Last tasted, 1/97.

1993— A successful wine for Lafite, this dark ruby/purple–colored 1993 is tightly
•   wound, medium bodied, with a closed set of aromatics that reluctantly reveal
88   hints of sweet black currant fruit, weedy tobacco, and lead pencil scents. Polished and elegant, with Lafite's noble restraint, this is an excellent, classy, slightly austere wine. Anticipated maturity: 2004–2020. Last tasted, 1/97.

1992— In 1992 only 36% of the harvest was utilized, resulting in a deeply colored
•   wine with a nearly exceptional cedary, chocolatey, cassis character, medium
89   body, surprisingly concentrated flavors, as well as the classic Lafite aromatic

profile. Readers should take the opportunity to experience Lafite's finesse in a softer, more precocious vintage. The 1992 Lafite should drink well in 2–3 years and should last for 12–20. Last tasted, 11/94.

1991 — Lafite's light-bodied 1991 possesses moderate ruby color, a solid inner core
•   of fruit, as well as potentially excessive tannin for its size and constitution.
86?   The wine exhibits Lafite's subtle personality with a leafy, tobacco, lead pencil nose intertwined with sweet aromas of cassis. Dry, austere, and lacking length, it should turn out to be a good representation of Lafite-Rothschild in this so-so year. Last tasted, 1/94.

1990 — The 1990 is ripe, rich, and well textured, but mouth-searing tannin and a
•   closed personality make it hard to fully assess. The wine possesses excellent
92+   richness, a hint of the unmistakable Lafite perfume of minerals, cedar, lead pencil, and red fruits, medium to full body, moderate weight, admirable richness and overall balance, and a tough finish. Give it a decade of cellaring to shed some tannin and evolve; it may be a 40- to 50-year Lafite. As outstanding as I believe it will ultimately turn out to be, I do not think the 1990 Lafite will ever match the sheer class, quality, and complexity of the 1988, 1986, and 1982. Anticipated maturity: 2006–2035. Last tasted, 11/96.

1989 — The 1989 Lafite is outstanding, but closed, with the tannin more elevated,
•   and the wine so stubbornly reticent as to make evaluation almost impossible.
90+   Lafite's 1989 was far easier to taste and understand several years ago. It appears to have gone completely to sleep. This medium ruby–colored, medium-bodied wine reveals new oak in the nose and a spicy finish. It is a quintessentially elegant, restrained, understated style of Lafite. Anticipated maturity: 2006–2025. Last tasted, 11/96.

1988 — Broodingly backward and in need of considerable bottle age, the 1988 is a
•   classic expression of Lafite. This deeply colored wine exhibits the telltale
94   Lafite bouquet of cedar, subtle herbs, dried pit fruits, minerals, and cassis. Extremely concentrated, with brilliantly focused flavors and huge tannins, this backward yet impressively endowed Lafite-Rothschild may well turn out to be the wine of the vintage! Anticipated maturity: 2000–2035. Last tasted, 10/94.

1987 — I would not be surprised to see this wine fill out with several additional years
•   in the bottle, largely because Lafite is a notoriously bad performer in the first
87   few years after bottling. Out of cask, the 1987 was the most complex wine I tasted from this vintage, but now the nose seems only a fraction of what it was from cask. The lead pencil, vanillin-scented, leafy, cedary bouquet is just beginning to emerge. In the mouth, the wine is light, displaying a soft, supple texture, some acidity, but little tannin. It will probably improve and may ultimately merit a higher score. Anticipated maturity: Now–1999. Last tasted, 10/90.

1986 — The prodigious 1986 possesses outstanding richness, a deep color, medium
•   body, a graceful, harmonious texture, and superb length. The penetrating
100   fragrance of cedar, chestnuts, minerals, and rich fruit is a hallmark of this wine. Powerful, dense, rich, and tannic, as well as medium to full bodied,

with awesome extraction of fruit, this Lafite has immense potential. Patience is still required. Anticipated maturity: 2000–2030. Last tasted, 4/96.

1985—The 1985 Lafite should be better, but for followers of fashion, its star-studded
•   price will fetch you a moderately intense, cedary, woody, herb-and-leather-
87   scented bouquet, and attractive, very forward, developed flavors displayed in a medium-bodied format. The finish is softly tannic, and after a pensive sip, one is likely to ask, Is this all there is? Anticipated maturity: Now–2008. Last tasted, 3/91.

1984—The personality of Lafite comes through in the 1984 vintage. An elegant
•   bouquet of herbaceous, cedary fruit is first class. New oak dominates the
84   palate, and some hard tannins exhibit a dryness at the finish. The 1984 is a light but well-balanced wine. Anticipated maturity: Now. Last tasted, 1/88.

1983—Finally, the 1983 Lafite is beginning to shed its tannin. The wine exhibits a
•   deep ruby/garnet color with only a slight lightening at the edge. The intoxicat-
93   ingly perfumed nose of lead pencil, *pain grillé*, red and black fruits, minerals, and roasted herbs is provocative. In the mouth, this wine displays considerable body for a Lafite, plenty of power, and a fleshy, rich, sweet midpalate. Long, elegant, plump, and surprisingly fleshy, this outstanding example of Lafite seems largely forgotten given the number of high-quality vintages during the golden decade of the eighties. Anticipated maturity: Now–2030. Last tasted, 3/97.

1982—Still extraordinarily backward and youthful, this large-scaled (massive by
•   Lafite's standards) wine should prove to be the greatest Lafite made after the
100   1953 and 1959. It continues to offer an exceptionally intense, compelling bouquet of herbs, black currants, vanilla, lead pencil, and cedar. The wine reveals considerable tannin as well as amazing, atypical power and concentration for Lafite. The hallmark elegance of this wine has not been compromised because of the vintage's tendency to turn out powerful and unctuously textured, thick, juicy wines. Rich, full, and still youthful and unyielding, this should prove to be a fabulous Lafite-Rothschild—but only for those readers prepared to wait until 2003–2005. It should easily last through the first 3 decades of the next century. A potential 100-point wine! Last tasted, 9/95.

1981—This wine is close to full maturity, but it is capable of holding for another 2
•   decades. It reveals the classic Lafite bouquet of red and black fruits, cedar,
91   fruitcake, and tobaccolike aromas. In the mouth, this medium ruby/garnet–colored wine displays a delicacy of fruit and sweet attack, but subtle, well-defined flavors ranging from tobacco, cigar box, cedar, and fruitcake. This is a savory, soft Lafite-Rothschild that is pleasing to both the intellect and the palate. Anticipated maturity: Now–2018. Last tasted, 3/97.

1980—A lightweight, agreeable wine from Lafite, the 1980 has a moderately intense
•   aroma of cassis and fresh tobacco and soft, charming flavors. A success for
83   the vintage. Anticipated maturity: Now. Last tasted, 6/87.

1979—I over-rated this wine when it was young and have not been as pleased with
•   its evolution in the bottle. The wine has retained a cool-climate high acidity,
87   giving it a more compressed personality than I had envisioned. The color

remains a dark ruby/garnet, but the nose has taken on a more vegetal, earthy note to go along with the new oak and sweet red and black currant personality. The wine's crisp acidity keeps its tannic edge aggressive. There is already some amber at the edge of the wine's color. Anticipated maturity: Now–2012. Last tasted, 10/97.

1978—This wine is distinctively herbaceous and cedary, with surprisingly high
•   acidity and aggressive tannin in the finish. Its medium garnet color and
87   smoky, roasted herb-scented nose are followed by a wine with good fruit on the attack, but an angular, sharp finish. The wine appears to be closer to full maturity than its younger sibling, the 1979. Anticipated maturity: Now–2010. Last tasted, 10/97.

1976—The 1976 Lafite clearly stands far above the crowd in this vintage. A beautiful
•   bouquet of seductive cedarwood, spices, and ripe fruit precedes a very con-
93   centrated, darkly colored wine, with great length and texture. Some amber is just beginning to appear at the edge. The 1976 has turned out to be the best Lafite of the seventies. It is gorgeous to drink at present. Anticipated maturity: Now. Last tasted, 9/96.

1975—Why is it that Lafite-Rothschild is often so distressingly irregular from bottle
•   to bottle? Much of the inconsistency during the sixties and mid-seventies can
92?   be explained by the relaxed bottling schedule, which saw the wines blended and bottled over an unusually long period (12+ months, compared with the estate's modern-day bottling operation, which never takes longer than 2–4 weeks). I have had some great bottles of the 1975 Lafite, most of them in the wine's first 15 years of life. Since then I have seen wines that appeared cooked and stewed, with a Barolo tarlike aroma, as well as others with the classic Pauillac, lead pencil, cedar, cassis, and tobacco aromatic dimension. The 1975 is a powerful Lafite, and troublesome bottles tend to reveal more tannin and funkiness than others, which have a roasted character, combined with a gravelly, mineral underpinning. As this wine has aged, it appears to be less of a sure bet. In most cases it has been an outstanding wine, as the bottle tasted in December 1995 suggested. The aromatics indicate the wine is fully mature, but the tough tannin level clearly underscores the dark side of the 1975 vintage. This wine will undoubtedly last for another 30+ years, but I am not sure the fruit will hold. It is a perplexing wine that may still turn out to be an exceptional Lafite. In contrast, the 1976 has always been much more forward and consistent. However, I would still take the 1975 over the over-rated, mediocre 1970, 1966, and 1961. Last tasted, 6/98.

1974—It was very difficult to make good wine in 1974, but certainly a first-growth is
•   expected to make a strict selection of its best lots and sell only the best. This
56   wine is browning badly, has a tired, stale, flat taste, and is inexcusably diluted and very short and thin on the palate. Quite poor. Last tasted, 11/82.

1973—One of the charming 1973s, this light, somewhat watery, thin wine has Lafite's
•   classic perfumed bouquet, short, compact, agreeable flavors, and little tannin.
72   That was in 1980, the last time I tasted it. Anticipated maturity: Now–probably in serious decline. Last tasted, 12/80.

1971—Another disappointment for Lafite, the 1971 has always tasted flat, is quite
  •   brown in color, with a stewed, slightly dirty, rusty, nondescript bouquet sug-
 60   gesting a poor *élevage* (the French term for bringing up the wine). Now close
         to its demise, this wine is of no value except to those who care only for labels.
         Last tasted, 11/82.

1970—Lafite's 1970 has consistently left me disappointed. The wine is beginning to
  •   reveal some of the classic Lafite nose of cedar, lead pencil, dried red and
 85   black fruits, and spice. The wine's bouquet would merit an outstanding rating
         if it were slightly more intense. On the palate, the annoyingly high acidity
         continues to be problematic, largely because the wine does not possess the
         flesh, fat, and extract to cover its angular structure. I have had some sour,
         acidic bottles of the 1970 Lafite, but this offering had better balance than
         previous examples. This is a wine that has far greater value on the auction
         block than on the dinner table. Last tasted, 6/96.

1969—The 1969 Lafite has been consistently unusual to smell, with a cooked, burnt
  •   aroma, short flavors that suggest coffee and herbs, and a hollow framework.
 62   This is a poorly made, ungracious wine that is unpalatable. Last tasted,
         11/78.

1967—A vintage in which Lafite could certainly have done better. Light ruby with
  •   browning very much in evidence, this wine in the mid-1970s had a fragrant,
 72   spicy, charming bouquet, easygoing, simple fruity flavors, and light tannins.
         Now it is quite tired, with old, faded, fruit flavors. Drink up! Anticipated
         maturity: Now–probably in serious decline. Last tasted, 12/80.

1966—With a light to medium ruby/garnet color, this wine exhibited a classy, weedy,
  •   herbal, Cabernet-dominated nose, soft, washed-out flavors, and little body
 84   and length. It is also beginning to dry out. I suppose if one were to taste a
         30-year-old Cabernet from Monterey County, California, it might reveal simi-
         lar characteristics. The 1966 Lafite-Rothschild has consistently been a major
         disappointment from what is an irregular but very good vintage. Last tasted,
         12/95.

1964—Given the overblown praise for the 1961, 1966, and 1970 Lafites, it seems as
  •   though the 1964, a wine obviously made after the rains, has taken more
 80   criticism than it deserves. Not that it is sublime or profound, but it has
         consistently shown a chunky, fruity character and a whiff of some of Lafite's
         fabulous bouquet. Anticipated maturity: Now. Last tasted, 7/82.

1962—The 1962 Lafite-Rothschild exhibited the château's telltale cedary, cigar box–
  •   like, understated bouquet, and light-bodied, delicate flavors. Although it is
 88   soft, round, and delicious, like so many Lafites, its stiff price always makes
         me think that the quality of Lafite is rarely proportional to the wine's cost.
         Last tasted, 12/95.

1961—This wine has a phenomenal reputation. However, I have now tasted the wine
  •   on 8 separate occasions where I found it to be shockingly light, too acidic,
 84   disturbingly austere, and surprisingly ungenerous for a 1961. Moreover, re-
         cent tastings have suggested that the wine was clearly drying out. The color
         is light ruby with a brownish cast. The wine does have the penetrating "cigar

box" Lafite bouquet, yet even it seems shy, given the legendary status of this wine. Lacking the weight, concentration, and majesty of the great 1961s, this is a wine that far too many writers have euphemistically said "needed time" or was "elegant" or "not properly understood," when they should have used the words "overrated" and "disappointing." In the context of the vintage and the estate of Lafite-Rothschild, it represents an indifferent winemaking effort. Caveat emptor. Anticipated maturity: Now–2000. Last tasted, 12/89.

ANCIENT VINTAGES

The 1959 (99 points; last tasted 10/94) is unquestionably the greatest Lafite-Rothschild that has approached full maturity. It remains to be seen whether vintages such as 1982, 1986, and 1990 will reach a similar height. The superaromatic bouquet of flowers, black truffles, cedar, lead pencil, and red fruits is followed by one of the most powerful and concentrated Lafites I have tasted. Medium to full bodied, velvety textured, rich, and pure, it is a testament to what this great estate can achieve when it hits the mark. This youthful wine will last for another 30 or more years. On two occasions I rated the 1953 100 and on another occasion nearly perfect. According to some old-timers, the wine has been fully mature for almost 30 years. It possesses that extraordinary Lafite fragrance of minerals, lead pencil, cedar, and spice. It is velvety textured, wonderfully round, and sweet, but so well delineated and balanced. It is best purchased today in magnum and larger formats unless you can be assured the wine came from a cold cellar and has not been traded frequently.

Most vintages of the nineteenth century have tended to be quite exhilarating, in contrast with most Lafites of the twentieth century. Consider the following. The 1832 Lafite-Rothschild (76 points; last tasted 9/95) offered a cigar box-, iced tea-, herbal-scented nose, fragile, light-bodied, round, diluted flavors, and a quick, hard finish. The fact that this wine still retained some fruit was remarkable.

Michael Broadbent has long claimed that the 1848 Lafite-Rothschild was one of the great wines of the last century. In his last tasting in 1988, he awarded it 5 stars. Seven years later it was again extraordinary! (I rated it 96 points in December, 1995.) The color was light ruby/garnet, but the exceptionally penetrating bouquet of sweet cedar, ripe, jammy fruit, earth, fruitcake, and lead pencil was followed by a remarkably dense yet elegant wine with exceptional expansion and a velvety texture. It was wonderfully concentrated, sweet, and ripe, with neither acidity nor tannin showing through the wine's quantity of fruit. It could easily pass for a 45–50-year-old wine. Quite stunning, this is truly a legendary wine with an unmistakable Lafite character!

The amber/ruby–colored 1864 Lafite-Rothschild (92 points; last tasted 9/95) possessed a Mouton-like nose of cedar and cassis, accompanied by surprising intensity and ripeness. In the mouth, the wine revealed remarkable freshness, sweet fruit, surprisingly high alcohol, and wonderful, exotic, Asian spice, tobacco, and Graves-like flavors. There was surprising power and intensity in the finish of this totally delicious, compelling wine! The 1865 Lafite-Rothschild (98 points; last tasted 9/95) was otherworldly. The first word I wrote after smelling it was "Wow!" The color was a medium garnet, with considerable rust and orange at the edge. The wine possessed an extraordinary fragrance, great density, and fabulous intensity of chocolate, herb, and cedarlike flavors with a wonderful, sweet, inner core of opulent fruit. The finish was long and velvety, with no hard edges. It is hard to imagine a 130-year-old wine (made when American Civil War adversaries Robert E. Lee and Ulysses S. Grant were alive) tasting so extraordinary, but I was there —I saw it, I smelled it, I tasted it, and I drank it! Unreal!

After two disappointing tastings of the immortal 1870 Lafite-Rothschild (96 points; last tasted 9/95), the Hardy Rodenstock tasting in Munich in September 1995 finally provided me a provocative, compelling, profound bottle of this legendary wine. The color is a healthy dark garnet, and the huge nose of freshly sliced celery, mint, cedar, and cassis unfolded quickly but held in the glass during the 30–40 minutes it remained there before it became just a mere component of my bodily fluids. The wine exhibited sweet fruit, surprising glycerin and opulence for a Lafite, and a sweet, jammy, powerful finish. It is an extraordinary wine!

For all of these superlative wines, my Lafite scorecard is dotted with far more disappointments than successes. The 1950, 1952, and 1955 are uninspiring. The 1957, while not great, is nevertheless surprisingly good (twice I have rated it in the 86–88 range). In the forties, the 1947 is disappointing, the 1949 good but far from profound, and the 1945 excessively astringent and out of balance. Among the ancient vintages, I have very good notes only for one vintage in the thirties (not a good decade for Bordeaux). The 1934 (rated 90), drunk from magnum in 1986, was wonderful.

In April 1991 I had the opportunity to taste (from a friend's cellar in Bordeaux) the 1929, 1928, 1926, and 1924. The wines had been purchased in the thirties and kept in a cold Bordeaux cellar until this tasting. All of them were disappointing, with scores of 59 for the 1929 (faded and sickly), 68 for the 1928 (some elegance, but attenuated and short as well as the only Lafite ever pasteurized), 67 for the 1926 (hard, dried out), and 69 for the 1924 (slightly more freshness than the 1926). Yet I was stunned by the 1921 (93 points; last tasted 9/95). The 1921's garnet color, with considerable amber on the edge, and sweet, over-ripe nose of red and black fruits, cedar, herbs, and spices were followed by a medium-bodied, remarkably well-preserved wine with a roasted character. Some acidity began to appear in the finish as the wine sat in the glass, but this is a sweet, fragrant, delicious Lafite that has probably been fully mature for 40–50 years.

LATOUR   OUTSTANDING

Classification: First-growth 1855
Location of vineyards: Pauillac
Owner: François Pinault
Address: 33250 Pauillac
Telephone: 33 5 56 73 19 80; telefax: 33 5 56 73 19 81
Visits: By appointment only
Contact: Severine Camus

VINEYARDS (red)
Surface area: 160.5 acres (116.1 acres just around the château are called l'Enclos and are included in the grand vin)
Average age of vines: 40 years (l'Enclos) and 37 years (for the rest)
Blend: 80% Cabernet Sauvignon, 15% Merlot, 5% Cabernet Franc and Petit Verdot
Density of plantation: 10,000 vines per hectare
Average yields (over the last 5 years): 45–50 hectoliters per hectare (grand vin) and 55–60 hectoliters per hectare (for the rest)
Total average annual production: 380,000 bottles

GRAND VIN (red)
Brand name: Château Latour
Appellation: Pauillac
Mean annual production: 220,000 bottles
Upbringing: Grapes are hand-picked, totally destemmed, and put into temperature-controlled stainless-steel vats of 200 hectoliters.
Fermentations and *cuvaisons* last 3 weeks, and malolactics occur in vats. After malolactics, the wines are transferred into new oak casks for 20–26 months depending upon the vintage. They are racked every 3 months and fined (with egg whites) during the winter season that just precedes bottling.

SECOND WINE
Brand name: Les Forts de Latour
Average annual production: 140,000 bottles
(Les Forts de Latour is usually composed of 70% Cabernet Sauvignon and 30% Merlot)

THIRD WINE
Brand name: Pauillac
Average annual production: 20,000 bottles
(Designated from those cuvées not deemed of sufficiently good quality to make either the grand vin or Les Forts de Latour)

Evaluation of present classification: Should be maintained
Plateau of maturity: Before 1983, 15–40 years following the vintage;
since 1983, 10–25 years following the vintage

NOTE: The plot of 116 acres just around the château is called l'Enclos.
Planted with old vines, these are replaced only when needed, and it is
this parcel that is the primary component of the grand vin. The harvest is
done in two goes; there is a first *passage de nettoyage* to pick the grapes
from the young vines, which usually go into Les Forts de Latour or
generic Pauillac, and the harvest is completed for the grand vin when the
berries are at perfect maturity.
    Les Forts de Latour is made

1. from young vines of l'Enclos;
2. from the cuvées of l'Enclos that do not seem fit, after tasting, to go into
   the grand vin;
3. from the plots of land outside l'Enclos, called "Comtesse de Lalande,"
   "Petit Batailley," and "Sainte-Anne," some of which have belonged to
   the domaine for more than a century.

Normally Les Forts de Latour is composed of 70% Cabernet Sauvignon
and 30% Merlot, one-third of which comes from the young vines and
two-thirds from the vines outside l'Enclos. These vines were planted in
1964. It is therefore untrue to consider this as a second wine coming
only from young vines. As the vines outside l'Enclos get older, the
quality of Les Forts de Latour is increasing steadily.

Impressively situated on the Pauillac/St.-Julien border, immediately north of
the walled vineyard of Léoville-Las Cases, Latour's vineyard can be easily
spotted from the road because of the creamy-colored, fortress-like tower.
Notably depicted on the wine's label, this formidable tower overlooking the
vineyards and the Gironde River remains from the seventeenth century, when
it was built on the site of a fifteenth-century fortress used by the English to
fend off attacks by pirates.

    Latour is one of a handful of major Bordeaux châteaux to have been
controlled by foreign interests. Between 1963 and 1994, Latour was under
English ownership, but in 1994 François Pinault purchased this estate, re-
turning it to French ownership.

    The wine produced here has been an impeccable and classic model of
consistent excellence, both in great, mediocre, and poor vintages. For that
reason, many have long considered Latour to be the Médoc's finest wine.
Latour's reputation for making Bordeaux's best wine in mediocre or in poor
vintages—such as 1960, 1972, 1974—has been totally justified, although in

the recent poor Bordeaux vintages—1977, 1980, and 1984—Latour's wines were surprisingly light and eclipsed in quality by those of a number of other châteaux. The wine of Latour also has a remarkable record of being a stubbornly slow-developing wine, requiring a good 20–25 years of bottle age to shed its considerable tannic clout and reveal its stunning power, depth, and richness. This style, often referred to by commentators as virile, masculine, and tough, may have undergone a subtle yet very perceptible softening up between 1983 and 1989. This was adamantly denied by the staff at Latour, but my tastings suggest a more gentle and accessible style. Fortunately this ignoble trend was quickly abandoned, as Latour has once again been producing blockbuster wines since 1990.

While the 1982, and to a lesser extent the 1986, are undeniably great Latours, on the whole the estate did not have a distinguished decade. It was no secret that the *cuverie* was too small to handle the gigantic crop sizes of 1983, 1985, and 1986. As a consequence, the fermentation tanks had to be emptied too soon in order to make room for the arriving grapes. The underground cellars and *cuverie* were subsequently enlarged—just in time to handle 1989, the largest vintage ever harvested in Bordeaux. However, an objective tasting analysis of the 1983, 1985, 1988, and 1989 Latours leaves one with the impression that in these years, Latour is a significantly lighter, less powerful and concentrated wine than it was in any decade earlier in this century. The charge cannot be sustained given the Latours produced in 1990, 1994, 1995, and 1996.

Latour remains one of the most concentrated, rich, tannic, and full-bodied wines in the world. When mature, it has a compelling bouquet of fresh walnuts and leather, black currants, and gravelly, mineral scents. On the palate, it can be a wine of extraordinary richness, yet it is never heavy.

VINTAGES

1997—Like so many of the 1997s I tasted, Latour's offering is an extremely evolved,
•   soft, precocious-tasting wine that is easy to comprehend. Latour's dynamic
90–   duo of Frédéric Engerer and Christian Le Sommer suggested that the 1997
92   Latour may evolve along the lines of the brilliant 1967 (one of the two or three finest wines of that vintage, and one that continues to provide immense pleasure at 31 years of age). Latour's 1997 (49% of the production made it into the final blend) is composed of 76% Cabernet Sauvignon, 19% Merlot, 4% Cabernet Franc, and 1% Petit Verdot. The harvest began early (September 8) and proceeded intermittently over the following two weeks, ending on September 25. In contrast to the blockbuster 1996, the 1997 is an expressive, open-knit wine that is already fun to drink. This deep ruby/purple–colored claret offers up evolved aromas of cranberry jam intertwined with black currants and Latour's telltale, intense minerality. By Latour's standards it is neither immense nor massive, but, rather, elegant with a sweet, ripe attack,

velvety tannin, medium body, and a round, graceful, stylish finish. This beautifully knit, harmonious Latour is already evolved for such a young age. Anticipated maturity: 2002–2018. Last tasted, 3/98.

1996—The 1996 is a fabulous wine that should rival, and (in 15–20 years) possibly
• eclipse the extraordinary 1995. The 1996 Latour is a huge, massive, block-
96– buster example of this wine, the likes of which are distinct and original. The
98+ wine boasts an opaque ruby/purple color, as well as extraordinary, thick, monster-sized fruit, glycerin, and extract on the palate, and a finish that lasts for 40+ seconds. As I indicated last year, 56% of Latour's production went into the 1996, which is a blend of 78% Cabernet Sauvignon, 17% Merlot, and 5% Cabernet Franc. In addition to being a classic Pauillac, it is a textbook Latour, with formidable power, compelling purity, and remarkable presence on the palate. The nose is just beginning to offer some of the mineral, roasted herbs, grilled meats, cassis, and blackberry character of this great first-growth. Full bodied and layered, with amazing power and richness, but no sense of heaviness, this is a wine to buy for your children. Anticipated maturity: 2015–2040. Last tasted, 3/98.

1995—I have been blown away by this wine on recent occasions, and all of my hopes
• for its being a prodigious example of Latour after bottling have proven to be
96+ correct. The wine is a more unctuously textured, sweeter, more accessible Latour than the 1996. Wow! What a fabulous, profound wine this has turned out to be. It is unquestionably one of the great wines of the vintage, and will probably need 10–12 years of cellaring before it can be approached. The wine reveals an opaque purple color, and a knockout nose of chocolate, walnuts, minerals, spice, and blackberry and cassis fruit. Exceptionally full-bodied, with exhilarating levels of glycerin, richness, and personality, this wine, despite its low acidity, possesses extremely high levels of tannin to go along with its equally gargantuan proportions of fruit. It is a fabulous Latour that should age effortlessly for 40–50 years. Last tasted, 11/97.

1994—This is an interesting as well as great vintage for Latour. 1994 possesses an
• atypically high percentage of Merlot (27%) in the final blend. Because of this,
94 the wine appears to have a sweeter, more fleshy texture than is typical for a young Latour, but do not make the mistake of thinking this will be a commer-cially styled, easy to drink wine. It exhibits an opaque dark ruby/purple color and a backward, intense textbook nose of walnut and cassis scents complemented by smoky *pain grillé* notes that build in the glass. This full-bodied, powerful, layered Latour reveals high tannin, but no bitterness or astringency. The superb purity, fabulous precision, and remarkable length should ensure 35–40 years of longevity. Readers will find more fat, flesh, and glycerin than usual for a young Latour (save for such great vintages as 1982 and 1990), but don't be deceived: this wine requires 8–10 years of cellaring. Anticipated maturity: 2005–2035. Last tasted, 1/97.

1993—A terrific wine for the vintage, Latour's 1993 reveals an opaque purple color,
• a backward nose offering scents of cedar, black walnut, cassis, and earth,
90+ medium to full body, gorgeously rich, concentrated fruit, moderately high

tannin (but no astringency), and a sweet, long, powerful finish. The wine does not possess any of the vegetal, green pepper characteristics of the vintage, nor any hint of hollowness or harshness. This wine may prove to merit an even higher rating. Anticipated maturity: 2007–2025. Is this vintage the modern-day clone of the 1967 and 1971? Last tasted, 1/97.

1992 — Only 50% of the 1992 harvest went into the grand vin. The result is a sweet,
●　　　expansive, rich, medium-bodied, surprisingly supple Latour with the telltale
88+　　English walnut-, black currant-, and mineral-scented nose, very good to excellent flavor concentration, low acidity, and moderate tannin in the finish. This is an extremely well-made, approachable style of Latour that should age well for 10–15 years. It may develop even further, thus justifying a higher score. Last tasted, 11/94.

1991 — After Latour's exquisite performance in 1990, the 1991 is somewhat of a
●　　　letdown. Nevertheless, it is a candidate for the wine of the vintage because of
89　　　its concentration and class. After a strict selection, only 11,500 cases were made. The wine offers a dense, dark ruby color and a reticent but promising bouquet of black cherries, cassis, minerals, roasted nuts, spices, and subtle herbs. Medium bodied, with excellent richness, fine glycerin, and aggressive tannin, this ripe, muscular, beefy 1991 needs 5–6 years to shed its tannin; it should last for 15 or more. Last tasted, 1/94.

1990 — There is no doubting the 1990 Latour is a potential candidate for the wine of
●　　　the vintage. It is remarkably youthful, with a deep purple color and full-
98+　　bodied, powerful, massive richness, and everything is held together by high levels of tannin. Fortunately the tannin is sweet and ripe, making evaluation easy. The finish, which lasts for 35–40 seconds, reveals layers of flavor as well as impressive purity. This backward 1990 requires another 7–10 years of cellaring. It is a wine for drinking between 2005 and 2035. Last tasted, 11/96.

1989 — I am still disappointed by the 1989, wondering how this château produced an
●　　　elegant, medium-weight wine that seems atypically restrained for Latour. The
89　　　deep ruby color is followed by a wine with surprisingly high acidity and hard tannin, but not the depth, richness, and power expected from this great estate. This closed wine is admittedly in need of 5–6 years of cellaring, but what is so alarming is its lack of weight, ripeness, and intensity, particularly when compared to the 1990. I suspect there is more than what has been revealed in recent tastings, but this looks to be an excellent as opposed to outstanding wine. In the context of the vintage, it is a disappointment. Last tasted, 11/96.

1988 — The 1988 Latour is deep in color, has a complex bouquet of mineral, hickory
●　　　wood, leafy, and black currant scents, medium body, nicely extracted flavors,
89　　　but ferocious tannins in the finish. Patience will most definitely be required. Developing more richness and character than I had previously anticipated, it is certainly more classic and typical of Latour than several of the property's more recent vintages, such as 1983, 1985, and 1989. Anticipated maturity: 2000–2025. Last tasted, 1/93.

1987—The 1987 Latour was made from 75% Cabernet Sauvignon and 25% Merlot,
  •   without any Cabernet Franc or Petit Verdot used in the blend. The wine has
 86   a deep ruby color and a surprisingly backward yet promising bouquet of black
       currants, spicy oak, and herbs. In the mouth, it is medium bodied, exhibits
       more power and tannin than many wines in this vintage, and finishes with
       surprising authority. It is one of the few 1987s that I find not ready to drink.
       It and Mouton-Rothschild are the only two wines that will actually last more
       than 15 years. The 1987 is a notable success for Latour, comparable with
       their 1983 and 1985. Anticipated maturity: Now–2010. Last tasted, 4/91.

1986—This wine has developed in a perplexing manner, although it still needs
  •   another 5–10 years of bottle age before it reaches that magical plateau of
 90   maturity. The color remains a dark murky garnet with some purple at the
       edges. The nose has developed Latour's classic aromas of black currants and
       walnuts, as well as scents of tar, earth, and a touch of peppery herbs. This
       medium- to full-bodied wine possesses high tannin and excellent to outstand-
       ing concentration. Given the top quality level achieved by many other north-
       ern Médoc 1986s, Latour will always, I suspect, be considered somewhat of a
       disappointment for the vintage. It is well behind its rivals—Château Margaux,
       Lafite-Rothschild, and Mouton-Rothschild. Anticipated maturity: 2000–
       2015. Last tasted, 1/97.

1985—This has always been a weak, open-knit, fruity, light-styled Latour. The wine
  •   exhibits a deep ruby color with some lightening at the edge. There is a jammy,
 87   berry fragrance intertwined with herbs and earth. In the mouth, the wine is
       surprisingly light and has always been accessible. There is little grip, tannin,
       or extract in the finish, which quickly disappears. Anticipated maturity: Now–
       2008. Last tasted, 1/97.

1984—Curiously, the 1984 tastes nearly as fine as the lightish 1985. Spicy, woodsy,
  •   mineral, herbal scents and ripe fruit swell in the glass. It has good length and
 84   grip, plus adequate tannin for 5–9 years of further cellaring. Anticipated
       maturity: Now. Last tasted, 3/89.

1983—Another disappointing example of Latour, although as a wine it is certainly
  •   very good. A soupy, muddled character is atypical for Latour, even in some of
 87   the most difficult vintages. A medium garnet color with amber at the edge is
       followed by aromas of roasted walnuts and berry fruit, as well as a touch of
       tar and spice. In the mouth, this round wine is surprisingly light (actually
       medium bodied), with soft tannin and not much of a finish. Again, the 1983
       Latour is not equal to the performance of its first-growth stablemates—Châ-
       teau Margaux, Lafite-Rothschild, and Mouton-Rothschild. Anticipated matu-
       rity: Now–2005. Last tasted, 1/97.

1982—Guess which of the 1982 so-called "Bordeaux Big 8" (the 5 first-growths plus
  •   Ausone, Cheval Blanc, and Pétrus) tastes the most profound in 1998? For the
100   last 3 or 4 years, the 1982 Latour has begun to look like a clone of the
       magnificently opulent, powerful 1961. The 1982 continues to surge in quality,
       moving from strength to strength. If I were going to pull the cork for pure
       pleasure on any of the Big 8, it would be on this wine. Still an infant in terms

of development, the wine displays extraordinary richness, ripeness, and the beginning of that compelling Latour perfume of cassis, cedar, walnuts, and minerals. Extremely full bodied, concentrated, and thick, this viscous, chewy, large-scaled wine is also amazingly soft. Huge levels of tannin are concealed behind the layers of fruit. More and more I am convinced that this is another unqualified legend of the vintage. Today, it outperforms even the likes of Cheval Blanc for pure hedonistic appeal. There is a possibility that this wine could begin to close up, but it shows no signs of doing so, even though the color is reminiscent of an 18-month-old barrel sample. If readers only have 1 or 2 bottles stashed away, I suggest waiting until 2002–2003 before doing the deed. Save the other until about 2020. This could be a 50–60-year wine. A tour de force! Last tasted, 3/98.

1981 — The 1981 tastes remarkably velvety and supple for such a young Latour—
  •   not that this is a malevolent occurrence—because the excellence, complexity,
  88   and richness of the wine are still present. The color is dark ruby, the bouquet offers plenty of ripe cassis and spicy oak, and the flavor is generous, silky, moderately tannic, and long in the finish. This Latour may turn out to be similar to the 1971. Anticipated maturity: Now–2005. Last tasted, 9/90.

1980 — In the mediocre vintages of the fifties, sixties, and early seventies, Latour
  •   frequently made the best wine in the Médoc. Not so in 1980. The wine is
  83   clearly well above average for the vintage but lacks weight and richness. Fruity, charming, supple, with a pleasant fruitiness, it is slightly short on the palate. Anticipated maturity: Now. Last tasted, 11/84.

1979 — This wine has been difficult to evaluate, as evidenced by multiple tasting notes
  •   that varied greatly in terms of the wine's style and quality. In most examples,
  88?   the 1979 Latour has been backward and astringent, with medium body and reasonably good fruit. Two examples have been quite rich, with noticeable acidity, medium body, and the classic Latour mineral, walnut, and black fruit character. As I have said before, this wine is a light-bodied version of the outstanding 1971 Latour. Anticipated maturity: Now–2005. Last tasted, 1/97.

1978 — One of the great wines of the vintage, the 1978 Latour has reached full
  •   maturity. While it does not possess the extraordinary concentration of the
  94   massive 1970, or the power of the 1975, the 1978 offers a stunningly fragrant nose of roasted herbs, sweet, jammy black fruits, nuts, and minerals. There is almost an iron taste, as if it were a vitamin supplement. The wine is medium- to full-bodied, with fat, rich, concentrated flavors of black fruits, earth, and smoke. Although it has been delicious for some time, this wine reveals no signs of weakening. Anticipated maturity: Now–2010. Last tasted, 1/97.

1976 — I have had my share of arguments with Latour's staff over the relative merits
  •   of this wine, which I deem slightly shallow, lacking depth, and, for a Latour,
  83   somewhat hollow and angular on the palate. Of course, the château thinks differently, but the proof is, as always, in the bottle. The wine succeeds for the vintage, but this Latour is not likely to get better, only worse as the fruit continues to fade and the harsh tannins ascend. Anticipated maturity: Now. Last tasted, 2/87.

1975 — Cream always comes to the top, and so it is with Latour. Given enough time,
   •   Latour always seems to emerge as the leader of the Pauillac first-growths. The
  93+   1975 appears to be one of the few sure bets among the relatively hard,
        disappointing 1975 Pauillacs. The color remains a healthy dark ruby, opaque
        garnet. The nose offers up classic walnut, cedar, minerals, tobacco, and
        cassis aromas. Although this full-bodied wine is still excruciatingly tannic, I
        detected plenty of glycerin, extract, and richness, which gives me cause for
        optimism. Nevertheless, it will always be a wine with a firm, tannic edge.
        Drinkable if decanted several hours in advance, this wine should be cellared
        until the turn of the century and drunk during the following 3 decades. Last
        tasted, 12/95.

1974 — In this mediocre year of rather green, stalky, hollow wines, Latour produced
   •   one of the very best wines of the vintage. Still not fully mature, this dark ruby
  86   wine has good fruit, a medium body, surprising depth and ripeness for the
        vintage, and a sinewy, tannic finish. It avoids the telltale harshness and fruit
        deficiency found in so many 1974s. Anticipated maturity: Now–2000. Last
        tasted, 10/90.

1973 — A featherweight for Latour, even considering the watery, diluted character of
   •   most wines from this vintage, the 1973 Latour still offers light, charming,
  78   somewhat complex drinking, as it has held together much better than I would
        have suspected. Soft, ripe, moderately intense flavors seem dominated by
        Merlot and exhibit no tannin. This atypical Latour requires immediate drink-
        ing. Anticipated maturity: Now. Last tasted, 2/87.

1972 — A disastrous vintage for Bordeaux, yet Latour produced a rather big, deeply
   •   colored, somewhat disjointed, and clumsy wine, but one with good fruit,
  75   an herbaceous, cedary bouquet, and good flavor concentration. Drink now!
        Anticipated maturity: Now–may be in decline. Last tasted, 12/83.

1971 — I was lucky to be able to buy several cases of this wine at a low price. Every
   •   bottle has been consistently outstanding and the wine seemingly better with
  93   each tasting. The 1971 Latour may still not have reached its plateau of
        maturity (although I have drunk most of my collection). The color is a dark
        garnet with good saturation and some lightening at the edge. The nose offers
        abundant aromas of iron, mineral, black fruits, smoke, and roasted herbs. The
        wine is medium bodied, with a fleshy, chewy texture, a sweet mid-palate, and
        admirable length. More and more this looks to be the wine of the vintage in
        the Médoc. Anticipated maturity: Now–2010. Last tasted, 1/97.

1970 — One of the top 2 or 3 wines of the vintage (Pétrus and Trotanoy are noteworthy
   •   rivals), this young, magnificent Latour is still 5–10 years away from full
  98+   maturity. The opaque garnet color is followed by a huge, emerging nose of
        black fruits, truffles, walnuts, and subtle tobacco/Graves-like scents. Full
        bodied, fabulously concentrated, and intense, with a sweet inner core of fruit
        (a rarity in most 1970 Médocs) and high but well-integrated tannin, this
        enormously endowed, massive Latour should hit its prime by the end of the
        century and last for 2–3 decades thereafter. This will be the longest-lived
        and potentially most classic wine of the vintage. Last tasted, 6/96.

1969—In this ungracious vintage Latour produced an acceptable wine of average
•　　　color and concentration, but lean, angular, and charmless. Anticipated matu-
74　　rity: Now—may be in decline. Last tasted, 6/76.

1967—Unquestionably the best wine produced in the Médoc in 1967, the La-
•　　　tour has dark ruby color with some browning at the edges, a medium- to
88　　full-bodied feel, plenty of black currant fruit, and some light, soft tan-
　　　nins still present. Head and shoulders above the other first-growths, this
　　　wine has the classic Latour bouquet of black walnuts, black currants,
　　　mineral scents, and cedarwood. Anticipated maturity: Now. Last tasted,
　　　1/85.

1966—The 1966 Latour is the wine of the vintage! Very dark ruby colored with an
•　　　amber edge, the wine boasts a top-notch bouquet of leather, spices, tobacco,
96　　and ripe fruit. Quite concentrated, rich, and powerful, this full-bodied wine
　　　has shed much of its ferocious tannin and is easily the best wine produced by
　　　Latour in the sixties, omitting, of course, the monumental 1961. Anticipated
　　　maturity: Now—2008. Last tasted, 1/97.

1964—In 1964, as in 1966 and 1967, Latour was the best wine in the Médoc. The
•　　　1964 is drinking beautifully now, but it should hold for at least another
90　　decade. The bouquet is powerful, spicy, and filled with aromas of minerals,
　　　black fruits, and licorice. Rich, round, supple, generous flavors show excel-
　　　lent concentration. Soft tannins and a silky, rich, very long finish make this a
　　　sumptuous, even opulent Latour. Anticipated maturity: Now—2005. Last
　　　tasted, 5/91.

1962—Latour, once again, produced one of the great wines of the vintage. This is a
•　　　wine that seemingly has gotten more powerful and put on weight, richness,
94　　and complexity with age. The color is a murky dark garnet with very little
　　　lightening at the edge. The fabulous nose may not be as exotic as the 1962
　　　Mouton-Rothschild or as compellingly perfumed as the 1962 Lafite-
　　　Rothschild, but it exhibits plenty of intense sweet fruit, a roasted character,
　　　and attractive truffle scents in the background. The wine is a rich, heavy-
　　　weight, full-bodied style of Latour with exceptional extraction, a thick, glyc-
　　　erin-endowed palate, and a stunningly long finish. Still extraordinarily
　　　vibrant, it is capable of lasting another 20+ years. Anticipated maturity:
　　　Now—2015. Last tasted, 1/97.

1961—I have been fortunate to have this wine on eleven separate occasions, with
•　　　many of the tastings being held over the last several years. I have had it from
100　　both regular bottles and magnum. It has scored a consistent 100 points at
　　　every tasting, whether it has been tasted on the other side of the Atlantic or
　　　in the United States. The wine is a full-bodied, monumental Pauillac that
　　　tastes like syrup of Cabernet. The portlike, unctuous, chewy texture is to
　　　die for. The color remains an opaque purple/garnet. The nose offers up
　　　celestial quantities of black fruits, truffles, leather, cedar, and minerals. On
　　　several occasions, because of the jammy sweetness of the aromatics, I have
　　　thought this to be a Pétrus (how embarrassing in terms of the different
　　　nature of the wines). The 1961 Latour is still gorgeously sweet, rich, and

showing absolutely no amber at the edge, or other signs of aging. It is a massive, extraordinary mouthful of Bordeaux that is certainly one of the greatest wines I have ever tasted. Anticipated maturity: Now–2040. Last tasted, 6/97.

ANCIENT VINTAGES

The 1959 Latour (98+ points; last tasted 9/96) from Imperial could have been a 1993 California Cabernet Sauvignon—it tasted that young, thick, and rich. Soft, with beautifully integrated tannin, it possessed an opaque purple color, huge body, and massive richness and intensity.

The 1949 Latour (100 points; last tasted 10/94) is one of those wines that can take a taster's breath away. It is a wine of extraordinary richness, yet it is perfectly balanced. It has extraordinary extraction, layers of flavor, and a finish that is both supple and authoritative. Drink it over the next 25 years. The 1948 (94 points; last tasted 10/94) boasts a forceful, exotic nose of mint, cassis, walnuts, and leather that jumps from the glass. The wine exhibits impressive richness, density, and body, as well as a long, soft finish. Fully mature, it is capable of lasting another 15–25 years. Two other bottles revealed a more inky color and greater flavor depth and richness.

I have experienced extraordinary discrepancy in the quality of the 1945 Latour. In a tasting in 1995 (rated 89), it revealed a healthy garnet color with light amber/orange at the rim. The textbook Latour bouquet of cassis and black walnuts was apparent, but in the mouth the fruit was drying out, and the tannin dominated the wine's full-bodied, austere personality. It is a powerful wine, but this slightly rustic and tannic example was excellent rather than sublime. A superb bottle consumed with friends in December 1995 at Gérard Pangaud's excellent Washington, D.C., restaurant was significantly richer, meriting a 96–97-point rating.

Purchased from the Nicolas cellars, a bottle of 1928 Latour (100 points; last tasted 10/94) was absolute perfection. The wine exhibited an astonishing bouquet of hickory wood, smoke, walnuts, and gobs of sweet black truffle– and raspberry-scented fruit. Full bodied, with layers of sweet, expansive fruit, with no hard edges, this large-scaled wine still possesses phenomenal flavor concentration as well as marvelous aromatic and flavor dimension. One of the great wines of the century, it is a winemaking tour de force! It revealed little tannin and appeared completely mature. I found it to be in superb condition at 65 years of age, so who among us would argue that it will not last another 20–25 years? A bottle of 1926 Latour (93 points; last tasted 10/94), which clearly demonstrates the fact that there are no great wines, just great bottles, was in far better shape than another bottle of 1926 Latour I tasted in Bordeaux in March 1991. At first the aromas were muddled, but with breathing they offered up the classic Latour scents of walnuts, black fruits, herbs, and oak.

Surprisingly, in the mouth the wine was muscular and rustic, with considerable tannin, plenty of richness, and amazing freshness. Given that it is fully mature, with some amber and brown hues in its color, as well as acidity in the finish, I would opt for consuming this wine over the near term. My first experience with the 1924 Latour came at a blind tasting held several years ago in Bordeaux. The wine had been purchased by my host's father, and although cellared impeccably, it was astringent and disappointing. This example (94 points; last tasted 10/94) was profound, with a sensational fragrance of leafy tobacco, damp earth, cedar, and fruit. Intensely spicy for a Latour, this medium- to full-bodied wine displayed crisp acidity but little tannin and only medium body. Most of the wine's complexity and character emanated from its fragrant bouquet, which did not fade with airing. Quite impressive!

The 1921 Latour (90 points; last tasted 9/95) exhibited a moderately dark ruby/garnet color with an amber/orange rim. Tannin dominated the high alcohol flavors. This wine revealed a port-like texture, with notes of fruitcake, coffee, tobacco, and over-ripe fruit. Although it is losing its balance as the tannin becomes dominant (at the expense of the wine's fruit), this is still a flavorful, full-bodied, intriguing example of Latour that has remained an outstanding wine.

SECOND WINE

LES FORTS DE LATOUR * (unclassified)   VERY GOOD

Evaluation: The quality equivalent of a fourth-growth

The staff at Latour have always maintained that the "second" wine of Latour was equivalent in quality terms to a "second-growth" in the 1855 classification. In fact, they claim that blind tastings of Forts de Latour are held at Latour against the wines produced by the second-growths. If Forts de Latour does not do extremely well, then a decision must be made whether to declassify it as a Pauillac. In specific vintages, for example, 1978 and 1982, I would agree with their assessment, but in more objective terms, the wine is comparable to a fourth-growth in quality, which still establishes this wine as the finest "second" wine produced in Bordeaux.

The wine, which is vinified exactly the same way as Latour, comes from three vineyards called Petit Batailley, Comtesse de Lalande, and Les Forts de Latour. Additionally, selected lots of Latour (often from young vines) not considered quite "grand" enough are also blended with the wine from the aforementioned vineyards. The character of Forts de Latour is astonishingly similar to Latour itself, only lighter and quicker to mature. Les Forts de Latour is certainly among the finest of the second labels, or *marques*, produced by the well-known châteaux in Bordeaux.

* Because Les Forts de Latour is widely regarded as the finest of all the "second wines" and, in tastings, frequently rated above more famous Pauillacs, its stature is such that it merits separate coverage.

VINTAGES

1997—The 1997 reveals a rich blackberry, jammy (the French call it *confituré*) nose
•   nicely intermingled with spice and earth. Soft, with low acidity, medium body,
87–   and good length, this plump, precocious-tasting Les Forts de Latour should
88   drink well during its first decade of life. Last tasted, 3/98.

1996—The 1996 Forts de Latour (a blend of 73% Cabernet Sauvignon and 27%
•   Merlot) is a very fine effort. This wine possesses excellent sweetness, crisp
91–   acidity, and a deep, black/purple color. It is much more forward than the
93   *grand vin*, but it still needs 7–8 years of cellaring; it will last for 25 or more
      years. Last tasted, 3/98.

1995—A ripe, mineral-, crushed stone-, black currant-scented nose is followed by a
•   dense, medium- to full-bodied wine with coarse tannin and gobs of fruit,
88   glycerin, and ripeness. It will benefit from 6–8 years of cellaring and last for
      20 years. Last tasted, 1/97.

1994—Dark purple colored, with a moderately intense walnut-, black currant-, and
•   mineral-scented nose, this is a formidably tannic, backward wine with fine
87   density. It needs another 7–10 years of cellaring, after which it may merit an
      even higher score. Last tasted, 1/97.

1993—This wine reveals a healthy opaque purple color, dense, concentrated fruit,
•   and moderate tannin, but the wine's flavors were marred by a slight filter pad,
?   musty smell. Perhaps I saw a defective bottle. Last tasted, 1/97.

1992—The 1992 Forts de Latour is supple and fruity, with fine color and low acidity.
•   Although surprisingly light and easygoing, this classy wine will offer ideal
85   drinking over the next 5–9 years. Last tasted, 11/94.

1991—In keeping with the high quality of Latour's 1991, the property's second wine
•   is a graceful, elegant, medium-weight wine with moderate tannin, a spicy,
86   berry-scented nose, fine length, and enough tannin to give it grip and struc-
      ture. Drink it over the next 7–8 years. Last tasted, 1/94.

1990—The rich, well-endowed 1990 possesses round, generous, surprisingly concen-
•   trated flavors. It will make ideal drinking over the next 10–15 years. This is
90   the most complete second wine made at the property since their glorious
      1982; over one-half of the crop was relegated to this wine. Anticipated matu-
      rity: Now–2005. Last tasted, 1/93.

1989—Once past the bouquet of black fruits, cedar, and oak, the 1989 is round,
•   generously endowed, surprisingly supple (even for the second wine of Latour),
87   and low in acidity, with a fleshy, heady finish. Anticipated maturity: Now–
      2004. Last tasted, 1/93.

1988—The medium-bodied, somewhat austere, noticeably oaky and tannic 1988
•   Forts de Latour possesses good aging potential but lacks charm, complexity,
84   and concentration. Nevertheless, it is an elegant, understated wine. Antici-
       pated maturity: Now–2002. Last tasted, 1/93.

1987—The delightful 1987 Forts de Latour is, to my taste, a better wine than
•   the 1988. The forward yet intriguing bouquet of walnuts, spicy oak,
86   cedar, and herbs is followed by a surprisingly concentrated, generously
       fruity, medium- to full-bodied wine with excellent balance and depth. It
       is a top-notch success for the vintage. Anticipated maturity: Now. Last tasted,
       4/90.

1986—This wine has consistently exhibited a great deal of oak and peppery,
•   mineral-scented black currant fruit in its blossoming nose. In the mouth,
86   it exhibits the tannic ferocity that characterizes many 1986s but is sur-
       prisingly lighter than I would have expected. A good effort, but it
       could use more depth and concentration, particularly if one compares
       it with the 1982 or 1989. Anticipated maturity: Now–2005. Last tasted,
       4/90.

1985—Latour made one of the lightest wines I have ever tasted from this property in
•   this very good vintage. Not surprisingly, their second wine is also forward.
84   Soft, with only medium body, and a surprisingly short, undistinguished finish,
       this smooth, lightweight Latour should be drunk over the next 5–6 years.
       Anticipated maturity: Now. Last tasted, 4/91.

1984—A weedy, cedary bouquet lacks fruit. In the mouth, the wine is light, has some
•   annoyingly high acidity and some vague, curranty, cedary fruitiness. The
80   relatively high acidity will keep the wine alive, but I doubt that it will ever
       be enjoyable. Anticipated maturity: Now. Last tasted, 12/89.

1983—Quite soft and fully mature, with a hint of the famed Latour bouquet of
•   minerals, walnuts, and black currants, this medium-bodied, round, moder-
84   ately concentrated wine should be drunk over the next 5–7 years. It makes
       an interesting comparison with the enormously concentrated, more backward
       1982. Anticipated maturity: Now. Last tasted, 7/90.

1982—The 1982 is the finest Forts de Latour I have ever tasted. It continues to offer
•   a glimpse of what potential magic will be forthcoming from its larger and
92   more forceful sibling, the great Latour. Delicious since its release, the 1982
       Forts de Latour offers a healthy saturated ruby/purple color with no signs of
       age. A classic nose of walnuts, cassis, and spices is followed by a rich,
       full-bodied, beautifully concentrated, velvety-textured wine exhibiting the
       vintage's great ripeness and opulent texture. It will continue to offer a
       complex, classy mouthful of wine for at least another decade. Last tasted,
       9/95.

1981—While this wine lacks muscle, weight, and the compelling concentration of
•   the 1982, it is still an elegantly wrought, stylish wine that indeed resembles
85   the grand vin. Medium to deep ruby color, with an emerging bouquet of wet
       stones, cassis, and oak, this medium-bodied, gracefully made Latour is just
       beginning to drink well but should last for another 5–7 years. It is restrained,

but attractive and well balanced. Anticipated maturity: Now. Last tasted, 4/88.

1978—Still quite dark with a rich, intense, cassis, oaky nose, ripe, moderately
  •   tannic, yet supple flavors, and excellent length, this wine is fully mature but
  87   will keep for another decade. After the 1982, this is my favorite vintage.
       Anticipated maturity: Now–2000. Last tasted, 10/89.

1976—Forward, smooth, and showing ripe fruit and less tannin than its big brother,
  •   this wine can be drunk now but is quite ordinary in the total Bordeaux scheme
  76   of things. Anticipated maturity: Now. Last tasted, 10/89.

1975—True to the vintage and to Latour, this wine is tannic, lean, aggressive, and
  •   still in need of bottle age. The color remains impressive, the richness and
  85   depth appear to be present, but the tannins refuse to yield. Anticipated
       maturity: Now–2000. Last tasted, 10/89.

1974—Latour made one of the top wines of the vintage, so it is not surprising to find
  •   Forts de Latour better than many a more famous classified growth. A trifle
  74   austere and lean, but spicy, with good fruit, a hard, tough personality, yet a
       short, soft finish, this wine seems to suggest potential for improvement, but
       the personality of the entire vintage scares me off. Respectable given the
       year. Drink up. Anticipated maturity: Now–may be in decline. Last tasted,
       1/83.

1972—Surprisingly dark colored, with an amber/brownish edge, this soft, chunky,
  •   somewhat rugged wine offers good chocolatey, herbaceous, stemmy fruit, a
  74   good palate impression, and a short finish. Drink up. Anticipated maturity:
       Now–may be in serious decline. Last tasted, 4/80.

1970—This very fine wine is fully mature and ideally requires consumption. Very
  •   dark ruby, with a smooth, round, ripe black currant and cedar bouquet,
  84   savory, full, generous flavors, and a slightly tart, acidic finish that detracts
       from an otherwise fine performance in 1970. Drink now. Anticipated maturity:
       Now. Last tasted, 1/85.

1967—The 1967 was beginning to fade in the eighties. For a number of years, this
  •   wine could lay claim to giving wine enthusiasts on a budget a good introduc-
  84   tion to the style of Latour. Drink up. Anticipated maturity: Now–may be in
       decline. Last tasted, 3/82.

1966—The 1966 Forts de Latour is a textbook Pauillac, which displays near perfectly
  •   proportioned scents of black currants, spices, leather, and cedar, ripe yet
  85   supple flavors, a long fruity texture and palate impression, and light tannins.
       It is now at its zenith. Drink up! Anticipated maturity: Now–may be in
       decline. Last tasted, 12/88.

LYNCH-BAGES   EXCELLENT

Classification: Fifth-growth in 1855
Location of vineyards: Pauillac
Owner: Cazes family
Address: 33250 Pauillac

Telephone: 33 5 56 73 24 00; telefax: 33 5 56 59 26 42
Visits: Every day of the week from April 1 to October 13, and from
Monday to Friday the rest of the year, between 9 A.M. and
12:30 P.M., and 2 P.M. and 6:30 P.M.
Contact: Isabelle Faurie at the above telephone and fax numbers

VINEYARDS (red)
Surface area: 222 acres
Average age of vines: 35 years
Blend: 73% Cabernet Sauvignon, 15% Merlot, 10% Cabernet Franc, 2%
Petit Verdot
Density of plantation: 9,000 vines per hectare
Average yields (over the last 5 years): 45 hectoliters per hectare
Total average annual production: 30,000–35,000 cases

GRAND VIN (red)
Brand name: Château Lynch-Bages
Appellation: Pauillac
Mean annual production: 25,000 cases
Upbringing: Grapes are picked manually and totally destemmed.
Fermentations last 15–17 days normally (except in 1996, 20
days) in temperature-controlled stainless-steel vats. Malolactics
occur in tanks except for a small proportion of the yield that
goes into cask. All wines are then transferred to oak barrels, of
which 60% are new, for 12–15 months. They are fined and filtered
only once prior to bottling. Racking every 3 months from barrel to
barrel.

SECOND WINE
Brand name: Château Haut-Bages Averous
Average annual production: 10,000 cases

VINEYARDS (white)
Surface area: 11.1 acres
Average age of vines: 10 years
Blend: 40% Semillon, 40% Sauvignon Blanc, 20% Muscadelle
Density of plantation: 7,500 vines per hectare
Average yields (over the last 5 years): 55 hectoliters per hectare
Total average annual production: 2,500–3,000 cases
Brand name: Blanc de Lynch-Bages
Appellation: Bordeaux
Mean annual production: 2,500–3,000 cases

Upbringing: *Macération pelliculaire* for 13–15 hours, and upbringing in new oak barrels. Wines are both fined and filtered prior to bottling.

Evaluation of present classification: Should be upgraded to a second-growth
Plateau of maturity: 6–25 years following the vintage

This château is located just west of Bordeaux's Route du Vin (D2) as one approaches the dull, commercial town of Pauillac from the south. It is situated on a small ridge that rises above the town and the adjacent Gironde River, called, not surprisingly, the Bages plateau. The luxury hotel/restaurant Château Cordeillan-Bages sits directly in front of Lynch-Bages. Until recently the kindest thing that could be said about the buildings was that they were utilitarian. However, Lynch-Bages has benefited enormously from a major face lift and renovation. The château now sports a new facade, new cellars exhibiting large stainless-steel tanks, and a state-of-the-art tasting room.

Except for these recent changes, this large estate has remained essentially intact since the sixteenth century. Half the name is taken from the plateau upon which the château and cellars are located, and the rest results from 75 years of ownership (during the seventeenth and eighteenth centuries) by Thomas Lynch, the son of an Irish immigrant whose family ran the property. After Thomas Lynch sold Lynch-Bages, it passed through the hands of several wine merchants before being purchased in 1937 by Jean Charles Cazes, the grandfather of the current-day proprietor, Jean-Michel Cazes. In his time, Jean Charles Cazes was already a renowned proprietor and winemaker, having directed the fortunes of one of the leading Cru Bourgeois of St.-Estèphe, Château Les-Ormes-de-Pez. He continued to handle both châteaux until 1966, when his son André, a prominent politician who had been the mayor of Pauillac for nearly two decades, took control. André's reign lasted until 1973, when Jean-Michel Cazes assumed control of both Lynch-Bages and Les-Ormes-de-Pez. Jean-Michel, who spent several years in America, had developed an international perspective of wine as well as of business. He made perhaps the smartest decision of his business career in 1976 when he hired the brilliant Daniel Llose as director of Château Lynch-Bages and Les-Ormes-de-Pez.

After the great success Lynch-Bages enjoyed under Jean-Michel's father, André, in the fifties (1952, 1953, 1955, 1957, and 1959 were all among the top wines of that decade) and in the sixties (1961, 1962, and 1966), Jean-Michel's inheritance consisted of a disappointing 1972 still in cask. Even his first vintage, 1973, was largely a washout. This was followed by another disappointing year in 1974 and, for Lynch-Bages, less than exhilarating wine from the sometimes troublesome vintage of 1975. Jean-Michel Cazes recognized that the old wooden vats created sanitation problems and also made it difficult to control the proper fermentation temperature in both cold and hot years. At the same time (the late seventies), Cazes flirted with a newer style, producing several vintages of Lynch-Bages that were lighter and more elegant. Longtime fans and supporters of Lynch-Bages were dismayed. Fortunately, after Jean-Michel Cazes installed 25 large stainless-steel vats in 1980, the slump in quality between 1971 and 1979 came to an abrupt end. Lynch-Bages produced a very good 1981 and continued to build on that success with highly successful wines in nearly every vintage since.

The vineyard itself is located midway between Mouton-Rothschild and Lafite-Rothschild to the north, and Latour, Pichon-Longueville–Comtesse de Lalande, and Pichon-Longueville Baron to the south. Despite the enormous amount of modernization and rebuilding that has taken place at Lynch-Bages, the general philosophy of making wine remains quite traditional. Since 1980, as I have mentioned, the vinification has taken place in new steel tanks. After that, the wine is put directly into small French oak casks. The percentage of new casks has increased from 25% in the 1982 vintage to 60% in more recent vintages. Lynch-Bages spends an average of 12–15 months in these oak casks, is fined with egg whites, and lightly filtered prior to bottling. Now that the vineyards are fully planted, production has soared from an average of 20,000–25,000 cases in the seventies to nearly 35,000 cases in abundant years. In addition, from 20%–30% of the harvest is relegated to the second wine of Lynch-Bages, Haut-Bages-Averous.

In 1990 Cazes began making a dry, rich white Bordeaux from a vineyard in the northern Médoc. The wine, a blend of 40% Semillon, 40% Sauvignon Blanc, and 20% Muscadelle, was fermented in new oak and aged in cask for nearly 12 months prior to bottling. The debut vintage was remarkably impressive, with a level of quality reminiscent of a top white Graves. In the famous 1855 Classification of the Wines of Gironde, Lynch-Bages was positioned in the last tier as a fifth-growth. I know of no professional in the field today who would not argue that its present-day quality is more akin to a second-growth. Englishman Oz Clarke lightheartedly argues that those responsible for the 1855 classification must have been essentially Puritans because they "couldn't bear to admit that a wine as openheartedly lovely as Lynch-Bages could really be as important as other less-generous growths."

Just as it is difficult not to enjoy a bottle of Lynch-Bages, so is it difficult not to appreciate the affable, seemingly always open and gregarious Jean-Michel Cazes, the architect behind Lynch-Bages's more recent stratospheric rise to international prominence. The confident Cazes, who, having attended school in America, speaks English like a native, has a global vision, and anyone who talks with him knows he wants his wines to be lusty, open, and direct yet also reflect the class and character of a top Pauillac. For that reason he always prefers vintages such as 1985 and 1982 to more tannic and severe years such as 1988 and 1986. He is also an untiring ambassador not only for his own wines, but for the wines of the entire Bordeaux region. There rarely seems to be a conference, symposium, or international tasting of Bordeaux where one does not encounter Monsieur Cazes. There is no other producer in Pauillac (with the possible exception of Madame Lencquesaing of Pichon Lalande) who travels so extensively and who pleads his case so eloquently for these wines.

VINTAGES

1997—A very successful effort for the vintage, this hedonistically styled Lynch-
• Bages delivers copious quantities of ripe, fat, black currant fruit intermixed
87– with sweet oak. Low acidity combined with high pH results in a chewy, fleshy,
90 up-front wine that will make many friends when it is released in a year and a half. The color is a healthy dark purple, and the wine is perfumed, expansive, round, and crammed with black fruit. The glycerin level is high, the tannin sweet and unaggressive, and the overall style provides considerable satisfaction and thrills. If this wine takes on more weight and adds a nuance or two of complexity, look for it to merit an outstanding rating when released. Anticipated maturity: 2000–2012. Last tasted, 3/98.

1996—The wine is low in acidity, but it possesses an opaque black/purple color, as
• well as extraordinary sweet, full-bodied, cassis fruit aromas intermixed with
90– cedar, fruitcake, and licorice scents that soared from the glass at each tasting.
93 With superlative structure, a boatload of ripe tannin, massive body, and dazzling intensity and power, this may be the greatest Lynch-Bages produced since the 1989 and 1990. Anticipated maturity: 2001–2025. Last tasted, 3/98.

1995—On the three occasions I tasted the 1995 out of bottle it came across in an
• elegant, restrained, 1985/1953 Lynch-Bages style. While attractive and soft,
90 with obvious tannin in the background, the 1995 is not made in the blockbuster style of the 1996, 1990, 1989, or 1986. Deep ruby-colored, with an evolved nose of sweet, smoky, earthy, black currant fruit, this fleshy, round, seductive, fat and fruity Lynch-Bages should drink well young, yet age for two decades. Anticipated maturity: 2000–2015. Last tasted, 11/97.

1994—Deep ruby colored with a purple center, this wine displays ripe black cur-
• rant fruit, with no vegetal or weedy notes. Medium to full bodied and ripe,
88 with surprising softness, fatness, and precociousness for a wine from this vintage, Lynch-Bages's 1994 possesses well-integrated toasty oak, as well as an attractive, hedonistic style that should please the followers of this corpulent Pauillac. It should drink well now and over the next 12–15 years. Last tasted, 1/97.

1993—Once past the herbal, dill pickle-, and green pepper-scented nose, this dense
• ruby/purple–colored wine offers good structure, medium body, and soft, ripe,
86 alluring flavors possessing fat, glycerin, and fruit. It is possible that the herbal

aromas will develop a more cedary character with another 1–2 years of bottle age. There is plenty of black currant, jammy fruit in the wine's flavor profile. Anticipated maturity: Now–2008. Last tasted, 1/97.

1992—Lynch-Bages has produced an impressively colored 1992. The wine has not
• begun to display much complexity in its cassis-, damp earth-, and spicy-
86 scented nose. There is fine fatness and ripeness, medium body, and light tannin in the finish. This is a very good, spicy, cedary Lynch-Bages for drinking over the next 6–8 years. Last tasted, 11/94.

1991—Lynch-Bages has fashioned an attractive, medium bodied, soft wine in 1991.
• It would make a noteworthy bargain if it were selling for under $18 a bottle.
86 The color is dense, and the nose offers up bold cassis aromas intertwined with earth and new oak. The wine is moderately deep, reveals some tannin, but finishes quickly. It is a good, ripe, light- to medium-weight Lynch-Bages that is best drunk over the next 7–8 years. Last tasted, 1/94.

1990—The 1990 is a forward, flattering, and delicious to drink wine, in contrast
• with the more massive, backward, tannic, and potentially superior 1989.
93 Lynch-Bages 1990 offers sweet, beefy, leathery, black currant aromas inter-mingled with smoky, toasty oak, and roasted herbs. The wine offers a hedonis-tic turn-on of fruit, extract, and high levels of glycerin, all crammed into a full-bodied, supple-textured, rich, powerful Lynch-Bages with no hard edges. It can be drunk now and over the next 20–25 years. Last tasted, 11/96.

1989—The opaque purple–colored 1989 is less evolved and showy than the 1990.
• However, it looks to be a phenomenal example of Lynch-Bages, perhaps the
95+ finest vintage in the last 30 years. Oozing with extract, this backward, muscu-lar, dense wine possesses great purity, huge body, and a bulldozer-like power that charges across the palate. It is an enormous wine with unbridled quanti-ties of power and richness. The 1989 requires 5–8 years of cellaring; it should last for 3 decades. Last tasted, 11/96.

1988—Undoubtedly, the 1988 Lynch-Bages is the biggest wine produced in the
• northern Médoc in this vintage. The saturated black/ruby/purple color sug-
90 gests excellent ripeness and plenty of concentration. The oaky bouquet exhib-its roasted black raspberries and currants, as well as an earthy, robust character. The wine is full bodied, rich, with an attractive cedary, herbaceous, black fruit character. This fleshy, broad-shouldered wine characterizes the style of the château. Anticipated maturity: Now–2010. Last tasted, 1/93.

1987—The 1987 Lynch-Bages is a densely colored, herbaceous, rich, medium-
• bodied, soft, supple wine for current drinking. Anticipated maturity: Now.
82 Last tasted, 11/89.

1986—What remarkable tastings should occur in the twenty-first century between
• the opulent, seductive 1982 and 1985 and the powerful, brawny, tannic,
90 dense, muscular 1986 and 1989 Lynch-Bages. The results will make interest-ing reading for decades. At present, I have a strong preference for the 1982 and 1989, but I would not want anyone to shortchange the immense, huge, behemoth 1986 or the seductive, flashy 1985. The 1986 is black/purple in color and extremely rich and tannic. But are the tannins too prominent and

astringent? I doubt that anyone will be capable of answering that question for
at least a decade. As for now, this wine is more admirable for remarkable size
and weight than for charm and enjoyability. Anticipated maturity: Now–2020.
Last tasted, 5/94.

1985— This has been a deliciously charming, seductive wine since its birth. Fully
•   mature, it offers a fragrant bouquet of sweet black currant fruit intermixed
91   with smoky toasty oak and roasted herbs. Medium bodied (with far less girth,
        weight, and richness than the 1989, 1986, and 1982), the 1985 Lynch-Bages
        is a gorgeously fleshy, well-proportioned wine that should continue to drink
        well for another decade. Its low acidity, corpulent fleshiness, and sweet tannin
        make for a charming mouthful of wine. Anticipated maturity: Now–2007. Last
        tasted, 10/97.

1984— One of the top successes of the vintage, the 1984 Lynch-Bages, which is
•   nearly 100% Cabernet Sauvignon, is a forceful, fleshy, supple wine with
82   plenty of herbaceous-scented, ripe fruit, a round, generous texture, and good
        length. Anticipated maturity: Now. Last tasted, 10/89.

1983— A success for this very good, yet surprisingly inconsistent vintage, the Lynch-
•   Bages 1983 is a full-blown, big, ripe, gutsy Pauillac, with an intense bouquet
88   of ground beef and black currant fruit and deep, rich, briery flavors. Quite
        full bodied, alcoholic, and long, this substantial wine has a heady, alcoholic
        finish with the tannins quickly melting away. Anticipated maturity: Now–
        2002. Last tasted, 3/89.

1982— The 1982 Lynch-Bages continues to develop well. Delicious since age
•   5–6, it remains a husky, forceful, grapey, exuberant wine with gobs of
93   cassis fruit presented in an unctuously textured, thick, succulent style.
        The wine has not developed much complexity aromatically, but it is a weighty,
        textbook example of a wine from this popular estate. Full bodied, soft,
        and supple, it will continue to drink well for 15–20 more years. Last tasted,
        9/95.

1981— After a period in the late seventies where Lynch-Bages seemed to be taking
•   suppleness in winemaking too far, I detected with the 1981 a partial return to
85   the very rich, robust, ripe, huge extract style of the great Lynch-Bages wines
        like the 1970, 1962, and 1961. Certainly the monumental 1982 and excellent
        1983 will eclipse the 1981 in stature, but this wine is quite good, and the
        best Lynch-Bages since 1975. Very dark ruby, with a strong, aggressive
        bouquet of black currants, cedar, and new oak, this ripe wine has surprising
        density on the palate, with plenty of tannin. The 1981 shows lots of gutsy
        character. Anticipated maturity: Now. Last tasted, 12/88.

1980— Somewhat variable from bottle to bottle, this lightweight Lynch-Bages has a
•   cedary, fruity, somewhat stalky, herbaceous aroma, light-intensity flavors, and
78   a short, greenish, unripe finish. Anticipated maturity: Now–may be in de-
        cline. Last tasted, 4/87.

1979— Made in a period when Lynch-Bages was flirting with a lighter, more preco-
•   cious, supple style, this wine is attractive but atypical for what fans of Lynch-
79   Bages expect. Medium bodied with soft, crisp, berryish flavors, light tannins,

and some pleasing spicy, oaky notes, it is quite drinkable now. Anticipated maturity: Now. Last tasted, 6/88.

1978—The 1978 is very similar to the 1979: round, fruity, and straightforward in
•   style, with soft, spicy black currant flavors of moderate intensity. Ready to
82   drink now, this wine should continue to drink well for another 5–6 years. A good but not particularly noteworthy effort from Lynch-Bages. Anticipated maturity: Now. Last tasted, 1/88.

1976—Fully mature and beginning to lose its fruit, the 1976 Lynch-Bages is still
•   fruity, but diffuse, with no grip or "attack," and displaying disturbing brown-
72   ing at the edge. Owners of this vintage of Lynch-Bages should run, not walk, to the wine cellar and consume it immediately. Anticipated maturity: Now– may be in decline. Last tasted, 3/86.

1975—The 1975 Lynch-Bages exhibits significant amber/orange at the edge, fol-
•   lowed by a dusty, herbaceous, cedary nose with some ripe fruit. Full bodied
86   but slightly hollow, the wine exhibits more sweetness and expansiveness than I expected. This above average wine is beginning to reach full maturity. Given the number of washed-out, excessively tannic examples of 1975 Lynch-Bages I have tasted, I am now more optimistic about this wine. Drink it between 2000 and 2010. Last tasted, 12/95.

1974—A surprisingly weak effort from Lynch-Bages, this watery, hollow wine fades
•   remarkably fast in the glass, and the shallow, pale colors suggest a wine
60   that was diluted significantly by rain and perhaps overcropping. Anticipated maturity: Now–may be in decline. Last tasted, 2/80.

1973—Disappointing for Lynch-Bages, this light, feeble wine has a washed-out color,
•   a chaptalized bouquet of hot, burnt fruit, and thin, nondescript flavors. It was
55   at its best in 1978. Last tasted, 2/78.

1971—Lynch-Bages was clearly in a slump during this period. A number of very fine,
•   graceful, fruity 1971 Pauillacs were produced, but not here. Now decrepit and
58   very brown, with a musty, faded, dead vegetal bouquet and short, sharp acidic flavors. A failure for the vintage. Last tasted, 10/79.

1970—I have had nearly two cases of this wine and have consistently rated it in the
•   low to mid-nineties. It is a classic Pauillac, more like a downscaled version
93   of Latour than the "poor man's Mouton-Rothschild," as it is often called. It reveals a fabulously saturated opaque color (only Latour can match Lynch-Bages for color saturation in the 1970 vintage) with no amber at the edge. The nose offers up scents of cedar, saddle leather, smoked meat, fruitcake, tobacco, and spices. Although youthfully rich and tannic, this massive, thick wine has always been supple enough to be considered close to maturity. The finish goes on and on. The 1970 Lynch-Bages can be drunk now and over the next 20 years. It is one of the greatest wines from this estate in the last 30– 40 years. It remains to be seen whether or not the 1982, 1986, 1989, or 1990 will surpass it. Last tasted, 6/96.

1966—Dark ruby with a slight amber edge, this wine appears to have the requisite
•   concentration and structure, yet for whatever reason the wine tastes dull,
84   lacks complexity and character, and finishes in a one-dimensional, tannic

manner. It is capable of aging, but it mysteriously does not sing. Anticipated maturity: Now–2000. Last tasted, 9/90.

1964—The 1964 Lynch-Bages is a failure, not so much because of faulty winemak-
•   ing, but as a result of the château's decision to pick late to obtain max-
55   imum ripeness in the grapes. Such decisions always run the risk of foul weather, and in 1964 Lynch-Bages was one of the châteaux to get caught badly in the deluge that ensued. Thin, old, watery, and uninteresting. Last tasted, 1/91.

1962—One of the all-time popular wines of the château, this wine has been drinking
•   beautifully since 1970 and continues to be delightful. It indicates just how
89   long a top-class Bordeaux can remain at its apogee. However, the regular bottle size seems to be losing some of the exuberant, unabashed, gutsy fruiti-ness. Cedary and black currant aromas still prevail, and this wine maintains the wonderful, silky voluptuousness that has made it so pleasurable. Owners are advised to catch the wonderment now or risk losing its pleasure altogether. Anticipated maturity: Now. Last tasted, 11/89.

1961—This is the best Lynch-Bages made during the sixties, with rich, cedary,
•   massive aromas of black currants and leather still present in plentiful
94   amounts. Not terribly refined, but deep, powerful, concentrated, alcoholic, and extremely long on the palate, this huge wine has been at its apogee since the late seventies but will hold for another 10 years. Anticipated maturity: Now–2000. Last tasted, 12/89.

ANCIENT VINTAGES

A tasting in December 1995 revealed a relatively strong showing for the 1945 Lynch-Bages (92 points). This wine exhibited a minty, cassis-scented nose that did indeed seem reminiscent of the "poor man's Mouton-Rothschild." A dense, opaque ruby/garnet color was followed by a full-bodied, powerful, but tough-textured, hard, astringently tannic wine that may lose its fruit before the tannin fully melts away. Although impressive for its overall size and intensity, this wine will never win any awards for grace and harmony. It will keep for another 15–20 years.

Lynch-Bages also enjoyed a glorious decade of the fifties, producing super-lative wines in 1959 (94 points), 1957 (88 points), 1955 (92 points), 1953 (90 points), and 1952 (91 points). Such consistent brilliance was not again evi-dent until the succession of superperformances that began in 1982.

LYNCH-MOUSSAS

Classification: Fifth-growth in 1855
Location of vineyards: Pauillac
Owner: Héritiers Castéja
Address: 33250 Pauillac

Mailing address: Domaines Borie-Manoux, 86, Cours
Balguerie-Stuttenberg, 33082 Bordeaux
Cedex
Telephone: 33 5 56 00 00 70; telefax: 33 5 57 87 60 30
Visits: By appointment only, except on Saturdays
Contact: Domaines Borie-Manoux

VINEYARDS (red)
Surface area: 86.5 acres
Average age of vines: 25 years
Blend: 65% Cabernet Sauvignon, 30% Merlot, 5% Cabernet Franc
Density of plantation: 7,000 vines per hectare
Average yields (over the last 5 years): 55 hectoliters per hectare
Total average annual production: 20,000 cases

GRAND VIN (red)
Brand name: Château Lynch-Moussas
Appellation: Pauillac
Mean annual production: 20,000 cases
Upbringing: Grape picking is done manually, and grapes are totally
destemmed. Fermentations last 4 weeks in temperature-controlled
stainless-steel tanks. Wines undergo malolactics in tanks and are
transferred to oak casks in December for 12–16 months. Sixty
percent new oak is used. Wines are fined using egg whites but
not filtered.

SECOND WINE
None produced.

Evaluation of present classification: Should be downgraded to a Cru
Bourgeois
Plateau of maturity: 4–10 years following the vintage

Lynch-Moussas is owned and controlled by the Castéja family, who operate
the well-known Bordeaux *négociant* business Borie-Manoux. The wines of the
firm of Borie-Manoux have demonstrated considerable improvement in vintages since the early eighties, particularly their famous estates in Pauillac
(Château Batailley), in St.-Emilion (Château Trotte Vieille), and in Pomerol
(Domaine de L'Eglise). However, this estate continued to turn out light, often
diluted, simple wines that lacked character and stature, but in 1994 quality
began to turn around. The 1995 was well made, and the 1996 is the finest
Lynch-Moussas I have ever tasted.

VINTAGES

1997—Interestingly, I prefer this wine to its bigger, more renowned stablemate,
•   Batailley. The cleanly made 1997 Lynch Moussas exhibits a dark, ruby/purple
85–   color, and ripe black currant and cassis notes. In the mouth, the wine reveals
86   moderate intensity, good sweetness (from glycerin and ripeness, not sugar),
      and a short but adequate finish. This wine should be ready to drink at bottling
      and last for 7–8 years. Last tasted, 3/98.

1996—The most promising Lynch-Moussas ever? Dense dark ruby/purple-colored,
•   with a textbook cassis nose with scents of smoky new oak and minerals, this
87–   focused wine exhibits layers of rich fruit, full body, and an excellent chewy
88+   texture without an excess of acidity or hard tannin. Long and impressively
      endowed, this wine may merit a close to outstanding score. Wow! Anticipated
      maturity: 2003–2016. Last tasted, 3/98.

1995—After bottling, the 1995 Lynch-Moussas is a very good wine, with a dark ruby
•   color, spicy, cedary, cassis fruit in its moderately endowed nose, good ripeness
86   and flesh on the attack, and a dry, clean, moderately tannic finish with grip
      and delineation. Anticipated maturity: 2002–2016. Last tasted, 11/97.

1994—A palatable effort, this deep ruby–colored wine exhibits a sweet bouquet with
•   scents of ripe red currant, cedar, herbs, and spice. Medium bodied, soft, and
82   fruity, this is a cleanly made, straightforward Pauillac to drink over the next
      7 years. Last tasted, 1/97.

1993—A green, herbaceous vegetal wine, the 1993 Lynch-Moussas is lean, harsh,
•   and likely to dry out over the next decade. Last tasted, 1/97.
76

1989—The 1989 is pleasant and cleanly made, but uncommonly light and soft for
•   such a well-placed vineyard. Drink it over the next 4–5 years. Last tasted,
79   1/93.

1988—Light, yet fruity and medium bodied, with good concentration, the soft, some-
•   what one-dimensional 1988 should be drunk over the next 4–6 years. Last
80   tasted, 1/93.

1986—The 1986 is a stern yet light wine, without enough richness and fruit to hold
•   up the tannins. Nevertheless, if you like your claret on the leaner, tougher
77   side, you may prefer the 1986 more than I do. Anticipated maturity: Now.
      Last tasted, 11/89.

1985—The wines of Lynch-Moussas tend to be light and early maturing, and the
•   1985 displays those characteristics, in addition to being soft, fruity, and
78   one-dimensional. Anticipated maturity: Now. Last tasted, 4/89.

MOUTON-ROTHSCHILD   OUTSTANDING

Classification: First-growth, June 21, 1973
Location of vineyards: Pauillac
Owner: Baronne Philippine de Rothschild G.F.A.
Address: 33250 Pauillac

Mailing address: Baron Philippe de Rothschild S.A., B.P.117, 33250
Pauillac
Telephone: 33 5 56 73 20 20; telefax: 33 5 56 73 20 44
Visits: By appointment only
Contact: Marie Françoise Parinet: telephone 33 5 56 73 21 29; telefax 33
5 56 73 21 28

VINEYARDS (red)
Surface area: 185.3 acres
Average age of vines: 42 years
Blend: 80% Cabernet Sauvignon, 10% Cabernet Franc, 8% Merlot, 2%
Petit Verdot
Density of plantation: 8,500 vines per hectare
Average yields (over the last 5 years): 55 hectoliters per hectare
Total average annual production: 25,000–30,000 cases

GRAND VIN (red)
Brand name: Château Mouton-Rothschild
Appellation: Pauillac
Mean annual production: 25,000 cases
Upbringing: Grapes are picked manually. Fermentations occur in wooden
vats. Wines are aged for 19–22 months in 100% new oak barrels. They
are fined.

SECOND WINE
Brand name: Le Petit Mouton de Mouton-Rothschild
Average annual production: extremely variable depending upon the
vintage, but usually well under 10% of the total production.

VINEYARDS (white)
Surface area: 14.8 acres
Average age of vines: 9 years
Blend: 48% Semillon, 38% Sauvignon Blanc, 14% Muscadelle
Density of plantation: 9,000 vines per hectare
Average yields (over the last 5 years): 45 hectoliters per hectare
Total average annual production: 1,500–2,000 cases

GRAND VIN (white)
Brand name: Aile d'Argent
Appellation: Bordeaux
Mean annual production: 1,500–2,000 cases
Upbringing: Fermentations occur in oak casks, 50% of which are new
and 50% of which have been used once, after *pressurage* direct or

macération pelliculaire. They remain on lees with a weekly *bâtonnage* and are transferred to vats a short time before bottling. The whole process lasts 12–14 months. Wines are both fined and filtered before bottling.

Evaluation of present classification: Should be maintained
Plateau of maturity: 12–40 years following the vintage

Mouton-Rothschild is the place and wine that the late Baron Philippe de Rothschild singularly created. No doubt his aspirations for Mouton, beginning at the age of 21 when he acquired the estate, were high. However, through the production of an opulently rich and remarkably deep and exotic style of Pauillac, he has been the only person able to effectuate a change in the 1855 classification of the wines of the Médoc. The baron died in January 1988, and his daughter, Philippine, is now the spiritual head of this winemaking empire. She continues to receive extraordinary assistance from the talented Mouton team led by Patrick Léon.

In 1973 Mouton-Rothschild was officially classified a "first-growth," which permitted the flamboyant baron to change his defiant wine labels from *"Premier ne puis, second ne daigne, Mouton suis"* ("First I cannot be, second I will not call myself, Mouton I am") to *"Premier je suis, second je fus, Mouton ne change"* ("First I am, second I was, Mouton does not change").

There is no question that several of the greatest bottles of Bordeaux I have ever drunk have been Moutons. The 1929, 1945, 1947, 1953, 1955, 1959, 1982, 1986, 1995, and 1996 are stunning examples of Mouton at its best. I have also experienced too many mediocre vintages of Mouton that are embarrassing for a first-growth to produce and obviously irritating for a consumer to purchase and taste. The 1980, 1979, 1978, 1977, 1976, 1974, 1973, 1967, and 1964, however, fell well below first-growth standards. Even the 1990 and 1989, two renowned vintages, produced wines that were surprisingly austere and lacking the concentration expected from a first-growth in a superb vintage.

The reasons for the commercial success of this wine are numerous. To begin with, the labels of Mouton are collector's items. Since 1945 the Baron Philippe de Rothschild has commissioned an artist to do an annual painting, which is depicted on the top of the label. There has been no shortage of masters to appear on the Mouton-Rothschild labels, from such Europeans as Miró, Picasso, Chagall, and Cocteau to the Americans Warhol, Motherwell, and, in 1982, John Huston. Second, the opulence of Mouton in the great vintages differs significantly in style from the austere elegance of Lafite-Rothschild and the powerful, tannic, dense, and muscular Latour. Third, the impeccably kept château itself, with its superb wine museum, is the Médoc's (and possibly the entire Bordeaux region's) top tourist attraction. Last, there was the baron himself, who did so much to promote not only his wines, but all the wines of Bordeaux. His daughter, Philippine, appears more than capable of continuing her father's legacy.

VINTAGES

1997—Mouton has been experimenting with malolactic fermentation in barrel (20%
•   of the 1997 was vinified in this manner). The 1997, which possesses some
90–   characteristics similar to the 1985, but is ultimately different, is a blend of
92   81% Cabernet Sauvignon, 13% Merlot, 3% Cabernet Franc, and 3% Petit
       Verdot. Only 60% of Mouton's harvest made it into the grand vin. This is a
       hedonistic, forward Mouton (hence the comparison with the 1985) with a deep
       ruby/purple color, ripe tannin, and the telltale Mouton cassis in its aromatics
       and flavors. Mouton's Merlot harvest took place on September 11, and was
       then stopped until September 16, concluding with the very late picked
       Cabernet Sauvignon on October 5. Approachable, without the massiveness of
       the two preceding vintages, the 1997 Mouton exhibits a soft mid-palate, loads
       of pure fruit, nicely integrated smoky new oak, and surprising length for the
       wine's initial attack. There is moderate tannin in this offering. This will be
       one of the few 1997s that will warrant a short-term cellaring of 3–4 years
       before consumption. I would not be surprised to see this wine last for two
       decades or more, making it one of the longer-lived 1997s. Last tasted, 3/98.
1996—Made from a blend virtually identical to the 1995 (72% Cabernet Sauvignon,
•   20% Merlot, and 8% Cabernet Franc), the 1996 has taken on weight and
94–   richness since I tasted it in spring 1997. An opaque purple color is accompa-
96   nied by an impressive, somewhat undeveloped but gorgeously pure crème de
       cassis nose with Asian spices, licorice, and smoky oak in the background.
       Sweet, full-bodied, powerful, and rich, with formidable extract, ripe tannin,
       and a layered impression, this wine builds to a blockbuster finish. I am
       super-impressed by this wine's evolution during 1997, as it now looks to be a
       great Mouton which I underrated when I first tasted it. Anticipated maturity:
       2006–2030. Last tasted, 3/98.
1995—Bottled in June 1997, this profound Mouton is more accessible than the more
•   muscular 1996. A blend of 72% Cabernet Sauvignon, 19% Merlot, and 9%
95+   Cabernet Franc, it reveals an opaque purple color, and reluctant aromas of
       cassis, truffles, coffee, licorice, and spice. In the mouth, the wine is "great
       stuff," with superb density, a full-bodied personality, rich mid-palate, and a
       layered, profound finish that lasts for 40+ seconds. There is outstanding
       purity and high tannin, but my instincts suggest this wine is lower in acidity
       and slightly fleshier than the brawnier, bigger 1996. Both are great efforts
       from Mouton-Rothschild. Anticipated maturity: 2004–2030. Last tasted,
       11/97.
1994—The 1994 appears to be the finest Mouton-Rothschild made following the
•   1986 and before the 1995's conception. The wine exhibits a dense, saturated
91+   purple color, followed by a classic Mouton nose of sweet black fruits intermin-

gled with smoke, *pain grillé,* spice, and cedar. Medium to full bodied, with outstanding concentration, a layered feel, plenty of tannin, and rich, concentrated fruit, this wine is similar to the fine 1988. Anticipated maturity: 2005–2025. By the way, the Dutch artist Appel has created a gorgeous label for the 1994. Last tasted, 1/97.

1993 — This beautifully made wine could be considered a sleeper of the vintage. The
 •   wine boasts a dark purple color, followed by a sweet bouquet of *pain grillé,*
 90   roasted nuts, and cassis that is just beginning to open. In the mouth, the wine may not possess the body and volume of a vintage such as 1990 or 1989, but there is more richness of fruit and a sweet, ripe, pureness to the wine, as well as medium body and outstanding balance. This moderately tannic, well-focused, surprisingly rich 1993 is capable of 15–20 years of evolution. Anticipated maturity: 2004–2015.

Readers should note that this wine comes with two labels. The original label, with its delicate yet unprovocative portrait nude of a preadolescent by Balthus, was not used as a result of protests from America's neopuritans. What has resulted is considerable speculation in the original label, which is selling at $50 more than the blank creamy white label that is "officially" sported by those bottles of Mouton-Rothschild imported to America. Last tasted, 1/97.

1992 — In 1992 Mouton has fashioned a flattering, soft, opulently styled wine with me-
 •   dium body, a healthy dark ruby/purple color, and a big, fragrant nose of jammy
 88   cassis, smoky oak, and roasted herbs and nuts. The wine offers a sweet, expansive midpalate and a lush, velvety-textured finish. It is an ostentatious, flashy Mouton for drinking over the next 10–12 years. Last tasted, 11/94.

1991 — The 1991 exhibits a moderately dark ruby/purple color as well as a promising
 •   and complex nose of such classic Pauillac aromas as lead pencil, roasted
 86+   nuts, and ripe cassis. The initial richness is quickly obliterated by frightful levels of tannin and a tough, hard finish. Although there is an interesting and alluring dimension to this wine, the tannin level is excessively high and the wine is likely to dry out after 10–15 years of cellaring. Readers who admire austere, fruitless wines will rate it higher. Last tasted, 1/94.

1990 — The 1990 is a hard, lean, austere, tannic style of Mouton that I predict will
 •   never shed enough tannin to attain complete harmony and balance. The wine
 87   exhibits a deep ruby color, less noticeable sweet oak than it possessed 2–3 years ago, hints of ripe black currant fruit, and an attenuated, angular, tough style that is uncharacteristic of this château's winemaking or the character of the 1990 vintage. This wine needs at least 10–15 years of cellaring, but don't expect a balanced Mouton when the tannin fades away—the wine is not that concentrated. In the context of a great vintage, Mouton's 1990 is a disappointment, something the Baroness agreed with when we shared it over dinner in Bordeaux. Anticipated maturity: 2006–2020. Last tasted, 3/98.

1989 — The 1989 Mouton-Rothschild is the superior wine, but in no sense is this a
 •   compelling wine if compared with the Moutons produced in 1995, 1986, and
 90   1982. The 1989 displays a dark ruby color that is already beginning to

reveal significant lightening at the edge. The bouquet is surprisingly evolved, offering up scents of cedar, sweet black fruits, lead pencil, and toasty oak. This elegant, medium-bodied, restrained wine is beautifully made, stylish, and not dissimilar to the 1985. It is an excellent to outstanding Mouton that should be close to full maturity in 4–5 years; it will drink well for 15–20. Last tasted, 11/96.

1988—The 1988 Mouton has an attractive aroma of exotic spices, minerals, coffee,
  •   black currants, and sweet oak. Much like the 1989, the bouquet is staggering,
 89   but the flavors are distinctly less profound. In the mouth, it is a much firmer, tougher, more obviously tannic wine than the 1989, with medium body and outstanding ripeness. This is a beautifully made 1988 that will last 20–25 years, but its short finish keeps it from being sublime. The 1988 is somewhat reminiscent of the 1985, but with more tannin. Anticipated maturity: Now– 2020. Last tasted, 1/93.

1987—This would appear to be a sure bet for the wine of the vintage. Certainly it is
  •   the most complete and backward 1987, with at least 10–15 years of aging
 88   potential. The touching dedication from the late Baron Philippe de Roth- schild's daughter on the label is almost worth the price of one bottle. Addi- tionally, 1987 was the last vintage of the baron and thus will probably fetch a fortune in 40 or 50 years. One of the deepest and most opaque wines of the vintage, with a tight yet promising bouquet of cedar and black currants, this wine exhibits surprising depth, medium to full body, and plenty of tannin in the finish. Anticipated maturity: Now–2010. Last tasted, 11/90.

1986—An enormously concentrated, massive Mouton-Rothschild, comparable in
  •   quality, but not style, to the 1982, 1959, and 1945, this impeccably made
 100 wine is still in its infancy. Interestingly, when I was in Bordeaux several years ago, I had this wine served to me blind from a magnum that had been opened and decanted 48 hours previously. Even then it still tasted like a barrel sample! I suspect the 1986 Mouton-Rothschild requires a minimum of 15–20 more years of cellaring; it has the potential to last for 50–100 years! Given the outrageously high prices being fetched by so many of the great 1982s and 1990s (and, lest I forget, the 1995 Bordeaux fu- tures), it appears this wine might still be one of the "relative bargains" in the fine wine marketplace. I wonder how many readers will be in shape to drink it when it does finally reach full maturity? A compelling wine! Last tasted, 3/98.

1985—This estate compares their 1985 to their 1959, but to me it is more akin to
  •   their 1962 or 1953. The rich, complex, well-developed bouquet of Oriental
 90+ spices, toasty oak, herbs, and ripe fruit is wonderful. On the palate, the wine is also rich, forward, long, and sexy. It ranks behind both Haut-Brion and Château Margaux in 1985. I am surprised by how evolved and ready to drink this wine is. Readers looking for a big, boldly constructed Mouton should search out other vintages, as this is a tame, forward, medium-weight wine that is close to full maturity. It is capable of lasting another 15+ years. Anticipated maturity: Now–2012. Last tasted, 3/98.

1984—During the decade of the eighties, Mouton was the hottest first-growth in
•   Pauillac. The 1984, which is almost 100% Cabernet Sauvignon, will be one
80   of the longest-lived wines of this vintage. Full bodied, tannic, concentrated,
         and rich in extract, this wine should have a surprisingly long life. It is a
         considerable surprise in a generally poor vintage. Anticipated maturity: Now—
         2005. Last tasted, 3/90.

1983—The classic Mouton lead pencil, cedary nose has begun to emerge. Medium
•   dark ruby, this elegant, medium-bodied wine will never be a great or legend-
90   ary Mouton. The flavors are ripe and moderately rich. With good depth and
         some firm tannins to resolve, this offering from Mouton is bigger and richer
         than the 1981, 1979, or 1978. Austere by the standards of Mouton and the
         vintage, the 1983 resembles the château's fine 1966. Anticipated maturity:
         Now–2015. Last tasted, 10/90.

1982—I find the saturated purple-colored Mouton-Rothschild to be the most back-
•   ward and unevolved wine of the 1982 vintage. It flaunted a knockout, fabu-
100   lously rich and ostentatious personality during its first 5–6 years after
         bottling. Since the late eighties it has gradually closed down, and it is hard to
         estimate when this wine might reemerge. The thick, unctuously textured,
         jammy fruit and enormous flavor concentration that are the hallmarks of the
         vintage are present, but the wine is extremely unevolved and behaves like a
         young barrel sample. This massive, powerful example of Mouton exhibits
         huge tannin and immense body. Significantly richer than the 1970 or 1961, it
         is not farfetched to suggest that it is comparable to either the 1959 or the
         1945! Owners who do not want to commit infanticide should cellar it for
         another 5–10 years. Like Latour, the 1982 Mouton-Rothschild is a potential
         50–60-year wine.
             The last two times I had this wine, I actually decanted it the morning of
         the day before I intended to drink it. The wine will reveal its extraordinary
         potential with approximately 30 hours of breathing in a closed decanter. It is
         a remarkable effort that still looks like a barrel sample more than a finished
         wine. A legend! Last tasted, 4/98.

1981—This has always been an uninspiring Mouton, but it has become increasingly
•   attenuated, with a frightfully austere personality. The color is a medium dark
79   ruby with some amber at the edge. The nose is composed largely of earth,
         wood, and dusty, dried red fruit aromas. In the mouth, this compact wine
         reveals medium body, excruciatingly high tannin, and little fruit. In my opin-
         ion, it is drying out and in large measure is a huge disappointment. Antici-
         pated maturity: Now. Last tasted, 10/97.

1980—This is an uninspiring effort from Mouton, notwithstanding the vintage condi-
•   tions that were unfavorable. Medium ruby color, with a stemmy, stalky, unripe
74   aroma, lean, austere, overly tannic flavors, and an astringent finish. Time may
         help, but I have my doubts. Anticipated maturity: Now. Last tasted, 10/83.

1979—This is another wine that has never quite developed, and, sadly, additional
•   time in the bottle does it no favors. It is a high-acid Mouton that has always
76   been austere, and what black currant fruit it possessed in its youth now seems

to have disappeared or evaporated. It is the tannin, acidity, alcohol, and wood that make up much of the uninspiring aromatics and flavors. The 1979 Mouton is an uninteresting wine that has no place to go. Anticipated maturity: Now. Last tasted, 10/97.

1978—A vegetal, cedary, coffee- and berry-scented Mouton, the 1978 is pleasant but
  •   lacks the concentration and depth expected of a first-growth. The wine is
  85   medium bodied, with a slight greenness to its curranty, earthy flavors and moderately astringent, bitter tannin in the finish. It is a pleasant wine that is unlikely to develop additional complexity or richness. Anticipated maturity: Now. Last tasted, 10/97.

1977—Thin, vegetal, stemmy, and charmless, this medium ruby wine should have
  •   been declassified completely rather than sold as a "first-growth" to unsus-
  66   pecting consumers. Last tasted, 4/81.

1976—Medium to dark ruby, with some browning at the edges, this wine is ap-
  •   proaching maturity and exhibits an interesting, moderately intense bouquet
  85   of ripe plums, spicy oak, and leather. Plenty of tannin is still evident, but the overall balance and depth of fruit suggest that the tannin will clearly outlive the fruit. It lacks the depth and concentration to be great, but for the vintage it is a respectable Mouton for drinking over the next decade. I must say that the wine's evolution has been much slower than I would have suspected. Anticipated maturity: Now–2000. Last tasted, 3/98.

1975—This wine has finally begun to reveal some potential. It has been closed and
  •   frightfully tannic for the last decade. The wine exhibits a good dark ruby/
  90?   garnet color, a sweet nose of cedar, chocolate, cassis, and spices, good ripe fruit and extraction, and a weighty, large-scaled, tannic finish. Although still unevolved, it is beginning to throw off its cloak of tannin and exhibit more complexity and balance. I remain concerned about how well the fruit will hold, but this wine will undoubtedly hit its plateau around the turn of the century. Putting it in the context of what is a largely disappointing range of Mouton-Rothschilds in the decade of the seventies, great bottles of the 1970 are superior to the 1975, but this is clearly the second-best Mouton of the decade. Last tasted, 12/95.

1974—A below average effort from Mouton, this wine has the telltale hollowness of
  •   the vintage, a stale, flat bouquet, and deficiency in rich fruitiness. Anticipated
  69   maturity: Now–probably in serious decline. Last tasted, 5/81.

1973—The year Mouton was officially made a "first-growth" was celebrated by a
  •   beautiful label done by Pablo Picasso. Whether judged by an art or wine
  65   critic, the label clearly surpasses the wine. Very oaky and woody, with rapidly fading fruit, this is a wine worth having only for the historic significance of the bottle's label. Anticipated maturity: Now–probably in serious decline. Last tasted, 2/82.

1971—This wine, which was a medium-weight, charming example in its youth,
  •   continues to develop well. Recent bottles have been the finest I have tasted
  88   of the 1971 Mouton-Rothschild. The color remains a deep dark garnet with some amber at the edge. The wine offers up a classic Pauillac nose of cedar,

black currant, and lead pencil aromas. On the palate, it reveals a savory, sweet, cedary, currant flavor profile with good freshness, adequate acidity, and ripe tannin. The wine is fully mature but is capable of lasting for another 5–10 years. Anticipated maturity: Now–2006. Last tasted, 10/97.

1970— I have had a remarkable number of opportunities to taste this wine. One of
• the most frustratingly irregular wines I have ever encountered, the 1970
93? Mouton can range from pure nectar to a wine that is angular, austere, and frightfully hard and tannic. This bottle (one of the Reserve du Château bottlings that was mistakenly released by the estate and labeled with the letters "R.C." rather than a number) was impossible to assess when decanted, owing to its hard, tough, impenetrable style. Nearly 8 hours later the wine had opened magnificently to reveal a classic bouquet of sweet cassis, tobacco, minerals, and exotic spice aromas. Opulent, full bodied, thick, and juicy, this particular wine would make a persuasive argument for long-term decanting given such an extraordinary evolution. After being perplexed throughout much of this wine's evolution, I was reassured by this bottle. No doubt Mouton's high Cabernet Sauvignon content causes this wine to go through a tight, hard, ungenerous stage, and the 1970 requires 5–7 more years of cellaring. Last tasted, 6/96.

1967— I tasted one agreeably fruity, fairly simple, medium-weight, and fully mature
• 1967 Mouton in 1974. More recently the wine has shown itself to be shallow,
70 hollow, and in decline. In the late eighties, a musty, mushroomy quality emerged. Drink up! Anticipated maturity: Now–probably in serious decline. Last tasted, 1/91.

1966— This review may be generous, but I have always liked this wine, even though
• it borders on being slightly too dry, austere, and restrained. Nevertheless, the
90 dark garnet color and classic sweet, spicy, tobacco, coffee, and black currant aromas are enticing. The wine still has powerful tannin in the finish, which contributes to the dry, austere character this example has always exhibited. One of the more intellectually styled Moutons, the 1966 is a classic example of the vintage, as well as of the château's Cabernet Sauvignon–dominated style. Anticipated maturity: Now–2008. Last tasted, 3/98.

1964— The 1964 Mouton is a notable failure because it was picked late in the deluge
• of rain that wiped out those châteaux that were waiting for extra ripeness.
55 One wonders why Bordeaux's best châteaux do not declassify the entire crop when they produce a wine such as this. A sweet, cooked bouquet is followed by equally sweet, disjointed, flabby flavors. Last tasted, 1/91.

1962— In earlier editions of this book I complained about bottle variation, but three
• tastings over the last several years from bottles that had been perfectly stored
92 revealed a splendid wine. The 1962 is extremely fragrant, with a dark garnet color revealing lightening at the edge. A sweet nose of jammy black fruits, cedar, and smoke is followed by a velvety-textured, medium- to full-bodied wine with no hard edges. It is a compellingly rich, opulent Mouton that appears to have gained character and complexity with age. Anticipated maturity: Now–2008. Last tasted, 10/97.

1961—I have found the 1961 Mouton-Rothschild to be distressingly variable in
 •   quality, much like the consistently inconsistent 1970. At its best the wine is
98?   a great Mouton. Huge, cedary, cassis, lead pencil, menthol-like aromas soared
        from the glass. The black/purple color revealed no signs of lightening or
        amber at the edge. Full bodied, rich, and superintense, this was a profound
        bottle of 1961 Mouton that would have stood up against the compelling 1959.
        Last tasted, 3/98.

ANCIENT VINTAGES

I am always blown away by the 1959 Mouton (100 points; last tasted 3/98),
one of the greatest Moutons ever made. Every time I have this wine it is
undeniable that Mouton made a richer, more persuasive wine in 1959 than in
1961. Astonishingly young and unevolved, with a black/purple color, the wine
exhibits a youthful nose of cassis, minerals, and new oak. Exceptionally
powerful and superextracted, with the fruit supported by high levels of tannin
and some lusty quantities of alcohol, this mammoth, full-bodied Mouton-
Rothschild should continue to evolve for another 20–30 years. It may well be
a 100-year wine! The 1955 (97 points; last tasted 3/98) should be a vintage
to buy at auction, as I suspect the price is more reasonable than what such
acclaimed vintages as 1959 and 1961 fetch. The color reveals no amber or
rust, only a slight lightening of intensity at the edge. The nose offers up that
explosive Mouton perfume of mint, leather, cassis, black olives, and lead
pencil. In the mouth, there is stunning concentration, magnificent extraction
of fruit, and plenty of tannin in the long finish. The wine still tastes remarkably young and could easily last another 20–30 years. Amazing! I remember
a friend of mine decanting a magnum of the 1953 (95 points; last tasted
10/94) and sticking it under my nose to share with me the incredible bouquet.
In addition to the exotic aromas of soy sauce, new saddle leather, cassis,
herbs, and spices, the 1953 offers a deep ruby color with some amber at the
edge. Sweet and fat, with voluptuously textured fruit, this low-acid wine has
no noticeable tannin. While it may be living dangerously, it is a decadent
treat if it is drunk immediately after decanting.
    The 1949 (94 points; last tasted 10/94) was always considered to be the
late baron's favorite vintage. While I find it a formidable Mouton, I have a
preference for the 1945, 1947, 1959, 1982, 1986, 1995, and 1996. The
bouquet offers copious amounts of sweet, ripe cassis fruit, herbs, spicy oak,
and a touch of coffee and cinnamon. Medium bodied, with moderate tannin
still noticeable, this compact, dark garnet, opaquely colored wine possesses
superb concentration and a remarkably long finish. It appears to be fully
mature, yet the balance, length, and tannin level suggest this wine could last
for another 20 years.
    I have never had anything but extraordinary, decadent, fabulously rich,

concentrated bottles of the 1947 Mouton-Rothschild (98 points; last tasted 3/98). The exotic, ostentatious bouquet of ginger, mint, coffee, cedar, and gobs of cassis fruit is followed by a syrupy, viscously textured, thick, juicy Mouton that is bursting with fruit. Although drinkable since I first tasted it over a decade ago, it exhibits no signs of fruit loss or color deterioration. It is one of the most exotic and opulent Mouton-Rothschilds I have ever tasted, but it needs to be consumed.

A consistent 100-point wine (only because my point scale stops at that number), the 1945 Mouton-Rothschild (last tasted 8/97) is truly one of the immortal wines of the century. This wine is easily identifiable because of its remarkably exotic, over-ripe, sweet nose of black fruits, coffee, tobacco, mocha, and Asian spices. An extraordinarily dense, opulent, and rich wine, with layers of creamy fruit, it behaves more like a 1947 Pomerol than a structured, powerful, and tannic 1945. The wine finishes with more than a 60-second display of ripe fruit, extract, and sweet tannin. This remarkably youthful wine (only light amber at the edge) is mind-boggling! Will it last another 50 years?

I know of no great Moutons from the thirties, but the 1929 (rated 86 in April 1991) is still drinkable, though only a shadow of what it was. The 1928, 1926, and 1924, all tasted in April 1991, were fading badly. None of them merited a score above the mid-seventies. The 1921 Mouton-Rothschild (72 points) offered a ruby/garnet color and an old, musty nose with hints of cedar, ginger, and jammy fruit. In the mouth, the wine was acidic, sinewy, compact, and angular, with no charm, fat, or fruit. Moreover, there was excessive tannin in the finish. Interestingly, the minty side of Mouton was still noticeable in the wine's aromatics.

PIBRAN

Classification: Cru Bourgeois
Location of vineyards: Pauillac
Owner: AXA Millésimes
Administrator: Jean-Michel Cazes
Address: 33250 Pauillac
Telephone: 33 5 56 73 17 17; telefax: 33 5 56 59 64 62
Visits: By appointment only
Contact: Suzanne Calvez at above telephone and fax numbers

VINEYARDS (red)
Surface area: 25 acres
Average age of vines: 30 years
Blend: 60% Cabernet Sauvignon, 30% Merlot, 10% Cabernet Franc

Density of plantation: 9,000 vines per hectare
Average yields (over the last 5 years): 45 hectoliters per hectare
Total average annual production: 4,500 cases

GRAND VIN (red)
Brand name: Château Pibran
Appellation: Pauillac
Mean annual production: 4,500 cases
Upbringing: Grapes are picked manually and totally destemmed.
Fermentations last 15–17 days normally (except in 1996, 20 days) in
temperature-controlled stainless-steel vats. Malolactics occur in vats, and
wines are transferred to casks, of which one-third are new, for 12–15
months. They are fined and filtered prior to bottling, and racking is done
every 3 months from barrel to barrel.

SECOND WINE
None produced.

Evaluation of present classification: The quality equivalent of a Cru
Bourgeois Exceptionnel
Plateau of maturity: 4–12 years following the vintage

Pibran, which is usually well colored, is aged in oak casks and has a dense, concentrated, moderately tannic style. If it lacks complexity and finesse, it more than compensates for that with its power and muscular personality. Given its moderate price, it provides one with a good introduction to the wines of Pauillac. Since Jean-Michel Cazes and his winemaker, Daniel Llose, took over responsibility for the making of Pibran, the wine has become more noticeably fruity, plump, and tasty. Both the 1988 and 1989 exhibited a more modern style than previous vintages and, no doubt because of their fat, fruity style, will have considerable crowd appeal.

VINTAGES

1996—This wine, which performed surprisingly well, may turn out to be one of the
•   better Pibrans I have tasted. The color is saturated purple. The nose offers
(85–   convincingly rich, cassis scents interwoven with spicy vanillin from new
87?)   barrels. The wine is medium bodied, with a good attack, but the tannin kicks
       in and the wine narrows out, tasting slightly astringent. If it fleshes out, it will
       merit an 87-point score, but it is too soon to know if that will happen. Last
       tasted, 3/97.
1995—The 1995 exhibits good color, ripeness, spice, flesh, and sweet fruit. It is an
•   easygoing, soft wine that will be ready to drink early and will keep for 7–8
85   years. Last tasted, 3/96.

1994—Pibran's 1994 is a tough-textured, tannic wine with average concentration
•   and a compressed, short finish. Last tasted, 3/96.
80

1992—Pibran's 1992 offers an impressively saturated color, but little else. The
•   acidity is too high, the tannin too noticeable, and the absence of fruit too
74   glaring. The result is a hollow, tough-textured wine with no charm. Last
        tasted, 11/94.

1991—The straightforward, deep ruby–colored 1991 exhibits little bouquet and hard
•   tannin in its tough-textured, medium-bodied finish. It will no doubt dry out
76   before any real charm emerges. Last tasted, 1/94.

1990—The 1990 Pibran is a clone of the 1989, although slightly fatter and richer.
•   Drink it over the next 6–9 years. Last tasted, 1/93.
88

1989—This Pauillac Cru Bourgeois has turned in a strong effort in 1989. It is deep
•   ruby/purple, with a fine nose of smoky new oak followed by copious quantities
87   of cassis fruit. The low-acid finish is fat and mouth-filling. Drink it over the
        next 5–7 years. Last tasted, 1/93.

1988—The 1988, a plump, tasty, ripe, amply endowed Pauillac, lacks complexity,
•   but it does have gobs of sweet fruit and offers immediate appeal. Anticipated
86   maturity: Now. Last tasted, 1/93.

PICHON-LONGUEVILLE BARON   EXCELLENT

Classification: Second-growth in 1855
Location of vineyards: Pauillac
Owner: AXA Millésimes
Administrator: Jean-Michel Cazes
Address: St.-Lambert, 33250 Pauillac
Telephone: 33 5 56 73 17 17; telefax: 33 5 56 73 17 28
Visits: Every day from 9 A.M. to 12:30 P.M., and 2 P.M. to 6 P.M. (on Friday
until 5 P.M.)
Contact: Susanne Calvez

VINEYARDS (red)
Surface area: 168 acres
Average age of vines: 35 years
Blend: 70% Cabernet Sauvignon, 25% Merlot, 5% Cabernet Franc
Density of plantation: 9,000 vines per hectare
Average yields (over the last 5 years): 45 hectoliters per hectare
Total average annual production: 35,000 cases

GRAND VIN (red)
Brand name: Château Pichon-Longueville Baron
Appellation: Pauillac

Mean annual production: 24,000 cases
Upbringing: Grapes are picked manually and are totally destemmed.
Fermentations last 15–17 days normally (except in 1996, 20 days) and
occur in temperature-controlled stainless-steel tanks. Malolactics occur
in vats, except for a very small portion of the yield that goes into oak
casks. Wines are transferred in December to barrels, 70% of which are
new, for 12–15 months (bottling is done in springtime). They are fined
and filtered. Racking is done every 3 months from barrel to barrel.

SECOND WINE
Brand name: Les Tourelles de Longueville
Average annual production: 12,000 cases

Evaluation of present classification: Should be maintained, particularly
since 1986
Plateau of maturity: 8–25 years following the vintage

This noble-looking château opposite Pichon-Longueville–Comtesse de Lalande and Latour, which made a modest comeback in wine quality in the
early eighties, was sold in the late 1980s by its owners—the Bouteiller family
—to the insurance conglomerate known as AXA. To the company's credit,
they hired Jean-Michel Cazes of Château Lynch-Bages to oversee the vineyard and winemaking. The Cazes touch, which included later picking dates,
a stricter selection, the introduction of a second wine, and the utilization of a
higher percentage of new oak casks, has made for a dramatic turnaround in
quality. As a consequence, Pichon-Longueville, frequently called Pichon
Baron, now merits its prestigious second-growth status.

The vineyard is superbly situated on gravelly soil with a full southerly
exposure. Much of the vineyard is adjacent to that of Château Latour. It has
been speculated that the lack of brilliance in many of Pichon Baron's wines
in the sixties and seventies was a result of both casual viticultural practices
and poor cellar management. I remember passing by the cellars on a torridly
hot afternoon in July, only to see the newly bottled vintage stacked up outside
the cellars, roasting in the relentless sunshine. Under the Cazes team, such
recklessness has no doubt stopped.

Rhetoric and public relations efforts aside, the best evidence that Pauillac
once again has two great Pichons are the wines that have been produced at
Pichon Baron since 1986. This château should prove to be one of the great
superstars of the nineties. Great wines also emerged from the estate in 1988,
1989, and 1990. If the 1988, 1989, and 1990 are indicative of the style
Jean-Michel Cazes has in mind for Pichon Baron, expect a powerful, bold,
intensely concentrated wine.

VINTAGES

1997—Seventy percent new oak casks were utilized for this 80% Cabernet Sauvi-
•   gnon/20% Merlot blend. Not a heavyweight, it is a medium-bodied, dense
87–   purple-colored claret with low acidity and moderate tannin. Well-focused and
90   delineated for a 1997 (most wines of this vintage are open-knit and round),
        this offering is characterized by copious quantities of sweet black currant fruit
        intermixed with toasty *pain grillé* scents. In the mouth, there is a well-focused
        feeling, moderate tannin, and a moderately long finish. This was one of the
        lesser-evolved 1997s I tasted, so it will probably need 2–3 years of cellaring
        when it is released. It should keep for 15 years. Last tasted, 3/98.

1996—An impressive wine with enough potential to merit an outstanding score, but
•   more tannic and austere than the 1995, the 1996 Pichon Baron reveals a
88–   dense ruby/purple color, and sweet cassis fruit and toasty new oak in the
90+   nose. The wine offers attractive chocolatey, cassis, and blackberry fruit in its
        finish, and appears to be fleshing out as it ages in cask. I expect this wine to
        be every bit as good as the 1995 with additional longevity. Anticipated
        maturity: 2004–2018. Last tasted, 3/98.

1995—A stylish, elegant, more restrained style of Pichon Baron, with less obvious
•   new oak than usual, this deep ruby/purple-colored wine offers a pure black
90   currant-scented nose with subtle aromas of coffee and smoky toasty oak. In
        the mouth, the wine displays less weight and muscle than the 1996, but it
        offers suave, elegant, and rich fruit presented in a medium- to full-bodied,
        surprisingly lush style. Anticipated maturity: 2001–2016. Last tasted, 11/97.

1994—Dark ruby/purple colored, with a crushed, pure cassis aroma, this excellent,
•   medium- to full-bodied wine reveals sweet fruit on the attack and plenty of
88   tannin, but not the inner core of richness and density exhibited by such other
        1994 Pauillacs as Pichon Lalande, Grand-Puy-Lacoste, and Pontet-Canet. To
        its credit, the 1994 Pichon-Longueville does not reveal any vegetal notes. It
        should evolve nicely for 10–15 years, representing an attractive, well-made,
        medium-bodied, classically rendered Bordeaux. Anticipated maturity: 1999–
        2014. Last tasted, 1/97.

1993—An evolved dark garnet color is followed by vegetal, green pepper–like
•   aromas and some sweet, red curranty fruit. Given the laudable consistency of
84   Pichon-Longueville since the late eighties, the 1993 is mediocre. It is soft,
        vegetal, and easy to drink, but uninteresting. Anticipated maturity: Now–
        2006. Last tasted, 1/97.

1992—This is one of the legitimate stars of the vintage. In all the tastings done
•   during my 10-day sojourn immersed in tasting the 1992 and 1993 Bordeaux
89   in November 1994, this wine stood out every time I tasted it. The wine
        exhibits a saturated dark ruby/purple color and a big, flashy, bold bouquet of
        jammy black currants, cedar, and smoky oak. Medium to full bodied, with
        wonderful sweet, rich, concentrated fruit, and moderate tannin, this highly
        extracted, gorgeously made wine is low enough in acidity to be drunk now yet
        promises to evolve gracefully for 12–15 years. It is a terrific effort for the
        vintage! Last tasted, 11/94.

1991 — The 1991 exhibits a formidable, opaque, dark purple color and a tight but
  •   promising nose of licorice, minerals, and black currants. The attack offers
 86+   wonderfully ripe fruit in a medium-bodied format, but the finish is dominated
        by hard, tough tannin. Is there sufficient fruit? I think so. It is one of the most
        promising wines of the vintage, but backward. This wine needs a good 2–3
        years of cellaring; it should last for 15 or more. Last tasted, 1/94.

1990 — The 1990 Pichon-Longueville exhibits the roasted overripeness of this vintage,
  •   but it manages to keep everything in perspective. The wine is opulent and
 96   flamboyant, with lower acidity and noticeably less tannin than the 1989. It is
        equally concentrated, with a more evolved nose of cedar, black fruits, earth,
        minerals, and spices. On the palate, the wine offers sensational quantities of
        jammy fruit, glycerin, wood, and sweet tannin. It is far more fun to taste and
        drink (more hedonistic, perhaps?) than the more structured, backward, yet ex-
        ceptional 1989. Ideally readers should have both vintages in their cellars. The
        1990 can be drunk now as well as over the next 25+ years. Last tasted, 11/96.

1989 — The 1989 Pichon-Longueville exhibits an opaque, dense purple color that
  •   suggests a massive wine of considerable extraction and richness. The dense,
 95+   full-bodied 1989 is brilliantly made, with huge, smoky, chocolatey, cassis
        aromas intermingled with scents of toasty oak. Well layered, with a sweet
        inner core of fruit, this awesomely endowed, backward, tannic, prodigious
        1989 needs another 5–6 years of cellaring; it should last for 3 decades or
        more. It is unquestionably a great Pichon-Longueville. Last tasted, 11/96.

1988 — The 1988 Pichon-Longueville promises to be one of the half dozen superstars
  •   of this vintage. Surprisingly large scaled for a 1988, with a bouquet of oak,
 90   cassis, and licorice, it is deep in color, rich, softly tannic, and medium to full
        bodied. The wine should reach maturity early on but keep for 15–20 years.
        Anticipated maturity: Now–2010. Last tasted, 1/93.

1987 — This is a fine wine for the vintage. Rich, long, supple, and fat, this tasty,
  •   generously endowed Pauillac should drink well for another 5–7 years. Antici-
 84   pated maturity: Now. Last tasted, 11/90.

1986 — Deep black/ruby in color, with a fragrant, expansive bouquet of oak and
  •   black currants, this brawny, full-bodied, rich wine has plenty of tannin yet,
 88   atypically for the vintage, a pleasing suppleness that permits it to be drunk
        now. Anticipated maturity: Now–2005. Last tasted, 10/90.

1985 — The 1985 Pichon-Longueville is fruity and agreeable, but diffuse, slightly
  •   flabby, and unstructured. It is a tasty but essentially one-dimensional wine.
 83   Anticipated maturity: Now. Last tasted, 10/90.

1983 — The 1983 is certainly a better-structured wine than the 1982, but as it has
  •   aged, it has, curiously, become less interesting. Dark ruby, with a spicy,
 85   cassis-and-herb-scented bouquet, this medium-bodied wine still has plenty
        of tannin but appears to be maturing rapidly. Anticipated maturity: Now–
        2005. Last tasted, 3/89.

1982 — I certainly bungled the early reviews of this wine! In barrel and early in
  •   bottle, it was a big, ripe fruit bowl of a wine with virtually no acidity or
 92   structure in evidence. However, it is safe to say the one component Bordeaux

never lacks, even in the ripest, fattest vintages is tannin. As this wine has evolved it has become much more delineated as well as classically proportioned. In fact, it is an exceptional example of Pichon-Longueville produced during a period when this estate was best known for the mediocrity of its wines. The 1982 reveals a dense, opaque ruby/purple/garnet color, and a huge nose of cedar, sweet cassis, and spice. The wine's full body, marvelous concentration, that 1982-like opulence and unctuosity, and a thick, jammy, moderately tannic, superb finish, all combine to offer a splendid drinking experience. Given its sweet, creamy personality, this wine can be drunk now or cellared for 20 more years. Last tasted, 9/95.

1981 — The 1981 is overtly oaky, without any great depth or intensity. With average
  •   concentration of fruit, and somewhat short in the finish, this Pichon-
  83   Longueville is a charming, agreeable, precociously styled wine that is ideal
       for consumption over the next 5–6 years. Anticipated maturity: Now. Last
       tasted, 2/87.

1980 — Thin, vegetal, unripe fruity flavors reveal deficiencies in aroma, flavor, and
  •   length. Last tasted, 2/83.
  60

1979 — For whatever reasons, the 1979 Pichon-Longueville is gloriously supple and
  •   ready to drink. It has ample velvety, black currant fruit, a spicy, tarry, oaky
  84   bouquet, and soft, precocious flavors. Anticipated maturity: Now. Last tasted,
       3/88.

1978 — Fat, plump, jammy, and one-dimensional, the 1978 Pichon-Longueville lacks
  •   grip and backbone, has a loosely knit structure, and exhibits a sweet, short
  82   finish. It has reached full maturity. Anticipated maturity: Now. Last tasted,
       7/88.

1975 — A very medicinal, unusual nose suggesting burnt coffee is offputting. Chapta-
  •   lized, sweet, unstructured flavors dissipate and fade in the glass. A soft,
  64   uncharacteristic, and disjointed 1975. Anticipated maturity: Now—probably
       in serious decline. Last tasted, 8/90.

1971 — A poor effort from Pichon-Longueville, this dried-out, hollow wine exhibits a
  •   washed-out brownish color, an artificial, sugary ripeness of fruit, and a poor,
  65   astringent, tannic finish. Quite disappointing. Anticipated maturity: Now—
       probably in serious decline. Last tasted, 9/78.

1970 — Decently colored, but rather light in weight with an astringent, very tannic
  •   feel on the palate, this medium-bodied wine does not appear to have the fruit
  73   to outdistance the tannin. Only a gambler would bet on it. Anticipated matu-
       rity: Now. Last tasted, 3/86.

1966 — Rather imbalanced and perplexing to taste, the 1966 Pichon-Longueville has
  •   good, dark ruby color, with just a little amber at the edge, a spicy, aggressive,
  82   cedary, black currant bouquet intermingled with decaying vegetation smells.
       Big, fleshy, but disjointed on the palate, with an excess of tannin, this wine
       can be drunk now. No doubt the 1966 will age for another decade or more,
       but the wine is coarse and rustic. Anticipated maturity: Now–2000. Last
       tasted, 2/87.

1961—After having some mediocre bottles of this wine, the last several times I
 • tasted it, it performed well. Still dark ruby with an orange edge, the 1961
86 Pichon-Longueville has a big, spicy, damp-earth, cedary bouquet, and rich,
fat, substantial flavors that lack the multidimensionality of the finest 1961s.
Anticipated maturity: Now–2000. Last tasted, 2/88.

ANCIENT VINTAGES

The finest old vintages of Pichon-Longueville I have tasted included the 1959
(better as well as less evolved than the 1961, and a wine I have rated between
87 and 90), a fine, dense 1955 (rated 87), and a robust, fragrant, fully
mature 1953 (rated 89). I have tasted the following vintages once, but I was
disappointed with the 1949, 1947, and 1945.

PICHON-LONGUEVILLE–COMTESSE DE LALANDE OUTSTANDING

Classification: Second-growth in 1855
Location of vineyards: Pauillac and St.-Julien (for 11 hectares)
Owner: Madame May-Elaine de Lencquesaing
Address: 33250 Pauillac
Telephone: 33 5 56 59 19 40; telefax: 33 5 56 59 29 78
Visits: By appointment only
Contact: Sophie Ferrère at above address and numbers

VINEYARDS (red)
Surface area: 185.3 acres
Average age of vines: 35 years
Blend: 45% Cabernet Sauvignon, 35% Merlot, 12% Cabernet Franc, 8%
Petit Verdot
Density of plantation: 9,000 vines per hectare
Average yields (over the last 5 years): 50 hectoliters per hectare
Total average annual production: 450,000–500,000 bottles

GRAND VIN (red)
Brand name: Château Pichon-Longueville–Comtesse de Lalande
Appellation: Pauillac
Mean annual production: 35,000 cases
Upbringing: Grapes are picked manually and totally destemmed. After a
light destemming and crushing, they are placed into 33 temperature-
controlled stainless-steel vats. Fermentations last 18–24 days, and
malolactics occur in vats. *Assemblage* takes place in December, and
wines are transferred, half in new oak barrels and half in 1-year-old
barrels for a period of 18 months. Racking is done every 3 months, and
wines are fined with egg whites and bottled after a slight filtration.

SECOND WINE
Brand name: Réserve de la Comtesse
Average annual production: 6,000 cases

THIRD WINE
Brand name: Domaine de Gartieu
Average annual production: 6,000 bottles
The product of the younger vines that is not good enough to make either
the grand vin or Réserve de la Comtesse is bottled under this label.

Evaluation of present classification: The quality equivalent of a
first-growth
Plateau of maturity: 5–25 years

NOTE: Selection at Pichon-Comtesse: Each year, at the time of the
assemblage, all the cuvées, without exception, are tasted blind by
Madame de Lencquesaing, her immediate staff, and the oenologists, so as
to pick out those that best reflect the style of Pichon-Comtesse for the
vintage. Usually the young vines are eliminated because of the
herbaceous character.

At present, Pichon-Longueville–Comtesse de Lalande (Pichon-Lalande) is
unquestionably the most popular and, since 1978, one of Pauillac's most
consistently brilliant wines. In many vintages it rivals and occasionally
surpasses the three famous first-growths of this commune. The wines of
Pichon-Lalande have been very successful since 1961, but there is no question that in the late seventies and early eighties, under the energetic helm
of Madame de Lencquesaing, the quality has risen to an extremely high
plateau.

The wine is made in an intelligent manner and is darkly colored, supple,
fruity, and smooth enough to be drunk young. It has the distinction, along
with Château Palmer in Margaux, to be one of the most famous Médoc estates
that utilizes a significant quantity of Merlot in the blend. Yet Pichon-Lalande
has the requisite tannin, depth, and richness to age gracefully for 10–20
years. The high proportion of Merlot (35%) no doubt accounts for part of the
wine's soft, fleshy characteristic.

The property was once part of a single estate called Pichon-Longueville,
which was divided in 1850. Madame Lencquesaing's father, Édouard Miailhe,
purchased it in 1924, but it is his daughter who has been responsible for the
current fame. Significant investments were made during the eighties. A new
cuvier was built in 1980, a new barrel-aging cellar and tasting room (with a
spectacular vista of neighboring Château Latour) in 1988, and in 1990, the
renovations of the château were completed. Madame Lencquesaing resides at

the château, which sits across the road from Pichon-Longueville Baron. Its vineyards lie both in Pauillac and St.-Julien, the latter characteristic often given as the reason for Pichon-Lalande's supple style.

VINTAGES

1997—It seems to me that Pichon-Lalande aimed for an elegant style of wine in
•   1997, avoiding any attempt to overextract. Consequently, it turned out a wine
87–   with more depth, but also astringent tannin. It is an elegant, medium-bodied
88   Pichon-Lalande that will drink well young. If it puts on a bit more weight and intensity, it will merit a slightly higher score. This estate's harvest took place between September 19 and early October. Only 40% of the production was considered good enough for the grand vin. A blend of 55% Cabernet Sauvignon, 30% Merlot, 5% Cabernet Franc, and a whopping 10% Petit Verdot, the wine exhibits a dark ruby color, followed by a forward, sweet black cherry and cassis-scented nose, and fleshy, medium-bodied, open-knit, low acid flavors. The finish is slightly short, but the wine is stylish, graceful, and easy to drink and understand. It should age well for 10–12 years. An expressive wine aromatically, with light tannin in the finish, Pichon-Lalande's 1997 is a captivating and pleasing wine, but to put it in perspective, it is not comparable to the fabulous 1996 and 1995, or even the underrated, impressive 1994. Last tasted, 3/98.

1996—The 1996 Pichon-Lalande exhibits extraordinary *sur-maturité* due to the ex-
•   ceptional ripeness the Médoc's Cabernet Sauvignon achieved in this vintage.
94–   The wine has tightened up since my tasting in the spring, but it remains an
96+   opaque purple-colored example with a smoky, blueberry, blackberry, and cassis-scented nose that is to die for. Medium to full bodied, with huge extract as well as extraordinary elegance, and a perfect marriage between new oak, fruit, and tannin, this is one of the more structured and tannic Pichon-Lalandes I have ever tasted, yet the wine's triumph is a result of its sweetness of tannin. An atypically high percentage of Cabernet Sauvignon (75%) was used in the blend, with an abnormally small percentage of Merlot (5%). In most vintages Pichon-Lalande contains 30%–40% Merlot, so the 1996 may be the most Cabernet Sauvignon-based wine made at this estate in memory. A profound success, the 1996 is one of the finest examples made under the regime of Madame de Lencquesaing. Anticipated maturity: 2002–2025. Last tasted, 3/98.

1995—What sumptuous pleasures await those who purchase either the 1996 or 1995
•   Pichon-Lalande. It is hard to choose a favorite, although the 1995 is a
96   smoother, more immediately sexy and accessible wine. It is an exquisite example of Pichon-Lalande with the Merlot component giving the wine a coffee/chocolatey/cherry component to go along with the Cabernet Sauvignon and Cabernet Franc's complex blackberry/cassis fruit. The wine possesses an opaque black/ruby/purple color, and sexy, flamboyant aromatics of *pain grillé*, black fruits, and cedar. Exquisite on the palate, this full-bodied, layered, multidimensional wine should prove to be one of the vintage's most extra-

ordinary success stories. Anticipated maturity: 2001–2020. Last tasted, 3/98.

1994—One of the stars of the vintage, this opaque purple–colored wine possesses a
•   gorgeously perfumed, exotic, smoky, black currant, Asian spice, and sweet
91   vanillin bouquet. It is followed by thick, rich, moderately tannic flavors that
       exhibit medium to full body, good structure, outstanding purity, and a classi-
       cally layered, long, pure finish. This terrific Pichon-Lalande should evolve
       effortlessly for 18–20 years. Anticipated maturity: 2001–2020. Last tasted,
       1/97.

1993—Pichon-Lalande's 1993 is not as fruity and soft as I expected. The wine
•   exhibits light to medium body, an herbal, sweet, currant nose, disjointed,
85   awkward flavors, and an evolved personality with a pervasive greenness to its
       aromas and flavors. The wine is best consumed over the next 5–6 years. Last
       tasted, 1/97.

1992—The 1992 is the most disappointing wine made at this estate in nearly a
•   decade. The wine reveals medium ruby color, a disjointed, awkward personal-
79   ity with compact, attenuated flavors, a stewed, tannic character, and harsh
       tannin in the short finish. The color is sound, but there is no charm or ripe
       fruit, resulting in a wine that is all structure, tannin, and alcohol. Three
       tastings after bottling, with nearly identical notes to those from cask tastings,
       confirm this wine's performance. Last tasted, 11/94.

1991—Pichon-Lalande's 1991 is among only a handful of 1991s worthy of being the
•   "wine of the vintage." Only 30% of the harvest went into the final wine,
89   resulting in a deeper-colored, richer, more concentrated, and complex wine
       than the 1990, which was atypically light—even for the elegant Pichon-
       Lalande style. The 1991, which possesses plenty of tannin, displays an
       opaque, deep ruby/purple color and a sweet nose of chocolate, cedar, and
       ripe, plummy, black currant fruit. Round, medium to full bodied, and opulent
       (atypical for a 1991), this wine finishes with considerable length and author-
       ity. Drink it over the next 10–15 years.

1990—I have been consistently disappointed by my tastings of the 1990 Pichon-
•   Lalande. Yet never have I rated it as low as I did in this blind tasting. The
79   wine is unmistakably vegetal, austere, and lacking the seductive, sweet,
       ripe fruit this estate produces in top years. Something clearly went awry for
       Pichon-Lalande to miss so badly in an exceptional vintage. In this tasting,
       the wine was lean, diluted, intensely herbaceous, and lacking sweetness,
       depth, ripeness, and charm. Apologists who have badly overrated this wine
       will no doubt insist that its owners give it additional cellaring, but aging will
       only exaggerate this wine's lack of balance. Like its northern neighbor in
       Pauillac, Mouton-Rothschild, this wine is a major disappointment. As I have
       said before, the 1991 Pichon-Lalande, from a decidedly weak vintage, is a
       superior wine! Last tasted, 4/98.

1989—Pichon-Lalande's 1989, although not as profound as the 1995, 1994, 1986,
•   1983, or 1982, is a beautifully made wine. It exhibits a deep ruby/purple
92   color, and a sweet, roasted nose of rich cassis fruit, herbs, and vanilla. Lush

and round, this medium- to full-bodied, nicely textured, layered Pichon-Lalande possesses low acidity, outstanding ripeness, and beautiful purity and balance. It is already drinking surprisingly well, so owners should not hesitate to pull a cork. It should continue to offer rich, seductive drinking for another 15+ years. Last tasted, 11/96.

1988 — Dark ruby, with a full-intensity bouquet of new oak, black fruits, vanillin, and
• spring flowers, this silky smooth, full-bodied 1988 has excellent extraction of
90 fruit, plenty of glycerin, and a sense of elegance. Seductively precocious, it should drink superbly over the next 10–15 years. Anticipated maturity: Now–2008. Last tasted, 4/98.

1987 — This wine typifies Pichon-Lalande with graceful, velvety texture, rich, cassis-
• scented and cassis-flavored fruit, medium body, and a satiny finish. It is
86 faithful to the style of wine sought by the château. Offering a fragrant, velvety mouthful of wine, it should be drunk up immediately. It was one of my favorite wines of the vintage, and while still delicious, increasingly fragile. Anticipated maturity: Now–2000. Last tasted, 4/98.

1986 — The 1986 is the most tannic, as well as the largest-framed Pichon-Lalande
• between the 1975 and the 1996. Whether it will ultimately eclipse the 1982
94 is doubtful, but it will be longer-lived. Dark ruby/purple, with a tight yet profound bouquet of cedar, black currants, spicy oak, and minerals, this full-bodied, deeply concentrated, exceptionally well balanced wine is, atypically, too brawny and big to drink young. Anticipated maturity: Now–2015. Last tasted, 4/98.

1985 — The 1985 Pichon-Lalande is an outstanding wine, but I do not think it reaches
• the same level of quality as the 1996, 1995, 1994, 1989, 1986, 1983, or
90 1982. It has a deep ruby color and a ripe, oaky, curranty bouquet with a trace of herbaceousness. On the palate, the wine is rich, elegant, supple, and not unlike the style of either the 1979 or 1981, but fatter. It is a lovely wine. Anticipated maturity: Now–2002. Last tasted, 4/98.

1983 — A stunning wine, Pichon-Lalande's 1983 has been gorgeous to drink for a
• number of years. It is one of the finest 1983s, especially for a northern Médoc.
94 The color remains a dark ruby/purple, with slight lightening at the edge. The knockout nose of roasted herbs, sweet, jammy black currants, and *pain grillé* is followed by a full-bodied, gorgeously concentrated and well-proportioned wine with low acidity, plenty of glycerin, and a savory, highly extracted, fleshy mouth-feel. This has always been one of the stars of the vintage. Anticipated maturity: Now–2005. Last tasted, 4/98.

1982 — This has been the most sumptuous, delicious, and profound 1982 to drink
• over the last 5–6 years. It has never gone through any kind of dormant stage,
99 and it continues to be the odds-on favorite to emerge first in any blind tasting of the top 1982s. It reveals a classic Pauillac aromatic profile of sweet black currant fruit intermingled with scents of herbs, cedar, and toast. However, on the palate it performs more like a great Pomerol. Given its unctuous texture and lavish quantities of fruit, glycerin, and alcohol, this is a thick, supple, velvety-textured, gloriously decadent, and hedonistic Pichon-Lalande that

should continue to drink well for another 10–12 years. If readers need just one wine with which to impress someone, close a deal, or just experience the pleasures of wine, make it the 1982 Pichon-Lalande. Last tasted, 4/98.

1981 —This has always been one of the sexiest, most delicious wines from the 1981
• 　　vintage. It still possesses a dark ruby/purple color. While the 1981 is less
89 　　powerful than the 1982 and 1983, it reveals copious quantities of sweet black currant fruit, good flesh for the vintage, and a pure, nicely textured and balanced style. This wine remains vibrant and youthful. Anticipated maturity: Now–2002. Last tasted, 6/97.

1980 —A lovely, medium-weight wine that has been very well vinified, the 1980
• 　　Pichon-Lalande is delightful for current drinking. The bouquet offers spicy,
84 　　cedary scents intermingled with copious ripe aromas of black currants. This is a soft, velvety, very nicely concentrated wine from a vintage considered poor to mediocre. Anticipated maturity: Now. Last tasted, 12/88.

1979 —Undoubtedly a top success for the vintage, Pichon-Lalande's 1979 exhibits a
• 　　dark garnet color, with some amber at the edge. It offers a fragrant bouquet of
90 　　cedar, roasted herbs, and cassis. Rich, with medium body, well-integrated tannin, and some acidity, this is the quintessentially elegant style of Bordeaux that is found nowhere else in the world. Anticipated maturity: Now–2004. Last tasted, 6/97.

1978 —An excellent 1978 (one of the top wines of the vintage), Pichon-Lalande's
• 　　offering displays an aromatic profile consisting of roasted herbs, chocolate,
92 　　cedar, tobacco, and ripe currant fruit. Medium bodied, with low acidity, some tannin, and a round, attractive personality, this wine has reached its plateau of maturity, where it should remain for another decade. Anticipated maturity: Now–2007. Last tasted, 6/97.

1976 —Lacking the concentration and character of the best years, this wine is,
• 　　nevertheless, highly successful for the vintage. The color is medium ruby,
84 　　with some brown and amber at the edges. A gentle, suave, interesting, mature bouquet and soft, round, curranty flavors have provided pleasure since the late seventies. Yet the wine refuses to fade. Still at its peak. Anticipated maturity: Now. Last tasted, 2/88.

1975 —This wine reached full maturity early and has taken on an increasing amount
• 　　of amber/orange. It exhibits a dusty, herbaceous side as it sits in the glass.
90 　　Although the wine is beginning to dry out, it is still an excellent claret, with classic, cedary, currant fruit combined with herbs and spices. Medium bodied, with some sweetness on the attack, the wine narrows out and tastes more compressed and compact after it sits in the glass for 5–10 minutes. I would opt for drinking it over the next 5–6 years. At a tasting in spring 1998, the wine performed exquisitely, making me think that well-stored bottles of this vintage may be undervalued. Last tasted, 4/98.

1974 —Now past prime by a good decade, the 1974 Pichon-Lalande is light ruby/
• 　　amber in color with a frail, dissipated bouquet and soft, very faded flavors.
67 　　Last tasted, 9/80.

1973—Again completely gone, the light ruby, brown–colored wine was at its best in
  •   1978, but like so many light, diluted 1973s, it is now thin and empty. Last
  62   tasted, 10/80.

1971—The 1971 is an attractive wine, although I have not retasted it recently. The
  •   last note I have (from a magnum) suggested the wine had a mature, spicy,
  81   caramel-scented, ripe, complex bouquet. Soft, gentle, spicy flavors exhibited
          good concentration. Quite pleasant, but this wine, I believe, should have been
          drunk by the mid-1980s. Last tasted, 2/83.

1970—The 1970 Pichon-Lalande appears to be losing its fruit and is in decline. The
  •   color revealed considerable rust and amber. The wine exhibited some vegetal,
  87   tobacco, cedary, black currant scents, but on the palate the sweet fruit in the
          attack dissipated quickly to reveal acidity, tannin, and alcohol as well as a
          tough finish. I have had better examples, but this wine has been fully mature
          for many years. Well-stored bottles should consistently rate in the upper
          eighties. Last tasted, 4/98.

1967—The 1967 was best in 1975, when it had some charm and just enough fruit to
  •   balance out the acidity and tannins. Not tasted recently, but given the light,
  75   frail character, the wine is most likely to have faded badly. Last tasted, 7/78.

1966—Now ready to drink, this moderately dark ruby–colored wine has a rich,
  •   toasty, peppery, somewhat minty bouquet and firm, fleshy, tannic flavors.
  88   Medium bodied, with good concentration and the austerity that marks the
          vintage, the 1966 Pichon-Lalande should be drunk over the next decade.
          Anticipated maturity: Now–2000. Last tasted, 3/88.

1964—A delicious yet chunky, foursquare sort of wine, the 1964 Pichon-Lalande
  •   continues to evolve in the bottle. It exhibits an appealing black-currant-and-
  85   herb-scented, earthy, spicy, almost Graves-like bouquet. In the mouth, the
          wine has soft, nicely endowed, ripe flavors that have reached full maturity.
          Anticipated maturity: Now. Last tasted, 3/88.

1962—Quite flavorful, elegant, and deliciously charming, as so many of the 1962s
  •   have proven to be, this fully mature wine has a moderate- to full-intensity
  85   bouquet of ripe, black currant fruit, cedar, and mineral scents. It is medium-
          weight on the palate, with a good measure of fruit and charm still in evidence.
          It should continue to drink delightfully for the near term. Anticipated matu-
          rity: Now. Last tasted, 3/88.

1961—In 1978 I had the 1961 Pichon-Lalande from a magnum in which it was quite
  •   unready, but since then I have had the wine four times from a regular bottle
  95   (most recently at a spring 1998 tasting in Baltimore), where it was equally
          impressive and approaching its apogee. Dark, almost opaque in color, with a
          huge, ripe, plummy bouquet and savory scents of cedar, toffee, and chocolate,
          the 1961 Pichon-Lalande is rich, full bodied, viscous, and deep on the palate,
          with a luscious, silky finish. Stylistically, it is reminiscent of the 1982. This
          wine will continue to drink well for 4–6 years. Anticipated maturity: Now–
          2004. Last tasted, 4/98.

ANCIENT VINTAGES

Pichon-Lalande has rarely been a star performer in tastings of older wines, adding evidence to the claim by some that the greatest wines made at the property are those being produced today. The finest vintages, for me, have been the gloriously decadent 1952 and 1953 (both drunk in 1988 and rated in the high 80s). However, both wines quickly fell apart in the glass, suggesting that they have begun to decline. The 1959, 1955, 1949, and 1947 have left me decidedly unmoved, but the 1945 (tasted in January 1989 and rated 96) was worthy of that vintage's reputation. The bottle I had would have lasted for another decade in a cool cellar. In spring 1998 a 1926 (rated 76) was tired, but still holding some cedar, coffee, and currant scents.

PONTET-CANET   EXCELLENT SINCE 1994

Classification: Fifth-growth in 1855
Location of vineyards: Pauillac
Owner: Guy Tesseron family
Address: 33250 Pauillac
Telephone: 33 5 56 59 04 04; telefax: 33 5 56 59 26 63
Visits: By appointment only
Contact: Alfred and Michel Tesseron at above telephone and telefax numbers

VINEYARDS (red)
Surface area: 296.4 acres in all, but only 192.3 acres are planted in vines
Average age of vines: 37 years (for the grand vin)
Blend: 63% Cabernet Sauvignon, 32% Merlot, 5% Cabernet Franc
Density of plantation: 9,800 vines per hectare
Average yields (over the last 5 years): 55 hectoliters per hectare
Total average annual production: 35,000–42,000 cases

GRAND VIN (red)
Brand name: Château Pontet-Canet
Appellation: Pauillac
Mean annual production: 21,000 cases
Upbringing: Harvest is done manually. Winemaking is traditional, and fermentations last 3 weeks. Only old Merlot vines undergo malolactics in barrels; others complete malolactics in vats. Wines are aged in casks, 40%–45% of which are new, for 16–18 months. They are fined and filtered.

SECOND WINE
Brand name: Les Hauts de Pontet
Average annual production: 20,000 cases

Evaluation of present classification: Since 1994 should be elevated to a third-growth
Plateau of maturity: 8–30 years following the vintage

NOTE: The harvest is always carried out manually. For those parcels that give the grand vin, eventual young vines are harvested first and separately, and the older vines are harvested afterward, when they are deemed fully mature. The grapes are sorted on a table that has been specially designed for the château.

With the largest production of any classified growth wine of the Médoc, and with the enviable vineyard positioned directly across from Mouton-Rothschild, one would expect the quality and stature of the wines of Pontet-Canet to be exceptionally high. Yet take a close look at the track record of Pontet-Canet over the period 1962–1983. While the wines were sound and competent, they have lacked that special ingredient called excitement. In the last several years a renewed vigor and commitment, as evidenced by the new ownership, has commenced. A totally new vinification cellar was constructed, a secondary label for weaker vats was launched, and a higher percentage of new oak was inaugurated. Mechanical harvesting has been discontinued.

Until 1975, the ubiquitous Cruse firm owned Pontet-Canet and tended to treat the wines as a brand name to be used for promotional purposes, rather than as a distinctive, individual, estate-bottled wine from Pauillac. The wine was not château bottled until 1972, and for years batches of the wine were sold to the French railways without a vintage date yet always marketed as Pontet-Canet. In 1975 the Cruse firm was forced to sell Pontet-Canet as a result of a trial that had found the firm negligent in blending and labeling practices. Guy Tesseron, a well-known Cognac merchant, purchased Pontet-Canet and has delegated responsibility for the management of this estate to his son, Alfred. I believe everyone in Bordeaux agrees that Pontet-Canet possesses a vineyard with enormous potential, provided it is carefully managed and exploited. If the initial wines from Guy and Alfred Tesseron lacked the character expected, recent vintages, notably those since the late eighties, give strong signs that Pontet-Canet is serious about challenging the elite of Pauillac. In particular, the 1994, 1995, and 1996 were fantastic efforts.

VINTAGES

1997—Only 36% of the crop made it into this surprisingly structured, powerful
• 1997. If the wine puts on a bit more fat and length, it will be a candidate for
87– an outstanding score. However, I do not see it ever approaching the extraordi-
89+ nary quality of the 1996, 1995, and 1994, a brilliant trilogy of vintages for
Pontet-Canet. As for the 1997, it reveals an impressively saturated ruby/
purple color, and sweet cassis fruit and minerals in the nose, along with a
hint of toasty oak. In the mouth, the wine is medium to full bodied, with a
powerful personality offering surprisingly intense tannin in the finish. This is
one 1997 that is a *vin de garde*, with an aging potential of 15 or more years.
Anticipated maturity: 2003–2015. Last tasted, 3/98.

1996—A classic Pauillac, the 1996 continues to flesh out, revealing an opaque
• purple color, and a magnificent crême de cassis nose reminiscent of the
91– superb vintages of Mouton-Rothschild (Pontet-Canet's neighbor). The wine is
95 full-bodied, as well as extraordinarily rich, ripe, and powerful, with layers of
sweet black fruits intertwined with earth, minerals, and spicy oak. Massive
on the palate, with lofty tannin, but equally high extract, this is a profound
Pontet-Canet that may turn out to be even more classic and longer-lived than
the 1995 and 1994. Terrific stuff! Anticipated maturity: 2006–2035. Last
tasted, 3/98.

1995—An old style Pauillac, yet made with far more purity and richness than
• the estate's ancient vintages, this broad-shouldered, muscular, classic wine
92 exhibits a saturated purple color, and sensationally dense, rich, concentrated,
cassis flavors that roll over the palate with impressive purity and depth. The
wine is tannic and closed, but powerful and rich. It appears to possess length
and intensity similar to the 1996. This is a great young Pauillac. Anticipated
maturity: 2005–2025. Last tasted, 3/98.

1994—One of the finest as well as longest-lived wines of the vintage, this opaque
• purple–colored 1994 needs 7–10 years of cellaring. A rich, impressive,
93 full-bodied wine, it represents the finest Pontet-Canet produced since the
1961. This purely made wine is crammed with black currant fruit and is
forbiddingly tannic and backward. Anticipated maturity: 2005–2025. Last
tasted, 1/97.

1993—Among the least herbaceous of the 1993 non-first-growth Pauillacs, Pontet-
• Canet's offering reveals a subtle, tobacco, leafy component in its otherwise
86+ attractive, ripe, rich, cassis fruit. The wine is dark ruby/purple colored,
medium to full bodied, dense, tannic, and potentially a long-lived example
from the 1993 vintage. Although closed, it is well made, pure, muscular, and
large-sized for the 1993 vintage. Anticipated maturity: 2001–2017. Last
tasted, 1/97.

1992—This wine was unimpressive from cask. Tasted four times from bottle in
• November, the wine exhibited very good ripe cassis fruit and a round,
85? medium-bodied, soft, juicy personality on two occasions and a lighter-bodied,
more simplistic, tannic character at two other tastings. It is a large estate, so
perhaps there is some unexpected bottle variation, but this wine can be a

reasonably good value and an attractive 1992 for drinking over the next 5–6 years. The question mark signifies the confusing array of evaluations I experienced. Last tasted, 11/94.

1991—The light-bodied, fruity, soft, decently colored 1991 Pontet-Canet offers gen-
•   tle, cedary, cassis fruit, a sense of elegance, and a velvety finish. Drink it
84   over the next 5–6 years. Last tasted, 1/94.

1990—The 1990 is as impressive as the similarly styled 1989. Dense purple in color,
•   with a huge, smoky, cassis-scented nose, this well-constituted wine is very
89   tannic, admirably deep, and in need of 5–8 years of cellaring. Anticipated
        maturity: Now–2015. Last tasted, 1/93.

1989—The 1989 exhibits an impressive deep ruby/purple color, a highly scented
•   nose of exceptionally ripe cassis fruit and licorice, full body, an excellent
89   midpalate, and a rich, intense, relatively tannic finish. Anticipated maturity:
        2000–2015. Last tasted, 1/93.

1988—The 1988 Pontet-Canet typifies many of the Médocs in this vintage with its
•   fine color, narrowly constructed personality, and green tannins. Relatively
83   lean and austere, this wine will age well, but it will always lack charm and
        flesh. Last tasted, 1/93.

1987—Pontet-Canet's 1987 is a success in this difficult vintage. An attractive spicy,
•   vanillin-scented, and cassis-dominated bouquet is followed by soft, smooth,
84   easy to drink flavors. This medium-bodied wine should be drunk up over the
        near term. Anticipated maturity: Now. Last tasted, 4/90.

1986—The 1986 is dark ruby in color, with an intense bouquet of sweet oak and
•   cedary black currants. This wine has excellent depth and richness, full body,
88   and sensational extraction of fruit. It lingers and lingers on the palate, with
        quite a tannic finish. This wine should not be touched before the mid-1990s
        and is capable of lasting for 15–20 years thereafter. Thirty percent new oak
        casks were used. Along with the 1989, it represents the finest Pontet-Canet
        since 1961. Anticipated maturity: Now–2012. Last tasted, 4/90.

1985—An elegant, tasty, stylish wine, the 1985 Pontet-Canet is well colored, with a
•   moderately intense black currant, toasty oak bouquet. While not nearly as
86   concentrated as the 1986, it should still evolve nicely. Anticipated maturity:
        Now–2001. Last tasted, 4/90.

1984—Hard and austere, this is, with its fruit buried beneath abundant tannins, a du-
•   bious 1984, Anticipated maturity: Now–may be in decline. Last tasted, 4/90.
74

1983—A good vintage for Pontet-Canet, the 1983 is moderately dark ruby in color,
•   with a sweet, ripe black currant fruitiness and briery, concentrated flavors
86   that linger on the palate. The tannins have melted away faster than I would
        have thought. Anticipated maturity: Now–2003. Last tasted, 4/90.

1982—This is a chunky, husky style of wine with an astringent side to its tannin. It is
•   robust, with plenty of depth as well as an annoying coarseness. There is some
86+?   lightening of the color, but the wine is still a young, spicy, monolithic style of
        Pauillac that may emerge and reveal greater complexity and class or remain four-
        square and compact. Give it another 2–4 years of cellaring. Last tasted, 9/95.

1979—The 1979 is an undistinguished Pauillac, with a bland, moderately intense,
•   black currant aroma, soft, charming, round flavors, medium body, and light
80   tannins in the finish. Anticipated maturity: Now. Last tasted, 4/90.

1978—In contrast with the 1979, a much more tannic, reserved wine for long-term
•   cellaring, the 1978 Pontet-Canet has dark ruby color and a spicy, ripe, yet
82   generally tight and closed bouquet. While certainly a good wine, it seems to
       be missing length and complexity. Anticipated maturity: Now–2000. Last
       tasted, 4/90.

1976—Not particularly outstanding, the Pontet-Canet, like so many 1976 Bordeaux,
•   is quite mature, with an amber, brownish color. Medium bodied, with good,
75   soft, round, fruity flavors, this wine is slightly deficient in acidity and length,
       but very agreeable. Anticipated maturity: Now–may be in decline. Last
       tasted, 10/84.

1975—A good, solid, slightly rustic 1975 with a well-developed toasty, cedary,
•   caramel-and-tobacco-scented bouquet, Pontet-Canet lacks the tremendous
85   grip and size of the best 1975 Pauillacs but has good fruit and a firm, long,
       alcoholic finish. The best Pontet-Canet of the seventies? Anticipated maturity:
       Now–2000. Last tasted, 4/90.

1971—An ambivalent sort of wine, with both positive and negative attributes, this
•   fully mature, somewhat brownish-colored wine has an interesting, spicy,
81   fruity, complex bouquet and a savory, satisfying sweet palate impression.
       However, sharp acidity in the finish detracts considerably from the overall
       impression. Drink up. Anticipated maturity: Now–probably in serious de-
       cline. Last tasted, 7/82.

1970—Good, dark ruby color still exists. The bouquet of wood and ripe plums is
•   enjoyable but lacks complexity. In the mouth, the wine has plump, chunky,
82   fruity flavors of good intensity but seems to miss the mark when it comes to
       interest and length. Hopefully it will get better, but I am unsure. Anticipated
       maturity: Now. Last tasted, 4/90.

1966—The 1966 Pontet-Canet is a leaner styled, tight, hard wine that to this day re-
•   mains firm and closed. It is also beginning to lose its fruit. The wine is moder-
77   ately ruby, with some amber, a restrained, cedary, black currant bouquet, and
       an austere, astringent finish. Anticipated maturity: Now. Last tasted, 4/90.

1964—I prefer the 1964 Pontet-Canet to the 1966 simply because of the supple,
•   lush fruitiness and straightforward, gustatory pleasure. Browning at the edge,
84   with virtually all of the tannin gone, this wine requires consumption. Antici-
       pated maturity: Now–probably in serious decline. Last tasted, 5/83.

1961—Pontet-Canet produced a great 1961, although a distressingly high incidence
•   of variation as a result of the numerous English bottlings is undoubtedly a
94?   problem. The best bottles exhibit rich, deep color, with a full-blown, ripe,
       deep bouquet of spices and plums, viscous, round, supple flavors, and the
       sumptuous length that typifies this great vintage. Now fully mature, the good
       examples of this wine will last a decade. Certainly the best Pontet-Canet I
       have ever tasted. The wine performed splendidly at a vertical tasting at
       Pontet-Canet in 1990. Anticipated maturity: Now–2005. Last tasted, 4/90.

ANCIENT VINTAGES

My notes reveal a satisfying 1959 (rated 85), a dull, tough, still-dense, charmless 1955 (rated 76), and a magnificent 1945 (rated 93 in April 1990) with a stupendous Oriental spice bouquet and smashing concentration. Last, the 1929 (rated 90 at the same tasting) had an orange brownish color but tasted sweet, opulent, and remarkably deep. Very few of the vintages prior to 1975 were estate bottled, so buyers should exercise considerable caution.

OTHER PAUILLAC ESTATES

LA BÉCASSE

Classification: None
Location of vineyards: Pauillac
Owner: Georges and Roland Fonteneau
Address: 2, rue Edouard de Pontet, 33250 Pauillac
Telephone: 33 5 56 59 07 14; telefax: 33 5 56 59 18 44
Visits: By appointment only, secured 2 days before
Contact: Roland Fonteneau at above address and numbers

VINEYARDS (red)
Surface area: 10.4 acres
Average age of vines: 35 years
Blend: 55% Cabernet Sauvignon, 36% Merlot, 9% Cabernet Franc
Density of plantation: 8,000 vines per hectare
Average yields (over the last 5 years): 56 hectoliters per hectare
Total average annual production: 28,000 bottles

GRAND VIN (red)
Brand name: Château La Bécasse
Appellation: Pauillac
Mean annual production: 28,000 bottles
Upbringing: Grapes are picked manually. Fermentations last 3 weeks, and wines are aged in oak barrels (renewed by one-third each year) for 18 months. They are fined with egg whites but not filtered.

SECOND WINE
None produced.

Evaluation of present classification: Should be maintained
Plateau of maturity: 5–15 years following the vintage

I owe a great deal of thanks to Bernard Ginestet, who first told me about this Pauillac gem that has previously been known only to a fiercely loyal group of insiders who buy the production. In the handful of vintages I have tasted, the wine possessed excellent concentration and aging potential.

BELLEGRAVE

Classification: Cru Bourgeois Supérieur
Production: 1,500 cases
Blend: 80% Cabernet Sauvignon, 15% Merlot, 5% Petit Verdot
Secondary label: None
Vineyard size: 7.5 acres
Proprietor: Henry J. Van der Voort
Time spent in barrels: 14–18 months
Average age of vines: 18 years

Evaluation of present classification: The quality equivalent of a Cru Bourgeois
Plateau of maturity: 3–10 years following the vintage

The tiny production of this property, owned by the San Francisco–based Van der Voort family, which also import wines from France under the name Bercut-Vandervoort, is rarely seen. The vineyard and winemaking are both in good hands, as they are looked after by Pierre Peyronie, the owner of the nearby Château Fonbadet. The few vintages I have tasted of Bellegrave have been competent, straightforward examples of a Pauillac.

BERNADOTTE

Classification: Cru Bourgeois Supérieur

Evaluation of present classification: Should be maintained
Plateau of maturity: 2–7 years following the vintage

NOTE: This estate was purchased by Pichon-Longueville–Comtesse de Lalande in 1997.

The first vintage of Bernadotte to be estate bottled was the 1983. I have been unimpressed by the light, somewhat diluted, one-dimensional, and indifferent style of the wines.

LA COURONNE

Classification: Cru Bourgeois Exceptionnel
Location of vineyards: Pauillac
Owner: Madame Brest-Borie (sister of Jean-Eugène Borie)
Address: 33250 Pauillac
Mailing address: c/o J.-E. Borie S.A., 33250 Pauillac
Telephone: 33 5 56 59 05 20; telefax: 33 5 56 59 27 37
Visits: No visits

VINEYARDS (red)
Surface area: 10 acres
Average age of vines: 25 years
Blend: 70% Cabernet Sauvignon, 30% Merlot
Density of plantation: 10,000 vines per hectare
Average yields (over the last 5 years): 46 hectoliters per hectare
Total average annual production: 20,000 cases

GRAND VIN (red)
Brand name: Château La Couronne
Appellation: Pauillac
Mean annual production: 2,000 cases
Upbringing: Grapes are picked manually and totally destemmed.
Fermentations occur in temperature-controlled stainless-steel tanks for
15–18 days. Wines are aged for 12–14 months in oak casks, 20% of
which are new. They are fined and undergo light filtration before bottling.

SECOND WINE
None produced.

Evaluation of present classification: The quality equivalent of a Cru
Bourgeois
Plateau of maturity: 4–10 years following the vintage

This small vineyard, created in 1879, is located inland and is run by Xavier
Borie, the son of Jean-Eugène Borie and also the proprietor of Grand-Puy-
Lacoste. For whatever reason, the Bories' magic winemaking touch that is
evident at their other properties has not worked at La Couronne. The wine
tends to be one-dimensional and simple. I have tasted virtually all of the
vintages in the eighties and there is not one that I would serve enthusiastically
to friends.

LA FLEUR MILON

Classification: Cru Bourgeois in 1932
Location of vineyards: Pauillac
Owner: Héritiers Gimenez
Address: 33250 Pauillac
Telephone: 33 5 56 59 29 01; telefax: 33 5 56 59 23 22
Visits: Monday to Friday, between 8 A.M. and noon, and 1:30 P.M. and
5:30 P.M.
Contact: Mr. or Mrs. Claude Mirande at above numbers

VINEYARDS (red)
Surface area: 32 acres
Average age of vines: 45 years
Blend: 65% Cabernet Sauvignon, 25% Merlot, 10% Petit Verdot and
Cabernet Franc
Density of plantation: 8,000 vines per hectare
Average yields (over the last 5 years): 54 hectoliters per hectare
Total average annual production: 6,000–8,000 cases

GRAND VIN (red)
Brand name: Château La Fleur Milon
Appellation: Pauillac
Mean annual production: 6,000 cases
Upbringing: Grapes are hand-picked and totally destemmed.
Fermentations last 3–4 weeks in temperature-controlled cement vats.
Malolactics occur in vats. Wines are then transferred for 18 months to
oak barrels, one-third of which are new. They are fined with egg whites
but not filtered prior to bottling.

SECOND WINE
Brand name: Chantecler Milon
Average annual production: 1,000–2,000 cases

Evaluation of present classification: The quality equivalent of a Cru
Bourgeois
Plateau of maturity: 5–12 years following the vintage

I rarely see the wines from this producer, but the vineyard, which consists of
a number of small parcels, is located on the high plateau north of the town of
Pauillac, near both Mouton-Rothschild and Lafite-Rothschild.

GAUDIN

Classification: None
Location of vineyards: St.-Lambert, Pauillac
Owner: Madame Capdeville
Address: 2–8, route des Châteaux, B.P.12, 33250 Pauillac
Telephone: 33 5 56 59 24 39; telefax: 33 5 56 59 25 26
Visits: By appointment only
Contact: Mrs. Capdeville or Mr. Bibian—telephone 33 5 56 59 06 15 and
the above numbers, too

VINEYARDS (red)
Surface area: 25 acres
Average age of vines: 40 and 90 years
Blend: 85% Cabernet Sauvignon, 10% Merlot, 5% Petit Verdot
Average yields (over the last 5 years): 54 hectoliters per hectare
Total average annual production: 6,000 cases

GRAND VIN (red)
Brand name: Château Gaudin
Appellation: Pauillac
Mean annual production: 6,000 cases
Upbringing: Fermentations last 30 days, and wines then spend 18 months
in cement vats and 2-year-old barrels. They are fined and filtered.

SECOND WINE
None produced.

Evaluation of present classification: The quality equivalent of a Cru
Bourgeois Exceptionnel
Plateau of maturity: 5–12 years following the vintage

This is a serious estate, with an excellently situated vineyard near the village
of St.-Lambert, between the more famed vineyards of Pichon-Lalande and
Lynch-Bages. The proprietor, who had his wine vinified by the cooperative of
Pauillac until 1968, produces a relatively old-style, traditional Pauillac, with
a month's *cuvaison*, the use of a small percentage of new oak casks, and at
least 24 months of barrel aging so the wine does not have to be filtered prior
to bottling. The three vintages I have tasted, 1982, 1985, and 1986, all had
plenty of stuffing, concentration, and fullness, suggesting they were capable
of lasting 10–15 more years. This is a relatively unknown estate that merits
a closer look.

HAUT-BAGES-MONPELOU

Classification: Cru Bourgeois in 1932
Location of vineyards: Pauillac
Owner: Héritiers Castéja
Address: 33250 Pauillac
Mailing address: Domaines Borie-Manoux, 86, cours
Balguerie-Stuttenberg, 33082 Bordeaux Cedex
Telephone: 33 5 56 00 00 70; telefax: 33 5 57 87 60 30
Visits: By appointment only
Contact: Domaines Borie-Manoux

VINEYARDS (red)
Surface area: 37 acres
Average age of vines: 25 years
Blend: One-third each of Cabernet Franc, Cabernet Sauvignon, and
Merlot
Density of plantation: 8,000 vines per hectare
Average yields (over the last 5 years): 55 hectoliters per hectare
Total average annual production: 5,000 cases

GRAND VIN (red)
Brand name: Château Haut-Bages-Monpelou
Appellation: Pauillac
Mean annual production: 5,000 cases
Upbringing: Harvest is done mechanically. Grapes are totally destemmed.
Fermentations last 3 weeks in temperature-controlled stainless-steel
tanks. Malolactics occur in tanks. Wines are bred in oak casks, 40% of
which are new, for 12 months. They are fined but not filtered.

SECOND WINE
None produced.

Evaluation of present classification: Should be maintained
Plateau of maturity: 2–8 years following the vintage

This vineyard, located inland near that of Grand-Puy-Lacoste, has been
owned by the Castéja family since 1947. The wines, light, fruity, and generally
undistinguished, are commercialized exclusively by Mr. Castéja's *négociant*
firm, Borie-Manoux.

PÉDESCLAUX

Classification: Fifth-growth in 1855
Location of vineyards: Near those of Mouton, on the plateau of Pauillac
Owner: Jugla family
Address: Padarnac, 33250 Pauillac
Telephone: 33 5 56 59 22 59; telefax: 33 5 56 59 22 59
Visits: No visits

VINEYARDS (red)
Surface area: 59.3 acres
Average age of vines: 38 years
Blends: 50% Cabernet Sauvignon, 40% Merlot, 10% Cabernet Franc
Density of plantation: 8,400 vines per hectare
Average yields (over the last 5 years): 60 hectoliters per hectare
Total average annual production: 12,000–13,000 cases

GRAND VIN (red)
Brand name: Château Pédesclaux
Appellation: Pauillac
Mean annual production: 7,000 cases
Upbringing: Grapes are picked mechanically and totally destemmed.
Fermentations last 3 weeks in temperature-controlled stainless-steel
tanks. Malolactics occur in vats, and wines spend 12–14 months in oak
casks, of which 80% are new (100% new next year). They are fined and
filtered.

SECOND WINES
Chateau Bellerose, Grand Duroc Milon, and Haut Padarnac
These 3 wines are sold as Cru Bourgeois. They originate from different
plots of land.

Evaluation of present classification: Should be downgraded to a Cru
Bourgeois
Plateau of maturity: 3–10 years following the vintage

Pédesclaux gets my nod as the most obscure classified growth in the 1855
classification of the wines of the Gironde. Much of the wine is sold in Europe,
particularly Belgium. I have never been impressed, finding it robust but
straightforward, lacking depth, and, to my taste, having an excess of tannin.

PLANTEY

Classification: Cru Bourgeois in 1932
Location of vineyards: Pauillac
Owner: Madame Gabriel Meffre
Address: 33250 Pauillac
Telephone: 33 5 56 59 06 47; telefax: 33 5 56 59 07 47 or
33 4 90 65 03 73
Visits: By appointment only
Contact: Claude Meffre

VINEYARDS (red)
Surface area: 64.2 acres
Average age of vines: 25 years
Blends: 50% Cabernet Sauvignon, 45% Merlot, 5% Cabernet Franc
Density of plantation: 6,600 vines per hectare
Average yields (over the last 5 years): 47 hectoliters per hectare
Total average annual production: 12,000–14,000 cases

GRAND VIN (red)
Brand name: Château Plantey
Appellation: Pauillac
Mean annual production: 10,000 cases
Upbringing: Picking is done by hand and by machine. Fermentations last
21 days in cement vats, no temperature control. Malolactics occur in vats.
Wines are afterward aged in oak barrels (not new) and in vats for 12
months before bottling. Wines are fined and filtered.

SECOND WINE
Brand name: Château Artigues
Average annual production: 4,000 cases

Evaluation of present classification: Should be maintained
Plateau of maturity: 3–8 years following the vintage

This wine has always impressed me as a standard-quality, fruity, supple, easy
to drink Pauillac of no great distinction or aging potential. The most successful recent vintages have been 1982 and 1989.

LA ROSE PAUILLAC

This cooperative, consisting of 125 vineyard owners who control 272
acres of vineyards in Pauillac, was created in 1932. At present it is the
most successful cooperative in Bordeaux, with 6,000 private clients as
well as significant sales to many of Bordeaux's most prestigious

négociants. The cooperative produces three cuvées, the majority of which is labeled La Rose Pauillac. In addition, two domains that vinify their wines at the cooperative, Château Haut-Milon and Château Haut-St.-Lambert, sell their wines under their own label, but it is entirely made and bottled at the cooperative. The cooperative has been using increasing percentages of small oak barrels, with a tiny percentage of them new. The wines exhibit a soft, agreeable, clean, but not particularly distinguished style. These wines should be drunk in their first 5–7 years of life.

SAINT-MAMBERT

Classification: None
Location of vineyards: Pauillac
Owner: Domingo Reyes
Address: Bellevue, St.-Lambert, 33250 Pauillac
Telephone: 33 5 56 59 22 72; telefax: 33 5 56 59 22 72
Visits: Every day
Contact: Domingo Reyes at above telephone and fax numbers

VINEYARDS (red)
Surface area: 1.3 acres
Average age of vines: 50 years
Blend: 65% Cabernet Sauvignon, 20% Cabernet Franc, 15% Merlot
Density of plantation: 10,000 vines per hectare
Average yields (over the last 5 years): 58 hectoliters per hectare
Total average annual production: 3,800 bottles

GRAND VIN (red)
Brand name: Château Saint-Mambert
Appellation: Pauillac
Mean annual production: 58 hectoliters per hectare
Upbringing: Grapes are hand-picked and totally destemmed. Fermentation of all 3 varietals lasts 3 weeks in 1 tank only (with a system of temperature control). Wines are aged for 18 months in oak casks, 15% of which are new and others are 1 year old. Malolactics occur in casks, and the wines are bottled after fining with egg whites but without filtration.

SECOND WINE
None produced.

ST.-JULIEN

If Pauillac is famous for having the Médoc's largest number of first-growths, and Margaux for being the most widely known appellation, St.-Julien is the Médoc's most underrated commune. The winemaking in St.-Julien—from the lesser-known Cru Bourgeois châteaux such as Terrey-Gros-Cailloux and Lalande Borie to the three flagship estates of this commune, Léoville-Las Cases, Ducru-Beaucaillou, and Léoville-Barton—is consistently both distinctive and brilliant. St.-Julien starts where the commune of Pauillac stops, and this is no better demonstrated than where Léoville-Las Cases and Latour meet at the border. Heading south from Pauillac on D2, Léoville-Las Cases is on the right, followed by Léoville-Poyferré on both the left and right, Langoa and Léoville-Barton on the right, Ducru-Beaucaillou on the left, Branaire-Ducru on the right, and Beychevelle on the left. At normal driving speeds, the time necessary to pass all of these illustrious properties is no more than 5 minutes. Farther inland and lacking a view of the Gironde are the large estates of Gruaud-Larose, Talbot, Lagrange, and St.-Pierre.

There is no commune in the Médoc or, for that matter, in Bordeaux, where the art of winemaking is practiced as highly as in St.-Julien. Consequently the wine consumer has the odds stacked in his or her favor when purchasing a St.-Julien. In addition to a bevy of fine wines from the Cru Bourgeois châteaux of St.-Julien, the eleven classified growths are all turning out wonderfully crafted wines, yet all vary greatly in style.

Léoville-Las Cases is the most Pauillac-like of the St.-Juliens for two main reasons. The vineyards sit next to those of Pauillac's famous first-growth, Latour, and owner Michel Delon makes a deeply concentrated, tannic wine marked by the scent of vanillin oakiness. In most vintages, this wine needs a minimum of a decade to shed its cloak of tannin. No other St.-Julien is this stubbornly backward at the outset; the other top properties seem to make wines that do not require as much patience from the consumer.

Léoville-Las Cases is one of a trio of St.-Julien estates with the name Léoville. At present, all of them produce superb wines, but Las Cases is the best of the three, largely because its proprietor is a perfectionist. Of the other two, Léoville-Poyferré has immense potential and, fortunately, has begun to exploit it. Like Léoville-Las Cases, the office and wine *chai* sit in the tiny, sleepy town of St.-Julien-Beychevelle. Poyferré's record was less than brilliant

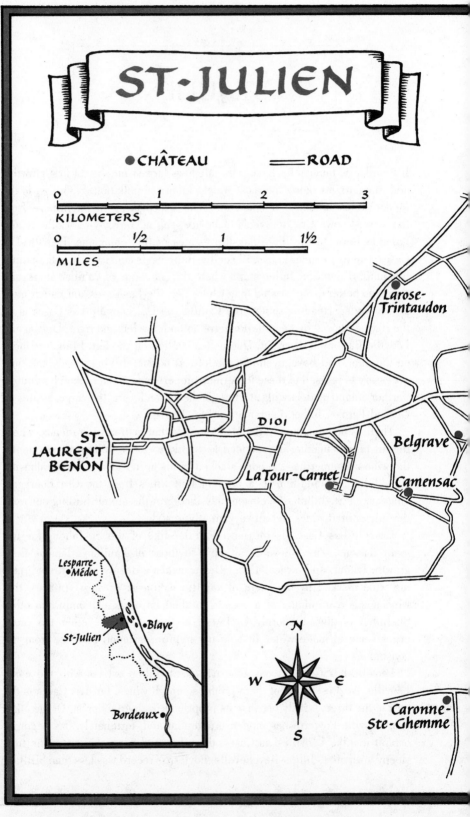

ST-JULIEN

●CHÂTEAU   ══ROAD

KILOMETERS
0   1   2   3

MILES
0   ½   1   1½

Larose-
Trintaudon

ST-
LAURENT
BENON

D101

Belgrave

La Tour-Carnet

Camensac

Lesparre-
●Médoc

●Blaye

St-Julien

Bordeaux●

N
W   E
S

Caronne-
Ste-Ghemme

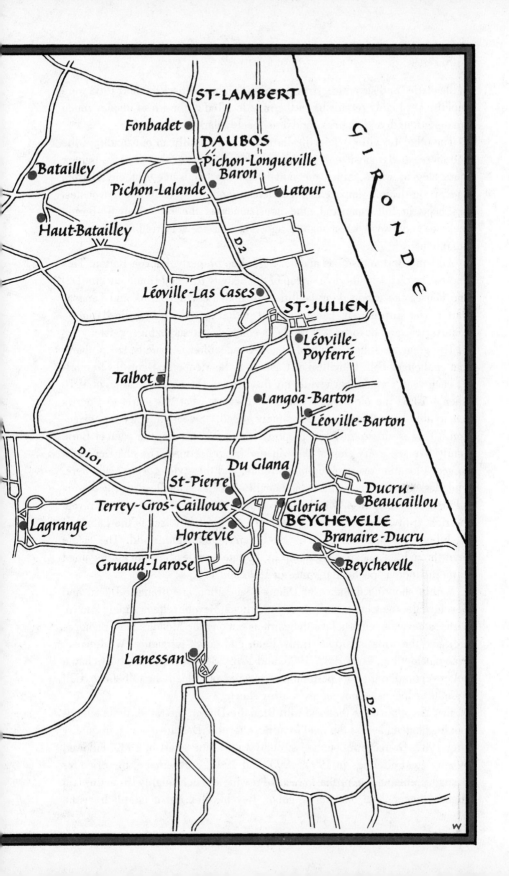

in the sixties and seventies, irregular in the eighties (the 1982 and 1983 were superb), yet highly promising in the nineties. Today the wines display much greater strength and richness and a noticeably darker color.

The other Léoville is Léoville-Barton. It is generally an outstanding wine and increasingly consistent, particularly in the vintages that produce lighter, more elegant wines. Since the mid-1980s the handsome Anthony Barton, one of Bordeaux's impeccable gentlemen and most charming advocates, has been in full command, and consistency is the rule. Léoville-Barton reeks of cedarwood when mature and is a classic, very traditionally made St.-Julien.

Anthony Barton also has another St.-Julien property, Langoa-Barton. This impressive château sits right on top of the heavily traveled Route du Vin (D2) and houses the winemaking facilities for both Léoville-Barton and Langoa-Barton. Not surprisingly, Langoa is very similar in style to Léoville-Barton—cedary, rich, and flavorful, yet rarely as concentrated as its bigger sister.

The great St.-Julien estate of Ducru-Beaucaillou is usually the property that challenges both Léoville-Las Cases and the Médoc first-growths in quality each year. I remember vividly my first visit to Ducru-Beaucaillou in 1970 when I asked the old cellar master, M. Prévost, what the secret to Ducru's remarkable consistency was. He simply stated, "Selection, selection, selection." This is an expertly run property where the owners, the genteel Borie family, oversee every step of the winemaking procedure. The château has a gorgeous location overlooking the Gironde, and the style of wine made here, while less massive and tannic than Léoville-Las Cases and less overtly powerful than Gruaud-Larose, is a classic St.-Julien that needs 8–10 years to reveal the rich, fruity, elegant, suave flavors. If Léoville-Las Cases is the Latour of St.-Julien, Ducru-Beaucaillou is St.-Julien's Lafite-Rothschild. The estate went through an unexpected slump in the late eighties but quickly regained form, producing spectacular wines in 1995 and 1996.

Within shouting distance of Ducru-Beaucaillou are Branaire-Ducru and Beychevelle, the two most southern St.-Juliens. Beychevelle is widely known, perhaps because tourists love the gardens (among the Médoc's most photogenic), and the wine is supple, fruity, light, and quick to mature. While good, even outstanding, as in 1982, 1986, and 1989, Beychevelle has always had a better reputation than its performance record would lead one to believe. Call it Château Inconsistency on my scoring sheet.

Just the opposite is the case with Branaire-Ducru, the rather drab, sullen-looking château across the road from Beychevelle. Despite a slump in quality after 1982, Branaire rebounded strongly with a fine effort in 1989, followed by very good offerings in 1994, 1995, and 1996. Furthermore, the price for Branaire remains one of the lowest for a wine of such quality. Branaire is a slightly bigger wine than its neighbor, Beychevelle, but it is still from the finesse school of winemaking. It possesses an unmistakable exotic, richly scented bouquet of cedar and chocolate. Branaire will never have the aging potential of the three Léovilles or Ducru-Beaucaillou, but between the ages of 8 and 20, Branaire can be an opulently rich, distinctive style of wine.

Two other potentially excellent wines of St.-Julien are made at Gruaud-Larose and Talbot. For years these two estates were owned by the Cordier family. They have now been sold, and that is reflected in somewhat different styles of wine emerging from the new proprietor. Gruaud-Larose sits back off the river behind Beychevelle and Branaire-Ducru. Until the recent change in proprietors, Gruaud-Larose and stablemate and immediate northern neighbor Talbot produced densely colored, rich, fruity wines. Gruaud was usually superior to Talbot, which has a tendency to sometimes be lean, but the quality of these two wines, while historically quite good, was brilliant between 1978 and 1990. Furthermore, because they both produce in excess of 35,000 cases of wine, fetching a price per bottle that always appeared modest, Gruaud-Larose and Talbot immensely satisfied both the purse and the palate. In particular, Gruaud-Larose often performed at a first-growth-quality level between 1961 and 1982. Although critics of Gruaud-Larose suggest that it can lack the great complexity and staying power of a true first-growth, such charges have proved baseless when the wine is compared in blind tastings against the first-growths. Under the new proprietors, the wine appears to be made in a supple, more fruity and accessible style, yet still very powerful. Talbot, under a different owner, looks also to be producing a more forward, fruitier wine than the older Cordier-styled offerings.

The remaining two St.-Julien classified growths, Lagrange and St.-Pierre, both have undergone significant personality changes. Lagrange, lowly regarded for decades, took on new owners from Japan, and with some expert start-up advice from Michel Delon of Léoville-Las Cases, the improvements have been remarkable. This is now one of St.-Julien's great wines—powerful, full bodied, very concentrated, and obviously ageworthy. Moreover, its price is still reasonable.

St.-Pierre has always been a terribly underrated property. The style of wine produced is rich in color and extract, full bodied, sometimes a bit rustic, but always satisfyingly fat, robust, and fruity. Now the property and the wine are under the watchful eye of the late Henri Martin's son-in-law, Jean-Louis Triaud, also manager of St.-Julien's most famous Cru Bourgeois, Gloria. The transition to a "Martinized" style of St.-Julien was readily apparent with their first vintage, the 1983, a richly fruity, almost sweet, easy to drink, supple wine that has huge popular appeal. St.-Pierre, probably St.-Julien's most lavishly oaked, exotic, and flamboyant wine, has also been on a qualitative hot streak and merits considerable interest.

St.-Julien is not without some wonderful Cru Bourgeois properties. In addition to the excellent Gloria, there are the very good Terrey-Gros-Cailloux and Hortevie; the stylish, elegant Lalande Borie; the rather commercial, sometimes dull, sometimes good du Glana; and a bevy of good *deuxième* or second wines from the major châteaux. The best of these is the Clos du Marquis from Léoville-Las Cases.

St.-Julien is a good commune for treasure hunting when Bordeaux has a poor or mediocre vintage. In fact, St.-Julien's soil is similar to the light, gravel-based earth of Margaux, except that it is richer in clay. This affords the wines more body and viscosity. Since most of the major vineyards are close to the Gironde, they tend to have excellent, well-drained, deep beds of gravel soil. In 1992, 1987, 1984, and 1980, all difficult years, St.-Julien produced more acceptable wines than elsewhere in Bordeaux.

In the excellent-to-great vintages, St.-Juliens are quintessential Médocs. The 1996, 1995, 1990, 1989, 1986, 1985, 1982, 1978, 1970, 1961, and 1959 from St.-Julien are the truly great vintages for this appellation, followed by 1988, 1983, 1979, 1976, 1966, and 1962.

ST.-JULIEN
(An Insider's View)

Overall Appellation Potential: Excellent to Superb (from top to bottom the most consistent appellation of Bordeaux)

The Most Potential for Aging: Ducru-Beaucaillou, Gruaud-Larose, Lagrange, Léoville-Barton, Léoville-Las Cases, Léoville-Poyferré

The Most Elegant: Ducru-Beaucaillou

The Most Concentrated: Ducru-Beaucaillou, Gruaud-Larose, Lagrange, Léoville-Barton, Léoville-Las Cases

The Best Value: Branaire, Gloria, St.-Pierre, Talbot

The Most Exotic: Branaire, St.-Pierre

The Most Difficult to Understand (when young): Ducru-Beaucaillou

The Most Underrated: Lagrange, St.-Pierre, Talbot

The Easiest to Appreciate Young: Gloria, Talbot

Up-and-Coming Estates: Lagrange, St.-Pierre

Greatest Recent Vintages: 1996, 1995, 1990, 1989, 1986, 1985, 1982, 1961

ST.-JULIEN—AN OVERVIEW

Location: In many ways the centerpoint of the Médoc, lying to the north of Margaux, bordered on the south by the village of Cussac-Fort-Médoc and on the north by Pauillac; it is approximately 22 miles north of the city of Bordeaux

Acres under Vine: 2,175

Communes: St.-Julien is the major commune, along with small parcels of

Cussac and St.-Laurent; some of the St.-Julien commune actually sits within Pauillac

Average Annual Production: 490,000 cases

Classified Growths: Total of 11: 5 second-growths, 2 third-growths, and 4 fourth-growths; there are 8 Crus Bourgeois

Principal Grape Varieties: Cabernet Sauvignon, followed by Merlot and Cabernet Franc

Principal Soil Type: St.-Julien's soil consists of extremely fine gravel, especially for the great vineyards adjacent to the river. Farther inland, there is considerable gravel but more clay.

A CONSUMER'S CLASSIFICATION OF THE CHÂTEAUX OF ST.-JULIEN

OUTSTANDING
Ducru-Beaucaillou
Léoville-Barton
Léoville-Las Cases

EXCELLENT
Branaire
Gruaud-Larose
Lagrange
Léoville-Poyferré
St.-Pierre
Talbot

VERY GOOD
Beychevelle
Gloria
Hortevie
Langoa-Barton

GOOD
Lalande Borie
Terrey-Gros-Cailloux

OTHER NOTABLE ST.-JULIEN PROPERTIES
La Bridane, Domaine Castaing, du Glana, Domaine de Jaugaret, Lalande, Moulin de la Rose, Teynac

BEYCHEVELLE   VERY GOOD

Classification: Fourth-growth in 1855
Location of vineyards: St.-Julien and Cussac Fort Médoc
Owners: Grands Millésimes de France (GMF/Suntory) 90% and Scribe
2010 (10%)
Address: Beychevelle, 33250 St.-Julien-Beychevelle
Mailing address: Same as above
Telephone: 33 5 56 73 20 70; telefax: 33 5 56 73 20 71
Visits: By appointment only during the winter season (from November to
March); from April to March, Monday to Friday, between 9:30 A.M. and
noon, and 2 P.M. and 5 P.M.; in July and August the château is opened on
Saturdays, also.

VINEYARDS (red)
Surface area: 222.3 acres in all, but only 192.7 are entitled to the
appellation St.-Julien
Average age of vines: About 25 years
Blend: 60% Cabernet Sauvignon, 28% Merlot, 8% Cabernet Franc, 4%
Petit Verdot
Density of plantation: 8,300–10,000 vines per hectare
Average yields (over the last 5 years): 55 hectoliters per hectare
Total average annual production: 500,000 bottles

GRAND VIN (red)
Brand name: Château Beychevelle—Grand Vin
Appellation: St.-Julien
Mean annual production: 300,000 bottles
Upbringing: Grapes are hand-picked and totally destemmed after severe
sorting. Fermentations last 21–24 days, at temperatures of 28–30
degrees centigrade, in 165-hectoliter tanks (stainless steel and cement).
The *vins de presse* are kept separate. Wines are transferred, after
assemblage in December, to oak barrels, 55%–60% of which are
new, for about 16–18 months. They are fined, but not filtered, prior
to bottling.

SECOND WINE
Brand name: Amiral de Beychevelle
Average annual production: 150,000 bottles

Evaluation of present classification: Should be maintained
Plateau of maturity: 7–20 years following the vintage

Tourists visiting Bordeaux are unlikely to miss Château Beychevelle because it is the first major château passed on the D2 road leading north into the commune of St.-Julien. The beautiful flowering gardens that face the road have caused many speeding drivers to stop and take photographs.

Although consistently inconsistent, the wines of Beychevelle can also be beautifully produced. During the decades of the sixties and seventies, quality from vintage to vintage was a problem. Moreover, the wine has been disappointing in mediocre years, such as 1974, 1987, 1992, and 1993, and sometimes uninspiring in great years (1990). Even in top years, Beychevelle tastes uncommonly smooth, supple, and drinkable at a young age. This seems to give purists and traditionalists cause for unnecessary concern. Most recent top vintages of Beychevelle, while fully mature by the time they are 10 years old, have the requisite stuffing to age well for 15 or more years. However, this is generally not a property whose wines require laying away for decades.

In the early eighties the owners began to realize that the ultrasmooth style of Beychevelle was, as the English say, "not making old bones." Since 1982 there has been an increasing reliance on the firmer, more muscular Cabernet Sauvignon in the blend, a lengthening of the all-important *cuvaison* period, the increased usage of new oak, and the introduction of a second label for lighter vats of wine. These techniques have significantly improved the quality of Beychevelle, with fine efforts in 1982, 1986, and 1989. The light, supple, elegant, quick-maturing style of wine made in the sixties and seventies has, since 1982, moved to a firmer constructed, more concentrated type of St.-Julien without, however, sacrificing any of the wine's flattering up-front style, charm, and finesse.

Beychevelle is not one of St.-Julien's most expensive wines, selling at a price level well below that of Léoville-Las Cases and Ducru-Beaucaillou.

VINTAGES

1997— Green pepper, weedy tobacco, and herb-tinged red currant fruit dominate the
•   aromatics of this lean, medium-bodied, yet soft-styled wine. There is some
83–   spice, but essentially the wine is compact and one-dimensional in comparison
85   to many of its peers. Anticipated maturity: 2002–2008. Last tasted, 3/98.

1996— Slightly sweeter Cabernet Sauvignon fruit distinguishes the 1996 from the
•   1995. It reveals medium body, good but not terrific ripeness, clean winemak-
85–   ing, and toasty oak. It provides a narrowly constructed, elegant, but unmoving
86   drinking experience. There is firm tannin in the finish, so bottle age may help
         a bit. Anticipated maturity: 2001–2015. Last tasted, 3/98.

1995— This wine performed better from cask. Out of bottle, it displays a medium
•   ruby color, and a distinctive nose of underbrush, damp earth, and loamy-
85   tinged black currant fruit. Moderately tannic, with medium body and some
         angularity, the 1995 possesses good extract, but not much soul or character.
         Anticipated maturity: 2001–2012. Last tasted, 11/97.

1994—This light- to medium-weight wine exhibits a dark ruby color and a straight-
•   forward, red currant–scented nose with toast and earth in the background.
85   Low acidity, high tannin, and sweet fruit result in a good but uninspiring
      impression. The 1994 Beychevelle should drink well for a decade. Last
      tasted, 1/97.

1993—A dark ruby color is followed by a wine revealing plenty of new oak, a touch
•   of pepper, but very little of the vegetal character found in many Médoc 1993s.
82   Spicy fruit is present, but the wine is austere and tannic, although elegant
      and subtle. Anticipated maturity: Now–2006. Last tasted, 1/97.

1992—The herb-tinged 1992 is a straightforward, compact wine with its tannin
•   dominating its fruit. Light bodied and angular, but attractively supple with
81   low acidity, the 1992 Beychevelle needs to be drunk over the next 3–4 years.
      Last tasted, 11/94.

1991—This is an estate where the 1991 has outperformed the 1992. The 1991
•   offers an attractive, curranty, sweet, oaky nose, soft, round, elegant flavors,
85   admirable ripeness, low acidity, and a plush finish. Although not a big wine,
      it is graceful, fruity, and tasty. Drink it over the next 5–6 years. Last tasted,
      1/94.

1990—The dark ruby–colored 1990, always an uninspiring effort, continues to reveal
•   a greenness to its tannin, a hollowness in the mid-palate, and coarse tannin
81   in the finish. It is not a top effort. Last tasted, 11/96.

1989—The 1989 Beychevelle, which usually performs better than it did in the
•   recent tasting, is an elegant, medium-bodied wine with soft tannin, copious
89   quantities of ripe, herb-tinged, black currant fruit, some evidence of toasty
      oak, and a generous, velvety-textured finish. It appears to be evolving quickly
      and can be drunk now as well as over the next 15 years. Last tasted, 11/96.

1988—Relatively light and lacking concentration, with an under-ripe green streak to
•   its flavors, the 1988 Beychevelle will age well, but it lacks the depth and
84   ripeness to provide excitement. Anticipated maturity: Now–2002. Last tasted,
      1/93.

1987—Light, with a two-dimensional bouquet of vanillin oak and herbs, this me-
•   dium-bodied wine is soft, slightly diluted, yet ideal for drinking young. Antic-
78   ipated maturity: Now. Last tasted, 11/90.

1986—While quite outstanding and deserving to be in any conscientiously stocked
•   wine cellar, the 1986 Beychevelle does not quite have the extraordinary
92   concentration and potential for longevity that I had thought it would. Never-
      theless, this is still one of the best Beychevelles in the last 30 years. With its
      black/ruby color and huge bouquet of roasted fruit, this full-bodied, concen-
      trated, rich wine should now be ready for drinking. Anticipated maturity:
      Now–2010. Last tasted, 4/98.

1985—The 1985 admirably reflects the character of this charming vintage. Deep
•   ruby, low in acidity, ripe, round, fruity, and precocious, this medium-bodied,
87   supple wine is very tasty and displays the cedary, black currant fruit so
      common in the wines of St.-Julien. Anticipated maturity: Now–2000. Last
      tasted, 3/90.

1984—The 1984 has turned out well for the vintage. A raspberry-scented, spicy nose
•   is followed by a medium-bodied wine with high acidity and some underlying
79   greenness. Anticipated maturity: Now. Last tasted, 10/89.

1983—Dark ruby with some amber at the edge, this wine has a ripe, intense, cassis
•   smell. Moderately rich and tannic on the palate, with good depth, the 1983
85   continues to exhibit an aggressive texture and a long, rough finish. This is a
       good rather than profound Beychevelle. Anticipated maturity: Now–2002.
       Last tasted, 1/89.

1982—The 1982 Beychevelle has not developed as quickly as I had anticipated. It
•   is an atypical Beychevelle, an estate known for the delicacy and elegance of
91   its wines and, lamentably, its inconsistency. The 1982 is a powerful, full-
       bodied, intensely concentrated wine that has revealed far greater potential for
       extended cellaring than I expected. It has lost some of its baby fat, and those
       unctuously thick, forward flavors have settled down to reveal a more classic
       bouquet of cedar, herb, and black currant scents, along with aromas of new
       saddle leather and truffles. Monolithic, but powerful, rich, and surprisingly
       backward, this is a broad-shouldered, brawny Beychevelle that may not de-
       velop as much finesse as the 1989. It will always be a richer, more powerful
       wine. Although approachable, I would hold it for another 2–3 years and drink
       it over the subsequent 15–20 years. Along with the more forward and flat-
       tering 1989 and the backward, tannic 1986, the 1982 is one of the most
       impressive Beychevelles produced over recent decades. Last tasted, 9/95.

1981—The 1981 is significantly lighter than either the 1982 or 1983. Forward, quite
•   fruity, with a straightforward, oaky, fruity bouquet, medium bodied, with a
83   healthy color, this is a supple, soft, charming wine that already provides
       pleasant drinking. Anticipated maturity: Now. Last tasted, 1/88.

1979—Diffuse and soft in style, this medium-bodied, moderately ruby-colored wine
•   has been drinkable for at least 5–6 years. The fruit is holding nicely, but the
81   wine lacks excitement. Anticipated maturity: Now–may be in decline. Last
       tasted, 10/83.

1978—Dark ruby/garnet with some amber at the edge, the 1978 Beychevelle tastes
•   close to maturity. A lovely bouquet of ripe berry fruit, oak, and spice is
85   followed by a wine that is slightly sweet, soft, and savory, with some unre-
       solved tannins. It remains a bit chunky but is still satisfying and flavorful.
       Anticipated maturity: Now. Last tasted, 1/89.

1976—Technically the 1976 Beychevelle is not the most perfect wine. The acidity is
•   low and the pH high, but statistics aside, this wine has retained its immensely
85   enjoyable, plummy, fat, fruity character. I would have thought it to be in
       decline now, but this seductive effort from Beychevelle continues to provide
       surprising pleasure. Anticipated maturity: Now. Last tasted, 11/90.

1975—Early in this wine's life, it tasted precocious and forward for the normally
•   tannic, hard wines of the vintage. However, this wine has now firmed up, and
86   it should turn out to be the longest-lived Beychevelle of the seventies. Dark
       ruby, with a ripe, spicy, leather-and-black-currant-scented bouquet, this full-
       bodied, weighty, muscular Beychevelle is atypically powerful. Whether it will

ever resolve all the tannins remains debatable. Anticipated maturity: Now–
2005. Last tasted, 10/89.

1974—Beychevelle made a good showing in 1974, producing a supple, easygoing,
•   fruity, gentle wine that is now fully mature. Anticipated maturity: Now–
77   probably in serious decline. Last tasted, 3/79.

1973—Now totally faded and dissipated, this light wine should have been drunk by
•   1980. Last tasted, 2/81.
65

1971—Quite attractive and fully mature, the 1971 Beychevelle, while not classically
•   structured, but rather loosely knit and too soft, nevertheless has a savory,
83   spicy, fruity clout, with moderately intense flavors and light tannin. Antici-
     pated maturity: Now–may be in decline. Last tasted, 2/83.

1970—Fully mature with a spicy, plum-like bouquet and some caramel aromas, the
•   1970 Beychevelle is round, fruity, quite silky and soft, and nicely concen-
85   trated. It lacks complexity and the depth of the best 1970s but is still quite
     attractive. Anticipated maturity: Now. Last tasted, 4/88.

1967—In the early and mid-1970s, this wine was attractive, flavorful, and spicy, with
•   above average fruity intensity for the vintage. Now the wine has lost that
70   exuberant fruitiness and begun to fade badly. Some fruit still remains, but
     this wine should have been drunk up prior to 1980. Last tasted, 3/81.

1966—One of my favorite Beychevelles, this wine has constantly shown well in
•   tastings of the 1966s. Quite mature, with an expansive, complex, ripe, fruity,
86   spicy, cedary bouquet and supple, soft, velvety flavors, this Beychevelle has
     consistently exhibited good concentration as well as the tough, tannic firm-
     ness of the 1966 vintage. Although fully mature for over a decade, it displays
     no signs of decline. Anticipated maturity: Now. Last tasted, 1/88.

1964—Beginning to crack up ever so slightly, the 1964 Beychevelle still has a good
•   measure of chunky fruitiness, a rustic, medium- to full-bodied feel on the
83   palate, and a creeping brownish cast to the color. The bouquet is particularly
     spicy for Beychevelle. Anticipated maturity: Now–may be in decline. Last
     tasted, 1/81.

1962—This is another example of a Beychevelle that has not stood the test of time.
•   My notes reveal I had a good example in a Bordeaux restaurant in 1970, but
74   more recent tastings have displayed a tired and fatigued wine, with some fruit
     and character still remaining, but most definitely on the slide. Anticipated
     maturity: Now–probably in serious decline. Last tasted, 7/79.

1961—The 1961 Beychevelle continues to age gracefully, but it is not in the top
•   league of 1961s. I have always regarded it as a fruity, concentrated wine that
88   has a voluptuous, expansive, even sweet taste. The wine has been fully mature
     for over a decade. Anticipated maturity: Now. Last tasted, 1/88.

ANCIENT VINTAGES

For unexplainable reasons, Beychevelle does not frequently appear in my
tasting notes of older vintages. The 1959 and 1952, each tasted only once,
were solid but hardly inspiring. A 1953 (rated 92 in 1987) was terrific, the

second-best Beychevelle I have ever tasted. The finest mature Beychevelle (I have high hopes for the 1982, 1986, and 1989) I have tasted was the 1928, drunk in March 1988. I rated it in the upper 90s and found it to have at least a decade of life left.

BRANAIRE   EXCELLENT

Classification: Fourth-growth in 1855
Location of vineyards: Beychevelle
Owner: Maroteaux family (president of the group: Patrick Maroteaux)
Address: 33250 St.-Julien-Beychevelle
Mailing address: Same as above
Telephone: 33 5 56 59 25 86; telefax: 33 5 56 59 16 26
Visits: By appointment only, from Monday to Friday, between 9 A.M. to 11 A.M., and 2 P.M. and 5 P.M.
Contact: Mr. Philippe Dhalluin

VINEYARDS (red)
Surface area: 123.5 acres
Average age of vines: 30 years
Blend: 70% Cabernet Sauvignon, 22% Merlot, 5% Cabernet Franc, 3% Petit Verdot
Density of plantation: 10,000 vines per hectare
Average yields (over the last 5 years): 47 hectoliters per hectare
Total average annual production: 22,000 cases

GRAND VIN (red)
Brand name: Château Branaire (Duluc-Ducru)
Appellation: St.-Julien
Mean annual production: 15,000 cases
Upbringing: Grapes are hand-picked and destemmed. Fermentations last 3 weeks. One-third of the yield undergoes malolactics in new oak barrels and the rest in tanks. After malolactics, the whole yield is aged for 18–24 months in oak barrels, 50% of which are new. The wines are fined with egg whites but not filtered prior to bottling.

SECOND WINE
Brand name: Château Duluc
Average annual production: 7,000 cases

Evaluation of present classification: Should be upgraded to a third-growth
Plateau of maturity: 5–15 years following the vintage

I have always found Branaire-Ducru to be curiously underrated, undervalued, and somewhat forgotten whenever Bordeaux enthusiasts discuss their favorite wines. Travelers passing through St.-Julien have no doubt noted the drab beige building directly opposite Beychevelle on the Médoc's main wine road. Several of the recent vintages, particularly 1975, 1976, 1982, and 1989, have been magnificently scented, deep, rich wines that are as good as the other top wines of St.-Julien. However, the estate is no model of consistency, with a dubious series of indifferent wines produced in the eighties and nineties. Does this reflect overly abundant crop sizes and less than strict selection? The construction of a new cellar and introduction of a new winemaking team, as well as a second label, appear to have been the necessary cures to get Branaire back on track, as evidenced by very strong efforts in 1994 and 1995.

The vineyards of Branaire, like those of many Bordeaux châteaux, are spread out in a morcellated fashion throughout the commune of St.-Julien.

The wines of Branaire have a distinctive character. For a St.-Julien they are particularly spicy, with an almost exotic aroma of spice, oak, and vanillin. On the palate, the wine often has a pronounced, distinctive chocolatey component that makes Branaire relatively easy to spot in blind tastings. This personality trait is especially noticeable in the great vintages of 1975, 1976, 1982, and 1989.

VINTAGES

1997—This is an elegant, pleasingly textured Branaire with a dark ruby/purple color,
•   and telltale aromas of vanillin, lead pencil, minerals, black raspberries, and
87–   cherries. The wine has sweet fruit, low acidity, plenty of cherry liqueur/
89   cassislike flavors, no hard edges, and excellent to outstanding purity. It will
          be delicious young, yet keep for 10–15 years. Last tasted, 3/98.

1996—My notes on this wine have been shockingly similar, almost to the point of
•   being word for word, despite the fact I have had the 1996 a half-dozen
90–   different times. Obviously I am proud of how consistent my palate is, but I
92?   was struck by the identical descriptions given this wine on multiple occa-
          sions. There are very positive attributes to the 1996 Branaire, from its dark
          purple color, to its chocolatey, cherry, lead pencil, and toasty aromas and
          flavors. However, the wine is extremely tannic, somewhat austere, and al-
          though the ripeness and palate impression offer excellent purity, medium-
          bodied richness, and fine ripeness, the wine still seems disjointed and
          awkward. I would not bet against this St.-Julien because there are too many
          positive things going on, but it is not the sure thing that many other 1996
          Médocs appear to be. Anticipated maturity: 2005–2015. Last tasted, 3/98.

1995—A beauty in the elegant, restrained, finesse school of winemaking, the dark
•   ruby/purple-colored 1995 Branaire exhibits a floral, cranberry, cherry, and
90   black currant-scented nose intermixed with high quality toasty new oak.

Medium bodied, with excellent definition, supple tannin, and an attractive, alluring personality, this pleasant, measured yet complex wine should drink well young, and keep for two decades. Last tasted, 11/97.

1994— One of the most stylish, complex, and remarkably delicious wines of the
•   vintage, this charmer possesses a dark ruby/purple color and an excellent,
89   sweet nose of cassis, spice, and an intriguing floral component. Soft and savory, with pure, toasty, black fruit flavors, this luscious, low-acid wine has managed to avoid the vintage's tough tannin. I'm not sure this wine has the potential to be outstanding, but it is very close. It is one of the vintage's more attractive values for a top-classified growth. It should drink well for 12–16 years. Last tasted, 1/97.

1993— This medium-bodied wine offers spicy, tea-like aromas, diluted, austere fla-
•   vors, and enough tannin in the finish to make the wine's balance suspect.
84?   Anticipated maturity: Now–2006. Last tasted, 1/97.

1992— A spicy, light, vaguely fruity nose is followed by some evidence of ripe fruit,
•   medium body, and low tannin. The wine delivers some oak-tinged, ripe berry/
82   curranty fruit in a soft, easygoing style. Drink it during its first 4–6 years of life as a picnic or luncheon wine. Last tasted, 11/94.

1991— I admire the charm, elegance, and sweet ripe fruit of Branaire's 1991. It is an
•   elegant, stylish wine with adequate ripeness, medium body, a soft, velvety
85   texture, and fine balance. Already delicious, it will drink well for 4–5 years. Last tasted, 1/94.

1990— The 1990 has turned out to be a very good wine, with attractive, plump,
•   chocolatey, smoky, black cherry, and cassis aromatic and flavor profiles.
88   Although it is medium to full bodied, with delicious fruit, ripeness, and glycerin, it does not possess the complexity and focus of the 1989. Perhaps that will emerge with further cellaring, since many 1990s are performing even better than I had predicted. Give this wine 2–3 more years of cellaring and drink it over the subsequent 15 years. Last tasted, 11/96.

1989— The 1989 was exhibiting far more power and intensity than I expected. It has
•   always been an impressively crafted, elegant, seamless wine with cassis
92   fruit nicely dosed by high-quality oak. The wine is currently revealing more expansiveness, fuller body, and plenty of lusty richness, a surefire formula for producing a crowd pleaser. There are no hard edges to this opulently textured, rich, ripe, complex, savory style of wine. Drink it over the next 12–15 years. Last tasted, 11/96.

1988— The 1988 is light, angular, and pleasant, but one-dimensional. Drink this
•   acceptable claret now. Last tasted, 1/93.
81

1986— Branaire was in the midst of a slump when the 1986 was conceived. The
•   culprit would appear to be overproduction and lack of a strict selection
84   process. However, restaurants will love the 1986, which offers surprisingly ripe, forward, cedary, herbaceous black currant fruit, married nicely with plenty of sweet, vanilla-scented, toasty oak. The wine is medium bodied and somewhat atypical for the vintage given the suppleness and precocious ap-

peal, but it is an attractive, easy to like and understand wine. Anticipated maturity: Now–2000. Last tasted, 3/90.

1985— The 1985 is a spicy, plummy, tasty wine with undeniable appeal because
• of precocious fruitiness. Once past all the up-front charm and makeup,
85 there is not much depth or tannin. Anticipated maturity: Now. Last tasted, 3/81.

1984— The 1984 Branaire has adequate color, but the texture and flavors are not
• generous. The acidity is high and the finish short and tannic. I doubt if
74 cellaring will add more charm. Anticipated maturity: Now. Last tasted, 3/88.

1983— Somewhat soft for Branaire, with a medium-weight texture and relatively lush
• fruit, the 1983 is a moderately tannic, compact wine that is similar to the
84 1981 Branaire, only less elegant and charming. Anticipated maturity: Now. Last tasted, 6/84.

1982— Inconsistent tasting notes range from austere, fruitless wines to those that
• have been gorgeously elegant, expansive, complex, and satisfying. Wines
90 tasted from my cellar have consistently been rich, well-colored, textbook St.-Juliens with less body and unctuosity than is exhibited by the finest examples of the vintage. Always seductively supple and precocious, the wine has opened beautifully, exhibiting classic cedar, mineral, and cassis aromas in a medium- to full-bodied, supple, rich format. This wine has reached its plateau of maturity and should continue to drink well for another 12–15 years —where well stored. Last tasted, 12/95.

1981— Somewhat understated in personality, the 1981 Branaire is quite successful
• but forward, precociously supple, and fruity. The bouquet is already showing
85 expansive, complex, chocolatey, cedary components. Anticipated maturity: Now. Last tasted, 11/84.

1980— A pleasant, fruity, soft, round wine without any of the vintage's unripe vegetal
• greenness present, the 1980 Branaire-Ducru is fully mature. Anticipated
78 maturity: Now–may be in decline. Last tasted, 2/83.

1979— Ready to drink, as full maturity seems very close, the 1979 Branaire has a
• full-intensity, spicy, cedary, ripe black currant bouquet. On the palate, the
84 wine is soft and supple, with generous silky fruitiness, light to moderate tannins, and good length and weight. A very stylish, round, elegant wine. Anticipated maturity: Now. Last tasted, 9/90.

1978— The 1978 is not up to the quality level of the 1979. The wine has good color
• and an attractive, spicy, ripe bouquet, but on the palate it has a sharpness
80 and angular quality that gives it an attenuated feel. Anticipated maturity: Now. Last tasted, 11/88.

1976— This Branaire has been fully mature and delicious to drink since its release
• in 1979. Medium ruby, with some browning at the edge, the 1976 Branaire
87 has a full-blown, captivating bouquet of spicy oak, ripe fruit, caramel, and toffee scents. In the mouth, the wine is soft, silky, and admirably concentrated for a 1976. It has a round and generous finish. Despite low acidity and overall fragility, the wine continues to drink beautifully. However, don't push your luck. Drink up. Anticipated maturity: Now. Last tasted, 12/89.

1975—Branaire-Ducru has consistently been one of the finest 1975s. I have come to
  •   the conclusion that it will never resolve all of the tannin, but the wine has
 91   such a large-scaled, muscular, rich, concentrated personality that the tannin
          level is acceptable. There is plenty of cedar, sweet cassis fruit, vanilla, and
          lead pencil notes to this powerful Branaire-Ducru. The wine's deep ruby color
          displays some amber at the edge. I enjoyed drinking this wine young, but it
          has not budged in its development, continuing to display freshness, richness,
          and the telltale tannin of the vintage. It should continue to evolve and last for
          another 10–15+ years. Last tasted, 12/95.

1974—One of the very best St.-Juliens produced in this poor vintage, the 1974
  •   Branaire is now fully mature and quite good. A complex bouquet of spicy
 82   oak, flowers, and ripe black currant fruit has the depth of a much better
          vintage. Medium bodied, with good fruit and just a trace of brown at the edge,
          this is a noteworthy success for the vintage. Drink up! Anticipated maturity:
          Now—may be in decline. Last tasted, 3/80.

1971—A mediocre wine for Branaire, with a diffuse, somewhat watery character,
  •   rust/brown color at the edges, and light body and extract. It should have been
 71   drunk up by 1980. Last tasted, 10/79.

1970—The 1970 is a dark ruby wine that is now approaching maturity. This Branaire
  •   is a plump, somewhat fat wine, with good, chewy fruit, some coarse, dusty
 84   tannins, and plenty of oak aromas. Big and powerful rather than elegant, it is
          a good but not excellent wine for the château. Anticipated maturity: Now.
          Last tasted, 2/83.

1966—This has always been a beautiful Branaire. It is now fully mature but in
  •   no danger of falling off for at least another couple of years. The 1966 is
 88   dark ruby, with some amber at the edge. It has the telltale big, intense,
          spicy, black currant-, tarry-, truffle-scented bouquet, soft, silky, ripe, rich,
          deep, savory flavors, and a long finish. The flavors appear to have become
          more sweet and expansive in the late eighties. It is a lovely success from
          St.-Julien for the 1966 vintage. Anticipated maturity: Now. Last tasted,
          2/89.

1964—The 1964 has only been tasted once, and that was in the early seventies. At
  •   that time, the wine was chunky and fruity, without much direction or charac-
 70   ter, and browning prematurely. Probably well past its prime. Last tasted,
          4/72.

1962—Branaire usually can be counted on to age extremely well; however, this wine
  •   was brown, fading badly, and very sweet and sugared when last tasted in
 58   1986. It had little redeeming interest, and I suspect it has completely col-
          lapsed by now. Last tasted, 5/86.

1961—This is a very good Branaire but, to my thinking, not as good as the fine 1966
  •   or nearly as successful as the outstanding wines made in 1975, 1982, and
 83   1989. Good, dark ruby color with amber at the edges indicates maturity. On
          the palate, the wine is full bodied, flavorful, and deep, but the tannin is
          coarse, and the dusty texture lacks elegance and finesse. Anticipated matu-
          rity: Now. Last tasted, 2/83.

ANCIENT VINTAGES

Curiously, I have tasted only one vintage of Branaire-Ducru older than the 1961. The 1959 did not distinguish itself when I had it in 1988. Lacking fruit and too alcoholic, it appeared to be cracking up.

DUCRU-BEAUCAILLOU   OUTSTANDING

Classification: Second-growth in 1855
Location of vineyards: St.-Julien-Beychevelle
Owner: Jean-Eugène Borie and family
Address: 33250 St.-Julien-Beychevelle
Mailing address: same
Telephone: 33 5 56 59 05 20; telefax: 33 5 56 59 27 37
Visits: By appointment only, Monday to Friday, between 9 A.M. and noon, and 2 P.M. and 5 P.M. (except in August and during the harvest, when the château is closed)
Contact: François-Xavier Borie

VINEYARDS (red)
Surface area: 123.5 acres
Average age of vines: 38 years
Blend: 65% Cabernet Sauvignon, 25% Merlot, 5% Cabernet Franc, 5% Petit Verdot
Density of plantation: 10,000 vines per hectare
Average yields (over the last 5 years): 42 hectoliters per hectare
Total average annual production: 22,000–25,000 cases

GRAND VIN (red)
Brand name: Château Ducru-Beaucaillou
Appellation: St.-Julien
Mean annual production: 210,000 bottles
Upbringing: Grapes are hand-picked. Fermentations last 17–21 days, depending upon the vintage, and occur half in stainless-steel and half in cement temperature-controlled tanks. Wines are transferred after malolactics to oak barrels, 45%–65% of which are new, for 18–20 months aging. They are fined with egg whites and lightly filtered prior to bottling.

SECOND WINE
Brand name: La Croix de Beaucaillou
Average annual production: variable, around 60,000 bottles in 1995 and 1996

Evaluation of present classification: Should be upgraded to a first-growth
Plateau of maturity: 10–30 years following the vintage

Ducru-Beaucaillou, sitting among an outcropping of trees, with a splendid view of the Gironde River, enjoys a picture-postcard setting. The property belongs to Jean-Eugène Borie, one of the Médoc's few resident proprietors. He inherited the estate from his father, who purchased it in 1941. In the last three decades, he has brought the quality of Ducru-Beaucaillou up to a level where vintages such as 1961, 1966, 1970, 1973, 1976, 1978, 1981, 1982, 1985, 1995, and 1996 can challenge any of the Médoc first-growths. Passion for his wine, an obsessive commitment to quality, remarkable modesty, and numerous trips abroad as ambassador for Bordeaux have made him one of this region's most respected wine personalities.

The wine of Ducru-Beaucaillou is the essence of elegance, symmetry, balance, breed, class, and distinction. It is never one of the most robust, richest, or fruitiest wines of St.-Julien and by its nature is a stubbornly slow developer. Most of the finest vintages of Ducru-Beaucaillou usually take at least 10 years to reveal their stunning harmony of fruit and power. Ducru-Beaucaillou is a great wine for a number of reasons. The meticulous attention to detail, the brutal selection process—whereby only the finest grapes and finest barrels of wine are permitted to go into the bottle—and the conservative viticultural practices all play major roles in the success of this wine.

That being said, Ducru-Beaucaillou had a problem with bottles of 1988, 1989, and 1990. The question marks that accompany my tasting notes reflect the fact that many bottles from these vintages had a musty component in the aromatics, probably attributable to some noxious aromas given off by the insulation in the old *chai* at Ducru. This *chai* was completely rebuilt and the source for the off smells eliminated. This problem, which does not affect all bottles of 1988, 1989, and 1990, has been eradicated.

Ducru-Beaucaillou is one of Bordeaux's most expensive second-growths, reflecting the international demand for the wine and the consistently high quality.

VINTAGES

1997—After the phenomenally successful and prodigious Ducrus of 1995 and 1996,
• it is easy to be unmoved by the performance of the 1997. While the 1997 is
87– obviously below the quality of the previous two vintages, it is a well-made,
89 elegant wine. In terms of aromatic profile, weight, and texture, it is reminiscent of the beautiful 1981, but riper and more developed. The 1997 exhibits a deep ruby color, as well as sweet, ripe black raspberry and blue berry-like fruit, medium body, dry tannin in the finish, and a firm, closed personality that is somewhat at odds with this vintage's style. I had the wine on three separate occasions with consistent notes, and I believe it is very good to excellent, but I do not see it evolving into an outstanding wine. Moreover, it will be one of the few 1997s that will warrant 2–3 years of cellaring when released. Anticipated maturity: 2001–2014. Last tasted, 3/98.

1996— This extraordinary wine may be the most complete Ducru-Beaucaillou I have
• ever tasted. For now, let's call it the finest wine made at this estate since
95– 1982. Moreover, it is developing in such a manner that it may even eclipse
96 that renowned vintage. The 1996 boasts an opaque black/ruby/purple color,
as well as a glorious, complex nose of lead pencil, licorice, weedy cassis, and
subtle *pain grillé* notes. Exquisite rich fruit is presented in a medium-bodied,
undeniably elegant yet gloriously intense, pure format. The wine, which coats
the palate with glycerin and intense fruit, displays a floral quality that suggests both blueberries and blackberries in its flavor profile. There is copious
tannin, but it is largely overwhelmed by the wine's glycerin, fruit, and overall presence in the mouth. The 1996 Ducru-Beaucaillou is a surreal beauty
that should age effortlessly. Anticipated maturity: 2005–2030. Last tasted,
3/98.

1995— Once again, this wine is of first-growth quality, not only from an intellectual
• perspective, but in its hedonistic characteristics. More open-knit and accessi-
94 ble than the 1996, Ducru's 1995 exhibits a saturated ruby/purple color,
followed by a knockout nose of blueberry and black raspberry/cassis fruit
intertwined with minerals, flowers, and subtle toasty new oak. Like its younger
sibling, the wine possesses a sweet, rich mid-palate (from extract and ripeness, not sugar), layers of flavor, good delineation and grip, but generally
unobtrusive tannin and acidity. It is a classic, compelling example of Ducru-
Beaucaillou that should not be missed. Anticipated maturity: 2003–2025.
Last tasted, 11/97.

1994— A top-notch effort in this vintage, Ducru-Beaucaillou's 1994 displays a dark
• purple color, a textbook cassis, mineral, licorice, and floral-scented nose,
90 medium body, outstanding extract and purity, moderate tannin, and a persuasively rich, sweet, spicy finish. Everything is well-integrated (including the
tannin). This should prove to be a classic St.-Julien. Anticipated maturity:
2004–2022. Last tasted, 1/97.

1993— Spicy red and black currant aromas compete with peppery, cedary notes.
• Sweet, rich, ripe fruit hits the palate in a soft, pretty style. A tannic finish
87 does not detract from the precocious, flattering personality of this elegant,
herbaceous but delicious, medium-bodied, supple Ducru-Beaucaillou. A very
good effort for the vintage, it should be drunk over the next 7–10 years. Last
tasted, 1/97.

1992— An excellent 1992 that reveals impressive concentration, this vintage of
• Ducru boasts fine structure, as well as an attractive berry-scented, floral nose.
87+ Rich and authoritative, with firm tannin, medium body, and a spicy, long
finish, this impressive wine begs for 2–3 years of cellaring. It is a candidate
for 10–15 years of positive evolution. This is one of the most complete wines
of the vintage. Last tasted, 11/94.

1991— At present, the concentrated, promising 1991 is a backward, tannic, young
• wine, a textbook Ducru in that sense. It will benefit from 4–5 years of
86+ cellaring and will last for 15 years. It has plenty of depth, and with time,
Ducru's elegance and complexity are sure bets to emerge. Last tasted, 1/94.

1990—Many bottles of 1990 Ducru-Beaucaillou have exhibited a damp, musty,
  •   cardboard component in the nose that obliterated the wine's fruit. The color
  ?   was a healthy deep ruby/purple, and the wine possessed moderate weight and
            length, but, as I have written in the past, too many bottles seem musty, giving
            the impression of being corked. Interestingly, a bottle served at a friend's
            house on New Year's Day, 1996, was unquestionably a 90-point wine, exhib-
            iting no off aromas. Fortunately, this was the last year for the musty problem
            in Ducru's wines. Last tasted, 1/96.

1989—Ducru's tannic, backward 1989 is cleanly made and well crafted, with plenty
  •   of black raspberry and cassis fruit nicely touched by minerals and a fragrant,
89+?   floral component. Medium bodied, elegant, and well endowed, this is a poten-
            tially outstanding wine if all the tannin melts away over the next 5–6 years.
            One of the least flattering 1989s to drink at present, it requires 4–5 more
            years of cellaring. Anticipated maturity: 2001–2020. Last tasted, 11/96.

1988—The 1988 Ducru is a medium-bodied wine, without the profound depth and
  •   sheer intensity of fruit of the 1989. Possessing high tannins and good ripe-
88?   ness, with an overall sense of compactness and toughness, it recalls the style
            of the best 1966 Médocs. Anticipated maturity: Now. Last tasted, 1/93.

1987—Some attractive ripe fruit can be found in this successful, elegant, yet surpris-
  •   ingly tannic and closed Ducru. It should prove to be one of the longer-lived
83   1987s. Anticipated maturity: Now–2000. Last tasted, 4/91.

1986—This wine remains backward, tannic, and in need of another 5 or more years
  •   of bottle age. The 1986 Ducru possesses a dark ruby color with purple
92   nuances. Initially the bouquet is restrained, but with coaxing it reveals scents
            of lead pencil, sweet cranberry, and black currant fruit nicely intertwined
            with aromas of steel, minerals, and earth. Rich and medium to full bodied,
            but excruciatingly tannic, this is an intensely concentrated Ducru-
            Beaucaillou with formidable aging potential. Readers should note that 1986
            is the first vintage where some bottles were marred by off aromas of damp
            cardboard. The last three times I tasted the wine the bottles were totally pure,
            with no evidence of this disturbing irregularity. Anticipated maturity: 2002–
            2030. Last tasted, 3/97.

1985—For sheer elegance, charm, and finesse, the 1985 Ducru-Beaucaillou has it
  •   all. The wine is close to full maturity yet retains a vibrancy and youthfulness
92   that is unusual for a 1985. The generous flavors are soft but not flabby. The
            wine possesses outstanding concentration yet is elegant and refreshing. This
            is a beautifully knit, harmonious Ducru. Anticipated maturity: Now–2010.
            Last tasted, 3/97.

1984—The 1984 is soft and has some attractive, weedy Cabernet Sauvignon fruit,
  •   but it tails off in the mouth. It is light and, I suppose, elegant. Anticipated
79   maturity: Now. Last tasted, 4/91.

1983—This wine possesses an austerity and aggressiveness to its tannin, but it is a
  •   very good to excellent Ducru-Beaucaillou with an earthy, peppery nose of
87   black fruits, earth, and minerals. The wine's attack and mid-palate are ripe,
            with smoky, black currant fruit. I doubt the 1983 will ever fully shed its

tannic astringency, but it is a savory, medium- to full-bodied wine that has reached full maturity. Anticipated maturity: Now–2006. Last tasted, 3/97.

1982— Flawless from cask, the bottled wine has finally emerged from a long dor-
•   mancy when it was forbiddingly backward and impenetrable. I do not think
94   the estate has produced any wine since that can be said to be as complete and concentrated as the 1982. Although the 1982 is beginning to reveal some lightening at the edge, it still exhibits an impressively saturated ruby/purple color. The wine offers a classic St.-Julien/Pauillac aromatic profile—intense cedar, some black currants, a touch of oak, and good spice. Rich and more full bodied than normal, this chewy, concentrated, moderately tannic Ducru can be drunk with considerable pleasure, but ideally it should be cellared for another 3–4 years. It should last through the first 2 decades of the next century. Last tasted, 9/95.

1981— One of the Médoc's more successful wines, the 1981 has reached full maturity.
•   It exhibits a dark ruby/purple color and a moderately attractive nose of
88   minerals and jammy cranberry fruit intermixed with black currants. In the mouth, this wine has lost its baby fat, revealing medium body and an elegant, measured personality. Pure, with well-integrated tannin, this is a stylish, graceful Ducru-Beaucaillou. Anticipated maturity: Now–2007. Last tasted, 3/97.

1980— Ducru can often be counted on in off vintages, but the 1980 lacks charm and
•   fruit; it has good structure yet finishes short and is a bit harsh. Anticipated
74   maturity: Now. Last tasted, 4/91.

1979— Ducru has produced so many exceptional wines in the last several decades
•   that when the château does not produce a wine that is among the top dozen
84   or so best wines of the Médoc, I am quite surprised. This offering is a good but not great Ducru. Medium ruby in color and noticeably lighter in style than previous efforts, this moderately intense, soft, pleasant wine should evolve quickly. Anticipated maturity: Now. Last tasted, 4/91.

1978— An outstanding 1978, Ducru-Beaucaillou's effort displays a fragrant, well-
•   developed bouquet of licorice, earth, black currants, and underbrush. Rich
90   for a 1978, with none of the vegetal character now found in many wines of this vintage, this fully mature, medium-bodied wine exhibits soft tannin, excellent concentration and purity, and a sweet, elegant finish. Anticipated maturity: Now–2010. Last tasted, 3/97.

1977— One of the more attractive 1977s, with surprisingly ripe character, and not
•   marred by too much acidity or vegetal aromas, the 1977 Ducru will continue
78   to improve. Good solid fruit, yet not complex, this medium-bodied wine has some charming attributes to it. Anticipated maturity: Now–may be in decline. Last tasted, 2/84.

1976— This is a lovely Ducru that retains much of the silky, elegant personality of a
•   top-class St.-Julien. However, it does not have the concentration and richness
85   of the 1982, 1978, 1970, or 1961. Now fully mature, this medium-weight, firm, yet rich, savory, and well-constituted 1976 has plenty of character and elegance. Anticipated maturity: Now. Last tasted, 2/89.

1975—I have never been a fan of this wine. I lost confidence in it when it was around
•   10 years of age because of its hard, angular, austere, tannic style. In the most
87+   recent tasting, the wine exhibited more ripe fruit than I had previously noticed. There is still plenty of astringent, aggressive tannin, but the balance is
better, and the wine reveals a complex, earthy, cedar, curranty nose with dried
fruit and herb components, full body, and a classic, old-style personality. It
displays more finesse and character than it did at a younger age. Like many
1975s, it will keep for 20+ years . . . but will the fruit hold up? Last tasted,
12/95.

1974—A bit hollow, noticeably vegetative, yet spicy and still palatable—barely—
•   this is a wine that should be consumed. Anticipated maturity: Now—may be
70   in decline. Last tasted, 3/88.

1973—The 1973 Ducru is certainly one of the best wines of this watery vintage. It
•   drank well for 15 years before beginning to fade. Holding it any longer would
79   be senseless. The 1973 Ducru was fully mature by 1978 but miraculously
retained its fruit until 1988. It has just begun to fade. Drink up. Anticipated
maturity: Now—probably in serious decline. Last tasted, 12/88.

1971—For whatever reason, the 1971 vintage for Jean-Eugène Borie's Ducru-
•   Beaucaillou was not as good as it should have been. Now fully mature,
78   the bouquet exhibits light-intensity, cedary, vanillin aromas. The flavors are
satisfying, but the coarse texture and astringent tannins are cause for concern.
Anticipated maturity: Now—may be in decline. Last tasted, 10/87.

1970—This wine has been fully mature and delicious for many years. It has always
•   been an outstanding wine for the vintage—complex, rich, savory, and the
92   quintessentially elegant Bordeaux. This beauty continues to reveal the fragrance and finesse that one expects from Lafite-Rothschild but so rarely
finds. A fragrant, complex bouquet of cedar, herbs, vanillin, fruitcake, and
coffee is followed by a soft, gentle, graciously constructed wine with sweet
layers of fruit. I am not sure how much longer the 1970 Ducru will keep, but
from regular bottle, it is delicious and should be consumed. Last tasted,
6/96.

1967—For Ducru, the 1967 is a rather coarse, bland, obviously chaptalized wine,
•   without the graceful fruit and spicy exuberance normally found in wines from
74   this estate. Drink up. Anticipated maturity: Now—probably in serious decline.
Last tasted, 10/78.

1966—A very flavorful wine now in full maturity, the 1966 Ducru-Beaucaillou de-
•   fines such wine adjectives as elegant, graceful, and well bred. Medium dark
87   ruby with an amber edge, the bouquet is spicy, cedary, and subtly herbaceous.
Velvety, round, medium-bodied flavors exhibit good concentration. Drink it
over the next 5 years. Anticipated maturity: Now. Last tasted, 11/87.

1964—Solid, rustic, amiable, and pleasantly full and firm, the 1964 Ducru-
•   Beaucaillou lacks complexity and character but offers a mushroom-scented,
78   robust, round mouthful of claret. The fruit is just beginning to fade. All
things considered, this was a success for a 1964 northern Médoc. Anticipated
maturity: Now. Last tasted, 2/87.

1962—I have inconsistent notes for the 1962 Ducru-Beaucaillou. My early notes
•   suggested the wine was beginning to lose its fruit. Two tastings in the early
85?   eighties revealed a wine with a light to medium ruby color, a mature, fruity,
        damp cellar, woody bouquet, and soft flavors that appeared to be beginning to
        fade. Two tastings in the late eighties were much more successful. The wine
        was deeper colored, richer, with an attractive cedary aroma and long, velvety
        flavors. Will the real 1962 Ducru-Beaucaillou please come forward? Antici-
        pated maturity: Now. Last tasted, 11/89.

1961—Fully mature, yet continuing to exhibit gobs of rich, lush, expansive fruit, this
•   dark ruby wine has amber/orange edges and possesses an exotic bouquet of
96   ripe fruit, vanillin, caramel, mint, and cedar. Fat, rich, and loaded with
        sweet, highly extracted fruit, this velvety, beautifully crafted wine has a 60–
        75-second finish. It is a brilliant wine that should hold up nicely for up to a
        decade. Anticipated maturity: Now–2005. Last tasted, 5/91.

ANCIENT VINTAGES (text from 1991 edition)

The greatest old vintages of Ducru-Beaucaillou I have tasted include a magnificently opulent 1947 drunk in 1987 (rated 93, although slightly volatile), a
quintessentially elegant and perfumed 1953 (rated 93; last tasted 1988), and
a solid, but well endowed, yet atypically muscular 1959 (rated 90). Whether
it is the condition of the bottles or the vintages I am not sure, but I have
unenthusiastic tasting notes for the 1957, 1955, and 1945.

GLANA

Classification: Cru Bourgeois in 1832
Location of vineyards: St.-Julien-Beychevelle
Owner: G.F.A. Vignobles Meffre
Address: 33250 St.-Julien-Beychevelle
Mailing address: J.-P. Meffre, c/o Vignobles Meffre, 84810 Aubignan
Telephone: 33 5 56 59 06 47; telefax: 33 4 90 65 03 73
Visits: Preferably by appointment
Contact: Jean-Paul Meffre, at above telephone and fax numbers

VINEYARDS (red)
Surface area: 111.2 acres
Average age of vines: 25 years
Blend: 65% Cabernet Sauvignon, 5% Cabernet Franc, 30% Merlot
Density of plantation: 7,000 vines per hectare
Total average annual production: 20,000 cases

GRAND VIN (red)
Brand name: Château du Glana and Château du Glana Vieilles Vignes
Appellation: St.-Julien

Mean annual production: 150,000 bottles and 50,000 bottles
Upbringing: Grapes are picked by hand and mechanically. Fermentations
last 18–21 days in temperature-controlled vats (internal system of
regulation). Wines are then aged in oak barrels, 20% of which are new,
for approximately 15–18 months. They are fined with fresh egg whites
but not filtered prior to bottling.

SECOND WINE
Brand name: Château Sirène
Average annual production: 30,000 bottles

Evaluation of present classification: Should be maintained
Plateau of maturity: 2–8 years following the vintage

It has been said that Glana produces a blatantly commercial wine—soft,
overtly fruity, and too easy to drink. Yet the prices are reasonable and the
wine is ripe, cleanly made, and ideal for newcomers to Bordeaux. Some
vintages tend to be jammy—1982, 1985, 1989, and 1990, for example—but
in tastings people always seem to enjoy this plump St.-Julien. It must be
drunk within its first decade of life, preferably before it turns 8 years old.

VINTAGES

1996—Vieilles Vignes: A tasty, plump, fruitball, this dark ruby/purple–colored St.-
•   Julien reveals copious amounts of lusty black cherry and currant fruit, sur-
(85–   prisingly low acidity, and moderate tannin that gives the wine a tough,
87)   structured feel in the finish. This will be a wine to drink in its youth. It will
      last for 10–12 years. Last tasted, 3/97.

GLORIA   VERY GOOD

Classification: None
Location of vineyards: St.-Julien-Beychevelle
Owner: Françoise Triaud
Address: Domaines Martin, 33250 St.-Julien-Beychevelle
Mailing address: 33250 St.-Julien-Beychevelle
Telephone: 33 5 56 59 08 18; telefax: 33 5 56 59 16 18
Visits: By appointment only, from Monday to Friday, between 8 A.M. and
12:30 P.M., and 2 P.M. and 6 P.M.
Contact: Jean-Louis Triaud

VINEYARDS (red)
Surface area: 123.5 acres
Average age of vines: 41 years

Blend: 65% Cabernet Sauvignon, 25% Merlot, 5% Cabernet Franc, 5% Petit Verdot
Density of plantation: 10,000 vines per hectare
Average yields (over the last 5 years): 50 hectoliters per hectare
Total average annual production: 2,500 hectoliters

GRAND VIN (red)
Brand name: Château Gloria
Appellation: St.-Julien
Mean annual production: 240,000 bottles
Upbringing: Grapes are hand-picked. *Cuvaisons*, after alcoholic fermentation, last 15–30 days, depending upon the vintage. The whole process occurs in temperature-controlled stainless-steel tanks, starts at 28 degrees centigrade and finishes at 32 degrees centigrade. There are 4 pumping-overs daily, with airing. Wines are then transferred into oak barrels (which are renewed by half at every vintage) for 18 months aging. They are fined and filtered prior to bottling.

SECOND WINE
Brand name: Château Peymartin
Average annual production: 50,000 bottles

Evaluation of present classification: Should be upgraded to a fourth-growth
Plateau of maturity: Since 1978, 5–10 years following the vintage; prior to 1978, 5–18 years following the vintage

Gloria has always been used as an example of why the 1855 classification of the Médoc wines is so outdated. Not included in the original classification are wines Gloria has made (from vineyards purchased from neighboring classified châteaux) over the last 25 years that in vintages such as 1961, 1966, 1970, 1971, 1975, 1976, 1982, 1985, 1986, 1989, 1994, 1995, and 1996 are certainly as good as many of the wines produced by many of the classified growths. Shrewd merchants and consumers have long known Gloria's quality, and the wine has been widely merchandised in America and abroad.

The late Henri Martin, Gloria's owner, died in February 1991. He was one of the Médoc's legendary figures. His wines were no doubt made for sheer crowd appeal. They were round, generous, and slightly sweet, with wonderful cedary, spicy, almost exaggerated bouquets. Nothing is likely to change under the management of his son-in-law, Jean-Louis Triaud. Interestingly, the wine is matured primarily in large oak *foudres* rather than the more conventional 55-gallon barrels. They perform surprisingly well young but can age for up to 12–15 years. The Gloria style of the sixties and early seventies changed after the mid-1970s. Gloria vintages from 1978 through 1993 definitely appear to be wines that are lighter, more obviously fruity, and less tannic than those made previously. However, the 1995 and 1996 were clearly beefier, richer wines, perhaps foreshadowing a return to the pre-1978 style. Gloria remains, in either style, a gloriously exuberant, delicious St.-Julien that continues to sell at a price well below its actual quality level.

VINTAGES

1997—Recent vintages of Gloria have pushed the level of quality even higher. There
•   is no doubting this cunningly made wine that offers mouth-filling levels of
87–   black cherry, herb-tinged, cassis fruit. There is plenty of glycerin in this
88   velvety-textured, medium-bodied Gloria. Pure, plump, and succulent, it is all
       a young, exuberant claret should be. However, do not expect it to age long;
       this is a wine to drink during its first decade of life. A sleeper of the vintage.
       Last tasted, 3/98.

1996—One of the perennial winners in the under-$30 range Bordeaux, Gloria's 1996
•   looks to be the finest wine they have produced since the 1990 and 1982.
87–   Made in a hedonistic, low-acid, plump, juicy (gobs of fruit) style, the 1996 is
89   hard to resist. The color reveals more saturation than usual. The fruit is fat
       and ripe—surprising for a vintage known more for its structure than opu-
       lence. This exceptionally well-made St.-Julien should drink well for 10–15+
       years. Last tasted, 3/97.

1995—The 1995 builds on the success of the 1994, offering more fatness, glycerin,
•   and extraction, a deeper color, more alcohol, and lower acidity, thus empha-
88   sizing the wine's opulence, charm, and up-front character. It is a delicious,
       juicy, succulently textured Gloria that should drink well during its first de-
       cade of life. Given this estate's pricing policy, the 1995 is unquestionably a
       sleeper of the vintage. Last tasted, 3/96.

1994—This well-known estate appears to be aiming for greater richness and ripeness
•   without sacrificing the wine's up-front, flattering precociousness or opulent
87   texture. The 1994 exhibits a deep ruby color with purple nuances. It pos-
       sesses excellent ripeness for the vintage, medium body, spicy oak, and a soft,
       lush, jammy, open-knit texture. The wine's low acidity suggest it should be
       drunk over the next 7–8 years. Last tasted, 3/96.

1990—Surprisingly light and lacking a mid-palate and flavor extraction, the 1990
•   Gloria is still a pleasant, middle-of-the-road, commercial wine that should be
84   drunk over the next 5–7 years. Last tasted, 1/93.

1989—The 1989 Gloria is a fat, plump, deliciously agreeable wine with a consider-
•   able alcoholic kick in the finish. Fruity, with soft tannins, it will be a fine
86   wine to drink over the next 7–10 years. Anticipated maturity: Now–2000.
       Last tasted, 1/93.

1988—The 1988 is an unabashedly fruity, exuberant, herb-and-cassis-scented wine,
•   with a smooth texture and easy to understand and enjoy flavors. No wonder
85   Gloria is called a beginner's Bordeaux. Anticipated maturity: Now. Last
       tasted, 1/93.

1987—Light, soft, intensely herbaceous, this medium-bodied wine should provide
•   near-term drinking. Anticipated maturity: Now. Last tasted, 10/89.
78

1986—Gloria has graced many tables in America, and, of course, the de facto
•   ascendancy of this Cru Bourgeois to the quality of a classified growth was
86   proprietor Henri Martin's lifelong ambition. The 1986 has as much structure
       as any Gloria in the last 15 years, a deep ruby color, and plenty of tannin,
       but I had to ask myself if it really, in fact, had as much fruit as it needed to
       balance out the hard tannins in the wine. This should certainly be a very fine
       Gloria, but it will need at least 5–6 years to soften, unusual for a wine from
       this property. Anticipated maturity: Now–2002. Last tasted, 10/90.

1985—The 1985 displays fine depth and richness. Deep in color, with a weedy,
•   herbaceous, cedary, black currant bouquet, it offers up a rich mouthful of
86   succulent claret. Drink it over the next decade. Anticipated maturity: Now.
       Last tasted, 10/90.

1984—Very light and vegetal to smell, this light- to medium-bodied wine is diffuse
•   and watery. Anticipated maturity: Now–may be in decline. Last tasted, 9/89.
72

1983—A forward, typically spicy, herbaceous-scented, fruity Gloria, the 1983 has
•   more noticeable tannin than the 1982 but less rich, glossy fat fruit. Antici-
82   pated maturity: Now. Last tasted, 1/89.

1982—The 1982 Gloria is proving to be one of the most pleasant surprises of the
•   vintage. Recent bottles have been beautifully rich, with classic black currant
88   fruit intertwined with scents of spice, herbs, and cedar. Full bodied, with a
       lovely concentrated feel, this is the richest Gloria since the tannic 1975 and
       glorious 1970 (now in decline). The 1982 could have been bought for a song
       when released (I purchased it for $7.29 a bottle). When it was young, it was
       just a big ball of juicy fruit, but it has developed well. While seemingly fully
       mature, this wine will easily last for another 7–10 years. Last tasted, 9/95.

1981—Very similar to the stylish yet mature 1979, this wine offers supple cedary,
•   olive-tinged flavors, medium body, and a more austere character than the
80   1979. The Gloria telltale sweetness on the palate is present. Anticipated
       maturity: Now. Last tasted, 1/88.

1980—Light, slightly vegetal, and lacking the roundness and fruity character one
•   expects from Gloria, the 1980 is a mediocre wine. Anticipated maturity:
73   Now–probably in serious decline. Last tasted, 3/84.

1979—Very forward and quite ready to drink, this wine has an attractive fruity
•   character, a medium-bodied, nicely ripe, savory, sweet, lush texture, and little
82   or no tannins present. This wine will hold for a few more years, but other than
       some further bottle bouquet development, it is ready now. Anticipated matu-
       rity: Now. Last tasted, 4/87.

1978—Round, flavorful, fruity, with a bouquet suggestive of herbs and cinnamon,
•   this wine is deliciously mature. The sweetness and fruitiness on the palate
83   are almost Burgundian. It should be drunk up. Anticipated maturity: Now.
       Last tasted, 1/88.

1976—Gloria's huge, plummy, spicy bouquet is enticing. Dark ruby/garnet, with plenty
• of sweet, ripe fruit in evidence, this medium- to full-bodied wine is deep and
84 very fruity and has been ready to drink since the late seventies. It appears to be
in no danger of losing its fruit. Anticipated maturity: Now. Last tasted, 1/88.

1975—This has always been a very good 1975. Atypically powerful and muscular
• for Gloria, it exhibits as much fruit as many of the top wines. The opaque
87 garnet color reveals slight amber at the edge. The wine offers a classic
St.-Julien/Pauillac aromatic profile (tobacco, cedar, currants) combined with
more earthy, dusty notes than usual (blame that on the 1975 vintage). A
sweet, rich, chewy attack is followed by a dense, concentrated wine that may
suffer from a lack of complexity and finesse but more than compensates for
that deficiency with plenty of muscle, extract, ripeness, and body. Drink it
over the next 5–7 years. Last tasted, 12/95.

1973—In the mid-1970s, this wine could be enjoyed for light, fruity, simple charms.
• It has now faded badly. Anticipated maturity: Now–probably in serious de-
72 cline. Last tasted, 4/81.

1971—A beautiful wine, the 1971 Gloria has been fully mature since 1979 but has
• not lost a thing, although amber, brownish colors are becoming more apparent.
86 The bouquet is highly perfumed, exhibiting scents of cedar, plums, vanillin
spice, and sweet oak. On the palate, the wine is silky, gentle, and very fruity
and sweet. An unquestioned success. I have not tasted this wine since 1984.
Anticipated maturity: Now–may be in decline. Last tasted, 10/84.

1970—Another triumphant success for Gloria, the 1970 is richer and fuller than the
• lovely 1971, with longer-term keeping possibilities. Dark ruby color with
87 some amber at the edge, a fully mature bouquet of sweet fruit, cedar, and a
spicy, vanillin oakiness, this wonderful, rich, fruity, medium-bodied wine
remains impressive. The finish is gentle and soft. This is a voluptuous, decadently fruity Gloria. Anticipated maturity: Now. Last tasted, 1/88.

GRUAUD-LAROSE   EXCELLENT

Classification: Second-growth in 1855
Location of vineyards: St.-Julien-Beychevelle
Owner: Jacques Merlaut
Address: 33250 St.-Julien-Beychevelle
Mailing address: B.P.6, 33250 St.-Julien-Beychevelle
Telephone: 33 5 56 73 15 20; telefax: 33 5 56 59 64 72
Visits: By appointment only, from Monday to Friday, between 9 A.M. and
noon, and 2 P.M. and 5 P.M.
Contact: François Peyran

VINEYARDS (red)
Surface area: 326 acres in all, but only 202.5 are currently under vine
Average age of vines: 45 years

Blend: 57% Cabernet Sauvignon, 30% Merlot, 7% Cabernet Franc, 4% Petit Verdot, 2% Malbec
Density of plantation: 10,000 vines per hectare
Average yields (over the last 5 years): 54 hectoliters per hectare
Total average annual production: 500,000 bottles

GRAND VIN (red)
Brand name: Château Gruaud-Larose
Appellation: St.-Julien
Mean annual production: 300,000 bottles
Upbringing: Grapes are hand-picked. Fermentations last between 18 and 35 days (depending upon the vintage) in temperature-controlled wooden and cement tanks. Twenty-five percent of the yield goes into oak barrels for malolactics. Wines are then entirely aged in oak barrels, 30% of which are new, for 18 months. They are fined with egg whites and undergo a very light filtration prior to bottling.

SECOND WINE
Brand name: Sarget de Gruaud-Larose
Average annual production: 200,000 bottles

Evaluation of present classification: Should be maintained
Plateau of maturity: 10–35 years following the vintage

ADDITIONAL INFORMATION

IN THE VINEYARDS
- Use of chemicals for treatment against diseases is restricted. All treatments are carried out taking weather conditions into consideration —the estate has its own meteorological station. To fight against grape-worm, experiments are being carried out.
- Yields are reduced by extensive green pruning.
- Computerization of all data relating to the 66 parcels of the estate ensures better control of treatments and of the harvest.
- A very good drainage system has been installed.

IN THE CELLARS
- The harvest is sorted out twice (in the vineyards and at the winery) as it moves on a conveyor belt. It undergoes a *saignée* just as it comes into the winery and is fermented in stainless-steel or cement vats.

> • A new cellar has been built with 14 oak *foudres* of 200 hectoliters
> capacity each. Another temperature-controlled cellar has been
> constructed to store the wines while they are still in barrels (first- and
> second-year aging).

For decades, Gruaud-Larose produced St.-Julien's most massive and backward wine. Under the new proprietor, Jacques Merlaut, there has been an
obvious trend to produce a more refined, less rustic and tannic style of
Gruaud. I expect this recent winemaking direction to continue. The production is large and the quality consistently high. Gruaud-Larose produced wines
of first-growth quality in vintages such as 1979, 1982, 1983, 1985, 1986, and
1990. The beautiful château, which sits on the plateau of St.-Julien rather
than riverside, is not likely to be seen unless the visitor to the Médoc turns
off the main Route du Vin (D2) at the town of St.-Julien-Beychevelle and
takes Route D101 in a westerly direction.

Those critics of Gruaud-Larose who found the wine too chunky, solid, and
massive may want to revisit this wine now that it is taking on more finesse
and elegance.

VINTAGES

1997—This is the most impressive Gruaud-Larose since the 1990. Under the new
•   ownership of Jacques Merlaut, this property seems set to recapture its glory
90–   days of the sixties and eighties. The wine possesses a saturated purple color,
92   and a knockout nose of jammy blackberries, cassis, earth, and vanillin. Rich
      in the mouth, with outstanding purity, super extraction, and well-integrated
      tannin, this wine has low acidity but more delineation than many of the
      bigger-styled wines of the vintage. Some chocolate and cassis flavors linger
      for over 30 seconds on the palate of this impressively endowed, medium- to
      full-bodied, outstanding Gruaud-Larose. Moreover, unlike many vintages of
      Gruaud-Larose, the 1997 will drink superbly when young. Anticipated matu-
      rity: 2001–2015. Last tasted, 3/98.

1996—The 1996 appears to be a potential sleeper of the vintage, and may merit an
•   outstanding score. It is a powerful, bulky style of Gruaud-Larose, with a dark
88–   ruby/purple color, and plenty of cassis, spicy new oak, and roasted herbs
91   in the jammy nose. On the palate, the wine has lost much of the forward
      precociousness it was revealing last spring, now boasting loads of tannin in
      its powerful, muscular flavors. It seemed much softer when I first tasted it,
      but the wine has put on weight and gained considerable structure. It now
      appears this husky wine has the potential for long-term cellaring. Anticipated
      maturity: 2005–2020. Last tasted, 2/98.

1995—Revealing more grip and tannin since bottling, the 1995 Gruaud-Larose
•   exhibits a dark ruby color, and a nose of sweet black cherries, licorice, earth,
89   and spice. Rich, with medium to full body, high tannin, and subtle oak in the

background, the 1995 is nearly as structured and tannic as the 1996. The two vintages are more similar than dissimilar. Anticipated maturity: 2005–2020. Last tasted, 11/97.

1994 — The 1994 performed better prior to bottling. It appears to have dropped much
 • of its mid-palate sweetness and fatness, tastes greener than my cask-tasting
82? notes suggested, and finishes with a searing degree of harsh, bitter tannin. Perhaps I caught it in a dormant, unflattering state of evolution, but it is currently revealing less ripeness, fruit, and texture. This wine's future is suspect, as the wine lacks harmony. Last tasted, 1/97.

1993 — This is an attractive wine for the vintage. The provocative nose of grilled
 • meats, smoked herbs, olives, and earthy, truffle-scented black fruits is intense
86 (perhaps too fragrant for many tasters). The wine is soft, ripe, and medium bodied, with surprising levels of sweet fruit and glycerin, as well as low acidity. This is one Gruaud-Larose that is best drunk during its first decade of life. Last tasted, 1/97.

1992 — The black/purple–colored 1992 gives evidence that Gruaud-Larose may have
 • returned to the forceful, robust, muscular style that made the estate famous.
. 86 In general, the 1992 vintage did not produce big, rich wines, but this effort from Gruaud-Larose is a reassuringly large-scaled, dense, powerful, rich, thick wine. The 1992 is more cleanly made than the leathery, "brett"-tinged 1991, exhibits gobs of earthy, rich, peppery, black currant, and herbal fruit flavors, low acidity, and a thick, chewy, lush finish. The wine's tannin is noticeable but well integrated, making this wine appealing today yet capable of 8–10 years of evolution. Last tasted, 3/95.

1991 — The 1991, with its dark color and leathery, smoked meat, tar, and licorice-
 • scented nose, is a return to the estate's bold, intense style. Spicy, with sweet
85 fruit, low acidity, and a soft, plump texture, it will last for another 8–10 years. Last tasted, 1/94.

1990 — This superb wine exhibits a thick-looking, plum/purple/garnet–like color.
 • A sensational nose of jammy black cherries, earth, cedar, and herbs has
93 become far more intense and striking. The wine displays sensational richness and power, but not quite the burly, monstrous size and hulking weight of the 1986 or 1982. Nevertheless, it reveals impressive stuffing and power. The low acidity emphasizes the thick, juicy, succulent fruit in this backward yet rich, chewy wine. This was the finest showing yet for the 1990 Gruaud-Larose. Anticipated maturity: 1999–2020. Last tasted, 11/96.

1989 — The 1989 was excellent, nearly outstanding. The herbal side of Gruaud-
 • Larose was more noticeable, but the wine revealed a deep ruby/purple color
89 (but not the opaqueness of the 1990), more obvious tannin, without the mid-palate and sweet inner core of fruit exhibited by the 1990. It is a big, tannic, spicy wine, with plenty of potential but not the sweetness and chewy texture of the 1990. The 1989 needs more time to shed its cloak of tannin; give it 5–8 years of cellaring and drink it over the following 20+ years. Last tasted, 11/96.

1988 — The 1988 Gruaud-Larose is probably a 30-year wine. Dark plum/garnet, this
•　　surprisingly powerful, rich, concentrated, wine is long and full-bodied for a
88　　1988. Reminiscent of the 1975, only less savage, it has copious quantities of
　　　meaty, herb-tinged chocolate and berry flavors in addition to moderate tannin.
　　　Anticipated maturity: 2000–2025. Last tasted, 4/98.

1987 — Typical of most of the Cordier wines in 1987, this is a surprisingly muscular,
•　　robust, chunky wine, with plenty of concentrated, weedy, cassis fruit hiding
84　　under a veneer of hard tannins. Medium to full bodied, intense, and powerful,
　　　this is a wine to consider purchasing by parents who have children born in
　　　1987. Anticipated maturity: Now–2005. Last tasted, 10/90.

1986 — There seems to be no doubt about the quality of the 1986 Gruaud-Larose,
•　　which in 20 years should rival the extraordinary 1990, 1982, 1961, 1949,
94+　and 1928 made at this vast estate. From the first time I tasted this wine in
　　　cask, I have thought it to be among the blockbusters of the vintage. It has a
　　　black/purple color, mammoth structure, a fabulous wealth of fruit, and a finish
　　　that seems to last several minutes. This is indeed first-growth quality, but
　　　then when, in the last decade, has a Gruaud-Larose not matched the quality
　　　of the first-growths? Given the enormous structure, impressive concentration,
　　　and massive tannins, one must wonder when this wine will be ready to drink.
　　　That may preclude a number of consumers from actually deciding to buy it.
　　　For many readers this is probably a wine to lay down for their children rather
　　　than to realistically consider drinking in their own lifetimes. Anticipated
　　　maturity: 2000–2030. Last tasted, 7/97.

1985 — The dark ruby/garnet–colored 1985 Gruaud-Larose has evolved beautifully.
•　　It exhibits a lovely, sweet, fragrant bouquet of berry fruit, truffles, earth, and
90　　smoky oak. On the palate, the wine is fat, long, forward for Gruaud, medium
　　　to full bodied, and deep. This is one of the few Gruauds to drink well
　　　extremely young. Anticipated maturity: Now–2005. Last tasted, 6/97.

1984 — All the Cordier wines were successful in 1984, but what else is new? The
•　　1984 Gruaud is almost 100% Cabernet. It is a big, virile, rich, tannic, spicy,
83　　densely colored, powerful, somewhat hard-edged wine that will age for 10
　　　years. Anticipated maturity: Now–2000. Last tasted, 10/89.

1983 — This dark garnet–colored, unctuous, rather viscous, deep wine has reached
•　　full maturity. The 1983 Gruaud-Larose exhibits a provocative nose of roasted
90　　herbs, animal fat, jammy blackberries, licorice, and cedar. It is a big, fat,
　　　juicy, and succulent wine, with sweet tannin in the finish. Anticipated matu-
　　　rity: Now–2010. Last tasted, 9/97.

1982 — When I most recently tasted this wine I mistook it for a first-growth Pauillac.
•　　It gets my nod as the greatest Gruaud-Larose of the last half century. With
96　　decanting of 1 hour (the wine's heavy sediment makes it necessary), this
　　　opaque black/garnet–colored wine offers up staggeringly intense aromas of
　　　licorice, tar, overripe cassis, olives, and new saddle leather. Extremely full
　　　bodied, with an unctuous texture and layers of concentrated fruit that
　　　ooze from the glass, this is a spectacularly rich, thrilling Gruaud-Larose.
　　　Still youthful, it exhibits no signs of age except for the fact that it

has shed considerable amounts of tannin. This large-scaled, massive St.-Julien should hit its plateau of maturity in several more years and last through the first 20+ years of the next century. This is a whopper! Last tasted, 4/98.

1981—A top success for the vintage, the 1981 Gruaud-Larose is dark ruby, with
•   a full-intensity bouquet of ripe black currants, spicy oak, plums,
88   leather, smoked meat, and violets. This wine is concentrated on the palate, with rich, tannic, lingering flavors. The tannins are melting away, and the wine is close to maturity. Anticipated maturity: Now–2005. Last tasted, 10/89.

1980—Unusually variable from bottle to bottle, the 1980 Gruaud-Larose can be soft,
•   fruity, spicy, and attractive. It is short in the finish and lean, as well as overtly
72?   herbaceous, hard, and acidic. It should be drunk up. Anticipated maturity: Now. Last tasted, 6/87.

1979—This is a typical Gruaud-Larose: dark colored, ripe, with fat, fruity, meaty
•   flavors suggestive of herbs, plums, and black cherries. In the mouth, the wine
88   has full body, medium-soft tannins, and a supple, smooth finish. Because of its forward charms, it is undeniably appealing now. Anticipated maturity: Now–2000. Last tasted, 1/91.

1978—In 1978, Gruaud-Larose produced a dark-colored wine with gobs of aggres-
•   sive tannins. Built for long-term cellaring, the 1978 Gruaud-Larose has a
87   big, briery, tar-and-herb-scented bouquet, deep, intense, ripe, relatively hard flavors, and a full-bodied, long finish. The 1978 has taken longer to mature than the 1979, and it is slightly inferior in quality. Anticipated maturity: Now–2005. Last tasted, 10/90.

1976—Not one of the better efforts for Gruaud-Larose, the 1976 lacks the rich, soft,
•   silky fruitiness that characterizes the top wines of this irregular vintage. It
73   seems to have an imbalance of tannin and an annoying acidity in the finish. Drink it up. Anticipated maturity: Now. Last tasted, 2/83.

1975—This massive, backward wine appears to resist aging. Still bitterly tan-
•   nic, impressively colored (dark garnet with no amber), and monstrous on
89+?   the palate, this wine will either turn out like the outstanding 1928 and begin to reveal some charm and character around age 40 or it will dry out, much like the 1948. It needs another 5–10 years of cellaring. The excru-ciatingly painful level of tannin makes this wine an enigma. It is likely to be appreciated only by the most patient Bordeaux enthusiasts. I would not be surprised to see some wine writer touting its greatness around 2025, long after most of it has been consumed and found to be pleasure-less. Owners should try not to touch a bottle before 2005. Last tasted, 12/95.

1974—Now fully mature, and not likely to hold together for more than a few more
•   years, this off-year Gruaud has surprisingly good color, with a pleasingly
76   mature, moderately intense bouquet of cassis and spices, medium body, tart acidity, and a vegetal aspect to its fruit. The wine is becoming more attenuated. Anticipated maturity: Now–may be in decline. Last tasted, 7/87.

1973—Soft and fruity, but fading badly, this wine has held together longer than I
  •   would have ever expected. It requires immediate drinking offering simple,
 67   straightforward, one-dimensional, washed-out flavors. Anticipated maturity:
       Now—probably in serious decline. Last tasted, 7/86.

1971—Gruaud-Larose represented a good example of the 1971 vintage. It has been
  •   fully mature for over a decade and now reveals the telltale brown color of
 81   approaching decline. This vintage of Gruaud was fruity, plummy, spicy, soft,
       and agreeable. It has now begun to dry out. Anticipated maturity: Now. Last
       tasted, 12/88.

1970—This is a typically tough, muscular, closed, angular, acidic 1970, seemingly
  •   without the extract and concentration to balance out the tannin. The 1970
86?   Gruaud-Larose remains dusty and coarse, with considerable brett (the spoil-
       age yeast that technocrats find appalling). I am not sure this wine will ever
       become fully mature. While it offers an attractive leathery, smoky, earthy
       nose, the flavors remain hard and coarse. Last tasted, 6/96.

1967—At peak in the mid-1970s, this wine was effusively fruity, ripe, round, and
  •   sweet. Now the color has taken on a brownish cast, the flavors seem to be at
 74   odds with each other, and the wine tastes as if it is cracking up. Some of my
       friends claim to have drunk much better bottles, so perhaps I have been
       unlucky. Anticipated maturity: Now—may be in decline. Last tasted, 3/89.

1966—A classic vintage for Gruaud-Larose, the 1966 remains surprisingly young,
  •   relatively unevolved, but austere, with a black currant, cedary, earthy fruiti-
 88   ness, and firm tannins. The finish is dry, but long and still youthful. In style
       and texture, the 1966 Gruaud-Larose resembles a big Pauillac. Will the 1966
       Gruaud-Larose ever shed its tannic toughness? Anticipated maturity: Now–
       2015. Last tasted, 1/89.

1964—One of only a handful of vintage successes in the Médoc, Gruaud-Larose
  •   continues to taste uncommonly fruity, deep, and round. There is no evidence
 87   of dilution from the heavy rains that ruined many others. This is a succulently
       textured, generous, perfumed wine with medium to full body. The 1964 Gru-
       aud-Larose has been fully mature for over a decade without drying out. A
       sleeper! Anticipated maturity: Now. Last tasted, 12/88.

1962—A surprisingly big, darkly colored wine that continues to perform admirably,
  •   the 1962 Gruaud-Larose remains concentrated for the vintage, with deep,
 87   black curranty, cedary, and herbaceous flavors, full body, and a satiny finish.
       This intensely fruity wine has drunk well and been fully mature for over 2
       decades. It has yet to exhibit signs of cracking up—a testament to how long
       well-balanced Bordeaux can last at its apogee. Anticipated maturity: Now–
       2000. Last tasted, 11/89.

1961—The 1961 is among the greatest mature wines of Gruaud-Larose I have drunk.
  •   This powerful, rich, densely concentrated wine remains young, fresh, and
 96   vigorous, with a full decade of life ahead. It continues to exhibit a dark garnet
       color with some amber, a wonderfully fragrant quality (minerals, tar, cedar,
       soy sauce, and licorice), a viscous texture, sensational depth of fruit, and a
       fabulous, albeit alcoholic, finish. This is claret at its most decadent. Antici-
       pated maturity: Now–2015. Last tasted, 10/94.

ANCIENT VINTAGES

The 1945 (96+ points; last tasted 10/94) is a remarkably young, backward, massive Gruaud-Larose, similar in style to the 1961, 1975, 1982, and 1986. Still opaque, garnet/black colored, with a tight but promising nose of licorice, black fruits, and herbs, this full-bodied, meaty, chewy wine exhibits huge reserves of fruit and a spicy, powerful, tannic finish. While it can be drunk now (I would suggest decanting of at least an hour), it is another immortal 1945 that will last for an additional 20–30 years. The 1953 (93 points; last tasted 3/98) is another gem.

The 1928 Gruaud-Larose (97 points; last tasted 10/94) is an amazingly intact wine as it approaches 70 years of age. It exhibits a huge, earthy, sweet, truffle, cedar, and spicy nose, massive body, noticeably high tannin, and stunning concentration. A slight austerity creeps in at the finish. The dark garnet color with only light amber is remarkable given the wine's age. The 1921 Gruaud-Larose (70? points; last tasted 12/95) was a disjointed, clumsy, closed, astringently tannic wine with little fruit remaining.

HORTEVIE　　　　　　　　　　　　　　　　　　　VERY GOOD

Classification: Cru Bourgeois
Location of vineyards: St.-Julien-Beychevelle
Owner: Henri Pradère
Address: 33250 Beychevelle
Mailing address: c/o Château Terrey-Gros-Cailloux, 33250 St.-Julien-Beychevelle
Telephone: 33 5 56 59 06 27; telefax: 33 5 56 59 29 32
Visits: No visits

VINEYARDS (red)
Surface area: 8.6 acres
Average age of vines: 40 years
Blend: 70% Cabernet Sauvignon, 25% Merlot, 5% Petit Verdot
Density of plantation: 10,000 vines per hectare
Average yields (over the last 5 years): 50 hectoliters per hectare

GRAND VIN (red)
Brand name: Château Hortevie
Appellation: St.-Julien
Upbringing: Grapes are hand-picked. Fermentations last 3 weeks. Wines are then aged in tanks, oak casks, and barrels (20% of which are new). They are fined but not filtered prior to bottling.

SECOND WINE
None produced.

Evaluation of present classification: The quality equivalent of a Grand
Bourgeois Exceptionnel
Plateau of maturity: 3–10 years following the vintage

The tiny production of Hortevie comes from a vineyard owned by Henri
Pradère, who also owns Terrey-Gros-Cailloux. Although both these wines are
made by identical methods from the same vineyard, Hortevie is said to be
produced from older vines and is treated as somewhat of a *tête de cuvée* of
Terrey-Gros-Cailloux. Pradère's tendency to pick late has always resulted in
rich, concentrated, low-acid wines that begged for some structure from new
oak casks. These were finally introduced at Hortevie in the late eighties,
although much of the production of both Hortevie and Terrey-Gros-Cailloux
is still aged in tank until the proprietor deems it ready for bottling. Hortevie
is a consistently good St.-Julien and has long represented a fine value. While
not long-lived, the top vintages, such as 1982, 1986, 1989, 1995, and 1996,
are capable of aging well for 10–15 years.

VINTAGES

1997—This consistently attractive, juicy, succulent wine is very approachable. Con-
•   sequently, 1997 is an ideal vintage for this plump, precocious winemaking
86–   style. The deep ruby/purple-colored 1997 Hortevie offers gobs of juicy black
87   currant fruit intertwined with herbs and earth. Lush, low acid flavors exhibit
        fine ripeness, as well as a layered feel on the palate. There is no aggressive-
        ness, harshness, or sharp edges to any component in the wine's pliant person-
        ality. Drink it over the next 5–6 years. Last tasted, 3/98.

1996—Performing well, the deep opaque purple-colored 1996 offers sweet, ripe
•   jammy cassis and cherry fruit, and fleshy, full-bodied flavors with moderate
87–   tannin in the finish. The tannin is sweet, ripe, and mature, so this wine will
89   not require an inordinate amount of patience. It is a potential sleeper of the
        vintage. Anticipated maturity: 2001–2012. Last tasted 3/98.

1995—This dense purple-colored wine displays a delicious personality, from its no
•   holds barred, uncomplicated, but intense, creamy, black currant, cedar, and
87   smoky-scented nose, to its deep, chewy, spicy, fleshy flavors. Fruit, glycerin,
        body, and tannin are the major components of this St.-Julien, which can be
        drunk young or cellared. Anticipated maturity: 2000–2012. It is another
        sleeper of the vintage. Last tasted, 11/97.

1994—The 1994 exhibits a deeper hue to its dark ruby color, as well as a cedary,
•   spicy nose intertwined with scents of vanilla (presumably from new oak
87   barrels). The wine is soft and medium bodied, with fine concentration and
        length and more noticeable tannin than the 1993. This wine is meant to be
        drunk during its first 7–8 years of life. Last tasted, 1/97.

1993—Undoubtedly a sleeper of the vintage, the 1993 Hortevie may turn out to be
•   as good as its two successors. The wine reveals an excellent deep ruby color,
87   Hortevie's telltale, sweet, tarry, jammy, black currant aromas, and surprisingly
        soft, round flavors, with no hard tannin or herbaceousness—characteristics
        of the less successful 1993s. This low-acid wine offers rich, delicious drinking
        now and over the next 5–7 years. Last tasted, 1/97.

1990—The 1990 is a rich, velvety-textured, deliciously jammy wine that will make
•   ideal drinking over the next 7–8 years. Although it lacks complexity and
86   grip, it is plump and tasty. Anticipated maturity: Now–1999. Last tasted,
        1/93.

1989—The 1989 is an excellent wine, rich, powerful, concentrated, and alcoholic,
•   with a long, heady finish. It should prove to be this property's finest wine
87   since 1982. Anticipated maturity: Now–2000. Last tasted, 1/93.

1988—The 1988 is typical of the vintage—tannic, lean, austere, and in need of 2–3
•   years of cellaring. It is well made, but lighter and less complete than either
85   the 1989 or 1990. It should drink well from now until the end of the decade.
        Last tasted, 1/93.

1986—Only 1,500–1,800 cases were made of this very reliable, rich, full-bodied,
•   chunky, fleshy wine that provides immense satisfaction rather than great
87   finesse and complexity. The 1986, deep ruby/purple in color, has a plummy,
        licorice-scented bouquet, fat, fleshy flavors, and plenty of solid tannins in the
        finish. It is a sleeper of the vintage. Anticipated maturity: Now–2001. Last
        tasted, 9/89.

1985—The 1985 Hortevie is deep in color, fat, supple, big, and chunky, with a
•   full-intensity bouquet of road tar and blackberries. It is a meaty, hefty wine,
85   short on finesse but big on flavor. Anticipated maturity: Now. Last tasted,
        4/89.

1984—Thin, hard, and very tannic, the 1984 Hortevie does not have enough fruit to
•   cover its bones. Last tasted, 4/86.
73

LAGRANGE   EXCELLENT

Classification: Third-growth in 1855
Location of vineyards: St.-Julien-Beychevelle
Owner: Château Lagrange S.A. (Suntory Ltd.)
Address: 33250 St.-Julien-Beychevelle
Mailing address: Same as above
Telephone: 33 5 56 73 38 38; telefax: 33 5 56 59 26 09
Visits: By appointment only, Monday to Friday, between 9 A.M. and
11 A.M., and 2 P.M. to 4:30 P.M., on Fridays to 3:30 P.M.
Contact: Catherine Munck

VINEYARDS (red)
Surface area: 270 acres
Average age of vines: 27 years

Blend: 64.8% Cabernet Sauvignon, 27.9% Merlot, 7.3 % Petit Verdot
Density of plantation: 8,500 vines per hectare
Average yields (over the last 5 years): 53.35 hectoliters per hectare
Total average annual production: 50,000–55,000 cases

GRAND VIN (red)
Brand name: Château Lagrange
Appellation: St.-Julien
Mean annual production: 23,500 cases
Upbringing: Grapes are hand-picked. Fermentations last 15–25 days, at
28 degrees centigrade, in temperature-controlled stainless-steel tanks of
220-hectoliter capacity. Only indigenous yeasts are used. Pumping-overs
last 20 minutes twice daily. Wines are transferred to oak barrels, which
are renewed by half at each vintage, for about 20 months aging. They are
both fined and filtered before bottling.

SECOND WINE
Brand name: Les Fiefs de Lagrange
Average annual production: 31,000 cases

VINEYARDS (white)
Surface area: 9.8 acres
Average age of vines: 3 years (actually these are grafts on vines of age 10)
Blend: 53% Sauvignon, 36% Semillon, 11% Muscadelle
Density of plantation: 8,500 vines per hectare
Average yields (over the last 5 years): Debut in 1997
Total average annual production: (Debut in 1997)

GRAND VIN (white)
Brand name: Les Arums de Lagrange
Appellation: Bordeaux
Mean annual production: Debut vintage 1997
Upbringing: Pressing and racking of the must. Fermentations occur in oak
barrels, 50% of which are new. Wines remain on lees for 12 months, with
regular *bâtonnages*, before bottling. They are fined and filtered.

Evaluation of present classification: Since 1983 should be upgraded to a
second-growth
Plateau of maturity: 7–20 years following the vintage

Prior to 1983, Lagrange (a third-growth) had suffered numerous blows to its
reputation as a result of a pathetic track record of quality in the sixties and
seventies. The well-situated vineyards represent a rare unmorcellated property adjacent to Gruaud-Larose, so there was no reason why good wine should
not have been produced.

In 1983 the huge Japanese company Suntory purchased Lagrange and began an extraordinary renovation of not only the château and the *chais,* but the vineyards as well. No expense has been spared, and such talented people as administrator Marcel Ducasse, and the property's young, enthusiastic oenologist, Kenji Suzuta, have begun to make stunning wines in an amazingly short period of time.

Not only has the quality of the wines been upgraded, but Lagrange is now a beautiful château with tranquil gardens and a lake teeming with wildlife.

If vintages from 1985 on reveal any particular style, it is one that favors an impressive depth of flavor welded to plenty of tannin, toasty new oak, and an underlying succulence and fatness that is no doubt due to a strict selection and the harvesting of very ripe fruit with an element of *sur-maturité.* Clearly the new proprietors seem intent on producing a wine that can age for 20 or more years yet have appeal when young.

While the world press has applauded the extraordinary turnaround made at Château Margaux by the Mentzelopoulos family, less has been written about the turn of events at Château Lagrange, although in 1990 *The Wall Street Journal,* amazingly, ran a front-page story about this showpiece property. Nevertheless, this wine currently remains considerably underpriced given the quality level of the wines that has emerged.

VINTAGES

1997—Tasted three separate times with consistent notes, Lagrange's 1997 exhibits a
 • dark ruby/purple color, copious quantities of toasty new oak in its aromas, me-
86– dium body, more structure and tannin than many of its peers, and a pure, oak/
88 cassis-driven flavor profile. This wine may not be as fat or low in acidity as others, but it is plump and soft. It should turn out to be a very good to excellent Lagrange that will be at its best between 2000–2012. Last tasted, 3/98.

1996.—A classic Bordeaux as well as a textbook St.-Julien, this dense, powerful yet
 • elegant 1996 is broodingly backward, but it does reveal considerable promise.
90– The dark purple color is accompanied by a nose that reluctantly offers up
91 aromas of sweet toasty oak, cassis, cedar, and minerals. The wine possesses full body and outstanding concentration, as well as an overall sense of elegance and equilibrium. Backward, but not aggressively tannic, the 1996 Lagrange should continue to flesh out and merit an outstanding rating. Anticipated maturity: 2005–2025. Last tasted, 3/98.

1995—The 1995 Lagrange is similar to the 1996, but the fruit is sweeter, the acidity
 • lower, and the wine less marked by Cabernet Sauvignon. The color is a deep
90 ruby/purple. The wine boasts a roasted herb, charcoal, black currant, mineral, and new oak-scented nose. Medium to full bodied and ripe, with copious quantities of jammy black cherry and cassis flavors presented in a low acid, moderately tannic style, this well-endowed, purely made wine requires cellaring. Anticipated maturity: 2003–2020. Last tasted, 11/97.

1994—In comparison with the more open-knit, flattering style of the 1993, the 1994
•   is a backward, less precocious, more tannic wine that needs another 5–7
88   years of cellaring. It is a wine that recalls the style of the more tannic vintages
       of the sixties and seventies. The healthy dark ruby/purple color is followed
       by copious quantities of smoky, toasty, new oak. There is an impression of
       ripe fruit, but for now, the wine's personality remains dominated by excruciat-
       ingly strong tannin. Give this wine 5–6 years of cellaring, as patience is
       definitely a requirement for purchasing the 1994 Lagrange. It should last for
       15–20 years. Last tasted, 1/97.

1993—A very good effort in this vintage (which produced a surprising number of
•   good wines considering the difficult conditions), the 1993 exhibits a dark
87   ruby/purple color accompanied by Lagrange's lavishly wooded, spicy, power-
       fully extracted, sweet, jammy, black currant–scented bouquet and flavors.
       This surprisingly dense, concentrated, medium-bodied wine possesses some
       tannin in the finish, but to the credit of this estate's winemaking, the tannin
       is unobtrusive. While it serves its structural purpose, it does not contain any
       astringency or bitterness. The 1993 Lagrange can be drunk now or cellared
       for 10+ years. It is a very good wine for the vintage. Last tasted, 1/97.

1992—This property is fashioning reasonably priced, rich, concentrated, lavishly
•   oaked wines. The 1992 is one of the top successes for the vintage. The color
87   is an impressive dark ruby, and the nose offers up scents of smoky, toasty new
       oak accompanied by surprisingly rich, black currant fruit scents. Medium
       bodied, concentrated, and soft, with a midpalate of ripe fruit, this sweet, sexy
       example of the vintage should drink well for 7–10 years. Last tasted, 11/94.

1990—The 1990 is a massive, highly extracted, boldly wooded, spicy, dark purple–
•   colored wine with high tannin, low acidity, and layers of jammy fruit. The
93   huge glycerin and massive mouth-feel in this unctuously textured wine are
       difficult to ignore. I suspect this wine will become more defined after it loses
       its baby fat. Although fun to taste at present, it does need 3–4 more years of
       cellaring; it should last for 20–25 years. Last tasted, 1/97.

1989—The 1989 is a smoky, tar, cassis, roasted herb, jammy style of wine, with a
•   dense purple color, sweet tannin, and low acidity. It is easy to drink, although
90   the bouquet has not changed since I tasted it several years ago. The wine is
       soft and fat, but not flabby. It should drink well for 15+ years, probably
       developing more focus as well as a more classical profile. The 1989 Lagrange
       is a big, rich, boldly flavored wine made in a California-like style. Last tasted,
       1/97.

1988—The 1988 exhibits a dark ruby/purple color and a closed but spicy, reticent
•   bouquet vaguely suggestive of cedar, plums, and green olives. This medium-
86   bodied, surprisingly hard and tannic wine will need 4–6 years of bottle age
       to soften. Last tasted, 1/97.

1986—Here is a classic example of a wine that is showing significantly more com-
•   plexity and richness from the bottle than out of cask, although it was certainly
92   a potentially outstanding wine when tasted from the barrel. In a vintage that
       produced a number of enormously structured, rich, concentrated wines,

Lagrange is another of the blockbuster wines that seems capable of lasting 30–35 years. Black/ruby in color, with a closed but burgeoning bouquet of spicy new oak, black fruits, and flowers, this muscular, full-bodied, tannic wine is packed with fruit and is clearly one of the great long-distance runners from this vintage. I admire how the significant investment made by the Japanese owners in this property has paid off with a thrilling, albeit amazingly backward, wine. The finest Lagrange to date! Anticipated maturity: 2000–2025. Last tasted, 1/97.

1985 — Lagrange's recent vintages are powerfully constructed wines made to survive
 • 　　several decades of aging with grace and complexity. The dark ruby–colored
89 　　1985 is deep, rich, long, and, for a 1985, surprisingly backward and tannic.
 　　　Medium bodied, elegant, and packed with fruit, it is a long-distance runner.
 　　　Anticipated maturity: Now–2010. Last tasted, 1/97.

1984 — Take a lot of yen (remember, a Japanese concern owns this property), per-
 • 　　suade a perfectionist such as Michel Delon of Léoville-Las Cases to help
82 　　consult with respect to the making of the wine, and just like that you have
 　　　the ingredients for instant stardom. The 1984 is moderately ruby, and tannic,
 　　　exhibits plenty of new, toasty oak and good fruit, and is a success for this
 　　　minor vintage. Anticipated maturity: Now. Last tasted, 3/89.

1983 — Potentially a sleeper of this vintage, Lagrange is deep in color, spicy, and
 • 　　rich, with full-bodied, briery, cassis flavors, good firm tannins, and a long
86 　　finish. If the wine resembles the style of Léoville-Las Cases, it's not surpris-
 　　　ing, because Michel Delon, the gifted winemaker at Las Cases, oversaw the
 　　　vinification of Lagrange in 1983. Anticipated maturity: Now–2000. Last
 　　　tasted, 3/89.

1982 — This was a successful vintage for Lagrange, as well as the last wine made
 • 　　under the old regime. Perhaps the 1982 is not the equal of the excellent
85 　　1983, but it is still an improvement over previous efforts from Lagrange. Dark
 　　　ruby, with a well-developed bouquet of ripe berry fruit and vanillin oak, the
 　　　wine is also precocious on the palate, displaying rich, lush, nicely concen-
 　　　trated flavors and full body. Anticipated maturity: Now–2000. Last tasted,
 　　　1/85.

1979 — The 1979 is a bit too herbaceous and stalky, but once past the rather unim-
 • 　　pressive bouquet, the wine shows good ripe fruit, a supple, soft texture, and a
78 　　spicy finish. It will be ready early. Anticipated maturity: Now–may be in
 　　　decline. Last tasted, 3/83.

1978 — Dark ruby in color, with a ripe berry bouquet suggestive of Merlot, the
 • 　　1978 has generous, straightforward, fruity flavors, light to moderate tannins,
80 　　medium body, and a pleasant finish. A good, if unexciting, wine. Anticipated
 　　　maturity: Now–may be in decline. Last tasted, 3/83.

1975 — The color is dark ruby, yet one is hard-pressed to find any fruit behind a wall
 • 　　of abrasive tannins. Very severe and bitter on the palate, with an excess of
70 　　tannins, this will require a lengthy stay in the cellar just to soften. However,
 　　　my guess is that the fruit will never be adequate enough to balance out the
 　　　harsh qualities of this wine. Anticipated maturity: Now. Last tasted, 4/84.

1973—A total failure—no fruit, no charm, just watery, thin flavors with entirely too
•   much acidity and tannin. Last tasted, 10/79.
·50

1971—A little wine, compact, a bit tannic, lean and short in the finish, the 1971
•   Lagrange is the kind of claret that is an embarrassment to the commune of
65   St.-Julien, as well as to Bordeaux. Charmless, coarse. Last tasted, 10/78.

1970—The 1970 is the best Lagrange of the seventies, as nothing of this quality
•   level was seen again until 1982 and 1983. Dark ruby, with chunky flavors,
84   good, ripe, black currant fruit, a solid, moderately long finish, and potential
for further evolution, this is a respectable effort from Lagrange. Anticipated
maturity: Now. Last tasted, 4/81.

1966—Light, fruity, simple, and one-dimensional, the 1966 Lagrange has been fully
•   mature for a number of years and seems totally devoid of the complexity,
72   breadth of character, and length one expects in a third-growth St.-Julien.
Drink up. Anticipated maturity: Now. Last tasted, 4/80.

1964—Lagrange's 1964 was pale in color and very stringy and skinny on the palate
•   when I first tasted it in 1980. It is a dubious effort for certain in this mixed,
60   rainy vintage. Anticipated maturity: Now–probably in serious decline. Last
tasted, 3/84.

1962—While the 1962 was reportedly a success for the vintage, my experience in
•   two separate tastings has shown the wine to have adequate color but too much
70   acidity, a harsh, aggressive finish, and little of the rich fruity charm one
expects from a St.-Julien. Drink up. Anticipated maturity: Now–probably in
serious decline. Last tasted, 2/81.

1961—Produced in a period when the wines of Lagrange were quite mediocre, the
•   1961 is a surprisingly good effort. Dark ruby with amber at the edge, this is a
85   chunky, flavorful wine, with some delicious black currant fruit, a pleasant
oaky spiciness, and very good suppleness and length on the palate. Anticipated maturity: Now. Last tasted, 2/84.

LALANDE BORIE   GOOD

Classification: Cru Bourgeois in 1932
Location of vineyards: St.-Julien
Owner: Borie family
Address: 33250 St.-Julien-Beychevelle
Mailing address: Same
Telephone: 33 5 56 59 05 20; telefax: 33 5 56 59 27 37
Visits: No visits

VINEYARDS (red)
Surface area: 44.5 acres
Average age of vines: 25 years
Blend: 65% Cabernet Sauvignon, 25% Merlot, 10% Cabernet Franc

Density of plantation: 10,000 vines per hectare
Average yields (over the last 5 years): 45 hectoliters per hectare
Total average annual production: 8,000 cases

GRAND VIN (red)
Brand name: Château Lalande Borie
Appellation: St.-Julien
Mean annual production: 90,000 bottles
Upbringing: Grapes are hand-picked. Fermentations last 15–18 days in
stainless-steel tanks. Wines are transferred, after malolactics, to oak
barrels, 25%–35% of which are new, for 14–16 months. They are fined
and lightly filtered before bottling.

SECOND WINE
None produced. The production not deemed good enough to bear the
grand vin label is sold in bulk.

Evaluation of present classification: Should be maintained
Plateau of maturity: 5–10 years following the vintage

This domain is a relatively recent creation. In 1970 Jean-Eugène Borie, the
proprietor of Ducru-Beaucaillou, purchased a parcel of 74 acres that had
at one time been part of Château Lagrange. Borie planted 18 hectares, or
slightly over 44 acres, in 1970, which today remains the size of the vineyard.

VINTAGES

1993—This dark ruby–colored wine exhibits attractive, chocolatey, sweet, curranty
•   fruit, fine ripeness, medium body, and a sense of elegance and grace. It is a
86   1993 that has managed to keep the tannin level well integrated and unobtru-
        sive. Drink it over the next decade. Last tasted, 11/94.
1989—The 1989 is a forward, deliciously black currant–scented wine that possesses
•   medium to full body, excellent concentration, and a long, heady, soft finish.
86   Anticipated maturity: Now–2004. Last tasted, 4/91.
1988—This is a good wine, somewhat tough textured yet spicy, with an attractive,
•   herbaceous fruitiness. Once the tannins in the finish begin to melt away, the
81   wine may merit a higher score. Anticipated maturity: Now–2000. Last tasted,
        4/91.
1986—With many 1986s, the questions continue to be, When will the tannins be
•   totally resolved? and Is the fruit sufficient to balance them out? This deep
85   ruby/purple wine is dense, huge, and backward on the palate but also has
        very aggressive tannins and appears a good decade away from maturity. This
        could turn out to be one of the sleepers of the vintage, but my reservations

about the level of tannins in the wine give me some cause for concern.
Anticipated maturity: Now–2005. Last tasted, 4/89.

1985—The 1985 Lalande Borie is very accessible, soft, fruity, pleasant, medium
•   bodied, and charming. Anticipated maturity: Now. Last tasted, 4/89.
84

LANGOA-BARTON   VERY GOOD

Classification: Third-growth
Location of vineyards: St.-Julien-Beychevelle
Owner: G.F.A. des Château Langoa et Léoville-Barton—Anthony Barton
Address: 33250 St.-Julien-Beychevelle
Mailing address: Same
Telephone: 33 5 56 59 06 05; telefax: 33 5 56 69 14 29
Visits: By appointment only, from Monday to Friday, between 9 A.M. and
11 A.M., and 2 P.M. and 4:30 P.M.
Contact: Miss Maud Frenoy

VINEYARDS (red)
Surface area: 37 acres
Average age of vines: 28 years
Blend: 70% Cabernet Sauvignon, 20% Merlot, 10% Cabernet Franc
Density of plantation: 9,000 vines per hectare
Average yields (over the last 5 years): 54 hectoliters per hectare
Total average annual production: 103,000 bottles

GRAND VIN (red)
Brand name: Château Langoa-Barton
Appellation: St.-Julien
Mean annual production: 85,000 bottles
Upbringing: Grapes are hand-picked. Fermentations occur in
temperature-controlled wooden vats of 200 hectoliters and last 2–3
weeks. Wines are then transferred to oak barrels, 50% of which are new,
for 18 months aging. They are fined and filtered prior to bottling.

SECOND WINE
Brand name: Lady Langoa
Average annual production: 18,000 bottles

Evaluation of present classification: Should be downgraded to a
fifth-growth
Plateau of maturity: 8–22 years following the vintage

Langoa-Barton is an impressively large château that sits directly on the well-traveled D2, or Médoc Route du Vin. The wine of the well-known second-growth Léoville-Barton is also made in the château's cellars. Both Langoa and Léoville-Barton are the properties of Anthony Barton, an Irishman whose family has had an interest in the Bordeaux area since 1821.

The late Ronald Barton, and now his handsome nephew Anthony have produced top-class wine that critics have called uncompromisingly traditional and classic. Both are St.-Julien wines with a distinctive Pauillac character and personality. Since the wines are made in the same wine cellar, by the same staff, the first question someone always asks is how they differ. In most years Léoville-Barton surpasses the quality of Langoa. Both are big, ripe, concentrated, spicy wines that frequently lack the youthful suppleness and commercial up-front fruit of some of their neighbors. Nevertheless, they age extremely well and, when mature, combine the savory, complex, graceful fruitiness of St.-Julien with the cedary toughness and virility of Pauillac.

Neither Léoville nor Langoa-Barton has ever enjoyed the reputation of Léoville-Las Cases and Ducru-Beaucaillou. That may now begin to change since Anthony Barton has full responsibility for the property, taking over when his uncle Ronald died in 1986. There is a new *régisseur*—Michel Raoul, a stricter selection, and the increased usage of new oak. These moves, plus a hard-headed, refreshingly realistic view that wine is not really sold until the consumer buys a bottle and drinks it, have all combined to make Langoa-Barton and Léoville-Barton grossly underpriced, particularly now that the quality level is close to the "super-second" level.

My only criticism of Langoa-Barton and Léoville-Barton is that in some of the lighter Bordeaux vintages, such as 1979, 1971, 1974, and 1973, the wines of these two châteaux taste less successful than many of their peers. Whatever the reason, both châteaux have excelled in top vintages such as 1996, 1995, 1990, 1986, 1985, 1982, 1975, 1970, 1961, 1959, and 1953. Langoa-Barton and its sister château produce wine for the true claret connoisseur.

VINTAGES

1997—The 1997 Langoa Barton reveals a *poivre vert*-scented nose, suggesting there
• 　was a slight lack of maturity in the Cabernet Sauvignon. The wine possesses
85– 　a deep ruby/purple color, as well as some of the vintage's up-front charm and
86 　softness, good purity, and a medium-bodied, ripe, rustic finish. It should drink
　　well reasonably early, in 3–4 years, and keep for 10–15. Last tasted, 3/98.

1996—My instincts suggest this wine may turn out to be slightly superior to the more
• 　monolithic 1995. The 1996 reveals a dark ruby/purple color, as well as plenty
85– 　of ripe Cabernet aromas of cassis and dried herbs, sweet fruit on the attack,
87+ 　medium body, and hefty tannin in the linear, compressed finish. If this wine's

flavor and texture expand, it will merit a score in the upper 80s. Anticipated maturity: 2006–2020. Last tasted, 3/98.

1995—
•
86+?
The 1995 Langoa-Barton has been perplexing to evaluate. It is woody, mono-lithic, and exceptionally tannic without the fruit and flesh necessary to pro-vide equilibrium. There are some positive components—a saturated dark ruby/purple color, hints of ripe fruit, and pure, clean flavors—but the wine's angularity/austerity is troublesome. It will probably be a good but old style claret that will never resolve all of its tannic bite. Anticipated maturity: 2003–2016. Last tasted, 11/97.

1994—
•
86+?
Dark ruby colored, with an unexpressive nose, this wine may turn out too austere and severe. It exhibits good power and fruit extraction, but the astrin-gent tannin may cause the fruit to dry out before the wine has shed its bitterness. Don't touch a bottle for 5–7 years . . . and keep your fingers crossed. Last tasted, 1/97.

1993—
•
86
There is no herbaceousness in this straightforward, medium-bodied, black currant-and-spicy-scented wine. It possesses solid fruit, some tannin, and a pleasant texture, with sweeter tannin and more precociousness than its sibling from Léoville-Barton. Drink it over the next decade. Last tasted, 1/97.

1992—
•
83
In 1992 both Barton estates turned out pleasant wines, although Langoa clearly does not possess the intensity of its sibling, Léoville-Barton. However, it is an attractively fruity, soft, charming, traditionally styled wine with some achingly painful tannin in the finish. The wine does not possess the fruit or depth to balance out its structure. Nevertheless, this is a cedary-, herb-, and curranty-flavored wine for drinking over the next 5–7 years. Last tasted, 11/94.

1991—
•
86
A successful 1991, Langoa-Barton's effort in this vintage produced a deeply colored wine with an attractive bouquet of cedar, cassis, and leather, medium body, firm flavors, admirable richness and depth, and a spicy, masculine finish. While drinkable now, it should last for a decade. Last tasted, 1/94.

1990—
•
87
The elegant, medium-bodied, tannic 1990 exhibits attractive ripe fruit as well as moderate depth and intensity. Anticipated maturity: Now–2005. Last tasted, 1/93.

1989—
•
86
The 1989 is a medium-bodied, pretty wine, but not as tannic, powerful, and concentrated as other St.-Juliens. The bouquet offers a pleasing tobacco, spice, and currant mélange. Well balanced, with a nice marriage of oak and red fruits, this wine displays surprisingly decent acidity. Anticipated matu-rity: Now–2005. Last tasted, 1/93.

1988—
•
85
The 1988 Langoa-Barton has some ripeness in its aroma but is austere, compact, and medium bodied. It should age well given the abundant tannins and firm framework. Drink it between now and the year 2000. Last tasted, 1/93.

1987—
•
84
A smaller-scaled wine, the 1987 is spicy and has a sense of elegance and breeding, medium body, some underlying greenness, but sound, ripe fruit. It is an attractive, delicious wine that is nearly as good as the 1988. Anticipated maturity: Now. Last tasted, 11/90.

1986—Ever so stubbornly, the 1986 Langoa-Barton is beginning to shed some of its
  •   enormously hard tannins to reveal a wine that has plenty of depth, full body,
  87   a spicy, burly texture, and 20–25 years of aging potential. The fruit does
          appear to be sufficient to hold up to the tannins, but again, patience is a
          required asset in order to fully appreciate this wine. Anticipated maturity:
          2000–2010. Last tasted, 11/90.

1985—The 1985 Langoa-Barton is a stylish wine, deep in color, medium bodied,
  •   with an elegant bouquet of black currant fruit and spicy oak. It is not a big,
  88   rich, blockbuster sort of wine, but rather a richly fruity, suave, and graceful
          St.-Julien. Anticipated maturity: Now–2003. Last tasted, 11/90.

1984—While the 1984 Langoa has good color, a spicy, somewhat closed bouquet,
  •   and firm yet malnourished flavors, it has turned astringent. It has no hope of
  72   further positive evolution. Anticipated maturity: Now. Last tasted, 2/90.

1983—From the cask, the 1983 Langoa-Barton was impressively deep in color, full
  •   bodied, admirably concentrated, but extremely tannic. However, although it
  84   appears to have the fruit to outlast the aggressive tannins, I feel this is a
          rustic, somewhat old-style, attenuated wine that comes across a bit clumsily.
          Anticipated maturity: Now–2005. Last tasted, 3/89.

1982—This is a top-class Langoa-Barton that is turning out better than the excellent
  •   1975. Comparable to the fine 1970, 1959, and 1948 yet fruitier, the 1982 has
  89   a rich, deep ruby color, an intense ripe, black currant bouquet, a big, tough,
          full-bodied framework, and exceptional potential. Very rich, tannic, big, and
          promising, this wine needs time. Anticipated maturity: Now–2010. Last
          tasted, 6/90.

1981—Like many vintages for the Barton-owned pair of Léoville and Langoa, it is
  •   often difficult to conclude which is the better wine since they are made and
  82   handled identically. The 1981 Langoa is medium bodied, with good color,
          a spicy, moderately fruity bouquet, and solid tannins that are beginning
          to soften. It is a trifle austere. Anticipated maturity: Now. Last tasted,
          10/90.

1980—One of the delicious wines of the vintage, the 1980 Langoa should be con-
  •   sumed. This wine is savory and spicy, with soft, round, attractively ripe, fruity
  81   yet monolithic flavors. Anticipated maturity: Now. Last tasted, 2/88.

1979—While the 1979 is an appealing wine, it lacks concentration, and tastes
  •   supple and light for Langoa-Barton. It is medium ruby/garnet, with a forward,
  78   supple, spicy bouquet, soft, average-intensity flavors, and a short finish. An-
          ticipated maturity: Now. Last tasted, 2/88.

1976—Very easy to drink, soft, and slightly sweet, with no abrasive tannin present,
  •   the 1976 Langoa has been fully mature for at least a decade. Now browning
  79   at the edges, this wine should be drunk up. Anticipated maturity: Now. Last
          tasted, 2/88.

1975—The 1975 Langoa-Barton tastes surprisingly open-knit, with a chocolatey,
  •   cedary, spicy, sweet nose, medium body, unobtrusive tannin for the vintage,
  87   and a round, gentle, elegant finish. This fully mature 1975 should be drunk
          over the next 5–7 years. Last tasted, 12/95.

1970—A wonderfully successful wine, the 1970 Langoa smells and tastes compara-
•   ble to a top Pauillac. A big yet restrained bouquet of cedar and black currants
88   is first rate. On the palate, the wine is ripe, weighty, rich, tannic, full bodied,
     and several years away from its zenith. This is Langoa at its best. Anticipated
     maturity: Now–2000. Last tasted, 2/88.

1966—Another unquestioned success for Langoa, the 1966, while very good, is not
•   up to the 1975 or 1982 quality level. Amber at the edge, with a solid ruby
87   color, the 1966 has a full-intensity, spicy, cedary, rich bouquet, lean, some-
     what austere flavors, but a good round, generous finish. Anticipated maturity:
     Now. Last tasted, 4/85.

1964—The tannin and acid seem clearly to outbalance the fruit in the 1964 Langoa.
•   Chunky, but a trifle lean and thin on the palate, the wine boasts an attractively
72   spicy, complex bouquet that somehow leaves the palate unfulfilled. Others
     have apprised me that good bottles of this wine do exist. Anticipated maturity:
     Now–may be in decline. Last tasted, 4/83.

1961—Tasted next to the 1959 at Anthony Barton's extravagant vertical tasting at
•   the International Wine Center in New York City, it was hard to pick which
89   wine was the best. The 1959 perhaps was more alcoholic, but the 1961 was
     filled with a richly scented smell of cedar, oak, vanillin, and ripe fruit. On
     the palate, the rich, round, sweet, ripe fruitiness of the vintage was capably
     displayed. Fully mature. Anticipated maturity: Now–may be in decline. Last
     tasted, 10/82.

ANCIENT VINTAGES

The 1959 (rated 90) Langoa-Barton has been marvelous on the two occasions
I have tasted it. The same could be said for the 1953 (a 90-point wine in
1988), the 1952 (88 and excellent, but tough), and the glorious 1948 (rated
93). I have never seen a bottle of the 1945 or anything older.

LÉOVILLE-BARTON   OUTSTANDING

Classification: Second-growth
Location of vineyards: St.-Julien-Beychevelle
Owner: G.F.A. des Châteaux Langoa et Léoville-Barton—Anthony Barton
Address: 33250 St.-Julien-Beychevelle
Mailing address: Same
Telephone: 33 5 56 59 06 05; telefax: 33 5 56 59 14 29
Visits: By appointment only, Monday to Friday between 9 A.M. and
11 A.M., and 2 P.M. and 4:30 P.M.
Contact: Mademoiselle Maud Frénoy

VINEYARDS (red)
Surface area: 116.1 acres
Average age of vines: 30 years

Blend: 72% Cabernet Sauvignon, 20% Merlot, 8% Cabernet Franc
Density of plantation: 9,000 vines per hectare
Average yields (over the last 5 years): 54 hectoliters per hectare
Total average annual production: 305,000 bottles

GRAND VIN (red)
Brand name: Château Léoville-Barton
Appellation: St.-Julien
Mean annual production: 20,000–22,000 cases
Upbringing: Grapes are picked manually. Fermentations occur in
temperature-controlled wooden vats of 200 hectoliters and last 2–3
weeks. Wines are transferred to oak barrels, 50% of which are new, for
18 months aging. They are fined and filtered prior to bottling.

SECOND WINE
Brand name: La Reserve de Léoville-Barton
Average annual production: 5,000 cases

Evaluation of present classification: Should be maintained
Plateau of maturity: 8–25 years following the vintage

Léoville-Barton is generally acknowledged to have an edge on its sibling,
Langoa-Barton. Both properties are owned by Anthony Barton. Unlike other
proprietors, Barton uses only a small amount of the supple, fleshy Merlot in
the blend (although it has been increased to 20% with plantings in the
mid-1980s), whereas the proportion of Cabernet Sauvignon is high not only
for the commune of St.-Julien, but for the Médoc in general.

Léoville-Barton is made at Langoa-Barton because there is no château at
Léoville. The main vineyard for Léoville-Barton sits immediately behind the
town of St.-Julien-Beychevelle and runs in a westerly direction, where it
intersects with the large vineyard of Château Talbot.

The inconsistencies of the seventies have been replaced by a consecutive
string of brilliantly successful wines in the eighties and nineties. Since 1985
Anthony Barton has refined rather than changed the traditional style of this
wine. Among all the top wines of St.-Julien, it represents the finest value.

VINTAGES

1997—Léoville-Barton's 1997, which was harvested between September 16 and 28
• (Anthony Barton claimed it "wasn't worth waiting" past the 28th to harvest
87– since the grapes had nothing more to gain), is a dense ruby/purple-colored
89 wine with more tannin and structure than many of its peers. There is plenty
of structure to this virile, more backward 1997. The sweet nose of peppery
fruit and black cherries intermixed with toast and cassis is alluring. The wine

has a soft middle, but the tannic power is noticeable. This is not exactly a *vin de garde*, but for the vintage it will be uncommonly long-lived. Moreover, it will not be a 1997 to drink immediately after bottling. Anticipated maturity: 2002–2016. Last tasted, 3/98.

1996—An enormous, masculine, backward wine, Léoville-Barton's 1996 exhibits an
• opaque black/purple color, and sweet, earthy, prune, and black currant
91– aromas intertwined with scents of licorice and Asian spices. Enormous and
94+ full bodied, with a sweet mid-palate and mouth-searing tannin in the finish, this exceptionally dense, powerful, layered wine will require significant patience. Its explosive power and richness may push this wine's ultimate rating into the mid-nineties. Anticipated maturity: 2007–2040. Last tasted, 3/98.

1995—Somewhat closed and reticent after bottling, but still impressive, this 1995
• possesses a dark ruby/purple color, as well as an oaky nose with classic
91 scents of cassis, vanillin, cedar, and spice. Dense and medium to full bodied, with softer tannin and more accessibility than the 1996, but not quite the packed and stacked effect on the palate, the 1995 is an outstanding textbook St.-Julien that will handsomely repay extended cellaring. Anticipated maturity: 2004–2025. Last tasted, 11/97.

1994—An impressive, serious, classic Bordeaux for collectors who are willing to
• forget about it for at least a decade, this well-endowed offering is a 30-year
90+ wine. The dense, murky, purple color, closed aromatics, massive flavor richness, and high tannin recall the old, noncompromised, beefy, blockbuster Médocs produced 30 years ago. However, this wine possesses sweeter tannin and was made under far more sanitary conditions. It is a classic, but patience is definitely required. Anticipated maturity: 2007–2030. Last tasted, 1/97.

1993—One of the biggest, richest, most impressive wines of the vintage, Léoville-
• Barton's 1993 reveals a saturated black/purple color, dense, foresty, rich,
88+ black currant, and chocolatey aromas and flavors, excellent ripeness and depth, good glycerin, and hard tannin in the finish. This is a backward, exceptionally well-endowed 1993 that needs another 5–7 years of cellaring. It should keep for 20 years. Last tasted, 1/97.

1992—This wine, which was impressive from cask, continues to prove that it is one
• of the finest wines of the vintage. It exhibits a dark ruby color, a bouquet that
87 offers up scents of spice, cedar, black cherry, and currants, rich, medium-bodied flavors with excellent ripeness, a sense of elegance, and a succulent, juicy personality. The wine reveals no signs of dilution, and the tannin is sweet rather than hard and astringent. Drink this noteworthy 1992 over the next 10–12 years. Last tasted, 11/94.

1991—If you are looking for a terrific value from a so-called off year, check out
• Léoville-Barton's 1991! It possesses a deep ruby color, a big, cedary, black
87 currant-and-herb-scented nose, and ripe, rich, medium-bodied flavors that offer impressive concentration, moderate tannin, and admirable length. This impressive Léoville-Barton is significantly better than vintages such as 1981 and 1979. It should drink well for 10–15 years. Last tasted, 1/94.

1990— The 1990 is dense, tannic, muscular, and virile. It offers an opaque purple
   •   color, but not much charm or openness. The nose reluctantly offers up aromas
  92+   of earth, spicy fruit, and wood. The wine is full bodied, powerful, and loaded
         with extract and glycerin. However, it is also revealing formidable quantities
         of tannin, as well as a closed, backward style. This is somewhat perplexing
         in view of previous tastings of this wine. I still believe the 1990 to be an
         exceptional Léoville-Barton, certainly the best wine made after the 1982
         and marginally superior to both the delicious 1985 and tannic 1986. How-
         ever, it needs another 7–10 years of cellaring. In its youth, it is one of
         the least approachable 1990s. Anticipated maturity: 2004–2025. Last tasted,
         11/96.

1989— The 1989 provides charming drinking with its soft, voluptuous texture, big,
   •   spicy, cedary nose, sweet, expansive fruit, medium body, and excellent rich-
  90   ness and purity. The wine reveals no amber at the edge, but it tastes surpris-
         ingly evolved and already delicious. I would not hesitate to drink it over the
         next 12–15+ years. Last tasted, 11/96.

1988— The 1988 Léoville-Barton is a classic example of the vintage. The tannins are
   •   hard, but the wine exhibits plenty of depth and juicy cassis fruit, firm struc-
  88   ture, and very good length. This is an excellent wine, with plenty of rich,
         deep, curranty fruit to balance out the tannins. Anticipated maturity: Now–
         2012. Last tasted, 1/93.

1987— The 1987 is maturing nicely, exhibiting a moderately sweet, curranty, oaky
   •   nose, round, gentle flavors, decent acidity, and a surprisingly long finish. It is
  85   an unqualified success for the vintage! Anticipated maturity: Now. Last tasted,
         11/90.

1986— In contrast with the elegant, graceful, finesse-filled 1985 (which may turn out
   •   to resemble the classic 1953 in 15 years), the 1986 is a great wine, but so, so
  92   backward and tannic. This huge, dense, medium- to full-bodied wine exhibits
         tremendously rich, classic, weedy, black currant fruitiness with airing and
         boasts the judicious use of new oak barrels. The tannins are elevated, but
         then this is a seriously concentrated, old-style, intense wine for long-term
         cellaring. The more I taste the 1986 Léoville-Barton, the more impressed I
         become with the wine's extraordinary power, density, and richness. However,
         it is not a wine for readers seeking immediate gratification. Although spectac-
         ular, it requires another 5–6 years of cellaring. It will easily last for half a
         century. Anticipated maturity: 2005–2030. Last tasted, 3/97.

1985— Anthony Barton's 1985 may turn out to be a remake of the château's splendid
   •   1953. Deep ruby/garnet with a complex, complete, and intense bouquet of
  92   sweet, superripe, curranty fruit, minerals, cedar, spice, and baked herbs, this
         medium-bodied wine has exceptional balance, fine length, gobs of fruit, and
         soft tannin in the velvety finish. This classic claret is a joy to drink. Antici-
         pated maturity: Now–2007. Last tasted, 9/97.

1984— Deeper on the palate than Langoa-Barton, the 1984 Léoville-Barton has a
   •   spicy, richly fruity nose, good body, length, and tannins, and plenty of new
  84   toasty oak smells. Anticipated maturity: Now. Last tasted, 3/88.

1983—Initially extremely tannic and hard, with a very deep color, plenty of alcohol,
•   and a rich, ripe, weighty fruitiness, this wine has matured much more quickly
86   than I would have expected. It is a good but not great wine that needs to be
     carefully monitored. Anticipated maturity: Now–2002. Last tasted, 3/89.

1982—One of the most traditionally styled wines of the vintage, the 1982 Léoville-
•   Barton is a throwback to the old, rough-and-tumble style of Bordeaux, with
93+   high tannin, huge extract, and an impenetrable personality. The wine has not
     budged in evolution since bottling. The color remains a murky, opaque pur-
     ple/garnet. The nose offers up aromas of cedar, licorice, spices, black truffles,
     and sweet, ripe fruit. Very unformed and unevolved, this full-bodied, tannic,
     intensely concentrated wine is thick and rich, but oh, so backward. In many
     respects this is a classic St.-Julien meant to be held for another 10–20 years
     before consumption. It should prove to be one of the great Léoville-Bartons,
     but it has more in common with a 1975 in terms of its glacial pace of
     development than with most 1982s. Anticipated maturity: 2005–2030. Last
     tasted, 9/97.

1981—This medium-bodied wine has an attractive spicy, black currant fruitiness,
•   melted tannin, and a decent finish. The 1981 is a good wine, but it lacks
84   excitement and is clearly outdistanced by several other St.-Juliens in this
     vintage. Anticipated maturity: Now. Last tasted, 2/89.

1980—A lovely wine and fine success for the vintage, the 1980 Léoville-Barton has
•   a surprisingly good color, a spicy, caramel-scented, deep bouquet, soft, ripe
83   fruity flavors, moderate tannins, and a good finish. This wine should be drunk
     up. Anticipated maturity: Now–may be in decline. Last tasted, 10/83.

1979—Surprisingly light and precociously fruity, with little grip or backbone, this
•   medium-bodied, moderately fruity wine has charm and a savory, easygoing
75   character but tastes a bit watery. It requires drinking. Anticipated maturity:
     Now. Last tasted, 1/88.

1978—This is a very attractive Léoville-Barton that seems to be developing at a
•   more accelerated pace than I had initially expected. A lovely, rather full, big
86   bouquet of smoky, berryish, ripe fruit is first class. On the palate, the wine
     shows a good cedary, spicy, deep fruity constitution, moderate tannins, and a
     long finish. Just about ready. Anticipated maturity: Now. Last tasted, 1/88.

1977—Although a trifle weedy and herbaceous to smell, the 1977 Léoville-Barton is
•   well above average in quality for the vintage, with soft, flavorful, fully mature
78   flavors. Anticipated maturity: Now–may be in decline. Last tasted, 10/82.

1976—A very successful wine, Léoville-Barton obtained much more fruit and stuffing
•   in its 1976 than did Langoa. Rich, fully mature, with a plummy fruitiness and
85   fat, lazy finish, this wine has a bouquet that seems to jump from the glass.
     Sweet, ripe, velvety fruit caresses the palate. It is a little low in acidity but
     delicious for drinking now. Anticipated maturity: Now. Last tasted, 7/87.

1975—For a 1975 Médoc, this wine has received surprisingly consistent notes.
•   While it has always revealed some of the severity and austerity of the vintage,
90   it has consistently possessed more depth, sweetness of fruit, and a more
     expansive texture. There is a firm, tannic framework, but the wine is admira-

bly concentrated, with classic scents of herb, cassis, cedar, tobacco, and spice, full body, an impressive palate, a youthful personality, and a long finish. There are no signs of color or fruit degradation. With 1–2 hours of decanting, this wine can be drunk now; it promises to age for another 15+ years. Last tasted, 12/95.

1971—Now fading badly, and best drunk up immediately, the 1971 Léoville-Barton
• has a sweet, caramel, candylike nose, soft, shallow flavors that show no
70 tannins, and a watery, weak finish. It will only become more astringent. Anticipated maturity: Now—may be in decline. Last tasted, 3/85.

1970—It seems that Barton excels in dry, hot years such as 1970. Deep ruby with an
• amber edge, the wine is rich and full on the palate, with excellent concentra-
87 tion, a full-intensity bouquet of black currants and cedar wood, and moderate tannins. A ripe wine that is now ready to drink, this muscular, larger-scaled Léoville should continue to age well. Anticipated maturity: Now—2000. Last tasted, 6/88.

1966—The 1966 is a good, reliable wine that, in view of the vintage, could perhaps
• have been better. A moderately intense, spicy, fruity bouquet that exhibits
84 plenty of oak is seductive enough. However, the palate impression is that austerity dominates the fruit. Fully mature, but capable of holding, this is a good but hardly top-rank 1966. Anticipated maturity: Now. Last tasted, 2/87.

1964—Darker in color, richer in flavor, and longer on the palate than the 1966, this
• chunky, fleshy wine shows impressive fruit, soft yet noticeable tannins, and a
86 ripe, fruity bouquet. Anticipated maturity: Now. Last tasted, 9/87.

1961—Several tastings in the early eighties must have been from less than per-
• fect bottles because I was never excited by this wine. Tastings in the late
92 eighties and nineties revealed a terrific, fully mature wine, splendidly per-fumed with cedar, herbs, and sweet black fruits, rich, full bodied, and long. Based on the best bottles, this wine is fully mature but is capable of lasting for another decade. Anticipated maturity: Now—2000. Last tasted, 9/97.

ANCIENT VINTAGES

Léoville-Barton had a strong decade from the late forties through the fifties. The powerhouse 1959 (94 points; last tasted 10/94) is fully mature but exhibits no signs of fading. It is large scaled and muscular, with a huge, cedary, earthy, black fruit–scented nose, gobs of glycerin and alcohol, and a heady, spicy finish with some noticeable tannin. Will the 1982 be its contem-porary counterpart? The 1953 (95 points; last tasted 10/94) is a seductive, voluptuously textured, gloriously fragrant, and fruity claret that has admirably stood the test of time. The wine is undoubtedly fragile from a regular bottling (as most 1953s tend to be), so purchasers should consider larger-format bottles, as I am sure it would be superb.

The 1949, 1948, and 1945 Léoville-Bartons are all great efforts. The 1949

(95 points; last tasted 10/94) is made in the mold of the 1953, although it is a more forceful, bare-boned wine with greater muscle, tannin, and body. The 1948 (96 points; last tasted 10/94) is an extraordinary wine from an under-rated vintage. It is still extremely powerful and young, offering a classic cedary, tobacco, curranty, full-bodied richness that suggests extremely low yields and ripe fruit. The blockbuster 1945 (98 points; last tasted 10/94) is one of the great wines of the vintage. It possesses extraordinarily thick, massive fruit and body that stand up to the formidable tannin level. All these wines will last for another 20 years.

LÉOVILLE-LAS CASES   OUTSTANDING

Classification: Second-growth 1855
Location of vineyards: St.-Julien
Owner: Jean-Hubert Delon and his sister, Geneviève d'Alton
Administrators: Michel and Jean-Hubert Delon
Address: 33250 St.-Julien-Beychevelle
Mailing address: Same as above
Telephone: 33 5 56 73 25 26; telefax: 33 5 56 59 18 33
Visits: By appointment only, from Monday to Thursday, between 9 A.M. and 11 A.M., and 2 P.M. and 4:30 P.M.; on Fridays, between 9 A.M. and 11 A.M. only; no visits during weekends and on public holidays

VINEYARDS (red)
Surface area: 240 acres
Average age of vines: 30 years
Blend: 65% Cabernet Sauvignon, 19% Merlot, 13% Cabernet Franc, 3% Petit Verdot
Density of plantation: 8,000 vines per hectare
Average yields (over the last 5 years): Confidential
Total average annual production: Confidential

GRAND VIN (red)
Brand name: Grand Vin de Léoville du Marquis de Las Cases
Appellation: St.-Julien
Mean annual production: Confidential
Upbringing: Fermentations last 12–20 days depending upon the vintage, with temperatures going up from 24 to 28 degrees centigrade, in different types of vats (wooden, cement, and stainless steel). The wines are transferred to oak barrels, 50%–80% of which are new (this percentage varies with the vintage), for 18–20 months. They are fined with egg whites prior to bottling, but there is no rule as to whether they are filtered or not.

> **SECOND WINE**
> Brand name: Clos du Marquis
> Average annual production: Confidential
>
> NOTE: A third wine is also produced.
>
> Evaluation of present classification: Should be upgraded to a first-growth
> Plateau of maturity: 8–30 years following the vintage

Léoville-Las Cases is unquestionably one of the great names and wines of Bordeaux. Situated next to Latour, Léoville-Las Cases's main vineyard of over 100 acres is the picturesque, enclosed vineyard depicted on the wine's label. The estate is one of Bordeaux's largest, and while the meticulous and passionate commitment to quality may be equaled by several others, it is surpassed by no one. The man responsible is Michel Delon, who succeeded his father, Paul. Over recent years his exuberant son, Jean-Hubert, has provided his father with valuable assistance. A proud man who is as admired as he is scorned, Michel Delon is the perfectionist architect behind the ascendancy of Léoville-Las Cases. His critics, and there are many, claim he plays games when selling his wines, doling out tiny quantities in great vintages, the critics claim, to artificially drive up the price. Yet no one can argue about the splendid quality of his wines, the product of an almost maniacal obsession to be the finest, not just in St.-Julien, but in the entire Médoc! Who else would declassify over 50% of their crop in an abundant vintage such as 1986 or an astonishing 67% in 1990? Who else would introduce not only a second wine, but a third wine (Bignarnon) as well? Who else would lavishly install marble floors in the air-conditioned *chais?* Like him or not, Michel Delon, ably assisted by Michel Rolland (not the Libourne oenologist) and Jacques Depoizier, is making one of the greatest wines in the Médoc.

The wines of Léoville-Las Cases have been excellent in the post–World War II era, yet the period from 1975 onward has witnessed the production of a string of successes that have come close to perfection in vintages such as 1975, 1978, 1982, 1985, 1986, 1990, 1994, 1995, and 1996. In fact, these wines are as profound as most of the Médoc's first-growths in those vintages.

In comparison with Ducru-Beaucaillou, its chief rival in St.-Julien, the wines of Léoville-Las Cases tend to be a shade darker in color, more tannic, larger scaled, more concentrated, and of course built for extended cellaring. They are traditional wines, designed for connoisseurs who must have the patience to wait the 10–15 years necessary for them to mature properly. Should a reclassification of Bordeaux's 1855 classification take place, Léoville-Las Cases, like Ducru-Beaucaillou and possibly Léoville-Barton, would merit and receive serious support for first-growth status.

VINTAGES

1997 — This great estate continues to turn out wines of first-growth quality and,

• increasingly, at first-growth price levels. The harvest took place between

91– September 18 and October 4, with only 40% of the production going into the

93 grand vin. The final blend consisted of 74% Cabernet Sauvignon, 13.5% Cabernet Franc, 9% Merlot, and 3.5% Petit Verdot. It is one of the more concentrated and complete, as well as best defined 1997s I tasted. It exhibits an opaque purple color, and the classic Las Cases aromatic profile (sweet black fruits, cherries, kirsch, vanillin, lead pencil, and minerals). Medium to full bodied, with silky tannin, low acidity, and layers of concentration, the wine reveals considerable intensity in both the mid-palate and finish. In contrast to the nearly perfect, prodigiously rich, massive yet phenomenally well balanced 1996, the 1997 has less weight and flavor dimension. Nevertheless, it is a compelling St.-Julien that should drink well in 2000–2020. This should turn out to be one of the most concentrated and longest-lived wines of the vintage. Last tasted, 3/98.

1996 — My tasting notes for this wine begin with the following words: "Wow, wow,

• wow!" I had been looking forward to retasting this 1996 since I had it in

98– spring 1997, and I was not disappointed by its evolution. The wine possesses

100 an opaque purple color, and an attention-getting, staggering sweet nose that offers the essence of black currant fruit, kirsch, and minerals as well as the essence of Léoville-Las Cases's personality. It is fabulously concentrated, with the *sur-maturité* (over-ripeness) of Cabernet Sauvignon, one of the wine's most undeniable hallmarks. When measured, the tannin level is extremely high, but you would never know that when tasting this wine because of the massive amount of extract, purity, and virtually perfect equilibrium. Despite its rare combination of unbridled power and complexity, this wine has *beaucoup de finesse*, as well as a finish that lasts close to 45 seconds. A candidate for a perfect rating, it is a modern day legend in the making. Will it surpass the 1986 and 1982? Time will tell. Only 40% of the total harvest was used in the 1996, with the final blend containing a slightly higher percentage of Cabernet Sauvignon than usual. Anticipated maturity: 2008–2030. Last tasted, 3/98.

1995 — If it were not for the prodigious 1996, everyone would be concentrating on

• getting their hands on a few bottles of the fabulous 1995 Léoville-Las Cases,

95 which is one of the vintage's great success stories. The wine boasts an opaque ruby/purple color, and exceptionally pure, beautifully knit aromas of black fruits, minerals, vanillin, and spice. On the attack, it is staggeringly rich, yet displays more noticeable tannin than its younger sibling. Exceptionally ripe cherry and cassis fruit, the judicious use of toasty new oak, and a thrilling mineral character intertwined with the high quality of fruit routinely obtained by Las Cases, make this a compelling effort. There is probably nearly as much tannin as in the 1996, but it is not as perfectly sweet as in the 1996. The finish is incredibly long in this classic. Only 35% of the harvest was of sufficient quality for the 1995 Léoville-Las Cases. Anticipated maturity: 2005–2025. Last tasted, 11/97.

1994—One of the more massive Médocs of the vintage, this opaque purple–colored
  •   wine exhibits fabulous richness and volume in the mouth. Layers of pure
  93   black cherry and cassis fruit are intermixed with stony, mineral-like scents
        as well as high-quality toasty oak. Medium to full bodied, with a sweet, rich
        entry, this wine possesses plenty of tannin yet fabulous extract and length.
        Léoville-Las Cases is one of the half dozen great wines of the Médoc in 1994.
        Anticipated maturity: 2002–2025. Last tasted, 1/97.

1993—This saturated purple–colored wine possesses remarkable sweetness, power-
  •   ful, chocolatey-and-cassis-scented aromas, and dense, medium- to full-
  90   bodied flavors with a superb inner core of fruit. Purity, balance, and
        superconcentration and intensity are hallmarks of this remarkable wine.
        Readers who find it difficult to believe that the 1993 vintage could turn out
        wines such as this need only to pull the cork on a bottle of the 1993 Léoville-
        Las Cases. Anticipated maturity: Now–2012. Last tasted, 1/97.

1992—The 1992 Léoville-Las Cases is one of the stars of what is overall a diluted
  •   vintage. Medium bodied, with attractive aromatics (red and black fruits,
  89–   minerals, and spicy oak), it is a forward, precocious Las Cases possess-
  90   ing grip and tannin. It can be drunk or cellared for 15+ years. Last tasted,
        3/95.

1991—A terrific success in this difficult vintage, Las Cases's forward 1991 is close
  •   to full maturity, revealing flattering scents of tobacco, cassis, and toasty
  89   oak. This medium-bodied wine possesses such excellent concentration and
        ripeness, it is hard to believe it could have come from a vintage such as 1991.
        Drink it now and over the next 12–15 years. Last tasted, 5/95.

1990—The 1990 continues to put on weight and richness, and it now clearly appears
  •   to be the superior vintage for Léoville-Las Cases. The 1990 reveals a dense,
  96   dark purple color, followed by a sweet, pure nose of black fruits, minerals,
        lead pencil, and vanillin. Broad, expansive flavors come across as rich, pure,
        and concentrated, but never heavy or coarse. Beautifully integrated tannin
        and acidity are barely noticeable in this classic, full-bodied, velvety-textured,
        youthful yet exceptional St.-Julien. The 1990 is more fun to taste than the
        1989, but readers should not interpret that comment to suggest it is ready to
        drink. This wine needs another 5–6 years of cellaring, after which it should
        last for 20–25 years. Last tasted, 11/96.

1989—The 1989 tasted California-like in its ripe, sweet, black cherry fruit, nicely
  •   integrated, toasty new oak, and clean, pure winemaking style. A tighter, more
  91   compact finish is the result of elevated tannin, but this is an outstanding,
        rich, medium-weight Las Cases that tastes less well endowed than I originally
        predicted. It is built more along the lines of the classy, elegant 1985 than the
        blockbuster 1982 and 1986. The wine is still youthful, with no amber at the
        edge of its healthy deep ruby/purple color. It will improve for another 8–12
        years and then plateau, offering very fine drinking over the subsequent 2
        decades. I overrated this wine from cask. As appealing as I still find it, it
        lacks the concentration and intensity I originally thought it possessed. Last
        tasted, 11/96.

1988—Remarkably, the 1988 Léoville-Las Cases has always been one of the most
•   successful wines of the vintage. With a rich, spicy nose of fruitcake, cedar,
92   and cassis, this medium-bodied, moderately tannic Las Cases offers attractive
sweetness and suppleness on the palate, a well-delineated and focused personality, and a moderately tannic finish. The wine is just beginning to reveal
some aromatic development. It will benefit from another 2–5 years of cellaring and will keep for 20+ years. Last tasted, 3/95.

1987—The 1987 is deep ruby colored, with a moderately intense bouquet of cassis
•   and spicy new oak. With no trace of underripeness, or any indication of
87   dilution, this is a rich, medium- to full-bodied wine that is probably better
than the château's 1981 and every bit as good as their excellent 1976. One of
the vintage's best! Anticipated maturity: Now–2000. Last tasted, 4/91.

1986—The 1986 Léoville-Las Cases, which Delon continues to believe is his finest
•   vintage in the eighties (even eclipsing the 1982), still exhibits a black/purple
98+   color with no signs of age. The nose offers up aromas of exceptionally ripe
cassis fruit intertwined with scents of vanillin, minerals, and spices. The wine
is full bodied, exceptionally well delineated, and phenomenally concentrated.
Still unevolved and youthful, this is one of the most profound Léoville-Las
Cases, but for my palate, it remains a notch behind both the 1982 and 1996.
Anticipated maturity: 2003–2030. Last tasted, 3/97.

1985—This is one of my favorite vintages of Las Cases for present-day consumption.
•   The wine reveals a youthful deep ruby/purple color, followed by a classic Las
93   Cases bouquet of *pain grillé,* lead pencil, minerals, and ripe black currants.
Medium to full bodied, with outstanding concentration and soft tannin, this is
a classic, fleshy 1985 that reveals none of the potential dilution noticeable in
many wines from this vintage. At one time I thought this might turn out to be a
modern-day clone of the 1953, but it possesses a lot more flesh and intensity.
Anticipated maturity: Now–2015. Last tasted, 3/97.

1984—This wine is very similar to the 1981 produced at Las Cases. Spicy, with the
•   vanillin touch of toasty oak, very good fruit, and medium to full body, this is
84   a very successful wine for the year. Anticipated maturity: Now. Last tasted,
1/90.

1983—The fully mature 1983 Léoville-Las Cases possessed a deep ruby color with
•   no signs of lightening. An open-knit, smoky, cassis-and-cedary-scented nose
91   was followed by a supple, rich, medium- to full-bodied wine with excellent
definition, outstanding ripeness and concentration, and a spicy, soft, velvety-
textured finish. Drink this wine over the next 12–15+ years. Last tasted,
3/95.

1982—The 1982 Léoville-Las Cases remains one of the awesome examples of this
•   great vintage. Rich, full bodied, and backward, this thick-looking, opaque
100   ruby/purple–colored wine is just beginning to display aromatic development.
Jammy aromas of cassis intertwined with scents of vanilla, lead pencil, cedar,
melted caramel, and toast are followed by a massively endowed, full-bodied
wine that will benefit from another 7–10 years of cellaring. This hugely
impressive, low-acid Las Cases is crammed with ripe fruit. It is the most

hedonistic and concentrated Léoville-Las Cases I have ever tasted, just eclipsing the otherworldly 1986. It is approachable now, but my instincts suggest more patience. Drink it between 2000 and 2030. It is a monumental wine! Last tasted, 9/97.

1981 — The 1981 Léoville-Las Cases appears close to full maturity, with an excellent
  •   deep ruby color, a spicy bouquet of cedar, tobacco, and currants, and good
  89   depth and ripeness. A classic, elegantly wrought wine, this is one vintage
         where the final blend was more complex but no better than the Cabernet
         Sauvignon cuvée. Last tasted, 3/95.

1980 — A solid, respectable effort for the year, but like many wines from this vintage,
  •   there is just not enough fruit to cover the bones. Anticipated maturity: Now–
  75   may be in decline. Last tasted, 10/84.

1979 — The 1979 Léoville-Las Cases is one of the leaner examples of this wine, with
  •   some hard tannin remaining in the finish. Nevertheless, it reveals good fruit,
  86   a stylish, curranty, mineral, and vanillin nose, medium body, some compact-
         ness, and a crisp, short finish. It is unlikely to improve, so drink it over the
         next 5–8 years. Last tasted, 3/95.

1978 — The 1978 Las Cases has taken on a garnet hue with some dark ruby tints.
  •   The nose is more complex and penetrating than the flavors. The wine offers
  90   classic, mineral, lead pencil, smoky, earthy scents, with plenty of ripe fruit
         and none of the vegetal herbaceousness that many 1978s have begun to
         exhibit. The attack offers good ripeness, medium to full body, higher acidity
         than many more recent vintages, and considerable tannin in the hard finish.
         Although this wine possesses outstanding complexity, the high tannin level
         may never fully melt away. While it will last another 15–20 years, the 1978
         is at its apogee and will slowly dry out over the next 2 decades. Last tasted,
         5/95.

1976 — One of the more successful offerings of the vintage, this wine was drinkable
  •   when released in 1979. It still possesses an attractive ruby/garnet color and
  86?   a spicy, roasted nose of jammy fruit, minerals, and spice. The flavors have
         become slightly disjointed, with the alcohol, acidity, and tannin beginning to
         peek through the wine's fruit. Although the 1976 is still healthy, it will not
         improve and should be consumed. The wine may merit a higher score out of
         larger-format bottles, such as a magnum. Last tasted, 5/95.

1975 — This is one of the great successes of the vintage. However, those with modern-
  •   day tastes for soft, easygoing, supple wines may not enjoy the 1975 Léoville-
  92+   Las Cases. Why? It is a tannic, backward, old-style wine cut from the mold
         of such vintages as 1948 and 1928. The color is a dark ruby/garnet, with a
         hint of amber at the edge. The nose offers up distinctive mineral, lead pencil,
         sweet, black currant scents with flinty overtones. Full bodied, thick, and
         concentrated, as well as atypically muscular and powerful, this should prove
         to be one of the longest-lived wines of the vintage. There are sensational
         levels of richness and intensity. While the vintage's tough tannin level ensures
         another 20–35 years of longevity, the wine may dry out by that time. I thought
         this wine would be at its peak by the mid-nineties, but it still needs another

5–8 years of cellaring. It is very impressive, albeit backward and hard. Last tasted, 12/95.

1974— The color is sound and still youthful looking, but the problem this wine has
• is the lack of fruit, which results in a short finish and an empty taste on the
70 palate. Time has helped soften the wine's astringency, but the fruit continues to fade. Anticipated maturity: Now–may be in decline. Last tasted, 7/85.

1973— Still drinkable, but clearly losing its freshness and lively, fruity character, the
• 1973 Las Cases is light, supple, and pleasant, but quite one-dimensional and
70 now beginning to fade. Drink up! Anticipated maturity: Now–probably in serious decline. Last tasted, 5/80.

1971— The 1971 is an unbalanced Léoville-Las Cases, exhibiting too much tannin,
• a loosely knit structure, and fruity flavors that seem to dissipate rapidly in
73 the glass. An austere, unyielding wine in which the tannin clearly has the edge over the fruit. Nevertheless, there is interest in the bouquet, and the color remains sound. Anticipated maturity: Now. Last tasted, 10/90.

1970— I have never had much fondness for this wine, and I continue to find it
• extremely austere, compact, and undernourished. The wine will undoubtedly
79 keep for another 15–20 years, but there is not much ripeness or intensity. It bears no resemblance to today's efforts from Léoville-Las Cases. The 1970 will continue to dry out and provide charmless drinking. Last tasted, 6/96.

1967— I rarely see this wine, but the only bottle from my cellar revealed a weak, ruby/
• garnet color and an earthy, rustic nose of spice, wet stones, and herbal, currant
74 fruit. This medium-bodied, rustic wine is in decline. Last tasted, 5/95.

1966— This may be the most successful wine produced by this estate during the
• decade of the sixties, although some bottles of the 1962 come close to offering
89 as much pleasure as the 1966. The wine may have turned the corner and begun its decline. I have never tasted it out of larger-format bottles, but I suspect magnums of this wine might merit an outstanding evaluation. The wine has always been a classic Bordeaux, with more fruit and body than many 1966s. There is a degree of austerity, but the dominant characteristics include a complex nose of tobacco, cedar, and red currants, medium body, excellent concentration and ripeness, and a spicy, long, moderately tannic finish. Drink it up, as it is unlikely to improve. Last tasted, 5/95.

1964— I never tasted this wine in the early seventies when it was reputedly at its
• best. Recent examples have been dry, astringent, acidic, and revealing a
71 glaring deficiency in fruit. Anticipated maturity: Now–probably in serious decline. Last tasted, 5/86.

1962— A strong performance for this wine, the 1962 Las Cases exhibits a light to
• medium ruby/garnet color and a seductive, intense fragrance that is often a
88 characteristic of the finest 1962s. The wine is soft, medium to full bodied, with excellent ripeness, gorgeous balance, and no hard edges. Don't push your luck with this vintage; drink it up. Last tasted, 5/95.

1961— I tasted this wine with Michel Delon after I told him I had never had a great
• bottle of the 1961. After tasting it again, my original assessment remains
85 unchanged. The wine reveals an austerity and under-ripeness that is reminis-

cent of the 1970. This fully mature Las Cases displays a garnet color with considerable amber at the edge and a spicy, earthy, tobacco-and-herb-scented nose. Some sweetness in the attack fades quickly to reveal a medium-bodied, tannic, compact wine that is good but uninspiring. It will keep for another 10 years, but don't expect any miracles to develop. Last tasted, 3/95.

ANCIENT VINTAGES

Slightly sweeter, riper, and richer when juxtaposed with the 1961, the ruby/garnet–colored 1959 (rated 86 in 3/95) exhibits a roasted character in the nose, as well as more fruit and a spicy, fleshy finish. Medium bodied, with supple, herb-tinged, curranty flavors, this low-acid wine will not improve. Owners of the 1959 should make plans for its consumption.

VINTAGES (CLOS DU MARQUIS)

1996— The quality level of the second wine of Léoville-Las Cases is unquestionably
  •   better than some of Bordeaux's famed 1855 classification's second- and third-
(90– growths. The 1996 Clos du Marquis boasts a thick black/purple color as well
 91) as a huge, soaring set of aromatics consisting of cherry liqueur and black
      currants. The wine is thick, rich, and tannic, but marvelously well balanced
      and long in the mouth. This wine will need 4–6 years of cellaring and keep
      for 2 decades. Readers may remember that I was equally amazed by the 1995
      Clos du Marquis. Michel Delon has done it again! Last tasted, 3/97.

1995— Dense purple colored with considerable intensity, this rich, high-quality,
  •   gorgeously extracted wine could easily pass for a top classified growth. A
 90   serious, well-endowed effort, the medium-bodied 1995 Clos du Marquis does
      indeed resemble the grand vin, Léoville-Las Cases. Anticipated maturity:
      2000–2012. Last tasted, 1/97.

1994— This deep ruby/purple–colored wine reveals the sweet, pure cassis fruit of
  •   Léoville-Las Cases, good fatness, medium body, low acidity, and no astrin-
 88   gency or harshness in the lush finish. It should drink well for 10–12 years.
      Last tasted, 1/97.

1993— A cedary, spicy, tobacco-and-black currant–scented nose offers plenty of
  •   attraction in this dark ruby–colored wine. Medium bodied, with excellent
 87   richness and a sweet, round palate impression, this is a delicious St.-Julien
      for drinking over the next 7–8 years. Last tasted, 1/97.

1992— An impressive 1992, it exhibits excellent ripeness, medium body, and plenty
  •   of richness in a soft, forward style. The finish boasts impressive depth and
86+ persistence, with no harshness. This is a noteworthy effort that should drink
      well for 7–10 years. It looks like a sure bet to be the best *deuxième* wine of
      the vintage. Last tasted, 11/94.

1991— Restaurants looking for an inexpensive, classy 1991 St.-Julien should check
  •   out Clos du Marquis. It displays fine ripeness, soft, round, complex fruit
 85   flavors, medium body, and a surprisingly long, soft finish. Drink it over the
      next 7–8 years. Last tasted, 1/94.

1990—The 1990 is equal to the 1989. The saturated color, intense black cherry,
•   oaky nose, and dense, rich, medium- to full-bodied flavors reveal fine concen-
88   tration and balance. Drink it over the next 5–12 years. Last tasted, 1/93.

1989—The 1989's complex bouquet of toasty new oak and cassis is followed by a
•   surprisingly rich, deep, well-built wine that resembles the great Léoville-Las
88   Cases. This beauty will support considerable cellaring. If you can neither
afford Léoville-Las Cases nor wait for it to lose all its tannins, consider this
offering from Clos du Marquis. Anticipated maturity: Now–2005. Last tasted,
1/93.

1988—The second wine of Léoville-Las Cases, the 1988 Clos du Marquis has good
•   fruit, a spicy, oaky character, medium body, and a fine core of black cherry
85   fruit. Firm and capable of supporting 8–10 years of cellaring, it is a good
effort, but the 1989 and 1990 are superior. Last tasted, 1/93.

1982—Although I enjoyed this wine more 3 or 4 years ago, it remains a vibrant,
•   exuberant, spicy, cedary, curranty claret with medium body, good depth, and
87   real class. The second wine of Léoville-Las Cases, it often performs at a
classified growth level. Owners should plan to drink it by the turn of the
century. Last tasted, 9/95.

LÉOVILLE-POYFERRÉ   EXCELLENT

Classification: Second-growth
Location of vineyards: St.-Julien
Owner: G.F.A. des Domaines de St.-Julien—Cuvelier family
Address: 33250 St.-Julien-Beychevelle
Mailing address: Same as above
Telephone: 33 5 56 59 08 30; telefax: 33 5 56 59 60 09
Visits: From Monday to Friday, between 8 A.M. and noon, and 2 P.M.
and 5 P.M.
Contact: M.-F. Dourthe for appointments

VINEYARDS (red)
Surface area: 197.6 acres
Average age of vines: 25 years
Blend: 52% Cabernet Sauvignon, 28% Merlot, 12% Cabernet Franc, 8%
Petit Verdot
Density of plantation: 8,500 vines per hectare
Average yields (over the last 5 years): 49 hectoliters per hectare
Total average annual production: 420,000 bottles

GRAND VIN (red)
Brand name: Léoville-Poyferré
Appellation: St.-Julien
Mean annual production: 250,000 bottles

Upbringing: Grapes are picked by hand. Fermentations last 7 days and macerations between 15 and 21 days. Thirty percent of the grand vin undergoes malolactics in new oak barrels. Wines are aged in oak barrels after malolactics for 18 months. Egg white fining is done, but there is no filtration prior to bottling.

SECOND WINE
Brand name: Château Moulin-Riche
Average annual production: 170,000 bottles

Evaluation of present classification: Should be maintained
Plateau of maturity: 8–20 years following the vintage

Talk to just about any knowledgeable Bordelais about the potential of the vineyard of Léoville-Poyferré, and they will unanimously agree that Poyferré has the soil and capacity to produce one of the Médoc's most profound red wines. In fact, some will argue that Léoville-Poyferré has better soil than any of the other second-growth St.-Juliens. But the story of Léoville-Poyferré since 1961, while largely one of disappointments, has the makings of a happy ending. Modernizations to the cellars, the introduction of a second wine, the elevated use of new oak, the increasingly watchful eyes of Didier Cuvelier, and the genius of Libourne oenologist Michel Rolland have finally pushed Léoville-Poyferré into the elite of St.-Julien. The two finest vintages of the eighties remain the prodigious 1982 and the gloriously fruity 1983. Both years exhibit the depth and richness that this property is capable of attaining. In the nineties, a top 1990 followed by strong efforts in both 1995 and 1996 suggest this estate has begun to finally exploit its considerable potential.

VINTAGES

1997—Proprietor Didier Cuvelier told me that the harvest at Léoville-Poyferré began
• and finished with the Petit Verdot grape. The harvest commenced on Septem-
89– ber 15 and lasted nearly three weeks concluding on October 5. Tasted on four
91 separate occasions, the 1997 is a beautifully made wine that, while not quite
as sensationally rich and textured as the 1996, is undoubtedly one of the
vintage's most successful wines. Poyferré, which used to be difficult to assess
at such a young age, began doing malolactic fermentation in barriques several
years ago. The results have been more advanced wines with better integrated
wood and thus can more readily be judged at a young age. The 1997 is a
sexy, open-knit, flamboyant wine with a dark ruby/purple color, and delicious
crème brûlée, coffee, black currant, and smoky notes that jump from the
wine's evolved aromatics. Expansive and fleshy, with good fat on the mid-
palate, this flashy styled Léoville-Poyferré should drink exceptionally well
young, yet keep for 15 or more years. Last tasted, 3/98.

1996—Extremely closed and backward, but oh, so impressive, the 1996 (as well as
  •   the 1995) is a wine that should be purchased only by patient Bordeaux
91–   connoisseurs. The 1996 offers a dark, dense ruby/purple color, followed by a
93+   reluctant but promising nose of cassis, licorice, spicy oak, and minerals.
         Powerful and medium to full bodied, with high tannin but a sensational
         finish (35+ seconds), this deep, serious, uncompromising claret will require a
         decade of cellaring. It is a brilliant wine, but long-term aging is warranted.
         Anticipated maturity: 2008–2040. Last tasted, 3/98.

1995—While not as backward as the 1996, the opaque purple-colored 1995 is a
  •   tannic, unevolved, dense, concentrated wine that will require 8–10 years of
90+   cellaring. The 1995 exhibits *pain grillé*, black currant, mineral, and subtle
         tobacco in its complex yet youthful aromatics. Powerful, dense, concentrated
         cassis and blueberry flavors might be marginally softer than in the 1996, but
         there is still plenty of grip and structure to this big wine. Anticipated maturity:
         2005–2030. Last tasted, 11/97.

1994—The dark ruby/purple–colored 1994 offers up scents of toasty vanilla and
  •   sweet black currant fruit. This medium-bodied claret possesses good fat,
87+   moderate tannin, and a traditional, backward feel. Although still youthful, the
         wine possesses enough fruit to balance out the tannin. This should develop
         into an excellent wine with 2–3 more years of cellaring. Anticipated maturity:
         2000–2015. Last tasted, 1/97.

1993—Dark ruby/purple colored, with sweet, perfumed, black currant fruit, this wine
  •   offers a round, supple entry on the palate, medium body, ripe fruit, not a great
87   deal of power or volume, but fine purity, some intriguing chocolate and smoky
         notes, and a velvety-textured, lush finish. A high percentage of Merlot was
         used in the final blend, a fact confirmed by this tasty, elegant wine. Last
         tasted, 1/97.

1992—Medium ruby colored, with an oak overlay, this wine lacks fruit and tastes
  •   monolithic, tannic, angular, and compact. It may improve with 2–3 years of
79   cellaring, but my instincts suggest it will dry out long before the tannin fades.
         Last tasted, 11/94.

1991—Léoville-Poyferré turned in a solidly made, muscular 1991 with good color,
  •   ripe fruit, plenty of tannin, and noticeable oak. The wine lacks charm and
84   finesse but should last for 12 or more years. It will benefit from 2–3 years of
         cellaring. Last tasted, 1/94.

1990—The two best Poyferrés of recent decades have been the 1982 and 1983, but
  •   the 1990 is superior. The wine exhibits a profoundly deep, opaque ruby/
96   purple color and a fabulous nose of jammy, sweet, cassis fruit intertwined
         with scents of minerals and toasty oak. Still youthful and full bodied, with
         low acidity, high tannin, and fabulous extract and purity, this is an awesomely
         endowed Léoville-Poyferré that is just beginning to evolve. It requires another
         decade of cellaring, and it should last 30+ years. Last tasted, 11/96.

1989—This has always been a very good wine, but somewhat abrasively tannic, with
  •   a coarse structure and degree of toughness that has been slow to subside. The
89+?   wine exhibits a youthful color, as well as attractive, sweet, cherry, and black

currant notes in its nose intermingled with a touch of earth and spice. The 1989 does not possess the body, weight, and richness of the 1990, coming across as more of a midweight, leaner style of wine. It is more austere, and the tough tannin that has been a worrisome component since its birth is still present. This wine could turn around and come close to being an outstanding example, but I suspect it will be a struggle for the fruit to overcome the tannin. Anticipated maturity: 2004–2018. Last tasted, 11/96.

1988 — The 1988 Léoville-Poyferré, which is austere and supercharged with tannin,
 •   exhibits leanness and a lack of fruit and charm. It will age well, but will it
82   ever provide much pleasure? Anticipated maturity: Now–2006. Last tasted, 1/93.

1987 — Thin, weedy, angular, and tough textured, the 1987 is not a success. Antici-
 •   pated maturity: Now. Last tasted, 11/90.
73

1986 — This is a good rather than dazzling 1986. On close examination, the wine is
 •   excessively tannic without the fruit to soften and balance its astringency.
87   Moreover, the wine's midrange palate is somewhat short, no doubt caused by the enormous crop size in the vintage. That criticism aside, what one gets is a wine with great color, a plummy, spicy bouquet, medium to full body, and very good length with considerable tannic clout. Anticipated maturity: Now–2010. Last tasted, 10/89.

1985 — The 1985 Léoville-Poyferré has good color, a soft, round, fruity, medium-
 •   bodied feel on the palate, a toasty, new oaky bouquet, ripe, melted tannins,
85   and a moderately long finish. Anticipated maturity: Now. Last tasted, 4/90.

1984 — Very tannic and hard, the 1984 Léoville-Poyferré seems to lack the requisite
 •   amount of fruit for the existing tannin. It is just too severe; perhaps in 2–3
75   years it will open. Anticipated maturity: Now. Last tasted, 6/88.

1983 — This is a beautifully made wine and certainly one of the two finest made at
 •   this estate during the eighties. The color is a healthy dark ruby/purple. A
90   classic nose of overripe black currants, plums, and sweet vanillin is followed by a wine with considerable opulence and a seductive, fleshy mouth-feel. The wine's low acidity and gorgeously pure, rich fruit with copious quantities of glycerin make for a beautiful tasting experience. Although the 1983 has reached full maturity, it exhibits no signs of drying out. Anticipated maturity: Now–2010. Last tasted, 3/97.

1982 — This is a classic Léoville-Poyferré as well as a backward 1982. The wine is
 •   not dissimilar from the 1982 Léoville-Barton—super-concentrated, extremely
93+   tannic, and a decade away from reaching its plateau of full maturity. The 1982 is an enormously concentrated, opaque ruby/purple–colored wine. Although it offers layers of sweet, jammy fruit, it remains closed but not out of balance. This wine possesses immense body, plenty of glycerin and sweet tannin, and a long finish. A massive example of Léoville-Poyferré, it requires another 8–10 years of cellaring and should last through the first 3 decades of the next century. Shrewd buyers should look to the auction market (there is a tendency for this wine, even in a great vintage like 1982, to be overlooked) to

snatch up this wine given the lack of confidence most investors have in Léoville-Poyferré. Last tasted, 9/95.

1981—Consistently perplexing to judge, the 1981 Poyferré has adequate tannin and
•   acidity, a soft, jammy midrange, and a short finish. Surely a good wine with
83   4–5 years of evolution ahead of it, but certainly not one of the leading St.-Juliens in 1981. Anticipated maturity: Now. Last tasted, 12/86.

1979—Medium to dark ruby, with an amber edge, this wine has an open-knit, ripe,
•   rather portlike bouquet. Soft, flabby flavors have modest appeal, but the wine
78   is quite loosely knit and diffuse in the finish. Anticipated maturity: Now. Last tasted, 5/84.

1978—Easygoing, with soft, charming, above-average-intensity flavors, medium
•   body, and very light tannins, this is a wine that has obviously been vinified
80   for near-term consumption. Anticipated maturity: Now. Last tasted, 4/82.

1976—Very soft, flabby, almost soupy, fruity flavors show good ripeness but little
•   structure, grip, or balance. This is a sweet, simple, fruity wine that can be
75   quaffed easily, but it does not deliver "classified growth" breed or character. Drink up. Anticipated maturity: Now—probably in serious decline. Last tasted, 6/83.

1975—This wine proved to be more irregular than even Lafite-Rothschild. The most
•   recent tasting revealed a spicy, cedar, good but uninspiring, tannic Médoc.
82? Previous bottles have exhibited impressive extract levels, but bottles tasted over the last 7–10 years have been tough and hard, displaying the more negative characteristics of the 1975 vintage. Last tasted, 12/95.

1971—Fully mature, simple, and straightforward, with a bouquet reminiscent of
•   cranberry juice, medium bodied, somewhat compact and lean, this is a pleas-
75   ant but hardly inspiring wine. Anticipated maturity: Now—probably in serious decline. Last tasted, 6/79.

1970—Foul barnyard aromas have long beset this wine, which otherwise shows a
•   good, dark ruby color, ripe, savory fruit, moderate tannins, and a decent
65   finish. I had once hoped that time would cause dissipation of the stinky smells, but they have only gotten worse. Last tasted, 10/83.

1966—Given the listless management that Poyferré was under during this period, it
•   is a wonder that the 1966 turned out as well as it did. Now fully mature, this
83   medium-bodied, stylish wine has good black currant fruit, a complex yet restrained bouquet of cedar and spices, and a good crisp, clean finish. Anticipated maturity: Now. Last tasted, 9/84.

1964—Some fruit can be found, but first one's palate must fend off abnormally high
•   acidity and harsh tannins. It is memorable only because of the obvious
55   deficiencies. Last tasted, 11/75.

1962—Much of the Léoville-Poyferré vineyard was replanted in 1962, and while the
•   young, infant vines may have been the reason for some of the lackluster wines
67   produced in the late sixties and early seventies, they had nothing to do with the mediocre 1962. Light, overly acidic, with some redeeming fruit flavors, this light- to medium-weight wine should be drunk up. Anticipated maturity: Now—probably in serious decline. Last tasted, 9/77.

1961—The 1961 is very good but not in the top class of wines from this vintage.
•   Certainly rich, flavorful, and concentrated with fruit, this wine represents a
87   rather rare phenomenon for Poyferré during a period of mediocrity. Dark ruby,
with an attractive cedary, spicy, mature bouquet on the palate, the 1961
Léoville-Poyferré is deep, supple, ripe, and long, but fully mature. Anticipated maturity: Now. Last tasted, 3/80.

ANCIENT VINTAGES

Unfortunately I have never tasted the legendary 1928 and 1929, but the
1945, 1953, 1955, and 1959, all drunk in the late eighties, were unexciting,
generally coarse, and rustic wines.

ST.-PIERRE   EXCELLENT

Classification: Fourth-growth in 1855
Location of vineyards: St.-Julien-Beychevelle
Owner: Françoise Triaud
Address: Domaines Martin, 33250 St.-Julien-Beychevelle
Mailing address: 33250 St.-Julien-Beychevelle
Telephone: 33 5 56 59 08 18; telefax: 33 5 56 59 16 18
Visits: By appointment only, from Monday to Friday, between 8 A.M. and
12:30 P.M., and 2 P.M. and 6 P.M.
Contact: Jean-Louis Triaud

VINEYARDS (red)
Surface area: 42 acres
Average age of vines: 41 years
Blend: 70% Cabernet Sauvignon, 20% Merlot, 10% Cabernet Franc
Density of plantation: 10,000 vines per hectare
Average yields (over the last 5 years): 48 hectoliters per hectare
Total average annual production: 8,000 cases

GRAND VIN (red)
Brand name: Château St.-Pierre
Appellation: St.-Julien
Mean annual production: 5,000 cases
Upbringing: Grapes are picked by hand. *Cuvaisons* last 15–30 days after
alcoholic fermentations, depending upon the vintage. Fermentations
occur in temperature-controlled stainless-steel tanks, starting at 28
degrees centigrade and finishing at 32 degrees centigrade. There are 4
pumping-overs daily, with airing. Wines are then transferred into oak
barrels, which are renewed by half for each vintage, and are aged for 18
months. They are fined and filtered prior to bottling.

SECOND WINE
Brand name: Sold in bulk
Average annual production: 3,000 cases
Evaluation of present classification: Should be maintained
Plateau of maturity: 7–20 years following the vintage

St.-Pierre is the least known of the classified-growth St.-Julien châteaux. Much of the production of St.-Pierre has traditionally been sold to wine enthusiasts in Belgium, no doubt because the former owners, Monsieur Castelein and Madame Castelein-Van den Bussche, were Belgian. In 1982 one of the Médoc's great personalities, Henri Martin, purchased the property. The vineyards of St.-Pierre are well located right behind the town of St.-Julien-Beychevelle, and a drive past them will reveal a high percentage of old and gnarled vines, always a sign of quality. The style of wine of St.-Pierre has tended to be rich and full bodied, even thick and coarse in some vintages. Always deeply colored, sometimes opaque, St.-Pierre is a big, rustic, dusty-textured wine. While it can lack the finesse and charm of many St.-Juliens, such as Ducru-Beaucaillou and Léoville-Las Cases, it compensates for that deficiency with its obvious (some would say garish) display of power and muscle.

Recent vintages, particularly those since 1985, have not sacrificed any of the wine's size but have added a forward, succulent character, and, I believe, more complexity. All in all, the wines of St.-Pierre, when compared with those of the top châteaux of St.-Julien, are vastly under-rated. This estate continues to languish in the shadows cast by the glamorous superstars of the St.-Julien appellation. Given the usually realistic price, consumers should put this lack of recognition to good use.

VINTAGES

1997—The under-rated estate of St.-Pierre deserves more attention. While the wines
• do not quite hit the heights of Léoville-Las Cases, Léoville-Barton, or Léoville-
87– Poyferré, they are remarkably consistent, chunky, husky Bordeaux with con-
89 siderable character. The 1997 reveals a nicely saturated ruby/purple color, and an earthy, spicy, fruit-driven bouquet (primarily jammy black currants) with subtle new oak in the background. Dense on the palate, and slightly backward, this fleshy, expansive but moderately tannic wine will be one of the few 1997s that will not be ready to drink upon release. However, it is approachable. Anticipated maturity: 2002–2013. Last tasted, 3/98.

1996—For whatever reason, this classified growth did not taste as impressive as its
• sibling, Gloria—usually a lesser wine that sells for a much lower price. On
86– the two occasions I had it, the wine exhibited a deep purple color, surprising
? softness for a 1996 Médoc, and an awkward character, with all of its compo-

nents in a discordant state. I think the wine possesses all the right stuff, it just needs to flesh out and find its identity. Anticipated maturity: 2002–2020.

1995—The 1995 reveals an opaque purple color, as well as good fatness, low acidity,
•　　and a slight disjointedness. Rich and full, with that sweet, ripe finish so
88　　prevalent in the top 1995s, it cannot be easily dismissed. If the wine develops more personality and its midsection fills out, it could easily merit a higher score. While it will be pleasant to drink young, it possesses the power and depth to last 12–16 years. Last tasted, 3/96.

1994—St.-Pierre's 1994 outshines the riper, slightly lower acid 1995. The former
•　　wine is a dense, rich, full-bodied, opulently textured, ostentatiously styled
89　　St.-Julien with outstanding concentration, gobs of toasty new oak, and plenty of fleshy flavor. It is an impressively saturated, full-bodied, concentrated, attractive wine. There is, however, some tannin lurking in the background, so I suspect this wine will begin to reveal more structure. Cellar it for 3–4 years and drink it over the following 15. Last tasted, 3/96.

1990—The lusty, richly oaky, deep, spicy 1990 appears designed to immediately im-
•　　press both critics and consumers. The color is dark, the big, vanillin, smoky
90　　aromas are intermingled with decadent quantities of black fruits, and the finish is lush, chewy, and soft. Anticipated maturity: Now–2007. Last tasted, 1/93.

1989—The 1989 is dark ruby/purple, with a smashing aroma of jammy, superripe
•　　black currants and new oak. This full-bodied, opulent wine offers a luscious,
89　　heady mouthful of low-acid fruit. The high alcohol combined with the wine's fragile balance will have to be monitored carefully. Anticipated maturity: Now–2010. Last tasted, 1/93.

1988—The 1988 St.-Pierre is a richly fruity, substantial wine, characteristics missing
•　　in many of the more compact, austere Médoc 1988s. Deep ruby and medium
87　　bodied, with an attractively long, well-balanced finish, it is a classic example from this vintage. Anticipated maturity: Now–1999. Last tasted, 1/93.

1986—The 1986 has turned out to be outstanding. It is a powerfully constructed,
•　　dark ruby–colored wine, with plenty of muscle and richness, an intriguing
90　　bouquet of exotic spices, sweet toasty oak, and plummy fruit. On the palate, the wine is very concentrated and tannic. This brawny, large-scaled wine has an underlying suppleness that suggests it should be drinkable at an earlier age than many of the other top 1986 Médocs. Anticipated maturity: Now–2012. Last tasted, 11/90.

1985—The 1985 St.-Pierre is rich, chewy, fat, and deep, with just the right amount
•　　of new oak. It reminds me of the fine 1981 made at this property. Anticipated
87　　maturity: Now. Last tasted, 11/90.

1984—A lightish, soft, fruity wine, the 1984 should be drunk over the next 3–4 years
•　　for the uncomplicated, yet pleasing, medium-bodied fruitiness. Anticipated
82　　maturity: Now. Last tasted, 10/87.

1983—Surprisingly similar in style to the 1982, fat, succulent, and very concentrated
•　　with a soft, rich, almost jammy concentration, this full-bodied, robust wine
87　　has a seductive lushness and will make excellent drinking. Anticipated maturity: Now. Last tasted, 3/89.

1982—A lovely, supple, ripe, savory, richly fruity wine with medium to full body and
 • a moderately intense bouquet of vanillin oakiness and ripe fruit, the 1982
88　St.-Pierre seems forward and lush but exhibits sufficient underlying tannin to
develop nicely. Anticipated maturity: Now–2000. Last tasted, 3/89.

1981—A top-notch wine, certainly one of the most successful wines of this vintage,
 • the 1981 St.-Pierre is impressively dark ruby and very aromatic, with the
88　scent of ripe berry fruit, cedar wood, and caramel. On the palate, it is quite
rich, medium to full bodied, long, lush, and moderately tannic. It is a big,
extroverted St.-Julien, with considerable personality. Anticipated maturity:
Now–2000. Last tasted, 11/88.

1979—A robust, virile wine for a 1979, this St.-Pierre has impressive color, a chunky,
 • satisfying, rich fruity character, some whiffs of cedar wood, and a solid,
85　moderately tannic finish. Not elegant, but nevertheless substantial and flavorful. Anticipated maturity: Now. Last tasted, 11/88.

1975—Impressive for sure, but as with so many 1975s, one wonders whether it will
 • live up to its potential. Still dark in color, with only a slight amber edge, this
86　full-bodied wine has ripe, chocolatey fruit, but also mouth-lashing, high
tannins that remain dry and astringent. The 1975 St.-Pierre is a robust,
muscular wine that still requires time in the bottle. Anticipated maturity:
Now–2005. Last tasted, 11/89.

1971—Ready to drink, this wine is quite spicy, with a plummy, cedary nose that
 • offers high expectations on the palate. The wine is good but less promising
83　than the fine bouquet suggests. The somewhat coarse, rough flavors are heavy-
handed and too aggressive. Anticipated maturity: Now. Last tasted, 6/82.

1970—A sleeper of the vintage, the 1970 St.-Pierre is dark ruby, is loaded with
 • spicy, black currant fruit, and has full body, plenty of round, ripe tannins and
87　substantial length on the palate. Fully mature, but made to last, the 1970
St.-Pierre can rival many of Bordeaux's best estates in 1970. Anticipated
maturity: Now–2005. Last tasted, 6/87.

1961—This is a fine 1961, with a fully mature, sweet, savory, plummy spiciness,
 • medium to full body, an expansive dark garnet color, and a long, alcoholic
87　finish. Anticipated maturity: Now. Last tasted, 7/85.

TALBOT　　　　　　　　　　　　　　　　　　　　　EXCELLENT

Classification: Fourth-growth in 1855
Location of vineyards: St.-Julien
Owner: Mrs. Rustmann and Mrs. Bignon
Address: 33250 St.-Julien-Beychevelle
Mailing address: Same
Telephone: 05 56 73 21 50; telefax: 05 56 73 21 51
Visits: By appointment only, Monday to Friday, between 9 A.M. and noon,
and 2 P.M. and 5 P.M.
Contact: Mr. Rustmann

VINEYARDS (red)

Surface area: 252 acres

Average age of vines: 30 years

Blend: 66% Cabernet Sauvignon, 26% Merlot, 3% Cabernet Franc, 5% Petit Verdot

Density of plantation: 7,700 vines per hectare

Average yields (over the last 5 years): 52 hectoliters per hectare

Total average annual production: 52,000 cases

GRAND VIN (red)

Brand name: Château Talbot

Appellation: St.-Julien

Mean annual production: 30,000–32,000 cases

Upbringing: The grapes are hand-picked and sorted twice, in the vineyards and at the winery, and are totally destemmed. Fermentations last 15–21 days in temperature-controlled stainless-steel and wooden vats of a total capacity of 9,200 hectoliters. Wines are transferred after *assemblage* in December to oak barrels, 40% of which are new, for 18 months. They are bottled without fining and after a very light filtration.

SECOND WINE

Brand name: Connétable de Talbot

Average annual production: 20,000 cases

VINEYARDS (White)

Surface area: 14.8 acres

Average age of vines: 25 years

Blend: 84% Sauvignon, 16% Semillon

Average yield (over the last 5 years): 55 hectoliters per hectare

Mean annual production: 3,000 cases

GRAND VIN (White)

Brand name: Caillou Blanc du Château Talbot

Appellation: Bordeaux

Mean annual production: 3,000 cases

Upbringing: Fermentations and upbringing last 9 months in all. Half the yield goes into new oak casks, and the other into 1-year-old barrels. Wines remain on lees all the time, with frequent stirring *(bâtonnage)*. They are not fined but lightly filtered prior to bottling.

Evaluation of present classification: Should be upgraded to a third-growth

Plateau of maturity: 7–25 years following the vintage

The huge single vineyard of Talbot is situated inland from the Gironde River, well behind the tiny hamlet of St.-Julien-Beychevelle and just north of Gruaud-Larose.

Talbot is named after the English commander John Talbot, the earl of Shrewsbury, who was defeated in battle at Castillon in 1453. The château made consistently fine, robust, yet fruity, full-bodied wines under the Cordier administration and deserves promotion should any new reclassification of the wines of the Médoc be done. The new administration appears to be moving in the direction of a softer, more elegant style.

A modest amount of delicious, dry white wine is made at Talbot. Called Caillou Blanc du Château Talbot, it is a fresh, fragrant white—one of the finest produced in the Médoc. It must, however, be drunk within 2–4 years of the vintage.

VINTAGES

1997—Fifty percent of Talbot's 1997 production was utilized in the grand vin. It is a
• potential sleeper of the vintage given its saturated purple color, and sweet,
87– earthy, leather, and cassis-scented nose. In the mouth, the wine is fat and
89 opulent, with low acidity. The finish is all glycerin, alcohol, and juicy fruit. It may be almost too low in acidity, but it is drinking well and can be expected to do so for another decade. It is a fine choice for readers who are unable to defer their gratification. Last tasted, 3/98.

1996—The 1996 Talbot is an excellent effort from this large St.-Julien estate.
• Black/ruby/purple-colored, with a pronounced nose of Provençal olives,
87– black currants, licorice, and Asian spices, this is a powerful, dense,
89 rich fruity wine with fine intensity, moderate tannin, and medium body. This attractive St.-Julien will be one of a handful of 1996s that can be drunk a few years after bottling. Anticipated maturity: 2002–2015. Last tasted, 3/98.

1995—This wine has turned out to be more impressive from bottle than it was in
• cask. It is a charming, intensely scented wine with a telltale olive, earth,
88 grilled beef, and black currant-scented bouquet soaring from the glass. Medium to full bodied, with low acidity, and round, luscious, rich fruity flavors, this is a meaty, fleshy, delicious Talbot that can be drunk now. Anticipated maturity: Now–2012. Last tasted, 11/97.

1994—A sweet, soft, commercially styled wine, the 1994 offers a medium deep ruby
• color, a smoky, berry-scented nose, supple, fruity flavors, medium body, no
85 hard tannin (a rarity for a 1994), and an easy to understand finish. Drink it over the next 4–8 years. Last tasted, 1/97.

1993—Talbot's 1993 exhibits a medium ruby color, a fragrant, smoky, herbal,
• green pepper-scented nose, light to medium body, no astringency or sharp-
84 ness, yet, sadly, unimpressive flavor concentration. The wine is ready to drink and should be consumed over the next 4–5 years. Last tasted, 1/97.

1992—I found this wine lacking fruit and tasting sinewy and tannic from cask, but I
• am delighted to say it is performing well from bottle. It will be a noteworthy
86 wine to purchase if it is discounted as much as I suspect it will be. Talbot's
1992 reveals an exotic nose of jammy black cherries, truffles, licorice, and
smoky, herbal scents. Following the extroverted bouquet, the wine offers a
medium-bodied, supple, juicy, succulent style with low acidity and plenty of
ripe fruit. This delicious wine promises to drink well for 6–7 years. Last
tasted, 11/94.

1991—Talbot's disappointing 1991 is an appallingly weak effort for this estate. The
• diluted medium ruby color is suspicious, and the weedy, vegetal, washed-out
72 herbal nose and flavors are lamentable. In the mouth the wine is odd, disjointed, and soft. Last tasted, 1/94.

1990—The medium-colored 1990 is an elegant, structured, more restrained style of
• wine than usual. There is admirable ripeness and length, but the wine lacks
85 the outstanding depth and flavor dimension of other top vintages of Talbot. Is
the style being changed? Anticipated maturity: Now–2008. Last tasted, 1/93.

1989—The 1989 is more elegant, with none of the herb, meaty, leathery aromas of
• the 1988. Opaque black/ruby, with a pronounced bouquet of black fruits and
88 spices, this extracted, medium- to full-bodied wine is voluptuous on the
palate, with a fine finish. The 1989 Talbot promises to drink well during its
first decade of life but keep for up to 20 years. Anticipated maturity: Now–
2015. Last tasted, 1/93.

1988—The 1988 Talbot is dark ruby, with a well-focused personality brimming
• with spicy, chocolatey, black currant, leathery, herbal fruit buttressed
89 by good acidity and high tannins. In the mouth, the wine has a game-like,
smoky, beefy character. If the tannins fade a little and the fruit takes over,
this will be an outstanding wine. Anticipated maturity: Now–2015. Last
tasted, 1/93.

1987—The 1987 Talbot is a surprisingly tannic, tough-textured wine but has a
• gorgeous nose of cedar and weedy, earthy black currants. Deep in color, with
85 a good deal of tannin and medium body, this is a vintage that will keep for
10–15 years. Anticipated maturity: Now–2000. Last tasted, 11/90.

1986—The 1982 Talbot is a marvelous wine, but it's my gut feeling that the 1986 is,
• along with the 1982, the finest Talbot made at this estate since the legendary
96 1945. The fact that there are 40,000 cases of this wine is good news for the
consumer, as there will be plenty to go around. The wine, which has been so
special since the first taste from cask, is classically structured, with a penetrating fragrance of peppery, spicy, weedy black currants, and tar, an enormous concentration of flavor on the palate, and staggering length. The tannins
are noticeable, but they are ripe tannins, somewhat softer than those found in
many of the 1986 Médocs. In comparison with stablemate Gruaud-Larose, the
Talbot is more developed and flattering to taste today. This should prove to be
an extraordinarily long-lived wine and, as are virtually all the Cordier wines,
a marvelous value for your money. Anticipated maturity: Now–2020. Last
tasted, 9/97.

1985 — The 1985 Talbot is a downsized version of their 1982 and is now flattering to
•   taste and drink. Very deep in color, with a ripe, rich, berry-like fragrance,
89   this supple, fleshy, medium-bodied wine has loads of fruit, a smooth, graceful
finish, and excellent balance. Anticipated maturity: Now–2000. Last tasted,
4/90.

1984 — The Cordiers seem to do well in the so-called off years (such as the 1968
•   Talbot and the 1974 Gruaud-Larose), so it is no surprise to see how good their
82   1984s are. The 1984 Talbot is 94% Cabernet Sauvignon and 6% Merlot. It is
quite elegant and stylish, with a lovely bouquet of spring flowers and ripe
currant fruit, medium to full body, and good tannins. Anticipated maturity:
Now. Last tasted, 3/88.

1983 — Full bodied, with a deep, almost opaque ruby/purple color, a forward, cassis-
•   scented aroma, and rich, lush flavors, the 1983 Talbot is a large-scaled wine
91   that is drinking surprisingly well. It is one of the great successes of the
vintage. Anticipated maturity: Now–2008. Last tasted, 3/89.

1982 — There have been some great Talbots—1945, 1953, and 1986—but I do not
•   think there has ever been a more satisfying or complex Talbot than the
96   1982. The wine tastes fully mature, although it is revealing no signs of
color degradation. My best guess is that this wine should easily hold for
another 10–15+ years. It has been delicious since the late eighties, exhibiting a saturated, nearly opaque purple/garnet color and a huge nose of
black truffles, licorice, herbs, meat, new saddle leather, and gloriously
sweet black fruit. Full bodied, yet surprisingly supple and fleshy, with
huge quantities of chewy fruit, this is a corpulent wine. The finish is all
glycerin, fruit, and alcohol, although there must be some tannin lurking
behind these components. This is one of the most seductive, complex,
and hedonistic 1982s for drinking between now and 2010. Last tasted,
10/97.

1981 — Attractive and well made, the 1981 Talbot exhibits surprising elegance and
•   suppleness for this property. Dark ruby, with a moderately intense bouquet of
85   cassis and meaty, leathery, tarry aromas, this medium-bodied wine has good
concentration and light tannins. It is drinkable now. Similar in style to the
1979, the 1981 is a shade fruitier and deeper. Anticipated maturity: Now–
2000. Last tasted, 4/89.

1980 — This wine offers solid, straightforward fruity flavors, none of the vegetal
•   characters found in the worst 1980s, and a solid, round, flavorful finish.
82   Anticipated maturity: Now–may be in decline. Last tasted, 6/83.

1979 — A richly fruity Talbot, with a precocious, forward appeal, this medium-bodied
•   wine has a velvety texture and a soft, round finish. Anticipated maturity: Now.
84   Last tasted, 2/84.

1978 — Developing very nicely in the bottle, the 1978 Talbot has a concentrated,
•   ripe, round, rich, herbaceous-scented, black currant fruitiness, a bouquet
87   suggestive of plums and cedary, toasty oak, a generous texture, and some
tannins in the finish. It has just reached its plateau of maturity. Anticipated
maturity: Now–2000. Last tasted, 10/90.

1976—The variable 1976 vintage reached its greatest heights in the commune of
 •   St.-Julien, where a number of fine wines were produced. Talbot is one of them.
86   Fully mature, but capable of holding for several more years, this immensely
       enjoyable wine has a lovely cedary, spicy, ripe plummy bouquet, soft, round,
       nicely concentrated flavors, and a velvety, satisfying finish. Anticipated matu-
       rity: Now. Last tasted, 11/87.

1975—The medium-bodied, hard, lean, austere 1975 Talbot revealed more fruit than
 •   in the past, an earthy, herbal, chocolatey, weedy-scented nose, good extrac-
84   tion, and the vintage's harshness and toughness in the finish. Although it will
       keep for another 10–15+ years, there is no reason to hold on to it that long.
       Last tasted, 12/95.

1971—One of the most stylish and complete wines of the vintage, the 1971 Talbot is
 •   now fully mature but showing no signs of fading. It has good concentration, a
86   lively, berryish, fruity quality, a deft touch of vanillin oakiness, and medium
       to full body. Very well structured for a 1971, it is without any brown color or
       soupy softness that afflicts many of the wines of this vintage. The 1971 Talbot
       is certainly a successful wine from this vintage. Anticipated maturity: Now.
       Last tasted, 3/89.

1970—My last bottle of the 1970 Talbot, from an ill-advised purchase in the early
 •   seventies, proved to be no better than the other eleven clunkers. Tannic,
76   angular, thin, and acidic, with harsh tannin and no fruit, this wine was
       astringent young, astringent in middle age, and astringent old. Last tasted,
       6/96.

1967—One of the more attractive wines of the vintage, the 1967 Talbot is now
 •   cracking up. Short, compact flavors now exhibit little of the rich, fruity,
75   robustness revealed in the mid-1970s. Anticipated maturity: Now. Last tasted,
       1/83.

1966—Age has given this wine some complexity as a result of bottle bouquet.
 •   However, this vintage did not produce a profound example of Talbot. Hard,
77   austere, lean flavors reveal little evidence that rich, ripe fruit is hidden
       behind a shield of tannin and acidity. The color is light, the fruit just ade-
       quate, the finish short. Anticipated maturity: Now. Last tasted, 9/84.

1964—This is an attractive, if uncomplex, 1964. Talbot is adequately fruity, chunky,
 •   a trifle hard and coarse in the finish, but overall a good mouthful of claret.
82   Anticipated maturity: Now–may be in decline. Last tasted, 3/79.

1962—An elegant Talbot, finely etched and reminiscent of the style of the 1971, this
 •   medium-bodied, flavorful, fully mature wine is holding up nicely in the bottle.
84   A fragrant, spicy, cedary bouquet is interesting and shows good fruit. Rather
       reserved on the palate, with polite flavors, some unresolved tannins still
       present, and above average length, this is a good rather than great Talbot.
       Anticipated maturity: Now–may be in decline. Last tasted, 2/83.

1961—One would naturally expect the 1961 Talbot to completely overwhelm the
 •   1962. When tasted side by side, the wines are more similar than not, a trait
85   that is abnormal given the different styles of these two vintages. The 1961,
       like the 1962, is a bit austere and lean, has medium to full body, a rather

stern, unyielding texture, and good rather than excellent concentration. The wine lacks the color and richness of the best 1961s but is still a good wine. In the context of the vintage, the 1961 Talbot must be viewed as a disappointment. Anticipated maturity: Now—may be in decline. Last tasted, 1/85.

ANCIENT VINTAGES

The delicious licorice-and-cassis-scented and -flavored 1953 Talbot (90 points; last tasted 12/95) was a lovely, complex, beautifully balanced St.-Julien with no hard edges and plenty of fruit. The profound 1945 (rated 94 in 1988) is the finest old vintage of Talbot I have tasted.

OTHER ST.-JULIEN ESTATES

LA BRIDANE

Classification: Cru Bourgeois in 1932
Location of vineyards: St.-Julien-Beychevelle
Owner: Bruno Saintout
Address: 33250 St.-Julien-Beychevelle
Mailing address: Bruno Saintout, Cartujac, 33112 St.-Laurent-du-Médoc
Telephone: 33 5 56 59 91 70; telefax: 33 5 56 59 46 13
Visits: From July 8 to August 31, Monday to Saturday, between 10 A.M. and noon, and 2 P.M. and 7:30 P.M.
Contact: Bruno Saintout

VINEYARDS (red)
Surface area: 37 acres
Average age of vines: 25 years
Blend: 38% Merlot, 30% Cabernet Franc, 30% Cabernet Sauvignon, 2% Petit Verdot
Density of plantation: 6,500 vines per hectare
Average yields (over the last 5 years): 48 hectoliters per hectare
Total average annual production: 50,000 bottles

GRAND VIN (red)
Brand name: Château La Bridane
Appellation: St.-Julien
Mean annual production: 50,000 bottles
Upbringing: Harvest is done mechanically. Fermentations last 4–5 weeks in temperature-controlled stainless-steel vats. Wines are transferred after malolactics to oak barrels, one-third of which are new, for 12 months. They are fined but not filtered before bottling.

SECOND WINE
None produced.

Evaluation of present classification: Should be maintained
Plateau of maturity: 5–14 years following the vintage

This solidly made wine usually has considerable power, weight, and a chunky fruitiness. What it frequently lacks are those elusive qualities called charm and finesse. Nevertheless, the wine keeps well and is usually reasonably priced.

DOMAINE CASTAING

Classification: None
Location of vineyards: St.-Julien-Beychevelle
Owner: Jean-Jacques Cazeau
Address: 39, Grand Rue, 33250 St.-Julien-Beychevelle
Mailing address: Same
Telephone: 33 5 56 59 25 60
Visits: By appointment only, from Monday to Thursday
Contact: Jean-Jacques Cazeau

VINEYARDS (red)
Surface area: 3.1 acres
Average age of vines: 50 years
Blend: 65% Cabernet Sauvignon, 25% Merlot, 10% Cabernet Franc and Petit Verdot
Density of plantation: 10,000 vines per hectare
Average yields (over the last 5 years): 50 hectoliters per hectare
Total average annual production: 6,200 cases

GRAND VIN (red)
Brand name: Domaine Castaing
Appellation: St.-Julien
Mean annual production: 6,200 cases
Upbringing: Fermentations last 20 days at least, and wines are transferred, after completion of malolactics, to oak barrels, which are renewed by one-third each vintage, for at least 20 months aging. They are fined but not filtered prior to bottling.

SECOND WINE
None produced.

DOMAINE DE JAUGARET

Classification: None
Location of vineyards: St.-Julien
Owner: Fillastre family
Address: 33250 St.-Julien-Beychevelle
Mailing address: Same as above
Telephone: 33 5 56 59 09 71; telefax: 33 5 56 59 09 71
Visits: By appointment only
Contact: Jean-François Fillastre

VINEYARDS (red)
Surface area: 3.2 acres
Average age of vines: More than 50 years
Blend: 70% Cabernet Sauvignon, 25% Merlot, 5% Malbec and Cabernet Franc
Density of plantation: 10,000 vines per hectare
Average yields (over the last 5 years): 40 hectoliters per hectare

GRAND VIN (red)
Brand name: Domaine de Jaugaret
Appellation: St.-Julien
Mean annual production: 5,200 cases
Upbringing: Alcoholic fermentations last 8 days and macerations 21 days. Wines spend 30–36 months in barrel (little or no new oak is used). They are fined but not filtered prior to bottling.

SECOND WINE
None produced.

LALANDE

Classification: None
Location of vineyards: St.-Julien-Beychevelle
Owner: Madame Gabriel Meffre
Address: 33250 St.-Julien-Beychevelle
Mailing address: Vignobles Meffre
Telephone: 33 5 56 59 06 47; telefax: 33 5 56 59 06 47, 33 4 90 65 03 73
Visits: By appointment only
Contact: Claude Meffre

VINEYARDS (red)
Surface area: 79 acres
Average age of vines: 26 years

Blend: 55% Cabernet Sauvignon, 40% Merlot, 5% Cabernet Franc
Density of plantation: 7,000 vines per hectare
Average yields (over the last 5 years): 45 hectoliters per hectare
Total average annual production: 14,000 cases

GRAND VIN (red)
Brand name: Château Lalande
Appellation: St.-Julien
Mean annual production: 11,500 cases
Upbringing: Grapes are picked both mechanically and by hand.
Fermentations last 25 days, and wines are aged in tanks for 12 months.
They are fined prior to bottling and are sometimes lightly filtered (only if
turbid, and upon client's request). (As of 1997, wines will be partly aged
in casks, proportion not known.)

SECOND WINE
Brand name: Marquis de Lalande
Average annual production: 2,500 cases

MOULIN DE LA ROSE

Classification: Cru Bourgeois in 1932
Location of vineyards: St.-Julien-Beychevelle
Owner: Guy Delon
Address: 33250 St.-Julien-Beychevelle
Mailing address: Same as above
Telephone: 33 5 56 59 08 45; telefax: 33 5 56 59 73 94
Visits: By appointment only
Contact: Guy Delon

VINEYARDS (red)
Surface area: 11.4 acres
Average age of vines: 30 years
Blend: 62% Cabernet Sauvignon, 28% Merlot, 5% Cabernet Franc, 5%
Petit Verdot
Density of plantation: 8,500 vines per hectare
Average yields (over the last 5 years): 50 hectoliters per hectare
Total average annual production: 30,000 bottles

GRAND VIN (red)
Brand name: Château Moulin de la Rose
Appellation: St.-Julien

Mean annual production: 30,000 bottles
Upbringing: Grapes are picked manually. Fermentations occur in temperature-controlled vats and last about 3 weeks, depending upon the vintage. There are frequent pumping-overs daily. The whole yield is aged in oak barrels, which are renewed by one-third each year, for about 20 months. Wines are racked 7 times during this period and fined with egg whites. No filtration before bottling.

SECOND WINE
None produced.

TERREY-GROS-CAILLOUX   GOOD

Classification: Cru Bourgeois
Location of vineyards: St.-Julien-Beychevelle
Owner: Annie Fort and Henri Pradère
Address: 33250 St.-Julien-Beychevelle
Mailing address: Same as above
Telephone: 33 5 56 59 06 27; telefax: 33 5 56 59 29 32
Visits: From Monday to Friday, between 9 A.M. and noon, and 2 P.M. and 5 P.M.
Contact: Mrs. Bergey or Mr. Henri Pradère

VINEYARDS (red)
Surface area: 34 acres
Average age of vines: 35 years
Blend: 70% Cabernet Sauvignon, Merlot 25%, 5% Petit Verdot
Density of plantation: 10,000 vines per hectare
Average yields (over the last 5 years): 50 hectoliters per hectare

GRAND VIN (red)
Brand name: Château Terrey-Gros-Cailloux
Appellation: St.-Julien
Upbringing: Grapes are picked by hand. Fermentations last 3 weeks. Wines are aged in tanks, casks, and barrels (20% of which are new). They are fined but not filtered prior to bottling.

SECOND WINE
None produced.

Evaluation of present classification: The quality equivalent of a Grand Bourgeois Exceptionnel
Plateau of maturity: 3–7 years following the vintage

The cellars of this well-run Cru Bourgeois are located just off the famous D2 in the direction of Gruaud-Larose and Talbot. They house not only Terrey-Gros-Cailloux, but also the wine of Hortevie. Terrey-Gros-Cailloux tends to be a richly fruity, round, occasionally full-bodied wine that offers delicious drinking if consumed within the first 7–8 years. It is not long-lived, but the decision by the proprietors in the late eighties to begin to use some new oak casks to give the wine more definition and structure should prove beneficial to the wine's longevity.

TEYNAC

Classification: None
Location of vineyards: St.-Julien-Beychevelle
Owners: Fabienne and Philippe Pairault
Address: Grand Rue, 33250 St.-Julien-Beychevelle (not far from Gruaud-Larose)
Mailing address: Same as above
Telephones: 33 5 56 59 93 04, 33 5 56 59 12 91, or 33 1 43 80 60 70; telefax: 33 5 56 59 46 12 or 33 1 46 22 38 00
Visits: By appointment only
Contact: Philippe Pairault or Patrick Bussier

VINEYARDS (red)
Surface area: 28.4 acres
Average age of vines: 45 years
Blend: 78% Cabernet Sauvignon, 20% Merlot, 2% Petit Verdot
Density of plantation: 8,000 vines per hectare
Average yields (over the last 5 years): 39 hectoliters per hectare
Total average annual production: Variable, normally around 50,000 bottles

GRAND VIN (red)
Brand name: Château Teynac
Appellation: St.-Julien
Mean annual production: 45,000 bottles (average)
Upbringing: Grapes are entirely hand-picked in *cagettes* and never stacked in a tub. Fermentations last around 3 weeks, with frequent pumping-overs and breaking of the cap with jets of carbon dioxide, in temperature-controlled stainless-steel and cement tanks. Wines are transferred to oak barrels, 36% of which are new, for 12–14 months. They are fined (albumin) and filtered before bottling.

SECOND WINE
Brand name: Château Les Ormes
Average annual production: about 15,000 bottles (variable)

MARGAUX AND THE SOUTHERN MÉDOC

Margaux is certainly the largest and most sprawling of all the Médoc's principal wine-producing communes. The 2,847 acres under vine now exceed those of St.-Estèphe. A first-time tourist to Margaux immediately realizes just how spread out the châteaux of Margaux are. Only a few sit directly on Bordeaux's Route du Vin (D2), and these are Dauzac, Prieuré-Lichine, Palmer, and Malescot St.-Exupéry. Château Margaux is just off the main road in the town of Margaux, but the other major châteaux are sprinkled throughout the five principal communes: Arsac, Labarde, Cantenac, Margaux, and Soussans.

Margaux has the greatest number of classified-growth châteaux (Crus Classés) in the 1855 classification. A total of twenty-one Margaux châteaux made the grade, which is four more than Pauillac's seventeen châteaux that were included, ten more than St.-Julien's eleven, and sixteen more than St. Estèphe's five châteaux.

From an outsider's view, Margaux thus appears to have the highest number of quality wine producers; however, nothing could be further from the truth. For much of the sixties, seventies, and eighties there were at least a half dozen estates in Margaux that had a dreadful record of performance and at least another four or five properties that would merit downgrading if a revised classification of the wines of the Médoc was done and the five-tiered hierarchy maintained. Since the late eighties, a number of these estates have improved the quality of their wines, but this remains Bordeaux's leading appellation of underachievers. Even the regal first-growth queen herself, Château Margaux, went through a period of mediocrity that was dramatically reversed when the Mentzelopoulos family purchased Château Margaux in 1977 from the Ginestets, who had inadvertently permitted this *grande dame* to slip considerably in quality but not price below first-growth standards.

Despite the irregularity and lackluster track record of many Margaux châteaux over the last 25 years, the fragrant bouquet and seductive charm of a few great Margaux wines are what set these wines apart from a St.-Julien or Pauillac. The bouquet of a fine Margaux is unquestionably more intense and compelling than those found in the wines of St.-Julien, Pauillac, and St.-Estèphe. This has been well chronicled in virtually all the writings on

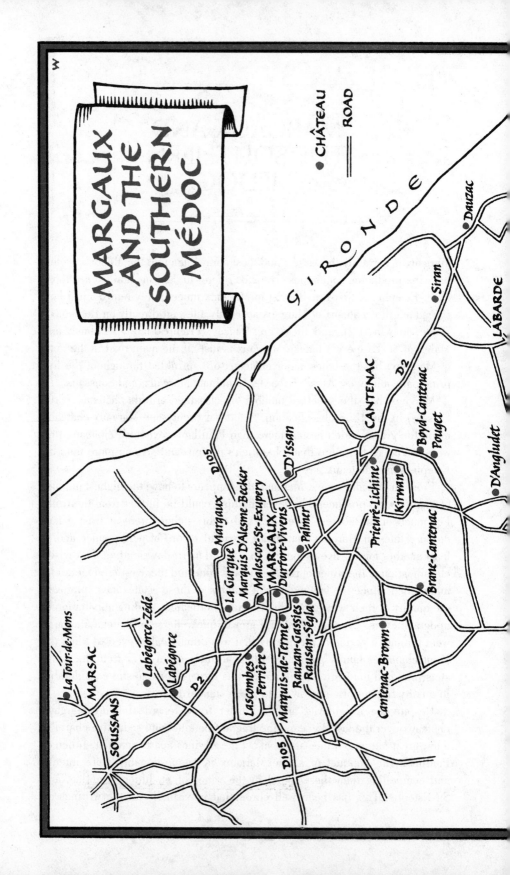

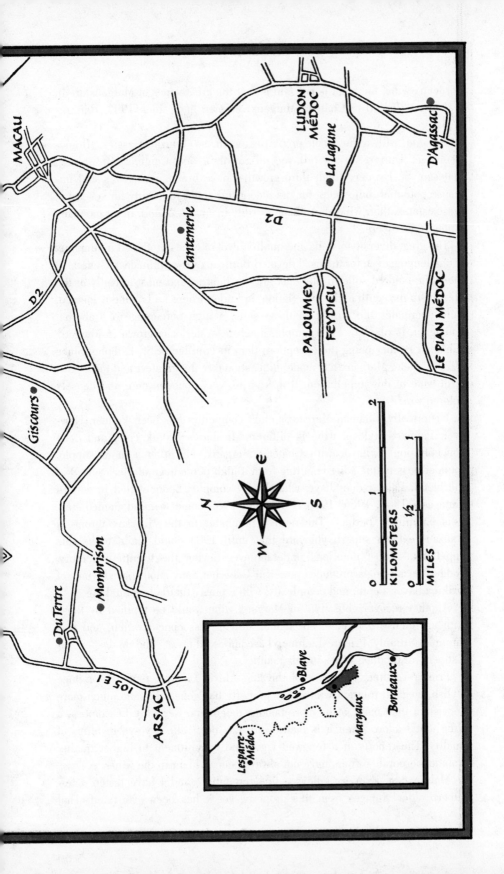

Bordeaux wine, but what is not said is that the great wines of Margaux are in real terms limited to Château Margaux, Palmer, and, since 1983, Rauzan-Ségla.

No one will argue that properties such as Rauzan-Gassies, Brane-Cantenac, Durfort-Vivens (all second-growths), and Cantenac-Brown and Malescot St.-Exupéry (both third-growths) have promising *terroirs* and immense potential, but except for the recent turnabout in quality for several of these estates, their wines have been terribly inconsistent and, in far too many vintages, mediocre.

The great diversity of soils and quality level of wines produced in Margaux is challenging even for the most devoted Bordeaux wine enthusiast. Generally, the white-colored soils in Margaux are the lightest and most gravelly of the Médoc. To the south of the appellation, in Ludon where La Lagune is located, sand dominates the *terroir.* In these soils, a high percentage of Cabernet Sauvignon is planted. For example, much less Merlot is grown in Margaux (Château Palmer being the exception) than in Pauillac or St.-Estèphe. Since 1977 Château Margaux has made unquestionably the greatest and most powerful wine of this appellation. It is a virile, very concentrated, and densely colored wine.

Historically, Château Margaux's chief competitor has been Palmer. However, Palmer's style of wine is different. It shares a dark color and deep concentration of flavor with Château Margaux, but it is a more supple, rounder, less tannic wine resulting from a high percentage of Merlot used in the blend. Palmer does have a fabulously complex bouquet that in certain vintages—1961, 1966, 1970, 1983, and 1989 come to mind immediately —is hauntingly perfect. The newest pretender to the Margaux throne is Rauzan-Ségla, a superb vineyard that until 1983 could claim to be this appellation's most notorious underachiever during the twentieth century. Today Rauzan-Ségla produces powerful Cabernet Sauvignon–based wines of striking flavor, depth, and complexity, with a purity that is breathtaking.

Another recognizable style of Margaux wine would be typified by those with an intense fragrance, but lighter weight, less concentration, and less tannin. Certainly Prieuré-Lichine, Lascombes, d'Issan, and Malescot St.-Exupéry all produce wines in this manner.

Prieuré-Lichine, the home of the late Alexis Lichine, tends to produce stylish, elegant, fragrant wines. The property has generally been much more consistent than many of its more famous neighbors. Certainly Lascombes, a wine that I adore when it is made well, has been like a yo-yo in terms of quality. The reports of a renewed vigor and commitment to higher quality from its corporate owners have not always been evident in the wines.

Malescot St.-Exupéry enjoys a fine reputation, and I have tasted a few superb older vintages from this property, yet it has been over-rated. That being said, vintages since 1990 have been impressive, giving reason for renewed interest in this estate.

Despite the number of mediocre wines produced by such noteworthy Margaux estates as d'Issan, Brane-Cantenac, Durfort-Vivens, Dauzac, and Kirwan in the sixties, seventies, and eighties, the encouraging thing is that all of these properties have halted their nosedives and, in the late eighties and mid-nineties, turned in some of their best winemaking efforts in more than a decade. Yet in spite of their improvements, no one could realistically argue that these estates should not be demoted in any new classification.

Both Brane-Cantenac and Durfort-Vivens have provided far too many unexciting, often flawed wines. As much as I enjoy the company of Lucien Lurton, the proprietor, the wines from these two estates throughout the sixties and seventies were terribly inconsistent. Because of a more careful selection process, the eighties have been kinder to both Brane-Cantenac and Durfort-Vivens, but both properties would have difficulties holding on to their second-growth status in any quality-based reclassification.

Dauzac's wines have also made progress since the late eighties, as have those of Kirwan. Yet both of these properties, even allowing for their improvements, rarely produce wines that provide exciting drinking. Hopefully, the encouraging efforts of both properties in the mid-nineties will reverse their fortunes.

There are a handful of other classified-growth Margaux estates. The most promising estate is du Tertre, which since 1978 has been making excellent wine under the capable hand of Madame Denise Capbern-Gasqueton. Cantenac-Brown, the producer of rustic, tannic, hard wines that appeal to those with nineteenth-century tastes, may move into the twentieth century in terms of its wine style now that Jean-Michel Cazes of Lynch-Bages has been hired by the château's new proprietor, AXA, to oversee the winemaking. To date, the results have been mixed. Rauzan-Gassies can be good but leans toward a chunky, full-bodied St.-Estèphe style of wine rather than a true Margaux. Furthermore, the property is terribly inconsistent. Marquis d'Alesme-Becker, hardly known and rarely seen, produces a light wine.

Two other classified châteaux, Giscours and Marquis-de-Terme, can make some of the richest and longest-lived wines of the appellation. Giscours was a proven performer during the sixties and seventies but declined seriously in the eighties. Recent vintages of Giscours suggest this property might be about to rebound. However, a potential scandal in June 1998 may have serious repercussions for Giscours. In contrast, Marquis-de-Terme, off form during the sixties and seventies, began to make more interesting wine, among the richest of the appellation, starting with the 1983 vintage.

Among the Crus Bourgeois in Margaux, most observers would say that three properties consistently make the finest wine. Angludet, Labégorce-

Zédé, and Siran are very good estates making typically elegant, perfumed, aromatic wine. Labégorce-Zédé's wine tends to be the most robust and richest of this trio, Siran the most masculine and tannic, and Angludet the most supple and charming.

Finally, two major properties and classified growths to the south of Margaux's appellation borders both make excellent wine. La Lagune is one of my favorite wines. Brilliantly made, the wine can resemble both a Pomerol and a Burgundy, but it is always deliciously rich, round, fruity, and complex. The quality is very consistent and the price surprisingly reasonable. Cantemerle is the other treasure of the southern Médoc, and after an uneven period in the late seventies, Cantemerle has been making superb wine, with the 1983 and 1989 its crowning achievements. Both La Lagune and Cantemerle, no doubt because they are not in the famous Margaux appellation, are considerably undervalued in the scheme of Bordeaux wine pricing.

Vintages for Margaux and southern Margaux can often be vastly different from those for the communes of St.-Julien, Pauillac, and St.-Estèphe, which sit a good distance to the north. This is not a region in which to look for good wines in off vintages. The light soils seem to produce thin wines in rainy years, although there are always exceptions. Also, extremely torrid, drought-like summers without adequate rainfall tend to stress those vineyards with high plantations of Cabernet Sauvignon in well-drained gravelly beds, retarding the ripening process while at the same time roasting the grapes. This explains why 1982, 1989, and 1990 were less successful in Margaux than in the northern Médoc. The finest vintages for Margaux wines have been 1996, 1995, 1986, 1983, 1979, 1978, 1970, 1966, and 1961.

MARGAUX AND THE SOUTHERN MÉDOC
(An Insider's View)

Overall Appellation Potential: Average to Outstanding

The Most Potential for Aging: Château Margaux, Palmer, Rauzan-Ségla

The Most Elegant: Cantemerle, Malescot St.-Exupéry, Château Margaux, Palmer

The Most Concentrated: Château Margaux, Rauzan-Ségla

The Best Value: Angludet, Cantemerle, Dauzac, La Lagune, du Tertre

The Most Exotic: Palmer

The Most Difficult to Understand (when young): Rauzan-Ségla

The Most Underrated: La Lagune, Malescot St.-Exupéry, du Tertre

The Easiest to Appreciate Young: La Lagune, Palmer

Up-and-Coming Estates: Dauzac, Kirwan, Malescot St.-Exupéry

Greatest Recent Vintages: 1996, 1990, 1983, 1961

MARGAUX—AN OVERVIEW

Location: Margaux is the southernmost of the four principal Médoc appellations, lying on the left bank of the Gironde, 13 miles north of the city of Bordeaux

Acres under Vine: 3,350

Communes: Arsac, Cantenac, Labarde, Margaux, Soussans

Average Annual Production: 640,000 cases

Classified Growths: Total of 21: 10 in the commune of Margaux, 8 in the commune of Cantenac, 2 in the commune of Labarde, and 1 in the commune of Arsac; the appellation has 1 first-growth, 5 second-growths, 10 third-growths, 4 fourth-growths, and 2 fifth-growths; 25 Crus Bourgeois

Principal Grape Varieties: Cabernet Sauvignon dominates, followed by Merlot, Petit Verdot, and tiny quantities of Cabernet Franc

Principal Soil Type: As a general rule, this large and diverse commune has thin top soil, and the top vineyards, situated close to the river, have fine, gravelly soils not much different than those found in Pessac-Léognan. Further inland, more clay and sand are found.

A CONSUMER'S CLASSIFICATION OF THE CHÂTEAUX OF MARGAUX AND THE SOUTHERN MÉDOC

OUTSTANDING

Margaux
Palmer
Rauzan-Ségla (since 1983)

EXCELLENT

La Lagune
Malescot St.-Exupéry (since 1990)

VERY GOOD

Angludet, Cantemerle, Marquis-de-Terme,
Prieuré-Lichine, du Tertre

GOOD

Brane-Cantenac, Cantenac-Brown, Charmant, Dauzac, Durfort-Vivens,
Giscours, La Gurgue, Kirwan, Labégorce-Zédé, Larruau, Lascombes,
Marsac-Séguineau, Monbrison, Siran

OTHER NOTABLE MARGAUX AND SOUTHERN MÉDOC PROPERTIES
Château d'Arsac, Bel-Air Marquis d'Aligre, Boyd-Cantenac, Desmirail,
Deyrem-Valentin, Ferrière, La Galiane, Haut-Breton Larigaudière, d'Issan,
Labégorce, Marquis d'Alesme-Becker, Martinens, Mongravey,
Paveil-de-Luze, Pontac-Lynch, Pontet-Chappaz, Pouget, Rauzan-Gassies,
Tayac, La Tour de Bessan, La Tour-de-Mons, Trois Chardons,
Les Vimières-Le Tronquera

ANGLUDET　　　　　　　　　　　　　　　　　　　VERY GOOD

Classification: Cru Bourgeois in 1932
Location of vineyards: Cantenac and Arsac
Owner: Peter Sichel
Address: 33460 Cantenac
Mailing address: Same as above
Telephone: 33 5 57 88 71 41; telefax: 33 5 57 88 72 52
Visits: By appointment only
Contact: Marie Pierre or Benjamin Sichel

VINEYARDS (red)
Surface area: 79 acres
Average age of vines: 25 years
Blend: 55% Cabernet Sauvignon, 35% Merlot, 10% Petit Verdot
Density of plantation: 6,666 vines per hectare
Average yields (over the last 5 years): 46 hectoliters per hectare
Total average annual production: 14,000–15,000 cases

GRAND VIN (red)
Brand name: Château Angludet
Appellation: Margaux
Mean annual production: 120,000 bottles
Upbringing: Grapes are picked mechanically. Fermentations take place in
cement tanks at temperatures of 28–32 degrees centigrade and last 21–
40 days, depending upon the vintage. Wines are transferred to oak
barrels in December for 12 months (20% new oak) and are kept for a
further 5 months in tanks prior to bottling. They are fined but not filtered.

SECOND WINE
Brand name: La Ferme d'Angludet
Average annual production: 20,000 to 30,000 bottles

Evaluation of present classification: The quality equivalent of a Médoc
fifth-growth
Plateau of maturity: 6–18 years following the vintage

The late Peter A. Sichel, (he died in early 1998), was a multifaceted individual. He was not only a highly respected Bordeaux wine broker, but was the past president of the promotional arm of the Bordeaux wine industry, the Union des Grands Crus. He was also a part owner of the famous Margaux estate of Palmer, as well as proprietor of his own château and residence, Angludet.

Sichel purchased this property in 1961 when it was in deplorable condition, and had been solely responsible for taking the property, which sits in the southwestern corner of Margaux on what is called the plateau Le Grand Poujeau (shared by three Margaux estates, Giscours, du Tertre, and Angludet), from virtual post–World War II obscurity to international prominence. It is irrefutable that the wine made at Angludet frequently surpasses some of its more illustrious siblings in the Margaux appellation.

The history of the estate is old, even by Bordeaux standards, and can be traced back to the early fourteenth century. The estate's wines had a good reputation, and appear numerous times in wine references from the sixteenth through the eighteenth centuries, but by the time of the famous classification of 1855, the property was in bad condition—a reason often offered as to why it was excluded from that classification.

The wines of Angludet have gone from one strength to another since the early eighties. This coincides with the fact that so much of the vineyard was replanted in the early sixties. Today, the wine is clearly of classified-growth quality, yet the price has remained extremely modest. Vintages prior to 1978 are generally undistinguished, but since that time there have been some marvelous to excellent wines, including a superb 1983, and excellent wines in both 1986 and 1989.

VINTAGES

1997—Sichel's last vintage, 1997, promises to be exciting, as he fashioned one of
  •   the finest wines of the vintage. An impressively saturated black/purple color
87–   is followed by an excellent blackberry, cassis liqueur, toast, and floral-scented
89+   nose. In the mouth, this medium-bodied wine is quintessentially elegant,
       with excellent sweetness, extract, length, and, most important, impeccable
       harmony. This wine may merit an outstanding rating if it evolves in a positive
       manner in cask. This is an impressively made claret that offers noteworthy
       homage to its recently deceased proprietor. Anticipated maturity: 2002–2012.
       Last tasted, 3/98.

1996—A sleeper of the vintage, Angludet's 1996 reveals an opaque purple color, as
  •   well as a powerful, rich, black currant-scented nose with cedar, weedy to-
88–   bacco, licorice, and earth in the background. Dense, backward, and atypically
90   powerful and unevolved for a wine from this well-run château, this boldly
       made, tannic, yet impressively endowed wine will have a long lifeline. Antici-
       pated maturity: 2001–2015. Last tasted, 3/98.

1995—In contrast to the powerful, tannic 1996, the 1995 is a silky, supple, charming,
•   forthcoming wine that is well above its cru bourgeois classification. The color
88   is a healthy saturated deep ruby/purple, and the wine offers up gobs of
jammy black fruits intermixed with subtle herbs, spice, and toast. In the
mouth, the wine displays excellent richness, a layered, medium-bodied
personality, well-disguised tannin and acidity, and a hedonistic mouth-feel.
Anticipated maturity: Now–2010. A sleeper of the vintage. Last tasted,
11/97.

1994—The 1994 Angludet possesses attractive black currant fruit, but since bottling,
•   it appears to have gone into a shell, revealing hard, astringent tannin that
84?   dominates the wine's fragilely concentrated sweetness and ripeness. The wine
is medium bodied and spicy but very austere. Will it return to its pre-bottling
form? Last tasted, 1/97.

1993—This medium ruby-colored wine exhibits light body, obvious dilution, and
•   hard tannin, resulting in a disappointing effort from this normally capable
76   estate. Last tasted, 1/97.

1992—Much of Angludet's herb-tinged fruit did not survive the fining, filtering, and
•   bottling process. Light ruby with a washed-out hollowness, this is a surpris-
73   ingly feeble effort from this estate. Drink it over the next 3–4 years. Last
tasted, 11/94.

1991—The excessively weedy, light-bodied, shallow 1991 needs more stuffing and
•   character. Last tasted, 1/94.
74

1990—Angludet's 1990 rivals their 1989. More noticeably tannic than the 1989,
•   without that vintage's sweet fruit and opulence, the 1990 is nevertheless a
85   fine wine. It exhibits deep color, rich herbaceous fruit, medium body, and
plenty of substance in its finish. Anticipated maturity: Now–2005. Last
tasted, 1/93.

1989—The 1989 Angludet is one of this property's best wines since their excellent
•   1983. It does not, however, appear to have the stuffing necessary to surpass
87   that wine. It is fat, plump, intensely fruity with a good ruby color, supple
texture, high alcohol, and soft tannins. Anticipated maturity: Now–2002. Last
tasted, 4/91.

1988—The 1988 is a sinewy, surprisingly light wine, medium bodied, low in extract
•   levels and tannins, and exhibiting straightforward, solid, but unexciting fla-
81   vors. Anticipated maturity: Now. Last tasted, 4/91.

1987—This is a delicious wine that should be drunk up. It exhibits fine ripeness,
•   light to medium body, very soft tannins, and an easygoing, smooth finish. One
84   can easily detect that the Merlot in Angludet has given this vintage attractive,
charming suppleness and an easygoing character. Anticipated maturity: Now.
Last tasted, 11/90.

1986—Dark ruby, with an attractive oaky, plummy nose, and medium body, this is
•   an aggressively tannic Angludet that exhibits good flavor depth, yet needs to
86   be kept for several years before it will be ready to drink. Anticipated maturity:
Now–2000. Last tasted, 11/90.

1985—The 1985 Angludet lacks depth and seems to have a slight hole in its
•   mid-range. Otherwise, it has good color, a plummy, spicy, obvious bouquet,
83   soft, medium-bodied flavors, fine ripe berry fruit, and light tannins in the
      finish. Anticipated maturity: Now. Last tasted, 11/90.

1983—The 1983 has aged beautifully, and has now reached full maturity. The color
•   is a dark, murky garnet with some lightening at the edge. Atypically powerful
88   for Angludet, this wine possesses a rich licorice, fennel, blackberry and
      cassis-scented nose with earthy overtones. Rich, fleshy, and full bodied, this
      mouthfilling, chewy Angludet is impressive for its size, ripeness, and extract.
      Anticipated maturity: Now–2006. Last tasted, 8/97.

1982—This wine was drinkable when released and has managed to hang on to much of
•   its fruit. It is not going to improve and is best consumed over the next several
83   years. Round and supple, with light amber at the edge, this loosely built wine
      exhibits some of the ripeness of the vintage, slightly above average depth, and
      easy-going, simple flavors and finish. Never impressive (the 1983 is signifi-
      cantly better), the 1982 Angludet is a wine to drink up. Last tasted, 9/95.

1981—Medium ruby, with some amber at the edge, the relatively tightly knit nose
•   reluctantly gives up aromas of dusty earth, old barrels, and some crisp,
81   currany fruit. In the mouth, it has the leanness and compactness that typifies
      the 1981 vintage. Close to maturity and well made, this is a lighter-styled, yet
      pleasant Angludet. Anticipated maturity: Now. Last tasted, 11/90.

1978—Fully mature, with a big, spicy, rich, plummy bouquet, this solidly built,
•   relatively fat, intense Angludet has shed its tannins and should be consumed.
85   Anticipated maturity: Now–may be in decline. Last tasted, 11/90.

1975—I finally worked my way through all the bottles I purchased of this wine, and
•   I did not enjoy any of them. The last bottle confirmed what all the others had
70   suggested—this is a wine with excessive tannin, not enough fruit, and a
      hollow, emaciated style. The color is a dark garnet with some rust at the edge.
      The nose displays some promise with earthy incense and roasted herb aromas,
      but in the mouth, the coarse, mouth-searing tannin obliterates what fruit
      remains. This wine will only dry out over subsequent years. Anticipated
      maturity: Now. Last tasted, 10/97.

BOYD-CANTENAC

Classification: Third-growth in 1855
Location of vineyards: Cantenac
Owner: G.F.A. du Château Boyd-Cantenac
Address: 33460 Cantenac
Mailing address: Same as above
Telephone: 33 5 57 88 90 82 or 33 57 88 30 58;
telefax: 33 5 57 88 33 27
Visits: By appointment only
Contact: L. Guillemet

VINEYARDS (red)
Surface area: 42 acres
Average age of vines: 35 years
Blend: 66% Cabernet Sauvignon, 22% Merlot, 8% Petit Verdot, 4%
Cabernet Franc
Density of plantation: 10,000 vines per hectare
Average yields (over the last 5 years): 42 hectoliters per hectare

GRAND VIN (red)
Brand name: Château Boyd-Cantenac
Appellation: Margaux
Mean annual production: 5,000 to 6,000 cases
Upbringing: Grape picking is done both by hand and machine.
Fermentations and macerations are rather long and take place in
epoxy-coated cement vats. Wines are afterward aged in oak barrels,
50% of which are new. They are fined and filtered at the time of
bottling.

SECOND WINE
Brand name: La Tour Hassac
Average annual production: 1,000 to 2,500 cases, depending upon the
vintage

Evaluation of present classification: Should be downgraded to a Cru
Bourgeois
Plateau of maturity: 8–20 years following the vintage

This is a distressingly inconsistent estate that, unfortunately, no longer merits its rank as a third-growth. It, and the nearby Château Pouget, have been owned by the well-known Guillemet family since the early 1930s. The proprietor lives at Château Pouget since there is no official château at Boyd-Cantenac, and the wines are vinified and cellared in a warehouse adjoining Pouget. It has always been a mystery why these wines are not better. For every good vintage of Boyd-Cantenac, there seem to be several where the wine falls well short of expectations. Perhaps a stricter selection, utilization of more wine for the second label, and a higher percentage of new oak might result in more consistency in the cellars. I have often found the wine impressive prior to bottling, but a bit coarse and attenuated in tastings afterward. As a consequence, this wine is never on my purchasing list, and I suspect many strangers to Bordeaux often confuse it with the two better-known, and now better-made, wines with the word Cantenac as part of their name, Brane-Cantenac and Cantenac-Brown.

VINTAGES

1997—Although there is some density in this wine, it comes across as somewhat
• savage and rustic, with an excessive amount of tannin for its delicate fruit.
82– The color is a healthy dark ruby, and the wine reveals attractive aromatics,
85 but there is a ferocious tannin level, and none of the charm or opulence found
in the top 1997s. Last tasted, 3/98.

1990—A successful wine, the 1990 exhibits an impressive deep black/ruby color, a
• spicy, rich, jammy nose, ripe, rich flavors, medium to full body, and plenty of
86 tannin in the low acid finish. Anticipated maturity: Now–2008. Last tasted,
1/93.

1989—The 1989 is a thick, unctuous, heavyweight wine, low in acidity, but enor-
• mously rich, fruity, and full. It has high alcohol and plenty of tannin, so it
86 should age well, yet be drinkable early. Anticipated maturity: Now–2003.
Last tasted, 4/91.

1988—The 1988 has a problem, at least those samples I tasted did. The disturbing
• nail-polish aroma suggested something was wrong. Otherwise, it is an atypi-
? cally big, brawny, rustic-styled 1988. Judgment reserved. Last tasted, 4/91.

1986—For some reason, Boyd-Cantenac tends to be a hard, sometimes dull wine and
• the 1986 has these characteristics plus diluted flavors, no doubt caused by the
78 excessive vineyard yields, as well as a lenient selection process at the château.
This medium-bodied, rather tannic wine should be consumed early in its life
because of the lack of extract. Anticipated maturity: Now. Last tasted, 3/90.

1985—The 1985 Boyd-Cantenac exhibits good ruby color and has a sweet, tasty,
• plummy fruitiness, medium body, low acidity, and a dull finish. It is good, but
83 not exciting. Anticipated maturity: Now. Last tasted, 3/89.

1984—Quite light, thin, and insubstantial, the 1984 is barely acceptable. It should
• be drunk up. Anticipated maturity: Now–probably in serious decline. Last
70 tasted, 6/87.

1983—In this very good vintage, Boyd-Cantenac has turned in one of its better
• efforts. Dark ruby in color, with a full-blown, spicy, ripe plummy aroma,
87 rich, full-bodied, concentrated flavors, and plenty of tannin, this big, robust
Margaux has begun to shed some of its tannins, but still needs 5 years to
reach maturity. Anticipated maturity: Now–2010. Last tasted, 11/89.

1982—Virtually identical in quality to the 1983 Boyd-Cantenac, but styled differ-
• ently, the 1982 has a dark ruby color with a trace of amber, a rich, fragrant,
86 ripe black cherry bouquet, unctuous, fat, fleshy flavors, full body, and moderate tannins. Anticipated maturity: Now–2005. Last tasted, 1/90.

BRANE-CANTENAC   GOOD

Classification: Second-growth
Production: 30,000–35,000 cases
Grape varieties: 70% Cabernet Sauvignon, 15% Merlot, 13% Cabernet
Franc, 2% Petit Verdot

Secondary labels: Château Notton and Domaine de Fontarney
Vineyard size: 210 acres
Owner: Lucien Lurton
Time spent in barrels: 18–20 months
Average age of vines: 25 years

Evaluation of present classification: Should be downgraded to a Médoc
fifth-growth, although the quality since 1982 has improved
Plateau of maturity: 5–15 years following the vintage

Brane-Cantenac is owned by one of the most famous winemaking families in Bordeaux. Lucien Lurton and his wife live in the modest château whose viticultural history traces back to the early part of the eighteenth century. This property enjoyed an outstanding reputation in the early nineteenth century when the wines were made by the owner who named it, the Baron de Branne. Once the owner of the famous Pauillac estate now called Mouton-Rothschild, Baron de Branne was a highly respected viticulturist whose political connections were so formidable that Brane-Cantenac was rated a second-growth in the 1855 classification despite some skeptics who felt that the vineyards did not produce wines that merited such a high standing. Today, the huge Lurton family, which includes Lucien's brother André—who has considerable holdings in the Graves and Entre-Deux-Mers—and a family of ten children, qualifies as the largest winemaking family of the region.

One of the Médoc's largest properties, Brane-Cantenac's extensive vineyards lie west of the village of Cantenac and well inland from the Gironde River. Because of the property's large production and a very friendly and charming owner, Lucien Lurton, the wines of Brane-Cantenac have enjoyed a large measure of commercial success throughout the world. This has occurred notwithstanding a record of mediocrity that was particularly acute throughout the period 1967–1981. Curiously, most wine writers turned their heads in the other direction rather than point out what were obvious flaws in the makeup of Brane-Cantenac's wines during this era. The most prominent problems with Brane-Cantenac during this slump were the wines' excessive lightness and frequent distressing barnyard aromas. One can only speculate, but such flaws must have been caused by a lack of selection and sloppy, as well as unsanitary, management of the cellars.

However, Brane-Cantenac's inconsistent track record has improved since the early eighties. Even with this renewed level of quality, the wines of Brane-Cantenac are made in a forward, fruity, soft style that makes the wine easily appreciated when young. Recent vintages have been fully mature within 5–6 years after bottling.

VINTAGES

1995—The 1995 Brane-Cantenac exhibits a dark ruby/purple color, low acidity, good
• ripeness, medium body, and attractive earthy red fruits in the nose and
86 flavors. A short, noticeably tannic finish suggests this wine will live for 10–
12 years. It is a competent rather than exciting effort for the vintage. Last
tasted, 3/96.

1994—This medium deep ruby-colored wine exhibits a nose of scorched earth,
• roasted herbs, spice, and red currants. In the mouth, it reveals some of the
82? 1994 vintage's negative features, such as astringent tannin, and a lack of fat
and ripeness. Nevertheless, there is good fruit on the attack, moderate acidity,
and a dry, austere finish. Anticipated maturity: 2000–2008. Last tasted,
3/97.

1993—I rarely have the opportunity to taste Brane-Cantenac before it is bottled. The
• 1993 cask sample revealed a high acid, hollow, diluted wine with herb-tinged,
72 washed-out fruit, and a medium-bodied, extremely tannic style. Last tasted,
11/94.

1990—A strong effort for Brane-Cantenac, this dark ruby-colored wine exhibits a
• sweet, jammy black cherry and currant nose intermingled with scents of herbs
86 and earth. This medium-bodied wine displays the ripeness, low acidity, and
fleshiness of the dry, hot growing season that shaped the 1990 vintage. Already accessible, it can be drunk with some pleasure. Anticipated maturity:
Now–2008. Last tasted, 3/97.

1989—I found the 1989 Brane-Cantenac to be similar to their 1982, only higher in
• alcohol and lower in acidity, with a loosely structured yet powerful, concen-
88 trated, fruity taste. Lots of new oak has given the wine much needed form and
focus. Although lacking in finesse, this wine offers a big, succulent mouthful
of juicy fruit along with a blast of alcohol in the finish. Anticipated maturity:
Now–2004. Last tasted, 1/93.

1988—Dark ruby-colored, the 1988 is intensely herbaceous, suggesting that the
• Cabernet Sauvignon was harvested too early. Medium bodied and lacking
77 concentration and class, it is another undistinguished effort from this
perennial underachiever. Drink it over the next 3–4 years. Last tasted,
1/93.

1986—The 1986 has wonderful opulence and fatness that is surprising to see,
• particularly in view of the tannic style of many of the 1986 Médocs. However,
88 there is no doubting its ability to age well, as it has plenty of tannin. This
full-bodied, impressive Brane-Cantenac displays loads of ripeness and is
deep and long on the palate with excellent balance. Along with the 1983, this
is one of the two best wines produced at the property since the 1961. Anticipated maturity: Now–2008. Last tasted, 10/90.

1985—The 1985 Brane-Cantenac, made in a succulent, forward, sweet, seductive
• style is oozing with scents of oak and velvety, super-ripe fruit. One might
87 argue that more grip and tannin could be expected, but the style of the
1985 vintage is well delineated in this attractive, precocious, tasty wine.
Anticipated maturity: Now. Last tasted, 10/90.

1984—Light to medium ruby, very spicy and herbaceous, but fruity, soft, and ideal
•   for near-term drinking. Anticipated maturity: Now. Last tasted, 11/89.
73

1983—Forward, seductive, and flavorful, the 1983 Brane-Cantenac has a fragrant,
•   plummy, coffee-and-chocolate-scented bouquet, a sweet, savory, round tex-
89   ture, light to moderate tannins, and a long, heady finish. Delicious and
       generously flavored, this wine has developed quickly, but should continue to
       evolve for another decade. Anticipated maturity: Now–1999. Last tasted,
       2/91.

1982—Except for the rather fecal, manure-like aromas, this wine offers fully mature,
•   herb-tinged, sweet, jammy fruit in a medium-bodied, smooth and supple
76   format. With airing, the nose becomes less objectionable, but this is not a
       clean wine. It is too funky and off-putting to evoke much excitement despite
       its soft, plush personality. Last tasted, 9/95.

1981—This is a charming, soft, fruity, straightforward wine, with medium body and
•   a clean, undistinguished finish. Anticipated maturity: Now–may be in de-
82   cline. Last tasted, 6/87.

1980—Light with an innocuous, faintly fruity aroma, this light-bodied wine has
•   shallow, yet clean, fruity flavors, and a short finish. Drink up. Anticipated
74   maturity: Now–probably in serious decline. Last tasted, 10/84.

1979—The 1979 is medium ruby, with an herbaceous, slightly dull, now washed-out
•   bouquet. Medium bodied and soft, the wine is beginning to dry out. Antici-
75   pated maturity: Now–may be in decline. Last tasted, 6/87.

1978—Made in a period when the wines of Brane-Cantenac were frequently disap-
•   pointing, the 1978 is a modest success. Medium ruby with a moderately
82   intense, berryish, earthy bouquet, very soft, round, plump flavors with little
       acidity or tannin present, this is one 1978 that is fully mature. Anticipated
       maturity: Now–probably in decline. Last tasted, 11/87.

1977—Light, faintly fruity, with shallow, somewhat herbaceous flavors, this medium-
•   bodied wine is medium ruby, with some tannin in the finish. Drink
67   up. Anticipated maturity: Now–probably in serious decline. Last tasted,
       4/81.

1976—Now fading and beginning to exhibit considerable brown at the edges, this
•   loosely knit wine lacks firmness, concentration, and structure. The round,
65   pleasant, soft, somewhat flabby, fruity flavors have become more unknit with
       the passage of time, and the barnyard dirtiness has become more pronounced.
       Drink it up. Anticipated maturity: Now–probably in serious decline. Last
       tasted, 11/87.

1975—Fully mature, the 1975 Brane-Cantenac has a generous, earthy, spicy, leath-
•   ery, mushroomlike bouquet, sweet, relatively soft, fruity flavors, medium body,
83   and adequate length. Anticipated maturity: Now–probably in serious decline.
       Last tasted, 11/87.

1971—Very dirty, barnyard smells predominate. On the palate, the wine is diffuse,
•   frail, very tannic and lean, weakly constituted, and just barely palatable.
62   Avoid. Last tasted, 3/84.

1970—After my first edition of *Bordeaux* I received several letters from readers
•   claiming that my ungenerous review of the 1970 Brane-Cantenac (I rated it
85?   65 and called it distressingly poor) was inconsistent with their tastings. I was
a participant in a Bordeaux tasting where the wine was served as part of a
horizontal tasting of the 1970 vintage. Two of the three bottles were deep ruby
in color, with a spicy, herbaceous, earthy scent (rather than the dirty barnyard
smell I described), and medium-bodied, with a soft, relatively concentrated
finish. Another bottle was not nearly as good as the other two but not nearly
as bad as the 1970 Brane-Cantenac I described in the 1985 edition of this
book. For whatever reason, there does appear to be a great deal of bottle
variation with this vintage; certainly the good examples are wines that merit
a score in the mid-eighties, the bad bottles are deplorable. Anticipated maturity: Now. Last tasted, 3/89.

CANTEMERLE

Classification: Fifth-growth in 1855
Location of vineyards: Macau-Ludon
Owner: S.M.A.B.T.P.
Address: 1, Chemin Guittot, 33460 Macau
Mailing address: c/o Château Cantemerle, 33460 Macau
Telephone: 33 5 57 97 02 82; telefax: 33 5 57 97 02 84
Visits: By appointment only
Contact: Ph. Dambrine

VINEYARDS (red)
Surface area: 165.5 acres
Average age of vines: 20 years
Blend: 40% Merlot, 40% Cabernet Sauvignon, 10% Cabernet Franc, 10%
Petit Verdot
Density of plantation: 9,600 vines per hectare
Average yields (over the last 5 years): 55 hectoliters per hectare
Total average annual production: 490,000 bottles

GRAND VIN (red)
Brand name: Château Cantemerle
Appellation: Haut-Médoc
Mean annual production: 280,000 bottles
Upbringing: Fermentations last 4–5 days (28–32 degrees centigrade) and
macerations around 30 days (25–27 degrees centigrade) in wooden tanks
of 175-hectoliters capacity. There are 2 pumping-overs daily. Twenty
percent of yield (Merlot) undergoes malolactics in oak barrels. Wines
are aged 12 months in oak barrels, 30% of which are new, in a

temperature-controlled cellar at 13–17 degrees centigrade. They are racked every 4 months, lightly fined with egg whites, assembled, and left to rest 2 months in vats. They remain unfiltered.

SECOND WINE
Brand name: Le Baron de Cantemerle
Average annual production: 200,000 bottles

Evaluation of present classification: Should be upgraded to a third-growth
Plateau of maturity: 5–18 years following the vintage

The lovely château of Cantemerle, sitting amidst a heavily wooded park just adjacent to the famous D2 (the major route leading from Bordeaux to the Médoc) has a winemaking history that goes back to the late sixteenth century. For most of the current century the property was owned by the Dubos family, who established this property's reputation for gloriously fragrant, elegantly rendered wines. However, financial problems, along with family quarrels, led to the sale of Cantemerle in 1980 to a syndicate. In the seventies the property was allowed to deteriorate and the wine suffered in vintages after 1975. Since the syndicate's acquisition, Cantemerle has been completely renovated with new cellars, a new winemaking facility, a state-of-the-art tasting room, and, most important, a greater commitment to quality.

Prior to 1980 there was also considerable bottle variation, and in a number of vintages the wines suffered from old barrel smells and a lack of fruit. The 1983 and 1989 are the two best wines made to date under the new management. Quality should only increase, as the vineyard, which has been significantly replanted, comes of age. The style of Cantemerle is a rich, supple fruitiness, and intensely fragrant bouquet. Given the lighter soils of their vineyards and high percentage of Merlot, this will never be a blockbuster wine. Cantemerle at its best always possesses a degree of fragrance and precociousness that give undeniable early appeal. Because of the improvements made during the eighties, this property now deserves a higher ranking than in the 1855 classification.

VINTAGES

1996—A fine effort from Cantemerle, the deep ruby/purple-colored 1996 exhibits an
• excellent mulberry, jammy cranberry, and currant-scented nose with floral
87– characteristics and high quality vanillin. In the mouth, the wine reveals rich,
90 sweet, ripe fruit on the attack, fine density, moderate tannin, and obvious balance. It will require 5–6 years of cellaring. Anticipated maturity: 2004–2018. Last tasted, 3/98.

1995—The 1995 does not possess the depth of the 1996 and reveals a more evolved
•   medium ruby color that is already lightening at the edge. Peppery, herb-tinged
86   red currant fruit aromas are pleasant but uninspiring. This medium-bodied,
straightforward wine lacks the depth, dimension, and power of a top-flight
classified growth. It will be at its best between 2001–2010. Last tasted,
11/97.

1994—Deep ruby-colored with purple nuances, Cantemerle's 1994 offers sweet
•   berry fruit in the nose, along with new oak and weedy notes. In the
86   mouth, the wine reveals moderate concentration and good body for the
vintage, but a dry, angular personality with astringent tannin in the finish. It is a gamble whether this wine will ever shed enough tannin to
come into complete harmony, but it is well made, and may turn out to be
surprisingly attractive. Anticipated maturity: 2000–2008. Last tasted,
3/97.

1993—I only tasted this wine once. It revealed a deep, ruby/purple color, more new
•   oak than Cantemerle generally possesses, admirable quantities of rich cassis
87   fruit backing up considerable tannin and structure, and an inner core of
sweetness and ripeness. This is an elegant, slightly austere 1993 for drinking
between 2000–2010. Last tasted, 11/94.

1992—The deeply colored 1992 offers spicy, ripe fruit and olive aromas, a supple,
•   ripe, smooth as silk palate, and plenty of juicy, uncomplicated fruit in the
86   finish. An elegant wine, it should be drunk over the next 4–6 years. Last
tasted, 11/94.

1991—Cantemerle's innocuous 1991 is disappointingly weedy, light-bodied, and
•   short in the finish. It exhibits some soft fruit flavors, but lacks substance. Last
76   tasted, 1/94.

1990—The 1990 offers soft, seductive, fragrant aromas that are obvious and pleasing.
•   A medium-bodied wine, with lush fruit, soft tannins, low acidity, and a
86   charming finish, it is already drinking well. Anticipated maturity: Now–1999.
Last tasted, 1/93.

1989—I believe the 1989 Cantemerle is this estate's finest wine since their monu-
•   mental 1983, 1961, and 1953. This ruby/purple wine has an explosive bou-
91   quet of crushed blackberry fruit and violets, an opulent, lush texture bolstered
by good alcohol levels and soft tannins. Anticipated maturity: Now–2010.
Last tasted, 1/93.

1988—The 1988 Cantemerle possesses adequate hard, dry tannins, but unlike many
•   Médocs, there is sufficient fruit. The classy bouquet of black fruits, minerals,
86   and spices is hard to resist. Medium bodied and elegant, with plummy,
mineral, and herb flavors, this stylish wine should be at its best between now
and the end of the century. Last tasted, 1/93.

1986—For whatever reason, the 1986 is an uncommonly tannic, rather stern and
•   hard-edged Cantemerle that seems at odds with the amount of fruit in this
82   light, delicately styled wine. Perhaps this wine will age better than I suspect,
but the tannins appear overwhelming. Anticipated maturity: Now. Last tasted,
4/90.

1985—The 1985 is Cantemerle at its most polite, stylish, and understated. Supple,
• medium ruby in color, with an open-knit bouquet of raspberries and oak, it
85 tastes more akin to a Volnay than a Médoc. Anticipated maturity: Now. Last
tasted, 11/90.

1984—The 1984 is a success for the vintage. It is a fruity, medium-bodied, gracefully
• assembled wine that should now be consumed. Anticipated maturity: Now.
79 Last tasted, 3/89.

1983—The first vintage of Cantemerle to be made in the new cellars, the 1983 is
• special, and one of the finest wines of this vintage. The color remains dark
91 ruby/purple and the bouquet explodes from the glass with scents of ripe
plums, flowers, and oak. On the palate, this generous wine is supple, concentrated, extremely long in the finish, with soft tannins. This is Cantemerle's
lushest and ripest style of wine. It has aged at a glacial pace, much like two of
this vintage's other stars, Château Margaux and Château Palmer. Anticipated
maturity: Now–2005. Last tasted, 9/97.

1982—This wine has turned out better than I would have thought. It is loosely
• structured, soft, and easy-going, but lacking the concentration and opulent
86 texture that are hallmarks of the vintage's finest wines. It is revealing some
amber, but no other degradation in the color or aromatics. The sweet, herb,
peppery, and berry-scented nose is followed by a friendly wine with round,
generous, medium-bodied flavors with no hard edges. Although it will not get
much better, it will drink well for another decade. It does not hold a candle
to the spectacular 1983, which remains gorgeously rich, young, and superconcentrated. Last tasted, 9/95.

1981—The 1981 has a ruby color, a pronounced vanillin, oaky component, a ripe
• cassis, fruity taste, moderate tannin, and a decent finish. This is a good, yet
82 relatively lean, compact wine. Anticipated maturity: Now. Last tasted, 1/89.

1979—Surprisingly ready to drink, Cantemerle's 1979 is charmingly fruity, soft,
• pleasant, and round but seems to lack grip and length. Anticipated maturity:
82 Now–may be in decline. Last tasted, 2/83.

1978—Medium dark ruby with some amber at the edge, the 1978 has begun to
• develop a musty, old-barrel aroma that detracts from the otherwise cedary,
81 spicy, black fruit character. In the mouth, there is a sense of fatness. The
astringent tannins in the finish suggest that perhaps there is not enough
fruit for the amount of tannin. Anticipated maturity: Now. Last tasted,
8/88.

1976—Unfortunately, the 1976 Cantemerle is in decline, exhibiting a brownish color
• and pale, weak, washed-out flavors that taste cooked and highly chaptalized.
60 Coming apart at the seams, this is a wine to drink up quickly. Last tasted,
4/84.

1975—The 1975 is still remarkably hard, tannic, and tough. Rustic, full bodied, and
• muscular on the palate, the wine exhibits plenty of concentration, but the
84 astringent, even severe tannins of the 1975 vintage continue to give rise to
doubts about how well this wine is evolving. Anticipated maturity: Now–
2005. Last tasted, 1/88.

1971—The 1971 has been fully mature for over a decade. Medium ruby with some
  •　　amber/orange color at the edges, this wine has a light-intensity, fragrant
  83　　bouquet suggestive of berry fruit and oak. On the palate, the flavors reveal
　　　adequate fruit and concentration, but the acidity is a bit sharp in the finish.
　　　Drink up. Anticipated maturity: Now—probably in serious decline. Last
　　　tasted, 10/83.

1970—This wine continues to evolve beautifully and has turned out to be one of the
  •　　sleepers of the vintage. The fragrant bouquet of plums, fruitcake, cedar, and
  87　　spicy oak is followed by a medium-bodied, concentrated wine with gobs of
　　　fruit, excellent length, and overall balance. The wine appears to have just
　　　entered the plateau of maturity. This is undoubtedly the best Cantemerle
　　　made during the seventies. Anticipated maturity: Now. Last tasted, 2/89.

1961—Still superb—in fact, even better than when I last tasted it in 1984—the
  •　　1961 is impressively opaque dark ruby with only some amber/orange at the
  92　　edge. The huge bouquet of smoky, earthy, black currant fruit, spring flowers,
　　　leather, and plums is followed by a lush, full-bodied, concentrated wine with
　　　that taste of *sur-maturité* (over-ripeness) that frequently characterizes the
　　　great vintages in Bordeaux. Still loaded and in fabulous condition, this unctu-
　　　ous, opulently styled wine should continue to drink well. Anticipated matu-
　　　rity: Now—2000. Last tasted, 1/88.

ANCIENT VINTAGES

The 1959 (rated 89) is not far off the pace of the glorious 1961. Somewhat
lighter, but decadently fruity, expansive, and even sweet in the mouth, this wine
was drinking beautifully and displaying no signs of deterioration when tasted in
Bordeaux in 1987. The finest Cantemerle I have ever tasted, however, is the
1953 (rated 94 in November 1996). It exhibited all the seductive charm one
expects from a vintage that apparently drank well when released in the mid-
1950s and, where well stored, has continued to delight Bordeaux enthusiasts.
Not as deep in color as the 1959 or 1961, yet wonderfully sweet and generous in
the mouth, this hauntingly perfumed, classic example of Cantemerle must be
the best wine made at the property in the last 40 years, although I have high
hopes that the 1983 and 1989 may ultimately turn out to be nearly as good. I
know the 1949 (89 points; last tasted 6/97) very well, having purchased a case
at auction in 1990. It is a fully mature, sweet, very fragrant, light- to medium-
bodied wine. Elegant and delicate, it requires consumption.

CANTENAC-BROWN　　　　　　　　　　　　　　　　　　　　GOOD

Classification: Third-growth in 1855
Location of vineyards: Cantenac
Owner: AXA Millésimes
Address: 33460 Margaux

Mailing address: Same as above
Telephone: 33 5 57 88 81 81; telefax: 33 5 57 88 81 90
Visits: By appointment, weekdays and weekends
Contact: José Sanfins

VINEYARDS (red)
Surface area: 104 acres
Average age of vines: 30 years
Blend: 65% Cabernet Sauvignon, 25% Merlot, 10% Cabernet Franc
Density of plantation: 8,500 vines per hectare
Average yields (over the last 5 years): 45 hectoliters per hectare
Total average annual production: 20,000 cases

GRAND VIN (red)
Brand name: Château Cantenac-Brown
Appellation: Margaux
Mean annual production: 15,000 cases
Upbringing: Grape picking is done by hand. Fermentations last 15 days
in temperature-controlled stainless-steel vats. Wines are then aged in oak
barrels, 50% of which are new, for 12–15 months. They are fined and
filtered before bottling.

SECOND WINE
Brand name: Château Canuet
Average annual production: 5,000 cases

Evaluation of present classification: Should be downgraded to a
fifth-growth
Plateau of maturity: Prior to 1980, 10–20 years following the vintage;
since 1980, 5–15 years following the vintage

Cantenac-Brown has had a checkered recent history. Sold in 1968 by the
famous Bordelais Jean Lawton to the Du Vivier family, the property was sold
again in 1980 to the huge Cognac house Rémy-Martin. More recently, the
property was sold once again to the huge insurance conglomerate AXA. They
had the intelligence to put Jean-Michel Cazes and his brilliant team of
winemakers, led by Daniel Llose, in charge.

The vineyard is not among the best situated in the commune of Cantenac
and has traditionally produced relatively hard, tannic wines that were often
too burly and muscular. Under the new management, the direction has tried
to move toward wines that are softer and less robust. The results have been
mixed. This is a positive development, yet far too many recent vintages of
Cantenac-Brown still possess an excess of tannin as well as a dry, charmless

character. The sad truth is that many of the estate's new vintages will lose their fruit long before their tannins. More skeptical observers claim the vineyard, which sits on deep, gravelly soil, will never produce wines of great elegance.

Visitors to the region are well advised, if for photogenic reasons only, to follow the well-marked road (right before the village of Issan) that passes in front of this exceptional Victorian château with its striking red-brick and Tudor decor. It is one of the more impressive edifices in the Médoc yet stands out as distinctly un-French in appearance, resembling an oversize English manor house more than a French château.

VINTAGES

1997—I liked Cantenac-Brown's 1997, a blend of 65% Cabernet Sauvignon, 25%
•   Merlot, and 10% Cabernet Franc. Whether it is the estate's terroir or the
85–   winemaking style, Cantenac-Brown tends to be a stern, tannic wine, but
87   the softness of the 1997 vintage has given this effort plenty of charm and
       precociousness. The color is a dark ruby/purple, and the wine offers up sweet
       black raspberry/cassis fruit intermixed with licorice, underbrush, and oaky
       aromas. The wine is medium-bodied, with a supple texture, good purity, and
       a low acid, plump finish. It could turn out to be one of the better Cantenac-
       Browns from recent vintages, as well as a candidate for an upper eighty point
       rating if it continues to develop well. Anticipated maturity: 2000–2014. Last
       tasted, 3/98.

1996—I know AXA, the huge umbrella corporation that owns many Bordeaux châ-
•   teaux, and Jean-Michel Cazes, have not been happy with my reviews of
85–   Cantenac-Brown, but I find the wine too tough-textured, tannic, and dry.
87   Therefore, I am happy to say the 1996, while tannic, looks to be one of the
       better balanced efforts to emerge under the AXA administration. The color is
       a deep ruby/purple. The wine offers simple but pleasing aromas of black
       currants, licorice, and vanillin. In the mouth, it is medium to full bodied,
       powerful, muscular, somewhat foursquare, but mouth-filling, rich, and with
       the potential to move up in score if more complexity develops. Anticipated
       maturity: 2004–2015. Last tasted, 3/98.

1995—Although the 1995 reveals a good color, it has been consistently angular,
•   austere, and too tannic. This is a lean, spartan style of claret that is likely to
78   dry out before enough tannin melts away to reach a balance with the wine's
       fruit. Anticipated maturity: 2000–2010. Last tasted, 11/97.

1994—This extremely tannic, medium-bodied wine's proportion of fruit to tannin is
•   out of balance. The color is a healthy dark ruby with a purple hue, but I
79   cannot see the tannin falling away sufficiently to give this wine charm or
       appeal. Masochists may enjoy it more than I did. Last tasted, 1/97.

1993—Dark ruby colored, with a mushroomy, herbal nose, this lean, austere, fruitless
•   wine will become only more attenuated with cellaring. Avoid. Last tasted,
74   1/97.

1992—This dark ruby–colored, lean 1992 exhibits adequate concentration and
•　　　length, but the austere, forbiddingly tannic and astringent style assaults the
78　　palate. I cannot imagine this wine ever achieving a balance between fruit and
　　　structure. Drink it over the next 4–5 years. Last tasted, 11/94.

1991—Cantenac Brown's 1991 is typical for this property—a hard, austere, tough-
•　　　textured, mean wine that will have a tendency to dry out before the tannins
74　　soften. In spite of its impressive color, it is a hollow wine lacking charm and
　　　finesse. Last tasted, 1/94.

1990—Slightly more structured and richer than the 1989, the opulent 1990 may lack
•　　　some complexity, but it offers gobs of rich, expansive, concentrated fruit in a
87　　full-bodied format. I especially admire the big, dramatic bouquet of smoke
　　　and cassis. Anticipated maturity: Now–2003. Last tasted, 1/93.

1989—For those who like an affable style of wine that is easy to drink, the 1989
•　　　offers generous amounts of soft, easygoing black currant fruit, medium
85?　body, some hollowness, and a smooth finish. It is deceptively easy to drink,
　　　but essentially unexciting. Anticipated maturity: Now–2001. Last tasted,
　　　1/93.

1988—The 1988 Cantenac-Brown is attenuated, with an elevated level of tannin.
•　　　This spicy, medium-bodied wine is well made, but it is not as impressive as I
82　　originally believed. Anticipated maturity: Now–2000. Last tasted, 1/93.

1986—The 1986 displays both power and elegance in a medium- to full-bodied
•　　　format. The color is deep ruby, and on the palate, the wine exhibits classic
85　　black currant fruit, with a toasty, spicy oak component. This foursquare,
　　　somewhat monolithic wine does not lack tannin. Anticipated maturity: Now–
　　　2010. Last tasted, 9/89.

1983—A typical effort from Cantenac-Brown, this dark-colored, ripe, robust, rich,
•　　　full-bodied, coarsely structured wine has good concentration and plenty of
85　　power, but, as is so often the case with this wine, it lacks charm and finesse.
　　　Anticipated maturity: Now–2005. Last tasted, 1/89.

1982—Thirteen years of cellaring have not been kind to this wine, which has lost
•　　　what little fruit it once possessed. The color is a murky ruby/garnet, and the
77　　nose offers up earthy, old cellar, damp cardboard aromas. Some fruit is
　　　noticeable in the attack, but the wine quickly dries out to reveal severe tannin
　　　and an unpleasant astringency. It has no place to go but down. Despite the
　　　enormous investment in this château over recent years, I am not sure recent
　　　vintages of this wine are any better. What does that say about *terroir?* Last
　　　tasted, 9/95.

1970—Dense ruby in color, with a big, black currant, cinnamon, herb, leather, and
•　　　mineral bouquet, this massive wine has huge tannins that refuse to melt away.
86　　At nearly 20 years of age, the 1970 remains a muscular wine that is impres-
　　　sive only for power and toughness. Anticipated maturity: Now–2010. Last
　　　tasted, 3/88.

1966—This is a compact, muscular, firm wine, with a dusty, rather coarse texture,
•　　　some spice and leathery aromas, and medium to full body, but it is deficient
83　　in richness and just too acidic and austere. Anticipated maturity: Now–may
　　　be in decline. Last tasted, 4/80.

DAUZAC   GOOD

Classification: Fifth-growth in 1855
· Location of vineyards: Labarde
Owner: André Lurton
Address: 33460 Labarde
Mailing address: c/o Les Vignobles André Lurton, Château Bonnet,
33420 Grezillac
Telephone: 33 5 57 25 58 58; telefax: 33 5 57 74 98 59
Visits: No visits permitted

VINEYARDS (red)
Surface area: 111 acres
Average age of vines: 18–20 years
Blend: 58% Cabernet Sauvignon, 37% Merlot, 5% Cabernet Franc
Density of plantation: 10,000 vines per hectare

GRAND VIN (red)
Brand name: Château Dauzac
Appellation: Margaux
Upbringing: Grapes are hand-picked. Fermentations last 3 weeks in
temperature-controlled stainless-steel tanks. Wines are then aged for
12 months in oak barrels, 50%–80% of which are new, depending upon
the vintage. They are racked every 3 months, fined, and filtered prior to
bottling.
Production: 23,000 cases

SECOND WINE
Brand name: La Bastide Dauzac

Dauzac's impressive new winery is one of the first major classified growths
the visitor to the Médoc encounters after passing through Macau on the
famous D2 heading north. Significant improvements have been made since
1978, including the installation of stainless-steel fermentation tanks, an extensive program of new vineyard plantings, and the increased usage of new
oak barrels. A noteworthy improvement of the wine has also occurred, particularly since 1993. At present, André Lurton, the well-known proprietor of
numerous Bordeaux châteaux, particularly in Pessac-Léognan, has taken full
control of Dauzac, and the future looks promising.

VINTAGES

1997—In spite of an attractive dark ruby/purple color, this wine came across as
•   extremely tannic, with a sweet and sour combination of low acidity, high
84–   tannin, ripe fruit, and some abrasiveness. It is hard to know which compo-
85+?   nents will win out, but it is usually the tannin, so this may develop into a

compact, austere 1997—atypical in view of the overall personality of the vintage. Am I being too kind? Anticipated maturity: 2002–2011. Last tasted, 3/98.

1996 — An impressively saturated black/purple color characterizes this classic Médoc
•   (the wine is slightly angular and austere), which reveals rich, weedy, cassis
85–   fruit, spice, earth, and nuances of new oak. This medium-bodied, well-
87   endowed, slightly compressed wine should prove to be very good, possibly excellent. Anticipated maturity: 2004–2016. Last tasted, 3/98.

1995 — A broodingly backward, tannic, dark ruby-colored wine, Dauzac's 1995 bor-
•   ders on being too austere, but there is enough sweet black currant fruit, as
86+   well as medium body and a fleshy mid-palate to elicit enthusiasm. While this will never be a great claret, it is a well-made, competent Margaux that will age nicely. Anticipated maturity: 2003–2015. Last tasted, 11/97.

1994 — The excellent 1994 Dauzac is one of the finest wines this estate has produced
•   in years. The color is a healthy, dense, dark ruby/purple. The wine's nose
87   suggests smoked herbs, toast, black cherries, olives, and spice. Medium bodied, with excellent concentration and moderately high tannin, this is a pure, well-structured, concentrated wine that should unfold with another 5–7 years of cellaring. It will keep for 20 years. Last tasted, 3/96.

1993 — The 1993 marks the beginning of the qualitative turnaround for Dauzac. This
•   ruby/purple–colored wine possesses a sweet, rich nose of cassis, licorice, and
88   toasty oak. The wine is pure, impressively extracted, medium bodied, and moderately tannic and has excellent balance. This should be one 1993 that ages well for 20 years but has the requisite depth and ripeness of fruit to balance out the wine's structure. My instincts suggest this wine will be at its best between 2002 and 2020. Last tasted, 11/94.

1992 — The thin, disjointed 1992 is, to be diplomatic, uninteresting. Last tasted,
•   1/94.
73

1991 — The 1991 is empty and hollow, with one-dimensional fruit flavors and no
•   finish. Drink it over the next 3–4 years. Last tasted, 1/94.
72

1990 — The 1990 is hard, austere, malnourished, and disappointing, especially in the
•   context of a great vintage. Last tasted, 1/93.
74

1989 — The unstructured, diffuse, shockingly light 1989 has some pleasant jammy,
•   berry fruit in evidence, but little else. Soft and low in acidity, it should be
76   drunk over the next 4–7 years. Last tasted, 1/93.

1988 — The 1988 Dauzac has a deep color, medium body, and an attractive bouquet
•   of spicy, herbal, red currant fruitiness bolstered by the smell and taste of new
83   oak. Will the hard tannins in the finish melt away before the fruit fades? Anticipated maturity: Now–2000. Last tasted, 1/93.

1986 — This wine tastes closed and hard. It is difficult to find sufficient fruit necessary
•   for balance. The finish is short and attenuated. Anticipated maturity: Now.
76   Last tasted, 3/90.

1985—The 1985 Dauzac is a compact, ruby-colored wine that is tightly knit and
•   concentrated. I found little charm, complexity, or substance. This is not Cru
77   class quality. Anticipated maturity: Now. Last tasted, 3/89.

DURFORT-VIVENS   GOOD

Classification: Second-growth
Production: 8,000 cases
Blend: 82% Cabernet Sauvignon, 10% Cabernet Franc, 8% Merlot
Secondary label: Domaine de Curé-Bourse
Vineyard size: 49.4 acres
Proprietor: Lucien Lurton
Time spent in barrels: 20 months
Average age of vines: 23 years

Evaluation of present classification: Should be downgraded to a Médoc
fifth-growth
Plateau of maturity: 6–18 years following the vintage

This famous second-growth is owned by Lucien Lurton, also the renowned
proprietor of another famed second-growth in Margaux, Château Brane-
Cantenac. The vineyards of Durfort-Vivens should produce better wine. Perhaps it is unfair to blame Lurton for the miserable track record of
Durfort-Vivens between 1961 and 1981. However, the vineyards are now a
respectable age and are certainly well placed within the appellation. One
wonders if the high percentage of Cabernet Sauvignon (the highest of any
southern Médoc) gives the wine less charm and more toughness than is ideal.

Vintages since 1982 have exhibited improvement, but this still looks to be
a château where the winemaker and owner could use a wake-up call.

VINTAGES

1995—The 1995 reveals a dark ruby color with purple tints. It exhibits moderate
•   ripeness as well as black cherry scents intermingled with earth, olives, and
86   oak. Moderately tannic, with medium body, this should be a midweight,
       unobtrusive style of claret that will drink well for 10–12 years. Last tasted,
       3/96.
1989—The 1989 Durfort-Vivens has proven to be admirably concentrated, low in
•   acidity, tannic, meaty, and potentially very good. Anticipated maturity: Now–
86   2005. Last tasted, 1/93.
1988—Medium ruby, with a spicy, dusty, very herbaceous bouquet, the 1988 Durfort-
•   Vivens has an astringent, pervasive vegetal character. No doubt the Cabernet
76   Sauvignon was picked before it had attained maturity, resulting in a short,
       compact, and attenuated wine. Anticipated maturity: Now. Last tasted, 1/93.

1986—The 1986 has considerable tannin as well as an impressive deep ruby color.
•   Yet it does not possess the ripeness, sweetness, or depth of fruit necessary to
84   back up the tannins. It is a good wine, but lower yields could have resulted
in something special. Anticipated maturity: Now–2000. Last tasted, 4/90.

1985—The 1985 Durfort-Vivens has a deep ruby color and a fragrant, spicy, rich,
•   and intense bouquet of fruit, olives, and oak. On the palate, the wine has a
87   creamy richness, medium to full body, light tannins, but fine length. This is
one of the best examples of Durfort I have ever tasted. Anticipated maturity:
Now. Last tasted, 4/89.

1983—A well-balanced, admirably constructed, muscular wine, the 1983 Durfort
•   is leaner and more austere than many of its Margaux counterparts. It has
86   concentrated, ripe, rich fruitiness, plenty of aggressive tannins, and good
length. Anticipated maturity: Now–2005. Last tasted, 2/91.

1982—The 1982 must be among the most seductive wines this estate has recently
•   made. It boasts a big, lovely, ripe, rich, black currant bouquet, deep, supple,
87   concentrated flavors, a long finish, and adequate tannin for another 5–8 years
of cellaring. The 1982 marked a dramatic turnabout in the quality of this
estate's wines. Anticipated maturity: Now–2000. Last tasted, 1/90.

GISCOURS   GOOD

Classification: Third-growth in 1855
Location of vineyards: Labarde and Arsac
Owner: The G.F.A. du Château Giscours owns the land, and the main
shareholder is Nicolas Tari. Eric Albáda is the principal shareholder of
the S.A.E.C.G., which leases the vineyards from the G.F.A.
Address: 10, route de Giscours, 33460 Margaux
Mailing address: Same as above
Telephone: 33 5 57 97 09 09; telefax: 33 5 57 97 09 00
Visits: Every day, from 9 A.M. to noon, and 2 P.M. to 5 P.M.
Contact: Vincent Rey

VINEYARDS (red)
Surface area: 197.6 acres
Average age of vines: 25 years
Blend: 65% Cabernet Sauvignon, 30% Merlot, 5% Cabernet Franc
Density of plantation: 8,300 vines per hectare
Average yields (over the last 5 years): 49 hectoliters per hectare
Total average annual production: 3,900 hectoliters

GRAND VIN (red)
Brand name: Château Giscours
Appellation: Margaux
Mean annual production: 300,000 bottles

Upbringing: Grapes are picked manually and sorted as they come into the winery (on a conveyor belt). Fermentations and macerations last 2–3 weeks in temperature-controlled tanks. There are 2–3 pumping-overs daily, temperatures are kept around 25 degrees centigrade, and yeasts are added to help fermentations. Malolactics occur in tanks, and wines are then transferred (in December) into oak barrels for aging. The proportion of new oak used is usually 30%–40%. The wines are racked every 3 months and are aged for approximately 17 months. They are fined with egg whites and filtered prior to bottling.

SECOND WINE
Brand name: La Sirène de Giscours
Average annual production: 120,000 bottles

Evaluation of present classification: Should be maintained
Plateau of maturity: 6–20 years following the vintage

Giscours is a vast estate of over 600 acres (less than a third are under vine) in the most southern portion of the Margaux commune known as Labarde. The estate, once in deplorable condition, was rescued in 1952 by the Tari family and has experienced a resurgence in quality and prestige. Pierre Tari began to assume more control in 1970 and has become one of the leading spokespersons for Bordeaux. Until the late eighties he was president of Bordeaux's Union des Grands Crus, an association of châteaux banded together for one common cause: to promote the virtues of Bordeaux wines.

The imposing château of Giscours is one of the largest of the Médoc and well worth a visit. It is set in a beautiful park with many ancient trees. The style of wine produced has been excellent in the last few decades. Except for the slump in quality during much of the eighties (the wine tasted too overtly commercial, flabby, and soft), Giscours has been characterized by a deep, often opaque color, gobs of concentration, and a muscular and rich construction with plenty of tannin. Furthermore, Giscours's record in "off" vintages is far superior to most other renowned Bordeaux châteaux. Part of the reason for that may be the apparatus used at Giscours, which, in years when the grapes are not ripe, heats the incoming grapes to 60 degrees centigrade for 30–60 seconds in order to extract color and fruit. While this procedure has been scoffed at by other proprietors, Giscours's record in less than great years has been admirable. In 1990 Giscours became one of the first Médoc properties to use high-tech equipment that removed excess water from the grapes by the process of reverse osmosis.

Just prior to the deadline for this manuscript, Château Giscours was charged with fraudulent winemaking practices by a Bordeaux magistrate. In essence, the charges were: 1) wine from outside the Margaux appellation was blended with Château Giscours; 2) different vintages were blended together; 3) excess sugar was used in the fermentation of the wines; and 4) wood chips, which are dumped in the wine to impart the flavor of wood (an inexpensive way of precluding the purchase of new oak barrels in which to age the wine), were added to some of the wine. At the time of writing, these charges were being investigated by the government agency known as the Service de Fraud. The Château issued a statement saying that these practices may have been utilized for its second wine, but not for the grand vin, Château Giscours. All of this will play out in court, but it is unfortunate for the new administrator, Eric Albáda Jelgersma, who has been trying to resurrect the quality of Giscours to the level it attained in the seventies under the former proprietor, Pierre Tari.

Giscours had a relatively impeccable track record in the mid- and late seventies, and a mixed record in the eighties, and has been trying to rebound in the nineties. Because of these allegations, its reputation will undoubtedly suffer, regardless of the outcome of the indictments.

VINTAGES

1997—Forward, fat, and appealing, the dark purple-colored 1997 Giscours offers
•   plenty of floral, blackberry, and cassis fruit in its aromas and flavors. Medium
87–   bodied, with light tannin in the finish, and low acidity, this wine comes across
88   as a modern day version of the excellent 1979, only softer, and obviously much lower in acidity. It is an attractive, endearing style of Giscours to consume during its first 8–9 years of life. Last tasted, 3/98.

1996—This wine possesses a deep ruby color with purple hues, attractive density,
•   medium body, and spicy, black fruit, and weedy tobacco scents. Overall it is
84–   a mid-weight, foursquare, but pleasant wine that should drink well young and
86   keep for 8–10 years. Last tasted, 3/98.

1995—An easygoing claret with plenty of crowd appeal, this dark ruby-colored
•   1995 exhibits roasted herb, meaty, black currant, and cherry fruit scents.
85   Underbrush and herbaceousness are intertwined with ripe fruit on the palate of this medium-bodied, spicy, pleasant, soft wine with some tannin in the finish. It will be ready for prime time drinking after another 1–3 years of bottle age. Anticipated maturity: 2000–2010. Last tasted, 11/97.

1994—The 1994 was revealing an open-knit, disjointed, soft, fleshy character with-
•   out the depth I had anticipated. This spicy, commercially oriented wine will
86   provide uncomplicated, straightforward drinking for the next 10–12 years. Last tasted, 3/96.

1993—The 1993's plump, corpulent style is typical for Giscours. Possessing more
•   fat than most wines of the vintage, this chunky, straightforward, mouth-filling
85   claret reveals moderate tannin as well as fine ripeness, body, and fruit. It should drink well over the next 7–10 years. Last tasted, 11/94.

1992—The 1992 Giscours is noteworthy for its saturated dark ruby/purple color, big,
•   plummy, licorice-and-Asian spice–scented nose, round, concentrated, chewy
86   flavors, medium body, and heady, alcoholic finish. It is a plump, rich, concentrated wine for a 1992. Drink it over the next 7–8 years. Last tasted, 11/94.

1991—The deeply colored 1991 offers an exotic nose of black cherries, coffee,
•   chocolate, and cinnamon, fine depth, and a chewy, cassis richness to its
86   fruit. Supple, with low acidity and a plump, fleshy feel, this medium-bodied,
attractively made, well-endowed wine should drink well for 7–8 years. Last
tasted, 1/94.

1990—The robust, exotic, rich, full-bodied 1990 offers low acidity, plenty of tannin,
•   and excellent richness and fruit. Anticipated maturity: Now–2005. Last
86   tasted, 1/93.

1989—The 1989 Giscours is the first reassuringly fine wine made at this property
•   since the 1981. It exhibits a black/ruby color and a big, forceful bouquet of
87   overripe plums and licorice. In the mouth, the wine has the telltale succulent
character of the vintage, a chewy texture, excellent concentration, high alcohol, low acidity, and a very long, opulent finish. It should prove seductive and
heady to nearly everyone. Anticipated maturity: Now–2008. Last tasted, 1/93.

1988—The 1988 Giscours is an extremely overripe wine, with aromas of prunes,
•   peaches, and apricots. Loosely structured, sweet, and flabby, this plump wine
78   does not have the tannin necessary to give it grip. It should be drunk over the
next 4–5 years. Last tasted, 1/93.

1986—Cask samples of the 1986 Giscours consistently tasted awkward and dis-
•   jointed, and after three bottle tastings, I remain worried about this wine's
74   potential. There is plenty of ripe fruit, but the pervading impression is one of
raisiny overripeness rather than balance. Aromas of peaches, apricots, and
prunes are followed by a wine that displays abundant spicy new oak, extremely low acidity, and a loosely knit, alcoholic, commercial character. Given
the immense production of Giscours, one wonders if there should have been
a stricter selection. Disappointing. Anticipated maturity: Now. Last tasted,
1/91.

1985—During much of the eighties, most of the structure of Giscours was sacrificed
•   in favor of a lighter, fruitier, ready-to-drink wine. This is especially evident
84   with the 1985 and 1986 vintages. The 1985 is light, fruity, agreeable, and
charming but lacks grip and length. It will be short-lived. Anticipated maturity: Now. Last tasted, 1/90.

1984—Giscours always manages to come out on top in off years—remember how
•   good their 1980 turned out to be? The 1984 is round, very fruity, fat, and, for
83   lack of a better word—just tasty. Anticipated maturity: Now. Last tasted,
11/88.

1983—Giscours was not as successful as many other Margaux châteaux in this
•   vintage. Medium ruby, with a soft, fruity, silky texture, light tannins, and
86   medium body, the 1983 Giscours will evolve quickly, as the acidity is low,
the pH high, and the wine lacking tannin and great depth. Anticipated
maturity: Now. Last tasted, 11/88.

1982 —This fully mature wine continues to offer a mouth-filling concoction of glyc-
   •   erin, over-ripe black cherry and cassis fruit, full body, and plenty of hefty
   86   alcohol. There is little complexity or grip to this chewy, meaty Giscours.
           Drink it over the next 5–6 years. Last tasted, 9/95.

1981 —This wine has been fully mature for a number of years, yet it reveals no sign
   •   of drying out. The color is a deep garnet, with some amber at the edge. The
   86   nose offers up roasted herbs and sweet black berry and currant fruit along
           with earthy notes. This medium-bodied wine is somewhat compressed on the
           palate but is true to the elegant, narrowly built style of most 1981s. It will
           never resolve all of its tannin, so my advice is to drink it up. The wine has
           more fragrance than fruit and appears to be increasingly spice and structure
           driven as opposed to fruit driven. Anticipated maturity: Now. Last tasted,
           5/97.

1980 —This was an outstanding success for such a mediocre vintage. It had sweet,
   •   ripe fruit but has now begun to dry out. Originally one of the best wines of
   79   the vintage, it should have been consumed during its first decade of life. Last
           tasted, 12/88.

1979 —Many Bordeaux lovers tend to bypass the 1979 vintage. It was a cool year, and
   •   the wines were irregular, but there were a number of unqualified successes
   89   for the vintage, including Giscours. This wine has consistently given me
           considerable pleasure, yet it still has a surprising vitality and youthfulness.
           The color remains a deep, dark ruby, with some lightening at the edge. The
           nose offers up floral scents intermixed with aromas of licorice, truffles, cedar,
           and peppery black fruits. This medium-bodied wine possesses excellent,
           nearly outstanding, concentration. It has come a long way in resolving some
           of its tannic bite. Although it will never be exceptional, this has been a
           consistently excellent wine that is still improving. Anticipated maturity:
           Now–2005. Last tasted, 10/97.

1978 —One of the unqualified successes of the vintage, and probably one of the two
   •   or three finest wines made from the Margaux appellation, the 1978 Giscours
   90   continues to offer delicious drinking. The color is a healthy, nearly opaque
           dark garnet. The wine reveals a fragrant bouquet of cedar, dried herbs, black
           fruits, earth, and spice. Medium bodied, with outstanding concentration, a
           sweet midpalate, and enough acidity to provide focus, this spicy, surprisingly
           rich as well as ripe 1978 continues to age marvelously well in the bottle. It is
           fully mature but capable of lasting. Anticipated maturity: Now–2008. Last
           tasted, 10/97.

1976 —Always one of my favorite 1976s, Giscours produced a deeply colored, plump,
   •   quite round, and generously fruity wine, with medium to full body and a lush
   81   texture. The wine has been fully mature for over a decade, yet when last
           tasted from a magnum, it was still delicious and plump. Drink up. Anticipated
           maturity: Now. Last tasted, 5/87.

1975 —The 1975 Giscours is one of the outstanding successes for the vintage. Close
   •   to full maturity, it exhibits a powerful, well-balanced style. The color remains
   92   a healthy dark garnet. The wine possesses rich, concentrated fruit, full body,

admirable ripeness, and an overall sense of balance despite strong tannin in the finish. This thick, rich Giscours may be the finest wine made between 1970 and 1994. It will continue to drink well for another 15+ years. Should readers see this wine at auction, it will probably sell for a low price. It is a classic, topflight 1975. Last tasted, 12/95.

1971—An impressively dark-colored wine for the vintage, the 1971 Giscours is
•   rather robust and chunky but lacking in polish and finesse. It makes a big
84   palate impression with its dusty, ripe, substantial fruit and weight, but it finishes coarsely. This is a brawny, oafish example of Giscours that is unlikely ever to come into harmony. Anticipated maturity: Now. Last tasted, 1/87.

1970—The 1970 Giscours continues to offer a large-scaled, spicy, licorice, earth,
•   cedar, curranty, and leathery nose backed up by muscular, full-bodied, tannic
88   flavors. This fully mature, fleshy, distinctive wine is unlikely ever to completely shed its tannin, but there is good size, fine ripeness, and an overall sense of balance. It is one of the better efforts from Giscours. Last tasted, 6/96.

1966—Since the last time I tasted this wine in 1984 it has nearly collapsed. The
•   dark ruby/amber at the edge has changed to medium ruby, with plenty of rust.
74   The wine's nose has begun to dry out, displaying old barrel and herbaceous, musty, fruit flavors. In the mouth, the wine is high in acidity and tannins and has lost nearly all of its fruit. This was once a wonderfully supple, big, tasty, corpulent wine, but it has now gone into serious decline. Last tasted, 1/91.

1962—Like the 1966 and 1967, this wine is past its prime. However, the bouquet
•   still exhibits spicy, floral-scented, ripe fruit. In the mouth, the wine lacks the
80   plump, rich fruity character of other Giscours and tails off in the finish. Anticipated maturity: Now—probably in serious decline. Last tasted, 1/81.

1961—This wine has held up nicely despite having been fully mature for well over
•   15 years. The color has lightened into a medium dusty ruby, but the rich, full,
87   earthy, superripe, curranty bouquet is still lively and penetrating. In the mouth, the wine has the foursquare, beefy, chunky character that often characterizes Giscours and a certain tarry, slightly oxidized character, but it finishes with plenty of richness and a heady alcohol content. This wine requires immediate consumption. Last tasted, 1/91.

ISSAN

Classification: Third-growth in 1855
Location of vineyards: Cantenac
Owner: Madame Emmanuel Cruse
Address: 33460 Cantenac
Mailing address: Same as above
Telephone: 33 5 57 88 35 91; telefax: 33 5 57 88 74 24
Visits: By appointment only, from September 15 to June 15, between
10:30 A.M. and 12:30 P.M., and 2 P.M. and 6 P.M.
Contact: Lionel Cruse

VINEYARDS (red)
Surface area: 74 acres
Average age of vines: approximately 25 years
Blend: 70% Cabernet Sauvignon, 30% Merlot
Density of plantation: 8,500 vines per hectare
Average yields (over the last 5 years): 45 hectoliters per hectare
Total average annual production: 150,000 bottles

GRAND VIN (red)
Brand name: Château d'Issan
Appellation: Margaux
Mean annual production: 125,000 bottles
Upbringing: Fermentations last 6 days, macerations 18–21 days,
depending upon the vintage. Wines are transferred, after malolactics, to
oak barrels, of which 35% are new, for 16 months aging. They are fined
but not filtered before bottling.

SECOND WINE
Brand name: Blason d'Issan
Average annual production: 25,000–40,000 bottles depending upon the
vintage

Evaluation of present classification: Should be downgraded to at least a
fifth-growth
Plateau of maturity: 5–15 years following the vintage
Château d'Issan also produces 70,000 bottles of Château de Candale
(Haut-Médoc) from 27.5 acres of vines; and 70,000 bottles of Moulin
d'Issan (Bordeaux Supérieur) from 27.5 acres of vines

The seventeenth-century Château d'Issan is one of the most strikingly beautiful estates in the Médoc. It is surrounded by a moat and has a Sleeping Beauty castle ambience. Since 1945 d'Issan has been owned by the famous Cruse family of Bordeaux, which exclusively controlled the marketing of this wine through their *négociant* business. Now the wine is freely sold to all *négociants* in Bordeaux. Undoubtedly the quality has improved, but I have had too many indifferent experiences.

When good (the 1900 is considered one of the greatest wines ever made in Bordeaux), d'Issan is prized for its soft yet delicate character and provocative perfume. Finding a d'Issan today with such characteristics is no easy task. The best recent vintages have been the 1996, 1995, and 1983.

Most vintages of d'Issan can be drunk at an extremely early age yet have the ability to last. At present, the property does not merit its status as a third-growth and objectively should be downgraded.

VINTAGES

1996—Perhaps a breakthrough effort for this beautiful, moated château in the
 •   Margaux appellation, the 1996 has fleshed out and put on more weight
87–   without losing any of its quintessentially elegant, finesse-styled charac-
89   ter. The wine exhibits a deep purple color, and a pretty, cherry, cassis,
      and floral-scented nose with subtle new oak in the background. In the
      mouth, there is an ephemeral lightness, yet wonderfully intense fruit, ex-
      cellent purity, and a graceful, stylish personality. This wine is intense, yet
      at the same time delicate. Anticipated maturity: 2002–2015. Last tasted,
      3/98.

1995—An excellent d'Issan, with more noticeable tannin than the 1996, the 1995
 •   possesses a deep ruby color, an excellent spicy, weedy, licorice, and black
87   currant-scented nose, sweet fruit on the attack, and very good purity, ripeness,
      and overall balance. The wine is well made and more backward than the
      1996, even though I suspect the latter wine has more tannin. Anticipated
      maturity: 2003–2014. Last tasted, 11/97.

1994—D'Issan's 1994 is a medium-bodied, moderately endowed wine with elegance,
 •   charm, crisp acidity, and a sense of compactness and compression. Some
84   obtrusive tannin in the finish may be a problem in 7–8 years, as this wine
      does not appear to possess the necessary richness to balance out the structural
      components. It does offer charm and elegance in a light- to medium-bodied
      style. Drink it over the next 10–12 years. Last tasted, 3/96.

1993—This light-bodied, vegetal, one-dimensional wine lacks concentration and is
 •   devoid of fruit and charm in the finish. Last tasted, 11/94.
73

1990—The 1990 d'Issan is a lighter-bodied, fragrant wine with medium ruby color,
 •   spicy, sweet berry scents, medium body, moderate tannin, and decent concen-
85   tration. Tasty and supple in a lighter, more delicate style, it should have 10–
      15 years of positive evolution in the bottle. Last tasted, 3/95.

1989—D'Issan is normally a light, delicate wine, so it is foolish to expect a
 •   powerful or blockbuster wine. Even so, lightness has its limits. The 1989
83   provides a fruity, straightforward, smooth, agreeable glass of wine, but
      there are Bordeaux Supérieurs that offer the same characteristics. It is
      ripe, but low in acidity. Anticipated maturity: Now–2002. Last tasted,
      3/95.

1988—The 1988 is unacceptably light, sinewy, and lacking fruit. Moreover, this
 •   medium-bodied wine has excessive acidity and tannin. D'Issan is normally a
75   light, delicate wine, so it is foolish to expect the power of a blockbuster wine,
      but this is a disappointment. Last tasted, 3/95.

1986—This wine is exhibiting considerable amber and orange at the edges of its
 •   uninspiring medium ruby/garnet color. The nose offers up old cellar smells
77   intermixed with earth and spice. Some sweet, diluted Cabernet Sauvignon
      fruit is present in the wine's attack, but it falls off, revealing significant
      dilution and thinness. There is also astringent tannin in the wine's finish.
      This wine will continue to become more attenuated with cellaring. Antici-
      pated maturity: Now–2005. Last tasted, 3/95.

1985—Along with the 1983, the 1985 is the finest d'Issan produced during the
  •   eighties. The wine exhibits a more saturated color than the 1986, al-
 86   though some lightening is noticeable at the edge. The nose is all berry
      fruit, flowers, and sweet earth. This delicately styled, medium-bodied,
      fruity, soft, measured wine will not appeal to those preferring a fuller-flavored
      Bordeaux, but it is stylish and purely made and reveals riper fruit than
      most d'Issan vintages. Anticipated maturity: Now–2003. Last tasted,
      3/95.

1983—This wine has reached full maturity, as evidenced by the amber edge to its
  •   medium dark ruby/garnet color. The nose offers up copious quantities of
 87   sweet earth, red and black currant fruit, cedar, and herbs. A plump, atypically
      fleshy style of d'Issan, the 1983 is nicely concentrated, attractive, round, and
      ideal for current drinking. Readers should contrast this fully mature 1983
      d'Issan with the backward, powerful, superconcentrated 1983 Château Mar-
      gaux and 1983 Château Palmer. Anticipated maturity: Now–2005. Last
      tasted, 3/95.

1982—Light to medium ruby, with significant lightening at the edge, the 1982 d'Issan
  •   is fully mature. The wine offers smoky berry fruit in its modest aromatics.
 84   Light to medium bodied and soft, with some tannin and acidity but not much
      depth, this is a pleasant but essentially one-dimensional wine. Drink it over
      the next 5–7 years. Last tasted, 9/95.

1981—This wine is in danger of becoming more attenuated and losing so much fruit
  •   that the charm and light-bodied appeal will disappear. Nevertheless, there is
 82   still enough ripe berry and plummy fruit, but the wine does appear to be ever
      so slightly drying out in the finish. Anticipated maturity: Now. Last tasted,
      3/89.

1979—This wine has developed considerably over the last 4–5 years and now has
  •   an amber edge to its medium ruby color. The slightly herbaceous, moderately
 78   intense, oaky, berryish nose is pleasant but not complex. In the mouth, the
      wine is light to medium bodied, with some elegance, but it finishes short and
      a bit hard. Anticipated maturity: Now. Last tasted, 3/89.

1978—Along with the 1983, this is probably my favorite d'Issan in the last 20 years.
  •   It exhibits a medium dark ruby color, with only some amber at the edge. The
 86   floral, intensely ripe, spicy aroma is followed by a relatively rich, medium- to
      full-bodied, concentrated wine with excellent depth and as much length as
      one is likely to ever find in a d'Issan. The tannins have nearly melted away,
      and the wine is close to reaching full maturity. Anticipated maturity: Now–
      1999. Last tasted, 3/89.

1976—I had several very mature, somewhat fading examples of this wine in the early
  •   eighties, but when I tasted it in a Bordeaux restaurant in 1988, it seemed
 76   much better. It was quite ripe, and there was some browning to the color, but
      there was that super-mature, heady fruitiness of the best 1976s, plenty of
      alcohol, and a soft, lush finish. Perhaps there is considerable bottle variation,
      but my last experience with this wine was pleasant. Anticipated maturity:
      Now. Last tasted, 3/88.

1975—One of the few classified growths that can be drunk now, the 1975 d'Issan
• has a good, dark ruby color, a spicy, chewy, muscular texture, good ripeness
82 of fruit, and medium body, but it tastes somewhat dull. Anticipated maturity:
Now–probably in serious decline. Last tasted, 5/84.

1970—This wine has always been relatively tight and unforthcoming, yet it continues
• to show no signs of drying out or fading. It is a solidly built, tightly knit,
79 muscular d'Issan with good color, a dusty, almost coarse fruitiness, and some
rough tannins in the finish. I had expected this wine to display greater
evolution by now, but it seems to be suspended in time. My question has
always been whether the fruit would outlast the tannins, and I am beginning to think it will not. Anticipated maturity: Now–2000. Last tasted,
3/89.

KIRWAN   GOOD

Classification: Third-growth in 1855
Location of vineyards: Cantenac
Owner: Schröder and Schÿler S.A.
President: Jean-Henri Schÿler
Address: 33460 Cantenac, Margaux
Mailing address: Same as above
Telephone: 33 5 57 88 71 42; telefax: 33 5 57 88 77 62
Visits: On weekdays from 9:30 A.M. to 5:30 P.M., and by appointment only
during weekends
Contact: Nathalie Schÿler, telephone 33 5 57 88 71 00

VINEYARDS (red)
Surface area: 86.5 acres
Average age of vines: 23 years
Blend: 40% Cabernet Sauvignon, 30% Merlot, 20% Cabernet Franc,
10% Petit Verdot
Density of plantation: 10,000 vines per hectare (for half the vineyards)
and 7,000 vines per hectare (for the other half)
Average yields (over the last 5 years): 46 hectoliters per hectare
Total average annual production: 20,000 cases

GRAND VIN (red)
Brand name: Château Kirwan
Appellation: Margaux
Mean annual production: 16,000 cases
Upbringing: Grapes are entirely hand-picked. Fermentations occur in 29
temperature-controlled stainless-steel tanks of 110 hectoliters to 140
hectoliters capacity each. One-third of the yield goes into new barrels
and casks for malolactics and the rest remains in tanks. *Assemblage* is

done after malolactics, and all the wines are then aged for about 18 months in oak barrels, which are renewed by one-third at each vintage. They are fined and lightly filtered before bottling.

SECOND WINE
Brand name: Les Charmes de Kirwan
Average annual production: 4,000 cases

Evaluation of present classification: Should be downgraded to a fifth-growth
Plateau of maturity: 5–14 years following the vintage

NOTE: The harvest is always hand-picked. Green pruning, at the end of July, helps reduce yields. One-third of the vineyards is located on clay soil with a gravelly subsoil, and the rest is situated on the plateau of Cantenac, where the soil is gravelly and the subsoil clay. The surface area currently under vine has practically not changed since the 1855 classification.

Kirwan is another Margaux estate that would have a hard time holding its position in Bordeaux's 1855 classification should a reclassification take place. Like many other Margaux classified growths, Kirwan has not had a very distinguished track record. While I have been a longtime critic of Kirwan's wines, consistently finding them too light, dull, and bland to justify the lofty classification and price tag, quality has rebounded in the decade of the nineties.

While Kirwan used to be a light-bodied, compact, acidic Bordeaux, the impressive performances during the nineties, often in difficult vintages, suggest a wine with more color, flesh, body, and intensity. Prices have not yet caught up with Kirwan's new level of quality, so readers who complain about the extravagant prices fetched by most classified-growth Bordeaux châteaux should take another look at Kirwan.

VINTAGES

1997—The younger generation has made great improvements with this wine. The
•   1997 exhibits an impressively saturated dark purple color, as well as an
86–   elegant, sweet, moderately intense blackberry fruit and spice-scented bou-
87+   quet, medium body, moderate tannin, and very good length. Still youthful and less evolved than many wines of the vintage, it should drink well between 2003–2014. Last tasted, 3/98.

1996—The 1996 Kirwan appears to be very good, and, given this château's lack of
•   recognition in the international fine wine marketplace, it could be an excel-
86–   lent buy. There is an element of overripeness (the French call it *sur-maturité*,
88   and it has a far more positive connotation in French than English) of the

Cabernet Sauvignon in this full-bodied, tannic, unevolved, powerful, and intense wine. There is good density and thickness, as well as gobs of new oak. If all of this comes together (and there is no reason to think that it won't), this wine may merit an even higher score than suggested. In any event, it will not be a commercial, soft wine to drink in its youth as a decade of cellaring is warranted. Anticipated maturity: 2006–2025. Last tasted, 3/98.

1995—I downgraded this wine because of the aggressive new oak and vanillin that
• dominate the wine's personality. This dark ruby/purple-colored wine displays
85 sweet cranberry and jammy black currant fruit on the attack but narrows in the mouth with a compressed personality. Nevertheless, there is fine purity, medium body, and plenty of tannin. This 1995 will merit a higher score if it turns out the fruit is deep enough to absorb the wood. Anticipated maturity: 2002–2018. Last tasted, 11/97.

1994—The impressively dark ruby/purple–colored 1994 exhibits medium body, good
• richness, plenty of structure, medium weight, and an overall ripe, concen-
86 trated, well-balanced mouth-feel. Combining power and elegance in a pure style, it is a noteworthy effort for Kirwan. Last tasted, 3/96.

1993—Kirwan is a Margaux classified growth that is making noticeable improvement.
• The 1993 possesses a dense, ruby/purple color and straightforward, clean,
86 ripe aromas of black fruits, herbs, and new oak. With medium body and above average ripeness and concentration, this moderately tannic, well-made wine requires 5–6 years of cellaring; it will age well for 15+ years. Last tasted, 11/94.

1992—The 1992 Kirwan is a good effort from this perennial underachiever. The
• color is a dark ruby/purple. The nose offers up plenty of toasty new oak and
85 black cherries. With some fatness, low acidity, and ripe fruit, this medium-bodied wine may be the best Kirwan in years. Drink it over the next 7–8 years. Last tasted, 11/94.

1991—The light-bodied, medium ruby–colored 1991 exhibits a bouquet reminiscent
• of herbal tea. Its fragile constitution, low acidity, and disjointed feel suggest
77 it should be drunk over the next 3–4 years. Last tasted, 1/94.

1990—The 1990 is a finesse-styled, light-bodied, tannic wine with medium color
• saturation. Though it finishes short on the palate, it should evolve and, per-
78 haps, improve over the next 7–8 years. Last tasted, 1/93.

1989—I was disappointed that the 1989 did not excite me more. Elegant, charming,
• and soft, but lacking some intensity and character, it represents a good
83 short-term claret. Anticipated maturity: Now–1999. Last tasted, 4/91.

1988—The 1988 is shallow but cleanly made and vaguely fruity, with some hard
• tannins in the finish. Anticipated maturity: Now. Last tasted, 4/91.
79

1986—1986 is not the type of vintage in which Kirwan would have been expected to
• excel. Much more powerful, intense, and tannic than the stylish, elegant
85 1985, the 1986 is a rich, intense, full-bodied wine with plenty of tannin. It should prove to be the longest-lived Kirwan in decades. Anticipated maturity: Now. Last tasted, 3/89.

1985 — Made during a period where Kirwan was sending out mixed messages concern-
  •　ing its qualitative intentions, the 1985 has turned out to be a correct, competent
  85　wine. The color is medium ruby, with some lightening at the edge. The wine
exhibits a mature earth-, spice-, and red currant/cherry–scented nose. Some
new oak is noticeable on the attack of this medium-bodied, soft, straightforward
yet pleasant claret. Anticipated maturity: Now–2000. Last tasted, 3/97.

1983 — Undoubtedly the finest Kirwan made during the eighties, the 1983 exhibits a
  •　dark ruby/garnet color with some amber at the edge. The nose reveals inter-
  87　esting scents of smoked herbs, charcoal, black currants, and weedy tobacco.
This medium-bodied, rustic, corpulent style of Kirwan has plenty of body and
flesh. Rustic tannin in the finish should melt away with another 1–2 years of
bottle age. Fortunately this wine's fruit and vigor remain lively. Anticipated
maturity: Now–2005. Last tasted, 9/97.　　•

1982 — A rather loosely knit wine with very good color, jammy, grapy fruit, low
  •　acidity, and a lush, supple texture, this medium- to full-bodied wine has
  84　a precocious personality and a charming fruitiness; it will evolve rapidly.
Anticipated maturity: Now. Last tasted, 3/89.

ANCIENT VINTAGES

The vintages of the sixties and seventies (I have tasted almost every top
vintage of Kirwan) were mediocre. The only ancient vintage with which I have
experience is the 1865, which I rated 86 points in December 1995. It exhibited a "youthful" orange-tinged, dark garnet color. Sweet cedar combined
with smoky, earthy notes were impressive. The wine possessed remarkably
ripe fruit and surprising density, but harsh tannin in the finish. It was somewhat monolithic, but given its age and what appeared to be an authentic
bottle, its condition was remarkable.

LABÉGORCE-ZÉDÉ　　　　　　　　　　　　　　　　　GOOD

Classification: Cru Bourgeois
Location of vineyards: Margaux, Soussans, and on the plateau of Marsac
Owner: G.F.A. du Château Labégorce-Zédé
Manager: Luc Thienpont
Address: 33460 Margaux
Mailing address: B.P. 33, 33460 Margaux
Telephone: 33 5 57 88 71 31; telefax: 33 5 57 88 72 54
Visits: On weekdays, from 8 A.M. to noon, and 2 P.M. to 6 P.M.
Contact: Luc Thienpont

VINEYARDS (red)
Surface area: 69.2 acres
Average age of vines: 40 years

Blend: 50% Cabernet Sauvignon, 35% Merlot, 10% Cabernet Franc, 5% Petit Verdot
Density of plantation: 10,000 vines per hectare and 6,600 vines per hectare (for a quarter of the surface)
Average yields (over the last 5 years): 50 hectoliters per hectare approximately
Total average annual production: 1,400 hectoliters

GRAND VIN (red)
Brand name: Château Labégorce-Zédé
Appellation: Margaux
Mean annual production: 80,000–90,000 bottles
Upbringing: Fermentations last approximately 10 days and macerations 10–15 days in temperature-controlled concrete vats. Pumping-overs are done twice a day. Malolactics occur in oak barrels, and wines are aged 18 months in 50% new oak. They are fined, but there is no rule as to whether they are filtered or not.

SECOND WINE
Brand name: Domaine Zédé
Average annual production: 80,000 bottles

Evaluation of present classification: Should be maintained

The Belgian Thienpont family owns and manages Labégorce-Zédé, and like the wine of their famous Pomerol estate of Vieux-Château-Certan, this is traditionally made. Since 1979, when young Luc Thienpont took over, the quality increased. Labégorce-Zédé, with a plain, drab farmhouse and vineyards in both the communes of Soussans and Margaux, usually requires 5–6 years to reach maturity but can retain fruit and harmony for 5–10 more years in top vintages. I personally prefer the wines of Labégorce-Zédé to Labégorce, given the extra measure of perfume and richness often found in the former.

VINTAGES

1997—A lovely, well-made Cru Bourgeois Margaux, the 1997 Labégorce-Zédé possesses good ripeness, sweet licorice, Asian spice, cherry, and black currant fruit, medium body, and light tannin in the supple finish. Drink it over the next 7–8 years. Last tasted, 3/98.
• 86– 87

1996—This Margaux Cru Bourgeois has turned out a surprisingly powerful, medium- to full-bodied, spicy, earthy, deeply extracted wine that should evolve nicely for 12–15+ years. It may always possess a slightly austere component, but there is no doubting the wine's sweet, rich, Cabernet-based personality. Give it 2–3 years of cellaring, and drink it over the following 12–15; I would not be surprised to see it last even longer. Last tasted, 3/97.
• 86– 87

1992—This 1992 exhibits too little ripeness and fruit to support its ferociously tannic
•　　personality. It will dry out within 4–5 years. Last tasted, 11/94.
75

1991—The rusty, rosé color of the 1991 Labégorce immediately raises suspicions
•　　about its quality. A weedy, vegetal, tea-like nose confirms the lackluster
70　　quality of this thin, short, malnourished wine. Last tasted, 1/94.

1990—Similar to the 1989, but even richer and denser, the opaque-colored, lavishly
•　　rich, spicy, oaky 1990 exhibits excellent fruit and length. It is an authorita-
88　　tive, boldly flavored wine that should drink well for the next 10–15 years.
　　　Last tasted, 1/93.

1989—The dark-colored 1989 offers an intense aroma of plums and licorice. This
•　　full-bodied, large-scaled wine has layers of fruit, soft, ripe, abundant tannins,
87　　and an impressively long finish. Anticipated maturity: Now–2005. Last
　　　tasted, 1/93.

1988—Lacking substance and length, the 1988 Labégorce-Zédé possesses a slightly
•　　hollow, underripe character as well as excessively herbal, nearly vegetal
78　　flavors. Last tasted, 1/93.

1986—This wine displays a moderately intense, flowery, currant-scented bouquet,
•　　medium body, attractive fruitiness, and moderate tannins in the finish. It is
84　　not of the same quality as the 1985 or 1983, but it is certainly a stylish,
　　　medium-weight 1986. Anticipated maturity: Now. Last tasted, 4/91.

LA LAGUNE

Classification: Third-growth in 1855
Location of vineyards: Ludon Médoc
Owner: Jean-Michel and Alain Ducellier
Address: 81, avenue de l'Europe, 33290 Ludon Médoc
Mailing address: Same as above
Telephone: 33 5 57 88 82 77; telefax: 33 5 57 88 82 70
Visits: By appointment—for professionals of the wine trade only

VINEYARDS (red)
Surface area: 173 acres
Average age of vines: 30 years
Blend: 50% Cabernet Sauvignon, 20% Merlot, 20% Cabernet Franc,
10% Petit Verdot
Density of plantation: 6,500 vines per hectare
Average yields (over the last 5 years): 43 hectoliters per hectare
Total average annual production: 400,000 bottles

GRAND VIN (red)
Brand name: Château La Lagune
Appellation: Haut-Médoc

Mean annual production: 300,000 bottles
Upbringing: Fermentations are traditional (maceration of grapes with skins) and take place in temperature-controlled vats. Wines are aged 15 months in oak barrels, 75% of which are new. They are fined and filtered before bottling.

SECOND WINE
Brand name: Château Ludon Pomies Agassac
Average annual production: 100,000 bottles

Evaluation of present classification: Should be maintained

Plateau of Maturity: 5–20 years

La Lagune is one of Bordeaux's shining success stories. In the 1950s the property was so run-down that numerous potential buyers, including the late Alexis Lichine, scoffed at the herculean task of replanting the vineyards and rebuilding the winery to reestablish La Lagune as a truly representative member of Bordeaux's elite group of 1855 Cru Classé châteaux. In 1958 George Brunet, an entrepreneur, acquired the property and totally replanted the vineyard and constructed what today remains one of the more sophisticated wineries in the Médoc. Brunet did not stay long enough to reap the accolades from his massive investment in the property; he moved to Provence, where he built, and again sold, one of that area's best wineries, Château Vignelaure. He sold La Lagune in 1962 to the Ayala Champagne firm, which has continued to renovate and manage La Lagune with the same fervor and passion. Their most revolutionary concept (which has remained uncopied) was the construction of a series of pipelines from the vats to the barrel-aging cellars for transporting the wine without any exposure to air.

La Lagune is the very first classified growth encountered on the famous D2 road to the Médoc from Bordeaux. It is less than 10 miles from the city. The vineyard is set on very light, gravel-like, sandy soils not unlike those of the Graves appellation south of Bordeaux. La Lagune was also the first château to position a woman, the late Jeanne Boyrie, as manager of the estate in 1964. In the chauvinist world of Bordeaux, this was a revolutionary development. While she was never able to penetrate the inner circle of the male-dominated wine society, no one took lightly her stern, formidable, meticulous personality, as she was undoubtedly one of the most conscientious and competent managers in all of Bordeaux. Following her mother's death in November 1986, Jeanne Boyrie's daughter, Caroline Desvergnes, assumed the responsibilities for running this property.

The style of wine produced at La Lagune has been described as both Pomerol-like and Graves-like. One notable connoisseur has called it "very

Burgundian." All three of these descriptions have merit. It can be a rich, fleshy, solid wine, with sometimes an overpowering bouquet of vanillin oak (it is one of the only non-first-growths to use 100% new oak barrels in nearly every vintage) and black cherries. The wine of La Lagune is usually fully mature by the tenth year of life, but will certainly keep 15 or 20 years. The quality and strength of La Lagune have improved significantly since 1966. As the vineyard has gotten older, La Lagune has continued to emerge as one of the great—and surprisingly reasonably priced—wines of the Médoc. They have been particularly strong since 1976, so cost-conscious consumers should certainly make themselves aware of this impeccably made wine that, of all the top Bordeaux classified growths, is irrefutably the region's greatest value.

VINTAGES

1997— One of my favorite value picks among the classified growths, La Lagune has
• turned out a weedy, somewhat herbaceous 1997. Lean, spicy, and light bod-
82– ied, this wine tasted unimpressive on the two occasions I sampled it. Last
84 tasted, 3/98.

1996— Tannic and austere, yet amply endowed, the dark ruby/purple-colored 1996
• La Lagune exhibits spicy new oak, attractive berry, plum-like fruit, and
87– toughness on the palate. I was impressed by the way the wine developed in
89+ the glass. It possesses sweet fruit, and expands on the palate. This wine could
turn out to merit an even higher rating. Anticipated maturity: 2004–2020.
Last tasted, 3/98.

1995— La Lagune's seductively styled 1995 displays a dark ruby color, as well as
• copious amounts of black cherry, kirsch, and plum-like fruit nicely dosed
88 with high quality smoky, toasty oak. This medium-bodied, elegant, round,
generous, charming wine can be drunk young, or cellared for a decade or
more. Anticipated maturity: 2000–2012. Last tasted, 11/97.

1994— Although La Lagune has provided me with many reasonably priced, delicious
• wines, both the 1994 and 1995 were a bit diluted, suggesting the selection
85 should have been more severe. The 1994 reveals this estate's telltale, pronounced oakiness in the nose, but the rich, ripe, black cherry fruit that is
almost Burgundian in its personality does not appear sufficient to stand up to
the wood. On the palate, there is some elegance, decent acidity, and a green,
peppery quality to the fruit. The wine narrows out to a short finish. Drink it
over the next 7–8 years. Last tasted, 3/96.

1993— La Lagune possesses a sweetness and suppleness of fruit rarely found in 1993
• Médocs. There is a layered density and ripeness, an attractive plum, cherry,
87 and oaky nose, and a soft, rich, tannic finish. This medium-bodied wine
should prove to be a charming, generous, and elegant La Lagune for drinking
over the next 10–15 years. Last tasted, 11/94.

1992— From both cask and bottle, the 1992 La Lagune has revealed a charming
• soft, round, medium-bodied personality, some attractive herb, vanillin, and
85 berry-scented fruit, and no hard tannin. The wine's weakness is its shortness.

For drinking over the next 6–7 years, this is a fruity, charming style of wine. Last tasted, 11/94.

1991—La Lagune's 1991 is a firm, compact wine with a deep ruby/purple color,
•   toasty, black cherry aromas, and an austere, compact flavor profile. Although
81   it should last for 10–15 years, it is unlikely to develop much charm. Last tasted, 1/94.

1990—Like so many 1990s, this wine appears to have put on more weight and added
•   a dimension or two to its personality. The color is dense ruby, with no light-
90   ening at the edge. The sweet nose of grilled nuts, smoked herbs, sweet, lavishly ripe black currant fruit, and chocolate is followed by a gutsy, medium-bodied wine that is about as fleshy as La Lagune can be. While the wine does not have the intensity, fat, and power of the 1982 (the greatest La Lagune I have ever tasted), it is a gorgeously proportioned, velvety-textured, sweet, and expansive wine that is already drinking well. Anticipated maturity: Now–2010. Last tasted, 9/97.

1989—I have always enjoyed the 1989 La Lagune. At first I thought it was marginally
•   superior to the 1990, but they are essentially equivalent in quality, although
90   the 1989 possesses less fat and a more ruggedly tannic structure. The color is a healthy dark ruby, and the wine offers up a smoky, sweet vanillin, jammy berry-scented nose with aromas of weedy tobacco. The wine is medium bodied, with excellent purity and richness and gobs of red and black currant fruit nicely dosed with new oak. The wine's grip is more noticeable than in the 1990, and the finish is more attenuated but still impressively long. Interestingly, the 1990 seems more evolved (or at least more drinkable) than the more obviously tannic 1989. Anticipated maturity: Now–2012. Last tasted, 9/97.

1988—La Lagune's 1988 has a streak of herbaceousness and tart, aggressive tannins
•   that appear to have the upper hand in the wine's balance. Medium bodied, spicy,
85   and straightforward, it lacks the flesh and chewy opulence of top vintages of La Lagune, but it should prove to be long-lived. The question remains, Is there enough fruit? Anticipated maturity: Now–2005. Last tasted, 1/93.

1987—Fully mature, ripe, surprisingly round and charming, this medium-bodied
•   wine requires drinking. Anticipated maturity: Now. Last tasted, 12/89.
82

1986—This wine has not evolved as well as I originally predicted. It displays a deep
•   ruby color and aromas of roasted herbs, sweet vanillin, earth, and black
88   cherries. In the mouth, the wine is big boned, but I am not sure it has the requisite sweetness and ripeness of fruit to stand up to the boatload of tannin as well as the wine's structure. Nevertheless, this is a youthful, promising, but slightly more attenuated La Lagune than I would have predicted. The wine's clean but tannic finish suggests another 2 decades of longevity. The question is, Will it reach a perfect marriage among all its component parts? Anticipated maturity: 2000–2015. Last tasted, 9/97.

1985—For whatever reason, this wine has always been loosely knit and exhibited less
•   than stellar concentration and an open-knit, commercial style. It possesses a
86   moderately intense, sweet, red currant–scented nose intermingled with earth,

herbs, and spice. On the palate, the wine begins well but lacks the concentration and ripeness expected in a top estate in a very good vintage. Some acidity
and tannin are present in the finish, but this wine has reached full maturity.
It's good, but unexciting. Anticipated maturity: Now–2004. Last tasted, 9/97.

1984—Less attractive now than from the cask, the 1984 is medium ruby, very oaky
•   (too woody?), tough, and stern on the palate, with more tannin than fruit. I
74   would not gamble on this wine. Last tasted, 12/89.

1983—Following the monumental wine produced at La Lagune in 1982, it is easy to
•   overlook the 1983, which is a very good, rather than great, wine. The late
87   Madame Boyrie compared it with the 1981, but with more substance and
      vigor. I agree. It is dark ruby, with a full-bodied texture, rich plummy fruit,
      and moderate tannins present. It is just beginning to open up. Anticipated
      maturity: Now–2000. Last tasted, 12/89.

1982—A beautifully made wine, the 1982 is my favorite La Lagune of the last 20
•   years. Again, I misjudged the aging potential of this wine, thinking it would be
92   fully mature by the early nineties. It can be drunk, given its sweet fragrance of
      toasty oak and ripe black cherries and currants. However, it is exhibiting
      more tannin and structure than I would have imagined. It is a powerful,
      full-bodied La Lagune with super-concentration and a thick, juicy personality.
      There are no signs of color degradation. The wine has some tannin to shed,
      so another 1–2 years of cellaring would be beneficial, particularly where the
      wine has been stored under ideal conditions. It is a classic 1982 that appears
      to be a synthesis in style between a right bank Pomerol and a more austere
      Médoc. Complex and rich, as well as more structured than I initially believed,
      this wine should achieve full maturity by the end of the decade and last
      through the first 20 years of the next century. Last tasted, 9/95.

1981—Bottle variation at first seemed a problem, but recent tastings of this wine
•   have been consistent. The 1981 is a medium-bodied, spicy, plummy,
83   cherryish-flavored wine, with good extract, an appealing texture, and pleasant
      finish. It could use more flavor dimension and depth, as the wine is compact.
      Anticipated maturity: Now. Last tasted, 12/89.

1979—The 1979 La Lagune is still youthful, but it is opening up and revealing an
•   oaky, ripe plummy fruitiness, a moderately intense, spicy, vanillin aroma, and
84   a clean, somewhat lean, dry finish. This is a satisfying but unexciting La
      Lagune. Anticipated maturity: Now. Last tasted, 12/89.

1978—The 1978 La Lagune remains deep in color, with no sign of maturity. The
•   expansive bouquet suggests roasted nuts, plums, and fresh new oak. On the
88   palate, the wine is tannic but lush and silky, with oodles of fruit present. It
      has been slow to evolve and, at its age, still tastes young and vigorous.
      Anticipated maturity: Now–2005. Last tasted, 12/89.

1976—In a vintage that produced numerous frail, diluted, fragile wines, the 1976 La
•   Lagune is a firmly made, concentrated, successful wine. Now fully mature,
88   this medium to dark ruby wine, with only a trace of amber at the edge, has a
      full-blown bouquet of vanillin oak, grilled nuts, and ripe plums. On the
      palate, it has an elegant, stylish texture, medium to full body, expansive,

sweet, lush fruit, and a heady, but silky finish. Oh, how I wish I had bought more of this wine! Anticipated maturity: Now. Last tasted, 12/89.

1975— Will the fruit outlast the tannin? This firm, austere, tannic wine exhibits
•   spicy, vanilla-tinged oak and ripe fruit, a good attack, and a medium-bodied,
86   elegant personality. Approaching full maturity, it will keep for another 10–15 years. Last tasted, 12/95.

1971— Fully mature, with an open-knit, aromatic, complex bouquet of cedar wood
•   and ripe fruit, this medium-bodied wine is silky, lush, and seductively
85   round and fruity. Anticipated maturity: Now–may be in decline. Last tasted, 3/82.

1970— Still surprisingly firm, but, I believe, fully mature, the 1970 La Lagune
•   has dark ruby color, a big, plummy, woodsy, and mushroom-like bouquet,
87   full-bodied, deep, concentrated, berryish fruit flavors, good tannins, and a long finish. This is a fine La Lagune that falls just short of being outstanding. Anticipated maturity: Now–2000. Last tasted, 1/91 (from a magnum).

1967— One of the best 1967s, at its apogee by 1976, this wine has a soft, round,
•   Burgundian character, quite a complex bouquet of truffles, caramel, and
83   raspberry fruit, and little tannin. Anticipated maturity: Now–probably in serious decline. Last tasted, 1/80.

1966— Fully mature, the 1966 is supple and fleshy, with an attractive plummy
•   fruitiness, medium body, and a soft, easy finish. Anticipated maturity: Now–
84   probably in serious decline. Last tasted, 4/78.

1962— Tasted only once, the 1962 La Lagune was browning badly and was quite soft
•   on the palate, with dissipated, washed-out, fruity flavors. It seemed to be
55   clearly coming apart at the seams. Pass it by. Last tasted, 8/78.

1961— An unusual wine, very peppery and Rhône-like, with an odd medicinal nose,
•   disjointed flavors, and a hot, alcoholic finish. A strange style of La Lagune
60   made ostensibly from very young vines. Last tasted, 10/77.

LASCOMBES   GOOD

Classification: Second-growth in 1855
Location of vineyards: Margaux and Soussans
Owner: Société BASS
Address: 33460 Margaux
Mailing address: B.P. 4, 33460 Margaux
Telephone: 33 5 57 88 70 66; telefax: 33 5 57 88 72 17
Visits: By appointment only, every day, between 9 A.M. and noon, and 2 P.M. and 4:30 P.M., except during the first weekend of each month
Contact: Géraldine Platon

VINEYARDS (red)
Surface area: 123.5 acres for Château Lascombes and 81.5 acres for Château Segonnes

Average age of vines: 25 years
Blend: 50% Cabernet Sauvignon, 40% Merlot, 5% Cabernet Franc,
5% Petit Verdot
Density of plantation: 8,000–10,000 vines per hectare
Average yields (over the last 5 years): 48 hectoliters per hectare
for Château Lascombes and 57 hectoliters per hectare for Château
Segonnes
Total average annual production: 4,275 hectoliters

GRAND VIN (red)
Brand name: Château Lascombes
Appellation: Margaux
Mean annual production: 240,000 bottles
Upbringing: Grapes are picked manually. Fermentations last 8–10 days
in temperature-controlled vats, macerations 10–20 days, depending upon
the vintage. Wines are transferred rather early to oak barrels (30%–60%
of which are new) for 16–18 months aging. They are fined but not filtered
prior to bottling.

SECOND WINE
Brand name: Château Segonnes
Average annual production: 240,000 bottles

Evaluation of present classification: Should be downgraded to a
fourth-growth
Plateau of maturity: 6–20 years following the vintage

NOTE ON CHÂTEAU LASCOMBES AND CHÂTEAU SEGONNES: As owner of
Château Lascombes, Alexis Lichine used to seize every opportunity
to buy neighboring plots of vines when they were for sale. In the
seventies, the Société BASS bought this estate and maintained
the same policy until the château controlled 205 acres of vine in all.
In 1982 a strict selection, as well as an extensive tasting of the
wines coming from the different plots, made it obvious that the grand
vin usually originated from the initial 123 acres that composed
Château Lascombes, and that the second wine currently came from the
newest acquisitions. As from this date, the estate is considered to be
formed of two distinctive parts, Château Lascombes and Château
Segonnes. The newest vines (81.5 acres) attached to Château Segonnes
are a little younger than those of Château Lascombes (average age 20–25
years), but the percentage of each *cépage* is nearly identical in both
cases.

Lascombes is one of the largest estates in the Médoc. The vineyards are not contiguous but consist of more than 40 separate plots of vines spread throughout the Margaux appellation. Because of this, the harvest at Lascombes can be one of the most difficult to manage and may, in part, help explain why the wines can be inconsistent.

Lascombes's onetime popularity was no doubt a result of the herculean efforts made by the late Alexis Lichine, who owned the property between 1951 and 1971. He oversaw a thorough renovation of the wine cellars, as well as an aggressive plan of vineyard acquisition from surrounding properties. Because of Lichine's commitment to high-quality wines, a succession of very good vintages of wine from Lascombes resulted.

Since 1971, when Lichine sold Lascombes to the English firm of Bass Charrington, the quality and consistency of Lascombes dropped noticeably. However, most vintages from 1982 onward reflect a more serious commitment to quality wine. Nevertheless, a lot remains to be done. In the nineties, however, the estate began a far stricter selection, as well as some malolactic fermentations in barrel—all designed to improve the richness and quality of Lascombes. As of 1998 Lascombes is on the rebound, but the wines, while good, still have a long way to go in order to be considered among the best of Bordeaux.

VINTAGES

1997—This medium ruby-colored wine lacks color saturation, and appears to be
   • more angular and higher in acidity than other wines of the vintage. It does
   79– possess attractive, sweet, herb-tinged, cherry, and currant fruit presented in
   84 a light to medium-bodied, measured style. Anticipated maturity: 2000–2007.
   Last tasted, 3/98.

1996—This dark ruby-colored wine reveals sweet fruit on the attack, medium body,
   • moderate tannin, a compressed, monolithic style, and a short finish. I am
   80– giving it the benefit of the doubt for now, but there is not much to get excited
   83 about. Anticipated maturity: 2000–2010. Last tasted, 3/98.

1995—Far less impressive after bottling than it was from cask, this wine is now a
   • candidate for drying out given its hollow middle and hard, austere, angular
   79? finish. The color is medium ruby, the wine has moderate weight and sweet
   fruit in the nose and on the attack, but it closes down to reveal a tart, spartan
   personality. Anticipated maturity: 2000–2008. Last tasted, 11/97.

1994—I remember how impressed I was when I tasted this wine at the château
   • and at several subsequent tastings. Lamentably, all examples of the 1994
   ? Lascombes tasted since bottling have exhibited an unusual musty wood character that initially made me think the wines were corked. The wine, which
   had exhibited fine potential from cask, seems disjointed and, at least for now,
   plagued by unattractive nonfruit aromas that could be related to bad corks or
   badly cured barrels. Judgment reserved. Last tasted, 1/97.

1993—A soft, elegant, light- to medium-bodied wine, the 1993 offers clean, fresh,
•   red currant and cranberry scents and flavors. Crisp acidity gives the wine
85   vibrancy, but it is a wine to drink during its first 5–6 years of life. Last tasted,
      1/97.

1992—This wine's medium ruby color and ripe curranty fruit intertwined with scents
•   of cedar are initially pleasing, but the dilution is apparent in the mouth,
82   where the tannin and wood dominate the wine's meager fruit. Perhaps more
      depth will emerge with aging, but it appears this wine should be drunk over
      the next 4–5 years. Last tasted, 11/94.

1991—The 1991 is well made given the vintage's limitations. The color is a sound
•   medium ruby, and the nose offers up attractive spicy, vanillin, berrylike
82   aromas. The wine possesses good body and an attractive ripe fruitiness and
      suppleness. Drink it over the next 4–5 years. Last tasted, 1/94.

1990—Exhibiting good tannin, the exotic, orange-scented 1990 offers up ripe aromas
•   of tropical fruits, cassis, and new oak. Rich, medium to full bodied, with
86   excellent concentration, low acidity, and a velvety, even voluptuous mouth-
      feel, this wine should provide delicious drinking over the next 8–10 years.
      Last tasted, 1/93.

1989—Lascombes's 1989 has an aroma of roasted peanuts, something I have fre-
•   quently found in Grenache-based Châteauneuf du Papes. A muscular, tannic
85   wine, it has a powerful, rich, alcoholic finish. I would not be surprised to see
      this exuberantly styled wine turn out much better than my projected rating.
      Anticipated maturity: Now–2002. Last tasted, 4/91.

1988—Deep ruby/purple, with a moderately intense bouquet of cedar, plums, and
•   currants, the 1988 Lascombes is a spicy, robustly styled Margaux. Medium to
85   full bodied and well balanced, it is not as excessively tannic as many 1988
      Médocs tend to be. Anticipated maturity: Now–2002. Last tasted, 1/93.

1986—The 1986 has been on a downhill slide since I first tasted it and rated it 83.
•   The wine is diluted and weedy, with no intensity or concentration. At present
78   it exhibits a shallow garnet color, with considerable lightening at the edge.
      The nose is filled with aromas of roasted vegetables and washed-out red
      currant and cherry fruit. Earth, tannin, and acidity dominate this meagerly
      endowed wine. It has no place to go but down. Anticipated maturity: Now.
      Last tasted, 3/97.

1985—This wine needs to be consumed, as it reached full maturity within 5–6 years of
•   the vintage. The medium garnet color is already revealing significant rust. The
85   wine displays sweet berry fruit intermingled with roasted herbs, chocolate,
      smoke, and licorice scents and flavors. This medium-bodied, soft, round wine
      is not very concentrated, but it is attractive, relatively elegant, and in need of
      consumption. Robust tannin in the finish makes me think the wine may already
      be beginning to dry out. Anticipated maturity: Now. Last tasted, 3/97.

1983—Medium to dark ruby in color, with a rich, spicy, berrylike aroma of some
•   intensity, this fat, concentrated, smoothly textured wine has reached maturity.
87   It appears to be one of the best wines made at the property in over a decade.
      Anticipated maturity: Now–2000. Last tasted, 3/89.

1982—An open-knit, diffuse, but delicious, fragrant wine, the 1982 Lascombe is low
  •   in acidity and borders on being disjointed and over-ripe; but it still offers an
  87   expansive, flavorful mouthful of herb-tinged, berry fruit combined with scents
       of coffee, earth, and vanilla. Drink it over the next 4–5 years. Last tasted,
       9/95.

1981—The 1981 has a light to medium ruby/orange color with a simple, somewhat
  •   herbaceous aroma, modest, meagerly endowed flavors, and a short finish. The
  72   wine is losing its fruit and becoming more attenuated. Anticipated maturity:
       Now—may be in decline. Last tasted, 3/89.

1980—Green and vegetal with an annoyingly high acidity level and shallow, diffuse,
  •   washed-out flavors. Ignore. Last tasted, 8/83.
  60

1979—While the commune of Margaux seemed to have produced a number of fine
  •   wines in 1979 (like those from Margaux, Palmer, and Giscours), Lascombes
  76   has consistently tasted light and diluted. Moderately concentrated fruit,
       plenty of oak, and increasingly noticeable tannin and acidity all suggest
       trouble ahead. Anticipated maturity: Now. Last tasted, 3/89.

1978—Surprisingly green (even vegetal), lean, and acidic without any of the plump,
  •   round, generous, ripe, rich fruit that is one of the landmarks of this vintage,
  76   the 1978 Lascombes lacks depth and richness and seems quite mediocre
       given the high quality of the vintage. Anticipated maturity: Now—may be in
       decline. Last tasted, 3/89.

1975—This wine possesses one of the most exaggerated aromatic profiles of the
  •   vintage. The 1975 Lascombes reveals an herbaceous, gingery, minty, spiced
  87   tealike nose that readers will either detest or find interesting. Tannic and
       loosely jointed, this fully mature wine (there is considerable amber/orange at
       the edge) exhibits the vintage's telltale tannin and structure, but the fruit is
       sweet and ripe. Consume it over the next 5–7 years before the fruit begins to
       dry out. This wine held up surprisingly well in an open decanter (2 days).
       Last tasted, 12/95.

1971—In the mid- to late 1970s, this was one of my favorite vintages of Las-
  •   combes. It has begun to tire badly, taking on a brown/rust color and los-
  80   ing some of its supple, intense fruitiness. This elegantly wrought wine still
       retains some vestiges of its complex, spicy, earthy, ripe plummy bouquet
       and soft, rich, yet fading, flavors. Anticipated maturity: Now. Last tasted,
       3/89.

1970—A fine example of Lascombes—darkly colored, ripe, full bodied, richly fruity,
  •   and fleshy—the 1970 is now fully mature but has the concentration of fruit
  87   and structure to hold for 4–6 more years. It is a spicy, fragrant, and altogether
       satisfying mouthful of amply endowed wine. Anticipated maturity: Now. Last
       tasted, 6/88.

1966—A top-notch effort from Lascombes, the 1966 is better than the 1970 and
  •   certainly more complete and charming than the 1975, and it has proven
  88   longer-lived than either the 1982 or 1983 will be—I think. Dark ruby with
       an amber edge, this wine has very good richness and length to go along with

its voluptuous, seductive bouquet. It has been fully mature for over a decade but continues to exhibit high class. It is one of my favorite 1966s. Anticipated maturity: Now. Last tasted, 3/89.

1962—A beautiful wine, fragrant, spicy, with a certain fat sweetness to its taste, this
•   textbook Margaux has a big, intense bouquet and wonderfully silky, lush
87   flavors. It has been fully mature since 1976. Anticipated maturity: Now—may be in decline. Last tasted, 11/81.

1961—A substantial Lascombes, but lacking complexity and the great depth associ-
•   ated with this vintage, the 1961 Lascombes is dark in color with an amber
85   edge. It possesses a smoky, earthy, ripe bouquet, a touch of raw acidity in the finish, and a good but unspectacular finish. Fully mature, the wine requires consumption. Anticipated maturity: Now—may be in decline. Last tasted, 10/79.

ANCIENT VINTAGES

I have no tasting notes on Lascombes from the thirties, forties, or early fifties, but I have two superb notes on the 1959 Lascombes (rated 90), which I have rated higher than any of the aforementioned Lascombes vintages. In 1988, from magnum, this wine had a huge mocha, cedary, plummy bouquet, full-bodied, remarkably intense, concentrated flavors (that seemed much younger and less evolved than the 1961), and a heady, cedary, spicy finish. It was a large-scaled, classic Margaux that is the finest Lascombes I have tasted.

MALESCOT ST.-EXUPÉRY   EXCELLENT

Classification: Third-growth in 1855
Location of vineyards: 90% in Margaux and 10% in Soussans
Owner: G.F.A. Zuger Malescot, Roger Zuger
Address: 33460 Margaux
Mailing address: Same as above
Telephone: 33 5 57 88 70 68; telefax: 33 5 57 88 35 80
Visits: On weekdays between 10 A.M. and noon, and 2 P.M. and
6 P.M. (except public holidays), and by appointment only during weekends

VINEYARDS (red)
Surface area: 58.2 acres
Average age of vines: 35 years
Blend: 50% Cabernet Sauvignon, 35% Merlot, 10% Cabernet Franc, 5% Petit Verdot
Density of plantation: 6,600–10,000 vines per hectare
Average yields (over the last 5 years): 52 hectoliters per hectare
Total average annual production: 13,500 cases

GRAND VIN (red)
Brand name: Château Malescot Saint-Exupéry
Appellation: Margaux
Mean annual production: 10,000 cases approximately
Upbringing: The harvest is picked by hand. Fermentations and macerations occur at rather warm temperatures in temperature-controlled vats and last 2–5 weeks (indigenous—natural—yeasts are used). Wines are transferred after malolactics to oak barrels (50% of which are new) for 12–14 months. They are fined with fresh egg whites and are not filtered.

SECOND WINE
Brand name: La Dame de Malescot
Average annual production: 3,500 cases approximately

Evaluation of present classification: Should be maintained (particularly since 1990)
Plateau of maturity: 5–15 years following the vintage

Changes at Malescot Saint-Exupéry:

- When Jean-Luc Zuger took over control of the estate, he asked Michel Rolland to join the team as technical adviser and consultant/oenologist.
- Variation in surface area: In 1994, 75 acres of vines were under control of the château; 17.5 acres, which were leased, have now returned to Château Marquis d'Alesme-Becker.
- Roger Zuger, having bought back the shares of his sister and brother, is now the sole owner of Malescot.

Malescot St.-Exupéry sits right in the town of Margaux, a few blocks north of Château Palmer on Bordeaux's main Route du Vin (D2). Malescot has long enjoyed a very favorable reputation, particularly for long-lived, traditionally made, firmly styled wines.

The Zuger family, the proprietors since 1955, claims that the style of Malescot will not be changed so as to be more supple and drinkable when released. However, it seems to me that recent vintages, particularly those since the late eighties, are not nearly as tannic or as hard as the wines of the sixties. The well-placed vineyards (some of them adjacent to those of Château Margaux) now tend to produce a medium-weight wine that can be compelling because of its combination of elegance and authoritative flavors. Since 1990 the undernourished, austere style of Malescot has taken on a great deal more richness and intensity. This is another property that has returned to form after a largely disappointing period during the sixties, seventies, and eighties.

VINTAGES

1997—This property has been making fine wines lately, so it was not surprising their
• 　　　1997 turned out to be a good effort. Depending on how it evolves, it could
85– 　　merit an even higher score. At present, it exhibits a dark ruby/purple color,
87 　　　and a forward, evolved, sweet black raspberry, cherry, herb, and floral-scented
　　　　nose. In the mouth, the wine lacks depth and length, but it is medium bodied,
　　　　elegant, charming, seductive, and easy to appreciate. Anticipated maturity:
　　　　2001–2010. Last tasted, 3/98.

1996—The continuing examples of high quality wine from Malescot St.-Exupéry are
• 　　　pleasing to see, as this is one of the more elegant, finesse-styled wines in the
89– 　　Médoc. The dense ruby/purple-colored 1996 exhibits rich, classic, floral and
91+ 　　weedy cassis aromas and flavors, fuller body and more power than typical for
　　　　this estate, and moderate tannin in the gutsy, intense finish. This wine cuts a
　　　　much bigger, more macho path than usual, but I suspect it will become more
　　　　civilized with further barrel aging. Given its candidacy for an outstanding
　　　　rating, and its reasonable price, it is somewhat undervalued in the over-
　　　　heated Bordeaux marketplace. Anticipated maturity: 2006–2025. Last tasted,
　　　　3/98.

1995—This wine merits an outstanding rating. It offers a classic Margaux combina-
• 　　　tion of elegance and richness. Medium bodied, with delicate, beautifully ripe,
90 　　　black currant and floral aromas that compete with subtle new oak, the 1995
　　　　Malescot hits the palate with a lovely concoction of fruit, nicely integrated
　　　　tannin and acidity, and a stylish, graceful feel. This quintessentially elegant
　　　　Bordeaux should continue to improve in the bottle. A beauty! Anticipated
　　　　maturity: 2002–2018. Last tasted, 11/97.

1994—A dark ruby color and an herbaceous, curranty, vanillin-scented nose are
• 　　　attractive, but what I find especially appealing about the 1994 Malescot
87+ 　　St.-Exupéry is its layered, richly fruity, beautifully pure style. It is not a big
　　　　wine, but it possesses good intensity, a sense of grace and balance, and the
　　　　impressive ability to open and expand after 5–10 minutes of airing. This
　　　　should turn out to be a stylish effort that may merit a higher score if the
　　　　herbaceousness turns into a cedary component after 3–4 years of bottle age.
　　　　Anticipated maturity: 2001–2016. Last tasted, 1/97.

1993—While some slight green pepper aromas are noticeable in this dark ruby–
• 　　　colored, medium-bodied wine, it remains an attractive, elegant, undersized
85 　　　but well-balanced claret that offers immediate charm. Drink it over the next
　　　　7–8 years. Last tasted, 1/97.

1992—The light- to medium-bodied 1992 Malescot St.-Exupéry exhibits herbaceous,
• 　　　curranty fruit, and oak scents in its bouquet, as well as rough tannin in the
82 　　　finish. The wine's graceful, fruity character suggests it should be consumed
　　　　over the next 4–5 years. Last tasted, 11/94.

1991—The 1991 is a stylish, herbaceous, moderately endowed wine with round,
• 　　　fruity flavors, a sense of elegance, and an immediate appeal. It should be
84 　　　drunk over the next 5–6 years. What it lacks in weight, power, and concentra-
　　　　tion it makes up for with its finesse. Last tasted, 1/94.

1990—This wine continues to develop impressively in the bottle. While not one
•   of the vintage's blockbusters, it possesses all the classic elegance, fra-
90   grance, and harmony one expects of a high-quality Margaux. The color
     remains a healthy dark ruby with a purple hue. The nose offers up lush,
     sweet, jammy black currant fruit intermixed with aromas of white flowers,
     spice, and a touch of smoky oak. Medium bodied, with a savory, expansive
     mouth-feel, this low-acid, rich, multilayered wine is approachable yet capa-
     ble of evolving gracefully. Anticipated maturity: Now–2010. Last tasted,
     3/97.

1989—Historically, I believe 1989 will be the vintage that marks the turnaround
•   in quality for Malescot St.-Exupéry. The 1989 is overshadowed by the
87   1990, as well as by the vintages of the mid-nineties, but it is a very good
     example, and far superior to much of what was produced during the six-
     ties, seventies, and eighties. The color is a dark ruby. The bouquet re-
     veals scents of roasted herbs, sweet black berry and red currant fruit,
     earth, and spice. The wine possesses moderately high tannin and some aus-
     terity, but a sweetness in the midpalate that comes from ripe fruit and
     attractive levels of glycerin. This is an elegant, soft Malescot St.-Exupéry
     that can already be drunk. Anticipated maturity: Now–2007. Last tasted,
     3/97.

1988—The 1988 is more classic, with a stylish mix of oak and black currants in its
•   bouquet. This elegantly wrought wine is medium bodied and austere, yet
84   backed up with sufficient fruit to age well. Anticipated maturity: Now–2005.
     Last tasted, 4/91.

1986—I found the 1986 Malescot to be herbaceous and cedary, but too light and
•   displaying the dilution caused by the enormous crop size. Perhaps a stricter
82   selection would have resulted in a wine with both finesse and flavor. Antici-
     pated maturity: Now–2001. Last tasted, 3/89.

1985—A dominating smell of leafy vegetation and new oak obscures any evidence of
•   ripe fruit that this medium-bodied, compact wine may have. Some of my
74   knowledgeable friends in Bordeaux have a high opinion of this vintage of
     Malescot, but I have yet to taste a persuasive example. Anticipated maturity:
     Now. Last tasted, 3/89.

1984—Very light, soft, fruity flavors characterize this elegant yet fragile wine. Its
•   meager charms will be fleeting. Anticipated maturity: Now. Last tasted,
76   11/89.

1983—The 1983 Malescot has a moderately dark ruby color, a ripe berryish bouquet,
•   hard, very astringent tannins, medium body, and a severe, compact finish.
83   The wine is tough textured and difficult to penetrate, as well as alcoholic.
     The question remains, Will the fruit outlast the tannins? Anticipated maturity:
     Now–2003. Last tasted, 3/89.

1982—Rarely tasted since bottling, this wine has exhibited a soft, fruity personal-
•   ity, with pleasant but undistinguished levels of fruit concentration. Drink
85   this round, supple, fully mature wine over the next 4–5 years. Last tasted,
     9/95.

1981—The 1981 is a lean, tight, unyielding wine that may develop better than I
•   anticipate. However, the wine seems to be deficient in fruit, although the
78   color is sound and the bouquet hints at an underlying ripeness. Anticipated
         maturity: Now–2000. Last tasted, 11/84.

1979—Soft, ripe-fruit, oaky aromas are charming and appealing on the palate. This
•   offering from Malescot is medium bodied, oaky, surprisingly soft and accessi-
83   ble, but well balanced in a lighter style. Anticipated maturity: Now. Last
         tasted, 10/89.

1978—Ripe black currant fruit and plenty of spicy vanillin oak dominate the bouquet
•   of this medium-bodied, increasingly attenuated, harder-styled wine. The oak
78   is apparent, and the wine appears to be losing its charm and fruit. It tastes
         awkward and out of balance. Anticipated maturity: Now. Last tasted, 6/88.

1976—A sound, fruity, straightforward 1976, with a ripe berrylike fruitiness, medium
•   body, a soft, round texture, and a short yet adequate finish. Fully mature for
78   nearly a decade, the 1976 Malescot should be drunk. Anticipated maturity:
         Now–may be in decline. Last tasted, 11/87.

1975—When Malescot St.-Exupéry is bad, it's really bad. The 1975's vegetal, tealike
•   aromas are followed by a washed-out, thin, emaciated wine with little re-
72   maining other than tannin, acidity, and alcohol. I did not enjoy this wine 10
         years ago, and I like it even less now. Last tasted, 12/95.

1970—This remains a coarse, somewhat old style of wine, with plenty of punch and
•   power, a dusty, rough texture, and a bouquet that suggests minerals, cedar,
82   and licorice. It still tastes austere and tough, yet the color is deep. It could
         use more fat and generosity. Anticipated maturity: Now–2000. Last tasted,
         1/88.

1966—Light and insubstantial in 1984, the 1966 has continued to dry out, displaying
•   tea, old-barrel, and barnyardlike aromas and flavors. The finish is marred by
67   excessive acidity. Over the hill! Last tasted, 4/88.

1964—The 1964 Malescot has an uncomplicated style, but given the number of
•   failures in the Médoc in 1964, it is a satisfactory wine. Chunky and darkly
82   colored, with a briery, spicy, cedary bouquet, tough, yet substantial flavors,
         and a coarse finish, this is a gutsy-styled wine. Anticipated maturity: Now–
         probably in serious decline. Last tasted, 10/78.

1961—Sampled twice since 1983, this is one of the two best Malescots I have ever
•   tasted. The rich, deep, black currant, spicy, cedary bouquet and long, fat,
92   tannic, concentrated flavors are explosive. It is amazing how remarkably
         young this large-scaled wine tastes. It can still evolve for another 10–15
         years. Even by the standards of the vintage, Malescot has turned in an
         outstanding effort. Remarkably, no recent vintage of Malescot even remotely
         resembles this wine, but 1990, 1995, and 1996 are closing the gap. Antici-
         pated maturity: Now–2005. Last tasted, 1/91.

ANCIENT VINTAGES

The fully mature yet splendid 1959 Malescot St.-Exupéry (rated 93 points
when tasted from an Imperial in December 1995) was an impressive, complex,

cedary, fragrant, classy wine with wonderful softness and harmony. The 1953 (rated 85) was a bit tired when I tasted it in 1988, but I could see that at one time it had been an excellent wine. The 1959 (rated 90) comes close to rivaling the superb 1961. It has the huge, full-bodied, muscular style of the vintage, a roasted nut and curranty nose, and plenty of concentration in an almost overwhelming style. It was amazingly fresh and vigorous when drunk in 1988.

MARGAUX   OUTSTANDING

Classification: First-growth in 1855
Location of vineyards: Margaux
Owner: S.C.A. du Château Margaux (main shareholders Mentzelopoulos/Agnelli)
Address: 33460 Margaux
Mailing address: Same as above
Telephone: 33 5 57 88 83 83; telefax: 33 5 57 88 31 32
Visits: By appointment only
Contact: Above telephone and fax numbers

VINEYARDS (red)
Surface area: 214.9 acres entitled to the appellation, but only 192.7 acres are currently under vine
Average age of vines: 35 years
Blend: 75% Cabernet Sauvignon, 20% Merlot, 5% Petit Verdot and Cabernet Franc
Density of plantation: 10,000 vines per hectare
Average yields (over the last 5 years): 40 hectoliters per hectare
Total average annual production: 400,000 bottles

GRAND VIN (red)
Brand name: Château Margaux
Appellation: Margaux
Mean annual production: 200,000 bottles
Upbringing: Grapes are hand-picked and severely sorted both in the vineyards and as they come into the winery. Fermentations last 3 weeks in oak vats equipped with an automatic temperature-control system. Malolactics occur in tanks, as a rule. Wines are transferred to oak barrels (100% new) in November. *Assemblage* occurs in February, and wines remain in barrels for approximately 18 months to 2 years (this depends on the vintage). They are fined with egg whites and racked every 3 months, but not filtered before bottling.

SECOND WINE
Brand name: Pavillon Rouge du Château Margaux
Average annual production: 200,000 bottles

VINEYARDS (white)
Surface area: 29.6 acres
Average age of vines: 25 years
Blend: 100% Sauvignon Blanc
Density of plantation: 6,600 vines per hectare
Average yields (over the last 5 years): 25 hectoliters per hectare
Total average annual production: 40,000 bottles

GRAND VIN (white)
Brand name: Pavillon Blanc du Château Margaux
Appellation: Bordeaux Blanc
Mean annual production: 40,000 bottles
Upbringing: Fermentation takes place in oak barrels, which are renewed
by one-third each vintage. Wines are aged in oak for 10 months before
they are bottled. They are not kept on lees, and there is no *bâtonnage*.
They are both fined (bentonite and treatment with caseine at bottling
time) and filtered.

Evaluation of present classification: Should be maintained
Plateau of maturity: 9–30 or more years following the vintage

After a distressing period of mediocrity in the sixties and seventies, when
far too many wines lacking richness, concentration, and character were produced under the inadequately financed administration of Pierre and Bernard
Ginestet (the international oil crisis and wine market crash of 1973 and
1974 proved their undoing), Margaux was sold in 1977 to André and Laura
Mentzelopoulos. Lavish amounts of money were immediately spent on the
vineyards and the winemaking facilities. Emile Peynaud was retained as a
consultant to oversee the vinification of the wine. Apprehensive observers
expected the passing of several vintages before the new financial and spiritual
commitments to excellence would be exhibited in the wines of Margaux.
It took just one vintage, 1978, for the world to see just how great Margaux
could be.

Unfortunately André Mentzelopoulos died before he could see the full
transformation of a struggling first-growth into a brilliantly consistent wine of
stunning grace, richness, and complexity. His elegant wife, Laura, and more
recently his savvy, street-smart daughter Corinne run the show. They are
surrounded by considerable talent, most notably Paul Pontallier. The immediate acclaim for the 1978 Margaux has been followed by a succession of other

brilliantly executed wines, so stunning, rich, and balanced that it is not unfair to suggest that during the eighties there was no better wine made in all of Bordeaux than that of Margaux.

The style of the rejuvenated wine at Margaux is one of opulent richness, a deep, multidimensional bouquet with a fragrance of ripe black currants, spicy vanillin oakiness, and violets. The wine is now considerably fuller in color, richness, body, and tannin than the wines made under the pre-1977 Ginestet regime.

Margaux also makes a dry white wine. Pavillon Blanc du Château Margaux is produced entirely from a 29.6-acre vineyard planted exclusively with Sauvignon Blanc. It is fermented in oak barrels and bottled after 10 months aging in cask. Trivia buffs will want to know that it is made at the small building, called Château Abel-Laurent, several hundred yards up the road from the magnificent château of Margaux. It is the Médoc's finest white wine, crisp, fruity, subtly herbaceous, and oaky.

VINTAGES

1997—Margaux, which made an outstanding wine in 1995, and a prodigiously monu-
•   mental wine in 1996, turned out an alluring, soft, delicious 1997 that will
90–   offer immediate appeal. The harvest occurred between September 15 and
93   October 2. Fifty percent of the crop made it into the grand vin, which is a
blend of 80% Cabernet Sauvignon, 15% Merlot, and 5% Petit Verdot. While
the administrator, Paul Pontallier, informed me that the 1997 has the same
amount of tannin as the 1985, the wines' texture and styles, while not totally
different, are dissimilar. The wine exhibits a dense purple color, followed by
an open-knit, charming nose of crème de cassis, *pain grillé*, and minerals. In
the mouth, the wine reveals beautifully ripe fruit, low acid, a suave, silky
texture, remarkable suppleness and complexity for such a young wine, and a
round, generous, moderately long finish. This wine will be drinkable when
released, but it will keep for 15–20 years. Think of it as a sweeter, fruitier
version of the 1985. Last tasted, 3/98.

1996—Two great wines were produced at Château Margaux in 1995 and 1996. The
•   1996 is a modern day legend. This wine, a blend of 85% Cabernet Sauvignon,
98–   10% Merlot, and 5% Petit Verdot, achieved a natural alcohol of nearly 13%.
100   The wine's acidity is low, largely because the estate harvested the Cabernet
Sauvignon extremely late, not completing the harvest until mid-October. The
wine, which was the single greatest wine I tasted from the 1996 vintage in
spring 1997, continues to give every indication of being one of the all-time
great clarets from this renowned wine region. The dense opaque purple color
possesses a thick, unctuous texture. The nose offers celestial aromas of cassis,
vanillin, and intriguing blackberry and floral scents in the background. Despite aging in 100% new oak, the fruit dominates the wine, with the oak
offering a minor background nuance. In the mouth, the wine is massive, but
not heavy, with extraordinary richness, perfect precision and equilibrium, an

opulent texture, and remarkably well-integrated tannin, acidity, and alcohol. Revealing dazzling sweetness at present, the 1996 may be the finest Château Margaux I have tasted in the two decades I have been visiting this property. Can it surpass the quality of the 1990, 1986, 1983, and 1982, not to mention the fabulous 1995? Anticipated maturity: 2006–2040. Last tasted, 3/98.

1995—Bottled very late (November 1997), the 1995 has continued to flesh out,
   •   developing into one of the classics made under the Mentzelopoulos regime.
   95   The color is opaque ruby/purple. The nose offers aromas of licorice and sweet smoky new oak intermixed with jammy black fruits and minerals. The wine is medium to full bodied, with extraordinary richess, fabulous equilibrium, and hefty tannin in the finish. In spite of its large size and youthfulness, this wine is user-friendly and accessible. This is a thrilling Margaux that will always be softer and more evolved than its broader-shouldered sibling, the 1996. How fascinating it will be to follow the evolution of both of these vintages over the next half century. Anticipated maturity: 2005–2040. Last tasted, 11/97.

1994—Château Margaux was one of the last estates to bottle their 1994 (September
   •   1996), hoping to soften the vintage's high, hard tannin level. The wine has
   92   turned out to be a classic, long-lived Margaux. The opaque purple color is followed by this estate's telltale aromas of flowers, black currants, licorice, and smoky oak. This dense, powerful, closed wine is a true *vin de garde*. It needs a decade of cellaring, but it should last for 25–35 years. Readers may find this wine reminiscent of the 1988, only riper and more powerful. Anticipated maturity: 2005–2030. Last tasted, 1/97.

1993—An excellent dark ruby/purple color accompanies a soft, smoky, black cur-
   •   rant–scented wine. Although round, generous, sexy, and alluring, the 1993
   89   does not possess enough length to justify an outstanding score, but I would not be surprised to see that develop with another 2–3 years of bottle age. It is a beautifully made, elegant, rich style of Margaux that can be drunk now or cellared for 15+ years. Last tasted, 1/97.

1992—The 1992 Margaux displays an impressively saturated, dark ruby/purple color
   •   and a fragrant bouquet of cassis, vanillin, and floral scents. The wine is
   89   smooth, supple, wonderfully ripe, and seductive, with medium body, low acidity, and light tannin in the finish. It is drinking extremely well. Some tasters will no doubt rate it even higher than I have, given its elegance and layers of ripe, generous fruit that are presented in a medium-bodied format. This impressive wine should drink well for 10–15 years. Last tasted, 11/94.

1991—Margaux's 1991 is a candidate for "wine of the vintage." It reveals a deep
   •   ruby color and a tight but promising nose of rich cassis, licorice, and toasty
   88   new oak. Dense, medium to full bodied, with plenty of depth, it possesses moderate tannin and a long, rich finish. Anticipated maturity: Now–2007. Last tasted, 1/94.

1990—The 1990 Margaux continues to be the quintessential example of this château.
   •   In addition to being profoundly concentrated, its ethereal bouquet of sweet
   100 black fruits, cedar, spices, flowers, smoke, and vanilla is remarkably well

formed and intense. In the mouth, there is not a hard edge to this classic wine, which is superconcentrated, soft, silky textured, and opulent. It displays an opaque ruby/purple color, a compelling bouquet, and exquisite layers of flavors that cascade over the palate without any notion of toughness or coarseness. The acidity is low, although sufficient enough to provide vibrancy and focus. This wine's significant tannin level is remarkably well concealed by the wealth of fruit. Although still an infant in terms of development, this fabulous Margaux is already drinkable. There have been so many great vintages of Margaux under the Mentzelopoulos regime that it is almost inconceivable that the 1990 could outrank the 1982, 1983, 1985, 1986, and 1995, but in my opinion, it possesses an extra-special dimension. While it is approachable, it will last for 25–30 years. Last tasted, 4/98.

1989— The 1989 seems to typify so many of the Médoc first-growths in this vintage
 •　　—excellent but undistinguished for its reputation. The wine possesses a
 89　　leathery, oaky nose, medium body, and good ripeness, but next to the 1990, the 1989 is dwarfed by that wine's richness, intensity, and length. The tannins come across as more elevated, as well as slightly greener and tougher. The 1989 may put on more weight and come together, much as the 1985 did after 4–6 years in the bottle, but for now this wine seems to follow the pattern of many 1989 Médoc first-growths, revealing an unexciting level of quality. Give it 5–6 more years of cellaring, and drink it over the following 20. Last tasted, 4/98.

1988— The 1988 has a classic bouquet of violets and black currants intertwined with
 •　　the vanillin scents of new oak. Medium bodied, concentrated, but extremely
 88　　hard and tannic, this elegantly wrought, yet surprisingly tough-textured wine should outlive the 1989. But will it ever provide as much pleasure? Anticipated maturity: 2000–2015. Last tasted, 4/91.

1987— While this is undoubtedly a success for the vintage, among the first-growths
 •　　I have a strong preference for Mouton-Rothschild, Lafite-Rothschild, and
 86　　Haut-Brion. The 1987 Margaux exhibits a much more herbal note than one normally finds, but there is good richness, as well as a solid texture, suggesting concentration and depth. The wine is a bit narrow and compact in the finish, which leads me to believe that it will continue to evolve and open up. It should turn out to be nearly as good as the other so-called off years of Margaux during this decade, 1984 and 1980. Anticipated maturity: Now– 2000. Last tasted, 1/91.

1986— The 1986 Margaux continues to be the most powerful, tannic, and muscular
 •　　Margaux made in decades. One wonders if the 1928 or 1945 had as much
 96+　power and depth as the 1986? The black/ruby/purple color reveals no sign of age. The reluctant nose offers up aromas of smoky, toasty new oak, and black currants, as well as a few flowers. The wine is mammoth, with extraordinary extract, superb balance, and a frightfully tannic finish. A Margaux of immense stature, it is made in a masculine, full-bodied style that is in complete contrast with the 1990. It should prove nearly immortal in terms of ageability, but will it fulfill the awesome potential I first predicted? Anticipated maturity: 2000–2050. Last tasted, 4/98.

1985—I consistently underestimated this wine when young. It gets better every
  •   time I retaste it, which happens with increasing frequency. While not as
  94   powerful and concentrated as the 1986, 1983, or 1982, the 1985 Mar-
        gaux is more charming and, at present, more complex than those more back-
        ward vintages. The color is a healthy dark ruby/purple. The seductive nose
        offers copious quantities of lavishly ripe black berry and cassis fruit inter-
        mixed with toasty oak and floral scents. Rich, expansive, and velvety textured,
        this wine has developed more length, and additional flavor dimensions over
        the last several years. It has always been a remarkably approachable and
        enjoyable wine, but it appears to be taking on more character and quality
        than I ever imagined. It is one of the most delicious and seductively opulent
        Margauxs of the last 2 decades. Anticipated maturity: Now–2010. Last tasted,
        4/98.

1984—One of the best wines of the vintage, the 1984 Margaux is rich in color and
  •   extract and has an attractive perfume of violets, black currant fruit, toasty
  87   oak, herbs, and licorice. Long, deep, and concentrated, for the vintage it is
        comparable to the property's 1980. Anticipated maturity: Now–2000. Last
        tasted, 1/91.

1983—The 1983 Margaux is a breathtaking wine. The Cabernet Sauvignon grapes
  •   achieved perfect maturity in 1983, and the result is an astonishingly rich,
  96   concentrated, atypically powerful and tannic Margaux. The color is dark ruby,
        the aromas exude ripe cassis fruit, violets, and vanillin oakiness, and the
        flavors are extremely deep and long on the palate, with a clean, incredibly
        long finish. This full-bodied, powerful wine remains stubbornly backward and
        at least 5–6 years away from maturity. Anticipated maturity: 2002–2030.
        Last tasted, 4/98.

1982—This is an atypically powerful, thick, ruggedly constructed Margaux that has
  •   been downgraded slightly because of a certain coarseness I have detected in
  98+   the tannin as the wine has evolved. Nevertheless, I would be thrilled to drink
        this wine—any time, any place. It may just be that the wine's tannin and
        structure are more noticeable than in the past. The opaque purple/garnet
        color is followed by an intense, sweet nose of truffles, cassis, smoke, flowers,
        and toasty oak. Full bodied, with impressive levels of glycerin, extract, and
        tannin, this large-scaled, robust Margaux may not possess the sheer class and
        breed of such other great Margaux vintages as 1983, 1986, and 1990, but it
        offers a huge, massive mouthful of thick, succulent wine. The elevated tannin
        in the finish suggests the wine should be cellared for another 5–7 years, but
        the thick, juicy chewiness so common in the top 1982s is hard to resist. Last
        tasted, 4/98. Anticipated maturity: 2002–2035.

1981—In weight and texture, the 1981 Margaux is closest in style to the 1979. It is
  •   an outstanding wine, even in the company of the monumental wines of 1982,
  91   1983, and 1986, although it does not have the power and weight of these
        vintages. Still very dark ruby/purple in color, the 1981 Margaux offers up
        aromas of ripe cassis fruit, spicy vanillin oakiness, and violets. On the palate,
        the wine is medium bodied, concentrated, tannic, and extremely long. It is

just beginning to open and evolve. Anticipated maturity: Now–2015. Last tasted, 12/96.

1980—Margaux, along with Pétrus, is unquestionably one of the best two wines
•   produced in the 1980 vintage. A wine of uncommon power, concentration,
88   richness, and beauty, the 1980 Margaux has a ruby color, fine extract, and a surprisingly long, supple palate. Medium bodied and still moderately tannic, this wine should continue to drink well for at least a decade. Anticipated maturity: Now–2000. Last tasted, 1/91.

1979—This wine is just now reaching full maturity, much later than I initially
•   expected. A classy, elegant example of Margaux, it has retained a dark ruby/
93   purple color and a moderately intense nose of sweet black currant fruit intermixed with minerals, vanillin, and floral scents. Medium bodied, with beautifully sweet fruit, this linear, more compressed style of Margaux possesses a good inner core of sweet fruit and a charming, harmonious personality. Although not a blockbuster, it is aging effortlessly and appears to take on more character with each passing year. Anticipated maturity: Now–2010. Last tasted, 12/96.

1978—For years I went back and forth as to which vintage I preferred—the 1978 or
•   1979. At present, I have a slight preference for the 1979. Although the 1978
92   is a more powerful, fuller-bodied style of Margaux, it is less charming and fruity than the 1979. The 1978's nose has moved from one of ripe fruit and spicy oak to tarry, truffle, earthy aromas that come across as slightly too masculine and meaty. Nevertheless, this is a rich, full-bodied, concentrated Margaux that suffers only in comparison with the great vintages produced under the Mentzelopoulos regime. Some of its rusticity may be due to tannins that were not totally ripe during the harvest. In any event, it remains one of the few great wines from the 1978 vintage. While I initially thought it would be fully mature within 2 decades of the vintage, it could still benefit from another 3–4 years of cellaring. Anticipated maturity: 2000–2020. Last tasted, 12/96.

1977—Fully mature, the 1977 Margaux is soft and has an herbaceous, black currant
•   fruitiness, no hollowness or bitterness, and a soft, supple, pleasant, yet undis-
78   tinguished finish. Anticipated maturity: Now–may be in decline. Last tasted, 4/81.

1976—A pre-Mentzelopoulos wine for certain, the 1976 is light, a trifle jammy
•   and fruity, but straightforward in style and terribly uncomplex. Anticipated
70   maturity: Now–probably in serious decline. Last tasted, 2/82.

1975—Displaying considerable amber at the edge, with an old saddle leather, earthy,
•   dusty nose, the 1975 Margaux has always been a disappointing effort. High
74   acidity, austere flavors lacking ripeness and charm, and harsh tannin contribute to the downfall of this mediocre wine. I have had worse bottles than this, so be forewarned. Last tasted, 12/95.

1973—Now in complete decline, this light brownish, ruby wine had some light-
•   intensity fruit and charm in 1978, but when last sampled it was decrepit and
55   bland. Last tasted, 3/80.

1971—Another mediocre wine produced during the Ginestet reign, the 1971 is best
 •   consumed immediately for what little fruit still remains. It is light ruby in
 70   color and browning badly at the edges, with a simple, light, fruity bouquet
        and diluted flavors that are hardly inspirational. This is definitely not what
        one expects from one of Bordeaux's fabulously expensive first-growths. Last
        tasted, 1/91.

1970—The 1970 is better than the 1971 or 1975 but certainly exceeded in quality
 •   by most of the classified growths of the Médoc, not to mention a good number
 76   of Crus Bourgeois. From a great vintage this is certainly the type of wine to
        foster consumer ill will toward expensive, presumably "great" first-growth
        Bordeaux. Compact, austere, lacking fruit and richness, this wine has ade-
        quate color and tannins, but not much flesh to cover the bones. Time may
        help, but then again, it may not. Anticipated maturity: Now—may be in
        decline. Last tasted, 9/83.

1967—Light, charming, and fruity in 1974, beginning to thin out and drop its fruit
 •   in 1978, and in total disarray in 1991, the 1967 Margaux is now way past its
 67   prime. Last tasted, 1/91.

1966—This has always been one of the best examples of Margaux during its period
 •   of mediocrity. Too light for a wine of first-growth standards, it has continued
 83   to exhibit some of the fabulous fragrance for which Margaux is famous. Soft,
        round, fruity flavors are suggestive of herbs, cedar, mushrooms, plums, and
        caramel. Fully mature, this wine should be drunk up. Anticipated maturity:
        Now. Last tasted, 1/91.

1964—The 1964 Margaux is a chunky specimen, with good color but a rather
 •   dumb, old grapy aroma, a fleshy, tannic texture, yet, quite curiously, no real
 78   resemblance to a wine from Margaux. Perplexing, but drinkable. Anticipated
        maturity: Now—probably in serious decline. Last tasted, 9/77.

1962—This wine should be enjoyed now for the gorgeous, fully mature, and quickly
 •   evaporating bouquet. It is beginning to decline for sure, but the full, intensely
 85   cedary, fruity bouquet has merits. The flavors are soft, and I detect some
        acidity beginning to poke its ugly head through. Drink up! Anticipated matu-
        rity: Now. Last tasted, 1/91.

1961—The 1961 is a topflight wine and unquestionably the last great Margaux until
 •   the Mentzelopoulos era began its remarkable string of great Margaux in 1978.
 93   An intense bouquet filled with the scents of ripe plums, flowers, toasted
        walnuts, and oak is divine. This expansive wine is silky, rich, very generously
        flavored, long, and full bodied on the palate. Fully mature, this wine will hold
        up for at least another decade. I have high hopes that the 1982, 1983,
        1986, 1990, 1995, and 1996 will ultimately surpass this vintage of Margaux.
        Anticipated maturity: Now. Last tasted, 1/98.

ANCIENT VINTAGES

The 1953 Margaux (98 points; last tasted 10/97) has been delicious for most
of its life. Bottles from the cold, damp Paris cellars of the French wine
merchant Nicolas have exhibited an impressively dark ruby/purple color with

only slight lightening at the edge. Its huge nose possesses rich scents of violets, sweet cassis fruit, and spices. Round and opulent, with a velvety texture and gobs of sweet, jammy fruit, this is Château Margaux at its most seductive.

In 1989 I had a chance to taste the 1947 on two occasions and the 1949 once. I was surprised at just how good the 1947 (rated 92) is because I had never been that impressed with most of the Médocs from that vintage. Among the first-growths in 1947, it is superior to Lafite and Latour and just behind the great Mouton. Quite perfumed, rich, and full bodied, the 1947 Margaux is capable of another decade of evolution. Moreover, there is none of the volatile acidity or harshness that often creeps into many of the Médocs from that year. The 1949 was disappointing, but perhaps it was the bottle I had.

Atypically powerful and masculine for a wine from this property, the deep garnet–colored 1928 Margaux (98 points; last tasted 10/94) offers a floral, perfumed bouquet, superrich, muscular, tannic flavors, and great presence and length in the mouth. It is amazing how much tannin is still left after 66 years of aging. The 1928 Margaux will last for a century. The 1921 Château Margaux (rated 79 in December 1995) revealed a light color with considerable rust and orange. Some melted road tar as well as maderized notes came out of this perfumed but dried-out wine. Rather light bodied (today's vintages are far more muscular and concentrated), this wine lacked balance and was slightly disjointed and losing its fruit.

The 1900 Margaux (100 points; last tasted 12/96) is one of this century's most renowned wines—assuming it is an authentic bottle! Interestingly, it was originally thought to lack aging potential because it was so drinkable by the time it was 10 or 12 years old. The production of 1900 Margaux was in excess of 30,000 cases, which is nearly identical to what was produced in 1982, a wine with shockingly similar acidity, alcohol, and extraction levels. Will the 1982 last 100 years? The 1900 Margaux is an immortal wine largely because it is still so young and fresh, with all the nuances and complexities that wine enthusiasts hope will develop. Splendidly rich, with a perfume that must fill a room, unbelievably unctuous, opulent, and well focused, this is a winemaking tour de force. The fact that it manages to balance power and high extraction of flavor with both finesse and elegance makes it stand out as one of the most extraordinary wines I have ever tasted. Not only will this wine live for another decade, I suspect it has the potential to last for 20–30 years into the next century. A breathtaking wine!

In April 1991 I had the 1926, 1928, and 1929 vintages of Margaux from a private collection in Bordeaux. The 1929 was fading badly, the 1926 was spicy, coarse, and unappealing, but the 1928 was once again magnificent. It is an immortal claret.

MARQUIS D'ALESME-BECKER

Classification: Third-growth in 1855
Location of vineyards: Margaux and Soussans
Owner: Jean-Claude Zuger
Address: 33460 Margaux
Mailing address: Same as above
Telephone: 33 5 57 88 70 27; telefax: 33 5 57 88 73 78
Visits: Monday to Friday, between 8 A.M. and noon, and 2 P.M. and 6 P.M.
Contact: Jean-Claude Zuger

VINEYARDS (red)
Surface area: 38.3 acres
Average age of vines: 30 years
Blend: 45% Merlot, 30% Cabernet Sauvignon, 15% Cabernet Franc,
10% Petit Verdot
Density of plantation: 10,000 vines per hectare
Average yields (over the last 5 years): 45 hectoliters per hectare
Total average annual production: 8,000 cases

GRAND VIN (red)
Brand name: Château Marquis d'Alesme
Appellation: Margaux
Mean annual production: 6,500 cases
Upbringing: Grapes are hand-picked. Selected yeasts are added to help
fermentations (8–10 days); macerations last 8–15 days depending upon
the vintage, in temperature-controlled stainless-steel tanks and at
temperatures not exceeding 30 degrees centigrade. Wines are transferred
after malolactics to oak barrels, 20% of which are new (renewed by
one-fifth each year), for 12–14 months aging. They are fined and
sometimes filtered (if they seem turbid) before bottling.

SECOND WINE
Brand name: Marquis d'Alesme
Average annual production: 1,500 cases

Evaluation of present classification: Should be downgraded
Plateau of maturity: 4–10 years following the vintage

This small vineyard produces one of the most obscure wines in the famous classification of 1855. The château itself is a beautiful Victorian mansion sitting
opposite the mayor's office in the village of Margaux. It has, since 1979, been
run by Jean-Claude Zuger, the brother of Roger Zuger, proprietor of the better-
known nearby Margaux château of Malescot St.-Exupéry. So little is known

about this wine in the export markets because virtually all the production is sold directly to private customers in France, Switzerland, and Belgium. On the occasions I have had to taste the wine, I have been surprised, given the high percentage of Merlot employed at this property, that the wine is not fuller and more plump. In fact, looking at the actual winemaking process, the maceration period is relatively long, and Zuger claims that the wine is rarely filtered prior to bottling. Why it does not have more extract and flavor remains a mystery. Nevertheless, Marquis d'Alesme-Becker does have admirers.

VINTAGES

1990—Deep in color, with a woody, nondescript nose, the spicy, hard, medium-
• bodied 1990 exhibits more tannin than ripe fruit. It possesses too much
79 structure and too little fruit for my taste. Drink it in its first 7–8 years of life.
Last tasted, 1/93.

1988—Medium ruby, with a one-dimensional, curranty, plummy bouquet, this rela-
• tively light, medium-bodied, monolithic Margaux should be consumed over
80 the next 5–7 years. Where is the famed Margaux fragrance and velvety,
enthralling texture? Anticipated maturity: Now. Last tasted, 1/91.

1986—Medium ruby, with a spicy, slightly herbaceous, relatively nondescript bou-
• quet, this medium-bodied, moderately tannic wine lacks charm as well as fat
78 and concentration. It appears to be the product of indifferent winemaking.
Anticipated maturity: Now. Last tasted, 1/91.

1985—Moderately dark ruby, the 1985 offers an attractive, yet light-intensity bou-
• quet of black currants, spring flowers, and spicy oak. In the mouth, the wine
83 is soft, medium bodied, and charming. Its relatively short finish suggests early
consumption. Anticipated maturity: Now. Last tasted, 1/91.

1983—Medium ruby with some amber at the edge, this spicy, medium-bodied wine
• has a curranty, slightly weedy bouquet, followed by flavors that are solid yet
83 uninspiring and somewhat dominated by acidity and tannin in the finish.
Anticipated maturity: Now. Last tasted, 1/91.

1982—The 1982 is solid and reliable, with an advanced, medium ruby color, a
• moderately intense blackberry, oaky bouquet, and soft, loosely knit flavors. It
81 requires drinking. Anticipated maturity: Now. Last tasted, 4/91.

1979—Ruby with some amber at the edge, the 1979 has a ripe curranty bouquet inter-
• mingled with the scents of tar, oak, and herbs. This medium-bodied wine is
78 beginning to reveal some astringent tannins in the finish and may be drying out.
Drink up. Anticipated maturity: Now–may be in decline. Last tasted, 1/91.

1978—A solid effort, the 1978 has an old woodsy aroma, a faint perfume of berry
• fruit, a round, charming, forward fruitiness, and a somewhat short finish.
80 Anticipated maturity: Now–may be in decline. Last tasted, 6/84.

1975—The 1975 is an average-quality wine, but somewhat bland and simple.
• Straightforward fruity flavors, some spicy oak aromas, and a rather hard,
77 sharp finish offer little excitement. Anticipated maturity: Now–may be in
decline. Last tasted, 5/84.

MARQUIS-DE-TERME

VERY GOOD

Classification: Fourth-growth in 1855
Location of vineyards: Margaux and Cantenac
Owner: S.C.A. Château Marquis-de-Terme
Address: 3, route de Rauzan, 33460 Margaux
Mailing address: Same as above
Telephone: 33 5 57 88 30 01; telefax: 33 5 57 88 32 51
Visits: By appointment only, Monday to Friday, between 9 A.M. and noon,
and 2 P.M. and 5 P.M.

VINEYARDS (red)
Surface area: 94 acres
Average age of vines: 35 years
Blend: 55% Cabernet Sauvignon, 35% Merlot, 3% Cabernet Franc,
7% Petit Verdot
Density of plantation: 10,000 vines per hectare
Average yields (over the last 5 years): 45 hectoliters per hectare
Total average annual production: 200,000 bottles

GRAND VIN (red)
Brand name: Château Marquis-de-Terme
Appellation: Margaux
Mean annual production: 150,000 bottles
Upbringing: Harvest is done manually. Fermentations last about 1 week,
at temperatures of 31–32 degrees centigrade, and macerations last 3–4
weeks. Wines are transferred to oak barrels for 18 months aging, and the
percentage of new oak varies between 30% and 50% depending upon the
vintage. Wines are fined with egg whites and filtered before bottling.

SECOND WINE
Brand name: Terme des Gondats
Average annual production: 25,000 bottles

Evaluation of present classification: Should be downgraded to a
fifth-growth
Plateau of maturity: 7–20 years following the vintage

One of the least known and—until several years ago—one of the most
disappointing classified growths of Margaux, Marquis-de-Terme has had an
infusion of much needed money to modernize the cellars and purchase at least
33%-50% new oak casks for each vintage. The owners have also instituted a
stricter selection policy with the introduction of a secondary wine.

The quality since 1983 has improved significantly. If the recent vintages since are indicative of the new style, claret enthusiasts should anticipate a deeply colored, more forceful, muscular style of Margaux that relies more on flesh, extract, and color than on elegance and finesse.

VINTAGES

1996— Three separate tastings suggested an exceptionally powerful, tannic, "St.-
• Estèphe-like" Margaux, with a black/purple color, masses of Cabernet Sauvi-
(89– gnon–dominated fruit, and mouth-searing tannin. Showing enormous weight,
90) structure, and ripeness, this wine is undoubtedly a sleeper of the vintage. However, it will require significant cellaring. Anticipated maturity: 2006–2025. Last tasted, 3/97.

1995— The deep-colored 1995 exhibits power and punch as well as low acidity and
• ripe fruit. Although the wine possesses admirable extraction and purity, hard,
86+ tough tannin in the finish raises concerns. Give it 4–5 years to soften, and drink it over the following 12–15 years. Last tasted, 3/96.

1994— The 1994's softness and sweetness of fruit offer initial up-front appeal. It also
• possesses a spicy, attractive black cherry–and-truffle-scented nose. Medium
83 bodied, with a short finish, this wine will provide correct but unexciting drinking for a decade. Last tasted, 3/96.

1993— The 1993 Marquis-de-Terme is a dark-colored, medium-bodied, concentrated
• wine. However, it did not escape the 1993 vintage's downside—compact
81 flavors and an excess of tannin. Some positive components—ripeness, extract, and purity—suggest this wine will last for 10 years or more. Last tasted, 11/94.

1992— Medium ruby colored, with a bouquet of wood, dusty earth, and herbs, this
• light-bodied, soft, insubstantial wine should be drunk over the next 4–5
76 years. Last tasted, 11/94.

1991— The light-bodied, short, compact, uninteresting 1991 reveals considerable
• dilution. Last tasted, 1/94.
74

1990— Spicy new oak and copious quantities of black fruits dominate the nose of the
• 1990. The wine exhibits medium body, an expansive, lush richness, plenty of
87 extract and glycerin, fine tannins, and a smooth finish. Anticipated maturity: Now–2002. Last tasted, 1/93.

1989— The 1989 is an excellent wine, dark ruby, medium to full bodied, fleshy, and
• chewy, with low acidity and high alcohol. The expansive, super-ripe, nearly
89 sweet-tasting flavors give this wine immense crowd appeal. It should develop quickly. Anticipated maturity: Now–2004. Last tasted, 1/93.

1988— Deep ruby/purple, with a spicy, oaky, relatively intense bouquet, the 1988
• Marquis-de-Terme has good body, fine extract levels, a moderately high level
86 of tannin, and good aging potential. Anticipated maturity: Now–2005. Last tasted, 1/93.

1986— Consistently impressive from its early days, the 1986 exhibits a nearly black
• color, enormous richness and depth, sensational extract, and an extremely
90? long finish. However, prospective purchasers should be aware that on four

occasions I have had bottles that were flawed by a smell of damp cardboard, which in my opinion suggests a problem with the corks. The wine is exceptional and clearly the finest made at this property in decades, but I wonder how much of the production has been affected by whatever is causing the off odor and taste. Anticipated maturity: Now–2015. Last tasted, 1/91.

1985—The 1985 displays a great concentration of fruit, full body, a super finish, and
• considerable aging potential. It has turned out to be one of the best examples
88 of 1985 Margaux. Anticipated maturity: Now–2003. Last tasted, 3/89.

1984—Rather tannic and hard for a 1984, this wine could use 2–3 years of bottle
• age to open up. It is medium to dark ruby in color, spicy yet tight, and the
79 flavors and impression in the mouth are of narrowness. Anticipated maturity:
Now. Last tasted, 10/88.

1983—This is a classic Bordeaux, with a deep ruby color, an emerging bouquet of
• vanilla, coffee, and black currants, rich, highly extracted fruit, medium body,
88 and a long, moderately tannic finish. Anticipated maturity: Now–2007. Last
tasted, 1/91.

1979—Given the château's reputation for producing rather tough, brawny wines, I
• would have expected this wine to be more backward and tannic. Not so.
82 Fragrant, earthy, berrylike aromas jump from the glass. Precocious, fruity,
and soft, this medium-bodied wine should be drunk up. Anticipated maturity:
Now. Last tasted, 4/84.

1978—This is an unimpressive wine from a vintage that was generally excellent for
• the wines of the Médoc. Dirty, musty, unclean aromas suggest an unkempt
50 wine cellar. On the palate, the wine is thin, tastes of mold, and is quite
unattractive. A flawed effort. Last tasted, 6/83.

1971—Pungent, earthy, smoky aromas intermingle with ripe black currant scents to
• provide a rather exotic bouquet. On the palate, the wine is fully mature,
80 soft, much lighter than one would expect from the bouquet, and ready to
drink. Anticipated maturity: Now–probably in serious decline. Last tasted,
2/80.

1970—Very backward, almost opaque ruby in color, with a rich, deep, intense
• bouquet of spicy oak, smoky fruit, and earthy scents. Dense, powerful, and
84 tannic, and perhaps too robust for its own good, this full-bodied wine should
age well for another 10–12 years. Anticipated maturity: Now–may be in
decline. Last tasted, 4/82.

MONBRISON   GOOD

Classification: Cru Bourgeois
Location of vineyards: Margaux
Owner: Mrs. E. M. Davis and Sons
Address: 1, allée de Monbrison, 33460 Arsac
Mailing address: Same as above
Telephone: 33 5 56 58 80 04; telefax: 33 5 56 58 85 33

Visits: By appointment only
Contact: Laurent Vonderheyden

VINEYARDS (red)
Surface area: 32.6 acres
Average age of vines: 30 years
Blend: 50% Cabernet Sauvignon, 30% Merlot, 15% Cabernet Franc,
5% Petit Verdot
Density of plantation: 6,500–10,000 vines per hectare
Average yields (over the last 5 years): 45 hectoliters per hectare
Total average annual production: 600 hectoliters

GRAND VIN (red)
Brand name: Château Monbrison
Appellation: Margaux
Mean annual production: 45,000–55,000 bottles
Upbringing: Fermentations and macerations last 3–4 weeks depending
upon the vintage and take place in temperature-controlled stainless-steel
tanks. There is no addition of yeasts. Wines are aged 14–18 months
in oak barrels, 35%–60% of which are new. They are racked from
barrel to barrel, are fined with egg whites, and remain unfiltered upon
bottling.

SECOND WINE
Brand name: Bouquet de Monbrison
Average annual production: 15,000–20,000 bottles

At the time of the first edition of this book a decade ago, Monbrison was
one of the up-and-coming stars among the Médoc's Cru Bourgeois estates.
Lamentably, much has changed, although the wine remains a good example
of the Margaux appellation. The architect behind the extraordinary resurrection of Monbrison was the late Jean-Luc Vonderheyden. His extraordinary
discipline in keeping production low and doing everything he could to produce a high-quality wine, won praise from everybody—from France's es-
teemed wine critic Michel Bettane to this author. However, Vonderheyden's
life was tragically cut short by cancer, and his brother is now in control of
Monbrison.

Laurent Vonderheyden's style appears to have moved toward a lighter,
more delicate wine, with more than a few hiccups in the early nineties. Such
recent vintages as 1995 and 1996 have been more impressive. Monbrison is
certainly a wine worth tasting, and should readers come across any of the
splendid wines made between 1986 and 1990 by the late Jean-Luc, they
should undoubtedly give them a taste.

VINTAGES

1996—The 1996 appears to be one of Monbrison's finer efforts over recent years,
•   although several samples exhibited a slight cardboardlike character in the
(85–   nose that could have been the result of defective corks. Assuming this is not
86+?)   an intrinsic problem, the wine offers a deep ruby/purple color, medium body,
         attractively ripe fruit, and an elegant, restrained, noteworthy format. Give this
         wine 4–5 years of cellaring, and drink it over the subsequent 12–15. Last
         tasted, 3/97.

1995—The 1995 Monbrison is a correct, medium-bodied, elegant, dark ruby–colored
•   wine with sweet fruit but a measured, polite style. Anticipated maturity:
86   2000–2006. Last tasted, 1/97.

1994—A tough-textured, charmless, lean, tannic wine—there is little hope that this
•   wine's fruit will survive its tannin. Last tasted, 1/97.
76

1993—Although somewhat herbaceous, this soft, spicy, medium-bodied wine re-
•   veals finesse and elegance in its measured, unsubstantial aromas and fla-
79   vors. It should offer straightforward drinking for 3–4 years. Last tasted,
         1/97.

1992—The 1992 is the most disappointing wine made at this estate in over a decade.
•   Lean, short, and woody, possessing excessive tannin and oak, and lacking
74   concentration, it will become only more extreme in style and is thus best
         consumed over the next several years. Last tasted, 11/94.

1991—Monbrison's 1991, a success for the vintage, displays spicy, toasty new oak,
•   solid color, ripe fruit, medium body, and a compact yet flavorful finish. It
85   should drink well for 4–5 years. Last tasted, 1/94.

1990—The softer 1990 is a lovely, rich, complex wine with an impressive dark ruby/
•   purple color, a smoky, floral-and-cassis-scented nose, medium- to full-bodied
88   flavors, and a nicely extracted, elegant finish. Anticipated maturity: Now–
         2007. Last tasted, 1/93.

1989—The black/purple–colored 1989 is fabulous. It reveals none of the problems
•   that many Margaux châteaux encountered in 1989. While extremely tannic
89   and backward, it has good acidity, stupendous concentration and length, and
         the potential to age for 20 or more years. Anticipated maturity: Now–2010.
         Last tasted, 4/91.

1988—The 1988 is indeed a special wine. Black/ruby in color, but not as opaque as
•   the 1989, this highly extracted, rich, concentrated wine surpasses most of the
90   classified growths of Margaux in quality. The use of 60% new oak commenda-
         bly supports the wine's richness and size. While the 1989 is a bigger wine,
         more alcoholic, more tannic, and more concentrated, I do believe the 1988 is
         equivalent but differently styled. Anticipated maturity: Now–2005. Last
         tasted, 4/91.

1986—The 1986 is a powerful, rich wine, with a great deal of spicy, new oak, aromas
•   of plums and licorice, full body, plenty of extract and flavor depth, and a deep
87   ruby/purple color. There is enough tannin to suggest extended cellaring is
         possible. Anticipated maturity: Now–2003. Last tasted, 4/91.

1985—The 1985 is rich and full but nicely balances deep fruit with an elegant
   •   bouquet of spicy oak and berries. On the palate, the wine is soft, creamy, and
   86   tasty. Anticipated maturity: Now. Last tasted, 11/89.

1984—A sleeper of the vintage? Rather amazingly good color for the year, the
   •   1984 Monbrison offers up an intense, ripe, herbaceous, black currant bou-
   86   quet followed by a smooth, velvety, concentrated wine with heaps of fruit,
         medium body, and an aftertaste. Anticipated maturity: Now. Last tasted,
         3/88.

1983—The 1983 Monbrison is the first in a series of very good to outstanding wines
   •   from this estate. The wine has shed much of the tannin and now reveals an
   86   open-knit, spicy, toasty, curranty nose, soft, nearly fat, round flavors, and
         ample body and alcohol in its moderate length. Anticipated maturity: Now.
         Last tasted, 3/90.

PALMER   OUTSTANDING

Classification: Third-growth in 1855
Location of vineyards: Margaux and Cantenac
Owner: S.C. du Château Palmer
Manager: Bertrand Bouteiller
Address: 33460 Margaux
Mailing address: Same as above
Telephone: 33 5 57 88 72 72; telefax: 33 5 57 88 37 16
Visits: By appointment only: October to March, Monday to Friday,
between 9 A.M. and 11:30 A.M., and 2 P.M. and 5:30 P.M.; from April to
October, on weekends and public holidays, too.

VINEYARDS (red)
Surface area: 111 acres
Average age of vines: 35 years
Blend: 55% Cabernet Sauvignon, 40% Merlot, 3% Petit Verdot,
2% others
Density of plantation: 10,000 vines per hectare
Average yields (over the last 5 years): 46 hectoliters per hectare
Total average annual production: 16,000–18,000 cases

GRAND VIN (red)
Brand name: Château Palmer
Appellation: Margaux
Mean annual production: 12,000–13,500 cases
Upbringing: Grapes are hand-picked. Fermentations last 21 days, and
wines are afterward aged in oak barrels for 18–24 months (35% new oak
is used). They are fined but not filtered prior to bottling.

SECOND WINE
Brand name: Réserve du Général
Average annual production: 4,000 cases

Evaluation of present classification: Should be upgraded to a Médoc
first-growth
Plateau of maturity: 5–25 years following the vintage

The impressive turreted château of Palmer is majestically situated adjacent to Bordeaux's Route du Vin (D2), in the middle of the tiny village of Issan. It is a worthy spot to stop for a photograph. More important to wine enthusiasts is the fact that the château also produces one of Bordeaux's greatest wines.

The château takes its name from an English general who served under Wellington and arrived in Bordeaux with his army in 1814. He subsequently purchased the property, which was then called Château de Gascq, and began an extensive program of land acquisition and vineyard planting. In less than 20 years the property became known as Château Palmer. Sadly, Charles Palmer, who did so much to create this estate, saw his fortune dissipate, became bankrupt, and had been forced out of Château Palmer by a bank foreclosure at the time of his death in 1836. The property has, since 1939, been owned by a syndicate involving the family of the late Peter A. Sichel, the Mahler-Besse family, and four other participants, the most notable of whom is Bertrand Bouteiller, who manages the day-to-day affairs of Palmer.

Palmer can often be every bit as profound as any of the first-growths. In vintages such as 1961, 1966, 1967, 1970, 1975, 1983, and 1989, it can be better than many of them. While Palmer is officially a third-growth, the wine sells at a price level between the first- and second-growths, no doubt reflecting the high respect Bordeaux merchants, foreign importers, and consumers throughout the world have for this wine.

Palmer is still a traditionally made wine, and the enviable track record of success is no doubt attributable to a number of factors. There is the dedication of the Chardon family, which has been making the wine and caring for the vineyard for over a century. Additionally, the *assemblage* (blend of grapes) at Palmer is unique in that a very high percentage of Merlot (40%) is used to make the wine. This high proportion of Merlot no doubt accounts for Palmer's Pomerol-like richness, suppleness, and generous, fleshy character. However, its compelling fragrance is quintessentially Margaux. Third, Palmer has one of the longest maceration periods (20–28 days), wherein the grape skins stay in contact with the grape juice. This explains the richness of color, excellent extract, and abundant tannins found in most vintages of Palmer. Finally, this is one of only a handful of Médoc properties that remain adamantly against the filtration of their wine.

Palmer consistently made the best wine of the Margaux appellation between 1961 and 1977, but the resurgence of Château Margaux in 1978, which has now taken the place at the top of the Margaux hierarchy, has—for the moment—left Palmer in the runner-up spot, although Palmer's 1989 is clearly superior to that of Margaux.

The style of Palmer's wine is one characterized by a sensational fragrance and bouquet. I have always felt that Palmer's great vintages (1961, 1966, 1970, 1983, 1989, and 1995) can often be identified in blind tastings by smell alone. The bouquet has the forward fruity richness of a great Pomerol but the complexity and character of a Margaux. The wine's texture is rich, often supple and lush, but always deeply fruity and concentrated.

VINTAGES

1997—Only tasted once, the 1997 Palmer did not perform impressively. The color is
•   medium dark ruby. The nose was closed, although some earthy, dusty, cherry/
82–   berry aromas emerged with coaxing. In the mouth, the wine lacks substance,
85?   seems short and hollow in the midpalate, with a hint of new oak, ripe plums, and
       cherries. The finish is lean and attenuated, with dry tannin. Can this wine really
       be this uninspiring? Anticipated maturity: 2000–2010. Last tasted, 3/98.

1996—Palmer has finally invested in a new state of the art winemaking facility, with
•   temperature-controlled stainless-steel tanks, and an impressive new *cuverie*.
88–   A blend of 55% Cabernet Sauvignon, 40% Merlot, and 5% Petit Verdot, the
91   1996 is a powerful, dense, backward wine that recalls the 1986. The wine is
       more difficult to judge because of the high Merlot component, and the fact
       that this wine has not yet totally fleshed out. It is an impressively built,
       medium- to full-bodied, muscular, rich claret. If it develops more complexity
       and puts on a bit of weight, it will be an outstanding Palmer, with less early
       charm than top vintages, but built for the long haul. Anticipated maturity:
       2005–2025. Last tasted, 3/98.

1995—Bottled in July 1997, this wine includes an extremely high percentage of
•   Merlot (about 43%). It is a gloriously opulent, low acid, fleshy Palmer that
90   will be attractive early and keep well. Dark ruby/purple-colored, with smoky,
       toasty new oak intertwined with gobs of jammy cherry fruit, and floral and
       chocolate nuances, this medium- to full-bodied, plump yet elegant wine is
       impressive. Anticipated maturity: 2002–2020. Last tasted, 11/97.

1994—I had hoped this wine would be better, but it has turned out to be a good yet
•   uninspiring Palmer. The medium dark ruby color is followed by a straightfor-
86   ward, sweet, berry-scented nose. In the mouth, the wine is medium bodied,
       with decent concentration, some noticeable tannin, and a spicy, short finish.
       It is a good wine, but disappointing for a Palmer. Anticipated maturity:
       1999-2010. Last tasted, 1/97.

1993—Despite a healthy dark ruby color, this diluted, thin, emaciated wine lacks
•   depth and body. High tannin in the finish will cause the wine to become
78   increasingly angular and, in all likelihood, dry out. Last tasted, 1/97.

1992—Palmer's 1992 revealed good ripeness and more concentration from cask
•　　samples. Now that it has been bottled, it is clear that the fining/filtration done
84?　　at bottling has removed some of the delicately constructed fruit and finesse.
　　　The color is a medium ruby, and the nose offers up aggressive aromas of
　　　toasty new oak and black cherry and black currant fruit. So far so good, but
　　　once past the charming, light to moderately intense bouquet, the wine's most
　　　obvious characteristics are its lightness, dilution of fruit, and lack of concen-
　　　tration. This medium-bodied, light wine possesses an extremely short finish.
　　　Drink it over the next 4–5 years. Last tasted, 11/94.

1991—Palmer's 1991 is a noteworthy effort. The deep ruby/purple color is followed
•　　by aromas of ripe black fruits and new oak. There is excellent definition, a
87　　sweet, creamy, medium- to full-bodied texture, noticeable fatness, and a lush,
　　　concentrated, rich finish. This seductive, hedonistic 1991 should drink well
　　　for 7–10 years. Last tasted, 1/94.

1990—The 1990 Palmer has put on some weight since I first tasted it. Typical of
•　　Palmer in hot, dry vintages, the wine is disjointed and expansive, with sweet
88　　fruit, but lacking the focus and inner core of extraction found in this estate's
　　　great vintages. The 1990 possesses low acidity and velvety tannin, but not
　　　the depth or length of the 1989. It can be drunk now as well as over the next
　　　15 years. For what it's worth, it took three bottles of the 1990 Palmer to find
　　　one that was not corked. Last tasted, 11/96.

1989—Palmer's 1989 is one of the vintage's great successes. The wine exhibits a
•　　dark ruby/purple color and a sweet, jammy nose of black fruits intermingled
95　　with floral scents, licorice, and a touch of truffles. Full bodied and supple,
　　　with low acidity, copious quantities of ripe fruit and glycerin, and a medium-
　　　to full-bodied, concentrated, harmonious, seamless texture, this is a gorgeous
　　　Palmer. It may turn out similar to this estate's brilliant 1962 and 1953.
　　　Although approachable, it will improve for another decade and last for 20–
　　　25 years. Last tasted, 11/96.

1988—Palmer's 1988 offers a promising sweet bouquet of ripe plums, has dense,
•　　rich, concentrated fruit, medium body, and possesses an expansive, lush,
87　　heady finish. This is one of the best and most delicious wines of the Margaux
　　　appellation in 1988. Anticipated maturity: Now–2006. Last tasted, 1/93.

1987—The 1987 Palmer is a star of the vintage in the Margaux appellation. It is a
•　　splendidly ripe, nearly opulent wine, exhibiting a great deal of toasty new
86　　oak, low acidity, excellent color, and medium body. No doubt the high per-
　　　centage of Merlot used by Palmer worked to their advantage in this charming,
　　　deliciously fruity wine. Anticipated maturity: Now–1999. Last tasted, 11/90.

1986—Like so many of the 1986 Médocs, this effort from Palmer has the capacity to
•　　test its purchasers' patience. The wine will not be a great Palmer, but I have
88+?　high hopes that it is going to merit the affixed numerical score and perhaps
　　　even turn out to be outstanding. By Palmer's more precocious standards, the
　　　1986 is tightly knit and closed. It reveals an impressive dark ruby/purple
　　　color, with a slight lightening at the edge. Aromatically the wine is tight, with
　　　some black fruit, floral, truffle, and cigar box scents emerging after extended

breathing. On the palate, the wine possesses excellent ripeness and richness, but all of it is submerged under layers of high tannin. The wine has been going through a compressed, ungracious stage and seems destined for a far shorter life than I originally projected. Anticipated maturity: 2000–2015. Last tasted, 9/97.

1985—This wine has consistently been attractive, elegant, and fruity, with a deep
•   ruby color that is now revealing some amber and orange at the edge. The
87   wine's low acidity has resulted in an up-front forwardness, but there is neither the depth nor the extract one expects in a top vintage of Palmer. Nevertheless, it is a well-made, richly fruity, fragrant wine with no hard edges that is ideal for present consumption. Anticipated maturity: Now–2004. Last tasted, 9/97.

1984—This is a good, solid wine, well colored, with a plummy bouquet. On the
•   palate, it lacks weight and finishes short, but there is ripeness to the fruit, a
82   seductive charm, and a precocious appeal. Anticipated maturity: Now. Last tasted, 4/90.

1983—One of the superb wines of the vintage, the 1983 Palmer continues to display
•   a saturated purple/garnet color and an intense perfume of jammy black fruits,
97   smoked meats, flowers, cedar, and Asian spices. Superconcentrated, powerful, and full bodied, this huge, unctuously textured wine is approaching its plateau of maturity. Because of the high Merlot content it can easily be drunk now yet promises to last for another 20–25 years. I remain convinced that the 1983 will be the most powerful Palmer since the compelling 1961. Last tasted, 9/97.

1982—The 1982 Palmer has turned out better than I had predicted. It has always
•   been a loosely knit, diffuse, but flavorful wine with low acidity and plenty of
88   soft, ripe black fruits intermixed with scents of flowers and herbs. Sweet, generous, and fleshy, without much grip, this medium-bodied, fully mature wine should continue to drink well for another decade. Very charming and delicious! Last tasted, 9/95.

1981—This is a relatively light, almost indifferent style of Palmer, lacking depth and
•   coming across as straightforward, with a simple plummy fruitiness intermin-
81   gled with scents and flavors of herbs, oak, and cedar. It is medium bodied and austere for a Palmer. Anticipated maturity: Now. Last tasted, 6/90.

1980—Light, fruity, and straightforward, the 1980 Palmer is ready to drink and
•   should be appreciated for its simple charms. One might call it a picnic
72   Palmer. Anticipated maturity: Now–probably in serious decline. Last tasted, 2/84.

1979—Palmer's 1979 has turned out to be one of the better wines of the vintage, but
•   it is not as profound as I had predicted. The wine has evolved slowly and is
89   just now approaching full maturity. The color remains a deep ruby with some lightening at the edge. The moderately intense bouquet of black fruits, earth, cedar, and herbs is followed by a wine with excellent richness, sweet tannin for the vintage, crisp acidity, and a medium-bodied, stylish personality. The wine still has tannin in the finish, but the midpalate and finish are silky and expansive. Anticipated maturity: Now–2008. Last tasted, 6/97.

1978—One of the Médoc's most successful 1978s, this wine has reached full matu-
   •   rity, but it reveals no signs of an early demise. The color is a dark ruby/garnet
   90   with only slight amber at the edge. The nose offers up black truffle, cassis,
         smoked herbs, and meaty aromas. In the mouth, there is a green pepper
         quality to the rich, sweet fruit. This medium-bodied, silky-textured wine
         is more spice driven than most Palmers, but attractive and mouth-filling.
         Anticipated maturity: Now–2006. Last tasted, 10/97.

1977—Rather thin, ungenerous, and too vegetal and herbaceous, the 1977 Palmer is
   •   medium bodied, somewhat fruity, and lightly tannic and shows no harsh or
   70   bitter qualities. Anticipated maturity: Now–probably in serious decline. Last
         tasted, 4/81.

1976—A deliciously supple, fruity, plump 1976 with a smooth, soft nature and little
   •   tannins, this Palmer is fully mature and has adequate fruit, unlike many frail,
   83   somewhat diluted wines of this vintage. Anticipated maturity: Now–may be
         in decline. Last tasted, 8/84.

1975—The 1975 Palmer has consistently been one of the top wines of the vintage.
   •   The color remains a dark ruby with no signs of amber. The wine reveals
   90   plenty of sweet fruit in the fragrant bouquet. Although more tannic than most
         top vintages of Palmer, this is a full-bodied, rich, concentrated wine with the
         vintage's toughness and high tannin well displayed. Yet I believe it possesses
         enough sweet fruit and extract to stand up to the tannin. Shockingly, the most
         developed bottle of 1975 Palmer I have tasted was from an Imperial several
         years ago. From my cellar, the wine is still very young, and in need of another
         5–7 years of cellaring. It has another 20+ years of evolution. Last tasted,
         12/95.

1974—In this poor vintage, Palmer produced a very mediocre wine with brownish
   •   color, a stringy, lean, weak, bland character, and little fruit in evidence. Last
   64   tasted, 2/78.

1971—While the 1971 is certainly not in the same class as the 1979, 1975, 1970,
   •   and 1966, Palmer's reputation for quality and finesse is hardly in danger as a
   86   result of this effort. Fully mature, with a good dark ruby color, this wine
         readily boasts the highly touted Palmer bouquet of berries, flowers, and
         cassis. A silky, lush wine, it has been at its peak for over a decade. Antici-
         pated maturity: Now. Last tasted, 12/88.

1970—Not yet fully mature, the 1970 Palmer is one of the great wines of the vintage.
   •   It exhibits a dark, opaque garnet color and an emerging, fabulously complex,
   95+   exotic nose of licorice, overripe plums and black currants, soy, cedar, and
         minerals. Rich and concentrated, with medium to full body, a sweet inner
         core of fruit, firm but silky tannin, and a long, rich finish, this remains a
         youthful, potentially superb Palmer. While approachable, it will benefit from
         another 3–5 years of cellaring and will keep through the first 10–15 years of
         the next century. Last tasted, 6/96.

1967—This wine has been a sleeper of the vintage—always providing surprisingly
   •   delicious drinking. The most recent tasting (from a magnum) revealed a wine
   87   that was not a blockbuster but, rather, the quintessentially elegant style of

claret that seems incapable of being replicated in the New World. The color is a mature garnet, with considerable rust at the edge. A sweet nose of cedar, fruitcake, berries, and tobacco is followed by a medium-weight, light-styled Pomerol that retains its fresh, ripe fruit as well as a vibrancy that seems unusual for the vintage. I have a half dozen tasting notes for the 1967, and they reveal I have consistently found this to be a charming, lightweight, but delicious claret. Anticipated maturity: Now. Last tasted, 12/96.

1966— The 1966 continues to be one of the greatest examples of Palmer I have ever
•   tasted. It is almost atypical for the 1966 vintage, which produced so many
96   austere, angular wines. Not only rich and full, it is also delicate and loaded with complexity and finesse. This wine gets my nod as one of the best of the vintage, rivaled only by Latour and Lafleur. The haunting bouquet is similar to the 1961's. It reveals a plummy, mulberry-like fruitiness, exotic spices, licorice, and a hint of truffles. Medium bodied, with a velvety richness, it has a long, ripe, lush finish and enough grip and focus to continue to drink well for another decade. Anticipated maturity: Now–2007. Last tasted, 5/96.

1964— A straightforward, somewhat awkward wine with none of Palmer's best quali-
•   ties—the great bouquet, the fleshy texture, and the generous, plummy fruiti-
75   ness—apparent in this medium-bodied, coarsely made wine. Anticipated maturity: Now–probably in serious decline. Last tasted, 2/78.

1962— This wine, like some of the finest 1962s, seems to have been underrated by
•   everybody, including the author. My last tasting, from a magnum with a top
91   shoulder fill, proved this can be a brilliant wine. The color was a dark garnet, with some lightening at the edge. The explosive perfume of red and black fruits, smoke, earth, and spring flowers lingered in the glass, revealing further nuances of incense and roasted meats. Sweet, round, and velvety textured, this medium-bodied, silky-smooth wine possesses a gorgeous inner core of ripe fruit as well as an opulent, round, generous finish. As is often the case with a well-balanced Bordeaux, its lifeline seems almost immortal. Antici-pated maturity: Now (but I have been saying that for years). Last tasted, 12/96.

1961— The 1961 Palmer has long been considered to be a legend from this vintage,
•   and its reputation is well deserved. The wine is at its apogee, with an extraor-
99   dinary, sweet, complex nose with aromas of flowers, cassis, toast, and miner-als. It is intensely concentrated, offering a cascade of lavishly ripe, full-bodied, opulent fruit, soft tannins, and a voluptuous finish. This is a decadent Palmer, unparalleled since in quality with the exception of 1983 and 1989. Last tasted, 10/94.

ANCIENT VINTAGES

Palmer's 1945 (97 points; last tasted 10/94) (never tasted stateside) is one of the few 1945s that can be called exceptionally opulent, super-rich, and fat in its chewy, nearly overripe fruit. It is a rich, succulent, decadently fruity, alcoholic wine that remains in top condition. The 1928 (96 points; last tasted 10/94) is another extraordinary wine from that vintage that has taken 50+

years to reach its plateau of maturity. Pity the consumer who purchased a wine from this vintage in the thirties thinking it would be consumed within their lifetime! The wine exhibits considerable rust and amber at the edge, as well as an intensely fragrant fruitcake, cedar, gingery nose, remarkably chewy, ripe flavors, and some of the vintage's renowned austerity and tannic bite. Where it has been well stored, it remains a terrific example of the vintage.

The 1900 Palmer (rated 96 in December 1995) is still remarkable— vibrant and well colored. Although there was significant amber at the edge, the color remained a healthy dark garnet in the middle. A huge nose of sweet, jammy fruit, flowers, and spices could have easily come from a 25– 30-year-old wine. Sweet and succulent on the palate, with what must be a high percentage of Merlot, this seductive, sprawling wine proves just how long great Bordeaux can not only survive, but develop. An astonishing bottle of 1900 Palmer!

POUGET

Classification: Fourth-growth in 1855
Location of vineyards: Cantenac
Owner: G.F.A. du Château Boyd Cantenac et Pouget
Address: 33460 Cantenac
Mailing address: Same as above
Telephone: 33 5 57 88 90 82 or 33 5 57 88 30 58;
telefax: 33 5 57 88 33 27
Visits: By appointment only
Contact: L. Guillemet

VINEYARDS (red)
Surface area: 25 acres
Average age of vines: 30 years
Blend: 60% Cabernet Sauvignon, 32% Merlot, 8% Cabernet Franc
Density of plantation: 10,000 vines per hectare
Average yields (over the last 5 years): 38 hectoliters per hectare

GRAND VIN (red)
Brand name: Château Pouget
Appellation: Margaux
Mean annual production: 3,000 cases
Upbringing: Fermentations last approximately 3 weeks in stainless-steel vats. Wines are then transferred into oak casks (50% of which are new) for 12–18 months. They are fined and lightly filtered (for additional safety) at the time of bottling.

> **SECOND WINE**
> Brand name: La Tour Hassac
> Average annual production: 1,000–2,500 cases depending upon the vintage
>
> Evaluation of present classification: Should be downgraded to a fifth-growth
> Plateau of maturity: 5–15 years following the vintage

Pouget is owned and managed by Pierre Guillemet, the proprietor of Boyd-Cantenac, a much more sizable and better-known Margaux estate. Pouget's wines are vinified in exactly the same way as Boyd-Cantenac. Therefore it is not surprising that the style of Pouget is sturdy and robust, deeply colored, somewhat coarse, but concentrated.

VINTAGES

1990—While there is considerable muscle, depth, and power in the 1990, there is
•   also a tough texture due to the high level of astringent tannin—giving the
82   wine a relatively hard, charmless taste. Anticipated maturity: 2000–2006.
        Last tasted, 1/93.

1989—Fat, chunky, and beefy, the 1989 lacks complexity but does offer a generous
•   mouthful of wine. Low acidity, soft tannins, and very high alcohol suggest that
85   this wine should be drunk early. Anticipated maturity: Now. Last tasted,
        11/90.

1988—The 1988 Pouget is compact and one-dimensional. Anticipated maturity:
•   Now. Last tasted, 1/93.
79

1986—Deep in color, with a dull, indifferent bouquet, this medium-bodied wine has
•   plenty of tannin, adequate depth, but little charm or complexity. Anticipated
75   maturity: Now. Last tasted, 3/90.

1978—A rather perplexing wine, the 1978 Pouget has a very deep, richly pigmented
•   color. On the palate, the wine offers little of the deep, rich fruit implied by
74   the color; rather, it has very woody, hard, tough flavors that seem unusually
        severe and backward. I suspect the fruit will fade before the tannins. Antici-
        pated maturity: Now. Last tasted, 3/88.

1975—The intriguing bouquet of ripe black currant fruit, spicy oak, and mineral
•   scents is top-notch. In the mouth, the wine is typically 1975, very tannic,
84   severe, hard, and remarkably backward. The color is dark and a good concen-
        tration of fruit is present, but one must wait a very long time for this wine to
        mature. Anticipated maturity: Now–2000. Last tasted, 5/84.

1974—A surprisingly attractive wine for this vintage, the 1974 Pouget has good fruit,
•   a chunky texture, some hard tannins to lose, but a healthy ruby color, a spicy,
79   currany bouquet, and an adequate yet firm finish. Drink up. Anticipated
        maturity: Now–probably in serious decline. Last tasted, 1/81.

1971—A lightweight, less tannic, less intense version of the 1970, the 1971 Pouget
  •   is mature, velvety, still holding its fruit, and very attractive, as well as being
 84   well made. Anticipated maturity: Now—probably in serious decline. Last
      tasted, 2/81.

1970—A big, rich, solidly constructed, deep, flavorful, somewhat forceful wine, the
  •   1970 Pouget has still not reached its maturity plateau. Lacking finesse in
 83   favor of power and robustness, this is a gutsy, rustic-styled Margaux. Antici-
      pated maturity: Now. Last tasted, 3/83.

PRIEURÉ-LICHINE　　　　　　　　　　　　　　　　VERY GOOD

Classification: Fourth-growth in 1855
Location of vineyards: Arsac, Cantenac, Margaux, Soussans, Labarde
Owner: Sacha Lichine
Address: 34, avenue de la Veme République, Cantenac, 33460 Margaux
Mailing address: B.P. 22, 33460 Margaux
Telephone: 33 5 57 88 36 28; telefax: 33 5 57 88 78 93.
Visits: All year through, except on Christmas and New Year's Day,
between 9 A.M. and 6 P.M.

VINEYARDS (red)
Surface area: 163 acres (under vine)
Average age of vines: 25 years
Blend: 54% Cabernet Sauvignon, 39% Merlot, 5% Petit Verdot,
2% Cabernet Franc
Density of plantation: 8,500 vines per hectare
Average yields (over the last 5 years): 48 hectoliters per hectare
Total average annual production: 31,000 cases

GRAND VIN (red)
Brand name: Château Prieuré-Lichine
Appellation: Margaux
Mean annual production: 23,000 cases
Upbringing: Grapes are hand-picked. Fermentations last 5–8 days,
macerations about 21–30 days, with temperatures going up to 31 degrees
centigrade. Pumping-over is done twice daily, followed by static
maceration. Wines are then transferred to oak barrels (40% of which are
new) for 18 months. They are racked every 3 months and fined with egg
whites. There is a light filtration at bottling.

SECOND WINE
Brand name: Château de Clairefont
Appellation: Margaux Cru Bourgeois
Average annual production: 7,000–8,000 cases

Other red wine produced: Haut Médoc du Prieuré—12,000 bottles annually

VINEYARDS (white)
Surface area: 3.9 acres
Blend: 80% Sauvignon, 20% Semillon
Total average production: 10,000 bottles

GRAND VIN (white)
Brand name: Blanc du Château Prieuré-Lichine
Upbringing: On lees
This white wine was first produced in 1990.

Evaluation of present classification: Should be downgraded to a fifth-growth
Plateau of maturity: 5–15 years following the vintage

The only major château in the Médoc open to tourists 7 days a week every week of the year, Prieuré-Lichine was the beloved home of Alexis Lichine, world-famous wine writer, wine authority, and promoter of the wines of Bordeaux, who died in June 1989. Lichine purchased Prieuré in 1951 and began an extensive program of improvements that included tripling the vineyard area. I have always thought that harvest-time here must be an incredibly complex operation because Prieuré-Lichine's vineyard is among the most morcellated in the Médoc, with in excess of several dozen parcels spread throughout the vast appellation of Margaux.

The wine of Prieuré tends to be made in a modern yet intelligent style. It is supple and quick to mature but has enough tannin and, in good vintages, substance to age well for 8–12 years. The price has always been reasonable.

Since the death of his father, the young Sacha Lichine has taken over the running of this lovely ivy-covered, onetime Benedictine priory. The young Lichine has indicated that he will be producing a wine with more concentration, body, and potential longevity, and his intentions appear confirmed with the 1989 vintage. This change is probably in response to a number of critics who have argued that many vintages of Prieuré-Lichine were somewhat light for the reputation of this classified growth. To accomplish his objectives, Lichine has increased the percentage of Merlot in the vineyards, and in 1990 he hired the famed oenologist Michel Rolland.

VINTAGES

1997—This has turned out to be a very good effort for the 1997 vintage. The saturated
•   dark ruby/purple color is followed by aromas of cigar box, fruitcake, sweet
86–   berry fruit, and loamy soil. In the mouth, this is an exceptionally elegant,
87   pure, medium-bodied wine with light tannin in the compact but attractive
      finish. Anticipated maturity: 2002–2011. Last tasted, 3/98.

1996—The 1996 is a very good Prieuré-Lichine, with some of the vintage's high tannin,
•   but plenty of berry and black currant fruit, Asian spices, and floral scents. A
86–   dark ruby-colored wine with purple nuances, this medium-bodied, attractive,
87   spicy, moderately tannic Margaux will require a few years of bottle age, atypical
      for Prieuré-Lichine. Anticipated maturity: 2003–2012. Last tasted, 3/98.

1995—I expected this wine to turn out better than it has. Hard tannin in the finish,
•   and a slight hollowness in the midpalate kept my score down. The wine
85   reveals a dark ruby color, light to medium body, good aromatics (earth,
      underbrush, sweet cherries, and vanillin), and pleasing ripe fruit on the
      attack. The severe finish is dry and austere. Anticipated maturity: 2000–
      2008. Last tasted, 11/97.

1994—This wine has declined since I first tasted it in March 1995. Subsequent
•   tastings that year and in 1996 suggested the wine was quickly losing its fruit.
?   Now that it is in the bottle, the 1994 Prieuré-Lichine tastes hard and lean,
      with an unusual sour, poorly cured oak barrel smell that overwhelms the
      wine's meager fruit. Tannin and acidity, the primary structural elements,
      dominate what remains. This is a dubious effort. Anticipated maturity: 2000–
      2006. Last tasted, 1/97.

1993—An attractive dark ruby color is followed by an herbaceous, aggressively tannic
•   wine with moderate weight, light body, ripeness, and sweet fruit. However, 5–6
83   years of cellaring will undoubtedly cause this fragilely constructed wine to be-
      come attenuated and austere. Drink it over the near term. Last tasted, 1/97.

1992—An unqualified success for the vintage, Prieuré-Lichine's 1992 exhibits a
•   saturated dark ruby color and a seductive bouquet of creamy black currant
87   fruit intertwined with aromas of smoky, vanillin-scented new oak. The wine is
      supple, velvety textured, and surprisingly concentrated, with medium body
      and an authoritatively long, extracted, rich finish. Proprietor Sacha Lichine
      has brought on the omnipresent, brilliant Libourne oenologist, Michel Rol-
      land, and the decision to make a stricter selection and to harvest later has
      resulted in a riper, more opulent style of wine. The 1992 should drink well
      for 7–8 years. Last tasted, 11/94.

1991—This 1991 offers solid color, medium body, soft, ripe, cedary, cassis, fruity
•   flavors, and a spicy, supple finish. It should drink well for at least 5–6 years.
84   It is better than many of the lightweight efforts Prieuré produced between
      1979 and 1985. Last tasted, 1/94.

1990—The deeply colored 1990, also rich, deep, and expansively flavored, offers a
•   spicy, cedary, fruitcake-scented nose, splendidly ripe, sweet, expansive fla-
89   vors, excellent depth and length, and a full-bodied, lush finish. Anticipated
      maturity: Now–2005. Last tasted, 1/93.

1989—The 1989 Prieuré-Lichine is one of the richest and fullest wines this property
  •   has made in the last 3 decades. Substantial in size, with gobs of ripe currant
 88   fruit, full body, soft, plentiful tannins, and a heady alcohol degree, this velvety
        wine should prove charming early in its life but easily last for 15 or more
        years. Sacha Lichine employed 60% new oak in 1989, which he believes is
        essential to support the rich fruit. Anticipated maturity: Now–2005. Last
        tasted, 4/91.

1988—The 1988 is a light- to medium-bodied wine that is perfumed and well
  •   balanced. It avoids the overly tannic character of many 1988 Médocs. Me-
 86   dium dark ruby, it has an attractive bouquet of wood, currants, herbs, and
        minerals. Anticipated maturity: Now–2003. Last tasted, 4/91.

1986—The thirty-fifth vintage of Alexis Lichine's beloved château should ultimately
  •   turn out to be one of the best wines he produced. In fact, the fragrance and
 88   elegance may, in 5 to 6 years, entitle it to an even better rating. With the
        exception of the 1989, it is the most concentrated Prieuré made in the
        eighties, and one would have to go back to the lovely 1978 or 1971 to find a
        Prieuré with such class and grace. Medium to dark ruby in color, with a very
        seductive, moderately intense bouquet of plummy fruit and sweet, toasty oak,
        this surprisingly supple yet still structured wine has good length and aging
        potential. Anticipated maturity: Now–2005. Last tasted, 11/90.

1985—The lightish, somewhat shallow 1985, while charming and fruity, lacks grip
  •   and depth, particularly for a classified growth. Anticipated maturity: Now.
 84   Last tasted, 11/90.

1984—Excessively light, with an aroma of faded teabags, this soft, shallow wine is
  •   now in complete decline. Last tasted, 2/89.
 67

1983—Dark ruby, with a moderately intense aroma of ripe black currants, herbs,
  •   cedar, and oak, this is a full-bodied, fleshy, yet supple Prieuré with a long,
 87   rich, softly tannic finish. Anticipated maturity: Now–2005. Last tasted,
        4/90.

1982—The last several times I tasted this wine it exhibited considerable dilution
  •   and seemed disjointed and perhaps heat damaged. None of it came from my
 74   cellar. In the most recent tasting, the wine appeared at the end of its useful
        life. The color revealed considerable amber. The nose offered roasted herb
        notes but very little fruit. Perhaps this was not the finest example available,
        but earlier tastings have consistently revealed a light-bodied, uninspiring
        wine. Drink it up. Last tasted, 9/95.

1981—Light but attractively fruity and pleasant when young, this wine has continued
  •   to lose fruit and taken on a lean, rather light-bodied and under-endowed
 75   personality. It is also beginning to lose charm, and the shallow flavors suggest
        that immediate drinking is warranted. Anticipated maturity: Now–may be in
        decline. Last tasted, 3/89.

1980—A light ruby–colored wine with very shallow, light-intensity flavors that sug-
  •   gest strawberries, the 1980 Prieuré is soft and one-dimensional. Anticipated
 70   maturity: Now–probably in serious decline. Last tasted, 6/84.

1979—Prieuré tastes particularly light in this vintage. Nevertheless, the wine is
•   medium bodied, with soft, pleasant flavors. However, it finishes short. Antici-
80   pated maturity: Now—probably in serious decline. Last tasted, 6/84.

1978—One of the best efforts from Prieuré-Lichine, the 1978 is fully mature and
•   exhibits a ripe, rather rich, fruity, oaky bouquet, with meaty and leathery
86   flavors, good concentration, melted tannins, and a long, satisfying finish.
       Anticipated maturity: Now. Last tasted, 6/91.

1976—This wine tasted rather unknit when young, but with age it has pulled itself
•   together (unlike many 1976s) and displays a good, ripe, cedary, fruity, spicy
82   bouquet and soft, fat, nicely concentrated flavors. Anticipated maturity: Now—
       may be in decline. Last tasted, 11/84.

1975—A typical 1975, tough, hard, and backward, the Prieuré has a leathery, ripe
•   fragrance. Full bodied and astringent with hard, tannic flavors, this wine is
83   just beginning to show signs of shedding its tannins and revealing some ripe,
       fleshy fruit. Anticipated maturity: Now. Last tasted, 11/84.

1971—One of the most enjoyable Prieuré-Lichines, the 1971 has for the last several
•   years provided immensely satisfying drinking. Fully mature and possibly just
86   beginning its decline, the 1971 is very perfumed and aromatic, with a bouquet
       redolent of spices, berry fruit, and oak. On the palate, it is soft, supple, and
       so, so velvety. Anticipated maturity: Now—may be in decline. Last tasted,
       10/89.

1970—A delightfully fat, fruity, concentrated, velvety Margaux, with soft, lush ber-
•   ryish, plummy flavors, some spicy oak, and light tannins. Fully mature, but
86   still capable of another 4–5 years of cellaring, this well-made, elegant wine
       is quite attractive. Anticipated maturity: Now—may be in decline. Last tasted,
       10/89.

RAUZAN-GASSIES

Classification: Second-growth 1855
Location of vineyards: Margaux
Owner: S.C.I. du Château Rauzan-Gassies, Jean-Michel Quié
Address: 33460 Margaux
Mailing address: Same as above
Telephone: 33 5 57 88 71 88; telefax: 33 5 57 88 37 49
Visits: On appointment only, Monday to Friday, from 9 A.M. to noon, and
2 P.M. to 5:30 P.M.
Contact: Jean-Marc Espagnet

VINEYARDS (red)
Surface area: 74 acres
Average age of vines: 25 years
Blend: 65% Cabernet Sauvignon, 25% Merlot, 10% Cabernet Franc
Density of plantation: 10,000 vines per hectare

Average yields (over the last 5 years): 40 hectoliters per hectare
Total average annual production: 12,500 cases

GRAND VIN (red)
Brand name: Château Rauzan-Gassies
Appellation: Margaux
Mean annual production: 12,500 cases
Upbringing: Grapes are hand-picked. Fermentations last about 3 weeks
in temperature-controlled stainless-steel tanks, with frequent
pumping-overs and addition of yeasts. Wines are afterward transferred to
oak barrels, of which 25% are new, for 14–18 months aging. They are
fined and filtered prior to bottling. No press wine is added into the grand
vin.

SECOND WINE
None produced.

Evaluation of present classification: Should be downgraded
Plateau of maturity: 8–20 years following the vintage

The vineyards of Rauzan-Gassies are situated on alluvial terraces. Sixty percent of them are situated just around the château itself, and the remaining vineyards (gravelly soils) border Château Margaux, Palmer, and Lascombes.

Historically, Rauzan-Gassies was part of Rauzan-Ségla until the French Revolution of 1789. Since 1943 it has belonged to the Quié family. In style, Rauzan-Gassies tends toward heaviness and corpulence for a Margaux, without the fragrance or finesse normally associated with the better wines of this commune. However, it can make fairly concentrated, powerful wines. In most vintages, the wines of Rauzan-Gassies have reached maturity surprisingly fast for a classified growth, usually within 7–8 years of the vintage. Reports continue to emanate from Bordeaux that the quality at Rauzan-Gassies is on the upswing. My tasting notes suggest that such pronouncements are excessively optimistic.

VINTAGES

1997—A perennial underperformer, Rauzan-Gassies turned in a competent effort in
•   1997. The wine has a deep ruby/purple color, and ripe black currant fruit
86–   intermixed with earth, minerals, and licorice. In the mouth, the wine narrows
87?   out somewhat but is highly extracted, muscular, and tannic. If everything
           comes into balance, look for this wine to merit a score in the 87–88 range. If
           it does not pull itself together, readers who like a good measure of tannin in
           their wines will appreciate this effort. Anticipated maturity: 2002–2010. Last
           tasted, 3/98.

1995—The dark purple–colored 1995 is one of the finest wines made at Rauzan-
•   Gassies in decades. It exhibits plenty of pure, ripe, black currant fruit, and
86   high-quality toasty oak. Medium bodied, with a sweet entry on the palate,
      good ripeness, and a layered, elegant style, this is a vast improvement over
      recent efforts. It will drink well young and last for 15 years. Anticipated
      maturity: 2002–2012. Last tasted, 1/97.

1994—This is a thin, tough-textured, angular style of wine, possessing little fruit but
•   plenty of tannin and acidity. Anticipated maturity: 2002–2008. Last tasted,
74   1/97.

1993—This dark ruby–colored wine offers a smoky, herbal nose, diluted fla-
•   vors, medium body, some charm, but not enough fruit to compensate for the
78   wine's tannin and acidity. Drink it over the next 3–4 years. Last tasted,
      1/97.

1992—Harsh, vegetal, light-bodied flavors accompanied by frightfully hard tannin
•   are unappealing. Last tasted, 11/94.
71

1990—Soft bodied, light, and fruity, the 1990 exhibits some tannin in the finish but
•   lacks depth and complexity. Drink it over the next 10–12 years. Last tasted,
73   1/93.

1989—Dusty, hard, even harsh flavors are obliterated by the abrasive tannins in the
•   1989. The impression created is one of hollowness, with only a skeleton of
72   acidity, wood, and tannin. A very disappointing wine. Anticipated maturity:
      Now–1999. Last tasted, 1/93.

1988—The 1988 is disappointing. Harsh tannins obliterate the fruit, and the overall
•   impression created is one of hollowness, with only a skeleton of acidity, wood,
66   and tannin. Caveat emptor! Last tasted, 4/91.

1984—Quite disappointing, the 1984 is a shallow, light, insipid wine with no future.
•   Last tasted, 3/89.
67

1983—Not complex, although this fat, grapy, tannic, and astringent wine exhibits
•   surprising power and presence in the mouth. Foursquare and chunky, the
86   1983 is typical of Rauzan-Gassies. It tastes like an old-style, robust St.-
      Estèphe. Anticipated maturity: Now–2000. Last tasted, 11/88.

1982—Fat, plummy, velvety, and precocious, with low acidity, this forward, tasty, but
•   loosely knit wine is charmingly fruity and straightforward. Anticipated matu-
85   rity: Now. Last tasted, 11/88.

1981—Surprisingly diffuse, flabby, and lacking depth, richness, and structure, the
•   1981 is a disappointment. Anticipated maturity: Now–may be in decline.
74   Last tasted, 6/84.

1979—A corpulent, straightforward, plausible wine, with good dark ruby color, a ripe
•   black cherry, oaky bouquet of moderate intensity, and soft, round, somewhat
82   jammy flavors. Anticipated maturity: Now. Last tasted, 4/83.

1978—I had several decent tasting notes on this wine in the early eighties, but when
•   tasted twice, the wine appeared out of balance, with a light to medium ruby
72   color, some dusty red fruit aromas, but high acidity, as well as a lack of

body and depth. All of this causes me great concern over the wine's future. Anticipated maturity: Now. Last tasted, 5/89.

1976— Diluted flavors and a lack of structure and grip have resulted in a wine that
•   tastes shallow, simple, and uninteresting. It is browning badly at the rim.
72   Anticipated maturity: Now–probably in serious decline. Last tasted, 4/83.

1975— A sleeper in this vintage, the 1975 Rauzan-Gassies may well be the best
•   wine produced in the Margaux appellation after Palmer and Giscours. It has
86   excellent dark ruby color, a deep, rich, oaky, black currant–fragrant bouquet, a chewy, full-bodied, very concentrated feel on the palate, and a tannic, long finish. Anticipated maturity: Now–2000. Last tasted, 5/84.

1970— The 1970 is a simple, one-dimensional, somewhat dull wine that has adequate
•   color, a compact bouquet of fruit and wood, and soft, average, concentrated fla-
78   vors. Anticipated maturity: Now–probably in serious decline. Last tasted, 4/83.

1966— Still quite lively, crisp, richly fruity, and full on the palate, the 1966 Rauzan-
•   Gassies has a spicy, mushroom-like aroma, robust, rather aggressive flavors,
81   and a rather hard, coarse finish. It is an interesting, rather rustic-styled wine. Anticipated maturity: Now–probably in serious decline. Last tasted, 4/83.

1961— The Rauzan-Gassies is less successful in this vintage than many of its second-
•   growth peers. Dark ruby, with significant browning at the edges, the wine
85   has an open-knit, fully mature, spicy, oaky, plummy, toffee-scented bouquet, moderately rich, soft, fruity flavors, and a supple, velvety finish. It is very attractive, but lighter in style than most 1961s. Anticipated maturity: Now. Last tasted, 4/83.

RAUZAN-SÉGLA   OUTSTANDING

Classification: Second-growth in 1855
Location of vineyards: Margaux and Cantenac
Owner: Chanel
Address: 33460 Margaux
Mailing address: Same as above
Telephone: 33 5 57 88 82 10; telefax: 33 5 57 88 34 54
Visits: By appointment only, Monday to Friday, between 9 A.M. and noon, and 2 P.M. and 5 P.M.
Contact: Hélène Affatato, telephone 33 5 57 88 82 15 and telefax 33 5 57 88 34 54

VINEYARDS (red)
Surface area: 121 acres
Average age of vines: 20 years
Blend: 61% Cabernet Sauvignon, 35% Merlot, 2% Petit Verdot, 2% Cabernet Franc
Average yields (over the last 5 years): 46 hectoliters per hectare
Total average annual production: 186,000 bottles

GRAND VIN (red)
Brand name: Château Rauzan-Ségla
Appellation: Margaux
Mean annual production: 96,000 bottles
Upbringing: Grapes are hand-picked. Fermentations and macerations last 18–24 days in temperature-controlled tanks (the musts are automatically cooled or heated when necessary). Wines are transferred after malolactics into oak barrels, 60% of which are new, for about 20 months of aging. They are fined but not filtered before bottling.

SECOND WINE
Brand name: Ségla
Average annual production: 90,000 bottles

Evaluation of present classification: Should be maintained
Plateau of maturity: 7–30 years following the vintage

Rauzan-Ségla can trace its history back to 1661, when the vineyard was created by Pierre des Mesures de Rauzan, who at the time was also the owner of the vineyards that now make up Pichon-Longueville–Comtesse de Lalande and Pichon-Longueville Baron. In 1855 Rauzan-Ségla was considered Bordeaux's best wine after the quartet of Premiers Grands Crus, Lafite-Rothschild, Latour, Margaux, Haut-Brion, and the top-ranked second-growth, Mouton-Rothschild. In 1973 Mouton-Rothschild was elevated, and now Rauzan-Ségla sits at the head of the class of the remaining fourteen second-growths. This position hardly seemed justified by the wines produced during the decades of the sixties and seventies, but the indifferent quality changed dramatically with the 1983 vintage.

There appear to be a number of valid reasons for the disappointing wines prior to 1983. First, many of the vintages were marred by a musty, damp, almost barnyard-like aroma that is believed to have come from a bacterial infection in the old wooden vats used to ferment the wine. These were replaced in the eighties with stainless steel. Second, there was major replanting after the killer frost of 1956 by then owner, Monsieur de Meslon. The replanting was largely of prolific clones of Merlot. Many of the wines made in the sixties and seventies no doubt reflected not only the young vines, but also a badly chosen clone. These plantings have been grubbed up in favor of more Cabernet Sauvignon and higher-quality Merlot. Last, the fact that Rauzan-Ségla was sold exclusively through Eschenauer—one of Bordeaux's famous *négociants*—resulted in the wine's exclusion from the comparative tastings that are common for wines sold on the open market. Obviously the incentive to improve quality is far greater when the wine is sold on the open market rather than through exclusive arrangements. Since 1983 the improvements have been remarkable. In that year, Jacques Théo, formerly the head of Alexis Lichine & Company, took over the running of Rauzan-Ségla. Additionally, Monsieur Pruzeau replaced the ailing Monsieur Joyeaux as *maître de chai*. The construction of a new *chai* and improvements to the winemaking facility —including the addition of the stainless-steel vats—an increased percentage of new oak, and Theo's severe selections ensuring that only the best of the crop appears in the wine have resulted in a succession of brilliant wines from Rauzan-Ségla. The quality of the recent wines puts this estate clearly in the elite group of Bordeaux super-seconds. Since 1983 Rauzan-Ségla has done only one thing wrong. Jacques Théo irritated many of his Bordeaux peers by declaring the 1987 Bordeaux vintage disappointing. Rauzan-Ségla became the first significant Médoc classified growth in decades to not produce a wine for a specific vintage—the 1987.

This is a splendid wine worth laying in, as prices have not yet caught up with the new level of quality at this famous old estate. The recent change in owner-ship (the property was acquired by Chanel) should only reinforce the generally held view that Rauzan-Ségla will continue to produce splendid wines.

VINTAGES

1997—Only 36% of the crop made it into the grand vin at Rauzan-Ségla. This estate, which has a tendency to turn out backward, tannic wines, produced a charming, elegant 1997 with a deep ruby color, and sweet berry and cassis fruit, intertwined with scents of flowers, herbs, and spice. Round and plush, with low acidity, ripe tannin, and excellent purity, this wine should firm up, and be drinkable when released. For statisticians, the Merlot harvest took place between September 17 and 20, and the Cabernet Sauvignon harvest between September 24 and 30. Yields were a modest 43 hectoliters per hectare. Last tasted, 3/98.

•
87–
88

1996—The dense purple-colored 1996 Rauzan-Ségla reveals a Cabernet Sauvignon-dominated nose of cigar box, cassis, floral, and vanillin scents. Long, struc-tured, tannic, and closed, with formidable power and muscle, and potentially outstanding purity and richness, this wine requires 10–12 years of cellaring. If it continues to flesh out and attain better balance between the tannin and fruit, this will be an outstanding effort from this estate. However, potential purchasers should have the discipline to wait a decade or more for it to reach its plateau of maturity. Anticipated maturity: 2007–2027. Last tasted, 3/98.

•
88–
90+

1995—This wine was consistently outstanding from cask, and I suspect it may eventually merit an even higher score. Unfortunately, it was one of the few wines that I was able to taste only once after bottling. Nevertheless, it is a classic *vin de garde*, with a saturated ruby/purple color, and a tight but promising nose of sweet plum and cassis fruit intertwined with underbrush, vanillin, and licorice scents. The wine is ripe, medium to full bodied, and

•
90

rich, as well as unyielding, ferociously tannic, pure, and layered. The finish
is extremely dry *(sec,* as the French would say), with a brooding angularity
and toughness. In spite of this, my instincts suggest the requisite depth is
present to balance out the structure. This effort will also require a decade of
cellaring. Anticipated maturity: 2007–2025. Last tasted, 11/97.

1994— A saturated dark purple color is accompanied by sweet, earthy, herb, and
• black currant aromas. The wine is dominated by its tannin and structure.
87? There is good weight, medium body, and an impression of ripeness and sweet
fruit, but patience will most definitely be required. The 1994 Rauzan-Ségla
was deeper and richer prior to bottling, so I suspect it may be going through
an ungenerous, postbottling dormancy. This muscular, virile style of Rauzan
should be at its peak of maturity between 2006 and 2020. Last tasted, 1/97.

1993— This is the last vintage for this property where Rauzan is spelled with an "s"
• as opposed to a "z." The opaque ruby/purple–colored 1993 is undoubtedly a
87? *vin de garde.* However, it is also frightfully tannic, austere, and lean, raising
some doubt as to whether it will ever achieve total harmony. Copious quantities of sweet cassis fruit do eventually emerge in the aromatics. Fruit and
extract can be detected in the attack, but the wine's personality quickly
narrows out with its formidable tannin lashing the back of the palate. As
always, the balance between fruit and tannin, especially critical with respect
to this vintage, may not favor a graceful evolution. Anticipated maturity:
2005–2015. Last tasted, 1/97.

1992— One of the stars of the vintage, Rausan-Ségla's 1992 is an uncommonly rich,
• opulent wine with an impressively saturated dark ruby/purple color and a
87 forceful, penetrating fragrance of black cherries, currants, spicy oak, smoke,
and flowers. The wine is medium to full bodied, with gorgeously sweet, rich
layers of fruit, ripe tannin, and a long, heady, voluptuously textured finish.
Only 50% of the production went into the 1992 Rausan-Ségla, resulting in a
brilliant wine for this tough vintage. Drink it over the next decade. Last
tasted, 11/94.

1991— Since the 1983 vintage Rausan-Ségla has been in top form, producing one of
• the top three or four Margaux wines. The 1991 is one of the vintage's stars.
87 The saturated dark ruby color is followed by a bouquet of spicy fruitcake,
cedar, cassis, and floral scents. Sweet and round, with excellent definition, layers of richness, and a long, supple finish, this well-endowed, concentrated, impeccably balanced wine should drink well for 10–15 years. Last
tasted, 1/94.

1990— I hope I am not too optimistic about the potential of the 1990 Rausan-Ségla,
• as it is one wine that requires a significant investment in patience. It reveals
93+ an opaque purple color, but the wine is broodingly backward, with a formidable tannin level. Closer examination, however, reveals large quantities of
sweet, earthy, cassis fruit, full body, and a leathery toughness. The wine is
pure, with huge flavor extraction, as well as mouth-searing tannin. In previous
tastings it displayed more openness and less aggressiveness. All the component parts appear to be present, but this massive wine has gone into a dormant

state. Give it 7–8 more years of bottle age; it may be a 30-year wine. Last tasted, 11/96.

1989—The 1989 Rausan-Ségla tasted slightly disjointed. My instincts suggested it
•   was a bit cooked, probably from being exposed to high heat somewhere along
89+?   its journey from Bordeaux to the United States. Based on previous tastings, the color seemed to be taking on more amber than I would have suspected. The wine revealed a sweet, black raspberry, herbal, earthy nose, tough tannin, a silky texture, medium body, ripe fruit, and a short finish. I have consistently rated this wine in the 89–92-point range, hence the question mark. Anticipated maturity: 2004–2020. Last tasted, 11/96.

1988—One of the vintage's most impressive as well as backward wines, Rausan-
•   Ségla's 1988 still exhibits a youthful, dark ruby/purple color and a tight but
91   promising nose of black fruits, minerals, and smoke. Full bodied, powerful, tannic, and rich, this is an intensely concentrated, muscular, brawny wine built for the long haul. Anticipated maturity: 2000–2015. Last tasted, 10/97.

1986—An extraordinary success for this estate (and also the finest wine they pro-
•   duced in the decade of the eighties), the 1986 remains extremely backward.
96   It reveals an impressively saturated dark purple color, followed by a tight but promising nose of sweet blackberries, cassis, licorice, earth, and smoke. Full bodied and excruciatingly tannic, with layers of concentration, this exceptionally endowed wine is still an infant in terms of its evolution. Anticipated maturity: 2002–2030. Last tasted, 10/97.

1985—The 1985 is richly fruity, supple, and precocious. If it lacks structure and
•   aging potential, there is little doubt that it offers delicious near-term drinking
87   in a medium-bodied, elegant, smooth-as-silk style. Anticipated maturity: Now. Last tasted, 11/90.

1984—With good color, and a fresh, spicy, herbaceous-scented bouquet, the 1984
•   Rausan-Ségla starts off well but seems to drop off in the mouth. One bottle
75   tasted seemed much richer. Anticipated maturity: Now. Last tasted, 3/90.

1983—Fully mature, this seductively rich wine offers a knockout nose of spring
•   flowers, black fruits, smoke, and roasted herbs. Expansive and round, with a
90   velvety texture, real opulence, and low acidity, this concentrated, deliciously layered and intense wine reveals no hard edges. It represents the beginning of Rausan-Ségla's rebound in quality. Anticipated maturity: Now–2008. Last tasted, 12/96.

1982—This soft, round, fully mature wine should be drunk over the next 2–3 years. It
•   exhibits herbaceous, black curranty aromas and flavors, medium body, and a
86   soft, disjointed finish with no real grip or tannin in evidence. Last tasted, 9/95.

1981—This mediocre wine is light, fruity, round, and one-dimensional. Hardly a
•   wine representative of its official Bordeaux pedigree, this meager Rausan-
65   Ségla should be drunk up. Anticipated maturity: Now–probably in serious decline. Last tasted, 6/84.

1980—The very thin, watery flavors, vegetal aroma, and little depth or length com-
•   bine to make this a very undistinguished effort. Last tasted, 3/83.
60

1979—Quite light, round, and fruity, the 1979 Rausan-Ségla resembles a simple
   •   Bordeaux Supérieur. Drink up. Anticipated maturity: Now–probably in seri-
   72   ous decline. Last tasted, 4/84.

1978—True to form for many of the wines that Rausan-Ségla produced in the seven-
   •   ties, the 1978 is fruity, round, and slightly charming, but devoid of flavor
   74   interest and complexity. Anticipated maturity: Now–probably in serious de-
         cline. Last tasted, 10/82.

1977—Intensely vegetal and thin, the 1977 Rausan-Ségla is a failure. Last tasted,
   •   11/81.
   50

1976—A leafy, weedy-scented wine, with light-intensity flavors, light to medium
   •   ruby/garnet color, and an awkward, unbalanced feel on the palate, this wine
   60   lacks richness and seems very sloppily vinified. Last tasted, 4/80.

1975—Very light in color, with a suspicious brownish cast, the 1975 Rausan-Ségla
   •   has a burnt, cooked-fruit aroma, shallow, very tannic and astringent flavors,
   55   and a short, nasty finish. This is a pitiful effort in such a fine vintage. Last
         tasted, 5/84.

1972—Ironically, in this disastrous vintage, Rausan-Ségla made one of the more
   •   successful wines. Surprisingly dark, yet now showing a brownish orange
   75   cast, the chunky, one-dimensional wine has good fruit and medium body.
         Anticipated maturity: Now–probably in serious decline. Last tasted, 7/82.

1971—Medium to light ruby, with some noticeable brown in the color, this wine,
   •   which was made during a dreadful period for Rausan-Ségla, still has some
   76   life to it. The herbaceous, cedary bouquet tends to fade quickly in the glass,
         but there is still enough fruit and ripeness in the wine to provide some degree
         of charm and pleasure. However, don't push your luck, as this wine is quite
         fragile and near collapse. Last tasted, 1/88.

1970—I am not sure this wine is ever going to open up and blossom. At age 21 it is
   •   still quite dark and opaque in color, with only a slight hint of amber at the
   82   edge. It is admirably big and full bodied, but rustic and coarsely textured,
         with entirely too much tannin in its finish. Perhaps I have consistently mis-
         read it, but having consumed three-fourths of the case I purchased, I have
         never gotten the pleasure from this wine that I expected. I guess the lesson is
         to always beware of those wines that taste hard and tannic when young. This
         one may still come around, but I doubt it. Anticipated maturity: Now–2000.
         Last tasted, 1/91.

1966—Similar in style to the 1970, only more austere and not quite as concen-
   •   trated, the 1966 has a ripe plummy, oaky fragrance of moderate intensity and
   84   graceful, yet still tough and firm flavors. Drinkable now, this fully mature
         wine will hold for 1–2 more years. Anticipated maturity: Now. Last tasted,
         4/79.

1962—This is an uncharacteristic wine for the 1962 vintage, which produced so
   •   many elegant, charming, round, fruity wines. The 1962 Rausan-Ségla is hard,
   75   lean, and austere, without much richness or charm, and its fruit has no
         chance of ever outdistancing the considerable tannins that are still pres-

ent. Anticipated maturity: Now—probably in serious decline. Last tasted, 2/78.

1961—Not a noteworthy 1961, Rausan-Ségla is a ripe, fruity, somewhat awkward
• and disjointed wine. While the wine tastes jammy, diffuse, and finishes flat,
81 it nevertheless has appeal as well as plenty of concentration and power.
Anticipated maturity: Now—may be in decline. Last tasted, 9/79.

ANCIENT VINTAGES

Displaying serious color degradation (rust, amber, and orange at the rim), the 1900 Rausan-Ségla (rated 88 in December 1995) still possessed an enticing, seductive, licorice, herb, old cedar nose with hints of ripe fruit. The wine revealed dry tannin but surprising body and even some sweet fruit. An intact, stylish wine that has survived the test of time, it is another testament to the longevity of Bordeaux.

The 1847 Rausan-Ségla (70? points; last tasted 9/95) (produced 100 years before I was born) revealed a pungent, barnyard-like, fecal aroma, and some sweetness, but it was largely unattractive, with stale incense-like smells, hard tannin, and little fruit. For me, blatant volatile acidity and high tannin ruined the 1852 Rausan-Ségla (51 points; last tasted 9/95). However, the 1858 and 1868 Rausan-Séglas were amazing wines. The 1858 (92 points; last tasted 9/95) displayed an orange/amber color, followed by a fragrant nose of orange marmalade, melted caramels, and curranty fruit. Sweet, with amazing ripeness, this medium-bodied, soft, round wine is alive and kicking, as well as delicious! The huge nose of cedar, chocolate, roasted coffee, and smoked herbs found in the 1868 Rausan-Ségla (96 points; last tasted 9/95) was followed by an astonishingly concentrated, sweet, full-bodied wine with high alcohol, layers of richness, and some well-integrated tannin in the finish. This could have easily been mistaken for a 50-year-old wine. The amount of fruit remaining had to be tasted to be believed.

Believe it or not, the 1865 Rausan-Ségla (rated 99+ in December 1995) displayed a deep, opaque garnet color with surprising intensity. It revealed a knockout nose of chocolate, cedar-tinged, cassis-like fruit. Extremely concentrated and powerful, as well as remarkably youthful (I would have thought the wine was 40–50 years old), this full-bodied, exceptionally rich, thick wine exhibits no signs of decline. Might this wine keep for another 30–50 years?

SIRAN   GOOD

Classification: None
Location of vineyards: Labarde
Owner: William Alain B. Miailhe
Address: 33460 Labarde, Margaux

Mailing address: Same as above

Telephone: 33 5 57 88 34 04; telefax: 33 5 57 88 70 05

Visits: Every day, between 10:15 A.M. and 12:30 P.M., and 2 P.M. and 6 P.M.

Contact: Mrs. Bourgine

VINEYARDS (red)

Surface area: 99 acres

Average age of vines: 30 years

Blend: 50% Cabernet Sauvignon, 30% Merlot, 13% Petit Verdot, 7% Cabernet Franc

Density of plantation: 10,000 vines per hectare (gravelly soils), 5,000 vines per hectare (in the other parcels)

Average yields (over the last 5 years): 50 hectoliters per hectare

Total average annual production: 200,000 bottles

GRAND VIN (red)

Brand name: Château Siran

Appellation: Margaux

Mean annual production: 100,000 bottles

Upbringing: Grapes are picked manually. Fermentations and macerations last about 25 days in all. Wines are transferred, after malolactics, into oak barrels, 60% of which are new and the rest of which are 1 year old. They are aged for 15 months, racked every 3 months (this is done from one barrel to another), and are both fined and filtered before bottling.

SECOND WINE

Brand name: Château Bellegarde

Average annual production: 20,000 bottles

Average age of vines: 38 years

Evaluation of present classification: The quality equivalent of a Médoc fifth-growth

Plateau of maturity: 5–15 years following the vintage

This outstanding property in Labarde in the southern part of the Margaux appellation is making consistently delicious, fragrant, deeply colored wines that are frequently on a quality level with a Médoc fifth-growth.

The estate is owned and managed by William Alain B. Miailhe, a meticulous grower, who produces in an average year 12,000 cases of rich, flavorful, polished wine that admirably reflects the Margaux appellation. The wine is also distinguished by a Mouton-Rothschild-like label that boasts a different artist's painting each year.

Siran's wine usually needs 5–6 years of bottle age to mature properly, and recent vintages have all been quite successful, even the light, mediocre vintage of 1980, where Siran outperformed virtually all of its Margaux peers save Margaux and Giscours. Above all, this is a wine that repays the patient consumer because of its ability to support extended cellaring. The long maceration period (15–25 days) and elevated percentage of the tannic Petit Verdot in the blend give the wine at least 15 years of aging potential in top vintages.

If a new classification of the wines of the Médoc were ever done, Siran would surely be given significant consideration for inclusion as a fifth-growth.

VINTAGES

1997—I thought this wine performed particularly well in my tastings. The color is a saturated dark ruby/purple, and the nose offers moderately intense aromas of licorice, cassis, violets, and earth. The wine's classic attack reveals black currant fruit nicely complemented by cedar, *pain grillé*, and spicy notes. Medium bodied, with sweeter tannin than most Sirans possess, this will be a charming, flavorful, complex wine that will be ready to drink when released; it will age well for a decade or more. Last tasted, 3/98.

•
86–
87+

1996—This backward wine possesses an attractive dark ruby/purple color with an opaque center, but extremely reticent aromatics, although some ripe Cabernet-scented cassis fruit is noticeable. Muscular, spicy, and less flattering than the 1995, the 1996 Siran, while neither opulent nor supple, appears to be a well-made, well-structured wine that is meant to go the long haul. Anticipated maturity: 2005–2016. Last tasted, 3/98.

•
86–
87

1995—A very good effort from Siran, this dark ruby-colored wine offers attractive aromas of vanillin, spicy new oak, and sweet, creamy cassis fruit interspersed with subtle fennel and spice box notes. Medium bodied and ripe, with savory richness, sweet tannin, and low acidity, this excellent, elegant Margaux is already accessible. Anticipated maturity: 2000–2014. Last tasted, 11/97.

•
87

1994—Siran's 1994 is a surprisingly extracted wine with medium body, deep color, and good purity and ripeness. Some astringent tannin in the finish raises questions as to how much of that component will melt away before the fruit begins to fade. Certainly the wine is well endowed as well as carefully made. It should turn out to be a good example of Margaux in this slightly firm vintage. Give it 3–4 years of cellaring, and drink it over the following 8–10. Last tasted, 3/96.

•
85+

1993—A perennial overachiever, Siran has a fine track record for producing long-lived, rich, structured wines. With its highly extracted, tannic style, the 1993 will unquestionably be an ageworthy effort. The color is an impressive ruby/purple. Although not complex, the wine has medium body, excellent concentration, high extract, and a beefy, chewy, muscular personality. It will require 5–7 years of cellaring and should drink well for 15–20 years. Last tasted, 11/94.

•
85

1990—The deeply colored 1990 reveals a tightly knit nose that offers aromas of
  •   black fruits, smoky oak, and earth. In the mouth, there is medium body,
  87   excellent ripeness, good acidity, and plenty of length in the moderately tannic
        finish. It should age nicely for 10–15 or more years. Last tasted, 1/93.

1989—The 1989 is a graceful, medium-bodied wine displaying the vintage's soft,
  •   silky texture, plenty of alcohol, low acidity, and aging potential of 4–8 years.
  86   It is hard not to admire its sweet, round, gentle nature. Anticipated maturity:
        Now–2000. Last tasted, 1/93.

1988— Deep ruby in color, with a spicy, black currant–scented bouquet, the full-
  •   bodied 1988 exhibits good depth and structure, but it will need 4–5 years in
  85   the bottle to shed its toughness. Anticipated maturity: Now–2005. Last tasted,
        1/93.

1986—With deep, dark ruby/purple color, plenty of body, and mouth-searing tannins
  •   in the finish, the 1986 Siran competently displays the personality characteris-
  88   tics of the vintage. Between the fragrant, tarry, spicy, curranty bouquet and
        the hard finish is plenty of depth and fruit. However, one must defer gratifica-
        tion for at least 7–8 years before drinking the 1986 Siran. Anticipated matu-
        rity: Now–2010. Last tasted, 11/90.

1985—The 1985 Siran is surprisingly powerful for the vintage, rich in fruit, elegant,
  •   long, and aromatic. It will age well. Anticipated maturity: Now–2000. Last
  86   tasted, 3/90.

1983—Approaching full maturity, the 1983 Siran has a smoky licorice-and-black
  •   currant–scented bouquet, rich, expansive flavors that offer more muscle and
  86   power than finesse, and a good finish. Anticipated maturity: Now. Last tasted,
        3/88.

TERTRE
VERY GOOD

Classification: Fifth-growth in 1855
Location of vineyards: Arsac
Owner: Eric Albáda; managed by Madame Capbern-Gasqueton
Address: 33340 Arsac
Mailing address: c/o Château Calon-Ségur, 33180 St.-Estèphe
Telephone: 33 5 56 59 30 08; telefax: 33 5 56 59 71 51
Visits: By appointment only
Contact: Mrs. Denise Capbern-Gasqueton at above telephone and fax
numbers

VINEYARDS (red)
Surface area: 121 acres
Average age of vines: 30 years
Blend: 65% Cabernet Sauvignon, 20% Merlot, 15% Cabernet Franc
Average yields (over the last 5 years): 40 hectoliters per hectare
Total average annual production: 225,000 bottles

GRAND VIN (red)
Brand name: Château du Tertre
Appellation: Margaux
Mean annual production: 180,000 bottles
Upbringing: Grapes are hand-picked. Fermentations last about 24 days in temperature-controlled tanks. Wines are transferred, after malolactics, to oak barrels, 30% of which are new, for 18 months aging. They are fined with egg whites but not filtered prior to bottling.

SECOND WINE
Brand name: Les Hauts du Tertre
Average annual production: 45,000 bottles

Evaluation of present classification: Should be maintained, although the quality since 1978 may justify elevation to a fourth-growth
Plateau of maturity: 6–15 years following the vintage

Du Tertre, located on one of the highest plateaus in the Margaux appellation, was acquired in 1961 by the late Philippe Capbern-Gasqueton, proprietor of the famous St.-Estèphe estate, Calon-Ségur. The property was in deplorable condition, and Gasqueton and his investors began an extensive plan to rebuild the château and replant the vineyard. Until 12 years ago, it was extremely easy to forget the wines of this property. The sandy-colored, plain yet elegant, two-story château is located in one of the most obscure areas of the Médoc (less than a kilometer from Arsac, near the appellation's top overachiever, Monbrison). In 1998, the estate was sold by Madame Gasqueton.

The vineyard is unusual because it is one contiguous parcel and not morcellated as so many Bordeaux château vineyards are. At first glance it is visually reminiscent of Domaine de Chevalier. In contrast with the relatively high percentage of Merlot planted at Calon-Ségur in St.-Estèphe, Gasqueton has chosen to utilize primarily Cabernet Sauvignon at du Tertre, taking advantage of the gravelly, sandstone soil that dominates his vineyard. The wine, since 1978, has been characterized by relatively deep color and a good bit of power and richness in the top vintages, but perhaps a lack of finesse and that extra-special fragrance that can make a Margaux so enthralling. Nevertheless, the wine continues to sell at a modest price, making it one of the most undervalued of the classified growths of Bordeaux.

As good as this wine now is, I would be curious to see if it could even be improved with the use of a slightly higher percentage of new oak and Merlot.

VINTAGES

1997—This wine performed well on the several occasions I tasted it. Du Tertre's dark
• ruby/purple-colored 1997 offers copious quantities of sweet blackberry and
86– currant fruit in the evolved nose. Soft, lush, and low in acidity, this medium-
88 bodied wine was tasting akin to a succulent fruit bomb. Anticipated maturity:
2000–2007. Last tasted, 3/98.

1996—A sleeper, du Tertre's 1996 exhibits a black ruby/purple color, a sweet black
• fruit-scented nose, medium to full body, well-integrated tannin, and fine
88– purity and depth. This wine should age nicely, yet have a degree of accessibil-
90 ity young. Anticipated maturity: 2004–2018. Last tasted, 3/98.

1995—A chocolatey, berry-scented nose with weedy cassis, licorice, and earth
• aromas is followed by a medium-bodied wine with fine concentration. Al-
86 though monolithic, the 1995 is well made, mouth-filling, and moderately
tannic. Anticipated maturity: 2003–2015. Last tasted, 11/97.

1990—The 1990 represents a strong effort for this property. It is surprisingly dark in
• color, with medium body, fine structure, plenty of depth and richness, and an
87 interesting bouquet of olives, smoky oak, and over-ripe black fruits. This wine
reminds me somewhat of a lighter version of the 1979. Anticipated maturity:
Now–2008. Last tasted, 1/93.

1989—The 1989 du Tertre is a charming, soft, medium-bodied wine that lacks
• concentration and structure. It is evolved, very perfumed (jammy black cur-
86 rants), low in acidity, and ideal for drinking during its first 6–8 years. Anticipated maturity: Now. Last tasted, 4/91.

1988—The 1988 du Tertre is a good example for the vintage. Medium deep ruby,
• with a curranty, smoky, oak-dominated nose, this wine continues to bear a
86 resemblance to this château's excellent 1979. It will drink well young, but
keep. Anticipated maturity: Now–2003. Last tasted, 1/93.

1987—This is another good example of how charming this vintage can be. Medium
• ruby, with an attractively projected bouquet of currants, spicy new oak, and
83 even a scent of spring flowers, in the mouth the wine is round, soft, with
surprising fat, low acid, and a gentle finish. Anticipated maturity: Now–may
be in decline. Last tasted, 11/90.

1986—The spicy, ripe, mineral, and curranty bouquet is followed by a wine with
• medium body and good grip. Approachable now, and evolving more rapidly
86 than I would have thought possible several years ago, this elegantly wrought
wine remains bargain priced for the vintage. Anticipated maturity: Now–
2005. Last tasted, 3/90.

1985—I have tasted the 1985 du Tertre nine times, five times from cask and
• four times from the bottle. While I have never seen a wine behave so
87 differently, the two most recent tastings have revealed positive results. The
last two examples (both tasted in France) exhibited a nice deep ruby/
purple color with no signs of age and a forward, earthy (truffles?),
curranty bouquet that was enticing. In the mouth, the wine possessed
plenty of fat, ripe, supple blackberry and curranty flavors, with just enough
soft tannins and acidity to give the wine grip and focus. This is a lus-

cious, very forward style of du Tertre. Anticipated maturity: Now. Last tasted, 11/90.

1983—Medium to deep ruby, with an intensely spicy, slightly herbaceous nose, du
  • Tertre's 1983 is rich and ripe, with medium-bodied flavors that exhibit good
 86 concentration and moderate tannins that are beginning to melt away. This is
     a very good, rather than exceptional, wine from the 1983 vintage. Anticipated
     maturity: Now–2001. Last tasted, 11/90.

1982—A wonderful, fragrant bouquet of violets, damp earth, cedar wood, black
  • currants, and white chocolate jumps from the glass. On the palate, the wine
 87 is lush, medium bodied, and concentrated, with ripe, fruity flavors. Like most
     Margaux of this vintage, it has reached its plateau of maturity. Anticipated
     maturity: Now. Last tasted, 1/90.

1981—Medium ruby in color, with a moderately intense, spicy, perfumed bou-
  • quet, the 1981 du Tertre is much leaner than the fat, generously flavored
 83 1982 or excellent 1979. It still possesses some tannin and, while pleasant,
     lacks weight and finishes short. Anticipated maturity: Now. Last tasted,
     7/88.

1979—This has always been one of the sleepers of the vintage. The 1979 du Tertre
  • continues to exhibit a marvelous tarry, rich, deep, berry-scented bouquet, fat,
 89 supple, very concentrated, fruity flavors, medium body, and fine length.
     Enough tannin remains for 5–7 more years of evolution. This is a bargain-
     priced wine to look for at the auctions. Anticipated maturity: Now. Last tasted,
     1/91.

1978—This wine has reached full maturity and exhibits a surprisingly earthy, almost
  • rustic bouquet filled with aromas of chestnuts, plummy fruit, and old, yet
 85 clean barrel smells. In the mouth, the wine is round, slightly herbaceous, but
     generously endowed and soft, with a smooth, heady finish. A touch of earthi-
     ness on the nose and in the flavors lowers the score. Anticipated maturity:
     Now. Last tasted, 1/91.

OTHER MARGAUX ESTATES

ARSAC

Classification: Cru Bourgeois in 1932
Location of vineyards: Arsac
Owner: Philippe Raoux
Address: 33460 Arsac
Mailing address: Same as above
Telephone: 33 5 56 58 83 90; telefax: 33 5 56 58 83 08
Visits: Between 10 A.M. and 6 P.M. on weekdays; by appointment only
during weekends
Contact: Hélène Schönbeck

VINEYARDS (red)
Surface area: 185.3 acres in all, with 44.5 acres in Margaux and the rest in appellation Haut-Médoc
Average age of vines: 15 years
Blend: 60% Cabernet Sauvignon, 40% Merlot
Density of plantation: 6,600 vines per hectare
Average yields (over the last 5 years): 55 hectoliters per hectare
Total average annual production: 550,000 bottles in all, 130,000 bottles of Margaux

GRAND VIN (red)
Brand name: Château d'Arsac
Appellation: Margaux
Mean annual production: 130,000 bottles
Upbringing: Grape picking is mechanical, but the grapes are sorted out when they come into the winery. Fermentations last approximately 3 weeks and are carried out in temperature-controlled stainless-steel tanks. Wines are transferred after malolactics into oak barrels, which are renewed by one-fourth each year. The wines are both fined and filtered before bottling.

SECOND WINE
None produced.

BEL-AIR MARQUIS D'ALIGRE

Classification: Cru Bourgeois Exceptionnel
Production: 5,000 cases
Blend: 35% Merlot, 30% Cabernet Sauvignon, 20% Cabernet Franc, 15% Petit Verdot
Secondary label: Bel-Air-Marquis de Pomereu
Vineyard size: 42 acres
Proprietor: Pierre Boyer
Time spent in barrels: 18–20 months
Average age of vines: 35 years

Evaluation of present classification: Should be maintained
Plateau of maturity: 4–12 years following the vintage

CHARMANT   GOOD

Classification: None
Location of vineyards: Margaux et Soussans
Owner: Christiane Renon
Address: 33460 Margaux
Mailing address: Same as above
Telephone: 33 5 57 88 35 27; telefax: 33 5 57 88 70 59
Visits: By appointment only
Contact: Christiane Renon

VINEYARDS (red)
Surface area: 12.4 acres
Average age of vines: 60 years
Blend: 50% Merlot, 45% Cabernet Sauvignon and Cabernet Franc,
5% Petit Verdot
Density of plantation: 8,300 vines per hectare
Average yields (over the last 5 years): 52 hectoliters per hectare
Total average annual production: 30,000 bottles

GRAND VIN (red)
Brand name: Château Charmant
Appellation: Margaux
Mean annual production: 30,000 bottles
Upbringing: Fermentations last 20–25 days at 28–30 degrees centigrade,
with frequent pumping-overs. Wines are afterward aged in oak barrels,
5% of which are new, for 15–18 months. They are fined but not filtered
before bottling.

SECOND WINE
None produced.

Evaluation of present classification: Should be maintained
Plateau of maturity: Unknown

This wine is highly prized by none other than Bernard Ginestet, who knows as much about the appellation of Margaux as any human being. The proprietor, Christiane Renon, believes in extremely old vines (half of his vineyard is over 100 years of age, a fact that makes his vineyard the oldest in Margaux in terms of vine age). Ginestet has told me this is the best Cru Bourgeois in the Médoc—high praise indeed.

DESMIRAIL

Classification: Third-growth
Production: 4,500 cases
Blend: 80% Cabernet Sauvignon, 10% Merlot, 5% Cabernet Franc,
5% Petit Verdot
Secondary label: Château Baudry
Vineyard size: 44.5 acres
Proprietor: Lucien Lurton
Time spent in barrels: 20 months
Average age of vines: 20 years

Evaluation of present classification: Should be downgraded to a Cru
Bourgeois
Plateau of maturity: 3–12 years following the vintage

This property, which currently has no attached château, was ranked a third-growth in the 1855 classification. However, following World War I most of the property was sold in a piecemeal fashion until little remained. The original château of Desmirail is now owned by the Zuger family, who have renamed it Marquis d'Alesme. The proprietor of Brane-Cantenac, Lucien Lurton, has, over the last several decades, purchased parcels of vines that originally composed the vineyard of Desmirail. The name was resurrected in 1980 when the last parcel, a 5-acre plot of the original vineyard, was acquired from Château Palmer. A *chai* and building that Lucien Lurton purchased in the village of Cantenac has now become known as Château Desmirail. Based on vintages in the eighties and early nineties, the wine hardly merits its third-growth ranking. Qualitatively it is the equivalent of a good Cru Bourgeois.

DEYREM-VALENTIN

Classification: Cru Bourgeois in 1932
Location of vineyards: Soussans
Owner: Jean Sorge
Address: 33460 Soussans
Mailing address: Same as above
Telephone: 33 5 57 88 35 70; telefax: 33 5 57 88 36 84
Visits: By appointment only, Monday to Friday, from 9 A.M. to noon, and
2 P.M. to 6 P.M.
Contact: Jean Sorge

VINEYARDS (red)
Surface area: 30.8 acres
Average age of vines: 30 years
Blend: 50% Cabernet Sauvignon, 45% Merlot, 5% Petit Verdot
Density of plantation: 9,000 vines per hectare
Average yields (over the last 5 years): 54 hectoliters per hectare
Total average annual production: 80,000 bottles

GRAND VIN (red)
Brand name: Château Deyrem-Valentin
Appellation: Margaux
Mean annual production: 40,000 bottles
Upbringing: Grapes are hand-picked and sorted as they come into the
winery. Alcoholic fermentations last 1 week and macerations 3 weeks in
temperature-controlled tanks. Wines are then aged for 18 months in
oak barrels, 35% of which are new. They are fined but not filtered before
bottling.

SECOND WINE
Brand name: Château Valentin or Château Soussans
Average annual production: Valentin (30,000 bottles), Soussans (10,000
bottles)

Evaluation of present classification: Should be maintained
Plateau of maturity: 4–10 years following the vintage

I have seen only a handful of the wines of Deyrem-Valentin. The vintages I
have tasted have had good color but seemed to be relatively straightforward,
compact wines, which were correctly and competently made but lacked excitement. If they were to be criticized, it would be because the wines were
aggressively tannic and severe in style. They must be drunk within their first
5–7 years of life.

FERRIÈRE

Classification: Third-growth in 1855
Location of vineyards: Margaux
Owner: S.A. du Château Ferrière
Address: 33460 Margaux
Mailing address: c/o Château Chasse Spleen, 33480 Moulis
Telephone: 33 5 56 58 02 37; telefax: 33 5 56 58 05 70

Visits: By appointment only, from Monday to Friday, between 9 A.M. and 4 P.M.
Contact: Claire Villars

VINEYARDS (red)
Surface area: 19.8 acres
Average age of vines: 35 years
Blend: 75% Cabernet Sauvignon, 20% Merlot, 5% Petit Verdot
Density of plantation: 10,000 vines per hectare
Average yields (over the last 5 years): 50 hectoliters per hectare
Total average annual production: 50,000 bottles

GRAND VIN (red)
Brand name: Château Ferrière
Appellation: Margaux
Upbringing: Grapes are picked manually. Fermentations and macerations last 15–20 days in temperature-controlled stainless-steel tanks. Wines complete their malolactic fermentation in oak barrels, half of which are replaced each vintage. They are aged in oak barrels for 16–18 months before bottling, fined with egg whites, but never filtered.

SECOND WINE
Brand name: Les Remparts de Ferrière

Evaluation of present classification: The quality equivalent of a Cru Bourgeois
Plateau of maturity: 5–10 years following the vintage

LA GALIANE

Classification: None
Location of vineyards: Soussans
Owner: Christiane Renon
Address: 33460 Soussans
Mailing address: Same as above
Telephone: 33 5 57 88 35 27; telefax: 33 5 57 88 70 59
Visits: Monday to Friday, between 9 A.M. and noon, and 2 P.M. and 6 P.M.
Contact: Christiane Renon

VINEYARDS (red)
Surface area: 12.4 acres
Average age of vines: 50 years
Blend: 50% Merlot, 45% Cabernet Sauvignon and Cabernet Franc, 5% Petit Verdot

Density of plantation: 9,300 vines per hectare
Average yields (over the last 5 years): 53 hectoliters per hectare
Total average annual production: 34,000 bottles

GRAND VIN (red)
Brand name: Château La Galiane
Appellation: Margaux
Mean annual production: 34,000 bottles
Upbringing: Fermentations last about 3 weeks at 28–30 degrees
centigrade, with frequent pumping-overs in lined cement vats. Wines are
afterward aged in oak barrels, 10% of which are new, for 15–18 months.
They are fined with egg whites and regularly racked but are not filtered
prior to bottling.

SECOND WINE
None produced.

LA GURGUE   GOOD

Classification: Cru Bourgeois in 1932
Location of vineyards: Margaux and Cantenac
Owner: S.C. du Château La Gurgue
Address: 33460 Margaux
Mailing address: Same as above
Telephone: 33 5 56 58 02 37; telefax: 33 5 56 58 05 70
Visits: By appointment only, Monday to Friday, from 9 A.M. to 4 P.M.
Contact: Claire Villars

VINEYARDS (red)
Surface area: 25 acres
Average age of vines: 25 years
Blend: 70% Cabernet Sauvignon, 30% Merlot
Density of plantation: 10,000 vines per hectare
Average yields (over the last 5 years): 50 hectoliters per hectare
Total average annual production: 60,000 bottles

GRAND VIN (red)
Brand name: Château La Gurgue
Appellation: Margaux
Mean annual production: 60,000 bottles
Upbringing: Harvest is done manually. Fermentations and macerations
last about 15 days in temperature-controlled stainless-steel tanks. Wines
are transferred to oak barrels, renewed by one-fourth each year, for 12–
16 months. They are fined but not filtered before bottling.

SECOND WINE
None produced.

Evaluation of present classification: Should be maintained
Plateau of maturity: 5–12 years following the vintage

With its well-placed vineyard just to the west of Château Margaux, this Cru Bourgeois has made considerable strides in quality since it changed owner-ship in 1978, when it was sold to Bernard Taillan and Chantovent.

In top vintages, La Gurgue is a wonderfully supple, deeply colored, rich, smoothly textured wine that is not meant to make old bones. Al-though for drinking in its first 10–12 years, it is rewarding. The price is also attractive. The finest recent vintages have been 1996, 1989, 1988, and 1986.

HAUT BRETON LARIGAUDIÈRE

Classification: Cru Bourgeois in 1932
Location of vineyards: Soussans and Arsac
Owner: S.C.E.A. du Château Haut Breton Larigaudière, Jacques de Schepper
Address: 33460 Soussans
Mailing address: Same as above
Telephone: 33 5 57 88 94 17; telefax: 33 5 57 88 39 14
Visits: By appointment only
Contact: Jean-Michel Garcion

VINEYARDS (red)
Surface area: 32 acres
Average age of vines: 22 years
Blend: 63% Cabernet Sauvignon, 31% Merlot, 4% Petit Verdot, 2% Cabernet Franc
Density of plantation: 10,000 vines per hectare
Average yields (over the last 5 years): 50 hectoliters per hectare
Total average annual production: 6,500 cases

GRAND VIN (red)
Brand name: Château Haut Breton Larigaudière
Appellation: Margaux
Mean annual production: 3,500 cases
Upbringing: Grape picking is entirely manual. Fermentations last approximately 3–5 weeks in temperature-controlled vats. Wines remain

in vats for 4–8 months and are transferred to oak barrels (70%–95% of which are new, depending upon the vintage) for 10–15 months aging. They are fined with egg whites but not filtered prior to bottling.

SECOND WINE
Brand name: Château du Courneau
Average annual production: 1,500 cases

LABÉGORCE

Classification: Cru Bourgeois
Location of vineyards: Margaux
Owner: Hubert Perrodo
Address: 33460 Margaux
Mailing address: Same as above
Telephone: 33 5 57 88 71 32; telefax: 33 5 57 88 35 01
Visits: All days of the week, from 8:30 A.M. to 6 P.M.
Contact: Maïté Augerot

VINEYARDS (red)
Surface area: 94 acres
Average age of vines: 25 years
Blend: 60% Cabernet Sauvignon, 35% Merlot, 5% Cabernet Franc
Density of plantation: 8,000 vines per hectare
Average yields (over the last 5 years): 45 hectoliters per hectare
Total average annual production: 190,000 bottles

GRAND VIN (red)
Brand name: Château Labégorce
Appellation: Margaux
Mean annual production: 150,000 bottles
Upbringing: Grapes are hand-picked. Fermentations last about 3–4 weeks in temperature-controlled vats. Forty percent of the grand vin completes malolactics in new oak barrels. All wines are aged for 12–15 months in oak casks, of which 30% are new. They are fined but not filtered prior to bottling.

SECOND WINE
Brand name: La Mouline de Labégorce
Average annual production: 25,000 bottles

Evaluation of present classification: Should be maintained
Plateau of maturity: 3–8 years following the vintage

Jean-Robert Condom took responsibility for the management of this property in 1978. After significant investments, encouraged by the huge *négociant* Dourthe (which controls much of the worldwide distribution of Labégorce), this has become a consistently well-made Cru Bourgeois in the appellation of Margaux. While it may lack the fragrance and suppleness of an excellent Margaux Cru Bourgeois such as La Gurgue, or the pure power and aging potential of a Monbrison, the wine has character and is fairly priced. In late 1989 the estate was sold to Hubert Perrodo.

Although many knowledgeable consumers are impressed with the wine's delicacy, Labégorce seems to me to have more of a St.-Estèphe style without the fragrance found in many Margaux. It is often as good as many of the Margaux classified growths as well as considerably less expensive. The best recent vintage has been 1983, followed by 1989 and 1986. Top years of Labégorce should be consumed within 8 years of the vintage.

LARRUAU   GOOD

Classification: Cru Bourgeois
Production: 1,000 cases
Blend: 66% Cabernet Sauvignon, 34% Merlot
Secondary label: None
Vineyard size: 7.5 acres
Proprietor: Bernard Château
Time spent in barrels: 18 months
Average age of vines: 15 years

Evaluation of present classification: Should be upgraded to a Médoc fifth-growth
Plateau of maturity: 5–12 years following the vintage

One of my personal goals is to taste more wines from Bernard Château, the young proprietor and winemaker of Château Larruau. He produces intensely concentrated wine, if the 1983 and 1986 are typical of the wines this tiny estate turns out. The property is also highly regarded by Margaux's most knowledgeable observer, Bernard Ginestet, who ranks Larruau as highly as such classified growths as Lascombes, Giscours, and Durfort-Vivens.

MARSAC-SÉGUINEAU   GOOD

Classification: Cru Bourgeois in 1932
Location of vineyards: Soussans
Owner: S.C. du Château Marsac-Séguineau
Address: 33460 Soussans

Mailing address: Same as above
Telephone: 33 5 56 01 30 10; telefax: 33 5 56 79 23 57
Visits: Exclusively by appointment and for professionals of the wine
trade only, from Monday to Friday, between 9 A.M. and noon, and 2 P.M.
and 5 P.M.
Contact: M. Cruse

VINEYARDS (red)
Surface area: 25.3 acres
Average age of vines: 29 years
Blend: 60% Merlot, 28% Cabernet Sauvignon, 12% Cabernet Franc
Density of plantation: 10,000 vines per hectare
Average yields (over the last 5 years): 56 hectoliters per hectare
Total average annual production: 5,500 cases

GRAND VIN (red)
Brand name: Château Marsac-Séguineau
Appellation: Margaux
Mean annual production: 3,800 cases
Upbringing: Harvest is done both by hand and by machine.
Fermentations last 21 days. Wines are transferred to oak casks for aging,
for 18–21 months. The percentage of new oak is usually 30%. Wines are
fined and filtered (for safety) at the time of bottling.

SECOND WINE
Brand name: Château Gravières-de-Marsac
Average annual production: 1,700 cases

Evaluation of present classification: An up-and-coming estate that is now
one of the best of the Margaux Cru Bourgeois
Plateau of maturity: 5–15 years following the vintage

I have had a chance to taste a half dozen vintages of Marsac-Séguineau, which
is controlled by the *négociant* Mestrezat. With a relatively high percentage of
Merlot in the blend, the wine is darkly colored, tannic, surprisingly intense,
and rich. The two most recent top vintages include a first-class 1990 and a
very smooth, large-scaled 1989. This property merits attention by consumers
looking for excellent wines from the under-achieving appellation of Margaux.
The entire 25-acre vineyard is located in the commune of Soussans.

MARTINENS

Classification: Cru Bourgeois in 1932
Location of vineyards: Cantenac
Owner: Mrs. Simone Dulos and her son, Jean-Pierre Seynat-Dulos
Address: 33460 Cantenac, Margaux
Mailing address: Same as above
Telephone: 33 5 57 88 71 37; telefax: 33 5 57 88 38 35
Visits: Preferably by appointment, from Monday to Saturday, between
9 A.M. and noon, and 2 P.M. and 6 P.M.
Contact: Jean-Pierre Seynat-Dulos

VINEYARDS (red)
Surface area: 77 acres in all, 59 in Margaux and 18 in Haut Médoc
Average age of vines: 35 years
Blend: 54% Merlot, 31% Cabernet Sauvignon, 11% Petit Verdot,
4% Cabernet Franc
Average yields (over the last 5 years): 55 hectoliters per hectare
Total average annual production: 12,500 cases

GRAND VIN (red)
Brand name: Château Martinens
Appellation: Argaux
Mean annual production: 100,000 bottles
Upbringing: Grapes are entirely hand-picked. Fermentations take place
in automatic temperature-controlled cement tanks and last 3 weeks.
Malolactics occur on warming. *Assemblage* is done after malolactics, and
wines are aged in oak casks, which are renewed by one-fourth each year,
for 18 months. They are racked every 3 months, fined with egg whites
(powder), and filtered before bottling.

SECOND WINE
Brand name: Château Bois du Monteil
Appellation: Haut-Médoc
Average annual production: 58 hectoliters per hectare

Evaluation of present classification: Should be maintained
Plateau of maturity: 3–10 years following the vintage

I have tasted this wine infrequently and have never tried an old vintage. Vintages such as 1989, 1988, 1986, and 1985, have all been abrasively hard, tough-textured wines lacking charm, fruit, and depth. The exceptionally high percentage of Petit Verdot (which rarely ripens except in years such as 1982 and 1989) may account for this wine's stern personality.

MONGRAVEY

Classification: None
Location of vineyards: Arsac
Owner: Régis Bernaleau
Address: 15, avenue de Ligondras, 33460 Arsac
Mailing address: Same as above
Telephone: 33 5 56 58 84 51; telefax: 33 5 56 58 83 39
Visits: By appointment only
Contact: Régis Bernaleau

VINEYARDS (red)
Surface area: 22 acres
Average age of vines: 18 years
Blend: 55% Cabernet Sauvignon, 45% Merlot
Density of plantation: 10,000 vines per hectare, 8,300 vines per hectare, and 6,500 vines per hectare
Average yields (over the last 5 years): 54 hectoliters per hectare
Total average annual production: 5,000 cases

GRAND VIN (red)
Brand name: Château Mongravey
Appellation: Margaux
Mean annual production: 40,000 bottles
Upbringing: Fermentations and macerations last 4–6 weeks depending upon the vintage. Wines are transferred to oak barrels for 12–18 months aging. One-third of the barrels is entirely new, one-third is 1 year old, and the other third is 2 years old. The wines are fined and filtered before bottling.

SECOND WINE
Brand name: Château Cazauviel
Average annual production: 24,000 bottles.

PAVEIL-DE-LUZE

Classification: Cru Bourgeois
Production: 10,000 cases
Blend: 70% Cabernet Sauvignon, 30% Merlot
Secondary label: De la Coste
Vineyard size: 60 acres
Proprietor: G.F.A. du Château
Time spent in barrels: 12–15 months
Average age of vines: 20 years

Evaluation of present classification: Should be maintained
Plateau of maturity: 3–9 years following the vintage

I have always found the wines of this estate to be bland and undistinguished. Tastings from vintages in the late eighties suggest nothing has changed. Baron Geoffroy de Luze and his three children administer this charming property that has been in the de Luze family for over a century.

PONTAC-LYNCH

Classification: Cru Bourgeois in 1932
Location of vineyards: Cantenac and Margaux; some vineyards are bordered by those of Châteaux Margaux, Palmer, and d'Issan, and some are located between those of Châteaux Margaux and Rauzan-Ségla
Owner: Bondon family
Address: Issan Cantenac, 33460 Margaux
Mailing address: B.P. 7, 33460 Margaux
Telephone: 33 5 57 88 30 04; telefax: 33 5 57 88 32 63
Visits: Preferably by appointment, from Monday to Friday, between 9 A.M. and noon, and 2 P.M. and 5 P.M.
Contact: Marie-Christine Bondon

VINEYARDS (red)
Surface area: 25 acres
Average age of vines: 20 years
Blend: 45% Merlot, 25% Cabernet Sauvignon, 20% Cabernet Franc, 10% Petit Verdot
Density of plantation: 10,000 vines per hectare
Average yields (over the last 5 years): 48 hectoliters per hectare
Total average annual production: 60,000 bottles

GRAND VIN (red)
Brand name: Château Pontac-Lynch
Appellation: Margaux
Mean annual production: 48,000 bottles
Upbringing: Grapes are hand-picked and sorted on conveyor belts installed in the vineyards at harvest-time. Fermentations last 10–14 days in temperature-controlled vats, and macerations last as long, depending upon the vintage. Wines are transferred for aging to oak barrels, one-third of which are new, for 12 months. They are fined with egg whites but not filtered prior to bottling. The wines are racked every 4 months.

SECOND WINE
Brand name: Château Pontac-Phenix
Average annual production: 12,000 bottles

PONTET-CHAPPAZ

Classification: None
Location of vineyards: Arsac
Owner: Vignobles Rocher Cap de Rive S.A., Roger Geens
Address: 33460 Margaux
Mailing address: c/o Château Rocher Bellevue, B.P. 89, 33350 St. Magne
de Castillon
Telephone: 33 5 57 40 08 88; telefax: 33 5 57 40 19 93
Visits: By appointment only
Contact: Isabel Teles Pinto

VINEYARDS (red)
Surface area: 17.3 acres
Average age of vines: 20 years
Blend: 70% Cabernet Sauvignon, 25% Merlot, 5% Petit Verdot
Density of plantation: 7,500 vines per hectare
Average yields (over the last 5 years): 55 hectoliters per hectare
Total average annual production: 4,000 cases

GRAND VIN (red)
Brand name: Château Pontet-Chappaz
Appellation: Margaux
Mean annual production: 2,300 cases
Upbringing: Fermentations last 28 days in temperature-controlled vats.
Wines are then aged in vats and oak barrels (20% of which are new) for
about 18 months. They are fined and filtered prior to bottling.

SECOND WINE
Brand name: Château Tricot d'Arsac
Average annual production: 180 hectoliters

TAYAC

Classification: Cru Bourgeois
Location of vineyards: Margaux
Owner: S.C. du Château Tayac
Address: 33460 Soussans
Mailing address: B.P. 10, 33460 Soussans
Telephone: 33 5 57 88 33 06; telefax: 33 5 57 88 36 06
Visits: Monday through Friday, from 10 A.M. to noon, and 2 P.M.
to 6 P.M.
Contact: Nadine Portet (director) or Yvette Favin

VINEYARDS (red)
Surface area: 91.4 acres
Average age of vines: 20 years
Blend: 65% Cabernet Sauvignon, 33% Merlot, 2% Petit Verdot
Density of plantation: 9,000 vines per hectare
Average yields (over the last 5 years): 60 hectoliters per hectare

GRAND VIN (red)
Brand name: Château Tayac
Appellation: Margaux
Mean annual production: 900 hectoliters
Upbringing: Fermentations and macerations last 21 days approximately
in temperature-controlled stainless-steel and concrete (lined with epoxy)
vats. Malolactics occur in tanks, and wines are transferred to oak barrels,
30% of which are new, for 12 months aging. They are fined but remain
unfiltered upon bottling.

SECOND WINE
None produced.

This is a large Cru Bourgeois with most of the vineyards in the commune of
Soussans. Based on the half dozen or so vintages I have tasted, the wine is
correctly made, but straightforward and lacking the fragrance and length that
the best wines of the Margaux appellation possess. Perhaps a stricter selection
and more elevated use of new oak might add to the wine's character and
complexity.

LA TOUR DE BESSAN

Classification: None
Location of vineyards: Soussans and Arsac
Owner: Marie Laure Lurton Roux
Address: 33460 Cantenac
Mailing address: S.C. Les Grands Crus Réunis, 33480 Moulis
Telephone: 33 5 57 88 83 33; telefax: 33 5 57 88 72 51
Visits: Not allowed
Contact: Marie Laure Lurton Roux

VINEYARDS (red)
Surface area: 42 acres
Average age of vines: 25 years
Blend: 58% Cabernet Franc, 28% Cabernet Sauvignon, 14% Merlot
Density of plantation: 6,000 vines per hectare

Average yields (over the last 5 years): 45 hectoliters per hectare
Total average annual production: 7,650 cases

GRAND VIN (red)
Brand name: Château La Tour de Bessan
Appellation: Margaux
Mean annual production: 100,000 bottles
Upbringing: Fermentations occur in stainless-steel vats. Wines are then
aged in oak barrels of 2–4 years for 6 months prior to bottling. They are
fined and filtered.

SECOND WINE
None produced.

Any declassified wine is sold in bulk to the trade.

LA TOUR-DE-MONS

Classification: Cru Bourgeois Supérieur
Location of vineyards: Soussans
Owner: S.C.E.A. La-Tour-de-Mons
Address: 33460 Soussans
Mailing address: Same as above
Telephone: 33 5 57 88 33 03; telefax: 33 5 57 88 32 46
Visits: By appointment only
Contact: Dominique Laux

VINEYARDS (red)
Surface area: 86.5 acres
Average age of vines: 30 years
Blend: 48% Merlot, 38% Cabernet Sauvignon, 8% Petit Verdot,
6% Cabernet Franc
Density of plantation: 8,000 vines per hectare
Average yields (over the last 5 years): 55 hectoliters per hectare
Total average annual production: 18,000 cases

GRAND VIN (red)
Brand name: Château La-Tour-de-Mons
Appellation: Margaux
Mean annual production: 18,000 cases
Upbringing: Fermentations last approximately 20 days in
temperature-controlled stainless-steel tanks. There are frequent
pumping-overs for better extraction. Wines are transferred after

malolactics to oak barrels, 30% of which are new, for 12 months aging. They are fined with egg whites but not filtered prior to bottling.

SECOND WINE
Brand name: Marquis de Mons
Average annual production: 600 hectoliters

Evaluation of present classification: Should be maintained
Plateau of maturity: 5–14 years following the vintage

This famous old estate, still run by the Clauzel-Binaud family (who at one time also controlled Château Cantemerle), is only a Cru Bourgeois, but some of its vintages, the 1949 and 1953, for example, are legendary. They have been rated among the best wines of those years. Like Cantemerle, however, the property was allowed to deteriorate in the late seventies and is only now beginning to regain its form. The vineyard, which is in the Margaux commune of Soussans, has an extremely ancient history, with origins tracing back to the late thirteenth century. All of the optimistic talk about the resurgence of La-Tour-de-Mons has not been reflected in my tasting notes. Certainly the wines are good, but nothing has emerged during the eighties that would merit an upgrading of this property to classified-growth status as some observers have suggested.

TROIS CHARDONS

Classification: None
Location of vineyards: Cantenac
Owner: Claude and Yves Chardon
Address: 33460 Cantenac, Margaux
Mailing address: c/o Yves and Claude Chardon, 2, route d'Issan, 33460 Cantenac
Telephone: 33 5 57 88 39 13; telefax: 33 5 57 88 33 94
Visits: By appointment only
Contact: Claude and Yves Chardon

VINEYARDS (red)
Surface area: 6.8 acres
Average age of vines: 30 years
Blend: 50% Cabernet Sauvignon, 45% Merlot, 5% Petit Verdot
Density of plantation: 10,000 vines per hectare
Average yields (over the last 5 years): 52 hectoliters per hectare
Total average annual production: 1,400 cases

GRAND VIN (red)
Brand name: Château des Trois Chardons
Appellation: Margaux
Mean annual production: 12,000 bottles
Upbringing: Fermentations and macerations last about 25 days. Wines are then transferred into oak barrels for 20 months of aging. They are fined but not filtered prior to bottling.

SECOND WINE
Brand name: None—sold in bulk if any.

LES VIMIÈRES-LE TRONQUERA

Classification: Cru Artisan
Location of vineyards: Soussans
Owner: A. M. and J. Boissenot
Address: 47, rue Principale, 33460 Lamarque
Mailing address: Same
Telephone: 33 5 56 58 91 74; telefax: 3 5 56 58 98 36
Visits: By appointment only, every day, between 9 A.M. and noon, and 2 P.M. and 6 P.M.
Contact: J. Boissenot

VINEYARDS (red)
Surface area: 1.1 acres
Average age of vines: 50 years
Blend: 100% Merlot
Density of plantation: 10,000 vines per hectare
Average yields (over the last 5 years): 39 hectoliters per hectare
Total average annual production: 3,000 bottles

GRAND VIN (red)
Brand name: Château Les Vimières-Le Tronquera
Appellation: Margaux
Mean annual production: 3,000 bottles
Upbringing: Fermentations last 18–20 days at temperatures of about 28 degrees centigrade. Wines are aged in oak barrels (60% new and 40% 1 year old) for 20 months. They are fined but not filtered before bottling.

SECOND WINE
None produced.

THE LESSER-KNOWN APPELLATIONS: MÉDOC, HAUT-MÉDOC, LISTRAC, AND MOULIS

There are hundreds of châteaux in the vast Médoc that produce notable wines of quality, character, and interest. They frequently offer astonishing values in good vintages and sensationally great values in excellent vintage years. A few of these estates make wine as good as (and in a few instances better than) many of the famous classified growths. However, most of these properties make solid, reliable wines, which, if never spectacularly exciting, are nevertheless sound and satisfying. In the very good to great vintages of Bordeaux —1961, 1970, 1975, 1982, 1985, 1986, 1989, 1990, 1995, and 1996—the wines from the best of these properties especially deserve seeking out.

No other wine regions of Bordeaux have made as much progress as the Crus Bourgeois of the Médoc, Haut-Médoc, Listrac, and Moulis during the last 20 years. To enjoy Bordeaux on a regular basis, knowledge of the best estates of these appellations is essential. The Médoc appellation refers to a vast area that now encompasses more than 11,610 acres of vineyards. The appellation name has caused some confusion because the entire region north of the city of Bordeaux, bordered on the west by the Atlantic Ocean and to the east by the Gironde River, is geographically called "the Médoc." However, in terms of the Médoc appellation, the area corresponds to the very northern part of the Bordeaux viticultural area that has long been called the Bas-Médoc. Most of the wines entitled to the Médoc appellation come from the seven communes of Bégadan, St.-Yzans, Prignac, Ordonnac, St.-Christoly, Blaignan, and St.-Germain d'Esteuil.

Making any generalizations about the wines of the Médoc appellation is impossible because of the huge variation in quality. However, in this remote, backwater region of Bordeaux, there has been a noticeable trend in the last several decades to plant more Merlot in the region's heavier, thicker, less porous soils. This has meant the wines possess more up-front charm and more fruit, as well as popular appeal. There also have been several classifications of the wines themselves, but for the purpose of this chapter, I have called everything a "Cru Bourgeois" because the classifications—observed objectively—appear to be political creations rather than any valid attempt to classify the châteaux by their commitment to quality.

The Haut-Médoc appellation also comprises just over 10,375 acres of vineyards. It is a massive area, stretching from the industrial suburb north of Bordeaux called Blanquefort, north to where the Bas-Médoc begins. This region, which skirts around the Médoc appellation, produces wines from fifteen communes, the most famous of which are St.-Seurin, St.-Laurent, Cussac, St.-Sauveur, Cissac, and Vertheuil. Many producers in the Haut-Médoc make wines that surpass some of the classified growths, and as in the Médoc, the quality of many of the Crus Bourgeois has improved immensely during this last decade.

Listrac is another obscure appellation of Bordeaux. It, like neighboring Moulis, sits well inland and covers just over 1,730 acres of vines. The wines justifiably have a reputation for being tough textured, dry, and astringent, with little charm and fruit. These characteristics have undermined the success of Listrac wines in export markets, but increasingly during the eighties this issue has been addressed by the proprietors. Today the wines are less rugged and tough than in the past, but they are still relatively tannic wines that could use more charm.

Moulis is, for me, the best of the lesser-known Bordeaux appellations. Perhaps this is because so many talented proprietors extract the highest quality possible from this small appellation of just over 1,420 acres. The wines from Moulis are among the longest lived of Bordeaux. In top vintages they are strikingly rich, full bodied, and powerful. There is a bevy of great châteaux in Moulis, including the likes of Chasse-Spleen, Gressier Grand-Poujeaux, Maucaillou, and Poujeaux. Many of the wines of Moulis can rival, at least in terms of longevity, the finest classified growths.

I have organized this chapter by listing the properties in alphabetical order. For those estates that I believe are making wines of classified-growth quality, specific tasting notes are provided. The best vintages of the other estates are mentioned, but tasting notes are not given.

LISTRAC—AN OVERVIEW

Location: This backwater appellation, southwest of St.-Julien, is 19 miles from Bordeaux's city center

Acres under Vine: 1,729

Communes: There are several specifically defined areas, but Listrac is the principal one

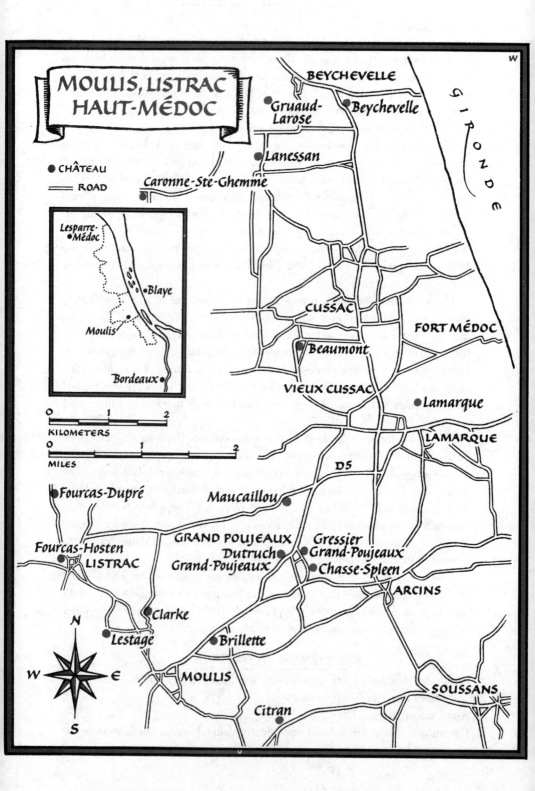

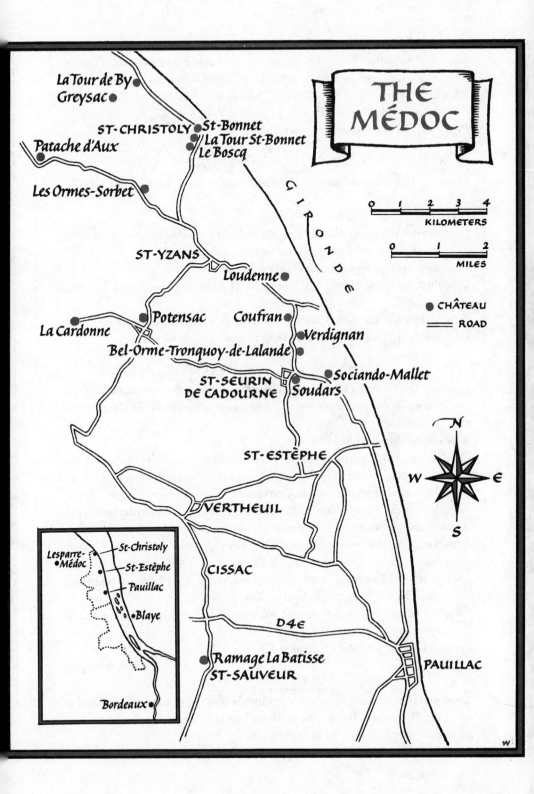

THE MÉDOC

La Tour de By
Greysac

ST-CHRISTOLY • St-Bonnet
La Tour St-Bonnet
Patache d'Aux • Le Boscq

Les Ormes-Sorbet

G I R O N D E

ST-YZANS
Loudenne

Potensac • Coufran
La Cardonne • Verdignan
Bel-Orme-Tronquoy-de-Lalande
ST-SEURIN • Sociando-Mallet
DE CADOURNE • Soudars

ST-ESTÈPHE

VERTHEUIL

CISSAC

D4E

Ramage La Batisse
ST-SAUVEUR

PAUILLAC

0 1 2 3 4
KILOMETERS

0 1 2
MILES

● CHÂTEAU
═══ ROAD

N
W E
S

Lesparre-
Médoc
St-Christoly
St-Estèphe
Pauillac
Blaye

Bordeaux

Average Annual Production: 300,000 cases

Classified Growths: None, but there are 29 Crus Bourgeois and 12 other estates, as well as 1 cooperative boasting 60 members

Principal Grape Varieties: Cabernet Sauvignon, followed by Merlot, with lesser quantities of Cabernet Franc and Petit Verdot

Principal Soil Type: Clay, limestone, and gravel

MOULIS—AN OVERVIEW

Location: 18 miles northwest of Bordeaux, northwest of the Margaux appellation

Acres under Vine: 1,420

Communes: Moulis-en-Médoc and a handful of estates located in specific areas of Arcins, Castelnau, Lamarque, and Listrac-Médoc

Average annual production: 285,000 cases

Classified Growths: None, but there are 31 Crus Bourgeois and 13 other estates

Principal Grape Varieties: Cabernet Sauvignon, followed by Merlot

Principal Soil Type: Limestone and sandy, gravelly, claylike soils

HAUT-MÉDOC—AN OVERVIEW

Location: Just north of the city of Bordeaux, the lower two-thirds of the entire Médoc peninsula encompasses what is known as the Haut-Médoc appellation

Acres under Vine: 10,375

Communes: From north to south, the communes include St.-Seurin-de-Cadourne, Vertheuil, Cissac, St.-Sauveur, St.-Laurent, Cussac-Fort-Médoc, Lamarque, Arcins, Avensan, Castelnau-de-Médoc, Arsac, Macau, Le Pian-Médoc, Ludon, Parenpuyre, Le Taillan, Blanquefort

Average annual production: In excess of 2 million cases

Classified Growths: Total of 5, including third-growth Château La Lagune, fourth-growth Château La Tour-Carnet, and 3 fifth-growths, Château Belgrave, Camensac, and Cantemerle; there are 140 Crus Bourgeois and 116 other estates, as well as 5 cooperatives

Principal Grape Varieties: Cabernet Sauvignon, followed by Merlot and Cabernet Franc

Principal Soil Type: Sandy, gravelly soil

MÉDOC—AN OVERVIEW

Location: The northern third of the peninsula north of Bordeaux is entitled to the Médoc appellation; its southern boundary begins approximately 30 miles north of the city of Bordeaux

Acres under Vine: 11,610

Communes: From north to south, they are Ste.-Vivien-de-Médoc, Jau-Dignac-et-Loirac, Vensac, Valeyrac, Queyrac, Bégadan, St.-Christoly-Médoc, Civrac-en-Médoc, Couqueques, Prignac, Gaillanen, Lesparre, Blaignan, St.-Yzans-de-Médoc, Ordonnac, St.-Germain-d'Esteuil

Average Annual Production: 2,550,000 cases

Classified Growths: None, but there are 127 Crus Bourgeois and 113 other estates, in addition to 5 cooperatives boasting over 400 members

Principal Grape Varieties: Cabernet Sauvignon dominates, followed by Merlot and, to a lesser extent, Cabernet Franc, Malbec, and Petit Verdot

Principal Soil Type: There is far more diversity in the Médoc appellation than in Haut-Médoc, with considerable gravel, limestone, and sandy soils.

A CONSUMER'S CLASSIFICATION OF THE CHÂTEAUX OF THE MÉDOC, HAUT-MÉDOC, LISTRAC, AND MOULIS

EXCELLENT

Charmail, Chasse-Spleen, Citran, Fourcas-Loubaney, Lanessan, Maucaillou, Potensac, Poujeaux, Sociando-Mallet, Tour Haut-Caussan, Tour du Haut-Moulin

VERY GOOD

Ducluzeau, Moulin-Rouge, Les Ormes-Sorbet, Peyredon-Lagravette, La Tour St.-Bonnet

GOOD

Anthonic, Arnauld, Beaumont, Belgrave, Le Boscq, Branas-Grand Poujeaux, Brillette, Camensac, Cissac, Clarke, Clément-Pichon, Coufran, Dutruch-Grand-Poujeaux, Fonréaud, Fourcas-Dupré, Fourcas-Hosten, Gressier Grand-Poujeaux, Greysac, Lamarque, Lestage, Liversan, Magnol, Malescasse, Mayne-Lalande, Moulin à Vent, Patache d'Aux, Plagnac, Sansarot-Dupré, Ségur, Semeillan-Mazeau, Sénéjac, Soudars, La Tour de By, Verdignan

OTHER NOTABLE PROPERTIES

d'Agassac, Bel-Orme-Tronquoy-de-Lalande, La Cardonne, Caronne-Ste.-Gemme, Clos des Demoiselles, Duplessis, Duplessis-Fabré, Hanteillan, Larose-Trintaudon, Loudenne, Moulis, Peyrabon, Ramage La Batisse, La Tour-Carnet, Villegeorge

AGASSAC

Classification: Cru Bourgeois
Location of vineyards: Ludon-Médoc
Owner: Groupama
Address: 15, rue du Château d'Agassac, 33290 Ludon Médoc
Mailing address: Same as above
Telephone: 33 5 57 88 15 47; telefax: 33 5 57 88 17 61
Visits: On weekdays, between 8:30 A.M. and 12:30 P.M., and 2 P.M.
and 5 P.M.
Contact: Jean-Luc Zell

VINEYARDS (red)
Surface area: 90.2 acres
Average age of vines: 20 years
Blend: 50% Merlot, 47% Cabernet Sauvignon, 3% Cabernet Franc
Density of plantation: 6,700 vines per hectare
Average yields (over the last 5 years): 36 hectoliters per hectare
Total average annual production: 175,000 bottles

GRAND VIN (red)
Brand name: Château d'Agassac
Appellation: Haut-Médoc
Mean annual production: 120,000 bottles
Upbringing: Fermentations and macerations last between 23 and 30 days
in temperature-controlled stainless-steel tanks. After malolactics in vats,
75% of the yield goes into oak barrels (renewed by a third at each
vintage), and the rest stays in vats for 18 months aging. Wines are
fined, but only press wines are filtered before being transferred to oak
barrels.

SECOND WINE
Brand name: Château Pomiès d'Agassac
Average annual production: 55,000 bottles

Evaluation of present classification: Should be maintained
Plateau of maturity: 4–9 years following the vintage

This property, one of only two (the other is La Lagune) to be located on the
sandy soils of Ludon, is in the southernmost part of the Médoc.

The wines of d'Agassac have had a track record of inconsistency despite
relatively low yields and a conservative and traditional vinification. The wine
is robust, frequently lacking charm and fruit. No new oak is used, and perhaps
that is an issue that should be addressed. This is a wine to drink within the
first decade of life. The best recent vintages have been 1990, 1989, and 1982,

which is now beginning to tire. I found the 1983, 1986, and 1988 indifferent winemaking efforts.

Visitors to the region are well advised to make a detour and go inland from the famous D2 to visit d'Agassac, as it represents a superb example of a medieval fortified castle. The edifice, accessible via multiple tours, is one of the most impressive in the Bordeaux region.

ANTHONIC   GOOD

Classification: Cru Bourgeois
Location of vineyards: Moulis
Owner: Pierre Cordonnier
Address: 33480 Moulis
Mailing address: Same as above
Telephone: 33 5 56 58 34 60; telefax: 33 5 56 58 06 22
Visits: On weekdays, between 9 A.M. and noon, and 2 P.M. and 5:30 P.M.; by appointment on weekends
Contact: Jean-Baptiste Cordonnier

VINEYARDS (red)
Surface area: 55.6 acres
Average age of vines: 20 years
Blend: Roughly 55% Merlot, 45% Cabernet Sauvignon (plus some Petit Verdot, negligible)
Density of plantation: 6,700 vines per hectare
Average yields (over the last 5 years): 53 hectoliters per hectare
Total average annual production: 150,000 bottles

GRAND VIN (red)
Brand name: Château Anthonic
Appellation: Moulis
Mean annual production: 130,000 bottles
Upbringing: Fermentations and macerations last approximately 21 days in stainless-steel tanks (temperatures of 33–35 degrees centigrade at the end of the fermentation process). After malolactics, wines are aged 12–15 months in oak barrels, which are renewed by a third at each vintage. They are fined and filtered.

SECOND WINE
Brand name: Château Le Malinay/Château La Grave de Guitignan
Average annual production: 20,000 bottles

Evaluation of present classification: An up-and-coming property that should be watched
Plateau of maturity: 3–10 years following the vintage

I have had the occasion to taste numerous vintages of Anthonic, and I have been duly impressed by the stylish, elegant character of these wines. The vineyard is still young, but it is well placed near the more famous Château Clarke. Proprietor Cordonnier utilizes stainless-steel tanks and 30% new oak each year.

ARNAULD   GOOD

Classification: Cru Bourgeois
Location of vineyards: Arcins
Owner: S.C.E.A. Theil-Roggy
Address: 33460 Margaux
Mailing address: Same as above
Telephone: 33 5 57 88 50 34; telefax: 33 5 57 88 50 35
Visits: Monday through Saturday, between 9 A.M. and noon, and 2 P.M. and 6 P.M.
Contact: François Theil

VINEYARDS (red)
Surface area: 59.3 acres
Average age of vines: 25 years
Blend: 50% Cabernet Sauvignon, 50% Merlot
Density of plantation: 6,666 vines per hectare
Average yields (over the last 5 years): 56 hectoliters per hectare
Total average annual production: 180,000 bottles

GRAND VIN (red)
Brand name: Château Arnauld
Appellation: Haut-Médoc
Mean annual production: 12,000 bottles
Upbringing: Fermentations and macerations last approximately 4 weeks in concrete and stainless-steel tanks. After malolactics in vats, wines are aged 12 months in oak barrels, which are renewed by 40 each year. They are fined and filtered.

SECOND WINE
Brand name: Le Comte d'Arnauld
Average annual production: 60,000 bottles

Evaluation of present classification: Should be maintained
Plateau of maturity: 3–8 years following the vintage

North on the famous D2, just past the village of Arcins, is Château Arnauld. This property is owned by the Theil-Roggy family, who long ago established the reputation of Château Poujeaux in nearby Moulis for one of the most distinctive wines of the Médoc.

The wine produced at Arnauld is less structured, no doubt reflecting the elevated percentage of Merlot (50%) used in the blend. Consequently, Arnauld, for all the attractive, rich fruit, is a wine to be drunk in its first 7–8 years of life. It has been well made since the early eighties, with the better Bordeaux vintages offering wines that are supple, exceptionally fruity, and with good color, yet with limited long-term aging potential. Prices, however, remain reasonable for this tasty wine.

BEL-ORME-TRONQUOY-DE-LALANDE

Classification: Cru Bourgeois in 1932
Location of vineyards: St.-Seurin-de-Cadourne
Owner: Jean-Michel Quié
Address: 33180 St.-Seurin-de-Cadourne
Mailing address: Same as above
Telephone: 33 5 56 59 31 29; telefax: 33 5 56 59 72 83
Visits: Preferably by appointment
Contact: Jean Philippe Caudouin

VINEYARDS (red)
Surface area: 74.1 acres
Average age of vines: 30 years
Blend: 60% Merlot, 30% Cabernet Sauvignon, 10% Cabernet Franc
Density of plantation: 6,500 vines per hectare
Average yields (over the last 5 years): 50–60 hectoliters
Total average annual production: 1,400–1,500 hectoliters

GRAND VIN (red)
Brand name: Château Bel-Orme-Tronquoy-de-Lalande
Appellation: Haut-Médoc
Mean annual production: 130,000 bottles
Upbringing: Fermentations and macerations last 3 weeks in concrete
tanks equipped with a temperature-control system (not automatic).
Malolactics occur in vats, and wines are aged 12–14 months in oak
barrels, 10% of which are new. They are fined with albumin and filtered
upon bottling. (No press wines are added to the grand vin.)

SECOND WINE
None produced; 200–300 hectoliters are sold in bulk.

Evaluation of present classification: Should be maintained
Plateau of maturity: 5–10 years following the vintage

I remember a profound 1945 Bel-Orme-Tronquoy-de-Lalande drunk on New Year's Day 1985. I also have good notes on the 1982 and, more recently, an opulent, chewy, full-bodied 1989 and 1990. But generally, my experience with this property, located in the very northern part of the Médoc near the village of St.-Seurin-de-Cadourne, has been uninspiring.

In the eighties the ancient style of winemaking, which combined immense power and excruciatingly painful tannin levels, gave way to a more supple style that often resulted in wines that lacked concentration and character.

BELGRAVE GOOD

Classification: Fifth-growth in 1855
Location of vineyards: St.-Laurent du Médoc
Owner: S.C. du Château Belgrave (farmed by Dourthe C.V.B.G.)
Address: 33112 St.-Laurent du Médoc
Mailing address: c/o C.V.B.G., B.P. 49, 35, rue de Bordeaux, 33290
Parempuyre
Telephone: 33 5 56 35 53 00; telefax: 33 5 56 35 53 29
Visits: By appointment only
Contact: C.V.B.G. at above telephone and fax numbers

VINEYARDS (red)
Surface area: 133.4 acres
Average age of vines: 22 years
Blend: 40% Cabernet Sauvignon, 35% Merlot, 20% Cabernet Franc, 5%
Petit Verdot
Density of plantation: 8,500 vines per hectare
Average yields (over the last 5 years): 55 hectoliters per hectare
Total average annual production: 3,000 hectoliters

GRAND VIN (red)
Brand name: Château Belgrave
Appellation: Haut-Médoc
Mean annual production: 250,000 bottles
Upbringing: Fermentations and macerations last approximately 3 weeks
in temperature-controlled tanks. There usually are 3–5 pumping-overs a
day. Malolactics occur partly in vats and partly in barrels, and wines are
aged in oak barrels, 50% of which are new, for 15–18 months depending
upon the vintage. They are fined with fresh egg whites and remain
unfiltered upon bottling.

SECOND WINE
Brand name: Diane de Belgrave
Average annual production: 120,000 bottles

Evaluation of present classification: Should be downgraded to a Cru
Bourgeois, although quality has improved since 1985
Plateau of maturity: 5–12 years following the vintage

When the huge firm of Dourthe (or C.V.B.G., as it is known in Bordeaux)
acquired this property in 1980, it was one of the Médoc's most neglected
estates. The owners made significant investments, and the property is now a
showpiece château that also provides lodging for Dourthe's best clients. Mi-

chel Rolland is the consulting oenologist, and there have been major replant-
ings of the vineyard to lower the exceptionally high percentage of Merlot and
increase the percentage of Cabernet Sauvignon.

There was little noticeable improvement in the wines, however, until the
mid-1980s, when Patrick Atteret—son-in-law of Jean-Paul Jauffret, the head
of Dourthe—was brought in to manage the property. At that time, Michel
Rolland, the famed Libourne oenologist, was also hired to provide counseling
for the winemaking. Since that time, Belgrave has taken on more color, depth,
and ripeness. The 1986 was a classically made wine, with excellent richness,
medium to full body, and good midterm aging potential. The 1988 was successful but, like so many Médocs, aggressively tannic. The 1989 looks generously endowed, super-ripe, and soft, a forward wine that should be consumed
within its first decade.

I still wonder whether or not Belgrave will improve to the point where it
again can be considered the qualitative equivalent of a fifth-growth.

LE BOSCQ   GOOD

Classification: Cru Bourgeois
Location of vineyards: St.-Christoly
Address: 1, route du 19 mars, 33340 Bégadan
Mailing address: Les Trois Châteaux, 1, route du 19 mars, 33340
Bégadan
Telephone: 33 5 56 41 50 18; telefax: 33 5 56 41 54 65
Visits: Monday through Friday, between 9 A.M. and 12:30 P.M., and 2 P.M.
and 5:30 P.M.
Contact: Patrice Ricard

VINEYARDS (red)
Surface area: 66.7 acres
Average age of vines: 20 years
Blend: 70% Cabernet Sauvignon, 20% Merlot, 10% Cabernet Franc
Density of plantation: 5,500 vines per hectare
Average yields (over the last 5 years): 59 hectoliters per hectare
Total average annual production: 200,000 bottles

GRAND VIN (red)
Brand name: Château Le Boscq Vieilles Vignes
Appellation: Médoc
Mean annual production: 70,000 bottles
Upbringing: Fermentations last 20–25 days in concrete, wooden, and
stainless-steel tanks. After malolactics in tanks, wines are aged 12

months in oak barrels, approximately 20% of which are new. They are fined but remain unfiltered upon bottling.

SECOND WINE
Brand name: Château Le Boscq
Average annual production: 130,000 bottles

Evaluation of present classification: Should be maintained
Plateau of maturity: 3–7 years following the vintage

This is a reliable Cru Bourgeois made from a vineyard sandwiched between the two excellent Cru Bourgeois vineyards of La Tour de By and La Tour St.-Bonnet near the village of St.-Christoly. The estate is managed by Jean-Michel Lapalu, who also owns the more famous Patache d'Aux. The style sought at Le Boscq is one of unbridled, up-front, in-your-face fruit and suppleness. Consequently this is a wine to drink in its first 3–7 years. The vineyard is harvested by machines, and the vinification and upbringing are designed to put a wine in the bottle that is drinkable immediately.

A Cuvée Vieilles Vignes was inaugurated in 1989.

BRANAS-GRAND POUJEAUX   GOOD

Classification: Cru Bourgeois
Location of vineyards: Moulis
Owner: Jacques de Pourquéry
Address: 33480 Moulis
Mailing address: Same as above
Telephone: 33 5 56 58 03 07; telefax: 33 5 56 58 02 04
Visits: By appointment only
Contact: Jacques de Pourquéry

VINEYARDS (red)
Surface area: 14.8 acres
Average age of vines: 30 years
Blend: 45% Merlot, 50% Cabernet Sauvignon, 5% Petit Verdot
Density of plantation: 6,600 vines per hectare
Average yields (over the last 5 years): 60 hectoliters per hectare
Total average annual production: 350 hectoliters

GRAND VIN (red)
Brand name: Château Branas-Grand Poujeaux
Appellation: Moulis
Mean annual production: 350 hectoliters

Upbringing: Fermentations last approximately 3 weeks in wooden and fiberglass vats. Malolactics occur in vats, and wines are aged 24 months, half in wooden vats and half in oak barrels. They are fined and filtered upon bottling.

SECOND WINE
Brand name: Clos des Demoiselles
Average annual production: 220 hectoliters

Evaluation of present classification: Should be maintained
Plateau of maturity: 6–15 years following the vintage

This is one of the smallest and least known of the Moulis properties. However, in the vintages I have tasted the wines have exhibited a great deal of full-bodied flavor concentration and the potential for 10–20 years of longevity. I wish I knew older vintages better, because there is no doubt that the 1985, 1986, and 1989 were enormously promising wines in their youth.

BRILLETTE   GOOD

Classification: Cru Bourgeois
Location of vineyards: Moulis-en-Médoc
Owner: Jean-Louis Flageul
Address: 33480 Moulis-en-Médoc
Mailing address: Same as above
Telephone: 33 5 56 58 22 09; telefax: 33 5 56 58 12 26
Visits: By appointment, on weekdays only
Contact: Sandrine Delmas or Laurent Crouzet

VINEYARDS (red)
Surface area: 90.2 acres
Average age of vines: 25 years
Blend: 50% Cabernet Sauvignon, 40% Merlot, 5% Cabernet Franc, 5% Petit Verdot
Density of plantation: 7,142 vines per hectare
Average yields (over the last 5 years): 45 hectoliters per hectare
Total average annual production: 220,000 bottles

GRAND VIN (red)
Brand name: Château Brillette
Appellation: Moulis-en-Médoc
Mean annual production: 110,000 bottles
Upbringing: Fermentations (28–30 degrees centigrade) and macerations

last 3–4 weeks in temperature-controlled vats. After malolactics, wines are aged 16–18 months in oak barrels, 30% of which are new. They are fined but remain unfiltered upon bottling.

SECOND WINE
Brand name: Château Haut-Brillette
Average annual production: 110,000 bottles

Evaluation of present classification: Should be maintained
Plateau of maturity: 7–10 years following the vintage

Just about 1 kilometer north of the town of Moulis-en-Médoc is the vast, 374-acre estate of Brillette, which has only 90 acres under vine and produces approximately 19,000 cases. The wines of Brillette are not yet well-known, but the quality of winemaking is high and the wines are made in a spicy, oaky, rich fruity style that appeals to many tasters.

Brillette's vineyard, which remains relatively young—with the great majority of it planted in the sixties and seventies—is one entire parcel located on gravelly, sandy soil. Since the early eighties the grapes have been harvested by machine. One-third new oak is used each year, which no doubt gives the wine a telltale smoky, toasty character.

This is a wine for those who admire a hefty dose of oak in their wines. It is best drunk within a decade of the vintage.

CAMENSAC   GOOD

Classification: Fifth-growth 1855
Location of vineyards: St.-Laurent du Médoc
Owner: G.F.A. du Château Camensac (Forner family)
Address: Route de St.-Julien, 33112 St.-Laurent du Médoc
Mailing address: Same as above
Telephone: 33 5 56 59 41 69; telefax: 33 5 56 59 41 73
Visits: By appointment and on weekdays only

VINEYARDS (red)
Surface area: 185.3 acres
Average age of vines: 35 years
Blend: 60% Cabernet Sauvignon, 40% Merlot
Density of plantation: 10,000 vines per hectare
Total average annual production: 28,000–30,000 cases

GRAND VIN (red)
Brand name: Château Camensac
Appellation: Haut-Médoc

Mean annual production: 20,000 cases

Upbringing: Fermentations last 15–21 days in temperature-controlled stainless-steel tanks. Most of the yield undergoes malolactics in vats (a very small proportion completes this process in oak), and wines are aged 18 months in oak barrels, 35%–75% of which are new, depending upon the vintage. They are fined and filtered before bottling.

SECOND WINE

Brand name: La Closerie de Camensac
Average annual production: 8,000–10,000 cases

Evaluation of present classification: Should be downgraded to a Cru Bourgeois
Plateau of maturity: 5–14 years following the vintage

Camensac is among the least known of the 1855 classified growths. No doubt its location well inland and west of St.-Julien in the commune of St.-Laurent explains in part the relative obscurity. In addition, the record of mediocrity, unchanged until the seventies, certainly added to a general lack of interest. However, things have changed for the better at Camensac.

The individuals responsible for the revival of Camensac are the Forner brothers, who purchased this estate in 1965 and set about the expensive task of replanting the vineyards and renovating the *chai* and winemaking facilities. The Forners are best known for the modern-style wines made at their winery called Marqués de Cacères, located in the Rioja region of Spain.

With the help of the omnipresent Bordeaux oenologist Emile Peynaud, Camensac's wines have lightened up in style and emphasize more suppleness and fruit. Even though Camensac is now making better wines, they are not representative of fifth-growth quality. They do have a certain St.-Julien-like personality, with good fruit, medium body, and enough tannin to warrant a decade of cellaring in good vintages. In my tastings during the late eighties many bottles had a damp cardboard-like smell, but that problem was rectified in the nineties. The wines possess good concentration and a straightforward, foursquare style.

LA CARDONNE

Classification: Cru Bourgeois
Location of vineyards: Blaignan and Ordonnac
Owner: S.N.C. Domaines C.G.R.
Address: Route de la Cardonne, 33340 Blaignan
Mailing address: 40, rue Notre Dame des Victoires, 75002 Paris

Telephone: 33 1 42 21 11 80; telefax: 33 1 42 21 11 85
Visits: Monday through Friday, between 9 A.M. and noon, and 1:30 P.M.
and 4:30 P.M.
Contact: Nathalie Figula, telephone 33 5 56 73 31 51 and telefax 33 5 56
73 31 52

VINEYARDS (red)
Surface area: 173 acres
Average age of vines: 35 years
Blend: 50% Merlot, 45% Cabernet Sauvignon, 5% Cabernet Franc
Density of plantation: 7,500 vines per hectare
Average yields (over the last 5 years): 55 hectoliters per hectare
Total average annual production: 3,800 hectoliters

GRAND VIN (red)
Brand name: Château La Cardonne
Appellation: Médoc
Mean annual production: 350,000 bottles
Upbringing: Fermentations and macerations are rather long (20–30 days)
and take place in temperature-controlled stainless-steel vats. Wines are
aged 12 months in oak barrels that are renewed by a third in each
vintage. They are fined and filtered.

SECOND WINE
Brand name: Cardus
Average annual production: Approximately 30% of the total production

Evaluation of present classification: Should be maintained
Plateau of maturity: 3–6 years following the vintage

Immense optimism sprang forth in 1973 when the Rothschild family (owners
of such famed Pauillacs as Lafite-Rothschild and Duhart-Milon) acquired this
property in Blaignan. It is a huge enterprise, and the wine is made in a
relatively light, indifferent, yet commercially correct style. I have always
maintained that the enormous yields and heavy reliance on filtration rob this
wine of much concentration and character. It is a wine that must be drunk
within 5–6 years of the vintage. Given the level of quality, it is overpriced,
but I did think the fine 1990 was the best wine I have yet tasted from this
estate. The Rothschilds sold the estate in the nineties, and it seems to me
that the quality has improved.

CARONNE-STE.-GEMME

Classification: Cru Bourgeois Supérieur in 1932 and Cru Bourgeois
Exceptionnel in 1966
Location of vineyards: St.-Laurent du Médoc
Owner: Jean and François Nony
Address: 33112 St.-Laurent du Médoc
Mailing address: c/o S.C.E. des Vignobles Nony Borie, 73, quai des
Chartrons, 33000 Bordeaux
Telephone: 33 5 57 87 56 81; telefax: 33 5 56 51 71 51
Visits: By appointment only
Contact: Vignobles Nony-Borie, at above telephone and fax numbers

VINEYARDS (red)
Surface area: 106.2 acres
Average age of vines: 30 years
Blend: 55% Cabernet Sauvignon, 43% Merlot, 2% Petit Verdot
Density of plantation: 10,000 vines per hectare
Average yields (over the last 5 years): 50 hectoliters per hectare
Total average annual production: 280,000 bottles

GRAND VIN (red)
Brand name: Château Caronne-Ste.-Gemme
Appellation: Haut-Médoc
Mean annual production: 220,000 bottles
Upbringing: Fermentations (28–32 degrees centigrade) and macerations
last 20–25 days, and wines are aged 16 months, after malolactics, in oak
barrels that are renewed by a quarter at each vintage. They are fined and
filtered.

SECOND WINE
Brand name: Château Lagrave Genesta
Average annual production: 60,000 bottles

Evaluation of present classification: Should be maintained
Plateau of maturity: 4–8 years following the vintage

This estate in St.-Laurent receives little publicity. For both tourists and
writers who desire to visit, the property is virtually impossible to find on the
back roads of the Médoc. Moreover, the wine is hardly an inspiring gustatory
pleasure. In my limited experience with this label, I have found the wine to
be generally dark in color, with surprisingly little bouquet and a solid, rather
rustic, almost coarse taste and an excess of tannin—in short, somewhat
austere and tannic.

CHARMAIL   EXCELLENT

Classification: Cru Bourgeois in 1932
Location of vineyards: St.-Seurin-de-Cadourne
Owner: Olivier Sèze
Address: 33180 St.-Seurin-de-Cadourne
Mailing address: Same as above
Telephone: 33 5 56 59 70 63; telefax: 33 5 56 59 39 20
Visits: Monday through Friday, from 9 A.M. to noon, and 2 P.M. to 6 P.M.
Contact: Olivier Sèze

VINEYARDS (red)
Surface area: 55.6 acres
Average age of vines: 22 years
Blend: 50% Merlot, 30% Cabernet Sauvignon, 18% Cabernet Franc, 2% Petit Verdot
Density of plantation: 6,666–6,700 vines per hectare
Average yields (over the last 5 years): 57 hectoliters per hectare
Total average annual production: 170,000 bottles

GRAND VIN (red)
Brand name: Château Charmail
Appellation: Haut-Médoc
Mean annual production: 110,000 bottles
Upbringing: Cold maceration, then fermentations take place at high temperatures, macerations are long (3½ weeks to 1 month), and wines are run off at 30–31 degrees centigrade. They are transferred to oak barrels, 25%–30% of which are new, for 12 months aging. They remain unfined and unfiltered.

SECOND WINE
None produced.

Evaluation of present classification: The quality equivalent of a Médoc fifth-growth
Plateau of Maturity: 2–10 years

These wines, fermented under cold nitrogen (at 5 degrees centigrade for 15 days), are revolutionary in their fruit intensity and richness for Haut-Médoc. Made from a blend of 50% Merlot, 30% Cabernet Sauvignon, 18% Cabernet Franc, and 2% Petit Verdot, from a property that does not possess one of the finest *terroirs*, these wines continue to amaze me with their inky intensity, purity, and richness. Given the high quality of recent efforts, this property is well on its way to meriting a position alongside the likes of Sociando-Mallet.

VINTAGES

1997—A sleeper of the vintage, this intriguingly made wine (a very long cold macera-
  •   tion of the fruit is practiced prior to the actual fermentation) possesses an
87–   opaque black/purple color, and gorgeously sweet black raspberry fruit inter-
 89   mixed with licorice and spice. Sweetness (from glycerin, not sugar), ripeness,
       low acidity and a fleshy finish make for a hedonistic wine. It should age well
       for 5–7 years. Last tasted, 3/98.

1996—The 1996 reveals an inky, opaque purple color, and stunningly sweet aromat-
  •   ics of creme de cassis, black raspberries, and licorice. Dense and full bodied,
88–   with amazing richness and purity, this wine has to be tasted to be believed. It
 90   could easily merit an outstanding rating after bottling. Anticipated maturity:
       2000–2010. Last tasted 3/98.

1995—The opaque purple-colored 1995 offers a moderately intense nose of jammy
  •   blackberries and currants, terrific fruit on the attack, medium to full body,
 88   outstanding purity, low acidity, and a fleshy texture. It can be drunk now as
       well as over the next decade. Last tasted, 11/97.

CHASSE-SPLEEN   EXCELLENT

Classification: Cru Bourgeois
Location of vineyards: Moulis
Owner: S.A. du Château Chasse-Spleen
Address: 33480 Moulis-en-Médoc
Mailing address: Same as above
Telephone: 33 5 56 58 02 37; telefax: 33 5 56 58 05 70
Visits: By appointment only, Monday through Friday, between 9 A.M. and
4 P.M.
Contact: Claire Villars

VINEYARDS (red)
Surface area: 197.6 acres
Average age of vines: 30 years
Blend: 70% Cabernet Sauvignon, 25% Merlot, 5% Petit Verdot
Density of plantation: 10,000 vines per hectare
Average yields (over the last 5 years): 50 hectoliters per hectare
Total average annual production: 500,000 bottles

GRAND VIN (red)
Brand name: Château Chasse-Spleen
Appellation: Moulis
Upbringing: Fermentations and macerations last 3–4 weeks in
temperature-controlled stainless-steel and concrete (epoxy-lined) tanks.
Wines are aged 14–18 months in oak barrels that are renewed by 40% at
each vintage. They are fined but remain unfiltered.

> **SECOND WINE**
> Brand name: L'Hermitage de Chasse-Spleen and L'Oratoire de Chasse-Spleen
>
> Evaluation of present classification: Should be upgraded to a Médoc fourth-growth
> Plateau of maturity: 5–18 years following the vintage

An impressive property, Chasse-Spleen has consistently produced fine wine that for the last 3 decades has often been as good as a third-growth. Even in poor and mediocre vintages, the wine is characterized by a very pronounced, deep ruby color, a bouquet of plummy ripeness, and rich, round, substantial flavors.

The great vintages for Chasse-Spleen, in which the wine can compare favorably with top Médoc classified growths, are 1966, 1970, 1975, 1978, 1985, 1986, 1989, and 1990.

Chasse-Spleen was owned by the Lahary family until 1976, when it was purchased by a syndicate whose controlling interest was the Société Bernard Taillan. The director of the firm, Jacques Merlaut, has made many intelligent decisions with respect to the administration of this château. The results have been increasingly inspired wines, with absolutely top-class wines in the late eighties. The vineyard, consisting of 4 parcels, sits on primarily deep, gravelly soil and boasts many old vines; their average age is an impressive 35 years. This is a property that still adheres to very traditional practices. It is one of only a handful in the Médoc that does not filter either after the malolactic fermentation or before bottling. In fact, the only compromise toward modern-day technology is that part of the crop gets harvested by machine. Improvements under Bernadette Villars are obvious with the introduction of a second wine, the increased usage of 50% new oak casks for aging, and the impeccable attention to every detail. Prices have jumped as the world has begun to discover that Chasse-Spleen was undervalued.

VINTAGES

1997—Dark ruby/purple–colored, with aromas of spice, black currants, vanillin, and
• berries, this medium-bodied wine reveals very good to excellent depth, fine
86– overall balance, ripe tannin, and not a great deal of acidity. It should drink
87+ well for 8–10 years. Last tasted, 3/98.

1996—I tasted this wine on three separate occasions, and although it possesses
• impressive structure and enough depth of fruit, it is disjointed and exhibits
86– an astringent finish—largely because of the high tannin level. If it fleshes out
87? and the tannin sweetens, the wine will merit a score in the upper 80s. For
now, it is a deep purple–colored, Cabernet Sauvignon–dominated wine with

medium body and strong tannin in both the flavor and finish. It is made in a style that will not provide much charm or pleasure for 7–8 years. It should keep for 2 decades. Last tasted, 11/97.

1995— This wine has everything in its aromatics and attack, and very little at the
•   back of the mouth—not a good sign for long-term aging. It possesses a
86   dark ruby/purple color, and black currant fruit intermixed with smoke and weediness. Drink it over the next 5–7 years. Last tasted, 11/97.

1993— This estate has produced a good, impressively colored, medium-bodied 1993
•   with the vintage's telltale firm, tannic structure as well as enough fruit and fat
86   for balance. The wine reveals fine ripeness, extraction, and purity, along with the black fruit character Chasse-Spleen routinely achieves. It should drink well between now and 2010. Last tasted, 11/94.

1992— This wine has turned out better than cask samples suggested. Light, with an
•   atypically herbaceous character, it offers good ripeness, a chunky, medium-
85   bodied personality, excellent color saturation, and light tannin in the attractive, firmly structured finish. It should drink well for 7–8 years. Last tasted, 11/94.

1990— The 1990 has evolved well and is displaying far greater intensity, medium to
•   full body, herb-and-black cherry–scented flavors, soft tannins, and good ripe-
88   ness and richness. It is not as super-concentrated as the brilliant 1989, but it is an immensely attractive, round, soft, well-made wine. Drink it over the next decade. Last tasted, 11/97.

1989— The 1989 Chasse-Spleen is the finest wine this property has produced
•   since their great 1949. This is a spectacularly rich, powerful, authorita-
91   tive example of the vintage that can compete with and even surpass many of the most famous names. Layer upon layer of concentrated, sweet, expansive, black currant fruit is wrapped in a frame of toasty new oak and decent acidity. An awesome wine! Anticipated maturity: Now–2015. Last tasted, 11/97.

1988— Chasse-Spleen made a good, elegant 1988. Displaying a generous, intense,
•   smoky, black currant bouquet and chewy, medium-bodied flavors, it has a
86   surprisingly long, spicy, soft finish. Anticipated maturity: Now–2001. Last tasted, 1/93.

1986— The black/ruby/purple color of the 1986 suggests a wine of remarkable rich-
•   ness and depth. And that is exactly what one gets. The huge bouquet of cassis
90   fruit is nicely backed up by a whiff of toasty, smoky oak. On the palate, the wine has sensational extract, full body, and massive texture; it should last for at least 15–20 years. I have rarely been more impressed by a young vintage of Chasse-Spleen than I have been with the 1986. Anticipated maturity: Now–2010. Last tasted, 11/90.

1985— The 1985 Chasse-Spleen is fabulously deep in color, with a full-intensity,
•   scented bouquet of spicy new oak, rich curranty fruit, and plums. In the
90   mouth, the wine is very concentrated, long, big framed, but impeccably balanced, with quite a finish. Anticipated maturity: Now–2005. Last tasted, 11/90.

1984—One of the better wines from this vintage, the 1984 has good color, an
 • attractive, ripe sweetness to its fruit, medium body, and a velvety texture.
 81 Anticipated maturity: Now. Last tasted, 3/88.

1983—Still deep ruby in color, with some amber creeping in at the edges, this
 • forward, round, generously endowed Chasse-Spleen has shed most of its
 86 tannins and offers a deliciously plump, fleshy mouthful of satisfying claret. I
 am surprised how quickly it has aged, but there is good depth, and the wine
 offers charm as well as complexity. Anticipated maturity: Now. Last tasted,
 12/89.

1982—The 1982 Chasse-Spleen has never been as impressive as the glorious series
 • of wines made under the late Bernadette Villars between 1985 and 1990.
 86 Nevertheless, the 1982 continues to behave well, exhibiting plenty of ripe,
 spicy, curranty fruit in its moderately intense nose, medium body, sweet,
 expansive fruit, and an easygoing finish. It is fully mature, so why wait? It
 should continue to drink well for another 4–6+ years. Last tasted, 9/95.

1981—Medium ruby, with an almost dusty, spicy, cedary nose, this austerely styled
 • Chasse-Spleen lacks the richness and concentration to ever be profound.
 79 It is medium bodied, a bit dry and tannic in the finish, but pleasant in a
 straightforward, foursquare way. Anticipated maturity: Now. Last tasted,
 11/88.

1979—Fully mature and drinking well, the 1979 exhibits an herbaceous, cassis-
 • scented bouquet, medium-bodied flavors, good concentration, and a soft finish
 83 with some acidity. Anticipated maturity: Now. Last tasted, 2/88.

1978—This was a successful vintage for Chasse-Spleen, and the wine has just now
 • reached full maturity. Much more opaque and deeper colored than the 1979,
 85 with a mushroomy, meaty, curranty bouquet, this full-bodied, powerful, muscular Chasse-Spleen still has some tannins to lose, but was immensely enjoyable to drink. Anticipated maturity: Now–2000. Last tasted, 3/89.

1976—Fully mature and beginning to take on considerable amber at the edge, this
 • spicy, soupy-textured Chasse-Spleen should be consumed over the next 3–4
 76 years. I detect the fruit beginning to fade and the alcohol becoming more
 noticeable. Quite soft and still perfumed, but beginning, I believe, to decline.
 Anticipated maturity: Now–may be in decline. Last tasted, 3/88.

1975—This has always been one of the top wines of an inconsistent vintage. Still
 • dense, even opaque, dark ruby, with only a slight amber edge, the 1975
 90 blossoms reluctantly in the glass to reveal scents of grilled nuts, minerals,
 licorice, and superripe black currants. In the mouth, it is full bodied
 and powerful, but the tannins, unlike in many 1975s, are noticeable, but
 not astringent or green. Just about ready to drink, this wine should easily
 last for another 10–20 years. Anticipated maturity: Now–2010. Last tasted,
 6/88.

OLDER VINTAGES

Anyone lucky enough to run across a bottle of the 1970 Chasse-Spleen (rated
90 in 1990) should snatch it up. This is a superb wine that after 20 years

was still youthful and capable of lasting another 5–10 years. Full bodied, ripe, and closer in style to the 1975 than any of the more recent vintages, this is a wine of true classified-growth quality. The price should also be reasonable.

Among the vintages in the sixties, I have good notes on the 1966 (rated 86), but it has been over a decade since I last tasted the wine. I have rarely seen any wines from the fifties, but the 1953 is highly regarded. I was fortunate to buy a case of the 1949 Chasse-Spleen that had been bottled in England. Every bottle was superb, one of the few times when buying an older vintage at a reasonable price paid immense dividends. I have high hopes the 1989, 1986, and 1975 will reach the heights of the 1949. For me, it is the most monumental Chasse-Spleen I have ever tasted and could have easily been confused with a first-growth from that vintage. I consistently rated it between 92 and 95.

CISSAC   GOOD

Classification: Cru Bourgeois Exceptionnel
Location of vineyards: Cissac Médoc
Owner: Vialard family
Address: 33250 Cissac
Mailing address: Same as above
Telephone: 33 5 56 59 58 13; telefax: 33 5 56 59 55 67
Visits: Monday through Friday, between 9 A.M. and noon, and 2 P.M. and 5 P.M.

VINEYARDS (red)
Surface area: 123.5 acres
Average age of vines: 30 years
Blend: 75% Cabernet Sauvignon, 20% Merlot, 5% Petit Verdot
Density of plantation: 7,500 vines per hectare
Average yields (over the last 5 years): 54 hectoliters per hectare
Total average annual production: 30,000 cases

GRAND VIN (red)
Brand name: Château Cissac
Appellation: Haut-Médoc
Mean annual production: 18,000 cases
Upbringing: Fermentations and macerations last 21–30 days in wooden tanks equipped with a temperature control. Wines are afterward aged 18 months in oak barrels, 30% of which are new. They are fined but not filtered.

SECOND WINE
Brand name: Reflets du Château Cissac
Average annual production: 12,000 cases

Evaluation of present classification: Should be maintained
Plateau of maturity: 7–10 years following the vintage

The proprietor of Cissac, Louis Vialard, is one of Bordeaux's most dedicated proprietors. Consequently, his beloved Château Cissac produces one of the best Bourgeois wines of the central Médoc.

Located just north of the town of Cissac, this property produces approximately 18,000 cases of very traditional, full-bodied, tannic, interesting, darkly colored wine. Normally unyielding and reserved when young, Cissac begins to show its true character at around age 6 and can easily age and improve in the bottle for 10–15 years in vintages such as 1975, 1985, and 1986.

The wine of Cissac is especially popular in England and seems to have a growing following among American connoisseurs who have the patience to wait for its slow (for a Cru Bourgeois) but sure evolution.

CITRAN   EXCELLENT

Classification: Cru Bourgeois in 1932
Location of vineyards: Avensan
Owner: S.A. du Château Citran
Address: 33480 Avensan
Mailing address: Same as above
Telephone: 33 5 56 58 21 01; telefax: 33 5 58 12 19
Visits: By appointment only
Contact: Claire Villars, telephone 33 5 56 58 02 37 and telefax 33 5 56 58 05 70

VINEYARDS (red)
Surface area: 222.3 acres
Average age of vines: 20 years
Blend: 58% Cabernet Sauvignon, 42% Merlot
Density of plantation: 6,666 vines per hectare
Average yields (over the last 5 years): 50 hectoliters per hectare
Total average annual production: 500,000 bottles

GRAND VIN (red)
Brand name: Château Citran
Appellation: Haut-Médoc

Upbringing: Fermentations and macerations last 2–4 weeks in temperature-controlled stainless-steel tanks. After malolactics, wines are aged in oak barrels, which are renewed by 40% at each vintage. They are fined but not filtered.

SECOND WINE
Brand name: Moulins de Citran

Evaluation of present classification: Since 1987 the wine is the quality equivalent of a Médoc fifth-growth; vintages before 1986 should be approached with considerable caution
Plateau of maturity: 6–10 years following the vintage

In the 10 years (1987–1997) following the acquisition of Citran by a Japanese syndicate, the quality of this estate's wines soared. In spite of their success, Citran was sold to the Société Bernard Taillan, run by the dynamic Jacques Merlaut. The renovation of the cellars, the commitment of the new owners, an increased percentage of new oak, a stricter selection process (and subsequent second wine), and excellent overall administration have resulted in glorious wines over recent years. If there is any criticism, it would be that the elevated use of new oak gives the wine such a dramatic, smoky, even charred character that those who admire claret for delicacy and subtlety might be put off by its flamboyant boldness.

Nevertheless, the new vintages should age well for up to a decade and are considerably more interesting and pleasurable than anything Citran previously produced. It should also be noted that prices have edged up to take into account the new designer bottle with its striking label that has replaced the old, traditional, somber Château Citran package.

VINTAGES

1996—Opaque ruby/purple, with plenty of intensity, fruit, body, glycerin, and tannin,
• the 1996 Citran is a forceful, muscular, broad-shouldered claret for drinking
86– between 2003 and 2015. Last tasted, 11/97.
87

1995—Softer than the 1996, the deep ruby/purple–colored 1995 reveals licorice,
• vanillin, and ripe black currant fruit presented in a straightforward but savory,
86 mouth-filling style. Drink it over the next 7–8 years. Last tasted, 11/97.

1993—I tasted this wine on four separate occasions. Although my notes were vari-
• able, there is no question that the wine is a densely colored purple/black with
85? lavish quantities of toasty new oak. My only reservation is whether the wine
will fill out or the tannin will get the upper hand and dominate the wine's
personality. There is some good red fruit, but is it enough to stand up to the
tannic bite? Last tasted, 11/94.

1992—The impressive black/purple–colored 1992 exhibits a tight and overtly woody
   •   nose. Spicy, with medium body, moderate tannin, and some length, this is an
   82   atypically pigmented, tannic, and woody 1992. If more fruit emerges, the
        wine will merit a higher score. It will keep for a decade. Last tasted, 11/94.

1991—The 1991 offers a bouquet of grilled nuts, new oak, and black currants. Spicy
   •   and ripe, this medium-bodied, soft, concentrated wine is a notable success.
   86   It will offer delicious drinking for at least 4–5 years. Last tasted, 1/94.

1989—The 1989 is terrific. Purple colored, with a huge nose of cassis, licorice, and
   •   smoky oak, this fleshy, huge wine is loaded with fruit, glycerin, and tannin. It
   88   should drink beautifully for 10–12 years. Last tasted, 1/93.

1988—Starting with the 1988 vintage, Citran has established itself as one of the
   •   stars among the Médoc Crus Bourgeois. Dark ruby/purple, with a smoky,
   86   roasted bouquet of cassis and lavish amounts of new oak, this cunningly
        made, ripe, overtly commercial wine will prove to be a crowd pleaser because
        of its direct, forward, plump character. Anticipated maturity: Now. Last tasted,
        1/93.

CLARKE   GOOD

Classification: Cru Bourgeois
Location of vineyards: Listrac
Owner: Compagnie Viticole des Barons Edmond et Benjamin de
Rothschild
Address: 33480 Listrac-Médoc
Mailing address: Same as above
Telephone: 33 5 56 58 38 00; telefax: 33 5 56 58 26 46
Visits: By appointment only
Contact: Hélène Cambabessouse

VINEYARDS (red)
Surface area: 135.9 acres
Average age of vines: 23 years
Blend: 45% Cabernet Sauvignon, 45% Merlot, 10% Cabernet Franc
Density of plantation: 6,600 vines per hectare
Average yields (over the last 5 years): 55–60 hectoliters per hectare
Total average annual production: 350,000 bottles

GRAND VIN (red)
Brand name: Château Clarke Baron Edmond de Rothschild
Appellation: Listrac-Médoc
Mean annual production: 200,000–250,000 bottles
Upbringing: Fermentations last approximately 2 weeks in
temperature-controlled stainless-steel vats at 30–31 degrees centigrade.
There are 4–8 pumping-overs depending upon the vintage. Wines are aged

12 months in oak barrels that are renewed by half at each vintage. They are fined and filtered upon bottling.

SECOND WINE
Brand name: Les Granges des Domaines Edmond de Rothschild
Average annual production: 100,000 bottles

Evaluation of present classification: Should be maintained
Plateau of maturity: 3–7 years following the vintage

One of the most remarkable developments in the Médoc has been the complete restoration and rejuvenation of the old vineyard of Château Clarke. The property boasts a history dating to 1750, and it took the considerable resources of a wealthy member of the famous Rothschild family—the late Baron Edmond de Rothschild—to accomplish the resurrection. In 1973 work began, and in the following 5 years the area under vine increased dramatically to 136 acres, large enough to have the potential to produce over 20,000 cases of wine. The first wines released, a 1978 and 1979, were given a great deal of hoopla from the wine press, but in actuality they were light, medium-bodied examples that clearly tasted like the product of a young vineyard. However, the commitment to high quality, the financial resources, and the management are all present, so as the vineyard matures, Château Clarke should become one of the more reliable wines made in Listrac.

Château Clarke also produces a delicious dry rosé and a kosher cuvée (made according to strict Jewish requirements) of its red wine.

CLÉMENT-PICHON   GOOD

Classification: Cru Bourgeois
Location of vineyards: Parempuyre
Owner: Clément Fayat
Address: 33290 Parempuyre
Mailing address: Same as above
Telephone: 33 5 56 35 23 79; telefax: 33 5 56 35 85 23
Visits: Monday through Friday, from 8 A.M. to noon, and 2 P.M. to 5:30 P.M.

VINEYARDS (red)
Surface area: 61.8 acres
Average age of vines: 20 years
Blend: 50% Cabernet Sauvignon, 40% Merlot, 10% Cabernet Franc
Density of plantation: 6,500 vines per hectare
Average yields (over the last 5 years): 48 hectoliters per hectare
Total average annual production: 160,000 bottles

GRAND VIN (red)
Brand name: Château Clément-Pichon
Appellation: Haut-Médoc
Mean annual production: 135,000 bottles
Upbringing: Fermentations take place in temperature-controlled
stainless-steel tanks (up to 30 degrees centigrade). Thirty percent of the
yield undergoes malolactics in oak barrels. Wines are aged 12–18
months in barrels that are renewed by a third at each vintage, fined with
fresh egg whites, and filtered before bottling.

SECOND WINE
Brand name: La Motte de Clément-Pichon
Average annual production: 25,000 bottles

Evaluation of present classification: Should be maintained
Plateau of maturity: 3–7 years following the vintage

This beautiful château, located just to the north of Bordeaux near the sprawling industrial suburb of Parempuyre, is owned by one of the most driven
proprietors of the region, Clément Fayat, an industrialist who also has been
responsible for the renaissance of the famed St.-Emilion vineyard La Dominique. Fayat totally renovated the château, which formerly was known as
Château de Parempuyre, and originally renamed it Château Pichon. However,
that caused legal problems with Madame de Lencquesaing, who felt the
name could be confused with her Château Pichon-Longueville–Comtesse de
Lalande. The name was then changed to Château Clément-Pichon.

The huge baroque and gothic château was constructed at the end of the
nineteenth century and is now inhabited by the Fayat family, who purchased
this domain in 1976. They totally replanted the vineyards, which consequently are extremely young. The Fayats were shrewd enough to ask their
oenologist at La Dominique, the famed Libournais Michel Rolland, to look
after the winemaking at Clément-Pichon. He has performed miracles with a
vineyard this young. No doubt Rolland realized the limitations of making a
true *vin de garde* and to date has emphasized wines with an up-front, exceptionally fruity, supple style that are meant to be consumed young.

CLOS DES DEMOISELLES

Classification: Cru Bourgeois
Appellation: Listrac
Address: 33480 Listrac-Médoc
Telephone: 5 56 58 05 12; telefax: 5 56 58 02 44

Production: 2,000 cases
Blend: 60% Cabernet Sauvignon, 40% Merlot
Secondary label: None
Vineyard size: 8.6 acres
Proprietor: Jacques de Pourquéry
Time spent in barrels: 16–20 months
Average age of vines: 16 years

Evaluation of present classification: Should be maintained
Plateau of maturity: 3–8 years following the vintage

The wines I have tasted from Clos des Demoiselles have been extremely tannic and hard, without sufficient fruit, charm, or balance. The vineyard is still relatively young, and there is no doubt that this well-placed vineyard could produce more interesting wines.

COUFRAN   GOOD

Classification: Cru Bourgeois
Location of vineyards: St.-Seurin-de-Cadourne
Owner: Jean Miailhe Group
Address: 33180 St.-Seurin-de-Cadourne
Mailing address: Same as above
Telephone: 33 5 56 59 31 02; telefax: 33 5 56 59 72 39
Visits: By appointment only
Contact: Eric Miailhe

VINEYARDS (red)
Surface area: 187.7 acres
Average age of vines: 35 years
Blend: 85% Merlot, 15% Cabernet Sauvignon
Density of plantation: 8,000 vines per hectare
Average yields (over the last 5 years): 58 hectoliters per hectare
Total average annual production: 48,000 cases

GRAND VIN (red)
Brand name: Château Coufran
Appellation: Haut-Médoc
Mean annual production: 45,000 cases
Upbringing: Fermentations and macerations last 1 month in stainless-steel vats equipped with a temperature-control system. Wines undergo malolactics in vats and are transferred to oak barrels, one-third

of which are new, for at least 12 months aging. They are fined and filtered before bottling.

SECOND WINE
None produced.

Evaluation of present classification: Should be maintained
Plateau of maturity: 3–12 years following the vintage

The large vineyard of Coufran is situated 3 miles north of the boundary of St.-Estèphe, contiguous to Route D2 after passing through the village of St.-Seurin-de-Cadourne. Since 1924 the property has been in the Miailhe family, a prominent name in the promotion of the quality among Crus Bourgeois of Bordeaux, and is now run by them.

The most distinctive aspect of Coufran is the high percentage of Merlot used in the blend, which the proprietors have decided succeeds well in the heavier, thicker soils common to this part of the Médoc. This has led some people to rashly conclude that the wine is drinkable upon release. I have not found that to be the case. In top vintages, Coufran is often supple and fruity in cask but can go into a dumb, tannic stage in the bottle. The wine is a good Médoc, but the yields are extremely high, and again, one wonders whether the property's use of machine harvesters has any effect on the ultimate quality.

Coufran's record in the eighties was somewhat spotty. The best vintages, 1982, 1986, and 1989, all had the potential for at least 10 years of evolution. I was unimpressed with the lean 1988 and straightforward 1985. In the nineties, 1990, 1995, and 1996 stand out for quality.

DUCLUZEAU   VERY GOOD

Classification: Cru Bourgeois in 1932
Location of vineyards: Listrac
Owner: Madame Jean-Eugène Borie
Address: 33480 Listrac-Médoc
Mailing address: Same as above
Telephone: 33 5 56 59 05 20; telefax: 33 5 56 59 27 37
Visits: No visits allowed

VINEYARDS (red)
Surface area: 12.1 acres
Average age of vines: 34 years
Blend: 90% Merlot, 10% Cabernet Sauvignon
Density of plantation: 10,000 vines per hectare

Average yields (over the last 5 years): 48 hectoliters per hectare
Total average annual production: 230 hectoliters

GRAND VIN (red)
Brand name: Château Ducluzeau
Appellation: Listrac
Mean annual production: 25,000 bottles
Upbringing: Fermentations and macerations last 15–18 days in
stainless-steel tanks. Malolactics occur in vats, and wines are aged 12–
14 months in oak barrels, 20% of which are new. They are fined and
lightly filtered.

SECOND WINE
None produced.

Evaluation of present classification: A high-quality Listrac that in certain
vintages can compete favorably with some classified growths
Plateau of maturity: 3–10 years following the vintage

This property, owned by Monique Borie, wife of the proprietor of Ducru-
Beaucaillou, Haut-Batailley, and Grand-Puy-Lacoste, has, to my knowledge,
the highest percentage of Merlot of any wine of the Médoc. The result is an
extremely supple yet deliciously round, seductive wine with a great deal of
charm and elegance. This wine has been estate bottled since 1976.

DUPLESSIS

Classification: Cru Bourgeois in 1932
Location of vineyards: Moulis
Owner: Marie-Laure Lurton Roux
Address: 33480 Moulis
Mailing address: Same as above
Telephone: 33 5 56 58 22 01; telefax: 33 5 56 88 72 51
Visits: By appointment only
Contact: Marie-Laure Lurton Roux

VINEYARDS (red)
Surface area: 44.5 acres
Average age of vines: 20 years
Blend: 60% Merlot, 26% Cabernet Sauvignon, 12% Cabernet Franc, 2%
Petit Verdot
Density of plantation: 10,000 vines per hectare and 6,600 vines per hectare
Average yields (over the last 5 years): 46 hectoliters per hectare
Total average annual production: 850 hectoliters

GRAND VIN (red)
Brand name: Château Duplessis
Appellation: Moulis
Mean annual production: 50,000–80,000 bottles
Upbringing: Fermentations and macerations take place in stainless-steel and concrete tanks lined with epoxy. Wines are aged 12 months in oak barrels, 10%–20% of which are new. They are fined and filtered before bottling.

SECOND WINE
Brand name: La Licorne de Duplessis
Average annual production: 20,000–30,000 bottles

Evaluation of present classification: Should be maintained
Plateau of maturity: 4–10 years following the vintage

This property, sometimes called Duplessis-Hauchecorne (after one of the former owners), now belongs to the ubiquitous family of Lucien Lurton. The wine is typical of an older-style Moulis—coarse, robust, and lacking charm and fruit.

DUPLESSIS-FABRÉ

Classification: Cru Bourgeois
Location of vineyards: Moulis
Owner: S.A.R.L. du Château Maucaillou
Address: 33480 Moulis-en-Médoc
Mailing address: Same as above
Telephone: 33 5 56 58 02 58; telefax: 33 5 56 58 00 88
Visits: Visits not allowed

VINEYARDS (red)
Surface area: 39.5 acres
Average age of vines: 19 years
Blend: 56% Merlot, 44% Cabernet Sauvignon
Density of plantation: 10,000 vines per hectare
Average yields (over the last 5 years): 52 hectoliters per hectare
Total average annual production: 9,000 cases

GRAND VIN (red)
Brand name: Château Duplessis-Fabré
Appellation: Moulis
Mean annual production: 9,000 cases

Upbringing: Fermentations (8 days in all) are kept, during the first 4 days, at 22 degrees centigrade, and temperatures go up to 30 degrees centigrade at the end of this process. Macerations last until the tannin index reaches 55–65. Wines are aged 18 months in oak barrels, 33%– 65% of which are new depending upon the vintage. They are fined and lightly filtered upon bottling.

SECOND WINE
None produced.

Evaluation of present classification: Should be maintained
Plateau of maturity: 5–10 years following the vintage

In 1989 this property was sold by the Pagès family to Philippe Dourthe of Château Maucaillou. There is plenty of potential for a more interesting wine to be produced, which should happen given the quality of this estate's bigger sibling, Maucaillou.

DUTRUCH-GRAND-POUJEAUX   GOOD

Classification: Cru Bourgeois Exceptionnel
Location of vineyards: Moulis
Owner: François Cordonnier
Address: 33480 Moulis-en-Médoc
Mailing address: Same as above
Telephone: 33 5 56 58 02 55; telefax: 33 5 56 58 06 22
Visits: By appointment only
Contact: François or Jean-Baptiste Cordonnier

VINEYARDS (red)
Surface area: 61.8 acres
Average age of vines: 30 years
Blend: Roughly 50% Merlot, 50% Cabernet Sauvignon (plus a little Petit Verdot)
Density of plantation: 8,500–10,000 vines per hectare
Average yields (over the last 5 years): 50 hectoliters per hectare
Total average annual production: 155,000 bottles

GRAND VIN (red)
Brand name: Château Dutruch-Grand-Poujeaux
Appellation: Moulis
Mean annual production: 140,000 bottles
Upbringing: Fermentations and macerations last approximately 21 days

in concrete and stainless-steel tanks equipped with a cooling system, and temperatures reach 31–34 degrees centigrade at the end of the fermentation process. After malolactics, wines are transferred to oak barrels, 25%–33% of which are new, for 15 months aging. They are fined and filtered before bottling.

SECOND WINE
Brand name: Château La Bernede Grand-Poujeaux
Average annual production: 15,000 bottles

Evaluation of present classification: Should be maintained, although certain vintages can compete favorably with a Médoc fifth-growth
Plateau of maturity: 6–12 years following the vintage

Dutruch-Grand-Poujeaux, like so many wines of Moulis, often lacks a great deal of charm when it is young. Unlike some neighbors, this is one wine that can have the requisite concentration and depth to stand up to the tannin. After 5–7 years' time, I have often been pleased by just how well this wine turns out. Part of the reason for the excellent concentration is not only the respectable age of the vines, but the fact that much of this vineyard is planted by the ancient system of 10,000 vines per hectare, as opposed to the more conventional 6,600 vines per hectare. This, of course, is believed to create more stress, resulting in more concentrated grapes.

This is an under-rated, impressively run property that merits more attention.

FONRÉAUD   GOOD

Classification: Cru Bourgeois Supérieur
Location of vineyards: Listrac-Médoc and Moulis
Owner: Jean, Elza, Katherine, and Caroline Chanfreau
Address: 33480 Listrac-Médoc
Mailing address: Same as above
Telephone: 33 5 56 58 02 43; telefax: 33 5 56 58 04 33
Visits: Monday through Friday, from 9 A.M. to noon, and 2 P.M. to 5:30 P.M.
Contact: Jean or Marie-Hélène Chanfreau

VINEYARDS (red)
Surface area: 79 acres in Listrac and 24.7 acres in Moulis
Average age of vines: 25 years
Blend: 58% Cabernet Sauvignon, 38% Merlot, 2% Cabernet Franc, 2% Petit Verdot

Density of plantation: 6,660 vines per hectare
Average yields (over the last 5 years): 55 hectoliters
Total average annual production: 290,000 bottles

GRAND VIN (red)
Brand name: Château Fonréaud
Appellation: Listrac-Médoc
Mean annual production: 130,000 bottles
Upbringing: Fermentations and macerations last 25–30 days, depending
upon the vintage, in temperature-controlled vats. Pumping-overs are
smooth, and macerations last at least 10 days after the end of the
alcoholic fermentations. Ninety percent of the yield is aged for 12 months
in oak barrels, 20%–25% of which are new. They are not systematically
fined or filtered.

SECOND WINE
Brand name: Les Tourelles de Fonréaud
Average annual production: 50,000–90,000 bottles
NOTE: This estate produces 50,000 bottles of Château Chemin Royal from
their vineyards in Moulis. This wine is vinified much in the same way as
the Listrac.
    Since 1989 they also produce a white wine called "Le Cygne de
Fonréaud" (all the white wines produced in Listrac at the beginning
of this century bore bird names—such as Le Merle blanc of Château
Clarke and La Mouette of Château Lestage). This white dry Bordeaux
is made from 5 acres of vines (60% Sauvignon, 20% Muscadelle,
and 20% Semillon). It is vinified and aged in oak barrels, 40% of which
are new. It remains on fine lees for 8–10 months with frequent
bâtonnages.

Evaluation of present classification: Should be maintained
Plateau of maturity: 5–7 years following the vintage

This impressively symmetrical white château, with a dominating center turret
and spire, sits on the left-hand side of Route D1 as one leaves the tiny village of Bouqueyran in the direction of Lesparre. Since 1982 the property has
been owned by the Chanfreau family, who also control the nearby Château
Lestage.
    The style emphasized is one of soft, fruity, immediately drinkable wines
that are limited to 6–7 years of aging ability. The high percentage of Merlot,
as well as the owner's decision to age the wine for 6 months in oak casks and
6 months in cuvées, results in a soft, round wine with immediate appeal. The
best recent vintages have been the 1989, 1990, 1995, and 1996.

FOURCAS-DUPRÉ

GOOD

Classification: Cru Bourgeois in 1932
Location of vineyards: Listrac-Médoc
Owner: S.C.E. du Château Fourcas-Dupré
Manager: Patrice Pagès
Address: 33480 Listrac
Mailing address: Same as above
Telephone: 33 5 56 58 01 07; telefax: 33 5 56 58 02 27
Visits: Monday through Friday, from 8 A.M. to noon, and 2 P.M. to 5 P.M.
Contact: Patrice Pagès

VINEYARDS (red)
Surface area: 108.7 acres
Average age of vines: 25 years
Blend: 44% Merlot, 44% Cabernet Sauvignon, 10% Cabernet Franc, 2%
Petit Verdot
Density of plantation: 8,500 vines per hectare
Average yields (over the last 5 years): 55 hectoliters per hectare
Total average annual production: 2,400 hectoliters

GRAND VIN (red)
Brand name: Château Fourcas-Dupré
Appellation: Listrac-Médoc
Mean annual production: 240,000–250,000 bottles
Upbringing: Alcoholic fermentations take place at approximately 30
degrees centigrade in temperature-controlled stainless-steel tanks or
epoxy-lined concrete tanks, with regular pumping-overs. Macerations last
15–21 days, and wines are transferred, after malolactics, to oak barrels
that are renewed by a third at each vintage, for 12 months aging (before
the 1996 vintage, only 25% new oak was utilized). Wines are usually
fined but filtered only if necessary.

SECOND WINE
Brand name: Château Bellevue-Laffont
Average annual production: 60,000–65,000 bottles

Evaluation of present classification: One of the best of the Cru Bourgeois
properties; should be maintained
Plateau of maturity: 5–10 years following the vintage

Until his death in 1985, Guy Pagès was responsible for elevating the quality
of the wines of Fourcas-Dupré. I purchased and cellared, with great satisfaction, the 1975 and 1978 and have been impressed more recently with the
1982, 1983, and 1986.

FOURCAS-HOSTEN GOOD

Classification: Crus Bourgeois in 1932
Location of vineyards: Listrac
Owner: S.C. du Château Fourcas-Hosten
Address: 2, rue de l'Eglise, 33480 Listrac
Mailing address: Same as above
Telephone: 33 5 56 58 01 15; telefax: 33 5 56 58 06 73
Visits: Monday through Friday, between 9:30 and noon, and 2 P.M. and
4:30 P.M.
Contact: Annette Monge

VINEYARDS (red)
Surface area: 114 acres
Average age of vines: 20 years
Blend: 45% Merlot, 45% Cabernet Sauvignon, 10% Cabernet Franc
Density of plantation: 8,500 vines per hectare
Average yields (over the last 5 years): 57 hectoliters per hectare
Total average annual production: 2,500 hectoliters

GRAND VIN (red)
Brand name: Château Fourcas-Hosten
Appellation: Listrac-Médoc
Mean annual production: 250,000–260,000 bottles
Upbringing: Fermentations take place at 30 degrees centigrade, and
macerations last 15–21 days in temperature-controlled stainless-steel
vats, with regular pumping-overs during the alcoholic fermentations.
After malolactics, wines are aged 12 months in oak barrels that are
renewed by a quarter at each vintage (starting with the 1997 vintage, they
will be renewed by a third). They are usually fined but filtered only if
necessary.

SECOND WINE
Brand name: La Chartreuse d'Hosten
Average annual production: 65,000–70,000 bottles

Evaluation of present classification: This is a fine Cru Bourgeois that
comes close in the top vintages to the quality of a Médoc fifth-growth
Plateau of maturity: 5–9 years following the vintage

The style of wine of Fourcas-Hosten has changed. The old Fourcas-Hosten
wines tended to be hard, tannic, robust, coarse wines, with impressive color and
body but often excessive tannins. The best of the old-style Fourcas-Hosten is
the 1970, a big, rich, generously flavored wine that is now approaching maturity.
Starting with the light vintage of 1973, the wines took on a pronounced sup-

pleness and fruitiness, with less abrasive tannins in evidence. The 1975 was a fine example of the new-style Fourcas-Hosten, possessing rich, deep, black currant fruit and aging potential of 10–20 years. The 1978 is very drinkable now, soft and flavorful, as is the lighter, more delicate 1979. After 1975, the best vintages are the 1982, 1985, 1986, 1989, and 1990.

FOURCAS-LOUBANEY   EXCELLENT

Classification: Cru Bourgeois in 1932
Location of vineyards: Listrac-Médoc
Owner: Consortium de Réalisation
Address: Moulin de Laborde, 33480 Médoc
Mailing address: Same as above
Telephone: 33 5 56 58 03 83; telefax: 33 5 56 58 06 30
Visits: Every day, between 2 P.M. and 6 P.M.
Contact: Yann Olivier

VINEYARDS (red)
Surface area: 30.9 acres
Average age of vines: 35 years
Blend: 55% Cabernet Sauvignon, 35% Merlot, 10% Petit Verdot
Density of plantation: 6,700 and 10,000 vines per hectare
Average yields (over the last 5 years): 45 hectoliters per hectare
Total average annual production: 80,000 bottles

GRAND VIN (red)
Brand name: Château Fourcas-Loubaney
Appellation: Listrac-Médoc
Mean annual production: 80,000 bottles
Upbringing: Fermentations and macerations last 4 weeks in
stainless-steel tanks equipped with a cooling system. Wines are aged 15–
18 months, after malolactics in oak barrels that are renewed by a third at
each vintage. They are fined and filtered.

SECOND WINE
None produced.

Evaluation of present classification: The quality equivalent of a Médoc
fifth-growth
Plateau of maturity: 5–12 years following the vintage

This is one of the very best, if not the finest, wine of the Listrac appellation. Unfortunately, the tiny production is rarely seen except by a small group of avid Bordeaux aficionados. Proprietor Michel Hostens believes in extremely small yields of no more than 45 hectoliters per hectare. Additionally, his vineyard is among the oldest in Listrac. The use of at least 35% new oak and minimal clarification techniques usually result in a surprisingly concentrated, rich wine that avoids the hard tannins and rustic feel of so many Listracs.

Although I have not tasted a fully mature vintage of Fourcas-Loubaney, the seven vintages I have tasted have been so impressive that this wine would merit inclusion in any revised classification of the wines of Bordeaux as a fifth-growth.

Fourcas-Loubaney is actually made at Michel Hostens's other Listrac château, Moulin de Laborde, which does not quite approach the quality level of Fourcas-Loubaney.

VINTAGES

1995—The 1995 reveals a saturated ruby/purple color, ripe fruit, good concentration,
•   and a smooth, medium-bodied, round feel on the palate. It is another 1995
87   that recalls the 1985 vintage, but with more depth and definition. It should
       drink well, and last for 7–8 years. Last tasted, 11/97.

1994—The 1994 exhibits a medium dark ruby color, plenty of toasty new oak in the
•   nose (not dissimilar from Haut-Marbuzet), medium body, soft tannin, and an
86   elegant, supple finish. It should be accessible, and will drink well for 5–6
       years. Last tasted, 3/96.

1990—The 1990 is deep in color, with a rich nose of cassis and oak. Dense,
•   concentrated, medium to full bodied, and tannic, it is an immensely impres-
88   sive wine. Anticipated maturity: Now–2008. Last tasted, 1/93.

1989—Soft and forward, with excellent color and a big, plummy, oaky nose, the 1989
•   lacks the concentration and grip of the 1990 and 1988. Yet it offers a gener-
85   ous, amply endowed mouthful of wine. Drink it over the next 4–6 years. Last
       tasted, 1/93.

1988—Black/ruby in color, with a full-intensity bouquet of superpure black currants,
•   herbs, and toasty new oak, this wine is splendidly concentrated for a 1988,
88   offers excellent balance, and has a long finish. Anticipated maturity: Now–
       2005. Last tasted, 1/93.

1986—The 1986 is one of the great sleepers of the vintage. Still splendidly dark
•   ruby/purple in color, with a blossoming bouquet of toasty new oak, cas-
89   sis, licorice, and some floral aromas, this full-bodied, impeccably bal-
       anced, admirably concentrated wine has loads of extract (no doubt from
       low yields and old vines) and a long, intense finish. Oh, how I wish I had
       bought more of this wine! Anticipated maturity: Now–2006. Last tasted,
       1/91.

1985—Just reaching its plateau of maturity, the 1985 Fourcas-Loubaney has a very
•   intense bouquet of black currants, subtle herbs, and new oak. In the mouth,
87   the wine is supple, expansive, and exhibits fine depth and length. It should
       be drunk over the next 5–6 years. Anticipated maturity: Now. Last tasted,
       1/91.

GRESSIER GRAND-POUJEAUX   GOOD

Classification: Cru Bourgeois
Appellation: Moulis
Proprietor: Bertrand de Marcellas
Address: 33480 Moulis-en-Médoc
Telephone: 33 5 56 58 02 51
Production: 11,000 cases
Blend: 60% Cabernet Sauvignon, 30% Merlot, 10% Cabernet Franc
Secondary label: None
Vineyard size: 54 acres
Time spent in barrels: 20–24 months
Average age of vines: 27 years

Evaluation of present classification: The quality equivalent of a Médoc
fifth-growth
Plateau of maturity: 7–20 years following the vintage.

This is a fascinating property to examine. The estate has been in the same family since it was purchased by Monsieur Gressier in 1724. The domain has a long track record of making wines that can last for 20–30 or more years, and it has not hesitated to declassify certain vintages such as 1963, 1965, and 1977 that were not up to its standards. The vineyard, which sits on some of the best gravelly soil of Moulis, has several parcels of extremely old vines where the production rarely exceeds 15 hectoliters per hectare. Additionally, a conservative pruning philosophy results in moderate yields. The wine, vinified in old oak fermentation tanks and aged in small casks, can be almost impossible to taste young, but I have become a believer in just how well this wine can last based on a tasting of the 1966, 1970 (a superb wine that I rated 90), and 1975. More recently, terrific wines were made in 1982, 1985, 1986, 1989, and 1990.

VINTAGES

1989—The dark, opaque, ruby/purple color of the 1989 suggests a serious level of
 •   extract and intensity. The bouquet remains tight, but with swirling, delivers
88   aromas of tar, spices, coffee, and black currants. In the mouth, the wine is
       packed with fruit, has high levels of glycerin, outstanding concentration, and
       plenty of tannin in the finish. While the acidity is low, the tannins are high.
       My guess is that this rustic, old-style wine needs another 8–10 years of
       cellaring. Anticipated maturity: 1999–2015. Last tasted, 1/93.

1988—Opaque ruby/purple, with a reticent but emerging bouquet of chocolate, cassis,
 •   and cedar, the 1988 is medium to full bodied, typically backward and rustic,
87   but filled with character. Anticipated maturity: Now–2008. Last tasted, 1/93.

1986—The 1986 Gressier Grand-Poujeaux is black/ruby/purple in color, with a
•   reticent but blossoming bouquet of minerals, licorice, and black currants. On
`89   the palate, the wine displays the judicious use of new oak barrels, outstanding
       richness and length, and a long, powerful, tannic finish. This is definitely a
       wine to lay away in your cellar for a minimum of 7–8 years. It could turn out
       to be one of the sleepers of the vintage. Anticipated maturity: Now–2020.
       Last tasted, 4/90.

1985—The 1985, a sleeper of the vintage, is a black/ruby–colored wine that is
•   loaded with extract and has a tremendous tannic clout, a long, rich finish, full
87   body, and 10–15 years of further evolution. This is a brilliant old-style wine
       that should be bought only by those who have patience and a fine, cool cellar.
       Anticipated maturity: Now–2010. Last tasted, 3/89.

1984—Quite a serious wine for a 1984, this dark-colored, ripe, rich, tannic, medium-
•   to full-bodied wine has plenty of extract and will reward those who try it.
84   Anticipated maturity: Now. Last tasted, 3/87.

1982—The bouquet is beginning to display signs of maturity. The big, almost roasted
•   chestnut, leather, mineral, and black currant bouquet precedes a powerful,
89   muscular, exceptionally concentrated wine that almost overpowers the palate
       but is impressive for its size, strength, and depth. This wine is not for the shy.
       Anticipated maturity: Now–2010. Last tasted, 3/88.

1979—Still remarkably young and backward, this dark ruby–colored, herbaceous,
•   peppery-and-currant-scented wine is medium bodied, with surprisingly strong
86   acidity and moderate tannins. It lacks the great depth this wine can achieve
       in top years and is a more streamlined and civilized rendition of Gressier
       Grand-Poujeaux. Anticipated maturity: Now–2001. Last tasted, 3/88.

1970—A spectacular bouquet of roasted nuts, minerals, tar, licorice, and black fruits
•   is clearly of classified-growth quality. In the mouth, the wine displays an
90   almost sumptuous richness, some moderate tannins in the finish, and great
       concentration and length. This wine has shed much of its hardness and is
       delicious to drink. It exhibits no signs of losing its fruit. In style and character
       it is reminiscent of the 1970 Lynch-Bages! Anticipated maturity: Now–2005.
       Last tasted, 3/88.

GREYSAC   GOOD

Classification: Cru Bourgeois in 1932
Location of vineyards: Bégadan (By)
Owner: EXOR Group
Address: By, 33340 Bégadan
Mailing address: Same as above
Telephone: 33 5 56 73 26 56; telefax: 33 5 56 73 26 58
Visits: By appointment only

VINEYARDS (red)
Surface area: 173 acres
Average age of vines: 25 years

Blend: 45% Merlot, 40% Cabernet Sauvignon, 10% Cabernet Franc, 5% Petit Verdot
Density of plantation: 7,600 vines per hectare
Average yields (over the last 5 years): 55 hectoliters per hectare
Total average annual production: 40,000 cases

GRAND VIN (red)
Brand name: Château Greysac
Appellation: Médoc
Mean annual production: 30,000 cases
Upbringing: Fermentations (27–32 degrees centigrade) last 4–5 days and macerations 25–30 days in temperature-controlled stainless-steel vats. Wines undergo malolactics in tanks and are transferred to oak barrels (20% of which are new) for 12 months aging. They are racked every 4 months, assembled in vats just before fining, and allowed to rest 2 months before bottling. They are not filtered.

SECOND WINE
Brand name: Domaine de By

Evaluation of present classification: Should be maintained
Plateau of maturity: 5–12 years following the vintage

Greysac has become one of the most popular Cru Bourgeois wines in the United States. High quality and the dynamic personality and marketing ability of the now deceased gregarious proprietor—Baron François de Gunzburg—were totally responsible for this wine's acceptance by Americans (who are normally so classification conscious when it comes to Bordeaux wines).

The style of wine at Greysac is one that I have always found very elegant, smooth, and medium bodied, with a complex bouquet filled with currant fruit and a true, mineral, soil-like aroma. Never an aggressive or overly tannic wine, Greysac is usually fully mature by its sixth or seventh year and keeps well for up to 12 years.

HANTEILLAN

Classification: Cru Bourgeois
Location of vineyards: Cissac
Owner: Catherine Blasco
Address: 12, route d'Hanteillan, 33250 Cissac
Mailing address: Same as above
Telephone: 33 5 56 59 35 31; telefax: 33 5 56 59 31 51

Visits: Monday through Friday, from 9 A.M. to noon, and 2 P.M. to 6 P.M.
Contact: Miss Brossard

VINEYARDS (red)
Surface area: 202.5 acres
Average age of vines: 20 years
Blend: 51% Cabernet Sauvignon, 40% Merlot, 5% Cabernet Franc, 4% Petit Verdot
Density of plantation: 6,500 and 8,500 vines per hectare
Average yields (over the last 5 years): 62 hectoliters
Total average annual production: 5,000 hectoliters

GRAND VIN (red)
Brand name: Château Hanteillan
Appellation: Haut-Médoc
Mean annual production: 450,000 bottles
Upbringing: Fermentations take place in stainless-steel tanks (blend separate), and in place of the traditional pumping-overs, the cap is "destructured" under pressure. Wines are aged, by rotation, half in concrete tanks and half in 1-vintage-old barrels (no new oak) for 6 months. They remain unfined and unfiltered.

SECOND WINE
Brand name: Château Laborde/Château Blagnac
Average annual production: 120,000 bottles/60,000 bottles

Evaluation of present classification: Should be maintained
Plateau of maturity: 4–8 years following the vintage

This is a highly promoted Cru Bourgeois that I have always found to be lacking in fruit and charm. It is classically made, with a high-tech *cuverie* designed to produce wines of quality. Nevertheless, the wine comes across as relatively tannic, austere, and compact. I thought I detected more charm and finesse with both the 1989 and 1990. There is a second wine for cuvées deemed not acceptable for Hanteillan.

LAMARQUE　　　　　　　　　　　　　　　　　GOOD

Classification: Cru Bourgeois
Location of vineyards: Lamarque
Owner: S.C. Gromand d'Evry
Address: 33460 Lamarque
Mailing address: Same as above

Telephone: 33 5 56 58 90 03 or 33 5 56 58 97 55;
telefax: 33 5 56 58 97 55
Visits: By appointment only, Monday through Friday, from 9:30 A.M. to
11:30 A.M., and 2 P.M. to 5 P.M.
Contact: Francine Prévot

VINEYARDS (red)
Surface area: 106.2 acres
Average age of vines: 30 years
Blend: 46% Cabernet Sauvignon, 25% Merlot, 24% Cabernet Franc, 5%
Petit Verdot
Density of plantation: 6,500 vines per hectare
Average yields (over the last 5 years): 52.83 hectoliters per hectare
Total average annual production: 245,000 bottles

GRAND VIN (red)
Brand name: Château de Lamarque
Appellation: Haut-Médoc
Mean annual production: 150,000 bottles
Upbringing: There is a *saignée* of 15%–20% of the volume before
alcoholic fermentation. Fermentations and macerations last 15–20 days
in epoxy-lined concrete tanks. Temperature control is manual. Free-run
wines undergo malolactics in vats, press wines in barrels. Wines are aged
12–14 months in oak barrels, one-third of which are new. *Assemblage* is
never done before the month of June following the vintage, at the time of
the second racking. (Note: Rackings are done from barrel to barrel.)
Wines are fined and lightly filtered.

SECOND WINE
Brand name: Donjon de Lamarque
Average annual production: 90,000 bottles

Evaluation of present classification: Should be maintained
Plateau of maturity: 4–7 years following the vintage

One of the outstanding medieval fortress castles in the Bordeaux region,
Lamarque, named after the town of the same name, sits just off the main
Route du Vin (D2) of the Médoc directly on the road to the ferry boat that
traverses the Gironde to Blaye.

Lamarque is a typically good, middle-weight, central Médoc wine. It seems
to have a touch of the St.-Julien elegance mixed with round, supple, soft, ripe
fruity flavors. The owners, the Gromand family, make the wine with great
care. Lamarque should be consumed within 7–8 years of the vintage. Prices
remain among the more reasonable for a Cru Bourgeois.

LANESSAN

Classification: Cru Bourgeois Supérieur in 1932
Location of vineyards: Cussac-Fort-Médoc
Owner: G.F.A. des Domaines Bouteiller
Address: 33460 Cussac-Fort-Médoc
Mailing address: Same as above
Telephone: 33 5 56 58 94 80; telefax: 33 5 56 58 93 10
Visits: Every day, between 9 A.M. and noon, and 2 P.M. and 6 P.M.

VINEYARDS (red)
Surface area: 98.8 acres
Average age of vines: 25 years
Blend: 75% Cabernet Sauvignon, 20% Merlot, 5% Cabernet Franc and
Petit Verdot
Density of plantation: 10,000 vines per hectare
Average yields (over the last 5 years): 55 hectoliters per hectare
Total average annual production: 2,800 cases

GRAND VIN (red)
Brand name: Château Lanessan
Appellation: Haut-Médoc
Mean annual production: 20,000 cases
Upbringing: Fermentations and macerations last 12–18 days in
temperature-controlled concrete tanks. After malolactics in vats, wines
are transferred to oak barrels, 5% of which are new, for 18–30 months
aging, depending upon the vintage. They are fined and filtered.

SECOND WINE
None produced.

Evaluation of present classification: At its best, Lanessan is the quality
equivalent of a Médoc fifth-growth
Plateau of maturity: 7–18 years following the vintage

Lanessan can be one of the outstanding wines of the Haut-Médoc appellation. The wine could probably be given serious consideration for fifth-growth status should any reclassification of the wines of the Médoc take place.

Lanessan, which is located in Cussac immediately south of the commune of St.-Julien, opposite the big vineyard of Gruaud-Larose, makes intensely flavored wines, with deep color, a robust, large-scaled frame, and chewy texture. If they can be criticized for lacking finesse, they more than compensate for that weakness with rich, gutsy, black currant flavors.

The 99 acres, which are being augmented each year with new plantings, produce in excess of 20,000 cases of wine. The property is owned and managed by the Bouteiller family. Lanessan ages extremely well, as attested by a delightful but tired 1920 I shared with a friend in 1983. Of more recent vintages, the top successes include the 1970, 1975, 1978, 1982, 1986, 1988, 1989, 1990, 1995, and 1996. The wines are powerful and individualized, somewhat similar in style and character to the fifth-growth Pauillac Lynch-Bages.

I have noted above that Lanessan can be inconsistent. Part of the spottiness of Lanessan's performance (the only criticism one could possibly make) is probably due to the château's insistence on using old barrels for aging the wine. Perhaps a small percentage of new barrels each year might prove beneficial for such a robust wine. For visitors to the region, this lovely château, which has been owned by the same family since 1890, is now a museum displaying numerous carriages and an assortment of harnesses. It is open to the public.

VINTAGES

1997—A sweet black currant and cherry-scented nose exhibits fine purity and matu-
•   rity. This is a savory, medium-bodied, fleshy, mouth-filling, satisfying wine
85–   that should drink well for 7–8 years. Last tasted, 3/98.
87

1996—The 1996 is an impressively built medium-bodied, deep ruby/purple–colored
•   wine with plenty of black currant, spice box, and cedar flavors. It is long in
86–   the mouth, with moderate but sweet tannin. Anticipated maturity: 2000–
88   2015. Last tasted, 3/98.

1995—The 1995 reveals less power and muscle but more elegance and fleshy,
•   weedy, tobacco-tinged red and black currant fruit presented in a soft, supple,
87   alluring, medium-bodied format. Anticipated maturity: Now–2008. Last
    tasted, 11/97.

1993—Another well-run Cru Bourgeois that has managed to tame the ferocious
•   tannin of the 1993 vintage, Lanessan has produced a plump, tasty, supple
86   wine with a forward, cassis, cedary, and herb nose, excellent ripeness, medium body, and a round, generous finish. It should drink well for 10–12 years. Last tasted, 11/94.

1992—Medium ruby colored, with an attractive herbal-scented nose of dusty red and
•   black fruits and earthy wood, this soft, medium-bodied, low-acid wine reveals
83   some tannin in the finish. Drink it over the next 4–5 years before it dries out. Last tasted, 11/94.

1990—The 1990 is opaque in color, with a huge, peppery, spicy, black cherry nose
•   intermingled with aromas of Provençal herbs. In the mouth, there is excellent
88   richness, a density and thickness to the texture, fine spice, tannin, and glycerin in the long finish. It should drink well for 10–12 or more years. Last tasted, 1/93.

1989—Lanessan's 1989 is herbaceous but also fat, richly fruity, and soft. A weighty,
•   rich, full-bodied wine, it offers gorgeous amounts of fruit, glycerin, and tan-
87   nin. Anticipated maturity: Now–2004. Last tasted, 1/93.

1988—The 1988 Lanessan is a full, rich, concentrated wine. Deep and ripe, with a
• complex bouquet of menthol, cedar and black currants intertwined with subtle
86 scents of oak, this plump, highly concentrated, full-bodied wine should drink
beautifully for 10–15 years. Last tasted, 1/93.

1987—Somewhat herbaceous and lean, the 1987 Lanessan has an open-knit bouquet
• and soft, round flavors exhibiting a greenness that is indicative of unripe
74 Cabernet Sauvignon. Anticipated maturity: Now. Last tasted, 4/90.

1986—This is probably the best Lanessan made in 2 decades. Still deep ruby/purple
• in color, with an emerging but reticent bouquet of herbs, leather, grilled
88 meats, and black currants, this full-bodied, tannic, powerful Lanessan should
be sought out by consumers who like their clarets well defined, tannic,
and impressively structured. Anticipated maturity: Now–2010. Last tasted,
3/90.

1985—Smoky, earthy, and ripe blackberry notes soar from the glass. On the palate,
• the 1985 Lanessan exhibits plenty of depth, lower acidity, and softer tannins
87 than normal but still offers a forceful, meaty mouthful of wine lacking a bit of
finesse and charm. It compensates for these shortcomings with robustness
and ripeness. Anticipated maturity: Now–2003. Last tasted, 3/89.

1984—A spicy, slightly vegetal bouquet is followed by a wine that is slightly sweet,
• rather disjointed, but adequate for drinking over the next 3–4 years. Antici-
76 pated maturity: Now. Last tasted, 4/89.

1982—Given the low acidity and a fat, loosely knit structure, this is not a typical
• example of Lanessan. However, there is no denying the forward, generously
86 endowed personality, gobs of earthy, black currant fruit, and soft, luscious
finish. Anticipated maturity: Now. Last tasted, 1/90.

OLDER VINTAGES

The 1906 (69 points; last tasted 12/95) exhibited a light amber/orange–like color, vague cedar notes in the nose that quickly turned to volatile acidity, and musty cellar smells. High acid and the absence of fruit made this wine a candidate for vintage vinegar. That being said, the nose was complex, at least for a brief period, but the fruit is dried out and the wine barely alive. Tasted at the same time, the 1914 Lanessan (76 points) was in slightly better shape, with an attractive sweet, curranty, cedarlike nose, high tannin on the palate, some fruit, and a medium-bodied, tart, acidic finish. There is a hole in the middle, but the wine has some life remaining.

LAROSE-TRINTAUDON

Classification: Cru Bourgeois
Location of vineyards: St.-Laurent-du-Médoc and Pauillac
Owner: A.G.F. since 1986
Address: Route de Pauillac, 33112 St.-Laurent-du-Médoc

Mailing address: Same as above
Telephone: 33 5 56 59 41 72; telefax: 33 5 56 59 93 22
Visits: By appointment only
Contact: Matthias von Campe or F. Bijon

VINEYARDS (red)
Surface area: 427.3 acres
Average age of vines: 25 years
Blend: 65% Cabernet Sauvignon, 30% Merlot, 5% Cabernet Franc
Density of plantation: 6,600 vines per hectare
Average yields (over the last 5 years): 55 hectoliters per hectare
Total average annual production: 1,150,000 bottles

GRAND VIN (red)
Brand name: Château Larose-Trintaudon
Appellation: Haut-Médoc
Mean annual production: 1,000,000 bottles
Upbringing: Fermentations and macerations last 3–4 weeks in
temperature-controlled stainless-steel vats. Wines are then aged
12 months in oak barrels, which are renewed by a quarter at each
vintage.

SECOND WINE
Brand name: Larose St.-Laurent
Average annual production: 130,000 bottles

Evaluation of present classification: Should be maintained
Plateau of maturity: 4–7 years following the vintage

The largest vineyard in the Médoc has for years produced a straightforward,
supple, correct wine of no great distinction.

LESTAGE   GOOD

Classification: Cru Bourgeois Supérieur
Location of vineyards: Listrac-Médoc and Moulis
Owner: Jean, Elza, Katherine, and Caroline Chanfreau
Address: 33480 Listrac-Médoc
Mailing address: Same as above
Telephone: 33 5 56 58 02 43; telefax: 33 5 56 58 04 33
Visits: Monday through Friday, from 9 A.M. to noon, and 2 P.M. to
5:30 P.M.
Contact: Jean or Marie-Hélène Chanfreau

VINEYARDS (red)
Surface area: 116 acres in Listrac and 16 acres in Moulis
Average age of vines: 28 years
Blend: 58% Merlot, 38% Cabernet Sauvignon, 2% Cabernet Franc, 2% Petit Verdot
Density of plantation: 6,660 vines per hectare
Average yields (over the last 5 years): 56 hectoliters
Total average annual production: 350,000 bottles

GRAND VIN (red)
Brand name: Château Lestage
Appellation: Listrac-Médoc
Mean annual production: 210,000 bottles
Upbringing: Fermentations and macerations last 20–31 days in temperature-controlled vats. Fermentations take place at 28–30 degrees centigrade and macerations at 30–32 degrees centigrade maximum. Seventy percent of the yield is aged in oak barrels, and 30% remains in vats (by rotation) for a period of 12 months. The wines are fined but not systematically filtered.

SECOND WINE
Brand name: La Dame de Coeur du Château Lestage
Average annual production: 32,000–50,000 bottles
NOTE: The 16 acres of Moulis produce a grand vin called Château Caroline, and the second wine is La Dame de Coeur du Château Caroline (35,000 bottles/year).

Evaluation of present classification: Should be maintained
Plateau of maturity: 3–8 years following the vintage

I have fond memories of many vintages of Lestage. They are supple, straightforward, richly fruity efforts, cleanly made and tasty. Until 1985 the entire production was aged in large vats, but in 1985 the proprietor began employing small oak barrels. That decision has resulted in wines with more structure and character. This is never a profound wine, and there is a tendency to produce too much wine per hectare, but this large vineyard in Listrac, with a charming three-story, nineteenth-century château, easily fulfills the needs of consumers looking for wines that offer immediate drinkability at a fair price.

LIVERSAN   GOOD

Classification: Cru Bourgeois
Location of vineyards: St.-Sauveur
Owner: S.C.E.A. du Château Liversan (belongs to Château Patache d'Aux)
Address: Route de Farpiqueyre, 33250 St.-Sauveur
Mailing address: Les Trois Châteaux, 1, route du 19 mars, 33340 Bégadan
Telephone: 33 5 56 41 50 18; telefax: 33 5 56 41 54 65
Visits: Monday through Friday, between 9 A.M. and 12:30 P.M., and 2 P.M. and 5:30 P.M.
Contact: Bruno Blanc, telephone 33 5 56 73 94 65

VINEYARDS (red)
Surface area: 98.8 acres
Average age of vines: 25 years
Blend: 49% Cabernet Sauvignon, 38% Merlot, 10% Cabernet Franc, 3% Petit Verdot
Density of plantation: 8,500 vines per hectare
Average yields (over the last 5 years): 56 hectoliters per hectare
Total average annual production: 290,000 bottles

GRAND VIN (red)
Brand name: Château Liversan
Appellation: Haut-Médoc
Mean annual production: 150,000 bottles
Upbringing: Fermentations last 20–25 days in concrete and stainless-steel tanks. Wines are then aged 12 months in oak barrels, approximately 20% of which are new. They are fined but are not filtered.

SECOND WINE
Brand name: Les Charmes de Liversan
Average annual production: 140,000 bottles

Evaluation of present classification: Should be maintained, but vintages since the mid-1980s are extremely close in quality to a Médoc fifth-growth
Plateau of maturity: 4–10 years following the vintage

Many Bordeaux observers have long considered the excellently placed vineyard of Liversan, which sits between the city of Pauillac and the hamlet of St.-Sauveur, to have the potential to produce wines of classified-growth quality. The construction of a new winery, increased use of new oak barrels, and conservative yields have resulted in a series of good to very good wines.

The style produced at Liversan aims for wines with a deep color, fine extract, soft tannins, and grip, concentration, and length. The owners attribute the quality of Liversan to the extremely dense plantations of 8,500 vines per hectare, which is 2,000 more vines per hectare than in most Bordeaux vineyards. This dense plantation causes the roots to push deeper into the earth, seeking nutrients and therefore producing wines with greater character and depth.

LOUDENNE

Classification: Cru Bourgeois
Location of vineyards: St.-Yzans-de-Médoc
Owner: W. & A. Gilbey
Address: 33340 St.-Yzans-de-Médoc
Mailing address: Same as above
Telephone: 33 5 56 73 17 80; telefax: 33 5 56 09 02 87
Visits: On weekdays, from 9:30 A.M. to 12:30, and 2 P.M. to 5:30 P.M.; by appointment only on public holidays and during weekends
Contact: Claude-Marie Toustou

VINEYARDS (red)
Surface area: 118.6 acres
Average age of vines: 28 years
Blend: 45% Cabernet Sauvignon, 45% Merlot, 7% Cabernet Franc, 2% Malbec, 1% Petit Verdot
Density of plantation: 5,000–6,500 vines per hectare
Average yields (over the last 5 years): 60 hectoliters per hectare
Total average annual production: 300,000 bottles

GRAND VIN (red)
Brand name: Château Loudenne
Appellation: Médoc
Mean annual production: 250,000 bottles
Upbringing: Fermentations and macerations last 3 weeks in stainless-steel or concrete tanks. Wines are aged 15 months in oak barrels renewed by a quarter at each vintage. They are fined and filtered.

SECOND WINE
Brand name: Château Lestagne
Average annual production: 40,000—60,000 bottles

VINEYARDS (white)
Surface area: 34.6 acres
Average age of vines: 19 years
Blend: 62% Sauvignon, 38% Semillon
Density of plantation: 5,000 vines per hectare
Average yields (over the last 5 years): 48 hectoliters per hectare
Total average annual production: 89,000 bottles

GRAND VIN (white)
Brand name: Château Loudenne
Appellation: White dry Bordeaux
Mean annual production: 40,000 bottles
Upbringing: After a short *macération pelliculaire* and cold settling of the musts, these are vinified at low temperatures (15–16 degrees centigrade) or fermented in oak barrels (21–22 degrees centigrade), with weekly stirrings, for 8 months. *Assemblage* is then done and the whole lot undergoes cold stabilization. Wines are bottled 10 months after the vintage. They are fined and filtered. (Since the 1995 vintage, more and more oak has been used for the vinifications. In 1997 the whole yield was fermented in oak barrels that are renewed by a quarter at each vintage.)

Evaluation of present classification: Should be maintained
Plateau of maturity: 3–6 years following the vintage

The lovely pink Château Loudenne has been owned by the firm of W. & A. Gilbey since 1875. The vineyard, planted on sandy, stony soils, is located at the very northern end of the Médoc, near St.-Yzans. While I have enjoyed the fruity, straightforward white wine, made from a blend of Sauvignon and Semillon, I find the red wine extremely light. Although it is correctly made, it lacks complexity, richness, and staying power.

Given the attention to detail exhibited at Loudenne, I have often wondered whether or not this area of the Médoc is capable of producing wines of staying power. Improvements in quality in the mid-nineties augur well for more complete and interesting red wines.

MAGNOL   GOOD

Classification: Cru Bourgeois in 1932
Location of vineyards: Blanquefort
Owner: Barton & Guestier
Address: Domaine de Magnol, 33290 Blanquefort

Mailing address: c/o Barton & Guestier, B.P. 30, 33292 Blanquefort
Cedex
Telephone: 33 5 56 95 48 00; telefax: 33 5 56 95 48 01
Visits: No visits allowed

VINEYARDS (red)
Surface area: 40.8 acres
Average age of vines: 20 years
Blend: 50% Merlot, 45% Cabernet Sauvignon, 5% Cabernet Franc
Density of plantation: 6,600 vines per hectare
Average yields (over the last 5 years): 50 hectoliters per hectare
Total average annual production: 825 hectoliters

GRAND VIN (red)
Brand name: Château Magnol
Appellation: Haut-Médoc
Mean annual production: 100,000 bottles
Upbringing: Fermentations and macerations last 4–5 weeks at 28–32
degrees centigrade in temperature-controlled stainless-steel tanks. Wines
are then aged 12 months in oak barrels, 25% of which are new. They are
fined and filtered.

SECOND WINE
None produced.

Evaluation of present classification: Should be maintained
Plateau of maturity: 3–5 years following the vintage

I have been impressed with the soft, fruity, easy to like, and easy to drink wines
of Château Magnol, a property owned by the huge firm of Barton & Guestier.
The vineyard is located just north of the city of Bordeaux, east of the sprawling
suburb of Blanquefort. The wine is extremely well made in a modern, commercial style, and there is no doubting its seductive, forward charms. Magnol is
not a wine to lay away in your cellar; it should be drunk early.

MALESCASSE
GOOD

Classification: Cru Bourgeois in 1932
Location of vineyards: Lamarque
Owner: Alcatel Alsthom
Address: 6, route du Moulin Rose, 33460 Lamarque
Mailing address: 6, route du Moulin Rose, B.P. 46, 33460 Lamarque
Telephone: 33 5 56 73 15 20; telefax: 33 5 56 59 64 72

Visits: Monday through Friday, from 9 A.M. to noon, and 2 P.M. to 5 P.M.
Contact: François Peyran

VINEYARDS (red)
Surface area: 91.4 acres
Average age of vines: 20 years
Blend: 55% Cabernet Sauvignon, 35% Merlot, 10% Cabernet Franc
Density of plantation: 8,500 vines per hectare
Average yields (over the last 5 years): 55 hectoliters per hectare
Total average annual production: 250,000 bottles

GRAND VIN (red)
Brand name: Château Malescasse
Appellation: Haut-Médoc
Mean annual production: 170,000 bottles
Upbringing: Fermentations and macerations last 24–30 days in
temperature-controlled stainless-steel tanks at rather high temperatures.
Malolactics occur in vats for 25% of the yield. Wines are aged 16 months
in oak barrels that are renewed by a quarter at each vintage. They are
racked every 3 months, fined with albumin and lightly filtered.

SECOND WINE
Brand name: La Closerie de Malescasse
Average annual production: 83,000 bottles

Evaluation of present classification: Should be maintained
Plateau of maturity: 4–8 years following the vintage

Malescasse is a well-situated vineyard located just to the north of the village
of Arcins and south of Lamarque. The vineyard was extensively replanted in
the early seventies, and the vines are now reaching maturity.

This is a seriously run Cru Bourgeois, and since the early eighties the
wines have been richly fruity, medium bodied, and ideal for drinking between
the ages of 4 and 8.

MAUCAILLOU   EXCELLENT

Classification: Cru Bourgeois in 1932
Location of vineyards: Moulis and Listrac
Owner: S.A.R.L. du Château Maucaillou—Philippe Dourthe
Address: 33480 Moulis-en-Médoc
Mailing address: Same as above
Telephone: 33 5 56 58 01 23; telefax: 33 5 56 58 00 88

Visits: Every day, from 10 A.M. to noon, and 2 P.M. to 6 P.M.
Contact: Magali Dourthe

VINEYARDS (red)
Surface area: 197.6 acres
Average age of vines: 28 years
Blend: 56% Cabernet Sauvignon, 35% Merlot, 7% Petit Verdot, 2% Cabernet Franc
Density of plantation: 8,000 vines per hectare
Average yields (over the last 5 years): 52 hectoliters per hectare
Total average annual production: 4,200 hectoliters

GRAND VIN (red)
Brand name: Château Maucaillou
Appellation: Moulis-en-Médoc
Mean annual production: 33,000 cases
Upbringing: Fermentations (8 days in all) are kept, during the first 4 days, at 22 degrees centigrade, and temperatures go up to 30 degrees centigrade at the end of this process. Macerations last until the tannin index reaches 55–65. Wines are aged 18 months in oak barrels, 33%–65% of which are new depending upon the vintage. They are fined and lightly filtered.

SECOND WINE
Brand name: Château Cap de Haut Maucaillou (Haut-Médoc)
Average annual production: 8,000 cases

Evaluation of present classification: Easily the equivalent of a fourth- or fifth-growth
Plateau of maturity: 4–12 years following the vintage

Maucaillou has consistently represented one of the best wine values in the Médoc. The wine is impeccably made by the robust and exuberant Philippe Dourthe. There is little to criticize at this estate. Maucaillou is a deeply colored wine, with a splendid ripe concentration of fruit, good body, soft tannins, and enough grip and extract to mature gracefully over a 10–12-year period. Since the early eighties the wines have been aged in as much as 60% new oak casks, with the remainder in 2-year-old casks purchased from prominent classified-growth châteaux.

It is not easy to make wines so rich and fat that they can be drunk young while maintaining their ability to age for up to a decade. Maucaillou has clearly succeeded in taming the soil of Moulis, which can render hard, tannic wine. They have produced exceptionally elegant, highly satisfying wines that are among only a handful of under-priced Bordeauxs. For the adventurous travelers who enjoy the back roads of the Médoc, I highly recommend a visit to Château Maucaillou, where there is an attractive wine-making museum. In addition, visitors have the opportunity to taste the new wine.

VINTAGES

1997—A fine effort from this property, Maucaillou's 1997 exhibits a saturated ruby/
 •   purple color, intense cassis and jammy cranberry fruit, fat, voluptuous flavors,
86– low acidity, and excellent purity. This delicious offering is a potential sleeper
87   of the vintage. Last tasted, 3/98.

1996—More concentrated than the lean, angular 1995, but still pushing the tannin
 •   limit, this saturated ruby-colored wine possesses berry, cassis fruit, good
84– spice, medium body, and ten years of ageability. Last tasted, 3/98.
85?

1989—The 1989 has a generous level of gorgeous black raspberry fruit in its bou-
 •   quet, followed by wonderfully rich, fleshy, highly extracted fruit flavors and a
87   velvety texture. It is pure seduction and finesse in the finish. Anticipated
      maturity: Now–2001. Last tasted, 1/93.

1988—The 1988 Maucaillou is an extremely attractive, oaky, plump, elegant, richly
 •   fruity, medium-bodied wine that should drink beautifully for the next 4–6
86   years. Last tasted, 1/93.

1986—The 1986 should prove to be slightly better than the 1985, as it is a deeper,
 •   fuller, and richer wine with a bit more tannin. The black cherry fruit is
86   complemented nicely by some toasty oak. Anticipated maturity: Now. Last
      tasted, 11/90.

1985—Of all the wines of Moulis, this one displays the most elegance and style,
 •   although it will never have the power and depth of a Chasse-Spleen or
85   Poujeaux. The 1985 is a stylish, rich, graceful wine with medium to full body,
      a perfumed, aromatic character, and long finish. Anticipated maturity: Now.
      Last tasted, 4/91.

MAYNE-LALANDE   GOOD

Classification: Cru Bourgeois
Location of vineyards: Listrac
Owner: Bernard Lartigue
Address: 33480 Listrac
Mailing address: Same as above
Telephone: 33 5 56 58 27 63; telefax: 33 5 56 58 22 41
Visits: Monday through Friday, from 8 A.M. to noon, and 2 P.M. to 6 P.M.
Contact: Bernard Lartigue

VINEYARDS (red)
Surface area: 39.5 acres
Average age of vines: 25 years

Blend: 45% Merlot, 45% Cabernet Sauvignon, 5% Cabernet Franc, 5% Petit Verdot

Density of plantation: 9,000 vines per hectare and 6,000 vines per hectare

Average yields (over the last 5 years): 40 hectoliters per hectare for the grand vin and 55 hectoliters per hectare for the second wine

Total average annual production: 95,000 bottles

GRAND VIN (red)

Brand name: Château Mayne-Lalande

Appellation: Listrac-Médoc

Mean annual production: 40,000–50,000 bottles

Upbringing: Fermentations (28–32 degrees centigrade) and macerations last approximately 30 days in tanks equipped with a cooling system. Wines are aged 12–15 months in oak barrels, 30%–40% of which are new. They are fined with fresh egg whites but are not filtered.

SECOND WINE

Brand name: Château Malbec Lartigue

Average annual production: 40,000 bottles

NOTE: This estate also produces a special cuvée called Grande Réserve du Château Mayne-Lalande. It is made in much the same way as the grand vin but is aged entirely in new oak, for 24–30 months. Production is 400 cases annually.

Evaluation of present classification: One of the least-known but best wines of Listrac, this château can, in some vintages, compete favorably with a Médoc fifth-growth

Plateau of maturity: 5–15 years following the vintage

This little-known Listrac property may emerge as one of the stars of the appellation. I had the opportunity to taste most of the vintages of the eighties, and I was especially impressed by the richness and intensity of the 1982, the finesse of the 1983, the power and surprising concentration of the 1985, and the potential for 15–20 years of longevity in the 1986. While the 1988 was slightly lean, both the 1989 and 1990 were among the best wines this property has made.

The key to their success at this estate is low yields and the dedication of proprietor Bernard Lartigue. For now, this wine remains known only to insiders and some of Bordeaux's most innovative restaurateurs, such as Jean-Pierre Xiradakis, who sells this wine at his well-known restaurant, La Tupina. The price has yet to take off, and therefore Mayne-Lalande appears to be undervalued at present.

MOULIN-ROUGE VERY GOOD

Classification: Cru Bourgeois in 1932
Location of vineyards: At the exit of Cussac-Fort-Médoc, in the direction of Beychevelle
Owner: Pelon and Ribero families
Address: 18, rue de Costes, 33460 Cussac-Fort-Médoc
Mailing address: Same as above
Telephone: 33 5 56 58 91 13; telefax: 33 5 56 58 93 68
Visits: Every day, from 9 A.M. to noon, and 2 P.M. to 6 P.M.
Contact: Laurence Ribero

VINEYARDS (red)
Surface area: 39.5 acres
Average age of vines: 25–30 years
Blend: 50% Merlot, 40% Cabernet Sauvignon, 10% Cabernet Franc
Density of plantation: 6,000 vines per hectare
Average yields (over the last 5 years): 50 hectoliters per hectare
Total average annual production: 90,000 bottles

GRAND VIN (red)
Brand name: Château du Moulin-Rouge
Appellation: Haut-Médoc
Mean annual production: 90,000 bottles
Upbringing: Fermentations and macerations last about 3 weeks in stainless-steel and concrete vats, equipped with a temperature control. Malolactics occur in vats, and wines are aged 12 months in oak barrels, 30% of which are new. They are fined with fresh egg whites but not systematically filtered.

SECOND WINE
None produced.

Evaluation of present classification: Should be maintained, but this is one of the better Crus Bourgeois
Plateau of maturity: 5–10 years following the vintage

Moulin-Rouge is one of my favorite Crus Bourgeois. The highly morcellated vineyard (there must be at least 6 separate parcels) is located north of the village of Cussac-Fort Médoc, just south of the appellation of St.-Julien. Not surprisingly, the wine often has the character of a good St.-Julien. It is always deep in color and in the eighties has been rich, fleshy, full bodied, and somewhat reminiscent of such wines as Hortevie and Terrey-Gros-Cailloux. Of course, Moulin-Rouge is significantly less expensive, since it is entitled only to the Haut-Médoc appellation.

This is one of the more solid, chunky, fleshy Crus Bourgeois, and while it may not have great finesse, it does offer considerable richness, muscle, and character.

MOULIN À VENT

GOOD

Classification: Cru Bourgeois in 1932
Location of vineyards: Moulis and Listrac
Owner: Dominique and Marie-Hélène Hessel
Address: Bouqueyran, 33480 Moulis-en-Médoc
Mailing address: Same as above
Telephone: 33 5 56 58 15 79; telefax: 33 5 56 58 12 05
Visits: Monday through Friday, between 9 A.M. and noon, and 2 P.M. and 6 P.M.; by appointment during weekends
Contact: Dominique Hessel

VINEYARDS (red)
Surface area: 61.8 acres
Average age of vines: 25 years
Blend: 65% Cabernet Sauvignon, 30% Merlot, 5% Petit Verdot
Density of plantation: 6,666 vines per hectare
Average yields (over the last 5 years): 49 hectoliters per hectare
Total average annual production: 150,000 bottles

GRAND VIN (red)
Brand name: Château Moulin à Vent
Appellation: Moulis
Mean annual production: 120,000 bottles
Upbringing: Fermentations and macerations last 3 weeks in concrete and stainless-steel vats. Pumping-overs are done daily. Wines are aged 20 months after malolactics by rotation in oak barrels (20%–25% of which are new) and vats (half the yield in each). They remain unfined and are lightly filtered upon bottling.

SECOND WINE
Brand name: Château Moulin de St.-Vincent
Average annual production: 30,000–40,000 bottles

Evaluation of present classification: Should be maintained
Plateau of maturity: 5–10 years following the vintage

This property continues to produce an older style of Moulis—dense, tannic, and requiring several years in the bottle to soften and evolve. The property uses a significant amount of press wine, resulting in a dark-colored, forceful, powerful style of Moulis that seems to be best when the grapes are fully ripe.

Overall, this is a property that has made considerable improvement in the quality of its wines since Dominique Hessel began to manage the estate's winemaking.

MOULIS

Classification: Cru Bourgeois in 1932
Location of vineyards: Moulis
Owner: Alain Darricarrère
Address: 33480 Moulis
Mailing address: Same as above
Telephone: 33 5 57 68 40 66
Visits: By appointment only
Contact: Alain Daricarrère

VINEYARDS (red)
Surface area: 42 acres
Average age of vines: 25 years
Blend: 50% Merlot, 50% Cabernet Sauvignon
Density of plantation: 6,660 vines per hectare
Average yields (over the last 5 years): 50 hectoliters per hectare
Total average annual production: 1,000 hectoliters maximum

GRAND VIN (red)
Brand name: Château Moulis
Appellation: Moulis
Mean annual production: 900 hectoliters
Upbringing: Fermentations and macerations last 3 weeks in stainless-steel tanks. Temperature control is manual. The wines undergo malolactics in vats. They are then aged 12 months, by rotation, in vats (75% of the yield) and oak barrels (25% of the yield). Very little new oak is utilized. The wines are fined and filtered.

SECOND WINE
Brand name: Château d'Anglas
Average annual production: Variable

Evaluation of present classification: Should be maintained
Plateau of maturity: 4–7 years following the vintage

Most vintages from Moulis have been deep in color but compact, relatively austere, straightforward wines without the complexity and charm one expects. Nevertheless, this is a well-situated vineyard, and the approach to the wine's vinification is traditional.

LES ORMES-SORBET

Classification: Cru Bourgeois in 1932
Location of vineyards: Couquèques
Owner: Jean Boivert
Address: 33340 Couquèques
Mailing address: Same as above
Telephone: 33 5 56 73 30 30; telefax: 33 5 57 73 30 31
Visits: Preferably by apppointment, Monday through Friday, from 9 A.M. to noon, and 2 P.M. to 6 P.M.
Contact: Jean Boivert

VINEYARDS (red)
Surface area: 51.9 acres
Average age of vines: 30 years
Blend: 60% Cabernet Sauvignon, 35% Merlot, 5% Carmenère and Petit Verdot
Density of plantation: 8,330 vines per hectare
Average yields (over the last 5 years): 50 hectoliters per hectare
Total average annual production: 140,000 bottles

GRAND VIN (red)
Brand name: Château Les Ormes-Sorbet
Appellation: Médoc
Mean annual production: 120,000 bottles
Upbringing: Fermentations and macerations last approximately 21 days in stainless-steel vats equipped with a temperature control. Wines are aged 22 months in oak barrels that are renewed by a third at each vintage. They are fined and remain unfiltered.

SECOND WINE
Brand name: Château de Conques
Average annual production: 20,000 bottles

Evaluation of present classification: Should be maintained, but since 1982 this has been one of the best Crus Bourgeois
Plateau of maturity: 6–12 years following the vintage

The current proprietor, Jean Boivert (who took over this estate in 1970), has since the mid-1980s produced one of the best wines in the northern Médoc. Boivert is the eighth generation of his family (since 1730) to run this vineyard near the sleepy village of Couquèques. The dense planting and Jean Boivert's decision in the seventies to increase the percentage of Cabernet Sauvignon have paid off with an excellent string of good vintages since 1982. The wine spends 18 months in oak casks, of which one-third are new, and there is minimal filtration done at bottling. The style that has emerged at Les Ormes-Sorbet is one of deep color and a pronounced toasty vanillin oakiness from excellent Troncalais barrels. They are wines that have the potential for a decade of longevity.

The best recent vintages include the sumptuous 1982, which is fully mature; a lighter but still tasty 1983; a delicious, intensely concentrated wine of classified-growth quality in 1985; another impeccably made wine in 1986; and an oaky, smoky, fat, and concentrated 1989. In the nineties, the 1990, 1994, 1995, and 1996 are all well-made wines. This is an up-and-coming domain in the northern Médoc.

PATACHE D'AUX   GOOD

Classification: Cru Bourgeois
Location of vineyards: Bégadan
Address: 1, route du 19 mars, 33340 Bégadan
Mailing address: Les Trois Châteaux, 1, route du 19 mars, 33340 Bégadan
Telephone: 33 5 56 41 50 18; telefax: 33 5 56 41 54 65
Visits: Monday through Friday, between 9 A.M. and 12:30 P.M., and 2 P.M. and 5:30 P.M.
Contact: Patrice Ricard

VINEYARDS (red)
Surface area: 106.2 acres
Average age of vines: 25 years
Blend: 70% Cabernet Sauvignon, 20% Merlot, 7% Cabernet Franc, 3% Petit Verdot
Density of plantation: 8,300 vines per hectare
Average yields (over the last 5 years): 59 hectoliters per hectare
Total average annual production: 330,000 bottles

GRAND VIN (red)
Brand name: Château Patache d'Aux
Appellation: Médoc
Mean annual production: 260,000 bottles
Upbringing: Fermentations last 20–25 days in concrete, wooden, and stainless-steel tanks. After malolactics in tanks, wines are aged 12 months in oak barrels, approximately 30% of which are new. They are fined but remain unfiltered.

> **SECOND WINE**
>
> Brand name: Les Relais de Liversan
> Average annual production: 70,000 bottles
>
> Evaluation of present classification: Should be maintained
> Plateau of maturity: 5–8 years following the vintage

Patache d'Aux produces wines that have an almost California-like herbaceous, juicy, black currant fruitiness, supple texture, and easy drinkability. In years where the Cabernet does not attain full ripeness, the wine has a tendency to be too vegetal. However, in ripe vintages, such as 1982, 1986, 1989, 1990, and 1995, this can be an immensely impressive Cru Bourgeois for drinking in the first 5–8 years of its life. It is often jammy and opulent, and rarely elegant, but for consumers looking for a well-made, reasonably priced Cru Bourgeois that does not require deferred gratification, this is a worthy choice.

PEYRABON

> Classification: Cru Bourgeois
> Appellation: Haut-Médoc
> Production: 25,000 cases
> Blend: 50% Cabernet Sauvignon, 27% Merlot, 23% Cabernet Franc
> Secondary label: Lapiey
> Vineyard size: 131 acres
> Proprietor: Jacques Babeau
> Time spent in barrels: 18–24 months
> Average age of vines: 20 years
>
> Evaluation of present classification: Should be maintained; an
> average-quality Cru Bourgeois
> Plateau of maturity: 3–5 years following the vintage

Because of this wine's wide availability, I would like to have something positive to say about it. The wine—which is made from a large vineyard near St.-Sauveur, sandwiched between Ramage la Batisse and Liversan—is straightforward and indifferently made, a soft wine of lesser character. Despite the reasonable price, I have never considered Peyrabon to represent good value.

PEYREDON-LAGRAVETTE   VERY GOOD

Classification: Cru Bourgeois in 1932
Location of vineyards: Listrac and Moulis (Médrac and Grand Poujeaux)
Owner: Paul Hostein
Address: 2062 Médrac Est, 33480 Listrac-Médoc
Mailing address: Same as above
Telephone: 33 5 56 58 05 55; telefax: 33 5 56 58 05 50
Visits: By appointment, from March to September 15, Monday through
Saturday, from 9 A.M. to 12:30 P.M., and 2 P.M. to 7 P.M.; from September
15 till end of February, from 9 A.M. to 6 P.M.
Contact: Paul Hostein

VINEYARDS (red)
Surface area: 17.3 acres
Average age of vines: 25 years
Blend: 65% Cabernet Sauvignon, 35% Merlot
Density of plantation: 9,091 vines per hectare
Average yields (over the last 5 years): 42 hectoliters per hectare
Total average annual production: 300 hectoliters

GRAND VIN (red)
Brand name: Château Peyredon-Lagravette
Appellation: Listrac-Médoc
Upbringing: Alcoholic fermentations last 5–8 days (28–30 degrees
centigrade) and macerations 21 days in temperature-controlled
stainless-steel vats. Pumping-overs are done twice a day. After
malolactics in vats, wines are aged 18 months in oak barrels, 25%–30%
of which are new. They are racked every 4 months, fined with albumin,
and lightly filtered.

SECOND WINE
None produced.

Evaluation of present classification: This is one of the better wines of
Listrac, close in quality to a Médoc fifth-growth.
Plateau of maturity: 6–15 years following the vintage

This excellent Listrac is not well-known, but if vintages such as 1982, 1983,
1986, 1989, 1990, and 1995 are any indication, this may be one of the best-kept
secrets of Listrac. The tiny vineyard sits to the east of most of the other Listrac
properties, adjacent to the appellation of Moulis. Two of the best Moulis vineyards, Chasse-Spleen and Maucaillou, are closer to Peyredon-Lagravette than
most of the other Listrac vineyards. The wine is very traditionally made with an

extremely long *cuvaison*. The result is an intensely concentrated, full-bodied, ripe, impressively built wine for drinking over 10–15 years.

The property itself is quite old, tracing its origin to 1546. The current proprietor, Paul Hostein, eschews the mechanical harvesters so frequently employed in this part of the Médoc, as well as all of the antibotrytis treatments that have become in vogue among the properties to fight mold and rot. Hostein prefers to use an organic method of winemaking. Additionally, his dense vineyard plantations of 9,000 vines per hectare represent many more vines per hectare than in most Bordeaux vineyards.

I have yet to taste a wine from Peyredon-Lagravette that has been fully mature, so this would appear to be one of the longer-lived Listracs, with a character more closely associated with Moulis than Listrac. More attention needs to be paid to Château Peyredon-Lagravette.

PLAGNAC   GOOD

Classification: Cru Bourgeois
Location of vineyards: Bégadan
Owner: Domaines Cordier
Address: 33340 Bégadan
Mailing address: c/o Domaines Cordier, 53, rue du Dehez, 33290 Blanquefort
Telephone: 33 5 56 95 53 00; telefax: 33 5 56 95 53 08
Visits: By appointment only
Contact: Domaines Cordier

VINEYARDS (red)
Surface area: 76.6 acres
Average age of vines: 25 years
Blend: 70% Cabernet Sauvignon, 30% Merlot
Density of plantation: 5,000 vines per hectare
Average yields (over the last 5 years): 55 hectoliters per hectare
Total average annual production: 1,650 hectoliters

GRAND VIN (red)
Brand name: Château Plagnac
Appellation: Médoc
Mean annual production: 1,650 hectoliters
Upbringing: Fermentations and macerations last 18–20 days in temperature-controlled stainless-steel vats. There are multiple pumping-overs during alcoholic fermentations, but they become less frequent during macerations. Wines are aged 12 months in oak barrels and *foudres*, with 20% new oak. Wines are fined and lightly filtered.

SECOND WINE
None produced.

Evaluation of present classification: A well-made Cru Bourgeois
representing excellent value
Plateau of maturity: 2–6 years following the vintage

Looking for a reasonably priced, soft, fruity, easy to drink, straightforward
Bordeaux? This wine, managed and looked after by the exceptionally talented
Cordier team, is the type of Bordeaux that pleases the crowd, and satisfies
both the palate and purse. It is meant to provide charm and immediate
drinkability. Drink this wine within its first 5–6 years of life.

POTENSAC   EXCELLENT

Classification: Grand Cru Bourgeois
Location of vineyards: Ordonnac
Owner: Jean-Hubert Delon and Geneviève Dalton
Address: 33340 Ordonnac
Mailing address: Same as above
Telephone: 33 5 56 73 25 26; telefax: 33 5 56 59 18 33
Visits: No visits allowed

VINEYARDS (red)
Surface area: 126 acres
Average age of vines: 35 years
Blend: 60% Cabernet Sauvignon, 25% Merlot, 15% Cabernet Franc
Density of plantation: 8,000 vines per hectare

GRAND VIN (red)
Brand name: Château Potensac
Appellation: Médoc
Upbringing: Fermentations and macerations last 15–18 days in concrete
and stainless-steel tanks at approximately 28 degrees centigrade. Wines
are then aged 12–16 months in oak barrels (new and up to 2 vintages
old). They are fined with fresh egg whites and remain unfiltered.

SECOND WINE
Brand name: Château Lassalle

Evaluation of present classification: Should be upgraded to a Médoc
fifth-growth
Plateau of maturity: 4–12 years following the vintage

Since the mid-1970s, Potensac, under the inspired and strong leadership of Michel Delon and his son, Jean-Hubert (also the proprietors of the famed Léoville-Las Cases in St.-Julien and Nenin in Pomerol), has been making wines that are clearly of classified-growth quality. This large vineyard, situated near St.-Yzans, produces wines so far above the level of quality found in this region of the Médoc that they are a tribute to the efforts of the Delons and the *maître de chai*, Michel Rolland.

The wine has a rich, cassis-and-berry-like character, excellent structure, a wonderful purity and balance that is characteristic of the Delons' wines, and surprising aging potential. This area of the northern Médoc is rarely capable of producing wines of this quality, but the Delons consistently manage to do that at Potensac.

Delon also owns another group of vineyards that make up the secondary labels for Potensac. A few years ago Potensac was somewhat of an insiders' wine, but that is no longer the case. Nevertheless, this is such a high-quality wine that any serious Bordeaux enthusiast would be making a mistake if he or she did not try it.

VINTAGES

1997—An outstanding bargain, this cru bourgeois estate consistently overperforms,
• thanks to the brilliant management of Michel and Jean-Hubert Delon. The
86– 1997 Potensac, a blend of 58% Cabernet Sauvignon, 24% Merlot, and 18%
88 Cabernet Franc, displays a deep, nearly opaque purple color, sweet, mineral-tinged, blackberry and cherry fruit in its aromatics and flavors, medium body, low acidity, and a plump, supple finish with gobs of glycerin and alcohol. Drink it over the next 7–8 years. Last tasted, 3/98.

1996—This wine is the finest Potensac I have tasted in the last two decades, perhaps
• the finest ever made. The dense opaque ruby/purple color is followed by
87– aromas of sweet black currant fruit intermixed with earth and minerals. Dense
89+ and rich, with sweet tannin, good but low acidity, and an accessible, supple personality, this is a surprisingly intense wine that should age well. It is a sleeper of the vintage. Anticipated maturity: 1999–2012. Last tasted, 3/98.

1995—Elegant, complex, and evolved, the saturated dark ruby–colored 1995 exhib-
• its herb-tinged, black currant/weedy cassis-like flavors that are supple, round,
87 generous, and appealing. This wine does not possess the power and density of fruit found in the 1996, but it is a delicious, reasonably priced claret that should have broad crowd appeal for a decade or more. A sleeper. Last tasted, 11/97.

1994—Potensac's 1994 appears to be one of the better efforts among the Cru Bour-
• geois of this vintage. The wine exhibits an excellent deep ruby color, followed
86 by a sweet, ripe nose of red and black fruits, earth, spice, and herbs. Medium bodied, with attractive fat, glycerin, and light tannin, this is a wine to drink during its first 7–8 years of life. Last tasted, 3/96.

1992—A lean, vegetal, medium-bodied wine with hard tannin but some ripe fruit
•   beneath the wine's structure, the 1992 Potensac is one of the least distin-
75   guished wines from this estate in the last decade. Drink it over the next 3–4
    years. Last tasted, 11/94.

1991—Potensac's 1991 is a lean, hollow, hard-style wine with little fruit. Its as-
•   tringence has the upper hand, so look for the 1991 to become more out of
74   balance as it ages. Last tasted, 1/94.

1990—Potensac's 1990 is almost as good as their 1989. It is deeply colored, with
•   plenty of body, an attractive, pure, curranty, earthy nose, medium to full body,
86   a classic structure, and a long finish. Drink this impressive wine over the
    next decade. Last tasted, 1/93.

1989—The 1989 Potensac is a big, intense, alcoholic wine with exceptional ripeness,
•   full body, and a long, chewy, fleshy finish. Anticipated maturity: Now–1999.
87   Last tasted, 1/93.

1988—Displaying an attractive ripeness in the nose, in the mouth, the 1988 Potensac
•   is soft, elegant, and well made. There is some pleasant new oak in evidence,
85   but the wine's roundness and precociousness suggest it should be consumed
    early in life. Last tasted, 1/93.

1986—Potensac made an excellent wine in 1986. In fact, in a blind tasting the wine
•   could easily be confused with a classified growth. Deep ruby/purple in color,
87   with an elegant, complex bouquet of herbs, minerals, spicy oak, and black cur-
    rants, this medium-bodied wine displays rich, well-focused fruit and plenty of
    tannin in the finish, but an overall harmony and complexity that is rare in a Cru
    Bourgeois. Anticipated maturity: Now–2000. Last tasted, 11/90.

1985—The 1985 is a lovely, elegant, supple wine imbued with a good measure of
•   black currant fruit, a deft touch of spicy oak, medium body, and fine length.
85   Anticipated maturity: Now. Last tasted, 3/90.

1984—Cleanly made and correct, the 1984 Potensac lacks the fruit and depth to
•   merit higher marks. Several years of cellaring may bring forth more character.
77   Anticipated maturity: Now. Last tasted, 3/88.

1983—Beginning to exhibit some amber at the edge, this spicy, cedary, surprisingly
•   herbaceous-scented Potensac has good body and an attractive ripeness but
84   has reached its plateau of maturity. It is a good, rather than inspirational,
    Potensac. Anticipated maturity: Now. Last tasted, 3/88.

1982—This wine has been fully mature for over 5 years, yet it continues to offer up
•   plenty of good, spicy, ripe black cherry fruit in its earthy, spicy, pleasing
87   personality. It is plump, tasty, and satisfying. It should be drunk up over the
    next 5–6 years. Last tasted, 9/95.

POUJEAUX   EXCELLENT

Classification: Cru Bourgeois Exceptionnel
Location of vineyards: Grand-Poujeaux in Moulis
Owner: Jean Theil S.A.
Address: 33480 Moulis-en-Médoc

Mailing address: Same as above
Telephone: 33 5 56 58 02 96; telefax: 33 5 56 58 01 25
Visits: Monday through Saturday, between 9 A.M. and noon, and 2 P.M. and 6 P.M.
Contact: Philippe or François Theil

VINEYARDS (red)
Surface area: 128.4 acres
Average age of vines: 30 years
Blend: 50% Cabernet Sauvignon, 40% Merlot, 5% Cabernet Franc, 5% Petit Verdot
Density of plantation: 10,000 vines per hectare
Average yields (over the last 5 years): 54 hectoliters per hectare
Total average annual production: 370,000 bottles

GRAND VIN (red)
Brand name: Château Poujeaux
Appellation: Moulis-en-Médoc
Mean annual production: 270,000 bottles
Upbringing: Fermentations and macerations last 4 weeks in wooden, concrete, and stainless-steel vats. Wines undergo malolactics in vats and are aged in oak barrels, which are renewed by half at each vintage, for 12 months. They are fined and filtered.

SECOND WINE
Brand name: Château La Salle de Poujeaux or Le Charme de Poujeaux
Average annual production: 100,000 bottles

Evaluation of present classification: Should be upgraded to a fifth-growth
Plateau of maturity: 6–20 years following the vintage

While there is a considerable rivalry among Poujeaux, Chasse-Spleen, and Maucaillou, most observers agree that year in and year out, these are the three best wines of Moulis. Poujeaux is one of the oldest estates, dating back to 1544, when the vineyards and surrounding area were called La Salle de Poujeaux. The property is now run by the Theil brothers, whose family acquired Poujeaux in 1920.

Poujeaux's style is typical of the wines of Moulis. It is dark ruby in color, tannic, and sometimes astringent and hard when young and therefore usually needs a minimum of 6–8 years to soften and mature. It is a slower-developing wine than neighbor Chasse-Spleen yet has the potential to be one of the longest lived. A splendid bottle of 1928 served to me in 1985 and again in 1988 proved just how magnificent, as well as ageworthy, Poujeaux can be.

Poujeaux is clearly a wine that deserves to be ranked as a fifth-growth in any new classification of the Bordeaux hierarchy.

VINTAGES

1997— One of the big-time sleepers of the vintage, the 1997 is one of the finest
• Poujeauxs I have ever tasted. It stands out in the vintage for its opulence,
89– wonderfully sweet, ripe, jammy black currant and cherry fruit, in addition to
91 copious quantities of glycerin, extract, fat, and lusciousness. Unctuously textured, thick and juicy, with low acidity, exceptional purity, and gobs of fruit, this knockout Poujeaux will be drinkable when released, yet will age well for 12–15 years. Kudos to the Theil family. Last tasted, 3/98.

1996— Opaque purple-colored, with moderately high tannin yet excellent sweet
• black currant fruit, this medium-bodied, well-structured, muscular, densely
86– packed Poujeaux will require 7–8 years of cellaring. Anticipated maturity:
87+ 2006–2015. Last tasted, 3/98.

1993— A very good wine, with grip, tannin, medium to full body, and excellent
• ripeness, this unevolved, backward yet promising Poujeaux needs cellaring.
87 There is some mineral-tinged, sweet black currant fruit in both the aromatics and flavors. Anticipated maturity: 2003–2015. Last tasted, 11/97.

1990— Oaky, with good fruit, the well-made, medium-bodied, moderately tannic,
• attractive 1990 will provide fine drinking over the next 10–12 years. Last
86 tasted, 1/93.

1989— The 1989 is an excellent wine, exhibiting a moderately intense bouquet of
• toasty new oak, spicy, black currant fruit, medium to full body, and attractive
86 ripeness and heady alcohol in the finish. Anticipated maturity: Now–2003. Last tasted, 1/93.

1988— The 1988 Poujeaux is a beautiful wine, superior, in my opinion, to both the
• 1989 and 1990. The oaky, classic, curranty bouquet exhibits both intensity
87 and ripeness. The wine offers plenty of toasty new oak, medium body, good acidity, excellent depth and definition, and firm tannins in the finish. Anticipated maturity: Now–2005. Last tasted, 1/93.

1987— This is a surprisingly strong effort, particularly for a so-called off year. Fully
• mature, this soft, round, charming wine is as smooth as silk. Anticipated
84 maturity: Now. Last tasted, 4/91.

1986— Only time will reveal whether the 1986 Poujeaux is better than the excellent
• 1982. With a deep, dark ruby color and a moderately intense bouquet of
89 weedy black currants, tobacco, and smoky oak, it is quite enticing. On the palate, the wine is very powerful, rich, full bodied, and capable of lasting at least 15–20 years. Anticipated maturity: Now–2008. Last tasted, 4/91.

1985— The 1985 Poujeaux is a lush, rich, full-bodied wine with soft tannins in the
• finish. It has matured quickly for a Poujeaux and can presently be drunk with
86 great pleasure. Anticipated maturity: Now. Last tasted, 4/91.

1984— The 1984 Poujeaux has adequate ripeness, a moderately intense, spicy, her-
• baceous, and oaky nose, some fruit and depth, and a decent finish. Antici-
76 pated maturity: Now. Last tasted, 4/91.

1983—Now fully mature, the 1983 still has a deep ruby color, an intense floral, pure
*   black currant bouquet, soft, medium-bodied flavors, and light tannins in its
86   heady finish. Anticipated maturity: Now–2000. Last tasted, 4/91.

1982—A delicious black raspberry–and–currant-scented wine, the 1982 Poujeaux
*   displays intense, medium- to full-bodied, sweet, round, generous flavor as well
88   as a corpulent, glycerin-endowed, rustic finish. Although fully mature, it exhib-
     its no signs of losing its fruit. Drink it over the next 5–7 years. Last tasted, 9/95.

RAMAGE LA BATISSE

Classification: Cru Bourgeois
Location of vineyards: St.-Sauveur
Owner: MACIF
Address: 33250 St.-Sauveur
Mailing address: Same as above
Telephone: 33 5 56 59 57 24; telefax: 33 5 56 59 54 14
Visits: By appointment, between 8 A.M. and noon, and 2 P.M. and 5 P.M.
Contact: Mr. Mechin

VINEYARDS (red)
Surface area: 150.8 acres
Average age of vines: 20 years
Blend: 50% Cabernet Sauvignon, 40% Merlot, 10% Cabernet Franc
Density of plantation: 7,550 vines per hectare
Average yields (over the last 5 years): 60 hectoliters per hectare
Total average annual production: 3,700 hectoliters

GRAND VIN (red)
Brand name: Château Ramage La Batisse
Appellation: Haut-Médoc
Mean annual production: 2,000 hectoliters
Upbringing: Alcoholic fermentations last 8–10 days and macerations
approximately 3 weeks. Fifteen percent of the yield completes its
malolactics in new oak barrels. *Assemblage* is done fairly early, 2 months
after the harvest. Wines are aged 18 months, 6 in vats and 12 in oak
barrels. Rackings are done every 3 months, and wines are fined and
filtered upon bottling.

SECOND WINE
Brand name: Château Tourteran
Average annual production: 1,000 hectoliters

Evaluation of present classification: Should be maintained; an
average-quality Cru Bourgeois
Plateau of maturity: 5–8 years following the vintage

The vineyards of Ramage La Batisse are located in St. Sauveur, a small wine-producing region situated inland and west from the small town of Pauillac. The vineyard has been completely replanted since 1961. The wines from the late seventies, particularly the 1978 and 1979, were quite impressive—supple, oaky, richly fruity wines of style and character. Even the 1980 was a notable success in a mediocre vintage. However, since then the wines of Ramage La Batisse have been inexplicably unimpressive. Even in top years such as 1982, 1983, 1985, and 1986, they have been excessively tannic, lean, and austere, with an oakiness that tended to obliterate the wine's fruit and charm.

This property is well placed and has the potential to turn out top wines, as it did in the seventies. Most vintages of Ramage La Batisse are best drunk between 5–10 years of age.

SANSAROT-DUPRÉ   GOOD

Classification: Cru Bourgeois in 1932
Location of vineyards: Listrac
Owner: Yves Raymond
Address: 33480 Listrac-Médoc
Mailing address: Same as above
Telephone: 33 5 56 58 03 02; telefax: 33 5 56 58 07 64
Visits: On weekdays, between 9 A.M. and 12:30 P.M. and 2 P.M. and 6 P.M.; by appointment during weekends

VINEYARDS (red)
Surface area: 32.1 acres
Average age of vines: 25 years
Blend: 60% Merlot, 30% Cabernet Sauvignon, 10% Cabernet Franc
Density of plantation: 6,666 vines per hectare
Average yields (over the last 5 years): 48 hectoliters per hectare
Total average annual production: 75,000 bottles

GRAND VIN (red)
Brand name: Château Sansarot-Dupré
Appellation: Listrac
Mean annual production: 60,000 bottles
Upbringing: Fermentations last 10 days and macerations 1 month in stainless-steel vats. Wines are aged for 12 months, after malolactics, in oak barrels, 15%–40% of which are new, depending upon the vintage. They are fined and lightly filtered.

SECOND WINE:
Brand name: Bouton Rouge de Sansarot-Dupré
Average annual production: 15,000 bottles

VINEYARDS (white)
Surface area: 4.3 acres
Average age of vines: 35 years
Blend: 50% Semillon, 40% Sauvignon, 10% Muscadelle
Density of plantation: 6,666 vines per hectare
Average yields (over the last 5 years): 50 hectoliters per hectare
Total average annual production: 10,000 bottles

GRAND VIN (white)
Brand name: Château Sansarot-Dupré
Appellation: White dry Bordeaux
Mean annual production: 8,000 bottles
Upbringing: Fermentations take place in barrels, and wines are aged 1
year, on lees, with regular stirrings. They are fined and lightly filtered.

SECOND WINE
None produced.

Evaluation of present classification: An extremely well-made Listrac that
occasionally comes very close to rivaling a Médoc fifth-growth
Plateau of maturity: 6–15 years following the vintage

The high percentage of Merlot ensures that in ripe vintages, such as 1982,
1985, 1989, 1990, and 1995, this wine has a degree of opulence and fullness
not often found in Listrac wines. The wine is usually dark ruby in color, with
a bouquet redolent of black fruits, such as plums, as well as licorice and
flowers.

Given the high extraction, ripeness, and intensity of the wines made at
Sansarot-Dupré, an elevated use of new oak could be beneficial. This is a wine
that needs 4–5 years to reach its plateau of maturity but can last for 12–15
years. To date, this château remains largely undiscovered in the export markets.

A delicious, dry white wine, made from 4.3 acres of Semillon, Sauvignon,
and Muscadelle, is produced at Sansarot-Dupré. I have never seen a bottle
outside of France, but it is a delicious Bordeaux Blanc.

SÉGUR

GOOD

Classification: Cru Bourgeois in 1932
Location of vineyards: Parempuyre
Owner: S.C.A. Château Ségur
Manager: Jean-Pierre Grazioli
Address: 33290 Parempuyre
Mailing address: Same as above

Telephone: 33 5 56 35 28 25; telefax: 33 5 56 35 82 32
Visits: Monday through Friday, between 8 A.M. and noon, and 1:30 P.M.
and 5 P.M.; by appointment on Saturdays
Contact: Jean-Pierre Grazioli

VINEYARDS (red)
Surface area: 93.9 acres
Average age of vines: 26 years
Blend: 42% Merlot, 35% Cabernet Sauvignon, 17% Cabernet Franc, 6%
Petit Verdot
Density of plantation: 6,666 vines per hectare
Average yields (over the last 5 years): 52 hectoliters per hectare
Total average annual production: 1,980 hectoliters

GRAND VIN (red)
Brand name: Château Ségur
Appellation: Haut Médoc
Mean annual production: 95,000 bottles
Upbringing: Fermentations and macerations are traditional and take place
in temperature-controlled stainless-steel vats. Wines remain in vats for 6
months and are afterward transferred to oak barrels, one-third of which are
new, for 12 months aging. They are fined with albumin and filtered.

SECOND WINE
Brand name: Château Ségur Fillon
Average annual production: 145,000 bottles

Evaluation of present classification: A solidly reliable, at times quite
good, Cru Bourgeois
Plateau of maturity: 4–5 years following the vintage

Since the mid-1980s Ségur has become one of the more reliable Cru Bourgeois wines. It can be a soft, deliciously fruity, attractive, ready to drink wine
that is best in ripe years such as 1985 and 1990. It is a successful wine,
although the quantities produced were tiny. With respect to either cuvée, this
is a wine to drink during its first 4–5 years of life.

SEMEILLAN-MAZEAU   GOOD

Classification: Cru Bourgeois
Location of vineyards: Listrac
Address: 33480 Listrac-Médoc
Mailing address: Same as above

Telephone: 33 5 56 58 01 12; telefax: 33 5 56 58 01 57
Visits: Monday through Friday, from 8 A.M. to noon, and 2 P.M. to 6 P.M.
Contact: Alain Bistodeau

VINEYARDS (red)
Surface area: 45.7 acres
Average age of vines: 20 years
Blend: 50% Merlot, 50% Cabernet Sauvignon
Density of plantation: 10,000 vines per hectare and 6,666 vines per
hectare for the younger vines
Average yields (over the last 5 years): 53 hectoliters per hectare
Total average annual production: 1,000 hectoliters

GRAND VIN (red)
Brand name: Château Semeillan-Mazeau
Appellation: Listrac
Mean annual production: 60,000 bottles
Upbringing: Fermentations last 3–4 weeks in stainless-steel tanks
equipped with a temperature control. Wines are then aged 18 months in
oak barrels, 30% of which are new. They are fined and filtered.

SECOND WINE
Brand name: Château Decorde
Average annual production: 60,000 bottles

Evaluation of present classification: Should be maintained, but it is one of
the better Listrac wines
Plateau of maturity: 5–15 years following the vintage

I have had limited experience with the wines of Semeillan-Mazeau, but
vintages since 1985 have exhibited a rich, highly extracted, old style of wine
with admirable power and tannin. My guess is that most of the wines from top
vintages can last for 10–15 years. This is another up-and-coming Listrac
vineyard that should be watched. Interestingly, the high-quality *négociant*
firm of Nathaniel Johnston assumed the exclusivity for distribution of this
wine several years ago. That in itself suggests this could be a name to watch
in the nineties.

SÉNÉJAC

GOOD

Classification: Cru Bourgeois
Location of vineyards: Le Pian-Médoc
Owner: Charles de Guigne
Address: 33290 Le Pian-Médoc

Mailing address: Same as above
Telephone: 33 5 56 70 20 11; telefax: 33 5 56 70 23 91
Visits: By appointment only
Contact: Bruno Vonderheyden

VINEYARDS (red)
Surface area: 61.8 acres
Average age of vines: 18 years
Blend: 60% Cabernet Sauvignon, 25% Merlot, 14% Cabernet Franc, 1% Petit Verdot
Density of plantation: 6,600 vines per hectare
Average yields (over the last 5 years): 48–52 hectoliters per hectare
Total average annual production: 1,500 hectoliters

GRAND VIN (red)
Brand name: Château Sénéjac
Appellation: Haut-Médoc
Mean annual production: 1,000 hectoliters
Upbringing: Fermentations and macerations last approximately 15 days. Fifteen percent of the yield undergoes malolactics in barrels, and wines are aged in oak barrels, 30% of which are new, 70% of which are one year old. They are fined but not systematically filtered.

SECOND WINE
Brand name: Artigue de Sénéjac or Bergerie de Sénéjac
Average annual production: 500 hectoliters

Evaluation of present classification: Should be maintained
Plateau of maturity: 4–6 years following the vintage

Sénéjac is located in the very southern part of the Médoc, west of the town of Parempuyre and just south of the village of Arsac. The vineyard sits on very light, sandy, gravelly soil and produces a soft, fruity red wine that is meant to be drunk young.

SOCIANDO-MALLET   EXCELLENT

Classification: Cru Bourgeois in 1932
Location of vineyards: St.-Seurin-de-Cadourne
Owner: Jean Gautreau
Address: 33180 St.-Estèphe
Mailing address: Same as above
Telephone: 33 5 56 73 38 80; telefax: 33 5 56 73 38 88
Visits: Monday through Friday, between 9 A.M. and noon, and 2 P.M. and 5 P.M.

VINEYARDS (red)
Surface area: 143.3 acres
Average age of vines: 20–25 years
Blend: 55% Cabernet Sauvignon, 40% Merlot, 5% Cabernet Franc and Petit Verdot
Density of plantation: 8,000 vines per hectare
Average yields (over the last 5 years): 48 hectoliters per hectare
Total average annual production: 380,000 bottles

GRAND VIN (red)
Brand name: Château Sociando-Mallet
Appellation: Haut-Médoc
Mean annual production: 230,000 bottles
Upbringing: Fermentations are traditional and last 25–30 days, with regular pumping-overs 2 or 3 times daily. Wines are aged for 11–13 months in oak barrels, 80%–100% of which are new depending upon the vintage. They remain unfined and unfiltered.

SECOND WINE
Brand name: La Demoiselle de Sociando-Mallet
Average annual production: 130,000–160,000 bottles

Evaluation of present classification: The quality equivalent of a Médoc third-growth
Plateau of maturity: 8–25 years following the vintage

Located in St.-Seurin-de-Cadourne, Sociando-Mallet is making uncompromising wines of extremely high quality that are meant to age gracefully for 10–25 years. The vineyards are superbly situated overlooking the Gironde, and the wine produced by the meticulous owner—Jean Gautreau, who purchased this run-down property in 1969—is inky black ruby in color, extremely concentrated, full bodied, and loaded with mouth-puckering tannin. Some observers have even claimed that Sociando-Mallet has the greatest potential for longevity of any wine in the Médoc. The keys to the quality of Sociando-Mallet are numerous. First there is the superb vineyard, with excellent exposure and well-drained, gravelly soil, a high density of vines per hectare (8,000), and manual-harvesting techniques. A fermentation temperature of 32–33 degrees centigrade, a 3-week or longer maceration period, the use of 80%–100% new oak, and no fining and filtration are further evidence of the château's high standards.

The result of all this is irrefutable. Sociando-Mallet is easily the equal of many of the classified growths, and its surging reputation among France's wine connoisseurs has already assured that much of it is purchased within that country.

VINTAGES

1997—I think I like this wine even more than the 1996. First of all, it is one of the
•   most forward, up-front Sociando-Mallets produced in the last decade. The
89–   color is a saturated opaque purple, and the wine extremely low in acidity, but
91   oh, so captivating. There are gorgeous layers of sweet cassis liqueur-like fruit
intermixed with vanillin, lead pencil, and mineral aromas. Medium bodied,
with outstanding concentration, and as smooth a texture as will ever be found
in such a young Sociando-Mallet, this wine will drink beautifully young and
will last for 12–15 years. Very impressive. Anticipated maturity: 2000–2014.
Last tasted, 3/98.

1996—An impressive cru bourgeois, Sociando-Mallet's opaque purple-colored 1996
•   displays a tight but nicely scented nose of minerals, licorice, cassis, and high
89–   quality vanillin from new oak barrels. In the mouth, the wine is dense and
90+   full bodied, with a boatload of tannin, as well as gobs of extract, glycerin, and
depth. This example will age at a glacial pace. However, it is unquestionably
of high quality, and the requisite fruit and depth are present to balance out
the wine's structural components. Anticipated maturity: 2007–2022. Last
tasted, 3/98.

1995—This accessible yet tannic example of Sociando-Mallet possesses a deep ruby/
•   purple color, and excellent aromatics consisting of jammy black cherries,
90   blackberries, and cassis, as well as subtle notes of minerals, earth, and new
oak. This is a deep, long, muscular, tannic wine that is structurally similar to
the 1996. Patience will be required from purchasers of this high-class wine.
Anticipated maturity: 2006–2025. Last tasted, 11/97.

1994—The 1994 is reminiscent of the 1985, with more structure and tannic ferocity.
•   The wine reveals a deep purple color and a tight but emerging nose of black
89   fruits, lead pencil, and well-integrated oak. Substantial on the palate, with
moderate tannin, this medium-bodied, classically built Bordeaux should be
at its peak between 2000 and 2010. Last tasted, 1/97.

1993—A more than competent effort was turned in by Sociando-Mallet in 1993. The
•   wine possesses a dense ruby/purple color, a surprisingly evolved, forward,
87   cedary, black cherry, currant, and mineral nose, spicy, fleshy flavors that
exhibit excellent texture, and, for this château, a beguiling suppleness for its
youthfulness. Jean Gautreau obviously handled the potential difficulties of
the 1993 vintage in a successful manner. This wine should drink well for 5–
10 years. Last tasted, 1/97.

1992—This exceptionally well-run estate has turned out a very fine wine for the
•   vintage. The color is an opaque ruby/purple and the nose offers up sweet,
87   ripe black currants intertwined with scents of minerals and wood. Medium
bodied and moderately tannic, with fine purity and sweetness, this is a firm,
well-built wine. It should be cellared for 3–4 years and drunk over the
subsequent 10–15. Last tasted, 11/94.

1990—The 1990 appears to be the finest Sociando-Mallet since the sensational
•   1982. The wine possesses an opaque purple color and a tight but promising
92   nose of thick, cassis, black currant fruit, subtle roasted herbs, smoke, licorice,
and minerals. Powerful, super-concentrated, and backward, with layers of

flavor and high tannin, this striking wine should evolve for 2–3 decades. Last tasted, 11/96.

1989—The 1989 reveals a youthful, unevolved purple color, followed by a sweet
• nose of black fruits, minerals, and vanillin. The wine is extremely young
90 (much more so than most 1989s), with medium to full body, good tannin, and not nearly as much of the vintage's soft, evolved personality in evidence. Dense, rich, and concentrated, this wine needs another 4–5 years of cellaring; it should keep for 20+ years. Last tasted, 11/96.

1988—The 1988 is medium bodied, somewhat lighter than one might expect from
• this property, but still concentrated and spicy, with a true sense of balance
87 and a long finish. It lacks the strength and highly extracted flavors seen in the top vintages, but it should last for 12–15 years. Last tasted, 1/93.

1986—Jean Gautreau's 1986 is a blockbuster of a wine. Enormously rich and full
• bodied, with awesome power, it is a classic Médoc with its extraordinary
90 depth and well-focused bouquet of minerals, black currants, violets, and spicy oak. It is an exquisite wine, but not for everybody. Do not expect to begin drinking this wine until after 2000. Anticipated maturity: 2005–2040. Last tasted, 1/91.

1985—The 1985 Sociando-Mallet is typically dense ruby/purple and has a rich,
• black currant, classically Médoc bouquet, full body, and sensational concen-
90 tration and balance. Anticipated maturity: Now–2015. Last tasted, 4/91.

1984—One of the darkest 1984s in color, Sociando-Mallet has loads of fruit, body,
• and tannin, as well as a life expectancy of 10–12 years. It is amazingly rich
84 and powerful for a 1984. Anticipated maturity: Now. Last tasted, 11/88.

1983—At one time I had high hopes for this wine, but the fruit does not seem nearly
• as ripe or as concentrated as it once was. Still medium to dark ruby, with a
85 spicy, mineral-like bouquet that lacks intensity and ripeness, on the palate, the wine is medium to full bodied, exhibits good rather than great concentra-tion, and has a somewhat sinewy, muscular texture and a good, long finish with moderate tannins. Anticipated maturity: Now–2001. Last tasted, 1/90.

1982—This amazing Cru Bourgeois estate produced a 1982 that remains young and
• vibrant, with little sign of evolution. Even from half bottles, the wine exhibits
92 a saturated dark purple color, with no lightening at the edge. The nose could be that of a 1990, revealing exuberant, pure, ripe black currant aromas intermixed with scents of minerals and spices. Full bodied, with high extrac-tion, copious quantities of glycerin, and huge tannin, this is a young, back-ward, impressively endowed Sociando-Mallet that may prove to be one of the longest agers of the vintage. Give this classic wine another 5–6 years of cellaring, and drink it through the first 2 decades of the next century. Last tasted, 9/95.

1981—The 1981 is a relatively compact, downsized Sociando-Mallet, with medium
• body, good concentration, but less tannin and a more supple, lower-acid
83 personality than one normally expects from this property. It has now reached its plateau of maturity, but this is not a wine that will decline rapidly. Antici-pated maturity: Now–2000. Last tasted, 3/89.

1979—Approaching full maturity, the 1979 is somewhat similar in texture, weight,
  •   and extract levels to the 1981. However, the 1979 seems a bit more marked
  80   by new oak and has a more aggressive and less impressive finish. Anticipated
       maturity: Now. Last tasted, 3/89.

1978—This is a beautiful wine that has matured much more slowly than many other
  •   1978 Médocs. Dark ruby, with no signs of age, the big, cedar-, mineral-, and
  87   cassis-scented bouquet is intense and enthralling. Medium bodied, concen-
       trated, exhibiting excellent ripeness with none of the herbaceous aromas that
       often mark the less ripe wines of this vintage, this wine offers a finish that is
       harmonious and moderately tannic. Anticipated maturity: Now–2003. Last
       tasted, 3/90.

1976—This may well turn out to be one of the three or four best wines of the vintage.
  •   The two best 1976s have consistently been Lafite-Rothschild and Ausone,
  88   but neither of those wines is as backward or as concentrated as Sociando-
       Mallet's 1976. Still opaque dark ruby, with an intense, almost explosive
       bouquet of black fruits and spices, this rich, full-bodied, opulently styled
       Sociando-Mallet comes closest in texture, ripeness, and headiness to the
       1982 but does not quite have the depth or tannins of that vintage. A superb
       success for the vintage, the 1976 displays none of the precocious, forward,
       quick to mature qualities of most Médocs or any of the dilution caused by the
       preharvest rains. Bravo! Anticipated maturity: Now–2002. Last tasted, 3/88.

1975—Still backward and tannic, but promising (after 20 years of life), this youthful,
  •   dark ruby/purple–colored, earthy, full-bodied, powerful, tannic wine pos-
  88+ sesses an intense concentration of fruit and a weightiness that suggests the
       component parts will turn out well balanced. Believe it or not, this wine
       requires another 5–6 years of cellaring. It will last for 20+ years thereafter.
       Last tasted, 12/95.

1973—Most 1973 clarets had one foot in the grave by the late seventies and were
  •   senile by the mid-1980s. Not the 1973 Sociando-Mallet. It is undoubtedly the
  86   most concentrated, most structured, and now most interesting wine of the
       vintage. Drinkable when relatively young, but still amazingly rich and deep
       in color, yet ripe and supple, this is another example of the dedication of
       proprietor Jean Gautreau. Anticipated maturity: Now. Last tasted, 3/88.

1970—Just now reaching its plateau of maturity, the 1970 Sociando-Mallet has a
  •   moderately intense bouquet of minerals, licorice, cedar, herbs, and black
  87   currants. Medium bodied and concentrated, with tannins that have now
       melted away, this luscious, complex wine has a long finish and provides
       immediate satisfaction. Anticipated maturity: Now. Last tasted, 3/88.

SOUDARS   GOOD

Classification: Cru Bourgeois
Location of vineyards: St.-Seurin-de-Cadourne
Owner: Eric Miailhe
Address: 33180 St.-Seurin-de-Cadourne

Mailing address: Same as above
Telephone: 33 5 56 59 31 02; telefax: 33 5 56 59 72 39
Visits: By appointment only
Contact: Eric Miailhe

VINEYARDS (red)
Surface area: 54.3 acres
Average age of vines: 18 years
Blend: 55% Merlot, 44% Cabernet Sauvignon, 1% Cabernet Franc
Density of plantation: 6,500 vines per hectare
Average yields (over the last 5 years): 60 hectoliters per hectare
Total average annual production: 14,000 cases of 12

GRAND VIN (red)
Brand name: Château Soudars
Appellation: Haut-Médoc
Mean annual production: 14,000 cases of 12
Upbringing: Fermentations and macerations last 1 month in
stainless-steel vats equipped with a temperature-control system. Wines
undergo malolactics in vats and are transferred to oak barrels, 40% of
which are new, for at least 12 months aging. They are fined and filtered
before bottling.

SECOND WINE
None produced.

Evaluation of present classification: An increasingly well-made, tasty,
supple Cru Bourgeois
Plateau of maturity: 3–6 years following the vintage

The high percentage of Merlot used at Soudars results in a wine that is
relatively fat, round, fruity, and easy to drink. Vintages since the early eighties
have been impeccably made by young Eric Miailhe. This is a wine not to lay
away for more than 5–6 years, but to drink in its youth. Soudars has a great
deal to offer at a reasonable price.

LA TOUR DE BY
GOOD

Classification: Cru Bourgeois
Location of vineyards: Bégadan and St.-Christoly
Owner: Mm. Pagès, Cailloux, and Lapalu
Address: 33340 Bégadan
Mailing address: Same as above

Telephone: 33 5 56 41 50 03; telefax: 33 5 56 41 36 10
Visits: Monday through Friday, from 8 A.M. to noon, and 1:30 P.M. to 5:30
P.M.; on Fridays, closing time at 4:30 P.M.; in July and August, open
during weekends, between 11 A.M. and 5 P.M.

VINEYARDS (red)
Surface area: 182.8 acres
Average age of vines: 35 years
Blend: 65% Cabernet Sauvignon, 30% Merlot, 3% Cabernet Franc, 2%
Petit Verdot
Density of plantation: 6,600 vines per hectare
Average yields (over the last 5 years): 55 hectoliters per hectare
Total average annual production: 530,000 bottles

GRAND VIN (red)
Brand name: Château La Tour de By
Appellation: Médoc
Mean annual production: 450,000–480,000 bottles
Upbringing: Alcoholic fermentations last 6–8 days (29–30 degrees
centigrade) and macerations 1 month (18–20 degrees centigrade). After
malolactics, wines are transferred to oak barrels, 20% of which are new,
for 14 months aging. They are fined with egg whites in January following
the vintage and are filtered.

SECOND WINE
Brand name: Cailloux de By and LaRoque de By
Average annual production: 50,000 bottles

Evaluation of present classification: A well-known and consistently good
Cru Bourgeois
Plateau of maturity: 5–10 years following the vintage

This is one of the best-known Crus Bourgeois for a number of reasons. One
is that the vast estate of 170 acres produces nearly 40,000 cases of wine.
The property was purchased in 1965 by well-known Médoc vineyard owners
Messieurs Cailloux, Lapalu, and Pagès, and they have built new cellars that
hold nearly 1,400 aging barrels. Given the huge production and yields of 55–
70 hectoliters per hectare, one might think this wine would lack stuffing, but
there is always a relatively severe selection process, as well as two secondary
labels where weaker vats and wine from younger vines are relegated.

La Tour de By produces well-colored, richly fruity, solid wines that only
lack complexity and intensity in the bouquet. The high percentage of Cabernet Sauvignon gives the wines their deep color and firm tannic background. I
do not remember tasting a badly made La Tour de By from any good vintage.

LA TOUR-CARNET

Classification: Fourth-growth in 1855
Location of vineyards: St.-Laurent-du-Médoc
Owner: Marie-Claire Pelegrin
Address: 33112 St.-Laurent-du-Médoc
Mailing address: 14, rue Labenne, 33110 Le Bouscat
Telephone: 33 5 57 22 28 00; telefax: 33 5 57 22 28 05
Visits: By appointment only
Contact: Marie-Claire Pelegrin or Olivier Dauga

VINEYARDS (red)
Surface area: 106.2 acres
Average age of vines: 25 years
Blend: 53% Cabernet Sauvignon, 33% Merlot, 10% Cabernet Franc, 4% Petit Verdot
Density of plantation: 8,000 vines per hectare
Average yields (over the last 5 years): 50–55 hectoliters per hectare
Total average annual production: 200,000–230,000 bottles

GRAND VIN (red)
Brand name: Château La Tour-Carnet
Appellation: Haut-Médoc
Mean annual production: 160,000–200,000 bottles
Upbringing: Fermentations and macerations last 25–30 days, depending upon the vintage, in stainless-steel and concrete tanks. Temperature control is manual. Malolactics occur in vats, and wines are transferred to oak barrels, up to 50% of which are new, for 12–16 months aging. They are fined with albumin but remain unfiltered.

SECOND WINE
Brand name: Le Second de Carnet
Average annual production: 60,000–80,000 bottles

Evaluation of present classification: Should be downgraded.
Plateau of maturity: 5–12 years following the vintage

La Tour-Carnet is located in St.-Laurent, and despite its inclusion in the 1855 classification, it has remained largely anonymous. This beautiful property has been restored completely and boasts a moated medieval castle. The wine has suffered considerably from, I suspect, extensive replanting in the sixties. More recent vintages, particularly the 1982, 1983, 1989, and 1990, are more promising. Yet based on this property's performance to date, it does not merit a fourth-growth classification, as the quality of the wine is no better than a Cru Bourgeois.

TOUR HAUT-CAUSSAN   EXCELLENT

Classification: Cru Bourgeois in 1932
Location of vineyards: Blaignan
Owner: Philippe Courrian
Address: 33340 Blaignan-Médoc
Mailing address: Same as above
Telephone: 33 5 56 09 00 77; telefax: 33 5 56 09 06 24
Visits: By appointment only
Contact: Véronique Courrian

VINEYARDS (red)
Surface area: 39.5 acres
Average age of vines: 21 years
Blend: 50% Merlot, 50% Cabernet Sauvignon
Density of plantation: 6,600 vines per hectare
Average yields (over the last 5 years): 60 hectoliters per hectare
Total average annual production: 56 hectoliters

GRAND VIN (red)
Brand name: Château Tour Haut-Caussan
Appellation: Médoc
Mean annual production: 120,000 bottles
Upbringing: Fermentations and macerations are rather long (3 weeks) and take place in concrete vats. After malolactics, 25%–30% of the yield goes into new oak and the rest into 1- and 2-vintage-old barrels. Wines are aged 15 months in new oak and stay only 12 months in the older barrels. They are fined but remain unfiltered.

SECOND WINE
Brand name: Château La Landotte
Average annual production: 15,000 bottles

Evaluation of present classification: A very good, occasionally excellent, Cru Bourgeois that in certain vintages—1982, 1988, 1989, and 1990—can compete favorably with a Médoc fifth-growth
Plateau of maturity: 6–15 years following the vintage

Philippe Courrian is the most recent proprietor from this family that has run this excellent Cru Bourgeois since 1877. Not surprisingly, the property takes its name not only from a beautiful windmill situated in the midst of the vineyards, but also from the nearest village, Caussan. The vineyard is located near the more famous properties of Potensac and La Cardonne. Everything about the winemaking is extremely traditional. The low yields of 40–60 hectoliters per hectare, the manual harvesting in an area where most vineyards are picked by machine, the declassifying of inferior lots to a second wine, and the policy against filtration all typify an estate dedicated to high quality. As Mr. Courrian has said many times, "Why filter? My wine does not contain anything bad."

VINTAGES

1996— The 1996 is less impressive than the 1995, although it is muscular and
•   structured, with tannin and deep fruit on the attack. However, it is more
84–   closed and angular and appears to be less charming than the 1995. It will
86   last for a decade. Last tasted, 11/97.

1995— This is a case where the 1995 may be better balanced and ultimately
•   more intriguing than the 1996. The 1995 possesses a deep ruby color,
86   excellent aromatics of earth, berry fruit, herbs, and spice, attractive ripeness, medium body, and moderate tannin. This is a seriously made wine that deserves respect. It should drink well for 7–8 years. Last tasted, 11/97.

1990— Powerful aromas of ripe fruit and minerals are followed by a deep, nearly
•   massive wine with significant glycerin, tannin, body, and depth. The color is
88   opaque. This brooding giant of a Cru Bourgeois should drink well for at least 10–15 years. It may turn out to be just as impressive as the 1989. Last tasted, 1/93.

1989— The 1989 is a more dramatic, alcoholic wine than the 1988, displaying an
•   abundant quantity of new oak in its nose, a robust, low-acid taste, and enough
88   tannin to support a decade's worth of aging. It is a surprisingly big, forceful wine that will reward those shrewd enough to buy it. Anticipated maturity: Now–2000. Last tasted, 4/91.

1988— The 1988 is much more evolved, with an elegant, cedary, spicy, curranty
•   bouquet, medium-bodied, stylish, well-balanced flavors, and soft tannins.
86   Nevertheless, it has the depth and overall equilibrium to last 4–7 years. Anticipated maturity: Now. Last tasted, 4/91.

1986— Still tightly knit, but promisingly deep in color, with a spicy, cedary, mineral
•   bouquet, this full-bodied, concentrated, impeccably made wine needs another
86   2–3 years to shed its tannins but should provide rewarding drinking. Anticipated maturity: Now–2002. Last tasted, 11/90.

1985— The 1985 is softer and not quite so opaque as the 1986. Its generous bouquet
•   offers up aromas of flowers, black fruits, spicy new oak, and cedar. Velvety
85   textured, full bodied, and admirably concentrated, this wine can be drunk now. Anticipated maturity: Now. Last tasted, 3/90.

1982— This wine is now fully mature and is the best I have tasted from Tour
•   Haut-Caussan. The big, ripe, robust nose faithfully reveals the superripeness
88   attained in 1982. Heady, velvety, flamboyant flavors that are present in a full-bodied format are attractive and long. Most of the tannins seem to have fallen away to reveal a big, juicy, succulent mouthful of Cru Bourgeois. Anticipated maturity: Now. Last tasted, 3/90.

TOUR DU HAUT-MOULIN   EXCELLENT

Classification: Cru Bourgeois
Location of vineyards: Cussac-Fort-Médoc
Owner: Lionel Poitou
Address: 7, rue des Aubarèdes, 33460 Cussac-Fort-Médoc
Mailing address: Same as above
Telephone: 33 5 56 58 91 10; telefax: 33 5 56 58 99 30
Visits: By appointment, Monday through Friday, from 9 A.M. to
11:30 A.M., and 2 P.M. to 5 P.M.

VINEYARDS (red)
Surface area: 76.6 acres
Average age of vines: 25 years
Blend: 50% Cabernet Sauvignon, 45% Merlot, 5% Petit Verdot
Density of plantation: 10,000 vines per hectare
Average yields (over the last 5 years): 55 hectoliters per hectare
Total average annual production: 200,000 bottles

GRAND VIN (red)
Brand name: Château Tour du Haut-Moulin
Appellation: Haut-Médoc
Mean annual production: 200,000 bottles
Upbringing: Fermentations and macerations last 3–4 weeks in concrete
vats (temperature control is done manually). Wines are then aged 15–18
months in oak barrels, 25% of which are new. They are fined but remain
unfiltered.

SECOND WINE
None produced.

Evaluation of present classification: An excellent Cru Bourgeois that can
be favorably compared with a Médoc fifth-growth in years such as 1990,
1989, 1988, 1986, and 1985
Plateau of maturity: 5–14 years following the vintage

The vineyards of this excellent Cru Bourgeois, located near Cussac, are
situated just to the north of Château Lamarque. There is no doubt that
proprietor Lionel Poitou produces one of the most concentrated and intensely
flavored wines among the Crus Bourgeois. He is not averse to letting the
fermentation temperature reach a dangerously high 34–35 degrees centigrade, and he favors a long *cuvaison* of nearly 1 month. Additionally, the
conservative yields from a densely planted vineyard of 10,000 vines per
hectare no doubt account for the impressively dark ruby/purple color of these

wines in top years, as well as their admirable depth and concentration. This is clearly one of the top Crus Bourgeois. In fact, in a blind tasting it would embarrass some classified growths.

VINTAGES

1996 — The austere 1996 exhibits jammy fruit, hard tannin, and some angularity. It
• will need 2–3 years of cellaring and will keep for a decade. Last tasted,
84– 11/97.
85+

1995 — The very good 1995 is sweeter than the 1996, with a deep ruby/purple color
• and excellent ripe black currant fruit intermixed with weedy earth and oaky
86 notes. Rich, with admirable purity and a layered, sweet finish, this wine
should drink well for 5–7 years. Last tasted, 11/97.

1990 — A traditional style of winemaking is evident in the dense, powerful, backward,
• yet well-structured and concentrated 1990. The color is impressive, and the
87 nose reluctantly offers up sweet aromas of fruit, earth, and minerals. There is
enough power and intensity to suggest this wine will still be going strong at
age 10. Last tasted, 1/93.

1989 — The 1989 is low in acidity, opulent, and alcoholic, yet highly extracted,
• flamboyant, and dramatic. The rich, full flavors marry well with the new oak.
88 Anticipated maturity: Now. Last tasted, 4/91.

1988 — The 1988 is a large-size wine with good definition and aggressive tannins.
• The wine has gobs of black currant fruit and a long, impressive finish.
87 Anticipated maturity: Now. Last tasted, 4/91.

1986 — The proprietor considers the 1986 one of the finest wines he has ever made.
• Dark ruby/purple, with a tight but emerging bouquet of spicy, herbaceous,
87 black currant fruit, this medium- to full-bodied wine is stuffed to the brim
with fruit but still has some dusty tannins to shed. It needs several more years
in the cellar. Anticipated maturity: Now–2001. Last tasted, 3/90.

1985 — This is an easily understood and satisfying wine to drink. It has not yet begun
• to exhibit any signs of reaching full maturity. Still deep ruby in color, but
86 round, smooth, and velvety textured, this immensely fruity yet straightforward
style of Tour du Haut-Moulin will display greater complexity with another
year or 2 of cellaring. Anticipated maturity: Now–2000. Last tasted, 3/90.

LA TOUR ST.-BONNET   VERY GOOD

Classification: Cru Bourgeois
Location of vineyards: St.-Christoly-de-Médoc
Owner: G.F.A. Tour St.-Bonnet
Manager: Jacques Merlet
Address: 33340 St.-Christoly-de-Médoc
Mailing address: Same as above
Telephone: 33 5 56 41 53 03; telefax: 33 5 56 41 53 03

Visits: By appointment, on weekdays between 9 A.M. and 11 A.M., and 3 P.M. and 6 P.M.
Contact: Nicole Merlet

VINEYARDS (red)
Surface area: 98.8 acres
Average age of vines: 30–35 years
Blend: 45% Merlot, 45% Cabernet Sauvignon, 5% Petit Verdot, 5% Malbec
Density of plantation: 9,000 vines per hectare
Average yields (over the last 5 years): 40–50 hectoliters per hectare
Total average annual production: 220,000 bottles

GRAND VIN (red)
Brand name: Château La Tour St.-Bonnet
Appellation: Médoc
Mean annual production: 200,000 bottles
Upbringing: Fermentations and macerations last approximately 3 weeks, and wines are aged in wooden vats for 18 months. They are fined but not systematically filtered.

SECOND WINE
Brand name: La Fuie St.-Bonnet
Average annual production: 20,000 bottles

Evaluation of present classification: A very good Cru Bourgeois that is frequently as good as a Médoc fifth-growth
Plateau of maturity: 6–14 years following the vintage

La Tour St.-Bonnet has always been one of my favorite Cru Bourgeois. The first vintage I tasted, and subsequently purchased, was the 1975. The vineyard of nearly 100 acres is well situated on a gravelly ridge adjacent to the Gironde River, near the village of St.-Christoly.

This is not a commercially made, supple, ready to drink Cru Bourgeois, but, rather, a deeply colored, firm, tannic, full-bodied wine with surprising concentration. Most vintages need at least 3–4 years to shed their tannins, and in top years, such as 1975, 1982 (the finest La Tour St.-Bonnet I have ever tasted), 1985, 1986, 1988, 1989, 1990, and 1995, they need 10 years or longer. The vineyard is machine harvested, and yields of 40–50 hectoliters per hectare are conservative by today's standards. Interestingly, the wine is aged not in small oak casks, but in larger oak *foudres*. The proprietor, the Lafon family, feels this preserves the wine's intensity and rich, concentrated fruit extract.

VERDIGNAN

Classification: Cru Bourgeois
Location of vineyards: St.-Seurin-de-Cadourne
Owner: Jean Miailhe Group
Address: 33180 St.-Seurin-de-Cadourne
Mailing address: Same as above
Telephone: 33 5 56 59 31 02; telefax: 33 5 56 59 72 39
Visits: By appointment only
Contact: Eric Miailhe

VINEYARDS (red)
Surface area: 148.2 acres
Average age of vines: 20 years
Blend: 48% Cabernet Sauvignon, 45% Merlot, 7% Cabernet Franc
Density of plantation: 7,500 vines per hectare
Average yields (over the last 5 years): 58 hectoliters per hectare
Total average annual production: 38,000 cases

GRAND VIN (red)
Brand name: Château Verdignan
Appellation: Haut-Médoc
Mean annual production: 29,000 cases
Upbringing: Fermentations and macerations last 1 month in
stainless-steel vats equipped with a temperature-control system. Wines
undergo malolactics in vats and are transferred to oak barrels, one-third
of which are new, for at least 12 months aging. They are fined and
filtered.

SECOND WINE
Brand name: Château Plantey de la Croix
Average annual production: 9,000 cases

Evaluation of present classification: An easygoing, amply endowed, fruity
Cru Bourgeois that merits its present standing
Plateau of maturity: 4–8 years following the vintage

Verdignan, another one of the Miailhe family's solidly run Cru Bourgeois
properties, has its château and vineyards located near the northern Médoc
village of St.-Seurin-de-Cadourne. A wine I have consistently enjoyed, it
is ripe, supple, and richly fruity and possesses a straightforward yet powerful black currant aroma. Made in a style designed for early drinking, it
is best drunk between 4–8 years of age. Since the early eighties the wine
has taken on more concentration and character. The vineyard is machine

harvested and averages 50–65 hectoliters per hectare. The price for Verdignan has remained reasonable, no doubt because of the significant production.

VILLEGEORGE

Classification: Cru Bourgeois Exceptionnel
Location of vineyards: Avensan and Soussan
Owner: Marie-Laure Lurton Roux
Address: Lieu-dit La Tuilerie, 33480 Soussans
Mailing address: S.C. Les Grands Crus Réunis, 33480 Moulis
Telephone: 33 5 57 88 83 83; telefax: 33 5 57 88 72 51
Visits: By appointment only
Contact: Marie-Laure Lurton Roux

VINEYARDS (red)
Surface area: 37 acres
Average age of vines: 20 years
Blend: 60% Merlot, 30% Cabernet Sauvignon, 10% Cabernet Franc
Density of plantation: 10,000 and 6,600 vines per hectare
Average yields (over the last 5 years): 36 hectoliters per hectare

GRAND VIN (red)
Brand name: Château Villegeorge
Appellation: Haut-Médoc
Mean annual production: 30,000–50,000 bottles
Upbringing: Fermentations and macerations take place in small stainless-steel tanks. Wines are aged in oak barrels, 10%–20% of which are new, for 6–18 months depending upon the vintage (1987—6 months, 1986—18 months). They are fined and filtered.

SECOND WINE
Sold in bulk until the 1996 vintage.

Evaluation of present classification: Should be maintained; an average-quality Cru Bourgeois
Plateau of maturity: 3–6 years following the vintage

In 1973 the omnipresent Lucien Lurton added this small property to his collection of Bordeaux châteaux. The wine is loosely knit, soft, pleasantly fruity, straightforward, and uninspiring. Perhaps the high yields and significant percentage of Merlot, which is planted in very gravelly soil, are the reasons this wine is relatively light and one-dimensional.

OTHER CRU BOURGEOIS ESTATES

ARCHE

Classification: Cru Bourgeois in 1932
Location of vineyards: Ludon-Médoc, in the center of the village, opposite
the church
Owner: Grands Vignobles de la Gironde
Address: Ludon-Médoc
Mailing address: c/o Mähler-Besse, 49, rue Camille Godard, 33026
Bordeaux Cedex
Telephone: 33 5 56 56 04 30; telefax: 33 5 56 56 04 59
Visits: By appointment only
Contact: Mähler-Besse

VINEYARDS (red)
Surface area: 22.2 acres under vine
Average age of vines: 30 years
Blend: 45% Cabernet Sauvignon, 40% Merlot, 15% Cabernet Franc, the
rest Petit Verdot and other varietals
Density of plantation: 9,000 vines per hectare
Average yields (over the last 5 years): 52 hectoliters
Total average annual production: 5,000 cases

GRAND VIN (red)
Brand name: Château d'Arche
Appellation: Haut-Médoc
Mean annual production: 4,000 cases
Upbringing: Fermentations and macerations take place in
temperature-controlled stainless-steel vats (rather long—3–4 weeks).
Wines undergo malolactics in vats before being transferred to barrels.
They are aged for 16 months in oak casks, 30% of which are new. They
are fined but remain unfiltered.

SECOND WINE
Brand name: Château Egmont
Average annual production: 500–1,000 cases

BEAUMONT

Classification: Cru Bourgeois in 1932
Location of vineyards: Cussac-Fort-Médoc
Owner: Grands Millésimes de France
Address: 33460 Cussac-Fort-Médoc
Mailing address: Same as above
Telephone: 33 5 56 58 92 29; telefax: 33 5 56 58 90 94.
Visits: Preferably by appointment, Monday through Friday from 8 A.M. to
noon, and 2 P.M. to 5 P.M.

VINEYARDS (red)
Surface area: 259.3 acres
Average age of vines: 15–20 years
Blend: 62% Cabernet Sauvignon, 30% Merlot, 5% Cabernet Franc, 3%
Petit Verdot
Density of plantation: 6,600 vines per hectare
Average yields (over the last 5 years): 50 hectoliters per hectare
Total average annual production: 55,000 cases

GRAND VIN (red)
Brand name: Château Beaumont
Appellation: Haut-Médoc
Mean annual production: 40,000 cases
Upbringing: Fermentations and macerations last 3–4 weeks, with regular
pumping-overs, which take place in temperature-controlled
stainless-steel tanks. Wines are then aged 12–16 months in oak barrels,
30% of which are new. They are fined and filtered.

SECOND WINE
Brand name: Château d'Arvigny
Average annual production: 15,000 bottles

BOUQUEYRAN

Classification: Cru Bourgeois
Location of vineyards: Moulis-en-Médoc
Owner: Philippe Porcheron
Address: 33480 Moulis-en-Médoc
Mailing address: S.A.R.L. des Grands Crus, 33480 Moulis-en-Médoc
Telephone: 33 5 56 70 15 40; telefax: 33 5 56 70 15 49
Visits: By appointment only
Contact: Philippe Porcheron

VINEYARDS (red)
Surface area: 32.1 acres
Average age of vines: 26 years (oldest were planted in 1949)
Blend: 57% Merlot, 41% Cabernets, 2% Petit Verdot
Density of plantation: 6,600 and 9,000 vines per hectare
Average yields (over the last 5 years): 48 hectoliters per hectare
Total average annual production: 8,000 cases

GRAND VIN (red)
Brand name: Château Bouqueyran
Appellation: Moulis-en-Médoc
Mean annual production: 4,000 cases
Upbringing: Fermentations and macerations last 18–25 days
in temperature-controlled stainless-steel vats, with frequent
pumping-overs. Wines are aged, after *assemblage*, in oak barrels
that are renewed by half at each vintage. They are fined but remain
unfiltered.

SECOND WINE
Brand name: Château Rose Cantegrit
Average annual production: 3,000 cases

CHANTELYS

Classification: Cru Bourgeois in 1932
Location of vineyards: Prignac—Médoc
Owner: Christine Courrian
Address: Lafon, 33340 Prignac
Mailing address: Same as above
Telephone: 33 5 56 09 00 16 or 33 5 56 58 70 58;
telefax: 33 5 56 58 17 20
Visits: By appointment only
Contact: Christine Courrian

VINEYARDS (red)
Surface area: 27.2 acres
Average age of vines: 30 years
Blend: 55% Cabernet Sauvignon, 40% Merlot, 5% Petit Verdot
Density of plantation: 8,500–10,000 vines per hectare
Average yields (over the last 5 years): 60 hectoliters per hectare
Total average annual production: 650 hectoliters

GRAND VIN (red)
Brand name: Château Chantelys
Appellation: Médoc
Mean annual production: 24,000 bottles
Upbringing: Fermentations and macerations last at least 5 weeks in concrete vats. The cap is kept immersed all the time. Wines are aged in oak barrels, 10% of which are new (the rest 1 and 2 vintages old), for 13–18 months depending upon the vintage. They are fined and filtered.

SECOND WINE
Brand name: Château Gauthier
Average annual production: 30,000 bottles

CLOS DU JAUGUEYRON

Classification: None
Location of vineyards: Cantenac
Owner: Farmed by Michel Théron
Address: 4, rue de la Haille, 33460 Arsac
Mailing address: Same as above
Telephone: 33 5 56 58 89 43
Visits: By appointment only
Contact: Michel Théron or Stéphanie Destruhaut

VINEYARDS (red)
Surface area: 1 acre
Average age of vines: More than 50 years
Blend: 60% Cabernet Sauvignon, 25% Merlot, 10% Petit Verdot, 5% Cabernet Franc
Density of plantation: 6,500 vines per hectare
Average yields (over the last 5 years): 45 hectoliters per hectare
Total average annual production: 2,500 bottles

GRAND VIN (red)
Brand name: Clos du Jaugueyron
Appellation: Haut-Médoc
Mean annual production: 2,500 bottles
Upbringing: Fermentations and macerations last between 3 and 6 weeks. Wines undergo malolactics in barrels and are aged in 25%–30% new oak for 20 months. They are fined and filtered.

SECOND WINE
None produced.

FONTIS

Classification: Cru Bourgeois in 1932
Location of vineyards: Ordonnac and Blaignan, on the plateau of
Potensac—formerly called Château Hontemieux
Owner: Vincent Boivert
Address: 33340 Ordonnac
Mailing address: Same as above
Telephone: 33 5 56 73 30 30; telefax: 33 5 56 73 30 31
Visits: Preferably by appointment, on weekdays
Contact: Vincent Boivert

VINEYARDS (red)
Surface area: 24.7 acres
Average age of vines: 20 years
Blend: 50% Merlot, 50% Cabernet Sauvignon
Density of plantation: 8,330 vines per hectare
Average yields (over the last 5 years): 55 hectoliters per hectare
Total average annual production: 72,000 bottles

GRAND VIN (red)
Brand name: Château Fontis
Appellation: Médoc
Mean annual production: 50,000 bottles
Upbringing: Fermentations and macerations last 15–20 days in
temperature-controlled stainless-steel vats. Wines are aged 22 months in
oak barrels that are renewed by a third at each vintage. They are fined
but remain unfiltered.

SECOND WINE
None produced.

GRIVIÈRE

Classification: Cru Bourgeois
Location of vineyards: Prignac
Owner: S.N.C. Domaines C.G.R.
Address: Route de la Cardonne, 33340 Blaignan
Mailing address: 40, rue Notre Dame des Victoires, 75002 Paris
Telephone: 33 1 42 21 11 80; telefax: 33 1 42 21 11 85
Visits: Monday through Friday, between 9 A.M. and noon, and 1:30 P.M.
and 4:30 P.M.

Contact: Nathalie Figula, telephone 33 5 56 73 31 51 and telefax 33 5 56 73 31 52

VINEYARDS (red)
Surface area: 62.2 acres
Average age of vines: 25 years
Blend: 55% Merlot, 40% Cabernet Sauvignon, 5% Cabernet Franc
Density of plantation: 7,000 vines per hectare
Average yields (over the last 5 years): 55 hectoliters per hectare
Total average annual production: 1,400 hectoliters

GRAND VIN (red)
Brand name: Château Grivière
Appellation: Médoc
Mean annual production: 120,000 bottles
Upbringing: Fermentations and macerations are rather long (20–30 days) and take place in temperature-controlled stainless-steel vats. Wines are aged 12 months in oak barrels that are renewed by a third at each vintage. They are fined and filtered.

SECOND WINE
Brand name: Malaire
Average annual production: Approximately 30% of the total production

LACHESNAYE

Classification: Cru Bourgeois Supérieur in 1932
Location of vineyards: Cussac-Fort-Médoc
Owner: G.F.A. des Domaines Bouteiller
Address: 33460 Cussac-Fort-Médoc
Mailing address: Same as above
Telephone: 33 5 56 58 94 80; telefax: 33 5 56 58 93 10
Visits: By appointment only, between 9 A.M. and noon, and 2 P.M. and 6 P.M.

VINEYARDS (red)
Surface area: 49.4 acres
Average age of vines: 20 years
Blend: 50% Merlot, 50% Cabernet Sauvignon
Density of plantation: 7,500 vines per hectare
Average yields (over the last 5 years): 57 hectoliters per hectare
Total average annual production: 1,400 cases

GRAND VIN (red)
Brand name: Château Lachesnaye
Appellation: Haut-Médoc
Mean annual production: 1,400 cases
Upbringing: Fermentations and macerations last 12 days in
temperature-controlled concrete tanks. After malolactics in vats, wines
are transferred to oak barrels (no new oak) for 12 months aging. They are
fined and filtered.

SECOND WINE
None produced.

LAMOTHE BERGERON

Classification: Cru Bourgeois in 1932
Location of vineyards: Cussac-Fort-Médoc
Owner: S.C. du Château Grand-Puy-Ducasse
Address: 33460 Cussac-Fort-Médoc
Mailing address: 17, cours de la Martinique, B.P. 90, 33027 Bordeaux
Cedex
Telephone: 33 5 6 01 30 10; telefax: 33 5 56 79 23 57
Visits: For professionals of the wine trade and by appointment only

VINEYARDS (red)
Surface area: 163 acres
Average age of vines: 25 years
Blend: 50% Cabernet Sauvignon, 37% Merlot, 13% Cabernet Franc
Density of plantation: 6,600 vines per hectare
Average yields (over the last 5 years): 55 hectoliters
Total average annual production: 3,460 hectoliters

GRAND VIN (red)
Brand name: Château Lamothe Bergeron
Appellation: Haut-Médoc
Mean annual production: 1,944 hectoliters
Upbringing: Fermentations and macerations last 3 weeks in
temperature-controlled stainless-steel vats. Wines are then aged in oak
barrels, 25% of which are new, for 16–18 months. They are fined and
filtered.

SECOND WINE
Brand name: Château Romefort
Average annual production: 1,420 hectoliters

LA LAUZETTE DECLERCQ (formerly Château Bellegrave)

Classification: Cru Bourgeois in 1932
Location of vineyards: In the village of Couhenne, north of Listrac
Owner: S.C. Vignobles Declercq
Manager: Jean-Louis Declercq
Address: B.P. 4, 33480 Listrac-Médoc
Mailing address: Gravenstafel, 32 Sneppestraat, 8860 Lendelede,
Belgium
Telephone: 33 5 56 58 02 40 or 32 51 30 40 81; telefax: 32 51 31 90 54
Visits: By appointment only
Contact: Jean-Louis Declercq

VINEYARDS (red)
Surface area: 37 acres
Average age of vines: 19.8 acres—35 years; 17.2 acres—15 years
Blend: 47% Cabernet Sauvignon, 46% Merlot, 5% Petit Verdot, 2%
Cabernet Franc
Density of plantation: 29.6 acres at 6,666 vines per hectare and 7.4 acres
at 10,000 vines per hectare
Average yields: 52 hectoliters per hectare
Total average annual production: 775 hectoliters

GRAND VIN (red)
Brand name: Château La Lauzette Declercq
Appellation: Listrac-Médoc
Mean annual production: 500 hectoliters
Upbringing: Fermentations and macerations take place in
temperature-controlled stainless-steel tanks; macerations never exceed
21 days. Wines undergo malolactics (at 20 degrees centigrade) in
concrete tanks and are aged 18 months in oak barrels, 25%–30% of
which are new. They are fined and lightly filtered.

SECOND WINE
Brand name: Les Galets de La Lauzette
Average annual production: 275 hectoliters (one-third of the yield
approximately)

MALLERET

Classification: Cru Bourgeois
Location of vineyards: Le Pian-Médoc
Owner: Farmed by G.V.G.
Address: S.C.E.A. du Château de Malleret, Domaine du Ribet, 33450 St.-Loubès
Mailing address: S.C.E.A. Domaine de Malleret, Domaine du Ribet, B.P. 59, 33450 St.-Loubès
Telephone: 33 5 57 97 07 20; telefax: 33 5 57 97 07 27
Visits: By appointment only
Contact: Eric Sirac, telephone 33 5 56 35 05 36

VINEYARDS (red)
Surface area: 79 acres
Average age of vines: 30 years
Blend: 55% Cabernet Sauvignon, 35% Merlot, 5% Cabernet Franc, 5% Petit Verdot
Density of plantation: 24 hectares at 10,000 vines per hectare and 8 hectares at 6,700 vines per hectare
Average yields (over the last 5 years): 55 hectoliters per hectare
Total average annual production: 1,760 hectoliters

GRAND VIN (red)
Brand name: Château de Malleret
Appellation: Haut-Médoc
Upbringing: Wines are aged 6 months in vats and 12 months in oak barrels, 20%–50% of which are new. They are fined but remain unfiltered.

SECOND WINE
Brand name: Château Barthez

MALMAISON BARONNE NADINE DE ROTHSCHILD

Classification: Cru Bourgeois
Location of vineyards: Moulis
Owner: Compagnie Viticole des Barons Edmond et Benjamin de Rothschild
Address: 33480 Listrac-Médoc
Mailing address: Same as above
Telephone: 33 5 56 58 38 00; telefax: 33 5 56 58 26 46

Visits: By appointment only
Contact: Hélène Cambabessouse

VINEYARDS (red)
Surface area: 59.3 acres
Average age of vines: 23 years
Blend: 55% Merlot, 45% Cabernet Sauvignon
Density of plantation: 6,600 vines per hectare
Average yields (over the last 5 years): 55–60 hectoliters per hectare
Total average annual production: 150,000 bottles

GRAND VIN (red)
Brand name: Château Malmaison Baronne Nadine de Rothschild
Appellation: Moulis
Mean annual production: 110,000–120,000 bottles
Upbringing: Fermentations last approximately 2 weeks in temperature-controlled stainless-steel vats at 30–31 degrees centigrade. There are 4–8 pumping-overs depending upon the vintage. Wines are aged 12 months in oak barrels, 20% of which are new, 50% 1 vintage old, and 30% 2 vintages old. They are fined and filtered.

SECOND WINE
Brand name: Les Granges des Domaines Edmond de Rothschild
Average annual production: 50,000 bottles

MOULIN DE LABORDE

Classification: Cru Bourgeois in 1932.
Location of vineyards: Listrac-Médoc
Owner: Consortium de Réalisation
Address: Moulin de Laborde, 33480 Listrac-Médoc
Mailing address: Same as above
Telephone: 33 5 56 58 03 83; telefax: 33 5 56 58 06 30
Visits: Every day, between 2 P.M. and 6 P.M.
Contact: Yann Olivier

VINEYARDS (red)
Surface area: 29.6 acres
Average age of vines: 25–30 years
Blend: 50% Cabernet Sauvignon, 50% Merlot
Density of plantation: 6,700 vines per hectare

Average yields (over the last 5 years): 55 hectoliters per hectare
Total average annual production: 75,000 bottles

GRAND VIN (red)
Brand name: Château Moulin de Laborde
Appellation: Listrac-Médoc
Mean annual production: 75,000 bottles
Upbringing: Fermentations and macerations last 4 weeks in
stainless-steel tanks equipped with a trickle cooling system.
Pumping-overs are done twice a day. Two-thirds of the yield is then aged
in oak barrels (2–3 vintages old) for 6–8 months by rotation. Wines are
fined and filtered.

SECOND WINE
None produced.

NOAILLAC

Classification: Cru Bourgeois
Location of vineyards: Médoc
Owner: Xavier and Marc Pagès
Address: 33590 Jau Dignac Loirac
Mailing address: Same as above
Telephone: 33 5 56 09 52 20; telefax: 33 5 56 09 58 75
Visits: Monday through Friday, between 8 A.M. and noon, and 1:30 P.M.
and 5:30 P.M.
Contact: Xavier Pagès

VINEYARDS (red)
Surface area: 101.3 acres
Average age of vines: 15 years
Blend: 55% Cabernet Sauvignon, 40% Merlot, 5% Petit Verdot
Density of plantation: 5,500 vines per hectare
Average yields (over the last 5 years): 68 hectoliters per hectare
Total average annual production: 2,500 hectoliters

GRAND VIN (red)
Brand name: Château Noaillac
Appellation: Médoc
Mean annual production: 150,000 bottles
Upbringing: Fermentations are traditional (approximately 3 weeks), and

wines are aged 1 year in oak barrels, 10% of which are new. They are fined and filtered.

SECOND WINE
Brand name: Château La Rose Noaillac
Average annual production: 60,000 bottles

RAMAFORT

Classification: Cru Bourgeois
Location of vineyards: Blaignan
Owner: S.N.C. Domaines C.G.R.
Address: Route de la Cardonne, 33340 Blaignan
Mailing address: 40, rue Notre Dame des Victoires, 75002 Paris
Telephone: 33 1 42 21 11 80; telefax: 33 1 42 21 11 85
Visits: Monday through Friday, between 9 A.M. and noon, and 1:30 P.M. and 4:30 P.M.
Contact: Nathalie Figula, telephone 33 5 56 73 31 51 and telefax 33 5 56 73 31 52

VINEYARDS (red)
Surface area: 58.5 acres
Average age of vines: 30 years
Blend: 50% Merlot, 50% Cabernet Sauvignon
Density of plantation: 6,000 vines per hectare
Average yields (over the last 5 years): 55 hectoliters per hectare
Total average annual production: 1,300 hectoliters

GRAND VIN (red)
Brand name: Château Ramafort
Appellation: Médoc
Mean annual production: 110,000 bottles
Upbringing: Fermentations and macerations are rather long (20–30 days) and take place in temperature-controlled stainless-steel vats. Wines are aged 12 months in oak barrels that are renewed by a third at each vintage. They are fined and filtered.

SECOND WINE
Brand name: Le Vivier
Average annual production: Approximately 30% of the total production

ROSE SAINTE-CROIX

Classification: Cru Bourgeois
Location of vineyards: Listrac
Owner: Philippe Porcheron
Address: Route de Soulac, 33480 Listrac
Mailing address: c/o S.A.R.L. des Grands Crus, 33480 Moulis-en-Médoc
Telephone: 33 5 56 70 15 40; telefax: 33 5 56 70 15 49
Visits: By appointment only
Contact: Philippe Porcheron, telephone 33 5 56 58 35 77

VINEYARDS (red)
Surface area: 24.7 acres
Average age of vines: 20 years
Blend: 55% Merlot, 44% Cabernet Sauvignon, 1% Petit Verdot
Density of plantation: 6,600 and 9,000 vines per hectare
Average yields (over the last 5 years): 50 hectoliters per hectare
Total average annual production: 5,000 cases

GRAND VIN (red)
Brand name: Château Rose Sainte-Croix
Appellation: Listrac-Médoc
Mean annual production: 3,000 cases
Upbringing: Fermentations and macerations last 18–25 days in
temperature-controlled stainless-steel tanks, with frequent
pumping-overs. Wines are transferred, after malolactics and *assemblage*,
to oak barrels (50% of which are new) for aging. They are fined but
remain unfiltered.

SECOND WINE
Brand name: Pontet Salanon
Average annual production: 2,000 cases

SAINTE-GEMME

Classification: Cru Bourgeois Supérieur in 1932
Location of vineyards: Cussac-Fort-Médoc
Owner: G.F.A. des Domaines Bouteiller
Address: 33460 Cussac-Fort-Médoc
Mailing address: Same as above
Telephone: 33 5 56 58 94 80; telefax: 33 5 56 58 93 10
Visits: By appointment only, between 9 A.M. and noon, and 2 P.M.
and 6 P.M.

VINEYARDS (red)
Surface area: 24.7 acres
Average age of vines: 15 years
Blend: 50% Merlot, 50% Cabernet Sauvignon
Density of plantation: 6,800 vines per hectare
Average yields (over the last 5 years): 59 hectoliters per hectare
Total average annual production: 750 cases

GRAND VIN (red)
Brand name: Château Sainte-Gemme
Appellation: Haut-Médoc
Mean annual production: 750 cases
Upbringing: Fermentations and macerations last 12 days in
temperature-controlled concrete tanks. After malolactics in vats, wines
are transferred to oak barrels (no new oak) for 12 months aging. They are
fined and filtered.

SECOND WINE
None produced.

THE RED AND WHITE WINES OF PESSAC-LÉOGNAN AND GRAVES

It was the wines of Graves that were the first Bordeaux wines to be made and exported. Barrels of Graves wine were shipped to England during the English reign over this region of France between 1152 and 1453. Even the Americans, led by the multi-talented Thomas Jefferson in 1785, seemed to think that the wines of Graves were among the best made in Bordeaux.

Times have changed, and no wine-producing region in Bordeaux has lost more ground, literally and figuratively, than the region of Graves.

Graves, which includes the appellation of Pessac-Léognan (created in 1987 for the most cherished *terroirs* of this sprawling area), gets its name

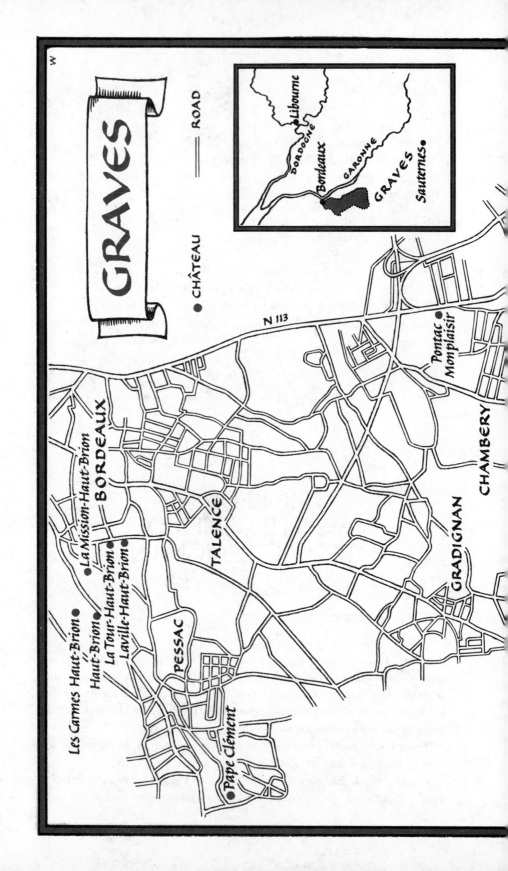

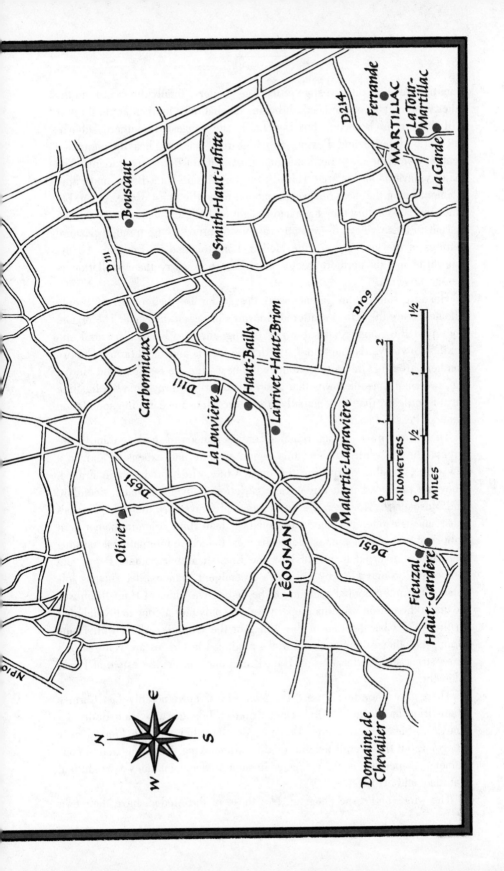

from the gravelly soil, a vestige of Ice Age glaciers. Totally different from the other wine regions of Bordeaux, it begins in what most tourists would think is still the city of Bordeaux but is actually the congested southern suburbs known as Talence and Pessac, two high-rise, modern, heavily populated centers of middle-class Bordelais and University of Bordeaux students. The major vineyards in this area, Haut-Brion, La Mission-Haut-Brion, and Pape-Clément being the most renowned, happen to be the finest of the region, but since the last century they have had to fight off both urban sprawl and blight. A visit to these vineyards will offer a noisy contrast to the tranquil pastoral settings of the vineyards in the Médoc, Pomerol, and St.-Emilion. All the vineyards in this northern sector of Graves now carry the appellation of Pessac-Léognan.

Heading south from Talence and Pessac for the better part of twenty kilometers are the widely scattered vineyards of Pessac-Léognan. The region, once past the commercial suburb of Gradignan, does become pastoral and rural, with vineyards intermingled with pine forests and small farms. The two southern areas of Graves that produce the best wine are Léognan and Martillac, two small bucolic towns that seem much farther away from the bustling city of Bordeaux than they actually are. These wines too carry the appellation name of Pessac-Léognan.

The entire Graves region produces and is famous for both red and white wines. The top white wines of this region are rare and expensive and, in a few cases, capable of rivaling the finest white wines produced in France. They are produced from three grape varieties, Sauvignon Blanc, Semillon, and Muscadelle. However, the finest wines of Graves are the reds. Graves's most famous estate, the American-owned Château Haut-Brion in the northern suburb of Pessac, was the first Bordeaux wine to receive international recognition. It was referred to in 1663 by the English author Samuel Pepys and between 1785 and 1789 by America's preeminent Francophile, Thomas Jefferson. The international acclaim for the distinctive wines of Haut-Brion was no doubt the reason why this property was the only non-Médoc to be included in the 1855 Classification of the Wines of the Gironde. Along with Haut-Brion, the other exceptional red wines produced in Graves are Haut-Brion's cross-street sibling, La Mission-Haut-Brion, and the nearby estate of Pape-Clément.

There are other fine Pessac-Léognan wines, most notably Les Carmes Haut-Brion in Pessac, La Tour-Haut-Brion in Talence, and Haut-Bailly, La Louvière, Smith-Haut-Lafitte, Domaine de Chevalier, and de Fieuzal near Léognan, but the overall level of quality winemaking, looked at from a consumer's perspective, is not as high as in such Médoc communes as St.-Julien, Pauillac, and St.-Estèphe.

The wines of Pessac-Léognan, like those of the Médoc, have their own quality classification. It, too, falsely serves as a quality guide to unsuspecting wine enthusiasts. The first classification occurred in 1953 and the most recent classification in 1959. The 1959 classification listed thirteen châteaux producing red wine, with Haut-Brion appearing first and the remaining twelve listed alphabetically. For the white wine producers (often the same châteaux), there were nine châteaux listed in alphabetical order, with Haut-Brion's minuscule production of white wine excluded at the château's insistence.

The personality traits of the northern Graves are individualistic and singular and not difficult to decipher when tasted blind in a comparative tasting with Médocs. While top wines such as Haut-Brion and La Mission-Haut-Brion differ considerably in style, they do share a rich, earthy, almost tobacco-scented (cigar box), roasted character. With the exception of La Mission-Haut-Brion, most of these red wines appear more fragrant, but lighter and more supple, than their Médoc counterparts. Yet the finest wines of this region almost always have a compelling fragrance. For my olfactory sense, there is no more provocative and profound bouquet in Bordeaux than that of a top vintage of Haut-Brion.

This particular characteristic reaches its most intense level with the Pessac vineyards of Haut-Brion, La Mission-Haut-Brion, Pape-Clément, and, to a lesser extent, Haut-Bailly, Domaine de Chevalier, Smith-Haut-Lafitte, and La Louvière.

Like two championship fighters staring down each other before a match, La Mission-Haut-Brion and Haut-Brion face each other across Route NP650. Neither the proprietors nor the winemakers of each property ever had many kind things to say about the other: the La Mission winemaking team called Haut-Brion's wines too light, over-priced, and over-manipulated; the Haut-Brion team accused La Mission of making overly big, alcoholic, savage, sometimes volatile wines that lacked finesse. This long-standing dispute came to an end in 1983 when Haut-Brion purchased La Mission, but the truth is that both properties produce profound, but different, wine.

La Mission-Haut-Brion tends to be a bigger, richer, more deeply colored wine than Haut-Brion. It has also been one of Bordeaux's most successful wines in mediocre or poor vintages. The 1957, 1958, 1960, 1967, 1972, 1974, 1987, and 1993 are vivid proof of that fact. When mature, the wine has the classic Graves bouquet of tobacco and earthy, mineral scents. Haut-Brion can be noticeably lighter, a trend particularly evident during the period 1966–1976, but before and after this era Haut-Brion has been a compellingly prodigious wine, and usually one of the most riveting first-growths. In particular, vintages since the mid-eighties have been spectacularly consistent.

Pape-Clément, since 1986, comes closer in style to Haut-Brion than to La Mission-Haut-Brion. Because of the high percentage of Merlot used in the blend and the thin, gravelly soil, Pape-Clément does, in top vintages, have the roasted, mineral, tobacco-scented nose and a smooth, supple, even opulent, plummy fruitiness that recalls a top Pomerol. It is cunningly made to be delicious young, yet the best vintages can last for up to 20 years.

Once away from the annoyingly noisy, traffic-cluttered roads of Pessac and Talence, the Graves region takes on more charm. This is the southern Graves, and the wines are less earthy, less smoky and tobacco scented than the Graves from Pessac and Talence. They are also lighter. Léognan is the center for the best southern Graves. The tiny Domaine de Chevalier, a relatively obscure vineyard hidden by thick forests, performs splendidly well, making minuscule quantities of outstanding white Graves and moderate quantities of the afore-mentioned smooth, very flavorful, rich, creamy, complex red wine, although recent vintages have been distressingly too woody in flavor.

Nearby is Haut-Bailly. Haut-Bailly produces an intensely fruity Graves wine that is usually ready to drink within 5–7 years of the vintage. Some of this château's wines can be long-lived, but this is one wine for which patience is not required. Nearby is de Fieuzal, which has made significant strides in quality since the eighties. The white wine has been among the most splendid examples of the appellation since 1985, and the red wine has also taken on more depth, size, and complexity. At present, de Fieuzal may be the most undervalued wine of the entire appellation.

One of the nineties' success stories is Smith-Haut-Lafitte. An under-achiever for decades, this beautiful estate was sold to the Cathiard family, who immediately turned this moribund producer into a bright, shining star.

There are, of course, numerous other wines, yet most of the other classified growths making red wine tend to produce light, rather one-dimensional wines that can be satisfying but will rarely offer much excitement. Malartic-Lagravière fits this mold nicely. Carbonnieux is more interesting and to my taste has the potential to be a higher-quality wine, if only the ownership would aspire to more lofty goals. Oddly enough, the white is consistently delicious, the red less so.

Pessac-Léognan and the larger area, Graves, are regions to investigate when Bordeaux has a mediocre or poor vintage. The drainage is excellent, and in years like 1994, 1993, 1987, 1974, 1964, and 1958, when many wines from the Médoc were diluted and disappointing, properties such as La Mission-Haut-Brion, Domaine de Chevalier, and Haut-Brion produced excellent wines from healthy, relatively mature grapes. On the other hand, exceptionally hot, drought-like years that often result in superb wines in the northern Médoc, St.-Emilion, and Pomerol tend to severely stress the vine-yards of Graves, causing a blockage in the grapes' maturity process. Most recently, particularly hot years such as 1982, 1989, and 1990 were less successful in Graves than elsewhere for this very reason. Recent outstanding vintages for Graves have been 1996, 1995, 1990, 1988 (better than 1990 and

1989 for some properties), 1987 (a sleeper year), 1985, 1983 (better than 1982), 1978, 1971, 1970, 1964, and 1961.

There are numerous properties in Graves, many of them not even classi-fied, that have been making significant qualitative progress and are, if any-thing, undervalued. Excellent producers such as La Louvière, Picque-Caillou, Larrivet-Haut-Brion, Clos Floridène, and Haut-Gardère will be names to take seriously.

GRAVES/PESSAC-LÉOGNAN
(An Insider's View—Red Wines)

Overall Appellation Potential: Average to Superb

The Most Potential for Aging: Haut-Bailly, Haut-Brion, La Mission-Haut-Brion, Pape-Clément, Smith-Haut-Lafitte

The Most Elegant: Haut-Bailly, Haut-Brion, Pape-Clément, Smith-Haut-Lafitte

The Most Concentrated: de Fieuzal, Haut-Brion, La Louvière, La Mission-Haut-Brion, Pape-Clément, Smith-Haut-Lafitte

The Best Value: Chantegrive, Les Carmes-Haut-Brion, Clos Floridène, La Garde, La Louvière

The Most Exotic: None

The Most Difficult to Understand (when young): Domaine de Chevalier

The Most Underrated: La Garde, La Louvière

The Most Difficult to Appreciate Young: Domaine de Chevalier

The Easiest to Appreciate Young: Les Carmes-Haut-Brion, Chantegrive, Clos Floridène, La Garde, La Louvière

Up-and-Coming Estates: La Garde, La Louvière, Smith-Haut-Lafitte

Greatest Recent Vintages: 1995, 1994, 1990, 1988, 1983, 1979, 1978

GRAVES/PESSAC-LÉOGNAN
(An Insider's View—White Wines)

Overall Appellation Potential: Average to Superb

The Most Potential for Aging: Domaine de Chevalier, Haut-Brion, Laville-Haut-Brion, Smith-Haut-Lafitte

The Most Elegant: Carbonnieux, Couhins-Lurton, La Garde, Pape-Clément, Smith-Haut-Lafitte, La Tour-Martillac

The Most Concentrated: de Fieuzal, Haut-Brion, Laville-Haut-Brion, La Lou-vière, Smith-Haut-Lafitte

The Best Value: Chantegrive, La Garde, La Louvière, Magneau, Rahoul, Rochemorin, La Vieille-France, Vieux-Château-Gaubert

The Most Exotic: Clos Floridène, La Tour-Martillac, La Vieille-France

The Most Difficult to Understand (when young): Domaine de Chevalier

The Most Underrated: Clos Floridène, La Garde, Magneau, Rochemorin, Smith-Haut-Lafitte, La Vieille-France

Up-and-Coming Estates: La Louvière, Smith-Haut-Lafitte

Greatest Recent Vintages: 1994, 1989, 1985

PESSAC-LÉOGNAN—AN OVERVIEW

Location: On the left bank of the Garonne River, this subregion of Graves covers the northernmost sector, which is essentially ten communes

Acres under Vine: 2,964

Communes: Cadaujac, Canéjan, Graignan, Léognan, Martillac, Mérignac, Pessac, St.-Medard-d'Eyrans, Talence, Villenave-d'Ornon

Average Annual Production: 560,000 cases, of which 80% is red and 20% is white

Classified Growths: Total of 16 in Graves/Pessac-Léognan, all of which are located in the sub-region of Pessac-Léognan; 6 are classified for both their red and white wines, 7 are classified for red wines, and 3 are classified for white wines

Principal Grape Varieties: Red—Cabernet Sauvignon and Merlot dominate, with Cabernet Franc playing a backup role; white—Sauvignon Blanc and Semillon, with a tiny quantity of Muscadelle

GRAVES—AN OVERVIEW

Location: A relatively large area located mostly to the south of the city of Bordeaux on the left bank of the Garonne River

Acres under Vine: 7,657

Communes: Nearly 30 separate communes, the most prominent being Cerons, Illats, Landiras, Langon, Podensac, Portets, and Saucats

Average Annual Production: 1,950,000 cases, of which 70% is red and 30% is white

Classified Growths: Total of 16 in Graves/Pessac-Léognan, none of which are located in the subregion of Graves

Principal Grape Varieties: Red—Merlot and Cabernet Sauvignon; white — Semillon and Sauvignon Blanc, with small quantities of Muscadelle

A CONSUMER'S CLASSIFICATION OF THE RED AND WHITE WINE-PRODUCING CHÂTEAUX OF GRAVES

OUTSTANDING

Domaine de Chevalier (white only)

Haut-Brion (red and white)

Laville-Haut-Brion (white only)
La Mission-Haut-Brion

EXCELLENT

Les Carmes Haut-Brion
de Fieuzal
Haut-Bailly
La Louvière
Pape-Clément (since 1986)
Smith-Haut-Lafitte (since 1991)

VERY GOOD

Bahans-Haut-Brion
Clos Floridène (white only)
Couhins-Lurton (white only)
La Garde Reserve du Château
La Tour-Haut-Brion

GOOD

Archambeau, Baret, Carbonnieux, Chantegrive, Chéret-Pitres, Domaine de
Chevalier, Coucheroy, Cruzeau, Ferrande, Gazin-Rocquencourt,
Graville-Lacoste, Haut-Gardère, Olivier, Picque-Caillou, Pontac-Monplaisir,
Rahoul, Rochemorin, Le Thil Comte Clary, La Tour-Martillac,
La Vieille-France

OTHER NOTABLE GRAVES PROPERTIES

Bardins, Bouscaut, Boyrein, Brondelle, Cabannieux, Caillou, Cantelys,
Chicane, Courreges-Segues du Château de Gaillat, La Fleur Jonquet, de
France, Gaillat, Jean Gervais, Grand-Abord, Grand-Bos, La Grave,
Haut-Bergey, Haut-Calens, Haut-Lagrange, Haut-Nouchet, l'Hospital,
Lafargue, Lamouroux, Landiras, Larrivet-Haut-Brion, Lespault, Magence,
Malartic-Lagravière, Mauves, Perin de Naudine, Pessan, Peyre Blanque,
Piron, St.-Jean des Graves. St.-Robert, Le Sartre, Seuil, Domaine de la
Solitude, La Tour de Boyrin, Tourte, Le Tuquet, Villa Bel Air

BOUSCAUT

Classification: Classified growth (for reds and whites)
Location of vineyards: Cadaujac
Owner: S.A. Château Bouscaut (managed by Sophie Lurton-Cogombles)
Address: 33140 Cadaujac

Mailing address: Same as above
Telephone: 33 5 57 83 10 16; telefax: 33 5 57 83 10 17
Visits: By appointment only
Contact: Sophie Lurton-Cogombles

VINEYARDS (red)
Surface area: 91.4 acres
Average age of vines: 35 years
Blend: 50% Merlot, 35% Cabernet Sauvignon, 15% Cabernet Franc and Malbec
Density of plantation: 6,600 vines per hectare
Average yields (over the last 5 years): 50 hectoliters per hectare
Total average annual production: 1,800 hectoliters

GRAND VIN (red)
Brand name: Château Bouscaut
Appellation: Pessac-Léognan
Mean annual production: 700 hectoliters
Upbringing: Fermentations last 2–3 weeks in all. Wines are then transferred to oak casks, of which one-third are new, for 18 months aging. They are fined and filtered.

SECOND WINE
Brand name: Château Valoux
Average annual production: 1,000 hectoliters

VINEYARDS (white)
Surface area: 19.8 acres
Average age of vines: 35 years
Blend: 65% Semillon, 35% Sauvignon
Density of plantation: 6,600 vines per hectare
Average yields (over the last 5 years): 40 hectoliters per hectare
Total average annual production: 300 hectoliters

GRAND VIN (white)
Brand name: Château Bouscaut
Appellation: Pessac Léognan
Mean annual production: 100 hectoliters
Upbringing: Fermentations occur in oak barrels (60% of which are new). Wines remain on lees for 12 months with frequent stirrings. They are fined but not filtered.

SECOND WINE
Brand name: Château Valoux
Average annual production: 200 hectoliters

> Evaluation of present classification: One of the classic underachievers of the Graves appellation; it no longer merits its status as a Cru Classé
> Plateau of maturity: (red) 4–12 years following the vintage; (white) 2–6 years following the vintage

It was widely believed that after the American syndicate sold Bouscaut in 1979 to the well-known Bordeaux château owner Lucien Lurton, the quality at Bouscaut would improve. It has not. This property, among all of the classified growths of Graves, remains content to turn out unexciting white and red wines. The eighteenth-century château, with a lovely pool, was restored completely in the 1960s and is one of the most attractive in the region. Tasting the wines leaves the impression that there is a lack of a selection process. Some claim the high percentage of Merlot in the red wine (from young vines) has been detrimental to the wine's quality. I do not agree with that; I simply think Bouscaut produces too much wine without a severe enough selection to put the best under the château's name. Observers are hoping that the proprietor, Sophie Lurton (who was given the property by her father, Lucien Lurton, in 1992), will increase the level of quality.

VINTAGES (red)

1990—Deep in color, with an appealing smoky, oaky, ripe berry–scented nose, the
•   1990 Bouscaut possesses less substance and aging potential than the 1989 or
78   1988. Last tasted, 1/93.

1989—The 1989 Bouscaut is light, medium bodied, and correct, but it has more
•   alcohol, extremely high tannins that appear excessive for its straightforward,
82   fruity personality, and a great deal of oak. If it fills out and develops a
       mid-palate (unlikely), this offering may merit a higher score. Anticipated
       maturity: Now. Last tasted, 1/93.

1988—The 1988 Bouscaut is a spicy, well-made, medium-bodied wine that is ideal
•   for drinking over the next 5–6 years. Last tasted, 1/93.
83

1986—This wine does not display much depth or complexity. It would appear to be
•   the product of an enormous crop size, as the soft, rather thin flavors fade
75   quickly on the palate. Anticipated maturity: Now. Last tasted, 3/90.

1983—This is an extremely supple, fleshy, medium-weight Graves, with plenty of
•   style and charm. Fortunately it lacks the abrasive tannin so common in many
84   wines of this vintage. Quite spicy on the nose, and nicely colored, this wine
       will be an early-maturing 1983. Anticipated maturity: Now. Last tasted, 3/88.

1982—The best Bouscaut in 2 decades, the 1982 is medium dark, with a vividly
•   rich, ripe berry aroma, fat, lush, concentrated flavors, plenty of tannins in the
85   long finish, and good aging potential of 10–12 years. This is a big-styled,
       impressive Bouscaut. Anticipated maturity: Now–2000. Last tasted, 1/85.

1981—The 1981 has a light-intensity, spicy, rather reserved bouquet followed by
   •   flavors that are quite unyielding, hard, and austere. Is there enough fruit to
   74   outlast the abrasive tannins? Probably not. Anticipated maturity: Now. Last
        tasted, 6/84.

1980—Not terribly different from the 1981, only lighter in color and body, the
   •   1980 Bouscaut is an acceptable but quite one-dimensional wine. Anticipated
   72   maturity: Now—probably in serious decline. Last tasted, 2/83.

1978—An average-quality Bouscaut, with a light-intensity, spicy, oaky aroma and
   •   modest, fruity, berryish flavors, this wine has a moderately tannic, firm fin-
   78   ish. Anticipated maturity: Now—probably in serious decline. Last tasted,
        12/82.

1975—Very closed, unyielding, and painfully tannic and harsh on the palate, the
   •   1975 Bouscaut has above average color and good weight, but I see no possi-
   75   bility that the fruit can outlive the tannin. Anticipated maturity: Now. Last
        tasted, 5/84.

1970—Hard and severe when young, this wine has not developed any richness or
   •   character but has remained sternly tannic, woody, and ungenerous, with little
   72   charm or fruit. Last tasted, 2/80.

VINTAGES (white)

1989—Dull, sterile, nearly nonexistent aromas are followed by thin, stripped, high-
   •   strung flavors that lack charm, flesh, and character. Anticipated maturity:
   71   Now. Last tasted, 4/91.

1988—This is an uninspired effort at turning out high-quality white wine. An innocu-
   •   ous, light-bodied, eviscerated wine, the 1988 Bouscaut should be drunk over
   72   the next 2–3 years. Last tasted, 11/90.

CARBONNIEUX   GOOD

Classification: Classified growth (reds and whites)
Location of vineyards: Léognan, Villenave d'Ornon, and Cadaujac
Owner: S.C. des Grandes Graves
Address: 33850 Léognan
Mailing address: Same as above
Telephone: 33 5 57 96 56 20; telefax: 33 5 57 96 59 19
Visits: By appointment only, Monday to Friday, from 8 A.M. to 11:30 A.M.,
and 2 P.M. to 5:30 P.M.
Contact: Anthony Perrin

VINEYARDS (red)
Surface area: 111.6 acres
Average age of vines: 30 years
Blend: 60% Cabernet Sauvignon, 30% Merlot, 7% Cabernet Franc, 2%
Malbec, 1% Petit Verdot

Density of plantation: 7,200 vines per hectare
Average yields (over the last 5 years): 55 hectoliters per hectare
Total average annual production: 300,000 bottles

GRAND VIN (red)
Brand name: Château Carbonnieux
Appellation: Pessac-Léognan
Mean annual production: Variable
Upbringing: Alcoholic fermentations occur in temperature-controlled stainless-steel tanks. Malolactics occur in vats for two-thirds of the yield and in oak barrels for one-third. Wines are aged in oak casks, which are renewed by a third every vintage, for 18 months. They are fined and filtered.

SECOND WINE
Brand name: Château La Tour-Léognan
Average annual production: Variable

VINEYARDS (white)
Surface area: 104 acres
Average age of vines: 32 years
Blend: 65% Sauvignon Blanc, 34% Semillon, 1% Muscadelle
Density of plantation: 7,200 vines per hectare
Average yields (over the last 5 years): 45 hectoliters per hectare
Total average annual production: 240,000 bottles

GRAND VIN (white)
Brand name: Château Carbonnieux
Appellation: Pessac-Léognan
Mean annual production: Variable
Upbringing: Fermentations occur in oak casks, which are renewed by a third each vintage. Malolactics are stopped by sulfiting. Wines are kept on lees for 10–11 months, never racked but frequently stirred (once a week). They are fined and filtered.

SECOND WINE
Brand name: La Tour Léognan
Average annual production: Variable

Evaluation of present classification: Since 1985 there has been significant progress with both the white and red wines, and the property now merits its Cru Classé status
Plateau of maturity: (red) 3–10 years following the vintage; (white) 3–12 years following the vintage

Carbonnieux, one of the largest estates of Graves, had until the mid-1980s fit into the pattern of many of the winemaking estates of the Pessac-Léognan area—the white wines were frequently delicious, but the red wines were innocuously light and bland. Since the mid-1980s that has changed for the better, with the white wine taking on even higher-quality aspirations and the red wine becoming tasty, elegant, supple, and well made.

The property is not only of historic significance, but is among the most scenic of the region. The history of the vineyards can be traced to the thirteenth century, but the modern era of Carbonnieux began in 1956 when Marc Perrin acquired the estate. His son, Tony, now oversees the winemaking. In the mid-1980s Tony Perrin hired the famed Denis Dubourdieu to give the whites even more fragrance and concentration. Additionally, the reds have taken on greater depth and intensity.

Most vintages of Carbonnieux, both the red and white wine, should be drunk in their first 7–10 years. Some of the white wine vintages have a remarkable potential to last for up to 2 decades.

VINTAGES (red)

1996—A less charming example of Carbonnieux than the pretty, delicious, seductive
• 　　 1995, Carbonnieux's 1996 is built more on structure and tannin. Neverthe-
86– 　 less, it is well made, with a spicy component, sweet strawberry, cherry, and
87 　　 currant fruit, moderate tannin, and a firm backbone. Some cellaring will be
　　　　required, but this wine will be drinkable at a relatively early age. Anticipated
　　　　maturity: 2003–2013. Last tasted, 3/98.

1995—An attractive, sexy effort from Carbonnieux, this medium-bodied, deep ruby–
• 　　 colored wine reveals subtle aromas of smoky oak intertwined with tobacco,
87 　　 kirsch, and black currant fruit. In the mouth, elegance, balance, suppleness,
　　　　finesse, and an overall allure characterize this round, lightly tannic, lush, and
　　　　captivating claret. Anticipated maturity: Now–2011. Last tasted, 11/97.

1994—Carbonnieux's 1994 displays a medium dark ruby color, a sweet, ripe nose of
• 　　 currants and cherries, spicy new oak, austere, lean flavors, and high tannin.
79 　　 There is a lack of complexity, fruit, and flesh in this dry, hard, woody wine.
　　　　Last tasted, 1/97.

1993—A dark garnet color is followed by weedy, tomato, cedary, new saddle leather
• 　　 aromas combined with the strong scent of green peppers. There is fruit in this
85 　　 soft, lean, pure, understated, lightly tannic, straightforward wine. Drink it
　　　　over the next 3–4 years. Last tasted, 1/97.

1992—The deeply colored 1992 exhibits an attractive bouquet of tobacco, toast, and
• 　　 black fruits. There is fine ripeness, solid body, light tannin, and an expansive,
86 　　 lush, silky personality. This is a delicious, pure, elegant 1992 that will
　　　　provide plenty of joy over the next decade. Last tasted, 11/94.

1991—The 1991 is one of the most seductive and graceful wines of the vintage. The
• 　　 medium ruby color is followed by a bouquet that soars from the glass, offering
86 　　 copious scents of tobacco, herbs, black fruits, and sweet oak. Medium bodied,
　　　　with gobs of rich, creamy-textured fruit, this elegant, well-balanced, smooth-

edged wine reveals soft tannin and a lush finish. Drink it over the next 7–8 years. Last tasted, 1/94.

1990—Behind the 1990's intensely oaky nose there appear to be good extract, a
•   forward, even flattering personality, and a charming, moderately endowed
85   finish. Anticipated maturity: Now–2008. Last tasted, 1/93.

1989—The 1989 is straightforward, pleasant, oaky, medium bodied, and tannic. It is
•   a serviceable, attractively fruity, medium-weight wine, but it is not distin-
83   guished. Anticipated maturity: Now–2000. Last tasted, 1/93.

1988—The 1988 Carbonnieux is an elegant, lighter-styled wine displaying charm,
•   medium body, sweet strawberry fruit, and plenty of oak. It is not a big wine,
83   but it is stylish, flavorful, and graceful. Drink it over the next 6–7 years. Last
       tasted, 1/93.

1986—The 1986 is impressive for its suave, graceful, cherry fruitiness, generous use
•   of toasty new oak, and soft flavors with some ripe tannins in the finish.
85   Anticipated maturity: Now. Last tasted, 3/90.

1985—The 1985 has sweet, soft, expansive flavors of cherries and toasty oak that
•   made me think of a Premier Cru Beaune, not a Graves. Anticipated maturity:
85   Now. Last tasted, 3/89.

1983—The 1983 is an attractive, plump, spicy, juicy wine, with an elegant cherry
•   fruitiness, soft, savory texture, light tannins, and a supple finish. Anticipated
85   maturity: Now–may be in decline. Last tasted, 1/88.

1982—I have had this wine only once in the last 10 years. Tasted at the château, it
•   revealed surprisingly delicious, ripe cherry fruit, a textbook Graves nose
86   (tobacco, minerals, herbs), fine sweetness, and a lush, medium-bodied, seduc-
       tive style. Although the wine has been drinkable most of its life, it exhibits
       no signs of decline. The color is just beginning to lighten at the edge. The
       1982 Carbonnieux should continue to drink well for another decade. Last
       tasted, 9/95.

1981—A light ruby–colored wine, the 1981 Carbonnieux is quite one-dimensional,
•   with spicy, soft, jammy fruit, a light-intensity bouquet, and a weak finish.
73   Anticipated maturity: Now–probably in serious decline. Last tasted, 11/84.

1978—Made during a period when Carbonnieux was not renowned for its red wines,
•   the 1978 has turned out to be a light, delicate, fruity Graves with some
79   herbaceous, earthy notes in the bouquet, and soft, round, medium-bodied
       flavors. Anticipated maturity: Now. Last tasted, 3/86.

VINTAGES (white)

1993—One of the benchmark producers for crisp, elegant, dry, white Graves, Car-
•   bonnieux has recently succeeded with wines that display even more richness
89   and weight without sacrificing any of their ethereal elegance and style. The
       1993 is a rich, honeyed wine with fine purity and attractive smoky oak that
       adds to the complexity of its otherwise waxy, melony, herb, and smoky fruit
       character. Drink it over the next 10–15 years. Last tasted, 11/94.

1992—Carbonnieux is striving for more fullness and richness in its dry white wine
•   program. This 1992 exhibits a spicy, rich, honeyed nose and medium-bodied
88   flavors with excellent ripeness and enough crisp acidity and toasty oak to

support this pure wine's richness. Carbonnieux's exuberant, fresh style makes it one of the most popular dry white Bordeaux. It should drink well for 10 or more years. Last tasted, 1/94.

LES CARMES HAUT-BRION   EXCELLENT

Classification: None
Location of vineyards: Pessac
Owner: Chantecaille family
Address: 197, avenue Jean Jaurès, 33600 Pessac
Mailing address: Same as above
Telephone: 33 5 56 51 49 43; telefax: 33 5 56 93 10 71
Visits: By appointment only
Contact: Mr. or Mrs. Didier Furt

VINEYARDS (red)
Surface area: 11 acres
Average age of vines: 30 years
Blend: 50% Merlot, 40% Cabernet Franc, 10% Cabernet Sauvignon
Density of plantation: 8,000 vines per hectare
Average yields (over the last 5 years): 49 hectoliters per hectare
Total average annual production: 2,000 cases

GRAND VIN (red)
Brand name: Château Les Carmes Haut-Brion
Appellation: Pessac-Léognan
Mean annual production: 1,800 cases
Upbringing: 80% of the yield completes malolactics in barrels and 20% in vats. Wines are aged for 18 months in oak barrels, 35% of which are new. They are sometimes filtered, depending upon the vintage.

SECOND WINE
Brand name: Le Clos des Carmes
Average annual production: 200 cases

Evaluation of present classification: Should be upgraded to a Graves Cru Classé
Plateau of maturity: 6–20 years following the vintage

In the early seventies I had the good fortune to walk into a wine shop that was discounting magnums of the 1959 Les Carmes Haut-Brion. I knew nothing about the wine, but I took a chance and bought two magnums. Both proved to be spectacular, and every effort I made to find the wine thereafter was futile. Little did I know then that this tiny jewel of a vineyard, situated on a gravelly knoll in the Bordeaux suburb of Pessac, near the famed Haut-Brion and La Mission-Haut-Brion, produces the most-obscure and least-known top-quality red wine of Pessac-Léognan.

The vineyard is named for the group of friars, called Les Carmes, who owned this vineyard between 1584 and 1789. During the French Revolution, the religious order was divested of ownership.

Les Carmes Haut-Brion is a rich, full wine, no doubt because the Merlot vines benefit from the gravelly and clay soil in which they are planted. A traditional approach to winemaking results in wines that are classic expressions of Graves, deeply colored, intense, and complex. Unfortunately, most of the wine from Les Carmes Haut-Brion is sold by Monsieur Chantecaille through his *négociant* business in Bordeaux to European markets. Since so little wine is made, the chances of finding any in America are remote.

This is a wine that comes closest to expressing the quality of Haut-Brion and La Mission-Haut-Brion, not surprisingly, as the vineyards and *terroir* are essentially the same. This small, consistently top-notch performer in Pessac is worth searching out.

VINTAGES

1997—I continue to enjoy the efforts from this little treasure buried in Bordeaux's
•   southern suburbs. A textbook Graves, this wine offers the tell-tale, gravelly,
87–   tobacco, sweet jammy cherry, and iron-laced aromatics. Soft and plump, with
88   low acidity and plenty of fruit and glycerin, this layered, elegant, silky-textured wine should be drunk during its first 5–7 years of life. It is captivating. Last tasted, 3/98.

1996—This wine continues to perform well, displaying an opaque ruby/purple color,
•   and an impressive nose of sweet tobacco, black currants, cherries, and smoke.
87–   A textbook Graves, with a sweet entry on the palate, medium body, silky
88   tannin, and a round, graceful finish, this is an accessible, low-acid, luscious 1996 that should provide near-term drinking. Anticipated maturity: Now–2009. Last tasted, 3/98.

1995—A classic example of Graves' smoky, tobacco-tinged, berry fruit, this small
•   jewel of an estate (not far from Haut-Brion and Pape-Clément) has produced
87   a medium-bodied, sweet, round, berry, complex, elegant, savory 1995 with no hard edges. Low acidity and a luscious, ripe Merlot component dominate the wine, giving it immediate appeal. This is a plump, delicious wine for consuming over the next decade. Last tasted, 11/97.

1994—The 1994 exhibits a medium to dark ruby color, a sweet, tobacco, smoky red
•   fruit–scented nose, medium body, soft tannin, low acidity, and a ripe, round
87   personality that slides easily down the gullet. It is a charming wine that should drink well for 7–8 years. Last tasted, 3/96.

1993—Les Carmes-Haut-Brion's 1993 offers a medium dark ruby color, a spicy,
•   earthy, berry-scented nose, soft, ripe flavors exhibiting fine concentration,
86   medium body, and a round finish. As with many 1993 Graves, the tannin

level is less severe than that found in many Médocs. I admired this wine's soft fruit and forward, precocious personality. Drink it over the next 5–7 years. Last tasted, 11/94.

1990—The 1990 reveals a classic Graves nose of sweet, weedy tobacco, roasted
  •   black fruits, and minerals. In the mouth, it is medium bodied, spicy, and rich,
 86   with adequate structure and a smooth, luscious texture. Drink it over the next 10–12 years. Last tasted, 1/93.

1989—The smoky, tobacco, mineral-like bouquet of the 1989 is enticing. The palate
  •   reveals a ripe, roasted, open-knit fruitiness with a finish that is alcoholic and
 86   soft. Anticipated maturity: Now. Last tasted, 1/93.

1988—The 1988 Les Carmes-Haut-Brion has a big, smoky, hickory-and-plum-
  •   scented bouquet, concentrated, soft, but structured flavors, and a long finish.
 87   An attractive textbook Graves with the characteristic cigar-box, mineral-scented aromas and flavors, it should be drunk over the next 4–6 years. Last tasted, 1/93.

1987—In a blind tasting in Bordeaux, I thought the 1987 Les Carmes Haut-Brion
  •   was Haut-Brion. Its intense, smoky, ripe, curranty nose is powerful and soars
 86   from the glass. In the mouth, the wine is rich and very soft, with an opulent finish. Anticipated maturity: Now. Last tasted, 3/90.

1986—This is a fleshy, full-bodied wine with an impressive deep ruby color. The
  •   high tannins should permit the wine to age well for at least 12–15 years. The
 88   bouquet has a sweet, plummy fruitiness, with a very pronounced mineral, tobacco character. Medium bodied, with good richness, this wine could well merit a higher score once the tannins soften. Anticipated maturity: Now–2005. Last tasted, 3/90.

1985—The 1985 is an admirably constituted wine and deep in color, with the
  •   unmistakable mineral, tobacco-scented bouquet so typical of the top wines of
 87   this appellation. It is supple, smooth, and easy to appreciate for the delicious, intense fruit and fine length. Anticipated maturity: Now–2000. Last tasted, 3/89.

ANCIENT VINTAGES

A magnum of 1959 Les Carmes-Haut-Brion (93 points) tasted in December 1995 revealed a singed, sweet, jammy, port-like nose intertwined with scents of tobacco and smoke. It reminded me that my palate tastes too little of this wine. Full, fleshy, opulent, and fully mature, it should continue to drink well for another decade.

CHANTEGRIVE   GOOD

Classification: None
Location of vineyards: Podensac, Illats, Virelade
Owner: Henri and Françoise Lévêque
Address: B.P. 14, 33720 Podensac

Mailing address: Same as above
Telephone: 33 5 56 27 17 38; telefax: 33 5 56 27 29 42
Visits: Monday to Friday, 8 A.M. to noon, and 2 P.M. to 6 P.M.; morning
only on Saturdays
Contact: Mrs. Soum-Lévêque

VINEYARDS (red)
Surface area: 104 acres
Average age of vines: 20 years
Blend: 50% Cabernet Sauvignon, 40% Merlot, 10% Cabernet Franc
Density of plantation: 6,200 vines per hectare
Average yields (over the last 5 years): 50 hectoliters per hectare

GRAND VIN (red)
Brand name: Château de Chantegrive
Appellation: Graves
Mean annual production 2,174 hectoliters
Upbringing: Vinifications are carried out under an electronic
temperature-control system. Wines are aged in new oak casks for 18
months. They are fined and lightly filtered.

SECOND WINE
Brand name: Mayne Lévêque
Average annual production: variable—depends upon the vintage

VINEYARDS (white)
Surface area: 123.5 acres
Average age of vines: 40 years
Blend: 50% Semillon, 40% Sauvignon, 10% Muscadelle
Density of plantation: 6,200 vines per hectare
Average yields (over the last 5 years): 50 hectoliters per hectare

GRAND VIN (white)
Brand name: Château de Chantegrive
Appellation: Graves
Mean annual production: 2,700 hectoliters
Upbringing: Fermentations occur in temperature-controlled
stainless-steel tanks for the normal cuvée. Wines are bottled after 9
months. They are fined and lightly filtered.

CUVÉE CAROLINE (luxury cuvée)
Selection on 34.6 acres of vines
Production: 50,000–60,000 bottles
Blend: 50% Semillon, 50% Sauvignon

Average age of vines: More than 30 years
Upbringing: *Macération pelliculaire* lasts 15 hours, and fermentations occur in new oak casks. Wines remain on lees for about 1 year and are stirred every 10 days. They are bottled 10–12 months after the vintage. They are fined and filtered.

SECOND WINE
Brand name: Mayne Lévêque
Average annual production: varies depending upon the vintage

Evaluation of present classification: The quality equivalent of a good Médoc Cru Bourgeois
Plateau of maturity: (red) 5–7 years following the vintage; (white) 5–7 years following the vintage

When I am eating in a Bordeaux restaurant, the red and white wines I often search out for value and quality are those made at the attractive Château Chantegrive, located just north of the village of Podensac, adjacent to Route Nationale 113. While proprietor Henri Lévêque can trace his family's wine heritage back to 1753, he alone resurrected this property from obscure standing in 1962 to one that is now recognized for high-quality red and white wines that represent excellent quality/price rapport.

This is one cellar where everything from barrel cellar to fermentation rooms are temperature and humidity controlled—a rarity in Bordeaux. In the mid-1980s a luxury cuvée of Lévêque's white Graves, the Chantegrive-Cuvée Caroline, was introduced. It is as good as some of the more renowned Crus Classés. Neither the white nor the red wine is meant to be long-lived, but rather to be drunk in the first 5–7 years of life. A strong argument can even be made for drinking the white wines before they reach the age of 5. Nevertheless, the wines are consistently well made, even in lighter-weight vintages, and are textbook examples of their appellation.

Frugal consumers looking for wines that satisfy both the palate and the purse should seek out this consistent overachiever in the southern Graves region.

VINTAGES (red)

1993—This light to medium ruby–colored wine displays a surprisingly advanced,
• nearly mature nose of soft cherry and cassis fruit, some oak, low acidity, and
81 a spicy, round finish. Drink it over the next 4–5 years. Last tasted, 11/94.

1990—Vanillin aromas from new oak are followed by a richly fruity, medium-bodied,
• nicely concentrated, low-acid wine that is delicious for drinking over the next
85 5–6 years. Last tasted, 1/93.

1990—Cuvée Edouard: The 1990 Cuvée Edouard is enhanced by more obvious
   •   toasty new oak and sweeter, riper fruit. The tannins are more present, and
   86   although this wine is drinkable now, it should age well for 7–8 years. Last
         tasted, 1/93.
1989—A big, pruny, plummy, spicy nose is followed by a light- to medium-bodied
   •   wine with luscious fruit and some shortness in the finish. Overall, it is a
   85   pleasing wine that should make for pleasant drinking over the next 2–3 years.
         Last tasted, 1/93.
1988—Cuvée Edouard: This well-run property has turned out a ripe, perfumed, tasty,
   •   medium-bodied 1988 wine that is fully mature. The nose and flavors of
   85   smoked nuts, tobacco, and red fruits is a delight. Anticipated maturity: Now.
         Last tasted, 3/94.

DOMAINE DE CHEVALIER   GOOD (WHITE, OUTSTANDING)

Classification: Classified growth (reds and whites)
Location of vineyards: Léognan
Owner: Bernard family
Administrator: Olivier Bernard
Address: 33850 Léognan
Mailing address: Same as above
Telephone: 33 5 56 64 16 16; telefax: 33 5 56 64 18 18
Visits: By appointment only during office hours, from Monday to Friday
Contact: Olivier Bernard and Rémy Edange

VINEYARDS (red)
Surface area: 74 acres
Average age of vines: 35 years and 12 years
Blend: 65% Cabernet Sauvignon, 30% Merlot, 5% Cabernet Franc
Density of plantation: 10,000 vines per hectare
Average yields (over the last 5 years): 48 hectoliters per hectare

GRAND VIN (red)
Brand name: Domaine de Chevalier
Appellation: Pessac-Léognan
Mean annual production: 7,000 cases
Upbringing: Fermentations occur in temperature-controlled tanks of 100
and 150 hectoliters capacity. Temperatures are kept relatively low.
Macerations are long and smooth to ensure extraction of the finest tannins
only. Wines are transferred to oak casks for 18–22 months aging. Half
the barrels are new, and the rest are 1 year old. Racking is done by
gravity from one barrel to another. Wines are fined with fresh egg whites
and lightly filtered.

SECOND WINE
Brand name: L'Esprit de Chevalier
Average annual production: 7,000 cases

VINEYARDS (white)
Surface area: 10 acres
Average age of vines: 30 years except for 2.47 acres of young vines (10 years)
Blend: 70% Sauvignon, 30% Semillon
Density of plantation: 10,000 vines per hectare
Average yields (over the last 5 years): 37 hectoliters per hectare

NOTE: Green pruning is carried out in July; only one cluster left on each shoot. In August, after the *véraison* (changing of the grapes' color to red), all the clusters that are not deemed good enough are cut off. There is sorting at harvest-time—only the first-generation grapes are picked. All berries that are not in perfect sanitary condition are removed from the cluster.

L'Esprit de Chevalier is not a selection *parcellaire*.

GRAND VIN (white)
Brand name: Domaine de Chevalier
Appellation: Pessac-Léognan
Mean annual production: 1,000 cases
Upbringing: Fermentations occur in barrels, and wines are kept on lees for 18 months. *Assemblage* is done in December. Wines are fined with bentonite and lightly filtered upon bottling.

SECOND WINE
Brand name: L'Esprit de Chevalier
Average annual production: 500 cases

NOTE: There can be as many as 4 or 5 "passages" (selective picking) in one particular plot of land to ensure that the grapes are picked at optimum maturity.

Evaluation of present classification: The quality equivalent of a Médoc third-growth
Plateau of maturity: (red) 5–20 years following the vintage; (white) 6–30 years following the vintage

The tiny estate of Domaine de Chevalier, tucked away in the midst of a forest on the southwest outskirts of Léognan, is a true connoisseur's wine. The production is tiny and the wines are among the most highly sought of Pessac-Léognan, but most important, the quality has been impeccably high—at least until the nineties.

Domaine de Chevalier's fame was no doubt due to the aristocratic Claude Ricard, who inherited the property in 1942 but because of family squabbles had to sell the estate in 1983 to the large Bernard distilling company. Claude Ricard was retained to run the property but finally turned over the reins of Domaine de Chevalier to Olivier Bernard.

The red wines of Domaine de Chevalier do not resemble the intense, rich, earthy style of Graves, best exemplified by Haut-Brion and La Mission-Haut-Brion. Until the nineties, the Domaine de Chevalier wines possessed a subtle, mineral, earthy aspect but were much lighter in body and tended to be more Médoc-like in style than the Graves wines from Pessac and Talence. Since the new owners acquired the property, there has been an intentional effort to produce a bigger, more structured and powerful wine. There are no problems with that, but the excessive oakiness in many recent vintages has often obliterated the wine's charm and finesse, telltale personality traits of Domaine de Chevalier.

The white Domaine de Chevalier is the only wine I know of in the Bordeaux region that spends over a year and a half in new oak casks. The production is tiny, and the wine, while fabulous when drunk from cask, usually closes up after bottling, not to blossom for 10 or more years. Yet it has the distinction of actually taking longer to mature, and aging even more gracefully, than the superb red wine.

Anyone who visits the southern portion of Pessac-Léognan (the northern sector of Graves) will have a difficult time finding Domaine de Chevalier. I became impossibly lost on my first trip to the property in the late seventies. The cream-colored château, surrounded on three sides by a pine forest, can be found by taking D109 east from Léognan in the direction of Cestas. Signs indicating the entrance to the vineyard of Domaine de Chevalier will guide the traveler to the château.

The soil of this relatively small vineyard has a gravel bed but also contains clay and iron. Two problems encountered here are that spring frosts and frequent hail can severely damage the crop. Inexplicably, no other major châteaux of the Bordeaux region suffer these two natural calamities as frequently as Domaine de Chevalier.

Domaine de Chevalier is an expensive wine, fetching prices similar to those of a Médoc second-growth.

VINTAGES (red)

1997—This is one of the finest Domaine de Chevaliers produced in the last 8–10
  • years. The saturated ruby/purple color is followed by aromas of sweet black
87– plums, cranberries, and currants intertwined with toasty oak, spice, and
88+ minerals. Excellent purity, combined with a medium-bodied, concentrated, sweet attack makes for a savory impression. There is some tannin in this reasonably well delineated 1997. This elegant, flavorful, nicely textured,

softer styled Domaine de Chevalier should be drinkable in 2–3 years. Anticipated maturity: 2001–2013. Last tasted, 3/98.

1996—This deep ruby–colored wine tastes somewhat stripped, overly wooded, and
• excessively tannic, but some berry fruit can be found underneath the abun-
84– dant wood and tannin. The wine possesses medium body, and good weight on
86 the palate, but the vintage's trademark hardness and astringency cannot be dismissed. This wine is a likely candidate to dry out over the next decade. Last tasted, 11/97.

1995—A shockingly high oak component obliterates any attempt at discerning the
• level of fruit that might be present. Yes, the wine is backward; yes, it is
80? light-bodied; yes, it hints at having some minerality: but where's the weight, ripeness, and fruit intensity? Last tasted, 11/97.

1994—A medium to dark ruby color is deceptive in view of the hollow, aggressively
• tannic wine that has emerged since bottling. The sweet, ripe fruit present in
77? cask has turned into a charmless wine of dubious balance. I cannot see it ever turning itself around. It reminds me of the 1975. Last tasted, 1/97.

1993—This is a frightfully lean, austere, ferociously tannic wine that is nearly devoid
• of fruit and charm. There is some spice and new oak in the nose, but very
76 little flavor and flesh to what is, in essence, a wine of all structure—acidity, alcohol, and wood tannin. Last tasted, 1/97.

1992—The 1992 offers copious toasty vanillin notes in its fruity nose, as well as a fine
• dark ruby color. While lighter and more one-dimensional than usual, it is con-
85 centrated, soft, and oaky. It should drink well for 7–8 years. Last tasted, 11/94.

1991—Domaine de Chevalier often makes attractive wines in off years, and the 1991
• is no exception. The wine reveals a deep ruby color, a spicy, oaky nose,
87 admirable structure, dense, ripe, sweet fruit, medium body, and a long, tannic finish. It will benefit from 2–3 years of cellaring. Last tasted, 1/94.

1990—I thought this wine had the potential to be outstanding, but it is typical of
• many recent vintages of this château—blatantly oaky! The color is a deep
88 ruby. The nose, in addition to the telltale blast of sweet, spicy new oak, offers the vintage's jammy cherry, curranty fruit intermixed with tobacco and herbs. A medium-bodied wine with good sweetness, excellent concentration, and moderate tannin, this is an elegant, stylish 1990 that should mature grace-fully. Anticipated maturity: Now–2010. Last tasted, 9/97.

1989—A plump, forward style of Domaine de Chevalier, the dark ruby–colored 1989
• displays smoky toasty oak that is better integrated than in more recent vin-
89 tages. A smoky, herb-tinged, sweet cherry–and–black currant–scented nose is followed by a medium-bodied wine with low acidity, ripe, fleshy fruit, moderate tannin, and a nice finish. The 1989 is less evolved than the 1990. Anticipated maturity: 1999–2010. Last tasted, 10/97.

1988—Domaine de Chevalier produced one of the finest wines of this vintage in
• 1988. Dark ruby, with an unevolved but generous bouquet of smoky new oak,
90 cassis, and flowers, this fleshy, generously endowed, medium-bodied wine is the finest effort from this property since their 1983. Anticipated maturity: Now–2008. Last tasted, 3/97.

1987—This domain consistently does fine work in off years, and the 1987 boasts an
•   intense, vanilla-scented, toasty, oaky bouquet, ripe raspberry and black cur-
86   rant flavors, medium body, surprising concentration, and ample, soft tannins
       in the finish. Drinkable now. Anticipated maturity: Now. Last tasted, 3/90.

1986—This wine has evolved less evenly than I hoped. The attractive nose of roasted
•   earth, herbs, minerals, and red and black fruits is pleasant. In the mouth, the
88   wine reveals unresolved, astringent tannin. Although short in the finish, it is
       a very good, possibly excellent, Domaine de Chevalier that should continue
       to evolve and, hopefully, fatten up over the next decade. Anticipated maturity:
       Now–2012. Last tasted, 11/95.

1985—The 1985 has the sweet, ripe, rich fruit that is the hallmark of this vintage,
•   but also more tannin than many Graves from this vintage. For a 1985 it will
86   be slow to mature, yet it does not have the concentration one usually expects
       of wines from this property. Anticipated maturity: Now–2005. Last tasted,
       3/90.

1984—The 1984 Domaine de Chevalier contains an unusually high amount of Caber-
•   net Sauvignon (90%). It is well marked by toasty new oak, but there is also
85   plenty of ripe fruit, as well as moderate tannins and fine depth. This is one of
       the few stars of the vintage. Anticipated maturity: Now. Last tasted, 3/89.

1983—The 1983 is the finest Domaine de Chevalier of the last 15 years. The wine
•   was tannic and hard in its youth, but the tannin has melted away, resulting in
91   a classic example of the elegance, authoritative sweetness, and compelling
       complexity this estate can achieve. The knockout nose of tobacco, sweet
       black fruits, smoke, licorice, and roasted herbs is intense. In the mouth, this
       wine is fleshy and medium bodied, with an expansive, savory mouth-feel.
       There are no hard edges, as all the tannin has become beautifully integrated
       into this opulently textured, seductive, luscious Domaine de Chevalier. Antic-
       ipated maturity: Now–2005. Last tasted, 10/97.

1982—The 1982 Domaine de Chevalier continues to be one of the vintage's major
•   disappointments. In cask the wine exhibited more fruit, but from 375-
71?   milliliter and 750-milliliter bottles, it reveals glaring fruit and extraction
       deficiencies, a hard, hollow personality with considerable astringent tannin,
       and too much weedy, underripe herbaceousness. Hail damaged part of the
       1982 crop at Domaine de Chevalier, and it appears the final wine has been
       tainted by those grapes. I have received reports of good bottles, and Michael
       Broadbent has rated it 4 out of 5 stars, so perhaps I have just been unlucky.
       Last tasted, 9/95.

1981—The 1981 Domaine de Chevalier is well made but lacks flavor dimension,
•   depth, and charm. A medium-bodied wine, it has a pronounced vanillin
83   oakiness, aggressive tannins, ruby color, and a lean finish. Will it ever blos-
       som and provide real pleasure? Anticipated maturity: Now–2000. Last tasted,
       3/89.

1980—A notable success in this mediocre vintage, Domaine de Chevalier has made
•   a deeply fruity, spicy, open-knit wine, with a bouquet dominated by the scent
84   of new vanillin oakiness. Medium bodied, with surprising concentration and

light tannins, this supple, classy wine is ideal for drinking over the next 5–6 years. Anticipated maturity: Now. Last tasted, 10/84.

1979— Very agreeable and drinkable from the time it was bottled, the 1979 Domaine
• de Chevalier is a charmingly supple, fruity, medium-bodied wine that refuses
85 to fall apart. A fragrant bouquet of ripe berry fruit and cedar is alluring. On the palate, the wine is supple, medium bodied, oaky, round, and long. Anticipated maturity: Now. Last tasted, 12/89.

1978— Along with the glorious 1970, this is my favorite vintage of Domaine de
• Chevalier during this decade. The 1978 has consistently been a textbook
92 Graves with a tobacco-tinged, smoky, sweet, cedary, berry-and-black currant– scented nose. Still lusciously fruity, round, and generous, this medium bodied, exceptionally stylish, elegant wine exhibits the exquisite levels of finesse Domaine de Chevalier can achieve without sacrificing flavor and concentration. Anticipated maturity: Now–2005. Last tasted, 10/97.

1977— One of the better 1977 wines, the Domaine de Chevalier is soft and fruity,
• with moderately intense, medium-bodied flavors that exhibit a pleasant berry
76 fruitiness. Anticipated maturity: Now–probably in serious decline. Last tasted, 3/81.

1976— An open, spicy, rather earthy, ripe, almost burnt bouquet is followed on the
• palate by a wine that is fully mature, soft, less concentrated than normal, but
78 fruity. Anticipated maturity: Now–may be in decline. Last tasted, 4/87.

1975— We all make mistakes, and a serious one I made was purchasing this wine
• before I tasted it. The 1975 has consistently proven to be disappointing. Hail,
68 much like in 1982, was again the undoing of the 1975 Domaine de Chevalier. The wine still has an impressive dark ruby, youthful-looking color, but in the mouth, it is hollow and extremely astringent, with mouth-searing tannins, and a hard, nasty finish. Perhaps this wine will exhibit more charm and fruit with aging, but I am increasingly skeptical. Anticipated maturity: Now–2000? Last tasted, 12/90.

1974— This is a flavorful, supple, fruity 1974, without any of the harshness or
• hollowness that afflicts so many wines from this vintage. It is drinkable now,
76 and the tannins and overall balance may keep this wine from declining for another 3–4 years. Anticipated maturity: Now–probably in serious decline. Last tasted, 6/80.

1973— I had this wine for the first and only time in 1990, and it was a revelation.
• Most 1973s were in serious decline by the end of that decade, but this wine,
87 drunk with a friend in Bordeaux, was still a deep ruby color, with only a slight amber edge. The explosively intense bouquet of plums, smoky vanillin oak, and minerals was delightful. In the mouth, it was pure velvet, with sweet, expansive, ripe fruit, and a long, heady, alcoholic finish. Can this really be a 1973? The best wine made on the left bank of Bordeaux in 1973! Anticipated maturity: Now. Last tasted, 4/90.

1971— Quite disappointing, this decrepit, prematurely senile wine has a very brown
• color, hot, almost cooked flavors, and a lean, short finish. It is now past its
67 prime. Last tasted, 3/81.

1970—The 1970 Domaine de Chevalier exhibits a classic, sweet, curranty, tobacco-
•   scented nose, followed by round, expansive, gentle Burgundian-like flavors.
90   Silky smooth, with no obnoxious acidity or tannin poking through, this wine
        has been fully mature since 1980, but well-stored examples (such as this one)
        continue to offer gorgeously elegant, complex drinking. The color reveals
        considerable rust, but there are no signs of oxidation or fruit loss in the
        flavors. Anticipated maturity: Now–2003. Last tasted, 6/96.

1966—Still tenuously holding on to its fruity component, the 1966 is beginning to
•   show a great deal of brown in its color and tastes a trifle dried out. However,
84   it still retains an elegant, aged, savory richness and spiciness that gives it
        plenty of appeal. Anticipated maturity: Now–may be in decline. Last tasted,
        8/82.

1964—When I wrote about this wine in the first edition of this book, I gave it
•   an adequate review. Two bottles tasted since were significantly better. Both
90   exhibited dark ruby color, with some amber/orange at the rim. Both had
        bouquets that displayed a roasted, rich, intensely concentrated character
        indicative of a hot vintage. In the mouth, the wine was extremely full bodied
        and alcoholic for a Domaine de Chevalier, but rich, full, intense, and velvety.
        Clearly I underrated this wine. While not as superb as the 1964 La Mission-
        Haut-Brion, the 1964 Domaine de Chevalier is still a gorgeously fragrant,
        hedonistic wine with gobs of plump, fat flavors. Anticipated maturity: Now.
        Last tasted, 11/89.

1961—Not unlike the 1964, the 1961 has better color but a coarser texture and
•   enough signs to indicate that it was in its prime in the early seventies. The
86   complex, aged bouquet of roasted fruit and nuts is classy, but on the palate,
        the wine does not deliver the expected richness and depth that characterize
        this vintage. A bottle tasted in 1989 had more fruit yet still did not impress
        me to the extent I would have thought given the vintage. Nevertheless, this is
        a very good, rather than great, Domaine de Chevalier. Anticipated maturity:
        Now. Last tasted, 11/89.

ANCIENT VINTAGES

The two vintages I tasted of Domaine de Chevalier from the fifties both proved
to be excellent wines. The 1959 (rated 89 in 1988) was a fuller, richer, more
muscular and tannic wine than the 1961. It will easily last through the end
of the century. Fully mature and exceptionally seductive in a 1970 or 1978
sort of style was the gloriously fragrant, voluptuous, and hedonistic 1953
(rated 92 in 1989). Holding on to this wine would be pushing one's luck, so
owners should consume it immediately.

VINTAGES (white)

1996—Extremely high acidity and high wood make it doubtful as to whether this
•   wine will ever provide a great deal of pleasure or charm. Undoubtedly it will
78   last 20–30 years given the mouth-searing levels of acidity, but there is not

much flesh covering the bones. Anticipated maturity: 2005–2015. Last tasted, 11/97.

1995— This is a solidly made, tightly knit, high-strung dry white wine with plenty of
•   sulfur, wood, and acidity. The wine is slowly fleshing out, so it may ultimately
85   deserve a higher rating, but the shrill levels of tart acid and pronounced
         oakiness give cause for concern. Nevertheless, it is a medium-bodied, reason-
         ably well-made dry white Graves that should age effortlessly for 2 decades.
         Anticipated maturity: 2005–2015. Last tasted, 3/97.

1994— This could turn out to be the finest Domaine de Chevalier since the 1983 and
•   1985. Displaying less oak than normal, the big, honeyed, cherry, smoky, and
91+   melon scents in the nose are followed by a full-bodied, powerful, dense,
         highly concentrated wine that lingers on the palate for nearly 45 seconds.
         This should be one of the bigger, more concentrated and powerful Domaine
         de Chevaliers made in the last 20 years. Given the performance of past top
         vintages, expect this wine to close up for 10–15 years after bottling. It will
         age well for 25–30+ years. Last tasted, 3/97.

1993— Domaine de Chevalier's 1993 does not yet reveal the chewy, rich, fat, muscu-
•   lar character of the outstanding 1992. The unformed, citrusy 1993 is
89   backward and unevolved, with abundant quantities of crisp, tart fruit comple-
         mented by lavish quantities of toasty new oak. Although the wine is tightly knit,
         firm, and certainly very good, my instincts suggest it is not as rich and complete
         as the 1992. It will last for 15–20+ years. Last tasted, 11/94.

1992— The 1992 exhibits a tight but promising nose of rich, melony, honeyed fruit
•   complemented nicely by smoky new oak. Well structured and concentrated,
90   with layers of fruit and an inner core of mineral, steely fruit, this formidably
         endowed, backward wine will need 7–12 years to open; it should last 25 or
         more years. Last tasted, 1/94.

1991— The 1991 reveals excellent fruit, an intense, mineral, oaky fruitiness, medium
•   body, and tremendous length. The wine, which is already beginning to close
89   up, explodes on the back of the palate, so this is one white wine that will
         keep for several decades. Even in light vintages, Domaine de Chevalier's
         white wines can last for 15–20 years. Last tasted, 1/94.

1989— This wine does not have the concentration of the 1988, and given my high ex-
•   pectations, I am disappointed by the showings to date. There is plenty of intense
86   vanillin oakiness in the bouquet, as well as some faint scents of minerals, herbs,
         and under-ripe apricots. However, the wine is medium bodied, and lacks con-
         centration and depth. Anticipated maturity: Now. Last tasted, 4/91.

1988— The 1988 is a classic Domaine de Chevalier. It exhibits a superb precision
•   and has a perfumed, oaky, mineral-like quality, an austere palate, and an
90   underlying profound richness and exceptional length. It is not a joy to drink
         now, but it should blossom in 7–8 years and last for 15 or more years.
         Anticipated maturity: Now–2005. Last tasted, 4/91.

1987— 1987 is a terribly underrated vintage for white Graves. This wine has more
•   depth, ripeness, and complexity than either the 1989 or 1986, the two vin-
88   tages that most casual observers would think to be superior. Pale straw in

color, with a more evolved, honeyed, herb-, mineral-, and orange-scented bouquet, this medium-bodied, surprisingly soft, forward Domaine de Chevalier has excellent depth, moderate acidity, and an oaky, alcoholic finish. Anticipated maturity: Now–2003. Last tasted, 11/90.

1986— Pale straw in color, with a decidedly oaky, ungenerous bouquet, the 1986 is
•   steely, tightly knit, extremely austere, and difficult to appreciate or assess. If
85   it develops more concentration and charm, it could merit a higher score, but my notes have been consistent since I first tasted it from barrel. Anticipated maturity: Now–2000. Last tasted, 3/90.

1985— This should turn out to be an extraordinary vintage for Domaine de Chevalier.
•   By the standards of this white Graves, it is sumptuous. While more closed
93   now than when I tasted it from barrel, the wine still cannot hide an exceptional degree of ripeness and richness. Full bodied, with good acidity, this brilliantly rendered, honeyed, fig-, melon-, and mineral-scented and -flavored wine should provide extraordinary drinking if one has the patience to wait it out. Anticipated maturity: Now–2010. Last tasted, 12/90.

1983— Domaine de Chevalier made the best white wine of the appellation in this
•   vintage, as well as one of the great successes of the eighties. Impossibly
93   closed when I last tasted it, the 1983 still reveals that profound mineral, honeyed bouquet, rich, intense, mouth-filling flavors that are exceptionally well knit, and a long, explosively rich finish. Nevertheless, the wine has budged little since its bottling and gives every indication of being one of the longest-lived white Domaine de Chevaliers of the last several decades. Anticipated maturity: Now–2015. Last tasted, 1/91.

1982— This is a more meaty, fleshy, and obvious example of a white Domaine de
•   Chevalier. It lacks the structure and precision, as well as the great depth and
87   haunting complexity, of the 1983, but it offers plenty of toasty vanillin oak, a big, fat, fleshy texture, and loads of alcohol and wood in the finish. Anticipated maturity: Now–2003. Last tasted, 3/90.

1981— Once past a surprisingly strong scent of sulfur, the 1981 displays narrowly
•   constructed mineral, melon, and herblike flavors, medium body, high acidity,
82   and plenty of wood, but not the generosity or overall balance and complexity of a typical Domaine de Chevalier. Anticipated maturity: Now–2005. Last tasted, 3/88.

1979— This is an example of just how slowly the white Domaine de Chevalier
•   matures. Most purchasers, I am sure, have consumed this wine, but it is just
88   beginning to open up and blossom. The rich aromas of melons, herbs, and oak gently ascend from the glass. In the mouth, this medium-bodied wine has excellent richness, a persistence on the palate, and a long, crisp finish. Anticipated maturity: Now–2000. Last tasted, 3/89.

1976— Advanced in color for a Domaine de Chevalier, this vintage produced a
•   medium gold–colored wine, with a relatively direct, open-knit, honeyed nose,
88   a great deal of body and glycerin in the mouth, and a long, alcoholic, fat finish. I find this wine delicious but atypical for Domaine de Chevalier. Anticipated maturity: Now–2000. Last tasted, 12/90.

1975—I wish I knew this vintage better, but this wine tastes extremely subdued and
•　　surprisingly light, and it lacks generosity, complexity, and length. Have I
84　　caught it in an ungenerous, closed stage of development? Anticipated maturity: Now. Last tasted, 12/90.

1971—Having had this wine several times, I am now convinced that it is a mediocre
•　　effort from Domaine de Chevalier. Straightforward, almost generic scents of
73　　no great distinction are followed by a medium-bodied, compact, one-dimensional wine that tastes nearly sterile. Anticipated maturity: Now. Last tasted, 12/90.

1970—This is a spectacular vintage for the white wine of Domaine de Chevalier.
•　　Medium golden in color, the wine offers a huge, flamboyant bouquet of spices,
93　　honeyed fruit, beer nuts, and figs; in the mouth it is full bodied, rich, luscious, even opulent, with a dramatically long, heady finish. With all of its concentration and flamboyance, what makes this wine so special is its super-acidity, which gives it delineation and precision. Anticipated maturity: Now–2005. Last tasted, 12/90.

1966—A classy bouquet of minerals and herbs is immediately apparent. In the mouth,
•　　the wine is medium bodied and still fresh and lively, with excellent generosity
88　　and a delicate, elegant personality. This is a lighter but interesting and enthralling Domaine de Chevalier. Anticipated maturity: Now. Last tasted, 3/86.

1962—The spectacularly fresh yet huge bouquet of spring flowers, melons, herbs,
•　　and minerals is hard to beat. Full bodied, exceptionally rich, creamy textured,
93　　yet impeccably balanced, this splendidly ripe Domaine de Chevalier has reached full maturity but displays no signs of age in either its color or freshness of fruit. It is quite a tour de force in white wine making. Bravo! Anticipated maturity: Now–2000. Last tasted, 3/87.

COUHINS-LURTON　　　　　　　　　　　　　　　　VERY GOOD

Classification: Classified growth (for whites only)
Location of vineyards: Léognan
Owner: André Lurton
Address: 33850 Léognan
Mailing address: c/o Château Bonnet, 33420 Grézillac
Telephone: 33 5 57 25 58 58; telefax: 33 5 57 74 98 59
Visits: No visits

VINEYARDS (white)
Surface area: 13.6 acres
Average age of vines: 15–18 years
Blend: 100% Sauvignon Blanc
Density of plantation: 6,500 vines per hectare

GRAND VIN (white)
Brand name: Château Couhins-Lurton
Appellation: Pessac-Léognan

Upbringing: Fermentations occur in oak barrels, 50% of which are new. Wines remain on lees for 12 months with frequent stirrings. They are fined and filtered before bottling.

SECOND WINE
None produced.

Evaluation of present classification: The quality equivalent of a Cru Classé in the white Graves classification
Plateau of maturity: 3–8 years following the vintage

André Lurton, another member of the ubiquitous Lurton family, enthusiastically runs this small gem of a property. Made from 100% Sauvignon Blanc, fermented in new oak, and aged for nearly 10 months prior to bottling, this is a consistently superb white Graves of surprising complexity, richness, and length. I would not age it past 7–8 years, but that reflects my personal predilection for drinking these wines relatively young and fresh. The price of Couhins-Lurton has not yet caught up to the quality, and enthusiasts of white Graves should be seeking out this difficult to find but impeccably made wine.

VINTAGES (white)

1995—One of the better efforts in the 1995 vintage, Couhins-Lurton's wine offers a
• citrusy, lemony nose with herbs and smoky oak in the background. Medium
87 bodied, with crisp, tart acidity, this is a tightly knit offering with hints of creaminess and richness. This should turn out to be a very good, possibly excellent, Couhins-Lurton that will drink well for a decade. Last tasted, 3/97.

1994—The delicate 1994 exhibits the pure, rich aromatics usually possessed by this
• wine. Scents of licorice, smoke, melon, and figs are followed by a medium-
90 bodied wine with wonderful intensity, a great midpalate of ripe fruit, and an elegant, dry, crisp finish. Anticipated maturity: Now–2006. Last tasted, 3/97.

1993—It is a shame so little of this wine is produced, as it is one of my favorite dry
• white Graves. Made from 100% Sauvignon Blanc, it possesses an intensity
91 and richness that suggest there is Semillon in the blend, but such is not the case. The 1993 is a classic, textbook white Graves with wonderful mineral, smoky, intense, honeyed flavors, medium to full body, great purity and vibrancy, and wonderful focus in the long finish. It should drink well for at least a decade. Last tasted, 11/94.

FIEUZAL   EXCELLENT

Classification: Classified growth for reds only
Location of vineyards: Léognan
Owner: S.A. du Château Fieuzal
Address: 124, avenue de Mont de Marsan, 33850 Léognan

Mailing address: Same as above
Telephone: 33 5 56 64 77 86; telefax: 33 5 56 64 18 88
Visits: By appointment only
Contact: Call above telephone number

VINEYARDS (red)
Surface area: 93.9 acres
Average age of vines: 30 years
Blend: 60% Cabernet Sauvignon, 33% Merlot, 4.5% Cabernet Franc,
2.5% Petit Verdot
Density of plantation: 8,300 vines per hectare
Average yields (over the last 5 years): 45 hectoliters per hectare
Total average annual production: 225,000 bottles

GRAND VIN (red)
Brand name: Château de Fieuzal
Appellation: Pessac-Léognan
Mean annual production: 140,000–150,000 bottles
Upbringing: Fermentations last 3 weeks in temperature-controlled
stainless-steel vats (lined with plastic). Malolactics occur partly in barrels
(approximately 20% of the yield) and partly in vats. Wines are transferred
to barrels in December for 18 months aging (60% new oak). They are
fined with egg whites and lightly filtered.

SECOND WINE
Brand name: L'Abeille de Fieuzal
Average annual production: 75,000–80,000 bottles

VINEYARDS (white)
Surface area: 25 acres
Average age of vines: 25 years
Blend: 50% Semillon, 50% Sauvignon
Density of plantation: 8,300 vines per hectare
Average yields (over the last 5 years): 45 hectoliters per hectare
Total average annual production: 60,000 bottles

GRAND VIN (white)
Brand name: Château de Fieuzal
Appellation: Pessac-Léognan
Mean annual production: 40,000 bottles
Upbringing: Harvest is done by hand, with selective picking.
Fermentations occur in oak barrels, 80% of which are new, and wines
remain on lees for 12 months with regular stirring. They are fined and
lightly filtered.

SECOND WINE
Brand name: L'Abeille de Fieuzal
Average annual production: 20,000 bottles

Evaluation of present classification: Now the quality equivalent of a
Médoc fourth-growth; since 1985 the white wine has been stunning and is
now capable of rivaling the best of the appellation
Plateau of maturity: (red) 5–20 years following the vintage; (white) 4–10
years following the vintage

De Fieuzal has always been one of the more obscure Graves, which is surprising given the fact that it is a relatively old property and is well recognized by the inhabitants of the region. The cellars are located in the rolling countryside adjacent to D651 on the outskirts of Léognan in the direction of Saucats. De Fieuzal's obscurity appears to have ended abruptly during the mid-1980s, when the wines became noticeably richer and more complex. This is not to say that older vintages were not well made. Many of them were, but they certainly did not have the dazzling character that more recent years have possessed.

Much of the credit for de Fieuzal's rise in quality must go to the enthusiastic administrator, Gérard Gribelin, who took over the running of the property in 1974. In 1977 stainless-steel, temperature-controlled fermentation tanks were installed, and there has been an increasing tendency in the eighties to prolong the maceration period and use more new oak. The breakthrough for the white wine of de Fieuzal came in 1985, when the property made the first of what was to be a series of stunning white Graves. Gribelin recognizes that his now retired technical director and winemaker, Monsieur DuPouy, contributed greatly to the restoration of de Fieuzal's reputation. DuPouy was, by any standard of measurement, a perfectionist and displayed remarkable talent and flexibility in supervising the winemaking at de Fieuzal. Amazingly, the high quality has not been accompanied by soaring prices, as de Fieuzal represents one of the best quality/price ratios in the entire Graves region. In 1994 de Fieuzal was acquired by a French insurance company (Fructivie), and to their credit, Gérard Gribelin was retained as the estate's administrator.

VINTAGES (red)

1997—Tasted four times, except for one musty sample, the 1997 De Fieuzal performed exceptionally well. One of the more saturated purple-colored wines of
• the vintage, it possesses copious amounts of intense cassis fruit married with
87– tobacco, herb, and tar-like scents. Impressively pure, medium bodied, and
88 rich, with moderate tannin, and an opulent attack, this wine should offer early

appeal (2–4 years of cellaring will be beneficial); it will last for 12–15 years. Anticipated maturity: 2002–2014. Last tasted, 3/98.

1996—If this wine fleshes out in the mid-palate, it will deserve a higher rating. A
•   lean, elegant, dark ruby/purple–colored Fieuzal, it possesses attractive
86–   smoky, lead pencil, black currant, and mineral fruit in the nose and flavors,
87+   medium body, moderately high tannin, and a spicy, aggressive finish. Antici-
       pated maturity: 2006–2020. Last tasted, 3/98.

1995—This quintessentially elegant wine reveals a deep ruby/purple color, and an
•   attractive smoky, black currant, mineral, and floral-scented nose. There are
90   sweet, ripe, lush flavors, medium body, ripe tannin, and a velvety texture that
       borders on opulence. There is no heaviness to the wine. Moreover, neither the
       tannin, acidity, nor alcohol are intrusive. This seamless, extremely well made
       claret is a candidate for early drinking, yet it possesses excellent aging
       potential. Anticipated maturity: 2003–2020. Last tasted, 11/97.

1994—Before bottling, the 1994 de Fieuzal appeared to be as good as, if not better
•   than, the 1993, but two bottles tasted after bottling exhibited moldy, wet
?   cardboard–like noses that made judgment impossible. It is rare to get two
       corked bottles in a row. Last tasted, 1/97.

1993—This is a successful 1993 red Graves. A saturated, inky purple color is more
•   reminiscent of a great year than a so-so vintage such as 1993. In addition to
87+   the impressive color saturation, the wine offers a penetrating, tobacco leaf,
       black currant, licorice, and smoky fragrance. Medium bodied, with moderate
       tannin, this well-endowed, youthful wine is approachable, but it will benefit
       from another 1–3 years of aging. It should be an atypically long-lived 1993.
       Anticipated maturity: 1999–2015. Last tasted, 1/97.

1992—This deep ruby/purple–colored 1992 exhibits ripe, sweet fruit and fine depth.
•   The wine is medium bodied, with plenty of juicy black fruit flavors wrapped
86   in smoky oak. This stylish, tasty, elegant, and flavorful Graves will benefit
       from 2–3 years of cellaring and last for a decade. Last tasted, 11/94.

1991—Characteristic of the vintage, the 1991 is compressed and compact, but it
•   possesses an excellent dark ruby color, a monolithic, spicy, toasty, earthy
82   nose, fine depth and ripeness, and a one-dimensional personality. Drink it
       over the next decade. Last tasted, 1/94.

1990—This wine has improved immensely in the bottle, making my earlier notes
•   look particularly stingy. The color is a healthy dark ruby/purple. Aromatically
88   the wine has opened considerably, revealing plenty of cranberry, black cherry,
       and cassis fruit. There are also notes of lavish new oak, earth, and cedar in
       the moderately intense bouquet. Medium bodied, with sweet fruit, gobs of
       glycerin (a hallmark of many 1990s), and soft tannin, this wine has fleshed
       out considerably, with the tannin becoming better integrated. It is still a
       youthful, promising wine. Anticipated maturity: 2000–2012. Last tasted,
       8/97.

1989—De Fieuzal's 1989 exhibits a deep ruby/purple color with some lightening at
•   the edge. This lavishly oaked wine displays copious quantities of toasty new
87   oak as well as earth/herb–tinged red and black currant fruit in its moderately

intense bouquet. On the palate, the wine reveals medium body, low acidity, and elevated tannin in the finish. It is a more compact, leaner style of wine than its slightly sweeter, fleshier sibling, the 1990. Anticipated maturity: 1999–2010. Last tasted, 3/97.

1988—The 1988 de Fieuzal is an extracted, darkly colored wine with an excellent
 • nose of sweet curranty fruit, medium body, and a compact, very tannic (nearly
 86 astringent) finish. The wine has closed up since its bottling and appears to need considerable time in the bottle. This wine seems to have been made in a style that will never shed its tannin, and it may always have a certain astringency and austerity. It is capable of lasting another 2 decades, but it will always remain an angular style of de Fieuzal. Anticipated maturity: Now– 2012. Last tasted, 1/97.

1987—Fieuzal's 1987 is surprisingly robust, richly fruity, fuller bodied, and more
 • muscular than the other top 1987s. There is low acidity, some soft tannins,
 86 and surprising alcohol and power in the finish. Although the wine is drink-able, it does not seem to have changed much from when I tasted it from cask. Anticipated maturity: Now–2000. Last tasted, 3/90.

1986—This vintage is decidedly mixed in the southern part of the Pessac-Léognan
 • appellation, but de Fieuzal has turned in a fine effort. The wine still retains a
 87 youthful, deep ruby/purple color. The nose is more backward than recent de Fieuzal vintages, displaying earth, spice, new oak, and moderately sweet black currant and cranberry fruit. A medium-bodied wine with high tan-nin, this de Fieuzal has evolved at a glacial pace and should have a long life. I expected it to be fully mature by now, but it appears to need another 4–5 years of cellaring. Anticipated maturity: 2001–2016. Last tasted, 1/97.

1985—The 1985 is just beginning to enter its plateau of maturity. The wine possesses
 • a deep ruby color, with noticeable lightening at the edge. A sweet nose of
 87 jammy fruit, herbs, smoke, and *pain grillé* is followed by an open-knit, plump, accessible wine with moderate weight, good richness, and a sweet finish with light tannin remaining. Anticipated maturity: Now–2006. Last tasted, 1/97.

1984—Surprisingly dark ruby in color, the 1984 de Fieuzal is a chunky, solidly
 • constructed wine with good depth and length. In need of 2–3 years of cel-
 85 laring, it reveals a strong, well-structured, Cabernet-dominated personality. It is an unqualified success for the vintage. Anticipated maturity: Now–2000. Last tasted, 3/89.

1983—The elegant, spicy, richly fruity nose is followed by a wine with good, firm
 • tannins. This medium-bodied 1983 has excellent concentration and good
 86 structure and length. De Fieuzal is a well-made, polished, and refined wine that has taken on weight and fat in the last 3–4 years. Anticipated maturity: Now–2001. Last tasted, 3/89.

1982—This has always been an attractive as well as deceptively forward wine that is
 • dark ruby, with a rich, chocolate, berry-like aroma, a prominent oakiness,
 86 and a toasty, smoky quality. For a de Fieuzal, this is a muscular, more intense

style than is usual. The 1982 should age well for at least a decade. It is reminiscent of the 1989 but less concentrated. Anticipated maturity: Now. Last tasted, 1/89.

1981—The 1981 has a pleasant herbaceous, berrylike bouquet, good acidity, medium
•   weight, and moderate tannin. It is a polite, restrained, compact style of wine.
80   Anticipated maturity: Now. Last tasted, 1/89.

1978—Deep ruby, with a slightly amber edge, de Fieuzal's 1978 has a surprisingly
•   unevolved, even reticent bouquet, some attractive ripe, smoky fruit, medium
82   body, good depth and length, but also plenty of tannin that has yet to melt
      away. Will the wine's fruit fade before the tannins fall off? Anticipated maturity: Now–2000. Last tasted, 1/89.

1975—This wine has begun to dry out, with more of the unsavory characteristics of
•   the 1975 vintage well displayed. The color is a dark garnet, with some amber/
78   orange at the edge. The nose offers up more spice and earth than fruit. The
      ferocious level of tannin, a downfall of many 1975s, runs unchecked across
      the palate. The wine possesses medium body and some concentration, but the
      brutal sharpness of the tannin makes for an unpleasant tasting experience.
      Anticipated maturity: Now–2005. Last tasted, 1/97.

1970—Several bottles tasted since the last edition of this book have shown the 1970
•   to be the finest de Fieuzal produced during the seventies. The wine possesses
87   a garnet color, with noticeable rust at the edge. The provocative, open-knit
      nose of tobacco smoke, red currants, and herbs is followed by a medium-
      bodied, round wine with savory flavors. There are no hard edges, bitterness,
      excessive dryness, or austerity in the wine's moderately long finish. Antici-
      pated maturity: Now–2002. Last tasted, 1/97.

VINTAGES (white)

1996—One of the stronger efforts from the 1996 vintage, de Fieuzal's dry white
•   exhibits a smoky, lavishly wooded nose with attractive sweet fruit. The wine
88   possesses high acidity, but also the requisite richness and creaminess in its
      texture to hold up to the wine's structure. It should close down and need 5–7
      years of cellaring. Although leaner and less opulent than the top vintages of
      de Fieuzal, it is one of the vintage's successes. Anticipated maturity: 2003–
      2012. Last tasted, 3/97.

1995—A highly successful effort from this vintage, which produced a number of
•   deceptively thin, light wines from the Pessac-Léognan and Graves regions, de
88   Fieuzal's medium-bodied 1995 displays an herb-tinged, citrusy, smoky nose,
      woody, medium-bodied flavors with good concentration, and fat and sweetness
      from a good glycerin level in the finish. Anticipated maturity: 2000–2010.
      Last tasted, 3/97.

1994—A terrific example from this estate that usually makes one of the best white
•   wines of Graves, with a citrusy, honeyed, smoky nose that soars from the
92   glass. Medium to full bodied, with exquisite concentration, superb focus, and
      a fresh, long, rich, structured finish, this fabulous de Fieuzal should age well
      for 15+ years. Last tasted, 3/97.

1993—The rich, powerful 1993 offers authoritative flavors presented in a full-bodied
•   style that is crammed with honeyed, waxy, melony fruit, and spicy new oak.
92   The wine possesses a chewy, thick texture and a long, crisp finish. De Fieuzal's white wines are made of 50% Semillon and 50% Sauvignon Blanc and
are vinified and aged in 100% new oak. This offering should last for at least
10–15 years. Last tasted, 1/97.

1992—The 1992 exhibits a big, creamy, rich nose of smoky new oak and ripe fruit,
•   medium to full body, excellent concentration, and a chewy finish. While it is
91   not as well delineated as some vintages, it offers a lusty mouthful of de
Fieuzal. Drink it over the next 7–8 years. Last tasted, 1/94.

1991—The 1991 has turned out well in what was a tough year. Although understated,
•   it possesses a sense of elegance, crisp, lemony/honeyed flavors, light to me-
86   dium body, toasty new oak, and a tasty, dry finish. Drink it over the next 5–6
years. Last tasted, 1/94.

1989—Like many 1989 white Graves, de Fieuzal does not quite have the grip
•   and delineation one expects because of the vintage's low acidity. Never-
90   theless, this has still turned out to be one of the most successful wines
of the vintage. It is a rich, honeyed, smoky-scented wine with wonderfully
ripe apple and melon flavors. Anticipated maturity: Now–2000. Last tasted,
3/93.

1988—This beautiful example of white Graves displays a full-intensity bouquet of
•   honey, flowers, and smoky new oak. In the mouth, it has an opulence and
92   richness that can only be the result of low yields and/or old vines. This is a
wonderfully precise, rich, classic white Graves. Anticipated maturity: Now–
2005. Last tasted, 1/96.

1987—Light gold, with a restrained yet provocative bouquet of figs, melons, smoky
•   new oak, and honey, in the mouth, this wine is less concentrated and full
88   when compared with the 1988, but delicate, with good acidity, complexity,
and an entirely satisfying finish. Anticipated maturity: Now. Last tasted,
4/91.

1986—I have never been a great admirer of the 1986 white Graves, and this effort
•   from de Fieuzal is more straightforward than usual, without the underlying
85   complexity and precision to its flavors. It is full but comes across as chunky
and foursquare. The wine remains slightly formless. Anticipated maturity:
Now. Last tasted, 4/91.

1985—To date, this is my favorite vintage of white de Fieuzal. It also marks the
•   breakthrough when de Fieuzal began making white wines that rivaled the
93   best of the region. Still young in color, the bouquet has that wonderfully
intense, honeyed, fig-, melon-, orange-, herb-, and oaky-scented nose. Full
bodied, rich, with substantial extract and length, this admirably endowed,
beautifully balanced white Graves is quite sensational. Anticipated maturity:
Now–2005. Last tasted, 7/97.

LA GARDE VERY GOOD

Classification: None
Location of vineyards: Martillac
Owner: Dourthe Frères (C.V.B.G.)
Address: 33650 Martillac
Mailing address: c/o Dourthe Frères, B.P. 49, 35, rue de Bordeaux, 33290 Parempuyre
Telephone: 33 5 56 35 53 00; telefax: 33 5 56 35 53 29
Visits: By appointment only
Contact: Above telephone number

VINEYARDS (red)
Surface area: 111 acres
Average age of vines: 20 years for the Cabernet Sauvignon and 23 for the Merlot
Blend: 65% Cabernet Sauvignon, 35% Merlot
Density of plantation: 6,500 vines per hectare
Average yields (over the last 5 years): 55 hectoliters per hectare
Total average annual production: 250,000 bottles

GRAND VIN (red)
Brand name: Château La Garde
Appellation: Pessac-Léognan
Mean annual production: 150,000 bottles
Upbringing: Harvest is done manually. Fermentations are carried out in temperature-controlled vats. Malolactics occur partly in vats and partly in barrels. Wines are transferred to oak barrels, 65% of which are new, for 15–20 months aging depending upon the vintage. They are fined with egg whites and are not filtered.

SECOND WINE
Brand name: La Chartreuse du Château La Garde
Average annual production: 100,000 bottles

VINEYARDS (white)
Surface area: 13.6 acres
Average age of vines: 15 years
Blend: 100% Sauvignon
Density of plantation: 6,500 vines per hectare
Average yields (over the last 5 years): 34 hectoliters per hectare
Total average annual production: 25,000 bottles

GRAND VIN (white)
Brand name: Château La Garde
Appellation: Pessac-Léognan

Mean annual production: 25,000 bottles
Upbringing: Harvest is done by hand. Selective picking. Cold settling of
the musts. Alcoholic fermentations and malolactics occur in oak barrels
renewed by a third at each vintage. Wines are kept on lees for 10–12
months and regularly stirred. They are fined but not filtered.

SECOND WINE
None produced.

Evaluation of present classification: The quality equivalent of a Médoc
Cru Bourgeois
Plateau of maturity: (red) 2–6 years following the vintage; (white) 2–4
years following the vintage

Since the huge *négociant* Dourthe became the new owner in 1990, this estate
has begun to turn out excellent wines, both white and red, which merit
considerable interest. They also represent excellent value.

VINTAGES (red)

1995—The 1995 reveals a sweet, open-knit, attractive, weedy, black currant–scented
• nose backed up by smoky, vanillin-scented new oak. Juicy, succulent, tasty,
88 and mouth-filling, this is an elegant red Graves for drinking over the next 7–
8 years. These are very fine wines that consumers have yet to discover. Last
tasted, 11/97.

1994—This property continues to make fine wines that deserve greater recognition
• in the marketplace. The 1994 is a textbook red Graves, exhibiting plenty of
88 smoky, tobacco, and sweet curranty fruit, medium to full body, a wonderful
sweet, round midpalate, and a lush texture. This delicious, pure, rich wine
should drink well for 7–8 years. Last tasted, 3/96.

1993—The 1993 exhibits well-integrated new oak, a moderately intense, pure nose
• of ripe cassis, a medium-bodied, elegant personality, and authoritative flavors.
87 The wine's tannin is neither aggressive nor astringent. This offering should
be drinkable when released and last for a decade. Last tasted, 11/94.

HAUT-BAILLY   EXCELLENT

Classification: Classified growth for reds only
Location of vineyards: Léognan
Owner: Robert G. Wilmers
Address: Route de Cadaujac, 33850 Léognan
Telephone: 33 5 56 64 75 11; telefax: 33 5 56 64 53 60
Visits: By appointment only
Contact: Jean Sanders, telephone 5 56 63 19 54, telefax 5 56 27 16 02;
or Serge Charitte at above telephone number

VINEYARDS (red)
Surface area: 69.2 acres
Average age of vines: More than 35 years
Blend: 65% Cabernet Sauvignon, 25% Merlot, 10% Cabernet Franc
Density of plantation: 10,000 vines per hectare
Average yields (over the last 5 years): 50 hectoliters per hectare
Total average annual production: 180,000 bottles

GRAND VIN (red)
Brand name: Château Haut-Bailly
Appellation: Pessac-Léognan
Mean annual production: 120,000 bottles
Upbringing: Fermentations usually last 3 weeks. Wines are transferred to oak casks (55% of the yield goes into new oak, the rest into older casks) for 12–14 months aging. Wines are neither fined nor filtered before bottling.

SECOND WINE
Brand name: La Parde de Haut-Bailly
Average annual production: 60,000 bottles (this figure varies with the vintage)

Evaluation of present classification: The quality equivalent of a Médoc third-growth
Plateau of maturity: 5–20 years following the vintage

By Graves standards, Haut-Bailly is a relative newcomer. The history, however, is not uninteresting. A Monsieur Bellot des Minières, who was the second owner of Haut-Bailly in 1872, apparently believed that the wine was greatly improved by the addition of copious quantities of cognac, which was left in the barrels after they were rinsed with this spirit. Today one hears rumors of Burgundy producers who fortify weaker vintages with *eau-de-vie* or brandy, but Monsieur Bellot de Minières was proud of his wine's "extra" dimension.

The Sanders family became the proprietors in 1955. According to the family, Daniel Sanders—a wine enthusiast from Belgium—was so astounded by the 1945 Haut-Bailly that after some investigation, he decided to buy the property. His son, Jean, who lives at the nearby estate of Château Courbon (which produces a pleasant, dry white Graves), has managed the property since his father's death. The property was sold to Robert G. Wilmers in July 1998.

Since the early sixties Haut-Bailly has had an inconsistent track record for quality. The 1961 was fabulous, as was the delicious 1964, but it was not until 1979 that the quality began to bounce back after a prolonged period of mediocrity. The decision to relegate as much as 30% of the crop to a second wine, the increase of new oak to 55%, and a conscious decision to harvest later in order to obtain riper grapes have all resulted in increasingly better wines for Haut-Bailly during the eighties.

When young, this is not the easiest wine to evaluate. I am not sure why, but it often comes across as a bit skinny and light yet seems to take on weight and depth in the bottle. When I asked Jean Sanders about this, he said he was not the least bit interested in making a wine to impress writers, particularly before it is bottled. He believes the extremely old age of his vineyard and his traditional winemaking style with absolutely no filtration (rare in modern-day Bordeaux) result in a wine that requires some time to reveal all of its charm and character. Haut-Bailly will never have the size or power of its nearby neighbor de Fieuzal, but it does exhibit exceptional elegance in the top vintages.

VINTAGES

1997—One of Bordeaux's most delicate, elegant, graceful wines, Haut-Bailly's 1997
• displays a deep ruby color, and already evolved sweet, spicy, red currant,
86– and tobacco aromas. The wine is medium bodied, subtle, richly fruity, and
87 harmonious. This soft, forward Haut-Bailly will be at its best between 2000–
2010. Last tasted, 3/98.

1996—More tannic, structured, muscular, and less charming than Haut-Bailly's
• 1995, the 1996 reveals intense red currant/cherry fruit, smoke, earth, and a
87– notion of truffles in the nose, intense fruit, light to medium body, moderate
88+ tannin, and a super-elegant style. While it is not as expressive as its older
sibling, the 1995, it is a well-made wine. Anticipated maturity: 2003–2018.
Last tasted, 3/98.

1995—A beauty, this deep ruby–colored wine offers a classic, smoky, cherry, red
• and black currant–scented nose, sweet, lush, forward fruit, medium body,
90 true delicacy and elegance (as opposed to thinness and dilution), perfect
balance, and a lovely, long, supple, velvety-textured finish. This is a ballerina
of a claret, with beautiful aromatics, lovely flavors, and impeccable equilibrium. Anticipated maturity: 2000–2018. Last tasted, 11/97.

1994—One of the finest 1994s from the Pessac-Léognan appellation, Haut Bailly's
• 1994 possesses a dark ruby color with purple hues. The sweet, black currant,
88 earthy, and mineral nose and ripe, medium-bodied, fleshy flavors represent
the quintessentially elegant style of red Graves. The wine is rich yet ethereal
in the mouth. This charming wine exhibits no hard edges (no small achievement in the 1994 vintage), as well as beautifully integrated acidity and new
oak. Anticipated maturity: Now–2005. Last tasted, 1/97.

1993—Haut-Bailly's dark ruby–colored 1993 offers a surprisingly intense, sexy,
• sweet, spicy, berry-scented nose. The wine exhibits a lightly tannic edge, but
87 this medium-bodied, ripe, excellent 1993 possesses charm, ripeness, richness, and a pure, well-balanced mouth-feel. Always a stylish wine, Haut-

Bailly should improve for 1–3 years and last through the first decade of the next century. This wine can be purchased for a reasonable price. Last tasted, 1/97.

1992—This estate has been coming on strong of late, with wines of undeniable
• 　finesse that are produced in an uncompromising fashion. The 1992 Haut-
86　Bailly displays a penetrating, elegant, cherry, smoky nose, ripe, round, gener-
　　ous, plump, fruity flavors (suggesting a high percentage of Merlot), and a soft,
　　velvety-textured, graceful finish. Haut-Bailly's classic elegance, combined
　　with admirable ripeness, flavor extraction, and depth, are well displayed. The
　　1992 should drink well for 7–10 years. An impressive 1992! Last tasted,
　　11/94.

1990—The 1990 Haut-Bailly, which I have always preferred slightly to the 1989,
• 　was once again the stronger vintage. It displays a richer, more saturated dark
92　ruby color, followed by a textbook bouquet of smoky tobacco, blackberry, and
　　cassis. Ripe, supple textured, and generous, with no hard edges, this is a
　　stylish, well-crafted wine with all the component parts in balance. Drink this
　　medium-bodied effort over the next 15 years. Last tasted, 11/96.

1989—The 1989 is a ripe, sweet, supple wine with a deep ruby color and an
• 　attractive nose of herbs, sweet berry fruit, and smoky tobacco. This soft,
89　low-acid wine is ready to drink now and should continue to evolve gracefully,
　　offering elegant, smooth as silk drinking for another 12+ years. Last tasted,
　　11/96.

1988—The 1988 is full and rich, with that profound, mineral, spicy, sweet oaky,
• 　currany aroma, gentle yet full-bodied, creamy-textured flavors, and a long,
89　smooth, marvelous finish. This wine may well turn out to be outstanding with
　　another 3–4 years in the bottle. Anticipated maturity: Now–2003. Last tasted,
　　1/93.

1986—Considering the strong, tannic personality of the vintage, Haut Bailly's 1986
• 　is a soft wine that can be drunk at a very early age. The full-intensity bou-
85　quet of sweet, smoky oak and ripe, plummy fruit is very attractive. On
　　the palate, this medium-bodied wine is long, rich in fruit, and supple, and
　　finishes surprisingly smoothly. Anticipated maturity: Now–2005. Last tasted,
　　1/97.

1985—There is not a great deal of depth to this Haut Bailly. Nevertheless, it offers
• 　charm, finesse, and a sweet black berry/currany fruitiness. Some of the new
86　oak and smokiness that were present when the wine was young has dissipated
　　to reveal a slight herbaceousness behind the new oak. The wine is medium
　　bodied, with soft tannin and some flesh on the attack that quickly narrows out
　　to a lighter-style, supple yet unexciting wine. Anticipated maturity: Now–
　　2002. Last tasted, 1/97.

1983—A typical Haut-Bailly, the 1983 is dark ruby in color, with a rich, voluptuous,
• 　ripe, black currant bouquet and some attractive vanillin oaky aromas. On the
87　palate, the wine is forward, with lush, silky, ripe, round tannins evident.
　　Medium bodied, with a Pomerol-like, silky, fat texture, this wine is already
　　fully mature. Anticipated maturity: Now. Last tasted, 1/91.

1982—I have always referred to this wine as the vintage's most frightfully inconsis-
• tent performer. In fact, recent bottles have been barely mediocre. The wine
? has lost much of its color, displaying a washed-out, rusty color and thin,
astringent, tannic flavors with no real fat, charm, or intensity. I have had some
delicious bottles, but none of them have been from recent tastings. I am
giving up on it. Last tasted, 9/95.

1981—The 1981 Haut-Bailly is neither profound nor intensely concentrated, but
• perfumed, elegant, spicy, soft, fruity, and remarkably easy to drink. It does
84 not have the punch and depth of the 1982, 1983, or 1979 but is agreeable
and pleasant in a lighter style. Anticipated maturity: Now. Last tasted, 12/87.

1979—Consistently one of the most delicious wines of this somewhat overlooked
• vintage, the 1979 Haut-Bailly has excellent deep ruby color, a rich, moder-
87 ately intense, smoky, oaky, ripe fruit bouquet, soft, silky, fat, plump, fruity
flavors, light tannins, and a velvety finish. It is harmonious and lovely. Anticipated maturity: Now. Last tasted, 3/88.

1978—For whatever reason, the now mature 1978, while fruity, quite charming, and
• soft, never quite had the depth and dimension of the 1979. Now taking on
81 some amber/orange color, this wine has an herbaceous, oaky fragrance, soft,
loosely knit flavors, and a smooth finish. Anticipated maturity: Now. Last
tasted, 1/91.

1976—Haut-Bailly is not a success in 1976. The intense heat prior to the harvest
• caused the grapes to become overripe. The wine is now mature, even old
62 looking, with a loosely knit structure, very low acidity, and diluted flavors.
Last tasted, 9/79.

1975—I have consistently rated this wine from the low 60s to the low 70s, so this
• was a relatively strong showing for this vegetal, thin, tannic wine. The nose
76 has opened to reveal some attractive weedy, curranty aromas, but there is not
much fruit, and the tannin still dominates this lightweight claret. It has no
future. Last tasted, 12/95.

1973—This wine has totally collapsed, exhibiting washed-out, vegetal, thin aromas,
• shallow, sweet, light flavors, and no grip, concentration, or length. It is educa-
55 tional in that it is a Bordeaux in complete decline. Last tasted, 9/88.

1971—Charming, but a little light and flabby, the 1971 Haut-Bailly is now in decline,
• taking on an even deeper and pronounced brownish cast. The velvety, soft,
75 fruity flavors are likable but fade quickly in the glass. Anticipated maturity:
Now—probably in serious decline. Last tasted, 12/83.

1970—In a 1970 claret tasting held several years ago, Haut-Bailly performed well,
• indicating that this is probably the best vintage for the château between 1964
87 and 1979. It still has that in-your-face, up-front, smoky, sweet, herbaceous
fruit, medium body, soft, velvety tannins, and a long, smooth, alcoholic finish.
Anticipated maturity: Now. Last tasted, 10/88.

1966—Fully mature, quite fruity, yet a little more reserved and sterner than the
• richer, more opulent 1970, the 1966 reveals some browning at the edge, good
85 concentration, earthy, fruity flavors, and a soft, round finish. Anticipated
maturity: Now—may be in decline. Last tasted, 4/82.

1964—I had the good fortune to taste this wine in Bordeaux and thought it to be
• excellent, nearly outstanding. The ripe, roasted bouquet of caramel, tobacco,
88 smoke, and black fruits was close to sensational. In the mouth, this plump,
generously endowed, velvety-textured Haut-Bailly probably has been fully
mature for at least a decade but exhibits no signs of losing fruit. It is heady,
soft, and totally seductive. Anticipated maturity: Now. Last tasted, 3/90.

1961—This wine is splendid, undoubtedly the finest Haut-Bailly I have ever tasted.
• It is even better than when I first tasted it nearly 6 years ago. The huge
93 bouquet of earthy, smoky tobacco and ripe berry fruit soars from the glass.
The opulent, nearly unctuous flavors are awesomely concentrated, thick, rich,
and powerful. There is not a bit of astringency and harshness left, but, rather,
relatively high alcohol and that splendidly intense, long, explosively rich
finish. How long will the 1961 last? I thought it would be in decline by now,
but this wine has the potential to keep for another decade or more. Anticipated maturity: Now–2001. Last tasted, 3/90.

ANCIENT VINTAGES

I have had some superb examples of the 1928 Haut-Bailly. For example, a
bottle drunk in December 1995 (rated 90) was in terrific shape. It exhibited
some amber/orange notes at the edge, but plenty of sweet, cedary, tobacco/
cigar box–like notes and plummy fruit presented in a velvety-textured, silky
format. It is a stylish and seductive wine without excessive tannin (unlike
many 1928s). On the dark side, a bottle of 1900 Haut-Bailly tasted in Paris
in March 1996 was, in my opinion, a total fake. The wine tasted like a grapey
young Spanish wine with lavish, even excessive, quantities of new oak and
a shockingly dark ruby/purple color. The bottle appeared authentic, but
the wine was clearly too simple, grapey, and one-dimensional to be from
1900.

HAUT-BRION   OUTSTANDING

Classification: First-growth in 1855
Location of vineyards: Pessac
Owner: Domaine de Clarence Dillon S.A.
Address: 33600 Pessac
Mailing address: B.P. 24, 33604 Pessac Cedex
Telephone: 33 5 56 00 29 30; telefax: 33 5 56 98 75 14
Visits: By appointment only
Contact: Carla Kuhn

VINEYARDS (red)
Surface area: 106.7 acres
Average age of vines: 36 years
Blend: 45% Cabernet Sauvignon, 37% Merlot, 18% Cabernet Franc

Density of plantation: 8,000 vines per hectare
Total average annual production: 18,000–22,000 cases

GRAND VIN (red)
Brand name: Château Haut-Brion
Appellation: Pessac-Léognan
Mean annual production: 14,000–18,000 cases
Upbringing: Harvest is done manually. Fermentations occur in temperature-controlled stainless-steel vats of 225 hectoliters. A computer system programs pumping-overs and temperature regulations according to the temperature of the must. Mean temperature is 30 degrees centigrade. Wines spend 22 months in new oak barrels and are fined with fresh egg whites.

SECOND WINE
Brand name: Bahans-Haut-Brion
Average annual production: 4,000 cases

VINEYARDS (white)
Surface area: 6.7 acres
Average age of vines: 27 years
Blend: 63% Semillon, 37% Sauvignon
Density of plantation: 8,000 vines per hectare
Total average annual production: 800 cases

GRAND VIN (white)
Brand name: Château Haut-Brion Blanc
Appellation: Pessac-Léognan
Mean annual production: 800 cases
Upbringing: Fermentations occur in 100% new oak barrels. Wines remain on lees for 13–16 months prior to bottling. They are fined with egg whites.

SECOND WINE
Brand name: Les Plantiers du Haut-Brion

Evaluation of present classification: Should be maintained
Plateau of maturity: (red) 6–35 years following the vintage; (white) 5–25 years following the vintage

Located in the bustling commercial suburb of Pessac, Haut-Brion is the only first-growth to be American owned. The Dillon family purchased Haut-Brion in 1935 in a very poor condition and invested considerable sums of money in the vineyards and wine cellars. This lovely property is now one of the show-piece estates of Graves.

The winemaking at Haut-Brion is managed by the articulate and handsome Jean Delmas (one of the wine world's most gifted administrators), who fervently believes in a hot, short fermentation. As Bordeaux wines go, Haut-Brion is kept a long time (up to 30 months) in new oak barrels. Along with Clinet in Pomerol, it is among the last châteaux to bottle its wine.

The style of wine at Haut-Brion has changed over the years. The magnificently rich, earthy, almost sweet wines of the fifties and early sixties gave way in the period 1966–1974 to a lighter, leaner, easygoing, somewhat simplistic style of claret that lacked the richness and depth one expects from a first-growth. Whether this was intentional or just a period in which Haut-Brion was in a bit of a slump remains a question in search of an answer. The staff at Haut-Brion is quick-tempered and sensitive about such a charge. Starting with the 1975 vintage, the wines have again taken on more of the customary earthy richness and concentration that existed prior to the 1966–1974 era. Haut-Brion today is undoubtedly making wine that merits its first-growth status. In fact, the wines from 1978 onward have consistently proven to be among the finest wines produced in the region, as well as a personal favorite.

Coincidence or not, the quality of Haut-Brion began to rebound from the 1966–1974 era when Douglas Dillon's daughter, Joan, became president of the company in 1975. After the death of her first husband, Prince Charles of Luxembourg, she married the duc de Mouchy in 1978. It was at this same time that the quantity of the crop relegated to Bahans-Haut-Brion was increased, a practice that has irrefutably improved the quality of Haut-Brion. Moreover, it appears that Jean Delmas has been given total responsibility for running the estate, and as almost everyone in Bordeaux will acknowledge, he is one of the most talented and knowledgeable winemakers/administrators in France. His extraordinary state-of-the-art research with clonal selections is unsurpassed in France. With the advent of the super-abundant crops during the decade of the eighties, Delmas began, much like his counterpart in Pomerol, Christian Moueix of Château Pétrus, to crop-thin by cutting off grape bunches. This has no doubt accounted for the even greater concentration, as well as the extraordinary quality, of the 1989, which at this early stage appears to be the most compelling Haut-Brion made since the 1959 and 1961.

It is interesting to note that in blind tastings Haut-Brion often comes across as the most forward and lightest of all the first-growths. In truth, the wine is not light, but just different, particularly when tasted alongside the oaky, fleshy, more tannic wines of the Médoc and the softer, Merlot-dominated wines from the right bank. Despite the precociousness, it has the ability to age for 30 or more years in top vintages, giving it a broader window of drinkability than any other first-growth.

Accompanying the increased level of quality in Haut-Brion since 1978 has been the increased quality of the second label, Bahans-Haut-Brion. This is now one of the best second wines of Bordeaux, surpassed in certain vintages only by the renowned second wine of Château Latour, Les Forts de Latour.

The white wine made at Haut-Brion continues to be rated the finest of the Graves region. However, at the request of the proprietors it has never been classified because the production is so tiny. Nevertheless, under Jean Delmas, who has sought to make a white Graves with the opulent texture of a prodigious Montrachet, the white wine has gone from strength to strength. Recent vintages such as 1994, 1989, and 1985 have been astonishing.

On a personal note, I should also add that after more than 30 years of intensely tasting as many Bordeaux wines as I can, the only general change I have noticed in my taste has been a greater and greater affection for Haut-Brion. The smoky, mineral, cigar box, sweet black currant character of this wine has increasingly appealed to me as I have gotten older and, as Jean Delmas would undoubtedly state, wiser as well.

VINTAGES

1997—A severe selection was employed for the *grand vin* at Haut-Brion, with only
•   45% of the production making it into the final blend. Only 35% of the
91–   remaining production went into the second wine. Bahans-Haut-Brion. Haut-
93   Brion's 1997 is an unqualified success, and among the finest of the first-
growths. The color is an opaque ruby/purple. The evolved nose offers up aromas of tar, tobacco, and sweet jammy plum and black currant fruit. Medium bodied, with exceptional harmony, low acidity, and sweet tannin, it boasts a surprisingly long, seductive, pure finish. As the wine sat in the glass, more chocolate, tobacco, and black fruits emerged. It is hard to compare this Haut-Brion with other vintages. Obviously it is not as powerful, packed, and stacked as the 1995 or 1996, yet the 1997 is a silky-textured, luscious Haut-Brion that will drink well when released, and will last for two decades. Last tasted, 3/98.

1996—Haut-Brion utilized only 60% of its production in the 1996 final blend (50%
•   Merlot, 39% Cabernet Sauvignon, 11% Cabernet Franc). While it is undoubt-
95–   edly true that the appellations of Pessac-Léognan and Graves were less suc-
96+   cessful in 1996 than the Médoc, the wines produced under the administration of Jean Delmas (i.e., Haut-Brion, La Mission-Haut-Brion, and La Tour-Haut-Brion) are brilliant in the 1996 vintage, continuing a trend that has made Haut-Brion one of the most consistent first-growths in Bordeaux (consider the superlative performances in such difficult vintages as 1993, 1992, and 1987). The 1996 Haut-Brion has put on weight, and was even sweeter and more fragrant in November than it was earlier in the year. The wine exhibits a dark ruby color with purple nuances. Haut-Brion's signature is most frequently its glorious perfume of tobacco, black fruits, smoke, and dried herbs, combined with sweet, supple fruit, all crammed into a concentrated wine that never has the weight or tannic power of a Médoc, or the thick unctuousness of a top

right bank wine. As I have frequently written, the one significant change to my palate over the last twenty years has been the fact that while I have always admired Haut-Brion, now I am addicted to its perfume and complexity. It is never the biggest of the first-growths, but it is usually among the most compelling wines of this elite group, with the most profound set of aromatics of any of its peers. That being said, the 1996 should turn out to be an exquisite wine, perhaps slightly more structured and backward than the superb 1995, but very rich, with gobs of smoky, cherry, tobacco-tinged fruit, medium body, exceptional purity and equilibrium, and a long, moderately tannic finish. The tannins taste extremely sweet. Anticipated maturity: 2004–2030. Last tasted, 3/98.

1995—This wine has been brilliant on every occasion I have tasted it. More accessi-
 •   ble and forward than the 1996, it possesses a saturated ruby/purple color, as
96   well as a beautiful, knockout set of aromatics, consisting of black fruits, vanillin, spice, and wood-fire smoke. Multidimensional and rich, with layers of ripe fruit, and beautifully integrated tannin and acidity, this medium- to full-bodied wine is a graceful, seamless, exceptional Haut-Brion that should drink surprisingly well young. Anticipated maturity: 2000–2030. Last tasted, 11/97.

1994—In contrast with the 1993's penetrating, up-front aromas, the 1994 is closed
 •   aromatically. With coaxing, some trufflelike, sweet, black fruit aromas, as
93   well as those of mineral/stones, come forward. This spicy, full-bodied, powerful wine is a more masculine, structured effort than the 1993, with a potentially more complex, richer character. It is superbly crafted, beautifully balanced, and as pure as a wine can be. The integration of new oak, acidity, and tannin is commendable. Anticipated maturity: 2002–2025. Last tasted, 4/98.

1993—One of the great wines of the vintage, Haut-Brion's 1993 possesses a dark
 •   garnet/plum/purple color, an expressive, fragrant, sweet, berry, black currant,
92   mineral, lead pencil, and earth-scented nose, and medium- to full-bodied, concentrated flavors that reveal none of this vintage's hardness or herbaceousness. This layered wine offers sweet tannin, good length, and outstanding purity. Its price is moderate when compared with those of more recent vintages of Haut-Brion. Give it 3–4 years of cellaring, and consume it between 2001 and 2020. Last tasted, 1/97.

1992—Forty percent of the 1992 harvest was eliminated from Haut-Brion's final
 •   blend. The result is a stylish yet authoritatively flavored wine that reminds
90   me of a slightly downsized version of the superb 1985. A beautiful deep ruby color is followed by a penetrating bouquet of black fruits, smoke, and minerals. Fine ripeness and outstanding richness allied to medium body, an elegant personality, and a supple, moderately tannic finish suggest this wine will be mature in 4–5 years and last for 15–20. A terrific success in 1992! Last tasted, 11/94.

1991—Haut-Brion's 1991 is austere, tannic, and closed. However, the wine does
 •   exhibit good dark ruby color and a tight but promising nose of black fruits,
86   minerals, and vanillin. It is spicy, with good depth and excellent definition.

Will this wine emerge from its shell to reveal more charm and finesse? If not, it may dry out before the tannin subsides. Anticipated maturity: Now–2008. Last tasted, 1/94.

1990—I have had a tendency to forget just how exceptional the 1990 Haut-Brion is
• because of the huge shadow cast by the 1989. However, in this blind tasting
96 the 1990 proved itself to be a great wine. Its price has not risen nearly as much as one might expect given its quality. The 1990 is a decadently ripe wine with much more evolution to its fragrant cassis, mineral, smoked-herb, hot rocks, tobacco, sweet, toasty nose. Fat, rich, and medium to full bodied, this superbly concentrated, forward, awesomely endowed wine requires 4–6 years of cellaring; it is capable of lasting for 20–25+ years. It is an unheralded, under-rated 1990 that deserves more attention. Last tasted, 4/98.

1989—The 1989 is one of a handful of truly profound wines from a vintage that
• tends to be over-rated, save for the Pomerols, a few St.-Emilions, and some
100 over-achievers in the Médoc. The prodigious 1989 Haut-Brion is one of the greatest first-growths I have ever tasted. It has always reminded me of what the 1959 must have tasted like in its youth, but it is even richer and more compelling aromatically. The wine exhibits an opaque ruby/purple color as well as a sweet nose of jammy fruit, tobacco, spicy oak, minerals, and smoke. Fabulously concentrated, with huge levels of fruit, extract, and glycerin, this wine is nearly viscous because of its thickness and richness. Low acidity gives the wine even more appeal and adds to its precociousness. The wine has not budged in development since it was first bottled, although it has always provided thrilling drinking because of its voluptuous texture. It needs another 5–6 years of bottle age before it will begin to develop Haut-Brion's fabulous fragrance. Expect it to hit its plateau of maturity around 2003–2005 and drink well for 15–25 years. Last tasted, 4/98.

1988—The 1988 Haut-Brion is built along the lines of the 1966, but it is more
• concentrated and powerful. The dense bouquet of tobacco, ripe, black fruits,
91 and spicy oak has just begun to develop. Medium bodied, rich, and tannic, with a good inner core of fruit, this wine will have to be cellared until the end of this century. Anticipated maturity: 2000–2025. Last tasted, 1/93.

1987—Oh, how I wish I had purchased more of this wine, given the low price for
• which it once sold. The 1987 has been delicious since bottling, exhibiting a
88 dramatic, earthy, singed-leather, sweet tobacco, and ripe black currant nose. Although not a blockbuster, it offers a medium-bodied, generous, sweet, rich fruitiness, as well as a seductive personality. Fragrant, round, elegant, and delicious, this Haut-Brion has been fully mature since the early nineties but reveals no signs of fading. However, owners should not push their luck much further. Anticipated maturity: Now. Last tasted, 1/97.

1986—The 1986 Haut-Brion, which I thought should be fully mature by now, remains
• a backward, highly concentrated, powerful wine with more noticeable tannin
96 than most top vintages. The wine does possess the telltale smoky tobacco and sweet black currant nose, in addition to subtle new oak and minerals scents. This medium- to full-bodied, rich, intensely smoky wine has still not reached

its plateau of maturity. It is unquestionably the wine of the vintage for Graves, and not far off the pace of the great 1986 first-growth Médocs. Anticipated maturity: 2000–2015. Last tasted, 5/98.

1985— This has always been one of the more seductive, savory, complex Haut-Brions
•   of the eighties. My notes have always suggested that it is the quintessentially
94   elegant, finesse-styled Haut-Brion. The color remains a deep ruby/purple, with slight lightening at the edge. The knockout nose of intense jammy black fruits, smoke, cedar, herbs, and new oak is followed by a generously concentrated, rich, gorgeously proportioned and layered Haut-Brion with no hard edges. Everything—alcohol, acidity, tannin—is beautifully integrated into the seamless personality of the 1985. Anticipated maturity: Now–2010. Last tasted, 10/97.

1984— Attractively perfumed with mineral scents, tobacco, and ripe fruit, the
•   medium-bodied 1984 Haut-Brion has surprisingly good depth and length. It
84   is not at all a big wine but is soft, creamy, and ideal for drinking young. Anticipated maturity: Now. Last tasted, 4/88.

1983— The fully mature 1983 is a very good wine that has fine depth, rich, soft, fat,
•   lush fruit, and a good measure of soft tannins in the finish. The overall
87   impression is of a forward, ripe, and voluptuous wine. It is successful, but by Haut-Brion's recent standards, the wine lacks excitement and has reached full maturity at an alarmingly fast pace. Of relatively mature Haut-Brions, this vintage, along with the 1978, has a distinctive melted road tar (asphalt) component in its aromatics. Anticipated maturity: Now–2004. Last tasted, 7/97.

1982— Administrator Jean Delmas continues to believe the 1982 is the modern-day
•   clone of the 1959 Haut-Brion. I am not willing to go that far, but it is certainly
94   a rich, seductive, medium- to full-bodied Haut-Brion that is beginning to reveal some of the telltale, mineral, tobacco, ripe, curranty fruit aspects of this fragrant, complex first-growth. The 1982 Haut-Brion is not, in my opinion, comparable to the perfect 1989, but it is a rich, full-bodied wine with well-integrated, sweet tannin, true class and character, and a sweet, expansive, long finish. The wine has been slow to throw off its cloak of tannin and reveal its true Haut-Brion-like personality. It should reach full maturity in 3–5 years and drink well through the first 2 decades of the next century. Last tasted, 9/95.

1981— My early notes on this wine were inconsistent, but two tastings of the 1981 in
•   the late eighties revealed a flattering, gentle, medium-bodied wine with a
85   smoky, vanillin oakiness, round, ripe flavors, and a soft, luscious finish. It lacks some guts and richness by the standards of most Haut-Brion vintages since 1978 but is nevertheless a charming, lighter-weight, forward wine that has reached its plateau of maturity. Anticipated maturity: Now–2000. Last tasted, 1/91.

1979— This wine has enjoyed a spectacular development in the bottle, and, while
•   drinkable upon release, it remains one of the most sumptuous, complex, and
93   satisfying Haut-Brions of the last 20 years. It is certainly the finest wine of

the vintage from Bordeaux's left bank. The wine has taken on a dark plummy/ garnet color and displays a magnificent *trés* Haut-Brion nose of jammy black fruits, earth, tobacco, smoke, and sweet fruitcake aromas. Rich and medium to full bodied, with impressive elegance, purity, and overall harmony, this is not a powerhouse or exceptionally opulent style of Haut-Brion (such as the 1989 and 1990), but, rather, a more structured yet authoritatively flavorful wine. It offers power, richness, and elegance in a wine with extraordinary equilibrium. Anticipated maturity: Now–2006. Last tasted, 10/97.

1978—As this wine has developed, it has taken on a pronounced roasted, melted
•   asphalt/tar–scented nose that in some ways is the essence of Graves, but it
90?   seems strikingly devoid of some of the other nuances so common in Haut-Brion. The wine is fully mature, with a deep garnet color. The asphalt-scented impression is verified in the mouth, where the wine reveals a lot of smokiness, tar, and sweet black fruit flavors. Surprisingly evolved, the wine has been fully mature for a decade or more. I would not push my luck with this vintage of Haut-Brion, preferring to consume it over the next 5–6 years. Anticipated maturity: Now–2003. Last tasted, 10/97.

1977—Haut-Brion was clearly outperformed by its neighbor La Mission-Haut-Brion
•   in this poor vintage. Medium ruby, with an aromatic, spicy, somewhat vegetal
74   aroma, lightish flavors, and some harshness in the finish, this wine is best drunk up over the next 5 years. Anticipated maturity: Now–may be in decline. Last tasted, 9/83.

1976—Medium ruby in color, with some amber creeping in at the edges, the 1976
•   Haut-Brion has been fully mature since the early eighties, yet it is still
86   drinking well. A spicy, earthy, oaky, moderately fruity bouquet offers elegance. On the palate, the wine is soft, round, medium bodied, and charming. It even seems to have put on some weight in the late eighties. However, do not push your luck; drink it over the next 4–5 years. Anticipated maturity: Now. Last tasted, 1/90.

1975—Blame me for completely misjudging this wine early in its life. I have since
•   purchased it at auction because of its price/quality ratio. Haut-Brion, which
93+   can begin life as a soft, light wine, never appeared to have much intensity when tasted beside the phenomenal La Mission-Haut-Brion and La Tour-Haut-Brion. However, over the last 5–7 years that has changed. Either the wine has put on considerable weight or I was off form the many times I tasted the 1975 when the wine was young. It has developed the hauntingly complex, tobacco, roasted herb, singed leather, smoky, sweet, fruity nose of a great Haut-Brion. Full bodied and intense, with noticeable ripe tannin, this is a wine of considerable richness and intensity. It offers delicious drinking after 1–2 hours of decanting, even though noticeable tannin remains. This wine is capable of another 15–20 years of cellaring. Yes, I did indeed underestimate this wine. I tasted it a half dozen times in 1995 and at each tasting it was a formidable wine. Do not be surprised to see this rating go even higher, as I do not believe the 1975 Haut-Brion has reached its pinnacle. Impressive! Last tasted, 12/95.

1974—Given the vintage, the Haut-Brion could be considered a modest success.
•   Now fully mature and a bit short in fruit, this wine has an open-knit, spicy,
76   earthy bouquet, somewhat angular, medium-bodied flavors, and a short finish.
        Anticipated maturity: Now—may be in decline. Last tasted, 3/79.

1971—For me, the 1971 is the best Haut-Brion produced between 1966 and 1975.
•   This fully mature 1971 has a sumptuous, sweet, ripe, earthy, richly fruity
88   flavor, medium to full body, a big, full-intensity, spicy bouquet, and a silky,
        supple texture. Very stylish and delicious, this wine should be drunk up. This
        wine has not been retasted since 1982, but I suspect it should still be in fine
        condition. Anticipated maturity: Now. Last tasted, 4/82.

1970—Although surprisingly light bodied, consistently pleasant, and enjoyable, this
•   is an undistinguished effort. The 1970 Haut-Brion has always come across as
85   angular and lacking the exceptional perfume and complexity this estate can
        achieve. In this tasting, the wine displayed vegetal, tobacco scents, good
        spice, some fruit, and a medium ruby color with significant amber. The tannin
        and acidity were too high for the amount of fruit, glycerin, and extract. Drink
        it up. Last tasted, 6/96.

1966—At its apogee, the 1966 Haut-Brion has an attractive, earthy, moderately
•   intense, fruity bouquet. It is medium in weight and richness and bordering on
86   being too lean and light. It is a satisfying, lighter-styled Haut-Brion that is
        quite attractive but not really of first-growth proportions. Drink over the next
        1–2 years. Anticipated maturity: Now. Last tasted, 11/84.

1964—This year, while a mixed vintage for the wines of the Médoc as a result of the
•   heavy rains that plagued many properties, was very good for the Graves
90   châteaux. Haut-Brion's 1964 is fully mature as evidenced by the amber edge
        to its color and has a splendidly rich, earthy, tobacco-and-mineral-scented
        bouquet. Ripe, deep, supple, voluptuous flavors are present on the palate.
        This full-bodied wine should be drunk up, as it is living dangerously. Antici-
        pated maturity: Now. Last tasted, 10/88.

1962—The 1962 has always been a very fine Haut-Brion, scoring between the upper
•   80s and low 90s. In this tasting it was spicy and sweet, with scents of tobacco,
88   roasted herb, and red and black fruit in the nose. The wine is lush, round,
        medium bodied, and fully mature. Last tasted, 12/95.

1961—The dark garnet–colored 1961 Haut-Brion is pure perfection, with gloriously
•   intense aromas of tobacco, cedar, chocolate, minerals, and sweet red and
100   black fruits complemented by smoky wood. This has always been a prodigious
        effort (it was the debut vintage for Jean Delmas). Extremely full bodied,
        with layers of viscous, sweet fruit, this wine is akin to candy. Consistently
        astonishing! Anticipated maturity: Now–2005. Last tasted, 3/97.

ANCIENT VINTAGES

When tasted in December 1995, the 1959 Haut-Brion (93 points) and 1947
Haut-Brion (86 points) did not live up to expectations. Most examples of the
1959 score in the 96–100-point range, as the wine easily competes with the
splendid 1961. Although the 1959 was outstanding, it seemed less concen-

trated, more disjointed, and more evolved than the 1961, displaying a more roasted aromatic profile and less sweetness and unctuousness than previous bottles. In January 1997 I had the exceptionally smoky, sweet, rich, impressively endowed 1957 Haut-Brion (90 points). The wine was fully mature, as evidenced by its dark garnet color with considerable rust. The wine was very aromatic, plump, and succulently textured, with fleshy flavors, plenty of glycerin, and sweet fruit. It is another example of an unheralded vintage producing a topflight wine. A dark ruby–colored wine with noticeable amber/rust, the 1955 Haut-Brion (97 points; last tasted 10/94) offers a huge, fragrant bouquet of walnuts, tobacco, wet stones, and smoky, cassislike fruit. Medium bodied, with extraordinary elegance and sweetness, this rich, concentrated wine exhibits no hard edges. Remarkably youthful, as well as concentrated and impeccably well balanced, it is capable of lasting for another 10–20 years. Haut-Brion's 1953 (95 points; last tasted 10/94) is best purchased today in magnums or larger-format bottles. Although it has been fully mature for decades, it has retained the hallmark, singed leather, tobacco leaf, super-ripe fragrance that makes Haut-Brion so distinctive. The wine is extremely soft, revealing considerable amber and rust at the edge, but it still possesses rich, creamy fruit and medium to full body. It does require drinking, so be very careful with regular-size bottles.

The 1949 Haut-Brion (91 points; last tasted 12/95) revealed some of the textbook cigar, ashtray, tobacco-scented notes, as well as scents of roasted herbs and ripe fruit. The color was a medium garnet, with considerable rust at the edge. Medium bodied, round, sweet, and soft, this wine is past its prime, although it remains exceptional. Drink it up. Neither Haut-Brion's 1948 nor its 1947 have ever left me with a favorable impression. The 1948 (75 points; last tasted 3/97), from a private cold cellar in Bordeaux, was attenuated, muddled, and extremely disjointed and unimpressive. Several tastings of the 1947 (my birth year) have always been too alcoholic, with high levels of acidity and not enough fruit and flesh to cover the wine's imposing structural components. The 1945 (100 points; last tasted 10/94) Haut-Brion is profound. It demonstrates the essence of Haut-Brion's style. The color remains a healthy, opaque garnet, with only slight amber at the edge. A huge, penetrating bouquet of sweet black fruits, smoked nuts, tobacco, and tar soars from the glass. The wine possesses extraordinary density and extraction of fruit, massive, full-bodied, unctuously textured flavors that reveal little tannin, and copious quantities of glycerin and alcohol. It is a fabulously rich, monumental example of a fully mature Haut-Brion that exhibits no signs of decline. Awesome! One of my more interesting tasting experiences was Haut-Brion's 1943 (89 points; last tasted 1/97). This was believed to be the finest vintage of the World War II years. The wine, bottled after the war ended, exhibited a deep garnet color and a scorched-earth/melted tar/aged beef–like aroma. The provocative aromatics were followed by a wine with copious quantities of sweet fruit, astringent tannin, and a dry, angular finish. Extremely complex, with most of the fruit remaining on the attack, this wine is just beginning to narrow out and become more austere and angular.

The 1937 vintage has a justifiable reputation for being hard, but one could see through the austere, still tannin-dominated 1937 Haut-Brion (89+? points; last tasted 12/95) to admire the healthy, dark, dense color with only some amber at the edge. Minerals, tobacco, cedar, and coffee aromas were followed by a muscular, medium-bodied wine with plenty of power and fruit. But the vintage's telltale hard tannin was still present. This particular magnum of 1937 Haut-Brion would have lasted another 20–30+ years. I have mixed tasting notes on the 1928 (97 points; last tasted 10/94). At its best, it is the most concentrated, port-like wine I have ever tasted from Haut-Brion. Its huge, meaty, tar, caramel, and jammy black fruit character is unctuously textured. The wine oozes out of the glass and over the palate. In some tastings it has been over-ripe, yet healthy and intact, but nearly bizarre because of its exaggerated style. There is a timeless aspect to it. The 1926 vintage, one of the best in the decade of the twenties, has always been overlooked in favor of the 1921, 1928, and 1929. Reputed to be one of the great wines of the vintage, the 1926 Haut-Brion (97 points; last tasted 3/98) is unusual in its roasted, chocolatey, sweet, dense, thick style. It reveals an impressive deep color with some orange at the edge and a huge nose of tobacco, mint, chocolate, grilled nuts, and smoked duck. Full bodied and powerful, with amazing thickness and unctuosity, but extremely tannic and rustic, this atypical Haut-Brion will last for another 20–30 years. The 1921 Haut-Brion (79 points; last tasted 12/95) possessed a dense, impressive color, extremely high tannin levels, and an old, sweaty, leathery, locker-room nose with vague coffee and chocolatey, roasted herb–like flavors. The astringent tannin gave the wine a coarse and disjointed personality.

VINTAGES (white)

1996—In a vintage that produced a lot of high-acid, emaciated dry whites, Haut-
•   Brion's 1996 is the wine of the vintage. It displays exceptional concentration,
93   tangy acidity, and gorgeously layered flavors of buttery citruslike fruit, olives,
         and smoke. This medium-bodied, concentrated wine is quite backward. It
         will need a considerable amount of bottle age to shed some of its structure.
         Anticipated maturity: 2010–2025. Last tasted, 11/97.

1995—In this vintage, the Haut-Brion Blanc contained less Semillon because Jean
•   Delmas thought the drought had negatively impacted this varietal more than
92   Sauvignon. Consequently the 1995 is less grandiose in its proportions but
         still one of the two best dry white Graves of the vintage. The wine possesses
         a light gold color and a citrusy, honeyed nose with subtle toasty oak. Medium
         bodied, with exquisite concentration and delineation, this beautifully pure

wine can be expected to close down and not reemerge from its dormant stage for a decade. Anticipated maturity: 2007–2025. Last tasted, 11/97.

1994—This spectacular dry white Graves is a likely candidate to rival the 1989
• produced at Haut-Brion. The harvest began at the end of August. The wine
98 possesses the texture of a great Burgundy Grand Cru given its thick unctuousness. The superb nose of honeyed fruits and smoky oak is far more developed and ostentatious than its sister, the more subtle and backward Laville-Haut-Brion. Awesomely rich, with a chewy texture and great purity and definition, this is a ravishingly intense, full-bodied, dry white wine that should age well for 30+ years. Last tasted, 7/97.

1993—Slightly superior to the sensational 1992 Haut-Brion-Blanc, the 1993 exhibits
• a flattering nose of oily, mineral-scented, ripe, honeyed fruit, full-bodied,
94 superconcentrated flavors, admirable acidity, great vibrancy and delineation, and a rich, long, dry, refreshing finish. It is a rich Haut-Brion-Blanc with more aromatic complexity than the muscular and chewy 1992. These wines are almost ageless. Like its older sibling, the 1993 will age effortlessly for 20–30 years. Last tasted, 11/94.

1992—This is another blockbuster Haut-Brion-Blanc, with a big, ostentatious bou-
• quet of sweet, honeyed fruit. Full bodied, with layers of richness, this creamy-
93 textured, fleshy wine is at present more evolved and dramatic than its sibling, the 1992 Laville. The wine possesses fine acidity and an explosively long, dry finish. This dazzling Haut-Brion-Blanc should drink well for 30+ years. Last tasted, 1/94.

1989—Whether this wine ultimately turns out to be better than the profound 1994
• and 1985 remains to be seen, but there is no doubt that this is the most
98 immense and large-scaled Haut-Brion Blanc I have ever tasted. Jean Delmas, administrator of the Dillon properties, felt the 1989 fully replicated the fleshy, chewy texture of a great Grand Cru white Burgundy. Only 600 cases were made of this rich, alcoholic, sumptuous wine. It is amazingly full and long in the mouth, with a very distinctive mineral, honeyed character. The low acidity would seemingly suggest a shorter life than normal, but I am convinced this wine will last 25 or more years. It is a real show-stopper! Anticipated maturity: Now–2025. Last tasted, 1/97.

1988—Tightly knit, with a reticent but light-intensity bouquet of minerals, lemons,
• figs, and melons, this tightly structured, relatively high-acid Haut-Brion
85 Blanc will no doubt prove to be a long-distance runner, but how much pleasure and character will evolve remains difficult to assess. Anticipated maturity: Now–2005. Last tasted, 4/91.

1987—This wine continues to evolve beautifully and offers up an elegant, moderately
• intense bouquet of herbs, creamy minerals, and fig-like fruit. Medium bodied,
88 wonderfully concentrated in a more delicate, yet still flavorful style, this impeccably balanced Haut-Brion Blanc should be drunk early on. Anticipated maturity: Now. Last tasted, 11/90.

1985—This has been a head turner since it was made. Unbelievably rich, with a
• velvety, fat consistency oozing with herb-, melon-, and fig-like fruit, this
97 voluptuously textured wine exhibits great length, richness, and character. It

never closed up after bottling and remains an exceptionally full-bodied, intensely concentrated, yet well-delineated white Graves. If you have the income of a rock superstar, this would be worth having to *fête* the turn of the century. Anticipated maturity: Now–2020. Last tasted, 1/97.

ANCIENT VINTAGES

I have virtually no tasting notes on older vintages of Haut-Brion Blanc. I did like, and gave a good rating (between 86 and 89) for the 1983, 1982, and 1981, and I remember once having an extremely powerful, full-bodied 1976. Other than that, this is a wine one rarely ever sees because of the tiny production.

BAHANS-HAUT-BRION   VERY GOOD

VINTAGES

1997—The 1997 Bahans-Haut-Brion exhibits a dark ruby color, as well as a subtle
•   mineral, tobacco, earthy, black plum and currant-scented nose. Light tannin
86–   is present in the finish, but this is an up-front hedonistic wine to drink during
87   its first 7–8 years of life. Last tasted, 3/98.

1996—The 1996 Bahans-Haut-Brion shares a similar, more structured character. It
•   looks to be another excellent second wine from this estate. The color is dark
87–   ruby, and the wine is medium bodied, sweet, rich, and already revealing some
89   of the evolved complexity of the Haut-Brion *terroir*. Last tasted, 11/97.

1995—The 1995 is an aromatic, round, complex, elegant wine that possesses all the
•   characteristics of its bigger, richer sibling but less depth, and more immediate
89   appeal. Very "Graves" with its smoky, roasted nose and sweet, smoke-infused
       black cherry and currant fruit, it should drink well for a decade. Last tasted,
       11/97.

1994—An excellent wine that has managed to avoid the vintage's telltale toughness
•   and occasional hollowness, this Bahans exhibits a dark ruby color, excellent,
88   sweet, spicy, black currant, smoky aromas, surprisingly ripe, concentrated
       flavors, a velvety texture and a delicious, easygoing finish. This top effort is
       superior to many more famous 1994 offerings. It should drink well for 5–8+
       years. Last tasted, 1/97.

1993—A complex wine, with some Haut-Brion character (a tobacco, earth, sweet
•   curranty nose is evident), this dark ruby–colored 1993 will never possess the
87   weight and aging ability of the *grand vin,* but it offers a charming, supple
       texture, textbook northern Graves aromatics, fine ripeness and spice, low
       acidity, and a soft finish. Drink it over the next 7–8 years. Last tasted, 1/97.

1992—Medium dark ruby with a curranty/herbal bouquet, this 1992 is supple,
•   medium bodied, charming, and harmonious. It should drink well for 4–6
85   years. Last tasted, 11/94.

1991—The 1991 is short, diluted, light bodied, and lacking color and fruit. Last
•   tasted, 1/94.
76

1990—The 1990 has put on weight since I first had it, although it is displaying some
 •   amber at the edge. The smoky, weedy tobacco, roasted herb, and black currant
 88   nose is followed by a fleshy, soft wine with well-integrated tannin and a
      jammy, low-acid finish. It should drink well for another 6–7 years. Last
      tasted, 11/96.

1989—I am amazed by just how delicious the 1989 Bahans-Haut-Brion continues to
 •   be. Although it is approaching full maturity, it reveals no signs of amber. The
 90   1989 is a textbook Graves in its sweet, black currant, tobacco, roasted herb
      nose. Medium to full bodied, with succulent texture, rich, fleshy flavors, and
      low acidity, it is a pure, beautifully made wine. It should continue to drink
      well for 5–8 years. Last tasted, 11/96.

1988—The 1988, a classic expression of Graves, offers up the telltale aromas of
 •   tobacco and black fruit. Medium bodied, soft, and round, this seductive wine
 86   should drink well for 5–6 years. Last tasted, 1/93.

1982—This wine was so easy to drink at age 2 that it is hard to believe it is still
 •   holding together. The color is medium ruby with amber at the edge. The nose
 85   is textbook Graves—minerals, spice, tobacco, and red and black fruits. With
      low acidity and medium body, this supple, attractive wine should be drunk
      up, as it is unlikely to improve. Last tasted, 9/95.

LARRIVET-HAUT-BRION

Classification: Grand Cru de Graves
Location of vineyards: Léognan
Owner: ANDROS S.A.
Address: 84, route de Cadaujac, 33850 Léognan
Mailing address: Same as above
Telephone: 33 5 56 64 75 51; telefax: 33 5 56 64 53 47
Visits: By appointment only, from Monday to Thursday, between 8:30 A.M.
and noon, and 1:30 P.M. and 5:30 P.M.; on Fridays, between 1:30 P.M. and
4:30 P.M.
Contact: Mrs. Gervoson or Mrs. Duval

VINEYARDS (red)
Surface area: 79 acres
Average age of vines: 20 years
Blend: 50% Merlot, 50% Cabernet Sauvignon
Density of plantation: 7,200 vines per hectare
Average yields (over the last 5 years): 55 hectoliters per hectare
Total average annual production: 200,000 bottles

GRAND VIN (red)
Brand name: Château Larrivet-Haut-Brion
Appellation: Pessac-Léognan

Mean annual production: 100,000 bottles
Upbringing: Fermentations last 3–4 weeks, depending upon the vintage, at temperatures of 26–28 degrees centigrade. Wines are aged in oak casks renewed by half in each vintage for 18 months. They are fined and filtered.

SECOND WINE
Brand name: Domaine de Larrivet
Average annual production: 100,000 bottles

VINEYARDS (white)
Surface area: 22 acres
Blend: 60% Sauvignon, 35% Semillon, and 5% Muscadelle
Total average annual production: 55,000 bottles

GRAND VIN (white)
Brand name: Château Larrivet-Haut-Brion
Appellation: Pessac-Léognan
Mean annual production: 25,000 bottles
Upbringing: Fermentations occur in new oak barrels. Wines are kept on lees for 12 months. They are fined and filtered prior to bottling.

SECOND WINE
Brand name: Domaine de Larrivet
Average annual production: 30,000 bottles

Evaluation of present classification: The quality equivalent of a Médoc Cru Bourgeois
Plateau of maturity: 3–10 years following the vintage

NOTE: Michel Rolland is the new oenologist, and Jean-Michel Arcaute is now consultant to the château.

Larrivet-Haut-Brion is well-known in European wine circles but is rarely seen in America. The vineyard, located in the southern section of Graves near Léognan, is adjacent to that of the much more famous Haut-Bailly. It has changed hands, and rumors abound in Bordeaux about a renaissance in quality.

VINTAGES (red)

1992—An attractive dark plum–colored wine with a moderately intense nose of
•   jammy black cherries and spicy fruitcake aromas, this soft, round, light- to
85   medium-bodied wine possesses pretty fruit, admirable purity, and a velvety

finish. This light yet flavorful wine is ideal for drinking over the next 3–5 years. Last tasted, 11/94.

1990— The reassuringly good 1990 is expressive of the Graves appellation. Deep
• ruby colored, with a smoky, herbal, cedary nose, the wine is supple, delicious,
86 and medium bodied, with gobs of cherry fruit in the smooth finish. Anticipated maturity: Now. Last tasted, 1/93.

1989— The medium-bodied 1989 has a suspiciously light color, and the tart green
• tannins are astringent and excessive. Frankly there is not much to this wine.
73 Last tasted, 1/93.

1988— Although the 1988 is light, it exhibits a good ruby color, an earthy, fruity
• nose, round, ripe, charming flavors, and soft tannins in the finish. It will be
85 ideal for drinking over the next 6–7 years. Last tasted, 1/93.

1986— The 1986 seems surprisingly light and somewhat diluted. This medium ruby–
• colored wine, with its soft strawberry and cherry fruitiness, should be drunk
78 over the next 4–5 years. Anticipated maturity: Now. Last tasted, 3/90.

1985— The 1985 has merit in the sense that the bouquet of tobacco and ripe fruit is
• textbook Graves. On the palate, one would have liked to see more flesh and
84 substance. Anticipated maturity: Now. Last tasted, 3/89.

VINTAGES (white)

1996— The high levels of shrill acidity are the undoing of this light-bodied, indiffer-
• ent dry white Graves. It will hold up to cellaring, but there is too little flesh
74 and ripeness. Anticipated maturity: 2000–2010. Last tasted, 3/97.

1995— This extremely acidic, tart, medium-bodied wine reveals plenty of oak, a
• surprisingly high level of SO_2, and an emaciated, austere palate. It will last
76 for 2 decades, but I wonder how much charm and fruit will emerge? Last tasted, 3/97.

1994— This light- to medium-bodied, smoky-, herb-, and honey-scented wine offers
• above average concentration, forward-tasting fruit, and a short, compact fin-
84 ish. Drink it over the next 5–6 years. Last tasted, 3/97.

1993— Flat, soft, low-acid flavors are diffuse and lack concentration. The wine tails
• off on the palate with significant dilution. Last tasted, 11/94.
75

1992— This is an excellent effort from Larrivet-Haut-Brion. A big, honeyed, ripe
• nose soars from the glass, offering up waxy, mineral, toasty scents suggestive
88 of Semillon. Rich and full bodied, with layers of fruit infused with considerable glycerin, this dry, corpulent, rich, full throttle, delicious white Graves
should be drunk in its first 5–7 years of life. Last tasted, 1/94.

LAVILLE-HAUT-BRION   OUTSTANDING

Classification: Classified growth (for whites)
Location of vineyards: Pessac
Owner: Domaine de Clarence Dillon S.A.
Address: 33600 Pessac

Mailing address: B.P. 24, 33604 Pessac Cedex
Telephone: 33 5 56 00 29 30; telefax: 33 5 56 98 75 14
Visits: By appointment only
Contact: Carla Kuhn

VINEYARDS (white)
Surface area: 9.1 acres
Average age of vines: 51 years
Blend: 70% Semillon, 27% Sauvignon, 3% Muscadelle
Density of plantation: 10,000 vines per hectare
Total average annual production: 1,100 cases

GRAND VIN (white)
Brand name: Château Laville-Haut-Brion
Appellation: Pessac-Léognan
Mean annual production: 1,100 cases
Upbringing: Fermentations occur in 100% new oak barrels at
temperatures of 20 degrees centigrade. Wines remain on lees for 13–16
months prior to bottling. They are fined with egg whites.

SECOND WINE
None produced.

Evaluation of present classification: Consistently one of the three best
white wines of Graves
Plateau of maturity: 10–45 or more years following the vintage

This tiny vineyard produces one of the most remarkably long-lived white
wines of France. The soil is less gravelly and heavier than the vineyard of La
Mission-Haut-Brion. The production is tiny, adding to the rarity value of this
white wine. Fermented and aged in new oak casks, Laville-Haut-Brion takes
on a waxy richness with aging. It is marvelous to taste from cask, but after
bottling, it closes up completely, not to reopen in some instances for 5–10
years. Reputation and a consistently high level of quality insure that it sells
for a frighteningly high price. Perhaps that explains why 95% of the production is exported.

VINTAGES (white)

1996—Laville's 1996 is one of the lighter-styled efforts from this estate in the
　•　　nineties. Nevertheless, it has managed to cram gorgeous levels of complexity
　90　　and elegance into a citrusy, melony, richly fruity format. While it does not
　　　　possess the weight and body of such blockbuster vintages as 1994, it is
　　　　impressive. There is good acidity, and the wine comes across as clean, crisp,

and stylish in an understated, restrained manner. This wine should drink well for 12–15+ years. Last tasted, 11/97.

1995— The 1995 Laville-Haut-Brion lacks some of the complexity and intensity of
•   the 1994 and other top years. The wine is tart, with ripe fig, melony, and waxy
88   fruit in the nose and flavors. Light to medium bodied, with high acidity and outstanding purity, this is a tasty, refreshing Laville to drink between 2000 and 2010. Last tasted, 11/97.

1994— This tightly knit, medium-bodied wine exhibits an intense, sweet nose of
•   toast, minerals, honey, and spices. There is ripe fruit and intensity on the
94   palate, but the overall impression is that of a backward, undeveloped wine. It has 20–25 years of aging potential. Last tasted, 3/97.

1993— While the 1993 Laville-Haut-Brion should rival the 1992 after a few more
•   years of cellaring, at present it is tight and lighter bodied than the fat, robust
90   1992. This stylish, backward yet finesse-styled Laville-Haut-Brion exhibits aromas of spicy, honeyed fruit and toasty new oak, crisp acidity, and a rich, firmly structured personality. Last tasted, 11/94.

1992— Laville's 1992 was the most backward, dry white Graves I tasted. It possesses
•   a medium straw color, a tight but promising nose of sweet waxy fruit, long,
91   rich, full-bodied flavors, adequate acidity, an opulent, chewy richness, and tremendous length. Although not as monumental as the 1989, this is a top-class Laville-Haut-Brion that should drink well for 20–30 years. Last tasted, 1/94.

1989— This utterly mind-blowing effort from Laville-Haut-Brion, with its decadent
•   bouquet of honeyed, superripe melons, figs, and toasty new oak, is a real
96   turn-on. In the mouth, the wine is stunningly rich, concentrated, and intense, with a texture more akin to a Grand Cru white Burgundy than an austere white Graves. Acidity is low and the alcohol level is high, suggesting this wine will have to be drunk in its first 10–15 years. For pure power, as well as a sumptuous texture, this may well be the most dramatic Laville-Haut-Brion ever produced. Production was tiny; only 900 cases were made. Anticipated maturity: Now–2020. Last tasted, 4/91.

1988— While lacking the personality of the blockbuster 1989, the 1988 is a beauti-
•   fully made, waxy, melon-scented wine with a touch of herbs and smoky oak.
87   It has better acidity and a more delineated personality than the 1989, but not the latter vintage's flamboyant character. Nevertheless, this should turn out to be an extremely long-lived Laville, and while it may not hit the heights of hedonism that the 1989 will, it still offers plenty of flavor in a more polite and civilized fashion. Anticipated maturity: 2000–2010. Last tasted, 3/97.

1987— The 1987 turned out to be a very good vintage for the white wines of Graves.
•   This is a lighter-weight Laville-Haut-Brion, but its wonderfully precise herb,
86   melon, and fig flavors are offered in a medium-bodied format with a great deal of charm and character. There is enough acidity to give the wine some lift and add focus to its medium-bodied flavors. Drink this charmer over the next decade. Anticipated maturity: Now–2001. Last tasted, 1/90.

1986—A Laville-Haut-Brion was made in 1986, but before it was officially released,
  •   the château, disappointed with the way it was tasting, declassified it.

1985—This is a sumptuous, rich, honeyed, full-bodied Laville-Haut-Brion that
  •   should drink beautifully for the next 2 decades. It is among the more powerful
  93   and richer wines produced by the château, yet it has the requisite acid to give
         it balance and freshness. Not quite as super-ripe and alcoholic as the 1989,
         it is perhaps more typical of Laville-Haut-Brion at its richest and fullest.
         Anticipated maturity: Now–2008. Last tasted, 12/90.

ANCIENT VINTAGES

I have not seen the 1984 since it was in cask, but the 1983 Laville-Haut-
Brion (rated 90) is an elegant, classy, textbook Laville, whereas the 1982 (87
points) is a chunky, foursquare, heavyweight Laville that lacks the finesse
and elegance of the 1983. Older vintages I have tasted include a powerhouse,
now fully mature 1976 (91 points), a classic, long-lived, tightly knit, well-
structured 1975 (90 points), and a glorious 1966 (92 points) and 1962 (88
points). In 1990 I finally had a chance to taste the Laville-Haut-Brion that
Michael Broadbent dubbed spectacular, the 1945 "Crème de Tête." In a blind
tasting against the regular cuvée of the 1945 Laville-Haut-Brion, there was
indeed a difference. The wines were stunning efforts that resembled old,
powerful Sauternes more than white Graves. Both were massive, rich, honeyed
wines that were quite dry, but because of their richness and fullness, they
had overwhelming impact on the palate. The Crème de Tête clearly was richer
and fuller. I rated it a 93.

LA LOUVIÈRE   EXCELLENT

Classification: Unclassified
Location of vineyards: Léognan
Owner: André Lurton
Address: 33850 Léognan
Mailing address: c/o Château Bonnet, 33240 Grézillac
Telephone: 33 5 57 25 58 58; telefax: 33 5 57 74 98 59
Visits: Monday to Friday, from 9 A.M. to noon, and 2 P.M. to 5 P.M.
Contact: Valérie Faure, telephone 33 5 56 64 75 87 and telefax 33 5 56
64 71 76

VINEYARDS (red)
Surface area: 79 acres
Average age of vines: 20–22 years
Blend: 64% Cabernet Sauvignon, 30% Merlot, 3% Cabernet Franc, 3%
Petit Verdot
Density of plantation: 6,500–8,500 vines per hectare

GRAND VIN (red)
Brand name: Château La Louvière
Appellation: Pessac-Léognan
Upbringing: Fermentations occur in temperature-controlled
stainless-steel tanks. Wines are aged in oak barrels, 50%–75% of
which are new, and are racked every 3 months. They are fined
and filtered.

SECOND WINE
Brand name: L. de la Louvière

VINEYARDS (white)
Surface area: 37 acres
Average age of vines: 20–22 years
Blend: 85% Sauvignon, 15% Semillon
Density of plantation: 6,500–8,500 vines per hectare

GRAND VIN (white)
Brand name: Château La Louvière
Appellation: Pessac-Léognan
Upbringing: Fermentations occur in barrels (50% of which are new)
and remain on lees for 12 months with stirring. They are fined and
filtered.

SECOND WINE
Brand name: L. de la Louvière

Evaluation of present classification: The quality equivalent of a Médoc
fourth-growth
Plateau of maturity: (red) 3–12 years following the vintage; (white) 2–6
years following the vintage

While unclassified, La Louvière in Léognan is now making wines superior to
many of the Crus Classés. In particular, recent vintages have been on a
quality level with a Médoc fourth-growth. The proprietor, André Lurton,
acquired the property in 1965 and has thoroughly rejuvenated the estate,
which has its vineyards impressively situated between Haut-Bailly and Carbonnieux.

The emphasis is on producing wines of immediate drinkability, but also
wines that are concentrated, fresh, and pure. Lurton has achieved all of that.
While it used to be true that the red wines could not match the brilliance of
the whites, that has changed since the mid-1980s, as both wines are now
excellent. Moreover, La Louvière remains notoriously undervalued, so consumers still have an opportunity to stock up on some delicious high-quality
wines that compete with many from the most renowned Graves properties.

VINTAGES (red)

1996—A tannic, harder, more masculine and structured style of La Louvière, the
•   1996 exhibits a dark ruby color with purple nuances. The nose offers aromas
86–   of leafy tobacco, smoke, black cherries and currants. In the mouth, this
87+   medium-bodied, tightly knit wine is closed, yet it reveals excellent potential
        for longevity. If it fleshes out, it will merit a score in the upper 80s. Antici-
        pated maturity: 2003–2014. Last tasted, 3/98.

1995—An exceptionally seductive, open-knit 1995, La Louvière's telltale tobacco,
•   smoky, leafy, herb-tinged red and black currant fruit jumps from the glass of
87   this aromatic wine. Exhibiting excellent ripeness, a supple texture, medium
        body, and a delicious, roasted fruitiness, this textbook Graves can be drunk
        now or over the next 10–12 years. Last tasted, 11/97.

1994—La Louvière is one of Pessac-Léognan's up-and-coming stars for both red and
•   white wines. One of the sleepers of the vintage, the 1994 is well worth buying.
89   Its deep ruby/purple color and smoky, black currant, herb-tinged nose are
        provocative. Rich, powerful, and dense, with moderate tannin, excellent to
        outstanding concentration, and admirable purity, this is an impressively en-
        dowed wine for drinking between 2000 and 2012. Last tasted, 3/96.

1993—The 1993 exhibits a saturated dark ruby/purple color and a tight but excellent
•   nose of ripe, black cherry and cassis fruit, minerals, and toasty new oak. The
87   wine possesses excellent flavor concentration and fatness (not a trait of many
        1993 clarets), a ripe, chewy texture, and a long, heady, rich, moderately
        tannic finish. The fruit and tannin suggest it should be drunk early; it should
        last for 10–15 years. Last tasted, 11/94.

1992—This property is turning out wonderful white wines and classic reds. Since
•   1988 they have released a bevy of highly successful wines, and the 1992 is
87   another fine La Louvière. It offers a dark, saturated, ruby/purple color, a big,
        spicy, sweet, cassis, herb, and tobacco nose, and smoky, black curranty
        flavors touched intelligently with oak for structure and sweetness. This lush,
        delicious, already complex, medium- to full-bodied wine should drink well
        for 7–10 years. Last tasted, 11/94.

1990—The 1990 exhibits a saturated purple color, an unevolved nose of black fruits,
•   smoke, and grilled meats, full body, low acidity, and intense, concentrated
90   fruit, all crammed into a layered, pure, sweet, fruity, ripe wine. While not yet
        mature, it is delicious to drink. The wine will hit its plateau of maturity in 2–
        3 years and last for 12–15 or more. Last tasted, 11/96.

1989—The soft, well-developed 1989 displays a dark ruby/purple color, with some
•   lightening at the edge. The wine offers a ripe, curranty nose intertwined with
88   scents of new oak, herbs, olives, and tobacco. Medium bodied, soft, and
        smoothly textured, this lush wine should drink well for 8–10 years. Last
        tasted, 11/96.

1988—Among the finest La Louvières I have tasted, the 1988 is a concentrated,
•   well-balanced wine possessing a delectable roasted, cassis fruitiness that
89   expands on the palate. Impressively concentrated, with an opulent texture
        and velvety tannins, this complete wine should provide delicious drink-

ing over the next decade. Anticipated maturity: Now–2002. Last tasted, 1/93.

1986— The red wine from La Louvière is made in a style that is meant to be drunk
• young, and the 1986 is no exception. It is a soft wine, but rich in flavor, with
85 a weedy, tobacco, spicy fruitiness, deep color, and fleshy, sweet, concentrated
   flavors. Anticipated maturity: Now. Last tasted, 3/89.

1985— The 1985 displays more structure than usual (somewhat surprising in view of
• the loose-knit character of the vintage), but it has generous portions of ripe,
85 plummy tobacco-scented and -flavored fruit in a medium-bodied format. Anticipated maturity: Now. Last tasted, 3/89.

1984— Too light and frail, without much grip and flavor, the 1984 is soft, fruity, and
• fresh, but shallow. Anticipated maturity: Now. Last tasted, 3/89.
74

1983— A notable success in 1983, La Louvière had one of the darkest colors of all
• the wines in a tasting of major Graves wines put on for me by the Union des
87 Grands Crus. This medium- to full-bodied wine has shed the tannins and now
   exhibits wonderful ripeness, excellent balance, deep, concentrated flavors,
   and a sweet, earthy, tobacco fragrance. Anticipated maturity: Now–2003. Last
   tasted, 1/88.

1982— This wine has tasted fully mature since bottling, yet it has lost none of its sweet,
• creamy, curranty fruit or tobacco and herb aromatics. Always a soft, low-acid
87 wine, it continues to provide delicious drinking in a supple style. Recent vintages of La Louvière have been more forcefully constructed, with greater extract, color, and intensity. Because of that, they are less charming in their youth.
   The 1982 should be drunk over the next 4–5 years. Last tasted, 9/95.

1981— The least successful of the La Louvière vintages of the early 1980s, the 1981
• is lean, a trifle austere, medium bodied, and relatively compact and bland in
75 taste. Anticipated maturity: Now. Last tasted, 6/84.

1978— Fully mature, the 1978 La Louvière is charmingly fruity, soft, round, and
• supple, with a pleasing, ripe berry-and-tobacco-scented character. Medium
83 to full bodied, with little tannins present, this precocious, easy to drink wine
   should be drunk up. Anticipated maturity: Now–may be in decline. Last
   tasted, 12/84.

VINTAGES (white)

1996— Mouth-searing levels of acidity, so common in the 1996 vintage, give this
• wine an attenuated, compact feel on the palate. There is excellent purity, as
79 well as attractive scents in the wine's aromatics, but the acidity is frightful.
   Perhaps it will soften with bottle age, but I do not hold much hope for that to
   occur. Anticipated maturity: 1999–2006. Last tasted, 11/97.

1995— An intriguing nose of buttery herbs, figs, smoky oak, and ripe fruit is followed
• by a medium-bodied wine with high acidity, an expansive texture, and clean,
87 ripe, rich fruit in the finish. The 1995 is not as expressive or rich as the 1994
   and 1993, but it is a successful effort for a white Graves in this vintage.
   Anticipated maturity: Now–2003. Last tasted, 11/97.

1994—Pungent scents of earth, minerals, and smoke combine with ripe fruit in
•   this medium-bodied, soft, supple, concentrated wine. The finish is long and
90   persuasive. It appears less structured than some of the other 1994s, so I
        would opt for drinking it during its first decade of life. Last tasted, 6/97.

1993—This estate is making very good red and white wines. It is, therefore, not surpris-
•   ing that the 1993 is a superb, medium- to full-bodied, smoky, honeyed wine
90   with layers of flavor, excellent purity, and the potential to last for up to a decade.
        Last tasted, 11/94.

1989—This is a relatively fat, open-knit, richly fruity La Louvière that lacks some
•   grip and delineation. There is no denying the foursquare, chunky fruitiness
86   and easygoing texture. It will not be long-lived. Anticipated maturity: Now.
        Last tasted, 4/91.

1988—This is a textbook example of just how delicious the white La Louvière can
•   be. It has just enough acidity to give it definition, and the general impression
87   is one of abundantly rich, honeyed, melony, fig-like fruit. There is a nice
        touch of toasty oak and even some flintiness in the wine's finish. It is a lovely,
        extremely well made white Graves for drinking over the next 4–5 years.
        Anticipated maturity: Now. Last tasted, 4/91.

1987—The 1987 is a terribly underrated vintage for white Graves. La Louvière
•   produced a tasty, honeyed, melony, fig-like wine with medium body, a touch
85   of oak, good acidity, and a crisp, long finish. Anticipated maturity: Now. Last
        tasted, 11/90.

MALARTIC-LAGRAVIÈRE

Classification: Classified growth (red and white)
Location of vineyards: Léognan
Owner: Alfred-Alexandre Bonnie
Address: 39, avenue de Mont de Marsan, 33850 Léognan
Mailing address: B.P. 7, 33850 Léognan
Telephone: 33 5 56 64 75 08; telefax: 33 5 56 64 53 66
Visits: By appointment only
Contact: Bruno Marly

VINEYARDS (red)
Surface area: 37 acres
Average age of vines: 28 years
Blend: 50% Cabernet Sauvignon, 25% Cabernet Franc, 25% Merlot
Density of plantation: 10,000 vines per hectare
Average yields (over the last 5 years): 47 hectoliters per hectare
Total average annual production: 84,000 bottles

GRAND VIN (red)
Brand name: Château Malartic-Lagravière
Appellation: Pessac-Léognan
Mean annual production: 60,000 bottles

Upbringing: Harvesting is done by hand, and grapes are sorted in the vineyards. Fermentations occur in temperature-controlled stainless-steel tanks and last 2–4 weeks. Malolactics occur in vats and partly in oak casks. Wines are aged in oak casks, one-third of which are new, for a period of 16–18 months. They are fined and filtered.

SECOND WINE
Brand name: Le Sillage de Martillac
Average annual production: 24,000 bottles

VINEYARDS (white)
Surface area: 10 acres
Average age of vines: 25 years
Blend: 85% Sauvignon, 15% Semillon
Density of plantation: 10,000 vines per hectare
Average yields (over the last 5 years): 45 hectoliters per hectare
Total average annual production: 24,000 bottles

GRAND VIN (white)
Brand name: Château Malartic Lagravière
Appellation: Pessac Léognan
Mean annual production: 12,000 bottles
Upbringing: Harvest is done manually. Racking of the must occurs in stainless-steel tanks. Fermentations take place in oak barrels, one-third of which are new, and wines are kept on lees for 8–9 months before being bottled. They are fined and filtered.

SECOND WINE
Brand name: Le Sillage de Martillac
Average annual production: 12,000 bottles

Evaluation of present classification: An average-quality Graves estate equivalent to a Médoc Cru Bourgeois
Plateau of maturity: (red) 5–12 years following the vintage; (white) 3–10 years following the vintage

NOTE: The estate, which used to belong to the Laurent Perrier Group, has been bought by Alfred Alexandre Bonnie. In September 1997 construction was begun on a new cellar and winery. The château will also be renovated. Yields have been lowered to 45 hectoliters per hectare, and selections will be carried more strictly (in 1996 the grand vin represented only 60% of the total production, versus 85% in former vintages). Michel Rolland and Athanase Fakorellis are advisers for red wines, Denis Dubourdieu for the whites.

One of the numerous estates in the southern Graves region of Léognan, Malartic-Lagravière is a property that makes much better white wine than red wine. Historically, the production per hectare at this estate has been high, as the former proprietor, Jacques Marly, held the minority point of view that young vines and high yields produced a better wine than low yields and old vines.

In stylistic terms, the red wine of Malartic-Lagravière is light, stern, tannic, and generally lacking richness and depth. Since it is unappealing when young, one would hope that age would fill it out and enhance its development. That has not been the case. The recent sale of the property and the installation of a new winemaking team should turn this moribund estate's fortunes upward.

VINTAGES (red)

1996—Dusty, hard tannin dominated this wine's seemingly lean, angular personality.
• The color was dark ruby, and the wine light to medium bodied with an
74– absence of depth and flesh. Last tasted, 3/98.
78

1995—There is excessive toasty new oak in this medium-bodied, straightforward,
• monolithic example. Soft plum and cherry fruit are present, but the wine is
76 too woody and tannic. Last tasted, 11/97.

1994—The 1994 displays less color saturation than the 1993. It appears stripped
• and eviscerated, with a hollow personality and only wood, alcohol, acidity,
74 and tannin in the finish. I cannot see this wine ever coming out of its
dormancy. Last tasted, 1/97.

1993—A terroir-dominated, earthy nose with a hint of red currants quickly fades in
• the glass. This dark ruby–colored wine reveals an herbaceous/olive/green
77 pepper–scented nose, high tannin, light body, and an average finish. Drink it
over the next 4–6 years. Last tasted, 1/97.

1992—Medium ruby colored, with a closed, nearly nonexistent bouquet that reluc-
• tantly offers up a few scents of dried, stale herbs and new wood, this compact,
71 stern, charmless wine reveals excruciatingly hard tannin, little fruit, and no
redeeming characteristics. Last tasted, 11/94.

1991—The 1991 exhibits a weak, watery color and a soft, vague bouquet of earthy
• red fruits and spice. There is little depth and only tannin and acidity in the
72 finish. Last tasted, 1/94.

1990—The 1990 is an excessively introverted, shy style of wine, as well as
• frightfully light colored. The weedy nose and flavors are also surprising.
73 Last tasted, 1/93.

1989—The 1989 is extremely subtle, light to medium bodied, forward, yet structured
• enough to last until the end of the century. Anticipated maturity: 2000–2007.
82 Last tasted, 1/93.

1988—The 1988 Malartic-Lagravière is lean, austere, light bodied, and too polite. A
• little excess would have been appreciated. Anticipated maturity: Now–2000.
77 Last tasted, 1/93.

1986—Medium ruby in color, the 1986 is pleasant but undistinguished and appears
  •   to have suffered somewhat from the huge rainstorms that hit the Graves area
  82   just prior to the harvest. Anticipated maturity: Now. Last tasted, 11/90.

1985—Ripe, modestly fruity, with a healthy dosage of new oak, the 1985 is a very
  •   pleasant wine, but it has little length or grip. Anticipated maturity: Now. Last
  84   tasted, 3/90.

VINTAGES (white)

1996—Given the number of high-acid, unimpressive white Graves in the 1996
  •   vintage, Malartic-Lagravière's effort is not as bad as the score indicates. The
  79   wine is light bodied, with crisp acidity, a fresh, grapefruity style, and tartness
        in the finish. It is a refreshing wine that will drink well for 10–12 years. Last
        tasted, 11/97.

1995—A high-strung, tart, medium-bodied wine, Malartic-Lagravière's 1995 exhibits
  •   crisp, herbaceous fruit flavors, medium body, good purity, and an intriguing
  86   mineral-like component. The oak adds definition to the wine's personality.
        Anticipated maturity: 2000–2007. Last tasted, 11/97.

1994—The finest white wine made at this estate in years, the 1994 includes Semillon
  •   in what used to be a 100% Sauvignon wine. The result is a richer, more
  89   intense, compelling example of white Graves. There is a honeyed melon,
        spicy, pungent, subtle herbaceousness, freshness, sweet fruit, and wonderful
        delineation to this medium-bodied wine. It should drink well for 15–20 years.
        Last tasted, 3/97.

1993—Extremely thin, watery, and light bodied, with green, overtly herbaceous
  •   flavors, this is an uninteresting offering. Last tasted, 11/94.
  72

1992—If you like the aroma of mashed green peas and unripe limes, you will admire
  •   this wine more than I did. While sharp and angular on the palate, its purity,
  76   lightness, and superausterity may offer some interest to masochists. It's not
        my style. Last tasted, 1/94.

1989—The decision to use 100% Sauvignon Blanc, ferment the wine in stainless-
  •   steel, and then age the wine for 7–8 months in vat is something I find curious.
  82   I say that because this property often produces a white wine with a shrill
        character that comes across as too lemony and tart. No doubt, given the high
        acidity, the wine will hold up. But if the question is the degree of pleasure it
        is capable of providing, Malartic-Lagravière fails. The 1989 is too tart, seem-
        ingly more akin to a Muscadet than a serious white Graves. It is light straw/
        green in color and reserved and has an unimpressive finish. Anticipated
        maturity: Now. Last tasted, 4/91.

1988—This is one of the best white wines I have ever tasted from this property.
  •   However, I should warn potential tasters that the compelling bouquet of
  87   minerals, green peas, and freshly mowed grass may be too intense for those
        who like their wines shy. In the mouth, this wine exhibits a crisp, melony
        richness but finishes with an austere lightness and slightly high acidity.
        Anticipated maturity: Now. Last tasted, 4/91.

1986—A bit dilute and light, yet crisp, tart, and refreshing in a low-keyed way, this
  •   pleasant, straw-colored wine has medium body and should be drunk over the
  81   next 7–8 years. Anticipated maturity: Now. Last tasted, 3/89.
1985—This is an attractive Malartic-Lagravière, with pronounced scents of mowed
  •   grass and green peas. Light straw in color with plenty of fruit (for a change),
  85   this medium-bodied, crisp, austere wine displays no signs of age. Anticipated
         maturity: Now–2000. Last tasted, 3/89.

ANCIENT VINTAGES

If this wine never becomes profound or compelling, it certainly stands the
test of time, as evidenced by examples of the 1971, 1975, 1978, and 1979 I
tasted in 1988. None of these wines was over-the-hill, and many had a
moderately attractive, herbaceous, slightly honeyed, melon-like character.
Nevertheless, there was also an impression of austerity and meagerness in
the finish. This distinctive style of white wine has admirers, but I must
confess, I am not one of them.

LA MISSION-HAUT-BRION   OUTSTANDING

Classification: Classified growth (red wines)
Location of vineyards: Pessac
Owner: Domaine de Clarence Dillon S.A.
Address: 33600 Pessac
Mailing address: B.P. 24, 33602 Pessac
Telephone: 33 5 56 00 29 30; telefax: 33 5 56 98 75 14
Visits: By appointment only
Contact: Carla Kuhn

VINEYARDS (red)
Surface area: 51.6 acres
Average age of vines: 21 years
Blend: 48% Cabernet Sauvignon, 45% Merlot, 7% Cabernet Franc
Density of plantation: 10,000 vines per hectare
Total average annual production: 7,000–10,000 cases

GRAND VIN (red)
Brand name: Château La Mission-Haut-Brion
Appellation: Pessac-Léognan
Mean annual production: 6,000–9,000 cases
Upbringing: Harvest is done manually. Fermentations occur in
temperature-controlled stainless-steel vats of 180 hectoliters capacity. A
computer system programs pumping-overs and temperature regulations
according to the temperature of the must. Mean temperature is 30

degrees centigrade. Wines spend 20 months in new oak barrels and are fined with fresh egg whites.

SECOND WINE
Brand name: La Chapelle de La Mission
Average annual production: 1,200 cases

Evaluation of present classification: The quality equivalent of a Médoc first-growth
Plateau of maturity: 8–40 or more years following the vintage

La Mission-Haut-Brion in Talence produces one of the greatest wines in the entire Bordeaux region. This estate sits across the road (RN 250), confronting its longtime rival, Haut-Brion, and has a record of virtually unmatched brilliance that covers much of the twentieth century.

The Woltner family acquired La Mission in 1919. It was they—particularly the late Frédéric and his son Henri—who were responsible for the ascendancy of La Mission-Haut-Brion's wine quality to a level that matched and frequently surpassed the first-growths of the Médoc and neighboring Haut-Brion.

Woltner's genius was widely recognized in Bordeaux. He was known as a gifted taster and oenologist and pioneered the installation of easy-to-clean, metal, glass-lined fermentation tanks in 1926. Many observers attributed the dense, rich, powerful, fruity character of La Mission to these short, squat vats that, because of their shape, tended to increase the grape skin-to-juice contact during the fermentation. These vats were replaced under the new administration with computer-controlled, state-of-the-art fermenters.

La Mission-Haut-Brion's style of wine has always been that of intense richness, full body, great color and extract, and plenty of tannin. I have had the pleasure of tasting all of the best vintages of La Mission back to 1921, and it is a wine that can easily last 30 or 40 years in the bottle. It has always been a much richer and more powerful wine than that of its one-time archrival, Haut-Brion. For this reason, as well as remarkable consistency in poor and mediocre vintages (along with Latour in Pauillac, it has had the finest record in Bordeaux for good wines in poor vintages), La Mission has become one of the most popular wines of Bordeaux.

Henri Woltner passed away in 1974, and until the sale of La Mission-Haut-Brion to the present owners of Haut-Brion in 1983, La Mission was managed by Françoise and Francis Dewavrin-Woltner. Internal family bickering over the administration of this property ultimately led to the sale of La Mission and two sister properties, La Tour-Haut-Brion and the white wine–producing estate of Laville-Haut-Brion. The Woltners live in Napa Valley, where they produce Chardonnay from the steep hillsides of Howell Mountain.

Since 1983 Jean Delmas has moved quickly to stamp his winemaking philosophy on the wines of this estate. After the property was sold in 1983, the winemaking staff was promptly dismissed and Delmas began to augment the percentage of new oak that had deteriorated because of the financial difficulties experienced by the Woltner regime. Now La Mission, like Haut-Brion, is aged in 100% new oak. In addition, the percentage of Merlot has been increased to 45%, with both the Cabernet Sauvignon and Cabernet Franc lowered.

The first vintages under Delmas were very good but lacked the power and extraordinary richness seen in La Mission in previous top years. They were technically correct wines but lacked a bit of soul and personality. With the installation of a state-of-the-art winemaking facility at the estate in time for the 1987 vintage, the quality of the wine has returned to that of its glory years. The wine is cleaner, and flaws such as elevated levels of volatile acidity that appeared in certain older vintages of La Mission are unlikely ever to rear their unpleasant heads under the management of Jean Delmas. Nevertheless, after a transitional period between 1983 and 1986, La Mission-Haut-Brion returned in the late eighties to produce one of the very best wines of the vintage in 1987, a beauty in 1988, and a sumptuous 1989, the latter wine undoubtedly the finest La Mission of the decade. Vintages of the nineties, while more vexing because of rainy Septembers, have all produced wines that are among the finest in Bordeaux.

It is unlikely that the newer style of La Mission will age as long as older vintages, but neither will it be as unapproachable and tannic in its youth. In the final analysis, La Mission-Haut-Brion remains a wine of first-growth quality.

VINTAGES

1997—Anyone who has recently visited La Mission-Haut-Brion's vineyard undoubt-
•　　edly noticed there has been considerable replanting. I am wondering if the
87–　average age of the vineyard having dropped may account for some of the
88　　narrowness and slight austerity of the 1997 La Mission-Haut-Brion. I do not
want to be too critical because this is certainly a very good wine, possibly excellent. The color is dark ruby/purple. The wine is medium bodied with aromas of black fruits, weedy tobacco, petrol, and earth. The dry, hard tannin in the finish is worrisome, but it appears to be balanced by the wine's depth and extract. While this is not a great La Mission, it is a very good one with moderate aging potential. Anticipated maturity: 2001–2012. Last tasted, 3/98.

1996—La Mission's 1996 is a true *vin de garde,* displaying a dense, opaque ruby/
•　　purple color, and a tight but powerful personality, with reluctant aromatics.
90–　This rich wine cuts a deep, medium- to full-bodied impression on the palate,
91+　and appears to need 7–8 years of cellaring. It is atypically backward for La

Mission-Haut-Brion, but the wine possesses exceptional depth, and the smoky, mineral, dried herb, rich, chocolatey, berry fruit that characterizes this brawny, muscular wine. Anticipated maturity: 2004–2025. Last tasted, 3/98.

1995—The 1995 La Mission-Haut-Brion was tight and closed when I tasted it, not
• revealing as much fragrance or forwardness as it did on the multiple occasions
91 I tasted it from cask. But don't worry, the wine is obviously high class, exhibiting a dense ruby/purple color, and a reticent but promising nose of roasted herbs, sweet, peppery, spicy fruit, medium to full body, and admirable power, depth, and richness. As outstanding as it is, readers should not expect the 1995 to tower qualitatively over vintages such as 1994. Anticipated maturity: 2003–2020. Last tasted, 11/97.

1994—This outstanding example of La Mission is surprisingly forward and velvety
• textured. The dark purple color suggests high extraction. The fragrant, smoky,
91 tobacco, leathery, roasted herb, and cassis nose is a real turn on. Voluptuous, round, medium to full bodied, and loaded with fruit, glycerin, complexity, and charm, this is a surprisingly open-knit (at least for now), intensely flavorful wine. Anticipated maturity: 1999–2015. Last tasted, 1/97.

1993—La Mission-Haut-Brion's 1993 is one of the vintage's most promising wines.
• Jean Delmas is justly proud of his accomplishments with all three of his
90 estates (La Tour-Haut-Brion, La Mission-Haut-Brion, and Haut-Brion) in this rain-plagued vintage. The 1993 La Mission exhibits a deep, dark, ruby/purple color and a provocative nose of black currants, minerals, smoke, and sweet oak. Medium bodied, with surprisingly sweet tannin, this is an elegant, rich wine. Although there is tannin lurking in the finish, the 1993 La Mission can be drunk with considerable pleasure. It is a complex, pure wine with no astringency or vegetal character. Anticipated maturity: 1999–2010. Last tasted, 1/97.

1992—An excellent wine for the vintage, La Mission-Haut-Brion's 1992 exhibits a
• dark ruby color, an intense, black currant, mineral, and floral nose, and
89 supple, medium-bodied flavors that cascade over the palate. The wine is soft and opulent, with plenty of glycerin and lusty alcohol in the gorgeous finish. Drink it over the next 10–12 years. Don't be surprised if this wine turns out to merit an even higher rating in a few years. Last tasted, 11/94.

1991—La Mission enjoyed considerable success in the 1991 vintage. This deep
• ruby–colored wine boasts a fragrant, smoky, mineral-and-berry-scented nose.
87 Suave, elegant, and rich, with noticeable fatness to its harmonious flavors, good balance, and a long, medium-bodied finish, the wine exhibits fine ripeness and a tasty, aromatic personality. This precocious La Mission should drink well for the next 6–10 years. Last tasted, 1/94.

1990—The 1990 is improving in the bottle, similar to the evolution of the 1990
• Haut-Brion. The 1990 La Mission performed well above my original score of
94+ 92. The wine is ostentatious, with a sweet, spicy, cedary, fruitcake, and roasted black fruit nose, admirable richness, a juicy, succulent, voluptuous texture, gobs of fruit and glycerin, low acidity, and a full-bodied, layered

finish. This splendidly chewy, intense La Mission-Haut-Brion will come close to matching the quality of the legendary 1989. It will continue to drink well for another 2 decades. Last tasted, 11/96.

1989—I am certainly not going to argue with anyone who believes La Mission-Haut-
 •   Brion's 1989 is every bit as profound as the 1989 Haut-Brion. It is a spectacu-
100   lar wine, and as it ages in the bottle, it is quickly becoming one of my all-time favorite La Mission-Haut-Brions, ranking alongside the 1982, 1975, 1961, 1959, and 1955. The 1989 boasts a dense, thick, purple color, followed by a sweet nose of roasted cassis and chocolate scents complemented by whiffs of tobacco, tar, and minerals. The wine is extremely full bodied, unctuously textured, sweet, jammy, and rich. Although it is still youthful and unformed, it is already delicious to drink. It should develop additional bottle bouquet by the turn of the century, after which it will drink well for 15–20 years. Last tasted, 11/96.

1988—Perhaps the high quality of Merlot (45% in this vintage's blend) has helped
 •   provide the 1988 with significant opulence and depth of fruit. The 1988
 90   has turned out to be a beautifully made, deep, full-bodied, concentrated, rich, well-structured wine that will last for 15–20 years. It is a big, deep, soft, concentrated wine. Anticipated maturity: Now–2012. Last tasted, 1/93.

1987—After having consumed almost two cases of this wine, I am upset that I did
 •   not buy more 1987 La Mission-Haut-Brion. No, it is not a phenomenal wine,
 87   but it is consistently one of the most perfumed, seductive examples of the vintage. It has always been a classic example of La Mission and of the exotic, tobacco, smoky, roasted herb character of a top-notch Graves. The wine is satiny smooth, with low acidity, lovely fresh, ripe black currant fruit, medium body, and a round finish. It has continued to hold at its plateau of maturity, revealing no signs of cracking up. Anticipated maturity: Now–2001. Last tasted, 7/97.

1986—There is a distinctive earthiness to this weedy, medium-bodied La Mission-
 •   Haut-Brion that still has some tannin to shed. The wine displays a youthful
 91   dark ruby/purple color and sweet cassis fruit in the reticent, still unevolved nose. There is admirable power in this wine that is driven more by its spice and structure than its sweetness of fruit. Still youthful, it should continue to develop and evolve for another decade. Anticipated maturity: 2000–2012. Last tasted, 5/97.

1985—If its younger sibling, the 1986, remains tightly knit and unyielding, the 1985
 •   is deliciously opulent, rich, and open knit. The color is a dark ruby/purple,
 92   with some garnet at the edge. The wine offers a sweet, smoky, melted road tar, and black currant nose, with toasty oak in the background. The 1985 has put on weight as it has evolved in the bottle and appears to be better than ever, with copious quantities of lush, jammy black fruits intermixed with the smoky, roasted character so prevalent in this appellation. The low acidity and loosely knit, medium- to full-bodied, fleshy character make for delicious drinking. Anticipated maturity: Now–2006. Last tasted, 10/97.

1984—A successful wine for the vintage, La Mission's 1984 has a moderately dark
• color and is round, herbaceous, fruity, and easy to drink. Anticipated matu-
82 rity: Now. Last tasted, 3/89.

1983—The first La Mission-Haut-Brion produced under Jean Delmas and his staff,
• the 1983 offers sweet asphalt, smoked meat, and animal scents in its provoca-
89 tive bouquet. Dark garnet colored, with spicy flavors of earth, truffles, and
jammy black currants laced with licorice, this medium-bodied wine has
evolved quickly. It is an excellent La Mission. Anticipated maturity: Now–
2005. Last tasted, 5/97.

1982—This wine has emerged from a dormant period to reveal the classic iron,
• tobacco, sweet black currant, and roasted herb nose of a great Graves. The
98 color remains an opaque purple, with a thick, viscous texture. Sweet, expansive, and chewy, with enormous concentration and fat, this wine has begun to
develop its secondary aromatics. It is already thrilling to drink, although it is
still very youthful. For pure complexity and class, the 1989 La Mission rates
higher, but the 1982 rivals the 1959 and 1961 for pure hedonistic appeal. It
may be the modern-day equivalent of the spectacular 1959. Drink it over the
next 25–30 years. Last tasted, 9/95.

1981—No doubt this vintage of La Mission-Haut-Brion was probably overlooked
• once the highly publicized 1982 vintage was conceived, but this wine has
90 always been, in my opinion, one of the stars of the vintage. It showed extremely well, with a big, rich, berry-and-smoky-scented bouquet, medium-
bodied, alcoholic, deep flavors, huge fruit, and a long finish. It has shed much
tannin and seems to be nearing its plateau of maturity, where I would
expect it to last for 10–15 years. Anticipated maturity: Now–2005. Last
tasted, 2/91.

1980—I had felt this wine would show a bit better than it did in this tasting, but it
• came across as extremely light, with a delicate, restrained, almost watery
72 bouquet, innocuous, medium-bodied flavors, and a short, rather diluted finish.
It should be drunk up before it fades any further. Anticipated maturity: Now.
Last tasted, 1/89.

1979—The 1979 is one of the few vintages in the seventies in which I find La Mission
• to be less successful than its neighbor, Château Haut-Brion. Nevertheless,
91 in this bountiful year La Mission made a wonderfully elegant, surprisingly
concentrated wine that stylistically resembles the 1971. While it lacks the
extraordinary depth and complexity that La Mission is capable of achieving
in great years such as 1982 or 1978, the 1979 is still a very fine wine,
with a life expectancy of 15 years. Anticipated maturity: Now–2005. Last
tasted, 2/91.

1978—The 1978 La Mission-Haut-Brion is a strong candidate, like the 1975, for
• the wine of the vintage. Deep ruby/purple colored with no signs of evolution,
96 it is much more backward than Haut-Brion. Intensely fragrant, it displays
a supple, smooth, velvety texture and well-developed, rich, cassis, gravel,
and smoky scents and flavors. Very full bodied, rich, and supple, this
layered, concentrated wine can be drunk now but promises to be even better

with additional bottle age. Anticipated maturity: Now–2010. Last tasted, 5/97.

1977—While this wine tasted highly chaptalized and extremely herbaceous, I was
  •   somewhat surprised that it was still palatable and, in its own way, easy to
  74   drink. There is no question that the wine is slightly too vegetal, but it is soft
         and fully mature, and for those who have any cellared, it should be consumed.
         Anticipated maturity: Now. Last tasted, 1/89.

1976—I never found the 1976 La Mission to be a very good wine, as it began to show
  •   age and take on an amber/brown color when only 4 years old. However, it
  76   seems to have changed little since I last tasted it. It is an alcoholic, loosely
         knit, rather flabby La Mission, with somewhat of a stewed, roasted character.
         Yet the wine does have ripe fruit, a good bit of alcohol, and very low acidity.
         Anticipated maturity: Now. Last tasted, 1/89.

1975—The 1975 La Mission has been the most consistent wine of the vintage.
  •   Super-concentrated, and now beginning to shed enough tannin so that it can
  100   be fully appreciated, this enormously constituted La Mission-Haut-Brion has
         developed that fabulous Graves set of aromatics—tobacco, black fruits, min-
         erals, roasted herbs, and cedar. Huge, massive, thick, and succulent, with
         moderate tannin and some amber at the edge, this wine will reach full
         maturity by the turn of the century and last for 30–40 years. An extraordinary
         La Mission, it comes closest in style to resembling the 1945, with a hint of
         the sweet, ripe 1959. Last tasted, 12/95.

1974—When I did my original tastings of the 1974s, the three wines that stood out
  •   in that mediocre vintage were Latour, Trotanoy, and La Mission-Haut-Brion.
  86   The 1974 is still very alive and has at least another 7–10 years of aging
         potential. It remains a tougher, more sinewy style of La Mission-Haut-Brion
         but exhibits an excellent deep, dark garnet color, a big, mineral-scented,
         smoky, earthy, spicy bouquet, medium to full body, very hard tannins, and
         very good flavor depth, particularly for a 1974. No doubt the deep guaunzian
         gravel and subsoil of La Mission's vineyard was responsible for producing
         such a successful wine in this rain-soaked vintage. Anticipated maturity:
         Now. Last tasted, 3/91.

1973—The spicy, somewhat watery bouquet fades after 30 or 40 seconds in the glass.
  •   On the palate, the wine is thin and hard. Last tasted, 1/89.
  58

1972—This vintage clearly demonstrates how well La Mission-Haut-Brion can do in
  •   an off year. The year 1972 was certainly the worst vintage of the decade, yet
  86   this wine displays a wonderfully fragrant, spicy, cedary, slightly herbaceous,
         berry-scented bouquet, ripe, round, spicy flavors, medium body, and an at-
         tractively lush finish. Delicious, this wine should be drunk up over the next
         2–3 years. It is an amazing success for this vintage. Anticipated maturity:
         Now. Last tasted, 1/89.

1971—1971 is a delicious La Mission that has been fully mature for the last 5–6
  •   years. This rustic wine has a big, earthy, cigar box, mineral-scented bouquet,
  87   generous yet coarse flavors, and a powerful, dusty finish. I would expect it to

continue to drink well for at least a decade. Anticipated maturity: Now–2000. Last tasted, 10/90.

1970—This wine has a well-deserved as well as notorious reputation for inconsis-
• tency, with many bottles marked by volatile acidity, while others taste cleaner
? and significantly better. My last three tastings, including this one, have placed the 1970 La Mission in a more negative light. The wine was unquestionably full bodied, admirably concentrated, muscular, thick, and rich, but the vola-tile acidity was more than a subtle component. This defect was especially noticeable and the wine disjointed and beginning to reveal some structural cracks. I have had outstanding examples, but none in the last 3 years. Last tasted, 6/96.

1969—A dull, hard, almost neutral bouquet reminded me of some of our modern-day
• California Cabernets that are sterile filtered. On the palate, the wine is hollow,
67 with hard, rough, coarse tannins that have obliterated what fruit may have once been present. While 1963 and 1968 were certainly much worse years for most châteaux, I continue to believe that 1969 may have turned out Bordeaux's least attractive wines in the last 30 years. Last tasted, 1/89.

1968—In the fifties, sixties, and seventies, La Mission-Haut-Brion and Latour were
• the two châteaux considered to be one's best gambles in the terrible vintages.
82 With the 1968, La Mission clearly proved its ability to turn out good wines in disastrous years. No vintage had worse climatic conditions than 1968. Yet this 1968 proved to be one of the surprises, even though it's hardly a great wine. A soft, warm, generously fruity, leather-scented bouquet is followed by a wine that is round and alcoholic (no doubt the wine was chaptalized quite a bit), with a velvety, oaky, sweet finish. The wine lacks complexity but still has fruit, and the high alcohol gives it a generous, warm, pleasant character. For those who might have any, it should be consumed, as it fades in the glass after 3–4 minutes. Anticipated maturity: Now–may be in decline. Last tasted, 1/89.

1967—In the early seventies the 1967 La Mission-Haut-Brion was one of the top
• eight or ten wines of this vintage from the Médoc and Graves. It has begun to
84 lose its fruit and has a coarse, chewy texture with some tough tannins that seem to be taking over the personality of the wine. There is still some fruit, and the wine has appeal, but I would suggest drinking it up immediately. Anticipated maturity: Now. Last tasted, 1/89.

1966—The 1966 La Mission-Haut-Brion, never quite as rich and deep as the 1964,
• is still a beautifully made, elegant La Mission, with a very cedary-and-leather-
89 scented, fruity bouquet, medium to full body, and a long, supple, velvety finish. I would advise those who have it in their wine collections to consume it over the next 4–5 years. It does not appear capable of getting any better and may, in fact, be just starting to lose the fruit. Anticipated maturity: Now–2000. Last tasted, 1/89.

1964—The year 1964 is one of those vintages that turned out to be great for Pomerol,
• St.-Emilion, and Graves, but most of the Médoc properties got caught with
91 their Cabernet Sauvignon unpicked when the heavy rains began to fall. La

Mission-Haut-Brion has always been one of the great successes of the vintage, but it has just turned the corner and is beginning a slow decline. I say that having cellared quite a few bottles of this vintage, which allowed me to taste it frequently. It displays a dark ruby color that is just beginning to show a trace of amber and orange. The bouquet is classic La Mission, with scents of cedar, leather, smoke, and even a trace of truffles in this vintage. It is still an expansively flavored wine, with a lovely, sweet ripeness to its fruit and a heady, alcoholic finish. Those who have it cellared should contemplate drinking it. Anticipated maturity: Now. Last tasted, 6/91.

1963 — For a vintage that many considered to be one of the two worst in the post–
 •   World War II era, La Mission-Haut-Brion certainly turned out to be a pleasant
 72   wine. There is nothing vegetal or diluted about the cedary, spicy, smoky, fruity, yet somewhat chaptalized bouquet. On the palate, the wine exhibits surprising body and vibrant fruit but has a hot, alcoholic finish. After several minutes in the glass, it fades completely. For the vintage, one would have to consider this a major success. Anticipated maturity: Now–probably in serious decline. Last tasted, 1/89.

1962 — I have never thought the 1962 to be a great success. It is an elegant, medium-
 •   bodied wine without a great deal of complexity or depth, but it exhibits a
 84   pleasant supple, cedary, smoky, cigar box character. There is also some pleasant plummy fruit and a soft finish. Still vibrant and alive, it should have no problem being cellared for another 2–7 years. Anticipated maturity: Now–may be in decline. Last tasted, 1/89.

1961 — One of the greatest 1961s, La Mission-Haut-Brion has been fabulous to drink
 •   for the last 5–10 years. Where well stored, this wine will continue to drink
 100   well for 10–20 years. More developed and drinkable than the 1959, it remains a thick, rich, super-aromatic wine with a textbook Graves bouquet of tobacco, barbecued meats, minerals, spices, and sweet red and black fruits. Dense, full bodied, alcoholic, and super-rich, this soft, opulently textured wine makes for a fabulous drink. Absolutely stunning! Last tasted, 10/94.

ANCIENT VINTAGES

It is interesting to note that many 1959s, much like the 1982s, were maligned for lacking both acidity and aging potential. How does one explain the fact that many 1959s are less evolved, as well as richer, fresher, and more complete, than many 1961s? For example, as great as the 1961 La Mission is, the equally perfect 1959 (100 points; last tasted 10/94) remains a less evolved and even richer, deeper-colored, more concentrated, and more powerful wine! It needs at least 3–5 more years of cellaring to reach its plateau of maturity. Spicy and super-concentrated, with a dense, plummy/purple color, this young, broodingly backward, formidably endowed wine should be at its best by the end of the century and drink well for the first 20–25 years of the next millennium. Even allowing for the greatness of Haut-Brion and Mouton-Rothschild, the 1955 La Mission (100 points; last tasted 10/94) is the "wine of the vintage." It possesses a sweet, cedary, clove, smoke, and black raspberry nose and rich, full-bodied, remarkably harmonious flavors that ooze with ripe fruit, glycerin, and heady alcohol. The tannin has totally melted away, and the wine reveals considerable rust at the edge, so it is unlikely that the 1955 will improve with further cellaring. There is no indication of any fragility or decline, so this wine can be safely drunk for 10–15 more years. It is an amazing, complex, superbly well-balanced La Mission-Haut-Brion! I have been told by a number of people who have followed the 1953 (93 points; last tasted 10/94) vintage from its youth that it drank exceptionally well in the late fifties. Apparently it has lost none of its hedonistic, supple, explosive fruit. It will not get any better, so consumption is recommended. It offers a delicious smoky, berry fragrance, a silky, creamy texture, and a long, heady finish. The low acidity provides vibrance, and the tannins have melted away. Should you be fortunate enough to have the beauty cellared, drink it over the next several years. La Mission also made a decent 1951 (81 points) and a great 1952 (93 points). Neither of these wines has been tasted since 1991. The 1950 (95 points; last tasted 10/94) possesses a huge nose of freshly brewed coffee, hickory wood, cedar, and chocolate. Super-rich and dense, with little evidence of its age (the color is still an opaque dark garnet), this full-bodied, concentrated wine is at its apogee. It should continue to drink well for another 15–20 years.

The 1949 (100 points; last tasted 10/94) exhibits an intense, singed nose of roasted herbs, smoky black currant fruit, and grilled meat aromas. Enormously rich yet sweet, soft, fat, and opulent, the fully mature 1949 La Mission is awesomely intense and long. It is a magnificent bottle of wine from the most harmonious Bordeaux vintage of the century. The 1948 (93 points; last tasted 10/94) offers up a powerful, roasted, rich bouquet of tobacco, ripe curranty fruit, and smoky chestnuts. It reveals no amber or brown, concentrated, highly extracted fruit, full body, and plenty of alcohol and tannin in the finish. The wine is clearly at its plateau of maturity and shows no signs of losing its fruit. It should last for another 10–20 years. A huge, portlike bouquet of chocolatey, cedary, earthy, plummy fruit demonstrates the extraordinary ripeness that was achieved in the 1947 (95 points; last tasted 10/94) vintage. Very alcoholic, powerful, and rich, but at the same time velvety and sweet, this wine was probably as close to a late harvest La Mission-Haut-Brion as one is likely to experience. It is an exceptional wine with great flavor dimension and length. The 1945 La Mission (94 points; last tasted 10/94) is certainly a great wine with fabulous concentration but also a leathery, tough, hard texture. It is very powerful, broodingly rich and opaque, but the tannin is extremely elevated, and one wonders what is going to fall away first, the fruit or the tannin? This wine still has the potential to last for another 20–25 years, and therein lies much of the mystique of this vintage.

The extraordinary 1929 (97 points; last tasted 10/94)—which may well have been the vintage of the century, with a style that old-timers compare to modern-day 1982s or, more recently, the 1990s—produced wines that were wonderfully opulent and unctuous. Henri Woltner wrote that the 1929 La Mission drank fabulously well in 1933, yet he doubted its ability to age well. How wrong he was! Still deep garnet in color, with only a trace of amber at the edge, this wine exhibits a fabulously exotic, sensual bouquet filled with aromas of tobacco, black currants, cedar, and leather. On the palate it reveals high alcohol, as well as the remarkably sweet, rich, expansive, staggering concentration of fruit necessary to stand up to the alcohol. This is a velvety, lush, full-bodied wine that it is an incredible privilege to drink.

VINTAGES (La Chapelle de la Mission)

1997—The soft, round, herb-tinged 1997 Chapelle-Haut-Brion (made from the youn-
•   gest vines) is up-front, easy to understand, fruity, straightforward, and simple.
83–   I would opt for drinking it during the first 4–5 years after release. Last tasted,
85   3/98.

1996—The 1996 is a soft, round, lovely, cedary, smoky, complex wine with medium
•   body, and luscious sweet fruit. It will not make old bones, but for a textbook
86–   Graves to drink over the next 7–8 years, this wine has considerable merit.
87   Last tasted, 3/98.

1995—The 1995 comes across as more extracted than the 1996, but offers a lovely,
•   rich, medium-bodied, well-endowed personality. The wine reveals much of
90   the character of La Mission-Haut-Brion in its sweet berry fruit intertwined
      with smoke, tobacco, and roasted herbs. Round, spicy, and generous, with no
      hard edges, it will provide ideal drinking over the next 7–8 years. Last tasted,
      11/97.

1993—Approximately 1,000 cases of this second wine of La Mission-Haut-Brion
•   were made. Not surprisingly, it is a tasty, rich, medium-bodied, soft wine that
86   is ideal for drinking over the next 7–8 years. The elimination of 18%–20%
      of the harvest is undoubtedly the reason both this wine and La Mission-Haut-
      Brion are superb in 1993. Last tasted, 11/94.

1992—This is the new second wine of La Mission-Haut-Brion. The 1992 is a soft,
•   fruity, attractively made, medium-bodied wine with a pure, ripe black cherry
86   fruit and smoky tobacco character. Drink it over the next 3–4 years. Last
      tasted, 11/94.

OLIVIER   GOOD SINCE 1995

Classification: Classified growth (red and white)
Location of vineyards: Léognan
Owner: Bethmann family
Administrator: J.-J. de Bethmann
Address: 33850 Léognan

Mailing address: Same as above
Telephone: 33 5 56 64 73 31; telefax: 33 5 56 64 54 23
Visits: By appointment only
Contact: Above telephone and fax numbers

VINEYARDS (red)
Surface area: 81.5 acres
Average age of vines: 20 years
Blend: 55% Cabernet Sauvignon, 35% Merlot, 10% Cabernet Franc
Density of plantation: 8,000–10,000 vines per hectare
Average yields (over the last 5 years): 45–50 hectoliters per hectare
Total average annual production: 18,000 cases

GRAND VIN (red)
Brand name: Château Olivier
Appellation: Pessac-Léognan
Mean annual production: Selection varies between 40% and 70% of total yield
Upbringing: Harvest is done manually. Fermentations last 10–30 days at 25–30 degrees centigrade in temperature-controlled lined stainless-steel vats. Wines are transferred after malolactics to oak casks that are renewed by a third each vintage, for 12 months aging. They are fined and filtered.

SECOND WINE
Brand name: Réserve d'O du Château Olivier
Average annual production: 30%–60% of total yield

VINEYARDS (white)
Surface area: 29.7 acres
Average age of vines: 30 years
Blend: 55% Semillon, 40% Sauvignon, 5% Muscadelle
Density of plantation: 8,000–10,000 vines per hectare
Average yields (over the last 5 years): 40–45 hectoliters per hectare
Total average annual production: 6,000 cases

GRAND VIN (white)
Brand name: Château Olivier
Appellation: Pessac-Léognan
Mean annual production: Varies between 40% and 70% of the total yield
Upbringing: Harvest is done manually. Wines are fermented in oak barrels, renewed by a third each vintage. They remain on lees for 12 months and are bottled after fining and filtration.

SECOND WINE

Brand name: Réserve d'O du Château Olivier

Average annual production: Varies between 30% and 60% of total yield.

Evaluation of present classification: Should be maintained, particularly since 1995.

Plateau of maturity: (red) 2–8 years following the vintage; (white) 2–4 years following the vintage

This estate is one of the oldest in the entire Bordeaux region, tracing back to the twelfth century. One of its most famous visitors in the fourteenth century was the Black Prince (son of King Edward III of England), the Bordeaux commander who led many of England's greatest knights in their battles against the French for control of the Aquitaine. Since the end of World War II, a family of German origin, the de Bethmanns, have been the proprietors. It has not been a management that has resulted in profound wines. Both the white and red wines vinified at Olivier have been mediocre in quality and unusually simple, light, and innocuous for a Cru Classé with vineyards so well placed in the Léognan region. Insiders in Bordeaux argue that the exclusivity the Bethmanns gave to the large *négociant* firm of Eschenauer often prevented the wine from being shown in comparative tastings, where its weaknesses would have been obvious. However, that exclusivity ended in the mid-1980s, and now the wine can easily be compared with that of its neighbors. Improvements are being made, but as my recent tastings continue to demonstrate, this property still has considerable unrealized potential.

I am convinced that live-in proprietor Jean-Jacques de Bethmann is in the process of making a major effort to improve the quality of Olivier's wines. The selection process has been increasingly strict in the nineties, and with the purchase of a concentrating machine (the reverse osmosis type) to be used in the 1998 vintage, readers can expect Olivier to become a far more interesting wine. Vintages from 1994 have been much better than prior ones.

VINTAGES (red)

1997—A splendidly moated fortress castle well-situated in Pessac-Léognan, Olivier's
• wines are on the upswing. The 1997 exhibits a dark ruby color with purple
85– nuances. Sweet blackberry, cassis, and toasty aromas are followed by a me-
87 dium-bodied, very open-knit and charming wine with light tannins and low
acidity. Not a big wine, but elegant and pure, this offering should drink well
for the next decade. Last tasted, 3/98.

1996—This is a harmonious, pure, light- to medium-bodied Graves with a dark ruby
• color, a soft supple style, and attractive cherry and dusty mineral-infused
85 fruit. Anticipated maturity: 1999–2010. Last tasted, 3/98.

1995—Compact, lean, tannic, and more austere than the 1996, the 1995 is a light-
*   to medium-bodied, competent but uninspiring effort. Anticipated maturity:
84   2000–2008. Last tasted, 3/98.

1994—Light to medium ruby–colored, the 1994 exhibits a spicy, cherry, and currant-
*   scented nose with toasty oak in the background. This medium-bodied wine
85   possesses reasonably good fruit, spice, and some of the earthy, mineral, and
         tobacco characteristics that come from wines made in this sector of Graves.
         Last tasted, 3/98.

1993—This wine's light to medium ruby color is adequate, and the pronounced
*   weedy, vegetal nose offers some spice but very little fruit. There is noticeable
74   dilution in this light-bodied, quaffable, but simple red Graves. Drink it over
         the next 3–4 years. Last tasted, 1/97.

1992—Although the 1992 offers impressive deep color and spicy notes in its oaky
*   bouquet, it lacks the fruit, concentration, and length of the 1991. A shal-
75   lowness becomes increasingly apparent as the wine rests on the palate. This
         is a wine that must be drunk in its first 2–3 years of life. Last tasted, 11/94.

1991—Olivier has turned in a meritorious performance in the tough 1991 vintage.
*   The deep ruby color is followed by a weedy, tobacco-scented, spicy, currany,
85   open, and easy to appreciate nose. Lavish quantities of new oak give the wine
         a forward, sexy, cosmetic appeal. Once past all the oak, attractive ripe fruit is
         presented in a soft, velvety-textured, medium-bodied format. Drink this
         charming wine over the next 4–5 years. Last tasted, 1/94.

VINTAGES (white)

1996—This narrowly constructed wine possesses sharp acidity and a lack of flesh and
*   concentration, making it a dubious candidate for extended cellaring. The abun-
75   dant use of smoky new oak is noteworthy only because it obliterates what little
         fruit the wine possesses. Anticipated maturity: Now–2005. Last tasted, 3/97.

1995—This is a shallow but pleasant dry white Graves with an herbal-scented nose.
*   Light intensity, honeylike flavors, and lavish quantities of new oak are present
82   on the palate of this medium-bodied wine. The acidity and wood are both
         high, but the wine is pleasant tasting. Anticipated maturity: Now–2006. Last
         tasted, 3/97.

1994—This intensely fruity white Graves offers honeyed citrus aromas, medium
*   body, a sense of elegance, and gobs of ripe fruit presented in a user-friendly
87   style. Drink it over the next 5–6 years. Last tasted, 3/95.

1993—Monolithic, with some toasty new oak, this light- to medium-bodied, re-
*   freshing, but simplistic dry white wine should be drunk over the next year.
81   Last tasted, 11/94.

1992—The delicate 1992 displays a citrusy, stony-scented nose, medium-bodied,
*   pleasant flavors, and a compact finish. Last tasted, 1/94.
84

1991—The diluted 1991 exhibits a sugary, cloying finish. Last tasted, 1/94.
*
76

PAPE-CLÉMENT

Classification: Classified growth (reds only)
Location of vineyards: Pessac
Owner: Société Montagne
Address: 216, avenue du Docteur Nancel Pénard, 33600 Pessac
Mailing address: B.P.164, 33607 Pessac Cedex
Telephone: 33 5 56 07 04 11; telefax: 33 5 56 07 36 70
Visits: By appointment only, Monday to Friday between 9 A.M. and noon,
and 2 P.M. and 5 P.M.
Contact: Bernard Pujol

VINEYARDS (red)
Surface area: 74 acres
Average age of vines: 38 years
Blend: 60% Cabernet Sauvignon, 30% Merlot, 10% Cabernet Franc
Density of plantation: 7,500 vines per hectare
Average yields (over the last 5 years): 40–45 hectoliters per hectare
Total average annual production: 140,000 bottles

GRAND VIN (red)
Brand name: Château Pape-Clément
Appellation: Pessac-Léognan
Mean annual production: 100,000–120,000 bottles
Upbringing: Fermentations last 20–24 days, and malolactics occur half in
stainless-steel tanks and half in barrels. Wines are transferred into oak
casks for 15–20 months aging. Percentage of new oak varies between
60% and 90% depending upon the vintage. Racking is done every 3
months, and wines are fined with fresh egg whites. They are bottled
unfiltered.

SECOND WINE
Brand name: Le Clémentin du Pape-Clément
Average annual production: 20,000–50,000 bottles

VINEYARDS (white)
Surface area: 6.2 acres
Average age of vines: 20 years
Blend: 45% Sauvignon, 45% Semillon, 10% Muscadelle
Density of plantation: 7,500 vines per hectare
Average yields (over the last 5 years): 30 hectoliters per hectare
Total average annual production: 8,000–10,000 bottles

GRAND VIN (white)
Brand name: Château Pape-Clément
Appellation: Pessac-Léognan

Mean annual production: 6,000–8,000 bottles
Upbringing: Racking of the must is done from barrel to barrel. Wines are kept on lees for 10 months with frequent stirring. Percentage of new oak varies between 20% and 40%. Wines are fined and filtered.

SECOND WINE
Brand name: Le Clémentin du Château Pape-Clément
Average annual production: 2,000–4,000 bottles

Evaluation of present classification: Since 1986 the quality equivalent of a Médoc second-growth
Plateau of maturity: (red) 5–20 years following the vintage; (white) 3–8 years following the vintage

Pape-Clément is located in the suburban sprawl of Pessac, several miles from the famed Château Haut-Brion. Historically Pape-Clément is among the most significant estates of the Bordeaux region. One of the original owners, Bertrand de Goth, purchased this country estate in 1300 and 6 years later became Pope Clément V. He was admired by the French for his bold decision to move the papacy to the sun-drenched, hallowed Provençal city of Avignon, where the historical period of the papacy became known as the Babylonian Captivity and the wine produced by Clément at his country estate outside Avignon became known as Châteauneuf du Pape. While Pope Clément V remained in Avignon, he turned over the vineyards of Pape-Clément to the church, where they remained undisturbed until divested during the French Revolution.

The vineyard is now controlled by the heirs of the late French poet Paul Montagne. While no one doubted the quality of Pape-Clément's wines in the fifties, sixties, and early seventies, lack of attention to detail and little investment in winemaking equipment or barrels resulted in a significant deterioration of quality at Pape-Clément after 1975. For the next decade the wines produced at the château were often musty, lacked freshness, and, in short, were poorly made. The succession of poor to mediocre results ended in 1985 subsequent to the hiring of the young, enthusiastic Bernard Pujol. Pujol was given total responsibility for resurrecting the quality of Pape-Clément, and the result, first evidenced with a profound 1986, has been a succession of wines that now come close to rivaling the great Haut-Brion and La Mission-Haut-Brion.

Pape-Clément, which sits on extremely light, gravelly soil, produces a wine that at its best has a fascinating and compelling bouquet offering up gobs of black fruits intermingled with strong smells of tobacco and minerals. Because of the relatively high percentage of Merlot, it is a wine that can be drunk extremely young yet can age easily for several decades in the best vintages. In the last half of the decade of the eighties, Pape-Clément became one of the stars of Bordeaux, producing profound wines in 1996, 1990, 1988, and 1986.

The new commitment to quality has also been evidenced by an increase in the vineyard area for their rare white wines. Previously, the microscopic production, usually less than 100 cases, was reserved for exclusive use by the château. The property now produces nearly 600 cases.

VINTAGES (red)

1997—One of the best wines from the Graves region, Pape-Clément's 1997 reveals a
•　　dark ruby color with purple nuances. The nose offers up scents of roasted
87–　herbs, cedar, tobacco, and fruitcake. Low in acidity, lush and charming, with
90　　medium body and plenty of fruit, this is a complex, savory, opulently textured wine that will provide gorgeous drinking early in life. It may merit an outstanding score if it develops more delineation and length. Anticipated maturity: 2001–2009. Last tasted, 3/98.

1996—Following a classic Graves aromatic profile of weedy tobacco, smoke, fruit-
•　　cake, and red and black currants, this dense, rich, medium-bodied 1996
90–　reveals outstanding purity and ripeness, as well as glorious levels of finesse
92　　and complexity. It is not a muscular, weighty wine but, rather, one of precision and delicacy. The tannin is sweet, but the 1996 Pape-Clément is capable of lasting two decades. Anticipated maturity: 2002–2020. Last tasted, 3/98.

1995—A softer, more accessible version of the more tannic 1996, Pape-Clément's
•　　1995 exhibits a deep ruby/purple color, and a lovely nose of spice, lead
90　　pencil, minerals, smoke, and tobacco-tinged black currants. Rich and ripe, with medium body, sweet fruit on the attack, and an overall sense of elegance and impeccable equilibrium, this beautifully knit, complex wine is already enjoyable. Anticipated maturity: Now–2015. Last tasted, 11/97.

1994—The 1994's medium ruby color is lighter than expected. The tobacco, red
•　　currant, and mineral aromatics are followed by a medium-bodied, restrained,
87　　measured wine with sweet fruit, no hard edges, and a suave personality. Drink this elegantly styled Pape-Clément over the next 7–8 years. Last tasted, 1/97.

1993—An unimpressive medium ruby color is followed by a textbook Graves nose of
•　　berries, tobacco, and spicy scents with that notion of scorched earth and hot
86　　rocks. This is a lighter wine than the great 1990, but within the style of the vintage it is well balanced, exhibiting sweet, red currant, plummy fruit, undeniable elegance and finesse, and a soft, round finish. The wine is more pleasurable than the score indicates. Drink it over the next 7–8 years. Last tasted, 1/97.

1992—Although the light to medium ruby color suggests dilution, this Pape-Clément
•　　offers a characteristically complex bouquet of tobacco, herbs, cedar, and
83　　sweet red and black fruits. Light bodied, with low acidity, this pleasant but short wine lacks concentration. It does possess enough of this well-run estate's

character to merit some attention. Drink it over the next 2–4 years. Last tasted, 11/94.

1991 — The excellent 1991 offers an intensely fragrant bouquet of cedar, tobacco,
• smoke, and black fruits. Medium bodied, with fine depth, sweet, jammy fruit,
87 wonderful elegance, and a soft, satiny-textured finish, this admirably long wine is already delicious; it should last for 7–8 years. Impressive! Last tasted, 1/94.

1990 — The 1990 is a rich, complete wine, with a deep ruby/purple color and a sweet
• nose of black fruits, tobacco, roasted herbs, and meats. This medium-bodied,
91 concentrated wine is surprisingly tannic and backward. While the outstanding 1990 appears to be one of Pape-Clément's top successes, rivaling what they produced in 1988 and 1986, it needs more bottle age (4–5 more years) than I originally predicted. Anticipated maturity: 2001–2019. Last tasted, 11/96.

1989 — The 1989 is tight, with a lean, austere personality and astringent tannin. It
• exhibited medium weight and ripe fruit, but the charm and suppleness this
87 wine displayed the first several years after bottling appears to have gone into hiding, replaced by the wine's structure. This impenetrable 1989 requires 4–5 years of cellaring. Whether the tannin will melt away sufficiently for the wine to exhibit complete harmony is doubtful. Last tasted, 11/96.

1988 — Possessing the quintessential Graves elegance and perfume, the 1988 is
• impressively deep in color for a Graves, with a thrillingly fragrant nose of
92 roasted chestnuts, tobacco, currants, and earthy stones. One notices that this is an atypically backward, full Pape-Clément, but there is wonderful ripeness and high, velvety tannins. The finish is all smoky-scented black cherries. Anticipated maturity: Now–2008. Last tasted, 1/93.

1987 — Similar to La Mission-Haut-Brion in the soft, seductive, velvety texture and
• easygoing flavors, this wine is a notable success for the vintage. It is charming
85 and fruity. Anticipated maturity: Now. Last tasted, 11/90.

1986 — The 1986 is a remarkable wine, which is amazing given the fact that this
• vineyard was inundated during the severe rainstorms prior to the harvest. No
91 doubt the very strict selection was responsible: as a result, only the later-picked grapes went into the 1986. It has a stylish black currant–and-mineral-scented bouquet backed up nicely by spicy new oak. Deep ruby/purple in color, medium bodied, with excellent ripeness and richness, this wine is not a blockbuster, but it does have a beautifully crafted, graceful texture and a long, stylish finish. It is undoubtedly the finest wine produced at this beautiful estate in Pessac between 1961 and 1988. Anticipated maturity: Now–2008. Last tasted, 2/91.

1985 — The 1985, the best Pape-Clément since the 1975, is a fragrant, supple, tasty
• wine with a great deal of finesse and charm. It is deeply concentrated,
87 medium bodied, long, and complex. Anticipated maturity: Now–2000. Last tasted, 3/89.

1983 — This is an adequate Pape-Clément. The wine is medium ruby, with an attrac-
• tive, herblike, spicy, ripe fruity nose somewhat dominated by vanillin oak and
78 tight, compact, rustic flavors. Anticipated maturity: Now–may be in decline. Last tasted, 3/89.

1982—My scores have ranged between the upper 50s and mid-60s for this distress-
  •   ingly ugly wine. It is mushroomy and moldy, with earthy, fecal scents, and
  62   washed-out flavors, and the only components left intact are acidity, tannin,
         and alcohol. This wine was made during a very difficult economic period for
         Pape-Clément. Fortunately a succession of gorgeous wines has been produced
         since 1986. Last tasted, 9/95.

1981—This wine has held up better than the 1982 but does display relatively weak,
  •   diluted, frail flavors, an earthy, dirty barrel, barnyard smell, and soft, fading
  65   flavors. Anticipated maturity: Now. Last tasted, 1/89.

1979—Medium bodied and one-dimensional, with only a hint of the famed tobacco,
  •   mineral-like bouquet, this is a light-bodied, austere, attenuated Pape-
  75   Clément. Anticipated maturity: Now. Last tasted, 1/89.

1978—This wine has dropped most of its fruit, taking on an earthy, stale mushroom
  •   like quality. The medium ruby color exhibits a great deal of amber and brown.
  72   The finish is marked by excessive acidity and a slight dirtiness. There is still
         some underlying fruit, but this wine seems to be collapsing quickly. Last
         tasted, 1/89.

1976—All the fruit has now faded from what was never a good example of this
  •   vintage. Last tasted, 7/88.
  62

1975—The best Pape-Clément of the seventies. A complex smoky, roasted chestnut,
  •   earthy bouquet is intense. On the palate, this dark garnet–colored, medium-
  87   bodied wine is lighter than many 1975s but has excellent concentration, a
         surprising suppleness, and a fine, spicy, mineral-flavored finish with a hint of
         truffles and charcoal. Do not expect all of the wine's tannin ever to fully melt
         away. Anticipated maturity: Now–2008. Last tasted, 10/97.

1970—While the 1970 was impressive when young, like many vintages of Pape-
  •   Clément made during the seventies it has not stood the test of time. Now
  84   becoming loosely knit and losing some fruit, this medium-bodied, very soft
         and supple wine has a classy, earthy, cedary, spicy bouquet and good flavors,
         but both fade quickly in the glass. Anticipated maturity: Now–probably in
         serious decline. Last tasted, 12/84.

1966—This wine has been fully mature since the early seventies and has always
  •   represented one of the best examples of this estate's style. Consistently ele-
  85   gant, with Pape-Clément's telltale bouquet of smoky tobacco and earthy,
         cedary, currant fruit, since the late seventies the 1966 has ever so slowly
         begun to lose some intensity and take on more amber color. The wine is still
         very good, but the acidity and tannins are more noticeable in the finish, and
         the fruit is less intense. This was once a beautiful, elegant wine that is now
         beginning to decline. Anticipated maturity: Now. Last tasted, 11/87.

1964—I purchased a half case of this wine and had five marvelous bottles, but the
  •   last bottle, tasted in 1979, had faded badly. However, in the late-1980s two
  88   bottles tasted in Bordeaux were excellent, nearly outstanding examples of
         what was always considered a top vintage for Pape-Clément. If this wine has
         been well stored, it should still reveal a big, smoky, roasted, truffle-and-

berry-scented bouquet, relatively fat, alcoholic flavors, and a long, lush finish. Look for this wine in larger formats at auctions because it is clearly one of the sleepers of the vintage. Anticipated maturity: Now—may be in decline. Last tasted, 3/88.

1961—Extremely rich and full bodied, with an opulent, almost roasted chestnut
•   fruitiness, layer upon layer of richness, and a long, silky, heady finish, this is
92   almost the essence of the mineral, tobacco, Graves-like style that most people associate with Haut-Brion. The wine is fully mature and seems to fade after 30 minutes in the glass—a sure sign that imminent consumption is required. Anticipated maturity: Now—2000. Last tasted, 6/97.

VINTAGES (white)

1996—In a year where white Graves had a tendency to be extremely acidic, Pape-
•   Clément's 1996 is well made. Although it does reveal some of the vintage's
88   tart acidity, there is a nice marriage of sweet citrusy fruit and herbs that go a long way toward concealing the wine's tartness. The wine's smoky spiciness and steely minerality make a refreshing and distinctive style of dry white. Given its high acidity and good flavor extraction, this wine should age well for 10–15 years. Last tasted, 11/97.

1995—While the 1995 is less successful than Pape-Clément's 1994, the wine avoids
•   the diluted, high-acid character found in many 1995 white Graves. The
87   citrusy, fig, and smoky aromatics are followed by a medium-bodied, well-concentrated wine with excellent purity and elegance. It possesses good acidity, a moderately long finish, and some aging potential. Anticipated maturity: 2000–2008. Last tasted, 11/97.

1994—A 10% Muscadelle, 35% Sauvignon, and 55% Semillon blend, the 1994 is
•   outstanding. The nose jumps from the glass, offering up copious scents of
91   tropical fruits, honeyed figs, and smoke. Rich, with superb purity and intensity, this medium-bodied, deliciously fruity, stylish white wine is hard to resist. It will keep for 10–15 years. Impressive! Last tasted, 3/97.

1993—The 1993 is the best white Pape-Clément yet made, exhibiting a fragrant,
•   wonderfully ripe nose of spicy fruit and well-integrated oak, rich, medium- to
90   full-bodied, crisp flavors of minerals, honey, and melons, and a lively, refreshing finish. It should drink well for 10–15 years. Last tasted, 11/94.

PICQUE-CAILLOU   GOOD

Classification: None
Location of vineyards: Mérignac
Owner: Denis family
Administrator: Paulin Calvet
Address: Avenue de Pessac, 33700 Mérignac
Mailing address: Same as above
Telephone: 33 5 56 47 37 98; telefax: 33 5 56 47 17 72

Visits: By appointment only
Contact: Nicolas Leclerc

VINEYARDS (red)

Surface area: 49 acres
Average age of vines: 25 years
Blend: 45% Merlot, 45% Cabernet Sauvignon, 10% Cabernet Franc
Density of plantation: 10,000 vines per hectare
Average yields (over the last 5 years): 35–40 hectoliters per hectare
Total average annual production: 100,000–110,000 bottles

GRAND VIN (red)

Brand name: Château Picque-Caillou
Appellation: Pessac-Léognan
Mean annual production: 60,000–70,000 bottles
Upbringing: Fermentations last 15–22 days in stainless-steel tanks.
Wines undergo malolactics in tanks and are aged in oak barrels, which
are renewed by a third each vintage, for 12–14 months. They are fined
and filtered.

SECOND WINE

Brand name: Château Chêne Vert
Average annual production: 30,000–40,000 bottles

VINEYARDS (white)

Surface area: 2.47 acres
Average age of vines: 6 years
Blend: 50% Sauvignon, 50% Semillon
Density of plantation: 10,000 vines per hectare
Average yields (over the last 5 years): 40 hectoliters per hectare
Total average annual production: 5,000 bottles

GRAND VIN (white)

Brand name: Château Picque-Caillou
Appellation: Pessac-Léognan
Mean annual production: 2,000 bottles
Upbringing: Racking of the musts occurs in stainless-steel vats and
fermentations occur in 1-year-old oak barrels. Wines remain 6–8 months
on lees, are fined, filtered, and bottled in July, following the vintage.

SECOND WINE

Brand name: Petit Caillou Blanc
Average annual production: 2,000–3,000 bottles

Evaluation of present classification: At its best, the quality equivalent of
a Médoc fifth-growth
Plateau of maturity: 3–12 years following the vintage

Picque-Caillou is the last surviving vineyard of the commune of Mérignac, which is now better known as the location of Bordeaux's ever-expanding international airport. The light, gravelly, stony soil, plus the high percentage of Cabernet Franc and Merlot in the blend, produce an aromatic, fruity wine that can be undeniably seductive when drunk young. The soil is not unlike the terrain of the famous Pessac châteaux of Haut-Brion and Pape-Clément. The quality of the winemaking is excellent, largely because of the Denis family, which has owned this property since 1920. No white wine is made.

VINTAGES (red)

1993—The only tasting I did of this offering revealed a strangely vegetal and under-
•   ripe wine. Last tasted, 11/94.
?

1990—This property rebounded in 1990 with a rich wine ripe with scents of smoke,
•   tobacco, oak, and earth. Lovely, rich, round fruit and good depth accompany
86   a smooth finish in this textbook, lighter-weight Graves. Drink it over the next
        5–6 years. Last tasted, 1/93.

1989—The disappointing 1989 is over-ripe, with a cooked, smoked component.
•   Anticipated maturity: Now. Last tasted, 1/93.
76

1988—The 1988 is, along with the 1985, Picque-Caillou's wine of the decade. Deep
•   ruby, with a pronounced earthy, curranty aroma, this fleshy, even opulent wine
86   is loaded with fruit; it should drink well for 6–7 years. Last tasted, 1/93.

RAHOUL   GOOD

Classification: None
Location of vineyards: Portets
Owner: Alain Thiénot
Address: Route du Courneau, 33640 Portets
Mailing address: Same as above
Telephone: 33 5 56 67 01 12; telefax: 33 5 56 67 02 88
Visits: Preferably by appointment, Monday to Friday, 9 A.M. to noon, and
2 P.M. to 5 P.M.
Contact: Nathalie Schwartz

VINEYARDS (red)
Surface area: 44 acres
Average age of vines: 20 years
Blend: 80% Merlot, 20% Cabernet Sauvignon
Density of plantation: 5,600 vines per hectare
Average yields (over the last 5 years): 55 hectoliters per hectare
Total average annual production: 125,000 bottles

GRAND VIN (red)
Brand name: Château Rahoul
Appellation: Graves
Mean annual production: 70,000 bottles
Upbringing: Harvest is done manually. Grapes are totally destemmed.
Fermentations take place in temperature-controlled stainless-steel
tanks and last about 20 days. Wines are aged for 15–18 months in oak
casks that are renewed by a third each vintage. They are fined and
filtered.

SECOND WINE
Brand name: Château La Garance
Average annual production: 55,000 bottles

VINEYARDS (white)
Surface area: 12.4 acres
Average age of vines: 25 years
Blend: 80% Semillon, 20% Sauvignon
Density of plantation: 5,600 vines per hectare
Average yields (over the last 5 years): 45 hectoliters per hectare
Total average annual production: 28,000 bottles

GRAND VIN (white)
Brand name: Château Rahoul
Appellation: Graves
Mean annual production: 18,000 bottles
Upbringing: Harvest is done manually. Fermentations take place in oak
barrels, half of which are new. Musts are clarified before being
transferred to barrels. Wines remain on fine lees in oak for 6–8 months.
They are not racked but fined and filtered.

SECOND WINE
Brand name: Château La Garance
Average annual production: 10,000 bottles

Evaluation of present classification: The quality equivalent of a Médoc
Cru Bourgeois
Plateau of maturity: (red) 5–12 years following the vintage; (white) 3–8
years following the vintage

NOTE: The owner of Château Rahoul, Alain Thiénot (a Négociant from
Champagne), also owns the Château de Ricaud (Loupiac) since 1981.
    The Château Rahoul also controls 7.5 acres in Cérons and produces
some 18,000 bottles of sweet wine annually.

This property near the village of Portets is highly regarded in some circles, but to date I have found the wines overwhelmingly oaky, as well as slightly out of balance. The vineyard is still young, and perhaps when mature the concentration of fruit in the wines will be sufficient to stand up to the wood. Certainly those readers who prefer more oaky-styled wines would rate these wines more highly. In 1991 Rahoul was sold to Alain Thiénot, a wealthy property owner from Champagne.

VINTAGES (red)

1995—The darker-colored 1995 reveals more ripeness in the nose than is found in
• the 1994. While there is more fat and alcohol, there is a slight disjointedness
83 and dilution in the midpalate and finish. Last tasted, 11/97.

1994—The 1994 exhibits a healthy, medium deep ruby color, soft, ripe, forward,
• berry, herb, and toasty aromas, low acidity, a gentle suppleness, and a me-
84 dium-bodied, clean, easygoing finish. Drink it over the next 5–7 years. Last
tasted, 3/96.

1993—This wine has turned out well. The 1993 Rahoul reveals a healthy dark ruby/
• purple color, and a smoky, jammy, rich, black cherry–and-toasty-scented
85 nose. Although the dense, powerful, concentrated flavors may lack complexity, that deficiency is compensated for by considerable intensity and power as
well as a supple, lightly tannic finish. It should drink well for a decade. Last
tasted, 11/94.

1992—The 1992 Rahoul has turned out much better than I would have thought.
• Graves was a consistently successful appellation in 1992, and this wine
85 possesses a medium to dark ruby color and an attractive nose of black
cherries, tobacco, and smoky new oak. It is straightforward, medium bodied,
soft, and ideal for drinking over the next 4–5 years. Last tasted, 11/94.

1991—Rahoul has fashioned an attractive 1991. The medium ruby color is followed
• by a sweet, ripe nose of cassis, tobacco, and spice. Soft, round, and ele-
83 gant, this nicely made 1991 should drink well for 3–4 years. Last tasted,
1/94.

1989—The 1989 exhibited a big, smoky, black cherry aroma, medium body, and a
• soft, exotic finish, although the alcohol was extremely noticeable and the
85 acids suspiciously low. Drink it over the next 4–5 years. Last tasted, 1/93.

1988—Compact, oaky flavors and a short, empty finish to the 1988 fail to elicit my
• interest. Last tasted, 1/93.
77

SMITH-HAUT-LAFITTE   EXCELLENT

Classification: Classified growth (reds only)
Location of vineyards: Martillac
Owner: Daniel and Florence Cathiard
Address: 33650 Martillac

Mailing address: Same as above
Telephone: 33 5 57 83 11 22; telefax: 33 5 57 83 11 21
Visits: By appointment only
Contact: Daniel or Florence Cathiard

VINEYARDS (red)
Surface area: 108.7 acres
Average age of vines: 30 years
Blend: 50% Cabernet Sauvignon, 35% Merlot, 15% Cabernet Franc
Density of plantation: 7,000–9,000 vines per hectare
Average yields (over the last 5 years): 36 hectoliters per hectare
Total average annual production: 1,500 hectoliters

GRAND VIN (red)
Brand name: Château Smith-Haut-Lafitte
Appellation: Pessac-Léognan
Mean annual production: 10,000 cases
Upbringing: Fermentations last 3–4 weeks and occur in
temperature-controlled stainless-steel vats, with temperatures of
28–32 degrees centigrade. Malolactics occur in casks, 50% of which
are new, and wines remain in casks for 15–18 months before bottling.
They are racked every 3 months, and remain both unfined and
unfiltered.

SECOND WINE
Brand name: Les Hauts-de-Smith
Average annual production: 3,000–4,000 cases

VINEYARDS (white)
Surface area: 27 acres
Average age of vines: 25 years
Blend: 95% Sauvignon Blanc, 5% Sauvignon Gris
Density of plantation: 7,000–9,000 vines per hectare
Average yields (over the last 5 years): 38–40 hectoliters per hectare
Total average annual production: 400 hectoliters

GRAND VIN (white)
Brand name: Château Smith-Haut-Lafitte
Appellation: Pessac-Léognan
Mean annual production: 3,000 cases
Upbringing: Pressing of the grapes is done with a bag press, racking of
the must in stainless-steel tanks at low temperatures. Fermentations
occur in casks (50% of which are new), and wines remain on lees for 12
months. They are fined with bentonite and filtered.

SECOND WINE
Brand name: Les Hauts-de-Smith
Average annual production: 1,000 cases

Evaluation of present classification: Since the early nineties this estate
has produced wines consistent with the quality of a second-growth
Plateau of maturity: (red) 5–25 years following the vintage; (white) 5–15
years following the vintage

For decades, while under the ownership of Bordeaux's Eschenauer family,
Smith-Haut-Lafitte was a perennial underachiever. However, this magnificent
estate was sold in 1991 to Florence and Denis Cathiard. Admittedly they had
the misfortune of having to deal with the rain-plagued vintages of 1991, 1992,
1993, 1994, and 1995, but through their extraordinary commitment to quality,
a ruthless selection process, and a long-term vision for this estate, they
produced better wines in the difficult vintages of the early nineties than the
previous owner was able to do in such exceptional years as 1990 and 1982.
Today Smith-Haut-Lafitte is one of Bordeaux's shining success stories, reflecting what hard work and conscientious proprietors can achieve in a short
period of time.

The style of both the white and red wines combines authoritative richness
with considerable elegance, finesse, and complexity. The international marketplace is often fickle, and it seems to me the prices fetched by recent
vintages of Smith-Haut-Lafitte are below what they ultimately will be once
the quality of these wines becomes known by the wine world.

VINTAGES (red)

1997—This winery continues to move from strength to strength under the committed
• leadership of Florence and Daniel Cathiard. Never a heavyweight or block-
88– buster, Smith-Haut-Lafitte tends to produce the quintessentially elegant style
90 of Bordeaux, offering an impressive marriage of intense flavors, finesse, and
complexity. The 1997 is a forward, beautifully made wine that may merit an
outstanding score by the time it is bottled. The color is deep ruby/purple, and
the wine is expressive aromatically. Chocolate, mineral, crème de cassis, and
subtle *pain grillé* notes soar from this wine. Sexy, with low acidity, medium
body, and beautifully etched flavors that linger on the palate, this is a totally
captivating Smith-Haut-Lafitte that should drink well young, yet last for 15
or more years. Last tasted, 3/98.

1996—A saturated deep ruby/purple color precedes a bouquet of smoke, vanillin,
• sweet cherry, and black currant aromas. Built along the lines of the 1995, but
90– more tannic and less forward, this medium-bodied wine possesses outstanding
92 concentration, purity, and equilibrium. It is a beautifully made, potentially

complex, perfumed, harmonious claret that should age gracefully. Anticipated maturity: 2004–2020. Last tasted, 3/98.

1995 — This wine is already showing exceptionally well, even though it is not close
• to its plateau of maturity. The deep ruby/purple color is followed by scents of
90 roasted herbs intermixed with sweet black currant fruit, truffles, vanillin, and minerals. Lush, with ripe cassis fruit on the attack, outstanding balance, medium body, and layers of intensity, this is an elegant, graceful, smoothly textured, beautifully made Bordeaux. Anticipated maturity: 2001–2018. Last tasted, 11/97.

1994 — Smith-Haut-Lafitte has managed to subdue the potential for astringent tannin
• in this vintage, producing a surprisingly soft, supple, velvety-textured 1994.
88 This wine possesses a healthy purple color, a smoky, spicy, black currant–scented nose, sweet, medium-bodied, well-endowed flavors, a youthfulness and grapiness that does not yet exhibit the complexity of the 1993, and a moderately tannic finish. The 1994 should reach maturity in 2–4 years and last for 15–18. Last tasted, 1/97.

1993 — A deep ruby/purple color is impressive for a 1993 Pessac-Léognan. The wine
• exhibits a textbook Graves nose of smoke, hot rocks, sweet currant and
87 mulberry fruit, and a touch of roasted herbs. Elegant yet flavorful, this medium-bodied, concentrated wine reveals a sweet ripeness and entry on the palate, light tannin, a beautiful dose of toasty new oak, and a suave, savory style. This wine defines what I mean when I say that French wines often possess intensity without significant weight. Drink this lovely offering over the next 6–7 years. Last tasted, 1/97.

1992 — The 1992 is unquestionably a successful wine for this vintage. It exhibits
• elegant, spicy, mineral-and-black cherry–scented notes in its smoky bouquet,
86 medium body, fine ripeness and extraction, a velvety texture, and light tannin in the finish. Drink it over the next 7–8 years. Last tasted, 11/94.

1991 — The 1991 reveals a dark ruby color, an attractive perfume of cassis, tobacco,
• herbs, and spices, excellent balance, considerable finesse, medium body,
85 admirable ripeness, and light tannin in the finish. A good effort for the vintage, it should drink well for 7–8 years. Last tasted, 1/94.

1990 — The 1990 is a surprisingly strong effort from this perennial underachiever.
• The color is dark ruby, and the nose offers attractive, seductive aromas of
86 sweet red fruits, vanillin, and spices. In the mouth, there is a smooth, velvety texture, fine ripeness, succulent fruit, attractive glycerin, and a heady, lush finish. This sexy, easy to drink Graves should provide delicious drinking for another 5–7 years. Last tasted, 1/93.

1989 — The 1989 is an example of a wine with a delicate, fruity character that was
• overwhelmed by the excessive use of new oak. The flavors of oak have crushed
81 much of the wine's finesse and elegance. Anticipated maturity: Now. Last tasted, 1/93.

1988 — Lean, tart, malnourished flavors reflect indifferent winemaking in the 1988.
• Moreover, it is too light and lacking in charm and balance. Caveat emptor!
75 Last tasted, 1/93.

VINTAGES (white)

1996—
•
87
In spite of the high acidity this wine possesses, Smith-Haut-Lafitte has turned out a complex, mellow wine with medium body and a moderately intense nose of grilled herbs, smoke, and ripe fruit (grapefruit and melons). It possesses excellent purity, an elegant, crisp personality, and a dry, refreshing finish. Anticipated maturity: 2000–2010. Last tasted, 11/97.

1995—
•
89
One of the vintage's more successful efforts, the 1995 possesses a smoky, buttery, fig/melony nose and medium-bodied, refreshing flavors with a powdered stone–like taste. Spicy, refreshing, and vibrant, this lively wine exhibits delicacy as well as intensity. Anticipated maturity: Now–2008. Last tasted, 11/97.

1994—
•
91
This 100% barrel-fermented Sauvignon offers gorgeous portions of rich, honeyed, fig, and melony fruit, great purity, and well-integrated new oak. Neither heavy nor excessively alcoholic, this charming, complex, beautifully made white Graves should drink well for 15 years. Last tasted, 3/97.

1993—
•
89
This property is pushing quality higher and higher, and the estate's white wines are among the finest being produced in Graves. The 1993, made from 100% Sauvignon Blanc, offers a rich, honeyed, melony nose with attractive notes of toasty new oak. The wine is fat and rich, with good underlying acidity and plenty of freshness and vibrancy. It should drink well for 3–4 years. Last tasted, 11/94.

1992—
•
87
The excellent 1992 combines all the herbaceous, melony, citrusy components of the 1991 with a touch of honey and smoky oak. The result is a rich, concentrated, medium-bodied wine with brilliant definition, gobs of fruit, and a crisp, long finish. Delicious now, it promises to last for 10 or more years. Last tasted, 3/96.

1991—
•
84
The 1991 is a light-bodied, melony, crisp, citrusy, dry, 100% Sauvignon with medium body and admirable purity, but its finish is too short to merit higher marks. Last tasted, 1/94.

LA TOUR-HAUT-BRION   VERY GOOD

Classification: Classified growth (red only)
Location of vineyards: Pessac
Owner: Domaine de Clarence Dillon S.A.
Address: 33600 Pessac
Mailing address: B.P. 24, 33602 Pessac
Telephone: 33 5 56 00 29 30; telefax: 33 5 56 98 75 14
Visits: By appointment only
Contact: Carla Kuhn

VINEYARDS (red)
Surface area: 12.1 acres
Average age of vines: 23 years

Blend: 42% Cabernet Sauvignon, 35% Cabernet Franc, 23% Merlot
Density of plantation: 10,000 vines per hectare
Total average annual production: 2,000–2,500 cases

GRAND VIN (red)
Brand name: Château La Tour-Haut-Brion
Appellation: Pessac-Léognan
Mean annual production: 2,000–2,500 cases
Upbringing: Harvest is done manually. Fermentations occur in
temperature-controlled stainless-steel vats of 180 hectoliters. A computer
system programs pumping-over and temperature regulations according to
the temperature of the must. Mean temperature is 30 degrees centigrade.
Wines spend 20 months in new oak barrels and are fined with fresh egg
whites.

SECOND WINE
None produced.

Evaluation of present classification: Since 1983, the quality equivalent of
a Médoc fifth-growth; prior to 1983, the quality equivalent of a Médoc
second-growth
Plateau of maturity: Since 1983, 5–10 years following the vintage; before
1983, 8–35 years following the vintage

La Tour-Haut-Brion was, until 1983, owned by the Woltner family, also the
proprietors of La Mission-Haut-Brion. In 1983 these two properties, plus the
white wine–producing Woltner property—Laville-Haut-Brion—were sold to
the American owners of Haut-Brion.

The wines of La Tour-Haut-Brion up to 1983 were vinified at La Mission-
Haut-Brion and handled identically. After both wines were completely finished with the secondary (or malolactic) fermentation, a selection process
commenced in which the most promising barrels were chosen for the wine of
La Mission-Haut-Brion and the others reserved for La Tour-Haut-Brion. In
vintages such as 1982 and 1975, the difference in quality between these two
wines was negligible. To give La Tour-Haut-Brion a unique personality, the
wine had more of the black/purple–colored, very tannic press wine added to
it than La Mission-Haut-Brion. The result was a wine with more size, tannin,
color, and grip than even La Mission-Haut-Brion. The addition of press wine
caused most vintages of La Tour-Haut-Brion to evolve slowly. In a few vintages
—notably 1973 and 1976—the wine turned out better than those of the more
famous sibling.

Since the Dillon family and Jean Delmas assumed control of the winemaking, the style of La Tour-Haut-Brion has changed considerably. It is no longer

the second wine of La Mission-Haut-Brion. Delmas has chosen to make La Tour-Haut-Brion in a lighter style from the property's own vineyards, which are now planted with relatively young vines. The result has been a less imposing, more supple wine that is significantly inferior not only to La Mission, but even to the second wine of Haut-Brion, Bahans-Haut-Brion. For admirers of the old beefy, muscular, brawny style of La Tour-Haut-Brion made before 1983, the new style must be disconcerting. Nevertheless, it is drinkable at an earlier age, and therein, I suppose, lies the modern-day rationale.

VINTAGES

1997 — Dark ruby–colored, with a distinctive nose of Provençal olives, green pepper,
•   tobacco, and red currants, this medium-bodied, slightly herbaceous, some-
85–   what angular La Tour-Haut-Brion reveals sweet fruit and spice on the attack,
86   but dry tannin appears in the finish. It should be drinkable early, and will
       last for a decade. Last tasted, 3/98.

1996 — Along with the 1995, this is one of the strongest efforts I have tasted of La
•   Tour-Haut-Brion since the property was acquired by the Dillon family, and
89–   the wines made by the administrator of Haut-Brion, Jean Delmas. The 1996
90   La Tour-Haut-Brion displays a distinctive Cabernet Sauvignon–dominated
       nose of cedar, fruitcake, spice, and black currants. The wine possesses excel-
       lent richness, a fat mid-palate, and surprising lushness and ripeness. The
       high percentage of Cabernet Sauvignon now used at this estate is evident in
       this attractive, medium-weight wine that should drink well during its first 10–
       15 years of life. This is seductive. Last tasted, 3/98.

1995 — One of the finest La Tour-Haut-Brions over the last 15 years, the 1995 offers
•   a heady perfume of coffee beans, tobacco, spice, smoke, grilled herbs, and
89+   sweet red and black fruits. It is long and round, with copious quantities of
       red currants, as well as good underlying acid, which gives the wine definition,
       and a spicy, lush, sweet finish with light but noticeable tannin. Anticipated
       maturity: 2001–2015. Last tasted, 11/97.

1994 — A surprisingly supple-textured, fragrant, rich, medium-bodied wine has been
•   produced in a vintage with a propensity to turn out stern, tannic, and occa-
89   sionally hollow wines. La Tour-Haut-Brion's 1994 possesses a deep ruby/
       purple color as well as that telltale, textbook Graves, smoky, weedy, tobacco-
       and-sweet black fruit–scented nose. The wine displays fine precision, a clean,
       crafted, pure winemaking style, and a smooth finish with well-integrated
       tannin. It can be drunk now as well as over the next 10–14 years. Last tasted,
       1/97.

1993 — This excellent La Tour-Haut-Brion reveals a medium dark ruby color, a spicy,
•   peppery, sweet black fruit–scented nose, pure, earthy, smoky tobacco flavors,
88   a sexy lushness and ripeness, medium body, and a soft, flattering finish.
       Already exhibiting complexity and considerable appeal, this wine should
       continue to drink well for 10–12 years. Last tasted, 1/97.

1992—This wine has turned out to be a success for the vintage. It offers a healthy,
•   medium dark ruby color, a pungent nose of smoky, earthy, tobacco, sweet
87   plum, and cherry aromas, attractive, supple flavors with fine concentration,
        and a sweet, elegant, ripe, expansive finish. Drink it over the next 5–6 years.
        Last tasted, 11/94.

1991—The 1991 displays a deep ruby/purple color, a sweet, spicy, mineral-and-
•   tobacco-scented nose, and excellent attack and richness, but there is some
85   shortness in the finish. This attractive, up-front wine should be consumed
        over the next 4–5 years. Last tasted, 1/94.

1990—Less concentrated than the 1989, the soft, fruity, earthy 1990 exhibits the
•   mineral, tobacco, roasted character one finds in wines from the northern
86   viticultural region of Graves. Plump and fleshy, it should be drunk over the
        next 7–10 years. Last tasted, 1/93.

1989—The 1989 La Tour-Haut-Brion is excellent. Primarily a Cabernet Sauvignon-
•   based wine (85% Cabernet, 15% Merlot), it exhibits a bold bouquet of
88   herbs, smoke, and cassis, plenty of ripeness, medium to full body, and a big,
        alcoholic, low-acid finish. Anticipated maturity: Now–2000. Last tasted,
        1/93.

1988—The 1988 La Tour-Haut-Brion has the telltale aggressive, hard tannins so
•   prominent in this vintage, good body, and adequate persistence on the palate.
83   Not charming, but austere and forceful, it should be at its best between now
        and 2003. Last tasted, 1/93.

1986—The 1986 has turned out to be a soft, supple, commercial wine that lacks
•   depth, dimension, and complexity. Anticipated maturity: Now–2002. Last
82   tasted, 11/90.

1985—The 1985 is good but a little short, a trifle too tannic for the amount of fruit
•   present, and lacking length and excitement. Anticipated maturity: Now–
84   2001. Last tasted, 3/89.

1984—Relatively light for this property, the 1984 La Tour-Haut-Brion is a straightfor-
•   ward, pleasant, fruity wine with some Graves character. It should be drunk
82   up. Anticipated maturity: Now. Last tasted, 3/88.

1983—A potentially good La Tour-Haut-Brion. However, it is lighter and more supple
•   in texture than previous vintages of this wine. The 1983 is a product of the
84   different approach to winemaking employed by the staff at Haut-Brion, who
        controlled the vinification for the first time in this vintage. Good medium to
        dark ruby color, spicy, soft, supple, and very approachable, this wine should
        mature fairly quickly. Anticipated maturity: Now. Last tasted, 3/89.

1982—This estate's offering has turned out to be more tannic than the 1982 La
•   Mission-Haut-Brion. The wine's color—forbiddingly dark ruby/purple—dis-
95   plays little evolution, while the nose offers up copious quantities of roasted
        earth and sweet black currant aromas intermingled with scents of herbs,
        leather, and spices. Full bodied, rich, and moderately tannic, La Tour-Haut-
        Brion does not possess the sweet, unctuous texture, extract, or intensity of La
        Mission. Give it another 2–4 years of cellaring. Anticipated maturity: 2001–
        2018. Last tasted, 9/95.

1981—The 1981 La Tour-Haut-Brion is a robust, aggressive, rather tannic wine, with
• plenty of power and guts but lacking in finesse. The color is impressively
85 dark, and the weight of fruit and body on the palate is considerable, but this
is not a wine for Bordeaux enthusiasts who want immediate gratification.
Anticipated maturity: Now–2005. Last tasted, 3/88.

1980—Rather light, slightly bitter, and underendowed, the 1980 La Tour-Haut-Brion
• has a smoky, earthy, interesting bouquet and straightforward flavors. Antici-
75 pated maturity: Now–may be in decline. Last tasted, 4/83.

1979—Somewhat similar in style to the 1981, only less tannic, more open knit and
• fruity, yet darkly colored, the 1979 La Tour-Haut-Brion has a spicy bouquet
85 and good weight, richness, medium to full body, and length on the palate. The
bouquet is beginning to mature, revealing earthy, Graves, smoky, mineral
scents. This is an attractively forward La Tour-Haut-Brion that can be drunk
now. Anticipated maturity: Now. Last tasted, 10/84.

1978—One of the top offerings of the 1978 vintage, this is a wine I try to purchase
• at auctions. La Tour-Haut-Brion's color remains a murky garnet/purple, and
95 an explosive nose offers up aromas of roasted meats and herbs, truffles,
licorice, Asian spices, and sweet black currant fruit. Powerful, muscular, and
full bodied, with considerable tannin, this profoundly rich wine is just beginning to reach its plateau of maturity, where it should remain for another 10–
20 years. It is a remarkable effort! Anticipated maturity: 2000–2020. Last
tasted, 4/98.

1976—Clearly better than the diffuse and diluted La Mission-Haut-Brion, yet really
• not very deep or complex for La Tour-Haut-Brion, this fully mature wine has
80 an open-knit, smoky, earthy bouquet, soft, rather diffuse flavors, medium to
full body, and a short, rather coarse finish. Anticipated maturity: Now. Last
tasted, 10/80.

1975—The 1975 La Tour-Haut-Brion has consistently been a great wine. As many
• wine enthusiasts have done, I have made the mistake of drinking it too early.
96 I have only two bottles (from a case and a half) remaining in my cellar. The
wine is more developed than La Mission-Haut-Brion, exhibiting a huge,
sweet, cedary, tobacco, mineral, chocolatey, smoky, cassis nose and flavors.
Massive and full bodied, with well-integrated tannin (because of its sweet,
jammy fruit), the wine exhibits good grip and that firm edge found in almost
all the 1975s. It is a wine of extraordinary extract and aging potential that
should drink well for another 20+ years. Last tasted, 10/97.

1974—Like the wine from sister château La Mission, La Tour-Haut-Brion is an
• unqualified success for the vintage. This is a robust, somewhat rustic, unpol-
83 ished, rich, hefty wine that lacks finesse but delivers plenty of punch and
taste. It is medium to full bodied, with good concentration. Anticipated maturity: Now–may be in decline. Last tasted, 7/82.

1971—More firm and tough than La Mission, with perhaps a little too much tannin
• and acidity for its own good, the 1971 La Tour-Haut-Brion has now been
84 mature for several years. A textbook mineral-scented, burnt tobacco bouquet
offers some interest. On the palate, the wine is medium to full bodied, a trifle

austere and hard, but big and robust. Anticipated maturity: Now. Last tasted, 2/83.

1970— While I have never had a problem with volatile acidity in what is supposedly
  •   the second wine of La Mission-Haut-Brion, La Tour-Haut-Brion has never hit
 88?   the high points given the fact that it is a burly, tannic, beefy, husky wine with
       considerable weight and power. The 1970 is more tannic and less well bal-
       anced than the great 1975. I do not think it will ever lose its coarseness. It
       may last another 20–30 years, but what's the point of holding it? Last tasted,
       6/96.

1966— Fully mature, with the telltale dark ruby, dense color of La Tour-Haut-Brion,
  •   punctuated only slightly by amber, this big, rich, spicy wine has a voluptuous
 88   bouquet of rich fruit and earthy, tobacco aromas. On the palate, it is less
       massive than some La Tour-Haut-Brions and has more finesse and overall
       balance. It is a very attractive Graves. Anticipated maturity: Now. Last tasted,
       3/81.

1961— Tasted only once, the 1961 La Tour-Haut-Brion exhibited remarkable concen-
  •   tration and richness and seemed to have a full 20 years of life ahead of it.
 95   Very dark in color, with just a touch of amber, this big, chewy, viscous wine
       had an opulent and exotic bouquet of ripe currants, cinnamon, tobacco, and
       truffles. Massively proportioned, with layers of fruit and oodles of tannin still
       present, the 1961 La Tour-Haut-Brion was a gustatory tour de force. Antici-
       pated maturity: Now–2030. Last tasted, 3/79.

ANCIENT VINTAGES

I would have loved to come across more examples of old vintages of La Tour-Haut-Brion, as those that I have tasted were extraordinary in quality. The 1947 (rated 95 in 1990) was magnificently rich, but the volatile acidity may put off purists. It possessed huge quantities of fruit, as well as a chewy, even viscous texture. It is a great wine that should continue to drink well for another decade. The other two great vintages of La Tour-Haut-Brion I have had an opportunity to taste include a massive, still backward, and frightfully young 1959. I last had this wine at a restaurant in Bordeaux in 1988, and it was still black/purple in color and at least a decade away from maturity. I rated it 92, but I am sure that when this wine has reached its apogee, it will merit a higher score. Last, the 1955 (rated 94 in 1990), while not having quite the blockbuster bouquet of its sibling—the 1955 La Mission—is still an enormously concentrated, chewy, old-style Graves that should continue to last for a minimum of 2 more decades. It is a shame that La Tour-Haut-Brion is no longer made in this style, but shrewd buyers at auctions are well advised to seek out top vintages of old La Tour-Haut-Brions that may show up from time to time.

LA TOUR-MARTILLAC   GOOD

Classification: Classified growth for reds and whites
Location of vineyards: Martillac
Owner: Kressmann family
Address: Chemin de la Tour, 33650 Martillac
Mailing address: Same as above
Telephone: 33 5 56 72 71 21; telefax: 3 5 56 72 64 03
Visits: Weekdays from 10 A.M. to noon, and 2 P.M. to 5 P.M.; by
appointment only during weekends
Contact: Mr. Tristan Kressmann

VINEYARDS (red)
Surface area: 69.2 acres
Average age of vines: 35 years
Blend: 60% Cabernet Sauvignon, 35% Merlot, 5% Cabernet Franc,
Malbec, and Petit Verdot
Density of plantation: 7,600 vines per hectare
Average yields (over the last 5 years): 45 hectoliters per hectare
Total average annual production: 165,000 bottles

GRAND VIN (red)
Brand name: Château La Tour-Martillac
Appellation: Pessac-Léognan
Mean annual production: 120,000 bottles
Upbringing: Fermentations last 3 weeks in temperature-controlled
stainless-steel vats. Part of the yield completes malolactics in new oak
barrels. Wines are aged in oak barrels, 50% of which are new, and
racked every 3 months. They are fined and lightly filtered.

SECOND WINE
Brand name: La Grave-Martillac
Average annual production: 45,000 bottles

VINEYARDS (white)
Surface area: 24.7 acres
Average age of vines: 40 years
Blend: 55% Semillon, 40% Sauvignon, 5% Muscadelle
Density of plantation: 7,600 vines per hectare
Average yields (over the last 5 years): 50 hectoliters per hectare
Total average annual production: 65,000 bottles

GRAND VIN (white)
Brand name: Château La Tour-Martillac
Appellation: Pessac-Léognan

Mean annual production: 45,000 bottles
Upbringing: Fermentation occurs in oak barrels, of which 50% are new.
Wines remain on lees for 15 months before bottling. They are fined and
filtered.

SECOND WINE
Brand name: La Grave-Martillac
Average annual production: 20,000 bottles

Evaluation of present classification: The red wine is the quality
equivalent of a Médoc Cru Bourgeois; the white wine, since 1987, is
excellent and merits its status as a Graves Cru Classé
Plateau of maturity: (red) 5–10 years following the vintage; (white) 3–7
years following the vintage

By the standards of other Graves properties, La Tour-Martillac is not an old
estate, as the history of the vineyard traces only to the mid–nineteenth
century. However, it has been owned by one of Bordeaux's most famous
families, the Kressmanns, since 1930, and is now managed by Tristan Kressmann.

The white wine has exhibited remarkable improvement since the 1987
vintage and now has become one of the most profound white Graves.
Unfortunately the same cannot be said for the red wine. It continues to
represent a straightforward, mediocre wine that usually has some correct
cherry fruit. Even in opulent vintages such as 1982 and 1989, it has a
compact, simple, undistinguished character. I know of no recent red wine
vintages that did not require consumption within the first 7–8 years of their
life.

VINTAGES (red)

1996 — This looks to be a very good, possibly excellent effort from La Tour-Martillac.
• The wine reveals a deep ruby/purple color, a moderately intense, mineral,
85– vanillin, black currant-scented nose, attractive flesh and texture on the attack,
87 excellent follow through in the mouth, and moderate tannin. It is not revealing
much complexity, but there is fine depth and overall balance. Anticipated
maturity: 2004–2012. Last tasted, 3/98.

1995 — An olive, tobacco, smoky, red currant, and cherry–scented nose is followed
• by an elegant, medium-bodied, soft, smoothly textured wine that can be drunk
86 now or over the next decade. Last tasted, 11/97.

1994 — The 1994 La Tour-Martillac's dark ruby/purple color suggests ripeness and
• decent extract, but aromatically this wine provides little interest. It is com-
81? pletely closed, compact, and hard on the palate, with only a hint of sweet
fruit. The finish consists of astringent tannin, acidity, wood, and alcohol. I am

not sure this wine will last over the long haul, but I feel there is more to it than it is displaying at present. Last tasted, 1/97.

1993 — A reasonably well-made 1993, this wine exhibits the textbook earth, vanillin,
• lead pencil, and cassis aromas of a young Bordeaux. With airing, some of the
84 herbal, green pepper notes of this vintage make their presence known. Spicy, with moderate tannin, medium body, and a tendency toward leanness and austerity, this wine should be drunk over the next 4–5 years before it dries out. Last tasted, 1/97.

1992 — There is no denying the impressive dark ruby, saturated color, but once past the
• color, the absence of any bouquet other than vague, earthy, weedy notes is cause
75 for concern. On the palate, the wine offers a blast of tannin, wood, and earth, but little fruit, ripeness, or charm. It should be drunk up over the next 4–5 years before it becomes even more out of balance. Last tasted, 11/94.

1991 — The light-bodied, aggressively herbal (nearly vegetal) 1991 needs to be drunk
• over the next 4–5 years. Last tasted, 1/94.
76

1990 — Although not a blockbuster, the 1990 is a light- to medium-bodied, elegant
• Graves with a fragrant, earthy, berry-and-mineral-scented nose and ripe fla-
85 vors. Exceptionally easy to drink, it exhibits soft tannins, good depth, and an overall sense of finesse and balance. Drink it over the next 7–8 years. Last tasted, 1/93.

1989 — There was clearly an attempt on the part of the proprietors to make a denser,
• richer wine in 1989. But in doing so, they appeared to have extracted an
80? unpleasant level of tannin. There is plenty of new oak, but the overall impression is one of toughness, a lack of charm, and excessively astringent tannin levels. Anticipated maturity: Now–2000. Last tasted, 1/93.

VINTAGES (white)

1996 — Built along the same lines as the 1995, but less concentrated and more acidic,
• the 1996 reveals smoky oak and a hint of lemony, melony fruit. The wine is
75 extremely acidic in the mouth, and I cannot see it developing much charm or pleasure. Last tasted, 11/97.

1995 — This aggressively woody, slightly acidic wine possesses herbal, lemony, cit-
• rusy aromas and flavors, medium body, and a short yet pleasant finish. Some
85 stoniness is apparent in the flavors and finish. This 1995 should age well for another 10–15 years given the higher than normal acidity level. Last tasted, 11/97.

1994 — This low-acid, plump, rich, well-endowed wine offers a generous and intense
• nose of smoky new oak, ripe fruit, and figs. Rich, with low acidity and an
90 unctuous texture, this wine offers considerable concentration in a slightly heavier style than many of its peers. It is a medium to full-bodied wine that can handle 8–12 years of aging. Last tasted, 3/97.

1993 — La Tour-Martillac has been producing excellent to outstanding dry white
• wines recently. The 1993 boasts gobs of rich, concentrated fruit, medium
89 body, wonderful purity, fine underlying acidity, and a long, smoky, honeyed finish. Drink it over the next 10–12 years. Last tasted, 11/94.

1992—The 1992 displays the big, rich, smoky, honeyed nose that is the result of
 • reasonable yields and barrel fermentation. This medium-bodied wine is
 90 loaded with rich, chewy fruit, wonderful purity and definition, and an
    excellent dry finish; it should drink well for another 7–9 years. Last tasted,
    1/94.

1991—The 1991 exhibits lovely fruit presented in a light- to medium-bodied, elegant
 • format. A stylish, light Graves, with a moderately intense nose, fine depth,
 86 and a lovely crisp finish, it should be drunk over the next 5–6 years. Last
    tasted, 1/94.

1989—While the 1989 is not as concentrated as the 1987 or 1988, it still possesses
 • an immensely attractive lemony, grassy, oaky nose, medium-bodied, soft,
 88 richly fruity flavors, and good length. It will not have extended aging potential
    given the low acidity, but it already provides great enjoyment. Anticipated
    maturity: Now. Last tasted, 4/91.

1988—This is an authoritative example of how delicious and complex a fine white
 • Graves can be. The honeysuckle, spicy, melony, figlike nose exhibits just
 90 enough oak to provide definition and complexity. In the mouth, the wine is
    medium bodied, long, and rich, with excellent focus and a surprisingly fresh,
    yet full-bodied, intense finish. Anticipated maturity: Now. Last tasted, 2/91.

1987—As I have said so many times, 1987 was an excellent year for white Graves,
 • although many observers dismissed the vintage, preferring to see things in
 88 black-and-white terms. This honeyed, herbaceous, smoky-scented white
    Graves has wonderfully precise, rich flavors, medium body, and a lush, long,
    zesty finish. Anticipated maturity: Now. Last tasted, 1/91.

OTHER GRAVES ESTATES

ARCHAMBEAU   GOOD

Classification: None
Location of vineyards: Illats
Owner: Jean-Philippe Dubourdieu
Address: 33720 Illats
Mailing address: Same as above
Telephone: 33 5 56 62 51 46; telefax: 33 5 56 62 47 98
Visits: Preferably by appointment, Monday through Friday, between 9
A.M. and noon, and 2 P.M. and 6 P.M.
Contact: Mrs. Dubourdieu

VINEYARDS (red)
Surface area: 47 acres
Average age of vines: 15 years
Blend: 45% Merlot, 40% Cabernet Sauvignon, 15% Cabernet Franc
Density of plantation: 5,500 vines per hectare

Average yields (over the last 5 years): 50 hectoliters per hectare
Total average annual production: 800 hectoliters

GRAND VIN (red)
Brand name: Château d'Archambeau
Appellation: Graves
Mean annual production: 400 hectoliters
Upbringing: Fermentations and macerations last 18 days, and malolactics occur in vats. Wines are aged 12 months by rotation in vats and oak barrels. They are fined and filtered.

SECOND WINE
Brand name: Château Mourlet
Average annual production: 300 hectoliters

VINEYARDS (white)
Surface area: 16.3 acres
Average age of vines: 20 years
Blend: 80% Sauvignon, 20% Semillon
Density of plantation: 5,500 vines per hectare
Average yields (over the last 5 years): 40 hectoliters per hectare
Total average annual production: 335 hectoliters

GRAND VIN (white)
Brand name: Château d'Archambeau
Appellation: Graves
Mean annual production: 200 hectoliters
Upbringing: Fermentations take place in oak barrels for one-third of the yield and in vats for the remaining two-thirds. Wines remain on lees, are sulfited and aged on fine lees. The whole process before bottling lasts 8–10 months. Wines are fined and filtered.

SECOND WINE
Brand name: Château Mourlet
Average annual production: 135 hectoliters

Evaluation of present classification: Equivalent to a well-made Cru Bourgeois
Plateau of maturity: (red) 2–5 years following the vintage; (white) 2–5 years following the vintage

I have seen only a few vintages of Archambeau's red wine. They were soft, somewhat commercial in orientation, but round and tasty.

The pride and joy of this small property in the commune of Cérons is the white wine, which comes from a gravelly, clay-like soil and is made under the auspices of the great white wine—making family of Dubourdieu. This means cold fermentation and the famed *macération pelliculaire* (prolonged skin contact with the fermenting juice). The results: wines that are remarkably fresh and fragrant, with a honeyed, creamy texture and a long, vividly fruity, generous finish. Consumers should search out recent vintages of this white Graves for drinking in their first 5 years of life.

Prices for Archambeau remain reasonable.

BARDINS

Classification: None
Location of vineyards: Pessac-Léognan
Owner: Yves de Bernardy de Sigoyer
Address: 124, avenue de Toulouse, 33140 Cadaujac
Mailing address: Same as above
Telephone: 33 5 56 30 75 85 or 33 5 56 30 71 51; telefax: 33 5 56 30 04 99
Visits: By appointment

VINEYARDS (red)
Surface area: 17.3 acres
Average age of vines: 23 years
Blend: 42% Cabernet Franc, 32% Merlot, 15% Cabernet Sauvignon, 11% Malbec, some Petit Verdot
Density of plantation: 6,000 vines per hectare
Average yields (over the last 5 years): 50 hectoliters per hectare
Total average annual production: 350 hectoliters

GRAND VIN (red)
Brand name: Château Bardins
Appellation: Pessac-Léognan
Upbringing: Fermentations and macerations last 3–5 weeks in temperature-controlled vats. Malolactics take place in vats, too, and wines are aged 12 months in oak barrels that are renewed by one-third in each vintage. They are fined, but there is no precision as to whether they are filtered.

SECOND WINE
None produced.

VINEYARDS (white)
Surface area: 0.86 acres
Average age of vines: 30 years
Blend: One-third each of Muscadelle, Semillon, and Sauvignon

Density of plantation: 6,000 vines per hectare
Average yields (over the last 5 years): 48 hectoliters per hectare
Total average annual production: 16.8 hectoliters

GRAND VIN (white)
Brand name: Château Bardins
Appellation: Pessac-Léognan
Mean annual production: 16.8 hectoliters
Upbringing: Fermentations take place in barrels, and wines are aged 10
months on lees with 50% new oak. They are fined but remain unfiltered.

SECOND WINE
None produced.

Evaluation of present classification: The quality equivalent of a Médoc
Cru Bourgeois
Plateau of maturity: (red) 3–7 years following the vintage; (white) 2–4
years following the vintage

I have seen only a handful of vintages from this tiny property in the commune
of Cadaujac, situated adjacently to the more renowned Château Bouscaut.
The proprietor has settled on an interesting percentage of grapes, with a very
high percentage of Cabernet Franc for the red wines to give them a soft, spicy,
herbaceous scent, and an extraordinarily high percentage of Muscadelle for
the white wines to make them richly fruity, soft, and ideal for drinking young.

BARET   GOOD

Classification: None
Location of vineyards: Villenave d'Ornon
Owner: Ballande family
Address: 33140 Villenave d'Ornon
Mailing address: c/o Maison Borie-Manoux, 86, Cours Balguerie
Stuttenberg, 33082 Bordeaux Cedex
Telephone: 33 5 56 00 00 70; telefax: 33 5 56 87 60 30
Visits: By appointment only
Contact: Mr. Philippe Castéja at Borie-Manoux

VINEYARDS (red)
Surface area: 104 acres in all, but only 49.4 are currently under vine for
red wines
Average age of vines: 30 years
Blend: 60% Cabernet Sauvignon, 35% Merlot, 5% Cabernet Franc

Density of plantation: 7,000 vines per hectare
Average yields (over the last 5 years): 50–52 hectoliters per hectare
Total average annual production: 6,500 cases

GRAND VIN (red)
Brand name: Château Baret
Appellation: Pessac-Léognan
Mean annual production: 4,500 cases
Upbringing: Fermentations last 4 weeks in temperature-controlled stainless-steel tanks. Malolactics occur in tanks, and wines are transferred to oak barrels (30% of which are new) in December for 12–18 months aging depending upon the vintage. They are fined but not filtered.

SECOND WINE
Brand name: Château de Camparian
Average annual production: 2,000 cases

VINEYARDS (white)
Surface area: 10 acres
Average age of vines: 25 years
Blend: 70% Sauvignon, 30% Semillon
Density of plantation: 7,000 vines per hectare
Average yields (over the last 5 years): 54–55 hectoliters per hectare
Total average annual production: 1,360 cases

GRAND VIN (white)
Brand name: Château Baret
Appellation: Pessac-Léognan
Upbringing: *Macération pelliculaire* lasts 12–24 hours, depending upon the vintage, in small concrete tanks of 40 hectoliters. Fermentations occur in barrels for 75% of the yield and in vats for 25%. Thirty percent new oak is used. Wines remain on fine lees for 6–8 months and are frequently stirred. They are unfined and unfiltered.

SECOND WINE
Brand name: Château de Camparian
Average annual production: 1,000 cases

Evaluation of present classification: The red wine has improved immensely since 1985; the white wine has come of age since 1987; this is increasingly one of the better-made but lesser-known Graves wines
Plateau of maturity: (red) 4–10 years following the vintage; (white) 2–5 years following the vintage

Significant changes have been made at Baret since 1981 when Philippe Castéja, one of the principals in the famous *négociant* firm of Borie-Manoux, assumed responsibility. The property, located just outside of Bordeaux in the commune of Villenave d'Ornon, is now making very good wines that deserve to be better known.

The red wine has become deeper, more fruity, and a great deal more interesting and pleasurable to drink than in the vintages of the sixties and seventies, when they were often coarse and hard. The white wines have improved in quality since 1987, with the addition of some barrel fermentation, extended lees contact, and a cooler fermentation. The results have been some excellent white wines that come close to rivaling all but the very best Graves.

BOYREIN

Classification: None
Location of vineyards: Roaillan
Owner: Jean Médeville and Sons
Address: Château Boyrein, 33410 Roaillan
Mailing address: c/o Château Fayau, 33410 Cadillac
Telephone: 33 5 57 98 08 08; telefax: 33 5 56 62 18 22
Visits: Preferably by appointment
Contact: Mr. Médeville

VINEYARDS (red)
Surface area: 54.3 acres
Average age of vines: 25 years
Blend: 50% Cabernet Sauvignon, 30% Merlot, 20% Cabernet Franc
Density of plantation: 5,000 vines per hectare
Average yields (over the last 5 years): 42 hectoliters per hectare
Total average annual production: 900 hectoliters

GRAND VIN (red)
Brand name: Château Boyrein
Appellation: Graves
Mean annual production: 9,200 cases
Upbringing: Fermentations last 12–15 days in stainless-steel tanks. Pumping-overs are done manually. Malolactics take place in cement tanks. Wines remain 18 months in underground tanks and are bottled after fining and filtration.

SECOND WINE
Brand name: Château Puy Boyrein
Average annual production: About one-third of total yield

VINEYARDS (white)
Surface area: 25 acres
Average age of vines: 18 years
Blend: 50% Sauvignon, 30% Semillon, 20% Muscadelle
Density of plantation: 5,000 vines per hectare
Average yields (over the last 5 years): 40 hectoliters per hectare
Total average annual production: 400 hectoliters

GRAND VIN (white)
Brand name: Château Boyrein
Appellation: Graves
Mean annual production: 200 hectoliters
Upbringing: Stabilization by cooling of the musts (4–5 days).
Fermentations occur at low temperatures (less than 20 degrees
centigrade). Wines are kept in underground tanks and filtered.

SECOND WINE
Brand name: Château Puy Boyrein
Average annual production: 200 hectoliters

BRONDELLE

Classification: None
Location of vineyards: Langon
Owner: Vignobles Belloc Rochet
Address: Château Brondelle, 33210 Langon
Mailing address: Same as above
Telephone: 33 5 56 62 38 14; telefax: 33 5 56 62 23 14
Visits: By appointment only
Contact: Jean Noël Belloc

VINEYARDS (red)
Surface area: 59.3 acres
Average age of vines: 20 years
Blend: 60% Cabernet Sauvignon, 40% Merlot
Density of plantation: 6,600 vines per hectare
Average yields (over the last 5 years): 53 hectoliters per hectare
Total average annual production: 170,000 bottles

GRAND VIN (red)
Brand name: Château Brondelle
Appellation: Graves

Mean annual production: 80,000 bottles
Upbringing: Fermentations last 3 weeks at temperatures of 28–30 degrees centigrade. Malolactics occur in vats after running off. Wines are aged for 12 months in oak casks, which are renewed by one-fourth each year. They are fined and filtered.

SECOND WINE
Brand name: Château La Rose Sarron
Average annual production: 40,000 bottles

VINEYARDS (white)
Surface area: 39.5 acres
Average age of vines: 20 years
Blend: 50% Semillon, 45% Sauvignon, 5% Muscadelle
Density of plantation: 5,000 vines per hectare
Average yields (over the last 5 years): 55 hectoliters per hectare
Total average annual production: 115,000 bottles

GRAND VIN (white)
Brand name: Château Brondelle
Appellation: Graves
Mean annual production: 40,000 bottles
Upbringing: *Macération pelliculaire* lasts 12 hours, followed by cold settling. Alcoholic fermentations occur in vats at 18 degrees centigrade. Wines are kept on fine lees in vats for 4 months before bottling. They are fined and filtered.

SPECIAL CUVÉE
Brand name: Cuvée Anais
Appellation: Graves
Production: 15,000 bottles
Upbringing: Fermentations occur in casks of which 60% are new (40% are 1 vintage old). Wines remain 10 months on lees, with regular stirrings (these are less frequent at the end of the process). They are fined and filtered.

SECOND WINE
Brand name: Château La Rose Sarron
Average annual production: 20,000 bottles

CABANNIEUX

Classification: None
Location of vineyards: Portets
Owner: Mrs. Régine Dudignac-Barrière
Address: 44, route du Courneau, 33640 Portets
Mailing address: Same as above
Telephone: 33 5 56 67 22 01; telefax: 33 5 56 67 32 54
Visits: By appointment only
Contact: Mrs Régine Dudignac-Barrière

VINEYARDS (red)
Surface area: 32.1 acres
Average age of vines: 30 years
Blend: 50% Merlot, 45% Cabernet Sauvignon, 5% Cabernet Franc
Density of plantation: 5,000 vines per hectare
Average yields (over the last 5 years): 58 hectoliters per hectare
Total average annual production: 740 hectoliters

GRAND VIN (red)
Brand name: Château Cabannieux
Appellation: Graves
Mean annual production: 650 hectoliters
Upbringing: Fermentations last about 3 weeks, and wines are aged in oak
barrels, 20% of which are new, for 18 months. They are fined and filtered.

SECOND WINE
Brand name: Château du Curcier and Château Migot
Average annual production: 100 hectoliters

VINEYARDS (white)
Surface area: 16 acres
Average age of vines: 20 years
Blend: 80% Semillon, 20% Sauvignon
Density of plantation: 5,000 vines per hectare
Average yields (over the last 5 years): 57 hectoliters per hectare
Total average annual production: 380 hectoliters

GRAND VIN (white)
Brand name: Château Cabannieux
Appellation: Graves
Mean annual production: 350 hectoliters
Upbringing: Fermentations last 15 days at low temperatures. Depending
upon the vintage, wines are either kept in stainless-steel vats until
bottling or kept for some time on lees in stainless-steel vats and

transferred for 3 months to oak barrels with stirring. They are fined and filtered.

SECOND WINE
Brand name: Château de Curcier and Château Haut-Migot
Average annual production: 30 hectoliters

Evaluation of present classification: An average-quality Graves that is the equivalent of a Médoc Cru Bourgeois
Plateau of maturity: (red) 2–8 years following the vintage; (white) 2–4 years following the vintage

CAILLOU

Classification: None
Location of vineyards: Cérons
Owner: S.A. Château du Caillou
Address: Route de Saint-Cricq, 33720 Cérons
Mailing address: Same as above
Telephone: 33 5 56 27 17 60; telefax: 33 5 56 27 00 31
Visits: By appointment only
Contact: Mr. Bayi

VINEYARDS (white)
Surface area: 7.4 acres
Average age of vines: 30 years
Blend: 50% Sauvignon, 50% Semillon
Density of plantation: 6,000 vines per hectare
Average yields (over the last 5 years): 40 hectoliters per hectare
Total average annual production: 120 hectoliters

GRAND VIN (white)
Brand name: Cuvée Saint-Cricq du Château Caillou
Appellation: Graves
Mean annual production: 45 hectoliters
Upbringing: Harvest is done by hand. Cold settling at 7 degrees centigrade; stabilization for 4–5 days. Fermentations start in vats, and wines are transferred to oak barrels, where they remain on lees for 7 months with frequent stirrings. They are fined but not filtered.

SECOND WINE
Brand name: Château du Caillou
Average annual production: 80 hectoliters

CANTELYS

Classification: None
Location of vineyards: Martillac
Owner: Daniel and Florence Cathiard
Address: G.F.A Malice, 4, chemin de Bourran, 33650 Martillac
Mailing address: Same as above
Telephone: 33 5 57 83 11 22; telefax: 33 5 57 83 11 21
Visits: By appointment only
Contact: Daniel or Florence Cathiard

VINEYARDS (red)
Surface area: 71.6 acres
Average age of vines: 10 years
Blend: 50% Merlot, 50% Cabernet Sauvignon
Density of plantation: 7,500 vines per hectare
Average yields (over the last 5 years): 30 hectoliters
Total average annual production: 1,500 cases

GRAND VIN (red)
Brand name: Château Cantelys
Appellation: Pessac-Léognan
Mean annual production: 1,500 cases
Upbringing: Fermentations last 3–4 weeks in temperature-controlled
stainless-steel vats. Temperatures are kept between 28 and 32 degrees
centigrade. Wines are transferred to oak barrels for 12–14 months aging.
They are neither fined nor filtered.

SECOND WINE
None produced.

VINEYARDS (white)
Surface area: 27.2 acres
Average age of vines: 10 years
Blend: 70% white Sauvignon, 20% Semillon, 10% grey Sauvignon
Density of plantation: 7,500 vines per hectare
Average yields (over the last 5 years): 30 hectoliters per hectare
Total average annual production: 10,000 bottles

GRAND VIN (white)
Brand name: Château Cantelys
Appellation: Pessac-Léognan
Mean annual production: 10,000 bottles
Upbringing: Harvest is done manually. Pressing is done with a bag press.
Racking of the must in stainless-steel vats occurs at low temperatures.
Fermentations take place in oak casks (50% of which are new), and

wines remain on lees for 10 months with regular stirring. They are fined with bentonite and filtered.

SECOND WINE
None produced.

CHERET-PITRES   GOOD

Classification: None
Location of vineyards: Portets, Virelade
Owner: Caroline and Pascal Dulugat
Address: 33640 Portets
Mailing address: Same as above
Telephone and Telefax: 33 5 56 67 27 76
Visits: Preferably by appointment, all days of the week
Contact: Pascal or Caroline Dulugat

VINEYARDS (red)
Surface area: 13.8 acres (plus 47.4 acres in appellation Bordeaux)
Average age of vines: 35 years
Blend: 60% Merlot, 40% Cabernet Sauvignon
Density of plantation: 5,500 vines per hectare
Average yields (over the last 5 years): 55 hectoliters per hectare
Total average annual production: 275 hectoliters

GRAND VIN (red)
Brand name: Château Cheret-Pitres
Appellation: Graves rouge
Upbringing: Wines are aged 18 months, with half the yield in
1-vintage-old barrels and the other half in concrete vats.

SECOND WINE
Brand name: Château Cheret

Evaluation of present classification: Easily the equivalent of a good
Médoc Cru Bourgeois
Plateau of maturity: 3–8 years following the vintage

I have frequently been satisfied by the smoky, tobacco, richly fruity character of the wines of Cheret-Pitres. I have enthusiastic tasting notes of the 1975, 1978, 1982, and 1985. It is not a well-known wine, but because of that it is often a super value. The vineyard is located in the commune of Portets, and no doubt the old vines and high percentage of Merlot give this wine its characteristic fatness and suppleness. No white wine is made at this property.

CHICANE

Classification: None
Location of vineyards: Toulenne, near Langon
Owner: François Gauthier
Address: 1, route de Garonne, 33210 Toulenne
Mailing address: La Magdelaine, 33490 St.-Pierre d'Aurillac
Telephone: 33 5 56 76 43 73; telefax: 33 5 56 76 42 60
Visits: By appointment only

VINEYARDS (red)
Surface area: 13.3 acres
Average age of vines: 20 years
Blend: 55% Cabernet Sauvignon, 35% Merlot, 10% Malbec
Density of plantation: 3,300–5,000 vines per hectare
Average yields (over the last 5 years): 45–50 hectoliters per hectare
Total average annual production: 28,000 bottles and 60 hectoliters of press wines

GRAND VIN (red)
Brand name: Château Chicane
Appellation: Graves
Mean annual production: 28,000 bottles
Upbringing: Fermentations last 3 weeks in temperature-controlled stainless-steel tanks. Wines are transferred to oak casks, which are renewed by one-quarter each vintage, for 12 months aging. They are fined and filtered.

SECOND WINE
Sold in bulk under the label Tourloumet.

NOTE: This estate was run by Pierre Coste until 1993. His nephew François Gauthier, an architect, has now taken over and brought in a number of changes:
• The vines are cultivated using the traditional methods (such as regular plowing).
• No herbicides are used.
• Severe pruning and green pruning are carried out if necessary.
• Vinifications: Grapes used to be fermented in concrete vats of 150–250-hectoliter capacity. Fermentations now occur in smaller stainless-steel tanks (50–80 hectoliter capacity).
• Denis Dubourdieu is consultant/oenologist to the estate

CLOS FLORIDÈNE   VERY GOOD

Classification: None
Location of vineyards: Pujols, Cirons, and Illats
Owner: Denis and Florence Dubourdieu
Address: Quartier Videau, 33210 Pujols, Ciron
Mailing address: Château Reynon, 33410 Béguey Cadillac
Telephone: 33 5 56 62 96 51; telefax: 33 5 56 62 14 89
Visits: By appointment only
Contact: Florence Dubourdieu

VINEYARDS (red)
Surface area: 12.4 acres
Average age of vines: 25 years
Blend: 80% Cabernet Sauvignon, 20% Merlot
Density of plantation: 5,500 vines per hectare
Average yields (over the last 5 years): 40 hectoliters per hectare
Total average annual production: 200 hectoliters

GRAND VIN (red)
Brand name: Clos Floridène
Appellation: Graves
Mean annual production: 180 hectoliters
Upbringing: Fermentations are rather long and occur at high
temperatures; there is intense extraction, with *saignées* at times. No press
wine is added to the grand vin. Wines are aged for 18 months in all. They
spend 12 months in oak casks, of which one-quarter to one-third are new.
They are fined and filtered.

SECOND WINE
Brand name: Château Montalivet
Average annual production: Variable

VINEYARDS (white)
Surface area: 29.6 acres
Average age of vines: 25 years
Blend: 40% Sauvignon, 40% Semillon, 20% Muscadelle
Density of plantation: 7,000 vines per hectare
Average yields (over the last 5 years): 37 hectoliters per hectare
Total average annual production: 480 hectoliters

GRAND VIN (white)
Brand name: Clos Floridène
Appellation: Graves
Mean annual production: 50,000–53,000 bottles

Upbringing: Fermentations occur in barrels, and wines are kept on lees for 11 months with frequent stirring. They are fined and filtered.

SECOND WINE
Brand name: Château Montalivet
Average annual production: 10,000 bottles

Evaluation of present classification: The quality equivalent of a white Graves Cru Classé
Plateau of maturity: 2–5 years following the vintage for the white wine

This small domain is owned by the white wine–making guru of Bordeaux, Denis Dubourdieu. He has long been given credit, and justifiably so, for revolutionizing white-wine-making in the Bordeaux region with his *macéra-tion pelliculaire* technique. The process permits a period of contact between the skins of the grapes and the juice at a relatively low temperature. This is done because of Dubourdieu's belief, now confirmed by other authorities, that it is the components in the grape's skin that give the wine its aromatic complexity and richness of fruit.

One taste of the wonderful wines he makes reveals that Clos Floridène is a superb white Graves, nearly matching the quality of such legends as Laville-Haut-Brion, Haut-Brion-Blanc, and Domaine de Chevalier. The price remains a relative steal, although Dubourdieu's talents have been recognized throughout Europe and Great Britain; Clos Floridène has indeed been discovered. This is a terribly underestimated, excellent wine that deserves to be a classified growth in the Graves firmament. A modest quantity of good, smooth, red wine is made, but it doesn't share the dazzling qualities of the white wine.

COUCHÉROY   GOOD

Classification: None
Location of vineyards: Martillac
Owner: André Lurton
Address: 33650 Martillac
Mailing address: S.C.E.A. Les Vignobles André Lurton, Château Bonnet, 33420 Grézillac
Telephone: 33 5 57 25 58 58; telefax: 33 5 57 74 98 59
Visits: Not allowed

VINEYARDS (red)
Average age of vines: 10–12 years
Blend: 50% Cabernet Sauvignon, 50% Merlot
Density of plantation: 6,500–8,500 vines per hectare

GRAND VIN (red)
Brand name: Château Couchéroy
Appellation: Graves
Upbringing: Fermentations last about 21 days in temperature-controlled
stainless-steel tanks. Malolactics occur partly in tanks and partly in oak
barrels. Wines are transferred for 12 months aging to oak barrels in
November (25%–30% new oak). The wines are fined and filtered.

SECOND WINE
None produced.

VINEYARDS (white)
Average age of vines: 10–12 years
Blend: 90% Sauvignon, 10% Semillon
Density of plantation: 6,500–8,500 vines per hectare

GRAND VIN (white)
Brand name: Château Couchéroy
Appellation: Graves
Upbringing: Fermentations occur partly in temperature-controlled
stainless-steel vats and partly in oak barrels. Wines remain on lees for
approximately 10 months and are fined and filtered before bottling.

SECOND WINE
None produced.

COURREGÈS-SÈGUES DU CHÂTEAU DE GAILLAT

Classification: None
Location of vineyards: St.-Pardon-de Conques
Owner: S.C.E.A du Château de Gaillat
Address: 3321 Langon
Mailing address: Same as above
Telephone: 33 5 56 63 50 77; telefax: 33 5 56 62 20 96
Visits: By appointment only
Contact: Hélène Bertrand-Coste

VINEYARDS (red)
Surface area: 3.7 acres
Average age of vines: 30 years
Blend: 75% Cabernet Sauvignon, 25% Merlot
Density of plantation: 6,800 vines per hectare

Average yields (over the last 5 years): 45 hectoliters per hectare
Total average annual production: 9,000 bottles

GRAND VIN (red)
Brand name: Courrèges-Sègues du Château de Gaillat
Appellation: Graves
Mean annual production: 9,000 bottles
Upbringing: Fermentations last 18 days at the highest possible
temperatures. Wines are aged in oak casks, 25% of which are new, for
12–18 months, depending upon the vintage. They are fined but not
filtered.

SECOND WINE
None produced.

CRUZEAU   GOOD

Classification: None
Location of vineyards: St.-Médard d'Eyrans
Owner: André Lurton
Address: 33850 Léognan
Mailing address: c/o Château Bonnet, 33420 Grézillac
Telephone: 33 5 57 25 58 58; telefax: 33 5 57 74 98 59
Visits: No visits

VINEYARDS (red)
Surface area: 123.5 acres
Average age of vines: 15–18 years
Blend: 55% Cabernet Sauvignon, 2% Cabernet Franc, 43% Merlot
Density of plantation: 6,500–8,500 vines per hectare

GRAND VIN (red)
Brand name: Château du Cruzeau
Appellation: Pessac-Léognan
Upbringing: Fermentations occur in temperature-controlled
stainless-steel tanks, and wines are aged in oak barrels (25%–35% of
which are new) for 12 months. They are fined and filtered.

SECOND WINE
None produced.

VINEYARDS (white)
Surface area: 76.6 acres
Average age of vines: 15–18 years

Blend: 85% Sauvignon, 15% Semillon
Density of plantation: 6,500–8,500 vines per hectare

GRAND VIN (white)
Brand name: Château de Cruzeau
Appellation: Pessac-Léognan
Upbringing: Fermentations occur in oak casks (25% new oak) for half the
yield and in stainless-steel tanks for the rest. The wines are bottled after
10 months (the wines in cask remain on lees). They are fined and filtered.

SECOND WINE
None produced.

Evaluation of present classification: Now equivalent to a good Cru
Bourgeois; should improve as the vines get older
Plateau of maturity: (red) 5–8 years following the vintage; (white) 2–6
years following the vintage

André Lurton, who has created quite a viticultural empire for himself in the
Graves region, purchased this property in 1973 and began extensive replanting in 1979. The new vineyard is young by Bordeaux standards, but the wine
has already begun to show promising potential. Using machine harvesters
for the red wine and producing a creamy-textured, open-knit, richly fruity,
smoky-scented red Graves have proven beneficial for attracting buyers looking for immediate gratification.

The white wine, made from grapes that are hand-harvested and -vinified
in stainless steel with no exposure to oak, has an almost California-like style,
with a great deal of fruit. However, the wine must be drunk within its first
several years of life.

Prices for the wines of Cruzeau are remarkably fair, and therein lies much
of this wine's appeal.

FERRANDE
GOOD

Classification: None
Production: 18,000 cases red; 4,500 cases white
Blend (red): 34% Merlot, 33% Cabernet Sauvignon, 33% Cabernet Franc
Blend (white): 60% Semillon, 35% Sauvignon, 5% Muscadelle
Secondary label: Lognac
Vineyard size: 109 acres
Proprietor: Delnaud family
Time spent in barrels: 15–18 months
Average age of vines: 28 years

Evaluation of present classification: The quality equivalent of a good Cru
Bourgeois
Plateau of maturity: (red) 3–10 years following the vintage; (white) 2–7
years following the vintage

This is a consistently reliable, if uninspiring, estate in the commune of
Castres. The property has been under the ownership of the Delnaud family
since 1954. I have found both the red and white wines of Ferrande to be
among the most earthy of the Graves region. In tastings I have noticed that
this characteristic can either be admired or disliked intensely.

The white wines have improved a great deal in the last decade and
now have much more charm and fruit in evidence. The white wine has a tendency to be not only aggressively earthy, but also extremely austere and
angular. The wines are priced fairly and age fairly well, particularly the
reds.

LA FLEUR JONQUET

Classification: None
Location of vineyards: Portets
Owner: Laurence Lataste
Address: Le Puy de Choyne, Arbanats, 33640 Portets
Mailing address: 5, rue Amélie, 33200 Bordeaux
Telephone: 33 5 56 17 08 18; telefax: 33 5 56 22 12 54
Visits: By appointment only
Contact: Laurence Lataste

VINEYARDS (red)
Surface area: 8.6 acres
Average age of vines: 10 years
Blend: 70% Merlot, 15% Cabernet Franc, 15% Cabernet Sauvignon
Density of plantation: 5,500 vines per hectare
Average yields (over the last 5 years): 50–55 hectoliters per hectare
Total average annual production: 20,000–22,000 bottles

GRAND VIN (red)
Brand name: Château La Fleur Jonquet
Appellation: Graves
Mean annual production: 18,000–20,000 bottles
Upbringing: Harvest is done manually or by machine, depending upon
the vintage. Fermentations last approximately 3 weeks in
temperature-controlled concrete vats. Malolactics occur in vats, and
wines are transferred afterward into oak barrels, renewed by a quarter in

each vintage. They are bottled after 12–15 months aging. They are fined and filtered.

SECOND WINE
Brand name: J de Jonquet
Average annual production: 2,000–4,000 bottles (the second wine is not always produced—the declassified lots are sometimes sold to the Négoce, depending upon the quality of the vintage)

VINEYARDS (white)
Surface area: 2.47 acres
Average age of vines: 45 years and 7–8 years
Blend: 40% Sauvignon, 50% Semillon, 10% Muscadelle
Density of plantation: 5,500 vines per hectare
Average yields (over the last 5 years): 45–50 hectoliters per hectare
Total average annual production: 6,000 bottles

GRAND VIN (white)
Brand name: Château La Fleur Jonquet
Appellation: Graves
Mean annual production: 6,000–7,000 bottles
Upbringing: Harvest is always done manually. Fermentations occur in barrels, which are renewed by a quarter in each vintage. They remain on lees with frequent stirrings for 11 months and are bottled after fining and filtration.

SECOND WINE
None produced.

FRANCE

Classification: None
Location of vineyards: Léognan
Owner: S.A. B. Thomassin
Address: 98, route de Mont de Marsan, 33850 Léognan
Mailing address: Same as above
Telephone: 33 5 56 64 75 39; telefax: 33 5 56 64 72 13
Visits: By appointment only, Monday to Thursday 8:30 A.M. to noon, and 1:30 P.M. to 5 P.M., and Fridays 8:30 A.M. to noon and 1:30 P.M. to 4 P.M.
Contact: Arnaud Thomassin

VINEYARDS (red)
Surface area: 70.4 acres
Average age of vines: 30 years

Blend: 60% Cabernet Sauvignon, 40% Merlot
Density of plantation: 5,000 and 6,950 vines per hectare
Average yields (over the last 5 years): 56 hectoliters per hectare
Total average annual production: 1,500 hectoliters

GRAND VIN (red)
Brand name: Château de France
Appellation: Pessac-Léognan
Mean annual production: 900 hectoliters
Upbringing: Fermentations last 3–4 weeks in temperature-controlled
stainless-steel tanks (30–32 degrees centigrade maximum). Wines are
aged in oak barrels, renewed by half in each vintage, for 12–18 months.
They are fined and filtered.

SECOND WINE
Brand name: Château Coquillas
Average annual production: 550 hectoliters

VINEYARDS (white)
Surface area: 8.6 acres
Average age of vines: 10 years
Blend: 70% Sauvignon, 20% Semillon, 10% Muscadelle
Density of plantation: 5,000 and 6,950 vines per hectare
Average yields (over the last 5 years): 50 hectoliters per hectare
Total average annual production: 130 hectoliters

GRAND VIN (white)
Brand name: Château de France
Appellation: Pessac-Léognan
Mean annual production: 100 hectoliters
Upbringing: Fermentations occur in oak barrels (renewed by half
in each vintage) at temperatures of 17 degrees centigrade. Wines
are bottled after 8 months. Frequent stirrings (once a week,
once every 2 weeks at the end of the process). They are fined and
filtered.

SECOND WINE
Brand name: Ganga Cata
Average annual production: 12 hectoliters

Evaluation of present classification: Since 1986 the quality has improved
immensely; it is now one of the obscure yet better wines of the region
Plateau of maturity: (red) 4–10 years following the vintage; (white) not yet
in production

Virtually the entire vineyard of this property, which is a neighbor of the more renowned Château de Fieuzal, has been replanted since 1971. The proprietor —an industrialist—has spared little expense in renovating the property and building a new winery with state-of-the-art stainless-steel fermentation tanks. The early results were not impressive, but in 1986 proprietor Thomassin began to do two things that have had a positive impact on the resulting wines. First, he decided to harvest as late as possible. Second, a severe selection of the finished wine was employed so that only the best vats were sold under the de France name.

GAILLAT

Classification: None
Location of vineyards: Langon
Owner: Coste family
Address: 3321 Langon
Mailing address: Same as above
Telephone: 33 5 56 63 50 77; telefax: 33 5 56 62 20 96.
Visits: By appointment only
Contact: Hélène Bertrand-Coste

VINEYARDS (red)
Surface area: 25.4 acres
Average age of vines: 30 years
Blend: 65% Cabernet Sauvignon, 30% Merlot, 5% Malbec
Density of plantation: 5,000–6,000 vines per hectare
Average yields (over the last 5 years): 50 hectoliters per hectare
Total average annual production: 70,000 bottles

GRAND VIN (red)
Brand name: Château de Gaillat
Appellation: Graves
Mean annual production: 60,000 bottles
Upbringing: Fermentations last 3–5 weeks depending upon the vintage, at the highest possible temperatures, with pumping-overs and *pigéage* (mashing the must). Wines are aged in oak barrels, 10% of which are new, for 12–18 months. They are fined and filtered.

SECOND WINE
Brand name: Aliénor de Gaillat
Average annual production: 10,000 bottles

VINEYARDS (white)
Surface area: 1 acre
Average age of vines: 30 years

Blend: 100% Semillon
Density of plantation: 6,800 vines per hectare
Average yields (over the last 5 years): 55 hectoliters per hectare
Total average annual production: 22 hectoliters

GRAND VIN (white)
Brand name: Château de Gaillat
Appellation: Graves

GAZIN ROCQUENCOURT   GOOD

Classification: None
Location of vineyards: Léognan
Owner: Jean-Marie Michotte and his sister Françoise Baillot-Michotte
Address: 74, avenue de Cestas, 33850 Léognan
Mailing address: Same as above
Telephone: 33 5 56 64 77 89; telefax: 33 5 56 64 77 89
Visits: By appointment only

VINEYARDS (red)
Surface area: 34.6 acres
Average age of vines: 24 years
Blend: 70% Cabernet Sauvignon, 20% Merlot, 10% Cabernet Franc
Density of plantation: 6,250 vines per hectare
Average yields (over the last 5 years): 50 hectoliters per hectare
Total average annual production: 680 hectoliters

GRAND VIN (red)
Brand name: Gazin Rocquencourt
Appellation: Pessac-Léognan
Mean annual production: 580 hectoliters
Upbringing: Fermentations last 3 to 4 weeks in stainless-steel vats with
frequent pumping-overs. Wines are then transferred to oak casks, which
are renewed by a quarter in each vintage, for 12 months aging. They are
fined and filtered.

SECOND WINE
Brand name: Les Granges de Gazin
Average annual production: 100 hectoliters

JEAN GERVAIS

Classification: None
Location of vineyards: Portets
Owner: Counilh family
Address: Vignobles Counilh et Fils, 51–53 route des Graves, 33640 Portets
Mailing address: Same as above
Telephone: 33 5 56 67 1 61; telefax: 33 5 56 67 32 43

Visits: Monday to Friday, from 9 A.M. to noon, and 2 P.M. to 6 P.M.
Contact: Denis Counilh

VINEYARDS (red)
Surface area: 69.2 acres
Average age of vines: 30 years
Blend: 60% Merlot, 40% Cabernet
Density of plantation: 6,000 vines per hectare
Average yields (over the last 5 years): 50 hectoliters per hectare
Total average annual production: 1,400 hectoliters

GRAND VIN (red)
Brand name: Château Jean Gervais
Appellation: Graves
Mean annual production: 80,000 bottles
Upbringing: Fermentations last 12–18 days in temperature-controlled stainless-steel vats, with frequent pumping-overs. Wines are transferred to lined cement tanks for 18 months aging. They are fined but not filtered.

SECOND WINE
Brand name: Château Lanette
Average annual production: 40,000 bottles

VINEYARDS (white)
Surface area: 32.1 acres
Average age of vines: 35 years
Blend: 80% Semillon, 15% Sauvignon, 5% Muscadelle
Density of plantation: 5,500 vines per hectare
Average yields (over the last 5 years): 60 hectoliters per hectare
Total average annual production: 650 hectoliters

GRAND VIN (white)
Brand name: Château Jean Gervais
Appellation: Graves
Mean annual production: 40,000 bottles
Upbringing: Fermentations last 18–22 days in temperature-controlled

tanks. Wines remain on lees for 3–6 months in rototanks and are transferred into lined concrete tanks for 9–12 months. They are fined but not filtered.

SECOND WINE
Brand name: Château Tour de Cluchon
Average annual production: 15,000 bottles

GRAND-ABORD

Classification: None
Location of vineyards: Portets
Owner: Vignobles M.C. Dugoua
Address: 56, route des Graves, 33640 Portets
Mailing address: Same as above
Telephone: 33 5 56 67 22 79; telefax: 33 5 56 67 22 23
Visits: Preferably by appointment
Contact: Colette Dugoua

VINEYARDS (red)
Surface area: 19.8 acres
Average age of vines: 40 years
Blend: 90% Merlot, 10% Cabernet Sauvignon
Density of plantation: 5,500 vines per hectare
Average yields (over the last 5 years): 50–55 hectoliters per hectare
Total average annual production: 390 hectoliters

GRAND VIN (red)
Brand name: Château du Grand-Abord
Appellation: Graves
Mean annual production: 50–55 hectoliters per hectare
Upbringing: Fermentations last 18 days in stainless-steel tanks at 28 degrees centigrade. Three hundred hectoliters are aged in stainless-steel and concrete tanks for 12 months (this makes the normal cuvée). Fifty hectoliters are aged for 12 months in new oak casks to make the Cuvée Passion. Wines are fined but not filtered.

SECOND WINE
Brand name: Château Bel Air
Average annual production: 390 hectoliters

VINEYARDS (white)
Surface area: 8.6 acres
Average age of vines: 35 years

Blend: 80% Semillon, 20% Sauvignon
Density of plantation: 5,500 vines per hectare
Total average annual production: 170 hectoliters

GRAND VIN (white)
Brand name: Château du Grand-Abord
Appellation: Graves
Mean annual production: 170 hectoliters
Upbringing: Fermentations occur at 18–20 degrees centigrade in
stainless-steel vats. Wines are fined and filtered.

SECOND WINE
None produced.

GRAND BOS

Classification: None
Location of vineyards: Castres and Portets
Owner: André Vincent and S.C. du Château du Grand Bos
Address: 33640 Castres
Mailing address: Same as above
Telephone: 33 5 56 67 39 20; telefax: 33 5 56 67 16 77
Visits: By appointment only
Contact: André Vincent

VINEYARDS (red)
Surface area: 25 acres
Average age of vines: 31 years
Blend: 45% Cabernet Sauvignon, 45% Merlot, 8% Petit Verdot, 2%
Cabernet Franc
Density of plantation: 5,600 vines per hectare
Average yields (over the last 5 years): 52.19 hectoliters per hectare
Total average annual production: 500 hectoliters

GRAND VIN (red)
Brand name: Château du Grand Bos
Appellation: Graves
Mean annual production: 3,000 cases
Upbringing: *Macération préfermentaire* occurs at 30 degrees centigrade,
and *macération postfermentaire* lasts 15–20 days. Malolactics occur in
vats, and wines are transferred to oak casks for aging (33% new oak).
They are racked every 3 months and bottled after 15–18 months. They
are fined but not filtered.

SECOND WINE
Brand name: Château Plégat La Gravière
Average annual production: 2,500 cases

VINEYARDS (white)
Surface area: 2.47 acres
Average age of vines: 27 years
Blend: 60% Semillon, 30% Sauvignon, 10% Muscadelle
Density of plantation: 5,600 vines per hectare
Average yields (over the last 5 years): 43.92 hectoliters per hectare
Total average annual production: 30 hectoliters

GRAND VIN (white)
Brand name: Château du Grand Bos
Appellation: Graves
Mean annual production: 350 cases
Upbringing: Pressing up is done slowly. Racking of the must is done at 10–12 degrees centigrade. Wines are fermented at low temperatures in oak casks and remain on lees for 8 months with frequent stirrings. There are usually 50% new oak and 50% 1-year-old barrels. Wines are fined and filtered.

SECOND WINE
None produced.

LA GRAVE

Classification: None
Production: 1,000 cases red; 500 cases white
Blend (red): 50% Cabernet Sauvignon, 50% Merlot
Blend (white): 100% Semillon
Secondary label: None
Vineyard size: 15 acres
Proprietor: Peter Vinding-Diers
Time spent in barrels: 20–22 months
Average age of vines: 28 years

Evaluation of present classification: The quality equivalent of a Médoc Cru Bourgeois
Plateau of maturity: (red) 3–8 years following the vintage; (white) 2–7 years following the vintage

GRAVILLE LACOSTE   GOOD

Classification: None
Location of vineyards: Pujols-sur-Cirons
Owner: Hervé Dubourdieu
Mailing address: c/o Château Roumieu Lacoste, 33720 Barsac
Telephone: 33 5 56 27 16 29; telefax: 33 5 56 27 02 65
Visits: By appointment only
Contact: Hervé Dubourdieu

VINEYARDS (white)
Surface area: 19.8 acres
Average age of vines: 52 years
Blend: 70% Semillon, 20% Sauvignon, 10% Muscadelle
Density of plantation: 6,500 vines per hectare
Average yields (over the last 5 years): 48 hectoliters per hectare
Total average annual production: 60,000 bottles

GRAND VIN (white)
Brand name: Château Graville Lacoste
Appellation: Graves Blanc
Mean annual production: 60,000 bottles
Upbringing: Cold stabilization of the musts. Fermentations occur in
temperature-controlled stainless-steel tanks at 18 degrees centigrade.
Wines are kept in tanks and racked 4 times before bottling. They are
fined but not filtered.

SECOND WINE
Brand name: Les Fleurs de Graville (100% Semillon—oldest vines of the
estate nearly 75 years of age)
Average annual production: 3,000 bottles

HAUT-BERGEY

Classification: None
Location of vineyards: Léognan
Owner: Sylviane Garcin-Cathiard
Address: 33850 Pessac-Léognan
Mailing address: Same as above
Telephone: 33 5 56 64 05 22; telefax: 33 5 56 64 06 98.
Visits: By appointment only, Monday to Friday, from 9 A.M. to noon, and 3
P.M. to 5 P.M.
Contact: Mrs. Sylviane Garcin-Cathiard

VINEYARDS (red)
Surface area: 56.6 acres in all, but only 43.2 acres are productive
Average age of vines: 28 years
Blend: 64% Cabernet Sauvignon, 35% Merlot, 1% Malbec
Density of plantation: 6,500 vines per hectare
Average yields (over the last 5 years): 45 hectoliters per hectare
Total average annual production: 100,000 bottles

GRAND VIN (red)
Brand name: Château Haut-Bergey
Appellation: Pessac-Léognan
Mean annual production: 70,000 bottles
Upbringing: Fermentations last 3 weeks in temperature-controlled
stainless-steel tanks. Wines are transferred to oak barrels, which are
renewed by a third at each vintage, for 12–18 months aging. They are
fined and filtered.

SECOND WINE
Brand name: Les Hauts de Bergey
Average annual production: 30,000 bottles

VINEYARDS (white)
Surface area: 7.4 acres in all, but only 3.7 are productive
Average age of vines: 7 years
Blend: 73% Sauvignon, 27% Semillon
Density of plantation: 6,800 vines per hectare
Average yields (over the last 5 years): 40 hectoliters per hectare
Total average annual production: 8,000 bottles

GRAND VIN (white)
Brand name: Château Haut-Bergey
Appellation: Pessac-Léognan
Mean annual production: 8,000 bottles
Upbringing: Fermentations occur in barrels, of which 70% are new.
Wines remain on lees for 10 months and are both fined and filtered.

SECOND WINE
None produced.

Evaluation of present classification: The quality equivalent of a Médoc
Cru Bourgeois
Plateau of maturity: 4–8 years following the vintage

HAUT CALENS

Classification: None
Location of vineyards: Beautiran
Owner: Albert Yung
Address: 33640 Beautiran
Mailing address: Same as above
Telephone: 33 5 56 67 05 25; telefax: 33 5 56 67 24 41
Visits: By appointment only

VINEYARDS (red)
Surface area: 22.2 acres
Average age of vines: 15 years
Blend: 50% Merlot, 50% Cabernet Sauvignon
Density of plantation: 3,300 and 5,000 vines per hectare
Average yields (over the last 5 years): 55 hectoliters per hectare
Total average annual production: 500 hectoliters

GRAND VIN (red)
Brand name: Haut Calens
Appellation: Graves
Mean annual production: 500 hectoliters
Upbringing: Fermentations last 21 days in temperature-controlled vats,
with pumping-overs twice daily. Wines are kept 24 months in
stainless-steel tanks before bottling.

SECOND WINE
Brand name: Château Belle Croix
Average annual production: 200 hectoliters

HAUT-GARDÈRE   GOOD

Classification: None
Location of vineyards: Léognan
Owner: S.A. du Château Fieuzal
Address: 33850 Léognan
Mailing address: Same as above
Telephone: 33 5 56 64 77 86; telefax: 33 5 56 64 18 88
Visits: By appointment only
Contact: call above telephone number

VINEYARDS (red)
Surface area: 49.4 acres
Average age of vines: 15 years

Blend: 55% Cabernet Sauvignon, 40% Merlot, 5% Cabernet Franc
Density of plantation: 8,300 vines per hectare
Average yields (over the last 5 years): 45 hectoliters per hectare
Total average annual production: 120,000 bottles

GRAND VIN (red)
Brand name: Château Haut-Gardère
Appellation: Pessac-Léognan
Mean annual production: 60,000–70,000 bottles
Upbringing: Fermentations last 3 weeks in temperature-controlled
stainless-steel vats. Malolactics occur in vats, and wines are transferred
to oak barrels in December for 18 months aging. Thirty percent new oak
is used. They are fined and lightly filtered.

SECOND WINE
Brand name: L'Abeille de Fieuzal
Average annual production: 50,000–60,000 bottles

VINEYARDS (white)
Surface area: 12.4 acres
Average age of vines: 15 years
Blend: 50% Sauvignon, 45% Semillon, 5% Muscadelle
Density of plantation: 8,300 vines per hectare
Average yields (over the last 5 years): 45 hectoliters per hectare
Total average annual production: 30,000 bottles

GRAND VIN (white)
Brand name: Château Haut-Gardère
Appellation: Pessac-Léognan
Mean annual production: 20,000 bottles
Upbringing: Harvest is done by hand. Selective picking. Fermentation
occurs in oak barrels, of which 80% are new, and wines are kept on lees
for 12 months before bottling. They are fined and lightly filtered.

SECOND WINE
Brand name: L'Abeille de Fieuzal
Average annual production: 10,000 bottles
This estate, once part of de Fieuzal, has been bought by the latter
château in August 1995. The new owner of both de Fieuzal and
Haut-Gardère is the Banque Populaire. Former owners Gribelin and
Negrevergne sold Fieuzal in 1994.

Evaluation of present classification: The quality equivalent of a Médoc
Cru Bourgeois
Plateau of maturity: (red) 2–6 years following the vintage; (white) 2–6
years following the vintage

This property is extremely well run. In spite of the youth of the vines, the last several vintages have produced generously rich, tobacco-scented, flavorful red wines and stylish white wines. The vineyard sits on a very fine outcropping of gravelly soil in the Léognan area. Prices are remarkably low, largely because word has not circulated about how good these wines can be. Before World War II Haut-Gardère had such a high reputation, it sold for the same price as Domaine de Chevalier, de Fieuzal, and Malartic-Lagravière.

HAUT-LAGRANGE

Location of vineyards: Léognan
Owner: Francis Boutemy
Address: 31, route de Loustalade, 33850 Léognan
Mailing address: Same as above
Telephone: 33 5 56 64 09 33; telefax: 33 5 56 64 10 08
Visits: By appointment only
Contact: Francis Boutemy

VINEYARDS (red)
Surface area: 33.3 acres
Average age of vines: 10 years
Blend: 55% Cabernet Sauvignon, 45% Merlot
Density of plantation: 7,000 vines per hectare
Average yields (over the last 5 years): 52 hectoliters per hectare
Total average annual production: 95,000 bottles

GRAND VIN (red)
Brand name: Château Haut-Lagrange
Appellation: Pessac-Léognan
Mean annual production: 95,000 bottles
Upbringing: Fermentations take place in temperature-controlled concrete tanks. Eighty percent of the yield is aged in vats and 20% in new oak barrels for 18 months. Wines are fined and filtered.

SECOND WINE
None produced.

VINEYARDS (white)
Surface area: 4.2 acres
Average age of vines: 10 years
Blend: 50% Semillon, 40% Sauvignon, 10% Sauvignon Gris
Density of plantation: 7,000 vines per hectare
Average yields (over the last 5 years): 50 hectoliters
Total average annual production: 11,000 bottles

GRAND VIN (white)
Brand name: Château Haut-Lagrange
Appellation: Pessac-Léognan
Mean annual production: 11,000 bottles
Upbringing: Cold settling of the must lasts 12–72 hours depending
upon the vintage. Fermentations start in vats, and 20% of the
yield is transferred to new oak barrels. Wines remain in vats for
9 months, with little racking. The wines in barrels remain on fine lees
for 9 months, too, and are stirred regularly. They are unfined but
filtered.

SECOND WINE
None produced.

HAUT-NOUCHET

Classification: None
Location of vineyards: Martillac
Owner: Louis Lurton
Address: 33650 Martillac
Mailing address: Same as above
Telephone and Telefax: 33 5 56 72 69 74
Visits: By appointment only
Contact: Call above telephone number

VINEYARDS (red)
Surface area: 69 acres
Average age of vines: 10 years
Blend: 72% Cabernet Sauvignon, 28% Merlot
Density of plantation: 6,600 vines per hectare
Average yields (over the last 5 years): 32 hectoliters per hectare
Total average annual production: 900 hectoliters per hectare

GRAND VIN (red)
Brand name: Château Haut-Nouchet
Appellation: Pessac-Léognan
Mean annual production: 6,500 cases
Upbringing: Fermentations are rather long (3–4 weeks) and occur in
stainless-steel tanks. Wines are transferred to oak casks (renewed by a
third at each vintage) after malolactics and are aged for 16 months. They
are fined but not filtered.

SECOND WINE
Brand name: Domaine du Milan
Average annual production: 3,500 cases

VINEYARDS (white)
Surface area: 27 acres
Average age of vines: 13 years
Blend: 78% Sauvignon, 22% Semillon
Density of plantation: 6,600 vines per hectare
Average yields (over the last 5 years): 21 hectoliters per hectare
Total average annual production: 230 hectoliters

GRAND VIN (white)
Brand name: Château Haut-Nouchet
Appellation: Pessac-Léognan
Mean annual production: 2,500 cases
Upbringing: Fermentations occur in barrels, renewed by a quarter at each vintage. Wines remain on lees for 6–8 months with regular stirring. They are fined and filtered.

SECOND WINE
Brand name: Domaine du Milan
Average annual production: Variable, depends on the vintage

NOTE: The vineyards are cultivated organically since 1992 (they have the ECOCERT certification label).

L'HOSPITAL

Classification: None
Location of vineyards: Portets
Owner: Marcel F. Disch
Address: Lieu-dit Darrouan, 33640 Portets
Mailing address: Same as above
Telephone: 33 5 56 67 54 73; telefax: 33 5 56 67 09 33
Visits: By appointment, on weekdays (except Wednesdays), between 11 A.M. and 6 P.M.
Contact: Danielle David

VINEYARDS (red)
Surface area: 17.3 acres
Average age of vines: 27 years

Blend: 78% Merlot, 10% Cabernet Sauvignon, 10% Cabernet Franc, 2% Malbec
Density of plantation: 7,000 vines per hectare
Average yields (over the last 5 years): 48–52 hectoliters per hectare
Total average annual production: 45,000 bottles

GRAND VIN (red)
Brand name: Château de l'Hospital
Appellation: Graves
Mean annual production: 30,000 bottles
Upbringing: Fermentations and macerations last 18–25 days in stainless-steel vats equipped with a temperature control (28–30 degrees centigrade). Wines are transferred to oak barrels, 25%–35% of which are new depending upon the vintage (the rest is 1 year old), for 12–18 months aging. They are fined and usually remain unfiltered.

SECOND WINE
Brand name: Château Thibaut-Ducasse
Average annual production: 15,000 bottles

VINEYARDS (white)
Surface area: 7.4 acres
Average age of vines: 27 years
Blend: 63% Semillon, 34% Sauvignon, 3% Muscadelle
Density of plantation: 7,000 vines per hectare
Average yields (over the last 5 years): 40 hectoliters per hectare
Total average annual production: 16,000 bottles

GRAND VIN (white)
Brand name: Château de l'Hospital
Appellation: Graves
Mean annual production: 9,000 bottles
Upbringing: The grapes are pressed with a pneumatic wine press. Cold settling of the musts and cold stabilization occurs at 7 degrees centigrade for 3–5 days. Fermentations take place in barrels, and wines are aged 6–8 months on fine lees with regular stirrings. They are fined with egg whites and remain unfiltered before bottling. Forty percent new oak and 60% 1-vintage-old barrels are utilized.

SECOND WINE
Brand name: Château Thibaut-Ducasse
Average annual production: 7,000 bottles

Evaluation of present classification: The quality equivalent of a Médoc Cru Bourgeois
Plateau of maturity: (red) 5–10 years following the vintage; (white) 3–8 years following the vintage

Lamentably, I have never been impressed with the wines from this property, whose château is classified as a historic monument under French law. The red wines tend to be stubbornly hard, austere, dusty, and not always the cleanest examples of winemaking. The minuscule quantity of white wine is flinty, smoky, sometimes overwhelmingly earthy and austere. They would seemingly benefit from a small quantity of Semillon to give the wines more fat, flesh, and charm. The wines of l'Hospital are seen in some marketplaces but are generally overpriced.

LAFARGUE

Classification: None
Location of vineyards: Martillac and Saint-Médard d'Eyrans
Owner: Jean-Pierre Leymarie
Address: 5, impasse de Dony, 33650 Martillac
Mailing address: Same as above
Telephone: 3 5 56 72 72 30; telefax: 33 5 56 72 64 61
Visits: Preferably by appointment, Monday to Friday, from 9 A.M. to 4 P.M.
Contact: Jean-Pierre Leymarie

VINEYARDS (red)
Surface area: 44.5 acres
Average age of vines: 19 years
Blend: 40% Cabernet Sauvignon, 40% Merlot, 15% Cabernet Franc, 2.5% Malbec, 2.5% Petit Verdot
Density of plantation: 6,500 vines per hectare
Average yields (over the last 5 years): 55 hectoliters per hectare
Total average annual production: 1,000 hectoliters

GRAND VIN (red)
Brand name: Château Lafargue
Appellation: Pessac-Léognan
Mean annual production: 600 hectoliters
Upbringing: Fermentations last approximately 1 month (carbonic maceration). Wines are aged for 12–15 months in oak casks, renewed by a third each year. They are fined and filtered.

SECOND WINE
Brand name: Château Haut de Domy
Average annual production: 400 hectoliters

VINEYARDS (white)
Surface area: 5 acres
Average age of vines: 8 years

Blend: 50% Sauvignon, 30% Sauvignon Gris, 20% Semillon
Density of plantation: 6,500 vines per hectare
Average yields (over the last 5 years): 55 hectoliters per hectare
Total average annual production: 110 hectoliters

GRAND VIN (white)
Brand name: Château Lafargue
Appellation: Pessac-Léognan
Mean annual production: 110 hectoliters
Upbringing: Fermentation occurs in new oak barrels. Wines remain on lees for about 6 months, with frequent stirring. They are fined and filtered.

SECOND WINE
None produced.

LAMOUROUX

Classification: None
Location of vineyards: Cérons
Owner: Mr. Lataste
Address: Grand Enclos du Château de Cérons, 33720 Cérons
Mailing address: Same as above
Telephone: 33 5 56 27 01 53; telefax: 33 5 56 27 08 86
Visits: By appointment only
Contact: Mr. Lataste

VINEYARDS (red)
Surface area: 5 acres
Average age of vines: 20 years
Blend: 50% Merlot, 50% Cabernet Sauvignon
Density of plantation: 6,000 vines per hectare
Average yields (over the last 5 years): 45 hectoliters per hectare
Total average annual production: 12,000 bottles

GRAND VIN (red)
Brand name: Château Lamouroux
Appellation: Graves
Mean annual production: 12,000 bottles
Upbringing: Fermentations last 15–20 days depending upon the vintage. Wines are aged for 16 months in 2- to 3-year-old oak barrels. They are fined and filtered.

SECOND WINE
None produced.

VINEYARDS (white)
Surface area: 59 acres
Average age of vines: 30 years
Blend: 60% Semillon, 40% Sauvignon
Density of plantation: 6,000 vines per hectare
Average yields (over the last 5 years): 40 hectoliters
Total average annual production: 60,000 bottles of dry white and 12,000
of sweet wine

GRAND VIN (white)
Brand name: Grand Enclos du Château de Céron
Appellation: Cérons
Mean annual production: 12,000 bottles
Upbringing: Fermentations occur in barrels renewed by a third at each
vintage, and wines are bottled after 18 months. They are fined and filtered.

SECOND WINE
Brand name: Château Lamouroux
Average annual production: 60,000 bottles of dry white wine

LANDIRAS

Classification: None
Location of vineyards: Landiras
Owner: S.C.A. Domaine La Grave, Peter Vinding-Diers
Address: 33720 Landiras
Mailing address: Same as above
Telephone: 33 5 56 62 44 70; telefax: 33 5 56 62 43 78
Visits: By appointment only
Contact: Peter Vinding-Diers

VINEYARDS (red)
Surface area: 3.6 acres
Average age of vines: 30 years
Blend: 67% Cabernet Sauvignon, 33% Merlot
Density of plantation: 5,000 vines per hectare
Average yields (over the last 5 years): 45 hectoliters per hectare

GRAND VIN (red)
Brand name: Château de Landiras
Appellation: Graves

Mean annual production: 200 cases
Upbringing: Fermentations are rather short and occur in stainless-steel vats. Wines undergo malolactics in barrels. Percentage of new oak depends upon the vintage. Wines are fined but not filtered.

SECOND WINE
Brand name: La Colombe de Landiras
Average annual production: 300 cases

VINEYARDS (white)
Surface area: 31.7 acres
Average age of vines: 7 years
Blend: 80% Semillon, 20% Sauvignon Gris
Density of plantation: 9,100 vines per hectare
Average yields (over the last 5 years): 40 hectoliters per hectare
Total average annual production: 500 hectoliters

GRAND VIN (white)
Brand name: Château de Landiras
Appellation: Graves
Mean annual production: 2,000 cases
Upbringing: Fermentations occur in casks, with indigenous yeasts. Wines are aged for 6–9 months (experiments going on for 18 months). They usually contain 3 grams per liter residual sugar, which accounts for the sterile filtration. They are not fined.

SECOND WINE
Brand name: La Colombe de Landiras
Average annual production: 3,000 cases

LESPAULT

Classification: None
Location of vineyards: Martillac
Owner: S.C. du Château Lespault, Jean Claude Bolleau
Address: SCF Domaines Kressmann, Chemin Latour, 33650 Martillac
Mailing address: Same as above
Telephone: 33 5 56 7 71 21; telefax: 33 5 56 72 64 03
Visits: Not allowed

VINEYARDS (red)
Surface area: 10 acres
Average age of vines: 40 years

Blend: 70% Merlot, 25% Cabernet Sauvignon, 5% Malbec
Density of plantation: 7,200 vines per hectare
Average yields (over the last 5 years): 45 hectoliters per hectare
Total average annual production: 30,000 bottles

GRAND VIN (red)
Brand name: Château Lespault
Appellation: Pessac-Léognan
Mean annual production: 30,000 bottles
Upbringing: Fermentations take place in temperature-controlled
stainless-steel tanks and last 3–4 weeks. Wines are aged in oak barrels,
25% of which are new, for 16 months. They are fined and filtered.

SECOND WINE
None produced.

VINEYARDS (white)
Surface area: 5 acres
Average age of vines: 35 years
Blend: 75% Sauvignon, 25% Semillon
Density of plantation: 7,200 vines per hectare
Average yields (over the last 5 years): 50 hectoliters per hectare
Total average annual production: 10,000 bottles

GRAND VIN (white)
Brand name: Château Lespault
Appellation: Pessac-Léognan
Mean annual production: 10,000 bottles
Upbringing: Harvest is done by hand. Grapes are pressed slowly.
Fermentations occur in oak barrels (25% of which are new), and wines
are kept on lees for 8 months. They are fined and filtered.

SECOND WINE
None produced.

MAGENCE

Classification: None
Location of vineyards: St.-Pierre de Mons
Owner: Guillot de Suduiraut, d'Antras
Address: 33210 St.-Pierre de Mons
Mailing address: Same as above

Telephone: 33 5 56 63 07 05; telefax: 33 5 56 63 41 42
Visits: Preferably by appointment, Monday through Friday, between 9
A.M. and 11 A.M., and 2 P.M. and 5 P.M.; weekends by appointment only

VINEYARDS (red)
Surface area: 52 acres
Average age of vines: 35 years
Blend: 45% Cabernet Sauvignon, 31% Merlot, 24% Cabernet Franc
Density of plantation: 5,500 vines per hectare
Average yields (over the last 5 years): 52 hectoliters per hectare
Total average annual production: 1,000–1,100 hectoliters

GRAND VIN (red)
Brand name: Château Magence
Appellation: Graves
Mean annual production: 100,000 bottles
Upbringing: Fermentations take place in temperature-controlled
stainless-steel vats of 200 hectoliters capacity. Alcoholic fermentations
last 8–10 days, with 2 daily pumping-overs. Macerations take place
in vats and last 20–30 days at 30–31 degrees centigrade maximum.
Wines are racked every month for the first 4 months. They are aged
24 months in stainless-steel tanks, fined with albumin, and filtered if
necessary.

SECOND WINE
Brand name: Château Brannens
Average annual production: 30,000 bottles

VINEYARDS (white)
Surface area: 35 acres
Average age of vines: 38 years
Blend: 50% Sauvignon, 50% Semillon
Density of plantation: 5,500 and 3,500 vines per hectare
Average yields (over the last 5 years): 50 hectoliters per hectare
Total average annual production: 700 hectoliters

GRAND VIN (white)
Brand name: Château Magence
Appellation: Graves
Mean annual production: 70,000 bottles
Upbringing: Fermentations take place, blend separate, in temperature-
controlled stainless-steel vats of 200 hectoliters capacity. Depending
upon the vintage, 0%–80% of the yield undergoes *macération pelliculaire*
for 12–18 hours (inert gas). Alcoholic fermentations last 5–8 days at

20–21 degrees centigrade maximum and wines remain 12 months in stainless-steel vats, *cépages* separate. They remain on lees for a maximum of 3 months, are assembled, and then kept at −5 degrees centigrade for 1 week before bottling. They are lightly filtered if necessary.

SECOND WINE (white)
Brand name: Château Brannens
Average annual production: 20,000 bottles

MAUVES

Classification: None
Location of vineyards: Podensac
Owner: Bernard Bouche
Address: 25, rue François Mauriac, 33720 Podensac
Mailing address: Same as above
Telephone: 33 5 56 27 17 05; telefax: 33 5 56 27 24 19
Visits: Preferably by appointment
Contact: Bernard Bouche

VINEYARDS (red)
Surface area: 49 acres
Average age of vines: 20 years
Blend: 70% Cabernet Sauvignon, 30% Merlot
Density of plantation: 4,000 vines per hectare
Average yields (over the last 5 years): 55 hectoliters
Total average annual production: 1,000 hectoliters

GRAND VIN (red)
Brand name: Château de Mauves
Appellation: Graves
Mean annual production: 1,000 hectoliters
Upbringing: Fermentations last 3–4 weeks in temperature-controlled tanks. Wines are aged in tanks for 2 years, fined, and filtered.

SECOND WINE
None produced.

VINEYARDS (white)
Surface area: 5 acres
Average age of vines: 40 years
Blend: 100% Semillon

Average yields (over the last 5 years): 50 hectoliters per hectare
Total average annual production: 100 hectoliters

GRAND VIN (white)
Brand name: Château de Mauves
Appellation: Graves
Mean annual production: 100 hectoliters
Upbringing: Fermentations are rather long, and temperatures are maintained at 18 degrees centigrade. Wines are bottled rather early—after 4–6 months. They are fined and filtered.

SECOND WINE
None produced.

PERIN DE NAUDINE

Classification: None
Location of vineyards: Castres
Owner: Olivier Colas
Address: 8, impasse des Domaines, 33640 Castres
Mailing address: Same as above
Telephone: 33 5 56 67 06 55 or 33 1 40 62 94 35; telefax: 33 5 56 67 59 68
Visits: By appointment only
Contact: Olivier Colas or Frank Artaud at above telephone numbers

VINEYARDS (red)
Surface area: 19.8 acres
Average age of vines: 20 years
Blend: 50% Merlot, 25% Cabernet Franc, 25% Cabernet Sauvignon
Density of plantation: 5,800 vines per hectare
Average yields (over the last 5 years): 60 hectoliters per hectare
Total average annual production: 30,000 bottles

GRAND VIN (red)
Brand name: Château Perin de Naudine
Appellation: Graves
Mean annual production: 25,000–30,000 bottles
Upbringing: Fermentations take place in temperature-controlled stainless-steel tanks, and wines are aged for 18 months in oak casks that are renewed by a quarter at each vintage. They are fined but not filtered.

SECOND WINE
Brand name: Sphinx de Naudine
Average annual production: 20,000 bottles

VINEYARDS (white)
Surface area: 5 acres
Average age of vines: 6 years
Blend: 60% Semillon, 30% Sauvignon, 10% Muscadelle
Density of plantation: 5,800 vines per hectare
Average yields (over the last 5 years): 60 hectoliters per hectare
Total average annual production: 120 hectoliters

GRAND VIN (white)
Brand name: Les Sphinx de Naudine
Appellation: Graves
Mean annual production: 16,000 bottles
Upbringing: Harvest is done manually. Cold settling. Fermentations occur
in new oak barrels, and wines remain on lees for 6 months. They are
fined and filtered.

SECOND WINE
None produced.

PESSAN

Classification: None
Location of vineyards: Portets
Owner: Mrs. Bitot
Address: 33 Portets
Mailing address: Château Fayau, 33410 Cadillac
Telephone: 33 5 57 98 08 08; telefax: 33 5 56 62 18 22
Visits: Preferably by appointment, especially during weekends; Monday
to Friday, from 9 A.M. to noon, and 2 P.M. to 5 P.M.
Contact: Mr. Medeville

VINEYARDS (red)
Surface area: 19.8 acres
Average age of vines: 25 years
Blend: 50% Cabernet Sauvignon, 30% Merlot, 20% Cabernet Franc
Density of plantation: 5,000 vines per hectare
Average yields (over the last 5 years): 48 hectoliters per hectare
Total average annual production: 380 hectoliters

GRAND VIN (red)
Brand name: Château Pessan
Appellation: Graves
Mean annual production: 50,000 bottles
Upbringing: Fermentations last 15 days in stainless-steel tanks. Wines are filtered after malolactics and aged in underground vats.

SECOND WINE
None produced.

VINEYARDS (white)
Surface area: 4.9 acres
Average age of vines: 20 years
Blend: 70% Sauvignon, 30% Semillon
Density of plantation: 5,000 vines per hectare
Average yields (over the last 5 years): 44 hectoliters per hectare

GRAND VIN (white)
Brand name: Château Pessan
Appellation: Graves
Mean annual production: 10,000 bottles
Upbringing: Grapes are pressed, but press wines are not included. After racking of the musts (24 hours), fermentations occur in temperature-controlled stainless-steel vats at low temperatures (less than 20 degrees centigrade). Bentonite is added during fermentations to fix up proteins. Wines are filtered and bottled rather early.

SECOND WINE
None produced.

PEYRE BLANQUE

Classification: None
Location of vineyards: Budos
Owner: Jean Médeville and Sons
Address: Château Peyre Blanque, 33 Budos
Mailing address: Château Fayau, 33410 Cadillac
Telephone: 33 5 57 98 08 08; telefax: 33 5 56 62 18 22
Visits: Preferably by appointment, especially during weekends; Monday to Friday, from 9 A.M. to noon, and 2 P.M. to 5 P.M.
Contact: Mr. Medeville

VINEYARDS (red)
Surface area: 17.3 acres
Average age of vines: 7 years
Blend: 90% Cabernet Sauvignon, 10% Merlot
Density of plantation: 5,000 vines per hectare
Average yields (over the last 5 years): 50 hectoliters per hectare
Total average annual production: 350 hectoliters

GRAND VIN (red)
Brand name: Château Peyre Blanque
Appellation: Graves
Upbringing: Fermentations last 15 days in stainless-steel tanks. Twenty
percent of the yield is aged in new oak barrels, and bottling is done after
18 months. Wines are filtered.

SECOND WINE
None produced.

VINEYARDS (white)
Surface area: 2.47 acres
Average age of vines: 7 years
Blend: 80% Muscadelle, 20% Sauvignon
Density of plantation: 5,000 vines per hectare
Average yields (over the last 5 years): 55 hectoliters per hectare

GRAND VIN (white)
Brand name: Château Peyre Blanque
Appellation: Graves
Upbringing: Grapes are pressed, but press wines are not included.
After racking of the musts (24 hours), fermentations occur in
temperature-controlled stainless-steel vats at low temperatures
(less than 20 degrees centigrade). Bentonite is added during
fermentations to fix up proteins. Wines are filtered and bottled early.

SECOND WINE
None produced.

PIRON

Classification: None
Location of vineyards: St.-Morillon
Owner: Paul Boyreau, G.F.A. du Château Piron
Address: 33650 St.-Morillon

Mailing address: Same as above
Telephone: 33 5 56 20 25 61; telefax: 33 5 56 78 48 36
Visits: By appointment only, all days of the week except on Sundays
Contact: Paul Boyreau

VINEYARDS (red)
Surface area: 14.8 acres
Average age of vines: 20 years
Blend: 50% Merlot, 50% Cabernet Sauvignon
Density of plantation: 5,000 vines per hectare
Average yields (over the last 5 years): 45 hectoliters per hectare
Total average annual production: 250 hectoliters

GRAND VIN (red)
Brand name: Château Piron
Appellation: Graves
Mean annual production: 25,000–30,000 bottles
Upbringing: Fermentations occur in stainless-steel tanks. Wines are aged
(in tanks) for 20–24 months. They are fined and filtered before bottling.

SECOND WINE
None produced.

VINEYARDS (white)
Surface area: 32 acres
Average age of vines: 25 years (some vines are 40–50 years old)
Blend: 50% Semillon, 50% Sauvignon
Density of plantation: 5,000 vines per hectare
Average yields (over the last 5 years): 45 hectoliters
Total average annual production: 500–700 hectoliters

GRAND VIN (white)
Brand name: Château Piron
Appellation: Graves
Upbringing: Fermentations occur in temperature-controlled
stainless-steel tanks. Part of the yield goes into oak casks of which half
are new. Wines are bottled within a maximum of 12 months. They are
fined and filtered.

SECOND WINE
Brand name: Château du Courreau

Evaluation of present classification: The quality equivalent of a Médoc
Cru Bourgeois
Plateau of maturity: (red) 2–6 years following the vintage; (white) 2–6
years following the vintage

PONTAC-MONPLAISIR GOOD

Classification: None
Location of vineyards: Villenave d'Ornon
Owner: Jean Maufras
Address: 33140 Villenave d'Ornon
Mailing address: Same as above
Telephone: 33 5 56 87 08 21; telefax: 33 5 56 87 35 10
Visits: By appointment only
Contact: Alain Maufras, telephone 33 6 09 28 80 88

VINEYARDS (red)
Surface area: 25.9 acres
Average age of vines: 25 years
Blend: 60% Merlot, 40% Cabernet Sauvignon
Density of plantation: 6,500 vines per hectare
Average yields (over the last 5 years): 58 hectoliters per hectare
Total average annual production: 450 hectoliters

GRAND VIN (red)
Brand name: Château Pontac-Monplaisir
Appellation: Pessac-Léognan
Mean annual production: 380 hectoliters
Upbringing: Fermentations and macerations last 3–4 weeks in
stainless-steel vats and concrete vats lined with enamel. Wines are aged
16–18 months in oak barrels, 30% of which are new (70% are 1 vintage
old). They are fined and remain unfiltered.

SECOND WINE
Brand name: Château Limbourg
Average annual production: 50 hectoliters

VINEYARDS (white)
Surface area: 10.3 acres
Average age of vines: 20 years
Blend: 50% Sauvignon, 50% Semillon
Density of plantation: 6,500 vines per hectare
Average yields (over the last 5 years): 60 hectoliters per hectare
Total average annual production: 270 hectoliters

GRAND VIN (white)
Brand name: Château Pontac-Monplaisir
Appellation: Pessac-Léognan
Mean annual production: 200 hectoliters
Upbringing: Fermentations start in stainless-steel vats (15 days) and
proceed in new oak barrels. Wines are aged in oak barrels, 35% of which

are new and 65% of which are 1 vintage old, for 10 months. They are kept on fine lees with regular stirrings, are fined, and remain unfiltered.

SECOND WINE
Brand name: Château Limbourg
Average annual production: 50 hectoliters

Evaluation of present classification: The quality equivalent of a Médoc Cru Bourgeois
Plateau of maturity: (red) 3–6 years following the vintage; (white) 1–4 years following the vintage

The vineyard of Pontac-Monplaisir sits on very sandy, light gravelly soil near Château Baret. The white wine from this estate is a textbook white Graves, with a pronounced intense, herbaceous, mineral character, medium body, and gobs of fruit. Some people find it almost too herbaceously scented. It is a wine not to lay away in the cellar, but to drink in its first 2–3 years. The red wine is of less interest—soft, straightforward, relatively light, but tasty and correctly made.

ROCHEMORIN
GOOD

Classification: None
Location of vineyards: Martillac
Owner: André Lurton
Address: 33650 Martillac
Mailing address: c/o Château Bonnet, 33420 Grézillac
Telephone: 33 5 57 25 58 58; telefax: 33 5 57 74 98 59
Visits: No visits

VINEYARDS (red)
Surface area: 153 acres
Average age of vines: 15–18 years
Blend: 60% Cabernet Sauvignon, 40% Merlot
Density of plantation: 6,500–8,500 vines per hectare

GRAND VIN (red)
Brand name: Château de Rochemorin
Appellation: Pessac-Léognan
Upbringing: Fermentations occur in temperature-controlled stainless-steel tanks. Wines are aged for 12 months in oak barrels (25%–35% of which are new) and racked every 3 months. They are fined and filtered.

SECOND WINE
None produced.

VINEYARDS (white)
Surface area: 56.8 acres
Average age of vines: 15–18 years
Blend: 90% Sauvignon, 10% Semillon
Density of plantation: 6,500–8,500 vines per hectare

GRAND VIN (white)
Brand name: Château de Rochemorin
Appellation: Pessac-Léognan
Upbringing: Fermentations occur in casks, 25% of which are new, and wines remain on lees for 10 months, with regular stirrings. They are fined and filtered.

SECOND WINE
None produced.

Evaluation of present classification: The quality equivalent of a Médoc Cru Bourgeois
Plateau of maturity: (red) 3–8 years following the vintage; (white) 2–5 years following the vintage

This is an up-and-coming estate in the commune of Martillac, one whose name is believed to have been taken from the Moorish expression for a fortified château. Many Graves observers feel the vineyard is one of the best placed of the appellation, sitting on high ground with superb drainage. The vineyard, however, remains relatively young, as André Lurton, the dynamic empire builder in the Léognan area of Graves and Entre-Deux-Mers, only acquired the property in 1973. Lurton has replanted the vineyard, which had become covered with large trees.

Among recent vintages, I have been impressed with the tobacco, mineral, spicy, richly fruity character of all the red wines since 1985, made in the straightforward, commercial style that Lurton prefers. The white wines have been wonderfully delicate and light, extremely dry and aromatic, but still classic expressions of a white Graves in a more austere, flinty style. This should be a property to search out when looking for impeccably made wines at reasonable prices.

SAINT-JEAN DES GRAVES

Classification: None
Location of vineyards: Pujols-sur-Cirons
Owner: Jean Gérard David
Mailing address: c/o Château Liot, 33720 Barsac
Telephone: 33 5 56 27 15 31; telefax: 33 5 56 27 14 42
Visits: By appointment only, Monday to Friday, from 9 A.M. to noon, and 2 P.M. to 5 P.M.
Contact: Mr. or Mrs. David

VINEYARDS (red)
Surface area: 22 acres
Average age of vines: 30–40 years
Blend: 70% Merlot, 30% Cabernet Franc
Density of plantation: 5,500 vines per hectare
Average yields (over the last 5 years): 50 hectoliters per hectare
Total average annual production: 450 hectoliters

GRAND VIN (red)
Brand name: Château St.-Jean des Graves
Appellation: Graves
Mean annual production: 3,800 cases
Upbringing: Half the yield is aged in oak casks (some new oak), the rest in tanks. The wines are fined and filtered.

SECOND WINE
None produced.

VINEYARDS (white)
Surface area: 27 acres
Average age of vines: 30–40 years
Blend: 50% Semillon, 50% Sauvignon
Density of plantation: 5,500 vines per hectare
Average yields (over the last 5 years): 45 hectoliters per hectare
Total average annual production: 450 hectoliters

GRAND VIN (white)
Brand name: Château Saint-Jean des Graves
Appellation: Graves
Mean annual production: 4,000 cases
Upbringing: Fermentations last 15 days in temperature-controlled vats. Wines are aged for 9 months in vats. They are not fined but are filtered.

SECOND WINE
None produced.

SAINT-ROBERT

Classification: None
Location of vineyards: Pujols-sur-Ciron
Owner: Foncier Vignobles
Address: Château St.-Robert, 33210 Pujols-sur-Ciron
Mailing address: Domaine de Lamontagne, 33210 Preignac
Telephone: 33 5 56 63 27 66; telefax: 33 5 56 76 87 03
Visits: Monday to Friday, from 8:30 A.M. to 12:30 P.M., and 2 P.M.
to 6 P.M.
Contact: Mrs. Poupot

VINEYARDS (red)
Surface area: 56.9 acres
Average age of vines: 20 years
Blend: 50% Merlot, 30% Cabernet Sauvignon, 20% Cabernet Franc
Density of plantation: 7,000 vines per hectare
Average yields (over the last 5 years): 50 hectoliters per hectare
Total average annual production: 1,100 hectoliters

GRAND VIN (red)
Brand name: Château St.-Robert and Cuvée Poncet-Deville
Appellation: Graves
Mean annual production: 100,000 bottles
Upbringing: Fermentations last 3 weeks. The special cuvée is aged 13
months in 100% new oak barrels. The Château Saint-Robert is aged 10
months in 25% new oak barrels. Both wines are fined and filtered.

SECOND WINE
None produced.

VINEYARDS (white)
Surface area: 17 acres
Average age of vines: 15 years
Blend: 60% Sauvignon, 40% Semillon
Density of plantation: 7,000 vines per hectare
Average yields (over the last 5 years): 50 hectoliters per hectare
Total average annual production: 350 hectoliters

GRAND VIN (white)
Brand name: Château St.-Robert and Cuvée Poncet-Deville
Appellation: Graves
Mean annual production: 40,000 bottles
Upbringing: The normal cuvée is fermented in vats and kept on lees
for 6 months. The special cuvée is fermented in oak casks and kept

on lees for the same period of time. Both wines are not fined but are filtered.

SECOND WINE
None produced.

LE SARTRE

Classification: None
Location of vineyards: Léognan
Owner: G.F.A. du Château Le Sartre
Address: 33850 Léognan
Mailing address: Same as above
Telephone: 33 5 57 96 56 20; telefax: 33 5 57 96 59 19
Visits: By appointment only, Monday to Friday, from 8 A.M. to 11:30 A.M., and 2:30 P.M. to 5:30 P.M.
Contact: Anthony Perrin

VINEYARDS (red)
Surface area: 44.5 acres
Average age of vines: 15 years
Blend: 70% Cabernet Sauvignon, 30% Merlot
Density of plantation: 7,200 vines per hectare
Average yields (over the last 5 years): 55 hectoliters per hectare
Total average annual production: 120,000 bottles

GRAND VIN (red)
Brand name: Château Le Sartre
Appellation: Pessac-Léognan
Mean annual production: 120,000 bottles
Upbringing: Fermentations occur in temperature-controlled stainless-steel tanks. Wines are aged in 20% new oak. They are fined and filtered.

SECOND WINE
None produced.

VINEYARDS (white)
Surface area: 17.3 acres
Average age of vines: 15 years
Blend: 70% Sauvignon, 30% Semillon
Density of plantation: 7,200 vines per hectare
Average yields (over the last 5 years): 45 hectoliters per hectare
Total average annual production: 35,000 bottles

GRAND VIN (white)
Brand name: Château Le Sartre
Appellation: Pessac-Léognan
Mean annual production: 35,000 bottles
Upbringing: Fermentations occur in oak casks, of which 20% are new. Wines remain on lees for 10 months with regular stirring but no racking. They are fined and filtered.

SECOND WINE
None produced.

SEUIL

Classification: None
Location of vineyards: Cérons
Owner: Mr. and Mrs. Bob Watts
Address: 33720 Cérons
Mailing address: Same as above
Telephone: 33 5 56 27 11 56; telefax: 33 5 56 27 28 79
Visits: By appointment only
Contact: Mr. Bob Watts

VINEYARDS (red)
Surface area: 111 acres
Average age of vines: 35 years
Blend: 50% Merlot, 40% Cabernet Sauvignon, 10% Cabernet Franc
Density of plantation: 5,550 vines per hectare
Average yields (over the last 5 years): 55 hectoliters per hectare
Total average annual production: 250 hectoliters

GRAND VIN (red)
Brand name: Château du Seuil
Appellation: Graves
Mean annual production: 33,300 bottles
Upbringing: Harvest is manual and mechanical. Fermentations occur in temperature-controlled stainless-steel tanks. Wines are aged in oak casks (30% of which are new) for 15 months. They are not fined but are filtered.

SECOND WINE
Brand name: Domaine du Seuil
Appellation: Premières Côtes de Bordeaux
Average annual production: 115 hectoliters

VINEYARDS (white)
Surface area: 7 acres
Average age of vines: 15 years
Blend: 80% Semillon, 20% Sauvignon
Density of plantation: 5,550 vines per hectare
Average yields (over the last 5 years): 55 hectoliters per hectare
Total average annual production: 150 hectoliters

GRAND VIN (white)
Brand name: Château du Seuil
Appellation: Graves
Mean annual production: 20,000 bottles
Upbringing: Sixty percent of the yield undergoes fermentation in
stainless-steel vats at low temperatures and wines remain on lees
3 months. Forty percent of the yield undergoes fermentation in
new oak barrels (selected yeasts are used). Wines remain on lees for
4–5 months and are stirred regularly. They are not fined but are
filtered.

SECOND WINE
Brand name: Domaine du Seuil
Appellation: Bordeaux Blanc Sec
Average annual production: 15,000 bottles

DOMAINE DE LA SOLITUDE

Classification: None
Location of vineyards: Martillac
Owner: Communauté Religieuse de la Sainte Famille (Convent)
Mailing address: c/o Domaine de Chevalier, 33650 Martillac
Telephone: 33 5 56 72 74 74; telefax: 33 5 56 72 74 74
Visits: By appointment only, Monday to Friday, 8:30 A.M. to 12:30 P.M.
Contact: Sister Evelyne Brel

VINEYARDS (red)
Surface area: 49 acres
Average age of vines: 30 years
Blend: 40% Merlot, 30% Cabernet Franc, 25% Cabernet Sauvignon, 5%
Malbec
Density of plantation: 5,500 vines per hectare
Average yields (over the last 5 years): 43 hectoliters per hectare

GRAND VIN (red)
Brand name: Domaine de la Solitude
Appellation: Pessac-Léognan
Mean annual production: 5,000 cases
Upbringing: Fermentations last 3 weeks in temperature-controlled vats—
maximum temperature 30 degrees centigrade. Wines are aged in oak
casks (1, 2, and 3 years old) for 15 months and are fined and filtered.

SECOND WINE
None produced.

VINEYARDS (white)
Surface area: 12.3 acres
Average age of vines: 30 years
Blend: 50% Sauvignon, 50% Semillon
Density of plantation: 5,500 vines per hectare
Average yields (over the last 5 years): 35 hectoliters

GRAND VIN (white)
Brand name: Domaine de la Solitude
Appellation: Pessac-Léognan
Mean annual production: 1,500 cases
Upbringing: Fermentations occur in oak barrels, 15% of which are new
(the rest are between 1 and 5 years old). Wines are kept on lees for 14
months and are bottled after fining and filtration.

SECOND WINE
None produced.
The Domaine de Chevalier has farmed this estate since 1993. The
Domaine de la Solitude belongs to the nuns of Martillac.

LE THIL COMTE CLARY   GOOD

Classification: None
Location of vineyards: Léognan
Owner: G.F.A. Le Thil
Address: 33850 Léognan
Mailing address: Same as above
Telephone: 33 5 56 30 01 02; telefax: 33 5 56 30 04 32
Visits: By appointment only
Contact: Jean de Laître

VINEYARDS (red)
Surface area: 21.2 acres
Average age of vines: 8 years
Blend: 70% Merlot, 30% Cabernet Sauvignon
Density of plantation: 6,700 vines per hectare
Average yields (over the last 2 years): 55 hectoliters per hectare
Total average annual production: 450 hectoliters

GRAND VIN (red)
Brand name: Château Le Thil Comte Clary
Appellation: Pessac-Léognan
Mean annual production: 3,700 cases
Upbringing: Fermentations last 3–4 weeks at temperatures of 27–31
degrees centigrade in temperature-controlled (electronic system)
stainless-steel tanks. Malolactics occur at 20 degrees centigrade. Wines
are transferred to oak barrels for 12 months aging (20% new oak). They
are racked every 3 months, then fined and filtered.

SECOND WINE
Brand name: Château Crigean
Average annual production: 1,300 cases

VINEYARDS (white)
Surface area: 7.6 acres
Average age of vines: 7 years
Blend: 50% Semillon, 50% Sauvignon
Density of plantation: 6,700 vines per hectare
Average yields (over the last 5 years): 50 hectoliters per hectare
Total average annual production: 150 hectoliters

GRAND VIN (white)
Brand name: Château Le Thil Comte Clary
Appellation: Pessac-Léognan
Mean annual production: 1,600 cases
Upbringing: *Macération pelliculaire*. Grapes are pressed out. Cold settling
at 10 degrees centigrade for 2 days. Temperature is controlled
electronically. Fermentations occur in stainless-steel tanks at 18 degrees
centigrade for the Sauvignon and in new oak barrels for the Semillon.
Sauvignon is kept on lees in tanks, and the Semillon is also kept on lees
but in new oak barrels with regular stirring. Bottling after 9 months.
Assemblage is done just before bottling. Wines are fined but not filtered.

SECOND WINE
None produced.

NOTE: The average yield indicated is over the last 2 years. The vineyards are located in between those of Château Carbonnieux, Smith-Haut-Lafitte, and Bouscaut. The estate has been "created" by Jean de Laître, formerly a doctor in Paris, in 1990. In 1994 the estate controlled 26 acres of vines.

To ensure perfect maturity of a healthy harvest, *effeuillage* is carried out on both sides and green pruning is done manually. The harvest is done manually; grapes are sorted twice, in the vineyards and at the winery.

The high percentage of Merlot is justified by the nature of the soil (gravelly) and subsoil (calcareous and clay).

LA TOUR DE BOYRIN

Classification: None
Location of vineyards: Roaillan and Langon
Owner: Jacques Goua
Address: 41, cours du Maréchal de Lattre de Tassigny, 33210 Langon
Mailing address: Same as above
Telephone: 33 5 56 63 18 62; telefax: 33 5 56 63 18 62
Visits: By appointment only
Contact: Mr. or Mrs. Jacques Goua

VINEYARDS (red)
Surface area: 27 acres
Average age of vines: 30 years
Blend: 60% Cabernet Sauvignon, 40% Merlot
Density of plantation: 5,000 vines per hectare
Total average annual production: 500 hectoliters

GRAND VIN (red)
Brand name: Château La Tour de Boyrin
Appellation: Graves
Mean annual production: 650 hectoliters
Upbringing: Fermentations last 21–25 days, and wines are aged in cement and stainless-steel tanks. They are fined and filtered.

SECOND WINE
None produced.

VINEYARDS (white)
Surface area: 22 acres
Average age of vines: 50 years

Blend: 70% Semillon, 20% Sauvignon, 10% Muscadelle
Density of plantation: 5,000 vines per hectare
Total average annual production: 300 hectoliters

GRAND VIN (white)
Brand name: Château La Tour de Boyrin
Appellation: Graves Supérieur
Mean annual production: 350–400 hectoliters
Upbringing: All of the wine is sold to the trade. No bottling is done at the château.

SECOND WINE
None produced.

TOURTE

Classification: None
Location of vineyards: Toulenne, near Langon
Owner: Hubert Arnaud
Address: Route de la Tourte, 33210 Toulenne (Langon)
Mailing address: c/o Mr. Hubert Arnaud, 44, rue de Fleurs, 75006 Paris
Telephone: 33 1 46 88 40 08; telefax: 3 1 46 88 01 40
Visits: By appointment only
Contact: Hubert Arnaud

VINEYARDS (red)
Surface area: 5 acres
Average age of vines: 30 years
Blend: 70% Merlot, 30% Cabernet Sauvignon
Density of plantation: 5,000 vines per hectare
Average yields (over the last 5 years): 35–40 hectoliters per hectare
Total average annual production: 70 hectoliters

GRAND VIN (red)
Brand name: Château du Tourte
Appellation: Graves
Mean annual production: 70 hectoliters
Upbringing: Fermentations last 3 weeks in temperature-controlled tanks. Wines are aged for 15 months in oak barrels, half of which are new. They are not fined but are filtered.

SECOND WINE
None produced.

VINEYARDS (white)
Surface area: 5 acres
Average age of vines: 30 years
Blend: 85% Semillon, 15% Sauvignon
Density of plantation: 5,000 vines per hectare
Average yields (over the last 5 years): 45 hectoliters per hectare
Total average annual production: 90 hectoliters

GRAND VIN (white)
Brand name: Château du Tourte
Appellation: Graves
Mean annual production: 90 hectoliters
Upbringing: Fermentations take place in temperature-controlled
stainless-steel vats. Wines are aged for 10 months in oak barrels, 30% of
which are new. They are both fined and filtered.

SECOND WINE
None produced.

LE TUQUET

Classification: None
Location of vineyards: Beautiran
Owner: Paul Ragon
Address: 33640 Beautiran
Mailing address: Same as above
Telephone: 33 5 56 20 21 23; telefax: 33 5 56 20 21 83
Visits: By appointment only, weekdays, between 8 A.M. and noon, and 2
P.M. and 6 P.M.
Contact: Paul Ragon

VINEYARDS (red)
Surface area: 86.5 acres
Average age of vines: 25 years
Blend: 45% Merlot, 35% Cabernet Sauvignon, 20% Cabernet Franc
Density of plantation: 5,000 vines per hectare
Average yields (over the last 5 years): 57 hectoliters
Total average annual production: 2,000 hectoliters

GRAND VIN (red)
Brand name: Château Le Tuquet
Appellation: Graves

Mean annual production: 100,000 bottles
Upbringing: Fermentations last 17–21 days, and wines are aged for 12 months in oak casks, 30% of which are new. Wines are fined and filtered.

SECOND WINE
Brand name: Château de Bellfont and Château Louloumey-Le Tuquet
Average annual production: 160,000 bottles

VINEYARDS (white)
Surface area: 38.3 acres
Average age of vines: 30 years
Blend: 70% Semillon, 30% Sauvignon
Density of plantation: 5,500 vines per hectare
Average yields (over the last 5 years): 48 hectoliters
Total average annual production: 750 hectoliters

GRAND VIN (white)
Brand name: Château Le Tuquet
Appellation: Graves
Mean annual production: 60,000 bottles
Upbringing: Fermentations occur at low temperatures and last 10–15 days. Wines are fined and filtered.

SECOND WINE
Brand name: Château de Bellefont—Château Louloumey-Le Tuquet
Average annual production: 40,000 bottles

LA VIEILLE FRANCE   GOOD

Classification: None
Location of vineyards: Portets
Owner: Michel Dugoua
Address: 1, chemin du Malbec, 33640 Portets
Mailing address: Same as above
Telephone: 33 5 56 67 19 11 or 33 6 11 70 15 24;
telefax: 33 5 56 67 17 54
Visits: Monday to Friday, from 9 A.M. to noon, and 2 P.M to 7 P.M.
Contact: Mrs. Dugoua

VINEYARDS (red)
Surface area: 21 acres
Average age of vines: 30 years

Blend: 75% Merlot, 25% Cabernet Sauvignon
Density of plantation: 5,500 vines per hectare
Average yields (over the last 5 years): 50.6 hectoliters per hectare
Total average annual production: 430 hectoliters

GRAND VIN (red)
Brand name: Château La Vieille France
Appellation: Graves
Mean annual production: 150 hectoliters
Upbringing: Fermentations last 17–21 days depending on the vintage.
Wines are then transferred to oak casks (renewed by a third each year)
for 12 months. They are fined but not always filtered.

NOTE: Blend of the grand vin is 50% Merlot and 50% Cabernet
Sauvignon.

SECOND WINE
Brand name: Château Cadet de la Vieille Ferme
Average annual production: 150 hectoliters

NOTE: Blend of the second wine is 75%–80% Merlot and 20%–25%
Cabernet Sauvignon, depending upon yields.

VINEYARDS (white)
Surface area: 10.9 acres
Average age of vines: 30 years
Blend: 80% Semillon, 20% Sauvignon
Density of plantation: 5,500 vines per hectare
Average yields (over the last 5 years): 50.6 hectoliters per hectare
Total average annual production: 250 hectoliters

GRAND VIN (white)
Brand name: Château La Vieille France
Appellation: Graves
Mean annual production: 3,000 bottles
Upbringing: Fermentations occur in new oak barrels. Wines remain on
lees with frequent stirrings for 7–8 months. They are fined and filtered if
necessary.

SECOND WINE
Brand name: Cadet La Vieille France
Average annual production: 15,000 bottles

VILLA BEL-AIR

Classification: None
Location of vineyards: St.-Morillon
Owner: Famille Cazes
Address: Villa Bel-Air, 33650 St.-Morillon
Mailing address: Same as above
Telephone: 33 5 56 20 29 35; telefax: 33 5 56 78 44 80
Visits: By appointment only
Contact: Guy Delestrac at above telephone and fax numbers

VINEYARDS (red)
Surface area: 59.3 acres
Average age of vines: 10 years
Blend: 50% Cabernet Sauvignon, 10% Cabernet Franc, 40% Merlot
Density of plantation: 7,500 vines per hectare
Average yields (over the last 5 years): 45 hectoliters per hectare
Total average annual production: 12,000 cases

GRAND VIN (red)
Brand name: Villa Bel-Air
Appellation: Graves
Mean annual production: 12,000 cases
Upbringing: Fermentations and macerations last about 15 days in
temperature-controlled stainless-steel tanks. Malolactics occur in vats,
and wines are transferred to oak barrels for 12 months aging. No new oak
is ever used. Wines are fined and filtered.

SECOND WINE
None produced.

VINEYARDS (white)
Surface area: 54.3 acres
Average age of vines: 10 years
Blend: 42% Sauvignon Blanc, 42% Semillon, 16% Muscadelle
Density of plantation: 7,500 vines per hectare
Average yields (over the last 5 years): 45 hectoliters per hectare
Total average annual production: 11,000 cases

GRAND VIN (white)
Brand name: Villa Bel-Air
Appellation: Graves
Mean annual production: 11,000 cases
Upbringing: Cold settling of the musts. Wines are fermented in new oak

casks, then remain on lees for 8 months, with regular stirring every 15 days. They are fined and filtered.

SECOND WINE
None produced.

THE WINES OF POMEROL

The smallest of the great red wine districts of Bordeaux, Pomerol produces some of the most expensive, exhilarating, and glamorous wines in the world. Yet Pomerol, whose wines are in such demand that they must be severely allocated, remains the only major appellation of Bordeaux never to have had its wines formally placed in a rigid hierarchy of quality. When members of the Bordeaux wine trade established the now famous and historic 1855 Classification of the Wines of the Gironde, they completely ignored Pomerol and St.-Emilion, both some 18 miles east of Bordeaux on the right bank of the Gironde River. These areas had developed reputations for high-quality wine, but because travel across the Gironde to Libourne was difficult (bridges were not built until after 1820), St.-Emilion and Pomerol developed most of their trade with northern France, Belgium, and Holland. In contrast, the larger wine-producing estates in the Médoc worked through brokers in Bordeaux. In many cases, these firms, called *négociants*, were run by transplanted English, as well as Irish, families that relied on existing contacts with the British wine trade. The 1855 classification was, in essence, a short list of well-known Médoc estates, plus the famous Haut-Brion in Graves. Why? Because these châteaux traditionally sold most of their production to Bordeaux brokers who then exported the wine to England. Since the brokers, who did little or no business with the châteaux of Pomerol and St.-Emilion until the late 1860s, were responsible for the 1855 classification, they were ignorant—or worse, self-serving—when they classified the top five dozen or so châteaux of the Bordeaux region.

Since 1855 the wines of St.-Emilion have been classified four times—first in 1954, with revisions in 1969, 1985, and 1997. The wines of Pomerol,

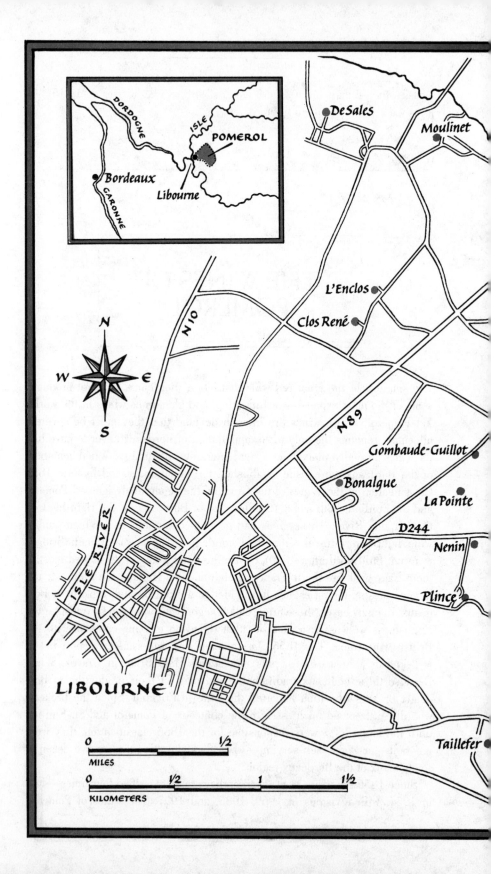

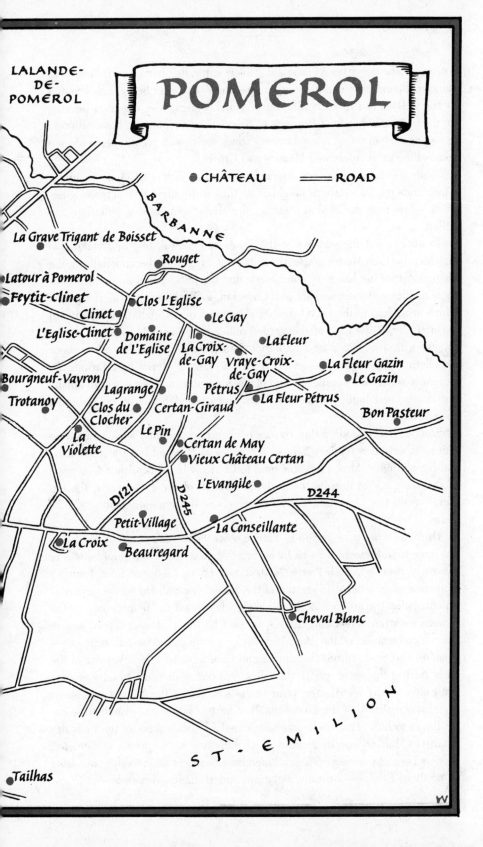

however, have never been classified. This is surprising because they began to gain great popularity and notoriety in the late 1940s, after being highly touted by the well-known English wine buyer Harry Waugh, who was then working for the respected house of Harvey's in Bristol. Their reputation has continued to soar to the point that many Pomerol wines are now in greater demand than some of the most celebrated Médocs and Graves.

While St.-Emilion covers an enormous area (with 13,434 acres under vine), Pomerol, its northern neighbor, is tiny, with only 1,939 acres of vine-yards—less than the total acreage for the Médoc's smallest appellation, St.-Julien.

To understand the success of the wines of Pomerol, one must take into consideration the Merlot grape (the dominant varietal of the appellation), the changing drinking habits of consumers, and the influence of an empire built by Jean-Pierre Moueix and his son, Christian. First, there is the Merlot grape, which according to the INAO (Institute National des Appellations d'Origine) accounts for 70%–75% of the grapes planted in Pomerol. Cabernet Franc follows with 20%–25% and Cabernet Sauvignon with 5%. No other major appellation of Bordeaux has as much Merlot planted. Merlot-based wines are generally softer, more opulently and obviously fruity and lush, lower in appar-ent tannin, and higher in alcohol than wines based primarily on Cabernet Sauvignon.

Second, many modern-day consumers (and restaurants) seek wines that can be drunk at a younger age, so the wines of Pomerol have a ready-and-waiting audience. Most Pomerols tend to be ready to drink within 4–6 years of the vintage. Yet despite the early maturation of these Pomerols, the top wines retain their fruit and evolve extremely well, frequently lasting 15–25 years.

Third, no other wine region in France owes its success to a single individ-ual more than Pomerol does to Jean-Pierre Moueix. In 1930, when he was in his early twenties, Jean-Pierre Moueix arrived in Libourne from France's Corrèze region, a desolate section of the Massif Central. He was regarded as an outcast by the aristocratic blue-bloods who traded in Médoc wines on the famous riverfront street called the Quai de Chartrons. Moueix turned east to the viticultural areas the Bordeaux brokers considered an afterthought—Pomerol and St.-Emilion. His timing and luck were bad, however, for in the early thirties the world was in the midst of a depression, not to fully emerge until after World War II. Yet, prior to the war, the young Moueix was smart enough to realize that the historic market for top Bordeaux—England—was off limits to him. That trade was dominated by the brokers of the quai des Chartrons, but no one there paid much attention to the wines of Pomerol. Moueix began by setting up a small merchant business and traveling regularly to northern Europe—Brittany, Belgium, and Holland—where he found enthusiastic buyers for his Pomerols. By 1937 he had established a *négociant* business in Libourne, the commercial town that today serves as Pomerol's port of entry. In the post–World War II years he purchased three properties in Pomerol—Trotanoy, Lagrange, and La Fleur Pétrus—and where he was unable to buy a property, he arranged to be the exclusive selling agent for that estate's wine.

In 1964 Moueix finally realized his dream and purchased a 50% interest in a vineyard he'd long coveted. The vineyard was called Pétrus. Moueix believed it was producing as great a wine as any of the first-growths in Bordeaux. In spite of Moueix's enthusiasm, Pétrus was not yet well-known in established wine circles. That would soon change.

Throughout the fifties and sixties Moueix was a tireless crusader (some would say an inexhaustible promoter) for the wines of Pomerol. His spectacular rise to a leadership position, and his achievement of enormous wealth was, in short, accomplished by working extremely hard and producing exceptional wines, particularly at his two flagship châteaux, Pétrus and Trotanoy. In the sixties and early seventies these two wines often surpassed the first-growths of the Médoc.

The extraordinary rise to prominence of both Moueix and his wines brought Pomerol attention and prestige that did not go unnoticed by other producers in this bucolic appellation. As a result, other properties began to upgrade the quality of their wines. Today, while no one can challenge the domination that Jean-Pierre Moueix's firm enjoys over the sale of the wines of Pomerol, there is an increasing number of challengers to the previously uncontested superiority of Pétrus.

The most celebrated Pomerol châteaux are located on the plateau of Pomerol. Pétrus sits on the highest elevation, and most of its acreage benefits from a soil base that is largely clay; the surrounding prestigious neighbors have much more gravel. Within shouting distance of Pétrus are La Fleur-Pétrus, Certan de May, Vieux-Château-Certan, Le Pin, La Conseillante, and l'Evangile. Immediately to the northwest are Lafleur, l'Eglise-Clinet, and La Fleur de Gay. Yet these vineyards' deep, gravelly soils (which also contain some clay) are excellent for both the Merlot and Cabernet Franc grapes, only Pétrus is planted with 95% Merlot and 5% Cabernet Franc. Other Pomerol properties, recognizing the fact that Cabernet grape varieties, especially Cabernet Franc, are well suited for this soil, plant somewhat higher percentages of Cabernet Franc.

Heading west, toward the end of the plateau of Pomerol, where Trotanoy is located, the soils become even more gravelly. Properties in this locale often excel in wet vintages because of the superb drainage provided by these deep beds. Farther west, in the direction of Route National N89 (connecting Libourne and Bordeaux), the soil changes to a mixture of gravel and sand, then to a light sandy, flint-based soil. These areas cannot support the production of long-lived wine, but many soft, fruity, extremely pleasant and supple Pomerols are made here. However, even the best of these wines will never have the strength, aging potential, or richness of the Pomerols from the gravel and gravel/clay/iron–based soils of the plateau.

For those familiar with the Médoc and Graves regions of Bordeaux, Pomerol—with its limited acreage and modest farmhouse "châteaux"—must come as a surprise. Pétrus itself is a remarkably humble building that truly stretches the definition of "château" to the limit. The appellation's largest estate, de Sales, is the only Pomerol property to have a building that could be said to resemble a Médoc château—and a modest one at that. The other three sizable vineyards of Pomerol are Nenin, Taillefer, and La Pointe. Not one of these three estates, however, could be accused of being in the top league of quality, although Nenin's purchase by Michel Delon (of Léoville-Las Cases) in 1997 should elicit plenty of excitement. Most of the best Pomerol vineyards encompass between 20 and 34 acres, but many are much smaller. For example, three current Pomerol superstars are true micro-estates. Lafleur, Certan de May, or l'Eglise-Clinet could sell their entire production within the Bordeaux city limits if they desired. None of these estates is larger than 15 acres.

What are the telltale characteristic traits of Pomerol wines? The dense ruby color, the intense berry fruit, plummy, sometimes truffle-and-mocha-scented, ripe, fruity, often black cherry and raspberry–dominated bouquet, and a lush, voluptuous, almost unctuous texture are typical—at least in the top vintages. Welcome to the glories of the Merlot grape.

As for the styles of wine produced in Pomerol, generally these are Bordeaux's most gentle, smooth, silky, lush, and richly fruity wines. However, that does not explain the diversity of styles that can be found; the individual producers do. The overall quality of winemaking in Pomerol is extremely high. Only in the Médoc appellation of St.-Julien is there as brilliant an overall level of talented winemakers.

Pétrus is frequently this appellation's greatest wine, as well as the most massively concentrated, rich, and long-lived. The heavy clay soil that the vineyard of Pétrus sits on results in a powerful wine. Yet until the early eighties Trotanoy was often indistinguishable from Pétrus in blind tastings and was clearly the most complete and demanded Pomerol (along with Lafleur) after Pétrus. Not surprisingly, Pétrus is made from 95% Merlot and Trotanoy 90%, and they are treated identically by the same winemaking team. The other Pomerol that has always rivaled, and in many vintages eclipsed, Pétrus, but is terribly obscure, is the tiny estate of Lafleur. Interestingly, Lafleur's vineyard sits adjacent to that of Pétrus on the plateau, and it, too, has extremely old vines that render small quantities of very concentrated, exotically flavored, highly structured grape juice.

If Pétrus, Trotanoy, and Lafleur have traditionally made Pomerol's richest, deepest-colored, most-massive wines, l'Evangile, La Conseillante, Petit-Village, La Fleur Pétrus, and l'Eglise-Clinet produce this appellation's most graceful, smooth, elegant, Burgundian-like wine. None of these properties can lay claim to making as massive or as rich a wine as Pétrus, Trotanoy, or Lafleur, but no Pomerol enthusiast would dare pass up the opportunity to lay away a few bottles or cases of any of these wines.

L'Evangile and La Conseillante justifiably have two of Pomerol's finest reputations but have been irregular performers. La Conseillante was a notorious underachiever during much of the sixties and seventies but came on strong in the eighties, making some of the greatest wines in its famed history. The 1981, 1982, 1983, 1985, 1989, and 1990 are decadently hedonistic beauties. L'Evangile has also been inconsistent. But when it makes superb wines, they rival the best that can be produced by Pétrus, Trotanoy, or Lafleur. L'Evangile made spectacular wines in 1947, 1950, 1961, 1975, 1982, 1985, 1990, and 1995. Given the fact that a major interest in L'Evangile was acquired by the Rothschild family (of Lafite-Rothschild) in 1989, this property may finally have the financial resources to challenge Pétrus, both in quality and price; the dreamy 1990 and sumptuous 1995 are cases in point.

La Fleur Pétrus has the right name for fame, yet it rarely seems to produce wines at a level its name suggests it could. With the acquisition of a parcel of old vines from Le Gay in the mid-nineties, this might change. Historically it is a very good, rather than superb, Pomerol, velvety, quick to mature, yet elegant and graceful.

Petit-Village lacked the meticulous care and concern that comes from a committed proprietor. This potentially great vineyard began to make topflight wines in the late 1970s under the guidance of Bruno Prats. Prats then sold the property, and Petit-Village improved in quality, with superb vintages in 1982, 1985, 1988, and 1989. More recently the wine has been very good but less consistent than I would have expected.

Since the release of their great 1985, l'Eglise-Clinet has been a rising superstar of the appellation. Historically l'Eglise-Clinet has had plenty to boast about. The 1921, 1929, 1945, 1947, 1948, 1949, 1950, 1957, and 1959 are amazingly rich wines that have stood the test of time. Yet an undistinguished period in the sixties and seventies caused many to forget this splendid estate. Possessing some of Pomerol's oldest vines, this traditionally run property produces an explosively fruity, densely colored Pomerol that seems always to taste like the essence of black fruits and minerals. Significantly, it is one of the few tiny Pomerol estates to employ a second wine for vats considered not rich enough for the grand vin.

A third style of Pomerol wine might also be called the "Médoc" style. One Pomerol estate, Vieux-Château-Certan makes a wine with a high percentage of Cabernet Sauvignon and Cabernet Franc (rather than Merlot), and their wines often have more Médoc-like characteristics than other Pomerols. Vieux-Château-Certan had a great reputation in the nineteenth century and first half of the twentieth century when it was considered among the greatest Pomerols. The 1947, 1948, and 1950 are legendary. However, this property's wines passed through an uninspired period in the sixties and seventies that resulted in a decline in their reputation. That has been reversed since the 1982 vintage.

A fourth school of Pomerols produces wines that are light and supple and offer immediate drinking. These wines rarely last more than a decade, but they do provide considerable value in an appellation whose wines are fetching higher and higher prices. Most of these Pomerols are located in the western part of the area on light, sandy soils. None of them have great reputations, but several of these estates, particularly l'Enclos, Clos René, and de Sales, make complete wines that satisfy the palate, the purse, and the impatient.

There are numerous other Pomerols, and perhaps the greatest story of the eighties was the emergence of such potential superstar estates as Certan de May, Clinet, La Fleur de Gay, and Le Pin.

La Fleur de Gay was inaugurated in the 1982 vintage by Dr. Alain Raynaud, the proprietor of the well-known Pomerol château La Croix de Gay. It is very unusual in Bordeaux to see a proprietor take a parcel of his very best vines (in this case a plot of 100% Merlot located near Pétrus and Lafleur) and make a separate wine from it. La Fleur de Gay, aged in 100% new oak casks, is a wine of astonishing richness and exotic super-ripeness. One sip of the 1990, 1989, 1988, 1987, 1986, 1985, or 1983 will make anyone a believer.

Clinet was another perennial underachiever until 1985, when the son-in-law of the proprietor, Jean-Michel Arcaute, assumed management of the property. In a remarkably short time, Clinet shed a cloak of mediocrity and started to produce wines that are among the most complex and profoundly concentrated of the appellation. This would now appear to be one of the titans of Pomerol, capable of challenging the very best. For example, virtually perfect expressions of wine were produced in 1989, 1990, 1994, and 1995.

The other superstar to emerge during the last two decades is the micro-estate of Le Pin. This wine, made from a tiny vineyard that is nearly 100% Merlot, is perhaps the most extraordinarily perfumed, hedonistic, kinky wine in Bordeaux. The proprietors, the Thienpont family, have clearly decided to make a wine in the image of Pétrus but even more exotic. The only question concerning Le Pin is how well it will age. Undeniably, it has become a cult wine for billionaires willing to pay the astronomical prices this wine fetches at auction.

Other topflight Pomerols include Latour à Pomerol, which has made some legendary wines (1947, 1950, 1959, and 1961), and Bon Pasteur, an estate run by two of the world's most gifted oenologists, the husband-and-wife team of Dany and Michel Rolland.

All things considered, Pomerol has fewer underachievers today than it did a decade ago. Nevertheless, there is no question that some of the larger properties, such as Nenin, Taillefer, and La Pointe, could make better wines. It is a shame they don't, since they are large vineyards by Pomerol standards and could provide a good introduction to the rich, fleshy, hedonistic wines of this appellation.

POMEROL
(An Insider's View)

Overall Appellation Potential: Average to Superb

The Most Potential for Aging: Clinet, l'Eglise-Clinet, l'Evangile, Le Gay, Gazin, Lafleur, Pétrus, Trotanoy

The Most Elegant: La Conseillante, Gazin, La Grave, Lafleur, Latour à Pomerol, Pétrus, Vieux-Château-Certan

The Most Concentrated: Clinet, l'Eglise-Clinet, l'Evangile, Le Gay, Gazin, Lafleur, Pétrus, Trotanoy

The Best Value: Bon Pasteur, l'Enclos, La Grave, La Loubière, de Sales

The Most Exotic: Le Pin, Clos l'Eglise (since 1997)

The Most Difficult to Understand (when young): Lafleur, Pétrus, Vieux-Château-Certan

The Most Underrated: None

The Easiest to Appreciate Young: La Conseillante, Petit-Village, Le Pin

Up-and-Coming Estates: La Fleur Pétrus, Nenin

Greatest Recent Vintages: 1995, 1990, 1989, 1982, 1975, 1970, 1964, 1961, 1950, 1949, 1948, 1947, 1945

POMEROL—AN OVERVIEW

Location: On the right bank of the Dordogne, Pomerol is bounded on the south by the railroad line between Libourne and Bergerac, as well as the city of Libourne, and on the north by the tributary named Barbanne

Acres under Vine: 1,939

Communes: Pomerol

Average Annual Production: 368,000 cases

Classified Growths: None; the wines of Pomerol have never been classified

Principal Grape Varieties: Merlot dominates, followed by small plantations of Cabernet Franc and even less of Cabernet Sauvignon

Principal Soil Types: Gravel with clay and iron dominates those vineyards on the plateau of Pomerol. Gravel with increasing amounts of sand is found in those vineyards that border Lalande de Pomerol

A CONSUMER'S CLASSIFICATION OF THE
CHÂTEAUX OF POMEROL

OUTSTANDING
Clinet
La Conseillante
l'Eglise-Clinet
l'Evangile
La Fleur de Gay
Lafleur
Pétrus
Le Pin
Trotanoy

EXCELLENT
Bon Pasteur
Certan de May
Clos l'Eglise (since 1997)
La Croix du Casse
La Fleur Pétrus
Gazin
Latour à Pomerol
Nenin (since 1997)
Petit-Village
Vieux-Château-Certan

VERY GOOD
Beau Soleil, Certan-Giraud, La Croix de Gay, Domaine de l'Eglise, l'Enclos,
Le Gay, Gombaude-Guillot, La Grave à Pomerol (formerly La Grave Trigant
de Boisset)

GOOD
Bellegrave, Bonalgue, Bourgneuf, Clos du Clocher, Clos René, La Croix,
Haut-Maillet, Rouget, de Sales, La Violette, Vraye-Croix-de-Gay

OTHER NOTABLE POMEROL PROPERTIES
Beauchene, Beauregard, de Bourgueneuf, La Cabanne, Le Caillou,
Cantelauze, Le Carillon, Clos du Pélérin, La Commanderie, Croix
St.-Georges, Croix Taillefer, Croix Toulifaut, Ferrand, Feytit-Clinet,
Feytit-Guillot, La Ganne, Guillot, Guillot Clauzel, Grand Moulinet, Grange
Neuve, Haut Cloquet, Haut Ferrand, Lafleur Gazin, Lafleur du Roy,

Lagrange, La Loubière, Mazeyres, Montviel, Moulinet, Nouvelle Eglise, La Patache, Plince, Plincette, La Pointe, Pont Cloquet, Prieurs de la Commanderie, Ratouin, Rempart, Renaissance, Reve d'Or, La Rose Figeac, St.-Pierre, Tailhas, Taillefer, Thibeaud-Maillet, Tour Robert, de Valois, Vieux Maillet, Vieux-Château-Ferron

BEAUREGARD

Classification: None
Location of vineyards: Catusseau
Owner: S.C. du Château Beauregard
Address: 33500 Pomerol
Mailing address: Same as above
Telephone: 33 5 57 51 13 36; telefax: 33 5 57 25 09 55
Visits: By appointment only, Monday through Friday, between 9 A.M. and noon, and 2 P.M. and 5 P.M.
Contact: Vincent Priou

VINEYARDS (red)
Surface area: 42 acres
Average age of vines: 30 years
Blend: 60% Merlot, 35% Cabernet Franc, 5% Cabernet Sauvignon
Density of plantation: 6,000 vines per hectare
Average yields (over the last 5 years): 45 hectoliters per hectare
Total average annual production: 100,000 bottles

GRAND VIN (red)
Brand name: Château Beauregard
Appellation: Pomerol
Mean annual production: 70,000 bottles
Upbringing: Fermentations last 2–4 weeks in temperature-controlled stainless-steel tanks, at temperatures between 25 and 33 degrees centigrade. Malolactics occur in oak barrels. Wines are aged for 15–20 months in oak barrels, 60%–75% of which are new, depending upon the vintage. They are fined but not filtered.

SECOND WINE
Brand name: Le Benjamin de Beauregard
Average annual production: 30,000 bottles

Evaluation of present classification: The quality equivalent of a Médoc fifth-growth
Plateau of maturity: 5–12 years following the vintage

As one leaves the tiny village of Catusseau, the vineyards of Beauregard are situated on the southern perimeter of the plateau of Pomerol. This is one of the few properties in the appellation that actually has a building grand enough to be called a château. The vineyard has significant potential. Most Pomerol observers consider the deep, gravelly soil to be ideal for producing high-quality wine. Until the mid-1980s most of the vintages produced quick-to-age, rustic wines. Since then administrator Paul Clauzel has been making finer wine, with better color and more ripeness and concentration. Moreover, greater attention is also being paid to sanitary conditions in the cellar. The Clauzel family sold the property in 1991 to Crédit Foncier de France, and the progression in quality has continued.

VINTAGES

1997 — Beauregard has been producing attractive wines over the last half dozen
• years, and the 1997 is an up-front, precociously styled wine with a *pain grillé*,
86– black cherry, and chocolatey-scented nose. The fruit is ripe and sweet, and
88 the wine is exceptionally supple with low acidity and a plump, easy-going finish. Already drinkable and surprisingly evolved for such a young Bordeaux, it should drink well between 1999 and 2006. Last tasted, 3/98.

1996 — Beauregard's 1996 reveals plenty of toasty new oak and a medium-bodied
• personality. The color is a healthy ruby/purple. Once past the vanillin, the
85– aromatics offer copious amounts of sweet cherry and straightforward black
86 fruits. The wine is fleshy, spicy, and well made in a straightforward, supple, oaky style. Anticipated maturity: Now–2008. Last tasted, 3/98.

1995 — An excellent wine, this 1995 offers an alluring deep ruby color with a smoky,
• vanillin, berry, chocolatey-scented nose. Medium bodied and ripe, with sweet
87 fruit, moderate tannin, and low acidity, this is a fine example of Beauregard. Anticipated maturity: Now–2010. Last tasted, 11/97.

1994 — Dark ruby/purple colored, with a closed, earthy, smoky, black fruit nose, this
• tightly knit, medium-bodied wine possesses very good to excellent concentra-
87 tion, but also high tannin. It has shut down since bottling and requires 3–4 years of cellaring. Anticipated maturity: 2001–2012. Last tasted, 1/97.

1993 — A sleeper of the vintage, this deep plum–colored wine offers up a sweet, smoky,
• hedonistic personality with lush black cherry, smoke-tinged flavors, a surpris-
87 ingly smooth, creamy texture, and lovely ripe fruit that gushes from the glass and hangs on the palate without any hard edges. This is a well-made, midweight, tasty Pomerol for drinking over the next 7–8 years. Last tasted, 1/97.

1992 — The 1992 is the best Beauregard in years. It offers a dark ruby color, an
• intensely spicy, fragrant, richly fruity nose, soft, fleshy flavors, medium to full
88 body, and a round, gentle finish. Drink it over the next 5–7 years. This is a surprisingly extracted and powerful 1992. Last tasted, 11/94.

1990 — This muscular, chunky, full-bodied wine offers considerable weight and inten-
• sity. While it was jammy and lacking individuality and complexity from
87 barrel, it has developed considerable personality. It is the finest Beauregard in years. Drink it over the next 7–8 years. Last tasted, 1/93.

BELLEGRAVE   GOOD

Classification: None
Location of vineyards: Lieu-dit René
Owner: Jean-Marie Bouldy
Address: Lieu-dit René, 33500 Pomerol
Mailing address: Same as above
Telephone: 33 5 57 51 20 47; telefax: 33 5 57 51 23 14
Visits: Monday through Saturday, from 8 A.M. to noon, and 2 P.M. to 7 P.M.
Contact: Jean-Marie Bouldy

VINEYARDS (red)
Surface area: 19.8 acres
Average age of vines: 35 years
Blend: 75% Merlot, 20% Cabernet Franc, 5% Cabernet Sauvignon
Density of plantation: 6,000 vines per hectare
Average yields (over the last 5 years): 45 hectoliters per hectare
Total average annual production: 360 hectoliters

GRAND VIN (red)
Brand name: Château Bellegrave
Appellation: Pomerol
Mean annual production: 40,000 bottles
Upbringing: Fermentations last 3–4 weeks, with half the yield in
stainless-steel tanks and the other half in concrete vats, both temperature
controlled. One-third of the yield undergoes malolactics in new oak
casks, and the rest of the wines are transferred into oak in November.
They are aged 22 months before bottling. They are fined with egg whites
and are not filtered.

SECOND WINE
Brand name: Château des Jacobins
Average annual production: 60–80 hectoliters (depending upon the
vintage)

Evaluation of present classification: The quality equivalent of a Médoc
Cru Bourgeois
Plateau of maturity: 3–8 years following the vintage

The Bellegrave vineyard, located west of RN 89, on light, sandy, gravelly soil, produces soft, easy to drink, and easy to understand wines that must be consumed in their youth. It would appear that the proprietor, Jean-Marie Bouldy, has a sensible view of what he is able to achieve in one of the less promising soil types of Pomerol. The results are cleanly made, fresh, fruity wines with mass appeal.

VINTAGES

1993—The 1993 Bellegrave is a pleasant, monolithic, fruity Pomerol with light
• tannin, fine body, and a solid but uninspiring finish. Drink it over the next 5–
80 7 years. Last tasted, 11/94.

1992—This up-and-coming property has recently begun fashioning better wine. The
• 1992 displays attractive raspberry/plum–like fruit, toasty new oak, and a
85 touch of herbal tea in its bouquet and flavors. Medium bodied, with sufficient
depth and a soft, easygoing finish, it should be drunk over the next 5–6 years.
Last tasted, 11/94.

1989—The 1989 Bellegrave is exceptionally low in acidity and very alcoholic. For
• those who like their wines fat, ripe, plummy, and obvious, this straightforward,
84 chunky, yet well-endowed Pomerol provides delicious drinking. Anticipated
maturity: Now. Last tasted, 11/90.

1988—The 1988 is lighter styled but manifests the same emphasis on straightfor-
• ward, ripe, tasty fruit in a medium-bodied, easy to appreciate style. Antici-
82 pated maturity: Now. Last tasted, 11/90.

1985—I found the 1985 Bellegrave attractively sweet, plummy, soft, medium bodied,
• and ideal for current drinking. Anticipated maturity: Now. Last tasted, 3/90.
83

BON PASTEUR   EXCELLENT

Classification: None
Location of vineyards: Maillet
Owner: Rolland family
Address: Maillet, 33500 Pomerol
Mailing address: 15, cours des Girondins, 33500 Libourne
Telephone: 33 5 57 51 10 94; telefax: 33 5 57 25 05 54
Visits: By appointment only
Contact: Dany Rolland at above telephone and fax numbers

VINEYARDS (red)
Surface area: 16.4 acres
Average age of vines: 30 years
Blend: 80% Merlot, 20% Cabernet Franc
Density of plantation: 6,000 vines per hectare
Average yields (over the last 5 years): 42 hectoliters per hectare
Total average annual production: 275 hectoliters

GRAND VIN (red)
Brand name: Le Bon Pasteur
Appellation: Pomerol
Mean annual production: 33,000 bottles
Upbringing: Fermentations last 25–35 days, depending upon the vintage,

in small stainless-steel vats of 70-hectoliter capacity. Malolactics occur in barrels, and wines are aged for 15–22 months in 80% new oak barrels. There is no general rule concerning fining and filtration.

SECOND WINE
None produced.

Evaluation of present classification: The quality equivalent of a Médoc fourth- or fifth-growth
Plateau of maturity: 5–14 years following the vintage

Bon Pasteur is the property of two of Bordeaux's most gifted oenologists, Dany and Michel Rolland, who have a laboratory in Libourne. Additionally, Michel boasts a list of clients that reads like a *Who's Who* of Pomerol, St.-Emilion, and the other major appellations of Bordeaux. His fame is such that he has been retained as the consultant for many of the world's leading wineries, from Ornellaia in Italy, to Casa Lapostolle in Chile, to the renowned Napa Valley treasure—Harlan Estate.

Michel Rolland's success, as well as the formation of an association of Pomerol estates called the Circle of Prestige of Pomerol, has given rise to two prevailing schools of thought about harvest dates and winemaking philosophies. One school—represented by the firm of Jean-Pierre Moueix and its two leading spokespeople, Christian Moueix and their oenologist, Jean-Claude Berrouet—believes that the Merlot grape should not be picked too late. Their argument is that early harvesting is essential to preserve the wine's stability and acidity. Furthermore, Moueix and Berrouet believe in shorter maceration periods to give the wines more elegance.

In contrast, Michel Rolland and his colleagues believe in harvesting as late as possible in order to obtain fruit that has an element of *sur-maturité* (overripeness). Rolland also believes in extended macerations to produce wines of profound color, richness, and aging potential. There is no doubt that Rolland's philosophy has caught the fancy of some of France's leading writers, particularly the outspoken Parisian Michel Bettane, probably Europe's finest taster and wine critic. He is a solid defender of Rolland, who he believes possesses the philosophy necessary to produce extraordinary wines. Interestingly, two of Rolland's clients, Clinet and La Fleur de Gay, are now turning out wines that compete with Pétrus.

The Bon Pasteur vineyard is not one of the best situated in Pomerol. The 17-plus acres are spread out in northeast Pomerol, near the village of Maillet. There are essentially two soil types, one gravel based and the other clay based, as well as lighter, deep gravel beds. Because of the extremely old vines, late picking, long maceration, and the use of 50% new oak, Rolland gets as much out of his vineyard as is possible. He made extraordinary wines in vintages such as 1982, 1988, 1989, 1990, 1995, and 1996.

VINTAGES

1997—A saturated dark ruby/purple color is followed by a hedonistic wine with
•   copious quantities of mocha-tinged, blackberry, and cherry flavors. Medium
89–   to full bodied, with an element of *sur-maturité,* this luscious, nicely textured,
91   nearly unctuous Bon Pasteur is already difficult to resist. With its low acidity, and copious quantities of fruit and glycerin, this offering will drink well early, but it possesses the requisite depth, and enough tannin to evolve for 10–12+ years. A sleeper of the vintage. Last tasted, 3/98.

1996—This wine, which continues on a favorable development track, is one of the
•   stronger efforts from Pomerol in this vintage. It possesses a dense ruby/purple
88–   color, and excellent aromatics, consisting of black cherries, mocha, and
90   sweet toasty new oak. Fat and rich for a 1996 Pomerol, as well as elegant and pure, this is a well-delineated, structured, moderately tannic, high-quality Pomerol that will age well. Anticipated maturity: 2002—2015. Last tasted, 3/98.

1995—This wine may turn out to be outstanding. It offers a dark plum color and
•   high-quality aromatics consisting of *pain grillé,* lead pencil, smoke, and black
90   cherry and currant fruit. In the mouth, this is a sweet, medium-bodied, round, spicy, succulently textured Bon Pasteur with a plump, fleshy finish. Anticipated maturity: 2001–2012. Last tasted, 11/97.

1994—A telltale Merlot/Pomerol nose of mocha, chocolate, tobacco, and sweet black
•   cherry/plummy fruit is followed by a medium-bodied wine with moderate
89   tannin, excellent purity, outstanding richness, and a sweet finish. This wine requires 2–3 years of cellaring. Anticipated maturity: 2000–2012. Last tasted, 1/97.

1993—This saturated dark garnet/plum/ruby–colored wine is a fine effort for the
•   1993 vintage, a year that still offers good value for readers looking for moder-
88   ately priced Bordeaux. The 1993 Bon Pasteur displays a sweet, smoky, coffee, black cherry nose, surprising fat, a soft texture, low acidity, and a spicy, chewy, medium-bodied finish. This is one of the most concentrated, delicious, and complex efforts of the vintage. Anticipated maturity: Now–2007. Last tasted, 1/97.

1992—The famed oenologist team of Dany and Michel Rolland has produced a lovely
•   1992 Bon Pasteur. Dark ruby colored, with a smoky, mocha/chocolate/black
86   cherry nose, this wine exhibits ripe fruit, medium body, a tannic backbone, satisfying depth, and more structure and length than many 1992s. It will drink well for 5–7 years, possibly longer. Last tasted, 11/94.

1990—This is a more complete wine than the 1989 Bon Pasteur; the 1990 has
•   greater fruit extract, a sweeter, richer, more expansive texture, a fine underly-
91   ing tannic structure, and impressive levels of mocha-tinged, chocolatey, jammy cherry fruit intermixed with aromas of smoke and vanilla. Full bodied, youthful, and seemingly far younger than the 1-year age difference would

suggest, this appears to be an outstanding Bon Pasteur that should drink well from the late 1990s through 2015. Last tasted, 11/96.

1989—Although the 1989 Bon Pasteur did not jump off retailers' shelves, I have had
•   it frequently, and the wine consistently scores in the 89–90-point category.
90   The nose offers up an interesting concoction of seaweed, salty ocean breezes, smoke, and sweet chocolate-covered cherry candy. There remains a firm, tannic edge to this medium- to full-bodied wine, but it is developing considerable complexity as well as additional richness and weight. This delicious 1989 should continue to drink well for 10–12 years. Last tasted, 11/96.

1988—Bon Pasteur's 1988 is a sure bet. Deep opaque dark ruby (darker than the
•   1989), with a huge bouquet of chocolate, plums, currants, and herbs, this
89   full-bodied, admirably extracted wine should prove to have considerable longevity. Anticipated maturity: Now–2008. Last tasted, 1/93.

1986—The 1986 Bon Pasteur is excellent. Proprietor Rolland is one of the few
•   producers with a significant percentage of Merlot planted in his vineyard
87   (90%) who was able to achieve a better wine in 1986 than in 1985. The 1986 has a deep ruby color, a forceful, big, rich, toasty, plummy bouquet, and luscious medium- to full-bodied flavors backed up by some sizable tannins. It should be ready to drink relatively soon but last for well over a decade. Anticipated maturity: Now–2000. Last tasted, 3/90.

1985—The 1985 is ready to drink, soft, fruity, and medium bodied but lacks the
•   concentration and structure of the top years. Anticipated maturity: Now. Last
84   tasted, 3/90.

1984—Quite acceptable, the 1984 Bon Pasteur is one of the better Pomerols of the
•   vintage. Moderately deep in color and extract, this plummy wine displays
80   what brilliant winemaker Michel Rolland can do in a terrible vintage. Anticipated maturity: Now. Last tasted, 3/90.

1983—The 1983 Bon Pasteur is a richly fruity wine, with a lovely perfumed bouquet
•   of black currants. Supple, lush, and precocious, this medium-bodied wine is
85   drinking well. Anticipated maturity: Now. Last tasted, 3/90.

1982—I have gone through several cases of this wine in half bottles, regular bottles,
•   and a handful of magnums. Except for one musty-smelling half bottle, the
96   wine has been thrilling from the day of its release in 1984. It is a classic Pomerol. In 1982 the renowned husband/wife proprietor/oenologist team of Dany and Michel Rolland raised Bon Pasteur's level of quality well above its *terroir* and, in doing so, caused one American wine critic to focus more closely on their work. The 1982 has always been thick and rich, with the creamy texture and splendid opulence that are hallmarks of this vintage. The wine has taken on some amber at the edge, but it reveals no signs of color or fruit degradation. The huge nose of toffee, caramel, sweet black fruit, spice, and cedar is a knockout. Rich, full bodied, and silky smooth, this exceptionally concentrated, large-scaled Bon Pasteur begs for consumption over the next 10+ years. It is one of those rare Bordeaux that has never gone through a "dumb" stage. Last tasted, 4/98.

1981—Supple, richly fruity, elegant, spicy, and soft, this medium-bodied wine has a
  •   jammy, mocha-flavored black currant fruitiness, a harmonious, lush texture,
  85   and immediate accessibility. It is fully mature. Anticipated maturity: Now.
         Last tasted, 12/90.
1980—Very well made in this difficult vintage, the 1980 Bon Pasteur is a soft,
  •   medium-weight wine with good ripeness and a savory, mellow personality.
  82   Anticipated maturity: Now—may be in decline. Last tasted, 6/84.
1979—The 1979 Bon Pasteur has always lacked the generous, ripe, richly fruity
  •   character I enjoy and associate so much with the wine from this estate. While
  78   well made, it remains austere and a little lean. Anticipated maturity: Now.
         Last tasted, 6/84.
1978—A successful 1978, Bon Pasteur has a caramel, toasty, herb, and coffee
  •   bouquet. The wine is amply endowed, rich, and concentrated, with layers of
  86   ripe Merlot fruit, and a long alcoholic, lush finish. It is one of the top Pomerols
         of this vintage. Anticipated maturity: Now. Last tasted, 1/90.

BONALGUE   GOOD

Classification: None
Location of vineyards: Pomerol
Owner: Pierre Bourotte
Address: Vignobles Pierre Bourotte S.A., 16, rue Faidherbe, 33502
Libourne Cedex
Mailing address: Vignobles Pierre Bourotte S.A., B.P.79, 33502 Libourne
Cedex
Telephone: 33 5 57 51 62 17; telefax: 33 5 57 51 28 28
Visits: By appointment only
Contact: Pierre Bourotte and Ludovic David

VINEYARDS (red)
Surface area: 16 acres
Average age of vines: 25 years
Blend: 80% Merlot, 20% Cabernet Franc
Density of plantation: 5,500 vines per hectare
Average yields (over the last 5 years): 45 hectoliters per hectare
Total average annual production: 2,500–3,000 cases

GRAND VIN (red)
Brand name: Château Bonalgue
Appellation: Pomerol
Mean annual production: 2,000–2,500 cases
Upbringing: Fermentations and macerations are rather long, and wines
are aged for 12–18 months in oak barrels that are renewed by half at
each vintage.

SECOND WINE
Brand name: Château Burgrave
Average annual production: 2,500 cases

Evaluation of present classification: The quality equivalent of a Médoc
Cru Bourgeois
Plateau of maturity: 4–10 years following the vintage

Bonalgue remains a relatively obscure Pomerol, but the quality is consistently sound and, in top vintages, very good. The vineyard, situated on a mixture of gravelly and sandy soil, just at the entrance of Libourne, behind the racetrack on RN 89, turns out deeply colored, chunky, fleshy wines that lack complexity but not character, fruit, or mouth-filling pleasure.

VINTAGES

1997— This is a consistently good source for plump, attractive, low-acid wines that
• drink well young yet age moderately well. The 1997 Bonalgue possesses
85– lower acidity and is more forward than other vintages, but it does offer a deep
86 ruby color, plenty of ripe prune and cherry fruit, a soft texture, good glycerin, and nearly an absence of tannin and grip in its open-knit finish. This wine should drink well for 4–5 years. Last tasted, 3/98.

1996— This is a relatively fat, forward style of Pomerol with new oak and nearly
• overripe flavors (suggested by a hint of prunes). A soft, ripe, surprisingly
85– oaky, medium-bodied, low-acid wine, the 1996 will require drinking during
86 its first 5–6 years of life. Last tasted, 3/98.

1995— A dark ruby–colored wine with sweet, spicy, berry fruit and a roasted peanut–
• scented nose, the 1995 Bonalgue is soft, round, and velvety-textured, with low
86 acidity and moderate weight. It is an attractive wine for near-term drinking. Anticipated maturity: Now–2004. Last tasted, 11/97.

1989— The 1989 is not far behind the 1982. Deep ruby/purple, with an obvious yet
• enticing bouquet of sweet, plump blackberries, this lush, deceptively easy, gen-
85 erously endowed wine goes down the throat far too easily for its 13% alcohol content. It will not be long-lived. Anticipated maturity: Now. Last tasted, 4/91.

1988— The 1988 has more tannin than the 1989, is spicy and harder in style, but
• has still managed to retain Bonalgue's rich black fruit character. It is a
83 medium-bodied wine that should be currently at its best. Anticipated maturity: Now. Last tasted, 4/91.

1986— The 1986 is a bit light and less impressive than I had hoped but offers
• straightforward, plummy fruit that displays decent extract and a soft, smooth
82 finish. Drink this wine over the next 3–4 years. Anticipated maturity: Now. Last tasted, 3/90.

1985— The 1985 displays a healthy dosage of toasty new oak and has lush, medium-
• bodied flavors that are packed with berry fruit and soft tannins in the finish.
85 Anticipated maturity: Now. Last tasted, 3/89.

1984—Quite spicy and robust, but a little coarse and charmless, the 1984 Bonalgue
  •   should drink decently for 2–4 more years. Anticipated maturity: Now. Last
  78   tasted, 3/88.

BOURGNEUF   GOOD

Classification: None
Location of vineyards: At Bourgneuf, in the very heart of Pomerol, next to
Trotanoy
Owner: Xavier Vayron
Address: 1, le Bourgneuf, 33500 Pomerol
Mailing address: Same as above
Telephone: 33 5 57 51 42 03; telefax: 33 5 57 25 01 40
Visits: Preferably by appointment, every day, between 9 A.M. and noon,
and 2 P.M. and 7 P.M.
Contact: Mr. and Mrs. Xavier Vayron

VINEYARDS (red)
Surface area: 22.2 acres
Average age of vines: 40 years
Blend: 90% Merlot, 10% Cabernet Franc
Density of plantation: 6,000 vines per hectare
Average yields (over the last 5 years): 40 hectoliters per hectare
Total average annual production: 380 hectoliters

GRAND VIN (red)
Brand name: Château Bourgneuf
Appellation: Pomerol
Mean annual production: 360–380 hectoliters
Upbringing: Fermentations occur slowly in temperature-controlled
concrete vats and last 15–20 days. Wines are transferred for 10–12
months aging in oak barrels that are renewed by one-fifth each vintage.
They are fined with egg whites and are lightly filtered. There are 22
months between the harvest and the bottling.

SECOND WINE
None produced.

Evaluation of present classification: The quality equivalent of a Médoc
Cru Bourgeois
Plateau of maturity: 5–10 years following the vintage

Given the well-situated position of Bourgneuf's vineyard in the center of the
appellation, on the plateau just to the west of Trotanoy, it has always puzzled
me why higher-quality wines do not emerge from this estate. Perhaps the
ruggedly impressive 1995 and 1996 signal better things. The production

yields are reasonable, and when one talks to the proprietors, it is clear that they pay a great deal of respect to a traditional vinification. All of this is perplexing, because what I continue to taste are monolithic, one-dimensional wines, with a great deal of body and tannin but an absence of underlying elegance, finesse, and what is subjectively called "breed." This is an ancient estate with vast potential.

VINTAGES

1997 — Bourgneuf has been producing better wines over recent vintages. Following
• successful efforts in both 1995 and 1996, the 1997 is a boisterous, flamboyant
86– Pomerol with plenty of body and flavor. A saturated deep purple color is
87 followed by a provocative spicy, roasted herb, vanillin, *pain grillé*, coffee, and plum/prune–scented nose. The wine possesses excellent ripeness, full body (unusual in this vintage), and a muscular, long finish. There is moderate tannin, so it may have more aging potential than most 1997s. Anticipated maturity: 2001–2012. Last tasted, 3/98.

1996 — The 1996 Bourgneuf has turned out to be an attractive Pomerol with a dark
• ruby/purple color, and sweet cherry aromas intertwined with scents of licorice
86– and vanillin. Excellent ripeness, good fat and flesh on the palate, and a
87 low-acid, lush, up-front appeal give this wine considerable charm. It will be a Bourgneuf to drink during its first 10–12 years of life. Last tasted, 3/98.

1995 — A sleeper of the vintage, Bourgneuf's 1995 may be the finest wine I have
• tasted from this estate. The color is an opaque purple, and the wine offers a
89 closed but promising nose of black cherries, raspberries, and coffee-tinged fruit. Packed and stacked, as they say in the vernacular, this medium- to full-bodied, powerful, mouth-filling Pomerol is big, bold, and boisterous. If additional complexity develops in this excellent, decadently rich wine, it will merit an outstanding rating. Anticipated maturity: 2000–2014. Last tasted, 11/97.

1994 — Tannic and lean, as well as big and structured, the 1994 may ultimately lack
• the fruit and extract needed to balance out the tannin. Anticipated maturity:
84 2000–2008. Last tasted, 1/97.

1993 — A certain coarseness and rusticity are accompanied by sweet fruit, medium
• body, chunky, fleshy flavors, good color, and a spicy finish. Drink the 1993
85 Bourgneuf over the next 5–7 years. Last tasted, 1/97.

1992 — With its medium ruby color and light-intensity bouquet consisting primarily
• of under-ripe fruit, this straightforward, one-dimensional wine suffers from
74 excessive tannin as well as a green, vegetal character. Unimpressive. It should be drunk up. Last tasted, 11/94.

1990 — With a deep ruby color and a huge plummy, spicy bouquet that borders on
• over-ripeness, this lush, rich, chewy-textured wine is the most impressive
87 Bourgneuf in years. Anticipated maturity: Now–2002. Last tasted, 1/93.

1989 — Bourgneuf's 1989 is a chunky, ripe, foursquare style of wine that has abun-
• dant quantities of fruit, good body, and soft tannins in its alcoholic finish.
84 Anticipated maturity: Now. Last tasted, 1/93.

1988—The 1988 lacks the fruit and heady qualities of the 1989 Bourgneuf-Vayron,
•   but it is a respectable, straightforward, medium-bodied Pomerol for drinking
82   over the next 5–7 years. Last tasted, 1/93.

1986—The 1986 Bourgneuf displays a judicious use of spicy, toasty oak, a lovely
•   supple, fleshy fruitiness, and good length. This is a straightforward-styled
84   wine. Anticipated maturity: Now. Last tasted, 3/90.

1985—The 1985 is typical of this estate. It is thick, plummy, and foursquare, but
•   essentially simple and grapey. Anticipated maturity: Now. Last tasted, 3/89.
82

LA CABANNE

Classification: None
Location of vineyards: Pomerol
Owner: J.-P. Estager
Address: 33500 Pomerol
Mailing address: 33 à 41, rue de Montaudon, 33500 Libourne
Telephone: 33 5 57 51 04 09; telefax: 33 5 57 25 13 38
Visits: By appointment only
Contact: François Estager

VINEYARDS (red)
Surface area: 24.7 acres
Average age of vines: 30 years
Blend: 94% Merlot, 6% Cabernet Franc
Density of plantation: 5,800 vines per hectare
Average yields (over the last 5 years): 47 hectoliters per hectare
Total average annual production: 470 hectoliters

GRAND VIN (red)
Brand name: Château La Cabanne
Appellation: Pomerol
Mean annual production: 60,000 bottles
Upbringing: Fermentations last 20 days in temperature-controlled
stainless-steel and epoxy vats. Malolactics occur in vats, and wines are
then transferred to oak barrels, 60% of which are new, for 14–18 months
aging. They are fined and filtered.

SECOND WINE
Brand name: Domaine de Compostelle
Average annual production: Varies with the vintage

Evaluation of present classification: The quality equivalent of a Médoc
Cru Bourgeois
Plateau of maturity: 5–12 years following the vintage

La Cabanne is run by one of Pomerol's true gentlemen, Jean-Pierre Estager. In addition to owning Château La Cabanne, he also owns property in Montagne-St.-Emilion (Château La Papeterie) and leases another estate in Pomerol (Château Haut-Maillet). La Cabanne, whose sizable production is distributed internationally, represents a solidly made, plump Pomerol that offers rustic aromas of dusty, cedary, plummy fruit, followed by a generous yet often coarse texture that can lack finesse and be overcharged with tannin. Nevertheless, if never dazzling, it is a reliably made wine that can stand the test of time. The vineyard is highly morcellated, but the château itself is situated in the heart of Pomerol, not far from the famed Château Trotanoy.

VINTAGES

1995—The 1995 is a softer, lower-acid, less well-defined version of the 1994. It has
• not yet filled out in the middle, and it does not appear to possess the power
86 and grip of its predecessor. Nevertheless, it is an attractive, medium-bodied wine with excellent purity and ripeness. If the wine develops more of a midpalate, it will merit a rating in the upper 80s. It will need to be drunk early in life, as it will not have the longevity of the 1994. Last tasted, 11/97.

1994—La Cabanne's 1994 is a surprisingly rich, powerful, concentrated wine that
• represents a new stylistic direction for this estate (long known for lighter-
87 styled Pomerols). Several months before bottling, the wine offers gobs of rich, chewy black cherry fruit, excellent color saturation, and plenty of depth and richness. With low acidity, good grip, and moderate tannin, it will be accessible young, but I suspect it will last for a decade. Last tasted, 3/96.

1993—Good, clean, spicy, light-intensity fruit is followed by a lean, tough-textured,
• tannic wine lacking depth and ripeness. Drink it over the next 7–8 years.
77 Last tasted, 11/94.

1992—La Cabanne's 1992 is typical of so many wines from the vintage. It offers an
• uncomplicated but attractively fruity, ripe nose, light to medium body, soft
80 tannin, and low acidity. It will last for 4–6 years. Last tasted, 11/94.

1990—The sweet, fruity, oaky aromas of the 1990 are followed by a wine with good
• depth, soft texture, and an adequate finish. Anticipated maturity: Now–2000.
84 Last tasted, 1/93.

1989—Because of the vintage, the 1989 carries more fruit, alcohol, and tannin than
• usual. Exhibiting some toasty new oak scents and a good dark ruby color, this
84 generously fruity, soft, medium-bodied Pomerol should drink well young. Anticipated maturity: Now. Last tasted, 1/93.

1988—La Cabanne tends to produce ready to drink, easygoing, lighter-styled Pomer-
• ols. The 1988 La Cabanne is a light, oaky wine, with a sound, unexciting
82 character. Drink it over the next 3–5 years. Last tasted, 3/93.

1986—The 1986 is extremely light, with watery, diluted flavors that point out the
• overabundant size of the Merlot crop in this vintage. Drink this lightweight,
73 medium-bodied wine over the next 3–4 years. Anticipated maturity: Now. Last tasted, 3/90.

1985—The 1985 has a light-intensity bouquet of cherry fruit and simple, pleasant,
- somewhat boring flavors. Last tasted, 3/89.
74

1984—A trifle austere, but certainly above average, the 1984 La Cabanne displays
- decent ripeness and fruit. Anticipated maturity: Now. Last tasted, 3/88.
80

1982—This lightweight wine has a precarious hold on life, revealing consider-
- able amber at the edge, dusty, washed-out aromas, and lean, compact fla-
72   vors that lack concentration and intensity. It is going nowhere. Last tasted,
      9/95.

CERTAN-GIRAUD   VERY GOOD

Classification: None
Location of vineyards: On the plateau of Certan in Pomerol
Owner: Société Civile des Domaines Giraud
Address: Château Certan-Giraud, 33500 Pomerol
Mailing address: 1, Grand Corbin, 33330 St.-Emilion
Telephone: 33 5 57 74 48 94; telefax: 33 5 57 74 47 18
Visits: By appointment only
Contact: Philippe Giraud

VINEYARDS (red)
Surface area: 18.5 acres
Average age of vines: 30 years
Blend: 80% Merlot, 20% Cabernet Franc
Density of plantation: 5,500 vines per hectare
Average yields (over the last 5 years): 52 hectoliters per hectare
Total average annual production: 394 hectoliters

GRAND VIN (red)
Brand name: Château Certan-Giraud
Appellation: Pomerol
Mean annual production: 394 hectoliters
Upbringing: Fermentations take place in open concrete tanks and last
approximately 3 weeks, depending upon the vintage. Wines are
transferred after malolactics into oak barrels for 12–14 months aging.
They are fined but not filtered.

SECOND WINE
None produced.

Evaluation of present classification: The quality equivalent of a Médoc
fifth-growth
Plateau of maturity: 3–10 years following the vintage

Given its immediate neighbors—Pétrus, Certan de May, and Vieux-Château-Certan—one would not be foolish to assume that the wines of Certan-Giraud have something special to offer. The vineyard, which is sandwiched between these much more famous properties on Pomerol's famed plateau, does indeed produce high-quality, typically rich, plump, fruity, Pomerol wine.

The wines of Certan-Giraud were steadily moving upward in quality until an unexplained slump began in 1984. Recent vintages suggest a return to the ripe, round, savory style that has made Certan-Giraud a popular wine both in France and abroad.

This property produces the least expensive Pomerol from the prestigious plateau section of the appellation. The vineyard's deep gravelly soils make for one of the most superbly located domains in Pomerol. Would the utilization of a higher percentage of new oak and a longer maceration period result in even greater wines? Some observers have claimed the Giraud family has allowed yields to soar out of control, which explained the indifferent quality of the wines after 1982. Nevertheless, this is an estate to take seriously. The owners also make the fine St.-Emilion Château Corbin.

VINTAGES

1997—The 1997 Certan-Giraud appeared to be grievously short of acidity (and I do
• not like high-acid wines). Excessively ripe pruny/earthy flavors have created
? a fat but shapeles wine that lacks definition and structure. It will be interesting to retaste this wine after 5–6 months of cask aging. Judgment reserved.
Last tasted, 3/98.

1996—I noticed some sample variation with this wine, but in the majority of tastings, it
• was a dense, low acid, fat, ripe Pomerol with a touch of prunes, jammy black
86– cherries, smoke, and dried herbs in its smoky, ripe, flamboyant nose. Plump,
87 succulent, medium- to full-bodied flavors are forward for the vintage, but appealing and delicious. Anticipated maturity: Now–2007. Last tasted, 3/98.

1995—Typical for this property, the 1995 has turned out to be a very good Pomerol
• with sweet, jammy flavors that border on over-ripeness. The wine displays a
87 deep ruby color with a flamboyant nose of smoke and black fruits. There is
noticeable glycerin on the palate, medium to full body, low acidity, and plenty
of power, intensity, and richness in this big, fleshy, mouth-filling, savory,
hedonistic Pomerol. Anticipated maturity: Now–2009. Last tasted, 11/97.

1994—This 1994 appears to have put on weight and is better defined and richer
• than the loosely knit 1995. It exhibits a dark plum color and a sweet, jammy
87 nose of pruny fruit, currants, and jammy cherries. Soft, plump, fleshy, and
hedonistic, this is a delicious Pomerol for drinking over the next 5–8 years.
Last tasted, 3/96.

1993—This property tends to fashion plump, slightly unfocused, but lusciously fruity,
• occasionally fat, juicy wines that are best drunk in their first 6–10 years of
86 life. Although monolithic, the mouth-filling, pure 1993 has good fruit and is
not burdened by excessive tannin. Drink it over the next 6–8 years. Last
tasted, 11/94.

1990 — The 1990, rather diffuse and fruity from the barrel, is markedly more impres-
•   sive from the bottle. Rich, dense, and well endowed, it is an opulent, chewy,
87   loaded wine that reminds me of the 1982. Consume it over the next 10–12
years. Last tasted, 1/93.

1989 — The 1989 is starting to look much better. Black/ruby in color, with an intox-
•   icatingly intense nose of cassis, this velvety, large-scaled, rich, alcoholic wine
87   has low acidity but high tannins. Anticipated maturity: Now–2001. Last
tasted, 1/93.

1988 — Ripe, medium bodied, fleshy, but simple, Certan-Giraud's 1988 is an attrac-
•   tive wine that should provide tasty drinking over the next 3–6 years. Last
85   tasted, 1/93.

1986 — The 1986 Certan-Giraud is watery, one-dimensional, and, given the lovely
•   wines made at this property over the last decade, disappointing. This wine
78   could have used a higher percentage of new oak, as well as a stricter selection,
or any selection process at all. Anticipated maturity: Now. Last tasted, 3/90.

1985 — The 1985 is loaded with fruit and very low in acidity, so take advantage
•   of its creamy-textured style and drink it. Anticipated maturity: Now. Last
84   tasted, 3/90.

1984 — Decent ruby color, spicy, soft, slightly metallic, this light-bodied wine should
•   be drunk up. Anticipated maturity: Now. Last tasted, 3/88.
78

1983 — One of the very top Pomerols of this vintage, Certan-Giraud is a dark ruby–
•   colored wine, with a big, ripe black cherry bouquet interlaced with the scent
87   of fresh garden herbs and over-ripe tomatoes. Dense, unctuous, full bodied,
and moderately tannic, this is a rich, fat, deeply concentrated wine that offers
considerable pleasure. Anticipated maturity: Now. Last tasted, 12/90.

1982 — I would have expected this wine to be showing more age based on how well it
•   drank during its first decade of life. However, it continues to exhibit a thick-
88   looking, dark ruby/purple/garnet color. The nose offers gobs of sweet, jammy,
earthy, tobacco, mocha, chocolatey, berry fruit. Full bodied, with an unctuous
texture, this chewy, lush wine is one of the finest Certan-Girauds made. I
originally thought it should be drunk up by 1995, but I am delighted to report
that it can be cellared for another 4–5 years. Last tasted, 9/95.

1981 — Not quite up to the quality of the 1982 and 1983, but still attractive, fruity,
•   and delicious, the 1981 Certan-Giraud is forward and ready to drink. Dark
84   ruby, with a moderately intense, plummy bouquet, this medium- to full-bodied
wine has very light tannins and a round, lush finish. Anticipated maturity:
Now–may be in decline. Last tasted, 6/84.

CERTAN DE MAY   EXCELLENT

Classification: None
Location of vineyards: Pomerol
Owner: Mrs. Barreau-Badar
Address: 33500 Pomerol

Mailing address: Same as above
Telephone: 33 5 57 51 43 53; telefax: 33 5 57 51 88 51
Visits: By appointment only
Contact: Jean-Luc Barreau or Mrs. Barreau-Badar

VINEYARDS (red)
Surface area: 12.3 acres
Average age of vines: 40 years
Blend: 70% Merlot, 25% Cabernet Franc, 5% Cabernet Sauvignon
Density of plantation: 5,500 vines per hectare
Average yields (over the last 5 years): 40 hectoliters per hectare
Total average annual production: 25,000 bottles

GRAND VIN (red)
Brand name: Certan de May de Certan
Appellation: Pomerol
Mean annual production: 40 hectoliters per hectare
Upbringing: Fermentations last 4–6 weeks in stainless-steel tanks. Wines
are then aged in oak barrels, 40% of which are new, for a period of
14–16 months. They are fined but not filtered.

SECOND WINE
None produced.

Evaluation of present classification: The quality equivalent of a Médoc
second-growth, particularly since 1979
Plateau of maturity: 6–20 or more years following the vintage

This tiny gem of a vineyard has become a star in the Pomerol firmament.
Certan de May's vineyard is superbly located on the highest ground of Pomerol, right between Vieux-Château-Certan and Pétrus. For years the wine was
made by another château, but since 1974 the present proprietors, Madame
Odette Barreau-Badar and her son, Jean-Luc, have been responsible for every
detail. The result has been a series of remarkably rich, concentrated Pomerols
that make Certan de May one of this appellation's stars.

There are a number of reasons why Certan de May has, since 1976,
emerged as one of Pomerol's most promising wines. In 1976 the old wooden
fermentation vats were replaced with stainless steel. Additionally, the increasing responsibilities given to Jean-Luc Barreau have resulted in several decisions that no doubt account for the higher quality of Certan de May. This
estate believes in harvesting as late as possible. Also, the extremely long
maceration—nearly 1 month—insures that the wines are super-extracted,
opaque black/purple colored, and loaded with tannin for a long evolution.

The use of 40% new oak casks seems to result in the perfect marriage between new oak and the ripe, concentrated fruit obtained by Certan de May.

However, this is not a Pomerol that can be drunk young. Most top vintages since the mid-1970s have needed at least 7–10 years of bottle age before they have exhibited a great deal of development. Sadly, Certan de May, which was once one of my favorite Pomerol estates, has become increasingly irregular since the late eighties.

VINTAGES

1997—This medium dark ruby–colored wine is quite vegetal, with pronounced
• aromas of green peppers, herbs, and olives. In the mouth, high tannin, and
78– an austere, angular personality seem devoid of charm and fruit. The wine is
83? medium bodied, but surprisingly green and unimpressive. Last tasted, 3/98.

1996—Dark ruby/purple–colored with garnet nuances, this is a tannic, muscular,
• chunky Certan de May with weedy, tobacco-tinged, berry fruit, medium to full
86– body, high tannin, and an austere, spicy, astringent finish. The wine is still
87 disjointed, and while it possesses ample strength and depth, the tannin level
is dry and hard. Anticipated maturity: 2003–2016. Last tasted, 3/98.

1995—An impressive Certan de May, the 1995 exhibits a dense ruby/purple color,
• and a moderately intense nose of black olives, cedar, raspberries, and cherry
90+ fruit intermixed with toasty new oak. In the mouth, the new oak is noticeable,
as is an elevated level of tannin. Notwithstanding the aggressive vanillin
flavors and powerful tannin, this wine has outstanding depth, and a layered,
concentrated style with considerable muscle and power. It is a big, backward,
formidably endowed Certan de May that may turn out to be the finest wine
made at this estate since the 1988, but patience is most definitely required.
Anticipated maturity: 2006–2020. Last tasted, 11/97.

1994—Dark ruby/purple colored with Certan de May's telltale roasted peanut, herbal,
• black cherry, curranty nose, this wine is reminiscent of the fleshy, open-knit
87 1983. There is moderate tannin, but the wine is surprisingly forward, soft,
and texturally appealing. However, readers must be willing to tolerate a strong
herbaceousness to enjoy this 1994. It will drink well for 10–12 years. Last
tasted, 1/97.

1993—Unfortunately, samples tasted displayed a musty, damp cellar, old, funky
• wood character that dominated the wine's aromatic personality. Lamentable,
? because otherwise Certan de May's 1993 possesses considerable color pig-
mentation, a ripe, full-bodied, powerful constitution, and moderate tannin in
a long, forceful, authoritatively flavored finish. Judgment reserved. Last
tasted, 11/94.

1992—First the good news. Certan de May's 1992 is obviously a powerful, concen-
• trated wine, with the intensely herbaceous side of Certan de May fortunately
87? subdued. The result is a wine with a forcefully rich, black currant nose
combined with scents of smoky new oak, tobacco, and herbs, medium to full
body, a soft, silky texture, excellent concentration, low acidity, and soft tan-

nin. It should be drinkable when released and age well for 10–12 years. The bad news is that some bottles reveal a damp, musty, cardboard character in the bouquet but not in the flavors. If it is not a cork problem, might this musty element relate to the use of steam in coopering or cleaning the barrels, with the steam's moisture trapped in the wood's interior, giving off unclean aromas of wood? Last tasted, 11/94.

1990—The 1990 offers loads of jammy, sweet, cedary, and herbaceous cassis scents
•   intermixed with a roasted herb, toasty wood character. Rich and full bodied,
91   as well as low in acidity and soft, the wine is already revealing some amber at the edge and a precocious, flattering personality. Drink it over the next 15 years. Last tasted, 11/96.

1989—I have expressed reservations about Certan de May's 1989, from its bizarre
•   showings prior to bottling to its more conventional yet loosely knit perfor-
87   mances afterward. This bottling revealed a raunchy, aged beef, gamey compo-nent that will prove to be controversial among tasters wishing to smell only new oak and fruit. While the wine possesses good concentration, its kinky, unusual aromatic profile and hard tannin dominate the concentration and fruit. Although distinctive, it does not live up to the quality of wines produced at Certan de May in such vintages as 1988, 1986, 1985, 1982, 1981, and 1979. Anticipated maturity: Now–2009. Last tasted, 11/96.

1988—A backward, still unevolved 1988, Certan de May has turned out a muscular,
•   powerful, deep ruby/purple–colored wine that exhibits little evolution. The
92+   wine holds exceptional promise given its tobacco leaf, spicy, cedary, black cherry, and currant nose. Roasted herb/meaty, fleshy, full-bodied flavors con-tinue to border on the exotic. This is an intense, rich, long-lived style of wine that still requires bottle age. Anticipated maturity: 2000–2015. Last tasted, 10/97.

1987—The 1987 Certan de May is one of the broadest-shouldered, most alcoholic,
•   massive wines of the vintage. It might deserve a higher rating, but there is no
87   denying the appeal, with a moderately intense, smoky, roasted, berry fruit aroma and concentrated, yet lush, herbaceous, fruity flavors. Drink this sump-tuously styled 1987 in its youth. Anticipated maturity: Now. Last tasted, 3/90.

1986—This wine is beginning to reveal ruby/orange at its edge. The nose of distinc-
•   tive weedy, black currant, tobacco-singed, smoky, oaky, and herb scents is
90   followed by a structured, medium- to full-bodied wine without the fat and flesh it exhibited a few years ago. Nevertheless, it possesses considerable vitality, muscle, and richness. This 1986 is behaving more like a Médoc than a Pomerol and requires a few more years of cellaring. Anticipated maturity: 2000–2015. Last tasted, 9/97.

1985—This is a flamboyant wine with a gaudy aromatic profile consisting of cedar
•   wood, smoke, licorice, jammy black fruits, and Asian spices. In the mouth, it
94   is fleshy and meaty, with a streak of roasted herbs running through the sweet, jammy, opulently textured black fruits, earth, and oak. Low in acidity and voluptuous, this wine has reached its peak of maturity, where it should

remain for at least another decade. Anticipated maturity: Now–2008. Last tasted, 9/97.

1983—Perhaps too tannic, oaky, and astringent for its own good, the 1983 Certan de
• May is a brawny, very powerful wine with a tough texture and excellent
86 concentration, but a coarse taste in the finish. The wine will take a long, long time to shed the tannins. Anticipated maturity: Now–2010. Last tasted, 3/85.

1982—Every time I have this wine in tastings outside my cellar, I have guessed it to
• be Pétrus, and I have rated it as one of the greatest 1982s. My scores have
96+ ranged from 96 to 100. From my cellar, the wine has always tasted fabulously concentrated, impressive, frightfully backward, and not nearly as flattering and open. This tasting note is based on a wine from my cellar—a cold, damp storage facility. The wine reveals no signs of age in its color, which remains an opaque, thick-looking ruby/purple. The nose offers up reticent aromas of super-ripe black fruits (jammy cherries), combined with earthy, truffle, cedar, and chocolate notes. Full bodied and super-concentrated, with high levels of extract, glycerin, and tannin, this remains an outrageously rich and compelling Pomerol that I find needs another 5 years until it begins to enter its plateau of maturity. It will easily last through the first 3 decades of the next century. It is a majestic Certan de May, as well as the finest young vintage of this wine I have tasted, but it is evolving at a glacial pace. Last tasted, 9/95.

1981—In a vintage that produced so many austere, spartan-style wines, Certan de
• May turned out one of the vintage's stars. The wine has retained a vigor and
90 youthfulness that makes me believe it will be one of the longer-lived examples of the vintage. The color remains a healthy dark ruby, with no lightening at the edge. A reticent aroma offers mineral, black cherry, earthy, and spice notes. On the palate, the wine is powerful and rich, somewhat austere, yet a remarkably layered, thick Pomerol that is atypical for the vintage. The wine can be drunk now, but it requires another 1–3 years of bottle age. Anticipated maturity: 1999–2012. Last tasted, 9/97.

1979—One of the two finest wines of Pomerol in 1979, Certan de May's effort has
• continued to provide exciting drinking. Still a thick garnet color with some
93 amber at the edge, this wine offers a flamboyant nose of roasted herbs, sweet jammy fruit, earth, minerals, smoke, and meat. In the mouth, this surprisingly full-bodied, intense, rich, and concentrated wine has shed most of its tannin yet retains remarkable freshness and palate presence. Anticipated maturity: Now–2010. Last tasted, 9/97.

1978—Unusually spicy, slightly peppery and herbaceous, but rich, dusty, ripe, and
• full bodied, the 1978 Certan de May has dark ruby color, very good extract,
85 but rather pungent Rhône-like flavors. Anticipated maturity: Now. Last tasted, 11/89.

1976—The 1976 Certan de May is an opulent, very ripe, rich, dense, full-bodied,
• alcoholic wine that has much more structure and richness than many wines
84 of this vintage. Drinkable and fully mature since 1980, the wine still shows no signs of losing its fruit. This big, corpulent wine is a delight to drink now and should hold for another 4–5 years. Anticipated maturity: Now. Last tasted, 7/90.

ANCIENT VINTAGES

After tasting the 1945 Certan de May (96 points; last tasted 10/94) blind I was convinced it was either Pétrus or a great vintage of Trotanoy. It exhibits an opaque garnet color and a huge nose of sweet plums, black raspberries, thyme, and grilled meats. Spectacular in the mouth, with a wonderful, sweet inner core of fruit and an unctuously textured, glycerin-imbued, heady, alcoholic finish, with enough concentration to conceal most of its tannin, this massive wine should drink well for 20 more years.

CLINET   OUTSTANDING

Classification: None
Location of vineyards: Pomerol
Owner: GAN Insurance Company (managed by Jean-Michel Arcaute)
Address: 33500 Pomerol
Mailing address: c/o Château Jonqueyres, 33750 Sant-Germain du Puch
Telephone: 33 5 56 68 55 88; telefax: 33 5 56 30 11 45
Visits: By appointment only

VINEYARDS (red)
Surface area: 22 acres
Average age of vines: 38 years
Blend: 80% Merlot, 10% Cabernet Sauvignon, 10% Cabernet Franc
Density of plantation: 6,600 vines per hectare
Average yields (over the last 5 years): 45 hectoliters per hectare
Total average annual production: 4,000 cases

GRAND VIN (red)
Brand name: Château Clinet
Appellation: Pomerol
Mean annual production: 3,500 cases
Upbringing: Fermentations and macerations may last up to 45 days (normally 30–40) in small stainless-steel vats equipped with a trickle-cooling temperature-control system. Wines are transferred to new oak barrels (for malolactics) for at least 24 to 28 months. *Assemblage* is done progressively when the wines are racked every 3 months. They are unfined and remain unfiltered.

SECOND WINE
Brand name: Fleur de Clinet
Production: 500 cases

Evaluation of present classification: Since 1988 the quality equivalent of a Médoc first-growth
Plateau of maturity: 7–18 years following the vintage

One of the appealing arguments often offered for the quality of a wine is the notion of *terroir*, that magical sense of a vineyard's soil giving a wine a particular character. However, Clinet, which does indeed possess a magnificent *terroir* at the summit of the plateau of Pomerol (not more than one-half mile from such superstars as Lafleur and Pétrus and immediately adjacent to l'Eglise-Clinet), is an example where a dedicated young man proved that the human commitment to quality can have greater influence than just relying on the vineyard's soil to turn out high-quality wine.

I am speaking of Jean-Michel Arcaute, who married the daughter of the proprietor, George Audy. In 1986 Arcaute assumed control of Clinet and in less than 4 years took this perennial underachiever to the very top of the Pomerol hierarchy. How did he do it? First, the famed oenologist Michel Rolland was given full responsibility regarding picking dates and style of vinification and *élevage*. This meant that Clinet would be harvested as late as possible. In fact, since 1987 the vineyards of Clinet have been among the last harvested in Pomerol. Moreover, the use of mechanical harvesters, utilized first with the 1982 vintage, was discontinued. The results have been a 1987 that is probably not only the wine of the appellation, but may well be one of the two best wines produced in the vintage (the other being Mouton-Rothschild), a glorious 1988, and compellingly great wines in 1989, 1990, and 1995. Arcaute macerates Clinet for up to a month and simultaneously has reduced the onetime high percentage of Cabernet Sauvignon to just under 15%.

Clinet has become one of the most exciting new wines not only of Pomerol, but of all Bordeaux and is worth every effort to find.

VINTAGES

1997 — Another outstanding example from this superbly run estate, Clinet's 1997 is
  •   extremely forward, with the telltale black/purple color and obvious signs of
90–   late-picked grapes (what the French call *sur-maturité*). The wine possesses a
93   jammy blackberry, blueberry, licorice, and smoky-scented nose, sweet, me-
       dium- to full-bodied, concentrated flavors, low acidity, a satiny, unctuous
       texture, and a plump, fleshy mouth-feel. This wine will drink gorgeously well
       when released, yet is capable of lasting for 12–15 years. Last tasted, 3/98.

1996 — An intriguing style of Clinet, the 1996 will be interesting to follow over its
  •   lifeline of at least 20–25 years. The wine exhibits an opaque black/garnet
91–   color. It possesses elements of what the French call *sur-maturité* (literally
93+   translated as "over-ripeness," but the word has a more positive connotation
       in French than in English), plenty of toasty, smoky new oak, and high levels
       of tannin. At the same time, compelling levels of fruit, extract, and glycerin
       are present. The wine is astringent and structured, with more of a Médoc-like
       austerity than other top vintages of Clinet, but there are gobs of sweet plum,
       black cherry, and blackberry fruit. The acidity is low, the tannin high, and

the concentration level exhilarating. This wine will not be accessible young, as it will undoubtedly tighten up even more, and need at least 6–8 years of cellaring. Anticipated maturity: 2006–2025. Last tasted, 3/98.

1995 — Another extraordinary wine made in a backward *vin de garde* style, the 1995
• Clinet represents the essence of Pomerol. The blackberry, cassis liqueur-like
96 fruit of this wine is awesome. The color is saturated black/purple, and the wine extremely full bodied and powerful with layers of glycerin-imbued fruit, massive richness, plenty of licorice, blackberry, and cassis flavors, full body, and a thick, unctuous texture. This is a dense, impressive offering. Anticipated maturity: 2006–2025. Last tasted, 11/97.

1994 — Inky purple/garnet colored, with an outrageously intense nose of black truf-
• fles, licorice, cedar, and black fruits, this phenomenally extracted wine bor-
92 ders on being too concentrated for its own good. This massive, huge wine possesses 25–30 years of potential longevity. The fruit's remarkable intensity and purity, as well as the liqueur-like richness and unctuosity, are something to experience. This is an exceptionally dense, massively endowed, controversial style of Pomerol that will reward those with patience. The tannins are strong, but so is the extract level. Anticipated maturity: 2004–2025. Last tasted, 1/97.

1993 — A saturated plummy color is followed by a wine with considerable fat, lush-
• ness, and power. One of the most concentrated 1993s, this wine is reminiscent
90 of the gorgeous 1987 Clinet. The 1993 offers copious amounts of jammy cassis/cherry aromas and flavors intermixed with earth, truffles, and tobacco. Smoke and licorice also make an appearance in the wine's flavor profile. This is a delicious, complex, medium- to full-bodied, surprisingly top-notch effort in a so-so vintage. Anticipated maturity: Now–2012. Last tasted, 1/97.

1992 — Since 1988 Clinet has surged to the forefront of quality in Pomerol. The
• backward, dense, opaque purple–colored 1992 is an impressive albeit back-
88+ ward wine for the vintage. In terms of body, extract, and ripeness, it is as well endowed as any 1992. Medium to full bodied, with superb purity and richness, an overall sense of balance, fine length, and low acidity, it is a candidate for an outstanding score in 3–4 years. It should drink well for 10–15 or more years. A very impressive 1992! Last tasted, 11/94.

1991 — An excellent wine in what was a disastrous year for most Pomerol estates,
• Clinet's 1991 may turn out to be the best wine of the appellation! Its surpris-
87 ingly deep ruby/purple color does not suggest the horrendous conditions under which the grapes were harvested. The bouquet of pure, rich, black raspberry fruit and subtle oak is followed by a medium-bodied wine with surprising ripeness, richness, and an especially long finish. It is difficult to imagine the effort that went into producing a wine this seductive and rich in 1991. It should drink well for 7–10 years. Last tasted, 1/94.

1990 — It is easy to overlook the 1990 Clinet given the fact that 1989 merits a perfect
• rating. Nevertheless, the 1990 has improved with each tasting. It started life
95 as an outstanding wine, although unfairly overshadowed by the massive 1989.

The 1990 exhibits an opaque purple color, followed by a fabulous sweet nose of jammy black fruits, violets, minerals, and toasty oak. Full bodied and rich, with fabulous purity, outstanding extract, and well-integrated acidity and tannin, this is a large-scaled, impressively endowed claret that is narrowing the gap between itself and the legendary 1989. Anticipated maturity: 2000–2020. Last tasted, 11/96.

1989—The 1989's aroma jumps from the glass, offering up pure scents of flowers,
•   black raspberries, currants, vanillin, and truffles. Full bodied, with a seamless
100   texture, fabulous concentration, a massive degree of richness, but no heaviness or awkwardness, this remains one of the most profound young wines I have ever tasted. Its sweetness of fruit and layers of flavor, combined with its remarkable texture, are the stuff of legends. Both the 1989 and 1990 are approachable (their high Merlot content ensures them softness), yet they remain largely unevolved. If readers like them young, do not hesitate to drink a bottle or two. Ideally, both vintages will benefit from 4–5 years of cellaring. Given the 1989's additional flavor extraction and length, it is a 25–30-year wine. Anticipated maturity: 2001–2030. Last tasted, 11/96.

1988—The 1988 is a dazzling example of Clinet. Its color is a deep black/purple,
•   and the bouquet exhibits the classic Pomerol scents of truffles, plums, subtle
90   herbs, and new oak. The wine has extraordinary extraction of fruit and a full-bodied, tannic finish. Anticipated maturity: Now–2010. Last tasted, 1/93.

1987—Dark ruby, with an emerging bouquet of licorice, black currants, herbs, and
•   toasty new oak, this surprisingly powerful, medium- to full-bodied, concen-
90   trated wine is an extraordinary success. Amazing! Anticipated maturity: Now–2000. Last tasted, 1/91.

1986—The 1986, while not so enticing a wine as the 1985, is certainly an excellent
•   success for the vintage. Medium dark ruby, with a pronounced spicy, oaky
88   bouquet, impressive flavor depth and length, and some hard tannin in the finish, this big wine should be drunk over the next decade. Anticipated maturity: Now–2002. Last tasted, 3/89.

1985—The 1985 represents the return of Clinet from the throes of mediocrity. Packed
•   and concentrated with jammy berry fruit encased in a veil of toasty oak, this
87   lusty, kinky, enticing fleshpot of a wine has broad, creamy flavors and is an absolute joy to drink, although its low acidity and over-ripe style suggest that it will be short-lived. Anticipated maturity: Now. Last tasted, 4/91.

1984—Aromas of tea and spicy fruit fill the nose. On the palate, the wine is dis-
•   jointed, soft, sweet, and adequate. Drink it up. Anticipated maturity: Now–
78   may be in decline. Last tasted, 3/88.

1982—Today Clinet is one of the most exciting wines of France, but in 1982 it
•   was one of that country's most conspicuous underachievers. In 1982 ma-
73   chine harvesters were used, yields were high, there was no selection, and little new oak was utilized. The results were mushy, diffuse, loosely constructed wines such as this 1982, which is approaching full collapse. Last tasted, 9/95.

ANCIENT VINTAGES

Clinet made so many mediocre wines in the sixties, seventies, and early eighties that it is easy to believe that the first top wines produced by this estate were the 1987 and 1988. However, as persuasively demonstrated by a magnum of 1947 Clinet drunk in December 1995, and rated 96 points, this vineyard has always possessed the potential to produce remarkable wines. In this flight, it was one of the most powerful, concentrated wines, as well as one of the youngest in terms of pure, youthful exuberance. Rich and dense, with an opaque garnet/purple color, this fragrant, intensely rich, overripe Clinet exhibited a huge, opulent texture, magnificent concentration and purity, and a long, blockbuster finish with some tannin still lurking behind the wine's massive extract. It should drink well for another 25–30 years.

CLOS DU CLOCHER   GOOD

Classification: None
Location of vineyards: Pomerol, at the center of the plateau, south of the church
Owner: G.F.A. du Clos du Clocher
Address: Ets. J.-B. Audy, 35, quai du Priourat, 33502 Libourne
Mailing address: Ets J.-B. Audy, B.P. 79, 33502 Libourne Cedex
Telephone: 33 5 57 51 62 17; telefax: 33 5 57 51 28 28
Visits: By appointment only
Contact: Pierre Bourotte—Ludovic David

VINEYARDS (red)
Surface area: 14.8 acres
Average age of vines: 25 years
Blend: 80% Merlot, 20% Cabernet Franc
Density of plantation: 5,500 vines per hectare
Average yields (over the last 5 years): 45 hectoliters per hectare
Total average annual production: 2,000–2,500 cases

GRAND VIN (red)
Brand name: Clos du Clocher
Appellation: Pomerol
Mean annual production: 1,500–2,000 cases
Upbringing: Fermentations and macerations are rather long, and wines are aged for 12–18 months in oak barrels, which are renewed by half at each vintage. They are fined and lightly filtered.

> **SECOND WINE**
> Brand name: Esprit du Clocher
> Average annual production: 500–1,000 cases
>
> Evaluation of present classification: The quality equivalent of a Médoc
> Cru Bourgeois
> Plateau of maturity: 5–12 years following the vintage

A terribly under-publicized property situated just south of the large church that dominates the landscape of Pomerol's vineyards, Clos du Clocher's 3,000-case production rarely makes its way outside Europe. The vineyard, planted with 80% Merlot and 20% Cabernet Franc, produces a generously flavored, full-bodied wine that lacks some polish and finesse but is quite attractive. Clos du Clocher consistently produces very Burgundian-style wines with a silky, supple texture that offer considerable charm and fruit.

All things considered, this is a slightly underrated Pomerol that in top vintages can produce excellent wines. Prices, however, have never been inexpensive because the tiny production is gobbled up by the enthusiastic fans of Clos du Clocher, whose traditional market has been in the Benelux countries.

VINTAGES

1996—This medium-weight Pomerol appears to be a good effort for the vintage. The
 • color is a healthy dark ruby with purple nuances. Sweet black cherry and
85– kirsch fruit are intermixed with chocolate and spice from new oak. Sweet and
87 round with good depth and overall equilibrium, this will not be a long-distance runner, but it will offer pleasant near-term drinking. Anticipated maturity: Now–2008. Last tasted, 3/98.

1995—A soft, well-made, attractive Pomerol, the 1995 offers smoky, dried herb,
 • black cherry aromas intermixed with earth and spicy oak. Round and fruity,
86 with moderate tannin in the finish, this is a medium-bodied, straightforward, yet pleasant Pomerol. Anticipated maturity: 2001–2010. Last tasted, 11/97.

1993—Medium ruby, with spicy, washed-out, fruity scents, this medium dark–col-
 • ored wine is dominated by its tannin and body rather than by ripeness and
80? fruit extraction. It is a likely candidate to dry out before any charm emerges. Last tasted, 11/94.

1992—A successful wine for the vintage, with plenty of sweet, ripe, mocha/cassis
 • fruit, this medium-bodied, chewy, fleshy wine exhibits fine ripeness and a
85? sense of elegance, but the astringent tannin in the finish gives cause for concern. I suggest drinking it over the near term—say, the next 4–5 years. Last tasted, 11/94.

1990—While one might quibble over the 1990's loose-knit structure and modest
 • aging potential, there is no doubting the impressive color, big, deep, rich,
87 chewy, chocolatey, herb, prune, and cassis flavors, and lusty, heady, pleasing

finish. Drink this beauty over the next 7–9 years. It makes for quite an unctuous, heady mouthful of wine. Last tasted, 1/93.

1989—The 1989 Clos du Clocher is the finest example of this property's wines I
• have tasted. It offers a deep purple/ruby color, with a penetrating blackberry
88 and vanillin fragrance. Highly extracted fruit is buttressed by supporting tannins, yet the acidity is low. This concentrated wine will provide impressive drinking early but should have the potential to last for 10–12 years. Last tasted, 1/93.

1988—The 1988 is a ripe, fleshy, chewy wine with some oak in evidence. For those
• looking for a forward, plump style of Pomerol, check it out. Anticipated
85 maturity: Now–1999. Last tasted, 1/93.

1986—The 1986 is a more muscular, tannic wine than the 1985, with less charm
• and up-front fruit, but for those who prefer a Médoc-like structure to their
84 Pomerols, it may turn out better than my rating indicates. Anticipated maturity: Now–1999. Last tasted, 3/90.

1985—The 1985 has vivid cherry fruit, a fragrant, enticing bouquet, medium body,
• an elegant feel in the mouth, and considerable charm. This is a wine that is
85 more satisfying to drink than my score might indicate. Anticipated maturity: Now. Last tasted, 3/88.

1984—The 1984 Clos du Clocher, a fragile wine, is light, sweet, spicy, but fully .
• mature. Anticipated maturity: Now–may be in decline. Last tasted, 3/88.
79

1982—Until the advent of the 1989, this was my favorite vintage of Clos du Clocher.
• The wine has reached full maturity and should be consumed. Dark ruby/
87 garnet, with only slight amber at the edge, this extroverted wine offers up a bouquet filled with scents of roasted chestnuts, ripe plums, and licorice. In the mouth, the wine is opulent, generously endowed, with low acidity, and a lush, heady finish. It makes for a seductive tasting experience. Anticipated maturity: Now. Last tasted, 11/90.

CLOS L'EGLISE   EXCELLENT SINCE 1997

Classification: None
Location of vineyards: Near Clinet
Owner: Sylviane Garcin-Cathiard
Address: Lieu-dit Clinet, 33500 Pomerol
Mailing address: c/o Château Haut-Bergey, 33850 Léognan
Telephone: 33 5 56 64 05 22; telefax: 33 5 56 64 06 98
Visits: By appointment only
Contact: Sylviane Garcin-Cathiard

VINEYARDS (red)
Surface area: 14.8 acres
Average age of vines: 25 years
Blend: 60% Merlot, 40% Cabernet Franc

Density of plantation: 6,500 vines per hectare
Average yields (over the last 5 years): 40 hectoliters per hectare
Total average annual production: 35,000 bottles

GRAND VIN (red)
Brand name: Clos l'Eglise
Appellation: Pomerol
Mean annual production: 35,000 bottles
Upbringing: Fermentations occur in temperature-controlled wooden vats
of 60-hectoliter capacity. Wines are then aged in new oak barrels for a
period of 24 months. They are fined but not filtered.

SECOND WINE
None produced.

Evaluation of present classification: The quality equivalent of a Médoc
Cru Bourgeois but significant improvement in quality began in 1997.
Plateau of maturity: 5–12 years following the vintage

The vineyard of Clos l'Eglise, one of the numerous châteaux in Pomerol
with the word *église* in its name (because so many of the vineyards abut the
large church that sits among the vines), is well situated on the plateau
adjacent to that of Château Clinet. While I have tasted some good vintages
from Clos l'Eglise (1964 is a favorite), the relatively high percentage of
Cabernet Sauvignon formerly used in the blend tended to give the wine a
Médoc-like austerity. In fact, it is this lack of richness and opulence in top
vintages that causes it to come across as anorexic. In years where the
Cabernet does not fully ripen, Clos l'Eglise can be herbaceous to the point of
being vegetal. The use of a mechanical harvester also seems at odds with a
high commitment to quality.

In 1997, the new proprietors hired Michel Rolland to make the wine, and
the result is the finest Clos l'Eglise I have ever tasted. Given the commitment
to excellence, this is now a Pomerol to take (and drink) seriously.

VINTAGES

1997 —Under new proprietor Gaston Garcin-Cathiard and his wife, Clos l'Eglise's
•   1997 vintage has proven to be a resounding success. A blend of 60% Merlot
89–   and 40% Cabernet Franc, this is the finest Clos l'Eglise I have ever tasted!
91   Historically, Clos l'Eglise has been an herbaceous, thin wine. Yet in one year,
         an ugly duckling has been transformed into a beauty. The color is dense ruby/
         purple. The knockout nose is evolved, but compelling. Aromas of sweet
         jammy black cherry liqueur and plump fruit are nicely complemented by
         smoky new oak. Round and medium to full bodied, with a voluptuous richness

and opulent texture, this hedonistic, low-acid, plump, fleshy Pomerol is sexy and hedonistic. Anticipated maturity: 2000–2012. Kudos to the new proprietors for turning around this moribound property. A big-time sleeper! Last tasted, 3/98.

1992 — Moderately intense aromas of oak and herbaceously scented, curranty fruit
•   are presented in a light-bodied, moderately tannic format. Drink the 1992
78   Clos l'Eglise over the next 4–5 years, as it does not possess the depth of fruit necessary to outlast the tannin. Last tasted, 11/94.

1990 — The 1990 is the best wine in years from this estate. It exhibits an excellent
•   bouquet of cassis, spicy new oak, and subtle herbs. In the mouth, it is
87   medium-bodied, with an attractive ripeness, elegance, and fleshy, surprisingly rich, long finish. Drink it over the next 7–10 years. Last tasted, 1/93.

1989 — The 1989 is light, intensely herbaceous, and short on the palate. Anticipated
•   maturity: Now–1999. Last tasted, 1/93.
76

1988 — The 1988, which is similar to the 1989 but with less alcohol and body, should
•   be consumed over the next 4–5 years. Last tasted, 1/93.
72

1986 — Because of the vintage, the 1986 demonstrates more class and richness than
•   the watery, lightweight 1985. Perhaps the late-picked Cabernet Sauvignon
81   has given the wine more depth, but it still comes up short in comparison with other Pomerols. There is an attractive oakiness, but overall this is a lightweight wine that could use more flesh and muscle. Anticipated maturity: Now. Last tasted, 3/90.

1985 — I found the 1985 to be light, medium bodied, and elegant, but a little short
•   on substance and length. Anticipated maturity: Now. Last tasted, 3/90.
78

1984 — Surprisingly deep in color, with a spicy, herbaceous nose, this wine's austere,
•   undernourished palate delivers enough fruit to provide decent drinking. An-
82   ticipated maturity: Now. Last tasted, 3/88.

1983 — Fully mature, with a moderately intense, herbaceous bouquet, this soft,
•   medium-bodied wine has shed its light tannins and now offers a spicy,
83   straightforward style of wine. Anticipated maturity: Now. Last tasted, 1/89.

1982 — Consistently one of my least favorite Pomerols, the 1982 Clos l'Eglise has
•   never exhibited much extract, intensity, or the trademark characteristics of
74   the vintage—sweet, expansive, ripe fruit and an opulent, chewy texture. The wine offers light-bodied, vegetal, tea-like aromas presented in a spicy, diluted format. It is clinging to life, but does anybody care? Last tasted, 9/95.

CLOS RENÉ   GOOD

Classification: None
Production: 6,800 cases
Blend: 60% Merlot, 30% Cabernet Franc, 10% Malbec
Secondary label: Moulinet-Lasserre

Vineyard size: 27 acres
Proprietor: Pierre Lasserre
Time spent in barrels: 22–24 months
Average age of vines: 30 years

Evaluation of present classification: The quality equivalent of a Médoc
fifth-growth
Plateau of maturity: 5–15 years following the vintage

Clos René sits well to the west of the major châteaux of Pomerol, in an area
that is just south of the appellation of Lalande de Pomerol. The wines made
in this area tend to be open knit in style, quite fruity, supple, and easy to
drink. While the style of Clos René is no exception to this rule, I have noticed
a perceptible change—starting with the 1981—to a wine that is a bit bigger
framed, darker colored, and a little more substantial and concentrated. Perhaps the counseling of Michel Rolland, the highly respected Libourne oenologist and proprietor of Bon Pasteur, has made the difference between a good,
round, fruity Pomerol and a very fine, more serious wine. Whatever the
reason, there is no doubt that the vintages of the eighties have produced the
best wines from Clos René in recent memory. Not one of the best-known
Pomerols, Clos René remains reasonably priced.

VINTAGES

1996—A light-bodied, medium-weight Clos René, the 1996 clearly reveals some of
• the problems Pomerol vintners experienced because of the heavy rains that
81– fell in late August and during the third week of September. Clos René's 1996
83 displays a medium ruby color and sweet berry fruit in the nose that is
reminiscent of Zinfandel. The wine possesses decent concentration and purity, but there is not a lot to it. Drink it over the next 5–7 years. Last tasted,
11/97.

1992—The 1992 Clos René is soft and watery, with ripe berry fruit and a strong note
• of roasted peanuts. Supple, even diffuse, this is a wine to drink over the next
75 2–4 years. Last tasted, 11/94.

1991—For drinking over the next 3–4 years, the smoked-herb- and tea-scented nose
• of the seemingly mature, shockingly evolved 1991 Clos René offers some
78 attraction. Although the wine displays ripeness and substance, it finishes
short. Overall, it is an acceptable effort for a right bank 1991. Last tasted,
1/94.

1990—The 1990's super-ripe aromas of prunes and plums are followed by a meaty,
• full-throttle style of wine with considerable power, low acidity, fleshy fruit,
88 and a smooth as silk texture. It is the most impressive Clos René in years.
Drink it over the next 10–15 years. Last tasted, 1/93.

1989— Clos René's 1989 reveals an alluring bouquet of super-ripe, almost sweet,
•   jammy, cassis fruit. In the mouth, the pleasant impression is dampened by a
85   wine that is slightly light, alcoholic, soft, and fruity. Anticipated maturity:
Now. Last tasted, 1/93.

1988— The 1988 Clos René, which has more tannin than the 1989, as well as more
•   structure, is a rich, complete wine. Anticipated maturity: Now–1999. Last
86   tasted, 1/93.

1986— The 1986 has good tannins, but the overall impression is one of softness and
•   supple, silky fruit. I prefer the 1985, but the 1986 merits attention if you
84   admire a lighter-weight Pomerol that requires drinking over the next 5–6
years. Anticipated maturity: Now. Last tasted, 3/90.

1985— The 1985 has broad, ripe, rich, plummy fruit, long, lush, medium- to full-
•   bodied flavors, a silky, lengthy finish, and impressive concentration. Antici-
87   pated maturity: Now. Last tasted, 3/90.

1983— Quite successful, the 1983 Clos René is atypically dense, full bodied, ripe,
•   corpulent, and loaded with layers of fruit. Rather viscous and jammy, but
86   intensely perfumed and decadently fruity, with soft tannins in the finish, this
wine presents a hedonistic mouthful. Anticipated maturity: Now. Last tasted,
3/90.

1982— Lush, rich, and fruity, but surprisingly not as deep or as big as the 1983,
•   the 1982 Clos René is a heady, supple, delicious wine, with some round,
86   nonaggressive tannins in the finish. Anticipated maturity: Now. Last tasted,
1/85.

1981— Supple, spicy, intensely fruity, with plenty of black currant flavors, the 1981
•   Clos René is a lovely, richly textured wine, with medium to full body and
84   light to moderate tannin. Anticipated maturity: Now. Last tasted, 6/84.

1979— The 1979 Clos René is rather bland and straightforward, with average inten-
•   sity, ripe berry-ish flavors, light body, and little tannin. Anticipated maturity:
74   Now–may be in decline. Last tasted, 6/83.

1978— The 1978 is a nicely concentrated, round, fruity wine that lacks grip and
•   complexity. However, it does offer ripe, fruity flavors in a medium-bodied
83   format. Anticipated maturity: Now. Last tasted, 4/84.

1976— Diffuse, over-ripe, loosely knit, and quite fragile, the 1976 Clos René is a
•   medium ruby–colored wine with some amber at the edges. It has a sweet,
73   candied flavor and overly soft, disjointed flavors. It was more attractive several
years ago and now is beginning to fade. Anticipated maturity: Now–probably
in serious decline. Last tasted, 12/84.

1975— This is a typical 1975, tannic, still youthfully hard and closed, though some-
•   what less weighty, concentrated, and authoritative than other wines from this
80   vintage. The wine is moderately dark in color, with the hard 1975-style
tannins still quite assertive. Anticipated maturity: Now. Last tasted, 5/84.

ANCIENT VINTAGES

It is a tribute to the 1947 vintage that Clos René, a mid-80-point performer in most top years, could have produced such a phenomenal wine.

For those lucky enough to run across a bottle at auction, it will undoubtedly sell at well below its true value. An under-rated achievement, Clos René's 1947 (95 points; last tasted 10/94) exhibited the viscosity possessed by many of the great Pomerols of this vintage. The thick-looking garnet color is followed by scents of apricots, coffee, and jammy black cherries. Full bodied, with layers of chewy fruit, this fully mature yet remarkably healthy, macho wine will continue to offer decadent drinking for another 10–15 years.

LA CONSEILLANTE   OUTSTANDING

Classification: None
Location of vineyards: Pomerol and St.-Emilion
Owner: Société Civile des Héritiers Nicolas
Address: Château La Conseillante, 33500 Pomerol
Mailing address: Same as above
Telephone: 33 5 57 51 15 33; telefax: 33 5 57 51 42 39
Visits: By appointment only
Contact: Above telephone number

VINEYARDS (red)
Surface area: 29.7 acres
Average age of vines: 40 years
Blend: 70% Merlot, 25% Cabernet Franc, 5% Malbec/Pressac
Density of plantation: 5,000–5,500 vines per hectare
Average yields (over the last 5 years): 47 hectoliters
Total average annual production: 5,000–6,000 cases

GRAND VIN (red)
Brand name: La Conseillante
Appellation: Pomerol
Mean annual production: 5,000–6,000 cases
Upbringing: Fermentations last 3 weeks in temperature-controlled stainless-steel vats. Wines are transferred, after malolactics, to oak barrels, 90% of which are new, for 21 months aging. They are fined but not filtered.

SECOND WINE
None produced.

Evaluation of present classification: The quality equivalent of a Médoc second-growth
Plateau of maturity: 5–20 years following the vintage

A very highly regarded Pomerol estate, La Conseillante produces some of this appellation's most elegant, lush, and delicious wines. On the negative side, many of the vintages during the seventies had a tendency to turn out diluted, and they matured at an overly rapid rate. This was especially notice-able between 1971 and 1980. La Conseillante, owned by the Nicolas family, has been brilliant in most vintages of the eighties, with the 1981, 1982, 1985, 1989, and 1990 among the finest wines produced in all of Bordeaux. The vineyard is superbly situated in eastern Pomerol next to l'Evangile, Petit-Village, and Vieux-Château-Certan, right on the boundary of the St.-Emilion/Pomerol appellations. In fact, the deep, gravelly soils intermixed with clay and iron deposits in this area are common not only to La Conseillante and its neighbor l'Evangile, but also to the two great St.-Emilion estates across the road, Figeac and Cheval Blanc.

La Conseillante is a meticulously made wine. It is vinified in stainless-steel tanks and aged in oak barrels of which 90% are new each year. In both 1989 and 1990, 100% new oak was employed. The wine is not so powerful in style as those of Pétrus, Trotanoy, Lafleur, or Certan de May, but it is always more supple and ready to drink sooner. Because La Conseillante never seems to show as well early on as it does after several years in the bottle, I have consistently under-rated it, only to find myself revising my ratings upward. Perhaps it is the ele-vated percentage of Cabernet Franc (25%) that makes the wine look lighter in its infancy than it ultimately turns out to be. Recent vintages have, as a general rule, reached full maturity within 6–8 years. Being highly prized, as well as occasionally profound, La Conseillante is an expensive wine, normally selling at a price well above most Médoc second-growths.

VINTAGES

1997—I am a fan of this estate, which turns out some of the most elegant yet
  •   sumptuous wines of Bordeaux. Moreover, they can be drunk at an extremely
86–   young age, yet have the capacity to last. I had mixed results in four tastings
89   of the 1997 La Conseillante. There is sweet raspberry fruit in this dark ruby–
      colored wine, but I also detected some green pepper herbaceousness, as if
      there were a lack of maturity in the estate's Cabernet Franc. Exhibiting good
      concentration and low acidity, this is a good, perhaps very good wine, but I
      do not believe it is up to the level of either the 1996 or 1995. Anticipated
      maturity: 1999–2008. Last tasted, 3/98.

1996—La Conseillante's 1996 is one of the vintage's more sexy, Burgundian-styled
  •   wines. The property's hallmarks—open, generously oaked, sweet, creamy
88–   textured raspberry and kirsch-like fruit—in addition to purity, roundness,
90   and precociousness, are well displayed. The wine also possesses admirable
      finesse and elegance, no hard edges, and a seamless, delicious style that is
      atypical in this tannic, powerful vintage. The 1996 should drink well when
      bottled and should last for 15 or more years. Last tasted, 3/98.

1995—It is tempting to give this wine an outstanding score because of its seductive-
  •   ness. However, I do not think it possesses quite the level of extract and
  89   concentration to merit an exceptional rating. Nevertheless, it is an extremely
       pleasing style of claret. The deep ruby color is followed by an open-knit,
       black cherry, raspberry, and smoky, roasted herb–scented nose. There is
       round, lush, ripe fruit, medium body, exceptional elegance and purity, and a
       soft, velvety-textured finish. Think of it as liquid charm and silk. Anticipated
       maturity: 2000–2014. Last tasted, 11/97.

1994—Dark ruby/garnet, with a backward, spicy, peppery, black fruit nose (also
  •   truffles?), La Conseillante's telltale sweet, charming, alluring fruit is pushed
  88   to the background by the 1994's tannin and austerity. The wine reveals more
       weight than the 1993, but also more structure. There is good fruit under the
       tannin, but the 1994, atypically for La Conseillante, requires another 1–3
       years of cellaring; it should keep for 10–12. Last tasted, 1/97.

1993—A well-made wine for the vintage, La Conseillante's 1993 displays an attrac-
  •   tive dark ruby color, a black raspberry, sweet vanillin, alluring bouquet,
  87   pretty, low-acid, fleshy, round flavors that caress the palate, and a finish
       with plenty of black fruit and glycerin. Already delicious and flattering, this
       moderately weighted wine should drink well for 7–8 years. Last tasted, 1/97.

1992—The 1992 La Conseillante displays light to medium body, an attractive but
  •   diluted raspberry-and-vanillin-scented nose, a supple texture, and a short,
  79   shallow, woody finish. Given the wine's lack of concentration, it should be
       drunk over the next 3–4 years. For one of the most elegant and stylish wines
       of Bordeaux (as well as a personal favorite), this is a disappointment. Last
       tasted, 11/94.

1991—La Conseillante's silky, soft, graceful style can be found in the light-bodied,
  •   delicate 1991. The medium ruby color is followed by a perfumed nose of
  83   toasty, smoky, new oak and raspberry fruit. Although the finish is short, there
       is some lovely fruit in the middle. Drink it over the next 4–5 years. Last
       tasted, 1/94.

1990—The 1990 is exhibiting all of its charms, with its deep ruby color and flam-
  •   boyant display of toasty new oak, black cherries, raspberries, kirsch, licorice,
  97   and Asian spices. Velvety textured, supple, sexy, and easy to drink, the
       low-acid 1990 La Conseillante is about as seductive a wine as readers will
       ever encounter. It admirably demonstrates why Pomerols are often called the
       Burgundies of Bordeaux. As flamboyant as the 1990 is, it remains youthful,
       in spite of its low-acid, precocious showing. While it can be drunk now, it
       will continue to develop for another 12–20 years. Last tasted, 4/98.

1989—This is an upper-90-point La Conseillante that is very much in the style of
  •   the 1990. In comparing the two vintages, the 1989 has slightly more notice-
  97   able tannin and structure, but it is a perfumed, exotic, sweet, expansive,
       yummy wine that is hard to resist. These two wines represent La Conseil-
       lante's quintessential smooth as silk style, which often leads consumers to
       believe the wines will not last. I remember feeling the same way about the
       1982 (which never tasted as stunning as either the 1989 or 1990). That wine

continues to get better and better. One of the unexplainable facts of Bordeaux wine drinking is that even the softer, delicious, up-front wines can age impeccably when well stored. Owners of the 1989 and 1990 La Conseillantes should not hesitate to enjoy them now as well as over the next 20 years. Last tasted, 4/98.

1988—La Conseillante's 1988 suffers in comparison with the 1989 and 1990, but it
•   is a fleshy, soft, charming, velvety-textured, medium-bodied wine for drinking
86   over the next 7–9 years. Anticipated maturity: Now–1999. Last tasted, 1/93.

1987—Better than the 1988, this expansive, Burgundy-style, deliciously fruity, soft,
•   charming wine makes for a seductive, succulent drink. No hard edges are
86   present given the absence of tannin and the low acidity. The ripe Merlot fruit
     is well displayed in a medium-bodied format. Anticipated maturity: Now. Last
     tasted, 4/91.

1986—This wine has matured rapidly. The wine reveals considerable orange and
•   rust at the edge of its medium dark garnet color. The fragrant nose of tobacco,
87   roasted herbs, berry fruit, and vanillin aromas is followed by a medium-
     bodied, silky-textured wine with generous, round, smoky, berry flavors, and
     light tannin in the finish. Anticipated maturity: Now–2005. Last tasted, 5/97.

1985—One of the truly glorious 1985 Pomerols, and a worthy candidate for the "wine
•   of the vintage," La Conseillante's 1985 has been fully mature since the late
94   eighties. The flamboyant aromatics consist of smoke, roasted herbs, and
     jammy black raspberry fruit intermingled with kirsch and *pain grillé*. In the
     mouth, an abundant concoction of berry, chocolate, coffee, and mocha
     emerges. This has always been a seductive, silky-textured, medium-bodied
     wine. Anticipated maturity: Now–2005. Last tasted, 4/98.

1984—A success for the vintage, the 1984 La Conseillante has a fragrant bouquet of
•   jammy raspberry fruit and spicy oak. On the palate, it is smooth, ripe, and
84   medium bodied. Anticipated maturity: Now. Last tasted, 4/91.

1983—This wine possesses a 90-point bouquet and 85-point flavors. It has been
•   fully mature for a number of years and should be drunk up. Considerable
87   amber and rust are creeping in at the edges. The sweet, jammy nose exhibits
     a distinctive floral, truffle, black cherry, earthy, smoky personality that soars
     from the glass. In the mouth, the wine's acidity and tannin are beginning to
     poke their way through the wine's flesh. A streak of herbaceousness has gotten
     stronger as the wine has aged, but it is a round, sexy, fully mature La
     Conseillante that needs to be consumed. Anticipated maturity: Now. Last
     tasted, 11/97.

1982—This wine has never tasted as thrilling from my cellar as it does from other
•   sources. None of my bottles have ever shown any evidence of heat damage
95? (poor fills, stained labels, raised corks), but from my cellar, the wine is (and
     has been) fully mature, with considerable amber to its color. Although it is an
     outstanding effort, other examples have revealed far more richness and inten-
     sity, making me think they were more typical of the heights achieved by La
     Conseillante in 1982. In several blind tastings I have mistaken it for Lafleur,
     which should tell readers just how great this wine can be. While I am not

prepared to say it rivals the heroic duo of 1989 and 1990, La Conseillante's fully mature 1982 boasts an exceptionally sweet nose of fruitcake, jammy cherries, and currants complemented by scents of sweet, toasty oak. Exhibiting this estate's hallmark silkiness and voluptuousness, this lush, rich, concentrated wine is impossible to resist. It has been delicious its entire life yet is capable of lasting another 10–15 years. With wines such as this, I see no reason to defer one's gratification. It is about as seductive, perfumed, and hedonistic as Bordeaux gets. Last tasted, 9/95.

1981—This wine has just begun its slide down the slippery slope. It was an outstand-
•   ing La Conseillante that drank beautifully young. Once the baby fat began to
89   fade in the mid-nineties, the wine was less enticing, although still excellent,
       and perhaps outstanding if drunk from larger-format bottles (such as a mag-
       num). The wine possesses a deep ruby color, with some lightening at the
       edge. The toasty, cherry, and raspberry nose is followed by smoky, roasted
       herb, sweet cherry and raspberry flavors judiciously infused with spicy oak.
       The acidity is adequate, and the tannin and fat have faded away. Anticipated
       maturity: Now. Last tasted, 11/97.

1979—Rather light and insubstantial, the 1979 La Conseillante is ready to drink,
•   has little tannin, not much body, and rather soft, somewhat diluted flavors,
78   but it is attractive and pleasant. Anticipated maturity: Now. Last tasted, 4/83.

1978—The 1978 is not terribly different from the 1979 and suffers from the same
•   ills—lack of depth, grip, and body. Medium ruby, with some amber at the
75   edge, this medium-bodied wine tastes soft, ripe, a trifle diffuse and unstruc-
       tured, and short and bland in the finish. Drink up! Anticipated maturity:
       Now—may be in decline. Last tasted, 6/87.

1976—The 1976 is very brown and on the verge of complete collapse. If one
•   rushes to drink the 1976 La Conseillante, there is still enough over-ripe,
72   jammy, soft fruit and velvety texture to produce enjoyment—but please
       hurry. Anticipated maturity: Now—probably in serious decline. Last tasted,
       6/84.

1975—Drinking extremely well (far better than I ever believed it would), the 1975
•   La Conseillante surprised me with its sweet, jammy, kirsch/black cherry/
89   flowery nose with vague scents of truffles. Medium bodied, sweet, and round,
       with hard tannin in the finish, this wine, which has often tasted disjointed
       and lacking depth, came through strongly in a January 1996 tasting. Fully
       mature, it is capable of lasting another 5–10 years. The color reveals consid-
       erable rust and orange, suggesting more advanced maturity than the aromatics
       and flavors display. Perhaps there is some bottle variation, but this was a
       stronger, more intense example of La Conseillante than I had previously
       tasted. Last tasted, 1/96.

1971—Quite charming, fruity, and seductively easy to drink in 1976, the 1971 La
•   Conseillante has now begun to fade, taking on more and more brown color
80   and losing its fruit. It still offers a supple, round mouthful, but the prime of
       its life is but a fleeting memory. Anticipated maturity: Now—probably in
       serious decline. Last tasted, 6/82.

1970—The 1970 La Conseillante exhibits the sweet, truffle, caramel, mocha, jammy
•   black cherry, and toasty nose of this renowned estate, as well as sweet, round,
93   concentrated flavors and a lush, velvety texture, with a heady, alcoholic, rich
finish. This was my last bottle out of what was a glorious case of wine. While
I may have drunk the other eleven too soon, every bottle was drained quickly
after the cork was pulled. Owners are advised to drink it up. Those who may
be fortunate enough to have larger-format bottles have another 10+ years to
enjoy this stunningly proportioned La Conseillante. Last tasted, 6/96.

1966—Almost Médoc-like with a cedary, tobacco-scented bouquet, the 1966 La
•   Conseillante has reached its apogee. However, it is unlikely to decline for
85   several years because of the firmness and structure. Medium ruby, with some
amber color at the edge, this is a rather restrained La Conseillante, yet it is
complex and interesting. Anticipated maturity: Now. Last tasted, 5/84.

1964—I had an excellent bottle of the 1964 La Conseillante in the late eighties that
•   proved to be better than I indicated in my tasting notes in the first edition of
88   this book. Medium ruby, with some amber at the edge, this wine has a
sensational nose of smoky, almost buttery, nutty, super-ripe, plummy fruit and
herbs. In the mouth, it is round, generous, even opulent, with a great deal of
concentration and a long, alcoholic finish. By the standards of the château,
this is a larger-framed, more muscular wine than usual. Anticipated maturity:
Now. Last tasted, 11/89.

1961—La Conseillante's 1961 appears to be dropping its fruit and drying out—ever
•   so slightly. It is more angular, with more amber/rust/orange in its color. The
87   tannin in the finish is also becoming aggressive, suggesting this wine has
turned the corner and is in decline. Last tasted, 12/95.

ANCIENT VINTAGES

I must confess I never dreamed so many 1959 Pomerols would turn out so
rich and concentrated. La Conseillante's 1959 (95 points; last tasted 10/94)
exhibits a fragrant bouquet of flowers, black raspberries, and smoke, medium
to full body, soft tannin, and wonderful, pure, sweet, expansive fruit. It is a
classic example of La Conseillante's ability to produce authoritatively rich
wines of extraordinary elegance and complexity.

It has been several years since I had the 1949 (97 points; last tasted
5/95), but having gone through a half case I purchased in outstanding condition, I must say that every bottle was exceptional, with a gorgeously ripe,
jammy nose of black fruits, sweet, expansive, medium-bodied flavors, and a
silky texture. It is interesting that La Conseillante, never the most tannic,
muscular, or powerful wine, appears to be drinkable at a remarkably young
age yet can hold its fruit for decades. A friend of the Nicolas family, the
proprietor, told me he consumed several cases of the 1949 in the early fifties
because it was so tasty—further proof that balance, not tannin, is often the
key to a graceful evolution. I have high hopes that the 1989 and 1990 will
prove to be as awesome and ageworthy as the 1949. The 1947 La Conseillante

(rated 92 in December 1995) has been fully mature for some time, but its color reveals only modest rust and orange at the rim. It is a more delicate, elegant style of wine, with medium body, sweet black raspberry fruit intertwined with scents of herbs, smoke, and cedar, and a long, alcoholic, soft finish. Drink it up.

LA CROIX   GOOD

Classification: None
Location of vineyards: Catusseau
Owner: S.C. Joseph Janoueix
Address: 33500 Pomerol
Mailing address: Maison J. Janoueix, 37, rue Pline Parmentier, B.P. 192, 33506 Libourne
Telephone: 33 5 57 51 41 86; telefax: 33 5 57 51 76 83
Visits: By appointment only
Contact: Maison Joseph Janoueix (at above telephone and fax numbers)

VINEYARDS (red)
Surface area: 24.7 acres
Blend: 60% Merlot, 20% Cabernet Franc, 20% Cabernet Sauvignon
Total average annual production: 4,500 cases

GRAND VIN (red)
Brand name: Château La Croix
Appellation: Pomerol
Mean annual production: 4,500 cases

Evaluation of present classification: The quality equivalent of a Médoc Cru Bourgeois
Plateau of maturity: 4–12 years following the vintage

La Croix, located on the outskirts of Libourne just off route D24, has a soil composition of gravel and sand. No wine made in this area ranks in the top dozen or so estates of Pomerol. Nevertheless, La Croix is a reputable property, producing big, dark-colored, tannic, full-bodied wines that can be criticized only for their lack of refinement and finesse. The best examples offer a mouth-filling, plump, rustic, simple pleasure and also repay 6–12 years of cellaring. I have noticed in some vintages that a musty quality does intrude, suggesting that the cellar's sanitary conditions could be improved. Fortunately this happens infrequently. The château never receives a great deal of press, and given the fact that La Croix can turn out wines that are representative of the appellation, it remains a somewhat undervalued estate.

VINTAGES

1993—This medium-bodied, straightforward, one-dimensional Pomerol reveals some
• earthy, herbal-tinged, berry fruit, some spice, and a moderately tannic finish.
78 Drink it during its first decade of life. Last tasted, 11/94.

1990—A rich, unctuous wine, with a rustic personality and thick, fruity flavors, this
• mouth-filling 1990 will make uncomplex but satisfying drinking over the next
87 10 years. Last tasted, 1/93.

1989—The 1989, a rich, unctuous, highly extracted wine, reveals layer upon layer
• of earthy, spicy fruit and a long, alcoholic finish. The wine lacks grip and
85 structure, but there is no doubting the overwhelmingly big, intense flavors. A
full-throttle, rustic style may not appeal to some tasters. Anticipated maturity:
Now–2005. Last tasted, 1/93.

1988—The 1988 La Croix has a soft, fruity, agreeable character and a round, user-
• friendly texture. Drink it over the next 2–4 years. Last tasted, 1/93.
82

1986—With an earthy bouquet filled with weedy scents of tobacco and cassis, the
• 1986 La Croix is quite attractive and already developed. In the mouth, the
84 wine is alcoholic, ripe, and somewhat fat, but with a tough, hard finish.
Anticipated maturity: Now–2000. Last tasted, 3/90.

1985—The 1985 is an exuberantly plump, fruit-filled wine with full body and a
• sweet, round, generous texture that offers a mouthful of clean, opulent, berry
84 fruit. Anticipated maturity: Now. Last tasted, 3/90.

1983—La Croix produced a very powerful wine in 1983, with nearly 14.8% alcohol.
• Deep ruby/garnet, with a dense, plummy, viscous, powerful presence on the
86 palate, this full-bodied wine is chewy and thick. What it lacks in finesse and
elegance, it compensates for with power. Anticipated maturity: Now. Last
tasted, 3/89.

1982—Another very successful wine, the 1982 La Croix is slightly less alcoholic
• than the big, massive 1983, but dark ruby, with layers of ripe, rich fruit, soft
86 tannins, and an impressively long, spicy finish. Anticipated maturity: Now–
2000. Last tasted, 1/91.

1981—The 1981 La Croix has been an inconsistent performer. Some bottles have
• shown a deficiency in color, whereas others have a rich, ripe cherry flavor,
84 with full body and hefty weight. The score reflects the better bottlings. Anticipated maturity: Now. Last tasted, 11/84.

LA CROIX DU CASSE   EXCELLENT

Classification: None
Location of vineyards: Pomerol
Owner: Arcaute-Audy families
Address: 33500 Pomerol
Mailing address: c/o Château Jonqueyres, 33750 Sant-Germain du Puch
Telephone: 33 5 56 68 55 88; telefax: 33 5 56 30 11 45
Visits: By appointment only

VINEYARDS (red)
Surface area: 22.2 acres
Average age of vines: 33 years
Blend: 80% Merlot, 20% Cabernet Franc
Density of plantation: 6,600 vines per hectare
Average yields (over the last 5 years): 48 hectoliters per hectare
Total average annual production: 4,600 cases

GRAND VIN (red)
Brand name: Château La Croix du Casse
Appellation: Pomerol
Mean annual production: 4,000 cases
Upbringing: Fermentations and macerations may last up to 45 days in
small stainless-steel vats equipped with an internal electronic
temperature-control system. Wines are transferred to oak barrels
(normally for malolactics), 60% of which are new, for 24 months aging.
Assemblage is done progressively when wines are racked every 3 months.
They remain unfined and unfiltered.

SECOND WINE
Brand name: Domaine du Casse
Production: 600 cases

Evaluation of present classification: Since 1986 the quality equivalent of
a Médoc fifth-growth
Plateau of maturity: 4–10 years following the vintage

Jean-Michel Arcaute, the manager who has taken Château Clinet from mediocrity to superstardom, administers this property and is also responsible for
resurrecting the quality. Located south of the village of Catusseau, on a
terrace of sand-and-gravel-based soils, this tiny Pomerol estate is not as
renowned or as well placed as that of Clinet. However, it would appear that
in the 1988, 1989, 1994, and 1995 vintages Arcaute has extracted as much
quality and character as is possible from the vineyard.

VINTAGES

1997—Another wine from the brilliant Jean-Michel Arcaute that is looked after by
•   the equally talented Michel Rolland, La Croix du Casse's 1997 is one of the
86–   more backward, tighter, and closed Pomerols. It possesses a saturated purple
88   color, an unyielding set of aromatics, and promising yet tight flavors consisting
of cassis, cherries, and *pain grillé*. Offering good depth and promise, there is
considerable room for optimism with this effort, but it is one of the few

Pomerols that will require 2–3 years of cellaring. Anticipated maturity: 2002–2012. Last tasted, 3/98.

1996— Inky/purple–colored with plenty of lead pencil, licorice, mineral, and black
•   currant fruit in its flamboyant nose, this dense, rich, medium-bodied wine
88–   possesses moderately high tannin, but enough flesh and sweet fruit to cover
89+   its structure. It is an impressive, backward and unevolved style of Pomerol
      that should be at its best between 2004 and 2012. Last tasted, 3/98.

1995— An outstanding wine, this dense ruby/purple–colored 1995 offers up a knock-
•   out nose of blackberries, cassis, minerals, and spicy new oak. Medium to full
90   bodied, with plenty of *pain grillé*-like flavors and abundantly sweet fruit
      imbued with glycerin and tannin, this wine possesses a long mid-palate, as
      well as a finish that builds in the mouth. It is an impressively built, pure,
      rich Pomerol that merits considerable attention. Anticipated maturity: 2000–
      2015. Last tasted, 11/97.

1994— Performing better after bottling than before (no fining or filtration is practiced
•   at La Croix du Casse), the dark plum–colored 1994 displays an exotic, coffee,
89   tobacco, sweet, jammy, black currant, and cherry nose, ripe, highly extracted
      flavors with surprising opulence (especially for a 1994), fine purity, low acid-
      ity, and moderate tannin. This medium-bodied, exciting 1994 can be drunk
      now as well as over the next 10–12 years. Last tasted, 1/97.

1993— An attractive dark ruby color is complemented by smoky, toasty oak, and
•   loads of sweet black curranty/cherry fruit. Lush and round, with low acidity,
86   this wine possesses good fat and ripeness as well as an up-front appeal. Drink
      it over the next 6–7 years. Last tasted, 1/97.

1992— La Croix du Casse has produced exceptionally well-made wines over recent
•   years. The ruby/purple–colored 1992 reveals a moderately intense bouquet
86   of sweet black cherries and toasty new oak, fine extraction of flavor, medium
      body, low acidity, and moderate tannin in the finish. Drink it over the next 5–
      8 years. Last tasted, 11/94.

1990— The 1990 is this estate's finest effort to date. It offers deep ruby/black
•   color, an expansive, sweet, cassis-scented nose, soft, luscious, opulent, su-
89   perbly endowed flavors, super length, low acidity, and a lush as well as
      long finish. It should be drunk within its first 7–9 years of life. Last tasted,
      1/93.

1989— The 1989 has a black/ruby/purple color, with a big, rich, expansive bouquet
•   filled with aromas of ripe plums, chocolate, cedar, and toasty new oak. It
87   offers splendid concentration, medium-bodied flavors, plenty of alcohol, and
      soft tannins in the finish and should provide delicious drinking over its first
      decade of life. Anticipated maturity: Now. Last tasted, 1/93.

1988— The 1988 La Croix du Casse exhibits deep, well-endowed, full-bodied, admi-
•   rably extracted flavors with good tannins, crisp acidity, and a satisfying,
86   moderately long finish. Anticipated maturity: Now–2000. Last tasted, 1/93.

1984— Not bad, this wine is spicy, has adequate fruit, and some intrusive alcohol.
•   Anticipated maturity: Now. Last tasted, 3/88.
77

LA CROIX DE GAY   VERY GOOD

Classification: None
Location of vineyards: Ten parcels throughout Pomerol
Owner: G. E. A. La Croix de Gay (Dr. Alain Raynaud)
Address: 33500 Pomerol
Mailing address: Same as above
Telephone: 33 5 57 51 19 05; telefax: 33 5 57 72 15 62
Visits: Every day, between 8 A.M. and noon, and 2 P.M. and 6 P.M.
Contact: Marie France Cubiller

VINEYARDS (red)
Surface area: 24.7 acres
Average age of vines: 40 years
Blend: 80% Merlot, 10% Cabernet Franc, 10% Cabernet Sauvignon
Density of plantation: 5,800 vines per hectare
Average yields (over the last 5 years): 50 hectoliters per hectare
Total average annual production: 60,000 bottles

GRAND VIN (red)
Brand name: Château La Croix de Gay
Appellation: Pomerol
Mean annual production: 40,000 bottles
Upbringing: Fermentations take place in temperature-controlled concrete
vats. Both alcoholic and malolactic fermentations take place in vats;
macerations last approximately 15 days. Wines are then aged 14 months
in oak barrels that are renewed by a third at each vintage. They are fined
with egg whites and lightly filtered.

SECOND WINE
Brand name: La Commanderie
Production: 20,000 bottles

Evaluation of present classification: The quality equivalent of a Médoc
fifth-growth
Plateau of Maturity: 3–17 years

La Croix de Gay, one of the greatest discoveries of Englishman Harry Waugh
in the late forties, proved to be an inconsistent, even inadequate, performer
in the seventies and early eighties. However, the proprietor, the handsome
Dr. Raynaud, has increasingly upgraded the quality and now produces one of
the most attractive and easy to drink Pomerols. In 1982 Dr. Raynaud
launched his luxury cuvée of La Croix de Gay—called La Fleur de Gay—
from a parcel of very old vines of Merlot planted between Pétrus and Lafleur.
This luxury cuvée of old vines (profiled separately, see page 847) is very rare

in Bordeaux, but it is one of the most magnificent wines of the appellation, rivaling the finest Pomerols in complexity and intensity. Some skeptics have argued that Dr. Raynaud's decision to make a special cuvée robs the primary wine, La Croix de Gay, of its best source of richness and backbone. Despite the addition of a luxury cuvée, one cannot ignore the fact that La Croix de Gay has improved immensely.

The vineyards of La Croix de Gay sit at the very northern section of Pomerol's plateau, immediately behind a cemetery and the tiny road called D245 that traverses the appellation. The soil in this area is gravel intermixed with sand.

VINTAGES

1997—
•
87–
88
This wine is almost Burgundian with its vivid display of sweet, pure black cherry fruit and spice. Far more concentrated and layered than the 1996, La Croix de Gay's 1997 exhibits a dark ruby color, and a lovely evolved nose of black fruits, vanillin, and spice. Open knit, round, and medium bodied, with no hard edges, and some defining tannin, this stylish, impeccably well made wine, while not a blockbuster, is satisfying. Anticipated maturity: 2000–2009. Last tasted, 3/98.

1996—
•
80–
82
Spicy oak intertwined with light intensity aromas of plums and cherries can be found in this compressed yet elegant, medium-bodied wine with tart acidity, and a pinched personality. It is crisp, fresh, and made in a lighter style than other recent vintages. Anticipated maturity: 1999–2007. Last tasted, 3/98.

1995—
•
87
This is a seductive, elegant, attractive Pomerol with a deep ruby color, plenty of sweet plum, cherry, and berry fruit intermixed with subtle toasty new oak. The wine is round and lush, with copious fruit and enough glycerin to provide a nicely layered texture in a stylish format. Anticipated maturity: 2002–2015. Last tasted, 11/97.

1994—
•
87+
A dense, saturated dark ruby/purple color suggests fine intensity and ripeness. Sweet berry fruit intermixed with vanillin, herbs, and spices emerges from the wine's aromatics. Medium bodied, with good richness and purity and a soft, fleshy attack, this stylish, concentrated wine should prove to be excellent. Anticipated maturity: 2000–2012. Last tasted, 1/97.

1993—
•
86
An attractive wine for the vintage, this dark ruby–colored 1993 reveals a sweet black cherry nose with attractive scents of new oak. Elegant, round, soft, and opulent, this delicious, low-acid Pomerol should be drunk over the next 6–8 years. Last tasted, 1/97.

1992—
•
86
The round, charming, seductive 1992 possesses sweet black currant fruit married intelligently with toasty oak. An elegant wine with fine depth, low acidity, and light tannin in the finish, this light- to medium-bodied wine is ideal for drinking over the next 5–6 years. Last tasted, 11/94.

1991—
•
82
The light 1991 reveals sweet fruit in the nose, toasty new oak, and a light-bodied, easygoing finish. Drink it over the next 4–5 years. Last tasted, 1/94.

1990—Nearly lavish aromas of sweet, toasty, vanillin oak, and ripe berry fruit soar
•   from the glass of the seductive 1990. In the mouth, one could wish for more
86   depth, but overall this is a richly fruity, soft, elegant, yet still interesting
      Pomerol that should drink beautifully for another 7–8 years. Last tasted,
      1/93.

1989—The 1989 La Croix de Gay is unusually deep, concentrated, and full bodied,
•   with excellent tannin and extract levels. The acidity is low, but the high
87   tannins and the elevated alcohol level should allow this wine to age well for
      6–15 years. It is the most impressive young La Croix de Gay I have tasted,
      reflecting this estate's increasing attention to detail and commitment to excel-
      lence. Anticipated maturity: Now–2005. Last tasted, 1/93.

1988—The 1988 displays a great deal of new oak, has good concentration, a smooth,
•   velvety, nearly opulent texture, and a sweet, smooth as silk finish. Anticipated
86   maturity: Now. Last tasted, 1/93.

1986—The 1986 displays a healthy use of new oak, a deep ruby color, medium body,
•   an attractive sweet, pure, plummy fruitiness, good length, and moderate tan-
85   nin in the finish. It will be ready to drink within several years. Anticipated
      maturity: Now–2000. Last tasted, 3/90.

1985—The 1985 is a success for La Croix de Gay, with a moderately intense, elegant,
•   ripe, spicy bouquet, attractive flavors wrapped gently in new oak, medium
85   body, and a velvety finish. Anticipated maturity: Now. Last tasted, 3/89.

1984—The 1984 is light but fruity, soft, round, and a delight to drink over the next
•   2–3 years. Anticipated maturity: Now. Last tasted, 3/89.
80

1983—Medium ruby, with some garnet at the edge, the 1983 La Croix de Gay has a
•   weedy, herbaceous, plum-scented bouquet, round, somewhat disjointed,
80   flabby, alcoholic flavors, and a hot, soft, unstructured finish. Fully mature, it
      should be drunk up. Anticipated maturity: Now. Last tasted, 11/90.

1982—Medium ruby, with some brown at the edge, the 1982 La Croix de Gay has a
•   monolithic, ripe bouquet of no great distinction, medium-bodied, slightly
77   watery, low-acid flavors, and a flabby, fully mature finish. Anticipated matu-
      rity: Now. Last tasted, 3/89.

1961—Although the 1961 La Croix de Gay (from a magnum) was elegant, round,
•   fruity, easygoing, and delicious, it was not comparable (qualitatively) with
85   other 1961s. Last tasted, 12/95.

ANCIENT VINTAGES

In 1995 I finally had the privilege of tasting the 1947 La Croix de Gay, the
wine Harry Waugh made legendary with his glowing accolades. It was superb,
with port-like intensity and a viscous, rich, roasted character. I rated it 92
points! The second-best ancient vintage I have tasted is the 1964 (rated 90
in 1990). Like so many Pomerols in what is clearly a great vintage for the
appellation, this full-bodied, rich, alcoholic wine is loaded with fruit and has
a sumptuous, opulent texture.

DOMAINE DE L'EGLISE   VERY GOOD

Classification: None
Location of vineyards: Pomerol
Owner: Castéja and Preben-Hansen families
Address: 33500 Pomerol
Mailing address: c/o Borie-Manoux, 86, cours Balguerie Stuttenberg,
33082 Bordeaux
Telephone: 33 5 56 00 00 70; telefax: 33 5 57 87 60 30
Visits: By appointment only
Contact: Maison Borie-Manoux, at above telephone and fax numbers

VINEYARDS (red)
Surface area: 17.3 acres
Average age of vines: 30 years
Blend: 80% Merlot, 20% Cabernet Franc
Density of plantation: 7,500 vines per hectare
Average yields (over the last 5 years): 47 hectoliters per hectare

GRAND VIN (red)
Brand name: Château du Domaine de l'Eglise
Appellation: Pomerol
Upbringing: Fermentations last approximately 3 weeks in
temperature-controlled tanks. After malolactics, wines are transferred to
oak barrels, 65% of which are new, for 16–18 months aging. They are
fined but not filtered.

SECOND WINE
None produced.

Evaluation of present classification: Since 1986 the quality equivalent of
a Médoc fifth-growth
Plateau of maturity: 5–15 years following the vintage

This beautifully situated vineyard is adjacent to the cemetery of Pomerol on
the high plateau and has a gravelly soil intermixed with some sand. The
château and vineyard are believed to be the oldest of Pomerol. The property
was run as a winemaking estate by the Hospitaliers de Saint-Jean de Jerusa-
lem, who managed a hospital in Pomerol for lepers long before the French
Revolution and was known as Domaine Porte Rouge. As with many church-
run properties, the revolution resulted in divestiture and placement in private
hands, where it has remained. It was acquired by the *négociant* firm of
Borie-Manoux in 1973.

Solid and reliable wines were made in the seventies and early eighties, but since the late eighties the quality has increased. Domaine de l'Eglise was particularly damaged during the 1956 freeze, and the vineyard was totally replanted. The lighter, more commercial style of wines produced in the seventies and eighties as well as nineties gave way in the late eighties to a richer, more profound and compelling product.

VINTAGES

1997—Intriguing roasted coffee, berry, chocolate, and toast aromas emerge from
• this medium dark ruby–colored wine. Round, plump, and succulent, with
85– moderately good concentration, and a short finish, this is a cleanly made,
86 competent Pomerol to drink over its first 4–7 years of life. Last tasted, 3/98.

1995—An impressive saturated black/purple color is followed by a wine with excel-
• lent black cherry and cassis fruit, medium body, fine purity, and surprising
87 opulence and unctuosness. If this wine is not excessively fined and filtered at
bottling, it should turn out to be an upper-80-point effort. Anticipated maturity: 2001–2016. Last tasted, 11/97.

1994—Dark ruby colored, with attractive, jammy, cherry, earth, and spicy scents,
• this midweight, pleasant, ripe 1994 displays no hard edges or vegetal notes.
86 It should drink well for 7–8 years. Last tasted, 1/97.

1993—This soft, diluted wine reveals a feeble, medium ruby color and easygoing,
• flat flavors that lack concentration and precision. Drink it over the next 4–5
78 years. Last tasted, 1/97.

1990—Sadly, overproduction and superripe fruit resulted in a soft, low-acid,
• medium-weight 1990. While round and tasty, it is essentially one-dimensional
82 and lacking grip and depth. Anticipated maturity: Now–2000. Last tasted,
1/93.

1989—The firm of Borie-Manoux has become deadly serious about the quality of its
• top wines. There is no better evidence of this than in the splendidly rich,
90 highly extracted, immensely impressive 1989 Domaine de l'Eglise. Black/
ruby in color, with fabulous, highly extracted flavors suggestive of prunes and
black plums, gobs of soft tannin as well as alcohol, yet decent acidity for the
vintage, this rich, broad-shouldered Pomerol is the most massive wine I have
yet tasted from the Domaine de l'Eglise. It is very soft and therefore should
be appealing young. Anticipated maturity: Now–2015. Last tasted, 1/93.

EGLISE-CLINET   OUTSTANDING

Classification: None
Location of vineyards: Pomerol
Owner: G.F.A. Château l'Eglise Clinet (Durantou family)
Address: 33500 Pomerol
Mailing address: Same as above
Telephone: 33 5 57 25 99 00; telefax: 33 5 57 25 21 96

Visits: By appointment only
Contact: Denis Durantou

VINEYARDS (red)
Surface area: 14.8 acres
Average age of vines: 40–45 years
Blend: 70%–80% Merlot, 20%–30% Cabernet Franc
Density of plantation: 6,500 vines per hectare
Average yields (over the last 5 years): 45 hectoliters per hectare

GRAND VIN (red)
Brand name: Château l'Eglise-Clinet
Appellation: Pomerol
Mean annual production: 1,800 cases
Upbringing: Fermentations last 15–21 days in concrete vats
(temperatures are not allowed to rise too much). Malolactics occur in
stainless-steel tanks, and wines are then transferred to oak casks, 40%–
70% of which are new, as soon as possible. They spend 15–18 months in
oak (2 winters, but bottling is always done before the second summer
begins). They are fined with egg whites and are not filtered.

SECOND WINE
Brand name: La Petite l'Eglise
Average annual production: 12,000 bottles

Evaluation of present classification: Since 1985 the quality equivalent of
a Médoc second-growth
Plateau of maturity: 5–15 years following the vintage

One of the least-known Pomerol estates, l'Eglise-Clinet often produces a
typically fat, succulent, juicy, richly fruity style of Pomerol. The wine is
admirably and traditionally made, but because of the tiny production, it is
not well known. The vineyard is well situated on the plateau of Pomerol
behind the church, where the soils are deep gravel beds intermingled with
sand, clay, and iron.

Eglise-Clinet is one of the few Pomerol vineyards that was not replanted
after the 1956 killing freeze, and consequently it has very old vines, a few of
which exceed 100 years in age.

Until 1983 Pierre Lasserre, the owner of the bigger and better-known
Pomerol property of Clos René, farmed this vineyard under the *métayage*
system (a type of vineyard rental agreement) and turned out a wine that was
rich, well balanced, supple, firm, and always well vinified. Since then the
winery has been run by the young, extremely dedicated Denis Durantou, who

is trying to take this tiny vineyard to the very top of the unofficial Pomerol hierarchy. The secret here is not only Durantou's remarkable commitment to quality, but vines that average 40–45 years in age, plus the fact that in abundant and/or difficult vintages one-fourth of the crop is relegated to the second wine called La Petite l'Eglise. One cannot applaud the efforts of Denis Durantou enough.

The price for a bottle of l'Eglise-Clinet is high, as connoisseurs recognize that this is one of the top dozen wines of the appellation.

VINTAGES

1997—Along with Pétrus, Lafleur, Trotanoy, Clinet, l'Evangile, Le Pin, Bon Pasteur,
•   and possibly Clos l'Eglise, the 1997 l'Eglise-Clinet is one of the most com-
91–   plete Pomerols of the vintage. This low acid, amazingly rich, black/purple–
95   colored wine offers intense aromas of black raspberries, cassis, kirsch liqueur, as well as subtle scents of underbrush, truffles, and toasty oak. Medium to full bodied and rich, with an unctuous texture, this is one of the vintage's few superstars. Anticipated maturity: 2001–2020. A remarkable wine for the vintage! Last tasted, 3/98.

1996—This wine has fleshed out considerably. While it was tasting exceptionally
•   fine in March 1997, it now appears to be one of the superstars of the right
93–   bank. Readers can thank proprietor Denis Durantou for the extraordinarily
95   strict selection that produced such an intense Pomerol. The opaque black/ purple color is followed by a wine with copious quantites of sweet blackberry and raspberry liqueurlike fruit that soars from the glass. Full bodied, with extraordinary fruit extraction, this is a large-scaled, broad-shouldered Pomerol with enough tannin to ensure 25–30 years of longevity. At present, the fruit dominates the wine, but there is considerable intensity to this 1996, which reveals layers of black fruits, in addition to a subtle dosage of smoky oak and black truffles. This large-scaled, massive l'Eglise-Clinet should be at its best between 2005 and 2025. Last tasted, 3/98.

1995—One of the vintage's most awesome wines, l'Eglise-Clinet's 1995 has been
•   fabulous from both cask and bottle. The color is opaque purple. The wine is
96   closed aromatically, but it does offer a concoction of black raspberries, kirsch, smoke, cherries, and truffles. Full bodied and rich, with high tannin but profound levels of fruit and richness, this dense, exceptionally well delineated, layered, multidimensional l'Eglise-Clinet only hints at its ultimate potential. This looks to be a legend in the making. I could not get over the extraordinary texture of this wine in the mouth. Intensity and richness without heaviness—a tour de force in winemaking! Anticipated maturity: 2008–2030. Last tasted, 11/97.

1994—The 1994 exhibits a saturated dark ruby/purple color as well as a tight but
•   promising nose of ripe cherries, mulberries, and currants, along with a vague
90   notion of black truffles. Medium to full bodied, with pure fruit, a layered impression, and stubborn tannin in the muscular finish, this wine is not as

charming as the more forward 1993. A larger-scaled, richer wine, the 1994 requires 5–6 years of cellaring. An impressive 1994. Anticipated maturity: 2002–2022. Last tasted, 1/97.

1993— This wine may merit a higher rating. I am not a fan of red wines with green
•   overtones, so perhaps the spicy, green peppery bouquet held my score down.
87   Nevertheless, this deep ruby/purple–colored wine possesses an undeniably
        grilled meat, smoky, peppery, sweet, fruity nose that is evolved and intense.
        The wine hits the palate with a nice display of sweet, ripe, soft fruit and low
        acidity. It is medium bodied, with the kirsch liqueur, black raspberry fruiti-
        ness that is a hallmark of this estate. The 1993 should be at its peak after 2–
        3 years of cellaring; it will last for 12–14 years. I would opt for drinking it on
        the young side, as the fruit may fade before the tannin. Last tasted, 1/97.

1992— Deep ruby colored, with a spicy, ripe, black cherry and smoky oak–scented
•   nose, concentrated, and ripe, medium-bodied flavors, l'Eglise-Clinet's 1992
85   reveals admirable intensity and a spicy, rich, fleshy finish. It should provide
        uncomplicated, delicious drinking for 5–7 years. Last tasted, 11/94.

1991— This 1991 is among only a handful of Pomerols that are supple, ripe, and drink-
•   able. It offers an enticing bouquet of red and black fruits, tobacco, tea, and
84   chocolate. Spicy, soft, and round, this medium-bodied wine is well endowed for
        a 1991 Pomerol. Drink it over the next 4–5 years. Last tasted, 1/94.

1990— The 1990, which continues to put on weight, is a rich, complete wine with an
•   opaque ruby/purple color. The wine offers up less evolved, sweet, jammy,
92   black cherry, smoky, chocolate aromas, followed by a full-bodied, layered,
        expansively flavored wine with low acidity, plenty of sweet fruit, and more
        depth and length than the 1989. It is also more backward. Give it another 2–
        3 years of cellaring, and drink it over the next 2 decades. Last tasted, 11/96.

1989— The 1989 has been variable in recent tastings. The most recent reveals a
•   deep garnet color with an amber edge. The wine exhibited sweet chocolate,
90?   jammy black cherry fruit, and lush, precocious, low-acid, heady flavors with
        excellent to outstanding concentration. Some spice and cedar notes emerged
        with breathing. This fleshy wine appears to be maturing at an accelerated
        pace. I would opt for drinking it now and over the next 15 years. This
        particular bottle was more advanced than several other bottles I had in 1996.
        Last tasted, 11/96.

1988— The 1988 is medium bodied and admirably concentrated, with a nose of
•   smoky oak and plums. It should be at its best between now and 2002. Last
88   tasted, 1/93.

1986— The 1986 l'Eglise-Clinet remains a young, densely colored wine with gobs of
•   fruit and intensity. I have always preferred it to such other vintages as the
92   1982, 1983, and 1989. The full-bodied 1986 exhibits excellent concentration
        and an over-ripe component. It can be drunk now or cellared for another 20–
        30 years. Last tasted, 12/95.

1985— In a vintage that has yielded fewer superb wines than originally predicted,
•   l'Eglise-Clinet may turn out to be one of the two longest-lived wines of
95   Pomerol (the other being l'Evangile). This wine is far more concentrated than

some of the appellation's superstars (Trotanoy and Pétrus, for example) and has retained a dense, opaque ruby/purple color as well as an unevolved but promising nose of kirsch, black raspberries, minerals, and truffles. Rich and medium to full bodied, with magnificent purity and a nicely layered feel on the palate, this youthful, intensely rich l'Eglise-Clinet is evolving at a glacial pace. Anticipated maturity: 2001–2020. Last tasted, 9/97.

1984 — Except for the hardness at the finish, this well-colored, decently made wine
•   has good fruit and displays impeccable winemaking. Give it 2–3 years of
81   cellaring. Anticipated maturity: Now. Last tasted, 3/89.

1983 — A success in 1983, l'Eglise-Clinet is dark ruby, with some amber at the edge.
•   It exhibits a dense, ripe, fat, black cherry bouquet, chewy, dense, ripe flavors,
86   full body, low acidity, and soft tannins. This big wine has matured quickly.
        Anticipated maturity: Now. Last tasted, 3/89.

1982 — Although the 1982 l'Eglise-Clinet exhibited plenty of plump, ripe fruit, it was
•   never one of the most compelling 1982s. The wine revealed more depth when
89   tasted in December 1995 than it did when I first tasted it from cask and follow-
        ing bottling. Rich, full bodied, chunky, and monolithic, it provides a mouthful
        of juicy claret, but it tastes uncomplicated and simple. Last tasted, 12/95.

1981 — Less powerful and rich than the 1982 and 1983, the 1981 l'Eglise-Clinet is a
•   light yet still very fruity, supple, spicy wine, with medium to full body,
84   moderate tannin, and a good finish. Anticipated maturity: Now. Last tasted,
        6/84.

1978 — The 1978 is fully mature, with a chocolatey, somewhat smoky, fruity bouquet.
•   It is a soft, round, moderately concentrated wine that is pleasant but lacks a
82   little weight and richness. Anticipated maturity: Now. Last tasted, 1/85.

1975 — The 1975 l'Eglise-Clinet is nearly as concentrated as l'Evangile and La
•   Mission-Haut-Brion, as well as extremely youthful, with a thick, dark ruby/
92   purple color revealing no signs of age. Sweet and expansive, with jammy fruit,
        huge body, and considerable tannin, this approachable but youthful wine
        should evolve effortlessly for another 25–30+ years. Last tasted, 11/96.

1971 — The 1971 l'Eglise-Clinet must certainly be one of the wines of the vintage. I
•   remember tasting it early in its life, but I never recognized its quality would
92   be this impressive. Rich and opulent, with extraordinary intensity and that
        viscous, thick, succulent Pomerol personality, this wine could easily rival the
        two greatest Pomerols of 1971—Trotanoy and Pétrus. Fully mature, it should
        keep for another decade. Last tasted, 12/95.

1964 — Sweet and delicious, with a deep ruby/garnet color revealing considerable
•   amber at the edge, the 1964 l'Eglise-Clinet possesses high alcohol and plenty
89   of ripe fruit, but not quite the intensity, richness, or complexity of the 1971.
        It should be drunk up. Last tasted, 9/95.

1961 — The 1961 l'Eglise-Clinet displayed a saturated, opaque garnet color, with
•   some amber/rust at the edge. A huge nose of soy sauce, grilled meats, mocha,
92   chocolate, and jammy cherry fruit is followed by a full-bodied wine with
        excellent richness, length, and balance. Drink this fully mature, velvety-
        textured wine over the next decade. Last tasted, 9/95.

ANCIENT VINTAGES

The 1959 l'Eglise-Clinet (96 points; last tasted 10/95) possessed immense body as well as a huge, knockout nose of over-ripe cherries, kirsch, Asian spices, fruitcake, and Häagen-Dazs Jamocha Chocolate Chip ice cream. Thick, sweet, and unctuously textured, this extremely viscous, youthful wine must be tasted to be believed. I would love to find some of this on the auction block! It should outlive the 1961 and continue to drink well for another 20–25 years.

Eglise-Clinet's 1950 (95 points; last tasted 9/95) is another masterpiece from an appellation and vintage that have been completely ignored. A superb vintage for Pomerol, this soft, velvety-textured, enormously concentrated, overripe wine is oozing with black cherry and cassis aromas intertwined with smoke, cedar, minerals, and vanilla. This thick, remarkably youthful 1950 l'Eglise-Clinet will offer a hefty, corpulent mouthful of chewy wine for another 10–20 years.

Virtually perfect, the 1949 l'Eglise-Clinet (99 points; last tasted 9/95) was one of a series of older vintages from this estate that possessed mind-boggling richness, extraordinary intensity, unctuosness, and that quintessential kirsch/ black cherry essence exhibited by its nearby neighbor Château Lafleur. The 1949 l'Eglise-Clinet revealed an opaque purple color, with no signs of lightening at the edge. In the glass, it looked more like port than a dry red table wine. There is extraordinary viscosity, thickness, and extract to this full-bodied, colossal l'Eglise-Clinet. Still young, it has no hard edges whatsoever because of its low acidity and ripe tannin. This must be one of the century's most underrated great wines. It should continue to drink well for another 25 years.

The 1947 l'Eglise-Clinet (100 points; last tasted 9/95) is a *tour de force* in winemaking. It is one of the greatest wines I have ever tasted. If only more than 100 points could be bestowed! Opaque purple colored, with a huge, knockout nose of black cherries, cassis, mocha, coffee, tobacco, and Asian spices, it is extremely full bodied, with layers of glycerin, extract, ripe fruit, and seriously high alcohol. This huge, massive wine is exceptionally well balanced.

The remarkable 1945 l'Eglise-Clinet (98 points; last tasted 9/95) revealed none of the harshness or astringency of many wines from this long-lived vintage. It exhibited a knockout nose of truffles, vanilla, chocolate, and gobs of black and red fruits, a viscous texture, awesome flavor extraction, massive body, and a finish composed of layers of fruit, glycerin, and alcohol. This is a remarkable wine with a blockbuster finish! Wow!

The 1921 (100 points; last tasted 9/95) displayed an opaque, dark ruby/ garnet color, gobs of sweet, jammy, opulent fruit, awesome concentration, high alcohol, and a vintage port-like character. Exhibiting few signs of age, it is a massive example of what Pomerol has done so exceptionally well for so long —make more hedonistic and decadent wines from Merlot and Cabernet Franc that taste better and hold their fruit longer than most Médocs! The 1921 l'Eglise-Clinet and 1921 Pétrus were two of the most profoundly great wines I have ever consumed.

ENCLOS
VERY GOOD

Classification: None
Location of vineyards: Some of the vineyards are situated near Libourne
Owner: G.F.A. du Château l'Enclos
Address: 1, L'Enclos, 33500 Pomerol
Mailing address: Same as above
Telephone: 33 5 57 51 04 62; telefax: 33 5 57 51 43 15
Visits: Preferably by appointment
Contact: Hugues Weydert

VINEYARDS (red)
Surface area: 23.5 acres
Average age of vines: 33 years
Blend: 82% Merlot, 17% Cabernet Franc, 1% Pressac
Density of plantation: 6,000 vines per hectare
Average yields (over the last 5 years): 46.97 hectoliters per hectare
Total average annual production: 4,400 cases

GRAND VIN (red)
Brand name: Château l'Enclos
Appellation: Pomerol
Mean annual production: 4,400 cases
Upbringing: Alcoholic fermentations occur in temperature-controlled tanks at a maximum of 32 degrees centigrade; malolactics occur in tanks at 24 degrees centigrade. Total equals 3–4 weeks. Wines are transferred at the end of the month of November to oak barrels, renewed by a third at each vintage, for 17 months aging. They are fined with egg whites and lightly filtered.

SECOND WINE
None produced.

Evaluation of present classification: The quality equivalent of a Médoc fifth-growth
Plateau of maturity: 3–15 years following the vintage

Located on sandy, gravelly, and flinty soil in the most western portion of the Pomerol appellation, l'Enclos is an unheralded property that produces very fine wine. Perhaps I have been lucky and seen only the best vintages of l'Enclos, but I have been impressed with this wine for the consistently smooth, velvety, rich, supple, nicely concentrated, pure blackberry fruitiness and for an overall harmony. In most vintages l'Enclos needs only 3–4 years of bottle age to reveal the opulent, rich, silky fruitiness, yet the wines hold up well in the bottle.

Most consumers think of Pomerols as expensive, which they are, because of the tiny vineyards and worldwide demand for these Merlot-based wines. However, l'Enclos represents one of the best quality/price rapport wines of any estate in the appellation.

VINTAGES

1997—An easy-going, low-acid, plump claret, l'Enclos' 1997 displays moderately
•   rich, chocolate, and mocha-tinged black cherry fruit, medium body, a supple
85–   texture, and a short finish. It is ideal for drinking over the next 5–6 years.
86   Last tasted, 3/98.

1995—The 1995's dark ruby/purple color is followed by a satiny-textured, mocha-,
•   coffee-, and cherry-scented and -flavored wine. Low acidity gives this wine a
86   forward, plump personality. Drink it over the next 7–8 years. Last tasted, 11/
       97.

1994—The 1994 l'Enclos is surprisingly light bodied, diluted, and vegetal, with no
•   real depth or ripeness. This can be an excellent estate, so I find this disap-
72   pointing performance puzzling. Last tasted, 3/96.

1992—Dilution and possibly a less than strict selection have resulted in an unchar-
•   acteristically poor performance. The 1992 l'Enclos is light, thin, and compact.
74   Drink it up. Last tasted, 11/94.

1991—One of my favorite Pomerol estates has turned in a disappointing effort. The
•   simple, diluted 1991 is lacking in fruit and personality. Last tasted,
72   1/94.

1990—The 1990 is even more structured and richer than the 1989. Very dark in
•   color, with enticing tobacco, plum, and coffee aromas and flavors presented
89   in a super-ripe, full-bodied format, this is the finest l'Enclos since the 1982.
       Drink it over the next 5–15 years. Last tasted, 1/93.

1989—The 1989 offers a hedonistic mouthful of plush, concentrated blackberry-
•   and-violet-scented fruit. Full bodied and silky smooth, the masses of rich
87   fruit nearly obscure some sizable tannins in the finish. This beautifully made,
       intensely perfumed wine should provide delicious drinking for the next 10–
       12 years. Last tasted, 1/93.

1988—The 1988 l'Enclos is a straightforward, fruity, soft-textured wine with ade-
•   quate concentration, an attractive, spicy, plummy, mocha-scented bouquet,
83   decent concentration, and a moderately long finish. It is already drinking well
       and can be expected to evolve pleasantly, if uninspiringly, for another 4–5
       years. Last tasted, 1/93.

1986—The 1986 is not quite as good as the 1975, 1979, or 1982, but it shares
·   with them the personality of l'Enclos. The style is one that produces a very
84   precocious, soft, fruity wine redolent of plums and black currants, with a
silky, smooth texture. Drink it over the next 4–5 years for its charm, not its
great depth or complexity. Anticipated maturity: Now. Last tasted, 11/90.

1985—The 1985 is delectably rich, long, expansive, velvety, and already a complete
·   pleasure to drink. Medium bodied, with oodles of caramel and berry fruit,
85   this Pomerol gives an impression not unlike biting into candy. Anticipated
maturity: Now. Last tasted, 3/90.

1983—The 1983 l'Enclos is a succulent, fat, juicy wine with a very forward, exuber-
·   ant, grapey appeal, round, ripe, lush flavors, and a velvety finish. Anticipated
86   maturity: Now. Last tasted, 3/89.

1982—Delicious since birth, the 1982 l'Enclos continues to offer attractive tea,
·   smoked duck, and cherry scents and flavors in its medium- to full-bodied,
87   lush, silky personality. Some amber at the edge along with the wine's low
acidity indicate it should be consumed over the next 4–5 years. Last tasted,
9/95.

1979—Deliciously fruity, with a lovely perfumed quality suggesting black currants,
·   this medium-bodied wine has a silky, velvety texture, light tannins, and a
85   round, generous finish. An extremely enjoyable style of wine, it has continued
to drink well and shows no signs of imminent decline. Anticipated maturity:
Now. Last tasted, 1/91.

1975—This is an outstandingly sweet, ripe, round, gentle, smooth wine, with oodles
·   of blackberry fruitiness, a complex berry-and-truffle-scented bouquet, and a
89   velvety finish. The 1975 l'Enclos is medium to full bodied and is drinking
well now, but this beautifully made wine can support additional cellaring. It
is a sleeper of the vintage. Anticipated maturity: Now–2001. Last tasted,
1/85.

1970—The 1970 l'Enclos is very similarly styled to the 1975 and 1982. Perhaps
·   more tannic, but nevertheless velvety, ripe, smooth, and polished, this dark
86   ruby wine is loaded with fruit and has a finish that caresses the palate.
Anticipated maturity: Now. Last tasted, 1/85.

EVANGILE   OUTSTANDING

Classification: None
Location of vineyards: Pomerol
Owner: S.C. du Château l'Evangile
Address: 33500 Pomerol
Mailing address: Same as above
Telephone: 33 5 57 51 15 30 or 33 5 57 51 45 95; telefax: 33 5 57 51 45 78
Visits: By appointment only
Contact: Mrs. Ducasse

VINEYARDS (red)
Surface area: 35.8 acres
Average age of vines: 40 years
Blend: 75% Merlot, 25% Cabernet Franc
Density of plantation: 5,600–6,300 vines per hectare
Average yields (over the last 5 years): 35 hectoliters per hectare
Total average annual production: 510 hectoliters

GRAND VIN (red)
Brand name: Château l'Evangile
Appellation: Pomerol
Mean annual production: 400 hectoliters
Upbringing: Fermentations last 12–14 days and maceration 15–20 days.
Malolactics occur in tanks. Wines are then transferred to oak casks,
35%–40% of which are new, for 16–20 months aging. They are fined but
not filtered.

SECOND WINE
Brand name: Le Blason de l'Evangile
Average annual production: 14,600 bottles

Evaluation of present classification: The quality equivalent of a Médoc
first-growth
Plateau of maturity: 6–25 years following the vintage

Anyone who has tasted the 1947, 1950, 1961, 1975, 1982, 1985, 1989, 1990, 1995, or 1997 l'Evangile knows full well that this property can make wines of majestic richness and compelling character. Bordered on the north by the vineyards of La Conseillante, Vieux-Château-Certan, and Pétrus and on the south by the great St.-Emilion Cheval Blanc, the 35-acre vineyard is brilliantly situated on deep, gravelly soil mixed with both clay and sand. With these advantages, I believe that l'Evangile (never a model of consistency) can produce wines that rival those of Pétrus and Lafleur.

That may well happen during the nineties, because in 1990 the Rothschild family (of Lafite-Rothschild) purchased a controlling interest. They are fully aware of the unlimited potential of this estate, and l'Evangile may soon be challenging Pétrus and Lafleur in both quality and, lamentably, price.

Certainly the late Louis Ducasse must have realized the distinctiveness of his vineyard because he often browbeat visiting wine critics with his observation that l'Evangile was every bit as good as, and even more complex than, neighboring Pétrus. The remarkable Madame Ducasse (93 years old in 1998) still runs l'Evangile on a day-to-day basis. I remember having lunch with this amazing woman in the early nineties, where she poured the 1964, 1961, and

1947 from her personal cellar. At the end of a sumptuous lunch of gigantic portions of truffles, *ris de veau,* and *filet de boeuf,* I noticed that the only person who had eaten everything, and who had finished the glorious wines even more quickly than the guests, was Madame Ducasse!

If the Rothschild winemaking team continues the late harvesting that produces such rich, concentrated grapes and additionally lowers the yields to under 45 hectoliters per hectare and increases the new oak to 50% or more, I predict l'Evangile will become one of the bright shining stars of Pomerol, not just in great vintages, but in less glamorous years as well.

VINTAGES

1997 — An outstanding success for the vintage, the 1997 l'Evangile, for my taste, is
• better than the estate's 1996. The 1997 verges on being over-ripe, but man-
90– ages to pull it off without any flabbiness or shapelessness. It boasts a dense
93 black/purple color, as well as sweet, exceptionally ripe aromas of blackberry liqueur, plummy jam, and a touch of prunes and truffles. Sweet, unctuously textured, and fat, with exceedingly low acidity, this chewy, fleshy, powerful, well-endowed wine should prove to be a hedonistic head-turner when bottled. It will be delicious young, and should age for 10–15 years. This is an exciting, distinctive claret. Last tasted, 3/98.

1996 — Readers may remember that because of its astringent tannin, I had some
• reservations after my initial tasting of this wine. Eight months later, the tannin
89– is less of a problem, but the wine still possesses a high tannic profile. The
91 dense ruby/purple color is followed by an emerging, exotic nose of prunes, black raspberries, earth, and truffles. The wine is backward, yet dense and powerful. This is an over-ripe style of l'Evangile with high tannin, prune-like notes to the black raspberry fruitiness, and plenty of weight and muscle. Although I find it slightly disjointed, I am optimistic that this wine will continue to come together, as it has evolved nicely over the last 7–8 months. Anticipated maturity: 2005–2018. Last tasted, 3/98.

1995 — Tasted three times, this wine is closed, backward, and marginally less impres-
• sive after bottling than it was from cask. It is still an outstanding l'Evangile
92+ that may prove to be longer-lived than the sumptuous 1990, but perhaps not as opulently styled. It remains one of the year's top efforts. The dense ruby/ purple color is accompanied by aromas of minerals, black raspberries, earth, and spice. The bottled wine seems toned down (too much fining and filtra-tion?), compared with the pre-bottling samples, which had multiple layers of flesh and flavor dimension. High tannin in the finish and plenty of sweet fruit on the palate suggest this wine will turn out to be extra special. Could it have been even better if the filters has been junked in favor of a natural bottling? I think so, yet that being said, the wine's ferocious tannin level cannot conceal its outstanding ripeness, purity, and depth. However, do not expect this Pom-erol to be drinkable for another 5–8 years, which is longer than I initially expected. Anticipated maturity: 2005–2020. Last tasted, 11/97.

1994—One of the vintage's most notable successes, l'Evangile's 1994 possesses a
   •   dense, saturated purple color, followed by a gorgeously sweet nose of fram-
  92   boise/cassis, with mineral and licorice notes in the background. This medium-
         to full-bodied wine reveals a seamless, opulent texture, fabulous purity to its
         layers of fruit, and superb extraction and equilibrium. This terrific wine is
         one of the few 1994s whose tannin is largely concealed by a wealth of fruit.
         It is a gorgeous l'Evangile. Anticipated maturity: 2001–2020. Last tasted,
         1/97.

1993—Dark ruby/purple colored with a sweet raspberry/black truffle/earthy nose,
   •   this low-acid, fleshy l'Evangile does not reveal any of the vintage's green
  89   pepper, vegetal characteristics. Soft, surprisingly powerful, and well focused
         for a 1993, it possesses a sense of elegance as well as sweet black fruits
         nicely presented in a medium-bodied, smooth, cedary-flavored format. This
         impressive 1993 can be drunk now as well as over the next 10–15 years. Last
         tasted, 1/97.

1992—Far more impressive prior to bottling, l'Evangile's 1992 has turned out to be
   •   a fruity, medium-bodied, soft, shallow wine that exhibits light body, hard
  78   tannin, and an obvious deficiency of both fruit and depth. Given the fine
         potential this wine displayed in cask, I wonder whether this is one more 1992
         that was eviscerated at bottling? It is disappointing in the context of the
         vineyard and the proprietor's commitment to excellence. Drink over the next
         5–6 years. Last tasted, 11/94.

1990—The 1990 remains one of the great modern-day l'Evangiles, rivaling such
   •   superb vintages as 1995, 1985, 1982, 1975, 1950, and 1947. It possesses a
  96   deep purple color and a youthful but promising nose of sweet black fruits,
         chocolate, caramel, truffles, and minerals. The wine is exceptionally rich and
         full bodied, with admirable glycerin and thickness. Its development in the
         glass indicates the wine is still in a youthful, dormant stage. The finish is full
         of sweet fruit, with the wine's extract concealing moderate tannin. The 1990
         is a fabulously pure, rich l'Evangile to drink between the turn of the century
         and 2020. Last tasted, 11/96.

1989—For me, the big surprises are the best bottles of 1989 l'Evangile. More
   •   forward, and revealing more maturity than the 1990, the dark ruby/purple–
  90   colored 1989 (some amber is just beginning to creep in at the edge) offers an
         exotic, sweet, chocolatey, toffee, roasted herb nose, thick, fat, ripe flavors, low
         acidity, and far more complexity and richness than I had originally imagined.
         This delicious wine is close to full maturity—perhaps that is why it is
         beginning to perform so well. This looks to be a terrific l'Evangile that is
         significantly better than I may have led readers to believe. I would opt for
         drinking it over the next 10 years, as I do not believe it possesses nearly the
         aging potential, weight, or force of the 1990. Last tasted, 11/96.

1988—Evangile's 1988 possesses this château's characteristic blackberry, plum-
   •   like nose, along with considerable grace, charm, depth, and harmony. It is
  87   precocious and should continue to drink well for 10–12 years. Last tasted,
         1/93.

1986—This fully mature wine displays an herbaceous, richly fruity nose with scents
•   of cedar and earth. Somewhat disjointed, it is just beginning to lose its fruit
87   and fat, so I would opt for drinking it over the next several years. Anticipated
        maturity: Now. Last tasted, 12/95.

1985—Evangile's 1985 remains relatively unevolved and youthful. The dark ruby
•   color exhibits no signs of age, and the hugely complex, multidimensional
95   bouquet of black currants, raspberries, exotic spices and oak requires coaxing
        from the glass. Rich, medium to full bodied, super-concentrated, well bal-
        anced, and tannic, this wine continues to evolve more slowly than other
        1985s. Anticipated maturity: Now–2015. Last tasted, 10/94.

1984—Soft, herbal-tea-like aromas fill the olfactory senses. In the mouth, the wine
•   is light, soft, and fruity but falls off and has a watery finish. Drink it up.
76   Anticipated maturity: Now. Last tasted, 3/89.

1983—Consistently an outstanding success for l'Evangile, the 1983 exhibits a dark
•   ruby/purple color, followed by a knockout nose of black raspberries, Asian
90   spices, and minerals. Not a blockbuster claret, it is an elegant, medium-
        bodied, beautifully knit Pomerol with a seductive perfume and soft, round,
        lush flavors with no hard edges. This wine remains remarkably fresh and
        vibrant, with good length. It should hold at its current plateau of maturity.
        Anticipated maturity: Now–2005. Last tasted, 12/95.

1982—I have never had less than a spectacular bottle of this wine, which continues
•   to evolve at a slow pace. Its pure thickness and exotic nose of saddle leather,
96   jammy black currants, licorice, smoke, grilled steak, and truffles have always
        been a turn-on. Thick, chewy, and opulent, with an impressive breadth of
        flavor and intensity, as well as an awesomely chewy, long finish, this colossal
        example of l'Evangile is reminiscent of the estate's 1961 and 1947. It should
        age effortlessly for 20+ more years. Last tasted, 9/95.

1981—Unexpectedly light, diffuse, and inadequately concentrated, the 1981 is well
•   below the standard for this excellent estate. It is medium ruby and just too
73   bland without much concentration to it. Drink up! Anticipated maturity: Now.
        Last tasted, 4/84.

1979—This wine has been fully mature since the mid-1980s. The 1979 l'Evangile is
•   a seductive, sensual wine with a soft, raspberry, black currant fruitiness,
88   a wonderful bouquet of violets, minerals, and spice, medium body, and
        a smooth, velvety finish. It is almost reminiscent of a Grand Cru from
        Chambolle-Musigny. Anticipated maturity: Now. Last tasted, 1/91.

1978—Attractively plump, spicy, and solid, but for whatever reason not terribly
•   complex, the 1978 l'Evangile has always struck me as a good, straightforward,
84   nicely concentrated wine, but nothing special. Anticipated maturity: Now.
        Last tasted, 4/84.

1975—The 1975 l'Evangile displayed a slight hint of amber, as well as a huge nose
•   of fruitcake, sweet cedar, and gobs of black fruits intermixed with scents of
96   truffles. The only other recent l'Evangile with a similar bouquet is the 1982.
        Powerful and forceful, with rich, jammy fruit buttressed by high tannin, this
        full-bodied, superbly extracted wine is soft enough to be approachable, but it

remains 2–3 years away from full maturity. Anticipated maturity: 2000–
2025. Last tasted, 12/95.

1971 — Beginning to decline, the 1971 l'Evangile is displaying an increasingly brown
•   color, and its bouquet has begun to suggest decaying vegetation. The wine is
70   also a trifle unstable on the palate. Medium ruby/brown, with a spicy, minty,
        somewhat burnt aroma and short, medicinal flavors. Anticipated maturity:
        Now–probably in serious decline. Last tasted, 3/80.

1970 — Fully mature, quite round, fruity, soft, elegant, and charming with l'Evangile's
•   telltale violet, raspberry-like bouquet, this medium-bodied, velvety wine
84   should be drunk up. Anticipated maturity: Now. Last tasted, 3/81.

1966 — Fully mature, yet seemingly longer-lived than the 1970, the 1966 has more
•   body and tannin, a vividly brilliant dark ruby color with just a touch of amber,
85   and a long, satisfying, rich, plummy finish. It is a harmonious, supple, very
        fruity wine. Anticipated maturity: Now. Last tasted, 3/79.

1964 — This is a corpulently styled l'Evangile, with a dark garnet color revealing
•   some amber at the edge. The wine offers sweet, smoky black fruits intermixed
87   with earth and smoke. In the mouth, the wine is round and generous, with no
        hard edges and plenty of intensity. There is more of a monolithic quality to
        the wine than its aromatics suggest. Fully mature, it should continue to hold
        (where well stored) for 5–7 years. Last tasted, 3/94.

1961 — The 1961 possesses a huge nose of coffee, sweet, jammy, black fruits, buttered
•   nuts, and truffles. The syrupy texture and fabulous concentration, viscosity,
99   and richness were unbelievable. Given its port-like richness, this full-bodied,
        massively endowed, fully mature wine is reminiscent of the great 1947.
        Interestingly, Madame Ducasse told me that two-thirds of the vineyard was
        replanted in 1957, so 66% of the blend is from 3-year-old vines! Readers who
        are fortunate enough to have bottles of this nectar should plan on drinking it
        over the next 10–15 years. Last tasted, 3/94.

ANCIENT VINTAGES

The 1947 l'Evangile can be a 100-point wine, but in a tasting in December
1995 I bestowed upon it a 97-point rating. An awesome bottle of wine—
thick, jammy, and full bodied, with extraordinary intensity, power, purity, and
layers of black fruits, truffles, and cedar—it represents the quintessential
style of l'Evangile. It should last for another 15–20 years.

FEYTIT-CLINET

Classification: None
Location of vineyards: In the center of Pomerol
Owner: Chasseuil and Domergue families (farmer Ets J.-P. Moueix)
Address: 33500 Pomerol
Mailing address: c/o Ets. J.-P. Moueix, 54, quai du Priourat, B.P. 129,
33502 Libourne Cedex

Telephone: 33 5 57 51 78 96; telefax: 33 5 57 51 79 79
Visits: By appointment and for professionals of the wine trade only
Contact: Frédéric Lospied

VINEYARDS (red)
Surface area: 14 acres
Average age of vines: 20 years
Blend: 85% Merlot, 15% Cabernet Franc
Density of plantation: 5,500–6,000 vines per hectare
Average yields (over the last 5 years): 60 hectoliters per hectare
Total average annual production: 2,000 cases

GRAND VIN (red)
Brand name: Château Feytit-Clinet
Appellation: Pomerol
Mean annual production: 2,000 cases
Upbringing: Fermentations last approximately 18 days in temperature-controlled concrete tanks. After malolactics in tanks, wines are transferred (in December–January) into oak casks, 20% of which are new (the rest are 2–4 years old), for 18 months aging. They are racked every 3 months, from barrel to barrel, fined but not filtered.

SECOND WINE
None produced.

Evaluation of present classification: The quality equivalent of a Médoc Cru Bourgeois
Plateau of maturity: 5–12 years following the vintage

Feytit-Clinet, despite the fact that the vineyard has been farmed under what is called a *métayage* agreement by the renowned firm of Jean-Pierre Moueix since 1967, tends to produce relatively straightforward, simple wines of no particular distinction. The vineyard, situated on the western section of the Pomerol plateau (next to Latour à Pomerol), should produce more interesting wine. Perhaps the yields are too high, but there is no firm in all of Bordeaux with more concern for crop management than that of Jean-Pierre Moueix. Most vintages of Feytit-Clinet are drinkable upon release. They can be cellared for 7–10 years.

VINTAGES

1993—Although this wine possesses excellent color, a vegetal, under-ripe fruit char-
•　　acter in both its aromatics and flavors render it a weak effort. Moreover, the
76　　dry, astringent finish suggests a problematic evolution. Last tasted, 11/94.

1992—The lush, ripe fruit of this estate's cask samples has been replaced by a green,
•   hard, tannic wine with an absence of charm. What happened? Last tasted,
76   11/94.

1990—The medium-bodied 1990 Feytit-Clinet reveals toasty vanillin-scented, su-
•   perripe aromas, gobs of rich, unctuous fruit, and a soft, chewy, smooth finish.
86   It is one of the best examples of Feytit-Clinet in years. Anticipated maturity:
Now. Last tasted, 1/93.

1989—The 1989 exhibits a moderately intense, ripe, spicy, straightforward bouquet,
•   medium to full body, lots of extract, and high, surprisingly hard tannins.
84   Anticipated maturity: Now–2002. Last tasted, 1/93.

1988—The 1988 Feytit-Clinet is a straightforward, spicy, ripe Pomerol that displays
•   fresh acidity, giving its flavors more precision and clarity. It also possesses an
84   elegant, plummy bouquet and a long, lush, spicy finish. While not a big
Pomerol when measured against the heavyweights of the appellation, Feytit-
Clinet is a charming, stylish wine that should be at its best between now and
2003. Last tasted, 1/93.

1985—The 1985 has an intense bouquet of bing cherries and toasty oak, good
•   richness, firm tannins, and some elegance. Anticipated maturity: Now. Last
84   tasted, 3/89.

LA FLEUR DE GAY   OUTSTANDING

Classification: None
Location of vineyards: The larger parcel of two is on the highest terrace of
Pomerol, near Pétrus
Owner: G.F.A. La Croix de Gay
Address: 33500 Pomerol
Mailing address: Same as above
Telephone: 33 5 57 51 19 05; telefax: 33 5 57 72 15 62
Visits: Every day, between 8 A.M. and noon, and 2 P.M. and 6 P.M.
Contact: Marie France Cubiller

VINEYARDS (red)
Surface area: 9.9 acres
Average age of vines: 40 years
Blend: 100% Merlot
Density of plantation: 5,800 vines per hectare
Average yields (over the last 5 years): 35 hectoliters per hectare
Total average annual production: 15,000 bottles

GRAND VIN (red)
Brand name: Château La Fleur de Gay
Appellation: Pomerol
Mean annual production: 15,000 bottles

Upbringing: Fermentations take place in temperature-controlled concrete vats. After a cold maceration at 12–15 degrees centigrade (1 week), alcoholic fermentations take place at temperatures not exceeding 32 degrees centigrade. Macerations last approximately 3 weeks (at 30 degrees centigrade) and malolactics take place in new oak barrels. Wines are aged in new oak barrels for 18 months, are fined with fresh egg whites, and remain unfiltered.

SECOND WINE
None produced.

La Fleur de Gay, the luxury cuvée of La Croix de Gay, was launched by Dr. Alain Raynaud in 1982 (see page 828). The wine comes from a small parcel of very old vines situated between Pétrus and Vieux-Château-Certan that is part of Dr. Raynaud's better-known estate called La Croix de Gay. Aged in 100% new oak, it is a wine that is characterized by a compelling opulence and sweetness, as well as exceptional purity of fruit. Michel Rolland oversees the vinification and upbringing of this luxuriously flavored, intense, full-bodied wine. Vintages to date give every indication of possessing 10–20 years of aging potential.

VINTAGES

1997—Deep ruby/purple–colored, with a reticent but promising nose of pure black
•　　raspberries, cassis, minerals, and toasty oak, this elegant, graceful wine pos-
86–　sesses excellent purity and concentration, in addition to overall fine balance.
88　　Only some shortness in the finish keeps it from meriting a higher score.
　　　Anticipated maturity: 2000–2009. Last tasted, 3/98.

1996—This is a more narrowly constructed, leaner, and more austere wine than
•　　typical for this estate. The wine is well made, with plenty of spicy oak and
86–　mineral-laden black currrant in the tightly compressed aromatics. High acid-
88　　ity and tannin as well as new oak dominate the palate of this medium-bodied,
　　　backward, spartan-styled wine. Some sweetness at the back of the palate and
　　　a weighty feel offer hope for further fleshing out of the fruit. This will be an
　　　interesting wine to taste after bottling. Anticipated maturity: 2004–2016.
　　　Last tasted, 3/98.

1995—The 1995 La Fleur de Gay has begun to shut down following bottling. The
•　　color is a healthy dense ruby/purple. The nose displays aromas of minerals,
90+　*pain grillé*, a touch of prunes, and gobs of black cherries and cassis inter-
　　　twined with vanillin from new oak casks. This medium-bodied wine exhibits
　　　fennel-like black currant flavors, high tannin, and impressive purity, depth,
　　　and length. However, patience will be required. Anticipated maturity: 2003–
　　　2018. Last tasted, 11/97.

1994—Dark ruby/garnet colored, with a sweet, spicy, oaky, black fruit–scented nose,
• this well-structured, moderately tannic, medium-bodied wine exhibits an ex-
89+ cellent underpinning of fruit, extract, and glycerin, but it needs 5–6 years of
cellaring. At present it is somewhat austere and backward. Anticipated maturity: 2003–2014. Last tasted, 1/97.

1993—This dark ruby–colored wine, with an overlay of spicy new oak and *pain*
• *grillé* notes, is tightly knit, but it gives every indication of aging well and
87 possibly meriting a slightly higher score than I have bestowed. The wine
possesses copious quantities of pure black cherry fruit intertwined with spice.
This beautifully made, medium-bodied, elegant, and concentrated 1993
needs 1–3 years of cellaring; it should age well for 10–12+ years. This wine
is not dissimilar to the excellent 1987 La Fleur de Gay. Last tasted, 1/97.

1992—This 1992 exhibits one of the most saturated purple colors of a wine from
• this vintage. With its ripe, black raspberry-and-plum-scented, toasty nose,
87 excellent concentration, medium to full body, moderate to high tannin level,
low acidity, and excellent length, this is a broodingly backward and structured
1992. It should drink well for 10–15 years. Bravo! Last tasted, 11/94.

1991—This 1991 has turned out well for the vintage, displaying a solid medium ruby
• color and a spicy, ripe, black currant–scented nose infused judiciously with
85 smoky new oak. Medium bodied, with low acidity, this pleasant, straightforward wine will drink well for 4–7 years. Last tasted, 1/94.

1990—I appear to have under-rated the 1990 La Fleur de Gay. This outstanding
• wine, which has put on weight, was not embarrassed when tasted next to the
92 1989. It offers an opaque purple color, a sweet, jammy nose of black fruits,
medium to full body, ripe tannin, and layers of extract and glycerin in its
pure, supple, low-acid finish. The development of the wine's character, complexity, and richness was surprising. Anticipated maturity: Now–2015. Last
tasted, 11/96.

1989—This wine remains backward and unformed, especially for a 1989, but it
• reveals a nearly opaque purple color and a sweet, pure nose of black raspber-
94+ ries, cassis, licorice, violets, and minerals nicely dosed with high-quality new
oak. There is great fruit on the palate, layers of richness, medium to full body,
and fabulous harmony and precision. Given its superb intensity and elegant
personality, it is a dazzling example of winemaking. The wine's finish goes on
for at least 35–40 seconds. Unlike many 1989 Pomerols, this wine requires
2–3 more years of cellaring; it should keep through the first 15+ years of the
next century. Last tasted, 11/96.

1988—Only limited quantities (1,000–1,500 cases) of the super 1988 are available.
• It is, however, worth whatever arm-twisting, retailer brow-beating one must
93 do to latch on to a few bottles. The 1988's black/ruby/purple color makes it
among the darkest-hued wines of the vintage. The bouquet is now shut down
compared with the terrific fragrance and opulence it displayed when young.
However, it takes no real talent to detect scents of smoky, toasty oak, black
plums, allspice and Oriental spices, as well as gobs of super-ripe fruit. Extremely concentrated on the palate, but structured, with considerable tannin,

this massive, full-bodied, more aggressive La Fleur de Gay will not have the sumptuous appeal of many Pomerols, but give it 4–5 years to mellow and it will provide a dazzling glass of decadent Pomerol. Anticipated maturity: Now–2010. Last tasted, 1/93.

1987—The 1987 La Fleur de Gay is fat, seductive, and lush, with expansive black-
•   berry flavors, low acidity, and light tannins. Its lush, gloriously rich, admira-
90   bly extracted flavors are nicely framed by the use of 100% new oak. This exotic crowd pleaser will have to be drunk over the next 5–7 years, but who cares? This is one of the few great wines of the 1987 vintage. Anticipated maturity: Now–2002. Last tasted, 4/91.

1986—I slightly over-rated this wine, which I had hoped would be outstanding. It
•   may still be, but its tendency to perform in a relatively one-dimensional
89+   manner has convinced me to lower the score. The wine possesses a deep ruby/purple color, with some lightening at the edge. The firm nose reveals plenty of new oak. It is followed by an austere, powerful, muscular wine that remains closed and unforthcoming. There is good weight and ripe fruit, but I would have liked to see more complexity and charm emerge now that the wine is 10 years old. Anticipated maturity: 1999–2012. Last tasted, 4/97.

1985—The 1985 exhibits super-richness, a stunningly intense bouquet, luxurious
•   flavors, full body, and melted tannins, giving it a satiny texture. Given the
89   softness, I hesitate to advise long-term cellaring, but drunk young, this trea-sure should provide memorable drinking. Anticipated maturity: Now. Last tasted, 1/91.

1983—This wine, which was at its peak several years ago, has begun to drop some
•   fruit and fat. The color remains a dark ruby/garnet with amber at the edge.
88   The nose offers scents of underbrush and sweet, jammy blackberry and cherry fruit intermixed with tea, smoke, and herbs. This medium-bodied wine is beginning to reveal astringent dried tannin in its finish. The fleshy, full-bodied character the wine possessed in its youth is drying out. Anticipated maturity: Now. Last tasted, 4/97.

1982—How things have changed! The debut vintage of this luxury cuvée from La
•   Croix de Gay, the 1982 has not turned out well. The color is taking on
79   considerable amber. The wine is spicy and earthy, with some of the vintage's ripeness but a diffuse personality. In addition, the wine lacks concentration and focus. Has it begun to fade? Last tasted, 9/95.

LA FLEUR-PÉTRUS   EXCELLENT

Classification: None
Location of vineyards: On the plateau of Pomerol, with Lafleur to the west and Pétrus to the south
Owner: S.C. du Château La Fleur-Pétrus (J.-P. Moueix)
Address: 33500 Pomerol
Mailing address: c/o Ets. J.-P. Moueix, 54, quai du Priourat, B.P. 129, 33502 Libourne Cedex

Telephone: 33 5 57 51 78 96; telefax: 33 5 57 51 79 79
Visits: By appointment, and for professionals of the wine trade only
Contact: Frédéric Lospied

VINEYARDS (red)
Surface area: 34 acres
Average age of vines: 30 years
Blend: 80% Merlot, 20% Cabernet Franc
Density of plantation: 5,500–6,000 vines per hectare
Average yields (over the last 5 years): 40 hectoliters per hectare
Total average annual production: 3,500 cases

GRAND VIN (red)
Brand name: Château La Fleur-Pétrus
Appellation: Pomerol
Mean annual production: 3,500 cases
Upbringing: Fermentations last 20 days in temperature-controlled
concrete vats. One-quarter of the yield undergoes malolactics in oak
casks and the rest in vats. Wines are aged in oak casks, 50% of which
are new (the rest are 2 vintages old), for 18 months. They are racked
every 3 months from barrel to barrel, fined and not filtered.

SECOND WINE
None produced.

Evaluation of present classification: The quality equivalent of a Médoc
third-growth
Plateau of maturity: 5–15 years following the vintage

Located on the eastern side of the plateau of Pomerol between Lafleur and
Pétrus (hence the name), where so many of the best estates are found, La
Fleur-Pétrus should be one of the most exquisite Pomerols. The famous firm
of Jean-Pierre Moueix purchased the estate in 1952, and the vineyard was
entirely replanted after 1956, when it was virtually destroyed by the winter
freeze. The wine at La Fleur-Pétrus is lighter in weight and texture than
other Moueix Pomerols such as Pétrus, Trotanoy, and Latour à Pomerol, but
connoisseurs prize it for elegance and a supple, smooth, silky texture. It
usually matures quickly and can be drunk as soon as 5 or 6 years after the
vintage. Recent vintages have produced very fine wines, but I cannot help
thinking that the quality could and should be higher. That may well happen,
because a small parcel of old vines formerly owned by Le Gay was purchased
by the Moueix firm for La Fleur-Pétrus.

    La Fleur-Pétrus, because of its name, quality, and small production, tends
to be expensive.

VINTAGES

1997—A lovely La Fleur-Pétrus, the 1997 continues this property's noticeable up-
•   swing in quality. With its dense ruby/purple color and luscious black cherry,
89–   kirsch, herb, fruitcake, and spicy nose, this is a seductive 1997. On the
91   palate, the wine is medium to full bodied and rich, with no hard tannin
       or unintegrated acidity. An opulent, rich wine with no hard edges, it will
       be delicious to drink upon release. Moreover, it possesses the extract and
       overall equilibrium to age well for 12–14 years. Impressive. Last tasted,
       3/98.

1996—One of the better Pomerols of the vintage, this wine has put on weight since I
•   first tasted it. It is deep ruby colored, with excellent aromatics, consisting of
87–   black plums, cherries, spices, and a hint of truffles. Backward and deep, with
90   excellent, possibly outstanding depth of fruit, this medium- to full-bodied,
       powerful, concentrated La Fleur-Pétrus is an impressive effort in this vintage,
       especially for a right bank wine that relies heavily on the Merlot grape.
       Anticipated maturity: 2004–2018. Last tasted, 3/98.

1995—Dazzling since birth, the 1995 has not lost a thing since bottling. A saturated
•   dark purple color suggests a wine of considerable depth and concentration.
93   The nose offers up gorgeous aromas of sweet kirsch intermixed with black
       raspberry, mineral, and smoky notes. Full bodied, with superb richness and
       purity, loads of tannin, and a layered, multidimensional personality, this
       terrific La Fleur-Pétrus is the finest wine I have tasted at this property in the
       twenty years I have been visiting Bordeaux. Readers may remember that I
       previously reported that a 10-acre old vine sector of Le Gay was sold to La
       Fleur-Pétrus, increasing the latter's vineyard to 33 acres. I believe this 10-
       acre acquisition has beefed up La Fleur-Pétrus, a fact particularly evident in
       this 1995. It is a splendid effort! Anticipated maturity: 2005–2025. Last
       tasted, 11/97.

1994—The attractive kirsch, cherry, *pain grillé* nose is followed by a medium-bodied,
•   restrained, pure, measured wine. The 1994 offers an impressively saturated
89+   color as well as an inner core of sweet, concentrated fruit and moderate tannin
       in the finish. All the richness, extract, and balance are present in this closed
       but impressively endowed wine. Drink it between 2003 and 2018. Last tasted,
       1/97.

1993—A high-quality offering for La Fleur-Pétrus, this is a medium-bodied, struc-
•   tured, backward-style Pomerol with a dark ruby/purple color, an attractive
87   floral-and-black fruit–scented nose, good spice, and fine length. Anticipated
       maturity: 2002–2016. Last tasted, 1/97.

1992—It is no secret that the Moueix family has been attempting to elevate the
•   quality of the wine produced at this vineyard that bears the name of two of
87   Pomerol's greatest wines—Lafleur and Pétrus. A new cellar has been built,
       crop thinning is routinely employed, and the age of the vines has become
       more respectable. Perhaps La Fleur-Pétrus will begin to live up to its grandi-
       ose name. The excellent 1992 offers a deep ruby/purple color and a big,
       sweet, jammy nose of black fruits, caramel, and vanillin. Ripe, rich, medium
       bodied, with excellent density, this concentrated, elegant, yet powerful wine

should drink exceptionally well during its first 8–15 years of life. Last tasted, 11/94.

1990— The 1990 is noticeably less concentrated than the 1989. The bouquet offers
•
88
aromas of tobacco, coffee, mocha, and red fruits intertwined with scents of new oak. In the mouth, the wine is medium bodied, moderately endowed, and admirably pure, with moderate tannins and crisp acidity—unusual for a 1990. Drink it over the next 10–12 years. Last tasted, 1/93.

1989— In 1989 50% of the grapes were cut off to reduce the crop size and to augment
•
91
the wine's intensity. The results may be the finest La Fleur-Pétrus since the 1950 and 1947. Dark opaque ruby, with a tight yet expressive bouquet of exotic spices, mocha, and deep, superripe black cherry fruit, this medium-bodied wine has an inner core of depth and length. Its admirable intensity of flavor is backed by a formidable degree of alcohol and tannin. Anticipated maturity: Now–2009. Last tasted, 1/93.

1988— The 1988 is a tasty, attractive, ripe, agreeable wine with adequate depth,
•
85
medium body, and enough length and tannin to warrant drinking over the next decade. Anticipated maturity: Now–2000. Last tasted, 1/93.

1987— This is one of the better examples from this château in recent years. Dis-
•
87
playing a surprisingly dark ruby/purple color, plenty of rich, ripe, plummy fruit, and a lush, alcoholic finish, it should be drunk young. A sleeper of the vintage. Anticipated maturity: Now. Last tasted, 11/90.

1986— I would have liked to taste a bit more flesh and depth in the insubstantial yet
•
83
still pleasant 1986. It is somewhat forward, slightly compact and attenuated, and quite evolved, with some light tannins in the finish. One wonders why it is not more concentrated given the winemaking team that produced it. Antici-pated maturity: Now. Last tasted, 3/90.

1985— The 1985 La Fleur-Pétrus is fruity, stylish, suave, and tasty. It exhibits
•
85
good ripeness, medium body, an aromatic bouquet, and a soft, velvety finish. Anticipated maturity: Now. Last tasted, 3/90.

1983— Rather light and fruity, but nevertheless charming, with medium body and an
•
81
open-knit, fruity, plummy, spicy, somewhat oaky bouquet, this is an indiffer-ent effort from La Fleur-Pétrus. It is ready to drink. Anticipated maturity: Now. Last tasted, 3/85.

1982— Inconsistent tastings have plagued the performance of this wine since bot-
•
90?
tling. At some tastings the wine has exhibited plummy/mulberry–like fruit with a touch of vanillin, a smooth, creamy texture, excellent aromatics, and outstanding concentration and personality. Other tastings revealed a more herbaceously scented and flavored wine with noticeable acidity and tannin. At the most recent tasting, the wine performed extremely well, but it tasted fully mature. Last tasted, 9/95.

1981— Very soft, a trifle jammy, and too supple, the 1981 La Fleur-Pétrus is still a
•
84
deliciously fruity, savory, medium-bodied wine that is ideal for drinking over the next 5–6 years. Anticipated maturity: Now. Last tasted, 10/84.

1979— The 1979 is an elegant, supple, very fruity wine, with the smell of ripe plums
•
85
and spicy, vanillin oak very prominently displayed. Medium bodied, with medium to dark ruby color and a lush, nicely concentrated texture, this is not

a big, hefty, rich Pomerol, but rather a suave, delicate, yet fruity, interesting wine. Anticipated maturity: Now. Last tasted, 2/83.

1978—Quite similar to the 1979, yet showing a more perceptible amber/brown edge
•   to it, the 1978 La Fleur-Pétrus has a supple, rich, fat, ripe Merlot fruitiness,
84   medium to full body, and light, round tannins. Anticipated maturity: Now. Last tasted, 2/85.

1977—In this poor vintage, La Fleur-Pétrus produced a decent, soft, fruity wine with
•   medium body, not too much annoying vegetal stalkiness, and a pleasant, clean
73   bouquet. Anticipated maturity: Now—probably in serious decline. Last tasted, 4/82.

1976—The 1976 La Fleur-Pétrus is quite mature, with some browning at the edges.
•   It is a charming, open-knit, very soft, round wine, with considerable appeal,
83   but like the great majority of 1976 Bordeaux, it is a trifle diluted and flabby, with low acidity. Anticipated maturity: Now—probably in serious decline. Last tasted, 1/80.

1975—This is an outstanding, restrained, still youthful wine with a healthy dark
•   ruby/purple color showing a bit of amber at the edge. The nose is more
90   restrained and less exuberant than in many 1975s. Sweet berry fruit is complemented by earth and new oak scents. Medium bodied, stylish, and concentrated, with forceful tannin and enough fruit, glycerin, and extract to support further aging, this youthful, delicious wine can be drunk over the next 10–15 years. Last tasted, 12/95.

1970—A top-notch success for the vintage, the 1970 La Fleur-Pétrus is now at its
•   apogee. It is very round and richly fruity, with medium body, a lush, vel-
87   vety texture, and a long finish. The predominant impression is one of rich, roasted black cherries and spices. Anticipated maturity: Now. Last tasted, 1/91.

1966—Fully mature, the 1966 La Fleur-Pétrus has a bouquet of oak, truffles, and
•   soft, ripe Merlot fruit. Medium bodied, with a touch of amber at the edge, this
84   is a wine that can be kept but is best drunk up. Anticipated maturity: Now— may be in decline. Last tasted, 1/80.

1964—The 1964 was a wonderful vintage for the wines of Pomerol and for the
•   properties of the firm of Jean-Pierre Moueix. Chunky and a trifle rustic for La
85   Fleur-Pétrus, this is a corpulent, jammy, ripe wine, full and flavorful, with good body, but a touch of coarseness does come through on the palate. Anticipated maturity: Now. Last tasted, 4/78.

1961—The 1961 La Fleur-Pétrus exhibited a sweet, black truffle aroma and
•   decent fruit and viscosity. Elegant, expansive, and ripe, with out-
92   standing balance, richness, and length, this is a fully mature, beautifully preserved wine for drinking over the next 10–15 years. Last tasted, 12/95.

ANCIENT VINTAGES

The 1947 La Fleur-Pétrus (90 points, last tasted 12/95) revealed a deep ruby/ garnet color, a spicy, floral-and-berry-scented nose, medium body, some of the unctuousness and viscosity expected in a wine from this vintage, and a soft, round, velvety finish. It has long been fully mature, so drink it up. Two other outstanding older wines include the 1950 (rated 95 in 1989) and the 1952 (rated 91 in 1989).

LE GAY   VERY GOOD

Classification: None
Location of vineyards: Pomerol
Owner: Marie-Geneviève Robin
Address: 33500 Pomerol
Mailing address: Same as above
Telephone: 33 5 57 51 12 43; telefax: none
Visits: By appointment

VINEYARDS (red)
Surface area: 19.8 acres
Average age of vines: 20 years and 5 years
Blend: 50% Merlot, 50% Cabernet Franc
Density of plantation: 5,900 vines per hectare
Average yields (over the last 5 years): 40 hectoliters

GRAND VIN (red)
Brand name: Château Le Gay
Appellation: Pomerol
Mean annual production: 2,000 cases
Upbringing: 18–20 months in oak casks

SECOND WINE
None produced.

Evaluation of present classification: The quality equivalent of a Médoc fourth-growth
Plateau of maturity: 10–25 years following the vintage

Just to the north of the Pomerol plateau is the run-down property of Le Gay, with its unkempt and rather poorly lit wine cellar. Since the death of her sister, Therese, several years ago, Marie Robin and her niece and nephew, Sylvie and Jacques Guinaudeau, own Le Gay and the adjacent vineyard of Lafleur. The Libourne firm of Jean-Pierre Moueix controls Le Gay's commercialization throughout the world.

Le Gay has been a vineyard of enormous potential, with old vines and minuscule yields of 15–20 hectoliters per hectare, but historically it has been inconsistent. Great raw materials from the vineyard are often translated into mediocre wine as a result of old and sometimes dirty barrels. Until 1982 the ancient barrels that housed the wine at Le Gay had to share space with flocks of chickens and ducks. In 1996 Le Gay sold what many considered its finest parcel of old vines to La Fleur-Pétrus. This is not likely to be a favorable development for Le Gay. Shrewd Pomerol enthusiasts should search out the ancient vintages of Le Gay as some are splendid. For example, the 1947 (rated 98 in 3/98) and the 1950 (rated 94 in 4/98) are two compelling examples of Le Gay.

The style of winemaking at Le Gay has resulted in powerful, rich, tannic, sometimes massive and impenetrable wines. In some years Le Gay can turn out to be coarse and overbearing, whereas in other vintages the power of Le Gay is in harmony and well balanced against ripe fruit, firm acidity, and tannin. Le Gay is almost always the least flattering Pomerol to taste at a young age, often needing 8–10 years of cellaring to shed its cloak of tannin. For those who prefer their claret soft and easy to drink, Le Gay is an intimidating sort of wine.

VINTAGES

1997—As I tasted this disappointing Le Gay, I couldn't help but remember a mag-
•   num of the 1947 I had in Paris in late March that easily scored in the upper
76–   90s. The latter Le Gay was a thrillingly opulent, viscously textured wine
78   loaded with glycerin and fruit. The same cannot be said for the 1997. It
       possesses a dark ruby color, but little charm, finesse, or ripeness. Extremely
       lean and attenuated, it is a sure-fire candidate to dry out over the next decade.
       Last tasted, 3/98.

1996—This monolithic, earthy, dense, tannic wine has some size and weight, but the
•   wine's astringency and forbidding structure make it a dubious bet for hedo-
85–   nists. While there is a lack of charm, the wine's size, density, and earthiness
86   might persuade others. Anticipated maturity: 2003–2015. Last tasted, 3/98.

1995—Lacking the depth, flesh, fruit, and charm that one expects in most Pomerols,
•   this dark ruby–colored wine exhibits an excess of tannin, body, and structure
82   for the amount of fruit it possesses. It will not provide near-term consumption
       given its severe personality. Anticipated maturity: 2005–2015. Last tasted,
       11/97.

1994—The 1994 is medium bodied, with a deep ruby/purple color and some spicy
•   oak, minerals, and black fruits in the nose. It is a beefy, muscular, tannic
86   wine with sufficient fruit to balance out the structure. Give it 1–3 years of
       cellaring, and drink it over the following 10. Last tasted, 3/96.

1992—An atypically light, diluted style for Le Gay, without this wine's typical
•   robustness and savage intensity. The medium ruby–colored 1992 is short,
78   lean, and tannic. Drink it over the next 4–5 years. Last tasted, 11/94.

1990—The 1990 possesses a coarseness and leathery astringence to its tannin that
•   lower its rating. The wine exhibits a deep ruby color, good spice, an earthy,
88   animal-like, meaty aroma, medium to full body, rustic tannin, and a spicy

finish. The 1990's edges are rougher and less velvety than the 1989's, but some of that roughness may dissipate with another 5–6 years of cellaring. It will unquestionably last for 2 decades. Last tasted, 11/97.

1989—This is one estate where the 1989 outshines the 1990. The 1989 displays a
•   youthful deep ruby/purple color and dense, tannic, muscular flavors that are
90   just beginning to reveal sweetness and opulence. Backward, youthfully tannic, and grapey for a 1989, this artisan-styled, robust, muscular Pomerol will benefit from another 2–3 years of cellaring. It should keep for 15–20 years. Last tasted, 11/97.

1988—The 1988 Le Gay is moderately rich, full bodied, deep, and oaky. It should
•   reach maturity, optimistically, by the turn of the century. Anticipated maturity:
86   Now–2010. Last tasted, 1/93.

1986—The 1986 Le Gay will appeal primarily to those with nineteenth-century
•   tastes for big, beefy, bulky wines that assault the senses and palate with
87   layer upon layer of tannin. It remains a closed and dense wine that only stubbornly offers up the ripe fruit that the deep color and weight of the wine suggest it possesses. It is a wine that will require a significant amount of time to pull itself together and smooth out. How many consumers will have the patience to wait? Anticipated maturity: Now–2010. Last tasted, 3/90.

1985—I have never enjoyed tasting Le Gay when young. With age, the finesse and
•   breed come through, but at the moment the 1985 is mean, moody, and murky,
86   as well as terribly tannic. It is full bodied and deep and exhibits good richness, but how long is one expected to wait? The rating may turn out to be conservative if this wine pulls itself together and smooths out. Anticipated maturity: Now–2008. Last tasted, 3/89.

1983—The 1983 is a good Le Gay—alcoholic, tannic, a little clumsy and awkward,
•   but powerful and ripe. Low acidity may prevent a long, graceful evolution,
83   but this wine will please many buyers for a direct, full-bodied, rich, aggressive style. Anticipated maturity: Now–2000. Last tasted, 9/87.

1982—Bottle variation/tasting irregularity continue to raise both hopes and concerns
•   about the 1982 Le Gay. The wine offers a dark ruby/garnet color, with only a
89+?   hint of amber at the edge. The pungent, earthy, spicy, green pepper, and sweet jammy fruit aromas are intense but controversial. Still broodingly backward and dense, this full-bodied wine has mouth-searing tannin as well as impressive length. However, the damp, musty aromas of some bottles are off-putting. Even healthy examples require another 4–5 years of cellaring, so don't rush to judgment on this one. Dr. Jekyll and Mr. Hyde—meet Monsieur Le Gay! Last tasted, 9/95.

1981—The deliciously fruity, supple, deep, cask samples of the 1981 Le Gay were
•   impressive, but in the bottle it has shown a remarkable degree of varia-
?   tion. Some bottles have dirty, flawed bouquets, while others are rich, fruity, and clean. It is impossible to tell which bottle is the clean one, so this wine is best avoided. Retasted twice in 1988 with similar results. Last tasted, 4/88.

1979—A success for Le Gay, the 1979 is richly fruity with the smell of black currants
•   and violets and earthy, truffle-scented aromas. This medium- to full-bodied
84   wine has light to moderate tannins and a good finish. Anticipated maturity:
         Now. Last tasted, 6/82.

1975—Although still backward, the 1975 Le Gay is an impressively extracted wine
•   that is beginning to reveal some aromatic development. Sweet, over-ripe
89+?   aromas of black cherries intermingled with scents of minerals and earth are
         followed by a powerful, muscular, tannic, large-scaled wine that remains
         immature. The color is a healthy dark garnet/ruby, with no amber at the edge.
         Although it is excruciatingly tannic, the high extraction of fruit remains a
         positive sign. This old-style, blockbuster wine is reminiscent of certain 1948s
         and 1945s. Whether it ever sheds its tannin and becomes completely harmo-
         nious is highly debatable (I don't think it will), but there are copious quanti-
         ties of sweet, exotic fruit. Perhaps in 20 years this will be a marvelous claret,
         but don't bet on it. Last tasted, 12/95.

1966—Mature and fully ready to drink, the 1966 Le Gay has an amber, moderately
•   dark ruby color, an earthy, austere Médoc-like, restrained bouquet, medium
83   body, and a solid, somewhat rustic finish. Anticipated maturity: Now—may be
         in decline. Last tasted, 9/82.

1962—Still firm, but mature, Le Gay's 1962 has a moderately intense bouquet of
•   ripe plums and mineral scents. On the palate, the wine is concentrated,
85   surprisingly well balanced, and interesting. Anticipated maturity: Now—may
         be in decline. Last tasted, 11/79.

1961—A disappointment in this great vintage, Le Gay has a bizarre, medicinal
•   bouquet and a loosely knit structure, harsh fruity flavors, and little balance.
68   Anticipated maturity: Now—probably in serious decline. Last tasted, 11/79.

GAZIN   EXCELLENT

Classification: None
Location of vineyards: Lieu-dit Gazin, Pomerol
Owner: G.F.A. du Château Gazin
Address: Lieu-dit Gazin, 33500 Pomerol
Mailing address: Same as above
Telephone: 33 5 57 51 07 05; telefax: 33 5 57 51 69 96
Visits: By appointment only
Contact: Nicolas de Baillencourt

VINEYARDS (red)
Surface area: 59.3 acres
Average age of vines: 35 years
Blend: 90% Merlot, 7% Cabernet Sauvignon, 3% Cabernet Franc
Density of plantation: 5,600 vines per hectare
Average yields (over the last 5 years): 43 hectoliters per hectare
Total average annual production: 90,000 bottles

GRAND VIN (red)
Brand name: Château Gazin
Appellation: Pomerol
Mean annual production: 70,000 bottles
Upbringing: Fermentations last 3 weeks in small temperature-controlled concrete tanks. Malolactics occur in barrels, and wines are aged for 15–18 months in oak barrels, which are renewed by half at each vintage. They are fined and sometimes filtered.

SECOND WINE
Brand name: Hospitalet de Gazin
Average annual production: 20,000 bottles

Evaluation of present classification: Since 1988 the quality equivalent of a Médoc classified growth
Plateau of maturity: 5–15 years following the vintage

Most commentators on Bordeaux have generally held Gazin in high regard, no doubt because the vineyard is ideally situated behind Pétrus. In fact, Gazin sold 12.5 acres of its vineyard to Pétrus in 1969. However, the track record for Gazin, one of the largest vineyards of Pomerol, has been mediocre throughout the sixties and seventies. Yet since the late eighties Gazin has rebounded impressively, producing a succession of topflight wines.

Strangely enough, Gazin has always been an expensive wine. A historic reputation and the strategic placement on the Pomerol plateau next to Pétrus and l'Evangile have served it well. The optimistic signs that began in 1988 and 1989 mark a new period of higher-quality wines from Gazin that should be greeted enthusiastically by consumers wanting a tasty, plump, succulent Pomerol.

VINTAGES

1997—I tasted this wine on three occasions and felt it was a very extracted style of
• 1997 that perhaps had been pushed to a point where some of the more
87– undesirable components (high, abrasive tannin) may have been picked up
88+? during the fermentation and *cuvaison*. In any event, there is plenty to admire in the 1997 Gazin, but it is still too early to pinpoint just where this wine might be going. Certainly one of the 1997 *vin de garde* efforts, it is a big, bruising, opaque ruby/purple–colored wine with a *pain grillé*, cherry liqueur, olive, and toasty oak-scented nose and flavors. The tannin level is surprisingly high, particularly for a 1997, and the wine is rich, medium to full bodied, and slightly rustic. It will require 2–3 years of cellaring before it becomes drinkable, and should last for 15 years. If the tannin becomes better integrated during the wine's sojourn in oak, it may merit an outstanding score. Last tasted, 3/98.

1996—A tannic, serious style of Gazin, the deep purple—colored 1996 reveals mod-
•   erately intense aromatics consisting of toast, black fruits, roasted herbs, lico-
89-   rice, and chocolate. Exotic, smoky, rich, medium- to full-bodied flavors
91+   possess powerful tannin, but this wine gives every indication of being loaded
and long-lived. The long finish builds in the mouth, offering copious quantities of black fruit, glycerin, and sweet tannin. However, Pomerol fanatics who
want their wines from this appellation to be immediately drinkable are going
to have to wait a few years for the 1996 Gazin to shed some tannin. Anticipated maturity: 2003–2020. Last tasted, 3/98.

1995—This deep ruby/purple—colored wine has shut down following bottling, and
•   while it hints at some of its exotic grilled herb and meat-like character, the
90+   reluctant nose reveals primarily new oak, smoke, spice, and background
jammy fruit. On the palate, the wine is deep, medium to full bodied, refined,
and except for some noticeably hard tannin in the finish, relatively seamless.
This expansively flavored wine offers plenty of spice, new oak, fruit, and
depth. Anticipated maturity: 2002–2018. Last tasted, 11/97.

1994—This opaque ruby/purple—colored, lavishly oaked wine displays a huge,
•   cedary, cassis, smoky, roasted meat—scented nose, unctuously textured,
90   chewy, thick flavors, and considerable power and richness in the muscular,
moderately tannic finish. This big, impressively structured Pomerol will
require patience. Anticipated maturity: 2003–2018. Last tasted, 1/97.

1993—One of the vintage's finest efforts, this dark-colored wine possesses an impres-
•   sive set of aromatics, including scents of black raspberries, cherries, mocha,
89   and Provençal olives. Deep and dense, with surprising fatness and glycerin
for a 1993, this is a lush, expansively flavored, medium-bodied, pure, rich,
concentrated 1993 that should offer gorgeous drinking for 10–12+ years.
Given the vintage's reputation, this should be one of the more affordable
wines from Bordeaux. Last tasted, 1/97.

1992—Gazin's 1992 is one of the vintage's most noteworthy wines. It displays an
•   opaque deep ruby/purple color and a bold, penetrating, sweet nose of caramel,
89   black cherries, vanillin, and smoke. With ripe, medium- to full-bodied, rich,
concentrated flavors and a succulent texture, this is an impeccably well-made
wine! Approachable now, it should improve for 3–4 years and last for a
decade or more. Gazin has been making a strong comeback over recent years
—readers take note. Bravo! Last tasted, 11/94.

1990—The powerful, rich, well-balanced 1990 Gazin reveals an opaque ruby/purple
•   color and a sweet, youthful nose of black cherries, chocolate, cedar, and
93   toasty oak. Rich, dense, and medium to full bodied, with moderate tannin,
layers of flavor, and that inner core of sweet, jammy fruit that is essential
for a wine's longevity, this complex, harmonious, youthful Gazin possesses
well-integrated tannin and acid. Anticipated maturity: Now–2016. Last
tasted, 11/96.

1989—The lovely, forward 1989 possesses a dark ruby color with no amber at the
•   edge. The big, sweet nose of cherry fruit, cedar, spice, herbs, and caramel is
89   followed by a supple wine with excellent concentration, low acidity, and sweet

tannin in the round, generous finish. The wine is close to full maturity yet promises to drink well for another decade. Last tasted, 11/96.

1988—After years of mediocrity, Gazin has begun to move in the right direction. The
•   turnaround started with the 1988, which is a wonderfully seductive, rich,
87   sweet, broad-flavored, hedonistic wine, with light tannins, a rich, savory
      texture, and a satiny, alcoholic finish. Moreover, who can ignore the big
      bouquet of herbs, mocha, and sweet fruit? Anticipated maturity: Now–2003.
      Last tasted, 1/93.

1986—The 1986, with a lightly vegetal, spicy, plum-like bouquet, seems to slip off
•   the palate, revealing only a trace of tannin and alcohol. Anticipated maturity:
79   Now. Last tasted, 3/90.

1985—The 1985 has adequate ripeness but is somewhat dull, medium bodied, and
•   overall a mediocre, one-dimensional wine. Anticipated maturity: Now. Last
76   tasted, 3/89.

1984—A very marginal wine, the 1984 Gazin is watery, light, and diffuse and should
•   be avoided. Last tasted, 3/88.
64

1982—Since the 1988 vintage, Gazin has been one of the up-and-coming stars of
•   Bordeaux. However, the 1982 was obviously made during an uninspiring
81   period when quality was not the château's highest priority. It exhibits an
      herbal, tealike, spicy, sweet, jammy cherry–scented nose, medium body, some
      dilution, and a round, easygoing style. It will not hold its fruit for more than
      another 4–5 years. This is a pleasant but undistinguished wine that should
      be drunk up. Last tasted, 9/95.

1961—The 1961 Gazin displayed a knockout, caramel/chocolate/coffee–scented
•   nose, medium to full body, sweet, expansive, exotic black cherry–and-
93   fruitcake-like flavors, and a chewy, fleshy, velvety-textured finish. This wine
      has been fully mature for some time, but it reveals no signs of fruit loss or
      color degradation. Anticipated maturity: Now. Last tasted, 12/95.

GOMBAUDE-GUILLOT   VERY GOOD

Classification: None
Location of vineyards: Near Clinet and Guillot
Owner: Mrs. Laval
Address: 3, Les Grands Vignes, 33500 Pomerol
Mailing address: Same as above
Telephone: 33 5 57 51 17 40; telefax: 33 5 57 51 16 89
Visits: By appointment only
Contact: From Monday to Friday, between 9:30 A.M. and 5:30 P.M.

VINEYARDS (red)
Surface area: 19.8 acres
Average age of vines: 35 years

Blend: 70% Merlot, 28% Cabernet Franc, 2% Malbec
Density of plantation: 6,000 vines per hectare
Average yields (over the last 5 years): 42.7 hectoliters per hectare

GRAND VIN (red)
Brand name: Gombaude-Guillot
Appellation: Pomerol
Mean annual production: 25,000–30,000 bottles
Upbringing: Fermentations last 3–4 weeks in temperature-controlled concrete tanks. Care is taken so that the harvest is done when the grapes (skins and seeds) are mature, but with no character of *sur-maturité*. Wines are then transferred to oak barrels, 30% of which are new. This percentage may vary with the vintage, however: for instance, in 1990 100% new oak was used, but 65% was judged enough in 1995. Also, the time the wines spend in barrels varies with each vintage, generally between 12 and 14 months. Wines are transferred to stainless-steel vats after fining. They are never filtered.

SECOND WINE
Brand name: Cadet de Gombaude
Average annual production: Maximum of 6,000 bottles

NOTE: The second wine is produced only when the vintage is too heterogeneous to allow a unique blend.

Evaluation of present classification: The quality equivalent of a Médoc fifth-growth
Plateau of maturity: 5–15 years following the vintage

This has become an intriguing property to follow. I remember tasting the wine in the early eighties and being unimpressed with the range of vintages I saw from the seventies; but a vertical tasting back through 1982 left me with the conclusion that in certain years Gombaude-Guillot can produce a Pomerol of very good quality.

The vineyard comprises three parcels made up of totally different types of soil. The only parcel from the plateau is heavier, dominated by clay and gravel with a great deal of iron in it. A second parcel is primarily sandy soil intermixed with some gravel, and a third parcel consists largely of gravel.

The old vines and relatively low yields that are 30% below those of many of the more prestigious names often result in strikingly rich, concentrated wines. Interestingly, in 1985 Gombaude-Guillot launched a Cuvée Speciale from a selection of wine that represented some of the best lots from their vineyards and aged it in 100% new oak. It was such an enormously successful wine that the château repeated this experiment in 1988 and 1989.

As the following tasting notes evidence, this is not a consistent wine, but when Gombaude-Guillot does everything right, it ranks as one of the top dozen Pomerols of the appellation.

VINTAGES

1990— With an attractive medium ruby color and a pronounced nose of cher-
• ries, smoke, and herbs, the round, exceptionally soft, fleshy 1990 regular
85 cuvée is low in acidity. However, it exhibits fine ripeness and gobs of up-
front, chewy fruit and glycerin. Drink it over the next 5–8 years. Last tasted,
1/93.

1989— The 1989 regular cuvée displays moderate ruby/purple color and an aroma of
• roasted black plums and cassis. In the mouth, it is concentrated and medium
86 bodied, with a silky opulence of fruit seen only in the best examples from this
vintage. Long, but low in acidity, with moderate tannins, this is a smooth
Pomerol. Curiously, I had rated it significantly higher prior to bottling. Anticipated maturity: Now–2005. Last tasted, 1/93.

1989— Cuvée Speciale: Aged in 100% new oak, this wine is richer and packed with
• fruit, although the difference between the two wines is less noticeable in 1989
87 than in prior vintages. Full bodied, sweet, and silky, it will be a Pomerol to
drink over the first 7–10 years of life. Last tasted, 1/93.

1988— The 1988 regular cuvée of Gombaude-Guillot has a ruby color, with a spicy
• bouquet and medium-bodied, adequately concentrated flavors. The finish has
84 some sharp tannins. The overall impression is of a wine with adequate rather
than great depth. Last tasted, 1/93.

1988— Cuvée Speciale: This luxury cuvée, aged in 100% new oak, surprisingly does
• not exhibit as much of a smoky, vanillin character in the nose as one might
89 suspect. Rich and full bodied, with intense aromas and flavors of black
currants, plums, and minerals, this beauty should have a graceful evolution.
Anticipated maturity: Now–2003. Last tasted, 1/93.

1987— This is a light, relatively soft, somewhat diluted, soundly made, but uninter-
• esting Pomerol. Anticipated maturity: Now. Last tasted, 11/90.
78

1985— Deep ruby/purple in color, with an intense bouquet of cassis and other black
• fruits, and rich, with an unctuous texture and gobs of sweet, super-ripe
88 fruit, this expansive, generously endowed wine is already delicious to drink.
Anticipated maturity: Now–2001. Last tasted, 4/91.

1985— Cuvée Speciale: Make no mistake about it, the 1985 Cuvée Speciale rivals
• the great Pomerols such as Lafleur, l'Evangile, l'Eglise-Clinet, and Pétrus. It
93 is still very young, as the opaque, purple/black color suggests. The huge
bouquet of minerals, super-ripe cassis, and smoky new oak is enthralling. In
the mouth, the wine is powerful, exceptionally concentrated, and well balanced, with a finish that must last for well over a minute. There are plenty of
tannins, but they are soft. Although this wine can be drunk now, it is still

undeveloped and needs a good 4–5 years of cellaring. Anticipated maturity: Now–2008. Last tasted, 1/91.

1982—This big, round, generously endowed, chewy-textured wine has reached full
•   maturity, as the amber at the edge suggests. The big nose of grilled nuts,
87   smoke, and super-ripe plums is followed by opulent, alcoholic, heady flavors. This hedonistic wine is ideal for current consumption. Anticipated maturity: Now. Last tasted, 12/90.

LA GRAVE À POMEROL (until the 1992 vintage
LA GRAVE TRIGANT DE BOISSET)   VERY GOOD

Classification: None
Location of vineyards: In the northwestern part of the plateau of Pomerol
Owner: Christian Moueix
Address: 33500 Pomerol
Mailing address: c/o Ets. J.-P. Moueix, 54, quai du Priourat, B.P. 129, 33502 Libourne Cedex
Telephone: 33 5 57 51 78 96; telefax: 33 5 57 51 79 79
Visits: By appointment and for professionals of the wine trade only
Contact: Frédéric Lospied

VINEYARDS (red)
Surface area: 20 acres
Average age of vines: 25 years
Blend: 90% Merlot, 10% Cabernet Franc
Density of plantation: 5,500–6,000 vines per hectare
Average yields (over the last 5 years): 50 hectoliters per hectare
Total average annual production: 3,500 cases

GRAND VIN (red)
Brand name: Château La Grave à Pomerol
Appellation: Pomerol
Mean annual production: 3,500 cases
Upbringing: Fermentations last 20 days, with half the yield in stainless-steel tanks and the other half in concrete vats (temperature-controlled). One-quarter of the yield undergoes malolactics in barrels. Wines are then transferred to oak casks, one-third of which are new (the rest are 2–4 years old), for 18 months aging. They are racked every 3 months, from barrel to barrel, fined, but not filtered.

SECOND WINE
None produced.

Evaluation of present classification: The quality equivalent of a Médoc fifth-growth
Plateau of maturity: 3–12 years following the vintage

La Grave is another of the relatively obscure Pomerol estates that is making better and better wine. Since 1971 the château has been owned by the meticulous and introspective Christian Moueix, who directs the business affairs of his father's firm in Libourne.

La Grave is located just to the east of Route Nationale 89, in the direction of France's truffle capital, Périgueux. It is adjacent to the border of Lalande-de-Pomerol and situated on unusually gravelly, sandy soil, which results in wines that are a little lighter and less powerful than those from the Pomerol plateau.

All the vintages from 1980 on have been successful, and the 1990 and 1982 are classics. Normally La Grave is a wine to drink after 5–6 years of bottle age, although in some vintages it can be cellared for 12–15 years. While not one of the most expensive Pomerols, neither is it one of the bargains of this appellation. However, given the increasing quality exhibited by this wine in recent vintages, this is a property to take more and more seriously.

VINTAGES

1997—A sexy cherry, berry, coffee, roasted herb, and cedary-scented nose is followed
•   by a seductive, charming wine. There are no hard edges to this round,
86–   medium-bodied, nicely concentrated, pure, silky-textured Pomerol. Drink it
88   within 7–8 years of its release. Last tasted, 3/98.

1996—A well-made, smoky, coffee, and cherry-scented wine, the 1996 La Grave
•   exhibits good concentration, nicely integrated acidity and tannin, and a
86–   round, attractive softness that makes it an ideal candidate for consuming in
87   its youth. Anticipated maturity: Now–2007. Last tasted, 3/98.

1992—One of the strongest efforts from this property (previously called La Grave
•   Trigant de Boisset) over recent years, this lovely, charming 1995 reveals a
86   deep ruby color, and plenty of sweet cherry fruit intertwined with high quality,
       spicy new oak. Medium bodied, with excellent concentration and a nicely
       layered, sexy personality, this is a textbook mid-weight Pomerol for drinking
       over the next 10–12 years. Last tasted, 11/97.

1990—The 1990 is the finest La Grave Trigant de Boisset I have tasted. Deep
•   ruby, with a fragrant bouquet of sweet black fruits, toast, and mocha, this
89   voluptuously textured wine gushes with fruit. Deep, juicy, and creamy, it
       makes for a gorgeously soft mouthful of wine. Anticipated maturity: Now–
       2001. Last tasted, 1/93.

1989—The 1989 is more concentrated, alcoholic, and structured than the 1988. The
•   excellent bouquet of spicy, toasty oak, black cherries, and plums is followed
87   by a medium-bodied wine, with a heady alcohol content, plenty of tannin,
       and good concentration. Anticipated maturity: Now–2002. Last tasted, 1/93.

1988—The 1988 boasts an intense, new oak–dominated bouquet, some spicy,
•   medium-bodied, ripe fruit, moderate tannins, sound acidity, and moderate
86   alcohol in the finish. It does not have the ampleness of the 1989, but those
       who like a more restrained, polite style of Pomerol may prefer the 1988.
       Anticipated maturity: Now–2001. Last tasted, 1/93.

1986—The 1986 displays more tannin than is usual, but the overall impression is
  •   one of lightness, delicate, understated fruit, and light to medium body. Antici-
  81   pated maturity: Now. Last tasted, 3/90.

1985—As usual, La Grave Trigant de Boisset's 1985 is an elegant, soft, fruity wine.
  •   Anticipated maturity: Now. Last tasted, 3/90.
  84

1983—A rather big, richly fruity wine for La Grave, the 1983 has a ruby/garnet
  •   color, surprisingly sound acidity for a 1983 Pomerol, a ripe, toasty, plummy
  85   fruitiness, and medium body. Anticipated maturity: Now. Last tasted,
       1/89.

1982—This wine has been fully mature since the late eighties. It offers an attractive,
  •   vegetal, fruity nose of olives, pepper, and mocha-tinged cherry fruit. Soft,
  86   medium bodied, and round, with an easygoing personality, this wine continues
       to drink well, although I see no reason for cellaring it any longer. Last tasted,
       9/95.

LAFLEUR   OUTSTANDING

Classification: None
Location of vineyards: Pomerol, on the plateau
Owner: Marie Geneviève Robin
Address: Château Grand Village, 33240 Mouillac
Mailing address: Same as above
Telephone: 33 5 57 84 44 03; telefax: 33 5 57 84 83 31
Visits: By appointment only
Contact: Sylvie and Jacques Guinaudeau

VINEYARDS (red)
Surface area: 11.1 acres
Average age of vines: Over 30 years
Blend: 50% Merlot, 50% Cabernet Franc
Density of plantation: 5,900 vines per hectare
Average yields (over the last 5 years): 38 hectoliters
Total average annual production: 170 hectoliters

GRAND VIN (red)
Brand name: Château Lafleur
Appellation: Pomerol
Mean annual production: Approximately 1,000 cases
Upbringing: Fermentations and macerations last 15–21 days depending
upon the vintage. Wines are transferred directly into oak barrels for
malolactics, where they remain for 18 months aging. One-third to
one-half of the barrels are new. Wines are fined with fresh egg whites but
not systematically filtered.

SECOND WINE
Brand name: Les Pensées de Lafleur
Average annual production: 250 cases

Evaluation of present classification: The quality equivalent of a Médoc
first-growth
Plateau of maturity: 8–40 years following the vintage

I have always had a personal attachment to this tiny Pomerol vineyard. In the mid-1970s, when I first started tasting the wines of Lafleur, I could find nothing written about them. Yet in my small tasting group we frequently found the wine to be every bit as compelling as Pétrus. I made my first visit to Lafleur in 1978, speaking very little French, and found the two elderly proprietors, the late Thérèse Robin and her sister, Marie, decrepit but utterly charming. The Lafleur château was, and remains today, more of a barn than a winery. Despite the advanced age of these two spinsters, they would ride their bikes out to Le Gay, the official reception center for both Lafleur and Le Gay. They were no doubt amused by my size, referring to me as Monsieur Le Taureau (Bull). I probably did look a bit oversize walking in the tiny *chai*, where the barrels, as well as a bevy of ducks, chickens, and rabbits, were housed. It always amazed me how wines of such great extraction and utterly mind-blowing character could be produced in such filthy conditions.

Only one Robin sister, Marie, remains alive, and she has given over the reins of running Lafleur to her niece and nephew, Sylvie and Jacques Guinaudeau. They took responsibility starting with the 1985 vintage and not only declassified the entire crop of 1987 Lafleur, but at the same time introduced a second wine, Les Pensées de Lafleur. This is rather remarkable given the tiny production of this micro-estate. The cellars remain the same, but they are now devoid of the ducks, chickens, and rabbits, as well as the dung they left behind. Additionally, Lafleur now benefits from 50%–66% new oak casks for each vintage.

Is the wine any better? Certainly Lafleur remains the only wine of the Pomerol appellation that is consistently capable of challenging, and in some cases surpassing, Pétrus. Even Jean-Pierre Moueix once admitted this to me, and I have been fortunate to have had Lafleur and Pétrus side by side enough times to know the former is a wine every bit as extraordinary as Pétrus. In many vintages, from an aromatic point of view, it is more complex than Pétrus, no doubt because of the Cabernet Franc.

Much of the greatness of Lafleur lies in the soil, which is a deep, gravelly bed enriched with iron and some sand but also characterized by extremely important deposits of phosphorus and potassium. Over the years the yields have been tiny, reflecting Lafleur's motto as quoted by the Robin sisters' father: "Quality surpasses quantity."

Old vintages of Lafleur are legendary, but the history of the property has not been without mixed results. The 1970 and 1971 should have been better, and more recently, the 1981 is flawed by the presence of fecal aromas. However, the wine is now being looked over by an oenologist, and even though the old vines (there was no replanting at Lafleur after the freeze of 1956) are having to be grubbed up, the average age is still impressive. Since 1982 (the 1982 and 1983 were made by Christian Moueix and Jean-Claude Berrouet) Lafleur has become less exotic and perhaps more influenced by modern-day oenologists with their obsession with wines that fall within certain technical parameters. Nevertheless, Lafleur, measured by the highest standards of Bordeaux, while now made within proper technical parameters, still remains one of the most distinctive, exotic, and greatest wines—not only from Pomerol, but in the world.

VINTAGES

1997—I liked the 1997 Lafleur more than the 1996. It is one of those rare Lafleurs
• that lucky purchasers will be able to drink at a young age. An impressively
91– saturated dense ruby/purple color is followed by the classic Lafleur aromas
93 —jammy black raspberries, kirsch liqueur, prunes, and minerals. Forward, full bodied, and sexy, with an unctuous texture, and gobs of sweet tannin, this is a luxurious, evolved Lafleur that will provide gorgeous drinking in 2–3 years and will last for two decades. The only other vintage of Lafleur that tasted this evolved and satiny at such a youthful age was the 1983. Last tasted, 3/98.

1996—In spite of being made primarily from Cabernet Franc, with little Merlot in
• the blend, this wine appears to be shaping into form, although it will undoubt-
90– edly require 15–20 years of cellaring. However, if you are looking for a wine
91+ to purchase for your children or grandchildren, read on. The color is a dense purple, and the wine is austere yet classic. The aromatics consist of cherry and black raspberry fruit intermixed with kirsch, minerals, and truffles. The wine is full bodied, ferociously tannic, and superbly concentrated, but the searing tannin is likely to scare off all but the most adventurous tasters. This Lafleur will probably age for 50–60 years. The question is . . . when will it ever be drinkable? My best guess is between 2020–2045. Last tasted, 3/98.

1995—This is another awesome Lafleur, but it is also an amazingly backward, tannic
• monster that will need more cellaring than any Médoc in this vintage. The
93+ wine boasts an opaque black/purple color, as well as a closed but promising nose that represents the essence of blackberry, raspberry, and cherry fruit. Intertwined with those aromas is the tell-tale mineral terroir of Lafleur, full body, blistering dry, astringent tannin, and a layered, weighty feel on the palate. This is the kind of young claret that I couldn't wait to rush out and buy two decades ago, but now I have to be content to admire it and wish I

were twenty years younger. It is formidable, prodigious, and oh, so promising, but I cannot see it being ready to drink before the end of the second decade of the next century! Anticipated maturity: 2020–2050. Last tasted, 11/97.

1994— For readers with 10–15 years of patience, this exceptionally concentrated,
•   massive, tannic, backward, opaque purple–colored Lafleur offers consider-
93+ able promise. The provocative nose of licorice, violets, black raspberry, and truffle-like fruit is followed by a huge, tannic, forbiddingly backward, super-concentrated wine that should be purchased only by those willing to wait until the end of the first decade of the next century. Anticipated maturity: 2008–2030. Last tasted, 1/97.

1993— Exhibiting a dark purple color with an opaque middle, Lafleur's 1993 is
•   structured, tannic, and almost charmless because of its huge power and
90+ structure. The wine offers up hints of gorgeously sweet, black raspberry, kirsch, and truffle aromas (similar to those possessed by l'Evangile), but after that, one has to be content with its unbridled power, medium- to full-bodied, layered richness, and ferocious tannin. This is a backward, dense, yet purely made wine. Anticipated maturity: 2005–2020. Last tasted, 1/97.

1992— Lafleur has fashioned a blockbuster wine in 1992 that must be tasted to be
•   believed. After seeing so many diluted, light, soft wines, I find it hard to
91   believe the level of concentration Lafleur achieved. Lafleur's color is an impressively saturated dark purple/black. The tight nose offers up sweet cassis and jammy black cherry scents intertwined with aromas of Asian spices and minerals. The wine possesses great richness, medium to full body, admirable density, layers of ripe fruit that linger on the palate, considerable tannin, and remarkable length. This would be a great wine in any vintage, but in 1992 it is a remarkable achievement. An amazing wine for the year! Anticipated maturity: 2000–2015. Last tasted, 11/94.

1990— The 1990 Lafleur is equally powerful, muscular, and super-concentrated, but
•   the tannin is riper as well as better integrated, resulting in a phenomenally
97   extracted wine revealing the 1990 vintage's over-ripeness. There are copious amounts of sweet black cherry fruit. My assistant, Pierre Rovani, remarked, "Why does this wine taste so much like Rayas [the renowned Grenache-based Châteauneuf de Pape]?" There is an unreal reality to such a comment, largely because both producers tend to pick their fruit at an over-ripe stage, producing an exotic, compelling wine. Despite its size, the 1990 Lafleur is more developed than the 1989, but it will easily be as long-lived given its massive weight, viscous texture, and profound mouth-feel and finish. It needs 5–10 more years of cellaring and will last for 4 decades. Last tasted, 11/96.

1989— Unfortunately, I have not seen as much of the 1989 Lafleur as I would
•   have liked. In this particular tasting, the wine had closed down and seemed
95+ somewhat muted and subdued when compared with my earlier notes. It is an enormous, full-bodied, tannic, powerful style of wine, with a dark purple color, an earthy, truffle, plum, licorice, and mineral nose, huge fruit and extract, and mouth-searing tannin in the finish. I would not open a bottle for 5–10 years. Anticipated maturity: 2005–2035. Last tasted, 11/96.

1988—A strong candidate for the wine of the vintage, Lafleur's 1988 is still extremely
 •   youthful, requiring another decade of cellaring. The color remains a dense
94   opaque plum, with no signs of lightening at the edge. The reticent but promis-
        ing nose of kirsch, minerals, violets, and Asian spices still needs to be coaxed
        out of the glass. Full bodied, dense, and concentrated, with exceptional power,
        layers of highly extracted fruit, and superb purity, as well as mouth-searing
        tannin, this is a wine for the true connoisseur. Anticipated maturity: 2003–
        2035. Last tasted, 7/97.

1986—One of the few right bank wines in this vintage that can stand up to the
 •   powerful Cabernet Sauvignon–based Médocs, Lafleur's 1986 is a structured,
94+   tannic, backward wine that needs another 5–8 years of cellaring. It possesses
        a jammy black cherry, herb, mineral, earthy nose and dense, rustic levels of
        tannin in its full-bodied power and richness. While it is not fun to drink, it
        sure is impressive. Will I always admire rather than enjoy this wine? Antici-
        pated maturity: 2005–2030. Last tasted, 7/97.

1985—The 1985 Lafleur is a much larger-scaled wine than the 1985 Pétrus. It pos-
 •   sesses a very special bouquet suggesting ripe plums, minerals, violets, and an
96   intensity that comes only from old vines. Deep ruby/purple, with an exceptional
        richness and depth of fruit, full body, and a powerful, long finish, this wine ranks
        with the mammoth-size vintages of Lafleur—1989, 1988, 1986, 1982, 1979,
        1975, and 1964. Anticipated maturity: Now–2015. Last tasted, 1/91.

1984—Certainly a success for the vintage, the 1984 Lafleur has a sweet, ripe nose
 •   and is obviously much lighter on the palate than usual, but I must admit I
84   was surprised by the depth of fruit and length. Anticipated maturity: Now.
        Last tasted, 2/89.

1983—Deep ruby colored, with noteworthy amber at the edge, this is the only Lafleur
 •   from a very fine year that has reached full maturity, at least from the last 2
93   decades. I have had this wine from both regular bottle and magnum, and it is
        an example of Lafleur at its kinkiest and most exotic. The soaring nose of
        jammy kirsch, plum, licorice, and Asian spices is superb. Soft, round, plump,
        medium- to full-bodied flavors coat the palate with considerable glycerin and
        sweet tannin. This open-knit, surprisingly evolved, luscious Lafleur should
        continue to drink well for 10–15 years. Anticipated maturity: Now–2010.
        Last tasted, 11/97.

1982—This wine is finally beginning to live up to my proselytization. Over the last
 •   several years it has begun to reveal its extraordinary richness. The wine's
97   fragrance of quintessential black cherry jam must be smelled to be believed.
        It is completely different from the thick, tannic, colossal 1975 or mammothly
        constituted wines of 1985, 1988, 1989, and 1990. The vintage that comes
        closest to resembling the 1982 is the 1990. The over-ripe, cherry liqueur
        character of the bouquet is unmistakable. The wine possesses a dark ruby
        color and a fabulous, exotic nose of incense combined with cherry jam. Thick,
        alcoholic flavors filled with glycerin and extract border on the surreal. Add a
        dosage of orange marmalade, soy, and juicy black cherry and plum-like fruit,
        and yes, the 1982 Lafleur is at your service. This thick, exotically flavored

wine is almost too intense and idiosyncratic for most tasters. But, wow, what a persuasive case for old-vine Merlot and Cabernet Franc. This wine was actually softer 10 years ago, but it has taken on more grip and tannin with age. I would never hesitate to drink a bottle now, but it will undoubtedly become even better over the next 5–10 years. It should last through the first 2 decades of the next century. Last tasted, 9/95.

1981— Considerable bottle variation seems to be the culprit with the 1981 Lafleur.
● The good examples exhibit a savory, supple, chewy, spicy, velvety, concen-
? trated fruitiness, medium body, and light tannins. The others display an annoying musty, fecal aroma that refuses to dissipate with aeration. Are you a gambler? Last tasted, 3/87.

1979— In the early nineties I began to think that the 1979 Lafleur would be the
● "wine of the vintage," particularly for serious collectors who judge a wine's
98+ quality not only by its potential for longevity, but also by its extraction of flavor and complexity. This wine, so atypical for the vintage, is phenomenally concentrated and thick, as well as massively full bodied and tannic. It is a different style of Lafleur from what emanated from this château in the early and mid-eighties. The 1979 is backward, with a reticent but promising bouquet of minerals, damp earth (truffles?), and super-sweet, rich blackberries and plums. One has to taste it to believe that in this vintage such awesome flavor, body, and lavish quantities of glycerin could be obtained. It remains the only great, potentially legendary, wine from this vintage. Do not touch a bottle before the end of the decade. It should age effortlessly through the first 3 decades of the next millennium. Last tasted, 10/94.

1978— More and more the 1978 Lafleur is looking like one of the two or three finest
● wines of the vintage, along with La Mission-Haut-Brion and Latour. This dark
93 plum/garnet–colored wine exhibits a knockout nose of black cherry fruit intermixed with licorice, minerals, cedar, and spice. Medium to full bodied, with powerful tannin remaining, this highly extracted wine is atypical for the 1978 vintage. It is a weighty, broad-shouldered, muscular, virile 1978 that is just beginning to reveal secondary nuances and complexity. I have always thought this wine could develop along the lines of the 1966, and I am more convinced than ever that it is a clone of that vintage. Anticipated maturity: 2000–2020. Last tasted, 11/97.

1976— Like many Pomerols of this vintage (which was marked by the intense heat
● and drought of that year's summer), Lafleur's 1976 exhibits an over-ripe
78 character. Diffuse in structure, with a flabby, soft texture, the 1976 Lafleur exhibits pleasingly plump and ripe flavors, but the acidity is quite low, and the tannin is fading quickly. Anticipated maturity: Now–probably in serious decline. Last tasted, 9/82.

1975— The 1975 Lafleur possesses a mind-boggling inner core of highly extracted
● fruit, something that was not achieved in such great Lafleurs as 1982, 1985,
100 1988, 1989, and 1990. Still extremely tannic, with an opaque purple/black/ garnet color, the wine exhibits a huge nose of jammy black fruits, earth, minerals, and spice. Massively proportioned, with a boatload of tannin to

shed, this is a wine for the twenty-first century. This monumental wine may behave like some of the great 1928s. If you own large stocks of the 1975 Lafleur, open a bottle and decant it for about 4–6 hours before drinking. However, if you have only a few bottles in your cellar, I recommend holding them until at least the turn of the century. This is a 50–75 year wine from an irregular, perplexing, yet sometimes exhilarating vintage. Last tasted, 12/95.

1971—Fully mature, this wine has an opulent, savory, cedary, spicy, slightly jammy,
• herbal bouquet. Soft, supple, broad flavors display a lot of ripe fruit and little
83 tannin. Anticipated maturity: Now–probably in serious decline. Last tasted, 2/84.

1970—The 1970 Lafleur has always been a muscular, big, full-bodied wine with
• funky, musty cellar aromas. The opaque garnet color is followed by aromas of
88? sweet, smoky, roasted, animal, and herb aromas, combined with damp earth and Asian spices. With an undeniable coarseness and toughness (because of its astringent tannin), this is a huge, immature wine that I am not sure will ever come into complete harmony. Drink it now and over the next 20 years. Last tasted, 6/96.

1966—The 1966 from magnum displays a deep ruby/purple color, with slight amber
• at the rim. It offers the essence of black cherry flavors intertwined with wet
96 stone and cold steel notes, full body, super-concentration, admirable structure, magnificent depth and delineation, massive reserves of fruit, and an amazingly long finish. It is approaching full maturity and should last for 20–25 more years. Last tasted, 10/94.

1964—Still dark colored, with just a slight rim of amber, the 1964 Lafleur is a big, rich,
• full-bodied, intense wine with oodles of extract and body. Still tannic, but begin-
89 ning to open up, this old-style, chewy, powerful wine lacks a little in complexity but delivers quite a mouthful. Anticipated maturity: Now. Last tasted, 6/84.

1962—The last three times I have had this wine it has consistently scored in the low
• 90s. There is a certain rusticity to its tough tannin, but the magnificent
91 bouquet of kirsch, roasted nuts, balsam wood, and earth is compelling. In the mouth, it is a plump, full-bodied, fat, concentrated wine with layers of extract and glycerin. Chewy and remarkably well preserved, this 1962 seems to just get better and better. Anticipated maturity: Now–2015. Last tasted, 12/96.

1961—I had poor luck with the 1961 Lafleur until several years ago. In four recent
• tastings, this wine has been at the upper end of my scale. This particular
98 bottle was extremely young, with an opaque garnet/black color and a powerful nose of black truffles, sweet, over-ripe cherry fruit, and grilled meats. A sensational wine, with huge body, massive extraction, great exuberance, and considerable tannin in the thick, exotic finish, it is not yet close to full maturity. Last tasted, 12/95.

ANCIENT VINTAGES

The 1959 (rated 88 in 12/87) is a ruggedly built, muscular, tough-textured wine that is impressive for its size and weight. But much like the 1964 and 1970, it lacks charm and finesse. It should continue to age well for another 10–15 years. I have always preferred the 1955 (rated 92 in 12/87). It possesses that exotic, mineral, black fruit character so typical of Lafleur, massive weight, an unctuous texture, and plenty of hard tannin still left in the finish.

Perhaps the greatest-kept secret in all of Bordeaux is how spectacular the 1950 vintage was in Pomerol. The 1950 Lafleur (100 points; last tasted 10/94) could easily pass for a 1947 or 1945 wine given its extraordinary level of concentration. The color remains black/purple, and the bouquet offers aromas of cedar, spices, and black fruits. The wine is unbelievably concentrated, massively full and rich, with sweet tannin in the finish. With a viscous, chewy texture, this pure wine could easily last for another 15–20 years. The 1949 Lafleur (96+ points; last tasted 10/94) offers a saturated purple/garnet color followed by a reluctant nose that with coaxing reveals intense, pure, cherry, jammy aromas intermingled with scents of minerals and licorice. Sensationally concentrated, with layers of thick, rich fruit and high tannin, this sweet, remarkably youthful wine is still not fully mature! It will last for another 20–30 years. There are many 1947s that were bottled in Belgium. I have had the 1947 Lafleur Belgian bottling, which ranges from very good to occasionally outstanding. As good as it is, the château bottling, from which this tasting note emanates, can leave you speechless. This is an extraordinarily profound wine that surpasses Pétrus and Cheval Blanc in this vintage, even though they can all be perfect wines. The 1947 Lafleur (100 points; last tasted 10/94) is more developed and forward than the 1949 and 1945. It reveals a thick, port-like color, with slight amber at the edge. The nose offers a smorgasbord of aromas, ranging from caramel to jammy black raspberries and cherries, honeyed nuts, chocolate, and truffles. The wine's unctuousness and viscosity are unequaled in any other dry wine I have tasted. There is neither volatile acidity nor residual sugar present, something that many of the greatest 1947s possess. This wine's richness and freshness are unbelievable. The finish, which lasts more than a minute, coats the mouth with layers of concentrated fruit. There have been many great Lafleurs, but the 1947 is the quintessential expression of this tiny yet marvelous vineyard that was ignored by wine critics for most of this century. To date, it is the only wine that has ever brought me to tears! Similar to the 1947 Lafleur in aromatic complexity and flavor, richness, and textural thickness, the 1945 (100 points; last tasted 10/94) is blacker in color and less evolved and possesses a more classic structural profile than the port-like 1947. The 1945 tastes young yet astonishingly unctuous, rich, and powerful. It will easily last for another 40–50 years. Will the 1975 turn out to be this memorable?

VINTAGES (Les Pensées de Lafleur)

1993—It appears that Lafleur's second wine (500 cases produced) was fashioned
 •   from this micro-estate's softer, more supple cuvées. The 1993 Pensées de
86   Lafleur exhibits impressive color, good ripeness, the exotic, jammy black
      cherry component found in top vintages of Lafleur, and moderate tannin. It is

far more accessible than its bigger sister. This wine can be drunk in 2–3 years and should keep for 10–15. Last tasted, 11/94.

1992—The 1992 second wine of the microscopic estate of Lafleur is dark ruby
• colored, with a sweet nose of black cherries, minerals, and earth. Although
86 the wine is tannic, it exhibits sweet, jammy fruit beneath its structure and toughness. After it sheds some tannin, it should be a good example of this vintage. I find it remarkable as well as admirable that an estate with a production of only 1,500 cases is willing to declassify 500 cases into its second wine to ensure that Lafleur is exceptional. Now that is a commitment to excellence! Last tasted, 11/94.

1991—No Lafleur was produced in 1991. Much of the production was declassified
• into this second wine, Les Pensées de Lafleur. It is easy to understand why.
74 The only positive thing the light, diluted, short, compact 1991 exhibits is some decent cherry fruit. Drink it over the next 4–5 years. Last tasted, 1/94.

1990—With plenty of tannin and a sense of over-ripe, jammy, cherry, kirsch-flavored
• fruit, the 1990 displays considerable power and a fleshy richness. It exhibits
89 surprising individuality, including an exotic, even flamboyant, personality. Anticipated maturity: Now–2002. Last tasted, 1/93.

1989—Can a second wine be this delicious? The unbelievable lengths to which
• the proprietors go in order to eliminate anything less than sublime from
89 their grand vin is evidenced by this 1989 from Lafleur. Amazingly rich, with incredibly deep, dense, cassis, mineral, and exotic flavors, this full-bodied, well-structured, highly concentrated wine should continue to evolve for at least 2 decades. Anticipated maturity: Now–2010. Last tasted, 1/93.

LAFLEUR-GAZIN

Classification: None
Location of vineyards: between Château Gazin and Château Lafleur
Owner: Mrs. Delfour-Borderie (farmer: Ets. J.-P. Moueix)
Address: 33500 Pomerol
Mailing address: c/o Ets. J.-P. Moueix, 54, quai du Priourat, B.P. 129, 33502 Libourne Cedex
Telephone: 33 5 57 51 78 96; telefax: 33 5 57 51 79 79
Visits: By appointment, and for professionals of the wine trade only
Contact: Frédéric Lospied

VINEYARDS (red)
Surface area: 18 acres
Average age of vines: 20 years
Blend: 80% Merlot, 20% Cabernet Franc
Density of plantation: 5,500–6,000 vines per hectare

Average yields (over the last 5 years): 50 hectoliters per hectare
Total average annual production: 3,000 cases

GRAND VIN (red)
Brand name: Château Lafleur-Gazin
Appellation: Pomerol
Mean annual production: 3,000 cases
Upbringing: Fermentations last 18–20 days in non-temperature-
controlled concrete tanks. After malolactics in vats, wines are transferred
to oak barrels, 20% of which are new (the rest are 2–4 years old), for 18
months aging. They are racked every 3 months, from barrel to barrel, and
fined but not filtered.

SECOND WINE
None produced.

Evaluation of present classification: The quality equivalent of a Médoc
Cru Bourgeois
Plateau of maturity: 5–10 years following the vintage

Lafleur-Gazin is situated between the two estates of Gazin and Lafleur. The
wine is produced by the firm of Jean-Pierre Moueix, which farms this property
under a lease arrangement. The wine is supple, round, and straightforward in
style. Given the vineyard's location, it remains perplexing that the wines are
so simple and light.

VINTAGES

1997—The 1997 is one of the finest examples of Lafleur-Gazin I have tasted over
• recent vintages. The exotic, roasted coffee, chocolatey, earthy nose is provoca-
86– tive. In the mouth, the wine is medium to full bodied and lush, with loads of
88 up-front, sexy appeal, good depth, attractive glycerin, and a husky, chunky
finish. Consume it within 7–8 years of its release. Last tasted, 3/98.

1993—A medium dark ruby color is followed by a green, herbal-scented wine with
• hard, austere, compact flavors and a lack of fruit, charm, and finesse. Last
74 tasted, 11/94.

1992—Impressively colored but closed, hard, and austere, this wine displayed far
• more fruit, body, and quality prior to bottling. The wine tastes gutted out,
72 hollow, and tough. Last tasted, 11/94.

1990—The 1990 has gained weight and now offers meaty, soft, fat flavors, rich,
• plummy fruit, and a juicy finish. Anticipated maturity: Now. Last tasted,
85 1/93.

1989—The performance of the 1989 Lafleur-Gazin suggests that the vineyard was
• harvested too early. The attenuated, higher than normal acidity levels and
78 green, hard, unripe tannins are not enjoyable. However, the wine does possess

noticeable alcohol and is otherwise well made. Anticipated maturity: Now–2000. Last tasted, 1/93.

1988—Initially the 1988 was tannic, austere, and lean, lacking both fruit and charac-
  •   ter. However, in the bottle, the wine has come alive, offering much richer
  84   fruit, a sexy, oaky component, and lush texture. Anticipated maturity: Now.
        Last tasted, 1/93.

LAGRANGE

Classification: None
Location of vineyards: Next to the church, on the plateau of Pomerol
Owner: Ets. J.-P. Moueix
Address: 33500 Pomerol
Mailing address: c/o Ets. J.-P. Moueix, 54, quai du Priourat, B.P. 129, 33502 Libourne Cedex
Telephone: 33 5 57 51 78 96; telefax: 33 5 57 51 79 79
Visits: By appointment, and for professionals of the wine trade only
Contact: Frédéric Lospied

VINEYARDS (red)
Surface area: 20 acres
Average age of vines: 28 years
Blend: 95% Merlot, 5% Cabernet Franc
Density of plantation: 5,500–6,000 vines per hectare
Average yields (over the last 5 years): 50 hectoliters per hectare
Total average annual production: 3,000 cases

GRAND VIN (red)
Brand name: Château Lagrange
Appellation: Pomerol
Mean annual production: 3,000 cases
Upbringing: Fermentations last 18–20 days in temperature-controlled concrete tanks. One-third of the yield undergoes malolactics in oak casks, the rest remaining in cement vats, and wines are transferred to oak casks for 18 months aging. Thirty percent of the casks are new, and the rest are up to 4 years old. Wines are racked every 3 months from barrel to barrel and fined but not filtered.

SECOND WINE
None produced.

Evaluation of present classification: The quality equivalent of a Médoc Cru Bourgeois
Plateau of maturity: 5–12 years following the vintage

One rarely sees the wine of Lagrange, another of the properties owned and managed by the firm of Jean-Pierre Moueix. Lagrange is well situated near the plateau of Pomerol, but the vineyard has been recently replanted significantly, with the composition changed to 90% Merlot and 10% Cabernet Franc. The wine tends to be a rather brawny, densely colored Pomerol, with significant power and tannins but not much complexity. Older vintages such as 1970, 1975, and 1978 have all proven to be stubbornly big, brooding, coarse wines that have been slow to develop. This is not a style of wine that I find attractive.

VINTAGES

1997—Surprisingly backward, closed, and hard (atypical for a 1997), the dark ruby–
 •   colored 1997 Lagrange reveals earthy, chocolatey, and berry fruit, good den-
86– sity, and a firm, angular personality. Time will tell whether more charm and
88   fruit emerge. Anticipated maturity: 2002–2009. Last tasted, 3/98.

1995—The 1995 possesses low acidity and a flattering, pure nose of jammy black
 •   cherries, chocolate, underbrush, and wood. With excellent concentration, low
86   acidity, and medium body, this is an attractively ripe, dense Pomerol that
     should drink well for 10–14 years. Last tasted, 11/97.

1994—The 1994 Lagrange exhibits plenty of sweet, plummy, black fruits intertwined
 •   with scents of smoky, toasty new oak. This sweet, medium- to full-bodied,
86   pure, well-made Pomerol should turn out to be a very good Lagrange with a
     more flattering personality than usual. Drink it over the next 10–12 years.
     Last tasted, 3/96.

1993—A medium dark ruby color is followed by spicy, damp, earthy notes in its nose
 •   and tough, medium-bodied, lean flavors. With cellaring, the high tannin level
77   will dominate the wine's fruit. Last tasted, 11/94.

1992—Dark ruby colored, with a spicy, tightly knit nose, Lagrange's 1992 suffers
 •   from a compact personality and considerable tannic toughness. There is good
84+ underlying fruit, resulting in a chunky, robust, coarsely styled wine that
     should be cellared for another 2–3 years. It should keep for a decade,
     assuming it does not dry out. Last tasted, 11/94.

1990—The 1990 has turned out well—in fact, much better than I had thought
 •   possible. Deep ruby colored, with a roasted cherry bouquet and fat, jammy,
86   chunky flavors, this corpulent Pomerol will make delicious drinking over the
     next 5–6 years. Last tasted, 1/93.

1989—The 1989 is typically rough edged, lean, austere, and too tannic for graceful
 •   aging. Anticipated maturity: Now–2000. Last tasted, 1/93.
75

1988—The 1988 is shallow, insipid, and undistinguished. Last tasted, 1/93.
 •
77

1986—This wine has consistently displayed a dull, one-dimensional character with
 •   barely adequate fruit, as well as a mouthful of tannin in the finish. Perhaps I
73   have missed something along the way, but I would opt for drinking it over the

near term because its balance is slightly suspect. Anticipated maturity: Now. Last tasted, 3/90.

1985—The 1985 is an easygoing, fruity, supple wine that offers immediate gratifica-
  • tion. Anticipated maturity: Now. Last tasted, 3/89.
83

LATOUR À POMEROL   EXCELLENT

Classification: None
Owner: S.C. du Château Pétrus
Address: 33500 Pomerol
Mailing address: c/o Ets. J.-P. Moueix, 54, quai du Priourat, B.P. 129, 33502 Libourne Cedex
Telephone: 33 5 57 51 78 96; telefax: 33 5 57 51 79 79
Visits: By appointment, and for professionals of the wine trade only
Contact: Frédéric Lospied

VINEYARDS (red)
Surface area: 20 acres
Average age of vines: 35 years
Blend: 85% Merlot, 15% Cabernet Franc
Density of plantation: 5,500–6,000 vines per hectare
Average yields (over the last 5 years): 40 hectoliters per hectare
Total average annual production: 3,000 cases

GRAND VIN (red)
Brand name: Château Latour à Pomerol
Appellation: Pomerol
Mean annual production: 3,000 cases
Upbringing: Fermentations last about 20 days in temperature-controlled concrete vats. Malolactics occur in vats, too. Wines spend 18 months in oak barrels, 50% of which are new and the balance 1–2 years old. They are racked every 3 months from barrel to barrel, fined but not filtered.

SECOND WINE
None produced.

Evaluation of present classification: The quality equivalent of a Médoc third-growth
Plateau of maturity: 6–20 years following the vintage

Latour à Pomerol produces splendidly dark-colored wine that usually represents a powerful, opulent, fleshy style of Pomerol. The vineyard comprises
two parcels. One is located near the church of Pomerol on a deep, gravelly
bed. The second, and smaller parcel, is located farther west near RN 89 on

sandier, lighter soil. The second parcel is closest to the vineyard owned by Christian Moueix called La Grave à Pomerol.

Latour à Pomerol can be a majestic wine and can often be one of the two or three greatest wines of the appellation in certain vintages. The 1947, 1948, 1950, 1959, 1961, and 1970 offer persuasive evidence that this estate can rival the greatest wines of Bordeaux, but except for the 1982, nothing in 30+ years recalls those legends. While some observers have claimed that Latour à Pomerol comes closest in weight and structure to Pétrus, that would not appear to be the case. This is a wine that, while rich and full, tends to have more in common with other Moueix-controlled properties such as Trotanoy than with Pétrus.

Latour à Pomerol is usually about one-fifth the price of Pétrus and about one-half the price of Trotanoy and Lafleur. For a limited-production Pomerol of such high quality, it remains a relative bargain.

VINTAGES

1997—This dark ruby–colored wine is a more masculine, lean, and tannic Pomerol
•   than I would have expected from such a soft, seductive vintage. The nose
85–   offers up earthy, truffle, and berry fruit scents, and there is good ripeness on
86   the attack, but on the palate, the wine quickly narrows out, becoming austere, reserved, and undistinguished. Anticipated maturity: 2002–2010. Last tasted, 3/98.

1996—A medium- to full-bodied wine with spicy, black cherry fruit, coffee, and toast
•   in the nose, this dark plum–colored 1996 displays good ripeness, moderate
86–   tannin, medium body, and an attractive texture. Although not profound, it is
88   unquestionably very good, and should be relatively accessible in its youth. Anticipated maturity: 2001–2015. Last tasted, 3/98.

1995—The 1995 Latour à Pomerol should develop into an outstanding wine, but it
⁹   was revealing considerable grip and structure following bottling. It possesses
89+   a dark ruby/purple color, as well as a distinctive nose of smoked herbs, black fruits, iron, mulberries, and spice. The wine is generous, ripe, and mouth-filling, with medium to full body, and excellent richness and purity, but the wine's tannic clout and slight bitterness kept it from receiving an outstanding score. Several years in the bottle could result in an excellent, perhaps outstanding Latour à Pomerol. Anticipated maturity: 2004–2020. Last tasted, 11/97.

1994—This wine possesses a deep dark purple color, a pungent, jammy, strawberry,
•   black cherry, weedy tobacco, and spicy nose, attractive fatness and ripeness,
89   medium body, low acidity, and a sweet, long, lusty finish. It is a delicious style of Latour à Pomerol that should drink well for 10–14 years. Last tasted, 1/97.

1993—A brilliant dark purple color and a fine mocha, richly fruity, spicy nose make
•   for a positive first impression. The wine exhibits impressive ripeness, medium
87   body, excellent overall balance, and 12–15 years of drinkability. Although not a blockbuster, it is a well-made, well-balanced, elegant style of Pomerol

with low acidity and plenty of ripe fruit. Anticipated maturity: 1999–2010. Last tasted, 1/97.

1992— This wine is a good example of what a conscientious winemaker should have
•   been attempting to do in a lighter-style vintage like 1992. Rather than aim
86   for power, intensity, structure, and ageability, it seems to me that the best
       strategy was to try to capture the charm and fruit of the vintage. Latour à
       Pomerol has done that, and the result is a seductive, easy to drink, pleasantly
       fruity, soft wine with a berry-, herb-, and coffee-scented nose, good ripeness,
       an attractive mid-palate, and a supple finish. Drink it over the next 4–6
       years. Last tasted, 11/94.

1990— The 1990 is super-ripe, supple, and already delicious. Made in an unctuous,
•   richer, more meaty style than the 1989, it exhibits fine ripeness, a generous
88   fruitiness, and flattering, sweet, plummy, oaky flavors. Anticipated maturity:
       Now–2004. Last tasted, 1/93.

1989— The 1989 Latour à Pomerol possesses a deep ruby/purple color and a full-
•   intensity bouquet of spices, new wood, plums, and cassis. This expansively
87   flavored, seemingly sweet (because of the fruit's ripeness), full-flavored wine
       has considerable tannin in the finish. Anticipated maturity: Now–2015. Last
       tasted, 1/93.

1988— The 1988 Latour à Pomerol exhibits an oaky, soft, fruity, tea, and berry
•   bouquet and rich, ripe, admirably concentrated flavors that display some
87   sweetness and length. This is a luscious style of wine for drinking over the
       next 7–9 years. Last tasted, 1/93.

1986— The 1986 is more burly and tannic than usual, with an excellent deep color,
•   full body, and a cedary, tea, and plum-like bouquet admirably backed up by
87   new oak. Given its tannic clout and power, I would want to cellar this wine
       for at least 3–5 years. Anticipated maturity: Now–2002. Last tasted, 3/90.

1985— I continue to see a resemblance in the rich, full-bodied, concentrated, ripe,
•   and sexy 1985 to the brilliant wine made at this estate in 1970. Full, long,
88   and powerful, this expansively flavored wine has considerable length and
       plenty of tannin and will require some cellaring prior to consumption. Antici-
       pated maturity: Now–2005. Last tasted, 3/89.

1984— This is a firm, tough, unyielding sort of wine that seems to have fruit lurking
•   beneath the tannins. Anticipated maturity: Now. Last tasted, 3/89.
82

1983— A top success for the vintage, the 1983 Latour à Pomerol is among the richest,
•   most powerfully constructed, broodingly opaque, and enormous Pomerols
88   from the 1983 vintage. It has remained big, brawny, ripe, and muscular,
       although the tannins have melted away. The bouquet, filled with scents of
       mocha, chocolate, and plums, is a delight. Anticipated maturity: Now–2005.
       Last tasted, 5/91.

1982— An astounding 50% of the *eight* bottles I have opened from my case of 1982
•   Latour à Pomerol have been corked (badly so). What really infuriates me is
94   that this is a spectacular wine! As gorgeous and rich as it is, it is a far cry
       from the legendary Latour à Pomerols produced in 1961, 1959, 1950, 1948,

and 1947. Fully mature, yet capable of lasting for another decade or more, the non-corked bottles offer a dark ruby/garnet–colored wine, with an intensely fragrant, forceful, spicy, sweet, *pain grillé*, black cherry, mocha, and herb bouquet. Lush, opulent flavors cascade across the palate with no astringency or tartness. It is a plump, fleshy, delicious wine that can be drunk now or held for another decade. I wonder if all the corked bottles from my case are typical of other readers' experience? Last tasted, 9/95.

1981—The 1981 is a fine example of Latour à Pomerol. However, it has subsequently
 • been eclipsed by both the 1982 and 1983 wines. Moderately dark in color for
 85 a 1981, with a dense, ripe, rich, medium-bodied texture on the palate, this well-balanced wine offers a velvety mouthful, but it is less impressive than I originally thought. Anticipated maturity: Now. Last tasted, 3/89.

1979—Precociously fat, supple, and easy to drink, this vintage of Latour à Pomerol
 • seems to have produced an amply endowed, charming, silky wine without
 85 much tannin. It is medium bodied, dark ruby in color, and quite forward. Anticipated maturity: Now. Last tasted, 10/84.

1978—Jammy, soft, ripe, and round, the 1978 Latour à Pomerol is ready to drink.
 • Like many Pomerols of this vintage, I detect a degree of over-ripeness and
 83 shortness in the finish, but nevertheless, this is a pleasant, fruity wine. Anticipated maturity: Now—may be in decline. Last tasted, 2/83.

1976—In 1976 this estate managed to produce a rich, flavorful, spicy, concentrated
 • wine while avoiding the over-ripe character that afflicted so many Pomerol
 86 estates. Lush, silky, creamy, fat, and fruity, this medium-bodied wine is complemented nicely by spicy oak. It has been fully mature for a decade, and no discernible tannins are remaining. Anticipated maturity: Now. Last tasted, 1/89.

1975—In a vintage where a number of Pomerols are superb, the 1975 Latour à
 • Pomerol is inexplicably disappointing. Severe, tannic, hollow, and totally
 67 charmless, this wine lacks fruit, substance, and color. Last tasted, 11/88.

1971—Beginning to fade ever so slightly, this lovely wine peaked in the middle
 • seventies. With some brown at the edges, the 1971 is soft, round, and medium
 82 bodied, with no tannins left. The classy bouquet still exhibits some cedary, spicy fruit, but it fades in the glass. Anticipated maturity: Now—probably in decline. Last tasted, 10/82.

1970—This wine has always offered an opulent, rich, concentrated, glorious mouthful
 • of Pomerol. Although there was considerable amber at the edge, this bottle
 93 exhibited loads of fruit, as well as a sweet, glycerin-dominated mid-section. With a complex, truffle, coffee, mocha, chocolatey, black cherry nose, this exotic, fat, ripe Latour à Pomerol remains one of the vintage's great successes. However, do not push your luck; it requires drinking. Last tasted, 6/96.

1966—The 1966 is an atypically ripe, rich, dense wine that, in style, seems an
 • anomaly in this vintage that produced lean, elegant, restrained wines. Still
 87 quite dark in color with an orange rim, the wine has a bouquet of ripe, deep fruit and oak, as well as a tarry, truffle-scented aroma. Powerful, full bodied, and rich, this wine should be drunk up. Anticipated maturity: Now. Last tasted, 4/81.

1961—Although the 1947 Cheval Blanc is widely considered to be the "wine of the
  •   century" among collectors, the 1961 Latour à Pomerol also merits a share of
 100   the title. Giving points to a wine such as this makes one think of Shake-
       speare's reflection that "comparisons are odious." To put it mildly, this wine
       is "off the charts." If I had only one Bordeaux to drink, the 1961 Latour à
       Pomerol would have to be at the top of my list (along with the 1947 Lafleur).
       Given its phenomenal richness and amazing precision and balance, it can
       bring tears to one's eyes. Still a saturated dark purple color with no signs of
       amber, orange, or rust, the nose offers extraordinarily rich, intense aromas of
       jammy plums, black currants, licorice, and truffles. Port-like, with remarkable
       viscosity and thickness, as well as a finish that lasts for more than a minute,
       this wine is in a class by itself. Even greater than the 1961 Pétrus and 1961
       Latour (two perfect wines), it is phenomenal. Given its youthfulness (it is the
       least evolved wine of the vintage), it has the potential to last for another 20–
       30 years. Last tasted, 12/96.

ANCIENT VINTAGES

The 1959 Latour à Pomerol (98 points; last tasted 12/95) exhibited a huge,
coffee, melted caramel, sweet jammy red and black currant/cherry–scented
nose and flavors. Unctuous, thick, and oh, so decadently rich, this blockbuster
Pomerol is fully mature and needs to be drunk up, an enticing proposition for
the fortunate few who still possess this wine.

   Two other prodigious vintages for Latour à Pomerol are 1950 and 1948.
The 1950 (98 points; last tasted 3/97) is still a well-preserved blockbuster.
Viscous, unbelievably rich and full bodied, with oodles of fruit, extract, and
glycerin, it is capable of lasting another 2 decades. The 1950 Pomerols are
clones of 1947! The 1948 (96 points; last tasted 3/96) came out first in a
blind tasting of 1948s in Bordeaux. It was exotic, perfumed, very rich, and
full, with abundant coffee/mocha/kirsch fruit displayed in a fully mature
personality. What a sleeper this wine must be!

   I have been blessed to have tasted the 1947 Latour à Pomerol several
times. Several times I have rated it a perfect 100, including my last tasting
in December 1995. It is a slightly older clone of the candidate for the wine of
the century—the 1961 Latour à Pomerol. The 1947 exhibited an extraordinary opaque purple color, with only some lightening at the edge. This exotic,
mammoth, seductive, awesomely concentrated wine goes and on in the
mouth. It is reminiscent of a cross between the 1947 Cheval Blanc and the
1947 Pétrus. Sweet, dense, and mind-boggling, what else can be said about
something so perfect and thrilling. Akin to eating candy, it should drink well
for another 20 years.

MOULINET

Classification: None
Location of vineyards: Pomerol
Owner: G.F.A. du Domaine Moulinet (directed by Armand Moueix)
Address: Château Moulinet, 33500 Pomerol
Mailing address: c/o Château Fonplégade, 333330 St.-Emilion
Telephone: 33 5 57 74 43 11; telefax: 33 5 57 74 44 67
Visits: No visits allowed

VINEYARDS (red)
Surface area: 44.5 acres
Average age of vines: 25 years
Blend: 60% Merlot, 30% Cabernet Sauvignon, 10% Cabernet Franc
Density of plantation: 5,400 vines per hectare
Average yields (over the last 5 years): 50 hectoliters per hectare
Total average annual production: 990 hectoliters

GRAND VIN (red)
Brand name: Château Moulinet
Appellation: Pomerol
Mean annual production: 600 hectoliters
Upbringing: Fermentations last approximately 3 weeks, with half the
yield in concrete vats and the other half in stainless-steel vats. Wines are
then aged for 18 months in oak barrels, renewed by a third at each
vintage. They are fined but not filtered.

SECOND WINE
Brand name: Clos Sainte-Anne
Average annual production: 390 hectoliters

Evaluation of present classification: The quality equivalent of a Médoc
Cru Bourgeois
Plateau of maturity: 3–8 years following the vintage

One of Pomerol's largest estates, Moulinet is located in the northwest section
of the Pomerol appellation near the large estate of de Sales. The soil in this
area renders lighter-style Pomerols, and Moulinet is certainly one of the
lightest. Unusually light in color and faintly perfumed, Moulinet is made in a
very commercial style by the owners, the Armand Moueix family. At best, in
vintages such as 1989 and 1982, it can be round, fruity, and elegant, but
frequently the wine is bland and innocuous, although clean and consistently
made.

VINTAGES

1996—Although this is a simple, straightforward Pomerol, aside from the wine's low
　•　acidity, it does not reveal any evidence of dilution. It exhibits a deep ruby
83–　color, plenty of sweet fruit in its attractive, moderately intense nose, round,
　85　silky-textured flavors, and light tannin. It is a Pomerol to drink over the next
　　　5–7 years. Last tasted, 11/97.

1990—An easygoing, lighter-styled, medium-bodied wine, Moulinet's 1990 exhibits
　•　soft tannins, noticeable alcohol, and little concentration or grip. At its best it
83　is charming and pleasant. Drink it over the next 5–6 years. Last tasted, 1/93.

1989—The 1989 is about as good a wine as Moulinet is capable of producing. It is a
　•　big, jammy, ripe, hedonistic wine lacking complexity but offering straight-
85　forward, chunky, luscious fruit, medium body, a soft texture, and an alcoholic
　　　finish. Anticipated maturity: Now. Last tasted, 1/93.

1988—Moulinet's 1988 will last longer than the 1989 but will never provide as much
　•　pleasure given its undernourished, lean, compact, short flavors. Last tasted,
79　1/93.

1986—The 1986 is austere and lean for a Pomerol. It should be drunk over the next
　•　5–6 years given its weight and character. Anticipated maturity: Now. Last
78　tasted, 3/90.

1985—The 1985 is an above-average-quality wine with a soft, somewhat obvious com-
　•　mercial fruitiness and medium body but agreeable, ripe, easy to appreciate, and
82　easy to understand flavors. Anticipated maturity: Now. Last tasted, 3/90.

NENIN　　　　　　　　　　　　　　　EXCELLENT SINCE 1997

Classification: No classification in Pomerol
Location of vineyards: Pomerol, Catusseau
Owner: S.C.A. du Château Nenin
Manager: Jean-Hubert Delon
Address: 33500 Pomerol
Mailing address: Same as above
Telephone: 33 5 57 51 00 01; telefax: 33 5 57 51 77 47
Visits: By appointment only, between 9 A.M. and 11 A.M., and 2 P.M. and
4:30 P.M.
Contact: Lionel Bares

VINEYARDS (red)
Surface area: 61.75 acres
Average age of vines: 28 years
Blend: 75% Merlot, 25% Cabernet Franc
Density of plantation: 6,000 vines per hectare

GRAND VIN (red)
Brand name: Château Nenin
Appellation: Pomerol

Upbringing: Not yet defined, but one can presume they will be done much in the same way as at Léoville-Las Cases and will respect very high standards. The wines will definitely be fined with fresh egg whites, and it appears they should stay 18 months in oak barrels, 30% of which are new (for the 1996 vintage).

SECOND WINE
Fugue de Nenin

Evaluation of present classification: The quality equivalent of a Médoc Cru Bourgeois . . . until 1997
Plateau of maturity: 5–15 years following the vintage

This is a historic estate of Pomerol, owned by the Despujol family between 1847 and 1997, when the property was sold to Michel and Hubert Delon, proprietors of Léoville-Las Cases. Obviously great things are anticipated. Nenin has a loyal following of wine enthusiasts, but I have never been able to quite figure out why. I was certainly taken by a bottle of their 1947 I tasted in 1983, but aside from that splendid wine, as well as an excellent 1975, I have always found Nenin to be good but unfortunately somewhat coarse and rustic.

Traditionally Nenin tends to be a firm, hard, chewy wine. Since 1976 the property has not performed well, turning out wines that have lacked intensity, character, and complexity. Were the yields too high? Did the decision to employ a mechanical harvester starting in 1982 negatively affect quality? To their credit, a serious effort has been made to bring Nenin out of their slump. The estate had the wisdom to bring in the brilliant Libourne oenologist Michel Rolland, who insisted that more new oak be used and that the sanitary conditions be improved. Yet Nenin continues to be machine harvested, and despite the presence of Rolland, recent vintages have been uninspiring. This will all change under the perfectionist regime of Jean-Hubert and Michel Delon.

VINTAGES

1997—
•
87–
89

This is the first vintage of Nenin produced under the new owners, the powerful father and son team of Michel and Jean-Hubert Delon. They are investing a significant fortune in resurrecting this famed vineyard from the throes of mediocrity. An entire drainage system is being installed in the vineyard, in addition to other large-scaled expenditures, all designed to take Nenin to the top of Pomerol's qualitative hierarchy. I do not doubt the Delons' ability to do just that. One-third of the harvest was relegated to the second wine, which will be called Fugue de Nenin. The 1997 Nenin is the finest wine from this estate over recent vintages, but I suspect it offers only a glimpse of the quality level that will ultimately emerge. A blend of 81.5% Merlot and 18.5%

Cabernet Franc, the wine possesses a deep ruby/purple color followed by a sexy, black cherry, mocha, and plum-scented nose, medium body, excellent ripeness and purity, soft, well-integrated tannin, and a moderately long finish. It is fleshy, yet surprisingly well-delineated for a Pomerol (the Médoc influence?). This wine should be at its best between 2001 and 2012. Last tasted, 3/98.

1996—This medium ruby–colored, thin, light-bodied wine reveals the adverse af-
•   fects of too much rain before and during the harvest. There is some fruit, but
76–   the wine is weak in comparison with other recent efforts. Drink it over the
78   next 5–7 years. Last tasted, 11/97.

1995—The 1995 exhibits a healthy, medium dark ruby color, plenty of sweet, jammy
•   cherry/plum–like fruit in the nose, medium body, low acidity, and a loosely
86   knit but attractively smooth texture and finish. It will require drinking within
       its first 5–7 years of life. Last tasted, 11/97.

1994—The excellent 1994 is the finest Nenin produced in 20 years. The dark ruby
•   color is accompanied by a forward, soft, supple wine with fine ripeness, sweet
87   tannin, and the caressing silkiness provided by Merlot fruit. The wine will be
       easy to drink when released, and it will last for 7–8 years. Last tasted, 3/96.

1993—The 1993 Nenin displays a healthy dark ruby/purple color, a sweet nose of
•   black raspberry and cherry fruit, medium body, and firm tannin in the finish.
86?   One sample I tasted displayed an element of musty wood, but the other
       examples were pure, healthy, ripe, and potentially very good. As with many
       1993s, the Nenin will benefit from several years of cellaring and will age for
       10–15 years. Last tasted, 11/94.

1990—The 1990, which exhibits surprisingly good color, is a wine with attractive
•   mineral, floral, and black fruit aromas, medium body, moderate tannins, and
84   a short, tough-textured finish. Anticipated maturity: Now–2001. Last tasted,
       1/93.

1989—The 1989 is frightfully light and simple for the vintage, resembling a generic
•   Bordeaux rather than one of the better-known estates of Pomerol. It possesses
78   soft tannins, a bit of fruitiness, and an innocuous character. Anticipated
       maturity: Now. Last tasted, 4/91.

1988—The 1988 is similar to the 1989, only more herbaceous, with an intrusive
•   mustiness that is cause for concern. Anticipated maturity: Now–2000. Last
76   tasted, 4/91.

1986—The 1986 is lighter than the 1985, with more tannin, but it is still a loosely
•   knit Pomerol for near-term drinking. Anticipated maturity: Now. Last tasted,
83   3/90.

1985—The 1985 displays good fruit, richness, and fine winemaking. It is not a
•   blockbuster Pomerol, but rather a charming, supple, fruity, medium-bodied
84   wine with an attractive, open-knit personality. Anticipated maturity: Now.
       Last tasted, 3/89.

1984—Medium ruby, with a sugary, overly chaptalized nose, this wine is soft, light,
•   but agreeable. Anticipated maturity: Now. Last tasted, 3/88.
75

1982—The 1982 was produced during a difficult period for Nenin (the wines are
 •   significantly better now), and the result is a light-bodied, soft, diluted wine
 76   already displaying signs of cracking up and drying out. The light to medium
      ruby color possesses considerable amber. The nose offers old, musty cellar
      aromas followed by a coarse, light-bodied wine with little depth. Drink it up.
      Last tasted, 9/95.

PETIT-VILLAGE   EXCELLENT

Classification: None
Location of vineyards: Pomerol
Owner: AXA Millésimes
Address: 33500 Pomerol
Mailing address: c/o Châteaux et Associés, 33250 Pauillac
Telephone: 33 5 56 73 24 20; telefax: 33 5 56 59 26 42
Visits: By appointment only
Contact: Stéphanie Destruhaut, telephone 33 5 56 59 66 12 and telefax
33 5 56 59 24 63

VINEYARDS (red)
Surface area: 27.2 acres
Average age of vines: 35 years
Blend: 80% Merlot, 10% Cabernet Sauvignon, 10% Cabernet Franc
Density of plantation: 7,500 vines per hectare
Average yields (over the last 5 years): 45 hectoliters per hectare
Total average annual production: 4,500 cases

GRAND VIN (red)
Brand name: Château Petit-Village
Appellation: Pomerol
Mean annual production: 4,500 cases
Upbringing: Fermentations and macerations last 22–35 days depending
upon the vintage, in temperature-controlled concrete vats. Wines undergo
malolactics in new oak barrels and are aged for 12–18 months before
bottling. They are racked every 3 months, fined with fresh egg whites,
and lightly filtered.

SECOND WINE
None produced.

Evaluation of present classification: The quality equivalent of a Médoc
fifth-growth
Plateau of maturity: 5–15 years following the vintage

Petit-Village is a Pomerol estate on the move. In 1971, when Bruno Prats, also the dynamic owner of the famous Médoc estate of Cos d'Estournel, took over responsibility for the making of the wine, the quality increased dramatically. Petit-Village had the benefit of significant capital investment, the care of a dedicated owner, and the state-of-the-art technology necessary for producing wine. The result was a succession of wines that ranged in quality from good to exceptional. In the late eighties Prats sold Petit-Village to an insurance conglomerate that installed Jean-Michel Cazes and his brilliant winemaking team, led by Daniel Llose, from Lynch-Bages as administrators.

The style of Petit-Village emphasizes the toasty, smoky character of new oak barrels, a fat, supple, black currant fruitiness, and impeccably clean winemaking and handling. Recent vintages have the ability to age for 10–15 years, although they are fully ready to drink by age 5 or 6. Older vintages (prior to 1982) have generally proven to be a disappointment, so wine enthusiasts are well advised to restrict their purchases to vintages since 1978.

It can be argued strongly that Petit-Village has joined the top hierarchy of Pomerol estates and now ranks as one of the top dozen wines of the appellation. Certainly the vineyard is superbly situated. Bordered by Vieux-Château-Certan and Certan de May on the north, La Conseillante on the east, and Beauregard on the south, the vineyard has plenty of gravel as well as an iron-rich subsoil intermixed with deposits of clay. The high percentage of Merlot insures a rich, voluptuous wine in years when the Merlot reaches full maturity and yields are reasonable. Petit-Village is a Pomerol to buy, as the price has not kept pace with its rejuvenated quality level.

VINTAGES

1997—This wine is almost devoid of acidity, giving it a round, excessively soft, *facile*
•   style. With jammy plum and berry fruit intermixed with herbs, *pain grillé*,
85–   and spice, this is a sexy, luscious wine, but I would not recommend much
87   cellaring. Drink it over the next 5–6 years for its undeniably up-front appeal. Last tasted, 3/98.

1996—Sample variation was not so severe that I could not get a good read on this
•   oaky, obvious, commercially styled wine. The color is deep ruby/garnet, and,
83–   in addition to plenty of oak, the aromatics consist of smoke and jammy berry
86   fruit intermixed with vanillin and chocolate. This medium-bodied, soft, round, richly fruity Pomerol is meant for near-term drinking. Anticipated maturity: Now–2005. Last tasted, 3/98.

1995—The 1995 is exhibiting more structure and definition than it did in cask. The
•   wine has an evolved dark garnet/ruby color, sweet, smoky, herb, and cherry
86   perfume, and fat, round, generously endowed, straightforward but satisfying flavors. This is a seductive, hedonistic, plump style of Pomerol that will offer uncritical drinking for the next 5–8 years. Last tasted, 11/97.

1994—Medium dark ruby colored, with a straightforward, earthy, spicy, curranty, and
•   cherry nose, this dull, hard wine lacks intensity, ripeness, and length. Drink
81   it over the next 6–7 years. Last tasted, 1/97.

1993—Dark ruby colored, with a vegetal, herbal nose, this thin, emaciated wine is
•   undistinguished. Drink it over the next 5–6 years. Last tasted, 1/97.
78

1992—The medium ruby colored 1992 reveals a soft, herbal, slightly oaky nose that
•   lacks fruit. Some black cherry flavors are apparent in the mouth, but the
79   wine's overall character is of straightforward, simple fruit wrapped in a me-
      dium-bodied, unfocused format. It should be drunk over the next 2–3 years.
      Last tasted, 11/94.

1991—The light ruby–colored 1991 offers a muted bouquet of herbal notes inter-
•   twined with scents of coffee, new oak, and berries. The wine has a decent
74   attack, but the primary impression is one of softness and herbal fruit. The
      flavors evaporate quickly, revealing a thin, short finish. Drink it over the next
      several years. Last tasted, 1/94.

1990—The 1990 is an in-your-face, ostentatious, super-delicious wine. This rich,
•   oaky, smoky, alcoholic, lusciously rich, hedonistic wine makes for a wonderful
90   drink. Drink this voluptuous, opulently textured, decadently smooth, ripe
      Pomerol over the next 8–12 years. Last tasted, 1/93.

1989—The 1989's sweet, round, in-your-face, obvious style is also delicious. Its
•   huge, chocolate, plum, and sweet oak bouquet roars from the glass. Expan-
88   sive, fat, hedonistic flavors coat the palate with plump, ripe fruit. A glaring
      lack of acidity and structure dictates that this generous wine is for consuming
      over the next 5–7 years. Anticipated maturity: Now. Last tasted, 1/93.

1988—The 1988 will not be a long-lived Petit-Village. Prospective purchasers
•   should consider the fact that it will probably have to be drunk within its first
92   decade of life. But oh, what pleasure it will provide! There is no doubting the
      sumptuous, seductive character of this super-concentrated yet velvety 1988.
      Its dark ruby/purple color suggests ripeness and extract. The huge aroma of
      exotic spices, bacon fat, jammy plums, and smoky, toasty new oak is a
      complete turn-on. This heady, concentrated, splendidly extracted Pom-
      erol is all velvet and suppleness. Anticipated maturity: Now–2000. Last
      tasted, 1/93.

1987—Oh, how delicious the 1987 Pomerols turned out to be. Consumers and
•   restaurants looking for immediately drinkable Pomerols would be well ad-
85   vised to reconsider the best 1987s. This soft, spicy, oaky, plum-scented wine
      has surprisingly good concentration, a round, satiny-smooth texture, and a
      heady, alcoholic, toasty finish. Drink it over the next 4–6 years. Anticipated
      maturity: Now. Last tasted, 2/91.

1986—Intense aromas of smoky new oak, herbs, and black fruits are immediately
•   enthralling. In the mouth, the wine is medium bodied and moderately con-
87   centrated, with soft tannins and perhaps more structure than other recent
      vintages of Petit-Village. Anticipated maturity: Now–2000. Last tasted,
      3/90.

1985 — This opulent, fully mature, fragrant, deliciously rich, soft wine lacks backbone
•   and grip but offers gobs of spicy, fat fruit that seduces the taster. There is a
89   wonderful, even explosive finish to this wine, without a rough edge to be
       found. Anticipated maturity: Now. Last tasted, 3/90.

1983 — Quite supple, fat, and richly fruity, this full-bodied, dark ruby/garnet–colored
•   wine is redolent of blackberries and toasty oak. On the palate, the wine is
87   precocious, sweet, ripe, fleshy, and delicious. Anticipated maturity: Now–
       2000. Last tasted, 7/88.

1982 — I began drinking this wine on a regular basis in the mid-eighties, as I could
•   not resist its dramatic, ostentatious display of roasted herbs, mocha, black
93   cherries, and smoky new oak scents and flavors. The wine has consistently
       been opulent, thick, juicy, and jammy. What's interesting is how much delin-
       eation and class the 1982 Petit-Village has begun to develop, although I do
       not see any reason for further aging. The wine displays a dark garnet color,
       with considerable amber at the edge. Its knockout nose is followed by corpu-
       lent, fat, ripe flavors exhibiting oodles of jammy fruit. Extremely low in
       acidity, this lush, chunky wine offers a gorgeous mouthful of thick, fleshy
       Merlot. If wine were a candy, Petit-Village would taste like a hypothetical
       blend of a Milky Way and Reese's Peanut Butter Cup. It should be drunk up.
       Last tasted, 9/95.

1981 — Definitely lighter and less concentrated than the powerful 1982 and deeply
•   fruity 1983, the 1981 Petit-Village does manifest a precocious, soft, ripe, fat,
85   Merlot fruitiness, ripe, round tannins, and a long, voluptuous finish. Antici-
       pated maturity: Now. Last tasted, 3/87.

1979 — The 1979 Petit-Village does not have the concentration of the 1981, 1982,
•   and 1983 but offers a ripe, moderately intense fruitiness, medium body, a
84   spicy, smoky bouquet, and a pleasant finish. Anticipated maturity: Now. Last
       tasted, 2/83.

1978 — Medium ruby, with a great deal of amber/brown at the edge, this wine has a
•   spicy, slightly herbaceous, oaky bouquet. The 1978 Petit-Village exhibits sup-
83   ple, moderately concentrated, fruity, berrylike, herbaceous flavors, light tan-
       nins, and a soft, round finish. Anticipated maturity: Now. Last tasted, 2/89.

PÉTRUS   OUTSTANDING

Classification: None
Location of vineyards: On the highest part of the plateau of Pomerol
Owner: S.C. du Château Pétrus
Address: 33500 Pomerol
Mailing address: c/o Ets. J.-P. Moueix, 54, quai du Priourat, B.P. 129,
33502 Libourne Cedex
Telephone: 33 5 57 51 78 96; telefax: 33 5 57 51 79 79
Visits: By appointment and for professionals of the wine trade only
Contact: Frédéric Lospied

VINEYARDS (red)
Surface area: 28.4 acres
Average age of vines: 40 years
Blend: 95% Merlot, 5% Cabernet Franc
Density of plantation: 5,500–6,000 vines per hectare
Average yields (over the last 5 years): 35 hectoliters per hectare
Total average annual production: 3,000 cases

GRAND VIN (red)
Brand name: Pétrus
Appellation: Pomerol
Mean annual production: 3,000 cases
Upbringing: Fermentations last 20–24 days in temperature-controlled
concrete tanks. Eighty percent of the yield undergoes malolactics in
tanks, 20% in new oak barrels. Wines are aged for 20 months in new oak
barrels, racked every 3 months from barrel to barrel, fined with egg
whites, and bottled unfiltered.

SECOND WINE
None produced.

Evaluation of present classification: The quality equivalent of a Médoc
first-growth
Plateau of maturity: 10–30 years following the vintage

The most celebrated wine of Pomerol, Pétrus has, during the last two decades, become one of Bordeaux's most renowned expensive red wines. Situated on a buttonhole of clay in the middle of Pomerol's plateau, the tiny 28.4-acre vineyard renders wines that are treated as well and as carefully as any wines produced on earth. After proprietor Christian Moueix makes his selection, most vintages of Pétrus turn out to be 100% pure Merlot.

There have been a tremendous number of legendary Pétrus vintages, which no doubt has caused prices to soar into the stratosphere. The 1921, 1929, 1945, 1947, 1948, 1950, 1961, 1964, 1970, 1971, 1975, 1982, 1989, 1990, 1994, and 1995 are among the most monumental wines I have ever tasted. Yet as Pétrus has become deified by much of the world's wine press, one must ask, particularly in view of this property's track record from 1976 on, "Is Pétrus as great today as it once was?" There is no doubt that Pétrus slumped a bit in vintages such as 1986, 1983, 1981, 1979, 1978, and 1976, but since 1989 Pétrus has been in top form, producing a succession of brilliant wines.

VINTAGES

1997—Only 2,500 cases (as opposed to 4,500 in a high quality, abundant year) of
 •   Pétrus were produced in 1997. The wine boasts an opaque ruby/purple color,
92–   as well as a knockout nose of sweet *pain grillé*, jammy cherries, plums, and
94   black raspberry scents. In the mouth, it is full bodied, with surprisingly high
       tannin, a sweet, opulently textured, unctuous mid-palate, and a structured,
       but overall forward finish. One of the most concentrated and complex wines
       of the vintage, it is a candidate for two decades of cellaring. The 1997 is hard
       to compare with any other Pétrus vintage. It is obviously far better than the
       wines made during the early and mid-eighties (the 1982 being the prominent
       exception), as well as more forward than the 1994, 1995, and 1996 Pétrus.
       Although I never tasted it at a young age, the 1997 may be reminiscent of the
       gorgeous 1967, which remains in dazzling shape (I had a superb magnum on
       December 31, 1997) despite the fact it comes from a light vintage that
       produced quickly maturing wines. For readers who like to keep records of
       such things, the Pétrus vineyard was harvested on three separate days, Sep-
       tember 11, 17 (the biggest haul), and 23. Some of the vines were harvested
       grape by grape rather than bunch by bunch because of the irregular ripening
       that afflicted nearly every estate in 1997. Last tasted, 3/98.

1996—Despite all the pessimism that emerged from proprietor Christian Moueix,
 •   this has turned out to be an exceptional effort. The wine possesses a dense,
91–   opaque purple color, a ripe, mulberry, cedar, and coffee-scented nose, and a
93   dense, powerful, medium- to full-bodied, tannic personality with plenty of
       spice, glycerin, and length. It will require time in the bottle. Pétrus's average
       production in a high quality vintage is approximately 4,500 cases, but due to
       Moueix's ruthless selection process, only 1,800 cases of 1996 Pétrus were
       produced. Anticipated maturity: 2006–2025. Last tasted, 3/98.

1995—It is interesting how this wine continues to evolve. Unquestionably one of the
 •   vintage's superstars, the 1995 Pétrus is taking on a personality similar to the
96+   extraordinarily backward, muscular 1975. This is not a Pétrus that can be
       approached in its youth (i.e., the perfect duo of 1989 and 1990). The wine
       exhibits an opaque ruby/purple color, followed by a knockout nose of *pain
       grillé*, jammy black fruits, and roasted coffee. On the palate, it possesses
       teeth-staining extract levels, massive body, and rich, sweet black fruits but-
       tressed by powerful, noticeable tannin. A formidably endowed wine with
       layers of extract, this is a huge, tannic, monstrous-sized Pétrus that will
       require a minimum of 10 years of cellaring. Forget all the nonsense about
       Merlot producing sweet, soft, ready to drink wines, because low-yielding old
       Merlot vines made in the way of Pétrus and other top Pomerols frequently
       possess as much aging potential as any great Cabernet Sauvignon–based wine
       in the world. Look for the 1995 Pétrus to last for 50+ years. Anticipated
       maturity: 2007–2050. Last tasted, 11/97.

1994—Opaque purple/black in color, with a sweet vanilla, *pain grillé*, jammy cherry
 •   and cassis nose, this full-bodied, densely packed wine reveals layers of flavor
93+   and an inner core of sweetness with huge quantities of glycerin and depth. A

tannic, classic style of Pétrus, with immense body, great purity, and a backward finish, this wine requires a decade of cellaring. Anticipated maturity: 2006–2035. Last tasted, 1/97.

1993—   A candidate for the most concentrated wine of the vintage, this 1993 exhibits
•   a saturated purple/plum color and a sweet nose of black fruits, Asian spices,
92+   and vanilla. Huge and formidably rich, this powerful, dense, super-pure wine is a *tour de force* in winemaking. For a vintage not known for wines of this immense richness and length, this brawny, splendidly endowed Pétrus possesses low acidity and high tannin, suggesting that 8–10 years of cellaring are required. This should be a 30-year wine, as well as the vintage's longest-lived effort. Very impressive! Last tasted, 1/97.

1992—   The 1992 Pétrus is clearly one of the two candidates for the "wine of the
•   vintage." The normal production of 4,500 cases was severely reduced to only
90+   2,600 cases, resulting in an atypically concentrated, powerful, rich wine with a dark, saturated ruby/purple color and a tight but promising nose of sweet black cherry fruit, vanillin, caramel, and herb-tinged mocha notes. Concentrated and powerful, with superb density of fruit and richness, as well as wonderful sweetness to its tannin, this is a brilliant effort for the vintage. The wine requires 3–5 years of cellaring and should keep for 15–20+.

Interestingly, the Pétrus vineyard, along with that of its sibling, Trotanoy, was covered with black plastic in early September 1992 to trap most of the rain rather than allowing it to saturate the vineyard's soil and dilute the grapes. It was a strategy that obviously paid off. Last tasted, 11/94.

1990—   A phenomenally rich, well-endowed wine, the 1990 Pétrus has been magical
•   from the first time I tasted it in cask. The color is a dense, jammy plum/
100   purple. The wine possesses a knockout nose of black fruits intertwined with aromas of toasty new oak, caramel, and flowers. Massively thick and full bodied, with slightly lower acidity and sweeter tannin than its older sibling the 1989, the 1990 is an extraordinarily rich, seamless wine with layers of flavor, and a finish that lasts for nearly 45 seconds. Although it is remarkably accessible because of its voluptuous texture, this wine has not begun to develop secondary nuances. It should hit its peak in 10–15 years and last for 3 decades. Anticipated maturity: 2006–2035. Last tasted, 6/98.

1989—   Multimillionaire collectors will have fun comparing the 1989 and 1990 Pé-
•   trus. The 1989 has a slightly more saturated color and seems more tightly
100   knit both aromatically and on the palate. However, this is splitting hairs, as this is another stunningly opulent, rich, full-bodied, amazingly concentrated, exotic, flamboyant Pétrus that remains remarkably youthful and in need of 7–8 more years of bottle age. Additionally, the tannins are slightly more elevated, at least from a tactile impression. However, the 1989 looks to be another 30-year wine, with extraordinary equilibrium between all of its component parts. An amazing effort! Last tasted, 6/98.

1988—   The 1988 Pétrus is reassuringly outstanding, but it is not a prodigious
•   Pétrus. The healthy dark ruby/purple color is followed by a young, back-
91   ward wine with high tannin levels, medium body, and an inner core of

sweet, ripe fruit. It needs another 7–10 years of cellaring. Last tasted, 12/95.

1987—Given the past performance of Pétrus in vintages such as 1980 and 1984, I
  •   would not be surprised to see the rating of the 1987 go up 3 or 4 points in 5–
  87   6 years. This is one of the most backward and full-bodied wines of the
         vintage, with a tremendous amount of tannic clout yet excellent underlying
         power and body. The problem is that it is impossibly closed, almost impene-
         trable, suggesting that my score may be entirely too conservative. If you are a
         millionaire who wants to buy wine for a child born in 1987, this one will still
         be in reasonable condition by the time he or she turns 21. Anticipated
         maturity: Now–2010. Last tasted, 11/90.

1986—The more I tasted this wine, the more I felt it left a lot to be desired. The
  •   wine has developed an herbaceous tea, smoky, cherry nose with new oak
  87   lurking in the background. The wine, which has lost its baby fat, sags a bit in
         the middle and reveals a Médoc-like austerity and tannic structure atypical
         for a Pomerol. It is closer to medium than full body and appears to be going
         through an awkward stage. Will it come around or continue to lose fruit?
         Anticipated maturity: Now–2010. Last tasted, 2/97.

1985—This wine was splendid from cask, but it was bottled during a period where
  •   Pétrus was probably fined and filtered entirely too much (since the late
  88   eighties, Pétrus is no longer filtered). The wine comes across as herbaceous,
         with medium body, good but uninspiring concentration, and a distinct weedy,
         cherry, berry fruitiness. The color is a diffuse ruby, with considerable amber
         at the edge. I would opt for drinking this wine over the next decade, or better
         yet . . . sell it! Anticipated maturity: Now–2010. Last tasted, 2/97.

1984—The 1984 Pétrus has turned out to be amazingly good. Deep in color, with an
  •   intense, jammy, herbaceous bouquet, medium to full body, fine length, and
  87   plenty of tannin, this wine needs 2–3 years to mature but will keep for 10–
         12 years. It is very impressive for the vintage. Anticipated maturity: Now.
         Last tasted, 11/90.

1983—The fully mature 1983 Pétrus (even from double magnums) is a weedy,
  •   herbaceous, vegetal-scented wine with plenty of sweet, somewhat disjointed
  87?   fruit flavors, medium to full body, and copious quantities of glycerin and
         alcohol that are not entirely balanced by fruit. It is just not as harmonious or
         well balanced as it should be. Drink it over the next 5–10 years. Last tasted,
         12/95.

1982—The 1982 Pétrus, while never quite living up to my predictions from cask (I
  •   thought it to be a perfect wine), is still a colossal Pétrus, exhibiting a back-
  98   ward, sweet, expansive nose of ripe fruit, Provençal herbs, chocolate, and
         spice. Full bodied, tannic, and super-concentrated, this wine requires another
         5–8 years of cellaring. It should keep for 25–30+ years. Last tasted, 6/98.

1981—I remember how thrilling the 1981 Pétrus was from cask, but it has never
  •   performed as well from bottle. I have continued to downgrade it. In this
  86   tasting, the wine exhibited an understated, light, washed-out personality, with
         vegetal cherry/coffee–flavored fruit in the nose intermingled with scents of

spicy oak. Tart, lean, and austere, this is a Médoc-like wine without any of the Pétrus sweetness, chewiness, or unctuosity. This must be one of the most overrated wines of the past 2 decades. As there was virtually no sediment in this 16-year-old wine, I wonder if it was excessively fined and/or filtered? Anticipated maturity: 2000–2015. Last tasted, 12/95.

1980—The 1980 Pétrus turned in a surprisingly strong performance. A roasted herb,
•   melted road tar, and sweet, jammy-scented nose is followed by a rich, me-
89   dium- to full-bodied wine with considerable length. It appears to have become more impressive with age. Could this wine really be superior to the 1981 and 1979? It is fully mature, so drink it over the next decade. Last tasted, 12/95.

1979—I remember how stunning the 1979 Pétrus was from cask, but it has never
•   lived up to its early potential. Even from an Imperial, the 1979 Pétrus is a
86   lean, compact, tannic, hard, austere wine lacking the richness and charm of the vintage's top Pomerols. The color was a healthy medium ruby. While the wine does not possess the vegetal overtones of the 1978, it leaves a great deal to be desired. Anticipated maturity: Now–2010. Last tasted, 12/95.

1978—I have never been a fan of the 1978 Pétrus, but even I was ready to give it
•   the benefit of doubt and be seduced when it was served out of an Imperial.
83   The wine revealed a medium ruby color, followed by an herb, underripe tomato, vegetal nose, medium body, and average flavor concentration and length. It is neither distinguished nor Pomerol-like. Anticipated maturity: Now–2006. Last tasted, 12/95.

1976—The 1976 Pétrus has been fully mature since it was released. The wine has
•   always possessed intense aromas of over-ripe tomatoes, roasted vegetables,
88   and red and black fruits touched by sweet toasty oak. It continues to be a pleasing, fat style of Pétrus, without the body, weight, and depth of a great year. It needs to be drunk up. Last tasted, 12/95.

1975—The 1975 Pétrus reveals a youthful, rustic, brutally powerful style, with an
•   opaque garnet/ruby/purple color and an emerging nose of over-ripe black
98+   cherries, mocha/chocolate, and truffles. Extremely full-bodied, ferociously tannic, but awesomely concentrated, the 1975 Pétrus can be drunk, provided readers have a penchant for slightly uncivilized wines. This behemoth Pétrus (the last made in this style) is at least a decade away from full maturity. It is potentially a 50-year wine, with exquisite concentration and intensity. Last tasted, 6/98.

1973—The wine of the vintage, this is the best Pétrus for immediate consumption
•   from those wines produced in the seventies. Given the prolific yield in 1973
87   and diluted quality of many wines, the Pétrus is sensationally concentrated, rich, supple, fat, and so, so flavorful. Friends tell me that it is still a delicious wine. Anticipated maturity: Now. Last tasted, 12/84.

1971—This is a sensational Pétrus that has drunk well since the mid-1970s. Plum/
•   garnet in color, with noticeable orange at the rim, the chocolate, mocha,
95   sweet, fruit-scented bouquet is followed by a rich, velvety, full-bodied wine with layers of silky fruit. The 1971 must surely be the wine of the vintage. Light to moderate tannins and high alcohol will continue to preserve this

plump, unctuous wine for another decade. This is Pétrus at its most seductive. Anticipated maturity: Now–2005. Last tasted, 6/98.

1970—The dark garnet, rust-rimmed 1970 Pétrus has developed magnificently over
  •   the last 4–5 years. Tight and reserved early in life, it has blossomed into a
 98+   true blockbuster. This massive, highly extracted, full-bodied, jammy, thick, unctuously textured wine possesses a huge, spice, tobacco, black cherry, mocha nose. It is a real turn-on. The wine is fully mature, but it has at least 20 years of life remaining. A spectacular Pétrus, it is now superior to the 1971, which outperformed it for nearly 2 decades. Owners of this wine have a true nectar in their cellars. Anticipated maturity: Now–2025. Last tasted, 6/96.

1967—In this vintage that produced so many lightweight wines, only the stablemate
  •   of Pétrus, Trotanoy, can compete with the great Pétrus. Fully mature, with
 92   good dark ruby color and minimal browning, this chunky, fleshy, warm, and generous wine has plenty of ripe Merlot fruit, a viscous, weighty texture, and fast-fading tannin. A lovely Pétrus, it is best drunk over the next decade. I recently drank a bottle of this wine with my wife to celebrate my fiftieth birthday, and it remains a beautiful, savory, complex, intense wine with a seamless texture. Anticipated maturity: Now–2005. Last tasted, 5/98 (from a magnum).

1966—Excellent, but even more highly regarded elsewhere than by me, the 1966
  •   Pétrus has a cedar, herbaceous, sweet, fruity bouquet and is full bodied, with
 89   very good viscous, ripe, berry flavors. A big, dense, somewhat coarse wine that seems just a trifle out of synch, the 1966 Pétrus has plenty of tannin, alcohol, and flavor, but they have never fully meshed. Anticipated maturity: Now–2002. Last tasted, 6/91.

1964—Deep, dark ruby/garnet colored, with a hint of orange and rust at the edge,
  •   the 1964 Pétrus offers a huge, smoky, roasted bouquet of jammy fruit, coffee,
 97   and mocha. This huge, massively endowed wine is packed with alcohol, glycerin, and high tannin. There is stupendous extraction of fruit and amazing length. The only criticism is that it is perhaps too big and robust for its own good. Lucky owners of well-stored bottles are advised to cellar it for a few more years. As they say, it's a tough job, but someone's got to do it! Anticipated maturity: Now–2025. Last tasted, 11/95.

1962—The fully mature 1962 is reminiscent of a Médoc, with its minty, chocolatey,
  •   herbal, cedary nose, medium-bodied, well-proportioned flavors, and struc-
 91   tured personality. The wine still possesses a healthy dark ruby color, with only slight amber at the edge. Although not that powerful or opulent, it is an outstanding example of Pétrus made in a more graceful, elegant manner. In a blind tasting I would never have picked it out as a Pomerol. Last tasted, 12/95.

1961—The fully mature 1961 Pétrus possesses a port-like richness (reminiscent of
  •   the 1947 Pétrus and 1947 Cheval Blanc). The color revealed considerable
100   amber and garnet, but the wine is crammed with viscous, thick, over-ripe black cherry, mocha-tinged fruit flavors. Extremely full bodied, with huge

amounts of glycerin and alcohol, this unctuously textured, thick wine makes for an awesome mouthful. Imagine a Reese's Peanut Butter Cup laced with layers of coffee and cherries and encased in a shell of Valrhona chocolate! Anticipated maturity: Now–2010. Last tasted, 6/98.

ANCIENT VINTAGES

The 1959 (rated 93 in December 1995) was unctuous, sweet, gloriously fruity, thick, and jammy, with gobs of glycerin, full body, and a viscous, long, heady finish. Fully mature, but revealing considerable intensity and life, this wine will drink well for another 10–15 years. It was the extraordinary 1950 Pétrus (99 points; last tasted 6/98), along with the 1950 Lafleur, first served to me years ago by Jean-Pierre Moueix, that made me realize how spectacular this vintage must have been in Pomerol. The wine is still a young, mammothly constituted Pétrus that is less evolved than more recent knockout vintages such as 1961. Massive and rich, with spectacular color saturation and the sweet, unctuous texture Pétrus obtains in ripe years, this wine will last for another 20–30 years.

While variable, the 1949 (95 points; last tasted 10/94) has always been a huge, thick, chewy, immense wine without the unctuosity and port-like quality of the 1947 or 1950. The first time I tasted it a decade ago it seemed to be chunky and one-dimensional but enormously rich. Since then the wine has begun to display the huge, exotic, fleshiness of Pétrus, as well as marvelously pure, plum, black cherry, mocha, and coffee-flavored fruit. It is developing well and remains remarkably youthful for a 45-year-old wine. The 1948 (95 points; last tasted 11/97) is another one of those vintages that was largely ignored by the press. Shrewd consumers would be smart to take a look at well-stored bottles of 1948s that might appear in the marketplace. In the past I have reported on some of the other great 1948s, such as Vieux-Château-Certan, La Mission-Haut-Brion, and Cheval Blanc, but the 1948 Pétrus has fooled me completely in blind tastings. The nose of cedar, leather, herbs, and cassis suggested to me that this was a first-growth Pauillac. The color is still dense, with only a moderate orange hue at the edge. The wine is rich, more austere and linear than usual, but full bodied, with considerable flavor and a spicy, moderately tannic finish. It has peaked but is clearly capable of lasting another 10–15 years. A word of caution: Some bottles possess excessive (even for this epoch) volatile acidity. The 1947 Pétrus (100 points; last tasted 6/98) is the most decadent "wine of the century." While not as port-like as the 1947 Cheval Blanc, it is a massive, unctuously textured, viscous wine with amazing power, richness, and sweet fruit. The nose explodes from the glass, offering jammy fruit, smoke, and buttery caramel scents. The wine's viscosity is reminiscent of 10 W-40 motor oil. It is so sweet, thick, and rich, one suspects a spoon could stand upright. The wine is loaded with dream-like quantities of fruit, as well as high alcohol, but there is no noticeable tannin. While drinkable now, given its amazing fruit extract and high levels of glycerin and alcohol, it is capable of lasting 2 more decades. While the 1947 Pétrus is a big, juicy, succulent, fruity wine, the 1945 (98+ points; last tasted 10/94) remains a backward, tannic colossus needing another 5–10 years of cellaring. The color reveals more purple hues than the 1947, and the nose offers aromas of black fruits, licorice, truffles, and smoked meat. Massively constituted, with formidably high tannin and extract levels, this sleeping giant may evolve into another perfect example of Pétrus.

The 1929 Pétrus (rated 100 in September 1995) displays a deep ruby/garnet color with some amber/orange at the edge. A huge, thick wine with extraordinary aromas of coffee, mocha, black cherries, herbs, and cedar, this unctuously textured, thick, tannic, massively concentrated wine was remarkably intact. It could have easily been mistaken for a 30–35-year-old wine. When I drank it in September 1995, the 1921 Pétrus (100 points) was, to state it mildly, out of this universe! The opaque color displayed considerable amber at the edge, but the blockbuster nose of black raspberries, freshly brewed coffee, and mocha/toffee–like candy was followed by one of the sweetest, most opulent, thick, juicy wines I have ever tasted. Extraordinarily rich and opulent, with interesting cedar notes to the succulent flavors, this huge, unbelievably concentrated wine could have been mistaken for the 1950 or 1947. In December 1996 I tasted what was believed to be a magnum of the 1900 Pétrus found in a private cellar in St.-Emilion. It was excellent rather than exceptional (I rated it 89), still revealing evidence of sweet cherry and blackberry fruit.

NOTE: Potential purchasers of Pétrus should be aware of the numerous examples of fraudulent bottles that exist in the marketplace. The most sought after vintages—1990, 1989, 1982, 1970, 1961, and 1947—are the most usual suspects. Provenance of any bottle purchased must be guaranteed.

LE PIN   OUTSTANDING

Classification: None
Location of vineyards: Pomerol, Lieu-dit Les Grands Champs
Owner: G.F.A. du Château du Pin (Thienpont family)
Address: 33500 Pomerol
Mailing address: Hof te Cttebeke, 9680 Etikhove, Belgium
Telephone: 33 5 57 51 33 99; telefax: 32 5 55 31 09 66
Visits: By appointment only
Contact: Jacques Thienpont

VINEYARDS (red)
Surface area: 4.94 acres
Average age of vines: 32 years
Blend: 92% Merlot, 8% Cabernet Franc
Density of plantation: 6,000 vines per hectare
Average yields (over the last 5 years): 30–37 hectoliters per hectare
Total average annual production: 600–700 cases

GRAND VIN (red)
Brand name: Château Le Pin
Appellation: Pomerol
Mean annual production: 600–700 cases
Upbringing: Fermentations and macerations are generally short, lasting about 15 days, and are done in stainless-steel tanks. Temperatures reach 32–36 degrees centigrade maximum and are manually controlled. Wines are transferred directly to oak barrels for malolactics and 14–18 months aging. *Assemblage* is done fairly early, and wines are racked every 3 months from barrel to barrel. They are fined with fresh egg whites but are not filtered.

SECOND WINE
None produced.

Evaluation of present classification: The quality equivalent of a Médoc first-growth
Plateau of maturity: 4–12 years following the vintage

The Thienpont family, who owns the neighboring and well-known estate Vieux-Château-Certan, acquired the miniature Le Pin vineyard, located in the heart of the Pomerol plateau, in 1979. Previously it had been owned by Madame Laubie, whose family acquired Le Pin in 1924. By their own admission they are trying to make a Pétrus-like wine of great richness and majesty. The first vintages had Pomerol enthusiasts jumping with glee, as this looks to be a splendidly rich, but noticeably oaky, big-styled Pomerol. It is not too early to say that Le Pin is one of the great wines of Pomerol, as well as the appellation's most exotic and expensive!

Much of the gaudy character of Le Pin is probably explained by the fact that it is one of only a handful of Bordeaux estates to actually conduct the malolactic fermentation of the wine in new oak casks. This is a labor-intensive procedure and can be done only by estates that have relatively small productions, where the wine can be monitored constantly. However, I believe it is this technique that gives Le Pin its huge, smoky, and exotically scented bouquet. Whatever the secret, no doubt the iron-enriched, gravelly soil on this part of the Pomerol plateau (which I have been told has the highest elevation of any vineyard) has helped to create a cult following for the microscopic quantities of Le Pin.

If Le Pin is to be criticized at all, it is because the wine may not fare well with extended cellaring. I have my reservations about its aging potential, but there is no denying that for sumptuous, complex drinking within the first 15 years of the vintage, there is no wine made in Pomerol, or even in Bordeaux —except for perhaps the decadently styled Haut-Marbuzet from St.-Estèphe —that rivals Le Pin for pure joy and hedonistic appeal.

VINTAGES

1997—Le Pin's evolved 1997 displays complex aromatics consisting of roasted cof-
•   fee, smoke, Provençal herbs, sweet kirsch liqueur, and black cherry fruit. In
90– the mouth, the wine is round, with a velvety texture, low acidity, and excellent
92   concentration and length. It is a succulent, juicy, captivating style of wine to
     consume during its first 10–11 years of life. Last tasted, 3/98.

1996—Only one-third of the harvest made it into the 1996 Le Pin, so this vintage
•   will be even more impossible to find than usual. The wine exhibits an even
92– denser, more saturated ruby/purple color than the 1995, as well as an exotic,
94   unformed but flamboyant vanillin, *pain grillé*, smoke, and jammy black
     cherry-scented nose. Ripe, dense, and atypically fleshy for a 1996 Pomerol,
     this is a sexy, medium-bodied, concentrated wine that should firm up be-
     fore bottling and age nicely. Anticipated maturity: 2000–2015. Last tasted,
     3/98.

1995—A dense ruby–colored Le Pin, the 1995 offers up aromas of lead pencil,
•   roasted nuts, smoke, spice, fruitcake, and black cherries intermixed with
93+ white chocolate. Luscious and full bodied, with low acidity, but plenty of grip
     and tannin in the finish, this wine, with its abundant cola, kirsch, and black
     raspberry flavors, is revealing far more structure since bottling than it did in
     cask. It appears to be every bit as structured and tannic as the 1996. The
     1995 Le Pin will take a few years to come around. Anticipated maturity:
     2002–2018. Last tasted, 11/97.

1994—Compared with its older sibling, the 1993, the 1994 Le Pin is a more reserved,
•   less flamboyant and ostentatious wine. It reveals a healthy dark ruby/purple
91+ color, spicy, sweet oak, and a silky, opulent entry, but it is a more structured,
     concentrated, medium- to full-bodied Le Pin with layers of fruit, moderate
     tannin, and a long, rich, jammy finish. Once again, new oak, outstanding
     purity, and a luscious mouth-feel account for the impressive showing of this
     wine in blind tastings. Last tasted, 1/97.

1993—The 1993 reveals the evolved dark plum/garnet color of Le Pin, as well as an
•   exotic, kinky, oaky, herb, coffee, jammy, black cherry nose. The exaggerated
90   aromatics are followed by a not surprisingly decadent, delicious, low-acid,
     medium-bodied wine crammed with fruit. Those of us who can remember as
     children gorging ourselves on lavishly rich banana splits, hot fudge sundaes,

and the like will no doubt appreciate that in wine terms, this is what Le Pin offers. Anticipated maturity: Now–2010. Last tasted, 1/97.

1992— This wine unquestionably possesses an excessive amount of toasty new oak
•   for its fragile, delicate constitution. The wine displays medium to dark ruby
82?   color, an aggressively woody, slightly smoky, herbal nose, and medium-
bodied, black cherry–like flavors that are insufficient to stand up to the
veneer of wood. Low in acidity, slightly diluted, and full of cosmetic smoke,
vanillin, and wood, it should be consumed over the next 5–6 years. Given the
frightfully high price asked for the 500+ cases of Le Pin (usually an exotic as
well as brilliant wine), this is a vintage when the proprietor should have
declassified the wine. Last tasted, 11/94.

1990— This is among the most profound Le Pins made to date. The wine exhibits a
•   dense, dark ruby/plum color and a spectacular, hedonistic aromatic profile
98   consisting of exotic spices, jammy kirsch, and other black fruits intermixed
with lavish quantities of *pain grillé*. On the palate, the wine is a velvety-
textured fruit bomb, with layers of concentration, fabulous ripeness, copious
glycerin, and well-integrated sweet tannin. It is a decadently rich, voluptuously textured, full-bodied wine that is impossible to resist, even though it
is still an infant in terms of development. Anticipated maturity: Now–2012.
Last tasted, 12/96.

1989— The 1989's dark ruby/purple color may have slightly more saturation than the
•   1990. The wine reveals a sweet, roasted herb, coconut, and jammy black
96   currant nose, with plenty of smoky new oak. Full bodied, with massive concentration, huge layers of glycerin, and more noticeable tannin than is found
in the 1990, this is a fabulous and fascinating wine, as well as one of
extraordinary singularity. It is unquestionably a compelling wine. But is it
worth the $4,000–$6,000 a bottle that top vintages of Le Pin were fetching at
auctions in late 1997? Anticipated maturity: 1999–2012. Last tasted, 12/96.

1988— This wine has developed nicely in the bottle. The color is a deep ruby with
•   purple nuances. The aggressive oakiness has melted away to reveal plenty of
92   *pain grillé* and sweet, rich black cherries, black currants, and a touch of
prunes. Chocolatey and rich, this medium- to full-bodied, super-concentrated
Le Pin possesses more structure and tannin than is noticeable in many
vintages. It is still a beautifully plump, hedonistic wine. Anticipated maturity:
2000–2010. Last tasted, 11/97.

1987— A big, exotic, perfumed, smoky, oaky bouquet is at first forceful and unre-
•   strained. However, as the wine sits in the glass, the ripe, red fruit character
88   emerges and is followed by a wonderfully lush, flattering, precocious wine
that should be drunk over the next 4–5 years. It is absolutely delicious—
another notable success for the 1987 vintage in Pomerol. Anticipated maturity: Now. Last tasted, 11/90.

1986— The 1986 Le Pin is a less flattering and opulent wine than the unctuous,
•   lavishly rich fleshpot of a wine produced in 1985, but it is no ugly duckling.
91   Its extraordinary nose of smoky oak and plummy fruit is followed by a wine
that is very concentrated and powerful, with the highest level of tannins

produced by this vineyard since the first vintage was conceived a decade ago. It will not provide the up-front, precocious charm that the 1985, 1983, and 1982 have done, but for those with patience, the 1986 is sure to be an attention getter in any tasting. Anticipated maturity: Now–2008. Last tasted, 11/90.

1985— This wine went through an unusual stage where it seemed disjointed, too
  •   oaky, and light, but that has all changed over the last 1–2 years. The wine is
  93   now a deep plum color, with some lightening at the edge. The nose soars from the glass, offering up an enticing fragrance of smoked herbs, sweet, jammy, curranty fruit, and toasty oak. In the mouth, caramel, toffee, and mocha blend with jammy cherry fruit to offer an unctuously textured, thick, satiny smooth wine that is impossible to resist. Anticipated maturity: Now–2008. Last tasted, 12/96.

1984— This must be one of the finest examples of the 1984 vintage. The sweet, oaky,
  •   herb, coffee, chocolatey aroma is a real turn-on. In the mouth, this round,
  87   opulent, shockingly ripe (particularly for the vintage) wine is loaded with fruit and finishes with a velvety, spicy taste. Anticipated maturity: Now. Last tasted, 11/90.

1983— The 1983 Le Pin offers a huge, soaring bouquet of smoky oak, spices, and
  •   sweet fruits. This splendidly opulent, voluptuously textured wine reveals
  98   the gorgeous sweetness and ripeness of fruit so much a hallmark of this estate. The 1983 Le Pin has low acidity, gobs of glycerin, superb extraction of fruit, and a sensational finish. It appeared lighter in its youth, with less aromatic and flavor dimension. Now that it has reached its plateau of maturity, it is one of my two or three favorite examples of this exotically styled, kinky wine. Drink it over the next 7–8 years. Last tasted, 10/94.

1982— This wine is off the charts and continues to provide a level of exotic drinking
  •   and unbridled opulence that must be tasted to be believed. The wine pos-
  100 sesses a spectacularly intense, penetrating fragrance of jammy red and black fruits, caramel, cocoa, soy, and vanilla. Extremely rich and thick, with layers of concentrated fruit, this sweet, expansive, preposterously concentrated and decadent wine is more delicious at present than the 1982 Pichon-Lalande. It also costs about $2,000 per bottle—if it can be found! It is as thrilling a wine as I have ever tasted. How much longer will it last? Given the wine's healthy color and extraordinary extract and balance, 10–15 years of further cellaring is not impossible—assuming anyone can resist its magnetic appeal. Last tasted, 9/95.

1981— The 1981 Le Pin has not lost any of its toasty new oak character. It offers a
  •   medium ruby color and some herbaceous, sweet, black cherry notes. Medium
  89   bodied, elegant, soft, and fully mature, it tastes very good rather than exceptional. Last tasted, 12/95.

NOTE: Le Pin is another luxury wine that has become the darling of criminals specializing in the production of phony bottles. In particular, the 1982 is a favorite of counterfeiters.

PLINCE

Classification: None
Location of vineyards: Next to Château Nenin and opposite Château La Pointe
Owner: G.F.A. du Château Plince
Address: 33500 Libourne
Mailing address: Same as above
Telephone: 33 5 57 51 20 24; telefax: 33 5 57 51 59 62
Visits: By appointment only
Contact: Michel Moreau

VINEYARDS (red)
Surface area: 20.6 acres (currently under vine)
Average age of vines: 30 years
Blend: 68% Merlot, 24% Cabernet Franc, 8% Cabernet Sauvignon
Density of plantation: 5,500 vines per hectare
Average yields (over the last 5 years): 53 hectoliters per hectare
Total average annual production: 440 hectoliters

GRAND VIN (red)
Brand name: Château Plince
Appellation: Pomerol
Mean annual production: 440 hectoliters
Upbringing: Fermentations last 3–4 weeks in temperature-controlled concrete tanks. Wines are transferred, after malolactics, to oak casks, 20% of which are new, for 15 months aging. They are fined and sometimes filtered, but only if necessary.

SECOND WINE
None produced.

Evaluation of present classification: The quality equivalent of a Médoc Cru Bourgeois
Plateau of maturity: 5–10 years following the vintage

Plince is a solid Pomerol, fairly rich, hefty, spicy, deep, and rarely complex, but usually very satisfying. The Moreau family, also owners of Clos l'Eglise, own this property, but the commercialization is controlled by the Libourne firm of Jean-Pierre Moueix.

I have found Plince to be a consistently sound, well-made wine. Though it may never have the potential to be great, it seems to make the best of its situation. It is a well-vinified wine in a big, chunky style that seems capable of aging for 8–10 years.

VINTAGES

1996—This is a monolithic but dense, dark ruby/purple–colored wine that is not
•   terribly expressive, but it does offer a corpulent, solid, medium-bodied
84–   mouthful of sweet, uncomplicated, plum and cherry fruit. It should be drunk
86   over the next 5–8 years. Last tasted, 11/97.

1993—This wine displays good color and density, but the tannin level dominates the
•   fruit. The wine's overall personality is one-dimensional and chunky. It should
80   last for 6–7 years. Last tasted, 11/94.

1992—I appreciated the uncomplicated robustness of this wine from cask, but now
•   that it has been bottled it has lost much of its charm and fruit. The wine is
76   dry, hard, and lean, with tough tannin and an old, stale, herb/black cherry–
      scented nose. Drink it over the next 2–4 years. Last tasted, 11/94.

1990—Straightforward, chunky, chewy fruit is offered in the medium-bodied, uncom-
•   plicated, monolithic 1990. With low acidity, this fat wine is too simple to
82   merit higher marks. Anticipated maturity: Now. Last tasted, 1/93.

1989—The 1989 reveals the super-ripe plum and black fruit character of the vintage.
•   It is a surprisingly intense and extracted wine, with a good amount of tannin
85   in the finish and an alcohol level of 13%–13.5%. It is one of the most
      impressive wines I have tasted from this vineyard. Anticipated maturity:
      Now–2000. Last tasted, 1/93.

1988—The 1988 Plince comes across as sinewy and charmless. However, because
•   of its high tannin level, it will age decently, lasting through the first 4–5 years
80   of the next century. Last tasted, 1/93.

1986—The 1986 Plince is surprisingly forward for the vintage, with a medium-
•   bodied, ripe, plummy fruitiness, adequate complexity, and a pleasant, yet
82   unspectacular finish. Anticipated maturity: Now. Last tasted, 3/90.

1985—The 1985 is a very ripe, succulent, plump wine with a fat, full-bodied texture,
•   low acidity, low tannins, and a tasty finish. Anticipated maturity: Now. Last
84   tasted, 3/89.

LA POINTE

Classification: None
Location of vineyards: Pomerol
Owner: Bernard d'Arfeuille
Address: 33500 Pomerol
Mailing address: Same as above
Telephone: 33 5 57 51 02 11; telefax: 33 5 57 51 42 33
Visits: By appointment only

VINEYARDS (red)
Surface area: 54.3 acres
Average age of vines: 25+ years
Blend: 75% Merlot, 25% Cabernet Franc

Average yields: 40–55 hectoliters per hectare
Total average annual production: 10,000 cases

GRAND VIN (red)
Brand name: Château La Pointe
Appellation: Pomerol
Mean annual production: 10,000 cases
Upbringing: Fermentations and macerations last 16–21 days in
temperature-controlled stainless-steel tanks. Malolactics occur in tanks,
after which the wine is moved to small oak barrels, of which
approximately one-third are new each year. The wines are fined
and usually filtered. Bottling takes place 15–18 months after the
harvest.

SECOND WINE
Brand name: Château La Pointe Riffat

Evaluation of present classification: The quality equivalent of a Médoc
Cru Bourgeois
Plateau of maturity: 3–10 years following the vintage

La Pointe has been an irregular performer. The wines can be round, fruity, simple, and generous, as in 1970, but far too frequently they are boringly light and unsubstantial. Older vintages, such as 1975, 1976, 1978, and 1979, were all uncommonly deficient in the rich, chewy, supple, zesty fruit that one finds so typical of a good Pomerol. The large production ensures that the wine is widely promoted. The owners have increased the percentage of Merlot significantly. All things considered, this is a mediocre Pomerol.

VINTAGES

1995—The 1995 possesses a healthy medium ruby color, sweet cherry fruit and toast
•   in the nose, medium body, a pleasant, well-balanced personality, moderate
83   flavor concentration, and low acidity. Both wines will have to be drunk during
      the first 5–7 years after bottling. Last tasted, 11/97.

1994—La Pointe's 1994 exhibits a medium cranberry–like color, weedy, oaky,
•   vaguely fruity notes, obvious dilution, and a light- to medium-bodied, lightly
76   tannic finish. Last tasted, 3/96.

1989—Medium ruby, with some dilution in color evident at its edges, this light-
•   bodied, simple, fruity, alcoholic 1989 leaves a great deal to be desired. It
74   should be drunk over the next 3–5 years. Last tasted, 1/93.

1988—The 1988 La Pointe is light, medium bodied, and one-dimensional. Drink it
•   over the next 4–5 years. Last tasted, 1/93.
76

1986—The 1986 could well be among the better wines. Displaying some spicy new
* oak, an attractive plummy fruitiness, medium body, and a good finish, it
84 clearly is meant to be drunk over the next 5–6 years. While Pomerols tend to
be expensive because of their small production, this wine is not unfairly
priced when one considers its quality. Anticipated maturity: Now. Last
tasted, 3/90.

1985—The 1985 La Pointe is quite light, but well balanced, richly fruity, and
* medium bodied; it is an agreeable luncheon or picnic wine. Anticipated
83 maturity: Now. Last tasted, 3/89.

ROUGET   GOOD

Classification: None
Location of vineyards: Pomerol
Owner: Labruyère family
Address: Château Rouget, 33500 Pomerol
Mailing address: Same as above
Telephone: 33 5 57 51 05 85; telefax: 33 5 57 51 05 85
Visits: By appointment only
Contact: Mr. Ribeiro

VINEYARDS (red)
Surface area: 43.4 acres
Average age of vines: 28 years
Blend: 85% Merlot, 15% Cabernet Franc
Density of plantation: 6,000 vines per hectare
Average yields (over the last 5 years): 35 hectoliters per hectare
Total average annual production: 450 hectoliters

GRAND VIN (red)
Brand name: Château Rouget
Appellation: Pomerol
Mean annual production: 29,000 bottles
Upbringing: Fermentations occur in temperature-controlled
stainless-steel vats. Wines are aged in oak barrels, renewed by a third at
each vintage, for approximately 15 months. (Starting in 1997, malolactics
occur in new oak barrels.)

SECOND WINE
Brand name: Vieux Château des Templiers
Average annual production: 29,000 bottles

Evaluation of present classification: The quality equivalent of a Médoc
Cru Bourgeois
Plateau of maturity: 5–15 years following the vintage

Historically, Rouget is one of Pomerol's most illustrious estates. In one of the early editions of Cocks et Féret's *Bordeaux et ses Vins,* the vineyard was ranked fourth among all the Pomerols. At present their reputation has been surpassed by numerous properties, but there is no question that Rouget can be a rich and interesting wine. For example, both the 1945 and 1947 vintages were dazzling wines that were both still drinking superbly in the late eighties. Until recently François-Jean Brochet ran this old yet beautiful estate that sits in the northernmost part of the Pomerol appellation on very sandy soil, with a lovely view of the Barbanne River visible through the trees. The wine was traditionally made by Brochet, who also maintained an immense stock of old vintages. Brochet's sale of the property to the Lambruyère family should result in improvements.

The style of Rouget is one that makes no concessions to consumers who want to drink their wine young. It is a darkly colored, rich, full-bodied, often very tannic wine that usually is in need of a minimum of 8–10 years of cellaring. It is sometimes too coarse and rustic, but almost always a delicious, rich, ripe, spicy wine. The vintages of the eighties and nineties have tasted more supple and less concentrated, giving rise to questions about a change in style.

Rouget is a good value among the wines of Pomerol, with even the old vintages being very fairly priced.

VINTAGES

1990—The 1990 exhibits more sweet fruit and fat than usual. It is medium bodied
• and surprisingly forward, with a soft, alcoholic finish. Drink it over the next
85 6–7 years. Last tasted, 1/93.

1989—The 1989 is an abundantly rich, medium-bodied wine, with dusty tannins,
• plenty of alcohol, fine ripeness, and a long, hard, tannic finish. It will never
84 be elegant, but for a more rough-and-tumble style of Pomerol, it should provide interesting drinking. Anticipated maturity: Now–2006. Last tasted, 1/93.

1988—A modest success for the vintage, the 1988 Rouget exhibits some black cherry
• fruit partially hidden behind the tannins, medium body, and a blossoming
84 bouquet of earthy fruit intertwined with the scents of minerals and herbs. Anticipated maturity: Now–2006. Last tasted, 1/93.

1986—For whatever reason, the 1986 Rouget seems to be made in a very forward,
• precocious, commercial style that I hope does not signal a new direction. It is
82 soft and fruity, but it is also quite simple, and that is not what Rouget could strive to achieve. Anticipated maturity: Now. Last tasted, 3/90.

1985—The 1985 showed considerably better from the cask, but after bottling, the
• wine has gone into a shell. It has a good ruby color, but the charm and depth
84 are concealed, maybe submerged, behind a wall of rustic tannins. By the standards of the vintage, it is tough and backward. Anticipated maturity: Now–2005. Last tasted, 3/89.

1983—Richly fruity, spicy, fat, and quite concentrated, the 1983 Rouget is a big,
•   full-bodied, moderately tannic wine that is drinking well now. Anticipated
82   maturity: Now–2000. Last tasted, 2/88.

1982—It appears that I over-rated the quality of the 1982 Rouget in my earlier
•   assessment of this wine. It is still relatively closed and hard, but I did not
85   find the rich, ripe, intense fruit that existed in the prebottling cask samples I
       tasted. Nevertheless, this is certainly a good wine, but those who own it may
       want to wait another 3–4 years before drinking it, as this property tends to
       produce wines that need a good decade of cellaring to reveal their full
       potential. Anticipated maturity: Now–2000. Last tasted, 1/91.

1981—Rouget's 1981 is good but seems to suffer in comparison with the more
•   powerful 1982 and grapy, fat, succulent 1983. Nevertheless, it has good
80   fruit, rather hard, aggressive tannin, and an adequate, but uninspiring finish.
       Anticipated maturity: Now. Last tasted, 6/83.

1978—A chunky, spicy, fruity, medium- to full-bodied wine, the 1978 Rouget is
•   attractive but a trifle awkward and clumsy on the palate. Moderate tannin is
82   present, so perhaps the wine will pull itself completely together. Anticipated
       maturity: Now. Last tasted, 6/83.

1971—Fully mature, the 1971 Rouget has a dusty texture, a spicy, earthy, cedary
•   bouquet, nicely concentrated flavors, but a somewhat coarse texture. This
80   medium amber, ruby–colored wine should be drunk up. Anticipated maturity:
       Now–may be in decline. Last tasted, 6/84.

1970—A big, rather fat, well-endowed wine, with full body and a cedary, rich black
•   currant fruitiness, the 1970 Rouget has roughly textured flavors and moderate,
84   aggressive tannin still very much in evidence. Anticipated maturity: Now.
       Last tasted, 6/84.

1964—The 1964 is a total success for Rouget. The predilection to wines with a
•   rough, big, tannic structure has—in this vintage—resulted in a wine with
87   more balance and harmony. Very deeply fruity, with earthy, black currant
       flavors in abundance, this full-bodied wine has power, symmetry, and surpris-
       ing length. Rouget is one of the better Pomerols in this vintage. Anticipated
       maturity: Now. Last tasted, 1/85.

SALES   GOOD

Classification: None
Location of vineyards: Part of the vineyards are located in the
northwestern part of Pomerol, and the rest are between Pomerol and
Libourne
Owner: G.F.A. du Château de Sales, de Lambert family
Address: 33500 Pomerol
Mailing address: Same as above
Telephone: 33 5 57 51 04 92; telefax: 33 5 57 25 23 91
Visits: Preferably by appointment
Contact: Bruno de Lambert

VINEYARDS (red)
Surface area: 117.4 acres
Average age of vines: A little more than 25 years
Blend: 70% Merlot, 15% Cabernet Franc, 15% Cabernet Sauvignon
Density of plantation: 5,600 vines per hectare
Average yields (over the last 5 years): 49.3 hectoliters per hectare
Total average annual production: 2,200 hectoliters

GRAND VIN (red)
Brand name: Château de Sales
Appellation: Pomerol
Mean annual production: 150,000–180,000 bottles
Upbringing: Fermentations and macerations last 17–22 days in
temperature-controlled concrete vats at maximum temperatures of 30
degrees centigrade. Pumping-overs vary according to the quality of
tannins. After completion of malolactics in vats, half the yield is
transferred to oak casks (no new oak is ever used), and the other half
goes into vats. At each racking, every 3 months, there is a rotation, and
wines move from cask to vats and vice-versa. They then spend 6 more
months in vats before bottling. They are fined with fresh egg whites and
lightly filtered.

SECOND WINE
Brand name: Château Chantalouette
Average annual production: 50,000–100,000 bottles (depending upon the
vintage)

Evaluation of present classification: The quality equivalent of a Médoc
Cru Bourgeois
Plateau of maturity: 3–10 years following the vintage

De Sales is the largest vineyard in Pomerol and boasts the appellation's only
grand château. The property is located in the northwestern corner of Pomerol,
with a vineyard planted primarily on sandy soil intermixed with gravel. The
owners and managers are the de Lambert family. The wines are increasingly
among the most enjoyable of the Pomerols. They are prized for their sheer,
supple, glossy, round, generous, ripe fruitiness and lush, silky personalities.
De Sales has always made good wine, but the recent vintages have been
particularly strong. It is never a powerful, aggressive, oaky, or big wine and
always offers immediate drinkability. In spite of a precocious style, it has a
cunning ability to age well for 10–12 years.

While consistently good, De Sales will never be a great Pomerol, but it has
rarely ever disappointed me. Its price remains modest, making it a good
value.

VINTAGES

1996— De Sales is on a comeback trail, which is good news for readers looking for a
• more reasonably priced Pomerol. An elegant, soft, berry, coffee-scented wine,
85– the 1996 De Sales exhibits medium body, low acidity, and attractive fruit.
86 This is a well-made, mid-weight Pomerol for consuming during its first 7–8
years of life. Last tasted, 3/98.

1995— This may turn out to be the best De Sales since the 1982. The wine displays
• a deep ruby color, and a seductive nose of jammy cherries, earth, kirsch, and
87 an intriguing balsam wood note. In the mouth, this supple wine possesses
very good concentration, a round, velvety texture, plenty of crowd appeal, and
a clean, lush, berry-infused finish. Already drinking well, this 1995 Pomerol
should keep for 7–8+ years. A sleeper. Last tasted, 11/97.

1993— Both the 1992 and 1993 de Sales have exhibited the same problem—odd,
• musty, damp wood/wet dog–like aromas. Judgment reserved. Last tasted,
? 11/94.

1990— The bold, rich 1990 has a bouquet similar to the 1989, with its sweet, forward,
• leathery, spicy, toffee, caramel, berry nose. There is plump, ripe fruit, medium
89 body, fine flesh, and a long finish. Drink it over the next 7–12 years. Last
tasted, 1/93.

1989— The 1989 is surprisingly full bodied for a De Sales, with a deep, intense,
• black cherry–scented bouquet intertwined with the scents of vanillin and
85 toast. In the mouth, the wine displays fine ripeness, a heady alcohol content,
and a long, tannic, rich finish. Anticipated maturity: Now–2003. Last tasted,
1/93.

1988— The forward 1988 will provide attractive drinking over the next 4–6 years.
• Last tasted, 1/93.
84

1986— The 1986 is light but does offer charm and appeal in a very light- to medium-
• bodied format. Anticipated maturity: Now. Last tasted, 4/91.
80

1985— The 1985 is a very soft, easygoing, supple, fruity wine meant to be drunk
• young. It could use more grip and length, but for uncomplicated quaffing at a
83 decent price, it is hard to beat. Anticipated maturity: Now. Last tasted, 4/91.

1984— An open-knit, engaging, soft, fruity character displays no vegetal or unripe
• components. Light to medium bodied, this wine should be drunk up. Antici-
78 pated maturity: Now. Last tasted, 4/91.

1983— Perhaps a little atypical for De Sales, the 1983 is a fat, jammy, alcoholic
• wine, with an opulent fruitiness, a ripe bouquet of black cherries and peaches,
85 and a soft, viscous texture. Low acidity seems to suggest that this wine should
be consumed quickly. Anticipated maturity: Now. Last tasted, 4/91.

1982— This wine has lasted far longer than I would have guessed. It has always been
• a tasty mocha-, root beer-, and cherry-scented and -flavored wine, with me-
85 dium body, a silky texture, and good fruit and flesh. It has taken on considerable amber at the edge and is just beginning to turn the corner and dry out.
Drink it up. Last tasted, 9/95.

1981—The 1981 de Sales is a notable success for the vintage. Quite lush and
• concentrated, with ripe, rich fruit, some spicy oak, medium body, and a long
86 finish, this is a graceful, savory wine. Anticipated maturity: Now. Last tasted,
11/84.

TROTANOY   OUTSTANDING

Classification: None
Location of vineyards: On the western edge and highest slope of Pomerol
(it is one of the estates that ring Pétrus)
Owner: S.C. du Château Trotanoy (Farmer Ets. J.-P. Moueix)
Address: 33500 Pomerol
Mailing address: c/o Ets. J.-P. Moueix, 54, quai du Priourat, B.P. 129,
33502 Libourne Cedex
Telephone: 33 5 57 51 78 96; telefax: 33 5 57 51 79 79
Visits: By appointment, for professionals of the wine trade only
Contact: Frédéric Lospied

VINEYARDS (red)
Surface area: 22 acres
Average age of vines: 30 years
Blend: 80% Merlot, 10% Cabernet Franc, 10% mixed varietals
Density of plantation: 5,500–6,000 vines per hectare
Average yields (over the last 5 years): 35 hectoliters per hectare
Total average annual production: 2,500–3,000 cases

GRAND VIN (red)
Brand name: Château Trotanoy
Appellation: Pomerol
Mean annual production: 2,500–3,000 cases
Upbringing: Fermentations last 7–10 days in small concrete
temperature-controlled vats, followed by 1-week maceration with the
skins. Thirty percent of the yield undergoes malolactics in new oak,
the rest remains in vats. Wines are then transferred to oak barrels,
two-thirds of which are new, for 18–20 months aging. They are
racked every 3 months, from barrel to barrel. Wines are fined but not
filtered.

SECOND WINE
None produced.

Evaluation of present classification: The quality equivalent of a Médoc
second-growth, occasionally a first-growth
Plateau of maturity: 7–20 or more years following the vintage

Trotanoy has historically been one of the great wines of both Pomerol and all of Bordeaux. Since 1976 Trotanoy has been the quality equivalent of a second-growth. In vintages prior to 1976 Trotanoy was often as profound as a first-growth.

Since 1953 Trotanoy has been owned by the firm of Jean-Pierre Moueix. The château is unmarked (it is the residence of Jean-Jacques Moueix). The vineyards of this modest estate, which lie a kilometer to the west of Pétrus between the church of Pomerol and the village of Catusseau, are situated on soil of clay and gravel. The wine is vinified and handled in exactly the same way as Pétrus, except only 66% new oak barrels are used each year.

Until the late seventies Trotanoy was an opulently rich, intense, full-bodied wine that usually needed a full decade of cellaring to reach its zenith. In some vintages the power, intensity, and concentration came remarkably close to matching that of Pétrus. It had an enviable track record of producing good, sometimes brilliant, wines in poor Bordeaux vintages. The 1967, 1972, and 1974 are three examples of vintages where Trotanoy was among the best two or three wines of the entire Bordeaux region.

In the late seventies the style became lighter, although Trotanoy appeared to return to full form with the extraordinarily opulent, rich, decadent 1982. Until 1995 there was a succession of good, rather than thrilling, wines. There is no question that there has been some major replanting of the micro-size vineyard of Trotanoy and that the production from these younger vines is being blended in. Whatever the case might be, Trotanoy no longer seems to be one of the top three or four wines of Pomerol and has been surpassed in the eighties (with the exception of the 1982 vintage) by such châteaux as Clinet, l'Eglise Clinet, Vieux-Château-Certan, Le Pin, Lafleur, La Fleur de Gay, l'Evangile, La Conseillante, and even Bon Pasteur in specific vintages. Given the competitiveness and talent of Christian Moueix and his staff, this situation is about to change. Recent vintages have all been very strong, including a sensational 1995.

Trotanoy is an expensive wine because it is highly regarded by connoisseurs the world over. Yet it rarely sells for more than half the price of Pétrus —a fact worth remembering since it does (in certain vintages) have more than just a casual resemblance to the great Pétrus itself.

VINTAGES

1997—A strict selection by Christian Moueix resulted in only 2,500 cases of 1997
•   Trotanoy. An impressively built and concentrated effort, it will be one of the
90–   vintage's longest-lived wines. The color is dense ruby/purple, and the nose
92   offers up scents of black truffles, plums, prunes, and ripe cherries. In the
      mouth, the wine reveals outstanding richness, a broad, expansive mouth-feel,
      moderate tannin, an excellent delineation (not a common characteristic of

many 1997s). This is a true *vin de garde* in a year that produced a plethora of wines requiring early consumption. Anticipated maturity: 2004–2015. Last tasted, 3/98.

1996—This is a broodingly backward *vin de garde,* dark ruby/purple–colored wine
•   with sweet truffle, mineral, and black cherry/raspberry fruit in the nose. In
90–   the mouth, it is medium to full bodied, with high tannin, plenty of muscle,
91+   and a chewy, old style intensity to its flavors, texture, and personality. The
       1996 does not possess the flamboyance or extraordinary intensity and poten-
       tial of the 1995, but it is a very competent effort in what was an irreg-
       ular vintage for Pomerol. Anticipated maturity: 2003–2020. Last tasted,
       3/98.

1995—A fabulous success for Trotanoy, this wine has considerable potential, and
•   may ultimately merit a higher score than I have bestowed it. The 1995 boasts
93+   a saturated deep purple color, followed by a knockout nose of black truffles,
       cherries, raspberries, and kirsch fruit intermixed with spicy oak and beef
       blood-like scents. Full bodied, dense, and as powerful and backward as its
       rival, Lafleur, this broad-shouldered, super-extracted Trotanoy is superb, but
       don't make the mistake of thinking it will provide easy-going drinking over
       the near-term. While splendid, this wine possesses extremely high tannin,
       and needs at least 7–8 years of cellaring. Anticipated maturity: 2005–2025.
       Bravo! Last tasted, 11/97.

1994—A dark ruby/purple color and a closed set of aromatics need to be probed to
•   find the sweet, ripe fruit that appears to have gone into hiding since bottling.
89+   The masculine 1994 Trotanoy is backward, powerful, and in need of 5–7
       years of cellaring. It is rich and medium to full bodied, with outstanding fruit
       extraction, beefy, burly, and a true *vin de garde.* Anticipated maturity: 2003–
       2020. Last tasted, 1/97.

1993—This is a wine to check out in the generally ignored 1993 vintage. Trotanoy's
•   offering exhibits a saturated purple color as well as a sweet, ripe nose of
90   black cherries, licorice, and earth. Top-class flavors, an opulent texture,
       medium to full body, moderate tannin, and an inner core of sweet, jammy,
       concentrated fruit make this a terrific effort for the 1993 vintage. Anticipated
       maturity: 2001–2018. A sleeper! Last tasted, 1/97.

1992—It offers a dense, saturated dark ruby color, an excellent sweet, black cherry,
•   mocha, mineral, vanillin nose, medium-bodied, concentrated flavors, a won-
88   derful succulence and suppleness to its fruit, and a long, heady, tannic, rich
       finish. This is an expansively flavored, moderately tannic Trotanoy that will
       benefit from another 2–3 years of cellaring and keep for 12–15 years. Last
       tasted, 11/94.

1990—This wine possesses more power, extract, alcohol, and glycerin, as well as
•   higher tannin levels, than the 1989. The deep ruby color reveals no signs of
91   amber. Aggressive tannin in the finish suggests the wine should last another
       10–15 years. Forward, with low acidity and sweet fruit, the 1990 is the
       richest Trotanoy made between 1982 and 1995. It is a reassuringly top wine
       from this great *terroir.* Drink it over the next 15 years. Last tasted, 11/96.

1989—Trotanoy's 1989 is an elegant, mature wine revealing a deep ruby color with
  •   some amber at the edge. Sweet, ripe fruit in the nose reveals hints of *herbes*
  88   *de Provence,* black olives, and cedar. Round, elegant, and medium bodied,
        this fruity, soft, easy to drink and understand wine should be consumed over
        the next 10–12 years. Last tasted, 11/96.

1988—The very good 1988 possesses an attractive plum and vanillin nose. On the
  •   palate, the wine exhibits fine concentration, firm, relatively hard tannins, and
  86   a spicy, long finish. While it is tasty, I would have preferred a more exciting
        style. Anticipated maturity: Now–2008. Last tasted, 1/93.

1986—I still do not care for this wine very much. Fully mature, it is an exceptionally
  •   vegetal wine with herbal tea/roasted aromatics. It reveals a medium ruby
  84   color, with amber at the edge. In the mouth, there is a big hole in the
        middle, although the wine does display sweet cherry fruit on the attack. The
        medium-bodied finish is relatively diluted. Anticipated maturity: Now–2005.
        Last tasted, 3/97.

1985—This wine is another disappointing offering that appears to be losing its fruit
  •   and fat at an accelerated pace. It possesses a medium ruby/garnet color, with
  85   considerable rust at the edge. The nose offers up aromas of olives, grilled vege-
        tables, and straightforward cherry fruit. In the mouth, the wine is medium bod-
        ied and soft, with some acidity and tannin poking through the meager flesh. This
        wine needs to be drunk up. Anticipated maturity: Now–2003. Last tasted, 3/97.

1984—Considering the difficulties posed by this vintage, this wine has turned out
  •   well. It is ripe, tannic, and firmly structured, with depth and length. Antici-
  84   pated maturity: Now. Last tasted, 3/89.

1983—The 1983 Trotanoy is a disappointment and is the first of a succession of
  •   vintages for this famous property that produced wines of lesser quality than
  81   one might expect. The 1983 is a bit dull and light and seems slightly out of
        balance, with an excess of tannin for the meager fruitiness. My rating may
        well turn out to be overly generous, as this wine continues to evolve, since it
        seems to be losing fruit rather than filling out, as I had hoped it might.
        Anticipated maturity: Now. Last tasted, 1/89.

1982—This fully mature, gorgeously seductive, fragrant, complex wine offers up
  •   intense aromas of jammy fruit, mocha, roasted herbs, and sweet toasty oak.
  94   Full bodied, with expansive, chewy concentration, gobs of fruit, and a soft,
        low-acid plushness, this is the most gorgeous Trotanoy made following the
        superb 1975. Although still young, it is soft, delicious, and ideal for drinking
        over the next 10–15+ years. Last tasted, 9/95.

1981—The 1981 Trotanoy is an elegantly wrought yet authoritative, moderately rich
  •   wine, with good, deep, ripe fruit, a spicy, oaky, leathery bouquet, medium
  85   body, decent concentration, and light tannins in the finish. Anticipated matu-
        rity: Now–2000. Last tasted, 12/90.

1979—Surprisingly precocious and charmingly supple and fruity, the 1979 Trotanoy
  •   continues to develop well in the bottle. Quite drinkable now, this is not a big
  86   or massive Trotanoy, but rather a round, ample, elegant wine with good overall
        balance. Anticipated maturity: Now. Last tasted, 12/90.

1978—The 1978 Trotanoy has matured rapidly. Ready to drink now, it has a full-
blown bouquet suggestive of herbs, fresh tomatoes, and black currants. On
84   the palate, the wine is medium bodied, soft, and velvety, without the depth of
fruit normally found in this wine. Little tannin remains in this loosely knit,
herbaceous, somewhat austere Trotanoy. Anticipated maturity: Now. Last
tasted, 12/90.

1976—Generally very highly regarded by other critics, I have enjoyed the 1976
Trotanoy, but it is now fully mature and showing signs of over-ripeness and a
84   jammy, low-acid character. Quite plummy, fat, even peppery, with a lovely
lush structure, this is an exotic style of Trotanoy that is delicious but lacks
backbone and structure. Anticipated maturity: Now—may be in decline. Last
tasted, 10/83.

1975—The exquisite 1975 Trotanoy gets my nod as one of the three finest wines
produced at this estate in the last 25 years (the others being 1970 and 1982).
95   This wine has been drinking splendidly for several years, exhibiting fabulous
mocha/toffee/jammy black cherry aromas in a complex, sweet, fragrant bouquet. Full bodied, splendidly concentrated, velvety textured, with a firm
finish, this is a weighty, rich, complex, great vintage for Trotanoy. Drink it
over the next 10–15 years. Like so many top Pomerols in the 1975 vintage,
there is a sweetness and jamminess to this wine's fruit that is not found in
most 1975 Médocs. This is a glorious Trotanoy! Last tasted, 12/95.

1974—One of the best wines of the vintage (clearly the best Pomerol), Trotanoy's
1974 is now fully mature and should be drunk over the next 2–3 years.
86   Uncommonly concentrated and surprisingly ripe and fruity, this medium- to
full-bodied wine has a smooth mocha, coffee, chocolate finish. Anticipated
maturity: Now. Last tasted, 2/91.

1971—I remember this dark garnet–colored wine being absolutely delicious in the
mid-1970s, and every time I go back to it, it seems to improve in the bottle.
93   It is still superb, with gobs of velvety, ripe, decadent Merlot fruit, an opulent
texture, and a long, full-bodied, heady finish. This is among the finest wines
of the vintage (eclipsed only by Pétrus). Given how long it has been able to
rest at its apogee, I may be wrong in saying it should be consumed. Anticipated maturity: Now–2002. Last tasted, 7/97.

1970—This wine has developed magnificently over the last 4–5 years. More backward and possibly even more concentrated than the 1970 Pétrus (as well as
96+   more tannic), this huge, old-style, massive, thick, rich wine is crammed with
concentrated, chocolatey, berry fruit with a hint of leather, smoked meat, and
licorice. The wine's opaque garnet color reveals no sign of amber. The nose is
just beginning to open. The flavors are so concentrated that I am going to go
out on a limb and say this may be the most concentrated Trotanoy made in
the post–World War II era. I suspect this wine can still be purchased for a
relatively good price. Owners should plan on drinking it between 2000 and
2030. One of the three greatest wines of the vintage, the 1970 Trotanoy is the
finest wine made at this estate save for the extraordinary 1961 and 1945. Last
tasted, 6/96.

1967—This is spectacular for the vintage. I would have thought it would be losing
• its fruit by now, but when last tasted the wine was still exuberantly rich,
91 crammed with fruit, and a total joy to drink. Full bodied and remarkably
concentrated, this multidimensional wine offers amazing opulence and richness for the vintage. A smashing success! Anticipated maturity: Now. Last
tasted, 12/90.

1966—I am beginning to wonder when this still tannic, tough, and closed-in wine,
• which remains impressively colored and concentrated, will open up. It is a
85 big, brawny Trotanoy that may very well lose its fruit before its tannin.
Anticipated maturity: Now. Last tasted, 1/87.

1964—This is an impressively big, deep, darkly colored Trotanoy, with only a trace
• of amber at the edge. The wine has outstanding ripeness and concentration,
90 with an almost port-like viscosity to its texture. The slight bitterness that I
mentioned in the first edition of this book has not been a problem the last two
times I tasted this wine. It is clearly an outstanding effort from Trotanoy in
1964. Fully mature, given its size and concentration, it should continue to
drink well for at least another decade. Anticipated maturity: Now–2002. Last
tasted, 11/90.

1962—The top Pomerol of the vintage, Trotanoy is still delicious, with a big, spicy,
• cedary, tobacco-scented bouquet and soft, generous, round flavors that linger
88 on the palate. Harmonious and attractive, this wine should be drunk up.
Anticipated maturity: Now. Last tasted, 1/83.

1961—The 1961, which I have consistently rated between 96 and 100, is unques-
• tionably the greatest Trotanoy in the post–World War II era. The wine's
98 saturated, thick, inky, plummy color reveals slight amber at the edge. The
magnificent bouquet of jammy black raspberries, smoke, cloves, tar, and
caramel is a knockout. With dense, unctuous, thick, sweet, rich flavors loaded
with glycerin and extract, this massive, full-bodied, stunningly rich, fully
mature wine is capable of lasting for another 10–20 years. Last tasted,
10/94.

VIEUX-CHÂTEAU-CERTAN   EXCELLENT

Classification: None
Location of vineyards: Pomerol, on the plateau
Owner: Thienpont family
Address: 33500 Pomerol
Mailing address: Same as above
Telephone: 33 5 57 51 17 33; telefax: 33 5 57 25 35 08
Visits: By appointment only
Contact: Alexandre Thienpont

VINEYARDS (red)
Surface area: 33.3 acres
Average age of vines: 35 years

Blend: 60% Merlot, 30% Cabernet Franc, 10% Cabernet Sauvignon
Density of plantation: 5,800 vines per hectare
Average yields (over the last 5 years): 40 hectoliters per hectare
Total average annual production: 60,000 bottles

GRAND VIN (red)
Brand name: Vieux-Château-Certan
Appellation: Pomerol
Mean annual production: 50,000–60,000 bottles
Upbringing: Alcoholic fermentations last 15 days in wooden tanks and
malolactics approximately 3 weeks in stainless-steel vats. Wines are then
transferred to oak barrels, renewed by half at each vintage, for 18–22
months aging. They are fined but not filtered.

SECOND WINE
Brand name: Gravette de Certan
Average annual production: Depends on the vintage

Evaluation of present classification: The quality equivalent of a Médoc
second-growth
Plateau of maturity: 5–20 or more years following the vintage

One of the most famous names in Pomerol is the pride and joy of the Thienpont family, the owners of Vieux-Château-Certan. In the nineteenth century,
as well as the early part of the twentieth century, Vieux-Château-Certan was
considered to produce the finest wine of Pomerol. However, following World
War II this distinction was surpassed by Pétrus. The two wines could not be
more different. Vieux-Château-Certan bases its style and complexity on a
high percentage of Cabernet Franc and Cabernet Sauvignon, whereas Pétrus
is nearly 100% Merlot. The vineyard, located in the heart of the plateau,
surrounded by much of the reigning aristocracy of the appellation, Certan de
May, La Conseillante, l'Evangile, Petit-Village, and Pétrus, has a gravelly soil
with a subsoil of iron-enriched clay. The wine that emerges from the vineyard
never has the strength of a Pétrus, or other Merlot-dominated wines of the
plateau, but it often has a perfume and elegance that recalls a top wine from
the Médoc.

A visit to the *chai* of Vieux-Château-Certan reveals a healthy respect for
tradition. The fermentation still takes place in old wooden vats, and the
château refuses to use more than 50% new oak for each vintage. The wine
rests in vats for up to 2 years, and according to the château, they do not filter
at bottling. For most of the post–World War II era, Vieux-Château-Certan was
made by Léon Thienpont, but since his death in 1985 the property has been
managed by his son, Alexandre, who apprenticed as the *régisseur* at the

St.-Emilion château of La Gaffelière. When the young, shy Thienpont took over the estate, old-timers scoffed at his lack of experience, but he asserted himself immediately, introducing crop-thinning techniques practiced by his neighbor Christian Moueix at Château Pétrus.

Because of its historic reputation for excellence, Vieux-Château-Certan is an expensive wine.

VINTAGES

1997—Typically elegant, suave, and graceful, Vieux-Château-Certan's 1997 exhibits
• a dark ruby color, an herb-tinged, berry, spicy-scented nose, well-balanced,
87– medium-bodied, refined flavors, good sweetness, and well-integrated acidity
88 and tannin. Nothing stands out in this unaggressive, measured, attractively styled wine. Anticipated maturity: 2000–2010. Last tasted, 3/98.

1996—This dark ruby–colored wine offers an intriguing nose of cedar wood, fruit-
• cake, Asian spices, smoke, and cassis. In the mouth, some olive notes reveal
87– the Cabernet Sauvignon component of this Pomerol. Medium bodied, with
90 excellent ripeness and considerable potential for complexity and elegance, this is a very good to excellent Vieux-Château-Certan that should provide fine drinking for two decades. Anticipated maturity: 2002–2016. Last tasted, 3/98.

1995—Frightful bottle variation left me perplexed about just where this wine fits in
• Bordeaux's qualitative hierarchy. I tasted the wine three times since bottling,
88? all within a 14-day period. Twice the wine was extremely closed and firm, with an evolved plum/garnet color, high levels of tannin, sweet black currant, prune, and olive-tinged fruit, and astringent tannin in the medium-bodied finish. Those two bottles suggested the wine was in need of at least 5–7 years of cellaring, and would keep for two decades. The third bottle was atypically evolved, with a similar color, but it was far more open-knit, displaying Provençal herbs, black cherry, and cassis fruit in a medium-bodied, jammy, lush style. I expect marginal bottle variation, but while the quality was relatively the same in all three bottles, the forward, open-knit example left me puzzled. Last tasted, 11/97.

1994—The 1994 is performing well, with no harsh tannin or vegetal characteristics.
• It displays a deep ruby color and a sweet nose of jammy cherry and Asian
88 spice scents with a touch of smoke. Dense, rich, medium-bodied flavors exhibit excellent concentration and fine purity. The wine possesses low acidity and plenty of flesh, so it should drink well between now and 2010. Last tasted, 1/97.

1993—Disappointing following bottling, this green-flavored, herbaceous, medium-
• bodied wine exhibits spice and red fruit notes, but it tastes under-ripe and
84 meagerly endowed. Anticipated maturity: Now–2006. Last tasted, 1/97.

1992—Medium ruby, with a light-intensity bouquet of herbaceous cherry fruit,
• this spicy, compact, medium-bodied wine reveals some tannin, but its finish
78 is short and insubstantial. Drink it over the next 4–5 years. Last tasted, 11/94.

1990—The 1990, which I previously rated several points higher, is backward and
•   tannic, but promising. I was surprised by the severe level of harsh tannin in
91   the wine, but I believe it is balanced out by sweet, jammy, coconut-scented,
spicy, earthy, black currant and cherry fruit. The wine is full bodied and
muscular, with a tannin level that is far more pronounced than in previous
tastings. Anticipated maturity: 2003–2020. Last tasted, 11/96.

1989—The austere, light-bodied 1989 reveals an amber/orange edge to its color. Al-
•   though the wine did not taste cooked, this bottle may have been exposed to
85   inhospitable temperatures sometime during its sojourn from Bordeaux to America. In any event, I look forward to tasting another bottle, hoping this tasting was
not an accurate representation of the 1989's quality. Last tasted, 11/96.

1988—The 1988 is a classic Vieux-Château-Certan. The huge bouquet of cassis,
•   herbs, and new oak is followed by a wine that is medium bodied, with deep,
91   black cherry flavors wrapped intelligently in toasty oak. Extracted, deep, yet
impeccably balanced, this well-delineated Pomerol should age well for 20–
25 years. Anticipated maturity: Now–2010. Last tasted, 1/93.

1987—The intense herbaceousness exhibited by this wine from the cask has now
•   calmed down. The result is a flattering, cedary, black currant-and-herb-
85   scented wine, with good depth, some light tannins, and a plump, satisfying
finish. Anticipated maturity: Now. Last tasted, 4/91.

1986—This wine is one of the finest efforts from Bordeaux's right bank in the 1986
•   vintage. It remains deep ruby-colored, with a complex nose suggesting cedar
92   wood, fruitcake, Asian spices, roasted herbs, and black currants. In the
mouth, there is moderate tannin as well as impressively concentrated flavors
that roll across all the palate's sweet spots. Medium to full bodied and rich,
this 1986 admirably marries power with finesse. The wine is still youthful but
is soft and developed enough to be enjoyed immensely. Anticipated maturity:
Now–2012. Last tasted, 3/96.

1985—Medium ruby/garnet colored, with some amber at the edge, this wine exhibits
•   a pronounced streak of roasted herbs, olives, and weedy tobacco. Some sweet
87   berry fruit does make an appearance in this medium-bodied, fragile, soft, yet
seductively charming wine. While not a blockbuster or terribly concentrated,
it is round, savory, and complex. Anticipated maturity: Now–2002. Last
tasted, 3/96.

1984—This is a lean wine, but there is an attractive spicy character, adequate fruit,
•   and 3–5 years of drinkability. Anticipated maturity: Now. Last tasted, 3/89.
78

1983—Vieux-Château-Certan is quite successful in this vintage. The wine is dark
•   ruby, with a rich, berry-like, slightly minty, oaky bouquet, plump, round, fat
88   flavors, good, round, tannin content, and medium to full body. Like most
Pomerols of 1983, it is slightly deficient in acidity, but it is round, generously
flavored, and precocious. Anticipated maturity: Now. Last tasted, 1/89.

1982—Notorious bottle variation has characterized all my tastings of the 1982 Vieux-
•   Château-Certan. Magnums have been outstanding, meriting 90–92 points.
88?   Regular 750-milliliter formats are soft and herbaceous, wonderfully delicious

and round, but not that complex or concentrated. While the wine is very good, it is not one of the stars of the vintage. The color is a healthy dark ruby, with some amber. The wine possesses a peppery, herb, olive, and vanillin nose, and jammy black cherry fruit. Lush and succulent, with medium to full body, excellent concentration, and a low-acid finish with no real tannin, this is a fully mature wine that begs to be drunk over the next 7–8 years. I prefer the 1986, 1988, and 1990 to the 1982 Vieux-Château-Certan. Last tasted, 9/95.

1981—The 1981 is extremely good, richly fruity, with a black currant, cedary bou-
•   quet interlaced with subtle, herbaceous scents. Rather Médoc-like in its firm,
87   well-structured feel, with medium body and tough tannins, this wine is well made and surprisingly generous for the vintage. Anticipated maturity: Now–2005. Last tasted, 7/91.

1979—Rather light for a wine of its reputation, the 1979 Vieux-Château-Certan is
•   medium ruby, with a moderately intense, cherryish, oaky bouquet, medium
78   body, soft, light tannins, and an adequate finish. Anticipated maturity: Now. Last tasted, 7/83.

1978—The 1978 Vieux-Château-Certan has much more color than the 1979, with
•   better concentration, a relatively rich, supple, medium-bodied texture,
82   light tannins, and a round, attractive finish. Anticipated maturity: Now. Last tasted, 7/83.

1976—Quite one-dimensional, with soft, ripe plummy fruit and some oaky aromas,
•   the 1976 has average concentration, no noticeable tannin, and a pleasant yet
75   uninteresting finish. Anticipated maturity: Now–may be in decline. Last tasted, 7/83.

1975—The best Vieux-Château-Certan of the seventies, the 1975 has excellent
•   power and richness as well as complexity and balance. Medium to dark ruby,
90   with a fragrant, ripe, rich, plummy, cedary, spicy bouquet, full body, big, concentrated flavors, and moderate tannin, the wine is just beginning to reach its apogee. Anticipated maturity: Now–2000. Last tasted, 12/88.

1971—The 1971 is a little wine, pleasant enough but lacking concentration, rich-
•   ness, character, and length. It has been ready to drink for some time and now
74   seems to be losing its fruit. Anticipated maturity: Now–may be in decline. Last tasted, 9/79.

1970—A Burgundy-like aroma of cherry fruit and earthy, oaky, spicy components is
•   satisfactory enough. On the palate, the 1970 Vieux-Château-Certan is moder-
80   ately concentrated, light, fruity, and charming. However, it has little of the power, richness, and depth expected. Anticipated maturity: Now. Last tasted, 4/80.

1966—The 1966 Vieux-Château-Certan is browning badly but is still solid and
•   showing moderately ripe fruit, medium body, a rather severe, unyielding
74   texture, and a short finish. Some astringent tannin still remains. This wine is very Médoc-like in character, but not very impressive. Last tasted, 2/82.

1964—A lovely wine that is round, generous, velvety, and deeply fruity, the 1964
•   has a very sweet, ripe bouquet of fruit, oak, and truffles, soft, amply endowed
90   flavors, medium to full body, and a long, silky finish. It remains a sumptuously

rich, intensely flavored wine (from a magnum). Anticipated maturity: Now. Last tasted, 3/91.

1961—This wine has gotten mixed reviews in my notes. Several years ago it was big
  • and powerful, but coarse, dumb, and totally lacking in finesse. At a vertical
  86 tasting of Vieux-Château-Certan, it was still a little rough around the edges but displayed rich, deep, youthfully scented fruit, full body, plenty of weight and power, and impressive length. The score reflects the better effort. Anticipated maturity: Now. Last tasted, 5/83.

ANCIENT VINTAGES

The 1952 Vieux-Château-Certan (94 points; last tasted 10/94) is in extraordinary condition. The wine, a sleeper, was sweet and cedary, with a huge, almost hickory, roasted, smoky nose that was reminiscent of a top Graves. Full bodied, with glorious concentration and richness, this wine still possesses plenty of tannin and youthfulness. It will easily keep for another 10–20 years. The 1950 (97 points; last tasted 10/94) is a remarkably rich, still youthful wine from this fabulous vintage in Pomerol. The color remains an amazing garnet/purple, and the nose offers sensationally ripe, chocolatey, cassis aromas intertwined with herbs, licorice, Asian spices, and coffee. Extremely full bodied with port-like viscosity similar to the 1947, this blockbuster wine must be one of the least-known profound wines of the century.

The 1948 Vieux-Château-Certan (98 points; last tasted 12/97) is another profoundly great wine from the forgotten vintage of the forties. I have tasted this wine four times in the last year, and it was exceptional in each tasting. The opaque dark purple/garnet color is followed by a huge, exotic nose of caramel, sweet cassis, soy sauce, walnuts, and coffee. Thick, chewy, fabulously concentrated flavors with low acidity and high tannin coat the palate. There is amazing glycerin and an elevated alcohol level to this super-concentrated wine. Although fully mature, it exhibits no signs of decline and will easily last for 15–20 more years. Remarkable! A dazzling wine, which I have tasted a number of times over the years, the 1947 Vieux-Château-Certan (97 points; last tasted 10/94) is typical of so many 1947 Pomerols. Its thick, viscous, port-like style and texture are the hallmarks of this vintage. More advanced than the 1948, it reveals a smoky, meaty, truffle, and black currant bouquet, as well as massive, chewy flavors loaded with glycerin, extract, and alcohol. It exhibits more amber at the edge than the 1948, but, wow, what a mouthful of wine! Like many 1947 Pomerols, its unctuosity and thickness make me wonder if a spoon would stand up in the glass without any support. Drink it over the next 10–12 years. Tasted twice and rated highly each time, the 1945 (98–100 points; last tasted 10/94) is an exceptional winemaking effort in what can be a frightfully tannic vintage. It exhibits a dark, murky, plum color, with little garnet at the edge. It also possesses a huge nose of smoked meats, black raspberries, plums, licorice, and tar. Dense, chewy, and powerful, with gobs of tannin, and amazing fruit extraction, this full-throttle wine must be at its plateau of maturity, yet I see no reason it cannot last for 2 more decades.

Dark garnet, with noticeable rust/amber at the edge, the spicy, peppery, herbaceous, sweet, caramel-and-black fruit–scented 1928 Vieux-Château-Certan (96 points; last tasted 10/94) possesses huge, chewy flavors, copious quantities of tannin, full body, and a rustic, astringent finish. Still in superb condition, it is capable of lasting 10–20 more years.

OTHER POMEROL ESTATES

BEAUSOLEIL   VERY GOOD

Classification: None
Location of vineyards: Pomerol
Owner: G.F.A. du Château Beausoleil—Arcaute-Audy families
Address: 33500 Pomerol
Mailing address: c/o Château Jonqueyres, 33750 St.-Germain du Puch
Telephone: 33 5 56 68 55 88; telefax: 33 5 56 30 11 45
Visits: By appointment only

VINEYARDS (red)
Surface area: 8.6 acres
Average age of vines: 35 years
Blend: 95% Merlot, 5% Cabernet Franc
Density of plantation: 6,600 vines per hectare
Average yields (over the last 5 years): 48 hectoliters per hectare
Total average annual production: 1,850 cases

GRAND VIN (red)
Brand name: Château Beausoleil
Appellation: Pomerol
Mean annual production: 1,850 cases
Upbringing: Fermentations and macerations may last up to 45 days in small stainless-steel vats equipped with an internal electronic temperature-control system. Wines are transferred to oak barrels (normally for malolactics), 80% of which are new, for 24 months aging. *Assemblage* is done progressively as the wines are racked every 3 months. They are fined with egg whites and remain unfiltered. This is a wine to take seriously given the involvement of Jean-Michel Arcaute and Michel Rolland.

SECOND WINE
None produced.

BEAUCHÊNE

Classification: None
Location of vineyards: Libourne
Owner: Leymarie family
Address: 15, impasse du Vélodrome, 33500 Libourne
Mailing address: Charles Leymarie & Fils, 90/92, avenue Foch, 33500 Libourne
Telephone: 33 5 57 51 07 83; telefax: 33 5 57 51 99 94
Visits: By appointment only
Contact: Gregory Leymarie

VINEYARDS (red)
Surface area: 24 acres
Average age of vines: 40 years
Blend: 65% Merlot, 30% Cabernet Franc, 5% Cabernet Sauvignon
Density of plantation: 5,500 vines per hectare
Average yields (over the last 5 years): 44 hectoliters per hectare
Total average annual production: 56,000 bottles

GRAND VIN (red)
Brand name: Château Beauchêne
Appellation: Pomerol
Mean annual production: 12,000 bottles
Upbringing: The best vat of Merlot is selected after alcoholic fermentation. It undergoes malolactics in new oak barrels, and wines are aged in 100% new oak barrels for 18 months. They are fined and lightly filtered.

NOTE: Château Beauchêne normally represents 12%–25% of the total production of the estate. The rest is bottled under Clos Mazeyres. It is a micro-vinification carried out on selected old Merlot vines (55–60 years old) of the Clos Mazeyres. The debut vintage was 1995.

SECOND WINE
Brand name: Clos Mazeyres
Appellation: Pomerol
Average annual production: 43,000 bottles
Upbringing: Fermentations and macerations last 15–30 days, depending upon the vintage, in temperature-controlled concrete vats. Wines are aged 18 months in tanks prior to bottling.

BOURGUENEUF

Classification: None
Location of vineyards: Pomerol
Owner: Meyer family
Address: S.C.E.A. Château de Bourgueneuf, Vignobles Meyer, 33500
Pomerol
Mailing address: Same as above
Telephone: 33 5 57 51 16 76; telefax: 33 5 57 25 16 89
Visits: On weekdays, from 8 A.M. to noon, and 2 P.M. to 6 P.M.
Contact: Mr. Meyer

VINEYARDS (red)
Surface area: 12.4 acres
Blend: 60% Merlot, 40% Cabernet Franc
Total average annual production: 25,000 bottles

GRAND VIN (red)
Brand name: Château de Bourgueneuf
Appellation: Pomerol
Mean annual production: 25,000 bottles
Upbringing: Fermentations last 3 weeks in stainless-steel and concrete
tanks. Wines remain in tanks for 8 months and are aged 12 months in
oak barrels. They are fined but not filtered.

SECOND WINE
None produced.

LE CAILLOU

Classification: None
Location of vineyards: Part of the vines are located on the plateau of
Pomerol, at "Le Caillou," and the rest are situated in the northwestern
part of the appellation
Owner: G.F.A. Giraud-Belivier
Address: c/o André Giraud, Château Le Caillou, 33500 Pomerol
Mailing address: Same as above
Telephone: 33 5 57 51 06 10; telefax: 33 5 57 51 74 95
Visits: Preferably by appointment (especially for groups), on weekdays
except Wednesdays, between 9 A.M. and noon, and 2 P.M. and
6 P.M.
Contact: Sylvie Giraud

VINEYARDS (red)
Surface area: 17.3 acres
Average age of vines: 25 years
Blend: 75% Merlot, 25% Cabernet Franc
Average yields (over the last 5 years): 46 hectoliters per hectare
Total average annual production: 40,000 bottles

GRAND VIN (red)
Brand name: Château Le Caillou
Appellation: Pomerol
Mean annual production: 40,000 bottles
Upbringing: Fermentations last 3–4 weeks, depending upon the vintage, in concrete tanks. Two-thirds of the yield are then transferred to oak casks and the rest into vats after malolactics. There is a rotation every 3 months, when racking is done. Wines are fined but not filtered.

SECOND WINE
None produced.

CANTELAUZE

Classification: None
Location of vineyards: Pomerol
Owner: Jean-Noël Boidron
Address: 6, place Joffre, 33500 Libourne
Mailing address: Same as above
Telephone: 33 5 57 51 64 88; telefax: 33 5 57 51 56 30
Visits: By appointment only
Contact: Jean-Noël Boidron

VINEYARDS (red)
Surface area: 1.9 acres
Average age of vines: 15 years
Blend: 90% Merlot, 10% Cabernet Franc
Density of plantation: 5,850 vines per hectare
Average yields (over the last 5 years): 22.5 hectoliters per hectare
Total average annual production: 18 hectoliters

GRAND VIN (red)
Brand name: Château Cantelauze
Appellation: Pomerol
Mean annual production: 18 hectoliters

Upbringing: Fermentations are rather long (3–4 weeks) and take place in temperature-controlled vats. There is no addition of yeasts. Seventy-five percent of the yield is aged in oak barrels, and the remaining 25% stays in vats. Wines are fined but not filtered.

LE CARILLON

Classification: None
Location of vineyards: Pomerol
Owner: Louis Grelot
Address: 33500 Pomerol
Mailing address: Same as above
Telephone: 33 5 57 84 56 61
Visits: By appointment only
Contact: Louis Grelot

VINEYARDS (red)
Surface area: 2.47 acres
Average age of vines: 8 years
Blend: 100% Merlot
Density of plantation: 5,500 vines per hectare
Average yields (over the last 5 years): 35 hectoliters per hectare
Total average annual production: 35 hectoliters per hectare

GRAND VIN (red)
Brand name: Château Le Carillon
Appellation: Pomerol
Mean annual production: 35 hectoliters
Upbringing: Fermentations are traditional (3 weeks) in wooden vats. Wines are transferred after malolactics to oak barrels (25% of which are new) for 18 months aging and sometimes more. They are fined but not filtered.

SECOND WINE
None produced.

CLOS DU PÈLERIN

Classification: None
Location of vineyards: Pomerol
Owner: Norbert and Josette Egreteau
Address: Clos du Pèlerin, 1, Grand Garrouilh, 33500 Pomerol

Mailing address: Same as above
Telephone: 33 5 57 74 03 66; telefax: 33 5 57 25 06 17
Visits: Preferably by appointment
Contact: Norbert and Josette Egreteau

VINEYARDS (red)
Surface area: 7.9 acres
Average age of vines: 30 years
Blend: 80% Merlot, 10% Cabernet Franc, 10% Cabernet Sauvignon
Density of plantation: 6,000 vines per hectare
Average yields (over the last 5 years): 44 hectoliters per hectare

GRAND VIN (red)
Brand name: Clos du Pèlerin
Appellation: Pomerol
Mean annual production: 150 hectoliters
Upbringing: Wines are aged both in vats and oak barrels (one-third new) and are bottled 2½ years after the vintage. They are fined but not filtered.

SECOND WINE
None produced.

LA COMMANDERIE

Classification: None
Location of vineyards: Catusseau, in the southern part of Pomerol
Owner: Marie-Hélène Dé
Address: 1, chemin de la Commanderie, 33500 Pomerol
Mailing address: Same as above
Telephone: 33 5 57 51 79 03; telefax: 33 2 35 69 65 15
Visits: By appointment only
Contact: Marie-Hélène Dé at above telephone and fax numbers

VINEYARDS (red)
Surface area: 13.6 acres
Average age of vines: 40 years
Blend: 80% Merlot, 20% Cabernet Franc
Density of plantation: 5,500 vines per hectare
Average yields (over the last 5 years): 50 hectoliters per hectare
Total average annual production: 300 hectoliters

GRAND VIN (red)
Brand name: Château La Commanderie
Appellation: Pomerol

Mean annual production: 240 hectoliters
Upbringing: Fermentations last 15–30 days in stainless-steel vats, and as far as possible no commercial yeasts are used to boost them up. Wines are aged partly in oak barrels (30% of which are new) and partly in vats for 2 years. They are fined and filtered.

SECOND WINE
Brand name: Château Haut-Manoir
Average annual production: 60 hectoliters

LA CROIX ST.-GEORGES

Classification: None
Location of vineyards: Between those of Vieux-Château-Certan, Petit Village, and Le Pin
Owner: S.C. Joseph Janoueix
Address: 33500 Pomerol
Mailing address: c/o Maison J. Janoueix, 37, rue Pline Parmentier, B.P. 192, 33506 Libourne
Telephone: 33 5 57 51 41 86; telefax: 33 5 57 51 53 16
Visits: By appointment only
Contact: Maison J. Janoueix (at above telephone and fax numbers)

VINEYARDS (red)
Blend: 95% Merlot, 5% Cabernet Franc

GRAND VIN (red)
Brand name: Château La Croix St.-Georges
Appellation: Pomerol
Upbringing: Fermentations and malolactics occur in temperature-controlled tanks. Wines are transferred for 12–15 months aging in oak barrels that are renewed by 40% at each vintage. They are fined with egg whites and racked 8 times before bottling.

LA CROIX TAILLEFER

Classification: None
Location of vineyards: In the southeastern part of Pomerol
Owner: S.A.R.L. La Croix Taillefer (managed by Marie-Claude Rivière)
Address: 33500 Pomerol
Mailing address: B.P. 4, 33500 Pomerol

Telephone: 33 5 57 25 08 65; telefax: 33 5 57 74 15 39
Visits: Preferably by appointment, on weekdays except Wednesdays, from
9 A.M. to noon
Contact: Maryse François

VINEYARDS (red)
Surface area: 5 acres
Average age of vines: 50 years
Blend: 100% Merlot
Density of plantation: 6,000 vines per hectare
Average yields (over the last 5 years): 48 hectoliters per hectare
Total average annual production: 12,000 bottles

GRAND VIN (red)
Brand name: La Croix Taillefer
Appellation: Pomerol
Mean annual production: 12,000 bottles
Upbringing: Fermentations last approximately 3 weeks in 70-hectoliter
stainless-steel temperature-controlled vats. Wines are then aged for 18
months in oak barrels, 40% of which are new (30% are 1 vintage old and
40% 2 vintages old). They are fined and filtered.

SECOND WINE
None produced.

LA CROIX TOULIFAUT

Classification: None
Location of vineyards: Between those of Château Beauregard in Pomerol
and Figeac in St.-Emilion
Owner: Jean-François Janoueix
Address: 33500 Pomerol
Mailing address: c/o Maison J. Janoueix, 37, rue Pline Parmentier, B.P.
192, 33506 Libourne
Telephone: 33 5 57 51 41 86; telefax: 33 5 57 51 76 83
Visits: By appointment only
Contact: Mr. and Mrs. Jean-François Janoueix at above telephone and fax
numbers

VINEYARDS (red)
Surface area: 3.9 acres
Average age of vines: 30 years
Blend: 100% Merlot

Density of plantation: 5,700 vines per hectare
Average yields (over the last 5 years): 42 hectoliters per hectare
Total average annual production: 70 hectoliters

GRAND VIN (red)
Brand name: Château La Croix Toulifaut
Appellation: Pomerol
Mean annual production: 70 hectoliters
Upbringing: Fermentations and macerations last approximately 3 weeks.
Wines are transferred to 100% new oak barrels for 18–20 months aging.
They are fined with egg whites but remain unfiltered.

SECOND WINE
None produced.

FERRAND

Classification: None
Location of vineyards: Pomerol and Libourne
Owner: Henry Gasparoux and Sons
Address: "Ferrand," Chemin de la Commanderie, 33500 Libourne
Mailing address: Same as above
Telephone: 33 5 57 51 21 67; telefax: 33 5 57 25 01 41
Visits: Monday through Friday, between 1:30 P.M. and 5:30 P.M.
Contact: Mrs. Petit

VINEYARDS (red)
Surface area: 29 acres
Average age of vines: 30 years
Blend: 50% Merlot, 50% Cabernet Franc
Density of plantation: 5,500 vines per hectare
Average yields (over the last 5 years): 50 hectoliters per hectare
Total average annual production: 80,000 bottles

GRAND VIN (red)
Brand name: Château Ferrand
Appellation: Pomerol
Mean annual production: 80,000 bottles
Upbringing: Fermentations are traditional and occur in temperature-controlled stainless-steel tanks. Wines are aged for 12–18 months in oak casks that are renewed by a third each vintage. They are fined and filtered.

SECOND WINE
None produced.

FEYTIT GUILLOT

Classification: None
Location of vineyards: Pomerol
Owner: Irène Lureau
Address: Catusseau, 33500 Pomerol
Mailing address: Same as above
Telephone: 33 5 57 51 46 58 or 33 5 56 63 19 37
Visits: By appointment only
Contact: Irène Lureau

VINEYARDS (red)
Surface area: 3.2 acres
Average age of vines: 25 years
Blend: 70% Merlot, 20% Cabernet Franc, 10% Cabernet Sauvignon and Malbec
Density of plantation: 5,000 vines per hectare

GRAND VIN (red)
Brand name: Château Feytit Guillot
Appellation: Pomerol
Mean annual production: 50 hectoliters per hectare
Upbringing: Fermentations occur in concrete vats. Wines remain in vats for 6 months and are then transferred to oak barrels for 14 months aging (these are 1-vintage-old barrels bought from Château Cheval Blanc). They are fined but not filtered.

SECOND WINE
None produced.

NOTE: Only part of the production is estate bottled (3–4 barrels). The rest of the production is sold in bulk to *négociants*.

LA GANNE

Classification: None
Location of vineyards: Pomerol
Owner: Michel Dubois
Address: 224, avenue Foch, 33500 Libourne
Mailing address: Same as above
Telephone: 33 5 57 51 18 24; telefax: 33 5 57 51 62 20
Visits: By appointment only, Monday through Friday and on Saturday mornings
Contact: Michel and Paule Dubois

VINEYARDS (red)
Surface area: 9.4 acres
Average age of vines: 35 years
Blend: 80% Merlot, 20% Cabernet Franc and Cabernet Sauvignon
Density of plantation: 6,000 vines per hectare
Total average annual production: 144 hectoliters

GRAND VIN (red)
Brand name: Château La Ganne
Appellation: Pomerol
Mean annual production: 120 hectoliters
Upbringing: Harvesting is manual. Fermentations and macerations
last 3–4 weeks in concrete tanks equipped only with a temperature-
control system. Malolactics occur in tanks, and wines are aged
for 12 months in oak barrels that are renewed by a third at
each vintage. They are fined with fresh egg whites but remain
unfiltered.

SECOND WINE
Brand name: Vieux Châteaubrun
Average annual production: 24 hectoliters

GRAND MOULINET

Classification: None
Location of vineyards: Lieu-dit Grand Moulinet, Pomerol
Owner: Jean-Pierre Fourreau
Address: Ollet-Fourreau, 33500 Néac
Mailing address: Ollet-Fourreau, Château Haut-Surget, 33500 Néac
Telephone: 33 5 57 51 28 68; telefax: 33 5 57 51 91 79
Visits: By appointment only, daily, between 8 A.M. and noon, and 2 P.M.
and 6 P.M.
Contact: Jean-Pierre and Patrick Fourreau

VINEYARDS (red)
Surface area: 5 acres
Average age of vines: 20 years
Blend: 90% Merlot, 5% Cabernet Franc, 5% Cabernet Sauvignon
Density of plantation: 5,500 vines per hectare
Average yields (over the last 5 years): 42 hectoliters per hectare
Total average annual production: 11,000 bottles

GRAND VIN (red)
Brand name: Château Grand Moulinet
Appellation: Pomerol
Mean annual production: 11,000 bottles
Upbringing: Fermentations last 15 days and macerations 1 month. Wines are then aged for 1 year in 100% new oak barrels. They are both fined and filtered.

SECOND WINE
None produced.

GRANGE NEUVE

Classification: None
Location of vineyards: In the western part of Pomerol
Owner: Mr. Gros
Address: Grangeneuve, 33500 Pomerol
Mailing address: Same as above
Telephone: 33 5 57 51 23 03; telefax: 33 5 57 25 36 14
Visits: By appointment only
Contact: Mr. Gros

VINEYARDS (red)
Surface area: 17.3 acres
Average age of vines: 40 years
Blend: 100% Merlot
Density of plantation: 6,700 vines per hectare
Average yields (over the last 5 years): 45 hectoliters per hectare
Total average annual production: 320 hectoliters

GRAND VIN (red)
Brand name: Château Grange Neuve
Appellation: Pomerol
Mean annual production: 30,000 bottles
Upbringing: Fermentations last about a month, with numerous pumping-overs. Wines are transferred to oak casks, which are renewed by a third at each vintage, in December (clarification occurs naturally with cold temperatures), and they are aged for 12–18 months, depending upon the vintage. They are fined with egg whites and are bottled after a light filtration.

SECOND WINE
Brand name: La Fleur des Ormes
Average annual production: 12,000–13,000 bottles

GUILLOT

Classification: None
Location of vineyards: Pomerol
Owner: G.F.A. Luquot Frères
Address: Les Grands Champes, 33500 Catusseau
Mailing address: 152, avenue de l'Epinette, 33500 Libourne
Telephone: 33 5 57 51 18 95; telefax: 33 5 57 25 10 59
Visits: By appointment, from Monday to Friday, between 9 A.M. and 7 P.M.
Contact: Jean-Paul Luquot

VINEYARDS (red)
Surface area: 11.6 acres
Average age of vines: 29 years
Blend: 71% Merlot, 29% Cabernet Franc
Density of plantation: 5,950 vines per hectare
Average yields (over the last 5 years): 52 hectoliters per hectare
Total average annual production: 240 hectoliters

GRAND VIN (red)
Brand name: Château Guillot
Appellation: Pomerol
Mean annual production: 29,000 bottles
Upbringing: Fermentations last 20–25 days in temperature-controlled concrete vats. Wines are then aged for 16 months in oak barrels that are renewed by a third at each vintage. They are fined but not filtered.

SECOND WINE
None produced.

GUILLOT CLAUZEL

Classification: None
Location of vineyards: Catusseau
Owner: Mr. and Mrs. Clauzel
Address: 33500 Pomerol
Mailing address: Same as above
Telephone: 33 5 57 51 14 09; telefax: 33 5 57 51 57 66
Visits: By appointment only (except during weekends)
Contact: Mrs. Clauzel

VINEYARDS (red)
Surface area: 4.2 acres
Average age of vines: 33 years
Blend: 60% Merlot, 40% Cabernet Franc
Density of plantation: 7,000 vines per hectare
Average yields (over the last 5 years): 30–35 hectoliters per hectare
Total average annual production: 650 cases

GRAND VIN (red)
Brand name: Château Guillot Clauzel
Appellation: Pomerol
Mean annual production: 350–400 cases
Upbringing: Fermentations last between 20 and 35 days, depending upon
the vintage (1992—3 weeks; 1995—5 weeks), and occur at temperatures
of 28–32 degrees centigrade. There are 3 pumping-overs daily, and
malolactics occur in barrels. Wines are brought up in oak barrels, 50%–
60% of which are new (the rest are 1 vintage old), for 12–15 months.
They are sometimes fined (depending upon the vintage) but not filtered.

SECOND WINE
Brand name: Château Graves Guillot
Average annual production: 250–300 cases

HAUT-CLOQUET

Classification: None
Location of vineyards: Pomerol
Owner: François de Lavaux
Address: 33500 Pomerol
Mailing address: c/o Ets. Horeau Beylot, B.P. 125, 33501 Libourne Cedex
Telephone: 33 5 57 51 06 07; telefax: 33 5 57 51 59 61
Visits: By appointment only

VINEYARDS (red)
Surface area: 7.4 acres
Average age of vines: 15–20 years
Blend: 50% Merlot, 30% Cabernet Sauvignon, 20% Cabernet Franc
Average yields (over the last 5 years): 40–45 hectoliters per hectare
Total average annual production: 18,000 bottles

GRAND VIN (red)
Brand name: Château Haut-Cloquet
Appellation: Pomerol

Mean annual production: 18,000 bottles
Upbringing: Fermentations and macerations last 18–23 days in temperature-controlled stainless-steel and concrete tanks. Malolactics usually occur in tanks (sometimes a very small percentage of the yield completes this process in oak barrels), and wines are aged for 8–12 months by rotation in oak barrels, 10%–15% of which are new (60% of the yield), and concrete tanks (40% of the yield). They are fined and filtered.

SECOND WINE
None produced.

HAUT-FERRAND

Classification: None
Location of vineyards: Pomerol and Libourne
Owner: Henry Gasparoux and Sons
Address: "Ferrand," Chemin de la Commanderie, 33500 Libourne
Mailing address: Same as above
Telephone: 33 5 57 51 21 67; telefax: 33 5 57 25 01 41
Visits: Monday through Friday, between 1:30 P.M. and 5:30 P.M.
Contact: Mrs. Petit

VINEYARDS (red)
Surface area: 11.1 acres
Average age of vines: 25 years
Blend: 70% Merlot, 30% Cabernet Franc
Density of plantation: 5,500 vines per hectare
Average yields (over the last 5 years): 45 hectoliters per hectare
Total average annual production: 20,000 bottles

GRAND VIN (red)
Brand name: Château Haut-Ferrand
Appellation: Pomerol
Mean annual production: 20,000 bottles
Upbringing: Fermentations are traditional and occur in temperature-controlled stainless-steel tanks. Wines are aged for 12–18 months in oak casks that are renewed by a third at each vintage. They are fined and filtered.

SECOND WINE
None produced.

HAUT-MAILLET

Classification: None
Location of vineyards: Pomerol
Owner: J.-P. Estager
Address: 33500 Pomerol
Mailing address: 33 à 41, rue de Montaudon, 33500 Libourne
Telephone: 33 5 57 51 04 09; telefax: 33 5 57 25 13 38
Visits: By appointment only
Contact: François Estager

VINEYARDS (red)
Surface area: 12.4 acres
Average age of vines: 23 years
Blend: 60% Merlot, 40% Cabernet Franc
Density of plantation: 5,800 vines per hectare
Average yields (over the last 5 years): 48 hectoliters per hectare
Total average annual production: 240 hectoliters

GRAND VIN (red)
Brand name: Château Haut-Maillet
Appellation: Pomerol
Mean annual production: 30,000 bottles
Upbringing: Fermentations last 20 days in temperature-controlled
stainless-steel tanks. Malolactics occur in vats, and wines are
then transferred to oak barrels, 30% of which are new, for 14–18
months aging, depending upon the vintage. They are fined and
filtered.

SECOND WINE
None produced.

Evaluation of present classification: The quality equivalent of a Médoc
Cru Bourgeois
Plateau of maturity: 4–10 years following the vintage

Jean-Pierre Estager, the well-known proprietor of La Cabanne, owns this tiny
vineyard situated on the outskirts of Pomerol, adjacent to Bon Pasteur. Very
little of their wine is ever exported since the estate consists of only 12.4
acres.

LAFLEUR DU ROY

Classification: None
Location of vineyards: Catusseau, in the southern part of Pomerol
Owner: Yvon Dubost
Address: 13, rue des Lavandières, Catusseau, 33500 Pomerol
Mailing address: Same as above
Telephone: 33 5 57 51 74 57; telefax: 33 5 57 25 99 95
Visits: By appointment only, Monday through Friday, between 9 A.M. and
noon, and 2 P.M. and 6 P.M.
Contact: Laurent Dubost

VINEYARDS (red)
Surface area: 7.9 acres
Average age of vines: 30 years
Blend: 80% Merlot, 10% Cabernet Sauvignon, 10% Cabernet Franc
Density of plantation: 5,500 vines per hectare
Average yields (over the last 5 years): 50 hectoliters per hectare
Total average annual production: 20,000 bottles

GRAND VIN (red)
Brand name: Château Lafleur du Roy
Appellation: Pomerol
Mean annual production: 20,000 bottles
Upbringing: Fermentations last 3 weeks in temperature-controlled
stainless-steel tanks. Wines are aged for 18 months in oak casks, 20% of
which are new. They are racked every 3 months, fined with egg whites
(in vats) and remain unfiltered.

SECOND WINE
None produced.

Evaluation of present classification: The quality equivalent of a Médoc
Cru Bourgeois
Plateau of maturity: 4–10 years following the vintage

I rarely see the wines of Lafleur du Roy, whose vineyard is located in the
southwestern section of the Pomerol appellation on sandy, gravelly soil, between Château Plince and Château Nenin. Most of the production is sold in
Belgium and Denmark. Monsieur Dubost is also the proprietor of the St.-
Emilion Grand Cru Vieux-Château-Carré.

LA LOUBIÈRE

Classification: None
Location of vineyards: In the southeastern part of Pomerol
Owner: Marie-Claude Rivière
Address: 33500 Pomerol
Mailing address: B.P. 4, 33500 Pomerol
Telephone: 33 5 57 25 08 65; telefax: 33 5 57 74 15 39
Visits: Preferably by appointment, on weekdays except Wednesdays, from
9 A.M. to noon
Contact: Maryse François

VINEYARDS (red)
Surface area: 6.2 acres
Average age of vines: 40 years
Blend: 100% Merlot
Density of plantation: 6,000 vines per hectare
Average yields (over the last 5 years): 45 hectoliters per hectare
Total average annual production: 14,000 bottles

GRAND VIN (red)
Brand name: La Loubière
Appellation: Pomerol
Mean annual production: 14,000 bottles
Upbringing: Fermentations last approximately 3 weeks in 87-hectoliter
stainless-steel temperature-controlled vats. Wines are then aged for 15
months in oak barrels that are renewed by a third at each vintage. They
are fined and filtered.

SECOND WINE
None produced.

MAZEYRES

Classification: None
Location of vineyards: In the southern and eastern part of the appellation,
on the commune of Libourne
Owner: Caisse de Retraite de la Société Générale
Address: 56, avenue Georges Pompidou, 33500 Libourne
Mailing address: Same as above
Telephone: 33 5 57 51 00 48; telefax: 33 5 57 25 22 56

Visits: By appointment only
Contact: Alain Moueix

VINEYARDS (red)
Surface area: 48 acres
Average age of vines: More than 33 years
Blend: 80% Merlot, 20% Cabernet Franc
Density of plantation: 6,000 vines per hectare
Average yields: 48 hectoliters per hectare
Total average annual production: Approximately 1,000 hectoliters

GRAND VIN (red)
Brand name: Château Mazeyres
Appellation: Pomerol
Mean annual production: Approximately 85,000 bottles
Upbringing: Fermentations last about 3 weeks in temperature-
controlled stainless-steel vats of small capacity (60–120 hectoliters).
One-third of the yield undergoes malolactics in new oak barrels,
and the other two-thirds are transferred to oak barrels (not new)
after completion of malolactics in vats. The wine remains for 18
months in oak and is lightly fined with fresh egg whites but not
filtered.

SECOND WINE
Brand name: Château Beaulieu
Average annual production: 20,000 bottles

Evaluation of present classification: The quality equivalent of a Médoc
Cru Bourgeois
Plateau of maturity: 3–8 years following the vintage

MONTVIEL

Classification: None
Location of vineyards: Pomerol
Owner: Yves and Catherine Péré-Vergé
Address: 1, rue du Grand Moulinet, 33500 Pomerol
Mailing address: 15, rue Henri Dupuis, 62500 St.-Omer
Telephone: 33 5 57 51 87 92; telefax: 33 3 21 95 47 74
Visits: By appointment only
Contact: Jean-Marie Bouldy at 33 5 57 51 20 47 and
telefax 33 5 57 51 23 14

VINEYARDS (red)
Surface area: 12.7 acres
Average age of vines: 25 years
Blend: 80% Merlot, 20% Cabernet Franc
Density of plantation: 6,000 vines per hectare
Average yields (over the last 5 years): 45 hectoliters per hectare
Total average annual production: 23,000 bottles

GRAND VIN (red)
Brand name: Château Montviel
Appellation: Pomerol
Upbringing: Fermentations last 4 weeks in temperature-controlled
stainless-steel tanks. Malolactics occur in oak barrels, and wines are then
aged for 18 months in oak barrels, 40% of which are new (the rest being
1 and 2 vintages old). They are fined but not filtered.

SECOND WINE
Brand name: La Rose Montviel
Average annual production: variable

NOUVELLE EGLISE

Classification: None
Production: 1,200 cases
Blend: 50% Merlot, 50% Cabernet Franc
Secondary label: None
Vineyard size: 6.9 acres
Proprietor: Servant-Dumas
Time spent in barrels: 18–24 months
Average age of vines: 25 years

Evaluation of present classification: The quality equivalent of a Médoc
Cru Bourgeois
Plateau of maturity: 4–8 years following the vintage

LA PATACHE

Classification: None
Location of vineyards: Lieu-dit La Patache, in Pomerol
Owner: S.A.R.L. de La Diligence
Address: La Patache, 33500 Pomerol

Mailing address: B.P. 78, 33330 St.-Emilion
Telephone: 33 5 57 55 38 03; telefax: 33 5 57 55 38 01
Visits: Preferably by appointment, Monday through Friday, from 8 A.M. to
6 P.M.
Contact: Philippe Lauret

VINEYARDS (red)
Surface area: 8.2 acres
Average age of vines: 35 years
Blend: 80% Merlot, 20% Cabernet Franc
Density of plantation: 6,600 vines per hectare
Average yields (over the last 5 years): 50 hectoliters per hectare

GRAND VIN (red)
Brand name: Château La Patache
Appellation: Pomerol
Mean annual production: 150 hectoliters
Upbringing: Fermentations (alcoholic and malolactic) occur in
stainless-steel tanks. Wines are then transferred to oak barrels, 50% of
which are new, for aging. They are fined but not filtered.

SECOND WINE
None produced.

PLINCETTE

Classification: None
Location of vineyards: Pomerol
Owner: J.-P. Estager
Address: 33500 Pomerol
Mailing address: 33–41, rue de Montaudon, 33500 Libourne
Telephone: 33 5 57 51 04 09; telefax: 33 5 57 25 13 38
Visits: By appointment only
Contact: François Estager

VINEYARDS (red)
Surface area: 5 acres
Average age of vines: 18 years
Blend: 70% Merlot, 30% Cabernet Franc
Density of plantation: 5,800 vines per hectare
Average yields (over the last 5 years): 48 hectoliters per hectare
Total average annual production: 96 hectoliters

GRAND VIN (red)
Brand name: Château Plincette
Appellation: Pomerol
Mean annual production: 12,000 bottles
Upbringing: Fermentations last 20 days in temperature-controlled stainless-steel vats. Malolactics occur in vats, too. Wines are then transferred to oak barrels, 20% of which are new, for 14–18 months aging, depending upon the vintage. They are fined and filtered.

SECOND WINE
None produced.

PONT CLOQUET

Classification: None
Location of vineyards: Pomerol
Owner: Stéphanie Rousseau
Address: Pont Cloquet, Petit Sorillon, 33230 Abzac
Mailing address: Same as above
Telephone: 33 5 57 49 06 10; telefax: 33 5 57 49 38 96
Visits: By appointment only
Contact: Stéphanie Rousseau

VINEYARDS (red)
Surface area: 1.2 acres
Average age of vines: 41 years
Blend: 80% Merlot, 20% Cabernet Franc
Density of plantation: 6,000 vines per hectare
Average yields (over the last 5 years): 27 hectoliters per hectare
Total average annual production: 27 hectoliters

GRAND VIN (red)
Brand name: Château Pont Cloquet
Appellation: Pomerol
Mean annual production: 27 hectoliters per hectare
Upbringing: Fermentations last 30 days (at 31 degrees centigrade maximum). Malolactics occur in barrels, and wines are aged for 18 months in new oak barrels. They are fined but not filtered.

SECOND WINE
None produced.

PRIEURS DE LA COMMANDERIE

Classification: None
Location of vineyards: Lieu-dit René, in Pomerol
Owner: Clément Fayat
Address: Lieu-dit René, 33500 Pomerol
Mailing address: c/o Château La Dominique, 33330 St.-Emilion
Telephone: 33 5 57 51 31 36; telefax: 33 5 57 51 63 04
Visits: None

VINEYARDS (red)
Surface area: 8.6 acres
Average age of vines: 30 years
Blend: 75% Merlot, 15% Cabernet Franc, 10% Cabernet Sauvignon
Density of plantation: 6,000 vines per hectare
Average yields (over the last 5 years): 40–42 hectoliters per hectare
Total average annual production: 140 hectoliters

GRAND VIN (red)
Brand name: Prieurs de la Commanderie
Appellation: Pomerol
Mean annual production: 15,000 bottles (maximum)
Upbringing: Fermentations last 3–4 weeks in temperature-controlled
stainless-steel vats, with temperatures maintained at 30–32 degrees
centigrade. Wines are transferred to oak casks (which are renewed
by a third at each vintage) as soon as possible (after 3–4 weeks)
for 12–18 months aging. They are fined with egg whites and
filtered.

SECOND WINE
Brand name: St.-André
Average annual production: 3,000 bottles approximately

Evaluation of present classification: The quality equivalent of a Médoc
Cru Bourgeois
Plateau of maturity: 3–8 years following the vintage

This vineyard, situated in the very western part of the appellation, used to
be called Château St.-André. It is now owned by Monsieur Fayat, the proprietor of the renowned St.-Emilion estate called La Dominique. I have
tasted only a few vintages of Prieurs de la Commanderie, and the wines were
sound, if uninspiring. The sandy, mineral-enriched soil of this area is
known for producing a lighter style of Pomerol that is meant to be drunk
early on.

RATOUIN

Classification: None
Location of vineyards: Pomerol
Owner: G.F.A. Family Ratouin
Address: Village de René, 33500 Pomerol
Mailing address: Same as above
Telephone: 33 5 57 51 47 92 or 33 5 57 51 19 58;
telefax: 33 5 57 51 47 92
Visits: By appointment only
Contact: Jean-François Beney

VINEYARDS (red)
Surface area: 6.2 acres
Average age of vines: 40 years
Blend: 80% Merlot, 20% Cabernet Franc
Density of plantation: 6,000 vines per hectare
Average yields (over the last 5 years): 50 hectoliters
Total average annual production: 14,000 bottles

GRAND VIN (red)
Brand name: Château Ratouin Cuvée Rémi (debut vintage 1995)
Appellation: Pomerol
Mean annual production: 1,800 bottles
Upbringing: Fermentations last 3 weeks. Only Merlot is used for this special cuvée. Wines are then aged for 1 year in 100% new oak barrels. They are fined and filtered.

SECOND WINE
Brand name: Château Ratouin
Average annual production: 12,000 bottles

DOMAINE DU REMPART

Classification: None
Location of vineyards: Pomerol, near Château Gazin
Owner: Paulette Estager
Address: Propriétés Jean-Marie Estager, 55, rue des 4 Frères Robert, 33500 Libourne
Mailing address: Same as above
Telephone: 33 5 57 51 06 97; telefax: 33 5 57 25 90 01
Visits: None

VINEYARDS (red)
Surface area: 4.9 acres
Average age of vines: 20 years
Blend: 100% Merlot
Density of plantation: 6,000 vines per hectare
Average yields (over the last 5 years): 50 hectoliters per hectare
Total average annual production: 100 hectoliters

GRAND VIN (red)
Brand name: Domaine du Rempart
Appellation: Pomerol
Mean annual production: 100 hectoliters
Upbringing: Fermentations occur in lined concrete vats and last
approximately 22 days. Wines remain in vats or are aged in ancient oak
casks for 2 years before being bottled. They are fined and filtered.

SECOND WINE
None produced.

LA RENAISSANCE

Classification: None
Location of vineyards: Pomerol
Owner: François de Lavaux
Address: 33500 Pomerol
Mailing address: c/o Ets. Horeau Beylot, B.P. 125, 33501 Libourne
Telephone: 33 5 57 51 06 07; telefax: 33 5 57 51 59 61
Visits: By appointment only

VINEYARDS (red)
Surface area: Approximately 7.5 acres
Average age of vines: 15–25 years
Blend: 85% Merlot, 15% Cabernet Sauvignon
Density of plantation: 5,500 vines per hectare
Average yields (over the last 5 years): 40 hectoliters per hectare
Total average annual production: 18,000 bottles

GRAND VIN (red)
Brand name: Château La Renaissance
Appellation: Pomerol
Mean annual production: 30,000 bottles
Upbringing: Fermentations and macerations last 18–23 days in

temperature-controlled stainless-steel and concrete tanks. Malolactics usually occur in tanks (sometimes a very small percentage of the yield completes this process in oak barrels), and wines are aged for 8–12 months by rotation in oak barrels, 10%–15% of which are new (60% of the yield), and concrete tanks (40% of the yield). They are fined and filtered.

SECOND WINE
None produced.

RÊVE D'OR

Classification: None
Location of vineyards: Lieu-dit Cloquet, Pomerol
Owner: Maurice Vigier
Address: Cloquet, 33500 Pomerol
Mailing address: Same as above
Telephone: 33 5 57 51 11 92; telefax: 33 5 57 51 87 70
Visits: By appointment only
Contact: Maurice Vigier

VINEYARDS (red)
Surface area: 17.3 acres
Average age of vines: 40 years
Blend: 80% Merlot, 20% Cabernet Sauvignon
Total average annual production: 280 hectoliters

GRAND VIN (red)
Brand name: Château Rêve d'Or
Appellation: Pomerol
Mean annual production: Approximately 1,500 cases
Upbringing: Fermentations and macerations last 3–4 weeks in temperature-controlled stainless-steel tanks. Wines are transferred to oak barrels, 30% of which are new, for 18 months aging. They are fined but not filtered.

SECOND WINE
Brand name: Château de Mayne
Average annual production: Approximately 18,000 bottles

LA ROSE FIGEAC

Classification: None
Location of vineyards: 1 hectare in the very northern part of Pomerol and
4.5 hectares in the extreme south of the appellation
Owner: D.F.A. Despagne-Rapin
Address: 33500 Pomerol
Mailing address: Maison Blanche, 33570 Montagne
Telephone: 33 5 57 74 62 18; telefax: 33 5 57 74 58 98
Visits: By appointment, Monday through Friday, during office hours
Contact: Gérard Despagne

VINEYARDS (red)
Surface area: 13.6 acres (being replanted)
Average age of vines: 40 years
Blend: 85% Merlot, 15% Cabernet Franc
Density of plantation: 5,350 vines per hectare
Average yields (over the last 5 years): 50 hectoliters per hectare
Total average annual production: 270 hectoliters

GRAND VIN (red)
Brand name: Château La Rose Figeac
Appellation: Pomerol
Mean annual production: 15,000 bottles
Upbringing: Fermentations last 15–20 days in epoxy-lined vats. Wines
are then transferred for 12–15 months aging in new oak barrels. They are
fined and filtered.

SECOND WINE
Brand name: Château Hautes Graves de Beaulieu
Average annual production: 3,000–4,000 bottles

ST.-PIERRE

Classification: None
Location of vineyards: Pomerol
Owner: De Lavaux family
Address: 33500 Pomerol
Mailing address: c/o Ets. Horeau Beylot, B.P. 125, 33501 Libourne
Telephone: 33 5 57 51 06 07; telefax: 33 5 57 51 59 61
Visits: By appointment only

VINEYARDS (red)
Surface area: 7.5 acres
Average age of vines: 35 years
Blend: 65% Merlot, 20% Cabernet Franc, 15% Cabernet Sauvignon
Density of plantation: 5,500 vines per hectare
Average yields (over the last 5 years): 30–40 hectoliters per hectare
Total average annual production: 15,000–18,000 bottles

GRAND VIN (red)
Brand name: Château St.-Pierre
Appellation: Pomerol
Mean annual production: 15,000–18,000 bottles
Upbringing: Fermentations and macerations last 18–23 days in
temperature-controlled stainless-steel and concrete tanks. Malolactics
usually occur in tanks (sometimes a very small percentage of the yield
completes this process in oak barrels), and wines are aged for 8–12
months by rotation in oak barrels, 10%–15% of which are new (60% of
the yield), and concrete tanks (40% of the yield). They are fined and
filtered.

SECOND WINE
None produced.

TAILHAS

Classification: None
Location of vineyards: Libourne
Owner: S.C. du Château Tailhas
Address: Route de St.-Emilion, Pomerol, 33500 Libourne
Mailing address: Same as above
Telephone: 33 5 57 51 26 02; telefax: 33 5 57 25 17 70
Visits: Preferably by appointment, Monday through Friday, between
9 A.M. and noon, and 2 P.M. and 6 P.M.; on Saturdays,
by appointment only
Contact: Luc Nebout

VINEYARDS (red)
Surface area: 26 acres
Average age of vines: 35 years
Blend: 70% Merlot, 15% Cabernet Franc, 15% Cabernet Sauvignon
Density of plantation: 5,600 vines per hectare

Average yields (over the last 5 years): 45 hectoliters per hectare
Total average annual production: 5,000 cases

GRAND VIN (red)
Brand name: Château du Tailhas
Appellation: Pomerol
Upbringing: Fermentations last 3 weeks in temperature-controlled
stainless-steel and concrete vats. Malolactics occur in barrels for
part of the yield. Wines are aged partly in new oak barrels and partly
in vats (there is a rotation). They usually remain in oak for
10–18 months, depending upon the vintage. They are fined and
filtered.

SECOND WINE
Brand name: Château La Garenne

Evaluation of present classification: The quality equivalent of a Médoc
Cru Bourgeois
Plateau of maturity: 3–10 years following the vintage

TAILLEFER

Classification: None
Location of vineyards: Libourne
Owner: Héritiers Armand Moueix
Address: 33500 Libourne
Mailing address: Same as above
Telephone: 33 5 57 25 50 45; telefax: 33 5 57 25 50 45
Visits: By appointment only
Contact: Sandrine Yonnet

VINEYARDS (red)
Surface area: 29.7 acres
Average age of vines: 25 years
Blend: 75% Merlot, 25% Cabernet Franc
Density of plantation: 6,000 vines per hectare
Average yields (over the last 5 years): 50 hectoliters per hectare
Total average annual production: 6,500 cases

GRAND VIN (red)
Brand name: Château Taillefer
Appellation: Pomerol
Mean annual production: 5,000 cases

Upbringing: Fermentations and macerations last 3–4 weeks in concrete vats. Wines are transferred after malolactics to oak casks, which are renewed by a third at each vintage, for 15 months. They are fined but not filtered.

SECOND WINE
Brand name: Château Fontmarty
Average annual production: 1,500 cases

Evaluation of present classification: The quality equivalent of a Médoc Cru Bourgeois
Plateau of maturity: 3–10 years following the vintage

Taillefer is a straightforward, fruity, medium-bodied wine without a great deal of complexity, but it is generally soundly made, round, and capable of evolving for 7–10 years before losing its fruit. Recent vintages have rendered consistently sound, attractive, cleanly made wines that are uninspirational but correct. The vineyard, which comprises a number of parcels surrounding the château, is situated to the extreme south of the appellation, along the frontier with St.-Emilion.

THIBEAUD-MAILLET

Classification: None
Location of vineyards: Pomerol
Owner: Roger and André Duroux
Address: 33500 Pomerol
Mailing address: Same as above
Telephone: 33 5 51 51 82 68; telefax: 33 5 57 51 58 43
Visits: Preferably by appointment, between 9 A.M. and noon, and 2 P.M. and 8 P.M.
Contact: Roger or André Duroux

VINEYARDS (red)
Surface area: 2.9 acres
Average age of vines: 25 years
Blend: 85% Merlot, 15% Cabernet Sauvignon
Density of plantation: 5,000 vines per hectare
Average yields (over the last 5 years): 50 hectoliters per hectare
Total average annual production: 6,000 bottles

GRAND VIN (red)
Brand name: Château Thibeaud-Maillet
Appellation: Pomerol

Mean annual production: 5,000–6,000 bottles
Upbringing: Fermentations last about 4 weeks in temperature-controlled tanks. Wines are then aged in oak casks, 50% of which are new, for a period of 16–18 months. They are fined and lightly filtered.

SECOND WINE
None produced.

TOUR ROBERT

Classification: None
Location of vineyards: In Libourne, between those of Château Mazeyres and Château de Sales
Owner: Dominique Leymarie
Address: Chemin de Grangeneuve, 33500 Libourne
Mailing address: Same as above
Telephone: 33 6 09 73 12 78; telefax: 33 5 57 51 99 94
Visits: By appointment, Monday through Friday, between 8 A.M. and 6 P.M.
Contact: Dominique Leymarie

VINEYARDS (red)
Surface area: 11.5 acres
Average age of vines: 30 years
Blend: 65% Merlot, 30% Cabernet Franc, 5% Cabernet Sauvignon
Density of plantation: 6,000 vines per hectare
Average yields (over the last 5 years): 43 hectoliters per hectare
Total average annual production: 26,000 bottles

GRAND VIN (red)
Brand name: Château Tour Robert
Appellation: Pomerol
Mean annual production: 6,000–8,000 bottles
Upbringing: Fermentations last 21–40 days, depending upon the vintage, in concrete vats at temperatures of 29–31 degrees centigrade. There are partial pumping-overs every 3 hours at the beginning of the process and *pigéage* toward the end. Wines are then aged in oak barrels, 60%–70% of which are new, for a period of 12–15 months. They are fined and filtered.

SECOND WINE
Brand name: Château Robert
Average annual production: 18,000–20,000 bottles

VALOIS

Classification: None
Location of vineyards: In Pomerol and Libourne, near Château Taillefer
and Tailhas, and also near the Châteaux La Croix and Beauregard
Owner: Mr. Leydet
Address: S.C.E.A. des Vignobles Leydet, Rouilledinat, 33500 Libourne
Mailing address: Same as above
Telephone: 33 5 57 51 19 77; telefax: 33 5 57 51 00 62
Visits: Monday through Friday, between 8 A.M. and noon, and 2 P.M. to
7 P.M.; till noon only on Saturdays
Contact: Mr. Leydet

VINEYARDS (red)
Surface area: 19.3 acres
Average age of vines: 30 years
Blend: 75% Merlot, 13% Cabernet Franc, 10% Cabernet Sauvignon,
2% Malbec
Density of plantation: 6,000 vines per hectare
Average yields (over the last 5 years): 45 hectoliters per hectare
Total average annual production: 45,000 bottles

GRAND VIN (red)
Brand name: Château de Valois
Appellation: Pomerol
Mean annual production: 45,000 bottles
Upbringing: Alcoholic fermentations last 7 days at temperatures between
30 and 33 degrees centigrade. Macerations last 4–6 weeks depending
upon the vintage, at temperatures not exceeding 22 degrees centigrade.
Wines are transferred to oak barrels for 14–16 months aging. Thirty-five
percent of the yield goes into new oak barrels, 20% remains in vats, and
the rest is aged in 1- and 2-year-old barrels. The wines are fined and
filtered.

SECOND WINE
None produced.

VIEUX MAILLET

Classification: None
Location of vineyards: Lieu-dit Maillet in Pomerol
Owner: G.F.A. du Château Vieux Maillet (directed by Isabelle Motte)
Address: 33500 Pomerol

Mailing address: Same as above
Telephone: 33 5 57 51 04 67; telefax: 33 5 57 51 04 67
Visits: By appointment only
Contact: Isabelle Motte

VINEYARDS (red)
Surface area: 6.5 acres
Average age of vines: 30 years
Blend: 80% Merlot, 20% Cabernet Franc
Density of plantation: 5,600 vines per hectare
Average yields (over the last 5 years): 48 hectoliters per hectare
Total average annual production: 15,500 bottles

GRAND VIN (red)
Brand name: Château Vieux Maillet
Appellation: Pomerol
Mean annual production: 15,500 bottles
Upbringing: Fermentations last 18–25 days, depending upon the vintage, in temperature-controlled concrete tanks. Malolactics occur in oak barrels. Wines are transferred for 12–16 months aging in oak barrels, 40%–50% of which are new (the rest are 1 and 2 years old). They are fined and filtered.

SECOND WINE
None produced.

VIEUX CHÂTEAU FERRON

Classification: None
Location of vineyards: Libourne
Owner: Garzaro family
Address: 36, route de Montagne, 33500 Libourne
Mailing address: c/o Château Le Prieur, 33500 Libourne
Telephone: 33 5 56 30 16 16; telefax: 33 5 56 30 12 63
Visits: By appointment only, Monday through Friday, between 10 A.M. and noon, and 2 P.M. and 6 P.M.
Contact: Pierre Étienne Garzaro

VINEYARDS (red)
Surface area: 9.8 acres
Average age of vines: 35 years
Blend: 90% Merlot, 10% Cabernet Franc

Density of plantation: 7,300 vines per hectare
Average yields (over the last 5 years): 47 hectoliters per hectare
Total average annual production: 25,000 bottles

GRAND VIN (red)
Brand name: Vieux Château Ferron
Appellation: Pomerol
Mean annual production: 15,000 bottles
Upbringing: Fermentations last 15–21 days in temperature-controlled
concrete and stainless-steel vats. Temperatures are maintained at
approximately 30 degrees centigrade for 3–4 days at the end of the
process. Wines are transferred after malolactics into 100% new oak
barrels for 12–14 months aging. They are fined but not filtered.

SECOND WINE
Brand name: Clos des Amandiers
Average annual production: 10,000 bottles

LA VIOLETTE

Classification: None
Production: 2,000 cases
Blend: 80% Merlot, 20% Cabernet Franc
Secondary label: None
Vineyard size: 10 acres
Proprietor: Servant-Dumas family
Time spent in barrels: 24 months
Average age of vines: 35 years

Evaluation of present classification: The quality equivalent of a Médoc
Cru Bourgeois
Plateau of maturity: 5–15 years following the vintage

This obscure Pomerol estate produces 2,000 cases of wine from a well-placed
vineyard near the church of Pomerol. While La Violette can be inconsistent,
it can also produce splendidly rich wine. While I have tasted these vintages
only once, the 1962, 1967, and 1982 all merited outstanding ratings for their
intensity, extract levels, complexity, and character. However, other vintages
exhibit a loosely knit, sometimes musty, old barrel smell and all too frequently
come across as rustic and disjointed.

VRAYE-CROIX-DE-GAY

Classification: None
Location of vineyards: Pomerol
Owner: Baronne Guichard
Address: 33500 Pomerol
Mailing address: S.C.E. Baronne Guichard, Château Siaurac, 33500 Néac
Telephone: 33 5 57 51 64 58; telefax: 33 5 57 51 41 56
Visits: By appointment only (usually during office hours)
Contact: Mr. Bartoletto

VINEYARDS (red)
Surface area: 9 acres
Average age of vines: 35 years
Blend: 80% Merlot, 15% Cabernet Franc, 5% Cabernet Sauvignon
Density of plantation: 5,500 vines per hectare
Average yields (over the last 5 years): 40 hectoliters per hectare
Total average annual production: 175 hectoliters

GRAND VIN (red)
Brand name: Château Vraye-Croix-de-Gay
Appellation: Pomerol
Mean annual production: 175 hectoliters
Upbringing: Fermentations last approximately 3–4 weeks. Wines are
transferred after malolactics into oak casks, 30% of which are new, for 18
months aging. They are both fined and filtered.

SECOND WINE
None produced.

Evaluation of present classification: The quality equivalent of a Médoc
Cru Bourgeois
Plateau of maturity: 5–12 years following the vintage

ST.-EMILION

St.-Emilion is Bordeaux's most aesthetically pleasing tourist attraction. Some will even argue that the walled, medieval village of St.-Emilion, which is perched on several hills amid a sea of vines, is France's most beautiful wine town.

The wine community of St.-Emilion is a very closely knit fraternity that maintains a fierce belief that their wines are the best in Bordeaux. They have always been sensitive and have felt slighted because the region was entirely omitted from the 1855 Classification of the Wines of the Gironde. This is the largest serious red wine appellation of Bordeaux, encompassing 13,434 acres.

St.-Emilion is only a forty-minute drive east from Bordeaux. Pomerol sits to the north, and the obscure satellite appellations of Montagne, Lussac, Puisseguin, and St.-Georges St.-Emilion, as well as the Côtes de Francs and Côtes de Castillon, border it on the east and south. The top vineyards are centered in distinctive and geographically different parts of St.-Emilion. Historically, St.-Emilion's finest wines tended to emerge from vineyards planted on the limestone plateau, the limestone hillsides (the so-called *côtes*), and the gravel terraces adjacent to Pomerol. Yet the decade of the nineties has established that other *terroirs,* if managed by perfectionist proprietors, can produce exceptionally fine wines. The vineyards called *"côtes St.-Emilions"* cover the limestone hillsides that surround much of the walled town of St.-Emilion. There are even a few vineyards located within St.-Emilion. Most of St.-Emilion's best-known wines—Ausone, both Beauséjours, Belair, Canon, Magdelaine, L'Arrosée, and Pavie—are located along these hillsides. Of the official thirteen Premier Grand Cru properties of St.-Emilion (the most recent classification took place in 1996), ten have at least part of their vineyards on these limestone hillsides. The wines from the *côtes* vineyards are all unique and distinctive, but they share a firm, restrained, and more austere character in their youth. However, with proper aging, as a general rule the youthful toughness gives way to wines of richness, power, and complexity.

Certainly Ausone, with its impressive wine cellars carved out of the rocky hillside and steep vineyard filled with very old, gnarled vines, is the most famous wine of the St.-Emilion *côtes.* This property was considered capable of making one of Bordeaux's best wines in the nineteenth century, but the wine of Ausone was surprisingly undistinguished until 1976, when a new winemaking team was installed. Ausone tends to be different from the other

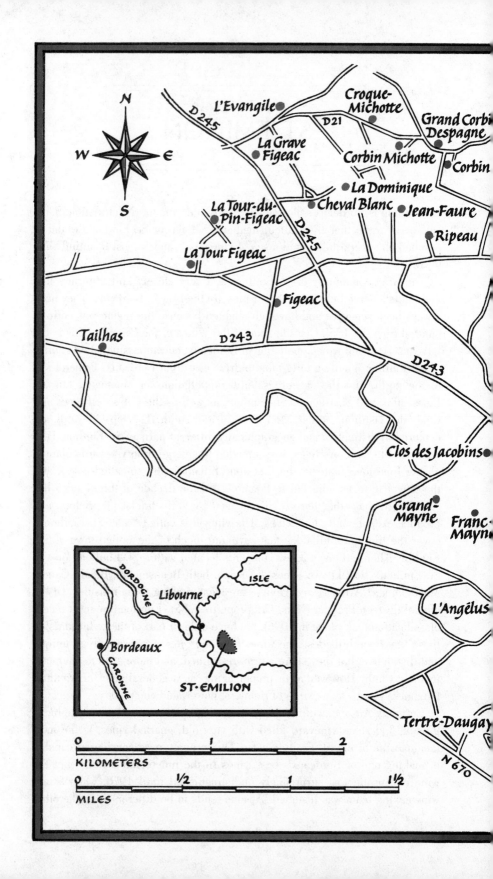

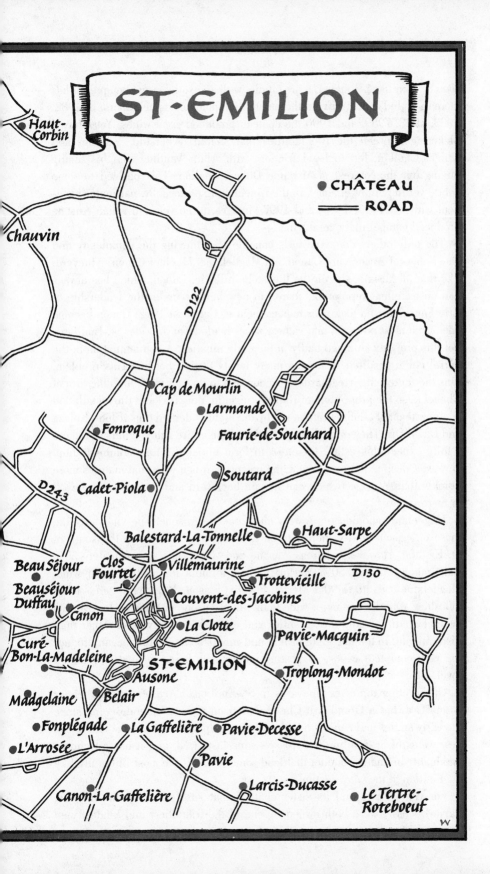

côtes St.-Emilions. Tougher, more tannic, with an exotic, sweet bouquet, it has more of a Médoc austerity on the palate than many of its neighbors. In 1982, 1983, 1988, 1989, and 1990 the château produced great wines. Yet internal bickering between the two families that shared ownership, Vauthier and Dubois-Challon, led to legal friction, with Alain Vauthier and his family buying out the interest of Madame Dubois-Challon. This has led to some subtle yet important changes in the winemaking philosophy, particularly evident with the 1995, 1996, and 1997 vintages, three years in which Ausone produced compellingly great wine.

The only other *côtes* vineyards capable of achieving the complexity and sheer class of Ausone are Canon and Magdelaine. Much of Canon's vineyard, like that of Ausone, sits on the limestone hillside. Canon, which has always had an excellent reputation, soared to new heights under the leadership of Eric Fournier, who took over management of Canon in 1972. Canon became one of the most powerful and richest wines made from the *côtes* St.-Emilions. Yet this property slumped badly in the early nineties. A contamination in the barrel cellar resulted in far too many musty-tasting bottles. This problem, plus the increasing irregularity of Canon, led to its sale in 1996 to the firm of Chanel (also the proprietors of Rauzan-Ségla in Margaux) and the installation of a new team of administrators, led by the highly talented duo of John Kolasa and David Orr. They immediately renovated the entire aging cellars of Canon. I fully expect this estate to return to form under the new administration. However, despite the excellent aging potential, it is a wine that matures more quickly than Ausone (which can remain backward and impenetrable for 30 or more years).

Magdelaine should be a worthy challenger to Ausone. The vineyard, like those of Ausone and Canon, sits on the limestone hillside to the south of St.-Emilion. However, whereas Ausone and Canon use approximately 50% Cabernet Franc and 50% Merlot in their formula for making great wine, Magdelaine uses up to 90% Merlot. For that reason, Magdelaine tends to be a fleshier, rounder, creamier wine than either Ausone or Canon. However, its general quality during the seventies and eighties was only good rather than inspirational. In the late eighties and mid-nineties Magdelaine began producing very complete wines, suggesting quality was being pushed to a higher level.

Of the other top *côtes* vineyards in St.-Emilion, L'Arrosée, not a Premier Grand Cru, but a Grand Cru Classé, has been making splendid wine since the early sixties and can often be counted on to produce one of the half dozen best wines of St.-Emilion. L'Arrosée's wine lasts well, and it has a richness and highly aromatic bouquet that lead some to call it the most Burgundy-like St.-Emilion of the *côtes* section.

For years Pavie and its sister château that sits farther up the hillside, Pavie-Decesse, were both owned by one of the friendliest and kindest men in St.-Emilion, Jean Paul Valette. Pavie is the Premier Grand Cru Classé, Pavie-Decesse the Grand Cru Classé, and both have always been good, yet lighter, more elegant, easygoing styles of St.-Emilion. Valette had been trying to make richer, bigger wines and during the eighties, particularly 1982, 1986, and 1989, and in 1990, he produced some of the finest wines ever made at these two estates. However, inconsistent efforts in the nineties from both châteaux were worrisome. In 1997 Pavie-Decesse was sold to Gérard Perse, the superdriven, high-quality proprietor responsible for the renaissance in quality at Monbousquet, another St.-Emilion estate. In 1998 he purchased Pavie, making Perse the most significant landholder in St.-Emilion.

Belair, the immediate neighbor of Ausone, rarely produces memorable wines. Lighter, more delicate, and earlier to mature than Ausone, Belair, when on form, can be a classy, stylish, medium-weight St.-Emilion that has the potential to reach lofty heights, as it did in 1983 and 1989; but more often than not this is a rather dull, uninspiring wine that seems most suitable for those who prefer their red wines to be austere and spartan.

Of the other famous *côtes* vineyards of St.-Emilion, a number of poor performers have just recently begun to turn things around and produce better and better wine. The Beauséjour estate of Duffau-Lagarrosse and Clos Fourtet of André Lurton have both improved dramatically in quality since the late eighties. Clos Fourtet's style of wine is the more commercial of the two, having abandoned its hard, tannic, stern, and unyielding *côtes* St.-Emilion in favor of a modern, supple, fruity, very easy to like and drink wine. Not so for Beauséjour, which has improved in quality but continues to emphasize the classic *côtes* style of St.-Emilion: tannic, firm, reasonably well colored, and ageworthy. Of note is the fact that this estate turned in three superlative efforts in 1988, 1989, and 1990, the latter wine a true blockbuster and one of the most profound young red wines I have ever tasted.

The other Beauséjour estate on the western slopes of St.-Emilion is owned by the Bécot family (Beau-Séjour Bécot). While its demotion from a Premier Grand Cru to Grand Cru in the 1985 classification of St.-Emilion wines didn't surprise me, I was impressed by the way the Bécots immediately began to fashion richer and more complex wines following their declassification. They were rewarded in 1996 by being promoted back to Premier Grand Cru Classé. In addition, they have begun to produce a 100% Merlot, old-vine cuvée called La Gomerie. The first vintages have been luxuriantly rich and intense in the style of Pomerol's mini-treasure, Le Pin.

Three other *côtes* St.-Emilions estates have the potential to produce some of the region's most profound wines but until recently have rarely done so. The Premiers Grands Crus Classés La Gaffelière and Trotte Vieille and Angélus have superb vineyard expositions and the soil necessary to make wonderful wine.

La Gaffelière has always been a perplexing wine and one of the perennial underachievers among the Premiers Grands Crus Classés of St.-Emilion. The location of the vineyard is superb, and in tasting through the wines from the sixties and seventies, one is struck by how wonderful the 1961 and 1970 are. But it was not until 1982 that the quality began to improve. Since the early eighties La Gaffelière has returned to form. While this will never be a blockbuster St.-Emilion, it is perhaps, along with Figeac, the most quintessentially elegant and finesse-styled St.-Emilion of all the Premiers Grands Crus Classés.

Trotte Vieille used to be another disappointing property, and it remains distressingly irregular, but under the leadership of Philippe Castéja, there has been progress since the late eighties. Angélus was a Grand Cru Classé until the recent 1996 reclassification, when it was justifiably promoted. This property, which went through a dreadfully mediocre period during the sixties and seventies, began to make good wines in the mid-eighties but has, since 1988, made remarkably intense, rich, even outstanding wines that are among the greatest not only of St.-Emilion, but of all Bordeaux. This estate, more than any other in Bordeaux, symbolizes what exceptional things can take place when an inspired person, in this case Hubert de Boüard, embarrassed by the shoddy wines of his predecessors, embarks on a program of producing a wine with no compromises. Angélus has been magnificent in the recent great vintages 1989, 1990, and 1995 and, perhaps more noteworthy, superb in difficult years, 1992, 1993, and 1994 being three salient examples.

These are not the only up-and-coming estates that are situated on either the limestone plateau or the hillside sections of St.-Emilion. One of the newest superstars of St.-Emilion is Canon-La-Gaffelière, which actually is one of the châteaux often referred to as being located on the *pieds de côtes,* meaning that its vineyard is situated at the foot of the hillsides. This property made profound wines in the late eighties and continues to be one of the stars of St.-Emilion in the nineties.

A property to watch carefully is Troplong-Mondot. The exciting quality of recent vintages of Troplong-Mondot has begun to be noticed outside St.-Emilion. The wine, produced by one of the leading ladies of Bordeaux, Christine Fabre, has all of the earmarks for becoming one of the great classics of St.-Emilion. This undervalued wine has been especially brilliant during the late eighties and nineties and, in my mind, should have been promoted to a Premier Grand Cru Classé in 1996.

Another Pavie worth considering seriously is Pavie-Macquin. This property, much like Angélus, Troplong-Mondot, Canon-La-Gaffelière, and Trotte Vieille, produced wines of mediocre quality during the decade of the seventies and into the early eighties. However, Pavie-Macquin finished the eighties with superb wines in 1988, 1989, and 1990 and has continued to build on this success with superb wines in the mid-nineties. It appears this is another up-and-coming star of the appellation. This organically farmed vineyard (a rarity in Bordeaux) is beautifully located on the plateau above the limestone hillside referred to as the Côte Pavie. One can taste the essence of low-yielding old vines in Pavie-Macquin.

Le Tertre-Roteboeuf is a tiny gem of a château located on the hillside section of St.-Emilion near its more famous neighbor, Larcis-Ducasse. Le Tertre-Roteboeuf has made monumental wines since the mid-eighties under the compulsive/obsessive eyes and hands of proprietor François Mitjavile. This property is the single greatest discovery I have ever made in the Bordeaux region. No compromises are made in producing the wine, and the result is the only St.-Emilion that can truly be called the Pétrus of St.-Emilion—it is that rich and compelling. Le Tertre-Roteboeuf should have been promoted to a Premier Grand Cru Classé in the 1996 classification, but too many influential people are jealous of this estate's star status.

Another section where St.-Emilion's best wines can be found is called the *graves terraces,* often referred to as *graves et sablés anciens* (or stones and ancient sand). Only 4 kilometers from the town of St.-Emilion and immediately to the northeast of Libourne, the area derives its name from the soil, a gravelly bed intermixed with some clay and sand. The top properties, Cheval Blanc, Figeac, La Dominique, Corbin, and Corbin-Michotte, produce a lush, more velvety, voluptuous wine that shows quite well when young. Yet in the top vintages these wines have excellent aging potential. These properties sit right on the southeastern border of Pomerol and often exhibit the same lush, supple fruitiness as the two closest Pomerol estates of l'Evangile and La Conseillante.

Many Bordeaux wine enthusiasts would argue that there is no greater St.-Emilion than Cheval Blanc. Even with the renaissance at Ausone, Cheval Blanc remains the quintessential St.-Emilion, opulent, decadently rich, exotic, surprisingly easy to drink when young, but capable of lasting 30 or more years in superb vintages such as 1982 and 1990. Cheval Blanc and Figeac are the only two Premiers Grands Crus from the graves section of St.-Emilion. An objective analysis of the top estates of this sector would reveal that La Dominique merits serious consideration for inclusion.

Cheval Blanc's vineyard is situated on deep gravelly soil with certain parts clay and sand as well as iron. Perhaps the most unique aspect of this wine is that nowhere else in Bordeaux does the Cabernet Franc grape produce such intoxicatingly perfumed and luxuriously rich, compelling wines. Cheval Blanc can be almost overpoweringly rich, deep, and fruity in vintages such as 1921, 1929, 1947, 1948, 1949, 1953, 1961, 1964, 1982, 1983, 1985, 1990, and 1995, and this fact, no doubt, explains why much of this wine is drunk before it ever achieves maturity. Figeac, the immediate neighbor of Cheval Blanc, is often compared with Cheval Blanc; however, Figeac is a very different style of wine. With a high percentage of Cabernet Sauvignon for a St.-Emilion and much sandier soil than Cheval Blanc, Figeac tends to be a more herbaceous-scented, lighter wine. However, Figeac's great vintages produce complex fruity, soft, charming, and concentrated wines that can be drunk when they are only 4–5 years old. Lamentably, only a handful of recent vintages—1964, 1970, 1975, 1982, and 1990—have exhibited the stuffing to suggest they can stand the test of time. Figeac has an extraordinary *terroir*, and when it hits the bull's-eye it is a wine of singular complexity and character, but, sadly, that occurs too infrequently.

La Dominique, an impressive wine and up-and-coming estate, sits just to the north of Cheval Blanc. La Dominique produces excellent wine with lush richness, a deep fruitiness, plenty of body, and aging potential of 10–20 years. It is a wine that might merit elevation to a Premier Grand Cru Classé. In some vintages—1955, 1970, 1971, 1982, 1989, and 1990—this property can produce wines rivaling the best in St.-Emilion.

It would be an over-simplification to think that the only fine wines of St.-Emilion come from the *graves* plateau and the hillsides or limestone plateau sectors of this appellation. There are other portions of St.-Emilion that have slightly different soils, and several properties in these sections of the appellation are capable of producing excellent wines.

On the sand-covered slopes, often called the plains of St.-Emilion, properties like Larmande, Cap de Mourlin, and Cadet-Piola are making excellent wine. The plateau that fans out to the east of St.-Emilion has predominantly clay and sand soil with a limestone base. Soutard is the outstanding estate in this area. Two other perennial overachievers are La Clotte and Balestard-La-Tonnelle; both are capable of producing fine wines.

Last, one property that is in none of the above geographic areas of St.-Emilion but makes excellent wine is Clos des Jacobins, a property located a kilometer northwest of St.-Emilion.

St.-Emilion developed its own classification of wine quality in 1954. On paper, the system developed by St.-Emilion should be the best of all the Bordeaux wine classifications. The classification is based on reputation, soil analysis, and tasting. Unlike the 1855 classification, which has been infinitely rigid and inflexible (except for the elevation of Mouton-Rothschild in 1973), the St.-Emilion classification is supposed to be revised every 10 years, so that in theory top vineyards can be promoted and poorly run vineyards demoted. However, the first major revision in 1969 changed very little. The 1969 classification established a four-tiered hierarchy. The hierarchy that was in effect until 1985 established at the top level twelve Premiers Grands Crus Classés, of which two were given recognition as the best. These were called Premiers Grands Crus Classés "A," and the remaining ten were labeled Premiers Grands Crus Classés "B." The second rung of this ladder of quality was the Grands Crus Classés, of which there were seventy-two. The third level of quality was for wines entitled to the status Grand Cru. The bottom level of St.-Emilion's quality hierarchy was for the wines that were entitled only to the appellation St.-Emilion. In the 1996 reclassification there were no demotions from the Premier Grand Cru level, yet two estates, Angélus and Beau-Séjour Bécot, were promoted—justifiably, in my view.

A trend that began in St.-Emilion (and may spread throughout Bordeaux) is a growing movement toward micro-vinifications of selected small vineyard parcels, usually comprising a high percentage of Merlot. The early performances of the following wines place them among the most ravishing, exotic, concentrated, and compelling wines being made in St.-Emilion. Only time will reveal how well they evolve and whether they justify their lofty, sometimes ridiculous, prices. Certainly there is no disagreement with the fact that these wines are the result of perfectionist proprietors pushing the envelope of quality as far as it can go. The first of these wines, Château Valandraud, is made from the assemblage of several different-vineyard parcels. The obsessive-compulsive, highly talented proprietor, Jean-Luc Thunevin, did not even make wine prior to 1991, Valandraud's debut vintage. The wine has become a cherished collector's dream, fetching prices that are undoubtedly surreal. Valandraud sells for prices far higher than Cheval Blanc or Ausone, which is no doubt unsettling to the ruling elite of St.-Emilion. These super-rich wines are made from exceptionally low yields as well as very ripe late harvested fruit, and they are bottled with neither fining nor filtration, a rarity in modern-day Bordeaux. They have been thrilling efforts, even in such difficult vintages as 1993 and 1994, and absolutely spectacular in vintages such as 1995 and 1996. The wines give every indication of lasting for 15–20 years, but since there is no track record, there is a degree of uncertainty about how well they will evolve despite their considerable promise.

Several other luxury-priced wines that are the product of micro-vinifications include La Gomerie, made by Gérard Bécot, proprietor of Beau-Séjour Bécot. Produced from 100% Merlot, the wine is fermented and aged in 100% new oak. Offerings thus far have been impressively rich, creamy-textured, blockbuster-style Merlots made from extremely ripe fruit and bottled without filtration. If they seem somewhat more forward than Valandraud, they do give every indication of lasting for 10–15+ years. Another newcomer to the microvinification, luxury-priced St.-Emilion sweepstakes is La Mondotte. While this wine was first made in 1995, it was the 1996 vintage (800 cases) that turned the wine world on its head. Nearly 100% Merlot, made from a 30-year-old parcel of vines located between Le Tertre-Roteboeuf and Canon-La-Gaffelière, and fermented and aged in 100% new oak casks, this is one of the most concentrated young Bordeaux wines I have ever tasted. It gives every indication of lasting for two decades or more. La Mondotte is made by

Comte Stephan Von Neipperg, the perfectionist proprietor of Canon-La-Gaffelière.

Other high-quality wines making waves among consumers include La Couspaude and Ferrand Lartigue. Both wines are made in very limited quantities, primarily from Merlot, although La Couspaude includes 30% Cabernet Franc. Both are given 100% new oak treatment. La Couspaude is made by the Aubert family, a well-known name in St.-Emilion, and while some have argued for a more controlled use of new oak with this wine, it is an exotic, flashy, flamboyant, exceptionally well made St.-Emilion. Made in the same hedonistic style is Ferrand Lartigue, a small estate that has turned out exquisite wines since the mid-nineties. Another wine made in the same style is Rol Valentin, made by proprietor E. Prisette. This is a sumptuous, exceptionally rich wine that offers lavish quantities of texture, fruit, and oak.

Given the extraordinary success of these limited-production wines to date, there is no reason to doubt that more imitators will be emerging from St.-Emilion, giving consumers plenty of wines to get excited about, assuming they can afford and find them.

St.-Emilion produces wines that have enormous crowd appeal. Fleshy, quick maturing, round, and generous, they are easy to like, easy to drink, and easy to understand. While the Premiers Grands Crus Classés are expensive, many of the Grands Crus Classés are significantly undervalued and can represent excellent bargains.

Since quality of the soils, the winemaking, and the combination of grape varietals planted in the vineyards are so diverse in St.-Emilion, it is exceedingly difficult to generalize about vintages in this vast appellation. Certainly the great vintages for St.-Emilion have been 1990, 1983, and 1982 (probably the three best vintages for this region in the post–World War II era). The other top vintages have been 1995, 1989, 1986, 1970, 1964, and, of course, 1961. The key to any excellent or great vintage for St.-Emilion is the healthy flowering and ripening to full maturity of the Merlot and Cabernet Franc grapes, the two most important grapes for this region.

Since this area has an enormous number of wine-producing estates, I have emphasized in my tastings and in this chapter the Premiers Grands Crus Classés and Grands Crus Classés. It may be arbitrary, even capricious, but given the sheer number of St.-Emilions that merit coverage from the two aforementioned categories, I have generally disregarded the generic St.-Emilions, except where their level of quality merits interest. Some of these wines can, in fact, be good, but they never have the consistency of the top estates.

ST.-EMILION
(An Insider's View)

Overall Appellation Potential: Average to Superb

The Most Potential for Aging: Angélus, L'Arrosée, Ausone, Beauséjour-Duffau, Canon-La-Gaffelière, Cheval Blanc, La Dominique, Magdelaine, La Mondotte, Pavie-Decesse (since 1997), Pavie-Macquin, Troplong-Mondot, Valandraud

The Most Elegant: Ausone, Belair, Chauvin, Figeac, La Gaffelière, La Plagnotte-Bellevue, Trotte Vieille

The Most Concentrated: Angélus, L'Arrosée, Ausone, Beauséjour-Duffau, Canon-La-Gaffelière, Cheval Blanc, Destieux, La Dominique, Larmande, Magdelaine, Monbousquet, La Mondotte, Moulin St.-Georges, Pavie-Decesse (since 1997), Pavie-Macquin, Troplong-Mondot, Valandraud

The Best Value: Corbin, Corbin-Michotte, Daugay, La Fleur de Jaugue, Lucie, Rolland-Maillet, Vieux Fontin

The Most Exotic: Cheval Blanc, La Couspaude, Ferrand Lartigue, La Gomerie, La Mondotte, Le Tertre-Roteboeuf, Valandraud, Rol Valentin, Gracia, l'Hermitage

The Most Difficult to Understand (when young): Ausone, Belair, Canon, Fonroque, Larcis-Ducasse

The Most Underrated: Clos des Jacobins, Clos de l'Oratoire, Faugères, Larmande, La Tour-Figeac, Monbousquet, Moulin St.-Georges, Pavie-Macquin

The Easiest to Appreciate Young: Dassault, Le Tertre-Roteboeuf

Up-and-Coming Estates: Barde-Haut, Chauvin, Clos de l'Oratoire, Grandes Murailles, Daugay, Destieux, Faugères, La Fleur de Jaugue, Grand-Pontet, Monbousquet, Pavie-Decesse, Rol Valentin

Greatest Recent Vintages: 1995, 1990, 1983, 1982, 1964, 1961

ST.-EMILION—AN OVERVIEW

Location:	This area, part of the right bank viticultural region of Bordeaux southeast of Pomerol, is approximately 20 miles from downtown Bordeaux
Acres under Vine:	13,434
Communes:	St.-Emilion, St.-Hippolyte, St.-Christophe des Bardes, St.-Laurent des Combs, St.-Pey d'Arnens, St.-Sulpice de Faleyrens, Vignonnet, St.-Etienne de Lisse
Average Annual Production:	2,800,000 cases
Classified Growths:	Total of 68: 2 Premiers Grands Crus Classés A,

11 Premiers Grands Crus Classés B, and 55 Grands
Crus Classés

Principal Grape
Varieties: Merlot, Cabernet Franc

Principal Soil
Types: Great diversity is the rule of thumb. On the southern
hillsides of the town of St.-Emilion are the limestone
outcrops. In the direction of Pomerol, clay, sand, and
gravel dominate the vineyards.

A CONSUMER'S CLASSIFICATION OF THE
CHÂTEAUX OF ST.-EMILION

OUTSTANDING

Angélus, Ausone, Canon-La-Gaffelière, Cheval Blanc, La Gomerie,
La Mondotte, Le Tertre-Roteboeuf, Troplong-Mondot, Valandraud

EXCELLENT

L'Arrosée, Beau-Séjour Bécot, Beauséjour (Duffau-Lagarrosse), Canon, Clos
de l'Oratoire, La Couspaude, La Dominique, Ferrand Lartigue, Figeac,
Grand-Mayne, L'Hermitage (since 1997), Larmande, Monbousquet (since
1994), Pavie-Macquin, Rol Valentin (since 1995), Soutard

VERY GOOD

Balestard-La-Tonnelle, Barde-Haut (since 1997), Cadet-Piola, Chauvin, Clos
Fourtet, Clos des Jacobins, Corbin-Michotte, Faugères, La Gaffelière,
Gracia (since 1997), Grand-Pontet, Magdelaine, Moulin St.-Georges,
Quinault-l'Enclos

GOOD

Béard, Belair, Bellefont-Belcier, Bergat, Cap de Mourlin,
Chante-Alouette-Cormeil, Clos la Madeleine, Clos St.-Martin, La Clotte,
Corbin, Couvent-des-Jacobins, Croque-Michotte, Curé-Bon, Dassault,
Daugay, Destieux, Faurie-de-Souchard, de Ferrand, Fleur-Cardinale, La
Fleur Pourret, Fonplégade, Fonroque, Franc-Mayne, Godeau, Haut Brisson,
Haut-Corbin, Haut-Sarpe, Jean-Faure, Le Jurat, Larcis-Ducasse, Laroze,
Lucie, Mauvezin, Pavie, Pavie-Decesse, Petit-Faurie-de-Soutard,
Pindefleurs, Ripeau, Rocher-Bellevue-Figeac, Rolland-Maillet,
St.-Georges-Côte Pavie, Tertre-Daugay, La Tour-Figeac, La Tour du
Guetteur, La Tour-du-Pin-Figeac-Moueix, Trotte Vieille

OTHER NOTABLE ST.-EMILION PROPERTIES

Bellevue, Berliquet, Bernateau, Bienfaisance, Jacques Blanc, La Bonnelle, Bouquey, Cadet-Bon, Cantenac, Capet-Guillet, Castelot, Cauze, Cheval-Noir, Clos Labarde, Clos Larcis, Clos Trimoulet, La Clusière, La Commanderie, Cormeil-Figeac, Côtes de Rol, Couronne, Coutet, La Croix-Figeac, La Croix de Jaugue, Cruzeau, La Fleur, Fombrauge, Fonrazade, Galius, La Grâce Dieu, La Grâce Dieu Les Menuts, La Grâce Dieu des Prieures, Grand-Corbin, Grand-Corbin-Despagne, Grand-Corbin-Manuel, La Grave-Figeac, Guadet St.-Julien, Haut-Mazerat, Haut-Quercus, Haut Villet, Lafleur-Vachon, Laniote, Laroque, Leydet-Figeac, Leydet-Valentin, Magnan La Gaffelière, Martinet, Matras, Monlot-Capet, Moulin Bellegrave, Moulin du Cadet, du Paradis, Pasquette, Patris, Pavillon-Cadet, Petit Figeac, Peyrelongue, Pipeau, Pontet-Fumet, Le Prieuré, Prieuré-Lescours, Puy-Blanquet, Puy-Razac, Quercy, Rocher, Rose-Pourret, Roylland, St.-Lô, Sansonnet, Tauzinat L'Hermitage, Tour Baladoz, La Tour-du-Pin-Figeac-Giraud-Bélivier, Trimoulet, Val d'Or, Vieux-Château-Carré, Vieux Sarpe, Villemaurine, Jean Voisin, Yon-Figeac

ANGÉLUS   OUTSTANDING

Classification: St.-Emilion Premier Grand Cru Classé B
Location of vineyards: St.-Emilion
Owner: De Boüard de Laforest and sons
Address: Mazerat, 33330 St.-Emilion
Mailing address: Same as above
Telephone: 33 5 57 24 71 39; telefax: 33 5 57 24 68 56
Visits: By appointment only

VINEYARDS (red)
Surface area: 57.8 acres
Average age of vines: 30 years
Blend: 50% Merlot, 47% Cabernet Franc, 3% Cabernet Sauvignon
Density of plantation: 6,500–7,000 vines per hectare
Average yields (over the last 5 years): 40 hectoliters per hectare
Total average annual production: 125,000 bottles

GRAND VIN (red)
Brand name: Château Angélus
Appellation: St.-Emilion Grand Cru
Mean annual production: 110,000 bottles
Upbringing: Fermentations and macerations last 2–3 weeks in temperature-controlled stainless-steel vats. Wines undergo malolactics in

barrels and are aged 18–22 months in 100% new oak. They are fined
with fresh egg whites and remain unfiltered.

SECOND WINE
Brand name: Carillon d'Angélus
Average annual production: 15,000 bottles

Evaluation of present classification: The quality equivalent of a Médoc
first-growth
Plateau of maturity: 4–12 years following the vintage

Angélus has always been a St.-Emilion with great popular appeal. With a
large production, much of it exported, a lovely label, and a charming, supple
style of wine, Angélus has been able to build a strong following among
enthusiasts of the wines of St.-Emilion. Angélus is located in the Mazerat
Valley, with vineyards planted on calcareous clay loam and clay/sandy
soil on the lower slopes. The entire vineyard enjoys a perfect southern exposure.

In the sixties and seventies Angélus produced a wine that started life with
a charming fruity intensity, then proceeded to disintegrate in a matter of a
few short years. This all changed in the eighties. The well-known Bordeaux
oenologist Michel Rolland was brought in to provide consultation, and he
insisted that the property age the wine in 100% oak casks. Previously the
wine had been aged in vats and saw no oak aging at all. The idea of fermenting
(malolactics) the wine in small oak casks (much like the Pomerol Le Pin)
tends to add an extraordinary amount of complexity and intensity to the wine.
This can be done only by small estates or by those committed to spending
huge sums of money on labor, because it is a time-consuming, back-breaking
process.

The results have been stunning. No doubt the young proprietor, Hubert de
Boüard de Laforest, is also making a much stricter selection of only the best
lots for the final wine. Angélus was denied elevation to Premier Grand Cru
status in the 1985 classification of the wines of St.-Emilion, but it did receive
that promotion in 1996.

The style of the "new" Angélus is one that still emphasizes early drinkability, with intense, rich, supple, fat fruitiness. However, the wine is now much
deeper colored and more concentrated and has more supportive tannins to
help it age better. Certainly the finest wines of the last 3 or 4 decades are the
profound 1988, 1989, 1990, 1994, 1995, 1996, and 1997. Older vintages,
prior to 1986, must be approached with extreme caution, as many of these
wines have fallen completely apart.

VINTAGES

1997— Since 1988 a persuasive argument can be made that no other St.-Emilion has
• been as consistently brilliant as Angélus. Even in such difficult vintages as
90– 1992 and 1993 Angélus produced wines of significant merit. In 1997 this
93 estate's harvest began on September 12 and finished on October 10. The final
blend is 60% Merlot and 40% Cabernet Franc. Not surprisingly, the 1997 is
another superlative effort. The opaque purple color is the most saturated of
any of the St.-Emilion Premiers Crus. The nose offers up thrilling quantities
of *pain grillé*, blackberries, truffles, vanilla, and other jammy fruit aromas.
Concentrated, with soft tannin, lavish concentration, and a luxurious, succulent, low-acid, unctuously textured personality, this super-endowed, undeniably captivating Angélus will be hard to resist in its youth. However, it should
prove to be long-lived for a 1997. Anticipated maturity: 2000–2015. Last
tasted, 3/98.

1996— Performing well in several tastings, this wine possesses a dense black/purple
• color, powerful aromatics of grilled meats, sweet blackberry, plum, and cur-
92– rant fruit, full body, plenty of tannin, and muscular, chewy flavors with excep-
94 tional intensity. New oak is present, but it is less lavishly displayed than in
other vintages of a similar age. This is a backward, 20–30-year wine, although
it is not as ferociously tannic as one might expect given the vintage. Anticipated maturity: 2003–2020. Last tasted, 3/98.

1995— A superb effort in this vintage, Angélus's opaque purple–colored 1995 is a
• massive, powerful, rich offering with plenty of ripe, sweet tannin. The wine's
95 aromatics include scents of Provençal olives, jammy black cherries, blackberries, truffles, and toast. A very full-bodied wine, it is layered, thick, and
pure. This is the most concentrated of the 1995 St.-Emilion Premiers Grands
Crus. Anticipated maturity: 2002–2025. Last tasted, 11/97.

1994— Another inky, purple/black–colored wine, the 1994 offers up heavenly scents
• of smoked meats, barbecue spices, hickory wood, and plenty of cassis and
92 kirsch liqueur. The fruit's phenomenal purity and denseness, as well as its
overall balance, are admirable in view of the massive, muscular personality
of this huge, full-bodied wine oozing with extract. It is a *tour de force* in
winemaking. Anticipated maturity: 2000–2020. Last tasted, 1/97.

1993— One of the four or five most concentrated wines of the vintage, this opaque,
• black/purple–colored 1993 offers an intensely fragrant nose of smoke, olives,
92 chocolate, black fruits, hickory, and sweet, spicy oak. Amazingly rich and full
bodied, with massive extract, it is almost unbelievable that this wine could
have been produced in a vintage such as 1993. Give it 3–4 years of cellaring,
and drink it over the following 15–18 years. Last tasted, 1/97.

1992— No estate has produced a more impressive array of wines since 1986 than
• Angélus. In what can be a light-bodied, sometimes dilute year, Angélus
89 has turned out one of the vintage's stars. Exhibiting a dark ruby/purple
color, a big, smoky, licorice-and-herb-scented nose, and gobs of ripe,
chocolatey, cassis fruit, the 1992 finishes with sweet tannin and no evidence of dilution. Charm, fatness, depth, purity, and suppleness are present

in this impressive wine. Anticipated maturity: Now–2004. Last tasted, 11/94.

1991 — One of the few successful wines of the vintage in St.-Emilion, the 1991
• reveals a complex bouquet of chocolate, coffee, toasty new oak, herbs, and
87 jammy red fruits. Lusciously ripe fruit is presented in a medium-bodied, sweet, round format that offers immediate gratification. It should drink well for another 5–6 years. Given how difficult the 1991 vintage was, this effort is noteworthy. Last tasted, 1/94.

1990 — The opaque purple–colored 1990 is softer (because of the vintage's great
• ripeness) as well as lower in acidity than the 1989, giving it a marginally more
96 forward and flattering set of aromatics and flavors. However, the impression is one of a big, beefy, thick, super-rich wine, offering that telltale Angélus nose of smoky vanillin oak, olives, jammy cassis, and spice. Last tasted, 11/96.

1989 — The 1989 possesses a huge finish, with more noticeable tannin than in the
• 1990. Picking a favorite between these two fabulous examples of their respec-
96 tive vintages is—for me—presently impossible. I will probably end up drink- ing the 1990 before the 1989, but both are 25–30-year wines, with the 1989 possibly reaching full maturity in 5–6 years and the 1990 needing several more years of cellaring. Last tasted, 11/96.

1988 — The 1988 is a rich, almost lusty St.-Emilion, with a full-throttle bouquet of
• licorice, spicy new oak, cassis, olives, and minerals. In the mouth, it is full
91 bodied, deep, and concentrated, with excellent extract and a long, heady, moderately tannic finish. Anticipated maturity: Now–2006. Last tasted, 4/91.

1986 — The 1986 has a dark ruby color, a broad, expansive, forward bouquet of ripe
• plums, spicy, smoky, new oak, and subtle herbs. On the palate, the wine
89 displays exceptional richness, fine length, and ripeness. While drinkable young, it has the potential to last another 10–15 years. Anticipated maturity: Now–2006. Last tasted, 3/90.

1985 — The 1985 is a seductively smooth, supple, broadly flavored wine with aromas
• and flavors of berry fruit and herbs. Full bodied, concentrated, but forward
87 and delicious, this is a luscious wine. Anticipated maturity: Now. Last tasted, 3/90.

1984 — Light in color, with an almost Burgundy-like bouquet of woodsy, cherry,
• mushroom-like fruit, the 1984 is soft and fully mature. It requires drinking.
72 Anticipated maturity: Now–may be in decline. Last tasted, 3/89.

1983 — Much like the 1982, this wine has matured all too quickly. Of course, it was
• made during a period when the raw materials were excellent, but the proprie-
83 tor was excessively fining and filtering the wine. (Both procedures were elimi- nated in the late eighties.) The 1983 is medium ruby with some amber at the edge, a weedy, cassis, oaky nose, and soft, loosely knit, nearly flabby flavors. The tannins have melted away, and this wine requires immediate consump- tion. Anticipated maturity: Now–may be in decline. Last tasted, 1/89.

1982 — Readers should remember that in 1982 there was no selection process and a
• completely different winemaking style and philosophy were in place. The
77 1982, soft and ripe after bottling, has deteriorated quickly. It reveals consid-

erable amber, orange, and rust colors and is diffuse and flabby; while it still reveals some sweet, jammy fruit, the wine exhibits an old, mushroomy, earthy note. It is clearly in decline and should be drunk immediately. Last tasted, 9/95.

1978—A typical pre-1985 Angélus, the 1978 is light, fully mature, and beginning to
•   exhibit plenty of brown in the color and lose its fruit. Pleasant and charming
75   in a light, picnic sort of style. Anticipated maturity: Now–probably in serious decline. Last tasted, 3/83.

1976—The 1976 Angélus is a total disaster—light, pale, no fruit, no character, no
•   charm, just alcohol and distant flavors of fruit. Last tasted, 6/80.
55

1975—The 1975 is a very poor wine, brown in color, with an old, decaying leafy,
•   vegetal aroma and hardly any ripe, fruity intensity. This wine is unacceptably
50   poor in what was an excellent, if somewhat irregular, vintage for the wines of Bordeaux. Last tasted, 3/86.

L'ARROSÉE   EXCELLENT

Classification: St.-Emilion Grand Cru Classé
Location of vineyards: St.-Emilion
Owner: G.F.A. du Château L'Arrosée (managed by François Rodhain)
Address: 33330 St.-Emilion
Mailing address: Same as above
Telephone: 33 5 57 24 70 47
Visits: By appointment only
Contact: François Rodhain

VINEYARDS (red)
Surface area: 24.7 acres
Average age of vines: 25 years
Blend: 50% Merlot, 30% Cabernet Sauvignon, 20% Cabernet Franc
Density of plantation: 5,500 vines per hectare
Average yields (over the last 5 years): 30–35 hectoliters per hectare
Total average annual production: 35,000–40,000 bottles

GRAND VIN (red)
Brand name: Château L'Arrosée
Appellation: St.-Emilion Grand Cru
Mean annual production: 35,000–40,000 bottles
Upbringing: Fermentations and macerations last 20–25 days in temperature-controlled concrete vats. Malolactics occur in vats, and wines are aged in 100% new oak for 12 months. They are racked every 3 months (manually), fined with fresh egg whites (in vats after assemblage), but not filtered.

> **SECOND WINE**
> None produced (except in 1987).
>
> Evaluation of present classification: Should be upgraded to a Premier
> Grand Cru Classé; the quality equivalent of a Médoc third-growth
> Plateau of maturity: 5–20 years following the vintage

One of the least known and publicized wines of St.-Emilion, L'Arrosée, which sits on the slopes or *côtes* of St.-Emilion, is destined to become more famous as the high quality of its wine becomes better known.

The estate was purchased by the Rodhain family in 1911 and since 1956 has been managed by François Rodhain. The production was, unfortunately, sold off in bulk to the local St.-Emilion cooperative for over 3 decades because the property had no winemaking facilities. Since the mid-sixties the entire production has been made and bottled at the château.

The style of L'Arrosée's wine is unique. Fleshy, yet firm and powerful, fragrant, as well as rich and full, it is a wine with plenty of character and has a style that seems at times to recall a southern Médoc property such as La Lagune. At other times—for example in 1985, 1986, 1989, and 1990—the wine resembles a rich, lusty Burgundy. In fact, the 1985 continues to remind me of a Henri Jayer Richebourg! L'Arrosée is a great wine that the renowned Dutch author Hubrecht Duijker called "the finest wine of the appellation."

VINTAGES

1997 — Although lighter than expected, this 1997 is intensely elegant, with plenty of
• L'Arrosée's black cherry–scented nose well displayed. This wine presents a
86– sweet, evolved, low-acid attack, medium body, and a clean, charming finish.
88 It is a stylish, understated L'Arrosée that will need to be drunk during its first
7–9 years of life. Last tasted, 3/98.

1996 — I lost some confidence in this wine based on my retastings, but I still believe
• it possesses the right ingredients to develop into an outstanding St.-Emilion
89– and one of the finest, most structured, tannic, and long-lived wines the estate
91+ has made since 1986. The wine was closed when I tasted it, without the
charm of the 1995 or 1990. However, it still reveals the vintage's force, power,
structure, and tannic presence. The wine is medium to full bodied, with the
sweet L'Arrosée nose of black cherries and high-quality toasty oak. Backward
and spicy, with noticeable tannin, this will be an atypical L'Arrosée in that it
will require 6–8 years of cellaring. The wine's purity and richness appear to
be sufficient to balance out the tannin, but I will be more certain of that after
bottling. Anticipated maturity: 2006–2015. Last tasted, 3/98.

1995 — With a medium dark ruby color and a complex, kirsch, *pain grillé*, smoky,
• deliciously complex, and fruity nose, this fragrant wine offers a wealth of
90 raspberry, currant, and cherry fruit. It is not a blockbuster, but, rather, an

elegant, multi-dimensional, round, velvety-textured wine with a lushness and sweetness of fruit that makes it irresistible. This is one of the more seductive wines of the vintage. Anticipated maturity: Now–2012. Last tasted, 11/97.

1994 — A deep ruby color and reluctant aromatics suggest a wine in a dormant
  •   state. On the palate, the wine offers little charm, yet it does possess dense,
87+   medium-bodied, concentrated, but closed and tannic flavors. The wine should evolve well, although the tough tannin apparent after bottling could prove troublesome in 7–8 years. Give the 1994 L'Arrosée 2–4 more years of cellaring; it should last for 15 years. Last tasted, 1/97.

1993 — An impressive effort for the vintage, L'Arrosée's 1993 possesses a medium
  •   dark ruby color, a complex, Burgundy-like nose of jammy cherry fruit, sweet,
88   smoky, toasty oak, and a touch of cedar. This medium-bodied wine reveals a sweet expansiveness reminiscent of a top-class Burgundy. It offers a silky, velvety texture and admirable complexity and elegance. Drink this evolved, well-made 1993 over the next 5–7 years. Last tasted, 1/97.

1992 — Only 36 hectoliters per hectare were produced by L'Arrosée in this abundant
  •   vintage. The result is one of the more hedonistic 1992s. True to the L'Arrosée
87   style, this wine offers generous amounts of smoky, toasty new oak and jammy black cherries and raspberries in both its aromatic and flavor profiles. Succulent, expansive, ripe, and smooth as silk, this is a delicious, up-front wine for drinking over the next 5–7 years. Last tasted, 11/94.

1990 — The impressive 1990 L'Arrosée offers up a provocative, penetrating, superfra-
  •   grant nose of minerals, truffles, black fruits (jammy raspberries), and high-
93   quality toasty oak. Rich, sweet, and full bodied, with well-integrated, moderate tannin, this lush, complex, and layered wine has turned out to be a super effort in this top-quality vintage. Anticipated maturity: Now–2015. Last tasted, 11/96.

1989 — The 1989 exhibits a dark ruby color, with slight lightening at the edge, as
  •   well as plenty of earthy, black cherry fruit nicely touched by sweet, toasty
88   oak. It exhibited more richness, glycerin, intensity, and precision than it has in previous tastings. It can be drunk now as well as over the next decade. Last tasted, 11/96.

1988 — The 1988 is also not up to previous standards. Medium bodied, spicy, and
  •   fruity, with good depth but not much length, this wine lacks complexity and
83   intensity. It saddens me to see this property, whose wines I adore, fall off the pace set by its recent past performances. Anticipated maturity: Now–2000. Last tasted, 4/91.

1986 — For L'Arrosée, this vintage has taken an atypically long time to round into
  •   shape. It has always possessed considerable power as well as a muscular,
92   concentrated style and hefty tannin. Beginning to shed its tannin, it reveals an intriguing dusty herb, black cherry, kirsch, and mineral nose, with subtle vanillin from new oak in the background. There are medium-bodied, concentrated flavors with some firm tannin, but by and large this is a very accessible wine. It remains youthful, with only a hint of amber at the edge of its deep ruby/purple color. This will undoubtedly be one of L'Arrosée's longest-

lived wines since their 1961. Anticipated maturity: Now–2012. Last tasted, 12/97.

1985— The 1985 has been fully mature for a number of years and should be con-
• sumed between now and 2004. The deep ruby color reveals some amber/
93 orange at the edge. The wine has always possessed a knockout set of aromatics, consisting of nearly over-ripe black cherries and raspberries intermingled
with high-quality *pain grillé* notes. Supple, with a layered, richly fruity texture
imbued with plenty of glycerin and heady alcohol, this sumptuous, luxuriously
styled, fully mature L'Arrosée should be drunk up. Anticipated maturity:
Now–2004. Last tasted, 12/97.

1984— The best wine of St.-Emilion in 1984? There is no question that M. Rodhain
• is one of those perfectionist owners who harvests very late in order to attain
86 super-ripeness. He also began using almost 100% new oak in this vintage.
The 1984 is a revelation. Broad, smooth, oaky, black cherry flavors seem to
suggest a Clos Vougeot more than a St.-Emilion. This is a ripe, fruity wine
with surprising depth. Anticipated maturity: Now. Last tasted, 3/89.

1983— This fully mature wine exhibits a certain rusticity to its aggressive tannin, a
• characteristic I do not believe will ever dissipate. Dark garnet colored with
88 amber at the edge, the wine offers forceful aromatics consisting of damp earth
(or is it a hint of black truffles?). It is medium bodied, with excellent fruit,
but coarse tannin in the finish keeps this wine from receiving an outstanding
rating. It should continue to drink well for another 7–8 years. Last tasted,
12/97.

1982— In the past I have rated the 1985 and 1986 L'Arrosée higher than the 1982,
• but my position on those evaluations is quickly losing validity. This is a
93 superb example of the 1982 vintage. Delicious and forward at 7–10 years of
age, the wine then took on more structure, weight, and delineation. Although
it can easily be drunk, it is unquestionably the most enormously concentrated
and richest L'Arrosée made during the exceptional decade of the eighties.
The color is an opaque ruby/purple/garnet. The nose offers knockout proportions of jammy red and black fruits, as well as herbs and sweet wood (although
it is less oaked than the 1985 or 1990). Full bodied, with the 1982 vintage's
opulence and unctuous texture well displayed, this is a stunningly rich,
complex, brilliant example of L'Arrosée that can be drunk now or cellared for
another 10–15+ years. Last tasted, 9/95.

1981— A classically proportioned wine of power and balance, the 1981 L'Arrosée is
• one of the better wines of St.-Emilion. Medium dark ruby, with an intense
85 perfume of ripe black cherries and spicy oak, this medium-bodied wine has
surprising power for the vintage, good tannin, and a moderately long finish.
Anticipated maturity: Now. Last tasted, 3/90.

1978— This is one of the very best St.-Emilions of this vintage. Many wines became
• too ripe in the very late harvest of 1978, but L'Arrosée is extremely well
87 structured and vinified. Dark ruby, with some amber at the edge, this wine
has a deep, rich, ripe fruity, oaky bouquet that suggests a Médoc more than a
St.-Emilion. On the palate, the wine is full bodied, concentrated, beefy, and

long in the finish. It is a big, substantial wine. Anticipated maturity: Now—
may be in decline. Last tasted, 1/85.

1970—This big, full-bodied wine has a dark ruby color, with some amber at the
• edge, a spicy, oaky, black cherry bouquet, medium body, rich, rustic, spicy,
85 long flavors, and a long but slightly astringent finish. Are the tannins too
excessive? Anticipated maturity: Now–1999. Last tasted, 3/89.

1964—Now fully mature, but in no danger of declining, this wonderfully fragrant
• wine has a big, rich, deep bouquet that develops in the glass. The wine is
87 quite fleshy, concentrated, and rich, with a chewy texture, substantial weight,
and a surprising amount of alcohol. Anticipated maturity: Now—may be in
decline. Last tasted, 6/84.

1961—I hope more recent vintages, such as 1982, 1985, and 1986, will ultimately
• rival this great wine. It challenges the finest St.-Emilions in this legendary
94 vintage. Medium ruby/garnet, with a huge, spicy, jammy, fruitcake sort of
bouquet crammed with intensity, the wine offers lush, expansive, generously
endowed flavors as smooth as silk. Fully mature for 5–6 years, it has an
opulent texture and a long, smoky, alcoholic finish. Anticipated maturity:
Now—may be in decline. Last tasted, 12/90.

AUSONE   OUTSTANDING

Classification: St.-Emilion Premier Grand Cru Classé A
Location of vineyards: St.-Emilion
Owner: Micheline, Alain, and Catherine Vauthier
Address: 33330 St.-Emilion
Mailing address: Same as above
Telephone: 33 5 57 24 68 88; telefax: 33 5 57 74 47 39

VINEYARDS (red)
Surface area: 17.3 acres
Average age of vines: 45–50 years
Blend: 50% Merlot, 50% Cabernet Franc
Density of plantation: 6,000–6,500 vines per hectare
Average yields (over the last 5 years): 35 hectoliters per hectare
Total average annual production: 230 hectoliters

GRAND VIN (red)
Brand name: Château Ausone
Appellation: St.-Emilion Grand Cru
Mean annual production: 20,000–25,000 bottles
Upbringing: Fermentations and macerations last 3–4 weeks in
temperature-controlled wooden vats. Malolactics occur in new oak
barrels, and wines are aged 19–23 months before being bottled. They are
generally fined with fresh egg whites (lightly) but remain unfiltered. They

are racked every 3 months. *Assemblage* is done normally in March following the vintage, and the blend is corrected if needed just before bottling.

SECOND WINE
Brand name: Chapelle Madeleine
Average annual production: 7,000 bottles (as from 1997)

Evaluation of present classification: Since 1976 it has merited its status as a Premier Grand Cru Classé and is the quality equivalent of a Médoc first-growth
Plateau of maturity: 15–50 years following the vintage

If the first-time visitor to Bordeaux had just one château and vineyard to visit, it should be the tiny Ausone property, perched on one of the hillsides outside the medieval walls of St.-Emilion. Ausone has a spectacular location, made all the more startling because of its tiny vineyard of very old vines and the extensive limestone caves that house the property's wine cellar. Ausone is named after the Roman poet Ausonius, who lived between A.D. 320 and 395. He was also known to have had a vineyard in the area (closer apparently to Bordeaux than to St.-Emilion), and while there are Roman ruins at Ausone, it is highly doubtful that Ausonius himself had anything to do with this estate.

Despite the great historical significance of Ausone and the fact that it has one of the most privileged locations for making wine in all of Bordeaux, the record of wine quality was mediocre—even poor—during the sixties and seventies. The turnabout in quality came in 1976, when the owners hired a new *régisseur*, Pascal Delbeck. While Ausone produced many dry, tired, and feebly colored wines in the forties, fifties, and sixties, Delbeck turned out one excellent wine after another, starting with the outstanding 1976, which is one of the two best wines of Bordeaux in that vintage.

The minuscule production of Ausone makes it almost impossible to find commercially. Even more rare than the famous Pomerol estate of Pétrus, yet considerably less expensive, Ausone has a style that is totally different from St.-Emilion's other famous estate, Cheval Blanc.

In spite of what appeared to be a cordial relationship between the two families that owned Ausone, Dubois-Challon and Vauthier, internal bickering and constant friction on the philosophy of winemaking resulted in the Vauthier family buying out Madame Dubois-Challon in the mid-nineties. Winemaker Pascal Delbeck was replaced by Alain Vauthier, who receives oenological consultation from Libourne's Michel Rolland. While partisans of the Dubois-Challon/Delbeck team complain that Ausone is being made in a more forward, commercial style, this is nothing more than the whining of those who have an ax to grind. The only changes made under Vauthier/ Rolland have been to harvest slightly later if weather conditions permit and do malolactic fermentation in barrel rather than tank. The first two efforts under the new regime (1995 and 1996) were spectacular wines, with all of Ausone's elegance, finesse, and extraordinary mineral-based personality, as well as greater concentration and intensity. In fact, the development of the 1995 Ausone during its *élevage* in barrel and bottle has been brilliant, and the wine has lost none of its "typicity," as the Dubois-Challon/Delbeck corner have argued. I expect Ausone to be more consistent and to reach even higher peaks of quality under the inspired leadership of Alain Vauthier.

VINTAGES

1997—
•
91–
94
It is clearly one of the vintage's superstars. The color is a healthy dark purple, and the wine offers up celestial aromas of black fruits, licorice, minerals, and roasted Côte Rôtie–like nuances. The wine's fascinating aromatics are matched by its exhilarating flavors. While not a powerhouse, and without the intensity, extraction, and richness of the 1996 and 1995, the 1997 is surreal in its display of complex aromas matched with intense but not heavy flavors. This medium-bodied wine reveals superb ripeness and glorious balance. It is a textbook example of how a wine can have remarkable flavor, intensity, and length without being tiring to drink. This Ausone is forward, particularly for a wine from this estate, yet it is capable of lasting for more than 2 decades. Anticipated maturity: 2005–2020. Last tasted, 3/98.

1996—
•
94–
95+
A brilliant Ausone, the 1996 displays this property's telltale mineral characteristic in its multi-dimensional bouquet. In addition, there is a plum-like liqueur intermixed with black currants, cold steel, floral, and crushed stone scents. Dense and rich, as well as extremely subtle, this medium-bodied Ausone possesses extraordinary richness yet no sense of heaviness. It takes the prize for having a rare equilibrium of flavor and structure. As the wine sat in the glass, I was convinced I smelled violets, or something that reminded me of the 1990 Comte de Vogüé Musigny. Undoubtedly one of the great wines of the vintage, the 1996 Ausone will require a decade of cellaring. Anticipated maturity: 2006–2050. Last tasted, 3/98.

1995—
•
93
The 1995 will be remembered as a historic vintage for Ausone. It is the first year where, after more than a decade of infighting among the owners, Alain Vauthier emerged as the sole proprietor and thus had complete control of the wine's viticulture, vinification, and upbringing. Ausone's extraordinary minerality is present in the 1995, yet there are more aromatics, a richer, more multi-dimensional palate impression, and a fuller texture—all with the *terroir* brilliantly expressed. The wine boasts a dense ruby/purple color and an emerging but tightly knit nose of spring flowers, minerals, earth, and black fruits. Rich, with an opulent texture, and surprising sexiness for a young vintage of Ausone, the medium-bodied 1995 displays exquisite balance among its acid, tannin, alcohol, and fruit. Although it is not yet seamless, all

the elements are present for an extraordinary evolution in the bottle. Given its backward style, this wine will require 5–7 years of cellaring and will age at a glacial pace for 30–40 years. Anticipated maturity: 2003–2045. Last tasted, 11/97.

1994 — Medium deep ruby colored, with a noticeably vanillin, stony minerality, this
• austere, medium-bodied wine possesses more ripeness and depth of fruit than
86? the 1993, but it still comes across as undersized and unimpressive. Give it 5–7 years to see if there is any substance behind the abrasive tannin. Last tasted, 1/97.

1993 — The understated style of the 1993 Ausone offers mineral, lead pencil scents
• with some red currant fruit in the restrained, backward bouquet. Austere and
85? medium bodied, this tannic, attenuated, lean wine will undoubtedly dry out long before the tannin melts away. It is a lightweight wine that is best drunk over the next 12 years—in spite of its astringency. Last tasted, 1/97.

1992 — Ausone's firmly structured, tannic 1992 reluctantly reveals a nose of dusty,
• flowery red fruits, wood, and minerals. Light bodied and shallow, with cherry
80? fruit flavors intermingled with the taste of herbs, this wine appears to lack a finish, depth, and intensity. Too tannic and sinewy to enjoy over the near
. term, Ausone's 1992 is a likely candidate to dry out before its tannins ever melt away. Last tasted, 11/94.

1990 — The 1990 is not a charming, precocious wine. It is closed, but the color is a
• dense, dark ruby, with no amber or orange at the edge. The fruit is sweeter,
92+ and the wine is more muscular, richer, and broader in the mouth, without losing Ausone's telltale minerality, spice, and curranty fruit. There is a good inner core of sweet fruit in this medium- to full-bodied wine that needs another 15–20 years of cellaring. Can the 1990 possibly rival the 1983 or 1982? Perhaps . . . but don't bet on it. Anticipated maturity: 2008–2030. Last tasted, 11/96.

1989 — The 1989 reveals amber at the edge and a green-tobacco-and-mineral-
• scented, hard-edged nose of musty wood and earthy fruit. This mid-weight
88 wine is spicy and elegant, with moderate body and a boatload of astringent tannin in the harsh finish. It requires a minimum of 10–15 more years of cellaring. Anticipated maturity: 2005–2020. Last tasted, 11/96.

1988 — The 1988 Ausone may need 20 years to reach its peak. Unlike a number of
• 1988s where the balance between tannin and fruit favors the former (always
91 a troubling sign), Ausone offers plenty of juicy red and black fruit extract in a medium-bodied, superbly concentrated, intense, and powerful format. Anticipated maturity: 2008–2040. Last tasted, 1/93.

1987 — This is a successful vintage for Ausone, which produced a wine with nearly 13%
• natural alcohol. Surprisingly ripe, with the exotic, mineral-scented character so
87 typical of this property, the 1987 Ausone is a medium-bodied, ripe, richly fruity, classy wine that should drink beautifully for another 12–20 years. If it continues to firm up and gain weight in the bottle, it may turn out to be as good as their wonderful 1976, as well as have 20 or more years of aging potential. A sleeper! Anticipated maturity: Now–2010. Last tasted, 12/90.

1986—Although an uninspiring effort from Ausone, the 1986 is a deeper, richer, and
  •   more interesting wine than the disappointing 1985. The 1986 displays a deep
 78?   ruby/garnet color, with light amber at the edge. The nose reveals a concoction
         of herbaceous cherry and earth-infused fruit with spice and mineral under-
         tones. Still tannic, with the wine's structure and astringency dominating its
         meager fruitiness, this Ausone is hollow in the middle, with little depth or
         richness. Even giving it the benefit of the doubt, I cannot imagine this wine
         ever being better than just above average in quality—if that. Anticipated
         maturity: 2000–2020. Last tasted, 11/97.

1985—I have never been impressed with this wine, which continues to muddle along,
  •   revealing little concentration, interest, complexity, or flavor dimension. The
 75?   light ruby/garnet color displays some amber at the edge. The uninspiring
         nose offers dusty aromas of dried fruits, earth, and spice. This light- to
         medium-bodied wine still possesses moderately high tannin, shallow fruiti-
         ness, and a tart, astringent finish. It is a strong candidate for drying out before
         the tannin fades away. Anticipated maturity: Now–2008. Last tasted, 11/97.

1983—Ausone's 1983 is a powerful, rich, full-bodied wine with a higher alcohol
  •   content than normal. Medium ruby, rich, and jammy, with low acidity but
 94   great concentration, as well as that glorious perfume of minerals and Asian
         spices, this wine should last 15–20 years but provide fine drinking early on
         —a rarity for Ausone. Anticipated maturity: Now–2010. Last tasted, 10/94.

1982—At last this wine is beginning to warrant the lavish praise and high score I
  •   gave it from cask, when it was one of the most extraordinary young wines I
 95+   had ever tasted. Its dormant stage has lasted for over a decade. When I last
         tasted it, the wine was taking on that provocative Ausone bouquet of minerals,
         spices, earth, and red and black fruits. Enormously constituted, with massive
         quantities of both extract and tannin, this powerful, still backward wine
         should prove to be one of the greatest Ausones made in the post–World War
         II era. It remains 5–10 years away from maturity. Although the exotic sweet-
         ness and lavish richness of the 1982 vintage is becoming more noticeable,
         readers should not touch a bottle before the turn of the century. It may turn
         out to be a 50-year wine. Last tasted, 9/95.

1981—This medium ruby wine remains closed but exhibits adequate ripeness of
  •   fruit. However, the hard tannins are cause for concern. A medium-weight
 82   wine, the 1981 Ausone has good concentration but will, I believe, always be
         an austere, tough-textured, charmless wine. It still needs 10 years to soften
         and develop. Anticipated maturity: Now–2010. Last tasted, 1/90.

1980—A lightweight wine from a lightweight vintage, the 1980 Ausone has medium
  •   ruby color, a minor, straightforward bouquet of plums and herbs, medium
 75   body, and average-intensity flavors. Anticipated maturity: Now. Last tasted,
         6/84.

1979—From the cask, I preferred the 1979 to the highly heralded 1978, but now the
  •   wine has closed up and seems unyielding and dumb. Light to medium ruby,
 87?   with a spicy, tight bouquet with hints of oak, ripe black cherries, spices, and
         charred earth, this medium-bodied wine continues to taste surprisingly

backward and austere. Will the marvelous fruit it exhibited when young reappear and outlive the tannins? Anticipated maturity: 2000–2015. Last tasted, 2/91.

1978—A classic Ausone, still backward and remarkably youthful, the 1978 has
•   a dark ruby color, an aroma of ripe fruit, and scents of minerals and spicy
88?   oak. Medium bodied, with high tannins and a long finish, this wine is austere, stubbornly slow to evolve, and obviously made for long-term cellaring. Will the fruit hold up? Anticipated maturity: Now–2015. Last tasted, 3/91.

1976—The finest Ausone of the seventies and, along with Lafite-Rothschild of Pauil-
•   lac, one of the two outstandingly great wines of this vintage, the 1976 Ausone
94   is indeed a profound wine. Surprisingly dark colored for the vintage, with a voluptuous, intense, complex bouquet of minerals, licorice, truffles, and ripe, spicy black currant fruit, this full-bodied, powerful, large-scaled Ausone has remarkable size given the vintage. Amazingly, it is a bigger wine than more recent Ausones such as the 1978, 1979, 1985, and 1986. It is a winemaking triumph for this difficult vintage. Anticipated maturity: Now–2010. Last tasted, 10/94.

1975—Extremely severe and hard, with an overwhelming scent of damp, dirty earth
•   and herbs, this austere, fruitless style of claret may last another 50 years, but
74   it is hollow and charmless. Interestingly, the spectacular 1976 is a candidate for the "wine of the vintage." Last tasted, 12/95.

1971—Light to medium ruby, with a rust-colored edge, this pleasant yet insubstantial
•   wine has a light perfume of spicy oak as well as scents of minerals and
78   decaying leafy vegetation. Not terribly concentrated, but adequately fruity in a savory, satisfying manner, the 1971 is a nice wine for drinking immediately. A magnum drunk at the château in 1988 merited a more enthusiastic review (86 points), but it was far from profound. Anticipated maturity: Now. Last tasted, 3/88.

1970—The 1970 Ausone is very light, with a bouquet that suggests old, faded
•   flowers and dusty fruit. Brown at the edges and beginning to dry out, this
69   medium-bodied wine is the poorest of the "Big Eight" of Bordeaux in this excellent vintage. Very disappointing. Last tasted, 1/87.

1967—A diluted, insipid bouquet is followed by a wine with bland, washed-out
•   flavors and significant browning to the color. Although not a complete failure,
65   it is extremely disappointing. Last tasted, 9/83.

1966—Tasted twice from well-stored bottles in Bordeaux, this wine reveals an amber/
•   rust overtone to its medium garnet color. At first the nose offers attractive
78   faded fruit, old leather, and dried herb–like aromas. In the mouth, the wine possesses sweetness on the attack that fades quickly to reveal astringency, harshness, and a medium-bodied, hollow personality. It is clearly in decline. Last tasted, 3/97.

1961—A ripe, port-like nose of dried fruits, herbs, old tea, and minerals made for an
•   intriguing set of aromatics. In the mouth, the wine reveals more sweetness
88   and fat than one expects from Ausone, but an underlying pruny quality suggested the fruit was more than merely over-ripe. Hard tannin, acidity, and

earthiness were noticeable in the background, but overall this was a good to excellent wine, with its positive attributes outweighing the more troublesome ones. Last tasted, 3/97.

ANCIENT VINTAGES

The kindest thing that can be said about many of the older vintages of Ausone, particularly those in the post–World War II era, is that they have survived. It is hard to find a vintage of Ausone from the forties or fifties that is not at least drinkable. In spite of the fact that Ausone often has longevity, the question remains as to how much pleasure these wines ultimately provide. Top vintages such as 1945, 1947, 1952, 1955, and 1959, while still alive, all represent the austere, under-nourished, and somewhat charmless style of Ausone. Why more richness and depth were not forthcoming escapes me, but there is no denying the high level of dry, astringent tannins in so many of these wines. My favorite older vintage of Ausone is the 1955, but even that wine is far from meriting an outstanding rating.

Tasted in September 1995, Ausone's 1949 (86 points) revealed a medium garnet color, with considerable rust at the edge. Some attractive mineral and black fruit aromas emerge from what is otherwise an austere, lean, light- to medium-bodied, high-acid wine—a textbook Ausone.

The 1874 Ausone (96 points) made me think that the reason I have never fully appreciated and understood Ausone is that I have never had the opportunity to wait 121 years for an Ausone to reach full maturity! When drunk in September 1995, the wine still possessed a sweet, tomato, herb, mineral, and black fruit bouquet, medium body, glycerin-dominated, chewy, fat flavors, and a gorgeously long, heady, mineral-dominated, sweet finish. This wine may drink well for another 30–40 years.

The first comment in my notes on the 1929 (96 points; last tasted 9/94) was "cedar city." Although lightly colored, with a rusty tint to the entire wine, the 1929 Ausone exhibits a fabulous bouquet of spices, cedar, and sweet, jammy fruit. It displays wonderful ripeness, as well as the telltale austerity and dry finish that often characterize Ausone. The wine remains rich, medium bodied, and intact, but I would not gamble on holding it any longer. However, it possesses more fruit, richness, and complexity than the shallow color suggests. The 1921 Ausone (92 points; last tasted 9/95) was elegant and less viscous but still remarkably rich and fragrant. It also revealed more tannin, as well as Ausone's trademark, Médoc-like style. Complex yet sweet aromas of berry fruit intertwined with minerals, dried flowers, and spices were followed by a medium- to full-bodied, concentrated, fully mature, well-balanced wine. As the wine sat in the glass, it quickly began to lose its fruit.

My notes indicate that the 1900 Ausone (94 points; last tasted 9/94) had a 90-point nose and 99-point flavors. Most Ausones are big on bouquet but short on flavor. It is unbelievable that a 94-year-old wine could have this much richness and flavor. The huge nose of roasted cloves, coffee, and honeyed red fruits is followed by a wine with super-sweetness, big, jammy, alcoholic, ripe flavors, and remarkable length with elevated alcohol. The light color is akin to a rusty-colored white Zinfandel. The extreme sweetness makes me think the fermentation halted and the wine has some residual sugar. This stunning wine remains fresh and lively.

BALESTARD-LA-TONNELLE　　　　　　　　VERY GOOD

Classification: St.-Emilion Grand Cru Classé
Location of vineyards: St.-Emilion
Owner: G.F.A. Capdemourlin
Address: 33330 St.-Emilion
Mailing address: Château Roudier, 33570 Montagne
Telephone: 33 5 57 74 62 06; telefax: 33 5 57 74 59 34
Visits: By appointment only
Contact: Jacques Capdemourlin

VINEYARDS (red)
Surface area: 26 acres
Average age of vines: 33 years
Blend: 65% Merlot, 20% Cabernet Franc, 10% Cabernet Sauvignon, 5% Malbec
Density of plantation: 5,400 vines per hectare
Average yields (over the last 5 years): 43 hectoliters per hectare
Total average annual production: 5,000 cases

GRAND VIN (red)
Brand name: Château Balestard-La-Tonnelle
Appellation: St.-Emilion Grand Cru
Mean annual production: 42 hectoliters per hectare
Upbringing: Fermentations and macerations last 3–4 weeks in stainless-steel tanks equipped with a temperature control (with Freon). After malolactics, 70% of the yield is transferred to oak barrels (40% of which are new), while the rest remains in stainless-steel vats. Wines are aged 18 months, fined, and filtered. Since 1997, part of the yield undergoes malolactics in barrels.

SECOND WINE
Brand name: Chanoine de Balestard
Average annual production: Variable—not systematically made

Evaluation of present classification: The quality equivalent of a Médoc fifth-growth
Plateau of maturity: 5–14 years following the vintage

I have always regarded Balestard-La-Tonnelle as a downsized Lynch-Bages of St.-Emilion. This property, owned by Jacques Capdemourlin, produces a densely colored, big, deep, rich, and chewy style of wine. It can sometimes be too big and alcoholic for its own good, but this is an immensely enjoyable style of St.-Emilion that can normally be drunk after 5 or 6 years of bottle age yet also evolve gracefully for 10 or more years.

The property takes its name from the writings of the fifteenth-century poet François Villon, who wrote about "drinking this divine nectar which carries the name of Balestard." The vineyard, enclosed by tall cypress (look for the windmill that sits on the knoll), is located on a limestone plateau adjacent to Château Soutard, to the east of the town of St.-Emilion. Balestard has been relatively successful since 1970. Given the realistic prices Jacques Capdemourlin charges for his wines, this is one of St.-Emilion's great bargains.

VINTAGES

1996—Dark ruby/purple colored, this tannic, astringent, austerely styled wine may
• possess an excess of structure and muscle for its level of fruit. It is hard,
80 tightly wound, and lacking charm. Anticipated maturity: 2003–2010. Last tasted, 11/97.

1995—The 1995 reveals the low acidity and jammy ripeness of the vintage, as well
• as medium to full body. However, it was disjointed on the three occasions I
86 tasted it. It is the type of wine that may pick up more definition and personality with 5–6 months in cask. My judgment may be conservative, as there is plenty of guts to this wine. Last tasted, 3/96.

1994—The 1994 continues to exhibit a healthy dark ruby color, a sweet, smoky,
• meaty, rich, black cherry, licorice nose, sweet, long, chewy flavors, excellent
85? purity, and moderate tannin in the finish. It is a concentrated, fleshy, husky style of St.-Emilion that should drink well for 10–12 years. Last tasted, 3/96.

1992—This light ruby–colored wine exhibits a spicy, dull nose, tannic, medium-
• bodied flavors, and a lean, tough finish. Readers can expect it to become even
75 more attenuated with cellaring. Last tasted, 11/94.

1990—The big, fat, oaky, chocolatey, herb-scented 1990 is admirable for its density,
• high alcohol, and in-your-face style. Anticipated maturity: Now–2002. Last
87 tasted, 1/93.

1989—The 1989 is a jammy, raspberry-and-blackberry-scented wine that is fat and
• lacks acidity but has high alcohol and a chunky, fleshy, mouth-filling feel.
86 If drunk young, this wine will provide a great deal of pleasure over the first 7–9 years of life. Given the resemblance to the 1982—a wine that has continued to develop more grip and structure over the last decade—this wine may well have greater longevity than I am predicting. It typifies the "house style" of Balestard. Anticipated maturity: Now–2005. Last tasted, 4/91.

1988—The 1988 is a narrowly constructed, compact, austere wine that should be
• consumed over the next 5–10 years. It certainly will last, but again, the
83 problem is the lack of balance between the excessive tannins and the amount of fruit present. Anticipated maturity: Now–2000. Last tasted, 4/91.

1986—This full-throttle powerhouse offers explosive levels of macho fruit and body
•   along with a chewy texture. It is never a delicate or particularly charming
85   wine, but one that tends to grab the taster's attention with intensity and
       muscle. The 1986 is typical of this estate but has a bit more tannin in the
       finish to go along with its ponderous, robust style. Anticipated maturity: Now–
       2001. Last tasted, 3/89.

1985—The 1985 is a hefty, fat, rich, but not ponderous wine, with plenty of gutsy,
•   meaty fruit and body. Anticipated maturity: Now–may be in decline. Last
86   tasted, 3/89.

1984—For a St.-Emilion from this vintage, the 1984 Balestard is a success. It is
•   fruity, soft, clean, and surprisingly fleshy and solid. Anticipated maturity:
77   Now–may be in decline. Last tasted, 3/88.

1983—A huge wine that may be too big for some tasters, the 1983 Balestard
•   has a black/ruby color and a ripe, full-blown bouquet of plums and
86   tarry, truffle scents. On the palate, the wine is powerful, dense, and alco-
       holic. This is a mammoth-styled anachronistic wine that is sure to pro-
       voke controversy in tasting circles. Anticipated maturity: Now. Last tasted,
       1/89.

1982—I remember purchasing this wine for about $7 a bottle, thinking it was terrific
•   for the price—opaque black/purple color, thick, rich, uncomplex, but chewy,
89   mouth-filling, and satisfying. Remarkably, the 1982 Balestard-La-Tonnelle
       reveals little age. It continues to offer a juicy, succulent, large-scaled mouth-
       ful of St.-Emilion. The wine oozes with glycerin and extract, and some unex-
       pected complexity has developed in the intense perfume of licorice, roasted
       meat, and jammy black cherries. Powerful, thick, and rich, it should continue
       to drink well and perhaps develop even more complexity for another decade.
       Last tasted, 9/95.

1981—I have always liked the uncomplicated fleshy texture and rich fruitiness of
•   Balestard. The 1981 has begun to lose its powerful, fruity gusto. Straight-
84   forward, generous, and full bodied, but beginning to tire, this wine requires
       consumption. Anticipated maturity: Now–may be in decline. Last tasted,
       3/87.

BARDE-HAUT   VERY GOOD SINCE 1997

Classification: St.-Emilion Grand Cru
Location of vineyards: Just at the border of St.-Emilion and
St.-Christophe des Bardes, near Troplong-Mondot
Owner: Dominique Philippe
Address: St.-Christophe des Bardes, 33330 St.-Emilion
Mailing address: Same as above
Telephone: 33 5 57 24 78 21; telefax: 33 5 57 24 61 15
Visits: By appointment only
Contact: Dominique Philippe or Bernard Lamaud

VINEYARDS (red)
Surface area: 42 acres
Average age of vines: 33 years
Blend: 75% Merlot, 25% Cabernet Franc
Density of plantation: 6,000 vines per hectare
Average yields (over the last 2 years): 38 hectoliters per hectare (bought in February 1996)
Total average annual production: 80,000 bottles

GRAND VIN (red)
Brand name: Château Barde-Haut
Appellation: St.-Emilion
Mean annual production: 40,000 bottles
Upbringing: Fermentations and macerations last approximately 21 days in temperature-controlled concrete tanks. Malolactics occur in 100% new oak barrels with 18–20 months aging. Wines are fined but generally not filtered.

SECOND WINE
Brand name: Le Vallon de Barde-Haut
Average annual production: 40,000 bottles

VINTAGES

1997— This impressive wine, made by Dominique Philippe, emerges from a vineyard
•   close to Troplong-Mondot. In 1997 Michel Rolland, Bordeaux's most influen-
88–   tial oenologist, was brought in to push the level of quality even higher.
91   The result is a splendidly rich, sexy St.-Emilion that deserves considerable
      attention. I was super-impressed on all three occasions I had it. The color
      is a saturated black/purple. The wine's knockout nose of licorice, cassis,
      blackberries, toast, and truffles is evolved and enticing. Powerful, with sur-
      prising structure for a 1997, the wine is ripe (elements of *sur-maturité* are
      evident), with medium body, layers of juicy, succulent fruit, and sweet tannin
      in the impressively endowed, long, well-balanced finish. This wine should
      merit an outstanding rating if it is not excessively fined and filtered at bottling.
      Anticipated maturity: 2000–2010. Bravo! A sleeper! Last tasted, 3/98.

BEAU-SÉJOUR BÉCOT   EXCELLENT

Classification: St.-Emilion Premier Grand Cru Classé B
Location of vineyards: On the plateau of St.-Emilion, near Château Canon, 200 meters away from the church
Owner: Gérard and Dominique Bécot
Address: Château Beau-Séjour Bécot, 33330 St.-Emilion

Mailing address: Same as above
Telephone: 33 5 57 74 46 87; telefax: 33 5 57 24 66 88
Visits: By appointment, Monday through Friday
Contact: Gérard or Dominique Bécot

VINEYARDS (red)
Surface area: 40.8 acres
Average age of vines: 35 years
Blend: 70% Merlot, 24% Cabernet Franc, 6% Cabernet Sauvignon
Density of plantation: 6,000 vines per hectare
Average yields (over the last 5 years): 42 hectoliters per hectare
Total average annual production: 90,000 bottles

GRAND VIN (red)
Brand name: Château Beau-Séjour Bécot
Appellation: St.-Emilion Premier Grand Cru
Mean annual production: 70,000–75,000 bottles
Upbringing: Fermentations and macerations last 20–28 days in
temperature-controlled stainless-steel vats. Wines are transferred to oak
barrels for malolactics and for 18–20 months aging. Depending upon the
vintage, 50%–90% new oak is used. Wines remain unfined and
unfiltered.

SECOND WINE
Brand name: Tourelle de Beau-Séjour Bécot
Average annual production: 15,000–20,000 bottles

Evaluation of present classification: Should be maintained
Plateau of maturity: 5–12 years following the vintage

The quality of Beau-Séjour Bécot has improved significantly since the mid-eighties. Ironically, Beau-Séjour Bécot was demoted in the 1985 classification of the wines of St.-Emilion, only to be promoted back to Premier Grand Cru Classé in the 1996 classification. The vineyard, which is well situated on a limestone plateau, produces wines that are rich and full bodied as well as supple and fleshy. No doubt the decisions to harvest very ripe fruit, utilize plenty of new oak, and bottle the wines naturally contribute to the wine's chewy texture and rich, hedonistic appeal. The château's consulting oenologist is the well-known Michel Rolland of Libourne.

The vineyard, situated on a limestone plateau, has since 1985 produced wines that are richer, fuller, and more obviously marked by new oak (100% new oak casks are employed).

VINTAGES

1997 — A trifle dominated by wood at present, Beau-Séjour Becot's 1997 possesses a
• deep ruby color, ripe cherry, berry, and currant aromas as well as flavors,
85– medium body, low acidity, and a plump, user-friendly, soft style. Anticipated
87 maturity: 1999–2007. Last tasted, 3/98.

1996 — This wine, which has consistently been impressive from barrel, may be shap-
• ing up as the finest wine made at this estate in many years. Although atypi-
89– cally ripe, intense, and powerful (especially for a right bank offering), it
92 possesses accessibility without the heavy overlay of tannin revealed by
some of this vintage's wines. Somehow proprietor Gérard Bécot was able to
achieve full extraction without any bitter tannin. The wine exhibits a saturated purple color and an exceptionally ripe nose of black raspberries
and kirsch intertwined with toasty sweet oak. Full bodied, muscular, and
rich, with layers of fruit, glycerin, and extract and a blockbuster finish, this
appears to be a wine with outstanding potential. Moreover, it is reasonably priced in the Bordeaux hierarchy, even though it is a St.-Emilion
Premier Grand Cru Classé. Anticipated maturity: 2003–2018. Last tasted,
3/98.

1995 — Beau-Séjour Bécot's sexy 1995 offers a dark plum color followed by a sweet,
• vanillin, spicy, black cherry, and currany nose that jumps from the glass. In
89 the mouth, this is a supple, round, hedonistically styled claret with copious
quantities of palate-pleasing plushness, no hard edges, and an impressively
endowed, rich finish. Although the wine is accessible, I recommend another
1–2 years in the bottle. Anticipated maturity: 2000–2014. Last tasted,
11/97.

1994 — Dark ruby, with the Bécots' lavishly oaked, toasty nose, this medium-bodied
• wine reveals more structure than the 1993 but less charm and precociousness.
87 Although qualitatively the equal of the 1993, as well as potentially longer
lived, I am not sure the 1994 will match the 1993 for pure, enjoyable drinking. Anticipated maturity: 1999–2012. Last tasted, 1/97.

1993 — This medium-bodied, delicious wine should be sought out by readers looking
• for a good buy in an unheralded vintage. The wine exhibits a deep ruby color,
87 followed by a forward, precocious, smoky, sweet, jammy, cherry-scented nose,
spicy, round flavors with good length and purity, and a sense of balance and
elegance. The finish is all silk. Drink it over the next 5 years. Last tasted,
1/97.

1992 — A solid, ripe, concentrated 1992, this deeply colored, oaky wine reveals a
• sweet, ripe, red and black fruit component, dramatic, spicy, lavishly oaked
86 flavors, low acidity, fine richness, and a medium-bodied, heady finish. It is
smooth enough to be drunk now and over the next 6–7 years. This St.-Emilion
estate is on its way up the quality scale. Last tasted, 11/94.

1990 — The 1990 is a highly successful effort, with an opaque dark ruby/purple color,
• a big, spicy, oaky, vanillin, and black cherry–scented nose, medium to full
88 body, good tannin and grip, and a surprisingly long, structured finish. Anticipated maturity: Now–2005. Last tasted, 1/93.

1989—Over the last several vintages, this wine has had a tendency to be overwhelm-
 •　ingly oaky in youth. In fact, if there is any criticism, it would be that the
87　proprietors may be using too much new wood. However, a high percentage of
　　new oak tends to work well in a vintage such as 1989, where the underlying
　　concentration and jammy, low-acid fruit character needs the structure of oak
　　to give the wine definition and focus. The 1989 has a dizzyingly high alcohol
　　level, luscious, concentrated, rich, jammy, black cherry fruit, an opulent
　　texture, and plenty of soft tannins in the finish. It should provide delicious
　　drinking early in its life. Anticipated maturity: Now–2002. Last tasted,
　　4/91.

1988—The 1988 is similar to the 1989 with its aggressive oak-scented bouquet.
 •　However, with airing, the oak seems to step back and the ripe, curranty fruit
85　emerges. The tannins are more aggressive than in the 1989, and the wine
　　appears to have good to very good concentration of fruit as well as length. In
　　all likelihood the 1988 will outlive the 1989, but will it provide as much
　　pleasure? Anticipated maturity: Now–2004. Last tasted, 4/91.

1986—Along with the 1989, the 1986 is the finest wine I have ever tasted from this
 •　property. It has an amazing level of smoky oak and dazzling quantities of
87　fruit. A very powerful, full-bodied, rich wine, with an impressive black/ruby
　　color, it has an undeniably seductive, even sexy, bouquet and a lush, opulent
　　texture. Anticipated maturity: Now–2005. Last tasted, 3/90.

1985—The 1985 is a rich, ripe, relatively alcoholic wine possessing a charming,
 •　precocious personality, medium to full body, low acidity, but plenty of flesh
85　and fruit. Anticipated maturity: Now. Last tasted, 3/90.

1983—The 1983 exhibits surprisingly good color, a ripe raspberry, oaky bouquet,
 •　lush, concentrated, soft flavors, and medium to full body. Anticipated matu-
86　rity: Now. Last tasted, 1/89.

1982—The 1982 was made during a period when the wines of Beau-Séjour Bécot
 •　were, to state it mildly—uninspiring. It remains a one-dimensional, soft,
72　compact wine with no depth or intensity. As I said over a decade ago, it will
　　last, but it will never develop into anything except a washed-out, meagerly
　　endowed St.-Emilion that is atypical of the 1982 vintage. Last tasted, 9/95.

1981—Suspiciously light in color, with an innocuous, barely discernible bouquet of
 •　fruit, the 1981 Beau-Séjour seems to be overly oaky, as well as hollow and
70　lean. Quite disappointing. Anticipated maturity: Now–probably in serious
　　decline. Last tasted, 9/84.

1979—For its class and obviously for the price, this skinny little wine leaves a lot to
 •　be desired. Medium ruby, with a simple, oaky, light-intensity, cherry bouquet,
72　medium body, and tannic, short flavors that tail off in the mouth, this wine is
　　palatable but outclassed by numerous generic St.-Emilions made by the
　　town's cooperative. Anticipated maturity: Now–probably in serious decline.
　　Last tasted, 11/82.

1978—A respectable effort from Beau-Séjour, the 1978, which is fully mature, is
 •　fruity, plummy, soft, adequately concentrated, and medium bodied. There is
78　no bitterness in the finish, and the wine has decent balance. Anticipated
　　maturity: Now–probably in serious decline. Last tasted, 10/82.

1976—Now totally faded and dried out, the 1976 has a vegetal, barnyard aroma, soft,
 •   diluted flavors, medium body, and a very short finish. Last tasted, 10/83.
 62

1975—An acceptable wine was produced by Beau-Séjour in 1975. Medium ruby,
 •   with an emerging bouquet of cherries and oak, this wine has tight, hard,
 75   tannic flavors, medium body, and a good finish. Anticipated maturity: Now.
      Last tasted, 5/84.

1971—Probably the best wine from this estate in the 1970s, this vintage has resulted
 •   in a soundly made wine, with an open-knit, plummy, oaky bouquet, soft,
 80   spicy, medium-bodied flavors that exhibit good ripeness, and light tannins
      present in the finish. Anticipated maturity: Now—may be in decline. Last
      tasted, 12/84.

1970—Tired and too tannic for its meager intensity of fruit, this lean, compact wine
 •   will only deteriorate further. Last tasted, 5/84.
 65

BEAUSÉJOUR (DUFFAU-LAGARROSSE)   EXCELLENT

Classification: St.-Emilion Premier Grand Cru Classé B
Location of vineyards: St.-Emilion Côtes
Owner: Heirs Duffau-Lagarrosse
Address: 33330 St.-Emilion
Mailing address: Same as above
Telephone: 33 5 57 24 71 61; telefax: 33 5 57 74 48 40
Visits: By appointment, Monday through Saturday, between 9 A.M. and
noon, and 2 P.M. to 7 P.M.
Contact: Jean-Michel Dubos

VINEYARDS (red)
Surface area: 17.3 acres
Average age of vines: 35 years
Blend: 65% Merlot, 25% Cabernet Franc, 10% Cabernet Sauvignon
Density of plantation: 6,500 vines per hectare
Average yields (over the last 5 years): 38–42 hectoliters per hectare
Total average annual production: 37,000 bottles

GRAND VIN (red)
Brand name: Château Beauséjour
Appellation: St.-Emilion Premier Grand Cru
Mean annual production: 37,000 bottles
Upbringing: Fermentations last 25–30 days in temperature-controlled
concrete and stainless-steel vats. Wines usually undergo malolactics in
vats and are then aged 16–18 months in oak barrels that are renewed by
half at each vintage. They are fined with fresh egg whites but remain
unfiltered.

SECOND WINE
Brand name: La Croix de Mazerat
Average annual production: Produced only in atypical vintages; the very
low yields and severe crop thinning allow the whole yield to be labeled as
the grand vin

Evaluation of present classification: Should be maintained; the quality
equivalent of a Médoc second- or third-growth
Plateau of maturity: 10–30 years following the vintage

There are two Beauséjour estates in St.-Emilion. Both are located on the *côtes*
of St.-Emilion. Both are among the crème de la crème of St.-Emilion's hierarchy—that of Premiers Grands Crus. However, the two wines could not be
more different. First of all, Beau-Séjour Bécot relies on unbridled jammy fruit
intertwined with tons of toasty new oak for much of its appeal. In contrast,
Beauséjour-Duffau, while also a dense, powerful wine, is much more reserved,
austere, and more mineral dominated. Beauséjour-Duffau leans more in the
direction of Ausone, whereas Beau-Séjour Bécot is more akin to La Dominique or Cheval Blanc.

Beauséjour-Duffau is run by Jean-Michel Dubos. He has improved the
quality significantly since the mid-eighties and has also introduced a second
wine for lesser cuvées. As the tasting notes indicate, the 1990 Beauséjour-
Duffau is one of the most profound young red wines I have ever had the
pleasure to taste. It should be one of the legends of the twentieth century.

The tiny vineyard, owned by the same family since the original vineyard
was divided in 1869, resulting in the two St.-Emilion Beauséjours, is planted
in a mixture of calcareous clay and limestone soil. Dubos's decisions to
harvest later and make a stricter selection have undoubtedly contributed to
the wine's greater richness and stature over recent years. However, this is not
a wine for those who are unable to defer their gratification, as Beauséjour-
Duffau normally requires a decade of cellaring before it begins to soften.

VINTAGES

1997—This is a pure, elegant, dark ruby–colored wine with the vintage's telltale
• softness. Moderately intense black raspberry fruit intermixed with minerals
86– and truffle-like scents are followed by a moderately tannic, medium-bodied,
87+ finesse-style wine that may turn out to be a trifle hard and angular. There are
sufficient meritorious components present for optimism. Anticipated maturity:
2003–2012. Last tasted, 3/98.

1996—This wine has a lot going for it, but the elevated tannin level prevents me
• from giving it an unequivocal endorsement. Nevertheless, I like the saturated
88– dark ruby/purple color as well as the alluring, intense black raspberry and
91 mineral scents in the wine's tight aromatics. In the mouth, there is good

weight and outstanding purity in this vividly delineated wine. To its credit, flavors and nuances unfold as the wine sits on the palate. However, in spite of all the potential joy, there is an aggressiveness and toughness to the wine's tannin that is unnerving. Given the 1996's style, it will be more instructive to taste following bottling. All the components are present for a top-notch effort, but considerable patience will be required. Anticipated maturity: 2008– 2025. Last tasted, 3/98.

1995— On numerous occasions this wine was gorgeous from cask, exhibiting a satu-
• rated dark purple color and a sweet kirsch, black cherry, mineral, and truffle
89+ character not dissimilar from the old-vine intensity found in the great Pomerol Lafleur. However, the wine is totally closed, with earth, minerals, and black fruits emerging after extended airing. In the mouth, the wine was completely shut down, with extremely high levels of tannin. Last tasted, 11/97.

1994— This has been a perplexing wine to evaluate. The color is a murky, dark
• garnet/plum. The nose exhibits a sweet, old-vine essence of cherries and
87? minerals, with some spice and earth in the background. Dense, as well as ferociously tannic and traditionally styled, the 1994 Beauséjour-Duffau may dry out if the fruit fades more quickly than the tannin. It is not a wine to buy by those seeking immediate gratification. Anticipated maturity: 2004–2016. Last tasted, 1/97.

1993— Dense ruby/garnet colored, this 1993 reveals a smoky, earthy, dark fruit
• character, medium body, moderate tannin, and good richness and balance.
87 After 2–3 years of cellaring, it will be an attractive, mid-weight wine for drinking between 2002 and 2010. Last tasted, 1/97.

1992— As evidenced by their excellent 1988, 1989, and blockbuster, rich, monu-
• mental 1990, this château is on a hot streak. This micro-estate's (less than
87+ 2,000 cases) 1992 is a stand-out effort among an undistinguished group of St.-Emilion Premiers Grands Crus Classés. The wine exhibits a deep, dark, opaque ruby/purple color and a heady bouquet of ripe black cherry fruit intermingled with scents of minerals, flowers, earth, and new oak. Surprisingly dense, medium to full bodied, concentrated, and noticeably tannic, this is a powerful, rich, ageworthy 1992 that needs 3–4 years to shed its tannin. It will last for 10–15 years. It is one of the most backward wines of the 1992 vintage, offering further evidence that Beauséjour-Duffau is producing one of Bordeaux's finest wines. Last tasted, 11/94.

1990— I have had the 1990 Beauséjour-Duffau a half dozen times since bottling. I
• believe this wine may, in 15–20 years, be considered to be one of the greatest
100 wines made this century. It is in a league with such legends as the 1961 Latour à Pomerol. Beauséjour-Duffau's 1990 has always been the most con- centrated wine of the 1990 vintage. The color remains an opaque murky purple. The nose offers up fabulously intense aromas of black fruits (plums, cherries, and currants), along with smoke, a roasted herb/nut component, and a compelling minerality. The wine is fabulously concentrated, with outstand- ing purity and a nearly unprecedented combination of richness, complexity, and overall balance and harmony. What makes this effort so intriguing is that as good as Beauséjour-Duffau can be, I know of no vintage of this estate's

wine that has come remotely close to this level of quality. In several blind tastings I have mistaken this wine for either the 1989 or 1990 Pétrus! However, the 1990 Beauséjour-Duffau is even more concentrated than those two prodigious efforts. It should be at its best between 2002 and 2030. Last tasted, 5/98.

1989— The 1989, which I had been told was close in quality to the 1990, comes
   • across as a smaller-scaled wine. The color is a moderately dark, opaque ruby/
   88 purple, and the nose offers up Grenache-like aromas of peanut butter and black cherries. This spicy, tannic, medium- to full-bodied 1989 is promising, but it does not possess the profound, unreal concentration and stature of the 1990. The 1989 requires 2–3 additional years of bottle age; it will last as long as the 1990, but it will never achieve the greatness of that vintage. Last tasted, 11/96.

1988— The 1988 has excellent depth and fullness, with a spicy, earthy, rich bouquet
   • filled with aromas of licorice, plums, spices, new oak, and subtle herbs.
   87 Exceptionally concentrated, with sound acidity and moderate alcohol, this beautifully made, complex wine should reach maturity by the mid-nineties and last through the first decade of the next century. Last tasted, 1/93.

1986— From both cask and bottle, the 1986 has never seemed to be anything more
   • than a lightweight, shallowly constructed, one-dimensional wine, with a lot of
   83 wood and tannin in the finish. Some fruit and charm has developed, but this is not one of the leaders in 1986. Anticipated maturity: Now–2012. Last tasted, 3/89.

1985— The 1985 did not exhibit as much depth as I would have expected. It is
   • lightweight and medium bodied, with a good spicy fruitiness, soft texture, and
   84 pleasant length. However, for its class, it is an uninspiring effort. Anticipated maturity: Now–2005. Last tasted, 3/89.

1983— This has turned out to be a very good example of Beauséjour. Medium dark
   • ruby, with some amber at the edge, the wine offers up a moderately intense
   86 bouquet of black fruits, smoke, licorice, and minerals. In the mouth, the wine is medium bodied and has some firm tannins to shed, but there appears to be very good extract. Almost fully mature, it should continue to evolve gracefully for at least another decade. Anticipated maturity: Now–2001. Last tasted, 1/89.

1982— The 1982 Beauséjour-Duffau surprised me with its youthfulness and tannic
   • ferocity. There is excellent, possibly outstanding, concentration behind the
   89+? wine's tough veneer. Still possessing a healthy dark ruby/purple color, with only a hint of garnet and lightening at the edge, the wine offers provocative aromas of over-ripe black fruits, minerals, and leather. Full bodied and rich, but tannic and atypically austere for a 1982, this is a difficult wine to fully grasp. Will the fruit continue to hold with the tannin softening, thus meriting an even higher rating, or will the wine remain forbiddingly tannic and backward without ever fully developing? I would gamble on it becoming at least excellent, perhaps outstanding—it is just a question of patience. Last tasted, 9/95.

1981—Medium ruby, with a firm, astringent, tough personality, the wine possesses
• an admirably tight structure, but I only wish there were a little more fruit and
82 depth. Anticipated maturity: Now. Last tasted, 11/84.

1979—Inexcusably light, feeble, frail, and lacking the richness and concentration
• one expects from wines of this class, Beauséjour's 1979 has no tannin, so it
74 is best consumed now. Last tasted, 7/83.

1978—A bigger, richer, more substantial wine than the pale 1979, the 1978, despite
• more flesh and weight, is flawed by a very metallic, bizarre bouquet that
61 seems atypical and foreign. If you can get past the smell, the wine exhibits
good structure and fruit. Anticipated maturity: Now–may be in decline. Last
tasted, 7/83.

1976—A satisfactory effort from Beauséjour, the 1976 has some ripe concentrated
• fruit, medium body, a little structure, and a charming, fruity bouquet. Not a
70 big wine, but cleanly made and pleasant. Anticipated maturity: Now–may be
in decline. Last tasted, 7/83.

1970—Extremely thin, hard, acidic flavors display none of the character of the 1970
• vintage. This wine is shockingly diluted and hollow; one cannot possibly
60 speculate what could have gone wrong. Last tasted, 7/83.

1964—In a year in which many St.-Emilions excelled, Beauséjour produced an
• insipid, dull, weakly colored, fruitless wine without charm or appeal. Quite
62 disappointing. Last tasted, 7/83.

BELAIR   GOOD

Classification: St.-Emilion Premier Grand Cru Classé B
Location of vineyards: St.-Emilion
Owner: Madame Hélyette Dubois-Challon
Address: 33330 St.-Emilion
Mailing address: Same as above
Telephone: 33 5 57 24 70 94; telefax: 33 5 57 24 67 11
Visits: By appointment, on weekdays, between 10 A.M. and noon, and
3 P.M. and 7 P.M.
Contact: Mrs. Delbeck

VINEYARDS (red)
Surface area: 30.8 acres
Average age of vines: 30 years
Blend: 75% Merlot, 25% Cabernet Franc
Density of plantation: 6,600 vines per hectare
Average yields (over the last 5 years): 39 hectoliters per hectare
Total average annual production: 490 hectoliters

GRAND VIN (red)
Brand name: Château Belair
Appellation: St.-Emilion Premier Grand Cru Classé

Mean annual production: 50,000 bottles

Upbringing: Fermentations are stimulated with indigenous yeasts obtained by biodynamic culture of part of the vineyards. Wines are aged 18–26 months in oak barrels, half of which are new (this varies according to the vintage). They are racked regularly, fined with fresh egg whites, and remain unfiltered. All transfers of the grapes and wine are done by gravity.

SECOND WINE
None produced.

Evaluation of present classification: The quality equivalent of a Médoc fifth-growth, particularly since 1979
Plateau of maturity: 5–15 years following the vintage

Belair, like so many other properties in Bordeaux, has emerged from a prolonged period of mediocrity. This property had a great reputation in the nineteenth century, and its history can be traced back as far as the fourteenth. Bernard Ginestet, a leading French writer on the wines of Bordeaux, boldly calls Belair "the Lafite-Rothschild among the hillsides of St.-Emilion." Is that overstating the case? The tiny vineyard of Belair is owned by the Dubois-Challon family, who were the former co-proprietors of Ausone, Belair's next-door neighbor. The level of wine quality at Belair has followed that of Ausone. The rehabilitation and renaissance of Ausone started with the 1976 vintage, and it was also during this time that higher-quality wines from Belair began to be produced. The same team that made Ausone (until the change in ownership in the mid-nineties)—Pascal Delbeck/Marcel Lanau/Jean-Claude Berrouet—is responsible for Belair, and as the tasting notes that follow demonstrate, this wine has improved, but it remains a tight, austere, reserved, and restrained style of wine. While part of the vineyard lies on the hillside, another part is squarely on the plateau. Could Belair be further improved?

VINTAGES

1997—Winemaker Pascal Delbeck appears to have produced an atypically soft,
•   forward, appealing 1997 that will not take long to come around. A dark ruby
86–   color is followed by aromas of sweet, mineral-infused, black cherry fruit,
87   medium body, and light tannin in the round, attractive finish. This wine
        requires 2–3 years of cellaring and should keep for 10–12 years. Last tasted,
        3/98.

1996—An angular, light-bodied, mineral-scented wine came across as austere and
•   spartan, lacking fruit, glycerin, and flesh. Anticipated maturity: 2003–2012.
80–   Last tasted, 3/98.
85

1995—This is a low-key claret with red and black currants competing with distinc-
  •   tive wet stone and mineral-like components. New oak is present in this
85   medium-bodied, hard, austere yet extraordinarily subtle and restrained St.-
       Emilion. It may be too polite for its own good. Anticipated maturity: 2002–
       2015. Last tasted, 11/97.

1994—This medium dark ruby–colored wine exhibits sweet, red currant and cherry
  •   fruit, low acid, light body, some of Belair's telltale earthiness, a spicy, tannic
85   personality, and a compact finish. Anticipated maturity: 2000–2007. Last
       tasted, 1/97.

1993—Medium garnet colored, with a musty, old barrel aroma, this wine is domi-
  •   nated by a powdered stone character, green, vegetal fruit flavors, and a lean,
76   light-bodied palate. Last tasted, 1/97.

1992—The light, washed-out color and weak, muted nose is followed by a wine lacking
  •   fruit, depth, and grip. There is little finish in this shallow, diluted wine. Three
74?   notes from cask samples revealed similar results. Last tasted 11/94.

1990—There is sweet, nearly over-ripe fruit, plenty of mineral/stony scents, and evi-
  •   dence of new oak underlying this medium-weight wine's backward personality.
89   The aromas of over-ripe cherries and prunes are vaguely reminiscent of the
       great Pomerol Lafleur. Anticipated maturity: Now–2010. Last tasted, 1/93.

1989—The 1989 exhibits a huge, smoky, roasted, exotic bouquet of plums and Asian
  •   spices. The wine exhibits surprisingly crisp acidity and plentiful but soft
88   tannins. The formidable level of alcohol and sensationally extracted, multi-
       dimensional fruit flavors make this a brilliant effort. Anticipated maturity:
       Now–2010. Last tasted, 1/93.

1988—The 1988 is a good rather than exceptional effort. Given the vintage, no one
  •   should be surprised that it is a leaner, more austere wine. But it does have a
85   good inner core of curranty fruit, fine tannins, and a general sense of elegance
       and grace. Anticipated maturity: Now–2010. Last tasted, 4/91.

1987—This elegant, ripe, supple, deliciously fruity, complex wine is, amazingly,
  •   better and paradoxically cheaper than the more highly touted 1988, 1986,
86   and 1985. There is plenty of extract, and the wine exhibits a long, ripe,
       seductive finish. A top success for a 1987 St.-Emilion, it should be drunk
       early in its life. Anticipated maturity: Now. Last tasted, 3/90.

1986—This is a disappointing effort from Belair. The medium ruby color appears
  •   slightly washed out, and the bouquet is closed but manages to offer up some
76   dusty, herbaceous, red fruit scents. In the mouth, the wine is astringent, too
       tannic, and very austere and finishes without any charm or concentration. Its
       future is suspect. Anticipated maturity: Now–2005. Last tasted, 3/90.

1985—I am perplexed by the 1985 Belair, as it seems somewhat light and lacking
  •   grip and intensity. Have I misinterpreted this wine from both cask and bottle?
77   Anticipated maturity: Now–2005. Last tasted, 3/89.

1983—Surprisingly powerful and rich for Belair, with excellent color and a deep,
  •   ripe, tannic, full-bodied texture, this is a big-styled wine that should prove to
88   be the longest-lived Belair in over 20 years. Quite impressive. Anticipated
       maturity: Now–2005. Last tasted, 2/89.

1982—For over a decade I have questioned which is the better vintage of Belair, the
•   forward, soft yet powerful 1983 or the more structured, exotic 1982. I am still
88   not sure. Certainly the 1982 has emerged from its "ugly duckling" stage and
        is beginning to reveal some mushroomy, leathery notes intermingled with
        scents of sweet black fruits, herbs, and minerals. The complex nose is fol-
        lowed by a wine with very good concentration. Although noticeably hard
        tannin is still in evidence, this is a nicely extracted, traditionally made
        St.-Emilion. The 1982, which rivals the 1983 Belair, possesses 10–15 more
        years of aging potential. Anticipated maturity: Now–2008. Last tasted,
        12/96.

1981—The 1981 is, as some Bordelais would enthusiastically say, "a finesse wine
•   with plenty of elegance." Light, fruity, and soft, this medium ruby–colored
74   wine has a pleasing texture and some hard tannins in the finish, but it seems
        unlikely to gain flavor or depth. Anticipated maturity: Now. Last tasted,
        3/87.

1979—The first attractive Belair in nearly 20 years, the 1979 has a perfume of ripe
•   black currant fruit, some spicy oak, and violets. On the palate, the wine is
85   medium bodied, with a lush, precocious fruitiness and light tannins. This is
        a deliciously soft, fruity, very elegant wine. Anticipated maturity: Now–may
        be in decline. Last tasted, 1/87.

1978—This wine is a trifle too light and fleeting on the palate, but it does offer
•   soft, pleasant, easygoing, fruity flavors, and it also finishes well. Anticipated
80   maturity: Now–may be in decline. Last tasted, 2/86.

1976—The 1976 is respectable, but perhaps it could have been better given the
•   excellence of Ausone in this vintage. Rather light, soft, fruity, and sweet,
75   displaying the obvious over-ripe quality of the vintage, the 1976 Belair has
        no discernible tannin. It was fully mature in the early eighties. Anticipated
        maturity: Now–may be in decline. Last tasted, 6/82.

1975—I have found this wine to be hollow and lacking fruit, with an excess of tannin
•   present. Medium ruby, with some brown at the edges, this medium-bodied
70   wine has a dusty, sparse texture, a leathery, hard bouquet, and a short, harsh
        finish. It appears to be one of the 1975s where the tannin content significantly
        outweighs the fruit. Last tasted, 5/84.

1971—Quite meagerly endowed, without much bouquet, this wine has a brownish
•   color, dry, astringent, hard flavors, and no charm. One rarely sees top proper-
65   ties today producing wines at this level of quality. Last tasted, 9/78.

1970—Adequately colored, with just a shade of brown, the 1970 Belair is hard and
•   spicy and finishes with a coarseness and bitterness. It is an atypical 1970.
68   Last tasted, 7/81.

BELLEFONT-BELCIER   GOOD

Classification: St.-Emilion Grand Cru
Location of vineyards: St.-Laurent-des-Combes
Address: 33330 St.-Laurent-des-Combes
Mailing address: Same as above

Telephone: 33 5 57 24 72 16; telefax: 33 5 57 74 45 06
Visits: Monday through Thursday, from 8:30 A.M. to 5:30 P.M.

VINEYARDS (red)
Surface area: 29.64 acres
Average age of vines: 30 years
Blends: 83% Merlot, 10% Cabernet Franc, 7% Cabernet Sauvignon
Average yields (over the last 5 years): 40 hectoliters per hectare
Total average annual production: 450 hectoliters

GRAND VIN (red)
Brand name: Château Bellefont-Belcier
Appellation: St.-Emilion Grand Cru
Upbringing: Malolactics occur in oak barrels, and wines are aged 18
months in 80% new oak. They are fined and filtered.

SECOND WINE
Brand name: Marquis de Bellefont
Average annual production: Variable

Evaluation of present classification: The quality equivalent of a Médoc
Cru Bourgeois
Plateau of maturity: 3–8 years following the vintage

This vineyard, well situated in the commune of St.-Laurent-des-Combes, not far from the outstanding *terroirs* of Tertre-Roteboeuf and Larcis-Ducasse, has begun to produce more interesting wine in the mid-nineties. The wine has historically been straightforward, soft, and easy to drink, lacking distinction and coming across as monolithic. However, the property began to harvest later, picking riper fruit, and has been more selective in what is being bottled under the château's name. The results have been very good wines in 1994, 1995, and 1996, all of which are superior to anything made previously.

VINTAGES

1997—This tasty, round easygoing wine with fat, texture, and length will drink well
•   for 3–5 years. Last tasted, 3/98.
84–
85

1996—The 1996 exhibits a complex, smoky, roasted herb, sweet black cherry, and
•   licorice nose that is surprisingly forward for a 1996. Soft, round, silky-
87   textured fruit flavors reveal low acidity as well as a succulent texture. Drink
     this chewy, lush St.-Emilion over the next 5–8 years. Last tasted, 11/97.

1995—The 1995 is somewhat of a sleeper, exhibiting a dense color and rich, jammy
•   black fruits intermingled with scents of herb, licorice, and toast. Thick, chewy
87   flavors reveal fine extraction and glycerin. This is a soft, low-acid, opulent

wine for drinking during the first 7–8 years after its release. Last tasted, 11/97.

1994—The 1994 Bellefont-Belcier is a solid, chunky, fleshy wine with moderate
•   quantities of fruit, glycerin, and extract. It is a wine to drink during its first
86   7–8 years of life. Last tasted, 3/96.

BERLIQUET

Classification: St.-Emilion Grand Cru Classé
Location of vineyards: St.-Emilion
Owner: Vicomte and Vicomtesse Patrick de Lesquen
Address: 33330 St.-Emilion
Mailing address: Same as above
Telephone: 33 5 57 24 70 48; telefax: 33 5 57 24 70 24
Visits: By appointment only, every day, between 9 A.M. and noon, and
2 P.M. and 6 P.M.

VINEYARDS (red)
Surface area: 22.2 acres
Average age of vines: Between 35 and 45 years
Blend: 67% Merlot, 25% Cabernet Franc, 8% Cabernet Sauvignon
Density of plantation: 5,500 vines per hectare
Average yields (over the last 5 years): 45 hectoliters per hectare
Total average annual production: 410 hectoliters

GRAND VIN (red)
Brand name: Château Berliquet
Appellation: St.-Emilion Grand Cru Classé
Mean annual production: 30,000 bottles
Upbringing: Fermentations and macerations last 30–40 days in
temperature-controlled vats. Malolactics occur in oak barrels (lots
separate), and wines are aged 14–16 months in oak barrels, 80% of
which are new. They are racked from barrel to barrel every 3 months,
fined but not filtered. *Assemblage* is done toward the end of the aging
process.

SECOND WINE
Brand name: Les Ailes de Berliquet
Average annual production: 24,000 bottles (approximate in 1996)

Evaluation of present classification: The quality equivalent of a Médoc
Cru Bourgeois
Plateau of maturity: 4–12 years following the vintage

This is a beautifully situated property with splendid underground caves and a superb exposition just outside the village of St.-Emilion. In fact, one could not ask for a better position on the limestone plateau of St.-Emilion, adjoining Canon, Magdelaine, and Tertre-Daugay. In 1985 Berliquet became the only château to be promoted to a Grand Cru Classé. Its fame, however, must have been far greater in the eighteenth century. In 1794 a well-known Libourne courtier wrote about the excellent quality of a wine in St.-Emilion called Berliquet.

Berliquet was content to stay in the background, as all of its wine, until the 1978 vintage, was made and produced by the huge cooperative in St.-Emilion. Although the staff at the cooperative oversees the production of Berliquet, since 1978 the wine has been made, matured, and bottled at the attractive château. While the quality has been solid rather than exciting, things may be changing. In 1997 Patrick Valette was hired to oversee the winemaking, and the result was a 1997 that I feel is the finest wine ever made at this estate.

VINTAGES

1997— The wine reveals an opaque purple color and reserved but promising aromas
•   of black currants, blackberries, oak, earth, and spice. Powerful, dense, and
86–   chewy, without the open-knit accessibility of many 1997s, this is a nicely
88   proportioned, hefty wine with moderate tannin in the finish. It will be drinkable within 3–4 years and last for 12 or more. It is an impressive showing for what has been a perennial St.-Emilion underachiever. Possibly a sleeper of the vintage. Last tasted, 3/98.

1996— This is an angular, tough-textured, tannic wine with insufficient fruit to balance out the wine's muscle and structure. It is likely to dry out over its
•
78   10–15-year evolution. Last tasted, 11/97.

1995— Medium deep ruby colored, with an earthy, tarry, spicy nose that dominates
•   the wine's meager fruit, this wine is compressed and pinched, with an angular
75   austerity and a lean, tannic, astringent finish. I do not see this wine ever coming around. Last tasted, 11/97.

1990— A soft, savory, herb-and-cherry-scented wine with attractive earth and spice
•   in the background, this medium-bodied, lush, fully mature St.-Emilion offers
86   a plump feel on the palate. It should drink well for 5–6 years. Anticipated maturity: Now–2003. Last tasted, 11/97.

1989— Medium ruby, with a spicy, earthy, ripe berry–scented bouquet, this medium-
•   bodied wine has surprisingly good acidity and grip for the vintage, but it lacks
82   the concentration and depth of the best wines of the appellation. It possesses some moderately astringent tannins. Anticipated maturity: Now. Last tasted, 4/91.

1988— This compact, relatively attenuated St.-Emilion could use more fat, depth,
•   and charm. It is spicy, but lean and anorexic. The finish is also surprisingly
79   short, but moderately tannic. Anticipated maturity: Now–may be in decline. Last tasted, 1/93.

CADET-PIOLA VERY GOOD

Classification: St.-Emilion Grand Cru Classé
Location of vineyards: In the northern part of the village, on a calcareous plateau
Owner: G.F.A. Jabiol
Address: 33330 St.-Emilion
Mailing address: B.P. 24, 33330 St.-Emilion
Telephone and telefax: 33 5 57 74 47 69
Visits: By appointment on weekdays, between 9 A.M. and 11 A.M., and 2 P.M. and 4 P.M.
Contact: Amélie Jabiol

VINEYARDS (red)
Surface area: 17.3 acres
Average age of vines: 30 years
Blend: 51% Merlot, 28% Cabernet Sauvignon, 18% Cabernet Franc, 3% Malbec
Density of plantation: 5,600 vines per hectare
Average yields (over the last 5 years): 38 hectoliters
Total average annual production: 36,000 bottles

GRAND VIN (red)
Brand name: Château Cadet-Piola
Appellation: St.-Emilion Grand Cru Classé
Mean annual production: 36,000 bottles
Upbringing: Fermentations and macerations last about 21 days in stainless-steel vats equipped with an internal temperature-control system. Wines are transferred after malolactics to oak barrels for 18 months aging (40% new oak, 30% of the barrels are 1 vintage old, and the remaining 30% 2 vintages old). Wines then spend 4 months in vats before being bottled. They are fined but not filtered.

SECOND WINE
Brand name: Chevaliers de Malte
Average annual production: This second wine is made only when the young Cabernet Franc is not deemed good enough to be blended into the first wine

Evaluation of present classification: Should be maintained; the quality equivalent of a Médoc fifth-growth
Plateau of maturity: 6–17 years following the vintage

It must be the small production of Cadet-Piola that has kept this wine's quality relatively secret for so long a time. Cadet-Piola, which is neither a *côtes* St.-Emilion nor a *graves* St.-Emilion, is just one-half kilometer north of the town. The château—with a splendid view overlooking St.-Emilion—is located on a rocky outcropping with a clay and limestone base; it is used only for making wine and not as a residence. The proprietors claim the microclimate is warmer than elsewhere in the appellation.

The owners, the Jabiol family (who are also the proprietors of the St.-Emilion estate of Faurie-de-Souchard), are conservative winemakers who produce a black/ruby–colored, rich and intense, full-bodied wine that over the last decade has outperformed many of the more famous and more expensive Premiers Grands Crus. Cadet-Piola is a great value, and hopefully consumer demand will result in more of this estate's wine being imported to America.

VINTAGES

1995 — The 1995 possesses an impressively saturated, ruby/purple color and a sweet
•   nose of blueberries and black raspberries intermingled with vague scents of
87   sweet oak and minerals. Ripe and medium bodied, but noticeably tannic, this
     well-endowed, muscular, backward wine will require 4–5 years of cellaring
     despite its low acidity. A very fine effort, it should keep for 10–12 years. Last
     tasted, 11/97.

1994 — Cadet-Piola's 1994 exhibits a healthy ruby/purple color, olive, licorice, and
•   sweet black cherry fruit in the nose, medium body, and a tough, tannic finish.
86   The wine may develop some Médoc-like austerity, but it is a good, solidly
     made, muscular St.-Emilion for drinking over the next decade. Last tasted,
     3/96.

1993 — Given the 1993 vintage's potential for tough, hard, tannic wines, and Cadet-
•   Piola's tendency to produce rustic, dense, tough wines, one would have ex-
85   pected a wine that would melt a tooth's enamel. Not so. This estate has
     produced a soft, fleshy, medium-bodied, supple, easygoing 1993 that will
     offer pleasant drinking over the next 5–7 years. Last tasted, 11/94.

1992 — The compact 1992 Cadet-Piola displays medium ruby color, an unimpressive,
•   watery bouquet, and short, soft, ripe, but insubstantial flavors dominated by
72   an astringent, dry, tannic taste. This wine will dry out in 4–6 years, so drink
     it young. Last tasted, 11/94.

1990 — The 1990 is a classic Cadet-Piola—highly structured, deep in color, forbid-
•   dingly backward, and nearly impenetrable. Black/ruby/purple colored, ex-
87   tremely tannic, and hard, it appears to possess the requisite concentration to
     balance out its tough personality. This is not a wine for those who lack
     patience. Anticipated maturity: Now–2010. Last tasted, 1/93.

1989 — The 1989 is probably a finer wine than my score suggests. This wine has
•   thick black/ruby color and is impressive, but the nose is closed. On the
87   palate, the wine is an overwhelmingly muscular, hard, tough-textured, tannic

behemoth that needs at least 7–10 years of cellaring but should last several decades. The muscular, backward style is typical of Cadet-Piola. Anticipated maturity: Now–2010. Last tasted, 4/91.

1988—The 1988 Cadet-Piola possesses excruciatingly high tannin levels, but the
•   big, rich, black cherry flavors intertwined with new oak, scents of chocolate,
86   and Provençal herbs gives me some basis for saying that the wine has the requisite depth to stand up to the tannin. A medium- to full-bodied wine, it should age well for up to 2 decades. Anticipated maturity: Now–2010. Last tasted, 1/93.

1986—The 1986 is an exceptionally backward, tannic, black-colored St.-Emilion. In
•   fact, I was a bit worried about the level of tannin, except for the gobs of rich,
85? long, chewy fruit one can easily sense when tasting it. The only question that remains is, when will enough of the excruciatingly high tannin content fall away to make this wine round and seductive? Will the fruit hold? Anticipated maturity: Now–2010. Last tasted, 11/90.

1985—The 1985 Cadet-Piola is a tannic, well-built wine for the vintage. Deep ruby,
•   with a spicy, plummy, intense bouquet, this is a full-bodied, dense, chewy
86   wine with plenty of character. It can be drunk now. Anticipated maturity: Now–2000. Last tasted, 3/90.

1983—Although not the success of the wonderful 1982, the 1983 Cadet-Piola is still
•   a darkly colored, ripe, full-bodied, admirably constructed St.-Emilion with
85   plenty of concentration, muscle, and power. Anticipated maturity: Now. Last tasted, 1/89.

1982—The 1982 Cadet-Piola continues to be a dark ruby/purple–colored wine with
•   admirable richness, mouth-searing tannin, and a promising yet still unevolved
87+ and backward set of aromatics (licorice, black fruits, herbs, and spice). Although full bodied, with excellent concentration, the wine reveals only a hint of complexity. It is more supple than it was a decade ago, but it remains a tannic mouthful of wine. Masochists might enjoy it now, but I recommend another 3–4 years of cellaring; it should keep through the first decade of the next century. Last tasted, 9/95.

CANON   EXCELLENT

Classification: St.-Emilion Premier Grand Cru Classé B
Location of vineyards: St.-Emilion Côtes
Owner: Wertheimer family—Chanel Inc.
Address: 33330 St.-Emilion
Mailing address: B.P. 22, 33330 St.-Emilion
Telephone: 33 5 57 55 23 45; telefax: 33 5 57 24 68 00
Visits: By appointment only, on weekdays, between 2 P.M. and 6 P.M.
Contact: John Kolasa or Mrs. Defrance

VINEYARDS (red)
Surface area: 44.5 acres
Average age of vines: 35 years

Blend: 55% Merlot, 45% Cabernet Sauvignon
Density of plantation: 6,500 vines per hectare
Average yields (over the last 5 years): 35 hectoliters
Total average annual production: 650 hectoliters

GRAND VIN (red)
Brand name: Château Canon
Appellation: St.-Emilion Premier Grand Cru
Mean annual production: 295 hectoliters
Upbringing: Fermentations and macerations last approximately 15 days
in temperature-controlled wooden vats. Wines are then aged 18 months in
oak barrels, 65% of which are new. They are fined but not filtered.

SECOND WINE
Brand name: Clos J. Kanon (used by the Fournier family, former owners
of the château; the new brand name has not yet been chosen and
registered)
Average annual production: Variable

Evaluation of present classification: Since 1982 the quality equivalent of
a Médoc third- or fourth-growth; prior to 1982 and in the early nineties,
the quality was inconsistent .
Plateau of maturity: 7–25 years following the vintage

One of the *côtes* St.-Emilions, Canon has a splendid location on the southwestern slopes of the town of St.-Emilion, where its vineyard is sandwiched between Premiers Grands Crus Classés vineyards such as Belair, Magdelaine, Clos Fourtet, and Beauséjour. This vineyard, which lies partly on the hillside and partly on the plateau, has several different soil types, ranging from limestone and clay to sandy soils on a limestone base.

Canon, the property of the Fournier family since 1919, was sold in the mid-nineties to the firm of Chanel. The name, however, comes from the eighteenth-century owner, Jacques Kanon. A very traditional, long, hot fermentation in oak vats suggests that the property pays little heed to consumers who want to drink supple Bordeaux wines. This is a tannic, powerful wine, built to last and last. It is marked by a pronounced oakiness that can, in lighter vintages, obliterate the fruit. This overzealous yet expensive use of new oak (a minimum of 65% is used in every vintage) is my only criticism of Canon. I adore this wine in vintages such as 1982, 1983, 1985, 1986, 1988, and 1989. In the eighties, under the leadership of Eric Fournier and his brilliant *maître de chai*, Paul Cazenove, Canon had attained a quality that often equaled, sometimes even surpassed, that of the St.-Emilion supergrowths Cheval Blanc and Ausone, but a miserable record of performances following the excellent 1990 led to a lack of confidence in Canon. This was further exacerbated by a contamination in the aging cellars that caused many of the wines produced between 1992 and 1996 to smell and taste excessively musty. The new proprietors immediately renovated the old *chai,* thankfully eliminating the cause of the off-putting smells.

At its best, Canon is a splendidly rich, deep, and concentrated wine, muscular and full bodied and, when mature, richly fruity, cedary, and often magnificent. It remains a mystery why this wine is not better known, because Canon has certainly been one of the top three or four St.-Emilions during the decade of the eighties, and it is likely to regain its lofty reputation under the new ownership.

VINTAGES

1997— I am expecting better things from Canon now that it is owned by Chanel and
• run by the capable team of John Kolasa and David Orr. However, the 1997
77– performed poorly the only time I tasted it. The wine revealed a dark ruby/
81 garnet color, an herbaceous earthiness, surprisingly high acidity, evolved
flavors, and light body. For now, this appears to be disappointing. Last tasted,
3/98.

1996— This medium ruby/plum–colored wine offers sweet notes of black fruits in
• the nose, but they quickly fade to reveal earth, loamy soil, mineral, oak,
78– and weedy scents. There is some pleasant richness on the attack of this
82? medium-bodied wine, but it closes down to display severe tannin and an
angular, lean personality. The acidity is high, the tannin excessive, and the
wine is a strong candidate to dry out. My rating may prove to be overly
generous. Anticipated maturity: 2002–2010. Last tasted, 3/98.

1995— I could not find any redeeming qualities in this sinewy, thin, austere, high-
• acid, ferociously tannic wine. As hard as I tried, I could not see any positive
74 side to the manner in which this wine is going to develop. Anticipated
maturity: 2000–2008. Last tasted, 11/97.

1994— In addition to being austere, lean, and unappealing on the palate, this wine
• is marred by damp wood, wet cardboard, musty, cork-like aromas that are
? similar to those afflicting the 1993. It is a very disappointing effort. Last
tasted, 1/97.

1993— In addition to unpleasant severe, tough tannin, a moldy, wet dog/musty card-
• board bouquet is present in this clipped, unattractive wine. Avoid. Last
? tasted, 1/97.

1992— From cask, I had thought the 1992 Canon to be one of St.-Emilion's most
• successful wines. Like many 1992s, the wine's fragile fruit appears to have
? suffered from its bottling. The results offer a perplexingly hard, tough, sculp-
tured wine that appears slightly eviscerated. The color is sound, the fruit
and attack begin well, but there is not much depth or length—just tannin,
alcohol, acidity, and wood. Is this wine closed or merely empty and hollow? No off odors were discernible at the most recent tasting. Last tasted,
11/94.

1990—The 1990 is not up to the quality of the 1989. Powerful and backward, it
•   displays astringent tannins as well as a tough-textured personality. Offering a
87   bouquet of black raspberry fruit intertwined with aromas and flavors of coffee
       and chocolate, this tannic, medium-bodied wine will require considerable
       patience. Anticipated maturity: 2000–2025. Last tasted, 1/93.

1989—The 1989 Canon will not approach the 1982 in terms of concentration and
•   complexity, yet it does resemble a synthesis in style between the 1985
92   and 1986. Deep ruby/purple in color, with a rich, spicy, new oak, black cur-
       rant bouquet of moderate intensity, this full-bodied, rather Burgundy-
       textured wine is tannic and deeply endowed. The flavor extraction as well
       as purity of taste is impressive. Anticipated maturity: Now–2008. Last tasted,
       5/95.

1988—The 1988's deep ruby/purple color is impressive and the spicy, mineral, tar,
•   and cassis bouquet is captivating. While there is an elevated level of tannins,
87   this wine possesses excellent concentration, plenty of length, and a sense that
       the yields were conservative, as there is good inner strength and depth. This
       is a less generous style of Canon, but it should age well for 2 or more decades.
       Anticipated maturity: 1999–2012. Last tasted, 1/93.

1987—Canon made a lovely wine in this sometimes underrated vintage. Medium
•   ruby, with a fragrant bouquet of black fruits and spicy oak, this is a supple,
85   easygoing, graciously endowed Canon. Anticipated maturity: Now. Last
       tasted, 3/90.

1986—This wine is still bound up by its high tannin content. It reveals a dark garnet/
•   ruby color, with no amber at the edge. The nose primarily offers minerals,
89+   earth, and smoke, with black plum and cassis fruit in the background. On the
       attack, the wine is rich, medium bodied, and elegant, with lofty tannin in the
       finish. Although approachable, it remains youthful and vibrant. Anticipated
       maturity: 1999–2015. Last tasted, 12/97.

1985—Just approaching full maturity, this St.-Emilion offers a delicious combination
•   of aromatics and flavors, including kirsch, cherries, minerals, and smoky oak,
89   as well as a soft, medium-bodied, lush, mellow, and nicely textured palate.
       This charming, rich, stylish wine is now at its plateau of maturity. Anticipated
       maturity: Now–2007. Last tasted, 12/97.

1983—The 1983 Canon has reached full maturity. The wine's dark garnet/ruby color
•   reveals some rust/amber at the edge. The nose is forthcoming, with scents of
88   leather, earth, spice, sweet plums and fruitcake. In the mouth, the wine
       possesses good richness, heady alcoholic clout, low acidity, and rustic tannin
       in the finish. This wine has matured quickly but should hold (if stored in a
       cool cellar) for another 10–12 years. Last tasted, 12/97.

1982—A consistently spectacular 1982, this wine provided sumptuous drinking the
•   first 5–6 years after bottling. Since the late eighties the wine has become
94   more structured without losing any of its power, fat, or concentration. It is
       capable of lasting for 20 more years, although I will not quibble with any
       readers who can no longer defer their gratification. The dense color reveals
       no amber. Young, primary aromas of black fruits, toasty oak, and flowers

dominate the wine's moderately intense nose. Thick, rich, full bodied, and multi-dimensional, this is unquestionably the most concentrated Canon I have ever tasted. This large-scaled, super-rich, sweet wine is one of the rare Canons that possesses more depth of fruit than tannin. Drink it over the next 25 years. Last tasted, 9/95.

1981—While Canon produced a good wine in 1978 and 1979 and a great, perhaps
•　　legendary, wine in 1982, and excelled in 1985, 1986, 1988, and 1989, the
75　　1981 falls way short of my expectations. The château's obsession with new oak barrels has rendered a wine that from its birth was too light and fragile to absorb the full impact of the tannin and vanillin from new barrels. The wine is overly tannic, lean, and out of balance. Time may help, but don't count on it. Anticipated maturity: Now–2000. Last tasted, 2/88.

1980—In this vintage I have found the 1980 Canon to have good fruit and average
•　　color, but excessive oak in its bouquet. One could call this a modest success
72　　for the vintage, yet I would like to see less of the annoying vegetal character and more of the pleasant, supple, black currant fruitiness. Anticipated maturity: Now–may be in decline. Last tasted, 7/87.

1979—One of the best St.-Emilions in this vintage, this Canon is impressively dark
•　　ruby in color without any amber and has tannic and youthful flavors. It
86　　exhibits good concentration, depth, and body, but the tannins are still foreboding. Canon's 1979 is a young, muscular wine with potential, but will the fruit hold up? Anticipated maturity: Now–2003. Last tasted, 1/91.

1978—Similar to the 1979, but leaner and more austere, the 1978 Canon still
•　　needs time to develop. Dark ruby with some amber, this relatively big, tannic
85　　wine has evolved much slower than I expected. It is a harder, less charming style of Canon than usual. Anticipated maturity: Now–2005. Last tasted, 1/91.

1976—Not one of my favorite Canons, the 1976 is diffuse and lacks both depth and
•　　structure. Browning, and overly tannic and oaky without supporting fruit for
70　　balance, this wine will only continue to get more awkward. It should be drunk soon, if ever. Last tasted, 10/82.

1975—The 1975 Canon is not evolving well. Still ferociously tannic, with the fruit
•　　beginning to fade, this wine clearly lacks the extract and concentration neces-
68　　sary to stand up to its astringent, hard personality. The color has changed from medium ruby to a strong amber/orange at the edge. The dusty tannins obliterate what fruit is left. The wine's future is dubious. Last tasted, 1/89.

1971—Disappointingly thin, attenuated, and lacking fruit and charm, this wine has
•　　become dried out, with a bitter, harsh finish. *Caveat emptor!* Last tasted,
65　　1/89.

1970—This is a good Canon, yet not nearly up to the quality that the young Eric
•　　Fournier, who took over direct management in 1972, produced in the period
84　　1978 through 1990. Fully mature, somewhat lighter, and less concentrated than expected, but fragrant and spicy, with a plummy, roasted character, this lightweight Canon has lost most of its tannin, so consume it now. Anticipated maturity: Now–may be in decline. Last tasted, 2/85.

1966—One of Canon's top efforts, this rich, intense, deeply concentrated wine is still
•   in top-notch shape, with a big, full-intensity bouquet of ripe fruit and melted
86   toffee. On the palate, the wine is in complete harmony, soft, rich, velvety, full
      bodied, and fleshy. Retasted from a half bottle in 1987, it appeared to be
      losing some of its fruit. Anticipated maturity: Now. Last tasted, 6/87.

1964—One of the finest wines made at Canon during the sixties, this full-bodied,
•   rich, still vigorous, and opulent wine has a roasted, spicy, tar, and plummy
88   bouquet, heady, alcoholic flavors, and considerable length. There's more mus-
      cle than finesse to this vintage of Canon. Anticipated maturity: Now. Last
      tasted, 4/91.

1961—This wine has been fully mature since I first tasted it over a decade ago. It is
•   an outstanding 1961, with a dark garnet color and exuberant, intense aromat-
88   ics consisting of smoked meats, jammy fruits, dried spices, and intriguing
      truffle and grilled vegetable–like aromas. Medium bodied, and still fresh with
      plenty of extract and full body, this wine has some tannin in the finish, which
      will undoubtedly remain after all of the fruit has faded. Anticipated maturity:
      Now–2002. Last tasted, 11/95.

ANCIENT VINTAGES

Due to the fact that the 1959 (95 points; last tasted 10/94) was undoubtedly made from relatively young vines (the 1956 freeze caused a significant loss of vines at Canon), this bottle performed spectacularly. The sweet, chocolatey, jammy, black cherry–scented nose and opaque garnet color revealed few signs of age. The wine exhibited an underlying herbaceous quality (young vines?), but its superb richness and chewy, viscous, thick flavors were sensational. There is enough richness and tannin for the wine to evolve for another 15–20 years. It is a magnificent example of Canon!

CANON-LA-GAFFELIÈRE   OUTSTANDING

Classification: St.-Emilion Grand Cru Classé
Location of vineyards: St.-Emilion Côtes
Owner: Comtes de Neipperg
Address: 33330 St.-Emilion
Mailing address: Same as above
Telephone: 33 5 57 24 71 33; telefax: 33 5 57 24 67 95
Visits: By appointment, on weekdays, from 9 A.M. to noon, and 2 P.M.
to 5 P.M.
Contact: Cécile Gardaix

VINEYARDS (red)
Surface area: 48.2 acres
Average age of vines: 32 years

Blend: 55% Merlot, 40% Cabernet Franc, 5% Cabernet Sauvignon
Density of plantation: 5,500 vines per hectare
Average yields (over the last 5 years): 40 hectoliters per hectare
Total average annual production: 100,500 bottles

GRAND VIN (red)
Brand name: Château Canon-La-Gaffelière
Appellation: St.-Emilion Grand Cru Classé
Mean annual production: 75,000–80,000 bottles
Upbringing: As of 1997, fermentations are long and may last up to 4
weeks in temperature-controlled wooden vats. Indigenous yeasts are used,
and pumping-over is done only for those vats that do not undergo any
pigéage. Malolactics occur in barrels, on fine lees with frequent
bâtonnages, and the first racking is done only 1 or 2 months after
completion of malolactics. Wines are aged in oak barrels that are
renewed by half at each vintage for 12–18 months. They are never
racked, but are provided with oxygen, called *micro-bullage.* They are
fined but remain unfiltered.

SECOND WINE
Brand name: Côte Migon-La-Gaffelière
Average annual production: 10,000 bottles

Evaluation of present classification: Since 1985 the quality equivalent of
a Médoc second- or third-growth; should be elevated to a St.-Emilion
Premier Grand Cru Classé
Plateau of maturity: 3–14 years following the vintage

Another of the *côtes* St.-Emilions, Canon-La-Gaffelière actually has most of
its vineyard on flat, sandy soil at the foot of the hills. For over 2 decades,
Canon-La-Gaffelière was widely promoted, offering light, bland, mediocre
wines at surprisingly high prices. That has changed dramatically since the
young, brilliant Stephan Von Neipperg assumed responsibility in 1985. In
fact, there is probably no St.-Emilion Grand Cru Classé that has exhibited
greater improvement than Canon-La-Gaffelière.

Changes that have led to the recent successes at this property include late
harvesting to ensure maximum maturity of the grapes, the introduction of a
second wine for weaker vats, and a longer maceration to extract more color
and intensity. The percentage of new oak utilized has also been increased.
The results of all these changes are some of the most opulent and flattering
wines of St.-Emilion. This is clearly one of the stars of the appellation, as
vintages since the late eighties so admirably attest.

VINTAGES

1997— This is one of the few 1997s that reminded me of how certain 1982s tasted at
•   a similar age. It is an explosive, opulently textured, knockout wine that coats
90–   the palate with superb levels of flavor and glycerin. The saturated black/
92   purple color is accompanied by evolved aromas and flavors of *pain grillé*,
     smoke, licorice, olives, and blackberries/cassis. Unctuous in the mouth, with
     superb concentration, low acidity, and a blockbuster finish, this is a luxuri-
     antly rich, decadent Canon-La-Gaffelière that should drink well young and
     last for 12 or more years. Very impressive! Sadly, the 1997 production was
     tiny, with less than 35% of the harvest going into proprietor Stephan Von
     Neipperg's grand vin. Last tasted, 3/98.

1996— An impressively extracted, opaque purple–colored wine, this flamboyant
•   St.-Emilion offers intense aromas of jammy black cherries, melted chocolate,
90–   *pain grillé*, and spice. Full bodied, rich, and huge in the mouth, with layers
91   of extract, glycerin, and tannin, this is an immense, exotic St.-Emilion that
     will require a half dozen years of cellaring. Anticipated maturity: 2004–2018.
     Last tasted, 3/98.

1995— A massive wine, with a cigar box, chocolatey, thick, black currant and cherry
•   nose, this full-bodied wine is crammed with layers of fruit, extract, glycerin,
91+   and alcohol. Spicy yet rich, with high tannin, the 1995 Canon-La-Gaffelière
     will need a minimum of 5–6 years of cellaring. The finish is long and rich
     and the tannin sweet rather than astringent. Anticipated maturity: 2004–
     2020. Last tasted, 11/97.

1994— A dense purple color is accompanied by strikingly pure aromas of Provençal
•   olives, jammy cassis, and smoky *pain grillé* notes. Ripe and fat, this medium-
90   to full-bodied, moderately tannic, muscular yet elegant wine needs another
     2–4 years of cellaring. It should keep for 16–17 years. It is an impressive,
     well-balanced 1994. Last tasted, 1/97.

1993— This 1993's saturated dark purple color is among the most impressive of the
•   vintage. Aromatically the wine offers copious amounts of dark, earthy,
88   plummy, licorice, smoke-tinged, rich fruit, a sweet, surprisingly ripe, glyc-
     erin-imbued entry, and medium to full body. With low acid, and the fruit and
     texture concealing the wine's light tannin, this appealing, attractive effort
     should drink well for 10–12 years. Moreover, it is a reasonable value from
     what is largely a forgotten vintage. Last tasted, 1/97.

1992— One of the bright, shining stars of Bordeaux's right bank appellation of
•   St.-Emilion, this impeccably run estate has produced an atypically rich,
87   concentrated, delicious 1992. Very dark ruby, with a spicy, toasty, black
     currant bouquet, ripe, medium- to full-bodied flavors, and excellent richness,
     this fine 1992 should spark considerable consumer interest. Drink it over the
     next 7–8 years. Last tasted, 3/96.

1990— The 1990 is a deep wine, with a saturated ruby/purple color exhibiting no
•   amber. The wine offers up copious aromas of grilled meat, black currants,
92   cedar, and sweet oaky scents. Full bodied, with moderate tannin, immense
     concentration, thickness, and richness, this low-acid yet structured wine

should reach full maturity by the end of the century and drink well for 10–15 years. Last tasted, 11/96.

1989— The 1989 is developing beautifully, although more quickly than I initially
•　　thought. The wine's dark garnet color reveals some amber at the edge. The
89　　wine possesses a big, lavishly wooded, herbal, olive, black fruit nose, attractive notions of soy and Asian spices, thick, juicy fruit, medium to full body, and a soft, supple texture. Drink it over the next 10–12 years. Last tasted, 11/96.

1988— The 1988 has everything the 1989 possesses, in addition to definition, struc-
•　　ture, and greater depth and concentration. This splendidly perfumed wine
90　　offers up a veritable smorgasbord of aromas, ranging from smoky, toasty, new oak, to jammy black currants and Asian spices. In the mouth, it is full bodied, seductively round, and expansively flavored, with a luscious and velvety, long, heady finish. This is a gorgeously made, rich, wonderfully pure, highly extracted wine that should drink well for the next 10–12 years. Anticipated maturity: Now–2004. Last tasted, 11/97.

1986— Except for the 1988 and 1989, the 1986 is the finest wine made at this
•　　property in over 3 decades and is certainly one of the sleepers of the vintage.
87　　It may eventually merit an even higher score. The use of 65% new oak, an extended maceration, and careful attention to detail have resulted in a wine that is black/ruby in color and has exceptional concentration and length, with a wonderful opulence and fatness in the midrange that makes for exciting drinking. I do not believe it will be the longest-lived St.-Emilion in 1986, but it does have more precocious appeal than many wines, and therein lies its value. Anticipated maturity: Now–2005. Last tasted, 3/90.

1985— The 1985 Canon-La-Gaffelière is a good, supple, richly fruity, tasty, expan-
•　　sively flavored wine. It requires drinking. Anticipated maturity: Now. Last
85　　tasted, 3/89.

1984— The 1984 is cleanly made, correct, simple, fruity, and mature. Anticipated
•　　maturity: Now–may be in decline. Last tasted, 7/89.
73

1983— Light, supple, fruity, spicy, and ready to drink, the 1983 Canon-La-Gaffelière
•　　displays a medium-bodied, spicy, easygoing charm and light tannins. Antici-
82　　pated maturity: Now–may be in decline. Last tasted, 3/85.

1982— Revealing considerable amber in its washed-out ruby color, this spicy, herb-
•　　scented wine still retains some fruit in its aromatics, but it is clearly past its
76　　apogee. The 1982 was made before young Stephan Von Neipperg began an intensive overhaul of this estate. Since 1988 Canon-La-Gaffelière has been one of the top dozen estates of St.-Emilion, making wines (even in lighter years) that are better than what was produced in 1982. This simple, uninteresting 1982 should be drunk up quickly, as time is not on its side. Last tasted, 9/95.

1981— A rather hollow wine, without adequate fruit to balance out the oak and
•　　tannins, the 1981 Canon-La-Gaffelière should be drunk over the next several
72　　years before it becomes more unbalanced. Anticipated maturity: Now–probably in serious decline. Last tasted, 2/83.

1979—Ready to drink, the 1979 Canon-La-Gaffelière is soft, slightly herbaceous,
•   medium bodied, pleasantly fruity, but undistinguished. Anticipated maturity:
75   Now—probably in serious decline. Last tasted, 2/84.
1978—The 1978 is fully mature, and given this wine's inclination to behave like a
•   Burgundy and die quickly, it is best drunk up. Light ruby, with some browning,
75   this round, soft, fruity wine is one-dimensional and light, but cleanly made.
     Anticipated maturity: Now—probably in serious decline. Last tasted, 2/84.

CAP DE MOURLIN   GOOD

Classification: St.-Emilion Grand Cru Classé
Location of vineyards: St.-Emilion, Pied de Côtes
Owner: G.F.A. Capdemourlin
Address: 33330 St.-Emilion
Mailing address: Château Roudier, 33570 Montagne
Telephone: 33 5 57 74 62 06; telefax: 33 5 57 74 59 34
Visits: By appointment only
Contact: G.F.A. Capdemourlin

VINEYARDS (red)
Surface area: 34.6 acres
Average age of vines: 35 years
Blend: 60% Merlot, 25% Cabernet Franc, 12% Cabernet Sauvignon,
3% Malbec
Density of plantation: 5,400 vines per hectare
Average yields (over the last 5 years): 45 hectoliters per hectare
Total average annual production: 6,000 cases

GRAND VIN (red)
Brand name: Château Cap de Mourlin
Appellation: St.-Emilion Grand Cru
Mean annual production: 40–45 hectoliters per hectare
Upbringing: Fermentations and macerations last 3–4 weeks in concrete
and stainless-steel vats equipped with a temperature-control system
(Freon). After malolactics, 60% of the yield is transferred to oak barrels
(50% of which are new) while the rest remains in stainless-steel tanks.
Wines are aged 12–18 months, depending upon the vintage, and are
fined and filtered.

SECOND WINE
Brand name: Capitan de Mourlin
Average annual production: Not systematically made

Evaluation of present classification: The quality equivalent of a fine
Médoc Cru Bourgeois
Plateau of maturity: 3–10 years following the vintage

The Capdemourlin family have been property owners in St.-Emilion for over 5 centuries. They also own the well-known St.-Emilion Grand Cru Classé Balestard-La-Tonnelle, as well as Petit-Faurie-de-Soutard and the excellent Montagne St.-Emilion, Château Roudier. Until 1983 there were two Grand Cru St.-Emilions with the name Cap de Mourlin, one owned by Jean Capdemourlin and one by Jacques Capdemourlin. These two estates have been united since 1983, and the confusion consumers have encountered in the past between these two different wines has ceased to exist.

Cap de Mourlin produces typically robust, rich, full-bodied St.-Emilions with a great deal of fruit and muscle. They sometimes fall short with respect to finesse, but they are consistently mouth-filling, satisfying wines. The vineyard is located on the flat, sandy, rocky soil of what is often called the *pieds de côtes*.

VINTAGES

1995—The medium ruby–colored 1995 displays a disjointed, hollow midsection and
• an absence of fruit and depth in the finish. For this reliable St.-Emilion, the
80 1995 looks to be a disappointment. Last tasted, 11/97.

1994—The 1994 is revealing an austere, tannic side, with hardness in the finish. It
• possesses good fruit, medium body, and depth, but the tannin dominates, and
84? I suspect it always will. Last tasted, 3/96.

1992—An element of menthol and jam in this wine's bouquet offers pleasure. The
• wine reveals a medium ruby color, light tannin, and a compact, muscular, yet
76 soft feel. There is an absence of depth and length. Drink it over the next 5–6
years. Last tasted, 11/94.

1990—If you are looking for a light wine with elegance and finesse, the blockbuster
• 1990 should be avoided. It is a big, beefy, rustic wine with more than enough
87 tannin to ensure a decade's worth of aging potential. The tannin is adequately
balanced by copious quantities of fat cassis fruit, sweet oak, and gobs of
glycerin and alcohol. Anticipated maturity: Now–2003. Last tasted, 1/93.

1989—The 1989 exhibits plenty of toasty, smoky, new oak and is full bodied, with high
• alcohol, low acidity, and a rich, jammy, long finish. There are plenty of tannins,
86 but they are soft. Anticipated maturity: Now–2006. Last tasted, 4/91.

1988—The 1988 has a more typical Bordelais feel to its lean, understated, more
• toughly knit texture. The tannins are high, but the wine is concentrated, and
85 this is one case where the fruit seems proportional to the amount of tannin.
Anticipated maturity: Now–2004. Last tasted, 4/91.

CHAUVIN   VERY GOOD

Classification: St.-Emilion Grand Cru Classé
Location of vineyards: St.-Emilion, near Cheval Blanc
Owner: Marie-France Février and Béatrice Ondet
Address: 1, Les Cabannes Nord, 33330 St.-Emilion

Mailing address: B.P. 67, 33330 St.-Emilion
Telephone: 33 5 57 24 76 25; telefax: 33 5 57 74 41 34
Visits: By appointment only
Contact: Marie-France Février and Béatrice Ondet

VINEYARDS (red)
Surface area: 38.8 acres
Average age of vines: 30 years
Blend: 80% Merlot, 15% Cabernet Franc, 5% Cabernet Sauvignon
Density of plantation: 5,500 vines per hectare
Average yields (over the last 5 years): 45 hectoliters per hectare
Total average annual production: 48,000 bottles

GRAND VIN (red)
Brand name: Château Chauvin
Appellation: St.-Emilion Grand Cru
Mean annual production: 40,000 bottles
Upbringing: Fermentations and macerations usually last 3–6 weeks in
temperature-controlled stainless-steel vats. Malolactics occur in oak
barrels for part of the yield (35%–50%), and wines are aged 12–15
months in oak barrels. They are fined, and filtration is employed if
laboratory tests suggest it is necessary.

SECOND WINE
Brand name: La Borderie de Chauvin
Average annual production: Varies between 4,000 and 15,000 bottles

Evaluation of present classification: Since 1989 the quality equivalent of
a Médoc Cru Bourgeois
Plateau of maturity: 3–10 years following the vintage

This property, a neighbor of Cheval Blanc, has made remarkable progress in
the last several vintages, particularly the 1995, 1996, and 1997. The decision
to harvest later, as well as to institute a stricter selection with a second wine,
has resulted in major improvements to the quality of the wines at this estate.
And yes, the omnipresent Michel Rolland is the oenologist in charge. Chauvin
may be an emerging star in St.-Emilion.

VINTAGES

1997—Extremely forward and delicious, this medium dark plum/purple–colored
  •   St.-Emilion reveals copious quantities of kirsch and cassis fruit. Soft, with
86–   low acidity, attractive levels of glycerin, and a fleshy, seductive mouth-feel,
87   this luscious wine is already drinking well. It should be consumed within its
       first 7–8 years of life. Last tasted, 3/98.

1996—This has turned out to be a very fine effort from Chauvin despite the presence
•   of high levels of tannin. The wine is dense and medium to full bodied, with
87–   plenty of tell-tale black cherry fruit intermingled with moderate quantities of
88   high-quality toasty oak. While the wine is textured, ripe, and impeccably well
       made, the tannin will require 4–5 years to melt away. Anticipated maturity:
       2002–2010. Last tasted, 11/97.
1995—Chauvin's 1995 is not dissimilar from the 1994. Deep ruby/purple colored,
•   with a sweet, nearly over-ripe, jammy nose of black fruits, oak, and spice,
87   this lush, attractively textured, plump St.-Emilion will need to be drunk over
       the next 6–10 years because of its extremely low acidity. Last tasted, 11/97.
1994—The purple-colored 1994 Chauvin displays super-jammy black cherries and
•   abundant sweet, toasty oak. Opulent, medium- to full-bodied flavors are low
87   in acidity, but moderately tannic. This could turn out to be a sleeper of the
       vintage if the wine's quality holds up after its *élevage* and bottling. Last tasted,
       3/96.
1993—The ruby–colored 1993 Chauvin is a light-bodied, fruity, soft-styled
•   St.-Emilion with attractive herb-tinged, cherry, curranty fruit, light tannin,
82   fine purity, and a short finish. Last tasted, 11/94.
1992—Medium ruby colored, with light intensity and charming fruit in the nose, this
•   moderately tannic wine lacks depth. The wine's ripeness and decent fruit will
79   provide uncritical, light drinking for 4–5 more years. Last tasted, 11/94.
1990—The explosively rich, fruity, unctuous 1990 exhibits plenty of velvety, smooth
•   tannins, excellent concentration, and medium to full body. This admirably
88   endowed, opulent, hedonistic Chauvin is the finest wine made at this estate
       in decades. Anticipated maturity: Now–2005. Last tasted, 1/93.
1989—The ubiquitous Libourne oenologist, Michel Rolland, had for the first time
•   full charge of overseeing the winemaking at Chauvin in 1989. The result is a
86   broad-flavored, hedonistic, concentrated, deeply extracted, luscious wine.
       Anticipated maturity: Now–2001. Last tasted, 4/91.
1988—Medium dark ruby, with a spicy, subtle plum-and-herb-scented bouquet,
•   this wine has good extraction of flavor, a nice, spicy, vanillin oakiness, and
84   medium-bodied, tightly knit flavors. It may outlive the 1989, but I do not see
       it ever providing the same degree of pleasure. Anticipated maturity: Now–
       2002. Last tasted, 4/91.

CHEVAL BLANC   OUTSTANDING

Classification: St.-Emilion Premier Grand Cru Classé A
Location of vineyards: Near Figeac and bordering Pomerol
Owner: Heirs Fourcaud-Laussac
Address: 33330 St.-Emilion
Mailing address: Same as above
Telephone: 33 5 57 55 55 55; telefax: 33 5 57 55 55 50
Visits: By appointment only
Contact: Nathalie Moussaire—Pierre Lurton (director)

VINEYARDS (red)
Surface area: 91.4 acres
Average age of vines: 40 years
Blend: 66% Cabernet Franc, 34% Merlot
Density of plantation: 6,000 vines per hectare
Average yields (over the last 5 years): 38 hectoliters per hectare
Total average annual production: 120,000 bottles

GRAND VIN (red)
Brand name: Château Cheval Blanc
Appellation: St.-Emilion Premier Grand Cru Classé A
Mean annual production: 80,000 bottles
Upbringing: Fermentations and macerations last 3–4 weeks in temperature-controlled stainless-steel and concrete vats. Malolactics occur in vats, and wines are transferred to new oak barrels for 18 months aging. They are racked every 3 months and fined with fresh egg whites but remain unfiltered.

SECOND WINE
Brand name: Petit Cheval
Average annual production: 30,000 bottles

Evaluation of present classification: The quality equivalent of a Médoc first-growth
Plateau of maturity: 5–20 or more years following the vintage

---

Cheval Blanc is undoubtedly one of Bordeaux's most profound wines. For most of this century it has sat alone at the top of St.-Emilion's hierarchy, representing the finest wine this appellation can produce. Since the renaissance began at Ausone in the mid-1970s, Cheval Blanc has had to share the limelight. Cheval Blanc is a remarkably distinctive wine. Sitting right on the Pomerol border, in the St.-Emilion *graves* sector, with only a ditch separating its vineyards from those of l'Evangile and La Conseillante, it has for years been accused of making a wine that is as much a Pomerol as it is a St.-Emilion.

Among the "Big Eight" of Bordeaux, Cheval Blanc probably has the broadest window of drinkability. It is usually delicious when first bottled yet has the ability in the top years to last and last. None of the Médoc first-growths, or Pétrus in Pomerol, can claim to have such flexibility. Only Haut-Brion comes close to matching Cheval Blanc's early drinkability and precociousness, as well as the stuffing and overall balance and intensity to age for 20–30 years. For me, Cheval Blanc is Cheval Blanc—it is like no Pomerol or other St.-Emilion I have ever tasted. The distinctive choice of grape varieties used at Cheval Blanc, two-thirds Cabernet Franc and one-third Merlot, is highly unusual. No other major château uses this much Cabernet Franc. Yet, curiously, this grape reaches its zenith in Cheval Blanc's gravelly, sandy, and clay soil that is underpinned by a bed of iron rock, producing an extremely rich, ripe, intense, viscous wine.

Cheval Blanc is also distinctive in that the property has been in the same family's hands since 1852. Until 1989 the Fourcaud-Laussac family's live-in owner was the towering Jacques Hébrard, who was obsessed with taking Cheval Blanc's reputation to even greater heights. Following Hébrard, Bernard Grandchamp was brought in to run the estate but resigned his position in 1990, fueling rumors of family infighting about the future of Cheval Blanc. At present, the estate is directed by Pierre Lurton, a very talented, highly respected administrator.

The style of wine produced at Cheval Blanc has no doubt contributed to its immense popularity. Dark ruby in color, in the very good vintages it is an opulently rich and fruity wine, full bodied, voluptuous, and lush, and deceptively easy to drink when young. The bouquet is especially distinctive. At its best, Cheval Blanc is an even more fragrant wine than Médoc first-growths such as Margaux. Scents of minerals, menthol, exotic spices, tobacco, and intense, as well as super-ripe, black fruits can overwhelm the taster. Many tasters, fooled by its cunning show of precocious charm, falsely assume that it will not age well. In the big, rich vintages, Cheval Blanc evolves exceptionally well, although one suspects that far too much of this wine is consumed long before its real majesty begins to emerge.

As the tasting notes demonstrate, Cheval Blanc can produce a decadently exotic wine of unbelievable depth and richness. However, in some vintages it has been one of the most disappointing wines of the "Big Eight" châteaux of Bordeaux. Cheval Blanc was not a strong performer during the decades of the sixties and seventies. However, with the increasing attention to quality and detail provided by administrator Jacques Hébrard, the quality of this wine during the eighties became more consistent. The consecutive vintages of the early eighties—1982 and 1983—were the finest Cheval Blanc since the splendid trilogy of 1947, 1948, and 1949.

Cheval Blanc, along with Haut-Brion, remains one of the two least expensive members of Bordeaux's "Big Eight."

VINTAGES

1997—Cheval Blanc's 1997 performed well. It is neither as super-extracted nor as
•   phenomenally rich as the 1990 or 1982, but it is exotic, seductive, and
90–   opulently textured. Yields were extremely low at this estate in 1997 (35
92   hectoliters per hectare), and the harvest, which began on September 8, did
      not finish until September 25. Because of their difficulties with the Cabernet
      Franc, this example of Cheval Blanc contains an atypically high proportion

of Merlot. The final blend, which represents 35% of the estate's total production, consists of 70% Merlot and 30% Cabernet Franc (contrast that with the more classic blend of 66% Cabernet Franc and 34% Merlot). The deep ruby/purple—colored 1997 offers a flamboyant, exotic nose of coconuts, coffee, jammy black cherries, and currants and high-quality *pain grillé* scents. This round, elegant, medium-bodied wine possesses gorgeously sweet fruit and absolutely no aggressiveness to any of its components. The acidity is low, the tannin soft and ripe, and the finish impressive. This will be an undeniably juicy, captivating Cheval Blanc to drink when it is released. It should keep for 12 or more years. Last tasted, 3/98.

1996— Typical for this estate's wines, the 1996 has put on considerable weight and
• flesh since I first tasted it. Forty percent of the 1996 crop was declassified,
90– but the quality of the Cabernet Franc (which often makes up 50%–60% of
94 the final blend) was high. Yields were 30–35 hectoliters per hectare. This deep garnet/plum—colored Cheval Blanc offers a gorgeously exotic, sweet, smoky, coconut, menthol, jammy raspberry and blackberry nose. Medium body, ripe fruit, outstanding concentration, and a succulent texture place this wine high up on the qualitative hierarchy. An intriguing coffee bean and chocolatey sweetness can be found in the wine's finish. This appears to be an impressive, savory, multi-dimensional Cheval Blanc that is growing in stature and weight as it ages in cask. Anticipated maturity: 1999–2020. Last tasted, 3/98.

1995— A pretty, attractive Cheval Blanc, the 1995 contains a higher percentage of
• Merlot in the final blend than usual (50% Merlot/50% Cabernet Franc). This
92 wine has not developed as much fat or weight as its younger sibling the 1996, but it appears to be an outstanding Cheval Blanc with an enthralling smoky, black currant, coffee, and exotic bouquet. Complex, rich, medium- to full-bodied flavors are well endowed and pure, with surprisingly firm tannin in the finish. Unlike the sweeter, riper 1996, the 1995 may be more structured and potentially longer-lived. Anticipated maturity: 2002–2020. Last tasted, 11/97.

1994— Dark ruby/purple colored, with a complex, spicy bouquet of tobacco, vanilla,
• black currant, mineral, and floral scents, the 1994 is a bigger, more structured
88+? wine than the 1993, its older sibling, but is it better? The wine finishes with mouth-searing tannin, which detracts from the otherwise impressive aromatics and sweet, medium-bodied, lush attack. As I have written many times in the past, Cheval Blanc has a tendency to fatten up, put on weight, and expand both aromatically and texturally with age, so perhaps this wine will move in that direction. If it does, my rating will appear unduly conservative. But if the tannin continues to taste astringent and the fruit begins to fade, then I will have overrated the 1994. Anticipated maturity: 2002–2017. Last tasted, 1/97.

1993— Dark ruby with a purple hue, this appealing style of Cheval Blanc offers the
• telltale nose of sweet black fruits, coconut, vanilla, and a touch of menthol.
87 The wine is medium bodied, elegant, and purely made, and while it lacks

volume and richness in the mouth, it is soft, delicious, and typical of this property's wines. This tasty, charming 1993 should drink well for 7–8 years. Last tasted, 1/97.

1992—A light-bodied, shallow wine for this great estate, the 1992 Cheval Blanc
  •   displays a vanillin-dominated nose with berry, jammy, herb, and coffee notes.
  77   There is not much depth, body, or length. Drink it over the next 4–5 years, as the hard tannin in the finish suggests that this wine will dry out quickly. Last tasted, 11/94.

1990—The 1990 is increasingly sumptuous with each additional tasting. The wine
  •   possesses all the hallmarks of a hot, ripe year—low acidity, super-ripe,
  99   (nearly over-ripe) fruit, an opulent, oily texture, great sweetness of fruit, and a long, voluptuous finish. In the most recent tasting I almost mistook it for Le Pin, given its showboat-like nose of coconut, toasty new oak, and gobs of smoky, black curranty, cherry fruit. The wine is full bodied, rich, and concentrated, with layers of extract and well-concealed tannin. I am increasingly convinced that this is the most profound Cheval Blanc since the legendary 1982. Because of its fleshy, low-acid character, the wine can be drunk, but it is still youthful, with a deeper purple color than the more mature-looking 1989. It should offer exotic opulence for at least another 15–20 years. A compelling Cheval Blanc! Last tasted, 6/98.

1989—Since its bottling, the 1989 has frequently tasted excellent, but it is uninspir-
  •   ing in the context of the vintage. In this tasting it showed better than it has
  89   over the last several years. The 1989 is not a great effort for this château. The color is already revealing an amber edge, and the lead pencil, cedar, spicy, black fruit, and vanillin nose is more reminiscent of a young Lafite than the exotic style associated with Cheval Blanc in a hot, dry, ripe year. This medium-weight, lightly tannic wine is very approachable. I have rated the 1989 Cheval Blanc consistently between 87 and 89, which is indicative of an excellent wine, but given the vintage and *terroir*, this is not one of the stars of 1989. It should continue to drink well for 10–15+ years, as there is moderate tannin in the wine's elegant framework, but readers should not expect any miracles. Last tasted, 11/96.

1988—The 1988 Cheval Blanc exhibits fine ripeness and a cool, almost menthol,
  •   plummy bouquet intertwined with aromas of smoke, tobacco, and new oak. In
  87   the mouth, there are some aggressive tannins, but the wine does not possess the depth one expects from renowned estates. It is a very good Cheval Blanc, but I had expected more. Anticipated maturity: Now–2002. Last tasted, 1/93.

1987—The 1987 Cheval Blanc is a successful wine for the vintage. The spicy,
  •   herbaceous, sweet nose is followed by a precocious, round, fat, fruity wine
  85   without much grip or structure. It does possess delicious, weedy, curranty fruit buttressed by gobs of sweet, smoky oak. It is a seductive wine. Anticipated maturity: Now. Last tasted, 3/90.

1986—At one time I thought the 1986 was better than the 1985, but the open-knit
  •   charm and exotic personality of the 1985 makes a more persuasive case than
  92   the more reserved, tannic, and backward 1986. The 1986 still has a youthful

dark ruby saturated color, with no amber at the edge. The wine possesses a developing bouquet that offers up weedy tobacco juxtaposed with sweet blackberry, raspberry, and cherry fruit. The new oak that was so obvious in the wine's youth has moved to the background, offering more of a cedary character than raw wood. Medium to full bodied, and moderately tannic, this is a delineated Cheval Blanc with more of a Médoc personality than typical St.-Emilion opulence. The wine is rich, intense, and well made but still requires a few more years of bottle age. Anticipated maturity: 1999–2012. Last tasted, 12/97.

1985—Fully mature, but capable of lasting another 10–15 years, this flamboyantly
• scented wine (jammy black fruits, licorice, Asian spices, herbs, grilled meats)
93 is a lusciously rich, opulent, medium- to full-bodied, fat, and juicy style of Cheval Blanc that seems to get better and better every time I taste it. Like so many Cheval Blancs, it has the uncanny ability to put on weight in the bottle. Anticipated maturity: Now–2005. Last tasted, 1/98.

1983—A classic example of Cheval Blanc's style, the 1983 continues to put on
• weight and develop favorably in the bottle. A saturated dark ruby color, with
95 some faint lightening at the edges, exhibits less age than most right bank 1983s. The huge nose of mint, jammy black fruits, chocolate, and coffee is sensational as well as surprisingly well developed. The wine offers lusty, rich, unctuous fruit presented in a medium- to full-bodied, low-acid, concentrated, rather hedonistic style. There are no hard edges to be found, but there is plenty of tannin in the lush finish. Gorgeous for drinking now, this is a great Cheval Blanc that should continue to drink well, and possibly improve, for another 20 years. It remains somewhat undervalued for its quality. Last tasted, 12/97.

1982—This wine has proven to be one of Bordeaux's modern-day legends. Absolutely
• spectacular for its first 7–8 years after bottling, the wine has gradually begun
100 to reveal more delineation, structure, and tannin. In 1998 the wine appeared even younger than it did 5–6 years earlier! It exhibits a thick, opaque garnet color, with light amber at the edge. The nose, which was ostentatious earlier in its life, was still offering up significant amounts of roasted fruit, coffee, melted chocolate, and decadently rich, sweet black fruits. This is an exotic, full-bodied, moderately tannic, massive example of Cheval Blanc noted for its sheer opulence and intensity. However, I find the wine more structured and delineated today than it was half a dozen years ago. It appears ready for a long evolution. I originally felt that the wine would be fully mature by 1993, but it now appears to require another 4–5 years to hit its plateau of maturity, where it should remain for 20+ years. The only question millionaire collectors should ask about the 1982 is whether the 1990 will rival it. Both are awesome wines. Last tasted, 4/98.

1981—I had this wine several times from the barrel and also twice in comparative
• tastings prior to bottling. I never gave it more than average marks. Tasted
90 numerous times after bottling, it is a different wine, relatively rich, spicy, plummy, with soft, silky, layered flavors, good concentration, and moderate

tannin. It continues to drink well, yet it has the potential to last for 5–7 more years. Not a blockbuster in the mold of the 1982 and 1983, it is nevertheless delicious and fully mature. Anticipated maturity: Now–2000. Last tasted, 10/90.

1980— The 1980 Cheval Blanc is a relative success for this mediocre vintage. Me-
• dium ruby, with a moderately intense bouquet of herbal, cedary, fruity scents,
80 this wine has medium body, adequate concentration, and a supple, soft finish.
Anticipated maturity: Now–may be in decline. Last tasted, 10/90.

1979— The 1979 Cheval Blanc is a charming, elegant wine that lacks some depth
• and richness (no doubt because of the prolific yields), but it displays moder-
84 ately intense, ripe plummy fruit, a cedary, herbaceous aroma, and soft, very
forward, easygoing, round flavors. This is a lightweight but well-made Cheval
Blanc that will age quickly. Anticipated maturity: Now. Last tasted, 3/89.

1978— This is a firmly built, concentrated Cheval Blanc that, curiously, has not
• displayed the precocious, fleshy, charming fruit in its early life typical of most
87 vintages of this estate. The wine is still dark ruby, with a relatively stubborn
and backward bouquet suggestive of rich, ripe black currants, mineral scents,
herbs, and grilled nuts. On the palate, the wine is tannic, medium bodied, and
admirably concentrated. It resembles the stylish, austere 1966 but appears
more concentrated. Anticipated maturity: Now–2008. Last tasted, 10/90.

1977— Cheval Blanc had a disastrous year in 1977, with over 75% of the crop lost
• because of the poor weather. The resulting wine should have been declassi-
68 fied. It is light in color, with a sweet vegetable aroma and shallow flavor, and
it has a nasty, harsh, astringent finish. Last tasted, 10/90.

1976— In this vintage marked by extreme drought, heat, and hope-crushing rains at
• harvest-time, Cheval Blanc has produced an open-knit, super-ripe, roasted
82 style of wine that is now fully mature. It has put on weight, and while there is
some browning at the edge, the 1976 Cheval Blanc has a full-blown bouquet
of ripe fruit, minerals, nuts, and toasty oak. On the palate, the wine is opulent,
even fat, with generous, savory, fleshy, plummy, fruity flavors. Low in acidity
and very soft, the 1976 Cheval Blanc has been drinkable since its release,
yet it continues to expand and develop. I initially underestimated this wine.
Anticipated maturity: Now. Last tasted, 10/90.

1975— Cheval Blanc was one of the more forward and fun to drink 1975s fifteen
• years ago, but its evolution has slowed considerably. It reveals some of the
90 kinky, exotic Cheval Blanc complexity, with chocolate, mint, cedar, and sweet
fruit filling the moderately intense bouquet. Although the color displays considerable amber at the edge, it has a deep ruby/garnet center, as well as
plenty of sweet, ripe fruit, with noticeable glycerin and extract. It is a rich,
firmly styled Cheval Blanc that juxtaposes power and tough tannin with plenty
of sweet jammy fruit. I admire and enjoy this fully mature wine, which is
capable of lasting for 15+ more years. Last tasted, 12/95.

1973— The 1973 Cheval Blanc has totally faded and is now just a pale, washed-out
• wine with a thin, diluted finish. Last tasted, 3/91.

55

1971—Somewhat of a disappointment, the 1971, while very good, has in the last
•   several years begun to brown badly. Nevertheless, the wine still has plenty of
84   sweet fruit, a burnt, roasted character to its bouquet, and medium body. The
       1971 is a pleasant, lowbrow Cheval Blanc that should be drunk over the next
       2–3 years. Anticipated maturity: Now. Last tasted, 10/90.

1970—A better wine than the 1971, the 1970 has been fully mature for over a
•   decade. Medium ruby/garnet, with some browning, this wine has a cedary,
85   sweet, tobacco bouquet, plump, ripe, round flavors that exhibit decent con-
       centration, and soft tannins. The wine is medium bodied and very soft, yet it
       lacks the focus and concentration a Premier Grand Cru Classé should pos-
       sess. It should be drunk up. Anticipated maturity: Now. Last tasted, 10/90.

1967—Now in decline, the 1967 Cheval Blanc drank well for the first decade of
•   life but has begun to take on a decaying, leafy component in an otherwise
77   tobacco-scented, plummy bouquet. In the mouth, the wine is soft and round
       but fades quickly. Anticipated maturity: Now–probably in serious decline.
       Last tasted, 4/90.

1966—A good, rather than great, effort from Cheval Blanc, the 1966 is now fully
•   mature. Medium ruby, with an amber edge, this is a restrained version of
85   Cheval Blanc, with a stylish, reserved bouquet of mineral scents, black cur-
       rants, and spicy oak. On the palate, the wine is medium bodied, moderately
       fleshy, but not so voluptuous or as concentrated as one expects Cheval Blanc
       to be in this highly regarded vintage. Anticipated maturity: Now. Last tasted,
       10/90.

1964—The 1964 is a wonderfully rich, thick, powerful, and concentrated wine that
•   is the most authoritative Cheval Blanc produced since the monumental wines
95   made by this château in 1947, 1948, and 1949. Opaque dark ruby, with only
       some amber and a powerful yet restrained bouquet of roasted ripe fruit, cedar,
       herbs, and gravelly, mineral scents, the wine remains amazingly young and
       tannic, with layer upon layer of ripe fruit. This is a heavyweight, old-style
       Cheval Blanc that should be pure nectar for at least another 10–15 years. It
       continues to evolve at a snail's pace. Anticipated maturity: Now–2010. Last
       tasted, 10/94.

1962—Compact, small sized, and disappointing, the 1962 Cheval Blanc has never
•   been one of my favorite wines from this under-rated vintage. Now in decline,
76   losing its fruit and drying out, the 1962 is a light, pretty wine, with some
       charm and round, gentle fruitiness. It is best drunk from large-format bottles,
       as I suspect the regular-size bottles are well past their prime. Friends of mine
       tell me they have tasted good examples of this vintage. Last tasted, 10/90.

1961—I have consistently mistaken this wine for a great Graves in tastings where it
•   has appeared. Opaque dark ruby/garnet, with a rust-colored edge, this wine
93   has a big, full-blown bouquet of burnt tobacco and earthy, gravelly scents. On
       the palate, it is sweet, ripe, full bodied, extremely soft and supple, and clearly
       at its apogee. I have noticed above normal bottle variation with the 1961
       Cheval Blanc, but the best bottles of this wine are marvelously rich, lush
       wines. Anticipated maturity: Now–2001. Last tasted, 10/90.

ANCIENT VINTAGES

In the fifties, the greatest vintage is the 1953 (95 points; last tasted 3/96). I am sure this wine has been fully mature for at least 15–20 years. Nevertheless, it has held its magic for that considerable period and is still the most fragrant and, from an aromatic perspective, the most compelling Cheval Blanc I have ever tasted. Perhaps the 1982 will turn out to be this profoundly perfumed. It is not a blockbuster, but it is incredibly seductive and so soft and silky. Another vintage of note during the fifties is the 1959 (92 points; last tasted 2/95), a denser, more structured wine than the 1961, although I am not sure it will ever hit the heights the 1961 has already achieved. However, it certainly appears to have the stuffing and muscle to outlive the 1961. The 1955 (90 points; last tasted 3/95) is a tougher-textured, fuller-bodied, less seductive style of Cheval Blanc. Nevertheless, it is immensely impressive, rich, and capable of another 5–10 years of evolution. It has been nearly a decade since I tasted it, but I loved the smooth as silk 1950, another top example from that underestimated vintage.

I have rated the 1949 Cheval Blanc as high as 100, but more consistently in the mid- to upper 90s. At the most recent tasting, in December 1995, I rated it 96 points. It is one of the great Cheval Blancs—not as port-like and syrupy as the 1947, but more classically rendered. But do not take that to mean this is a wimpish wine. It is an unbelievably rich, sweet, expansive, full-bodied style of Cheval Blanc, with enormous quantities of glycerin, fruit, alcohol, and extract. Although it has been drinkable for decades, it continues to offer that exotic, Asian spice, cedar, and huge, sweet fruit–scented nose. Unctuously textured, thick, rich, vibrant, pure, and compelling, it should drink well for another 10–20 years. The 1948 (96 points; last tasted 10/94) is the most backward Cheval Blanc among vintages of the forties. The wine retains an opaque plum/licorice–like color. A huge, earthy, soy, cedar, roasted herb nose is followed by a wine of immense power, body, intensity, and structure. It will easily last for another 20+ years. Having a 1947 Cheval Blanc (100 points; last tasted 11/97) served out of an impeccably stored magnum four times over the last 3 years made me once again realize what a great job I have. The only recent Bordeaux vintages that come even remotely close to the richness, texture, and viscosity of so many of these right bank 1947s are the 1982 and 1990. What can I say about this mammoth wine that is more like port than a dry red table wine? The 1947 Cheval Blanc exhibits such a thick texture, it could double as motor oil. The huge nose of fruitcake, chocolate, leather, coffee, and Asian spices is mind-boggling. The unctuous texture and richness of sweet fruit are amazing. Consider the fact that this wine is, technically, appallingly deficient in acidity and excessively high in alcohol. Moreover, its volatile acidity levels would be considered intolerable by modern-day oenologists. Yet how can they explain that after 50 years the wine is still remarkably fresh, phenomenally concentrated, and profoundly complex? It has to make you wonder about the direction of modern-day winemaking. Except for one dismal, murky, troubled, volatile double magnum, this wine has been either perfect or nearly perfect every time I have had it. But beware, there are numerous fraudulent bottles, particularly magnums, of 1947 Cheval Blanc in the marketplace.

The wine that has always enjoyed the greatest reputation of the vintage is Cheval Blanc's 1921. I had tasted this wine twice before and had been disappointed with both bottles, but at a tasting in December 1995, the wine (from a magnum) was unreal. I rated it 98 points. It offered an opaque color, with considerable amber at the edge, followed by remarkably fresh, sweet, jammy aromas of black fruits, Asian spices, coffee, herbs, and chocolate. Thick, unctuously textured, with oodles of fruit, this huge, massive, full-bodied wine must have possessed 14% alcohol. It could easily have been mistaken for the 1947 or 1949.

CLOS FOURTET   VERY GOOD

Classification: St.-Emilion Premier Grand Cru Classé B
Location of vineyards: Opposite the church of St.-Emilion
Owner: Lurton family
Address: 33330 St.-Emilion
Mailing address: Same as above
Telephone: 33 5 57 24 70 90; telefax: 33 5 57 74 46 52
Visits: By appointment
Contact: Tony Ballu and Jean-Louis Rivière

VINEYARDS (red)
Surface area: 47 acres
Average age of vines: 20 years
Blend: 72% Merlot, 22% Cabernet Franc, 6% Cabernet Sauvignon
Density of plantation: 6,600 vines per hectare
Average yields (over the last 5 years): 40 hectoliters per hectare
Total average annual production: 100,000 bottles

GRAND VIN (red)
Brand name: Clos Fourtet
Appellation: St.-Emilion Premier Grand Cru Classé
Mean annual production: 70,000 bottles
Upbringing: Fermentations and macerations last approximately 1 month in temperature-controlled stainless-steel vats. The whole yield undergoes malolactics in oak barrels, and wines are aged for 12–18 months depending upon the vintage. The percentage of new oak utilized may vary

between 60% and 100%. Wines are fined with fresh egg whites and remain unfiltered.

SECOND WINE
Brand Name: Domaine de Martialis
Average annual production: 30,000 bottles

Evaluation of present classification: Should be maintained; the quality equivalent of a Médoc fifth-growth
Plateau of maturity: 3–20 years following the vintage

This property is on the *côtes* of St.-Emilion, almost at the entrance to St.-Emilion, opposite the Place de l'Eglise and Hôtel Plaisance. Until recently the most interesting thing about Clos Fourtet was the vast underground wine cellars, among the finest in the Bordeaux region. This winery, like a number of highly respected yet over-rated St.-Emilion Premiers Grands Crus Classés, had been making wine over the last 2 decades that was good, but not up to the standards of its classification. The wines had been plagued by a bland, dull, chunky, dry, astringent fruitiness and a curious habit of getting older without getting better. In short, they did not develop well in the bottle. That has all changed for the better, as the Lurton family has made a serious attempt to upgrade the quality of this wine, evident since the 1989 vintage. Owners of numerous châteaux throughout Bordeaux, the Lurtons have made significant renovations at Clos Fourtet. Consequently this is an estate to follow (and buy) more seriously than ever before.

VINTAGES

1997—Clos Fourtet's 1997 reveals a saturated ruby/purple color as well as plenty of
•   sweet blackberry fruit intermingled with gravel/mineral-like and toasty oak
86–   nuances. Elegant and impressively sweet and ripe, Clos Fourtet may have
88   only two shortcomings: its so-so finish and a subtle herbaceousness in its
      flavors. Light to moderate tannin suggests 2–3 years of cellaring might be
      warranted. Anticipated maturity: 2001–2012. Last tasted, 3/98.
1996—Backward and tannic, but still impressive, Clos Fourtet's 1996 displays a
•   dense purple color that extends to the rim of the glass. The nose offers up
89–   sweet blackberry fruit intermixed with licorice and vanillin. Rich and impres-
91?   sive on the attack, the wine possesses medium body, potentially outstanding
      ripeness and extract, and admirable purity. However, the tannin is high and
      the wine angular and tough textured at present. This offering could go either
      way—developing the necessary equilibrium for an outstanding rating or be-
      coming more aggressively tannic and thus meriting a lower score. Anticipated
      maturity: 2004–2018. Last tasted, 3/98.

1995—A very fine effort from Clos Fourtet, the 1995 exhibits a medium dark plum
•   color, followed by sweet black cherry and kirsch fruit intertwined with miner-
88   als and toasty oak. Tightly wound on the palate, with medium body, excellent
      delineation and purity, and a spicy finish with plenty of grip, this example
      has closed down considerably since bottling, but it does possess excellent
      sweetness and depth. However, the tannin is more elevated, so this 1995 will
      require patience. Anticipated maturity: 2004–2018. Last tasted, 11/97.

1994—An impressive saturated purple color indicates a wine of strength and power.
•   In the mouth, it exhibits the vintage's high tannin level, but the tannins are
88   balanced by layers of ripe cassis fruit, attractive smoky elements, and fine
      glycerin and length. This is a forceful, impressively constituted, potentially
      outstanding Clos Fourtet that needs 3–4 years of cellaring. Anticipated matu-
      rity: 2002–2018. Last tasted, 1/97.

1993—A fine effort for the vintage, Clos Fourtet's 1993 exhibits a dense ruby/purple
•   color and attractive black cherry aromas intermingled with scents of minerals
86   and wood. The wine reveals some of the vintage's herbaceousness, but it is
      not annoying given the velvety texture and fleshy, sweet fruit. The wine's low
      acidity and forward character suggest drinking it now and over the next 7–8
      years. Last tasted, 1/97.

1992—I underestimated this wine from cask tastings. Exhibiting far more fruit,
•   ripeness, depth, and length than I had previously thought, Clos Fourtet's 1992
86   offers a dark ruby color, a pleasing jammy nose of black fruits and toast,
      medium body, sweet, expansive fruit, and a velvety texture. A fine effort, it
      should be consumed over the next 6–7 years. Last tasted, 11/94.

1990—The 1990 reveals an impressively deep black/ruby color and a dramatic nose
•   of black fruits, smoke, roasted nuts, flowers, and herbs. Medium to full
90   bodied, with a succulent texture and impressive concentration, this tannic
      and structured Clos Fourtet has a heady, concentrated, multi-dimensional
      finish. Bravo! Anticipated maturity: Now–2010. Last tasted, 1/93.

1989—The 1989 is an alcoholic, exuberantly styled, easy to drink wine, but its lack
•   of grip, definition, and tannin may be cause for some concern. Anticipated
86   maturity: Now–2004. Last tasted, 1/93.

1988—The 1988 has not fared well in comparative tastings. The fruit has faded, and
•   the tannins have become hard, lean, and noticeably aggressive. In fact, I
79   would argue that the 1988 is over-burdened with tannins to the detriment of
      its concentration and fruit. *Caveat emptor.* Last tasted, 4/91.

1986—The 1986 is one-dimensional and lacks grip and depth. Anticipated maturity:
•   Now. Last tasted, 3/90.
78

1985—The 1985 Clos Fourtet is the lightest of all the Premier Grand Cru Classé
•   wines. Medium ruby, with a supple, monolithic, fruity taste, and soft tannins,
84   it has an easy, agreeable finish. Anticipated maturity: Now. Last tasted, 3/90.

1983—This is a one-dimensional, soft, light-bodied wine with hardly any tannin, as
•   well as a short finish. It is one of the disappointments of the 1983 St.-Emilion
78   vintage. Anticipated maturity: Now. Last tasted, 3/89.

1982—This St.-Emilion estate that has long been in the throes of mediocrity pro-
• 　　　duced a satisfying wine in 1982. Medium ruby, with an attractive bouquet of
84　　vanillin oakiness and ripe, herb-scented, berry fruit, this medium-bodied
　　　　wine has a forward, precocious, rich, supple fruitiness that caresses the
　　　　palate. It is fully mature. Anticipated maturity: Now. Last tasted, 3/89.

1981—Another medium-weight 1981 St.-Emilion, the Clos Fourtet has above average
• 　　　fruit intensity, but the wood flavors dominate the frail composition of the wine.
78　　A nice ripe cherry component indicates good ripeness of the grapes, but the
　　　　wood tannins are entirely too pronounced. Anticipated maturity: Now. Last
　　　　tasted, 2/87.

1979—The 1979 is dark in color, with attractive, ripe fruit, medium to full body, and
• 　　　a good, clean finish. The wine's bouquet has opened, and this precocious
82　　wine has reached full maturity. Anticipated maturity: Now—may be in decline.
　　　　Last tasted, 6/84.

1978—The first wine in a line of good, rather than superb, Clos Fourtets, the 1978
• 　　　has settled down nicely in the bottle and reveals alluring scents of black
84　　currants, an open-knit, soft, ripe fruity texture, medium body, and a good
　　　　finish with moderate tannins present. Anticipated maturity: Now—may be in
　　　　decline. Last tasted, 5/83.

1975—This wine seems to have lost its fruit and dried out, revealing an excess of
• 　　　tannins and a charmless, hollow structure. Last tasted, 5/84.
70

1971—Well colored for a 1971, this wine has very little bouquet, a dull, tough, bland
• 　　　fruitiness, and very astringent tannin in the finish. There is just not enough
70　　fruit to balance the tannin. Anticipated maturity: Now—probably in serious
　　　　decline. Last tasted, 2/79.

1970—The 1970 has the same personality traits as the 1971. Even though it is a
• 　　　bigger, riper wine, it is one-dimensional, slightly coarse, and tannic, and just
72　　tastes boring. Anticipated maturity: Now—probably in serious decline. Last
　　　　tasted, 8/78.

CLOS DES JACOBINS　　　　　　　　　　　　　　　VERY GOOD

Classification: St.-Emilion Grand Cru Classé
Location of vineyards: St.-Emilion
Owner: Domaines Cordier
Address: 33330 St.-Emilion
Mailing address: Domaines Cordier, 53, rue du Dehez, 33290 Blanquefort
Telephone: 33 5 56 95 53 00; telefax: 33 5 56 95 53 01
Visits: By appointment only
Contact: Public relations service

VINEYARDS (red)
Surface area: 20.7 acres
Average age of vines: 40 years

Blend: 70% Merlot, 30% Cabernet Franc
Density of plantation: 6,000–6,500 vines per hectare
Total average annual production: 56,000 bottles

GRAND VIN (red)
Brand name: Château Clos des Jacobins
Appellation: St.-Emilion Grand Cru Classé
Mean annual production: 56,000 bottles
Upbringing: Fermentations and macerations last 16–18 days in epoxy-lined vats. Wines are then transferred to oak barrels, which are renewed by a third each vintage, for 18–20 months aging. They are racked every 3 months, fined with fresh egg whites, and filtered.

SECOND WINE
None produced.

Evaluation of present classification: The quality equivalent of a Médoc fifth-growth
Plateau of maturity: 3–12 years following the vintage

The large *négociant* firm of Cordier acquired this lovely ivy-covered château located just outside the gates of St.-Emilion in 1964. Clos des Jacobins, despite reasonably good wines, receives little publicity and is undoubtedly Cordier's least-known fine wine. It has been consistent over the last decade, producing a wine that is deeply colored, rich, round, creamy, and plummy, often with an opulence of ripe fruit. There is an absence of astringent, aggressive tannins, making Clos des Jacobins a wine that requires consumption within its first 10–12 years.

VINTAGES

1993—The well-colored, moderately tannic, one-dimensional 1993 Clos des Jacobins
•　　lacks the fat and charm this wine usually possesses. It is a candidate for up
83　　to 10 years of cellaring. Last tasted, 11/94.

1990—The 1990 exhibits soft tannins, a big herb-and-blackberry-scented nose, fat,
•　　luscious flavors, low acidity, and plenty of length and fruit that conceal the
86　　tannins. Anticipated maturity: Now–2002. Last tasted, 1/93.

1989—The 1989 exhibits a smooth, lush texture, abundant ripeness, and a short
•　　finish. Because of the high alcohol and low acidity, this wine must be drunk
86　　young. Anticipated maturity: Now–2000. Last tasted, 1/93.

1988—The 1988 Clos des Jacobins is a beautifully made, deep ruby–colored wine,
•　　with a bouquet of spring flowers, olives, smoky black currants, and licorice.
88　　In the mouth, there is plenty of rich, concentrated, opulent fruit, modest
　　　tannins, and good length. I prefer it to the 1989. Anticipated maturity: Now–
　　　2003. Last tasted, 1/93.

1986—Clos des Jacobins can often resemble the poor person's Figeac. Its cedary, her-
• baceous, black currant–scented bouquet seems to resemble that of the more
86 famous Figeac in blind tastings. The 1986 is a fairly muscular, alcoholic wine
with a good deal of soft tannin in the finish. The wine can be drunk now or
cellared for up to a decade. Anticipated maturity: Now–2000. Last tasted, 3/90.

1985—The 1985 is very soft, fruity, medium bodied, pleasant, and ideal for drinking
• over the next 3–4 years. It lacks the extract levels of more recent vintages.
84 Anticipated maturity: Now. Last tasted, 3/89.

1983—One of the top successes of the appellation in this very good, yet very irregular
• vintage, the 1983 Clos des Jacobins is dark ruby, with an intense, supple,
87 blackberry fruitiness, a lush, ripe, creamy, fat texture, moderate tannins,
plenty of alcoholic punch, and a long finish. It has matured quickly. Anticipated maturity: Now. Last tasted, 3/85.

1982—Probably the finest Clos des Jacobins I have ever tasted, the garnet-colored
• 1982 has an herbaceous, ripe, jammy bouquet that is filled with blackberry
89 fruit. On the palate, the wine is full bodied, sweet, and ripe, with layers of
satiny-textured fruit. This is a soft, decadently fruity, succulent, and delicious
wine. In blind tastings I have consistently mistaken it for Figeac. Anticipated
maturity: Now–2001. Last tasted, 5/97.

1981—The 1981 is a success for the vintage. However, this vintage of Clos des
• Jacobins gets overwhelmed in the company of the remarkable 1982 and
85 big-styled 1983 wines. The 1981 is precociously soft and intensely fruity,
with a complex cedary, herbaceous bouquet, medium body, and lush, nicely
concentrated flavors. Anticipated maturity: Now–may be in decline. Last
tasted, 11/90.

CLOS DE L'ORATOIRE   EXCELLENT SINCE 1990

Classification: St.-Emilion Grand Cru Classé
Location of vineyards: St.-Emilion
Owner: Comtes de Neipperg
Address: Château Peyreau, 33330 St.-Emilion
Mailing address: Same as above
Telephone: 33 5 57 24 71 33; telefax: 33 5 57 24 67 95
Visits: By appointment, on weekdays, from 9 A.M. to noon, and 2 P.M.
to 5 P.M.
Contact: Cecile Gardaix

VINEYARDS (red)
Surface area: 25.5 acres
Average age of vines: 25 years
Blend: 80% Merlot, 20% Cabernet Franc
Density of plantation: 5,500 vines per hectare, new plantations 7,100
vines per hectare

Average yields (over the last 5 years): 37 hectoliters per hectare
Total average annual production: 50,000–55,000 bottles

GRAND VIN (red)
Brand name: Clos de l'Oratoire
Appellation: St.-Emilion Grand Cru Classé
Mean annual production: 45,000 bottles
Upbringing: Since 1997, fermentations are long and may last up to 4
weeks in temperature-controlled wooden vats. Indigenous yeasts are used,
and pumping-overs are done only for those vats that do not undergo any
pigéage. Malolactics occur in barrels, on fine lees with frequent
bâtonnages, and the first racking is done only 1 or 2 months after
completion of malolactics. Wines are aged in oak barrels that are
renewed by half at each vintage for 12–18 months. They are never
racked but are provided with oxygen if needed. They are fined but remain
unfiltered upon bottling.

SECOND WINE
Brand name: Sold in bulk
Average annual production: Between 38 and 76 hectoliters depending
upon the vintage

Evaluation of present classification: The quality equivalent of a Médoc
fourth- or fifth-growth, particularly since 1990
Plateau of maturity: 3–8 years following the vintage

I have had some good experiences with this chunky, robust, fleshy St.-Emilion
that often lacks finesse but offers juicy, succulent flavors. The 1982, 1983,
and 1985, if one-dimensional, were still pleasurable because of their juicy,
crunchy fruit. Under the ownership of Comte de Neipperg, who acquired this
estate in 1991 (he is also the owner of Canon-La-Gaffelière and La Mondotte),
the wine has soared in quality.

The Clos de l'Oratoire vineyard is not as well situated as many in St.-
Emilion, located northeast of St.-Emilion on very light, less well-drained,
sandy soils.

VINTAGES

1997—Let me make it clear—this is the greatest Clos de l'Oratoire ever made!
•   Proprietor Stephan de Neipperg is doing remarkable things in St.-Emilion,
89–   not only with Clos de l'Oratoire, but with his flagship estate, Canon-La-
92   Gaffelière and, more recently, the luxury micro-estate of La Mondotte. This
       sensational effort is a lavishly rich, luxuriant, flamboyantly styled wine that
       scores high on the hedonistic charts. The wine boasts an opaque black/purple

color and a knockout nose of *pain grillé,* chocolate, cassis, and licorice. Full bodied, with layers of unctuously textured black fruits, this low-acid, thick, juicy wine is a thrill to drink. It should be delicious when released and offer compelling consumption for 10–15 years. Last tasted, 3/98.

1996—Opaque, purple colored with penetrating scents of jammy black cherries,
•   toasty new oak, Provençal herbs, and spices, this muscular 1996 provides
87–   copious quantities of red and black fruits on the attack, mid-palate, and
89   finish. This thick, tannic, medium- to full-bodied wine will require patience following bottling. Anticipated maturity: 2003–2015. Last tasted, 3/98.

1995—An impressive, possibly outstanding wine, the 1995 Clos de l'Oratoire is a
•   sleeper of the vintage. This dense ruby/purple–colored offering possesses
89   attractive, meaty, sweet cherry fruit in the nose intertwined with smoky, toasty oak. Medium to full bodied, spicy, and layered on the palate, the wine reveals fine delineation, grip, and tannin in the long, heady, impressively endowed finish. Some bottle age is warranted. Anticipated maturity: 2001–2015. Last tasted, 11/97.

1994—The 1994 is a dense, ripe, chewy, medium- to full-bodied St.-Emilion with
•   plenty of pure black cherry fruit intermingled with scents of Provençal herbs,
87   olives, and toasty oak. This low-acid, ripe claret is ideal for drinking over the next 7–8 years. Last tasted, 3/96.

1993—The saturated dark ruby color and the ripe, moderately intense bouquet
•   of black cherries, herbs, spicy oak, and earth are laudable. Medium to
86   full bodied, with an expansive, sweet, concentrated palate and light tannin, this well-made claret should drink well for 5–7 years. Last tasted, 11/94.

1990—An impressive wine, this sleeper of the vintage has an opaque deep ruby/
•   purple color, a jammy nose of super-ripe fruit and oak, and a full-bodied,
88   intensely flavored taste. This big wine should develop more finesse and age gracefully for 10–15 years. Last tasted, 1/93.

CLOS ST.-MARTIN   GOOD

Classification: Ste.-Emilion Grand Cru Classé
Production: 800 cases
Blend: 60% Merlot, 40% Cabernet Franc
Secondary label: None
Vineyard size: 3.2 acres
Proprietor: Reiffers family
Time spent in barrels: 18–20 months
Average age of vines: 25 years

Evaluation of present classification: The quality equivalent of a good Médoc Cru Bourgeois
Plateau of maturity: 5–10 or more years following the vintage

Colleagues of mine in France have long extolled the quality of the wines from this tiny St.-Emilion estate (the smallest Grand Cru Classé of the appellation) located on clay and limestone soil behind the church of St.-Martin, hence the name. Production is very tiny. The finest vintage I have tasted is the 1990. If the 1990 typifies the quality and style of wine produced at Clos St.-Martin, this property merits a more generous rating than I have given it. Libourne's famous Michel Rolland is the property's oenologist.

VINTAGES

1997—A muscular, concentrated, dark ruby/purple–colored wine, Clos St.-Martin
• has turned out a powerful example of the 1997 vintage that will need 2–3
86– years of cellaring. There are earth and mineral notes to the black cherry and
87+ cassis flavors. In the mouth, this medium-bodied wine displays moderately high tannin (unusual for a 1997), low acidity, and considerable glycerin and extract in its long finish. This may turn out to be a sleeper of the vintage. Anticipated maturity: 2002–2012. Last tasted, 3/98.

1995—Although the pleasant 1995 exhibits a deep ruby color and berry scents in
• the nose, it is soft and diluted. It should be drunk over the next 3–4 years.
81 Last tasted, 11/97.

1994—The medium ruby–colored 1994 Clos St.-Martin is a light-bodied, straightfor-
• ward wine, without much concentration or complexity. Drink it over the next
81 4–5 years. Last tasted, 3/96.

1993—This St.-Emilion possesses a Burgundy-like sweetness and expansiveness, as
• well as good ripeness, a round, fat, plump personality, and low acidity. Drink
85 it over the next 5–6 years. Last tasted, 11/94.

1992—This soft, round, richly fruity wine possesses a Burgundy-like smoothness
• and an amiable personality. Drink it over the next 3–4 years. Last tasted,
83 11/94.

1990—Dark in color, with a pure as well as dramatic bouquet, the 1990 displays
• massive extraction of fruit, full body, deep, multi-dimensional flavors, and a
89 long, spicy finish. The considerable depth of fruit nearly obscures the significant tannins. Anticipated maturity: Now–2010. Last tasted, 1/93.

1989—There are enough ripe tannins in the 1989 to warrant aging for 10–15 years,
• but considering this wine's harmony and luscious richness on the palate, most
86 readers will probably prefer to drink it in its first decade of life. Anticipated maturity: Now–2002. Last tasted, 1/93.

1988—The intense bouquet of herbs, black fruits, spices, and new oak offered in
• the 1988 is followed by a rich, supple, generously endowed wine that
86 adroitly marries power with finesse. Anticipated maturity: Now. Last tasted, 1/93.

LA CLOTTE   GOOD

Classification: St.-Emilion Grand Cru Classé
Location of vineyards: St.-Emilion
Owner: Héritiers Chailleau
Address: 33330 St.-Emilion
Mailing address: Same as above
Telephone: 33 5 57 24 66 85; telefax: None
Visits: By appointment only
Contact: Nelly Moulierac

VINEYARDS (red)
Surface area: 9 acres
Average age of vines: 43 years
Blend: 70% Merlot, 30% Cabernet Franc
Density of plantation: 6,000 vines per hectare
Average yields (over the last 5 years): 30 hectoliters per hectare
Total average annual production: 100 hectoliters

GRAND VIN (red)
Brand name: Château La Clotte
Appellation: St.-Emilion Grand Cru Classé
Mean annual production: Variable
Upbringing: Fermentations and macerations last 35–40 days in
temperature-controlled concrete tanks, at maximum temperatures of 32
degrees centigrade. There are 4 pumping-overs daily. Wines undergo
malolactics in oak barrels, where they are also aged for 18 months with
30% new oak. They are fined but remain unfiltered.

SECOND WINE
Brand name: Clos Bergat Bosson
Average annual production: Variable

Evaluation of present classification: The quality equivalent of a Médoc
Cru Bourgeois, sometimes even a Médoc fifth-growth
Plateau of maturity: 3–12 or more years following the vintage

---

The tiny vineyard of La Clotte is owned by the Chailleau family, who are
probably better known as the owners of the immensely popular restaurant
snuggled in a back alley of St.-Emilion, Logis de la Cadène. They have hired
the firm of Jean-Pierre Moueix to manage the vineyard, and in return the
Moueix firm receives three-fourths of the crop for selling on an exclusive
basis throughout the world. The rest of La Clotte's production is sold in the
restaurant. I have often enjoyed this wine and found it very typical of a

plump, fleshy, well-made St.-Emilion. Drinkable when released, it holds its fruit and develops for 10–12 years. The best recent vintages have included fine wines in 1975, 1982, 1983, 1985, 1986, 1988, 1989, and 1990. The vineyard is well situated on the edge of the limestone plateau, just outside the ancient town walls of St.-Emilion.

VINTAGES

1997 — This straightforward, chunky, low-acid, four-square wine offers immediate
• 　 appeal and reasonably abundant quantities of fruit, glycerin, and alcohol. Its
85– 　 spicy cherry fruit and easygoing style will have many admirers. Drink it over
86 　 the next 4–5 years. Last tasted, 3/98.

1993 — La Clotte consistently fashions supple, juicy St.-Emilions with attractive,
• 　 plummy, jammy black cherry, herb, and cedary personalities. The 1993 ex-
85 　 hibits medium body, good fruit and ripeness, light tannin, low acidity, and a
　 smooth as silk finish. Drink it over the next 7–8 years. Last tasted, 11/94.

1992 — The style offers enticingly ripe, jammy fruit in a supple format. The medium-
• 　 bodied 1992 is fruity, soft, and jammy. Drink it over the next 4–5 years. Last
85 　 tasted, 11/94.

1990 — The 1990 is a knockout. The seductive nose of jammy, berry fruit, herbs, and
• 　 vanillin grabbed my attention. Super-concentrated, with layer upon layer of
89 　 fruit, this multi-dimensional wine is loaded! Drink it over the next decade.
　 Last tasted, 1/93.

LA CLUSIÈRE

Classification: St.-Emilion Grand Cru Classé
Location of vineyards: St.-Emilion, on the Côte Pavie
Owner: Mr. and Mrs. Gérard Perse
Address: 33330 St.-Emilion
Mailing address: Same as above
Telephone: 33 5 57 55 43 43; telefax: 33 5 57 24 63 99
Visits: By appointment only
Contact: Laurence Argutti

VINEYARDS (red)
Surface area: 7.5 acres
Average age of vines: 30 years
Blend: 70% Merlot, 20% Cabernet Franc, 10% Cabernet Sauvignon
Density of plantation: 5,300 vines per hectare
Average yields (over the last 5 years): 48 hectoliters per hectare
Total average annual production: 19,000 bottles

GRAND VIN (red)
Brand name: Château La Clusière
Appellation: St.-Emilion Grand Cru Classé

Mean annual production: 19,000 bottles
Upbringing: Fermentations last approximately 10 days and macerations approximately 20 days in stainless-steel vats. Wines used to be aged in 1-year-old barrels from Château Pavie. Now, 18 months aging and malolactics are done in 100% new oak. They are fined but remain unfiltered.

SECOND WINE
None produced.

Evaluation of present classification: The quality equivalent of a Médoc Cru Bourgeois
Plateau of maturity: 6–15 years following the vintage

Anyone who has visited Château Pavie has probably been taken by the former owner, Jean Paul Valette, up the slope of Pavie to the underground cellars at the top of the hill. On this high ridge are the tiny vineyard and cellars of La Clusière. The wine that emerges from this vineyard tends to be surprisingly tough textured, with hard tannins and an ungenerous personality. One would suspect that moderate cellaring would soften the wine, but that has not been my experience. I have tasted too many wines that get older, but not better, and therein lies the problem I have with La Clusière. If you like sinewy, muscular, austere, even harsh clarets, you will enjoy this St.-Emilion more than I do. Given the fact that this estate was acquired by Gérard Perse in 1998, readers should expect a significant increase in quality.

VINTAGES

1997—This pleasant, one-dimensional, cleanly made wine lacks body and intensity.
•
77–
79
Undoubtedly, under the new proprietor, Gérard Perse, the 1998 will set a new level of quality for this perennial underachiever. Last tasted, 3/98.

1992—An earthy, herbal nose and moderately endowed, tight flavors display medium
•
76
body and muscle but little charm or fruit. This austere, ferociously tannic wine will undoubtedly dry out before any real grace or elegance emerges. Last tasted, 11/94.

1990—The 1990 is the most impressive La Clusière that I have tasted. Deep ruby
•
89
colored, with a bouquet that soars from the glass with scents of ripe raspberries and vanillin, this opulent wine offers layers of rich, sweet fruit, loads of glycerin, and a long, velvety finish. It is already delicious, but the necessary depth and balance are present for another 10–12 years of evolution. Last tasted, 1/93.

1989—The 1989's alcohol level is high, and the green, harsh, unripe tannins suggest
•
77?
that the grapes may have been analytically but not physiologically mature. It is a sinewy, charmless wine. Last tasted, 1/93.

1988—While the 1988 is slightly better than the 1989, it is still overwhelmingly
  •   tannic and mean-spirited, with an aggressive nature to its tannins that seems
 79   to obliterate any charm. Last tasted, 1/93.

CORBIN   GOOD

Classification: St.-Emilion Grand Cru Classé
Location of vineyards: St.-Emilion, Graves plateau
Owner: Société Civile des Domaines Giraud
Address: 1, Grand Corbin, 33330 St.-Emilion
Mailing address: Same as above
Telephone: 33 5 57 74 48 94; telefax: 33 5 57 74 47 18
Visits: By appointment only
Contact: Philippe Giraud

VINEYARDS (red)
Surface area: 31.3 acres
Average age of vines: 30 years
Blend: 71% Merlot, 29% Cabernet Franc
Density of plantation: 5,500 vines per hectare
Average yields (over the last 5 years): 51 hectoliters per hectare
Total average annual production: 645 hectoliters

GRAND VIN (red)
Brand name: Château Corbin
Appellation: St.-Emilion Grand Cru
Mean annual production: 645 hectoliters
Upbringing: Fermentations and macerations last about 3 weeks in open
concrete vats. Wines are then transferred to oak barrels, which are
renewed by a third each vintage, for 12–14 months aging. They are fined
but remain unfiltered.

SECOND WINE
None produced.

Evaluation of present classification: From time to time Corbin produces
wines of a Premier Grand Cru Classé status, but in general this is the
quality equivalent of a good Médoc Cru Bourgeois
Plateau of maturity: 3–12 years following the vintage

Corbin is clearly a property capable of making rich, deeply fruity, luscious
wines. My first experience with this wine was at a dinner party where the
1970 was served blind. It was an immensely enjoyable, round, full-bodied,
concentrated, delicious wine with plenty of fruit. Since then I have made it a
point to follow this estate closely. In the great vintages—for instance, 1970,

1975, 1982, 1989, and 1990—this wine can rival the best St.-Emilions. Its problem has been inconsistency.

Corbin sits on the *graves* plateau near the Pomerol border. Bordeaux's famed Professor Enjalbert argues that Corbin's vineyard is situated on a similar band of soil that underpins the vineyards of Cheval Blanc. The style of wine produced at Corbin reaches heights in hot, sunny, drought years when the wine is dark in color, fat, ripe, full bodied, and admirably concentrated. Unfortunately, Corbin is a moderately expensive wine, as it has long been popular in the Benelux countries and Britain.

VINTAGES

1997—A solidly made, plump, fruity St.-Emilion, with good depth, medium body,
• and robust spice and black cherry fruit, this wine will drink well for 4–5
84– years. Last tasted, 3/98.
85

1996—This wine possesses too much tannin for its uninspiring concentration of fruit.
• The medium ruby color is accompanied by a wine with cherry, herb, and
80? earth aromas. But the dusty tannin and other rustic character of this wine does not bode well for future development. It should keep for a decade, but there is not enough flesh or fruit to cover the wine's framework. Anticipated maturity: 2000–2006. Last tasted, 11/97.

1995—The 1995 exhibits a saturated color, as well as sweet fruit, low acidity, and
• good ripeness. It comes across as a forward, easygoing style of St.-Emilion for
86 drinking during its first 5–7 years of life. Last tasted, 11/97.

1994—The 1994 is revealing less intensity. It is a medium-bodied, fruity, pleasant,
• but essentially one-dimensional St.-Emilion for drinking during its first 5–6
85 years of life. Last tasted, 3/96.

1993—A correct, fruity, medium-bodied St.-Emilion, the 1993 Corbin reveals
• straightforward, tasty, currant fruit, and spicy notes, but it lacks complex-
80 ity and concentration. It should drink well for 5–6 years. Last tasted, 11/94.

1990—This wine has reached full maturity at an accelerated pace. Notwithstanding
• that, it is a delicious, plump Corbin with a dark garnet color already revealing
87 moderate quantities of rust and orange at its rim. It offers an attractive fruitcake, spice, and jammy-scented nose, followed by lush, soft, medium-bodied flavors with good levels of glycerin, flesh, and fat. The 1990 is similar to the 1989. It needs to be drunk up. Anticipated maturity: Now–2004. Last tasted, 11/97.

1989—The 1989 has extremely low acidity and soft tannins, but the overall impres-
• sion is one of power, an opulent, even unctuous texture, and precocious
87 drinkability. Assuming you like this big, over-ripe, Australian style of wine, and intend to drink it within its first decade of life, this wine will undoubtedly provide an enticing level of exhilaration. Anticipated maturity: Now–2004. Last tasted, 3/95.

1988—The 1988 is light and diluted, with a weedy, indifferent character. Last tasted,
- 4/91.

74

1986—The 1986 is too loosely knit and too soft and seems entirely unfocused, as
- well as over-cropped. It is a fruity, soft, pleasant wine that is easy to drink,

75　　but a bit more structure and concentration would be welcome. Anticipated
maturity: Now. Last tasted, 3/90.

1985—The 1985 exhibits the over-ripe character I find common in Corbin, a soft,
- exuberantly fruity, agreeable constitution and a finish that is a trifle short and

83　　too alcoholic. Anticipated maturity: Now. Last tasted, 3/90.

CORBIN-MICHOTTE　　　　　　　　　　　　　　VERY GOOD

Classification: St.-Emilion Grand Cru Classé
Location of vineyards: St.-Emilion, close to Pomerol, not far from Cheval
Blanc and Figeac
Owner: Jean-Noël Boidron
Address: 33330 St.-Emilion
Mailing address: Same as above
Telephone: 33 5 57 51 64 88; telefax: 33 5 57 51 56 30
Visits: By appointment only
Contact: Emmanuel Boidron

VINEYARDS (red)
Surface area: 17.3 acres
Average age of vines: 35 years
Blend: 65% Merlot, 30% Cabernet Franc, 5% Cabernet Sauvignon
Density of plantation: 5,850 vines per hectare
Average yields (over the last 5 years): 37 hectoliters per hectare
Total average annual production: 260 hectoliters

GRAND VIN (red)
Brand name: Château Corbin-Michotte
Appellation: St.-Emilion Grand Cru
Mean annual production: 260 hectoliters
Upbringing: Fermentations and macerations are rather long and take
place in temperature-controlled vats. Only indigenous yeasts are used.
Seventy percent of the yield is aged in new oak barrels, and the
remainder stays in vats for 24 months. Wines are fined but not
filtered.

SECOND WINE
Brand name: Château Les Abeilles
Average annual production: Variable

> Evaluation of present classification: From time to time this property
> produces wines of Premier Grand Cru Classé quality, but generally the
> quality is equivalent to a Médoc fifth-growth
> Plateau of maturity: 3–12 years following the vintage

Corbin-Michotte is one of five châteaux that sit along the Pomerol border with
"Corbin" in their name. This property has the potential to be one of the best
of the area. It is a small estate with relatively old vines that are planted on a
sandy, loam soil intermixed with fine gravel, and what the French call *crasse
de fer,* meaning a ferruginous iron-rich subsoil. The vineyard is also laden
with minerals, which the proprietor claims gives the wine's bouquet its extra
dimension. Unfortunately for American consumers, much of Corbin-Michotte
is sold directly to European clients and in Switzerland, which remains the
strongest market for this property. Vintages I have tasted have reminded me
more of a Pomerol than a St.-Emilion. They have been deeply colored wines,
with a very pronounced black fruit, plummy character and a luscious, opulent
texture.

VINTAGES

1997—One of my favorite St.-Emilions appears to have fallen on its face in the 1997
　•　vintage. While most wines reviewed in this issue were tasted two to four
78–　times, I saw Corbin-Michotte only once. At that particular tasting, it was light
82　bodied and weedy, with little color saturation and mediocre depth and extract.
　　It is one of the least impressive wines to emerge from this well-run estate
　　over the last decade. It will require consumption during its first 5–6 years of
　　life. Last tasted, 3/98.

1996—I liked the light, medium-bodied 1996 Corbin-Michotte's soft, sexy, berry and
　•　raspberry fruitiness, as well as the fact that the proprietor did not go for
83–　maximum extraction, thus avoiding a tannic, compressed wine. While this
86　offering is not a blockbuster, there is plenty of up-front appeal to this juicy,
　　succulent St.-Emilion. It will require near-term consumption. Anticipated
　　maturity: Now–2005. Last tasted, 3/98.

1995—A hedonistic effort from Corbin-Michotte, the 1995 reveals a deep ruby
　•　color, a jammy plum, cherry, and spice box nose, and medium-bodied, lush,
89　low-acid, juicy, opulently textured, fruity flavors. This is an exuberantly fruity,
　　tasty St.-Emilion that should be reasonably priced. On a pure scale of plea-
　　sure, it merits even higher marks. A sleeper! Anticipated maturity: Now–
　　2007. Last tasted, 11/97.

1994—The 1994 exhibits a dense ruby/purple color and a wonderfully expressive
　•　nose of jammy black currants, minerals, and flowers. Ripe, highly extracted,
89　medium to full bodied, with layers of flavor, this wine is undoubtedly a sleeper
　　of the vintage. It can be drunk upon release and over the next decade. Last
　　tasted, 3/96.

1990—The 1990 is similar to the 1989. Ripe but slightly deeper, it is a wine to
•   consume over the next 7–8 years. Last tasted, 1/93.
87

1989—The 1989 is a ruby/purple–colored wine, oozing with extract. Full bodied,
•   richly perfumed, with the scent of super-ripe plums and minerals, it has an
86   alcohol level of nearly 14%, relatively low acidity, but high tannins. Anticipated maturity: Now–2002. Last tasted, 1/93.

1988—The 1988 is a medium-bodied, pleasant, correct wine, with decent acidity
•   and length. It should be drunk over the next 5–7 years. Anticipated maturity:
83   Now. Last tasted, 4/91.

1985—Now fully mature, the 1985 Corbin-Michotte has a dark ruby color, with a
•   spicy, black currant-, plum-scented nose, lush, round, generously endowed
86   flavors, and a soft, silky texture. Anticipated maturity: Now. Last tasted,
11/90.

1982—This stunning example of Corbin-Michotte has matured rapidly and should
•   be consumed. It offers a roasted, plummy, mineral-scented bouquet, rich,
87   heady, alcoholic, fleshy, chewy flavors, considerable body, and abundant glycerin and alcohol in its soft finish. It makes for a hedonistic mouthful of
delicious St.-Emilion, but aging it any longer would be foolish. Anticipated
maturity: Now. Last tasted, 3/90.

LA COUSPAUDE   EXCELLENT

Classification: St.-Emilion Grand Cru Classé
Location of vineyards: St.-Emilion (*mono-terroir* situated on the heights of
St.-Emilion, less than 300 meters away from the very center of the town
on a rocky subsoil)
Owner: G.F.A. du Château La Couspaude
Address: 33330 St.-Emilion
Mailing address: B.P. 40, 33330 St.-Emilion
Telephone: 33 5 57 40 01 15 or 33 5 57 40 15 76;
telefax: 33 5 57 40 10 14
Visits: By appointment only
Contact: Jean-Claude Aubert

VINEYARDS (red)
Surface area: 17.3 acres
Average age of vines: 35 years
Blend: 70% Merlot, 18% Cabernet Franc, 12% Cabernet Sauvignon
Density of plantation: 6,500 vines per hectare
Average yields (over the last 5 years): 38–40 hectoliters per
hectare
Total average annual production: 3,000 cases approximately

GRAND VIN (red)
Brand name: Château La Couspaude
Appellation: St.-Emilion Grand Cru Classé
Mean annual production: 270–300 hectoliters
Upbringing: Alcoholic fermentations and macerations last 25–35 days in stainless-steel vats of small capacity (60 hectoliters).* Malolactics occur in new oak barrels, and 25% of the wines are again transferred to new oak barrels. Wines are aged 14–16 months in 100% new oak barrels. The wines are neither fined nor filtered.

SECOND WINE
Brand name: Junior
Average annual production: (Not produced yet)

Evaluation of present classification: The quality equivalent of a Médoc third- or fourth-growth
Plateau of maturity: 5–15 years following the vintage

* These will change to temperature-controlled wooden vats of 50-hectoliter capacity in 1998. These will be changed every 3 years.

This small, walled vineyard owned by the Aubert family has recently received significant attention because of its exotic, ripe, rich, sexy style. The wine was largely unimpressive until the last three or four vintages, which have all been made in a flamboyant, generously endowed style. While critics have complained that the wine is excessively oaky (and I would agree that oak is a prominent component of the wine), I believe the oak will be absorbed during the wine's evolution because of the richness and concentration possessed. That is already noticeable with the 1994 and is beginning to become noticeable with the 1995. Last, I predict the wines from this small estate will become increasingly expensive once the international marketplace recognizes the wines' quality.

VINTAGES

1997—This wine may have more potential than the numerical score suggests. During
•   the last 2 weeks of March, it was dominated by wood. The color is deep ruby.
86–   The wine is somewhat angular and over-oaked, but perhaps there is more
87   flesh and richness of fruit than was present the three times I tasted it. The
       extraction seems a bit pushed, and the wine possesses dry, tough tannin in
       the finish. Although disjointed and loosely knit when I sampled it, this is an
       impeccably run estate, so readers may want to give the wine the benefit of the
       doubt. Anticipated maturity: 2000–2007. Last tasted, 3/98.

1996—The saturated ruby/purple–colored 1996 La Couspaude reveals copious
•   quantities of sweet blackberry/cherry liqueur–like fruit in the nose, which
89–   also offers evidence of toasty new oak. This is a juicy, full-bodied, ripe, spicy
91   wine that takes the lavish new oak treatment to the limit but manages not to

exceed it. This 70% Merlot/30% Cabernet Franc blend (3,000 cases produced in 1996) is powerful, intense, and moderately tannic. While 100% new oak is utilized for the aging process, the malolactic fermentation is also done in new oak. Upon completion, 25% of that wine is then removed from those casks and aged in other new oak barrels. That portion of the cuvée is called "200% new oak *élevage*." Anticipated maturity: 2003–2018. Last tasted, 3/98.

1995—This is another offering from the exotic Le Pin school of St.-Emilions that
•   are made from extremely ripe fruit, aged in 100% new oak (the malolactic
90   fermentation is also done in new oak), and bottled without filtration. The 1995 La Couspaude exhibits a ripe, jammy kirsch, black currant, and licorice nose with plenty of smoky, *pain grillé* notes. Full bodied, with low acidity and a flamboyant personality, this wine will unquestionably cause heads to turn. Traditionalists may argue that it is too obvious and sexy, but this is a fun wine to taste, and no one can argue that it does not provide pleasure . . . and isn't that the ultimate objective of drinking this stuff? Moreover, it will age well and become even more civilized with cellaring. Anticipated maturity: 2000–2015. Last tasted, 11/97.

1994—The 1994 has put on more weight and may merit an outstanding score after a
•   few more years of bottle age. The wine reveals a deep ruby/purple color and
89   a big, toasty, smoky nose filled with the scents of Provençal herbs and jammy black cherries. Dense, rich, and fat, this well-endowed, oaky wine should drink well for 7–8 years. Last tasted, 3/96.

1993—The 1993's only weakness is a slight green pepper quality to its fruit. Other-
•   wise it is a darkly colored, dense, concentrated, and impressively endowed
86   wine with fine purity, ripeness, a natural, chewy texture, and a long finish. It should drink well for 10–12 years. Last tasted, 11/94.

1992—The 1992 has turned out to be a respectable effort in a tough year. The wine's
•   dark ruby color is followed by an attractive, ripe nose of black cherries and
85   smoky oak. Medium bodied, soft, and velvety, with fine purity and ripeness, this wine should be drunk over the next 3–4 years. Last tasted, 11/94.

COUVENT-DES-JACOBINS   GOOD

Classification: St.-Emilion Grand Cru Classé
Location of vineyards: St.-Emilion
Owner: Mr. and Mrs. Alain Borde
Address: Rue Guadet, 3333 St.-Emilion
Mailing address: Same as above
Telephone: 33 5 57 24 70 66; telefax: 33 5 57 24 62 51
Visits: By appointment only
Contact: Mr. or Mrs. Alain Borde

VINEYARDS (red)
Surface area: 26.4 acres
Average age of vines: 45 years

Blend: 65% Merlot, 25% Cabernet Franc, 10% Cabernet Sauvignon
Density of plantation: 6,000 vines per hectare
Average yields (over the last 5 years): 45 hectoliters
Total average annual production: 480 hectoliters

GRAND VIN (red)
Brand name: Couvent-des-Jacobins
Appellation: St.-Emilion Grand Cru
Mean annual production: 300 hectoliters
Upbringing: Fermentations and macerations last approximately 3 weeks
in temperature-controlled stainless-steel and concrete tanks. Wines are
transferred to oak barrels (renewed by a third each vintage) for 15–18
months of aging. They are fined but remain unfiltered.

SECOND WINE
Brand name: Château Beau-Mayne
Average annual production: 100 hectoliters

Evaluation of present classification: The quality equivalent of a Médoc
fifth-growth
Plateau of maturity: 4–14 years following the vintage

Couvent-des-Jacobins, named after the thirteenth-century Dominican monas-
tery that was built on this site, is an up-and-coming estate, meticulously run
by the Joinaud-Borde family, which have owned the property since 1902.

The vineyards are immediately situated adjacent to the town of St.-
Emilion, on a sandy, clay soil of the *côtes* that produces darkly colored, rich,
fairly alcoholic wines of substance and character. During the eighties the
quality of Couvent-des-Jacobins improved, largely because the owners introduced a second label for vats not considered rich enough for the grand vin.
They also increased the use of new oak casks to 33% for each vintage.

Couvent-des-Jacobins, located immediately to the left-hand side of the
main entrance to the town, has one of the most remarkable underground
cellars of the region. It is a showpiece property that would make for an
interesting visit even if the wines were not so distinguished.

VINTAGES

1990—Jammy, herb, and berry aromas dominate the 1990's spicy bouquet. In the
• mouth, there is fine ripeness, a lush, silky, fruity personality, and a smooth,
85 heady, sweet, but unstructured finish. Although it will not make old bones,
the 1990 Couvent-des-Jacobins will provide rewarding drinking early on.
Anticipated maturity: Now–2001. Last tasted, 1/93.

1989—The 1989 has a remarkable resemblance to the wonderful 1982. It is a
•   deeply colored, intensely perfumed, full-bodied wine with layers of extract,
86   an unctuous, plummy fatness, high alcohol, and very low acidity. Anticipated
      maturity: Now–2000. Last tasted, 4/91.

1986—The 1986 should prove to be one of the longest-lived wines from this property
•   in over 2 decades. Deep ruby/purple in color, with a pronounced spicy, oaky,
87   curranty bouquet intermingled with the scent of herbs, this wine displays a
      superripeness, medium body, and an excellent finish, with plenty of soft
      tannins. Anticipated maturity: Now–2001. Last tasted, 3/90.

1985—The 1985 is a textbook St.-Emilion—supple, generous, easy to appreciate,
•   with gobs of black currant fruit interlaced with a touch of toasty oak. This
86   medium- to full-bodied wine offers both complexity and a mouth-filling
      plumpness. Anticipated maturity: Now. Last tasted, 3/90.

1983—Nearly as concentrated and as deep as the 1982, the 1983 Couvent-des-
•   Jacobins is a soft, supple, fruity, medium-bodied, well-colored wine that is
85   fully mature. Anticipated maturity: Now–may be in decline. Last tasted,
      11/89.

1982—The 1982 Couvent still has an impressive dark garnet color and a complex,
•   berry bouquet of cedar, herbs, chocolate, and licorice. On the palate, this
87   fleshy wine is deep, rich, and full bodied, with a seductive, silky texture. It
      has attained full maturity. Anticipated maturity: Now–2001. Last tasted,
      12/96.

DASSAULT   GOOD

Classification: St.-Emilion Grand Cru Classé
Location of vineyards: St.-Emilion
Owner: S.A.R.L. Château Dassault
Address: 1, Couprie, 33330 St.-Emilion
Mailing address: Same as above
Telephone: 33 5 57 24 71 30; telefax: 33 5 57 74 40 33
Visits: By appointment only
Contact: Laurence Brun-Vergriette

VINEYARDS (red)
Surface area: 56.8 acres
Average age of vines: 30 years
Blend: 65% Merlot, 30% Cabernet Franc, 5% Cabernet Sauvignon
Density of plantation: 5,200 vines per hectare
Average yields (over the last 5 years): 40 hectoliters per hectare
Total average annual production: 150,000 bottles

GRAND VIN (red)
Brand name: Château Dassault
Appellation: St.-Emilion Grand Cru

Mean annual production: 80,000 bottles
Upbringing: Fermentations and macerations last a minimum of 20 days in temperature-controlled vats. Approximately 50%–70% of the yield undergoes malolactics in new oak barrels, and the rest is transferred to 1-vintage-old barrels after completion of the process. Wines are aged 18 months, fined but not filtered.

SECOND WINE
Brand name: Château Merissac
Average annual production: 70,000 bottles

Evaluation of present classification: The quality equivalent of a good Médoc Cru Bourgeois
Plateau of maturity: 3–9 years following the vintage

Dassault consistently produces smooth-textured, fruity, supple, straightforward wines that are meant to be drunk in their youth. They are very cleanly made and perhaps somewhat commercial in orientation, but there is no denying their attractive, uncomplicated style. The only caveat here is that aging rarely results in a better wine. As long as one is prepared to drink this wine at a relatively early age, it is unlikely that Dassault will be disappointing. The perfect restaurant St.-Emilion?

I hesitate to write it, but I have noticed that certain bottles of Dassault, particularly those following the consistently excellent 1990, occasionally possess a corky, moldy, damp cardboard-like aroma. This does not appear in all bottles, but it is something I have sometimes noticed in my tastings, both in samples prior to bottling and following the *mise en bouteille*.

VINTAGES

1996—This property, which tends to make soft, fruity, lighter-styled St.-Emilions,
• appears to have produced a forward, opulent, round wine with more depth
85– and weight than usual. Not as structured or tannic as many 1996s, it pos-
86 sesses deep kirsch, raspberry, and cassis fruit presented in a medium-bodied, pleasing, user-friendly style. Drink it over the next 6–8 years. Last tasted, 11/97.

1995—The wine offers a saturated purple color, a sweet, fleshy character, and plenty
• of guts and appeal. It remains to be seen how much of the mid-palate and
85 aromatics will be left after bottling. Anticipated maturity: 1999–2006. Last tasted, 11/97.

1994—This wine's austere character and tough tannin are two of the downsides of
• the 1994 vintage. It is astringent and lean, with good oak, but not enough
79 fruit. Last tasted, 1/97.

1993—Two samples of Dassault's 1993 exhibited the moldy cardboard aroma I have
 •   found in certain other Bordeaux wines. Multiple explanations have been
82?   offered for this problem, including badly cured barrels, the use of chlorine
       for cleaning in the winery (which vaporizes and contaminates the barrels),
       and bad corks and filter pads. Despite the musty cardboard-like nose, this
       commercial, light- to medium-bodied, easygoing wine offers cranberry fruit
       behind the defective nose. Drink it over the next 4–5 years. Last tasted,
       1/97.
1990—The 1990 is the strongest effort I can recall from Dassault. A precocious
 •   bouquet of sweet, plummy fruit, licorice, and black cherries is followed by a
87   wine that is bursting with fruit. Drink this succulent, fat, chewy 1990 over
       the next 7–8 years. Last tasted, 1/93.
1989—The 1989 is a loosely structured, grapy, expansively flavored, very soft and
 •   alcoholic wine that lacks structure and precision. However, it will offer a
84   deliciously smooth glass of wine if drunk young. Anticipated maturity: Now.
       Last tasted, 4/91.

DAUGAY   GOOD

Classification: None
Owner: Christian de Bouard de la Forest
Telephone: 33 5 57 24 78 12
Surface area: 13.8 acres
Blend: 50% Merlot, 48% Cabernet Franc, 2% Cabernet Sauvignon
Total average annual production: 2,500 cases
Time spent in barrel: 14–16 months
Average age of the vines: 25 years

Evaluation of present classification: The quality equivalent of a Médoc
Cru Bourgeois
Plateau of maturity: 3–12 years

This small estate is owned by the brother of Hubert de Bouard of Château
Angélus. In fact, until 1984 this vineyard was part of Angélus. The wine
is a very good St.-Emilion that is somewhat undervalued given modern-day
pricing.

VINTAGES

1996—Daugay's 1996 is a spicy, medium-bodied, Cabernet Franc–dominated wine
 •   with weedy, red and black currant, and tobacco notes, good depth, and more
85–   softness than many wines from this sector of St.-Emilion. Drink it over the
86   next 7–8 years. Last tasted, 3/98.

1995—The 1995 is meaty and ripe, with a deep ruby color, a sense of elegance,
•   herb-tinged black fruit, good ripeness, and a lush palate feel. Last tasted,
85   11/97.

1994—The 1994 Daugay displays less color saturation than the 1993, but it is made
•   in a similarly open-knit, smoky, richly fruity style, with good glycerin, me-
86   dium body, and a low-acid, fleshy finish. It should be drunk over the next 5–
       6 years. Last tasted, 1/97.

1993—An impressive wine for the vintage, this excellent, deep ruby/purple–colored
•   wine (a blend of 50% Cabernet Franc and 50% Merlot) offers up a sweet,
86   complex nose of herbs, black fruits, and smoke. With a supple texture, good
       to excellent concentration, low acidity, and fine ripeness (no bitter tannin or
       vegetal characteristics), this is a hedonistic sleeper of the vintage. Drink it
       over the next 5–7 years. Last tasted, 1/97.

DESTIEUX   GOOD

Classification: St.-Emilion Grand Cru
Location of vineyards: St.-Hippolyte
Owner: Christian Dauriac
Address: 33330 St.-Emilion
Mailing address: Same as above
Telephone: 33 5 57 24 77 44 or 33 5 57 40 25 05;
telefax: 33 5 57 40 37 42
Visits: By appointment only
Contact: Christian Dauriac

VINEYARDS (red)
Surface area: 19.8 acres
Average age of vines: 45 years
Blend: One-third Cabernets, two-thirds Merlot
Density of plantation: 5,000 vines per hectare
Average yields (over the last 5 years): 29 hectoliters per
hectare
Total average annual production: 30,000 bottles approximately

GRAND VIN (red)
Brand name: Château Destieux
Appellation: St.-Emilion Grand Cru
Mean annual production: 26,000 bottles
Upbringing: Alcoholic fermentations take place in vats and malolactics
in 100% new oak. Macerations are rather long and last approximately
3 weeks. Wines are aged 18 months in all, lightly fined but not
filtered.

SECOND WINE
Brand name: Château Laubarède

Evaluation of present classification: The quality equivalent of a good
Médoc Cru Bourgeois
Plateau of maturity: 5–15 years following the vintage

Located in the satellite commune of St.-Hippolyte, on clay and limestone
soils, in a particularly torrid St.-Emilion micro-climate, Destieux makes an
especially attractive, plummy, fleshy, tough-textured wine, with good concentration and plenty of alcohol.

The force behind the recent string of successes is both the owner, M.
Dauriac, and his talented consulting oenologist, Michel Rolland. The wines
of Destieux are among the deepest colored and most powerful and dense of
the appellation. If bulk and muscle were criteria for greatness, Destieux
would be near the top.

VINTAGES

1997— This well-made wine borders on over-ripeness but offers positive components
• of plum, prune, and sweet jammy cherry fruit in addition to a healthy ruby/
85– purple color. A round wine, with low acidity, and a nice texture, it will drink
86 well for 5–6 years. Last tasted, 3/98.

1996— This reasonably priced St.-Emilion estate has produced a dense black/pur-
• ple–colored 1996 with plenty of tannin and gutsy, meaty, concentrated fruit.
85– As always, this offering possesses plenty of personality, and while there
87 may be an excess of tannin, the wine is mouth-filling, dense, and pleasing.
Additionally, it is a good value as well as a potential candidate for 10–15
years of cellaring. Last tasted, 3/98.

1995— Well made, with a deep ruby/purple color and sweet, earthy, black currant
• aromas, this medium-bodied, moderately tannic wine reveals good fruit on
85 the attack, spice, leather, and iron in the flavors, and good depth, but some
hardness in the finish. Anticipated maturity: 2001–2010. Last tasted, 11/97.

1993— Destieux's wines always possess plenty of color, muscle, body, and tannin.
• What they lack is charm and finesse. The 1993 is typical in its hardness,
70 excessive tannin, and stern, chewy, essentially charmless style. Although the
wine will last 10–15 years, how much joy it is capable of providing is
debatable. Last tasted, 11/96.

1989— For much of the eighties I have been enthusiastic about the efforts of the
• proprietor of Destieux, Monsieur Dauriac, who tends to produce powerful,
85 dense, tannic wines with the potential to last for 10–15 years. At first unfocused and lacking definition, the 1989 has developed into a rich, highly
extracted, powerful, dense wine that may be too charged with tannin. Anticipated maturity: Now–2005. Last tasted, 4/91.

1988—The 1988 has a tremendously impressive ruby/purple color, but no charm or
　•　　finesse, as the overbearing tannins are so astringent and excessive that this
　77　 wine has little possibility of ever coming together and aging gracefully. Last
　　　　tasted, 4/91.
1986—The 1986 Destieux is a powerful, dense, tannic wine, with tremendous depth
　•　　of fruit, full body, and gobs of extract and tannin in the finish. It should prove
　86　 to be the longest-lived Destieux made in the last several decades. This
　　　　Destieux has the fruit necessary to hold up to the tannin. Anticipated matu-
　　　　rity: Now–2005. Last tasted, 3/90.
1985—The 1985 is another broodingly dense wine. Full flavored, it has a sumptuous
　•　　amount of ripe fruit, a voluptuous texture, and moderate aging potential.
　87　 Anticipated maturity: Now–2001. Last tasted, 3/90.

LA DOMINIQUE　　　　　　　　　　　　　　　　　　EXCELLENT

Classification: St.-Emilion Grand Cru Classé
Location of vineyards: St.-Emilion, adjacent to Cheval Blanc
Owner: Clément Fayat
Address: La Dominique, 33330 St.-Emilion
Mailing address: Same as above
Telephone: 33 5 57 51 31 36; telefax: 33 5 57 51 63 04
Visits: By appointment, Monday through Friday, between 8 A.M. and
noon, and 2 P.M. and 5:30 P.M.

VINEYARDS (red)
Surface area: 54 acres
Average age of vines: 25 years
Blend: 80% Merlot, 15% Cabernet Franc, 5% Cabernet Sauvignon
Density of plantation: 5,500 vines per hectare
Average yields (over the last 5 years): 45 hectoliters per hectare
Total average annual production: 990 hectoliters

GRAND VIN (red)
Brand name: Château La Dominique
Appellation: St.-Emilion Grand Cru Classé
Mean annual production: 100,000 bottles
Upbringing: Fermentations and macerations last between 21 and
28 days in small temperature-controlled stainless-steel tanks, with
temperatures going up to 29–32 degrees centigrade. Malolactics
occur in new oak casks, and wines are aged 18 months in oak
barrels, 50%–70% of which are new, depending upon the
vintage. They are fined with fresh egg whites and very lightly
filtered.

SECOND WINE
Brand name: St.-Paul de Dominique
Average annual production: 32,000 bottles

Evaluation of present classification: The quality equivalent of a Médoc
third-growth; should be upgraded to a St.-Emilion Premier Grand Cru
Classé
Plateau of maturity: 5–20 years following the vintage

This superbly situated estate, located near the border of Pomerol close to
Cheval Blanc, has a soil base composed of limestone gravel and sandy clay.
An intensive system of drain tiles installed in the mid-nineteenth century has
greatly enhanced this property's ability to produce fine wines in wet years.
The truly great wines made at La Dominique—1971, 1982, 1989, 1990, and
1995—should easily have qualified La Dominique for elevation to a Premier
Grand Cru Classé in the 1996 St.-Emilion classification. Sadly, that was not
the case. The property continues to lack the glamour and reputation of many
of the other Premiers Grands Crus Classés, a fact that can be put to advantage
by consumers looking for fairly priced St.-Emilions.

Proprietor Fayat, who purchased the Cru Bourgeois Château Clément in
the Médoc in 1978, utilizes the services of highly respected Libourne oenologist Michel Rolland to oversee the vinification and *élevage* of La Dominique.
The resulting wine is richly colored, intense, super-ripe, opulent, and full
bodied. It benefits immensely from the 33%–45% new oak barrels utilized
each vintage. The decision to make a second wine for less successful vats
and young vines has increased the quality even further.

La Dominique's wines continue to be undervalued.

VINTAGES

1997—With its exotic, flamboyant, blackberry liqueur and jammy black cherry nose,
the 1997 La Dominique is a turn-on. Medium bodied and soft, with well-
87– integrated, toasty new oak, this is a lavishly fruity, soft, plump wine to drink
88 during its first decade of life. Like so many 1997s, the wine tastes extremely
evolved. Last tasted, 3/98.

1996—The color is a dark ruby/purple, and the nose offers up a combination of
mineral, vanillin, black raspberry, and currant aromas. The wine has taken
87– on a more structured and tannic personality, with the tannin more aggressively
88+ astringent. This is a muscular, backward, unevolved La Dominique, but I am
concerned about the tannin level. Anticipated maturity: 2005–2014. Last
tasted, 3/98.

1995—While 1995 is also a tannic vintage for La Dominique, there is sweeter fruit
as well as more ripeness and intensity (at least at present) in the wine's
89 moderately intense nose of vanillin and blackberry and raspberry fruit. In the

mouth, there is good sweetness, medium to full body, moderate tannin, and a layered, rich, classic tasting profile. Anticipated maturity: 2003–2016. Last tasted, 11/97.

1994—The 1994 La Dominique reveals some of the vintage's tell-tale astringent
• toughness, but it is loaded with creamy, ripe, black raspberry and currant
88 fruit. My instincts suggest a balance between fruit and tannin has been struck. The wine is dense, dark ruby/purple colored, with a sweet-smelling, oaky, earthy, smoky, black currant–scented nose. This medium- to full-bodied, ripe 1994 possesses admirable concentration, moderately high tannin, and excellent purity. Anticipated maturity: 2002–2016. Last tasted, 1/97.

1993—This wine may turn out to be even better than my rating indicates. The
• extremely saturated opaque blue/purple color is followed by aromas of sweet,
86 over-ripe plum and cassis fruit, licorice, and toasty, smoky wood. Medium bodied, big, and rich, with no greenness or harsh tannin, this is an excellent, dense, richly endowed 1993 that will benefit from another 1–3 years of cellaring. Anticipated maturity: 1999–2012. Last tasted, 1/97.

1992—A ripe nose of herbs, cassis, and vanillin is fleeting but attractive. This
• medium-bodied wine offers straightforward cassis fruit, but the finish is short,
79 compact, and moderately tannic. It is vaguely reminiscent of this property's 1981 and 1979, but lighter and more austere. Last tasted, 11/94.

1990—The sweet 1990 exhibits *sur-maturité* (over-ripeness). It offers up a weedy,
• tobacco, jammy, cassis-scented nose intertwined with aromas of licorice and
92 earth. Dense, with a late harvest–like ripeness in the mouth, this full-bodied, low-acid, huge, chewy, fleshy wine is already too tasty to resist. Given its size and depth, it should have no problem aging well for 10–15 years. Last tasted, 11/96.

1989—I have drunk the 1989 multiple times since I purchased it for a modest price
• when it was offered as a future. The wine is typically forward, with an opaque
93 purple color and an intense, sweet black raspberry, cedary, toasty-scented nose. In the mouth, the wine defines the word "opulence" with its viscosity and superb levels of jammy black fruits nicely dosed with high-quality wood. Sweet and expansive, this is an exuberant, flamboyant St.-Emilion that should drink well for 10–15 years. Think of it as a wine built along the lines of the great 1971, only superior. Last tasted, 11/96.

1988—In some ways it is a shame that the 1989 is such a show-stopping effort,
• because it eclipses the 1988, which deserves a great deal of recognition. It is
87 a more typical (or, as the Bordelais would have you believe, "more classic") effort, with an alluring and precocious, big bouquet of plummy fruit and sweet vanillin-scented oak. In the mouth, there is not a hard edge to be found. This wine offers exuberantly rich, fruity, opulent flavors, medium to full body, and a long, satiny finish. Anticipated maturity: Now–2001. Last tasted, 4/91.

1986—The 1986 has a deep ruby/garnet color and a spicy bouquet of toasty new
• oak, rich, plummy fruit, and minerals. This is followed by a wine that is
88 full bodied and intense, with impressive extract and tremendous power and persistence in its finish. It does not have the opulence or precocious appeal

of vintages such as 1990, 1989, or 1982, yet it has reached full maturity. It is a firmer, structured, more Médoc-styled La Dominique. Anticipated maturity: Now–2005. Last tasted, 11/95.

1985—The 1985 La Dominique is a disappointment, tasting of green sap from
  •   improperly cured barrels and too large a crop. Its evolution in the bottle has
 74   not been beneficial. Avoid it. Last tasted, 12/88.

1983—This wine needs to be consumed over the near term. The color is a dark
  •   garnet, with considerable amber and orange at the edge. The wine possesses
 87   an enticing, expressive, herb, jammy fruit, earth, and vanillin nose. Some
       rustic tannin is noticeable on the palate, but this fleshy, soft, low-acid wine is
       fully mature, so readers should capture its intensity of fruit before it begins
       to fade, revealing more tannin, acidity, and alcohol. Anticipated maturity:
       Now–2000. Last tasted, 6/96.

1982—This wine was so inexpensive, I used to drink it 3–6 times a month—at least
  •   until my stocks began to be depleted. It is not as exceptional as the 1989 and
 91   1990 La Dominique, but the wine remains splendidly opulent, as well as
       more aggressively tannic. The color is still a deep, plummy ruby/purple, with
       only slight lightening at the edge. The nose of jammy black fruits intertwined
       with scents of licorice, smoke, and *pain grillé* is followed by a medium- to
       full-bodied, expansive, chewy wine with some tannin present in the finish.
       The wine has become far more delineated with cellaring. I would have thought
       it would be fully mature by 1995, but it is still an adolescent. Look for this
       delicious, beefy, chunky 1982 to hit its plateau of full maturity in 1–2 years
       and last for another 12–15. Last tasted, 6/98.

1981—La Dominique's 1981 is a complex, medium-weight, nicely balanced wine,
  •   with a tight but promising bouquet of new oak, ripe fruit, and herbal scents.
 84   Well made, this medium-bodied wine has reached full maturity but should
       hold nicely in the bottle for 4–6 years. Anticipated maturity: Now. Last
       tasted, 2/89.

1980—A success given the vintage in 1980, La Dominique produced a supple, fruity
  •   wine, with a slightly herbaceous, vegetal quality to its bouquet. On the palate,
 78   the wine displays good fruit, medium body, and a soft, pleasant finish. Antici-
       pated maturity: Now–may be in decline. Last tasted, 6/84.

1979—I have never been a great admirer of this wine. Consistently lean, austere,
  •   and lacking generosity, it is an acceptable wine, with an attractive bouquet,
 75   but for La Dominique a disappointment. Time may yield some hidden fruit,
       but I would not gamble on it. Anticipated maturity: Now. Last tasted, 11/88.

1978—Fully mature, this lovely, ripe, fleshy, fruity La Dominique has a cedary, spicy,
  •   herb-and-oak-scented bouquet, medium body, light tannins, and a soft, supple,
 85   spicy finish. This is a well-rendered wine that will keep and continue to drink
       well for another decade. Anticipated maturity: Now–2000. Last tasted, 1/91.

1976—A trifle loosely knit (as most 1976s are), but La Dominique has managed to
  •   produce a wine that avoids the soupy softness and unstructured feel of many
 83   wines of this vintage. A ripe, cedary, oaky, spicy bouquet is fully developed.
       On the palate, the wine is soft, nicely concentrated, and expansive. This is a

delightful medium-weight wine. Anticipated maturity: Now—may be in decline. Last tasted, 2/84.

1975—A typical 1975, hard, astringent, promising, but obnoxiously backward and
 •   tannic, this wine has remained closed and slightly dumb but exhibits very
79   good color, a hint of ripe, cedary, plummy fruit in its nose, and adequate
      weight and length in the finish. The fruit continues to take a backseat to the
      tannins. Anticipated maturity: Now. Last tasted, 3/88.

1971—One sip of the 1971 can turn a skeptic into an instant devotee of La Dominique.
 •   nique. A sensational wine for La Dominique, the 1971 is not only the best
90   St.-Emilion, but one of the top wines of the vintage. Medium garnet, with a
      concentrated, jammy, rich bouquet of herbs, cedar, Asian spices, and ripe
      berry fruit, this wine is lush and silky, with layer upon layer of ripe fruit and
      a lush, alcoholic finish. This is certainly one of the sleepers of the vintage.
      The wine has held at its plateau for over a decade, but why push your luck?
      Drink it up. Anticipated maturity: Now. Last tasted, 1/90.

1970—The 1970 is a very attractive, mature St.-Emilion that is in no danger of falling
 •   apart, but it is best drunk up over the next several years. Medium ruby with
88   some amber, this wine is soft, fragrant, ripe, and admirably concentrated, with a
      velvety finish. The wine has actually put on weight in the last several years.
      Drink it over the next 2–4 years. Anticipated maturity: Now. Last tasted, 1/91.

FAUGÈRES   VERY GOOD

Classification: St.-Emilion Grand Cru
Location of vineyards: St.-Etienne de Lisse
Owner: Corinne Guisez
Address: 33330 St.-Etienne de Lisse
Mailing address: Same as above
Telephone: 33 5 57 40 34 99; telefax: 33 5 57 40 36 14
Visits: By appointment, on weekdays, between 8 A.M. and noon, and
2 P.M. and 6 P.M.
Contact: A. Dourthe and S. Canfailla

VINEYARDS (red)
Surface area: 30.5 acres in 1997
Average age of vines: 30 years
Blend: 70% Merlot, 25% Cabernet Franc, 5% Cabernet Sauvignon
Density of plantation: 6,000 vines per hectare
Average yields (over the last 5 years): 45 hectoliters per hectare
Total average annual production: 110,000 bottles

GRAND VIN (red)
Brand name: Château Faugères
Appellation: St.-Emilion Grand Cru

Mean annual production: 110,000 bottles
Upbringing: Fermentations and macerations last 3 weeks in temperature-controlled cone-shaped stainless-steel vats. Twenty percent of the yield undergoes malolactics in barrels. Wines are aged 14–16 months in oak barrels, 50% of which are new. They are fined with fresh egg whites and filtered.

SECOND WINE
None produced.

Evaluation of present classification: The quality present equivalent of a Médoc fifth-growth
Plateau of maturity: 3–5 years

VINTAGES

1997—This property continues to display considerable potential, and it should be
  •   sought out by readers looking for a good value in high-quality wine. The 1997
87– exhibits a saturated purple color, pure, sweet, black cherry and berry fruit,
 88   well-integrated new oak, and a touch of minerals and licorice. Ripe, with low acidity, and admirable flat and chewiness, this plump, fleshy, low-acid, well-endowed wine will drink exceptionally well during its first 10 years of life, although I suspect it will last longer. A sleeper of the vintage. Last tasted, 3/98.

1996—Deep purple colored, with spicy new oak and black currant fruit in the nose,
  •   this medium-bodied, dense, muscular wine reveals dry tannin in the finish,
86– but abundant fruit, extract, and richness. If everything comes together, this
 87   will be an excellent wine, as well as a very good value. Anticipated maturity: 2003–2012. Last tasted, 11/97.

1995—Dark ruby/purple colored with a smoky, sexy nose of black cherry fruit,
  •   licorice, vanillin, and spice, this medium-bodied, elegant yet flavorful, mouth-
 87   filling St.-Emilion possesses excellent depth and fine overall balance. The long finish exhibits some tannin, but overall this is an accessible, up-front claret to consume over the next 7–8 years. It is also a reasonably good value. Last tasted, 11/97.

1993—This solidly made, ripe, medium-bodied wine reveals fine concentration,
  •   plenty of black fruits, and a spicy, moderately tannic finish. It should drink
 85   well for the next 7–8 years. Last tasted, 11/94.

1992—The 1992 Faugères reveals oak, spice, herbs, tannin, and ripe fruit presented
  •   in an easy to understand, medium-bodied format. It will drink well for 4–5
 85   years. Last tasted, 11/94.

FERRAND LARTIGUE   EXCELLENT

Classification: St.-Emilion Grand Cru
Location of vineyards: St.-Emilion
Owner: Mr. and Mrs. Pierre Ferrand
Address: 33330 St.-Emilion
Mailing address: Same as above
Telephone: 33 5 57 74 46 19; telefax: 33 5 57 74 49 19
Visits: By appointment only
Contact: Laurent Descos

VINEYARDS (red)
Surface area: 7.5 acres
Average age of vines: 40 years
Blend: 90% Merlot, 10% Cabernet Franc
Density of plantation: 5,900 vines per hectare
Average yields (over the last 5 years): 30 hectoliters per hectare
Total average annual production: 12,000 bottles

GRAND VIN (red)
Brand name: Château Ferrand Lartigue
Appellation: St.-Emilion Grand Cru
Mean annual production: 12,000 bottles
Upbringing: Fermentations last 10 days and macerations 10 days. Wines
are aged 20 months in oak barrels, 70% of which are new (30% are
1 vintage old). They are lightly fined with fresh egg whites and remain
unfiltered.

SECOND WINE
None produced.

Evaluation of present classification: The quality equivalent of a Médoc
fourth-growth
Plateau of maturity: 4–15 years

VINTAGES

1997—An impeccably run property, Ferrand Lartigue is one of the few 1997s that I
• was able to taste only once. It seemed to possess an excessive amount of new
85– oak for its delicate constitution. There is good extraction, cherry, strawberry,
86 and cassis fruit, copious evidence of *pain grillé*, medium body, and dry tannin
in the finish. Interestingly, the perfectionist proprietor picked grape by grape
(rather than bunch by bunch) to try to produce the finest wine possible. While
not as successful at such recent vintages as 1995 and 1996, the 1997 is
unquestionably a good wine that is overwhelmed by its wood at present. It
should drink well for 5–7 years. Last tasted, 3/98.

1996—A beautifully made offering from this tiny estate, the 1996 boasts a saturated
•   ruby/purple color, lavish quantities of toasty new oak, and enticing charcoal/
90–   smoky characteristics. The wine is well structured and rich, with layers of
91   jammy black cherry fruit intertwined with chocolate and cassis. In spite of
       what is a high tannin level for Ferrand Lartigue, the wine possesses both
       sweetness and accessibility. Once again this small estate has turned out one
       of the sleeper wines of the vintage. Anticipated maturity: 2000–2010. Last
       tasted 3/98.
1995—A sexy, open-knit wine, the 1995 Ferrand Lartigue exhibits a dark ruby/
•   purple color, a jammy, candied fruit and toasty-scented nose, ripe, velvety-
89   textured, complex, generous black cherry and cassis flavors, and low acidity.
       This medium-bodied, already delicious wine is ideal for drinking now and
       over the next decade. A sleeper of the vintage. Last tasted, 11/97.
1994—A powerful, medium- to full-bodied wine with a deep ruby/purple color, and
•   more noticeable size and weight, the fragrant (red and black fruits, smoke,
89+   and toast) 1994 is a smoothly textured, silky St.-Emilion for drinking during
       its first decade of life. This is a very sexy wine. Last tasted, 1/97.
1993—This elegant, complex wine offers a dark ruby/purple color as well as
•   sweet, toasty, smoky aromas coupled with ripe black currant and cherry fruit.
88   Medium bodied, with excellent purity and ripeness, this stylish, silky-
       textured wine can be drunk now and over the next 5–7 years. Last tasted,
       1/97.

FIGEAC   EXCELLENT

Classification: St.-Emilion Premier Grand Cru Classé B
Location of vineyards: St.-Emilion, on the gravel plateau
Owner: Thierry Manoncourt
Address: 33330 St.-Emilion
Telephone: 33 5 57 24 72 26; telefax: 33 5 57 74 45 74
Visits: By appointment only

VINEYARDS (red)
Surface area: 98.8 acres
Average age of vines: 35 years
Blend: 35% Cabernet Sauvignon, 35% Cabernet Franc, 30% Merlot
Density of plantation: 6,000 vines per hectare
Total average annual production: 18,500 cases

GRAND VIN (red)
Brand name: Figeac
Appellation: St.-Emilion
Mean annual production: 18,500 cases
Upbringing: 14–18 months in oak casks.

SECOND WINE
Brand name: La Grangeneuve de Figeac

Evaluation of present classification: The quality equivalent of a Médoc second-growth
Plateau of maturity: 3–15 years following the vintage

This moderately large property of just over 98 acres sits on the gravel plateau diagonally across the road from Cheval Blanc. (It once was even larger, including land holdings that are now part of Cheval Blanc.) Many observers have long felt Figeac produced St.-Emilion's second-best wine. Its proprietor, Thierry Manoncourt, believes it to be the finest wine of the appellation and unashamedly shares these feelings with all visitors. The fact that the wine from what is now Cheval Blanc's vineyard used to be sold as Vin de Figeac only seems to strengthen his case. Since the emergence of Ausone with the 1976 vintage and the heightened consumer awareness of the excellence of other St.-Emilions, Figeac has had to contend with increased competition.

The aristocratic-looking and amiable Thierry Manoncourt makes Figeac in a very popular style. In top vintages the wine is much closer in style and quality to its fabulously expensive neighbor Cheval Blanc than the price difference would seemingly suggest. Usually ruby colored, richly fruity, with a distinctive perfume of menthol, herbs, cedar, and black fruits, the precociously supple and charming Figeac tends to show well young and mature quickly, despite the fact that it has the highest percentage of tannic and astringent Cabernet Sauvignon used in any major St.-Emilion. Most recent vintages (even those admirably concentrated) have tended to be fully ready for imbibing by the time they were 5 or 6 years old. Only the finest years of Figeac had the ability to last well in the bottle for 15 or more years. This shortcoming has not gone unnoticed.

Figeac's critics claim the wine could be profound, perhaps the greatest wine of the appellation, if the vineyard were harvested later and the maceration stage extended beyond its surprisingly short period. One of Libourne's most talented oenologists once told me that if he were making the wine, Figeac could be superior to Cheval Blanc.

Figeac has had a good record in off vintages. The 1977, 1974, and 1968, while hardly inspirational wines, were considerably better than most of their peers. I often have difficulty judging Figeac when it is less than 1 year old. At this infant stage the wine frequently tastes thin, stalky, and overtly vegetal, only to fill out and put on weight in its second year in the cask. Perhaps the high percentages of Cabernet Sauvignon and Cabernet Franc from the vineyard's gravel-based soil account for this peculiar characteristic.

Figeac is generally priced at the high level of the best Médoc second-growths, but the price seems fair and realistic given the quality of wines produced.

Visitors to St.-Emilion would be remiss in not making an appointment to visit Monsieur Manoncourt at his château. Be prepared for a beautiful country estate with enormous, tastefully done underground cellars and a proprietor who fervently believes that Figeac should be spoken of not in the same breath as Cheval Blanc and Ausone, but before them!

VINTAGES

1997—A light medium ruby color is worrisome, but this estate generally aims for an
  •   elegant, understated style of wine. Already easy to drink, the 1997 Figeac is
81–   remarkably evolved and mature at 6 months of age! A peppery, herbaceous,
85   red currant nose is pretty but not intense. In the mouth, this light-bodied
      wine is soft and round, with low acidity. It displays obvious charm, but no
      real depth or intensity. I would opt for drinking it over its first 5–6 years of
      life. Last tasted, 3/98.

1996—This intriguing wine possesses 90-point aromatics and 75-point flavors. I love
  •   a great Figeac (like the 1990 and 1982), but too often this wine comes across
83–   as anorexic. The knockout nose of tobacco, fruitcake, Asian spices, and
86   incense is captivating. However, once the wine hits the palate it is angular,
      lean, and light bodied, without enough fruit and flesh to cover its structure. If
      it deepens and puts on weight, my score should rise significantly, but the
      astringent tannin and empty mid-palate are worrisome. Anticipated maturity:
      2000–2008. Last tasted, 3/98.

1995—The fiftieth anniversary release of the proprietors, the Manoncourt family, the
  •   1995 Figeac is a gorgeously complex, dark ruby–colored wine that is all
89   delicacy and complexity. The multi-dimensional, alluring, smoky, toasty,
      Asian spice, menthol, and cherry nose is followed by soft, round, rich, kirsch-
      like flavors intermixed with black currants, herbs, and weedy tobacco. While
      it is less impressive in the mouth, the nose is outstanding. This is a soft,
      forward style of Figeac that can be drunk young or cellared. Anticipated
      maturity: Now–2010. Last tasted, 11/97.

1994—The 1994's medium dark ruby color is followed by a nose of green pepper, olive,
  •   and black currant scents. The herbaceousness may develop a more cedary char-
84?   acter with 3–4 years of cellaring. Although too tannic, the wine is medium bod-
      ied, with ripe, sweet fruit, good purity, and a mid-weight feel in the mouth.
      Readers who have a fondness for austere wines will be more enchanted with this
      offering than I was. Anticipated maturity: 2000–2010. Last tasted, 1/97.

1993—Dark ruby colored, with a vegetal, green pepper–scented nose, this lean,
  •   tough-textured wine offers sweet fruit on entry, then dries out, revealing
79   severe tannin in its attenuated, light-bodied finish. Is this the wine of choice
      to accompany vegetable terrines? Drink it over the next 5–6 years. Last
      tasted, 1/97.

1990—The 1990 is a great Figeac, potentially a richer, more complete and complex
  •   wine than the 1982. The 1990 exhibits a saturated dark purple color (some-
  94   what atypical for Figeac) and a gorgeous nose of olives, fruitcake, jammy
        black fruits, minerals, and licorice. Medium to full bodied, with gobs of
        glycerin-imbued, sweet, jammy fruit, this wine is nicely buttressed by moder-
        ate tannin and adequate acidity. Fleshy and rich, as well as elegant and
        complex, it is approachable because of the wine's sweet fruit, but it promises
        even more pleasure with 2–4 more years of bottle age; it will last for 20 years.
        I predict the 1990 Figeac will have one of the most exotic and compelling
        aromatic profiles of the 1990s. It is a terrific wine! Last tasted, 11/96.

1989—The 1989 is an under-nourished, tough-textured, lean, herbaceous wine with
  •   a medium ruby color, little charm, and an absence of concentration and
  83   intensity. Given the high percentage of Cabernet Franc and Cabernet Sauvi-
        gnon in the blend, it is not surprising that the wine reveals a pronounced
        green, vegetal character, but the lack of intensity and flavor was even more
        pronounced than I remember. Last tasted, 11/96.

1988—Figeac's 1988 offers a moderate ruby color, high tannins, and a tart, lean,
  •   austere, overtly herbaceous character. The wine is light, with a surprisingly
  83   short finish. Anticipated maturity: Now–2000. Last tasted, 1/93.

1986—I over-rated this wine in its youth, believing that more fat and ripeness would
  •   emerge with aging. The wine has continued to possess an earthy, minty/
  87   herbaceous bouquet intermingled with scents of new oak and black fruits.
        The tannin is still present, but the wine has not fleshed out in the mid-palate
        and is somewhat austere, with noticeably hard tannin in the finish. This wine,
        which was delicious young, has continued to be a tasty, very good to excellent
        example of Figeac, but it has not turned out to be as outstanding as I initially
        predicted. Anticipated maturity: Now–2006. Last tasted, 11/97.

1985—Dark ruby/garnet colored, with some amber at the edge, this smoky, cedary,
  •   herbaceous wine reveals ripe fruit and obvious new oak. This 1985 has been
  86   mature for a number of years, and given its softness and amber/orange rim, it
        needs to be drunk over the next 5–6 years. The wine is medium bodied, soft,
        not terribly concentrated, but elegant and pleasant. Anticipated maturity:
        Now–2002. Last tasted, 11/96.

1983—Fully mature, this wine reveals an herbal, licorice, smoky, jammy, berry nose,
  •   smooth, fruitcake-like flavors, velvety tannin, and low acidity. Some alcohol
  87   is noticeable in the atypically hot finish. The wine is at the end of its plateau
        of maturity and is best drunk over the next several years before the fruit fades
        and the alcohol becomes more noticeable. Anticipated maturity: Now. Last
        tasted, 11/96.

1982—A marvelous example of Figeac, the 1982 is among the finest wine made at
  •   this estate. (I expect the 1990 to be a noteworthy rival.) The 1982 has been
  93   drinking deliciously for the last 4–5 years. Never a blockbuster, heavyweight
        wine, it exhibits exceptional perfume and complexity. The intense nose of
        berry fruit, Asian spices, and herbs is provocative. On the palate, this
        medium-bodied wine reveals no hard edges, wonderful ripeness, a silky

smooth texture, and that tell-tale Figeac olive, black currant, and vanillin-like fruitiness. It is hard to predict how long a wine such as this will last. It is clearly at its plateau of maturity and should keep for another 15 years. Last tasted, 9/95.

1981— Not terribly impressive, either from the cask or in the bottle, the 1981 Figeac
•   tastes like a rather dull, commercial sort of wine. It is herbaceous, very soft,
82   velvety, and medium bodied, with light tannins and a low acidity that points to a rapid maturation. Anticipated maturity: Now. Last tasted, 3/88.

1979— Now mature and fully ready to drink, the 1979 Figeac has a moderately
•   intense bouquet of soft, spicy, cedary fruit, adequate but unexceptional rich-
83   ness and concentration, medium body, and a soft finish, with no tannins present. Certainly good but, for Figeac's class and price, a bit disappointing. Anticipated maturity: Now–may be in decline. Last tasted, 2/84.

1978— Early in its life, the 1978 Figeac seemed very fruity, soft, rather straightfor-
•   ward, and destined to be drunk young. The evolution in the bottle has been
85   marked by a deepening of flavor, a more pronounced richness, and the emergence of more body. At present this wine is more impressive, but it is still a lightweight, fully mature Figeac that lacks concentration. Anticipated maturity: Now. Last tasted, 3/91.

1977— One of the few successes in this poor vintage, somehow Figeac has managed
•   to produce a fruity, soft, and velvety wine, with good body and adequate
75   length. Anticipated maturity: Now–probably in serious decline. Last tasted, 10/84.

1976— One of the top successes of the vintage, the 1976 Figeac was consistently
•   impressive in tastings. A big, deep, cedary, ripe fruity bouquet shows good
86   complexity. On the palate, this lush, rich, full-bodied wine avoids the soupy softness and diluted character of many wines produced in 1976. Round, concentrated, generous, and fully mature, this was a lovely wine from the 1976 vintage. Anticipated maturity: Now–probably in serious decline. Last tasted, 6/83.

1975— The advanced color suggests a 30–40-year-old wine. However, the 1975
•   Figeac possesses a knockout bouquet of cedar, ripe, jammy, cherry and cur-
87   ranty fruit, Asian spices, and herbal tea. The superb nose is followed by a wine that is beginning to dry out, with the tea component becoming more noticeable and the tannin beginning to have the upper hand on the wine's fruit. There are ripe cherry/herb/coffee–like flavors, but this wine may be at the end of its useful plateau of drinkability. Contradicting these observations, the 1975 held up for 2 days in a decanter before fading. Last tasted, 12/95.

1971— I had always thought this wine was lacking richness and depth and therefore
•   was disappointing in a vintage that was generally quite good for the right
84   bank communes of St.-Emilion and Pomerol. But in 1984 I saw two examples of the 1971 Figeac that were ripe, roasted, deep, and deliciously fruity, making me wonder about the abnormal degree of bottle variation. Anticipated maturity: Now–probably in serious decline. Last tasted, 12/84.

1970—This wine has been fully mature for at least a decade, but it continues to
•   exhibit an herb-, mineral-, plum-scented bouquet, with ripe, lush, expansive
90   flavors that appear to have put on a bit of weight and intensity since the
mid-1980s. The tannins have completely melted away, and the overall impression is of a round, generously endowed, silky-textured wine. I would opt for
drinking it over the next 3–5 years, but I have been wrong so many times in
the past about the aging potential of Figeac, this wine may last longer.
Anticipated maturity: Now. Last tasted, 1/91.

1966—A respectable effort from Figeac, nicely made, fruity, fragrant, with scents of
•   ripe fruit and cedar wood, this wine was fully mature when last tasted yet has
85   the stuffing and balance to age well. Not as big or as full bodied as either the
1964 or 1970, the 1966 is elegant and attractive. Anticipated maturity: Now.
Last tasted, 1/82.

1964—After having gone through numerous regular-size bottles and a case of mag-
•   nums, I can unequivocally say this is one of the two or three greatest Figeacs
94   I have ever tasted. It has drunk fabulously well since the early seventies and
is the type of wine that offers persuasive evidence that Figeac has one of the
broadest windows of drinkability of any Bordeaux wine. The wine is still a
great example of the 1964 vintage—opulent, with an intense, deep, rich,
fruitiness, a velvety texture, and a sensational bouquet of cedar, chestnuts,
plums, herbs, and smoke. Extremely smooth and ripe, it continues to defy the
laws of aging. Anticipated maturity: Now. Last tasted, 10/94.

1962—Still enjoyable, but beginning to lose its fruit and to brown significantly, the
•   1962 Figeac, a rather lightweight wine from this estate, should be drunk up.
80   Anticipated maturity: Now–probably in serious decline. Last tasted, 7/80.

1961—Several recent bottles of this wine were showing signs of cracking up and
•   losing their fruit. However, I had this wine out of magnum from a cold cellar
94?   stateside and was blown away by its extraordinary quality, proving the saying
about old Bordeaux wines: "There are no great wines . . . only great bottles."
From a pristinely stored magnum, the wine revealed a dark garnet color, with
moderate rust at the edge. Its huge, perfumed nose of fruitcake, cedar, jammy
plums, and other black fruits was followed by an opulently textured, luscious,
rich Figeac with sweet tannin in the finish. This particular bottle was fully
mature but capable of lasting another decade. Last tasted, 7/97.

ANCIENT VINTAGES

The 1959 (rated 91 in 1990) has not been retasted since the last edition of
this book, but I suspect well-stored bottles would still be impressive. It was a
powerful, rich, roasted Figeac that typified the torrid weather conditions of
the 1959 growing season. The 1955 (95 points; last tasted 10/94) is one of
those brilliant, unknown great wines of the century that no doubt appears
from time to time at auction and is undoubtedly sold for a song given the fact
that it has received so little press. From a château that tends to produce
quickly maturing wines, this offering is more backward than the fully mature

1964 and even richer than the 1982 and 1990 (at least as they appear today). The 1955 offers an extraordinary fragrance of ripe plums, cassis, mint, herbs, smoke, and spices. Dense and concentrated for a Figeac, with some tannin yet to melt away, this wine is a candidate for a half century of aging. Purchasing the 1953 (93 points; last tasted 10/94) can be a risky business if the bottle has not been stored impeccably. At its best, this wine exhibits a huge nose of smoky, earthy, herbal, mineral, fruity, and menthol scents, soft, velvety, medium-bodied flavors, no noticeable tannin, and heady alcohol in the finish. It has been fully mature for at least 2 decades, so it is unlikely to get any better. The 1950 (88 points; last tasted 12/96) is another fine wine from this under-rated vintage, which produced some very fine St.-Emilions and splendid Pomerols. The wine revealed a garnet color, with considerable orange/amber at the edge. The nose offered up intense smoky barbecue spice, cedar, and dried fruit aromas, which were followed by a medium-bodied, soft, round, supple-textured wine that had obviously been fully mature for a decade or more.

The splendid 1949 (94 points; last tasted 1/96) is one of the greatest Figeacs I have ever tasted. This wine possessed a cigar box/fruitcake aromatic profile, gorgeously rich, seamless flavors that flowed across the palate with no heaviness, yet extraordinary sweetness of fruit and plenty of glycerin. It is a glorious Figeac that I would love to encounter in large formats such as magnums! The 1947 (70 points; last tasted 11/96) revealed an old, dried fruit, vegetal nose that was in keeping with its amber, rusty, ancient-looking color. In the mouth, there was some dusty tannin, spiky alcohol, and an absence of any real flesh or fruit. It was disappointing for a wine from my birth year.

LA FLEUR

Classification: St.-Emilion Grand Cru
Location of vineyards: On a hill to the north of St.-Emilion
Owner: Madame Lacoste (owner of Pétrus)
Address: 33330 St.-Emilion
Mailing address: c/o Ets Jean-Pierre Moueix, 54, quai du Priourat,
B.P. 129, 3302 Libourne
Telephone: 33 5 57 51 78 96; telefax: 33 5 57 51 79 79
Visits: By appointment and for professionals of the wine trade only
Contact: Frédéric Lospied

VINEYARDS (red)
Surface area: 22 acres
Average age of vines: 20 years
Blend: 90% Merlot, 10% Cabernet Franc

Density of plantation: 5,500–6,000 vines per hectare
Average yields (over the last 5 years): 50 hectoliters per hectare
Total average annual production: 2,000 cases

GRAND VIN (red)
Brand name: Château La Fleur
Appellation: St.-Emilion Grand Cru
Mean annual production: 2,000 cases
Upbringing: Fermentations last approximately 18 days in
non-temperature-controlled concrete vats. Wines undergo malolactics in
vats and are transferred to oak casks, 20% of which are new, for 18
months aging. They are racked every 3 months from barrel to barrel,
fined, but remain unfiltered.

SECOND WINE
None produced.

Evaluation of present classification: The quality equivalent of a Médoc
Cru Bourgeois
Plateau of maturity: 2–8 years following the vintage

Christian Moueix, the co-proprietor of Château Pétrus, also runs this small
estate in St.-Emilion. For years the wines never exhibited a great deal of
character but were, rather, straightforward, soft, light, and easygoing. In the
mid-nineties I detected more fruit and depth, thus much more charm and
appeal. The wines are vinified and distributed by the firm of Jean-Pierre
Moueix. As a general rule, most vintages of La Fleur should be drunk in the
first 7–8 years after the vintage, as the wines rarely have exhibited the
stuffing necessary for extended cellaring.

VINTAGES

1997—A charming, richly fruity, up-front claret with no hard edges, La Fleur's 1997
 • 　　offers bing cherry fruit intermixed with herbs and spice. Already velvety
85– 　　textured, evolved, and ready to be consumed, it can be drunk from its release
86 　　until 2006.

1996—This soft, elegant, pleasant wine displays attractive berry fruit and currant
 • 　　and cherry flavors presented in an easygoing, drinkable, light-bodied, soft
84– 　　style. Although somewhat commercial, this is a good effort in what was a
85 　　tricky vintage in St.-Emilion. Anticipated maturity: Now–2004. Last tasted,
　　3/98.

1995—Consumers and restaurants looking for soft, seductive, richly fruity Bordeaux
 • 　　wines that are not priced like Tiffany jewelry should check out this seductive,
87 　　medium- to full-bodied, round, velvety-textured St.-Emilion. It is medium

deep ruby colored, with an evolved, lovely nose of jammy black cherries, strawberries, and spice. The supple palate is all finesse, fruit, and succulence. Drink this delicious 1995 La Fleur now and over the next 7–8 years. A sleeper. Last tasted, 11/97.

1994—A well-made wine in a vintage that favored the right bank more than the
• Médoc, La Fleur's 1994 exhibits a medium deep ruby color as well as attrac-
86 tive berry fruit intermixed with vanillin and spice. On the attack, the wine offers medium-bodied, concentrated flavors that are straightforward, pleasant, and pure, without any pretentiousness. This tasty, almost Burgundian-styled St.-Emilion should drink well during its first 5–8 years of life. Last tasted, 11/97.

1993—This estate has been producing better wines recently, so it is not surprising
• that the deliciously opulent 1992 has been followed by a more tannic and
86? structured, but still concentrated and promising 1993. The wine may possess too much tannin, but there is good depth and ripeness. After fining, it may be more approachable and supple. Last tasted, 11/94.

1992—This wine has turned out far better than I would have predicted. There is no
• need to defer your gratification with this plump, succulent, fat and juicy wine.
86 Bursting with jammy fruit and toasty oak, it is a lush, in-your-face claret that should drink well for 4–6 years. Last tasted, 11/94.

1990—The 1990 offers a decadent nose of sweet vanillin oak, jammy berry fruit, and
• flowers. It is all silky fruit, with a fat, chewy texture and soft tannins. Drink
86 it over the next 5–7 years. Not complex, but it is very delicious. Last tasted, 1/93.

FONPLÉGADE   GOOD

Classification: St.-Emilion Grand Cru Classé
Location of vineyards: St.-Emilion, southern slopes
Owner: Armand Moueix
Address: 33330 St.-Emilion
Mailing address: Same as above
Telephone: 33 5 57 74 43 11; telefax: 33 5 57 74 44 67
Visits: Preferably by appointment, every day except Tuesdays and Wednesdays, between 10 A.M. and 6 P.M.
Contact: Sébastien Nugues

VINEYARDS (red)
Surface area: 44.5 acres
Average age of vines: 35 years
Blend: 60% Merlot, 35% Cabernet Franc, 5% Cabernet Sauvignon
Density of plantation: 5,400 vines per hectare
Average yields (over the last 5 years): 50 hectoliters per hectare
Total average annual production: 990 hectoliters

GRAND VIN (red)
Brand name: Château Fonplégade
Appellation: St.-Emilion Grand Cru Classé
Mean annual production: 600 hectoliters
Upbringing: Fermentations last approximately 3 weeks, with half the
yield in stainless-steel tanks and half in concrete vats. Wines are
transferred to oak barrels (renewed by a third at each vintage) for 18
months aging. They are fined but remain unfiltered.

SECOND WINE
Brand name: Château Côtes des Trois Moulins
Average annual production: 390 hectoliters

Evaluation of present classification: The quality equivalent of a Médoc
Cru Bourgeois, although certain vintages are the quality equivalent of a
Médoc fifth-growth
Plateau of maturity: 3–12 years following the vintage

Fonplégade merits greater renown than it has received. The vineyard is
beautifully situated on the southerly slopes of St.-Emilion, not far from the
famous estate of Magdelaine. The château, built in the late nineteenth century
by the proprietor—a *négociant* by the name of Boisard—is one of the more
attractive of the appellation. Since 1953 the property has been owned by the
Armand Moueix family.

The style of wine produced at Fonplégade has not changed over the years.
One of the best wines from the Armand Moueix portfolio, it is usually darkly
colored, with a great deal of rich, plummy, black cherry fruit, a dash of smoky,
toasty, new oak, and a soft, luscious texture. It is a wine that can be drunk
young, but most vintages have the potential to last for 10 or more years. In
the St.-Emilion hierarchy, Fonplégade remains an underrated wine.

VINTAGES

1995—The 1995's color is a black/ruby/blue, and there are copious quantities of
•   sweet cassis fruit in the alluring aromatics. There are layers of fruit, good
86   glycerin, high extract, some spice, and a reassuringly long finish. Anticipated
        maturity: 2001–2012. Last tasted, 11/97.

1994—The 1994 is consistently stern, charmless, and angular before bottling and no
•   better afterward. Medium ruby colored with a watery rim and a dusty, filter
75   pad–scented nose, this short, clipped, uninteresting wine lacks sufficient
        fruit and depth to age well. Last tasted, 1/97.

1993—This attractive wine does not display any of the vegetal, green pepper charac-
•   ter found in many 1993s. There is a ripe plum, sweet fruit character in
85   this medium-bodied, dark ruby–colored Fonplégade. The wine's low acid,

lushness, and accessibility should provide sound, uninspiring, but tasty drinking for another 6–7 years. Last tasted, 1/97.

1992—Medium ruby/purple colored, with a spicy nose intermingled with scents of
• jammy cherries, this medium-bodied wine offers some tannin, low acidity,
80 and average concentration. It makes for a pleasant albeit uninteresting glass of wine. Drink it over the next 5–6 years. Last tasted, 11/94.

1990—The 1990 has excellent concentration, plenty of tannin, a saturated color,
• decent acidity, and a full-bodied robustness that characterizes this well-made
88 St.-Emilion. It is the finest Fonplégade in decades. Drink it over the next 8–12 years. Last tasted, 1/93.

1989—The 1989 is a generously fruity, alcoholic wine that should last for up to a
• decade. But it lacks the extra dimension of concentration and complexity the
85 top wines of the appellation achieved in this vintage. The wine is round, supple, and already a delight to drink. Anticipated maturity: Now–2002. Last tasted, 1/93.

FONROQUE   GOOD

Classification: St.-Emilion Grand Cru Classé
Location of vineyards: On the western slope of the hill, "Lieu-dit Cadet"
Owner: G.F.A. Château Fonroque
Address: 33330 St.-Emilion
Mailing address: c/o Ets Jean-Pierre Moueix, 54, quai du Priourat,
B.P. 129, 33502 Libourne
Telephone: 33 5 57 51 78 96; telefax: 33 5 57 51 79 79
Visits: By appointment and for professionals of the wine trade only
Contact: Frédéric Lospied

VINEYARDS (red)
Surface area: 45 acres
Average age of vines: 35 years
Blend: 70% Merlot, 30% Cabernet Franc
Density of plantation: 5,500–6,000 vines per hectare
Average yields (over the last 5 years): 45 hectoliters per hectare
Total average annual production: 6,500 cases

GRAND VIN (red)
Brand name: Château Fonroque
Appellation: St.-Emilion Grand Cru Classé
Mean annual production: 6,500 cases
Upbringing: Fermentations last about 18 days in temperature-controlled concrete tanks. Wines undergo malolactics in vats and are transferred to oak barrels, 25% of which are new, for 18 months aging. They are racked every 3 months from barrel to barrel, fined with egg whites, and bottled unfiltered.

SECOND WINE
None produced.

Evaluation of present classification: The quality equivalent of a Médoc
Cru Bourgeois
Plateau of maturity: 4–12 years following the vintage

Fonroque is situated in an isolated location north and west of St.-Emilion.
The vineyard is owned by the highly respected Libourne firm of Jean-Pierre
Moueix and run by Christian Moueix. While the Moueix name is more commonly identified with such famous estates of St.-Emilion and Pomerol as
Pétrus, Trotanoy, and Magdelaine, the wine of Fonroque usually represents
an excellent value and an interesting and distinctive style that is always
vinified properly.

In style it tends to be of the robust, rich, tannic, medium-bodied school of
St.-Emilions. It can take aging quite well and in good vintages actually needs
cellaring of at least 2–3 years before being consumed.

VINTAGES

1997—This medium ruby–colored wine is a rustic, animal, earthy style of St.-
  •   Emilion. It displays pure cherry fruit, medium body, moderate tannin, and a
84– so-so finish. A bit too austere and probably controversial, it is typical of many
86+ wines from this vineyard. Anticipated maturity: 2001–2009. Last tasted,
        3/98.

1996—Dark ruby colored, with earth, black cherry, tar, and weedy notes, this me-
  •   dium-bodied, elegant, moderately endowed wine reveals a dustiness to its
85– texture and a spicy, clean finish. There is sweet fruit on the attack, and the
86   tannin is unobtrusive, so I expect this wine to develop quickly and last for
        10–12 years. Last tasted, 3/98.

1995—This dark ruby–colored, spicy, medium- to full-bodied wine exhibits a firm
  •   but promising nose of iron, earth, jammy kirsch, and currant fruit, excellent
87   richness, a distinctive earth/truffle component throughout its flavors, and
        moderate tannin in the solid finish. Muscular but fleshy, this is a fine effort
        from Fonroque. Anticipated maturity: 2000–2012. Last tasted, 11/97.

1992—From cask, I thought Fonroque produced an excellent wine in 1992, with a
  •   deep ruby color, a big, spicy, earthy, meaty, roasted nose, and ripe, medium-
74? bodied flavors. Now that the wine has been bottled, it is savagely tannic,
        already devoid of fruit, and a sure bet to dry out over the next 3–4 years. A
        charmless wine, it is all muscle and no brains. Pass it by. Last tasted, 11/94.

1990—The 1990 is a big, chewy, sweet, opulent St.-Emilion with good body and
  •   intensity as well as a deep mouth-feel. There are gobs of fruit, plenty of spices
88   and herbs, and a nice touch of sweet vanillin from the new oak. Drink it over
        the next 10 years. It is the finest Fonroque in decades. Last tasted, 1/93.

1989—The 1989 is excellent, exhibiting the size, richness, and heady alcohol con-
  •   tent of the vintage, as well as an opulent, fleshy texture. This larger-scaled
 86   Fonroque should make delicious drinking for the next 5–9 years. Anticipated
         maturity: Now–2000. Last tasted, 4/91.
1988—The 1988 displays underlying ripe fruit, spicy new oak, good acidity, and
  •   some aggressive tannins in the finish. It is a pleasant but an essentially
 83   undistinguished effort. Anticipated maturity: Now–2000. Last tasted, 4/91.
1983—A typical Fonroque, broodingly dark with a high (but soft) tannin content,
  •   this wine has layers of ripe fruit and is medium bodied. Anticipated maturity:
 85   Now. Last tasted, 3/88.
1982—The 1982 Fonroque is made in an open-knit style, with an intensely fruity,
  •   spicy, plummy fruitiness. This full-bodied wine has a dark ruby color, with
 85   some amber, a velvety texture, and a soft, generous finish. It is big, plump,
         and decadently fruity with plenty of ripe tannins. It should be drunk over the
         next several years. Anticipated maturity: Now. Last tasted, 1/90.

FRANC-MAYNE   GOOD

Classification: St.-Emilion Grand Cru Classé
Location of vineyards: St.-Emilion
Owner: Georgy Fourcroy and others
Address: 33330 St.-Emilion
Mailing address: Same as above
Telephone: 33 5 57 24 62 61; telefax: 33 5 57 24 68 25
Visits: By appointment only
Contact: Lise Bessou

VINEYARDS (red)
Surface area: 17.3 acres
Average age of vines: 30–35 years
Blend: 90% Merlot, 10% Cabernet Franc
Density of plantation: 6,500 vines per hectare
Average yields (over the last 5 years): 50 hectoliters per hectare until
1995 and 43 hectoliters per hectare since 1996
Total average annual production: 40,000 bottles

GRAND VIN (red)
Brand name: Château Franc-Mayne
Appellation: St.-Emilion Grand Cru Classé
Mean annual production: 30,000 bottles
Upbringing: Fermentations and macerations last approximately 1 month
in temperature-controlled vats. Wines undergo malolactics in barrels and
are aged 15–18 months in oak barrels, 80% of which are new. They are
racked every 3 months, fined, but not filtered.

SECOND WINE
Brand name: Les Cèdres de Franc-Mayne
Average annual production: 10,000 bottles

Evaluation of present classification: The quality equivalent of a Médoc
Cru Bourgeois
Plateau of maturity: 3–8 years following the vintage

The huge insurance company AXA acquired Franc-Mayne in 1987. They very wisely hired the proprietor of Château Lynch-Bages, Jean-Michel Cazes, and his talented winemaker, Daniel Llose, to oversee the renovation of the estate and the making of the wine. In 1996 the property was sold to the Fourcroy family from Belgium.

Franc-Mayne is by far the best known of the St.-Emilion châteaux with the word "Franc" in their name. There are seventeen other châteaux with Franc as part of their name, although none produce wines of the quality level of Franc-Mayne. The vineyard is located in the northwest section of the St.-Emilion appellation, on the same hillside that runs into the appellation called the Côtes de Francs.

This has never been one of my favorite St.-Emilions, although improvements were made under the Cazes management and are expected to continue. This is a wine that requires consumption within the first 7–10 years of life.

VINTAGES

1996—A new proprietor has vastly improved the wines of Franc-Mayne, which
• previously had a tendency to be blatantly vegetal. While the 1996 possesses
84– a touch of herbs, the wine exhibits medium body and attractive ripe red and
86 black currant fruit presented in a slightly minty, forward, lush style. This
wine should be ready to drink in several years and last for a decade. Last
tasted, 11/97.

1993—Franc-Mayne always possesses an impressively saturated dark ruby/purple
• color, but the 1993's blatantly herbaceous, vegetal nose and hollow flavors
76 dominated by tannin, wood, and structure present a problem. This wine needs
more fruit, glycerin, and extract. It will require drinking over the near term,
as it will dry out quickly. Last tasted, 11/94.

1992—This dark ruby–colored 1992 reveals a pronounced herbal, vegetal compo-
• nent to its bouquet, light to medium body, hollow, shallow flavors, and exces-
76 sive tannin in the finish. This is not my style. Last tasted, 11/94.

1991—The 1991's aggressive, herbaceous nose reveals a lack of fruit and too much
• greenness. Some diluted, soft fruit flavors can be found, but this is a thin,
73 undistinguished effort. Last tasted, 1/94.

1990—Significantly richer than the top-notch 1989, the low-acid 1990 exhibits
   •   sensational ripeness and depth, a chewy, black cherry fruitiness, a viscous
   89   texture, and a dazzling finish. This is an explosively rich wine that might
        merit a higher rating in a few years. Anticipated maturity: Now–2007. Last
        tasted, 1/93.

1989—The purple-colored 1989 is a spicy, jammy-scented wine with oodles of ripe
   •   cassis fruit, a soft yet expansive texture, low acidity, and high alcohol in the
   87   finish. This decadent mouthful of juicy, succulent St.-Emilion should be
        drunk in its first 5–7 years of life. Anticipated maturity: Now–2000. Last
        tasted, 1/93.

1988—An attractive, spicy, intensely herbaceous nose is followed by a wine that is
   •   relatively hollow, attenuated, and short in the finish. The color is sound, but
   79   the overall impression is uninspiring. Anticipated maturity: Now–may be in
        decline. Last tasted, 4/91.

1986—The 1986 Franc-Mayne is a fruity, tasty, plummy St.-Emilion with an absence
   •   of complexity, yet satisfying flavors and immediate appeal. Anticipated matu-
   79   rity: Now–may be in decline. Last tasted, 3/89.

LA GAFFELIÈRE   VERY GOOD

Classification: St.-Emilion Premier Grand Cru Classé B
Location of vineyards: St.-Emilion, between the village and the train
station
Owner: Léo de Malet-Roquefort
Address: Château La Gaffelière, 33330 St.-Emilion
Mailing address: Same as above
Telephone: 33 5 57 24 72 15; telefax: 33 5 57 24 65 24
Visits: By appointment, every day, between 8 A.M. and noon, and 2 P.M.
and 6 P.M.
Contact: Eric Degliane or Jean-Marie Galeri

VINEYARDS (red)
Surface area: 54.3 acres
Average age of vines: 40 years
Blend: 65% Merlot, 30% Cabernet Franc, 5% Cabernet Sauvignon
Density of plantation: 5,800–6,600 vines per hectare
Average yields (over the last 5 years): 43 hectoliters per hectare
Total average annual production: 10,000 cases

GRAND VIN (red)
Brand name: Château La Gaffelière
Appellation: St.-Emilion Grand Cru Classé
Mean annual production: 41 hectoliters

Upbringing: Fermentations and macerations last 15–21 days in temperature-controlled stainless-steel tanks. Fifty percent of the yield undergoes malolactics in barrels, the rest remaining in vats until completion of this process. Wines are transferred to oak barrels (50% new and 50% 1 vintage old) for 16–18 months aging. They are racked every 4 months, fined with egg whites, and lightly filtered.

SECOND WINE
Brand name: Clos la Gaffelière
Average annual production: 5,000 bottles

Evaluation of present classification: Since 1985 La Gaffelière has merited its Premier Grand Cru Classé status; prior to 1985 the wine was inconsistent
Plateau of maturity: 5–15 years following the vintage

The impressive four-story château and cellars of La Gaffelière sit opposite each other just outside the walls of St.-Emilion. Historically this is one of the most distinguished properties in all of Bordeaux because the de Malet-Roquefort family has owned the property for over four centuries. The current proprietor, Comte Léo de Malet-Roquefort, is an experienced rider and hunter —not surprising, given that members of his family, descendants of the Normans, were honored by William the Conqueror for their heroism and fighting skills at the battle of Hastings.

La Gaffelière, however, has been a perplexing wine to evaluate. The wine was well made during the sixties, and the 1970 was impressive. However, after 1970 it took 12 years for another top-notch vintage of La Gaffelière to emerge from the cellars. I am not sure why this happened, because the vineyard is well situated on limestone/clay soils, and on every one of my visits I have been impressed by the cleanliness of the winemaking facilities and the dedication of the Count and his staff. Nevertheless, there were far too few wines to get excited about prior to the mid-1980s. Since then La Gaffelière has been making wines befitting its status as one of St.-Emilion's elite Premiers Grands Crus Classés.

The style aimed for at this estate is one of elegance and tenderness. This will never be a large-scaled, tannic monster of a wine, but when the wine is at its best, it will have a degree of finesse generally unmatched by other St.-Emilions.

Comte de Malet-Roquefort is also the proprietor of the St.-Emilion property Tertre-Daugay.

VINTAGES

1997—A fine effort from La Gaffelière, this may turn out to be one of the more
elegant, finesse-styled wines of the vintage. It is light to medium bodied,
with abundant quantities of high-class oak intermixed with ripe cherry fruit,
vanillin, and spice. There is a classic attack, with nicely integrated acidity
and tannin. In the mouth, there is an impression of intensity, but with considerable refinement and finesse. This wine does reveal light tannin in the
finish and is well delineated in a vintage where many wines are round and
"loosey-goosey." Anticipated maturity: 2001–2012. Last tasted, 3/98.

86–88

1996—Clearly a product of the finesse school of winemaking, La Gaffelière's 1996
appears to be in a transitional stage of its cask evolution. The wine exhibits an
attractive dark ruby color, along with spicy vanillin, cherry, strawberry, and red
and black currant fruit. Lean but pure, delicate, and medium bodied, this is a
well-made wine with elegance, as well as enough fruit for readers with hedonistic inclinations. If this offering sweetens and expands, it will merit a score in the
upper 80s. Anticipated maturity: 2000–2012. Last tasted, 3/98.

86–88

1995—This dark ruby–colored wine offers spicy, smoky oak and soft, ripe, cherry
and red currant flavors presented in a compressed but alluring, medium-
bodied, finesse-filled format. Some tannin is present, but the overall impression is one of pretty fruit and a dry, crisp finish. Anticipated maturity: 2000–
2010. Last tasted, 11/97.

87

1994—This is an understated, elegant, pretty wine with a light to medium ruby color
and decent crisp, tart, cherry, earthy flavors, but not much substance or flesh.
Based on cask samples, I was expecting more intensity and charm, but too
much fruit, glycerin, and extract have fallen out. Anticipated maturity: Now–
2006. Last tasted, 1/97.

84

1993—This wine has turned out lean, tight, earthy, light bodied, and somewhat
emaciated on the mid-palate and finish. Its lack of fruit, glycerin, and depth
suggests a dubious future. Last tasted, 3/96.

77

1992—The 1992 La Gaffelière reveals good fruit and toasty new oak presented in a
light- to medium-bodied, soft, supple-textured format. Round and graceful, it
is ideal for drinking over the next 5–6 years. It is a success for the vintage,
particularly for its seductive, smooth, finesse style. Last tasted, 11/94.

85

1991—The 1991 La Gaffelière possesses the hollowness typical of right bank 1991s.
Yet there is a sense of elegance, some ripeness, light to medium body, and a
spicy finish. Drink it over the next 4–5 years. Last tasted, 1/94.

78

1990—The deep ruby–colored 1990 offers up abundant aromas of sweet new oak,
ripe berry fruit, and floral scents. In the mouth, this stylish, medium-weight,
beautifully proportioned wine has excellent concentration, decent acidity,
moderate tannins, and a considerable sense of elegance and richness. It is
the finest La Gaffelière since the 1970 and 1947. Anticipated maturity: Now–
2008. Last tasted, 1/93.

90

1989—The 1989 displays an enthralling bouquet of black cherries, spring flowers,
minerals, and toasty new oak. Medium to full bodied, it possesses good acidity
for the vintage, soft tannins, and a long, velvety, rich finish. This is a stylish

89

yet authoritative La Gaffelière. Anticipated maturity: Now–2010. Last tasted, 1/93.

1988—The 1988 is well made, less impressively sized if compared with the 1989,
• but still an elegant, understated, charming wine that has avoided the excesses
87 of tannin so prevalent in many 1988s. Anticipated maturity: Now–2000. Last tasted, 4/91.

1986—The 1986 La Gaffelière has the potential to be one of the property's best
• wines. It is a rich, elegantly rendered wine with a bouquet of spicy new oak,
87 cedar, and black currants. Medium to full bodied, with wonderful focus and grip, this stylish, graceful wine should drink well for the next 12–15 years. Anticipated maturity: Now–2006. Last tasted, 3/91.

1985—The 1985 has a full-intensity, spicy, herbaceous, richly fruity bouquet, me-
• dium body, soft tannins, and a supple finish. Anticipated maturity: Now. Last
86 tasted, 3/91.

1984—Very light in color, with a faint perfume of candied, berry fruit and new oak,
• the 1984 is smooth and has decent ripeness. Anticipated maturity: Now. Last
76 tasted, 3/89.

1983—In early tastings this was certainly not one of the stars of the vintage, but it is
• a good wine, clearly better than many of the below par efforts from this
84 property in the seventies. Medium dark ruby, with a fine bouquet of crushed berry fruit, this is a medium-bodied, elegant, moderately tannic wine. Antici-pated maturity: Now. Last tasted, 1/89.

1982—The 1982 is one of the few successful wines made during a disappointing
• period for La Gaffelière. It displays the subtle, elegant style this estate favors,
88 as well as an attractive, graceful bouquet of sweet, toasty oak intermingled with ripe black cherries. Medium bodied and silky smooth, with plenty of spice, this low-acid wine has no hard edges. It should be drunk over the next 4–6 years. Last tasted, 9/95.

1981—This wine has lost what little fruit it once possessed and now comes across as
• unacceptably lean, attenuated, compact, and lacking charm and fruit. Its
72 future is suspect. Last tasted, 11/90.

1979—Fully mature, this relatively shallow-looking La Gaffelière has a moderately
• intense, berry, vanilla, herbaceous bouquet, round, pleasant, light-bodied
76 flavors, and a soft, clean finish. It is unlikely to get any better. Last tasted, 11/90.

1978—Extremely herbaceous to the point of being vegetal, with soft, muddled,
• inadequately concentrated flavors, this wine is beginning its decline and
67 should be consumed now if at all. Last tasted, 11/90.

1975—This wine has turned out far better than I initially thought it would. It
• has none of the hard tannins so typical of the 1975 vintage, but, rather,
79 a soft, elegant, medium-bodied, ripe, fruity nose and flavors, comple-mented nicely by some vanillin-scented new oak. The wine displays some amber at the edge, and given its lightness and softness, it should be consumed. Anticipated maturity: Now–may be in decline. Last tasted, 11/90.

1971—In the first edition of this book I indicated that this wine was on the verge of
 •   cracking up. It is now in full decline, as the decaying, mushroom-like, woody,
68   slightly oxidized bouquet suggests. In the mouth, the wine is feeble, lacks
      concentration, and finishes with noticeable alcohol and acidity. It is past its
      prime. Last tasted, 11/90.

1970—This has always been one of the best La Gaffelières produced during the
 •   sixties and seventies. The wine is still relatively rich and elegant, with a
86   bouquet of smoky, plummy fruit. In the mouth, the wine is round, with a silky
      texture and a lush, medium-bodied finish. It has been fully mature for well
      over a decade but has lost none of its fruit or charm. Anticipated maturity:
      Now—may be in decline. Last tasted, 11/90.

1966—A straightforward sort of wine, La Gaffelière's 1966 is lean, austere, with
 •   some elegance and charm, but compact and rather one-dimensional. It is fully
78   mature. Anticipated maturity: Now—may be in decline. Last tasted, 10/78.

1964—Diffuse, shallow, awkward flavors seem to struggle with each other. The me-
 •   dicinal, bizarre bouquet suggests something went afoul during the making of
60   this wine. Last tasted, 4/80.

1961—When I last wrote about this wine, I commented that it required drinking up,
 •   but a bottle I tasted in France in 1990 had more depth and freshness. It could
85   easily have held up for another 7–8 years. Medium ruby, with some amber/
      rust color at the edge, the wine exhibits a bouquet indicative of the vintage's
      tell-tale intensity and opulence. In the mouth, the wine is ripe and full, with
      an underlying spicy, mineral-like fruitiness. The finish is long and alcoholic.
      It should be drunk up, but based on the most recent bottle I tasted, it could
      hold up to another 4–5 years of cellaring. Anticipated maturity: Now—may be
      in decline. Last tasted, 11/90.

ANCIENT VINTAGES

The two finest old vintages I have seen of La Gaffelière included a deliciously
elegant, round, very perfumed 1953 (rated 89 in 1988) and a rich, fat,
surprisingly intense, full-bodied 1947 (rated 88 and drunk when I celebrated
my fortieth birthday in 1987).

LA GOMERIE   OUTSTANDING

Classification: St.-Emilion Grand Cru
Location of vineyards: St.-Emilion
Owner: Gérard and Dominique Bécot
Address: 33330 St.-Emilion
Mailing address: Same as above
Telephone: 33 5 57 74 46 87; telefax: 33 5 57 24 66 88
Visits: By appointment only
Contact: Gérard or Dominique Bécot

VINEYARDS (red)
Surface area: 6.2 acres
Average age of vines: 35 years
Blend: 100% Merlot
Density of plantation: 5,600 vines per hectare
Average yields (over the last 5 years): 37 hectoliters per hectare
Total average annual production: 9,000 bottles

GRAND VIN (red)
Brand name: La Gomerie
Appellation: St.-Emilion Grand Cru
Mean annual production: 9,000 bottles
Upbringing: Fermentations and macerations last 25–30 days in wooden
vats. Wines are then aged in 100% new oak barrels for 20 months. They
remain unfined and unfiltered.

SECOND WINE
None produced.

Evaluation of present classification: The quality equivalent of a Médoc
second-growth

This wine is made by Gérard Bécot, the proprietor of Beau-Séjour Bécot. It is
a micro-vinification/minuscule estate producing wine made from 100% Merlot, fermented and aged in 100% new oak. Not surprisingly, wines such as
this garner enthusiastic accolades from the wine press. The difficulty of
finding the wine and its high price aside, this is an impressive, rich, creamy-
textured, blockbuster Merlot that will seduce anybody who tries it. It seems
to me that Monsieur Bécot is trying—successfully, I might add—to produce
a luxury-priced wine similar to Pomerol's Le Pin. To date, only a few vintages
have been produced, but this is an impressive wine. How well will it age?
Time will tell.

VINTAGES

1997—Tasted three separate times with identical comments, this 100% Merlot is
• an up-front, plump, sexy, flashy St.-Emilion that will provide considerable
87– hedonistic pleasure over the next 7–9 years. The dark ruby/purple color is
89+ followed by soaring aromas of toasty vanillin from new oak and nearly over-
ripe prune, plum, and kirsch-like fruit. Plush, with an opulent texture, low
acidity, and outstanding purity, this is about as seductive a 1997 as one will
find. Already delicious, it should provide immense pleasure during its first
decade of life. Last tasted, 3/98.

1996—Explosively rich, this opaque purple–colored wine possesses amazing volume
• 　　 and intensity on the palate, with extraordinary thickness and ripeness of
92– 　 cherry and kirsch liqueur–like fruit, yet no sense of heaviness. A luxuriantly
94 　　 rich, 100% Merlot from a small parcel of vines owned by the Bécot family,
　　　　 this layered super-rich, exotic wine is compelling. Full bodied, with amazing
　　　　 extract, purity, and richness, it will be a treat to follow its evolution. Antici-
　　　　 pated maturity: 2002–2016. Last tasted, 3/98.

1995—The debut vintage for La Gomerie, the 1995 Le Pin look-alike, is show-
• 　　 ing fabulously well after bottling. The color is dense ruby/purple, and the
93 　　 nose offers up exotic aromas of Asian spices, soy, coffee, and ripe berry/
　　　　 cherry fruit. This full-bodied, thick, unctuously textured wine is marvel-
　　　　 ously concentrated, with plenty of sweet, well-integrated tannin. The acidity
　　　　 is low, which only adds to the voluptuous personality of this strikingly
　　　　 rich, head-turning effort. Anticipated maturity: Now–2012. Last tasted,
　　　　 11/97.

GRACIA *　　　　　　　　　　　　　　　　　VERY GOOD SINCE 1997

Classification: St.-Emilion Grand Cru
Location of vineyards: In the northwestern part of St.-Christophe des
Bardes, on clayey and calcareous soils
Owner: Michel Gracia
Address: St.-Christophe des Bardes, 33330 St.-Emilion
Mailing address: Same as above
Telephone: 33 5 57 24 77 98; telefax: 33 5 57 74 46 72
Visits: By appointment only
Contact: Michel Gracia

VINEYARDS (red)
Surface area: 3.3 acres
Average age of vines: 30 years for the Merlot and 10 years for the
Cabernet Franc
Blend: 75% Merlot and 25% Cabernet Sauvignon
Average yields (over the last 5 years): 20 hectoliters per hectare
in 1997
Total average annual production: 3,000 bottles

GRAND VIN (red)
Brand name: Château Gracia*
Appellation: St.-Emilion
Mean annual production: 3,000 bottles
Upbringing: Fermentations and macerations last approximately 21 days
in concrete tanks. Wines undergo malolactics in new oak barrels and
should be aged 12–18 months. Michel Gracia does not filter or fine.

SECOND WINE
None produced.
* NOTE: The proprietor has not yet made up his mind about the brand name.

VINTAGES

1997—Undoubtedly a sleeper of the vintage, this wine is the creation of Michel
• Gracia, a good friend of Ausone's Alain Vauthier and Valandraud's Jean-Luc
87– Thunevin. Their influence can be seen in the quality of this wine, which
90 comes from a tiny estate in St.-Emilion. The color is opaque purple, and the
wine is concentrated, hedonistic, and luxuriously rich. The nose reveals
nearly over-ripe aromas of kirsch liqueur and sweet berry fruit. The wine hits
the palate with a gush of rich, concentrated fruit and glycerin, in addition to
a nearly unctuous texture. Exceptionally low acidity adds to the knockout
effect of this wine's juicy, succulent personality. It is already hard to resist.
Anticipated maturity: 1999–2008. Last tasted, 3/98.

GRAND-CORBIN

Classification: St.-Emilion Grand Cru
Location of vineyards: St.-Emilion, near Pomerol
Owner: Ste. Familiale Alain Giraud
Address: 5, Grand Corbin, 33330 St.-Emilion
Mailing address: Same as above
Telephone: 33 5 57 24 70 62; telefax: 33 5 57 74 47 18
Visits: By appointment only
Contact: Philippe Giraud

VINEYARDS (red)
Surface area: 32.7 acres
Average age of vines: 35 years
Blend: 68% Merlot, 27% Cabernet Franc, 5% Cabernet Sauvignon
Density of plantation: 5,500 vines per hectare
Average yields (over the last 5 years): 51 hectoliters per hectare
Total average annual production: 687 hectoliters

GRAND VIN (red)
Brand name: Château Grand Corbin
Appellation: St.-Emilion Grand Cru
Mean annual production: 615 hectoliters
Upbringing: Fermentations and macerations last 3 weeks in open

concrete vats. Wines are aged 12–14 months in oak barrels that are renewed by a third at each vintage. They are fined and filtered.

SECOND WINE
Brand name: Château Tour du Pin Franc
Average annual production: 70 hectoliters

Grand-Corbin, a well-situated property on the Pomerol/St.-Emilion border, consistently produces round, chunky, generally well-colored St.-Emilions that require drinking in their first decade. The Girauds, an ancient family originally from Pomerol, own Grand-Corbin and, like their nearby neighbor Figeac, employ a relatively high percentage of Cabernet Franc in the blend. This works well when the Cabernet ripens fully, but in years that it does not, there is a tendency for Grand-Corbin to come across as too herbaceous, even vegetal. The best recent vintages I have tasted included a promising 1996, an excellent 1985, and a soft, alcoholic, fleshy 1989 that will not make old bones but will certainly provide delicious drinking in the first 7–8 years of life.

VINTAGES

1996—A strong performance for this estate, this opaque purple–colored wine
• offers a spicy, toasty, jammy fruit nose, rich, nicely concentrated flavors,
87– medium to full body, and plenty of power and length. Good acidity allied
88 with the wine's concentration suggest this wine will age for 12–15+ years. It
is one of the most structured Grand-Corbins I have ever tasted. Last tasted,
3/97.

1993—This full-bodied, opulently styled wine exhibits good color, a plump, roasted
• herb, coffee, black cherry, Merlot-like character, plenty of juicy fruit, low
86 acidity, and heady alcohol in the finish. It is a beefy, mouth-filling St.-Emilion
for drinking during its first 7–8 years of life. Last tasted, 11/94.

GRAND-MAYNE　　　　　　　　　　　　　　　　　　**EXCELLENT**

Classification: St.-Emilion Grand Cru Classé
Location of vineyards: East of the village of St.-Emilion
Owner: Jean-Pierre Nony
Address: 1, le Grand-Mayne, 33330 St.-Emilion
Mailing address: Same as above
Telephone: 33 5 57 74 42 50; telefax: 33 5 57 24 68 34
Visits: By appointment only
Contact: Mr. or Mrs. Nony

VINEYARDS (red)
Surface area: 47.3 acres
Average age of vines: 32 years
Blend: 67% Merlot, 25% Cabernet Franc, 8% Cabernet Sauvignon
Density of plantation: 5,550 vines per hectare
Average yields (over the last 5 years): 42 hectoliters per hectare
Total average annual production: 800 hectoliters

GRAND VIN (red)
Brand name: Château Grand-Mayne
Appellation: St.-Emilion Grand Cru
Mean annual production: 85,000 bottles
Upbringing: Fermentations and macerations last 21–30 days in
temperature-controlled stainless-steel vats. Eighty percent of the yield
undergoes malolactics in new oak barrels and 20% in vats. This latter
part is then transferred to 1-year-old barrels. Bottling is done after 19–20
months, and wines undergo both fining and filtration.

SECOND WINE
Brand name: Les Plantes du Mayne
Average annual production: 20,000 bottles

Evaluation of present classification: Grand-Mayne continues to do
everything right, and it easily competes with the better of the Premiers
Grands Crus Classés of St.-Emilion; a serious candidate for elevation in
any new classification of the wines of St.-Emilion; the quality equivalent
of a Médoc third-growth
Plateau of maturity: 5–15 years following the vintage

The famed authority on the soils of Pomerol and St.-Emilion, Professor Enjalbert, has made it very clear in his lectures and other works that Grand-
Mayne possesses one of the most privileged sites in all of St.-Emilion. The
exceptionally high altitude—55 meters above sea level—and soil base,
which consists primarily of clay and limestone intermixed with iron deposits,
make this vineyard potentially one of the best of the entire appellation.
Aesthetically the magnificent vanilla ice cream–colored château has been
totally renovated and is a striking sight to behold on a bright, blue-skied day.

The wines have gone from one strength to another during the eighties, with
the brilliant Libourne oenologist Michel Rolland asserting his winemaking
philosophy. The results are some of the most opulent and richest wines now
being made in St.-Emilion. This is a wine that can be exceptionally full
bodied, with gobs of glycerin because of the superb vineyard soil and great
exposition the vineyard enjoys. Since 1975 Grand-Mayne has been fermented

in temperature-controlled stainless-steel tanks. In the mid-1980s the percentage of new oak was increased to 70%, which—to me—seems like a perfect marriage to balance out the rich, intense fruit character of this wine.

Grand-Mayne is one of the up-and-coming stars of the appellation, yet prices have remained reasonable, a fact that should be put to good use by wine consumers. If my enthusiasm for Grand-Mayne seems excessive, consider the fact that the late Baron Philippe de Rothschild, after tasting the 1955 Grand-Mayne at a restaurant in Belgium, immediately placed an order for several cases, offering to replace the Grand-Mayne with a similar number of bottles of the 1955 Mouton-Rothschild!

VINTAGES

1997—Grand-Mayne has turned in a terrific performance in the 1997 vintage. It is
• one of my favorite 1997s because of its beautiful overall balance yet for-
90– ward, generous character. The wine reveals a saturated purple color and
91 gorgeously sweet black raspberry flavors with nicely integrated tannin. Sweet oak adds definition to this medium- to full-bodied, layered, concentrated yet elegant wine. Low acidity, ripe tannin, and copious amounts of fruit and glycerin will ensure this wine offers plenty of appeal at an early age. Anticipated maturity: 2001–2012. A dazzling sleeper of the vintage. Last tasted, 3/98.

1996—I enjoyed this wine's aromatics of black raspberries, minerals, licorice, and
• vanillin. In the mouth, the wine has taken on more tannin than it revealed
87– early last spring, but it still possesses copious quantities of black fruits,
89+ medium body, and a pure, clean, rich finish. If this 1996 fleshes out, look for the rating to rise. Anticipated maturity: 2002–2015. Last tasted, 11/97.

1995—An unqualified sleeper of the vintage, the opaque purple–colored 1995
• Grand-Mayne displays a sweet, creamy, black raspberry–scented nose with
90 subtle notes of smoky, toasty oak. Both powerful and elegant, this wine exhibits layers of richness, nicely integrated acidity and tannin, and an impressive full-bodied, long finish. This offering should be drinkable early and keep for over a decade. Anticipated maturity: 2000–2013. Last tasted, 11/97.

1994—Readers may remember my reservations about the three cask samples I tasted
• of this wine that revealed a musty, cardboard component. Three different
? tastings of this wine following bottling support the fact that something has flawed the wine's aromatics. Whether or not this mustiness will dissipate with cellaring remains to be seen. All of this is lamentable given the terrific efforts that the overachieving proprietors, the Nonyes, have produced at Grand-Mayne. Last tasted, 1/97.

1993—A deep ruby color and an oaky, vanillin, herbaceous nose are followed by a
• medium-bodied, astringent, austere wine offering a musty, damp wood, wet
? dog aroma that was detectable in two separate samples. Judgment reserved. Last tasted, 1/97.

1992—Grand-Mayne's 1992 has turned out to be a very good wine for the vintage,
•   with an attractive dark ruby color, a big, spicy, black currant-and-cherry-
86   scented nose, medium body, excellent ripeness, light tannin, and a lush,
      heady, succulent finish. Drink it over the next 5–6 years. Last tasted, 11/94.

1990—The 1990 offers an impressively saturated color, along with a black cherry,
•   mineral, smoky component, with a dash of roasted herbs. Spicy, rich, long,
90   and massive in the mouth, it is full bodied, sweet, jammy, and capable of
      lasting for 12–15+ years. Last tasted, 11/96.

1989—The 1989 can be drunk now, but it will be even better after another 1–3 years
•   of cellaring. It exhibits an opaque purple color, a sweet, black raspberry,
92   mineral, and toasty oak nose, dense, medium- to full-bodied flavors that
      possess terrific purity and harmony, and a spicy, long, sweet, tannic finish.
      This beautifully made, extracted wine is an ideal candidate for drinking over
      the next 12–15 years. Last tasted, 11/96.

1988—The 1988 Grand-Mayne is a big, alcoholic, obvious wine displaying an in-
•   tense, vanillin-scented, black plum–like fruitiness and fleshy, chewy flavors.
87   Anticipated maturity: Now–2003. Last tasted, 1/93.

1987—Grand-Mayne made one of the most successful wines of this unfairly maligned
•   vintage. Surprisingly dark ruby, with a pronounced, rich cassis bouquet and
85   soft, generously endowed flavors, soft tannins, and low acidity, this is a wine
      to drink over the near term. Anticipated maturity: Now. Last tasted, 4/91.

1986—The 1986 Grand-Mayne has performed extremely well, with a full-intensity
•   bouquet of cedary, ripe fruit and spicy oak that is followed on the palate by
87   excellent depth, plenty of extract, and a long, tannic, powerful, and impres-
      sive finish. Anticipated maturity: Now–2002. Last tasted, 3/90.

1985—The 1985 has very good color, a moderately intense bouquet of spicy oak and
•   ripe fruit, medium body, well-focused, expansive flavors, and an overall ele-
86   gant feel to it. Anticipated maturity: Now. Last tasted, 3/89.

GRAND PONTET   VERY GOOD

Classification: St.-Emilion Grand Cru Classé
Location of vineyards: Next to Beau-Séjour Bécot, on the western part of
the plateau of St.-Emilion
Owner: Bécot-Pourquet family
Address: 33330 St.-Emilion
Mailing address: Same as above
Telephone: 33 5 57 74 46 87 (or 88); telefax: 33 5 57 24 66 88
Visits: By appointment only
Contact: Gérard or Dominique Bécot

VINEYARDS (red)
Surface area: 34.6 acres
Average age of vines: 35 years

Blend: 75% Merlot, 15% Cabernet Franc, 10% Cabernet Sauvignon
Density of plantation: 600 vines per hectare
Average yields (over the last 5 years): 40 hectoliters per hectare
Total average annual production: 75,000 bottles

GRAND VIN (red)
Brand name: Château Grand-Pontet
Appellation: St.-Emilion
Mean annual production: 60,000–75,000 bottles
Upbringing: Fermentations and macerations last approximately 20–28
days in temperature-controlled stainless-steel vats. Malolactics occur in
new oak barrels for 60% of the yield; 40% remains in vats and is then
transferred to 1-vintage-old barrels for 12–18 months aging. The wine
generally remains unfined and unfiltered, except if too turbid, in which
case it is subjected to a light fining.

SECOND WINE
Brand name: Le Dauphin de Grand-Pontet
Average annual production: 5,000–15,000 bottles

Evaluation of present classification: For decades this was a perennial
underachiever, but since 1988 the quality has significantly improved and
it now merits its position in St.-Emilion's classification
Plateau of maturity: Before 1988, 3–7 years following the vintage; since
1988, 6–15 years following the vintage

Grand-Pontet, owned by St.-Emilion's Bécot family, is situated next door to
their more renowned property, Château Beau-Séjour. The vineyard sits in the
highly regarded western limestone plateau of St.-Emilion. For years many of
St.-Emilion's cognoscenti have suggested that this is a property that, with
improvements and a more strict selection, could emerge as a potential candidate for elevation to Premier Grand Cru Classé status. Improvements have
indeed been made, and vintages since 1988 have been quite impressive.

It is not unlikely that this property might merit elevation to Premier Grand
Cru Classé status in the next classification of St.-Emilion.

VINTAGES

1996—Opaque ruby/purple, with lavish quantities of sweet, smoky new oak, jammy
•   black cherry fruit, and spice in the nose, this highly extracted, tannic, me-
87– dium-bodied wine possesses an international style (largely because of the
90   lavish oak treatment), but I suspect more nuances and complexity will evolve
     with bottle age. Anticipated maturity: 2003–2012. Last tasted, 11/97.

1995—Dark ruby/purple colored with a forward, evolved nose of spice, black cher-
•　　ries, and toast, this supple, round, generous, medium- to full-bodied wine
88　　possesses low acidity and some tannin in the finish. There is good delineation
　　to this plump, succulently styled wine that can be drunk now as well as over
　　the next dozen years. Last tasted, 11/97.

1994—This medium- to full-bodied wine reveals the telltale oaky veneer that is so
•　　much a part of the wines made by the Bécot family. There is also plenty of rich,
88　　low-acid fruit, as well as a chewy texture, good purity and ripeness, and glycerin
　　in the muscular yet silky finish. Drink it over the next decade. Last tasted, 1/97.

1993—Shrewd readers should check out Grand-Pontet's 1993, as I suspect it is
•　　priced at an affordable level given this vintage's low esteem. This dark ruby–
87　　colored 1993 exhibits a sweet, ripe berry–scented nose that is boldly infused
　　with smoky, toasty new oak. Low in acidity, lusty, round, and supple, it is a
　　delicious, complex, oaky style of Bordeaux. Anticipated maturity: Now–2004.
　　Last tasted, 1/97.

1992.—A heady nose with noticeable alcohol, aggressive oak (too much?), and ripe
•　　fruit is followed by a light-bodied wine with a soft, chunky personality. This
82　　fleshy, obvious style of St.-Emilion will offer an uncomplicated mouth-filling
　　glass of wine over the next 3–5 years. Last tasted, 11/94.

1990—Lusciously fruity, with tons of sweet, smoky new oak, the 1990 fairly oozes
•　　unctuous flavors from the glass. The wine has copious quantities of fruit, a
89　　silky, full-bodied feel, and an opulent, splendidly long finish. For drinking
　　over the next 6–10 years, it will provide considerable pleasure. This is a
　　sleeper of the vintage! Last tasted, 11/95.

1989—The 1989 is lighter than many wines from this vintage. Displaying some
•　　dilution in the mid-palate, it is an alcoholic, chunky, softly styled St.-Emilion.
84　　Anticipated maturity: Now. Last tasted, 1/93.

1988—The 1988 Grand-Pontet has an indifferent bouquet of new oak and some
•　　vague spicy, ripe fruit. On the palate, it is soft, woody, nicely concentrated,
82　　but one-dimensional. Drink it over the next 3–4 years. Last tasted, 1/93.

1986—The 1986 Grand-Pontet is an obvious St.-Emilion, with soft, plummy fruit, a
•　　heady, alcoholic finish, and immediate appeal. Anticipated maturity: Now–
83　　2000. Last tasted, 3/90.

1985—The 1985 is a light, simple, fruity wine without a great deal of body, but with
•　　good, straightforward appeal. Anticipated maturity: Now–may be in decline.
77　　Last tasted, 3/89.

L'HERMITAGE　　　　　　　　　　　　EXCELLENT SINCE 1997

Classification: St.-Emilion Grand Cru
Location of vineyards: Adjacent to Matras
Owner: GFA du Château Matras (the Bernard family)
Address: 33330 St.-Emilion
Mailing address: Same as above
Telephone: 33 5 57 24 72 46; telefax: 33 5 57 51 70 19

Visits: By appointment only
Contact: Véronique Gaboriaud
Surface area: 7.5 acres
Average age of vines: 45 years
Average yield: 27 hectoliters per hectare
Density of plantation: 5,500 vines per hectare
Blend: 75% Merlot, 25% Cabernet Franc
Mean annual production: 10,800 bottles
Brand name: Château L'Hermitage
Appellation: St.-Emilion Grand Cru
Production: 10,800 bottles
Upbringing: Fermentations and macerations last approximately 3 weeks
in temperature-controlled stainless-steel vats. Wines undergo malolactics
in 100% new oak barrels and are aged 18 months afterward. They are
neither fined nor filtered.

VINTAGES

1997— This is the debut vintage of this luxury cuvée made by Château Matras in
• St.-Emilion. A blend of 75% Merlot and 25% Cabernet Sauvignon, it appears
87– to be a dazzling, possibly exceptional wine from the 1997 vintage. The color
90 is opaque purple, and the nose offers sweet, pure, blackberry and jammy
cherry aromas and flavors in an opulent, nearly unctuously textured medium-
to full-bodied format. It is a seriously concentrated, beautifully etched wine,
with the wood, acidity, and tannin seamlessly integrated into the wine's silky
texture. Look for this wine to drink beautifully upon release and age well for
10–12 years. A sleeper of the vintage. Last tasted, 3/98.

LARCIS-DUCASSE   GOOD

Classification: St.-Emilion Grand Cru Classé
Location of vineyards: St.-Emilion and St.-Laurent des Combes
Owner: Jacques-Olivier Gratiot
Address: 33330 St.-Emilion
Mailing address: Same as above
Telephone: 33 5 57 24 70 84; telefax: 33 5 57 24 64 00
Visits: By appointment, on weekdays, between 9 A.M. and noon, and
2 P.M. and 5 P.M.
Contact: Brigitte Séguin

VINEYARDS (red)
Surface area: 27 acres
Average age of vines: 35 years

Blend: 65% Merlot, 25% Cabernet Franc, 10% Cabernet Sauvignon
Density of plantation: 5,000 vines per hectare
Average yields (over the last 5 years): 45 hectoliters per hectare
Total average annual production: 500 hectoliters

GRAND VIN (red)
Brand name: Château Larcis-Ducasse
Appellation: St.-Emilion Grand Cru Classé
Mean annual production: 500 hectoliters
Upbringing: Fermentations and macerations last 15 days to 6 weeks
(depending upon the vintage) in temperature-controlled concrete tanks.
Wines undergo malolactics in vats and are transferred after a first racking
to oak barrels (renewed by a third each vintage) for 18 months aging.
They are racked 2 or 3 times a year, from barrel to barrel, fined with fresh
egg whites, and filtered.

SECOND WINE
None produced.

Evaluation of present classification: The quality equivalent of a Médoc
fifth-growth
Plateau of maturity: 8–20 years following the vintage

Larcis-Ducasse sits on the *côtes* of St.-Emilion, southeast of the town, with its vineyard abutting that of Pavie. The vines, planted on calcareous clay slopes, enjoy a full southerly exposure. This wine enjoys an excellent reputation, but until the early eighties the quality was unimpressive. Prior to 1982 too many wines consistently displayed a lean, austere, skinny taste and structure, although I have fond memories of a profound 1945. Since 1982 the quality of Larcis-Ducasse has improved, but my instincts suggest this wine could be ever finer.

VINTAGES

1997—Tasted on three separate occasions, this wine was light and disjointed, with
• herb-tinged, tea-like flavors reminiscent of green Chinese tea. Medium bod-
76– ied, with some cherry fruit and dusty, earthy flavors, this was not one of the
78 most impressive wines I tasted. Anticipated maturity: 1999–2007. Last
tasted, 3/98.
1996—One of St.-Emilion's great *terroirs* continues to produce uninspiring wines.
• The 1996 Larcis-Ducasse possesses a medium ruby color followed by a
84– forward, soft, commercially pleasing cherry-, herb-, and earth-scented nose.
86 The wine is medium bodied, straightforward, and simple. Drink it over the
next 7–8 years. Last tasted, 11/97.

1995—The 1995 exhibits a dark ruby/purple color with moderate saturation. A spicy,
• ripe, richly fruity nose with hints of earth and new oak is moderately intense.
87 Some tannin, good purity, medium body, and a firm, measured, elegant style
suggest this wine should last for 12 years but be fully drinkable in 2–3. Last
tasted, 11/97.

1994—A deep saturated ruby/purple color is accompanied by sweet, ripe, cherry,
• black currant, and Asian spice aromas. This medium-bodied, elegant, pretty
87 wine possesses a velvety texture, fine concentration, and no hollowness or
hard tannin (two characteristics that plagued many 1994s). Drink this well-
made, smooth wine over the next 8–10 years. Last tasted, 1/97.

1993—Medium dark ruby colored with a pink rim, this wine offers sweet, pure,
• cherry and red currant fruit in a gently suave, subtly spicy, medium-bodied
85 format. It is an elegant, restrained, smooth-textured, tasty 1993. The low
acidity and absence of any vegetal character and astringent tannin make this
a wine to drink over the next 6–7 years. Last tasted, 1/97.

1992—The light to medium ruby color lacks depth. The vegetal, herbaceous nose
• and hard, tannic, medium-bodied, fruitless flavors give further evidence of a
76 problematic vintage for this well-placed hillside St.-Emilion vineyard. This
wine will undoubtedly drop what little fruit it possesses over the next 3–4
years. Last tasted, 11/94.

1991—The 1991 is a pleasant, soft, light-bodied, herbaceous wine meant to be
• consumed over the next 4–6 years. Last tasted, 1/94.
76

1990—The 1990 is a wine of impressive richness, with a spicy, cedary, cassis-
• scented nose, a creamy, velvety texture, and rich, full-bodied flavors. There
90 are layers of fruit supported by moderate tannins. A little more concentration
and this wine could have been monumental. Anticipated maturity: Now–
2008. Last tasted, 1/93.

1989—The 1989, while filled with tannin and structured for aging up to 30 years,
• did not seem to have quite the inner core of fruit, depth, and intensity that
86 the 1988 possessed. Full and tannic, it will not be at its best until midway
through the first decade of the next century. This is an imposingly backward
style of wine that may ultimately merit a higher score—provided the fruit
does not dry out before the tannin fades. Anticipated maturity: Now–2010.
Last tasted, 4/91.

1988—Larcis-Ducasse made an excellent wine in 1988—full bodied and rich, with
• impressive ripeness and length and at least 20 years of potential evolution.
87 This is an admirable, old-style wine that will appeal to those who have
patience. Anticipated maturity: Now–2010. Last tasted, 1/93.

1986—The 1986 displays fine ripeness, long, rich, cedary, plummy flavors, medium
• to full body, and a concentrated, supple, alcoholic finish, with some serious
85 tannins present. Anticipated maturity: Now–2002. Last tasted, 3/90.

1985—The 1985 is over-produced, lacking focus, depth, and definition. It should be
• drunk up over the next 4–5 years. Excessive crop yields have left their mark
79 on this wine. Anticipated maturity: Now. Last tasted, 3/89.

1983—When I tasted this wine after bottling it never performed well. But more
• recently the wine has thrown off the bottle shock and appears much richer
86 and fuller than I would have ever imagined. Medium dark ruby, with a slight
trace of amber at the edge, with a big, spicy, cedary, herb- and red fruit–
scented bouquet, this wine offers both complexity and character. In the mouth,
the wine is classically structured, with medium body, plenty of tannin, and very
good extract. While drinkable now, it should continue to evolve for at least
another 7–10 years. Anticipated maturity: Now–2001. Last tasted, 3/90.

1982—Inconsistent tasting notes have plagued this wine since bottling. The finest
• examples (this particular tasting was one of them) exhibit a deep color with
87 minor lightening at the edge, an herbaceous, cherry, earthy, pungent nose,
and medium- to full-bodied, concentrated flavors. Noticeable astringent tannin does not present a problem given the wine's glycerin and sweetness. The
wine will last for another decade. Last tasted, 9/95.

1981—The 1981 is too angular and lacks flesh, generosity, and fruit. This is another
• so-so wine for near-term drinking from an estate with a good reputation.
75 Anticipated maturity: Now–may be in decline. Last tasted, 6/84.

1979—Medium ruby, with a spicy, fruity aroma of moderate intensity, this Larcis-
• Ducasse has average- to above-average-intensity flavors that are plainer scaled
78 than other St.-Emilions. The wine does have some underlying firmness and
texture. Anticipated maturity: Now–may be in decline. Last tasted, 11/83.

1978—Quite mediocre, this pale-colored, lightweight wine has a bouquet suggestive
• of strawberry and cherry fruit. On the palate, there is not much to find but
72 short, shallow, watery flavors, with some tannin and dry oaky flavors in the
finish. Anticipated maturity: Now–may be in decline. Last tasted, 9/82.

LARMANDE   EXCELLENT

Classification: St.-Emilion Grand Cru Classé
Location of vineyards: St.-Emilion
Owner: Groupe La Mondiale
Address: 33330 St.-Emilion
Mailing address: Same as above
Telephone: 33 5 57 24 71 41; telefax: 33 5 57 74 42 80
Visits: By appointment only
Contact: Marc Dworkin

VINEYARDS (red)
Surface area: 61.2 acres
Average age of vines: 30 years
Blend: 65% Merlot, 30% Cabernet Franc, 5% Cabernet Sauvignon
Density of plantation: 6,000 vines per hectare
Average yields (over the last 5 years): 41.5 hectoliters per hectare
Total average annual production: 1,120 hectoliters

GRAND VIN (red)
Brand name: Château Larmande
Appellation: St.-Emilion Grand Cru
Mean annual production: 890 hectoliters
Upbringing: Fermentations last about 3 weeks in temperature-controlled
stainless-steel vats. Two-thirds of the yield undergo malolactics in new
oak barrels. The remaining third is transferred to 1-vintage-old oak
barrels after malolactics. The aging process lasts 16–18 months. Wines
are racked every 3 months, fined with fresh egg whites, but not filtered.
Assemblage is done late, just before fining.

SECOND WINE
Brand name: Le Cadet de Larmande
Average annual production: 230 hectoliters

NOTE: The Groupe La Mondiale bought the Château Pavillon Cadet in
1993. This small estate of 2.5 hectares has been added to Château
Larmande by the 1996 classification of the St.-Emilion Grand Crus.

Evaluation of present classification: The quality equivalent of a Médoc
third-growth
Plateau of maturity: 4–15 years following the vintage

I remember when I first visited Larmande in the mid-1970s at the request of
the late Martin Bamford, one of Bordeaux's most knowledgeable observers.
He had told me that this would be one of the best wines made in St.-Emilion
because of the commitment to quality evidenced by the Mèneret family.
Larmande, situated in the northern area of St.-Emilion, is named after the
historic *lieux-dit* (place name) of the vineyard. It is one of the oldest vineyards
in St.-Emilion, with a wine-producing history going back to the thirteenth
century. For most of this century, however, the property was owned by the
Mèneret-Capdemourlin family and run with great enthusiasm by Philippe and
Dominique Mèneret. In 1991 the Mènerets sold the property to a large French
firm, and the quality has been maintained.

In the mid-1970s the entire *chai* was renovated with the introduction of
temperature-controlled stainless-steel tanks. The percentage of new oak utilized was also increased to nearly 66% in top vintages.

The key to Larmande's quality is late harvesting, a strict selection (the
production of a second wine was introduced during the 1980s), and relatively
low yields. As a consequence, Larmande's track record since the mid-1970s
has been impeccable. There are few Premiers Grands Crus Classés that can
boast such consistently fine wines.

VINTAGES

1997—This consistently well-run estate has fashioned a deeply saturated purple-
• colored 1997 with plenty of licorice, *pain grillé*, jammy black cherry, and
87– berry fruit. Soft, with sweet tannin and low acidity, the wine packs admirable
89 levels of glycerin and extract in a medium-bodied, supple format. Look for
this wine to be delicious upon release and drink well for a minimum of 10
years. A sleeper. Last tasted, 3/98.

1996—An exceptionally fine effort for the vintage, this dark ruby/purple–colored
• wine reveals lavish quantities of roasted herbs, smoky new oak, and black
88– fruit. The saturated deep purple color is followed by aromas of sweet licorice
89 and black currant fruit, as well as medium to full body, moderate tannin, and
surprising texture, richness, and, especially, accessibility, particularly for a
1996. Anticipated maturity: 2000–2014. Last tasted, 3/98.

1995—The 1995 is cut from the same mold as the 1996, except the 1995 possesses
• more accessible glycerin and fruit, as well as lower acidity. It offers a dense
88 ruby/purple color and an intense herb, *pain grillé*, jammy blackberry and
cassis nose intertwined with woodfire-like aromas. The wine is soft, round,
and medium to full bodied, with a sexy combination of glycerin, fruit, sweet
tannin, and heady alcohol. It should drink well for 10–12 years. Last tasted,
11/97.

1994—Since bottling, the 1994 Larmande has shut down, and it may under-perform
• my initial judgment. The wine exhibits a dark ruby/purple color, a tight, oaky,
86+? subdued nose, and a sweet, impressive entry, but hard, bitter tannin distracts
from an otherwise attractive, medium- to full-bodied, muscular effort. Atypically for Larmande, patience will be a valued asset with this wine. Anticipated
maturity: 2003–2015. Last tasted, 1/97.

1993—A dark ruby/purple color possesses fine saturation for the vintage. Made in a
• typical Larmande-like style, this lavishly oaked, smoky, black cherry–
86 scented wine exhibits a ripe entry, medium body, some distracting dry wood
tannin, and a firm, muscular, solid finish. I am not convinced enough tannin
will melt away to provide a velvety texture, but the 1993 is a rustic, oaky
St.-Emilion that should drink well between 1999 and 2004. Last tasted, 1/97.

1992—This well-run property has fashioned a 1992 with a California Cabernet
• Sauvignon–like mintiness and soft, ripe, pure, black currant fruit. Medium
85 bodied and round, with attractive new oak and tough tannin in the finish, it
can be drunk now as well as over the next 5–7 years. Last tasted, 11/94.

1990—The charming, personable 1990 Larmande displays fine color, excellent ripe
• plum and cassis fruit, full body, and considerable tannin in the finish. The
88 telltale signs of the 1990 vintage—high levels of hard tannins, plenty of
succulent, chewy fruit, and exceptionally low acidity—are all present. Anticipated maturity: Now–2003. Last tasted 1/93.

1989—The 1989 is nearly as structured and concentrated as the 1988. If you like
• wonderfully round, hedonistic, soft, alcoholic, luscious St.-Emilions, this
88 super-ripe, heady, and voluptuously textured wine will offer many thrills.
Anticipated maturity: Now–2001. Last tasted, 1/93.

1988—One of the vintage's more hedonistic wines, Larmande's 1988 was de-
•   licious young yet continues to mature evenly and impressively. The wine
90   remains a dark purple color, with only slight lightening at the edge. It
     offers an intense aromatic profile, with gobs of licorice, mineral, black-
     berry, and cherry fruit scents. Similar notes, in addition to a subtle tobacco
     weediness, can be detected on the palate of this full-bodied, rich, pure,
     spicy, smoky-style wine. Anticipated maturity: Now–2004. Last tasted,
     11/97.

1986—Typical of the vintage, Larmande's 1986 is an austere, structured wine, yet it
•   appears to have put on weight, exhibiting slightly more fruit and fat than it
87   did in its youth. The wine exhibits a dark ruby/purple color and earth,
     mineral, smoke, and ripe berry fruit in the nose, which still needs coaxing
     from the glass. On the palate, the wine is medium bodied, with noticeable
     tannin and excellent purity and ripeness of fruit presented in a linear style.
     Anticipated maturity: Now–2008. Last tasted, 11/97.

1985—Fully mature, this dark garnet–colored (with some amber at the rim) wine
•   reveals an earthy, sweet, weedy, spicy, black cherry nose that hints of over-
87   ripeness. Some vanillin is also still noticeable in the wine. In the mouth, it is
     soft and round, with no hard edges, low acidity, and delicious fruit, but this
     wine requires consumption over the near term. Anticipated maturity: Now–
     2001. Last tasted, 11/97.

1983—The 1983 Larmande is big, rich, full bodied, and luscious. This deeply
•   colored, powerfully built Larmande has shed its tannins and should continue
87   to drink well for another 5–6 years. Anticipated maturity: Now. Last tasted,
     1/89.

1982—Although the 1982 Larmande has reached full maturity, it has held at this
•   plateau without one sign of fruit loss—always a hallmark of a top Bordeaux.
88   Still dark garnet colored, with some amber at the edge, this wine reveals a
     sweet, jammy, herb, licorice, berry, and Asian spice nose and a thick, unctu-
     ous texture. Full bodied and juicy, with gobs of fruit, this is a soft, velvety
     Larmande, so why defer your gratification any longer? I expect it to last for
     another 7–8 years. Last tasted, 9/95.

1981—The lightest and most elegant of the three good vintages of the early eighties,
•   Larmande's 1981 has medium ruby color, a ripe, moderately intense, plummy,
83   slightly herbaceous bouquet, medium body, good concentration, and a fine
     crisp, clean finish. Anticipated maturity: Now–may be in decline. Last tasted,
     6/84.

1980—A success given the trying vintage conditions, Larmande's 1980 is fairly light
•   and supple but exhibits a fragrant, light-intensity bouquet of herbs, oak, and
75   cherry fruit, medium body, and soft, pleasant flavors. Anticipated maturity:
     Now–may be in decline. Last tasted, 6/84.

1978—Fully mature, the 1978 Larmande is a very stylish, elegant, fruity wine,
•   with medium body, a fine cedary, herbaceous, plummy bouquet of moderate
82   intensity, and nicely balanced, medium-bodied flavors. Anticipated maturity:
     Now–may be in decline. Last tasted, 6/84.

LUCIE　　　　　　　　　　　　　　　　　　　　GOOD

Classification: St.-Emilion Grand Cru
Location of vineyards: St.-Emilion
Owner: Michel Bartolussi
Address: 33330 St.-Emilion
Mailing address: 316, Grands Champs, 33330 St.-Sulpice de Faleyrens
Telephone: 33 5 57 74 44 42; telefax: 33 5 57 24 73 00
Visits: By appointment only
Contact: Michel Bartolussi at 33 5 57 24 72 63

VINEYARDS (red)
Surface area: 10.8 acres
Average age of vines: 30 years
Blend: 90% Merlot, 10% Cabernet Franc
Density of plantation: 6,500 vines per hectare
Average yields (over the last 5 years): 35 hectoliters per hectare
Total average annual production: 150 hectoliters

GRAND VIN (red)
Brand name: Château Lucie
Appellation: St.-Emilion Grand Cru
Mean annual production: 120 hectoliters
Upbringing: Fermentations and macerations last approximately 4 weeks
in concrete vats. Malolactics take place in 60% new oak barrels. Wines
are then aged 16 months. They remain unfined and unfiltered.

SECOND WINE
Brand name: Bord-Lartigue
Average annual production: 5,000 bottles

Evaluation of present classification: Quality equivalent of a good Médoc
Cru Bourgeois
Plateau of maturity: 4–10 years

VINTAGES

1997—This medium ruby–colored wine possesses attractive up-front fruit, but dry
　•　　tannin in the finish is cause for concern. Last tasted, 3/98.
84–
85

1996—This well-made, structured wine possesses medium body, moderate weight,
　•　　and sweet berry fruit intermixed with spice and toast. Some of the fleshy
85–　opulence it was displaying when last tasted has fallen away to reveal more
87　　tannin, but this will be an accessible, quick to mature wine requiring con-

sumption during its first 5–7 years of life. It is attractive and a fine value. Last tasted, 3/98.

1995—Deep ruby colored, with an herbaceous, jammy cherry and berry nose, this
•   soft, round, fruity, open-knit St.-Emilion displays a user-friendly personality
87   and a supple finish. It will provide ideal drinking over the next 3–5 years. A
     sleeper. Last tasted, 11/97.

MAGDELAINE   VERY GOOD

Classification: St.-Emilion Premier Grand Cru Classé B
Location of vineyards: Limestone terrace just outside the town of
St.-Emilion, next to Canon and Belair
Owner: Ets. J.-P. Moueix
Address: 33330 St.-Emilion
Mailing address: c/o Ets. Jean-Pierre Moueix, 54, quai du Priourat,
B.P. 129, 33500 Libourne
Telephone: 33 5 57 51 78 96; telefax: 33 5 57 51 79 79
Visits: By appointment and for professionals of the wine trade only
Contact: Frédéric Lospied

VINEYARDS (red)
Surface area: 24 acres
Average age of vines: 30 years
Blend: 90% Merlot, 10% Cabernet Franc
Density of plantation: 5,500–6,000 vines per hectare
Average yields (over the last 5 years): 40 hectoliters per hectare
Total average annual production: 3,000 cases

GRAND VIN (red)
Brand name: Château Magdelaine
Appellation: St.-Emilion Grand Cru Classé
Mean annual production: 3,000 cases
Upbringing: Fermentations and macerations last about 20 days in
temperature-controlled concrete vats. Wines undergo malolactics in vats
and are transferred to oak barrels, 50% of which are new, for 18 months
aging. They are racked every 3 months from barrel to barrel and fined
with fresh egg whites, but remain unfiltered.

SECOND WINE
None produced.

Evaluation of present classification: The quality equivalent of a Médoc
third-growth
Plateau of maturity: 7–20 years following the vintage

Magdelaine, one of the *côtes* St.-Emilions, with its vineyard beautifully situated on a limestone plateau overlooking the Dordogne Valley, has been one of the very best St.-Emilions since the early sixties. Since 1952 the famous Libourne firm of Jean-Pierre Moueix has been the sole proprietor of this property. Magdelaine has one of the highest percentages of Merlot (90%) of any of the renowned châteaux located on the St.-Emilion limestone plateau.

Most experts have considered this property to have outstanding potential, yet in the late seventies and much of the eighties, the quality of Magdelaine was very good but rarely inspiring. However, from 1989 the quality has been more impressive, with added layers of fruit, flesh, and complexity.

Nevertheless, Magdelaine remains a very distinctive St.-Emilion, largely because of the high proportion of Merlot. One would assume that the wine is soft, fleshy, and forward. It is not. Because of the relatively long fermentation, early harvesting, and the use of a small percentage of stems, Magdelaine is an extremely tannic, slow to evolve wine. It normally requires 5–7 years after bottling to reveal its character.

Given the small production and its historic reputation, as well as its ownership by the Moueix firm, Magdelaine has always been an expensive wine, selling at prices comparable to a top Médoc second-growth.

VINTAGES

1997—A severe selection (only 1,800 cases will be made) was implemented by this
•   Christian Moueix–run property. The wine may turn out to be somewhat light,
86–   but it reveals plenty of attractive components. The color is dark ruby, and the
88   nose offers up sweet kirsch/cherry fruit intermixed with herbs, earth, and spice.
      The excellent attack features elegance, ripeness, and sweet tannin. With medium body, delicacy, and refinement, this St.-Emilion will be ready to drink when released, and should mature gracefully for a decade. Last tasted, 3/98.

1996—The dark ruby/plum color of this elegant, delicate, finesse-styled Magdelaine
•   exhibits surprising evolution. On the attack, spicy, weedy, ripe cherries com-
86–   pete with currant and vanillin flavors for the taster's attention. The wine
87   displays excellent ripeness, medium body, a soft, sweet, round texture, and
      moderate tannin in the good finish. Anticipated maturity: 2000–2015. Last tasted, 3/98.

1995—A terrific effort from Magdelaine, the 1995 possesses a saturated ruby/purple
•   color and a sweet, kirsch, and black cherry–scented nose with notes of sexy
91   toast and vanillin. The wine is ripe, rich, and full bodied, with outstanding intensity, purity, and equilibrium. It is a beautiful, harmonious, long, surprisingly seductive and accessible Magdelaine that will have many admirers. Anticipated maturity: 2000–2020. Last tasted, 11/97.

1994—A dark ruby–colored wine with an opaque garnet middle, the 1994 Magde-
•   laine offers copious quantities of jammy black cherry fruit. Medium bodied
88   and elegant, with fine purity, this well-balanced, luscious, tannic wine should

provide stylish, savory drinking for 16+ years. Given Magdelaine's tendency, in spite of its high percentage of Merlot, to close down after bottling, I was surprised by how showy and flashy this wine was tasting. Anticipated maturity: 1999–2015. Last tasted, 1/97.

1993—Dark ruby colored, with sweet bing cherry fruit in its moderately intense
• nose, this elegant, medium-bodied, jammy, soft, mid-weight Magdelaine re-
87 veals pure fruit, obvious charm, and enough length and structure to support 10–12 years of cellaring. The 1993 should be given another 1–3 years of bottle age before pulling a cork. Last tasted, 1/97.

1992—Dark ruby colored, with a spicy, black cherry, oaky nose with a tea-like
• character, this medium-bodied, moderately tannic wine exhibits more depth
86 and ripeness than most Premier Grand Cru Classé St.-Emilions in this difficult vintage. There is moderate length and a modest amount of black cherry fruit in this classy, elegant St.-Emilion. It will keep well for 10–12 years. Last tasted, 11/94.

1990—The 1990 Magdelaine is among the most sumptuous examples of this estate's
• wine. The nose reveals interesting herb, berry, mineral, and vanillin scents.
92 Copious, even lavish, quantities of sweet tobacco, coffee, and orange tea-like flavors can be found in this super-ripe Merlot-based wine. The acidity is adequate, and the moderate tannins are firm. Magdelaine represents a different expression of St.-Emilion that tasters often find too austere. The opulent, even decadent, 1990 is an exception. Anticipated maturity: Now–2008. Last tasted, 3/96.

1989—Still a youthful deep ruby/purple color, the 1989 Magdelaine's aromatics are
• beginning to emerge after a period of dormancy. Sweet kirsch and black
90 cherry fruit intermixed with spice and a subtle herbaceousness and earthiness are present. On the palate, the wine is classic in terms of marrying elegance with ripeness and finesse. Moderate tannin remains in the finish. Overall, this is a measured, firmly structured, high-quality Magdelaine that still requires a few more years of cellaring, atypical for the 1989 vintage in this sector of Bordeaux. Anticipated maturity: 2000–2020. Last tasted, 3/97.

1988—The bouquet of the 1988 Magdelaine is understated, but the wine exhibits
• fine ripeness and intensity, along with attractive cherry fruit intertwined with
87 toasty new oak. Anticipated maturity: Now–2005. Last tasted, 1/93.

1986—This wine has been consistently mediocre in all my tastings. The color is a
• medium ruby, with garnet and amber at the edge. The wine reveals a distinc-
75 tive earthiness and herbaceousness that are far stronger components than either the wine's fruit or vintage character. There is plenty of tannin, but the mid-palate is hollow and unimpressive. This is an austere, empty wine with insufficient depth of fruit and flesh. It was made during a period when Magdelaine seemed to be off form. Last tasted, 3/95.

1985—What the 1985 possesses is soft, kirsch-like fruit in a compressed, medium-
• bodied format. Light and subtle, it reveals a Burgundian-like cherriness and
84 mineral earthiness. The wine could be called stylish and elegant, but that misses the point. This Magdelaine simply lacks concentration and is too

shallow and under-nourished for a wine of its class and irrefutably high-quality *terroir*. Anticipated maturity: Now–2003. Last tasted, 3/97.

1983—Brutally tannic, backward, and aggressive, the 1983 Magdelaine has excellent
•   color, full body, and plenty of rich, ripe fruit and weight, but the ferocious
85   tannins make it reminiscent of the 1975. Anticipated maturity: Now–2010.
       Last tasted, 1/90.

1982—Inconsistent tasting notes, plus a more linear, compact personality than I
•   would have expected, have caused me to slightly downgrade my impression
88+?   of the 1982 Magdelaine. This wine can often taste disarmingly fruity and soft
       from cask, only to be frightfully tannic and backward from bottle. The 1982
       has been stubbornly slow to develop. It appears to lack the sweet mid-palate
       of fruit necessary to merit an outstanding evaluation. The color is a healthy
       medium to dark ruby, and the nose offers up sweet cherry scents intertwined
       with aromas of oak, earth, and herbs. Medium bodied, polished, and exces-
       sively polite and understated, this wine does not appear to be living up to my
       high expectations. It needs an additional 2–3 years of cellaring and should
       last for 12–15 more years. Last tasted, 9/95.

1981—Here is an example of a wine that had a lovely, perfumed, soft, berry bouquet
•   and moderately intense flavors yet, because of extensive oak aging, now tastes
80   hard, astringent, tannic, and deficient in fruit. The color is very sound, and
       the bouquet suggests vanillin, woodsy aromas, but on the palate, the wine is
       unyielding and ungenerous. Perhaps time will unleash the fruit. Anticipated
       maturity: Now–2000. Last tasted, 3/87.

1979—Quite accessible, with round, gentle, forward, silky flavors, this medium-
•   bodied wine displays good concentration and light tannins. It is ready to
84   drink. Anticipated maturity: Now. Last tasted, 5/82.

1978—A very ripe wine, Magdelaine's 1978 is jammy and intensely fruity, with a
•   round, generous, nicely concentrated texture. Perhaps a little low in acidity,
86   but generally well balanced, with a spicy, vanillin oakiness, this is a forward-
       style Magdelaine. Anticipated maturity: Now. Last tasted, 3/86.

1975—Still evolving at a glacial pace, Magdelaine's 1975 remains a promising spicy,
•   mineral-laden, muscular wine with plenty of extract and a high level of
88   tannin. The wine exhibits a dark garnet color, with some amber at the edge.
       The nose offers up smoky, earthy aromas intermixed with plenty of sweet,
       highly extracted black fruits (particularly cherries). In the mouth, the wine is
       medium to full bodied and powerful, with some astringent tannin noticeable
       in the finish. The wine leaves a hefty impression on the palate, particularly
       for the normally elegant, stylish Magdelaine, and will benefit from another 2–
       3 years of cellaring. I doubt that the tannin will ever fully dissipate, but this
       is an impressive, somewhat old-style Bordeaux. Anticipated maturity: Now–
       2015. Last tasted, 10/96.

1970—The 1970 has taken nearly 25 years to reach its plateau of maturity. It
•   possesses an impressive dark garnet color, with only slight amber at the edge,
89   as well as a distinctive underbrush, earthy, currant-and-cherry-scented nose
       with plenty of minerals in the background. Powerful on the palate, with

medium to full body and gobs of spice, this meaty, fleshy, still tannic Magdelaine is unlikely ever to attain perfect harmony, but it provides a savory mouthful of complex claret. Anticipated maturity: Now–2010. Last tasted, 11/96.

1967—Always one of the best examples of the 1967 vintage, Magdelaine has begun
•   to fade but still offers an interesting chocolatey, cedary, minty bouquet and
82   soft, rich, surprisingly deep flavors marred by a slight astringence. Anticipated maturity: Now–probably in decline. Last tasted, 2/85.

1962—A lovely success for the vintage, the 1962 Magdelaine has been mature for quite
•   some time but seems to be holding its fruit. A full-blown bouquet of cedary,
85   herbal, spicy, ripe fruit is altogether impressive. Round, generous flavors exhibit good body and no tannins, and despite the brown color at the edges, this wine still has plenty of life. Anticipated maturity: Now. Last tasted, 1/81.

1961—The 1961 is one of the greatest Magdelaines I have ever tasted, although
•   bottle variation has always been present with this wine. The knockout nose
92   soars from the glass, offering up scents of fruitcake, cedar, and jammy currants, and cherries. Full bodied, rich, and exotic, with layers of fruit, this is an opulently textured, lush, compelling example of Magdelaine. Anticipated maturity: Now–2005. Last tasted, 3/97.

ANCIENT VINTAGES

Bottle variation, as one might expect, is a problem. In addition, many older vintages of Magdelaine were bottled in Belgium, as the practice of this property was to sell barrels of wine to their clients, who had them bottled outside the château. While I have had uninspiring examples of the 1953, 1955, and 1959, the best bottles of these vintages were all impressive. The 1953 (up to 88 points; last tasted 12/96), 1955 (87 points; last tasted 12/96), and 1959 (90 points; last tasted 11/96) have been impressive in their power and richness. The 1952, which I tasted only once, in 1991, was rated 88. It appeared to have the stuffing and structure to last another 10–15 years, but the providence and condition of the bottle are everything with respect to most vintages older than 20 years.

MONBOUSQUET   EXCELLENT SINCE 1994

Classification: St.-Emilion Grand Cru
Location of vineyards: St.-Emilion
Owner: Mr. and Mrs. Gérard Perse
Address: 33330 St.-Emilion
Mailing address: Same as above
Telephone: 33 5 57 24 67 19; telefax: 33 5 57 74 41 29
Visits: By appointment only
Contact: Laurent Lusseau

VINEYARDS (red)
Surface area: 79 acres
Average age of vines: 35 years
Blend: 60% Merlot, 30% Cabernet Franc, and 10% Cabernet Sauvignon
Density of plantation: 5,400 vines per hectare
Average yields (over the last 5 years): 30 hectoliters per hectare
Total average annual production: 128,000 bottles

GRAND VIN (red)
Brand name: Château Monbousquet
Appellation: St.-Emilion Grand Cru
Mean annual production: 128,000 bottles
Upbringing: Fermentations last 2 weeks and macerations approximately
4 weeks in stainless-steel vats. Wines are aged in 100% new oak barrels
for 18 months. They remain unfined and unfiltered.

SECOND WINE
Brand name: L'Angélique de Monbousquet

Evaluation of present classification: Since 1993 the quality equivalent of
a Médoc third- or fourth-growth
Plateau of maturity: Before 1993, 3–8 years following the vintage; since
1993, 5–20+ years following the vintage

Monbousquet, a large estate, was the pride and joy of the Querre family, who produced a fruity, supple style of St.-Emilion that had broad commercial appeal and was always fairly priced. It was a wine to drink within its first 5–6 years of life.

In the early nineties the Querre family sold Monbousquet to Gérard Perse, who had made a fortune in the supermarket business. Perse immediately renovated the cellars, hired Michel Rolland as a consulting oenologist, and began to produce what has become one of St.-Emilion's most concentrated and fascinating wines. Yields were cut to under 2 tons of fruit per acre in the 1994, 1995, 1996, and 1997 vintages. The first example of Perse's commitment to high-quality wine emerged from the difficult 1993 vintage, as Monbousquet's 1993 was one of the finest wines of the appellation. This property is now turning out exciting wines that will reward connoisseurs looking for multi-dimensional, complete St.-Emilions that will age for 2 decades or more.

This is an emerging superstar from St.-Emilion. The middle-aged readers of this book who purchased Monbousquet in the seventies (myself included) may remember this château as producing soft, innocuous, commercially styled wines, but that has all changed under the passionate leadership of the estate's new proprietor.

VINTAGES

1997—The opaque purple–colored 1997 ratchets up the level of hedonism to consid-
  • erable heights. It is an impressively endowed wine with layers of jammy black
90– currant, cranberry, and cassis fruit, well-integrated toasty *pain grillé* scents,
92 and an unctuous texture that conceals moderate levels of sweet tannin. Unlike
   many 1997s with that "loosey-goosey" feel, this is a well-delineated, full-
   bodied, powerful, classic claret. Anticipated maturity: 2002–2018. Last
   tasted, 3/98.

1996—Small yields of 24 hectoliters per hectare have resulted in a wine with
  • extraordinary richness, power, and tannic ferocity. This is unquestionably a
90– wine for true collectors, but patience will be required. The opaque purple
91+ color is followed by sweet, pure aromas of cassis, blueberries, and smoky,
   toasty new oak. Massive, full bodied, and powerful with layers of ripe fruit,
   remarkable depth, and a hefty, blockbuster feel, this is a classic yet muscular
   vin de garde that will require significant cellaring. Anticipated maturity:
   2007–2020. Last tasted, 3/98.

1995—Although similar to the 1996, the 1995 possesses more accessible fruit, and
  • while the tannin is elevated, it is buffered by lower acidity as well as more
92 glycerin and fat. The 1995 offers an opaque purple color and a glorious nose
   of new oak, spice, and abundant black fruits. This full-bodied, super-
   extracted, multi-layered wine must be tasted to be believed—especially for
   readers who remember Monbousquet as the soft, innocuous, commercially
   styled St.-Emilion it was for many decades. The 1995 has more accessibility
   than its blockbuster younger sibling, but it still requires 4–5 years of cellaring. Anticipated maturity: 2003–2022. Last tasted, 11/97.

1994—Opaque purple colored, with a tight but promising nose of cherry jam, black
  • currants, smoked herbs, and grilled meats, this dense, chewy, medium- to
90 full-bodied wine exhibits the vintage's tough tannin. However, this 1994
   possesses enough fruit, glycerin, and extract to counterbalance the wine's
   structure. It will need 2–3 years of cellaring yet promises to keep for 15
   years. Last tasted, 1/97.

1993—One of the sleepers of the vintage, this lavishly oaked, dense purple–colored
  • wine reveals gobs of sweet black cherry and cassis fruit intertwined with
89 aromas of smoke and new oak. Extracted and rich, with no hard edges, this is
   a fat, glycerin-endowed, chewy, pure St.-Emilion that can be drunk young or
   cellared for 10–12 years. Last tasted, 1/97.

LA MONDOTTE   OUTSTANDING SINCE 1996

Classification: None
Location of vineyards: St.-Laurent des Combes, east of Troplong-Mondot
and west of Tertre-Roteboeuf
Owner: Comtes de Neipperg
Address: 33330 St.-Emilion

Mailing address: c/o Château Canon-La-Gaffelière, 33330 St.-Emilion
Telephone: 33 5 57 24 71 33; telefax: 33 5 57 24 67 95
Visits: No visits—being restructured
Contact: Cécile Gardaix

VINEYARDS (red)
Surface area: 10.3 acres
Average age of vines: 35 years
Blend: 75% Merlot, 25% Cabernet Franc
Density of plantation: 5,500–6,500 vines per hectare
Average yields (over the last 5 years): 35 hectoliters per hectare
Total average annual production: 20,000 bottles

GRAND VIN (red)
Brand name: Château La Mondotte
Appellation: St.-Emilion
Mean annual production: 20,000 bottles
Upbringing: Since 1997, fermentations are long, and may last up to 4
weeks in temperature-controlled wooden vats. Indigenous yeasts are used,
and pumping-overs are done only for those vats that do not undergo any
pigéage. Malolactics occur in barrels, on fine lees with frequent
bâtonnages, and the first racking is done only 1 or 2 months after
completion of malolactics. Wines are aged in new oak barrels for 12–18
months. They are never racked but are provided with oxygen if needed.
They are fined but remain unfiltered.

SECOND WINE
None produced.

Evaluation of present classification: If the 1996 and 1997 typify what La
Mondotte is capable of achieving, this wine is the quality equivalent of a
Médoc first- or second-growth

La Mondotte is one of the most concentrated young Bordeaux I have tasted.
Whether it is trying to be the Pétrus or Le Pin of St.-Emilion is irrelevant, for
this wine, made by the superbly talented Comte Stephan Von Neipperg,
proprietor of Canon-La-Gaffelière and Clos de l'Oratoire, is a showcase offering that is already turning heads and leading to some uncalled-for jealousy.

VINTAGES

1997—The 1997 La Mondotte is undoubtedly the wine of the vintage from Bordeaux's
•   right bank (St.-Emilion and Pomerol), as well as a candidate for the wine of
93–   1997. Much like its 1996 counterpart, the 1997 is the most concentrated
95   wine I tasted. On the two occasions I had it, I was blown away by its quality.

From its saturated opaque black/purple color to its extraordinarily intense jammy blackberry/cassis liqueur–scented nose, this is a fabulous claret. Expansive and full bodied, with exhilarating levels of extract, an opulent, unctuously textured feel, extremely low acidity, and a 40+-second finish, this is a prodigious effort. While not quite as well defined as the 1996, and perhaps slightly less concentrated (I'm splitting hairs here), this medium- to full-bodied, showy, unbelievably dense and rich wine is another *tour de force* in winemaking. Projected maturity: Now–2014. Last tasted, 3/98.

1996—Unquestionably one of the superstars of the 1996 vintage, the wine is atypi-
•   cally powerful and unctuously textured, especially for a 1996 right bank
95–   offering. It boasts an opaque ruby/purple color as well as celestial aromas of
98   jammy black fruits, truffles, licorice, coffee, and smoky new oak. In the mouth, the wine is full bodied and seamless, with gorgeously integrated acidity, alcohol, and tannin. Still remarkably thick, layered, and extravagantly rich, this wine possesses considerable tannic clout in the blockbuster finish. If it continues to improve as it did between spring and late fall, it may merit an even higher rating. Amazing stuff! Anticipated maturity: 2005–2025. Last tasted, 3/98.

MOULIN DU CADET

Classification: St.-Emilion Grand Cru Classé
Location of vineyards: On the hillside next to Fonroque
Owner: S.C. du Château Moulin du Cadet
Address: 33330 St.-Emilion
Mailing address: c/o Ets. Jean-Pierre Moueix, 54, quai du Priourat, B.P. 129, 33502 Libourne
Telephone: 33 5 57 51 78 96; telefax: 33 5 57 51 79 79
Visits: By appointment and for professionals of the wine trade only
Contact: Frédéric Lospied

VINEYARDS (red)
Surface area: 12 acres
Average age of vines: 25 years
Blend: 85% Merlot, 15% Cabernet Franc
Density of plantation: 5,500–6,000 vines per hectare
Average yields (over the last 5 years): 50 hectoliters per hectare
Total average annual production: 2,500 cases

GRAND VIN (red)
Brand name: Château Moulin du Cadet
Appellation: St.-Emilion Grand Cru
Mean annual production: 2,500 cases
Upbringing: Fermentations and macerations last about 20 days in

temperature-controlled concrete tanks. Twenty percent of the yield undergoes malolactics in casks. Wines are then transferred to oak barrels (40% of which are new) for 18 months aging. They are racked every 3 months and fined with fresh egg whites, but remain unfiltered.

SECOND WINE
None produced.

Evaluation of present classification: The quality equivalent of a Médoc Cru Bourgeois
Plateau of maturity: 3–8 years following the vintage

Moulin du Cadet is a micro-estate of 12 acres located on the plateau north of St.-Emilion. It tends to produce rather fragrant, lighter-style wines lacking depth but displaying attractive bouquets. With the famous firm of Jean-Pierre Moueix attending to the estate's winemaking, one can expect to see more richness and depth.

VINTAGES

1993—Looking for a 1993 that is all chewy, fleshy, succulent fruit presented in an
• 　　opulent, voluptuously textured style? Check out Moulin du Cadet's 1993
86　　offering. This ripe, fruity, low-acid, medium-bodied wine is ideal for readers
　　　who are unable to defer their gratification. Last tasted, 11/94.
1990—The lavishly fruity, medium-bodied 1990 gushes with fruit. Fat and supple,
• 　　this tasty, disarming wine should be drunk over the next 3–5 years. Last
86　　tasted, 1/93.
1989—The 1989 possesses rich, sweet, expansive flavors and exhibits good concen-
• 　　tration and length. Anticipated maturity: Now. Last tasted, 4/91.
85

MOULIN ST.-GEORGES　　　　　　　　　　　　　　　　　　VERY GOOD

Classification: St.-Emilion Grand Cru
Location of vineyards: St.-Emilion, at the base of Ausone
Owner: Catherine and Alain Vauthier
Address: Moulin St.-Georges, 33330 St.-Emilion
Mailing address: Same as above
Telephone: 33 5 57 24 70 26; telefax: 33 5 57 74 47 39
Visits: No visits

VINEYARDS (red)
Surface area: 17.3 acres
Average age of vines: 20 years

Blend: 66% Merlot, 34% Cabernet Franc and Cabernet Sauvignon
Density of plantation: 5,500 vines per hectare
Average yields (over the last 5 years): 42 hectoliters per hectare
Total average annual production: 35,000–40,000 bottles

GRAND VIN (red)
Brand name: Moulin St.-Georges
Appellation: St.-Emilion Grand Cru
Mean annual production: 35,000 bottles

Upbringing: Fermentations and macerations last 3–4 weeks in temperature-controlled stainless-steel vats. Malolactics occur in new oak barrels for 80%–90% of the yield, the rest remaining in vats until completion of this process. Wines are aged 15–20 months, fined depending upon the vintage, but never filtered.

SECOND WINE
None produced.

Evaluation of present classification: The quality equivalent of a Médoc third- or fourth-growth

Ausone's owner, Alain Vauthier, also owns this small, well-situated estate (situated between Ausone and La Gaffelière) from which he has been fashioning terrific wines. Readers should think of Moulin St.-Georges as a junior version of the great Ausone.

VINTAGES

1997—Over the last several years it has consistently been one of the sleeper wines
• of the vintage. The 1997 is another success, albeit more forward with more
87– limited aging potential than its two predecessors. Nevertheless, there is plenty
89 to like in this up-front, hedonistically oriented wine. The color is a healthy dark purple. The aromatics consist of jammy black raspberries and cherries infused with aromas of woodsmoke. Ripe, with copious quantities of glycerin on the attack, this generously rich, silky-smooth, nearly unctuously textured wine should drink well young yet keep for 7–8 years. A sleeper of the vintage. Last tasted, 3/98.

1996—A tannic, dense, concentrated wine with plenty of extract as well as an
• intriguing mineral, blackberry, earth, truffle, and vanillin nose, this medium-
89– bodied wine is crammed with ripe fruit and tannin. It is not unfair to consider
91+ this wine as a downsized verson of the great Ausone. The wine is more forthcoming than a young vintage of Ausone but still high toned and tightly wound. This wine possesses outstanding purity and concentration, and if the tannin becomes better integrated, it is a sure bet for a 90+ rating after

bottling. Anticipated maturity: 2003–2020. A sleeper of the vintage. Last tasted, 3/98.

1995—A gorgeous wine, and another sleeper of the vintage, Moulin St.-Georges's
  •   1995 exhibits a dense purple color and a sweet, black raspberry and currant
 90   nose intertwined with high-quality toasty oak and minerals. Deep, rich, impressively pure, ripe, elegant, and harmonious, this gorgeous, persuasive St.-Emilion has a bright future. Anticipated maturity: 2001–2016. Last tasted, 11/97.

PAVIE   GOOD

Classification: St.-Emilion Premier Grand Cru Classé B
Location of vineyards: St.-Emilion, Côte Pavie
Owner: Mr. and Mrs. Gérard Perse
Address: 33330 St.-Emilion
Mailing address: Same as above
Telephone: 33 5 57 55 43 43; telefax: 33 5 57 24 63 99
Visits: By appointment only
Contact: Laurence Argutti

VINEYARDS (red)
Surface area: 91.4 acres
Average age of vines: 45 years
Blend: 55% Merlot, 25% Cabernet Franc, 20% Cabernet Sauvignon
Density of plantation: 5,300 vines per hectare
Average yields (over the last 5 years): 48 hectoliters per hectare
Total average annual production: 180,000 bottles

GRAND VIN (red)
Brand name: Château Pavie
Appellation: Premier Grand Cru Classé
Mean annual production: 180,000 bottles
Upbringing: Fermentations last approximately 10 days and macerations 20 days. Wines are then aged with 50% new oak. They are fined but remain unfiltered. Beginning in 1998, malolactics will be in 100% new oak barrels, with approximately 18 months of aging.

SECOND WINE
None produced.

NOTE: Several changes under the new ownership: A new *cuvérie* has been built and a new cellar (for *élevage* in barrels) has also been constructed.

Evaluation of present classification: The quality equivalent of a Médoc fourth- or fifth-growth
Plateau of maturity: 7–20 years following the vintage

Pavie has the largest vineyard of all the St.-Emilion Premiers Grands Crus Classés. With a production seven times the size of one of its neighbors, Ausone, and twice that of the adjacent vineyard, La Gaffelière, Pavie is widely known throughout the world.

The vineyard is superbly situated just to the southeast of St.-Emilion (a 5-minute drive), on the eastern section of the hillsides of the town. Therefore it is one of the *côtes* St.-Emilions.

Until 1998, Pavie was owned and run by Jean Paul Valette, who had been at Pavie since 1967 after giving up ranching in Chile. He was one of St.-Emilion's friendliest proprietors, and his hospitality, combined with the fact that Pavie has some of the region's most interesting limestone caves for storing wine, made this a must stop for tourists to the area.

Pavie, despite the large production and popularity, has not been a top performer among the St.-Emilion first-growths. In many vintages the wine has been too light and feebly colored, with a tendency to brown and mature at an accelerated pace. Valette was well aware of these problems, and there was a strong movement to a more densely concentrated, deeper-colored, fuller-bodied Pavie with the vintages of 1979 onward. This is not to suggest that all of the wines of Pavie produced before 1979 were insipid and weak; but far too many vintages—for example, 1976, 1975, 1974, and 1966—were well below acceptable standards. Fortunately, this period of inconsistency is past history. However, this is not a St.-Emilion to drink young; most vintages, particularly in the eighties and early nineties, have been stubbornly hard at their outset, and a minimum of 7–10 years of bottle age is required for mellowing. The wine was particularly disappointing during the early nineties, and this undoubtedly played a role in the decision of Mr. Valette to sell the estate.

Pavie is fairly priced for a Premier Grand Cru Classé St.-Emilion. The large production has guaranteed that the price to date has remained realistic. I expect great wines to emerge under the new administration of Gérard Perse.

VINTAGES

1997—The dark ruby–colored 1997 is herbal and earthy, with a lean palate and
•   none of the charm, fat, or richness of the appellation's better wines. Its dry
83–   tannin, medium body, and overall size and depth suggest it should be drunk
85   during its first 7–8 years of life. Last tasted, 3/98.

1996—The dark ruby–colored 1996 Pavie exhibits a pinched, tart personality with
•   moderate quantities of red currant fruit in the nose, along with earth and
84–   spice. Although it exhibits good, clean winemaking, this understated, lean,
86   angular wine does not possess much stuffing, flesh, or length. It should keep
      for 10–15 years. Anticipated maturity: 2000–2012. Last tasted, 3/98.

1995—Medium plum/ruby in color, with a distinctive peppery, leafy, spicy nose
•   with vague hints of red cherry and currant fruit, this is a rigid, austere
78   wine with an angular personality and severe tannin. There is some ripe

fruit on the attack, but that is quickly dominated by the wine's structural components. This may turn out to be a pleasant wine, but my best guess is that it will dry out. Anticipated maturity: 2000–2010. Last tasted, 11/97.

1994—This is a severe, light- to medium-bodied Pavie lacking fruit, texture, and
•　　charm. Mouth-searing tannin in the finish ensures that this wine's fruit will
80?　never survive 8–10 years of cellaring. Last tasted, 1/97.

1993—Dark ruby colored, with an earthy, nondescript nose offering vague red fruit
•　　and green pepper aromas, this sinewy, highly structured, hard, astringent
75　　wine will dry out long before the tannin fades. Last tasted, 1/97.

1992—In 1992 Pavie has produced a light-bodied, compact, structured wine with an
•　　excess of tannin that gives the wine a tough texture and rough finish. There
78　　is not enough fruit to balance out the structure, thus the end result is a wine
　　　that may keep for 10 years or more but will become more attenuated, with the
　　　fruit drying out over the next 4–5 years. Last tasted, 11/94.

1991—At this property the 1991 is better than the 1992. Pavie is one of a hand-
•　　ful of St.-Emilion Premiers Grands Crus Classés to produce a 1991. While
82　　it is hardly a stellar effort, the wine does offer medium ruby color, a spicy,
　　　attractive, bing cherry, vanillin nose, ripe, medium-bodied flavors, light tan-
　　　nin, and adequate depth. Drink it over the next 7–8 years. Last tasted,
　　　1/94.

1990—The impressive 1990 Pavie exhibits a deep, saturated ruby/garnet color as
•　　well as a sweet, expressive bouquet of truffles, Asian spices, black cherries,
92　　and smoked herbs. Full bodied and powerful, with a meaty, beef blood–like
　　　richness, this backward, intense, deep, concentrated, muscular St.-Emilion
　　　needs 3–4 more years of cellaring; it should age well through 2018. Last
　　　tasted, 11/96.

1989—The 1989 displays a deep ruby/garnet color, with no signs of amber at the
•　　edge. It offers up an exotic, spicy, fruitcake, earthy, chocolatey nose with
89+　sweet woodsy aromas in the background. Long and youthful, with noticeably
　　　hard tannin, this medium-bodied, concentrated 1989 appears to be a slowly
　　　evolving wine. With another 2–3 years of bottle age, it may merit an outstand-
　　　ing score. Anticipated maturity: 2003–2016. Last tasted, 11/96.

1988—The backward 1988 Pavie is a structured, tannic wine, balanced nicely by
•　　elegant, ripe, tobacco-and-black-cherry-scented fruit, good acidity, and
86　　a long, spicy, tannic finish. Anticipated maturity: Now–2005. Last tasted,
　　　1/93.

1986—Excluding the 1961 and 1990, the 1986 is the finest Pavie made in the
•　　last 3 decades. It is a full-bodied, deep, tannic, highly extracted wine,
90　　with a bouquet that displays a great deal of sweet, toasty oak and a
　　　finish that goes on and on. There are noticeable tannins in the wine,
　　　so expect to defer your gratification for some time while waiting for this
　　　wine to mature. Quite impressive, Pavie is clearly one of the stars of the
　　　St.-Emilion appellation in 1986. Anticipated maturity: Now–2010. Last
　　　tasted, 3/90.

1985—The 1985 is firm, tannic, and unyielding, particularly for a wine from this
•   vintage. Deep in color, ripe, medium bodied, but needing time, this wine will
86   provide graceful drinking if cellared. Anticipated maturity: Now–2005. Last
    tasted, 3/90.

1983—Now reaching full maturity, the 1983 Pavie has an attractive bouquet of rich
•   raspberry and plummy fruit intermingled with the scents of new oak and
88   herbs. The color is still medium dark ruby, but some amber has crept in at
    the edge. On the palate, the wine is crammed with rich, opulent, expansive,
    red fruit flavors but has enough acidity and tannin to give it grip and focus.
    This is a surprisingly drinkable, exuberantly styled Pavie that should con-
    tinue to evolve for at least another 10–15 years. Anticipated maturity: Now–
    2005. Last tasted, 3/91.

1982—Pavie's 1982 is beginning to shed its tannin and open. The wine exhibits an
•   impressive saturated garnet/ruby color, a textbook, Médoc-like nose of cedar,
89   black currants, vanillin, and roasted herbs, medium body, excellent concen-
    tration, and moderate tannin still in evidence. This is an elegant, measured
    style of wine that can be drunk now, although it will not hit its plateau of
    maturity for another 2–4 years. It will keep through the first decade of the
    next century. Last tasted, 9/95.

1981—This vintage of Pavie has developed fast. A classy and complex bouquet of
•   spicy, vanillin oak, and ripe cherries is attractive. In the mouth, the wine is
85   medium bodied and flavorful, with a sweet, oaky component that has blended
    in well with the wine's fruit. In short, Pavie's 1981 is a very good, elegant,
    medium-weight wine. Anticipated maturity: Now–may be in decline. Last
    tasted, 11/90.

1979—This is an attractive Pavie that is nearing maturity. The 1979 has surprisingly
•   dark ruby color with only a trace of amber, a toasty, smoky, herb-and-berry-
85   scented bouquet, medium body, good power and weight, and moderate tan-
    nins. It is a tasty but compact wine. Anticipated maturity: Now–2000. Last
    tasted, 3/91.

1978—A loose, open-knit style of wine, the 1978 Pavie lacks concentration, struc-
•   ture, and firmness but offers a sweet, ripe (possibly overripe) Merlot fruitiness
78   and one-dimensional charm. I also detected a vegetal quality to the bouquet.
    Anticipated maturity: Now. Last tasted, 4/82.

1976—Quite disappointing, the 1976 Pavie is an insipid, dull, diluted wine, with
•   marginal flavor interest, a vegetal, overly spicy, woody aroma, and pale,
56   shallow flavors. Last tasted, 9/80.

1975—A minor wine in this vintage, the 1975 Pavie exhibits sweet, ripe, lightly
•   concentrated, fruity flavors, medium body, and surprisingly little tannin. A
72   compact little wine, the 1975 Pavie should be drunk up. Anticipated maturity:
    Now–probably in serious decline. Last tasted, 5/84.

1971—The 1971 Pavie is a graceful, well-balanced, fruity, soft, elegant wine that
•   always impressed me as being among the most restrained and subdued
81   of the 1971 St.-Emilions. Now beginning to lose its fruit, this medium-
    bodied wine still has charm and finesse but is displayed in an under-

stated way. Anticipated maturity: Now—may be in decline. Last tasted, 3/86.

1970—Produced in a period when Pavie was obviously in a performance slump, the
• 1970 is still a modest success for the vineyard. Not terribly complex, but
83 chunky, straightforward, and foursquare (as I suspect Michael Broadbent
would say), this wine has a roasted, ripe cherry bouquet and full, oaky, yet
one-dimensional flavors. It is a good effort. Anticipated maturity: Now. Last
tasted from a magnum, 3/88.

1961—The first few times I tasted this wine I was unimpressed, but in 1988 at a
• blind tasting, the wine revealed a huge, spicy, cedary, black plum nose, rich,
90 concentrated, opulent flavors, amazing youthfulness, and plenty of tannin and
alcohol in the finish. I was shocked when I learned it was the 1961 Pavie.
The bottle I saw could easily last for another 10–15 years. It bore no resemblance to the relatively tired examples I had tasted previously. Will the real
1961 Pavie please come forward? Anticipated maturity: Now–2005. Last
tasted, 2/88.

PAVIE-DECESSE   GOOD

Classification: St.-Emilion Grand Cru Classé
Location of vineyards: St.-Emilion
Owner: Mr. and Mrs. Gérard Perse
Address: 33330 St.-Emilion
Mailing address: Same as above
Telephone: 33 5 57 55 43 43; telefax: 33 5 57 24 63 99
Visits: By appointment only
Contact: Laurence Argutti

VINEYARDS (red)
Surface area: 23 acres
Average age of vines: 40 years
Blend: 60% Merlot, 25% Cabernet Franc, 15% Cabernet Sauvignon
Density of plantation: 5,400 vines per hectare
Average yields (over the last 5 years): 24 hectoliters per hectare
Total average annual production: 28,000 bottles

GRAND VIN (red)
Brand name: Château Pavie-Decesse
Appellation: St.-Emilion Grand Cru Classé
Mean annual production: 28,000 bottles
Upbringing: Fermentations last approximately 15 days and macerations
about 5 weeks. Wines are then aged in 100% new oak for 18 months.
Since 1997, malolactics are in new oak for 100% of the yield. Wines
remain unfined and unfiltered.

NOTE: The yields have been cut down drastically under the new ownership. A new *cuvérie* has been built, equipped with wooden tanks. Macerations are longer, and the percentage of new oak has been increased.

SECOND WINE
None produced.

Evaluation of present classification: The quality equivalent of a Médoc fifth-growth
Plateau of maturity: 5–15 years following the vintage

Between 1971 and 1997 this small estate was owned by Jean Paul Valette, the proprietor of the Premier Grand Cru Classé Pavie, which sits several hundred feet farther down the hill below Pavie-Decesse. In 1997 Valette sold the estate to Gérard Perse, the ambitious young proprietor of Monbousquet. This is a *côtes* St.-Emilion, with a vineyard situated on chalky, clay, and limestone soils. The quality at this estate has followed that of its bigger, more famous sibling, Pavie. Consequently, after some mediocre wines in the seventies, the vintages from 1979 onward have been inconsistent. However, my first look at the 1997, produced by the new owners, left me with the impression that great things can be expected from Pavie-Decesse.

For visitors to the area, I highly recommend a visit not only to Pavie, but also to Pavie-Decesse. It is reached by a long and winding road farther up the hill from Pavie. The view of the vineyards from Pavie-Decesse is breathtaking.

VINTAGES

1997—The first vintage under the total control of proprietor Gérard Perse, the 1997
•   is the finest Pavie-Decesse I have ever tasted. Unlike the lean, sinewy,
89–   emaciated wines produced under the previous regime, this opaque purple–
92   colored example possesses fabulously sweet, black currant and cherry fruit
       intermixed with minerals and subtle new oak. Full bodied, powerful, and
       highly extracted, yet intense, without any heaviness, this is a beautifully pure,
       layered, well-endowed Pavie-Decesse, that will require 4–5 years of cellaring
       following bottling. Anticipated maturity: 2003–2018. Bravo to Gérard Perse!
       Last tasted, 3/98.

1996—This wine performed reasonably well from cask, but on two subsequent occa-
•   sions it was totally closed, with severe tannin levels, a frightful austerity, and
?   an absence of fruit. Judgment reserved. Last tasted, 3/98.

1995—I may have badly misled readers when I last rated this wine (giving it an 86–
•   88 range of score). Now that it has been bottled, the 1995 Pavie-Decesse is
82?   extraordinarily austere, with elevated tannin levels, some sweet black currant,
       cranberry, and cherry fruit, but a hollow midpalate and a dry, sharp finish

with noticeable astringent tannin. I liked this wine much better from three separate cask tastings, but two tastings from bottle have made me question my earlier reviews. Anticipated maturity: 2002–2010. Last tasted, 11/97.

1994— The 1994's saturated dark purple color suggests good intensity, but this wine
• is dominated by its acid and bitter tannin. It is a big, structured, charmless
82? wine in need of more glycerin, midpalate, and depth. Perhaps 4–5 years of cellaring will be beneficial, but I suspect this will turn out to be an attenuated, compact wine with 12–15 years of aging potential. Last tasted, 1/97.

1993— This was a surprisingly good performance for a Pavie-Decesse, which has a
• tendency to be astringent and austere early in life. The 1993 possesses a
86 deep ruby color. There is plenty of tannin, as well as nicely extracted, ripe cherry and plum fruit backed up with spicy oak, herbs, and wood. There is good purity, as well as a medium-bodied, firmly knit build to this midweight St.-Emilion. Anticipated maturity: 2000–2008. Last tasted, 1/97.

1992— Cask samples and two tastings following bottling offer convincing evidence
• that in 1992 Pavie-Decesse, the less expensive sibling of Pavie, produced the
84 better wine. The dark ruby color is followed by some spicy, earthy fruit in the nose to go along with subtle wood and herbaceous notes. Spicy in the mouth, this medium-bodied, narrowly constructed, austere, muscular St.-Emilion will benefit from 1–2 years of aging and last for 5–6 years. Last tasted, 11/94.

1991— Although light, the 1991 Pavie-Decesse displays attractive ripeness, decent
• body, soft, moderately endowed flavors, and a quick finish. Drink it over the
78 next 3–4 years. Last tasted, 1/94.

1990— The 1990 offers powerful aromas of sweet fruit, minerals, chocolate, and
• herbs that are followed by a low-acid wine with a huge, chewy texture, gobs
90 of tannin, and plenty of extract and depth. This is an exceptionally powerful wine that should prove to be sensational. Anticipated maturity: Now–2010. Last tasted, 1/93.

1989— The 1989 Pavie-Decesse is a dense, tannic, full-bodied, rich, and, not sur-
• prisingly, backward wine for the vintage. It displays an herbaceous, mineral-
88 scented, black cherry fruitiness, full body, and crisp acidity. Anticipated maturity: Now–2010. Last tasted, 1/93.

1988— The 1988 Pavie-Decesse has fine concentration, good length, an enticing
• bouquet of earthy, mineral, and exotic fruit, but tremendous tannin in the
86 finish. Cellaring is most definitely needed. Anticipated maturity: Now–2009. Last tasted, 1/93.

1986— An extremely impressive wine that is very tannic and powerful, the 1986 will
• require long-term cellaring. It is almost opaque in color and very reserved
89 and backward in terms of development, but with the requisite patience to wait at least a decade, it should prove to be one of the sleepers of the vintage. Anticipated maturity: 1999–2010. Last tasted, 4/91.

1985— The 1985 Pavie-Decesse has turned out to be even better than Pavie. Very
• deep in color, with an intense aroma of black currant fruit, toasty oak, and
88 tarlike scents, this rich, long, very big and structured wine has loads of fruit that is tightly bound in a full-bodied format. It should be a very long-lived 1985. Anticipated maturity: Now–2005. Last tasted, 3/90.

PAVIE-MACQUIN   EXCELLENT

Classification: St.-Emilion Grand Cru Classé
Location of vineyards: St.-Emilion, on Côte Pavie
Owner: Corre-Macquin family
Address: 33330 St.-Emilion
Telephone: 33 5 57 24 74 23; telefax: 33 5 57 24 63 78
Visits: By appointment only
Contact: Contact the château

VINEYARDS (red)
Surface area: 37 acres
Average age of vines: 25–35 years
Blend: 70% Merlot, 25% Cabernet Franc, 5% Cabernet Sauvignon
Density of plantation: 6,000–7,000 vines per hectare
Average yields (over the last 5 years): 39 hectoliters per hectare
Total average annual production: 6,500 cases

GRAND VIN (red)
Brand name: Château Pavie-Macquin
Appellation: St.-Emilion Grand Cru
Mean annual production: 35–45 hectoliters per hectare
Upbringing: The wine spends 18–20 months in barrel.

SECOND WINE
Brand name: Les Chênes de Macquin

Evaluation of present classification: Since 1988 the quality equivalent of
a Médoc third- or fourth-growth
Plateau of maturity: 5–20 years following the vintage

Pavie-Macquin takes its name from Albert Macquin, who was the leading
specialist of his time in grafting European vines onto American root stocks, a
practice that became essential after the phylloxera louse destroyed most of
the vineyards of Bordeaux in the late nineteenth century. The vineyard is well
situated on what is frequently referred to as the Côte Pavie, adjacent to
the more renowned vineyards of Troplong-Mondot and Pavie. The wines of
Pavie-Macquin, which were frequently disappointing in the seventies and
eighties, made a significant leap in quality beginning with the 1988, 1989,
and 1990 vintages, largely because the Corre family hired the brilliant Nicolas Thienpont (of Vieux-Château-Certan) to look after the estate and viticulture. Moreover, the additional hiring of Libourne oenologist Michel Rolland
to look after the vinification and *élevage* have completely turned around the
fortunes of this well-placed St.-Emilion. This estate, organically farmed, has
become one of the stars of St.-Emilion.

VINTAGES

1997—After tasting this wine on three separate occasions, I am confident that it is
•   one of the superstars of the vintage. In fact, it is the finest Pavie-Macquin I
91– have ever tasted. This wine has never lacked intensity, as it is always one of
93   the more concentrated wines in Bordeaux, but at times the tannin level can
be severe, giving the wine a rustic, or what the French call *sauvage*, component. The 1997 is a blockbuster effort in a year that produced no shortage of
soft, undelineated, tasty, but commercial wines. The color is opaque purple/
black, and the nose offers up celestial aromas of black raspberries, cassis,
and mineral notes reminiscent of wines from the renowned Pomerol estate
Lafleur or, more recently, the prodigiously perfect 1990 Beauséjour-Duffau.
The 1997 Pavie-Macquin reveals exceptional old-vine intensity and more
structure than many wines of the vintage, but the tannin is sweet and silky.
Full bodied, with layers of extract, an unctuous texture, and a finish that lasts
for 40+ seconds, this is a profoundly great wine from a good vintage. Anticipated maturity: 2005–2020. Bravo! Last tasted, 3/98.

1996—Dense purple colored, with a tight but promising nose of blackberries, raspber-
•   ries, and mineral-tinged cherry fruit, this full-bodied, massive wine hits the
89– palate with a boatload of tannin, extract, and power. The 1996 Pavie-Macquin
90? possesses an austere, angular, tough personality, as well as impressive fruit extraction, excellent purity, and a long finish. The question is, when will this monster ever be drinkable? Anticipated maturity: 2010–2025. Last tasted, 3/98.

1995—Made in a style similar to the 1996, the 1995 reveals copious quantities of
•   black fruits, obvious old-vine intensity (note the minerals and deep mid-
89+? palate), but mouth-searing levels of tannin will be enjoyed only by masochists.
There are many good things about this wine, but the elevated tannin level is
cause for concern. If the tannin melts away and the fruit holds, this will be
an outstanding effort. Anticipated maturity: 2008–2025. Last tasted, 11/97.

1994—The dark ruby–colored 1994 reveals a Musigny-like nose of violets, black
•   cherries, and powdered stone. This tough-textured, tannic, muscular wine
88? exudes personality and character, but it needs 6–8 years of cellaring. It may
turn out to be an outstanding wine, but since bottling, the wine has become
dominated by its structure and tannin and is less of a sure thing than I
thought last year. While it possesses plenty of personality and richness, it is
questionable as to whether this wine will evolve gracefully or eventually dry
out. A tough call. Anticipated maturity: 2005–2020. Last tasted, 1/97.

1993—A dark ruby/purple color is followed by a kirsch, earthy, truffle nose. This
•   jammy, full-bodied, powerful, backward 1993 needs 7–10 years of cellaring.
89+ Atypically rich, brawny, and muscular for a 1993, this Pavie-Macquin possesses 20–25 years of cellaring potential. How many readers possess the
discipline to wait years for old-style, impressively endowed wine to attain full
maturity? Anticipated maturity: 2005–2020. Last tasted, 1/97.

1992—This property has been making top-notch wines recently. The soft, tasty,
•   elegant 1992 is light to medium bodied, with fine ripeness and balance and a
84   pleasing, gentle finish. Drink it over the next 4–5 years. Last tasted, 11/94.

1990—The 1990 Pavie-Macquin is fat, sweet, and ripe, with its pronounced smoky
  • oak component intertwined with jammy black raspberry and curranty aromas
  91 and flavors. The wine's sweet fruit (from ripeness, not sugar) and concentrated, medium- to full-bodied, low-acid style suggests early maturity, but the
wine is still youthful and unevolved. While already delicious, this wine will
benefit from another 2–3 years of cellaring. It will be at its peak between
2000 and 2008. Last tasted, 11/96.

1989—The 1989 continues to be one of that vintage's sleepers. The color remains a
  • youthful ruby/purple. The bouquet offers copious quantities of black rasp-
  90 berry and cassis fruit nicely touched by stony/mineral and floral scents. The
spicy, vanillin component is subtle. This full-bodied, highly extracted, elegant
wine should reach full maturity in 2–3 years; it will last through the first 15
years of the next century. Last tasted, 11/96.

1988—The 1988 Pavie-Macquin is an excellent wine. Deep in color, with a spicy,
  • black fruit–scented bouquet caressed gently by sweet vanillin oak, this
  87 medium-bodied, concentrated, classy wine offers considerable generosity, as
well as finesse and length. It should be drunk over the next 8–10 years. Last
tasted, 1/93.

QUINAULT-L'ENCLOS   VERY GOOD SINCE 1997

Classification: St.-Emilion Grand Cru
Location of vineyards: Libourne
Owner: Alain and Françoise Raynaud
Address: 30, boulevard de Quinault, 33500 Libourne
Mailing address: Same as above
Telephone: 33 5 57 74 19 52; telefax: 33 5 57 25 91 20
Visits: Every day, between 8 A.M. and noon, and 2 P.M. and 5 P.M.
Contact: Françoise Raynaud

VINEYARDS (red)
Surface area: 37 acres
Average age of vines: 50–70 years
Blend: 80% Merlot, 10% Cabernet Franc, 10% Cabernet Sauvignon
Density of plantation: 5,800 vines per hectare
Average yields (over the last 5 years): 48 hectoliters per hectare
Total average annual production: 80,000 bottles

GRAND VIN (red)
Brand name: Château Quinault-L'Enclos
Appellation: St.-Emilion Grand Cru
Mean annual production: 50,000 bottles
Upbringing: Cold maceration of 1 week at 10 degrees centigrade.
Fermentations at 30 degrees centigrade, macerations (rather warm

temperatures) last 5 weeks, and malolactics occur in barrels. Wines are aged 18 months in entirely new oak barrels. They remain unfined and unfiltered.

SECOND WINE
Brand name: Château Quinault "La Fleur"
Average annual production: 30,000 bottles (wines are aged in 50% new oak and 50% 1-vintage-old barrels)

Evaluation of present classification: Likely the quality and equivalent of a Médoc third- or fourth-growth
Plateau of maturity: Too soon to know

A great deal is expected of this St.-Emilion Grand Cru located in the heart of the city of Libourne. The property possesses extremely old vines and now an exceptionally talented and committed proprietor. This should turn out to be a name to be considered by serious buyers of Bordeaux.

VINTAGES

1997—This is the debut vintage from what will undoubtedly turn out to be an
•   exceptionally promising St.-Emilion estate. Dr. Alain Raynaud and his wife,
87–   Françoise, have resurrected this property, which is essentially an enclosed
88   vineyard within the city limits of Libourne. While it might be expected to fall within the Pomerol appellation, it is actually a St.-Emilion. The Raynauds have invested heavily in constructing a new *cuverie* and *chai*, and the first vintage is indeed a classy wine. It is dark ruby/purple colored, with sweet *pain grillé* notes competing for the drinker's attention with ripe raspberries, cherries, and spice. In the mouth, this graceful, pure wine reveals a smooth texture, medium body, and admirable balance. It is an impressive debut effort from the Raynauds, who are also the proprietors of La Croix de Gay and La Fleur de Gay. Look for Quinault-L'Enclos to be even better in future vintages. Anticipated maturity: 2000–2010. Last tasted, 3/98.

ROL VALENTIN   EXCELLENT SINCE 1995

Classification: St.-Emilion Grand Cru
Location of vineyards: On the northwestern part of the plateau of St.-Emilion
Owner: Eric Prisette
Address: 33330 St.-Emilion
Mailing address: Same as above
Telephone: 33 5 57 74 43 51; telefax: 33 5 57 74 45 13
Visits: By appointment only
Contact: Eric Prisette

VINEYARDS (red)
Surface area: 8.6 acres
Average age of vines: 40 years
Blend: 90% Merlot, 5% Cabernet Franc, and 5% Cabernet Sauvignon
Density of plantation: 6,000 vines per hectare
Average yields (over the last 5 years): 38 hectoliters per hectare
Total average annual production: 15,000–18,000 bottles

GRAND VIN (red)
Brand name: Château Rol Valentin
Appellation: St.-Emilion
Mean annual production: 7,000–9,000 bottles
Upbringing: Fermentations (8 days) and macerations (3–4 weeks) take
place in temperature-controlled concrete vats. Malolactics take place in
100% new oak barrels, and wines are aged 14–18 months depending
upon the vintage. They are fined but remain unfiltered. Beginning next
year, fermentations will take place in wooden tanks.

SECOND WINE
Brand name: Les Valentines
Average annual production: 5,000–7,000 bottles

VINTAGES

1997—It is a shame that this property is so small, because this beautifully made
  • wine merits broader attention. Made from a blend of 90% Merlot, 7% Caber-
90– net Sauvignon, and 3% Cabernet Franc, the 1997 Rol Valentin is crafted in
92 the flamboyant, concentrated style favored by many of the new generation of
  St.-Emilion growers. The wine exhibits a dark ruby/purple color, a wonderfully sweet, kirsch, black currant, and *pain grillé* aromatic profile, medium to
  full body, a creamy, expansive, chewy texture, low acidity, and exceptionally
  ripe tannin. Elements of *sur-maturité* can be found in this layered, purely
  made, rather ostentatious wine. Drink it over the next 10–12 years. Last
  tasted, 3/98.

1996—Young proprietor Eric Prisette is attempting to produce a Valandraud-style
  • St.-Emilion at Rol Valentin. The 1996 is a well-endowed, full-bodied, opaque
90– ruby/purple–colored wine with lavish quantities of new oak, outstanding
91 purity, and layers of fleshy, jammy red and black fruits, glycerin, and body.
  The tannin is sweet and the wine broad shouldered and potentially outstanding. This is a wine to purchase quickly, before the price soars out of control.
  Anticipated maturity: 2002–2016. Last tasted, 3/98.

SOUTARD   EXCELLENT

Classification: St.-Emilion Grand Cru Classé
Location of vineyards: St.-Emilion, northern sector
Owner: Des Ligneris family
Address: 33330 St.-Emilion
Mailing address: Same as above
Telephone: 33 5 57 24 72 23; telefax: 33 5 57 24 66 94
Visits: By appointment, on weekdays only, between 8 A.M. and noon, and
2 P.M. and 6 P.M.
Contact: François des Ligneris

VINEYARDS (red)
Surface area: 54.3 acres
Average age of vines: 35 years
Blend: 65% Merlot, 35% Cabernet Franc
Density of plantation: 5,500 vines per hectare
Average yields (over the last 5 years): 48 hectoliters per hectare
Total average annual production: 130,000 bottles

GRAND VIN (red)
Brand name: Château Soutard
Appellation: St.-Emilion Grand Cru Classé
Mean annual production: 120,000 bottles
Upbringing: Fermentations and macerations are long (in 1997, 40–45
days) and take place at low temperatures. Sometimes malolactics are not
completed by July, in which case there is no addition of sulfites to the
wines. These are aged for 1 year in oak barrels (several sizes and
different types of wood) that are renewed by a third each vintage. They
remain on lees during the winter and are unfined and unfiltered.

SECOND WINE
Brand name: Clos de la Tonnelle
Average annual production: 10,000 bottles

Evaluation of present classification: Should be upgraded to a St.-Emilion
Premier Grand Cru Classé; the quality equivalent of a Médoc third- or
fourth-growth
Plateau of maturity: 10–25 or more years following the vintage

This is one of the oldest St.-Emilion estates and has been owned by the same
family since 1785. Situated in the northern part of the appellation, the vineyard is located on a soil base composed primarily of limestone.

Soutard is highly prized in the Benelux countries, but the wine has largely
been ignored outside Europe. That is a shame, because this is one of the most

traditionally made and longest-lived wines in St.-Emilion, rivaled only by Ausone and a handful of other St.-Emilions in terms of potential longevity. Most vintages can easily last for 25 or more years and are often unapproachable for a decade.

The property employs at least one-third new oak for aging the wine and often bottles it much later than other St.-Emilion châteaux. Soutard is usually an opaque dark ruby color (there is no fining or filtration) and possesses a powerful, tannic ferocity that can be off-putting when the wine is young. Nevertheless, this is one of St.-Emilion's best-kept secrets. For consumers looking for wines capable of lasting 20 or more years, Soutard should be seriously considered.

VINTAGES

1993—This estate, which tends to march to the beat of a different drummer
•   when it comes to bottling (later than most), has fashioned a full-bodied,
87   concentrated, ripe 1993 with surprising suppleness, good underlying structure, and moderate tannin. It offers plenty of juicy Merlot fruit and a jammy personality. More tannin and delineation should emerge with age. This big, beefy, mouth-filling wine appears to be an excellent example of the vintage; it is capable of 10–15 years of cellaring. Last tasted, 3/96.

1992—Soutard's 1992 displays a medium ruby color, weedy, smoky, berry fruit in the
•   nose, modest proportions in the mouth, and hard tannin in the finish. It should
77   be drunk over the next 4–5 years before the tannin begins to dominate the fragile fruit. Last tasted, 11/94.

1991—Soutard should have had second thoughts about placing its 1991 on the
•   market. This hollow, light, disappointing, vapid, vegetal offering is nearly
64   undrinkable. Last tasted, 1/94.

1990—The 1990, which is close in quality to the 1989, is a typical Soutard, with
•   its massive proportions, gobs of tannin, highly structured, old-style, intense
88   concentration, and a powerful, tannic, rich finish. Anticipated maturity: Now– 2010. Last tasted, 1/93.

1989—As one might expect, Soutard's 1989 is one of the most backward wines of
•   the vintage. Impressively opaque ruby/purple, with a spicy, vanillin-scented,
90   plum and licorice bouquet, this full-bodied, muscular, and densely concentrated wine needs at least 7–10 years of bottle aging. It may well merit an outstanding rating by the turn of the century. Look for it to last at least 20 or more years. One of the most impressive wines of the vintage, it may well be the longest-lived St.-Emilion produced in 1989. Anticipated maturity: 2000– 2020. Last tasted, 4/91.

1988—Backward, dense, concentrated, and unforthcoming, the powerful, herba-
•   ceous, vanillin-and-black-currant-scented 1988 Soutard has plenty of extract,
87   although it is buried beneath considerable quantities of tannin. It is a worthy candidate for 20 or more years of cellaring. Anticipated maturity: Now–2020. Last tasted, 1/93.

1986—Soutard remains one of the longest-lived wines in the appellation of
•   St.-Emilion. There is no doubt that the proprietors intentionally packed this
86   wine with gobs of extract and mouth-searing tannins, making it a sure bet
       to last 20 years. The 1986 is a very backward, unyielding wine, with tremen-
       dous tannin levels but also rich, highly extracted, concentrated fruit. Antici-
       pated maturity: Now–2015. Last tasted, 3/90.

1985—The 1985 Soutard is a sensationally rich, tannic, deep, multi-dimensional
•   wine that balances muscle and grace. It is more supple than usual but is still
90   capable of 20 or more years of longevity. Anticipated maturity: Now–2010.
       Last tasted, 3/90.

1982—The 1982 is an old-style St.-Emilion made to last and last. It belongs with
•   enthusiasts who have the patience to lay it away for a decade or more. The
87   1982 is typically huge, backward, almost abrasively tannic. However, this
       wine—which is now quite closed—has a broodingly dark color and excellent
       richness, ripeness, and weight on the palate and will no doubt receive a
       higher score circa 2000, but it is brutally tannic. Anticipated maturity: 2000–
       2025. Last tasted, 3/89.

1981—The 1981 is closed in but exhibits ripe, spicy, plummy fruit, a tight, firm
•   structure, and plenty of weight and richness. Soutard has made an impressive
84   wine in 1981, but once again one needs patience. Anticipated maturity: Now–
       2005. Last tasted, 6/84.

1979—A very successful 1979, but unlike most wines from this vintage, Soutard is
•   backward and tannic, with a deep ruby color and a big-framed structure. It is
84   still raw and undeveloped and tastes like a barrel sample rather than a
       5-year-old wine. Anticipated maturity: Now–2005. Last tasted, 6/84.

1978—Totally different in style from the 1979, the 1978 Soutard tastes much softer
•   and riper and has more mid-range fruit, full body, relatively low acidity, and a
84   good, lush, moderately tannic finish. For Soutard, this wine will develop much
       more quickly than normal. Anticipated maturity: Now. Last tasted, 6/84.

1975—A very impressive wine, the 1975 Soutard is still youthfully dark ruby, with
•   rich, savory, ripe, full-bodied flavors, plenty of mouth-coating tannins, and a
87   long finish. This is a big, typical Soutard that will continue to evolve very
       slowly. Anticipated maturity: Now–2005. Last tasted, 10/84.

1966—Not so big or so intense as one might expect, the 1966 Soutard is fully mature
•   and has a dark color with some brown at the edge, a ripe, harmonious, sweet
82   palate impression, and some light tannins in the finish. This vintage of Sou-
       tard is surprisingly elegant and lighter than expected. Anticipated maturity:
       Now–may be in decline. Last tasted, 6/81.

1964—This is one of the few great Soutards that can be said to have reached full
•   maturity. The huge bouquet of roasted cassis, grilled nuts, and smoky oak
90   also has a touch of volatile acidity that adds rather than detracts from its
       appeal. In the mouth, it has a voluptuous, full-bodied, opulent texture, gobs
       of fruit, and plenty of alcohol in its heady finish. This is a dense, old-style,
       and superbly concentrated wine that should continue to drink well for another
       10–15 or more years. Anticipated maturity: Now–2005. Last tasted, 3/90.

ANCIENT VINTAGES

The only old Soutard I had the privilege of tasting was the 1955 (rated 88 in 1989). I am sure at one time it was an unbearably rustic wine, but the tannins have largely melted away, even though the wine is still relatively firm. The result is a rich, full-bodied, mineral-scented wine offering gobs of black fruits (plums) in its taste.

TERTRE-DAUGAY   GOOD

Classification: St.-Emilion Grand Cru Classé
Location of vineyards: St.-Emilion
Owner: Léo de Malet-Roquefort
Address: 33330 St.-Emilion
Mailing address: Same as above
Telephone: 33 5 57 24 72 15; telefax: 33 5 57 24 65 24
Visits: By appointment only
Contact: E. Degliade or Jean-Marie Galeri

VINEYARDS (red)
Surface area: 38.3 acres
Average age of vines: 25 years
Blend: 60% Merlot, 40% Cabernet Franc
Density of plantation: 6,600 vines per hectare
Average yields (over the last 5 years): 40 hectoliters per hectare
Total average annual production: 550 hectoliters

GRAND VIN (red)
Brand name: Château Tertre-Daugay
Appellation: St.-Emilion Grand Cru Classé
Mean annual production: 500 hectoliters
Upbringing: Fermentations last approximately 3–4 weeks.
Wines are aged in oak barrels 30% of which are new (the
rest being 1 and 2 vintages old). They are fined and
filtered.

SECOND WINE
Brand name: Château de Roquefort
Average annual production: 50 hectoliters

Evaluation of present classification: The quality equivalent of a good
Médoc Cru Bourgeois
Plateau of maturity: 5–15 years following the vintage

This was a property that, because of sloppy winemaking and lack of effective management, lost complete credibility during the sixties and seventies. In 1978 the proprietor of La Gaffelière, Comte Léo de Malet-Roquefort, purchased the property and has made significant improvements both to the vineyards and to the wine cellar. It has taken some time for the vineyard to rebound, but both the 1988 and 1989 were more promising, particularly after such a prolonged period of mediocrity.

Historically, Tertre-Daugay is one of the most ancient properties in St.-Emilion. It is located on the hillside near most of the Premiers Grands Crus Classés. The actual name is derived from the Gascon term *Daugay*, which means "lookout hill." The excellent exposure enjoyed by the vineyard of Tertre-Daugay ensures maximum ripening of the grapes. The soil, a combination of clay and limestone with significant iron deposits in the subsoil, is claimed to give the wines great body and concentration.

VINTAGES

1997—This woody, dark ruby–colored wine reveals some ripeness and cherry/berry
  •   fruit on the attack, but it becomes more attenuated, compact, and angular in
79–   the mouth. Drink this light-bodied 1997 during its first 5–7 years of life. Last
82   tasted, 3/98.

1993—The 1993 is a light-bodied, undernourished wine with excessive tannin and
  •   little ripe fruit in evidence. Last tasted, 11/94.
75

1990—The 1990 exhibits fine concentration, a deep, dark ruby color, low acidity, a
  •   multi-dimensional personality, and a long, luscious finish. For drinking over the
86   next 8–10 years, it will provide considerable enjoyment. Last tasted, 1/93.

1989—The 1989 is the best wine produced at the property in years. Concentrated,
  •   full bodied, with a heady alcohol content, this lavish, richly fruity, broad-
87   shouldered wine should be drunk in its first decade of life. Anticipated
       maturity: Now–2005. Last tasted, 1/93.

LE TERTRE-ROTEBOEUF   OUTSTANDING

Classification: St.-Emilion Grand Cru
Location of vineyards: St.-Laurent des Combes
Owner: François and Emilie Mitjavile
Address: 33330 St.-Laurent des Combes
Mailing address: Same as above
Telephone: 33 5 57 24 70 57; telefax: 33 5 57 74 42 11
Visits: By appointment only

VINEYARDS (red)
Surface area: 14 acres
Average age of vines: 32 years

Blend: 80% Merlot, 20% Cabernet Franc
Density of plantation: 6,000–7,000 vines per hectare
Average yields (over the last 5 years): 35 hectoliters per hectare
Total average annual production: 22,000 bottles

GRAND VIN (red)
Brand name: Château Tertre-Roteboeuf
Appellation: St.-Emilion
Mean annual production: 22,000 bottles
Upbringing: Fermentations and macerations are traditional and last
3–4 weeks in concrete tanks (temperature is manually controlled).
Malolactics take place in new oak barrels, and wines are aged in
100% new oak for 16–18 months. Fining and filtration depend upon
the vintage.

SECOND WINE
None produced.

Evaluation of present classification: The quality equivalent of a Médoc
second-growth
Plateau of maturity: 3–15 years following the vintage

It is unfortunate, but, I suppose, given the commercial world in which we live, totally understandable that there are just so few people in the wine world like François Mitjavile. While many famous producers push yields to such preposterous levels that they risk destroying any concept of *terroir* of the vineyard, or even muting the character of a vintage, here is one man whose talent and obsession for producing the finest possible wines are refreshing.

Le Tertre-Roteboeuf's micro-size vineyard now receives worldwide attention. It is no doubt justified, but one hopes nothing changes at this estate, which is run with single-minded determination by Monsieur Mitjavile. He makes no compromises. What Mitjavile has in mind is to make a wine from this splendidly situated vineyard that has the extract and intensity of wines such as Lafleur, Pétrus, and Certan de May in Pomerol. To do so, Mitjavile is one of the last to harvest, keeps his yields small, and since 1985 utilizes 100% new oak to harness the power of his wine. There is no doubt that recent vintages have had dazzling levels of fruit and a flashy flamboyance that have drawn numerous rave reviews from the European wine press.

The steep, sheltered vineyard (near Larcis-Ducasse) is named after the oxen that are necessary to cultivate the soil. When translated, the name means "the hill of the belching beef." Le Tertre-Roteboeuf is irrefutably one of Bordeaux's new superstars.

VINTAGES

1997—At this stage of life, Le Tertre-Roteboeuf's 1997, while impressive, is slightly

•　dominated by its toasty, *pain grillé,* oaky notes. Nevertheless, this is a round,

87–　ripe (*sur-maturité* is evident), medium-bodied, layered, opulently textured

90　wine with low acidity. Its garish display of toasty oak, jammy berry fruit, coffee, and chocolate flavors is admirable. This wine will be delicious young and probably best consumed during its first 7–8 years of life. Readers who remember the 1985 Le Tertre-Roteboeuf will find the 1997 comparable in style and drinkability. Last tasted, 3/98.

1996—In an irregular vintage for Bordeaux's right bank (Pomerol and St.-Emilion),

•　Le Tertre-Roteboeuf has fashioned a wine with luxuriously rich fruit and all

90–　the elements of *sur-maturité*—jammy plums, coffee, chocolate, and low acid-

93　ity. Fat, fleshy, dense flavors coat the palate with an unctuous texture. This is a luscious, rich, silky-textured wine bursting with fruit and personality. I expected this wine to become more structured and delineated with barrel age, but it has become even more decadently hedonistic. Anticipated maturity: Now–2012. Last tasted, 3/98.

1995—This is the third vintage (1989 and 1990 were the other two) where Le

•　Tertre-Roteboeuf exhibits a Le Pin–like exotic richness and opulence. The

95　wine exhibits a dense ruby/purple color and a compelling set of aromatics consisting of *pain grillé,* ripe black cherry and cassis fruit intermixed with truffles, mocha, and toffee. Dense and full bodied, with layers of intensely ripe fruit, this plump, gorgeously pure, expansively flavored, multi-dimensional wine is even better out of bottle than it was in cask. Anticipated maturity: 2001–2018. Last tasted, 11/97.

1994—This wine was increasingly stunning and supple each time I went back to it

•　as it evolved in cask, but it appears to have closed down. The wine exhibits a

90　dark saturated ruby/purple color and a tight, earthy nose that reluctantly gives up jammy black raspberry and cherry notes intermingled with grilled meats and smoky scents. Medium to full bodied, with more tannin in evidence than prior to bottling, this is a fat, dense, expansively flavored wine with outstanding purity, ripeness, and depth. However, I am always inclined to give the after-bottling tasting more weight than the half dozen or so tastings prior to bottling, because "it's what's in the bottle that counts." I may have caught this wine at an awkward stage, as it is unquestionably weighty, rich, and certainly outstanding, but I expected it to be even more intense. Antici-pated maturity: 1999–2012. Last tasted, 1/97.

1993—The 1993 Le Tertre-Roteboeuf's color is a deep ruby/purple. The nose offers

•　up backward, unevolved, sweet, plum, black cherry, and cassis aromas, with

90　a touch of earth and new oak. Dense, medium to full bodied, and moderately tannic, this is not the exotic, open-knit, flamboyant style of the 1989 and 1990, but it is an impressively endowed wine that will benefit from another 3–5 years of cellaring; it should keep for 15–20 years. It is an impressive 1993 that is selling for about one-fifth the price of the 1989 or 1990. Antici-pated maturity: 2001–2015. Last tasted, 1/97.

1992—I am an enthusiastic fan of the wines of Le Tertre-Roteboeuf, but even this
•   fanatically run property failed to triumph over the unkind hand dealt by
77   Mother Nature in September 1992. This light-bodied, soft, spicy, weedy, and
     diluted wine should be drunk up over the next 2–3 years. It is low in acidity
     and lacking depth. Last tasted, 11/94.

1991—Ironically, the 1991 reveals more depth, ripeness, and fruit than the exces-
•   sively woody, diluted, light-bodied 1992. The soft, berry, oaky, medium-
83   bodied 1991 will provide pleasant drinking for 4–5 years. Last tasted, 1/94.

1990—The 1990 has been so stunning the last several times I tasted it that it is
•   inching its way up the scoring ladder. In fact, I am close to running out of
98   points. The sweet nose of coffee, jammy berry fruit, smoke, caramel, and
     spice soars from a glass of this marvelously concentrated, viscous, layered,
     smooth wine. Whatever tannin this show-stopping, flashy wine possesses (I
     am sure if analyzed, the level is respectable) is buried beneath the jammy
     fruit and glycerin. The 1990 is so dazzling that I would be a fool to suggest
     owners refrain from consuming it. It should continue to drink well for 10–15
     years. Last tasted, 6/98.

1989—A great Le Tertre-Roteboeuf, the 1989 is a massively endowed wine with
•   full-blown aromas of bacon fat and sweet fruit. As someone once said, tasting
95   these wines is akin to swallowing liquefied chocolate-covered, over-ripe cher-
     ries. The 1989 will benefit from another 2–3 years of cellaring; it will last for
     2 decades. It may turn out to be the more classical wine of this duo, but not
     necessarily superior. Last tasted, 12/97.

1988—Mitjavile's 1988 is extraordinary and, once again, super-concentrated, with a
•   dazzling level of extract and a powerful, full-bodied, concentrated finish. It is
91   less flashy and unctuous than the 1989, and those who like their Bordeaux a bit
     more linear and obviously tannic may prefer the 1988. It is a spectacular, rivet-
     ing wine from one of the most driven winemakers in the world. I know the wine
     has now become hard to find, but producers like this deserve consumers' sup-
     port, even allegiance. Anticipated maturity: Now–2010. Last tasted, 4/91.

1986—The 1986 is a prodigious wine, aged in 100% new oak, with fabulous ripeness
•   and richness as well as an amazingly long, opulent, fleshy finish. The wine is
91   immensely seductive and full bodied and, despite its precocious appeal,
     should age well for at least a decade. Anticipated maturity: Now–2002. Last
     tasted, 3/91.

1985—The 1985 Le Tertre-Roteboeuf has an astonishing level of richness, the per-
•   fume of a wine costing three to four times as much, full body, an opulent
90   texture that recalls a great 1982, and a penetrating fragrance and taste that
     are top class. Anticipated maturity: Now–2000. Last tasted, 11/96.

1984—A successful 1984, this wine is meaty, cleanly made, soft, and well colored.
•   Anticipated maturity: Now. Last tasted, 3/91.
81

1983—This wine has reached full maturity and has taken on a slightly amber edge
•   to its deep ruby color. The big, spicy, ripe nose offers up gobs of mineral
87   scents and super-ripe black fruit. In the mouth, this fleshy, chewy, full-bodied

wine has excellent extract, a velvety texture, and a long, heady, alcoholic finish. Anticipated maturity: Now–2000. Last tasted, 3/90.

1982—The 1982 was the first vintage of Le Tertre-Roteboeuf I tasted and that was
  •   made before proprietor François Mitjavile began to use new oak casks and
 87   make a selection. Certainly the raw materials were among the finest he has ever had, but the wine could use more grip and structure, which would have occurred if new oak had been employed. The wine offers plenty of pleasure, with considerable quantities of nearly over-ripe cherry fruit intermingled with scents of caramel, herbs, and earth. Soft, supple, and fat, this is a wine to drink over the next 3–4 years. Last tasted, 9/95.

LA TOUR-DU-PIN-FIGEAC-MOUEIX   GOOD

Classification: St.-Emilion Grand Cru Classé
Production: 4,000 cases
Blend: 60% Merlot, 30% Cabernet Franc, 10% Malbec
Secondary label: None
Vineyard size: 22 acres
Proprietor: Armand Moueix
Time spent in barrels: 16–22 months
Average age of vines: 20 years

Evaluation of present classification: The quality equivalent of a Médoc Cru Bourgeois
Plateau of maturity: 3–12 or more years following the vintage

La Tour-du-Pin-Figeac-Moueix is situated on a sandy, clay, gravelly soil base on the Pomerol border between Cheval Blanc and La Tour-Figeac.

The wine of La Tour-du-Pin-Figeac-Moueix is made in a straightforward, fleshy, fruity style, with good body and an aging potential of 6–12 years. Few vintages of this wine will improve beyond their twelfth birthday.

VINTAGES

1995—Another sexy, up-front, flattering wine, the 1995 La Tour-du-Pin-Figeac is not
  •   complex, but it possesses low acidity, gobs of ripe fruit, and medium body
 87   presented in a delicious, soft, enchanting style. Drink it over the next 7–8 years. Last tasted, 11/97.

1994—Similar to the 1993, with more raspberry, kirsch-like fruit, this medium-bodied,
  •   luscious, fruity, soft, low-acid wine has managed to avoid this vintage's high
 87   tannin and astringency. Drink it over the next 6–7 years. Last tasted, 1/97.

1993—This soft, fruity, strawberry-and-cherry-scented wine makes no pretense
  •   of being complex or intellectually challenging. Drink this medium ruby–
 86   colored, pretty, deliciously fruity, low-acid wine over the next 4–5 years. Last tasted, 1/97.

1990—The seductive, impressive, black/ruby–colored 1990 is another exhilarating
  •   St.-Emilion. Densely colored, this wine's huge bouquet of jammy fruits (plums
89   and raspberries), meaty, full-bodied texture, and lavish quantities of fruit all
     combine to make this an impressive effort. Anticipated maturity: Now–2008.
     Last tasted, 1/93.

1989—The 1989 is a concentrated, powerful, full-bodied wine, with gobs of extract
  •   and a penetrating bouquet of black fruits, new oak, and subtle herbs. A
88   powerhouse of a wine, it is well balanced, with decent acidity for the vintage
     and a super finish. Anticipated maturity: Now–2003. Last tasted, 1/93.

1988—The 1988 from this estate is a worthy competitor to the 1989, with excellent
  •   extract, more elegance but less power, and a rich, toasty, plummy bouquet
87   intertwined with scents of licorice, toast, and spring flowers. Full bodied and
     intense for a 1988, it should be at its best between now and 2004. Last tasted,
     1/93.

1986—The 1986 is packed with oodles of berry fruit, is full bodied, and has signifi-
  •   cant tannins in the finish. While it lacks the charm of the excellent 1985, it
87   should last for at least 2 decades. Anticipated maturity: Now–2005. Last
     tasted, 3/90.

1985—The 1985 is an impressive St.-Emilion, with grip and very fine balance.
  •   Powerful, concentrated, rich, opaque in color, full bodied, and soft enough to
87   drink now, this boldly flavored wine will keep well for another decade. Antici-
     pated maturity: Now–2000. Last tasted, 3/89.

1982—One of the best efforts in years from this property, the 1982 is dark ruby, with
  •   an attractive ripe berryish, spicy bouquet. On the palate, the wine is silky,
85   velvety, and medium to full bodied, with light to moderate tannins and a good,
     lush finish. Anticipated maturity: Now. Last tasted, 1/85.

TROPLONG-MONDOT   OUTSTANDING

Classification: St.-Emilion Grand Cru Classé
Location of vineyards: St.-Emilion
Owner: G.F.A. Valette (directed by Christine Valette)
Address: 33330 St.-Emilion
Mailing address: Same as above
Telephone: 33 5 57 55 32 05; telefax: 33 5 57 55 32 07
Visits: By appointment only

VINEYARDS (red)
Surface area: 74 acres
Average age of vines: 40 years
Blend: 80% Merlot, 10% Cabernet Franc, 10% Cabernet Sauvignon
Density of plantation: 6,000 vines per hectare
Average yields (over the last 5 years): 41.89 hectoliters per hectare
Total average annual production: 130,000 bottles

GRAND VIN (red)
Brand name: Château Troplong-Mondot
Appellation: St.-Emilion Grand Cru Classé
Mean annual production: 100,000 bottles
Upbringing: Alcoholic fermentations and macerations take place
in temperature-controlled stainless-steel vats. Wines undergo
malolactics in oak barrels (70% of which are new and 30% of which
are 1 vintage old) and are aged for 12–24 months depending upon
the vintage. They are fined with fresh egg whites but remain
unfiltered.

SECOND WINE
Brand name: Mondot
Average annual production: 30,000 bottles

Evaluation of present classification: Since 1985 should be elevated to a
St.-Emilion Premier Grand Cru Classé; the quality equivalent of a Médoc
second- or third-growth
Plateau of maturity: 5–15 or more years following the vintage

This lovely château, with a magnificent view overlooking the town and vine-yards of St.-Emilion, sits on a slope facing the Côte de Pavie. There are numerous old vines. Since the mid-1980s, when Michel Rolland was brought in as the oenologist and Christine Valette began assuming more control, the quality of the vintages has soared. There is an extended maceration in stainless-steel vats and aging of the wine for at least 18 months in oak casks, of which 70% are new. The wine is fined but never filtered.

I should also note that the introduction of a secondary label has resulted in weaker vats being relegated to that wine, which has only served to strengthen the wine that appears under the label Troplong-Mondot.

St.-Emilion and Pomerol have had their share of famous, even legendary, female proprietors. There was Madame Fournier at Château Canon and, of course, the well-known Madame Loubat of Pétrus. Now the appellation boasts Christine Valette, whose extraordinary commitment to quality is especially evident in great wines produced at Troplong-Mondot in the 1988, 1989, 1990, 1994, 1995, and 1997 vintages.

VINTAGES

1997—I much prefer this effort from the impeccably run Troplong-Mondot to the
• château's tannic 1996. The impressive 1997 is one of the vintage's top wines.
90– The color is saturated black purple, and the nose offers up blackberry, cassis,
92 olive, and licorice scents along with nicely integrated toasty new oak. In the

mouth, there is impeccable balance, gorgeously sweet layers of ripe fruit, medium body, fabulous concentration, and sweet, velvety tannin. This should be a charming, seductive Troplong-Mondot that can be consumed early. Anticipated maturity: 2001–2015. Last tasted, 3/98.

1996— This wine still offers plenty of promise but also raises numerous questions
• about its overall balance. Although the wine's blue/black color, high-class
88– aromatics of black fruits, toasty new oak, licorice, and minerals are outstand-
90? ing, the excruciatingly severe level of tannin is worrisome. This is a medium-bodied, concentrated, but unevolved, backward claret. Will the tannin melt away and make this vintage of Troplong-Mondot less austere than it appears to be? Anticipated maturity: 2006–2020. Last tasted, 3/98.

1995— Closed but immensely promising, this dark purple–colored wine exhibits
• a reticent but intriguing nose of underbrush, jammy black fruits, minerals,
92 and vanillin. Deep, rich, and medium to full bodied, with outstanding extract and purity, the wine possesses a seamless personality with sweeter, more integrated tannin than in the 1996. This is a *vin de garde* to cellar for another 7–8 years. It is not far off the splendid level of quality achieved in both 1989 and 1990. Anticipated maturity: 2005–2020. Last tasted, 11/97.

1994— Opaque ruby/purple colored, with a tight but promising nose of toasty new
• oak, black fruits, licorice, and spice, the 1994 Troplong-Mondot is built for
90 the long haul. The wine possesses high tannin levels as well as outstanding concentration and ripeness. It is largely closed except for some explosive sweetness and ripeness that appear at the back of the palate. Prospective purchasers should realize this wine requires 7–8 years of cellaring before it rounds out. Anticipated maturity: 2005–2015. Last tasted, 1/97.

1993— This dark ruby–colored wine with a purple center exhibits a spicy, toasty,
• plum, black cherry, and cassis nose and medium-bodied, tannic flavors, with
87+ good sweetness, purity, and ripeness. The wine is a backward 1993 that will require 2–4 years of cellaring; it will keep for a dozen or more years. Anticipated maturity: 2001–2012. Last tasted, 1/97.

1992— At three separate bottle tastings, Troplong-Mondot's 1992 blew away much of
• the St.-Emilion competition and embarrassed many of the Premier Grand Cru
89 Classés. The wine boasts a saturated black/purple color and a huge, sweet, ripe nose of black currant fruit intermingled with scents of toasty new oak, herbs, and licorice. It is amazingly concentrated for the vintage, with superb denseness and ripeness of fruit, moderate tannin, and a long, pure, beautifully proportioned finish. It will benefit from 2–3 years of cellaring and last for 15 years. Once it has more bottle age, it may merit an outstanding score. Last tasted, 11/94.

1991— In a disastrous vintage for Pomerol and St.-Emilion, the 1991 Troplong-
• Mondot stands out for its medium dark ruby color and spicy, ripe nose of
85 cassis, vanillin, licorice, and toast. With elegant, medium-bodied, attractive, rich flavors, this supple, well-endowed wine should drink well for 4–6 years. Last tasted, 6/95.

1990—The amazing performance of the 1990 Troplong-Mondot came as no surprise.
•　　This broodingly backward, opaque purple–colored wine with masses of fruit,
98　　extraction, and power reveals a chocolatey, black currant, weedy tobacco-
　　　scented nose and classic, full-bodied, powerful flavors. It possesses a massive
　　　finish that coats the mouth with extract, glycerin, and tannin. I suspect the
　　　1990 will mature rather quickly because of its lower acidity. Anticipated
　　　maturity: Now–2020. Last tasted, 12/97.

1989—The 1989 Troplong-Mondot is an extraordinary wine. It is slightly less evolved
•　　than the 1990, with more muscle and tannin, but equally rich and compelling.
96　　The color is an opaque dark ruby/purple, and the wine offers up aromas of
　　　licorice, prunes, black cherries, and sweet cassis fruit intermingled with
　　　high-quality toasty new oak and smoke. This is a full-bodied, rich, layered,
　　　concentrated wine that should evolve more slowly than the 1990. It is a
　　　spectacular achievement in this vintage! Anticipated maturity: 2003–2025.
　　　Last tasted, 12/97.

1988—The 1988 Troplong-Mondot is a beautifully made, elegant wine with a deep
•　　ruby/purple color, a fascinating bouquet of plums, spicy new oak, and miner-
89　　als, rich, multi-dimensional flavors, and fresh acidity. Another example of a
　　　young proprietor committed to making a strict selection. Anticipated maturity:
　　　Now–2007. Last tasted, 12/96.

1986—The 1986 is a more structured version of the elegant, complex 1985. There
•　　is a good lashing of toasty new oak, medium body, a moderately intense bou-
89　　quet of cedary, black currant fruit, excellent length, and complete harmony
　　　among the wine's elements. Anticipated maturity: Now–2005. Last tasted,
　　　3/90.

1985—The 1985, with a deep ruby color and a complex bouquet of spicy oak and
•　　ripe currants, offers extremely well-balanced and well-delineated flavors,
87　　medium body, excellent depth, and firm, but soft tannins. Anticipated matu-
　　　rity: Now–2005. Last tasted, 3/90.

1984—Very light, dilute, short on the palate, but drinkable, the 1984 Troplong
•　　should be drunk up. Anticipated maturity: Now–may be in decline. Last
73　　tasted, 3/87.

1982—This is a soft, simple, one-dimensional wine that was made before proprietor
•　　Christine Valette began to take Troplong-Mondot to the heights of the Bor-
79　　deaux hierarchy. The soft, herbal, pleasant 1982 is beginning to lose some of
　　　its fruit, with the acidity, tannin, and alcohol starting to dominate. Drink
　　　it up. Last tasted, 9/95.

1981—Not much different from the 1982, the 1981 is perhaps less fleshy, ripe, and
•　　concentrated, but it has a light- to medium-bodied feel on the palate, soft,
79　　fruity flavors, and some light tannins in the finish. Anticipated maturity:
　　　Now–may be in decline. Last tasted, 1/85.

TROTTE VIEILLE   GOOD

Classification: St.-Emilion Premier Grand Cru Classé B
Location of vineyards: St.-Emilion
Owner: Castéja—Preben-Hansen families
Address: 33330 St.-Emilion
Mailing address: c/o Maison Borie Manoux, 86, cours Balguerie
Stuttenberg, 33082 Bordeaux Cedex
Telephone: 33 5 56 00 00 70; telefax: 33 5 57 87 60 30
Visits: By appointment only
Contact: Borie-Manoux at above telephone and fax numbers

VINEYARDS (red)
Surface area: 24.7 acres
Average age of vines: 40 years
Blend: 50% Merlot, 45% Cabernet Franc, 5% Cabernet Sauvignon
Density of plantation: 7,500 vines per hectare
Average yields (over the last 5 years): 46 hectoliters per hectare

GRAND VIN (red)
Brand name: Château Trotte Vieille
Appellation: St.-Emilion Premier Grand Cru Classé
Upbringing: Fermentations last about 3 weeks. Wines undergo
malolactics in barrels and are aged in oak barrels (90% of which are new)
for 12–18 months. They are fined but not filtered.

SECOND WINE
None produced.

Evaluation of present classification: Since 1986 the wines justify Trotte
Vieille's rating as a Premier Grand Cru Classé; previously the wine was
the quality equivalent of a Médoc Cru Bourgeois
Plateau of maturity: 5–20 years following the vintage

One of the celebrated Premiers Grands Crus Classés of St.-Emilion, Trotte
Vieille is located east of St.-Emilion in a relatively isolated spot on clay and
limestone soil. Since 1949 it has been the property of Borie-Manoux, the
well-known firm of Bordeaux *négociants*. This firm also owns Batailley, the
fifth-growth Pauillac, and Domaine de l'Eglise, an up-and-coming Pomerol,
as well as a bevy of lesser-known Bordeaux châteaux.

Trotte Vieille is a wine with which I have had many disappointing experiences. Until the mid-1980s the property produced wines that were among the
most mediocre of St.-Emilion. Prior to 1985 Trotte Vieille too frequently

lacked concentration and character and was often disturbingly light and dull; in some vintages it was also poorly vinified.

Since the mid-1980s the indifferent winemaking at Trotte Vieille has come to a halt. I suspect the dedication of Philippe Castéja is largely responsible for the remarkable turnaround in the quality of this estate's wines. The stricter selection process, the use of 90% new oak, and the decision to harvest later and extend the maceration has resulted in a relatively profound wine that now appears capable of challenging the best of the appellation.

VINTAGES

1997—This is a pretty, lighter-styled, medium-bodied wine with a healthy dark ruby/purple color and attractive, sweet *pain grillé*, licorice, and black currant aromas and flavors. Soft, plump, and easy to understand and drink, the wine offers low acidity and moderate concentration that suggest it will be best consumed over the next 7–8 years. Last tasted, 3/98.

• 85– 87

1996—Impressive before bottling, the 1996 Trotte Vieille was put through malolactic fermentation in barrel, which has resulted in a wine with a creamier texture and better integration of new oak. This wine possesses a dark ruby/purple color as well as an attractive nose of sweet black fruits and vanillin. There is admirable expansiveness, texture, and flavor, sweet black cherry and currant fruit, spicy oak, medium body, and soft tannin—especially for a 1996. The wine should be drinkable early yet keep. Anticipated maturity: 2000–2012. Last tasted, 3/98.

• 87– 88

1995—I have very good tasting notes of this wine before bottling, but tasted twice after bottling, the wine has revealed an evolved medium ruby color already displaying amber at the edge. Additionally, the wine came across as austere, hard, tannic, and out of balance. This is completely at odds with prebottling samples, so I prefer to reserve judgment. Last tasted, 11/97.

• ?

1994—Dark ruby colored, with a gentle, cedary, herb-infused, cherry-scented bouquet, this soft, medium-bodied wine gives conflicting signals with its low acidity and high tannin. The attack is soft, but the tannin then kicks in, resulting in an attenuated, short finish. This wine should evolve for 8–10 years. Last tasted, 1/97.

• 85

1993—Better than many of the disappointing St.-Emilion Premiers Grands Crus Classés, the 1993 Trotte Vieille exhibits a medium ruby color, sweet, cherry fruit, a touch of *herbes de Provence*, an austere palate, and more definition, fat, and ripeness than its peer group. It should drink well for 5–7 years. Last tasted, 1/97.

• 84

1992—This light-bodied, soft wine avoids the harsh tannin and vegetal character of so many 1992s, but it offers no real density or depth. Nevertheless, there is some pleasant, straightforward charm in the wine's berry fruit and gentle, easygoing, diluted, Burgundy-like character. Drink it over the next 4–5 years. Last tasted, 11/94.

• 78

1991—This property is high on its 1991, but I cannot understand why. It is diluted
• and thin, with some vegetal fruitiness but little grip or concentration. Last
72 tasted, 1/94.

1990—The 1990 is at least very good. A backward, oaky, tannic wine in need of
• some bottle age, this full-bodied St.-Emilion exhibits plenty of power and
88 guts. Anticipated maturity: Now–2005. Last tasted, 1/93.

1989—The 1989 is an immensely impressive wine, exhibiting an opaque black color
• and a sensational bouquet of licorice, chocolate, and super-ripe plums. In the
90 mouth, the wine displays immense size, enormous concentration, a tremendous level of tannins, and an intense, alcoholic, long, opulent finish. Given
the size of this wine, the acidity seems sound, and the fact that it is now aged
in 100% new oak suggests that the wine will have the proper marriage of
toasty oak for balancing out its awesomely concentrated fruit flavors. The
1989 could well turn out to be the finest Trotte Vieille made in the last 3 or 4
decades. Anticipated maturity: Now–2015. Last tasted, 4/91.

1988—This is a very good, but exceptionally tannic, backward style of wine that
• needs a good 5–6 years in the bottle to shed its toughness. There is plenty of
86 ripe, extracted fruit, the color is dark ruby, and there is a feeling of weight
and length, but the tannins dominate the wine at present. Anticipated maturity: Now–2008. Last tasted, 4/91.

1987—One of the better efforts for a well-known St.-Emilion estate, the 1987 has an
• herbaceous, spicy, blackberry-scented nose, soft, oaky, ripe flavors, and a
85 smooth texture with some surprising power. Anticipated maturity: Now. Last
tasted, 4/91.

1986—The 1986 Trotte Vieille has a deep ruby color and a relatively well-developed
• and forward, big, plummy, herbaceous bouquet that displays a considerable
87 measure of smoky oak. On the palate, the wine is tannic, oaky, full bodied,
and concentrated. One might ask for a bit more complexity from one of the
very top vineyards in St.-Emilion. Anticipated maturity: Now–2008. Last
tasted, 3/90.

1985—The 1985 displays very ripe berry aromas, some evidence of new oak, a
• sweet, supple, round, and generous texture, medium to full body, and soft
86 tannins in the finish. Anticipated maturity: Now. Last tasted, 3/90.

1983—In comparative tastings against the other St.-Emilion Premiers Grands Crus
• Classés, Trotte Vieille came off as one of the weaker wines of the vintage. It
75 is decently colored, but a stewed, bizarre bouquet and diffuse, awkward
flavors exhibited little promise of anything exciting. Anticipated maturity:
Now–may be in decline. Last tasted, 2/87.

1982—Fully mature, the 1982 is a bit diffuse and lacks focus and grip. It does offer
• straightforward, chunky, fleshy, velvety smooth, cassis fruit and plenty of
79 alcohol in the finish. I see no point in holding on to the wine any longer.
Anticipated maturity: Now–may be in decline. Last tasted, 1/90.

1981—Lacking color, fruit, body, and uncommonly bizarre to smell, this is a feeble,
• lightweight wine without any substance to it. Disappointing. Last tasted,
70 4/84.

1979—A reasonably good effort from Trotte Vieille, the 1979 displays adequate
• color, a medium- to full-bodied, nicely concentrated feel on the palate, moder-
84 ate tannin, and good ripeness. This is a rare success for this estate. Anticipated maturity: Now. Last tasted, 2/84.

1978—Quite frail, beginning to brown, and seemingly on the edge of cracking up,
• this loosely knit, shallow, lean wine has little to offer. Last tasted, 2/84.
64

1976—A failure, the 1976 Trotte Vieille was apparently picked when the grapes
• were over-ripe and waterlogged. Unstructured, with a watery, jammy quality
55 and an unusually harsh finish, this is a most unattractive wine. Last tasted,
9/80.

1975—There is certainly not much to get excited about here—light, under-endowed,
• medium bodied, and tannic or, as several English wine writers would say,
70 "not enough flesh to cover the bones." Last tasted, 5/84.

VALANDRAUD   OUTSTANDING

Classification: None
Location of vineyards: In St.-Emilion and St.-Sulpice de Faleyrens
Owner: Ets. Thunevin (managed by Jean-Luc Thunevin)
Address: 1, rue Vergnaud, 33330 St.-Emilion
Mailing address: Same as above
Telephone: 33 5 57 55 09 13; telefax: 33 5 57 55 09 12
Visits: None

VINEYARDS (red)
Surface area: 6.2 acres
Average age of vines: 35 years
Blend: 75% Merlot, 20% Cabernet Franc, 5% Malbec
Density of plantation: 6,600 vines per hectare
Average yields (over the last 5 years): 35 hectoliters per hectare
Total average annual production: 950 cases

GRAND VIN (red)
Brand name: Château de Valandraud
Appellation: St.-Emilion Grand Cru
Mean annual production: 7,100 bottles (approx. 600 cases)
Upbringing: Fermentations and macerations last 8–10 days in wooden
vats (that are regularly renewed), with regular *pigéage* and pumping-
overs and maximum temperatures of 28–32 degrees centigrade.
Malolactics occur in new oak barrels, and wines are aged
21 months. They are racked every 3 months, and remain unfined
and unfiltered.

> **SECOND WINE**
> Brand name: Virginie de Valandraud
> Average annual production: 350 cases
>
> Evaluation of present classification: Should be promoted to a Premier
> Grand Cru Classé; the quality equivalent of a Médoc first-growth
> Plateau of maturity: 5–25 years following the vintage

The obsessive/compulsive, highly talented proprietor, Jean-Luc Thunevin, has the Cheshire Cat's grin these days given the publicity and prices his unfined, unfiltered, super-rich Valandraud is fetching. Along with his wife, Murielle, Thunevin has established a microscopic estate from selected parcels in St.-Emilion. Having had experience with running wine shops and restaurants in St.-Emilion, and also being involved in the wine trade, could not have hurt Thunevin with respect to his philosophy of what it takes to produce great wine.

Obviously the jury is still out as to how well Valandraud ages, but the wine is enormously rich, concentrated, and beautifully well delineated. It has been extraordinary, even in such difficult vintages as 1992, 1993, and 1994. More than any other St.-Emilion property, Valandraud has become the micro-treasure sought by billionaire wine collectors throughout the world.

VINTAGES

1997—Another outstanding effort from this small estate owned by Jean-Luc
•   Thunevin and his wife, the 1997 Valandraud is one of the most extracted
90– wines of the vintage, with elements of over-ripeness *(sur-maturité)*. The wine
91   possesses a dense purple color and an attractive nose of roasted Provençal herbs, *pain grillé*, black cherries, prunes, and cassis. Medium bodied, with more grip, delineation, and tannin than most wines of the vintage, this example provides outstanding purity, exceptional ripeness, and plenty of length. The wine, which a friend of mine appropriately called the "archetypical hedonistic wine," should be ready to drink when released yet age well for 15 years. Last tasted, 3/98.

1996—This opaque ruby/purple–colored wine is crammed with extract and power.
•   Chewy and thick, with extremely high tannin and a gorgeous, pure, natural
92– feeling and texture, it is more burly than the classic 1995, but, wow, what
94+ purity and flavor intensity this personality-filled wine possesses. Anticipated maturity: 2003–2020. Last tasted, 3/98.

1995—This splendid Valandraud ranks with the finest wines proprietor Jean-Luc
•   Thunevin has produced since his debut 1991 vintage. The wine exhibits an
95   opaque purple color and a sensational nose of roasted herbs, black fruits (cherries, currants, and blackberries), and high-class toasty oak (the latter component is more of a nuance than a dominant characteristic). Very concen-

trated, with layers of fruit, glycerin, and extract, yet seamlessly constructed, this wine contains the stuff of greatness and appears to be the finest Valandraud yet produced. The finish lasts for over 30 seconds. The wine's high tannin is barely noticeable because of the ripeness and richness of fruit. Anticipated maturity: 2003–2020. Last tasted, 11/97.

1994—
•
94+

An opaque purple color and a firm, closed set of aromatics (sweet black currant, woodsy, smoky aromas emerge with airing) are revealed in this blockbuster 1994. The wine possesses fabulous purity, great flavor intensity, a sweet inner core of fruit on the mid-palate, and a full-bodied, layered, viscous finish. It is unquestionably one of the finest wines of the vintage. Give it 5–7 years of cellaring. Anticipated maturity: 2002–2020. Last tasted, 1/97.

1993—
•
93

This is undoubtedly one of the most concentrated wines of the vintage. The color is an opaque purple, and the wine exhibits fabulously sweet, ripe, black cherry, and cassis fruit nicely infused with subtle oak and a touch of minerals and truffles. Full bodied, with exceptional density and no hard edges, the unbelievably concentrated 1993 Valandraud is a *tour de force* in a vintage that does not seem capable of producing wines such as this. Give it another 3–4 years of cellaring, and drink it over the following 15–20. Last tasted, 1/97.

1992—
•
88

This tiny estate, dedicated to becoming the "Le Pin of St.-Emilion," has turned out a strong effort in 1992. The Valandraud wines, all handcrafted and bottled unfiltered, will be difficult to find, but given what they have produced in 1992 and 1993, one can imagine what heights Valandraud might achieve in Bordeaux's next exceptional vintage. The 1992 reveals a saturated, opaque dark ruby/purple color, and a rich nose of sweet oak backed by gobs of jammy black currants and cherries. The wine possesses excellent richness, medium to full body, surprising opulence and chewiness (a rarity in the 1992 vintage), and a long, lusty, low-acid, concentrated finish. It should drink well for 7–10 years. Last tasted, 11/94.

1991—
•
83

The 1991 is exceptionally oaky, with the wood dominating the moderate quantities of sweet ripe fruit. Although it is a good wine, it is overpriced vis-à-vis its quality. Last tasted, 1/94.

VILLEMAURINE

Classification: St.-Emilion Grand Cru Classé
Location of vineyards: St.-Emilion (hillsides)
Owner: Robert Giraud S.A.
Address: 33330 St.-Emilion
Mailing address: Domaine de Loiseau, B.P. 31, 33240 St.-André de Cubzac
Telephone: 33 5 57 43 01 44; telefax: 33 5 57 43 33 17
Visits: By appointment only
Contact: Philippe Giraud

VINEYARDS (red)
Surface area: 17.5 acres
Average age of vines: 40 years
Blend: 85% Merlot, 10% Cabernet Franc, 5% Cabernet Sauvignon
Density of plantation: 6,000 vines per hectare
Average yields (over the last 5 years): 45 hectoliters per hectare
Total average annual production: 3,800 cases

GRAND VIN (red)
Brand name: Château Villemaurine
Appellation: St.-Emilion Grand Cru Classé
Mean annual production: 3,800 cases
Upbringing: Fermentations last 1 week and macerations 2 weeks in
temperature-controlled stainless-steel tanks. Malolactics occur in vats.
Wines are then aged in oak barrels, 33% of which are new, for 18
months. They are fined and filtered.

SECOND WINE
None produced.

Evaluation of present classification: The quality equivalent of a Médoc
Cru Bourgeois
Plateau of maturity: 3–10 years following the vintage

Villemaurine is one of St.-Emilion's most interesting vineyards. The property
gets its name from an eighth-century army of invading Moors who supposedly
set up camp on this site, which was called Ville Maure ("the City of Moors")
by the French. In addition, Villemaurine has enormous underground cellars
that merit considerable tourist interest. As for the wine, it is considerably
less interesting. Despite increasing promotional efforts by the proprietor,
Robert Giraud, also a major *négociant,* claiming that Villemaurine's quality
is improving, I have found the wines to lack richness and concentration, to
be rather diffuse, hard and lean, and to have little character.

VINTAGES

1997—Light and atypically high in acidity for a 1997, without much flavor, this wine
• 	has little to it. Last tasted, 3/98.
72–
74
1995—The sharp 1995 possesses high acidity, a compressed, charmless personality,
• 	and not much fruit. Last tasted, 3/96.
71

1994—The thin, high-acid 1994 exhibits straightforward, meagerly endowed flavors.
• Last tasted, 3/96.
69

1993—Copious aromas of new oak obliterate what little fruit this wine possesses.
• The combination of light body and high tannin does not result in a delicious
75 wine. The 1993 Villemaurine will dry out quickly. Last tasted, 11/94.

1990—Unbelievably dominated by new oak, the 1990 is light, with inadequate depth
• and character. Last tasted, 1/93.
75

1989—Black/purple in color, the 1989 displays a spicy, earthy, herb, and cassis
• nose. It is a big, chewy, monolithic wine that is impressively tannic but lacks
80 dimension. Anticipated maturity: Now–2003. Last tasted, 1/96.

1988—The 1988 exhibits abundant quantities of high tannin, a large, oaky, yet
• simple, ripe, plummy bouquet, and plenty of alcohol and size in the finish.
78 Anticipated maturity: Now–2002. Last tasted, 4/91.

OTHER ST.-EMILION PRODUCERS

BÉARD

Classification: St.-Emilion Grand Cru
Address: 33330 St.-Laurent des Combes
Telephone: 33 5 57 23 72 96; telefax: 33 5 57 24 61 88
Production: 3,000 cases
Blend: 65% Merlot, 35% Cabernet Franc
Secondary label: None
Vineyard size: 19.8 acres
Proprietor: Goudichaud family
Time spent in barrels: 16–20 months
Average age of vines: 30 years

Evaluation of present classification: The quality equivalent of a Médoc
Cru Bourgeois
Plateau of maturity: 3–8 years following the vintage

Unfortunately I have not had enough experience with Béard to form a strong opinion about their wines. However, the vintages I have tasted—1985, 1986, 1988, and 1989—were competently made wines that had good, pure fruit and a chunky, robust character. The domain, which can trace its existence to 1858, is now run by the Goudichaud family. The vineyard is situated in the commune of St.-Laurent des Combes, and the Goudichauds believe in hand harvesting, no herbicides, and a traditional vinification and *élevage*. While this estate is not in the top rung of St.-Emilions, it would appear to offer a reliable, reasonably priced alternative.

BELLEVUE

Classification: St.-Emilion Grand Cru Classé
Location of vineyards: Next to Beau-Séjour Bécot and facing Angélus
Owner: Société Civile du Château Bellevue (Jean de Coninck)
Address: 33330 St.-Emilion
Mailing address: Same as above
Telephone: 33 5 57 51 16 13 or 33 5 57 51 06 07;
telefax: 33 5 57 51 59 61
Visits: By appointment only
Contact: Jean de Coninck or Mrs. Cazenave

VINEYARDS (red)
Surface area: 14.8 acres
Average age of vines: 20–25 years
Blend: 67% Merlot, 16.5% Cabernet Franc, 16.5% Cabernet Sauvignon
Density of plantation: 5,700 vines per hectare
Total average annual production: 32 hectoliters

GRAND VIN (red)
Brand name: Château Bellevue
Appellation: St.-Emilion Grand Cru Classé
Upbringing: Fermentations and macerations last 15 days to 3 weeks in
temperature-controlled concrete tanks, depending upon the vintage.
Wines are then aged in oak barrels, 50% of which are new, for 12
months. They are fined but not filtered.

SECOND WINE
Brand name: Château Ramonet

Evaluation of present classification: The quality equivalent of a Médoc
Cru Bourgeois
Plateau of maturity: 3–8 years following the vintage

BERGAT

Classification: St.-Emilion Grand Cru Classé
Location of vineyards: St.-Emilion
Owner: Castéja—Preben-Hansen families
Address: 33330 St.-Emilion
Mailing address: c/o Borie-Manoux, 86, cours Balguerie Stuttenberg
33082 Bordeaux Cedex

Telephone: 33 5 56 00 00 70; telefax: 33 5 57 87 60 30
Visits: By appointment
Contact: Maison Borie-Manoux at above telephone and fax numbers

VINEYARDS (red)
Surface area: 9.9 acres
Average age of vines: 40 years
Blend: 55% Merlot, 35% Cabernet Franc, 10% Cabernet Sauvignon
Density of plantation: 7,500 vines per hectare
Average yields (over the last 5 years): 47 hectoliters
Total average annual production: 180 hectoliters

GRAND VIN (red)
Brand name: Château Bergat
Appellation: St.-Emilion Grand Cru Classé
Upbringing: Fermentations and macerations last approximately 3 weeks
in temperature-controlled stainless-steel tanks. Wines undergo
malolactics in tanks and are then transferred to oak barrels, 60% of
which are new, for 12–18 months aging. They are fined but not filtered.

SECOND WINE
Brand name: Enclos de Bergat

Evaluation of present classification: The quality equivalent of a Médoc
Cru Bourgeois
Plateau of maturity: 3–10 years following the vintage

BERNATEAU

Classification: St.-Emilion Grand Cru
Location of vineyards: St.-Etienne de Lisse, St.-Sulpice de Faleyrens,
Libourne
Owner: Mr. and Mrs. Régis Lavau
Address: 33330 St.-Etienne de Lisse
Mailing address: Same as above
Telephone: 33 5 57 40 18 19; telefax: 33 5 57 40 27 31
Visits: By appointment only
Contact: Régis Lavau

VINEYARDS (red)
Surface area: 43.2 acres
Average age of vines: 35 years

Blend: 80% Merlot, 15% Cabernet Franc, 5% Cabernet Sauvignon
Density of plantation: 5,500 vines per hectare
Average yields (over the last 5 years): 53 hectoliters per hectare
Total average annual production: 120,000 bottles

GRAND VIN (red)
Brand name: Château Bernateau
Appellation: St.-Emilion Grand Cru
Mean annual production: 85,000 bottles
Upbringing: Fermentations and macerations last 3 weeks minimum, and
wines are aged 12–14 months in oak barrels and in vats, with 15% new
oak. They are fined and filtered.

SECOND WINE
Brand name: Château Tour Peyronneau
Average annual production: 180 hectoliters

BIENFAISANCE

Classification: St.-Emilion Grand Cru
Location of vineyards: St.-Christophe des Bardes and St.-Emilion
Owner: Duval-Fleury family
Administrator: Patrick Baseden
Address: 33330 St.-Christophe des Bardes
Mailing address: Same as above
Telephone: 33 5 57 24 65 83; telefax: 33 5 57 24 78 26
Visits: By appointment, on weekdays
Contact: Christine Peytour

VINEYARDS (red)
Surface area: 34.6 acres
Average age of vines: 25 years
Blend: 80% Merlot, 15% Cabernet Franc, 5% Cabernet Sauvignon
Density of plantation: 6,500 vines per hectare
Average yields (over the last 5 years): 43 hectoliters per hectare
Total average annual production: 6,700 vines per hectare

GRAND VIN (red)
Brand name: Château de Bienfaisance
Appellation: St.-Emilion Grand Cru
Mean annual production: 48,000 bottles
Upbringing: Fermentations and macerations last 3 weeks minimum in

temperature-controlled concrete tanks. After malolactics, wines are aged 13–15 months in oak barrels that are renewed by a third at each vintage. They are fined with egg whites and are lightly filtered.

SECOND WINE
Brand name: Vieux-Château-Peymouton
Average annual production: 2,700 cases

JACQUES BLANC

Classification: St.-Emilion Grand Cru
Location of vineyards: St.-Etienne de Lisse
Owner: Mr. and Mrs. Pierre Chouet
Address: 33330 St.-Etienne de Lisse
Mailing address: Same as above
Telephone: 33 5 57 40 18 01; telefax: 33 5 57 40 01 98
Visits: By appointment, Monday through Friday, between 8:30 A.M. and noon, and 1:30 P.M. and 5:30 P.M.
Contact: Mr. and Mrs. Pierre Chouet

VINEYARDS (red)
Surface area: 49.4 acres
Average age of vines: 35 years
Blend: 66% Merlot, 32% Cabernet Franc, 2% Cabernet Sauvignon
Density of plantation: 5,000 vines per hectare
Average yields (over the last 5 years): 50 hectoliters per hectare
Total average annual production: 950 hectoliters

GRAND VIN (red)
Brand name: Château Jacques Blanc Cuvée du Maître
Appellation: St.-Emilion Grand Cru
Mean annual production: 35,000 bottles
Upbringing: Fermentations last 3 weeks in temperature-controlled stainless-steel vats. Only indigenous yeasts are used, regular breaking of the cap and experimentation with the process called *micro-bullage.* Malolactics take place in tanks, and wines are then aged in oak barrels, 30% of which are new, for 12–18 months depending upon the vintage. They are fined with egg whites and lightly filtered.

SECOND WINE
Brand name: Cuvée Aliénor
Average annual production: 60,000 bottles
NOTE: This estate is biodynamically farmed.

LA BONNELLE

Classification: St.-Emilion Grand Cru
Location of vineyards: St.-Pey d'Armens
Owner: F. Sulzer
Address: 33330 St.-Pey d'Armens
Mailing address: Same as above
Telephone: 33 5 57 47 15 12; telefax: 33 5 57 47 16 83
Visits: By appointment on weekdays, between 9 A.M. and noon, and 2 P.M.
and 7 P.M.
Contact: Olivier Sulzer

VINEYARDS (red)
Surface area: 24.7 acres
Average age of vines: 30 years
Blend: 70% Merlot, 20% Cabernet Franc, 10% Cabernet Sauvignon
Density of plantation: 5,500 vines per hectare
Average yields (over the last 5 years): 50 hectoliters
Total average annual production: 500 hectoliters

GRAND VIN (red)
Brand name: Château La Bonnelle
Appellation: St.-Emilion Grand Cru
Mean annual production: 300 hectoliters
Upbringing: Fermentations last 5 days and macerations another 15 days
in temperature-controlled stainless-steel tanks. Wines are aged by
rotation in oak and vats (concrete and stainless steel), for 12 months, the
oak barrels being renewed every 3 months. Wines are fined but remain
unfiltered.

SECOND WINE
Brand name: Château La Croix Bonnelle
Average annual production: 200 hectoliters

BOUQUEY

Classification: St.-Emilion Grand Cru
Location of vineyards: St.-Hippolyte, next to Château La Couronne
Owner: Mähectoliterser-Besse S.A.
Address: 33330 St.-Hippolyte
Mailing address: c/o Mähectoliterser-Besse, 49, rue Camille Godard,
33026 Bordeaux
Telephone: 33 5 56 56 04 30; telefax: 33 5 56 56 04 59

Visits: By appointment
Contact: Mähectoliterser-Besse at above telephone and fax numbers

VINEYARDS (red)
Surface area: 12.4 acres
Average age of vines: 25 years
Blend: 60% Merlot, 25% Cabernet Sauvignon, 15% Cabernet Franc
Density of plantation: 5,000 vines per hectare
Average yields (over the last 5 years): 50 hectoliters
Total average annual production: 120,000 bottles

GRAND VIN (red)
Brand name: Château Bouquey
Appellation: St.-Emilion Grand Cru
Mean annual production: 120,000 bottles
Upbringing: Alcoholic fermentations last 5 days and macerations up to 22 days in small conical temperature-controlled stainless-steel vats. Wines are aged either in oak barrels or in vats, depending upon the vintage. Aging in oak barrels (with little new oak) rarely exceeds 6 months. Aging in vats may go up to 2 years. Wines are fined with albumin but remain unfiltered.

SECOND WINE
Brand name: Château Les Fougères

CADET-BON

Classification: St.-Emilion Grand Cru Classé
Location of vineyards: St.-Emilion
Owner: S.A. Lorienne
Address: 1, Le Cadet, 33330 St.-Emilion
Mailing address: Same as above
Telephone: 33 5 57 74 43 20; telefax: 33 5 57 24 66 41
Visits: By appointment only
Contact: Marceline and Bernard Gans

VINEYARDS (red)
Surface area: 11.1 acres
Average age of vines: 35 years
Blend: 70% Merlot, 30% Cabernet Franc
Density of plantation: 6,660 vines per hectare
Average yields (over the last 5 years): 48 hectoliters per hectare
Total average annual production: 2,200 cases

GRAND VIN (red)
Brand name: Château Cadet-Bon
Appellation: St.-Emilion Grand Cru Classé (since 1996)
Mean annual production: 1,800 cases
Upbringing: Alcoholic fermentations take place in stainless-steel vats, and malolactic fermentations occur partly in new oak barrels. Wines are entirely aged in oak barrels that are renewed by a third each vintage. They are fined and remain unfiltered.

SECOND WINE
Brand name: Sold in bulk

Evaluation of present classification: The quality equivalent of a Médoc Cru Bourgeois
Plateau of maturity: 5–15 years following the vintage

CANTENAC

Classification: St.-Emilion Grand Cru
Location of vineyards: St.-Emilion
Owner: Nicole Roskam-Brunot
Address: R.D. 670, 33330 St.-Emilion
Mailing address: Same as above
Telephone: 33 5 57 51 35 22; telefax: 33 5 57 25 19 15
Visits: Preferably by appointment
Contact: Nicole Roskam-Brunot

VINEYARDS (red)
Surface area: 29.6 acres
Average age of vines: 21 years
Blend: 80% Merlot, 15% Cabernet Franc, 5% Cabernet Sauvignon
Density of plantation: 6,000 vines per hectare
Average yields (over the last 5 years): 52 hectoliters per hectare

GRAND VIN (red)
Brand name: Château Cantenac
Appellation: St.-Emilion Grand Cru
Mean annual production: 60,000 bottles
Upbringing: Fermentations and macerations last 21–28 days. Wines are then aged 18 months in oak barrels, 30% of which are new. They are fined and filtered before being transferred to barrels.

SECOND WINE
Brand name: Château Jean Melin
Average annual production: 18,000 bottles

CAPET-GUILLIER

Classification: St.-Emilion Grand Cru
Location of vineyards: St.-Hippolyte
Owner: Bouzerand and Galinou families
Address: 33330 St.-Hippolyte
Mailing address: Same as above
Telephone: 33 5 57 24 70 21; telefax: 33 5 57 24 68 96
Visits: Monday through Friday, between 9 A.M. and noon, and 2 P.M. and
5 P.M.; by appointment during weekends
Contact: Elisabeth Galinou

VINEYARDS (red)
Surface area: 37 acres under vines (49.5 acres in all)
Average age of vines: 35 years
Blend: 60% Merlot, 25% Cabernet Franc, 15% Cabernet Sauvignon
Density of plantation: 5,500 vines per hectare
Average yields (over the last 5 years): 52 hectoliters per hectare
Total average annual production: 806 hectoliters

GRAND VIN (red)
Brand name: Château Capet-Guillier
Appellation: St.-Emilion Grand Cru
Mean annual production: 480 hectoliters
Upbringing: Fermentations and macerations last approximately 3 weeks
in concrete vats. Wines are then aged 13 months in oak barrels (new and
1 vintage old).

SECOND WINE
Brand name: Château Grands Sables Capet
Average annual production: 326 hectoliters

CASTELOT

Classification: St.-Emilion Grand Cru
Location of vineyards: St.-Emilion, separated from Tertre-Daugay by the
Route Nationale 670A
Owner: Jean and Françoise Janoueix
Address: 33330 St.-Emilion
Mailing address: c/o Maison Janoueix, 37, rue Pline Parmentier,
B.P. 192, 33506 Libourne
Telephone: 33 5 57 51 41 86; telefax: 33 5 57 51 53 16
Visits: By appointment only
Contact: Maison J. Janoueix at above telephone and fax numbers

VINEYARDS (red)
Surface area: 22.2 acres
Average age of vines: 45–60 years
Blend: 70% Merlot, 20% Cabernet Franc, 10% Cabernet Sauvignon
Average yields (over the last 5 years): 48–50 hectoliters per hectare
Total average annual production: 400–450 hectoliters

GRAND VIN (red)
Brand name: Château Le Castelot
Appellation: St.-Emilion Grand Cru
Mean annual production: 65% of the total production (depending upon
the vintage)
Upbringing: Fermentations and macerations last 3–4 weeks in
temperature-controlled concrete vats. Wines are aged after malolactics in
oak barrels that are renewed by a third each vintage. They are bottled
after 2 years after fining with fresh egg whites. They remain unfiltered.

SECOND WINE
Brand name: Château Haut-Castelot
Average annual production: 35% of total production

CAUZE

Classification: St.-Emilion Grand Cru
Location of vineyards: St.-Christophe des Bardes
Owner: Bruno Laporte
Address: 33330 St.-Emilion
Mailing address: Same as above
Telephone: 33 5 57 74 62 47; telefax: 33 5 57 74 59 12
Visits: By appointment, on weekdays, between 8 A.M. and noon,
and 2 P.M. and 6 P.M.
Contact: Mr. Lladères, telephone 33 5 57 74 45 21

VINEYARDS (red)
Surface area: 49 acres
Average age of vines: 40 years
Blend: 90% Merlot, 10% Cabernets
Density of plantation: 5,500 vines per hectare
Average yields (over the last 5 years): 50 hectoliters per hectare
Total average annual production: 1,000 hectoliters

GRAND VIN (red)
Brand name: Château du Cauze
Appellation: St.-Emilion Grand Cru

Mean annual production: 130,000 bottles
Upbringing: Fermentations and macerations last approximately 5 weeks.
After malolactics, wines are transferred to oak barrels (for 12–18 months
aging) that are renewed by a quarter in each vintage. They are fined but
remain unfiltered.

SECOND WINE
None produced.

CHANTE-ALOUETTE-CORMEIL

Address: 33330 St.-Emilion
Telephone: 33 5 57 51 02 63; telefax: 33 5 57 51 93 39
Production: 3,500 cases
Blend: 60% Merlot, 20% Cabernet Franc, 20% Cabernet Sauvignon
Secondary label: None
Vineyard size: 20 acres
Proprietor: Yves Delol
Time spent in barrels: 20–24 months
Average age of vines: 20 years

Evaluation of present classification: The quality equivalent of a good
Médoc Cru Bourgeois
Plateau of maturity: 3–10 years following the vintage

CHEVAL-NOIR

Classification: St.-Emilion Grand Cru
Location of vineyards: St.-Emilion, near Château Angélus and
Cormeil-Figeac
Owner: Mahler-Besse
Address: 33330 St.-Emilion
Mailing address: c/o Mähectoliterser-Besse, 49, rue Camille Godard,
33026 Bordeaux
Telephone: 33 5 56 56 04 30; telefax: 33 5 56 56 04 59
Visits: By appointment
Contact: Mahler-Besse at above telephone and fax numbers

VINEYARDS (red)
Surface area: 12.4 acres
Average age of vines: 25 years

Blend: 60% Merlot, 20% Cabernet Sauvignon, 20% Cabernet Franc
Density of plantation: 5,000 vines per hectare
Average yields (over the last 5 years): 50 hectoliters
Total average annual production: 250 hectoliters

GRAND VIN (red)
Brand name: Cheval Noir
Appellation: St.-Emilion
Mean annual production: 250 hectoliters
Upbringing: Alcoholic fermentations last 5 days and macerations up to 22
days in small conical temperature-controlled stainless-steel vats. Wines
undergo malolactics in vats. Ninety percent of the yield remains in vats,
and 10% is transferred to oak barrels (with little new oak) for 2 years.
The wines are fined with albumin and filtered.

SECOND WINE
None produced.

CLOS LABARDE

Classification: St.-Emilion Grand Cru
Location of vineyards: St.-Laurent des Combes, Lieu-dit La Barde
Owner: Jacques Bailly
Address: Bergat, 33330 St.-Emilion
Mailing address: Same as above
Telephone: 33 5 57 74 43 69; telefax: 33 5 57 74 40 26
Visits: Monday through Friday, between 11 A.M. and noon, and 2 P.M. and
6 P.M.
Contact: Nicolas Bailly

VINEYARDS (red)
Surface area: 11.3 acres
Average age of vines: 35 years
Blend: 70% Merlot, 20% Cabernet Franc, 10% Cabernet Sauvignon
Density of plantation: 4,500 vines per hectare
Average yields (over the last 5 years): 46 hectoliters per hectare
Total average annual production: 210 hectoliters

GRAND VIN (red)
Brand name: Clos Labarde
Appellation: St.-Emilion Grand Cru
Mean annual production: 210 hectoliters

Upbringing: Fermentations and macerations last 28–30 days in temperature-controlled concrete tanks. Malolactics occur in vats. Two-thirds of the yield then remain in vats, while one-third is transferred to oak barrels (renewed by a third at each vintage) for 22 months aging (there is a rotation at each racking). Wines are fined and lightly filtered.

SECOND WINE
None produced.

CLOS LARCIS

Classification: St.-Emilion Grand Cru
Location of vineyards: Near Château Pavie and Larcis-Ducasse
Owner: Robert Giraud S.A.
Address: 33330 St.-Emilion
Mailing address: Domaine de Loiseau, B.P. 31, 33240 St.-André de Cubzac
Telephone: 33 5 57 43 01 44; telefax: 33 5 57 43 33 17
Visits: By appointment only
Contact: Philippe Giraud

VINEYARDS (red)
Surface area: 2.1 acres
Average age of vines: 40 years
Blend: 90% Merlot, 10% Cabernet Sauvignon
Density of plantation: 6,000 vines per hectare
Average yields (over the last 5 years): 45 hectoliters per hectare
Total average annual production: 416 cases

GRAND VIN (red)
Brand name: Clos Larcis
Appellation: St.-Emilion Grand Cru
Mean annual production: 416 cases
Upbringing: Fermentations last 1 week and macerations 2 weeks in temperature-controlled stainless-steel vats. Malolactics occur in vats. Wines are then aged in oak barrels, 50% of which are new, for 16–18 months. They are fined and filtered.

SECOND WINE
None produced.

CLOS LA MADELEINE

Classification: St.-Emilion Grand Cru (declassified in 1996)
Location of vineyards: St.-Emilion
Owner: S.A. du Clos La Madeleine
Address: La Gaffelière Ouest, 33330 St.-Emilion
Mailing address: B.P. 78, 33330 St.-Emilion
Telephone: 33 5 57 55 38 03; telefax: 33 5 57 55 38 01
Visits: By appointment, Monday through Friday, between 8 A.M. and
6 P.M.
Contact: Philippe Lauret

VINEYARDS (red)
Surface area: 4.9 acres
Average age of vines: 35 years
Blend: 50% Merlot, 50% Cabernet Franc
Density of plantation: 6,600 vines per hectare
Average yields (over the last 5 years): 45 hectoliters per hectare
Total average annual production: 89 hectoliters

GRAND VIN (red)
Brand name: Clos La Madeleine
Appellation: St.-Emilion Grand Cru
Mean annual production: 89 hectoliters
Upbringing: Fermentations and macerations last 3–4 weeks in
temperature-controlled stainless-steel vats. Malolactics take place in new
oak barrels for half of the yield; the rest remains in vats and is
transferred to 1-vintage-old barrels for 12–18 months aging. The wines
are fined but remain unfiltered.

SECOND WINE
None produced.

Evaluation of present classification: The quality equivalent of a Médoc
Cru Bourgeois
Plateau of maturity: 4–15 years following the vintage

CLOS TRIMOULET

Classification: St.-Emilion Grand Cru
Location of vineyards: 90% of the vineyards are in St.-Emilion and 10%
are over at St.-Christophe des Bardes and St.-Hippolyte
Owner: E.A.R.L. Appolot
Address: 33330 St.-Emilion

Mailing address: Same as above
Telephone: 33 5 57 24 71 96; telefax: 33 5 57 74 45 88
Visits: By appointment only, Monday through Friday, between 9 A.M. and
noon, and 2 P.M. and 6 P.M.; on Saturdays, morning only
Contact: Guy Appolot

VINEYARDS (red)
Surface area: 27.2 acres
Average age of vines: 30 years
Blend: 80% Merlot, 10% Cabernet Franc, 10% Cabernet Sauvignon
Density of plantation: 5,500 vines per hectare
Average yields (over the last 5 years): 55 hectoliters per hectare
Total average annual production: 600 hectoliters

GRAND VIN (red)
Brand name: Clos Trimoulet
Appellation: St.-Emilion Grand Cru
Mean annual production: 490 hectoliters
Upbringing: Fermentations and macerations last 3 weeks in
temperature-controlled vats. Seventy percent of the yield is aged in oak
barrels, 20% of which are new, and 30% of the yield remains in vats.
Wines are aged 14 months in all before bottling. They are fined and
filtered.

SECOND WINE
None produced.

LA COMMANDERIE

Classification: St.-Emilion Grand Cru
Location of vineyards: Lieu-dit Fortin
Owner: Domaines Cordier
Address: 33330 St.-Emilion
Mailing address: c/o Domaines Cordier, 53, rue du Dehez, 33290
Blanquefort
Telephone: 33 5 56 95 53 00; telefax: 33 5 56 95 53 01
Visits: By appointment only

VINEYARDS (red)
Surface area: 13.2 acres
Average age of vines: 25 years
Blend: 90% Merlot, 10% Cabernet Franc
Density of plantation: 6,000–6,500 vines per hectare
Total average annual production: 35,000 bottles

GRAND VIN (red)
Brand name: Château La Commanderie
Appellation: St.-Emilion Grand Cru
Mean annual production: 35,000 bottles
Upbringing: Fermentations and macerations last 18–20 days in concrete
tanks lined with epoxy. Wines are then transferred to oak casks (renewed
by a third each vintage) for 18–20 months aging. They are racked every 3
months, fined with egg whites, and filtered.

SECOND WINE
None produced.

CORMEIL-FIGEAC

Classification: St.-Emilion Grand Cru
Production: 4,000 cases
Blend: 70% Merlot, 30% Cabernet Franc
Secondary label: None
Vineyard size: 25 acres
Proprietor: Moreaud family
Time spent in barrels: 18–22 months
Average age of vines: 25 years

Evaluation of present classification: The quality equivalent of a Médoc
Cru Bourgeois
Plateau of maturity: 3–8 years following the vintage

This is a vineyard with potential, given the location adjacent to the famed
Château Figeac. However, its soils are more sandy than those of Figeac, and
one wonders what could be obtained if the selection were a bit stricter and
the proprietor used more new oak casks. From time to time there is an
underlying mustiness that is offputting. Otherwise the wines are supple,
fleshy, and generally well endowed.

CÔTES DE ROL

Classification: St.-Emilion Grand Cru
Location of vineyards: Several hundred meters northeast of St.-Emilion
Owner: Robert Giraud S.A.
Address: 33330 St.-Emilion
Mailing address: Domaine de Loiseau, B.P. 31, 33240 St.-André de
Cubzac

Telephone: 33 5 57 43 01 44; telefax: 33 5 57 43 33 17
Visits: By appointment only
Contact: Philippe Giraud

VINEYARDS (red)
Surface area: 7.4 acres
Average age of vines: 30 years
Blend: 80% Merlot, 10% Cabernet Sauvignon, 10% Cabernet Franc
Density of plantation: 6,000 vines per hectare
Average yields (over the last 5 years): 50 hectoliters per hectare
Total average annual production: 1,666 cases

GRAND VIN (red)
Brand name: Château Côtes de Rol
Appellation: St.-Emilion Grand Cru
Mean annual production: 1,666 cases
Upbringing: Fermentations last 1 week and macerations 2 weeks in temperature-controlled stainless-steel vats. Malolactics occur in vats. Wines are then aged in oak barrels, 25% of which are new, for 18 months. They are fined and filtered.

SECOND WINE
None produced.

LA COURONNE

Classification: St.-Emilion Grand Cru
Location of vineyards: St.-Hippolyte
Owner: EURL C.C.N.—Mahler-Besse
Address: 33330 St.-Hippolyte
Mailing address: c/o Mähectoliterser-Besse, 49, rue Camille Godard, 33026 Bordeaux
Telephone: 33 5 56 56 04 30; telefax: 33 5 56 56 04 59
Visits: By appointment
Contact: Mahler-Besse at above telephone and fax numbers

VINEYARDS (red)
Surface area: 22.2 acres
Average age of vines: 20 years
Blend: 60% Merlot, 25% Cabernet Sauvignon, 15% Cabernet Franc
Density of plantation: 5,000 vines per hectare
Average yields (over the last 5 years): 50 hectoliters
Total average annual production: 5,000 cases

GRAND VIN (red)
Brand name: Château La Couronne
Appellation: St.-Emilion Grand Cru
Mean annual production: 4,000 cases
Upbringing: Alcoholic fermentations last 5 days and macerations up to 22 days in small conical temperature-controlled stainless-steel vats. Wines undergo malolactics in vats and are transferred to oak barrels (30% of which are new) for 12 months aging. They are fined with albumin and remain unfiltered.

SECOND WINE
None produced.

COUTET

Classification: St.-Emilion Grand Cru
Location of vineyards: St.-Emilion
Owner: Jean and Alain David-Beaulieu
Address: 33330 St.-Emilion
Mailing address: Same as above
Telephone: 33 5 57 74 43 21; telefax: 33 5 57 74 40 78
Visits: By appointment only
Contact: Alain David-Beaulieu

VINEYARDS (red)
Surface area: 29.6 acres
Average age of vines: 38 years
Blend: 45% Merlot, 45% Cabernet Franc, 5% Cabernet Sauvignon, 5% Malbec
Density of plantation: 5,500 vines per hectare
Average yields (over the last 5 years): 42 hectoliters per hectare
Total average annual production: 500 hectoliters

GRAND VIN (red)
Brand name: Château Coutet
Appellation: St.-Emilion Grand Cru
Mean annual production: 45,000 bottles
Upbringing: Fermentations last 3–4 weeks in temperature-controlled stainless-steel tanks. They are aged 12 months in oak barrels that are renewed by a third at each vintage, fined, and filtered.

SECOND WINE
Brand name: Château Belles-Cimes
Average annual production: 20,000 bottles

LA CROIX-FIGEAC

Classification: St.-Emilion Grand Cru
Location of vineyards: The biggest parcel is situated on gravelly terraces, bordered to the north by Château Figeac and to the east by Lamarzelle
Owner: Mr. and Mrs. Dutruilh
Address: 33330 St.-Emilion
Mailing address: 14, rue d'Aviau, 33000 Bordeaux
Telephone and telefax: 33 5 56 81 19 69
Visits: By appointment only
Contact: Mr. and Mrs. Dutruilh

VINEYARDS (red)
Surface area: 13.6 acres
Average age of vines: 29 years
Blend: 80% Merlot, 20% Cabernet Franc
Density of plantation: 5,500–6,000 vines per hectare
Average yields (over the last 5 years): 47.5 hectoliters per hectare
Total average annual production: 165 hectoliters

GRAND VIN (red)
Brand name: Château La Croix-Figeac
Appellation: St.-Emilion Grand Cru
Mean annual production: 135 hectoliters
Upbringing: Fermentations and macerations last 4–5 weeks in stainless-steel vats. Forty percent of the yield undergoes malolactics in new oak, the rest remains in vats. Wines are aged 15–18 months in oak barrels (40% of which are new, 40% 1 year old, and 20% 2 years old). They are fined but remain unfiltered.

SECOND WINE
Brand name: Pavillon La Croix-Figeac
Average annual production: 4,000 bottles

LA CROIX DE JAUGUE

Location of vineyards: St.-Emilion
Owner: Georges Bigot
Address: 150, avenue du Général Leclerc
Mailing address: Same as above
Telephone: 33 5 57 51 51 29; telefax: 33 5 57 51 29 70
Visits: By appointment only
Contact: Georges Bigot

VINEYARDS (red)

Surface area: 11.24 acres
Average age of vines: 10–15 years for one-third of the vineyards;
35 years and over for the rest
Blend: 75% Merlot, 25% Cabernet Franc
Density of plantation: 6,500 vines per hectare
Average yields (over the last 5 years): 55–60 hectoliters per hectare
Total average annual production: 30,000 bottles

GRAND VIN (red)

Brand name: Château La Croix de Jaugue
Appellation: St.-Emilion
Mean annual production: 15,000–20,000 bottles
Upbringing: Fermentations and macerations last 20–28 days in concrete
vats equipped with a trickle cooling. Beginning in 1998 they will be
temperature controlled. Wines are aged 12–16 months in concrete and
stainless-steel tanks. They are fined and lightly filtered (plaque) upon
bottling.

PRESTIGE CUVÉE

Brand name: Château La Fleur de Jaugue
Average annual production: 12,000–15,000 bottles
Appellation: St.-Emilion Grand Cru

NOTE: This wine is made from a selection of the best cuvées, which
usually come from specific parcels of vines. The yields are usually lower
than for the normal cuvée—around 42–45 hectoliters per hectare.

Upbringing: Fermentations of 20–28 days in concrete tanks equipped
with a trickle cooling. Wines are then transferred to oak barrels, after
malolactics, for 12–13 months aging. The barrels are renewed by a third
each vintage. Wines are fined and lightly filtered.

Evaluation of present classification: The quality equivalent of a Médoc
Cru Bourgeois
Plateau of maturity: 3–8 years following the vintage

CROQUE-MICHOTTE

Classification: St.-Emilion Grand Cru
Production: 6,500 cases
Blend: 75% Merlot, 25% Cabernet Franc
Secondary label: None

Vineyard size: 34 acres
Proprietor: Madame Helene Rigal-Geoffrion
Time spent in barrels: 18–20 months
Average age of vines: 35 years

Evaluation of present classification: The quality equivalent of a good
Médoc Cru Bourgeois
Plateau of maturity: 4–12 years following the vintage

The vineyard of Croque-Michotte is well situated in the *graves* section of
the St.-Emilion appellation adjacent to the Pomerol border, close to the
better-known estates of Cheval Blanc and La Dominique. The wine produced
here is usually ready to drink within the first 5 or 6 years of a vintage,
and it rarely improves beyond a decade. Nevertheless, especially among
those who lack patience, this fleshy, sumptuous style of wine has many admirers.

CRUZEAU

Classification: St.-Emilion Grand Cru
Location of vineyards: Libourne
Owner: G.F.A. Luquot Frères
Address: 152, avenue de l'Epinette, 33500 Libourne
Mailing address: Same as above
Telephone: 33 5 57 51 18 95; telefax: 33 5 57 25 10 59
Visits: By appointment only, Monday through Friday, between 9 A.M. and
7 P.M.
Contact: Jean-Paul Luquot

VINEYARDS (red)
Surface area: 10.8 acres
Average age of vines: 26 years
Blend: 75% Merlot, 25% Cabernet Franc
Density of plantation: 5,500 vines per hectare
Average yields (over the last 5 years): 51 hectoliters per hectare
Total average annual production: 220 hectoliters

GRAND VIN (red)
Brand name: Château Cruzeau
Appellation: St.-Emilion Grand Cru
Mean annual production: 27,000 bottles

Upbringing: Fermentations and macerations last 20 days in
temperature-controlled concrete tanks. Wines are transferred after
malolactics to 2-vintage-old barrels for 16 months aging. They are fined
but remain unfiltered.

SECOND WINE
None produced.

CURÉ-BON

Classification: St.-Emilion Grand Cru Classé
Location of vineyards: St.-Emilion
Owner: S.A. Lorienne
Address: 9, Magdeleine, 33330 St.-Emilion
Mailing address: c/o S.A. Lorienne, 1, Le Cadet, 33330 St.-Emilion
Telephone: 33 5 57 74 43 20; telefax: 33 5 57 24 66 41
Visits: By appointment only
Contact: Marceline and Bernard Gans

VINEYARDS (red)
Surface area: 10.4 acres
Average age of vines: 30 years
Blend: 84% Merlot, 15% Cabernet Franc, 1% Petit Verdot and Malbec
Density of plantation: 6,660 vines per hectare
Average yields (over the last 5 years): 48 hectoliters per hectare
Total average annual production: 2,000 cases

GRAND VIN (red)
Brand name: Château Curé-Bon
Appellation: St.-Emilion Grand Cru Classé (since 1996)
Mean annual production: 1,500 cases
Upbringing: Alcoholic fermentations take place in stainless-steel vats,
and malolactic fermentations occur partly in new oak barrels. Wines are
entirely aged in oak barrels that are renewed by 40% at each vintage.
They are fined but remain unfiltered.

SECOND WINE
Brand name: Sold in bulk

Evaluation of present classification: The quality equivalent of a Médoc
fifth-growth
Plateau of maturity: 5–15 years following the vintage

This tiny estate has a splendid location on the *côtes* St.-Emilion, sandwiched between the famous vineyards of Canon, Belair, and Ausone. It is a wine with a very good reputation, but one that is rarely seen in export channels. My experience with Curé-Bon is very limited, but the wines I have seen have been surprisingly tannic and firmly structured St.-Emilions that can support considerable cellaring.

FAURIE-DE-SOUCHARD

Classification: St.-Emilion Grand Cru Classé
Location of vineyards: St.-Emilion
Owner: G.F.A. Jabiol-Sciard
Address: 33330 St.-Emilion
Mailing address: Same as above
Telephone: 33 5 57 74 43 80; telefax: 33 5 57 74 43 96
Visits: By appointment, Monday to Friday (except Wednesdays), between 9 A.M. and 4 P.M.
Contact: Françoise Sciard

VINEYARDS (red)
Surface area: 27.2 acres
Average age of vines: 25 years
Blend: 65% Merlot, 26% Cabernet Franc, 9% Cabernet Sauvignon
Density of plantation: 5,500 vines per hectare
Average yields (over the last 5 years): 45 hectoliters per hectare
Total average annual production: 58,000 bottles

GRAND VIN (red)
Brand name: Château Faurie-de-Souchard
Appellation: St.-Emilion Grand Cru Classé
Mean annual production: 58,000 bottles
Upbringing: Fermentations and macerations last approximately 3 weeks. Part of the yield undergoes malolactics in new oak barrels (33%); the rest of the yield remains in vats after running-off. Wines are aged 18–20 months in oak barrels that are renewed by a third at each vintage. They are fined and filtered.

SECOND WINE
Brand name: Souchard (not made each year)
Average annual production: 7,000 bottles in 1995

Evaluation of present classification: The quality equivalent of a good Médoc Cru Bourgeois
Plateau of maturity: 5–15 years following the vintage

Faurie-de-Souchard, one of the oldest properties in St.-Emilion, has been owned by the Jabiol family since 1933. The vineyard, located on both a limestone plateau as well as chalky clay and sandy soil, tends to produce relatively full-bodied, tannic, intense wines that require some patience in the bottle. Unlike many St.-Emilions, which are made to be drunk within their first 5–6 years, most vintages of Faurie-de-Souchard can last up to 10–15 years. If the wines are to be criticized at all, it is because their tannins often exceed the extraction levels of fruit.

FERRAND

Classification: St.-Emilion Grand Cru
Location of vineyards: St.-Hippolyte
Owner: Heirs to Baron Bich
Address: 33330 St.-Hippolyte
Mailing address: Same as above
Telephone: 33 5 56 74 47 11; telefax: 33 5 57 24 69 08
Visits: By appointment only
Contact: Jean-Pierre Palatin

VINEYARDS (red)
Surface area: 74.1 acres
Average age of vines: 30 years
Blend: 70% Merlot, 15% Cabernet Sauvignon, 15% Cabernet Franc
Density of plantation: 5,400 vines per hectare
Average yields (over the last 5 years): 50 hectoliters per hectare
Total average annual production: 200,000 bottles

GRAND VIN (red)
Brand name: Château de Ferrand
Appellation: St.-Emilion Grand Cru
Mean annual production: 1,000 hectoliters
Upbringing: Fermentations and macerations are rather long. Wines are aged 6 months in new oak barrels. They are fined but remain unfiltered.

SECOND WINE
Brand name: Château des Grottes
Average annual production: 500 hectoliters

Evaluation of present classification: The quality equivalent of a good Médoc Cru Bourgeois
Plateau of maturity: 4–12 years following the vintage

The late Baron Bich, celebrated for his "Bic" pens, purchased de Ferrand in 1978 and significantly increased the quality of the wine.

The vineyard itself is located in the commune of St.-Hippolyte on a plateau of limestone. The key to the success of many de Ferrand vintages has been an unusually late harvest and the use of a significant percentage of new oak, ranging from 50% to nearly 100%. De Ferrand makes wines with the potential for a moderately long evolution in the bottle.

FLEUR-CARDINALE

Classification: St.-Emilion Grand Cru
Location of vineyards: St.-Etienne de Lisse
Owner: Claude and Alain Asséo
Address: 33330 St.-Etienne de Lisse
Mailing address: Same as above
Telephone: 33 5 57 40 14 05; telefax: 33 5 57 40 28 62
Visits: By appointment only
Contact: Claude and Alain Asséo

VINEYARDS (red)
Surface area: 25 acres
Average age of vines: 35–40 years
Blend: 70% Merlot, 20% Cabernet Sauvignon, 10% Cabernet Franc
Density of plantation: 6,000 vines per hectare
Average yields (over the last 5 years): 45 hectoliters per hectare
Total average annual production: 5,000 cases

GRAND VIN (red)
Brand name: Château Fleur-Cardinale
Appellation: St.-Emilion Grand Cru
Mean annual production: 3,800 cases
Upbringing: Fermentations and macerations last 3–5 weeks at temperatures between 28 and 32 degrees centigrade. There are 3 pumping-overs a day. Approximately 40%–60% of the yield undergoes malolactics in new oak barrels, and the rest is transferred after completion of this process to oak barrels that are 1 year old. Wines are aged 13–16 months, are not systematically fined, and remain unfiltered upon bottling.

SECOND WINE
Brand name: Château Bois Cardinal
Average annual production: About 1,000 cases

Evaluation of present classification: The quality equivalent of a Médoc Cru Bourgeois
Plateau of maturity: 3–8 years following the vintage

Fleur-Cardinale is made in a very satisfying, round, generous style that offers immediate satisfaction. The wine is rarely complex but, rather, solid and robust. The vineyard, located in the commune of St.-Etienne de Lisse, is not well placed, but with a serious owner and the excellent counsel of the famed oenologist Michel Rolland, the quality of Fleur-Cardinale is consistent.

LA FLEUR POURRET

Classification: St.-Emilion Grand Cru
Production: 2,500 cases
Blend: 50% Merlot, 50% Cabernet Sauvignon
Secondary label: None
Vineyard size: 16 acres
Proprietor: AXA Insurance Group
Time spent in barrels: 18 months
Average age of vines: 25 years

Evaluation of present classification: Should be maintained
Plateau of maturity: 3–10 years following the vintage

I have been immensely impressed on the rare occasions when I have been permitted to taste this wine produced just outside the walls of St.-Emilion. The gravelly soil in this area is reputed to produce richly fruity, deeply colored, fleshy wines of surprising distinction and flavor extraction.

FOMBRAUGE

Classification: St.-Emilion Grand Cru
Location of vineyards: St.-Christophe des Bardes, St.-Etienne de Lisse, St.-Hippolyte
Owner: S.A. du Château Fombrauge
Address: 33330 St.-Emilion
Mailing address: Same as above
Telephone: 33 5 57 24 88 12; telefax: 33 5 57 24 66 95
Visits: By appointment only
Contact: Thérèse Polledri

VINEYARDS (red)
Surface area: 187.7 acres
Average age of vines: 27 years
Blend: 75% Merlot, 15% Cabernet Sauvignon, 10% Cabernet Franc
Density of plantation: 5,500 vines per hectare

Average yields (over the last 5 years): 40 hectoliters per hectare
Total average annual production: 26,000 cases

GRAND VIN (red)
Brand name: Château Fombrauge
Appellation: St.-Emilion Grand Cru
Mean annual production: 20,000 cases
Upbringing: Alcoholic fermentations last 5 -10 days and macerations 21
days. Wines are aged 16 months in oak barrels, 30% of which are new.
They are fined and filtered.

SECOND WINE
Brand name: Château Maurens
Average annual production: 6,000 cases

FONRAZADE

Classification: St.-Emilion Grand Cru
Location of vineyards: St.-Emilion, next to Angélus
Owner: Guy Balotte
Address: 33330 St.-Emilion
Mailing address: Same as above
Telephone: 33 5 57 24 71 58; telefax: 33 5 57 74 40 87
Visits: Every day except Sunday
Contact: Fabienne Balotte

VINEYARDS (red)
Surface area: 37 acres
Average age of vines: 30 years
Blend: 75% Merlot, 25% Cabernet Sauvignon
Density of plantation: 5,500 vines per hectare
Average yields (over the last 5 years): 45–48 hectoliters per hectare
Total average annual production: 600 hectoliters

GRAND VIN (red)
Brand name: Château Fonrazade
Appellation: St.-Emilion Grand Cru
Mean annual production: 40 hectoliters
Upbringing: Fermentations and macerations usually last more than
3 weeks in temperature-controlled concrete vats. Wines are aged
for 18 months in oak barrels that are renewed by half at each

vintage. They are racked every 3–4 months, fined with fresh egg whites, and not filtered.

SECOND WINE
Brand name: Château Comte des Cordes
Average annual production: 40 hectoliters

GALIUS

Classification: St.-Emilion Grand Cru
Location of vineyards: St.-Emilion, St.-Sulpice de Faleyrens and Vignonet
Owner: Union des Producteurs de St.-Emilion
Address: 33330 St.-Emilion
Mailing address: B.P. 27, Haut-Gravet, 33330 St.-Emilion
Telephone: 33 5 57 24 70 71; telefax: 33 5 57 24 65 18
Visits: Monday through Friday, between 8:30 A.M. and noon, and 2 P.M. and 6 P.M.
Contact: Patrick Foulon

VINEYARDS (red)
Surface area: 24.7 acres
Average age of vines: 30–37 years
Blend: 70% Merlot, 20% Cabernet Franc, 10% Cabernet Sauvignon
Density of plantation: 5,500 vines per hectare
Average yields (over the last 5 years): 50 hectoliters per hectare
Total average annual production: 66,000 bottles

GRAND VIN (red)
Brand name: Galius
Appellation: St.-Emilion Grand Cru
Mean annual production: 66,000 bottles
Upbringing: Alcoholic fermentations at 30 degrees centigrade, and malolactics last 15–20 days in temperature-controlled concrete vats. Wines are then aged 12 months in oak barrels, which are renewed by a third at each vintage. They are fined and filtered.

GODEAU

Classification: St.-Emilion Grand Cru
Production: 2,000 cases
Blend: 60% Merlot, 35% Cabernet Sauvignon, 5% Cabernet Franc
Secondary label: None

Vineyard size: 10 acres
Proprietor: Georges Litvine
Time spent in barrels: 18–22 months
Average age of vines: 25 years

Evaluation of present classification: The quality equivalent of a good
Médoc Cru Bourgeois, perhaps superior
Plateau of maturity: 5–15 years following the vintage

LA GRÂCE DIEU

Classification: St.-Emilion Grand Cru
Location of vineyards: St.-Emilion
Address: 33330 St.-Emilion
Mailing address: c/o S.C.E.A. Pauty, address same as above
Telephone: 33 5 57 24 71 10; telefax: 33 5 57 24 67 24
Visits: By appointment only
Contact: Mrs. Ghizzo

VINEYARDS (red)
Surface area: 32 acres
Average age of vines: 25 years
Blend: 70% Merlot, 15% Cabernet Franc, 15% Cabernet Sauvignon
Density of plantation: 6,000 vines per hectare
Average yields (over the last 5 years): 51 hectoliters per hectare
Total average annual production: 650 hectoliters

GRAND VIN (red)
Brand name: Château La Grâce Dieu
Appellation: St.-Emilion Grand Cru
Mean annual production: 560 hectoliters
Upbringing: Fermentations last about 20 days, and wines remain in
concrete vats for 16–18 months aging. They are fined and filtered.

SECOND WINE
Brand name: Château Etoile Pourret
Average annual production: 90 hectoliters

LA GRÂCE DIEU LES MENUTS

Classification: St.-Emilion Grand Cru
Location of vineyards: St.-Emilion
Owner: S.C.E.A. Vignobles Pilotte-Audier
Address: La Grâce Dieu, 33330 St.-Emilion
Mailing address: Same as above
Telephone: 33 5 57 24 73 10; telefax: 33 5 57 74 40 44
Visits: By appointment, on weekdays, between 9 A.M. and noon, and
2 P.M. and 7 P.M.
Contact: Mrs. Audier or Mr. Pilotte

VINEYARDS (red)
Surface area: 33.5 acres
Average age of vines: 35 years
Blend: 65% Merlot, 30% Cabernet Franc, 5% Cabernet Sauvignon
Density of plantation: 6,000 vines per hectare
Average yields (over the last 5 years): 50 hectoliters
Total average annual production: 650 hectoliters

GRAND VIN (red)
Brand name: Château La Grâce Dieu Les Menuts
Appellation: St.-Emilion Grand Cru
Mean annual production: 650 hectoliters
Upbringing: Fermentations last 20–25 days in temperature-controlled
vats (cap immersed). After malolactics, 80% of the yield is transferred to
oak barrels (renewed by a third each vintage) for 12 months aging.
Twenty percent of the yield remains in vats. Wines are assembled in vats,
fined but not systematically filtered.

SECOND WINE
Brand name: Vieux Domaine des Menuts
Average annual production: Variable—depends upon the vintage

LA GRÂCE DIEU DES PRIEURS

Classification: St.-Emilion Grand Cru
Location of vineyards: St.-Emilion
Owner: Laubie family
Address: La Grâce Dieu, 33330 St.-Emilion
Mailing address: Same as above
Telephone: 33 5 57 69 02 78 or 33 5 57 74 42 87;
telefax: 33 5 57 49 42 47

Visits: By appointment
Contact: Alain Laubie

VINEYARDS (red)
Surface area: 16.6 acres
Average age of vines: 35 years
Blend: 90% Merlot, 10% Cabernet Franc
Density of plantation: 5,000 vines per hectare
Average yields (over the last 5 years): 55 hectoliters per hectare
Total average annual production: 330 hectoliters

GRAND VIN (red)
Brand name: Château La Grâce Dieu des Prieurs
Appellation: St.-Emilion Grand Cru
Mean annual production: 200 hectoliters
Upbringing: Fermentations and macerations last 3 weeks in
temperature-controlled vats. Wines are then aged approximately
22 months in vats and oak barrels, 10% of which are new. They are
fined but remain unfiltered.

SECOND WINE
Brand name: Château Fortin
Average annual production: 130 hectoliters

GRAND-CORBIN-DESPAGNE

Classification: St.-Emilion Grand Cru (was declassified in 1996)
Location of vineyards: Just next to Pomerol, in the northern part of the
appellation
Owner: Despagne family
Address: 33330 St.-Emilion
Mailing address: Same as above
Telephone: 33 5 57 51 08 38; telefax: 33 5 57 51 29 18
Visits: By appointment, every day, between 8 A.M. and 7 P.M.
Contact: François Despagne

VINEYARDS (red)
Surface area: 65.5 acres
Average age of vines: 33 years
Blend: 75% Merlot, 20% Cabernet Franc, 5% Cabernet Sauvignon
Density of plantation: 6,200 vines per hectare

Average yields (over the last 5 years): 49 hectoliters per hectare
Total average annual production: 1,300 hectoliters

GRAND VIN (red)
Brand name: Château Grand-Corbin-Despagne
Appellation: St.-Emilion Grand Cru
Mean annual production: 650 hectoliters
Upbringing: Fermentations last 5–8 days and macerations 20–25 days in
temperature-controlled stainless-steel and concrete vats. Since 1996 the
whole yield is aged in oak barrels, 40% of which are new (the rest being
1 and 2 vintages old), for 12–18 months depending upon the vintage. The
wines are fined and filtered.

SECOND WINE
None produced.

Evaluation of present classification: The quality equivalent of a good
Médoc Cru Bourgeois
Plateau of maturity: 5–12 years following the vintage

GRAND-CORBIN-MANUEL

Classification: St.-Emilion Grand Cru
Location of vineyards: St.-Emilion
Owner: Pierre Manuel
Address: 33330 St.-Emilion
Mailing address: Same as above
Telephone: 33 5 57 51 12 47; telefax: Same
Visits: Preferably by appointment
Contact: Pierre Manuel

VINEYARDS (red)
Surface area: 17.3 acres
Average age of vines: 32 years
Blend: 55% Merlot, 25% Cabernet Sauvignon, 20% Cabernet Franc
Density of plantation: 6,000 vines per hectare
Average yields (over the last 5 years): 45 hectoliters per hectare
Total average annual production: 315 hectoliters

GRAND VIN (red)
Brand name: Château Grand-Corbin-Manuel
Appellation: St.-Emilion Grand Cru

Mean annual production: 315 hectoliters
Upbringing: Fermentations and macerations are rather long
(3–4 weeks) and take place in temperature-controlled vats. After
malolactics, wines are aged 2 years by rotation (1 year each) in
oak barrels (50% new oak) and vats. They are both fined and
filtered.

SECOND WINE
Brand name: Clos de la Grande Métairie
Average annual production: Variable

LA GRAVE-FIGEAC

Classification: St.-Emilion Grand Cru
Location of vineyards: St.-Emilion near Cheval Blanc and Figeac and
close to Château La Conseillante of Pomerol
Owner: Jean-Pierre Clauzel
Address: 1, Cheval Blanc Ouest, 33330 St.-Emilion
Mailing address: Same as above
Telephone: 33 5 57 51 38 47; telefax: 33 5 57 74 17 18
Visits: By appointment, every day
Contact: Jean-Pierre Clauzel

VINEYARDS (red)
Surface area: 15.8 acres
Average age of vines: 35 years
Blend: 65% Merlot, 35% Cabernet Franc
Density of plantation: 5,500 vines per hectare
Average yields (over the last 5 years): 43 hectoliters per hectare
Total average annual production: 36,000 bottles

GRAND VIN (red)
Brand name: Château La Grave-Figeac
Appellation: St.-Emilion Grand Cru
Mean annual production: 25,000 bottles
Upbringing: Fermentations and macerations last 20 or 25 days in
temperature-controlled concrete tanks. Wines are transferred to oak
barrels (renewed by a third at each vintage) for 12–18 months aging.
They are fined but remain unfiltered.

SECOND WINE
Brand name: Pavillon Figeac
Average annual production: 11,000 bottles

Evaluation of present classification: Until 1985 this was a perennial overachiever in the appellation; since 1985 the quality equivalent of a Médoc Cru Bourgeois

Plateau of maturity: 3–8 years following the vintage

This property proved to be quite a discovery when I first tasted the 1982 and 1983—both of which were still drinking beautifully in 1991. However, after 1983 the production soared and the wines became more loosely structured and lacked the concentration and character of the previous vintages. The vineyard is extremely well located on the Pomerol border near the great estates of Figeac and Cheval Blanc. In 1993 the property was sold to Jean-Pierre Clauzel, and I fully expect the quality to improve dramatically.

GUADET ST.-JULIEN

Classification: St.-Emilion Grand Cru Classé
Location of vineyards: St.-Emilion
Owner: Robert Lignac
Address: 4, rue Guadet, 33330 St.-Emilion
Mailing address: Same as above
Telephone: 33 5 57 24 63 50; telefax: 33 5 57 24 63 50
Visits: By appointment, Monday through Friday
Contact: Mrs. Lignac

VINEYARDS (red)
Surface area: 14.8 acres
Average age of vines: More than 35 years
Blend: 75% Merlot, 25% Cabernet Franc
Density of plantation: 5,200 vines per hectare
Average yields (over the last 5 years): 35 hectoliters
Total average annual production: 26,000 bottles

GRAND VIN (red)
Brand name: Château Guadet St.-Julien
Appellation: St.-Emilion Grand Cru Classé
Upbringing: Fermentations last 15–21 days. Wines are transferred to oak barrels, 40% of which are new, for 18–20 months aging. They are fined but remain unfiltered.

SECOND WINE
None produced.

Evaluation of present classification: The quality equivalent of a Médoc Cru Bourgeois
Plateau of maturity: 3–9 years following the vintage

This property's vineyard is located north of the town of St.-Emilion on the limestone plateau, but the cellars and winemaking facility are in St.-Emilion. The style of wine produced is soft, round, somewhat monolithic and straightforward, but pleasant and attractive in top vintages. Buyers are advised to drink the wine when it is young.

HAUT BRISSON

Classification: St.-Emilion Grand Cru
Production: 7,000 cases
Blend: 60% Merlot, 30% Cabernet Sauvignon, 10% Cabernet Franc
Secondary label: None
Vineyard size: 32 acres
Proprietor: Yves Blanc
Time spent in barrels: 18–20 months
Average age of vines: 22 years

Evaluation of present classification: The quality equivalent of a good Médoc Cru Bourgeois
Plateau of maturity: 3–10 years following the vintage

HAUT-CORBIN

Classification: St.-Emilion Grand Cru Classé
Location of vineyards: St.-Emilion
Owner: S.M.A.B.T.P.
Address: 33330 St.-Emilion
Mailing address: c/o Chateau Cantemerle, 33460 Macau
Telephone: 33 5 57 97 02 82; telefax: 33 5 57 97 02 84
Visits: By appointment only
Contact: Ph. Dambrine

VINEYARDS (red)
Surface area: 14.8 acres
Average age of vines: 40 years
Blend: 65% Merlot, 25% Cabernet Sauvignon, 10% Cabernet Franc
Density of plantation: 6,600 vines per hectare
Average yields (over the last 5 years): 50 hectoliters per hectare
Total average annual production: 40,000 bottles

GRAND VIN (red)
Brand name: Château Haut-Corbin
Appellation: St.-Emilion Grand Cru

Mean annual production: 30,000 bottles
Upbringing: Fermentations last 4–5 days (28–32 degrees centigrade) and
macerations 25–30 days (24–26 degrees centigrade) in concrete tanks of
90-hectoliter capacity. There are two pumping-overs daily. Thirty percent
of the yield undergoes malolactics in oak barrels. Wines are aged 12
months in oak barrels, 30% of which are new. They are racked every 3
months, lightly fined with egg whites, assembled, and left to rest 2
months in vats. They remain unfiltered.

SECOND WINE
Brand name: Sold in bulk
Average annual production: 10,000 bottles

Evaluation of present classification: The quality equivalent of a good
Médoc Cru Bourgeois
Plateau of maturity: 3–8 years following the vintage

HAUT-MAZERAT

Classification: St.-Emilion Grand Cru
Location of vineyards: Southwest of St.-Emilion, bordered by Beauséjour
(Duffau-Lagarosse), Canon, Angélus, and Berliquet
Owner: E.A.R.L. Christian Gouteyron
Address: 4, Mazerat, 33330 St.-Emilion
Mailing address: Same as above
Telephone: 33 5 57 24 71 15; telefax: 33 5 57 24 67 28
Visits: By appointment, Monday through Friday, between 9 A.M. and
6 P.M.
Contact: Christian Gouteyron

VINEYARDS (red)
Surface area: 14.8 acres
Average age of vines: 35 years
Blend: 60% Merlot, 30% Cabernet Franc, 10% Cabernet Sauvignon
Density of plantation: 5,700 vines per hectare
Average yields (over the last 5 years): 51 hectoliters per hectare
Total average annual production: 40,000 bottles

GRAND VIN (red)
Brand name: Château Haut-Mazerat
Appellation: St.-Emilion Grand Cru
Mean annual production: 310 hectoliters

Upbringing: Fermentations and macerations last 15 days in vats equipped with an internal temperature-control system. Maximum temperatures reached are 28–30 degrees centigrade. Wines are aged in oak barrels and vats (by rotation) for 18–20 months. They are fined and lightly filtered.

SECOND WINE
None produced.

HAUT-QUERCUS

Classification: St.-Emilion Grand Cru
Location of vineyards: St.-Emilion, St.-Christophe des Bardes,
St.-Etienne de Lisse, St.-Hippolyte, and St.-Laurent des Combes
(selection of hillside vineyards)
Owner: Union des Producteurs de St.-Emilion
Address: 33330 St.-Emilion
Mailing address: B.P. 27, Haut-Gravet, 33330 St.-Emilion
Telephone: 33 5 57 24 70 71; telefax: 33 5 57 24 65 18
Visits: Monday through Friday, between 8:30 A.M. and noon, and 2 P.M. and 6 P.M.
Contact: Patrick Foulon

VINEYARDS (red)
Surface area: 11 acres
Average age of vines: 30–37 years
Blend: 60% Merlot, 25% Cabernet Franc, 15% Cabernet Sauvignon
Density of plantation: 5,500 vines per hectare
Average yields (over the last 5 years): 50 hectoliters per hectare
Total average annual production: 30,000 bottles

GRAND VIN (red)
Brand name: Haut-Quercus
Appellation: St.-Emilion Grand Cru
Mean annual production: 30,000 bottles
Upbringing: Alcoholic fermentations at 30 degrees centigrade, and malolactics last 15–20 days in temperature-controlled concrete vats. Wines are then aged 11 months in oak barrels, which are renewed by one-third at each vintage. They are fined and filtered.

HAUT-SARPE

Classification: St.-Emilion Grand Cru Classé
Location of vineyards: Just to the northeast of Trottevieille on sandy, gravel soils.
Owner: Jean and Françoise Janoueix
Address: 33330 St.-Emilion
Mailing address: c/o Maison Janoueix, 37, rue Pline Parmentier, B.P. 192, 33506 Libourne
Telephone: 33 5 57 51 41 86; telefax: 33 5 57 51 53 16
Visits: By appointment only
Contact: Maison J. Janoueix

VINEYARDS (red)
Surface area: 52 acres
Average age of vines: 35 years
Blend: 70% Merlot, 30% Cabernet Franc
Density of plantation: 6,000 vines per hectare
Average yields (over the last 5 years): 46 hectoliters per hectare
Total average annual production: 10,000 cases

GRAND VIN (red)
Brand name: Château Haut-Sarpe
Appellation: St.-Emilion Grand Cru
Mean annual production: 550 hectoliters
Upbringing: Fermentations last 3–4 weeks in temperature-controlled concrete and stainless-steel vats. After malolactics, wines are aged 2 years in oak barrels, 30% of which are new. They are racked 8 times, fined with egg whites, but remain unfiltered.

SECOND WINE
Brand name: Now Château Vieux Sarpe (St.-Emilion Grand Cru), but prior to 1996, Le Second de Haut Sarpe (St.-Emilion *générique*)
Average annual production: 180 hectoliters

Evaluation of present classification: The quality equivalent of a good Médoc Cru Bourgeois
Plateau of maturity: 5–12 years following the vintage

Haut-Sarpe is a reliable St.-Emilion owned by the Libourne *négociant* firm of J. Janoueix. The château, which is one of the most beautiful of the region, sits to the northeast of St.-Emilion next to the highly regarded estate of Balestard-La-Tonnelle. The style of wine produced here is darkly colored, rustic, generously flavored, and usually firmly tannic. In good vintages the wine should be cellared for at least 5–6 years. It will keep for 12 or more.

HAUT-VILLET

Classification: St.-Emilion Grand Cru
Location of vineyards: St.-Etienne de Lisse
Owner: GFA du Château Haut-Villet
Address: St.-Etienne de Lisse, 33330 St.-Emilion
Mailing address: Same as above
Telephone: 33 5 57 47 97 60; telefax: 33 5 57 47 92 94
Visits: Every day, from 10 A.M. to noon, and 2 P.M. to 6 P.M.
Contact: Eric Lenormand

VINEYARDS (red)
Surface area: 18.5 acres
Average age of vines: 40 years
Blend: 70% Merlot, 28% Cabernet Franc, 2% Cabernet Sauvignon
Density of plantation: 5,500–6,400 vines per hectare
Average yields (over the last 5 years): 38 hectoliters
Total average annual production: 45,000 bottles

GRAND VIN (red)
Brand name: Château Haut-Villet
Appellation: St.-Emilion Grand Cru
Mean annual production: 30,000 bottles
Upbringing: Fermentations take place in temperature-controlled
stainless-steel tanks with frequent *remontages*. Wines are then aged 12
months in oak barrels, 40% of which are new. They are fined but remain
unfiltered.

SECOND WINE
Brand name: Château Moulin Villet
Average annual production: 10,000 bottles

SPECIAL CUVÉE
Brand name: Cuvée Pomone
Appellation: St.-Emilion Grand Cru
Mean annual production: 3,000 bottles
Upbringing: Fermentations take place in temperature-controlled
stainless-steel tanks with frequent *remontages*. Wines are then aged 12
months in 100% new oak barrels. They are fined but remain unfiltered.
(Since the 1997 vintage, malolactics occur in new oak and wines are aged
16 months minimum before bottling.)

JEAN-FAURE

Classification: St.-Emilion Grand Cru
Address: 33330 St.-Emilion
Telephone: 33 5 57 51 49 36
Production: 10,000 cases
Blend: 60% Cabernet Franc, 30% Merlot, 10% Malbec
Secondary label: None
Vineyard size: 49.4 acres
Proprietor: Michel Amart
Time spent in barrels: 18–22 months
Average age of vines: 30 years

Evaluation of present classification: The quality equivalent of a Médoc
Cru Bourgeois
Plateau of maturity: 3–12 years following the vintage

This is often a perplexing wine to evaluate given the extremely high percent-age of Cabernet Franc used in the blend. However, the proprietor has long argued that the sandy soils of Jean-Faure's vineyard near both Cheval Blanc and Figeac are perfect for this much Cabernet Franc.

LE JURAT

Classification: St.-Emilion Grand Cru
Location of vineyards: St.-Emilion
Owner: S.M.A.B.T.P.
Address: 33330 St.-Emilion
Mailing address: c/o Chateau Cantemerle, 33460 Macau
Telephone: 33 5 57 97 02 82; telefax: 33 5 57 97 02 84
Visits: By appointment only
Contact: Ph. Dambrine

VINEYARDS (red)
Surface area: 18.5 acres
Average age of vines: 30 years
Blend: 90% Merlot, 10% Cabernet Sauvignon
Density of plantation: 6,600 vines per hectare
Average yields (over the last 5 years): 50 hectoliters per hectare
Total average annual production: 50,000 bottles

GRAND VIN (red)
Brand name: Château Le Jurat
Appellation: St.-Emilion Grand Cru

Mean annual production: 40,000 bottles
Upbringing: Fermentations last 4–5 days (28–32 degrees centigrade)
and macerations 25–30 days (24–26 degrees centigrade) in concrete
tanks of 100-hectoliter capacity. There are 2 pumping-overs daily
and a cold maceration for 4–5 days at 8–10 degrees centigrade.
Wines are aged 12 months in oak barrels, 20% of which are new.
They are racked every 3 months, lightly fined with egg whites,
assembled, and left to rest 2 months in vats. They remain
unfiltered.

SECOND WINE
Brand name: Sold in bulk
Average annual production: 60–70 hectoliters

Evaluation of present classification: The quality equivalent of a good
Médoc Cru Bourgeois
Plateau of maturity: 3–10 years following the vintage

LAFLEUR-VACHON

Classification: St.-Emilion Grand Cru
Location of vineyards: St.-Emilion
Owner: Vignobles Raymond Tapon
Address: 33330 St.-Emilion
Mailing address: Same as above
Telephone: 33 5 57 74 61 20; telefax: 33 5 57 24 69 32
Visits: By appointment only
Contact: Nicole Tapon

VINEYARDS (red)
Surface area: 9.8 acres
Average age of vines: 35 years
Blend: 70% Merlot, 20% Cabernet Franc, 6% Cabernet Sauvignon,
4% Malbec
Density of plantation: 5,500 vines per hectare
Average yields (over the last 5 years): 48 hectoliters per hectare
Total average annual production: 180 hectoliters

GRAND VIN (red)
Brand name: Château Lafleur-Vachon
Appellation: St.-Emilion Grand Cru
Mean annual production: 20,000 bottles
Upbringing: Fermentations and macerations last 17–23 days in tanks

equipped with a trickle cooling. Wines are aged for 18–20 months in oak casks, 10%–20% of which are new. They are fined but not filtered.

SECOND WINE
None produced.

LANIOTE

Classification: St.-Emilion Grand Cru Classé
Location of vineyards: St.-Emilion
Owner: Arnaud de la Filolie
Address: 33330 St.-Emilion
Mailing address: Same as above
Telephone: 33 5 57 24 70 80; telefax: 33 5 57 24 60 11
Visits: By appointment for groups; otherwise every day of the week
Contact: Arnaud de la Filolie

VINEYARDS (red)
Surface area: 12.4 acres
Average age of vines: 35 years
Blend: 70% Merlot, 20% Cabernet Franc, 10% Cabernet Sauvignon
Density of plantation: 6,500 vines per hectare
Average yields (over the last 5 years): 49 hectoliters per hectare
Total average annual production: 32,000–35,000 bottles

GRAND VIN (red)
Brand name: Château Laniote
Appellation: St.-Emilion Grand Cru Classé
Mean annual production: 32,000–35,000 bottles
Upbringing: Fermentations last 3–4 weeks in temperature-controlled concrete vats, at temperatures of 22–24 degrees centigrade at the beginning and 31–32 degrees centigrade at the end of the process. Wines are transferred to oak casks, 35%–40% of which are new, for 12 months aging. Approximately 25%–35% of the yield is aged in 1-year-old barrels that have contained white wines (they are bought from estates such as Haut-Brion and Thieuley), the remainder being in 1-year-old barrels that have contained red wines. Wines are fined and filtered.

SECOND WINE
Brand name: La Chapelle de Laniote
Average annual production: Produced in 1992 only—5,000 bottles

Evaluation of present classification: The quality equivalent of a Médoc Cru Bourgeois
Plateau of maturity: 3–9 years following the vintage

I have had very limited experience with the wines from the tiny vineyard of Laniote. The property, located northwest of the town of St.-Emilion on rich clay, limestone, and iron-enriched soils, has been controlled by the same family for over 7 generations. The best wine I have tasted was the 1982, which was opulent and soft but fully mature by 1990. The 1981, 1983, and 1985 were above average in quality but unexciting.

LAROQUE

Classification: St.-Emilion Grand Cru Classé (from 1996)
Location of vineyards: St.-Christophe des Bardes
Owner: Beaumartin family
Address: 33330 St.-Emilion
Mailing address: Same as above
Telephone: 33 5 57 24 77 28; telefax: 33 5 57 24 63 65
Visits: Preferably by appointment
Contact: Bruno Sainson

VINEYARDS (red)
Surface area: 143 acres, but only 67 acres produce Château Laroque
Average age of vines: 30 years
Blend: 87% Merlot, 11% Cabernet Franc, 2% Cabernet Sauvignon
Density of plantation: 5,265 vines per hectare
Average yields (over the last 5 years): 44 hectoliters per hectare

GRAND VIN (red)
Brand name: Château Laroque
Appellation: St.-Emilion Grand Cru
Mean annual production: 150,000 bottles
Upbringing: Alcoholic fermentations and macerations with skins last approximately 4 weeks in temperature-controlled concrete vats. Wines are then run off from the lees. They are aged in oak barrels, which are renewed by a third or a half at each vintage, for 12 months and are blended in vats. They are bottled after 22 months, after both fining and filtration.

SECOND WINE
Brand name: Château Peymouton
Average annual production: 100,000 bottles

NOTE: They also produce 50,000–60,000 bottles of a third wine called Les Tours de Laroque.

Evaluation of present classification: The quality equivalent of a Médoc Cru Bourgeois
Plateau of maturity: 3–8 years following the vintage

LAROZE

Classification: St.-Emilion Grand Cru Classé
Location of vineyards: St.-Emilion
Owner: Meslin family
Address: 33330 St.-Emilion
Mailing address: Same as above
Telephone: 33 5 57 24 79 79; telefax: 33 5 57 24 79 80
Visits: By appointment only
Contact: Guy Meslin

VINEYARDS (red)
Surface area: 66.7 acres
Average age of vines: 20 years
Blend: 59% Merlot, 38% Cabernet Franc, 3% Cabernet Sauvignon
Density of plantation: 5,700 vines per hectare
Average yields (over the last 5 years): 48 hectoliters per hectare
Total average annual production: 120,000–150,000 bottles

GRAND VIN (red)
Brand name: Château Laroze
Appellation: St.-Emilion Grand Cru Classé
Mean annual production: 70,000–110,000 bottles
Upbringing: Fermentations last about 3 weeks in temperature-controlled stainless-steel tanks of small capacity. This allows the vinification of each parcel of vines separately. Only indigenous yeasts are used to start fermentations. Maximum temperatures reached are 30–34 degrees centigrade. Pumping-overs are frequent and slow. Malolactics occur in oak casks for 30% of the yield; the rest remains in vats and is transferred to oak casks. The wines are racked every 3 months, fined with egg whites, and not filtered. The aging process lasts 12–18 months.

SECOND WINE
None produced.

Evaluation of present classification: The quality equivalent of a good Médoc Cru Bourgeois
Plateau of maturity: 4–8 years following the vintage

While I have never considered the wines of Laroze to be that profound, there is something to be said for a style of wine that is fragrant, soft, fruity, and easy to drink. These are wines that require consumption within their first 4–8 years of life. If consumers keep that fact in mind, there is plenty of charm to be found with the wines of Laroze.

The vineyards do not possess one of St.-Emilion's better *terroirs*, being planted in light, sandy soil. The wines are vinified in a modern, up-to-date facility.

LEYDET-FIGEAC

Classification: St.-Emilion Grand Cru
Location of vineyards: Near Château La Tour-Figeac, not far from Figeac and Château Cheval Blanc
Owner: Mr. Leydet
Address: S.C.E.A. des Vignobles Leydet, Rouilledinat, 33500 Libourne
Mailing address: Same as above
Telephone: 33 5 57 51 19 77; telefax: 33 5 57 51 00 62
Visits: Monday through Friday, between 8 A.M. and noon, and 2 P.M. to 7 P.M.; on Saturdays, until midday only
Contact: Mr. Leydet

VINEYARDS (red)
Surface area: 9.5 acres
Average age of vines: 25 years
Blend: 70% Merlot, 15% Cabernet Franc, 15% Cabernet Sauvignon
Density of plantation: 6,000 vines per hectare
Average yields (over the last 5 years): 45 hectoliters per hectare
Total average annual production: 22,000 bottles

GRAND VIN (red)
Brand name: Château Leydet-Figeac
Appellation: St.-Emilion Grand Cru
Mean annual production: 22,000 bottles
Upbringing: Alcoholic fermentations last about 7 days (30–33 degrees centigrade), and macerations last 4–6 weeks depending upon the quality of the harvest. Malolactics occur in vats at controlled temperatures that do not exceed 22 degrees centigrade. Forty percent of the yield is aged in new oak barrels, 20% is kept in vats, and the remaining 40% is placed in 1- and 2-year-old barrels. Wines are fined and filtered.

SECOND WINE
None produced.

LEYDET-VALENTIN

Classification: St.-Emilion Grand Cru
Location of vineyards: In the northwestern part of St.-Emilion
Owner: Bernard Leydet
Address: Clos Valentin, 33330 St.-Emilion
Mailing address: Same as above
Telephone: 33 5 57 24 73 05
Visits: By appointment only
Contact: Bernard Leydet

VINEYARDS (red)
Surface area: 12.4 acres
Average age of vines: 20 years
Blend: 60% Merlot, 35% Cabernet Franc, 5% Malbec
Density of plantation: 5,500 vines per hectare
Average yields (over the last 5 years): 52 hectoliters per hectare
Total average annual production: 30,000 bottles

GRAND VIN (red)
Brand name: Château Leydet-Valentin
Appellation: St.-Emilion Grand Cru
Mean annual production: 30,000 bottles
Upbringing: Fermentations and macerations are traditional and rather
long in temperature-controlled concrete vats. Wines are aged 18–20
months in oak barrels, which are renewed by one-third in each vintage.
The wines are fined and filtered.

SECOND WINE
None produced.

MAGNAN LA GAFFELIÈRE

Classification: St.-Emilion Grand Cru
Location of vineyards: St.-Emilion
Owner: S.A. du Clos La Madeleine
Address: Magnan, 33330 St.-Emilion
Mailing address: B.P. 78, 33330 St.-Emilion
Telephone: 33 5 57 5 38 03; telefax: 33 5 57 55 38 01
Visits: By appointment, Monday through Friday, between 8 A.M. and
6 P.M.
Contact: Philippe Lauret

VINEYARDS (red)
Surface area: 19.8 acres
Average age of vines: 30 years
Blend: 75% Merlot, 25% Cabernet Franc
Density of plantation: 6,600 vines per hectare
Average yields (over the last 5 years): 53 hectoliters per hectare
Total average annual production: 425 hectoliters per hectare

GRAND VIN (red)
Brand name: Château Magnan La Gaffelière
Appellation: St.-Emilion Grand Cru
Mean annual production: 425 hectoliters per hectare
Upbringing: Fermentations and macerations last approximately 1 month
in temperature-controlled concrete tanks. Wines are then aged in vats.
They are fined but remain unfiltered.

SECOND WINE
None produced.

MARTINET

Classification: St.-Emilion Grand Cru
Location of vineyards: St.-Emilion
Owner: De Lavaux family
Address: 33330 St.-Emilion
Mailing address: c/o Ets. Horeau Beylot, B.P. 125, 33501 Libourne
Telephone: 33 5 57 51 06 07; telefax: 33 5 57 51 59 61
Visits: By appointment only

VINEYARDS (red)
Surface area: 49.4 acres
Average age of vines: 50 years
Blend: 65% Merlot, 35% Cabernet Franc
Density of plantation: 5,500 vines per hectare
Average yields (over the last 5 years): 40–45 hectoliters per hectare
Total average annual production: 120,000 bottles

GRAND VIN (red)
Brand name: Château Martinet
Appellation: St.-Emilion
Mean annual production: 120,000 bottles
Upbringing: Fermentations and macerations last 18–23 days in
temperature-controlled stainless-steel and concrete tanks. Malolactics

usually occur in tanks (sometimes a very small percentage of the yield completes this process in oak barrels), and wines are aged for 8–12 months by rotation in oak barrels, 10%–15% of which are new (60% of the yield), and concrete tanks (40% of the yield). They are fined and filtered.

SECOND WINE
None produced.

MATRAS

Classification: St.-Emilion Grand Cru Classé
Location of vineyards: Near Angélus, Beauséjour-Duffau, Canon, and Berliquet
Owner: GFA du Château Matras (the Bernard family)
Address: 33330 St.-Emilion
Mailing address: Same as above
Telephone: 33 5 57 24 72 46; telefax: 33 5 57 51 70 19
Visits: By appointment only
Contact: Véronique Gaboriaud

VINEYARDS (red)
Surface area: 22.2 acres
Average age of vines: 40 years (or more)
Blend: 60% Cabernet Franc, 40% Merlot
Density of plantation: 5,500 vines per hectare
Average yields (over the last 5 years): 45 hectoliters per hectare
Total average annual production: 400 hectoliters

GRAND VIN (red)
Brand name: Château Matras
Appellation: St.-Emilion
Mean annual production: 240 hectoliters
Upbringing: Fermentations and macerations last 3 weeks in temperature-controlled stainless-steel vats. Wines undergo malolactics in tanks and are then aged 18 months with 30% new oak. They are fined but remain unfiltered.

SECOND WINE
Brand name: L'Hermitage de Matras (produced from the younger vines)
Average annual production: 160 hectoliters

Evaluation of present classification: The quality equivalent of a Médoc Cru Bourgeois
Plateau of maturity: 3–10 years following the vintage

MAUVEZIN

Classification: St.-Emilion Grand Cru (declassified in 1996)
Location of vineyards: St.-Emilion
Owner: Pierre Cassat
Address: 33330 St.-Emilion
Mailing address: B.P. 44—33330 St.-Emilion
Telephone: 33 5 57 24 72 36; telefax: 33 5 57 74 48 54
Visits: By appointment, Monday through Friday
Contact: Olivier Cassat

VINEYARDS (red)
Surface area: 8.6 acres
Average age of vines: 40–45 years
Blend: 50% Merlot, 40% Cabernet Franc, 10% Cabernet Sauvignon
Density of plantation: 5,400 vines per hectare (1 hectare at 6,600 vines
per hectare)
Average yields (over the last 5 years): 40 hectoliters
Total average annual production: 130 hectoliters

GRAND VIN (red)
Brand name: Château Mauvezin
Appellation: St.-Emilion Grand Cru
Mean annual production: 15,000 bottles
Upbringing: Alcoholic fermentations last 10 days and macerations
3 weeks in temperature-controlled vats. Wines are aged 12 months in oak
barrels, 30%–80% of which are new depending upon the vintage. They
are fined and filtered.

SECOND WINE
None produced.

Evaluation of present classification: The quality equivalent of a good
Médoc Cru Bourgeois
Plateau of maturity: 3–10 years following the vintage

MONLOT CAPET

Classification: St.-Emilion Grand Cru
Location of vineyards: St.-Hippolyte
Owner: Bernard Rivals
Address: 33330 St.-Hippolyte
Mailing address: Same as above

Telephone: 33 5 57 24 62 32; telefax: 33 5 57 24 62 33
Visits: Monday through Friday, between 9 A.M. and 6 P.M.; by
appointment on weekends
Contact: Bernard Rivals

VINEYARDS (red)
Surface area: 42.7 acres
Average age of vines: 27 years
Blend: 70% Merlot, 25% Cabernet Franc, 5% Cabernet Sauvignon
Density of plantation: 5,000 vines per hectare
Average yields (over the last 5 years): 48 hectoliters per hectare
Total average annual production: 45,000 bottles

GRAND VIN (red)
Brand name: Château Monlot Capet
Appellation: St.-Emilion Grand Cru
Mean annual production: 45,000 bottles
Upbringing: Fermentations and macerations last 4–5 weeks in concrete
tanks at 27–30 degrees centigrade. Wines are aged 18 months in oak
barrels that are renewed by half at each vintage. They are fined and filtered.

SECOND WINE
None produced.

MOULIN BELLEGRAVE

Classification: St.-Emilion Grand Cru
Location of vineyards: Vignonnet, Saint-Pey-d'Armens, St.-Sulpice de
Faleyrens
Owner: Florian Perrier
Address: 33330 St.-Emilion
Mailing address: Same as above
Telephone: 33 5 57 74 97 08; telefax: 33 5 57 74 92 79
Visits: By appointment only
Contact: Florian Perrier

VINEYARDS (red)
Surface area: 39.5 acres
Average age of vines: 30 years
Blend: 60% Merlot, 20% Cabernet Franc, 20% Cabernet Sauvignon
Density of plantation: 5,000 vines per hectare
Average yields (over the last 5 years): 45 hectoliters per hectare
Total average annual production: 750 hectoliters

GRAND VIN (red)
Brand name: Château Moulin Bellegrave
Appellation: St.-Emilion Grand Cru
Mean annual production: 3,000 cases
Upbringing: Fermentations and macerations are conducted in
temperature-controlled stainless-steel vats. Malolactics occur in tanks,
after which the wines are transferred to oak barrels (20% new) for 6
months aging. They are fined and filtered.

SECOND WINE
Brand name: Château des Graves
Average annual production: 200 hectoliters

PARADIS

Classification: St.-Emilion Grand Cru
Location of vineyards: Vignonnet and St.-Emilion
Owner: G.F.A. Château du Paradis
Address: Vignobles Rany-Saugeon, B.P. 1, 33330 St.-Emilion
Mailing address: Same as above
Telephone: 33 5 57 84 53 27; telefax: 33 5 57 84 61 76
Visits: Preferably by appointment, Monday through Friday, between
10 A.M. and 6 P.M.
Contact: Janine Rany-Saugeon

VINEYARDS (red)
Surface area: 64.2 acres
Average age of vines: 25 years
Blend: 75% Merlot, 20% Cabernet Franc, 5% Cabernet Sauvignon
Density of plantation: 5,000 vines per hectare
Average yields (over the last 5 years): 47 hectoliters per hectare
Total average annual production: 1,200 hectoliters

GRAND VIN (red)
Brand name: Château du Paradis
Appellation: St.-Emilion Grand Cru
Upbringing: Fermentations and macerations last 3–4 weeks in
temperature-controlled vats. Wines remain in vats for 18 months aging.
They are fined and filtered.

SECOND WINE
None produced.

PASQUETTE

Classification: St.-Emilion Grand Cru
Location of vineyards: At the foot of the hillsides, near Tertre-Daugay and L'Arrosée
Owner: G.F.A. Jabiol
Address: 33330 St.-Emilion
Mailing address: B.P. 24, 33330 St.-Emilion
Telephone: 33 5 57 74 47 69; telefax: Same
Visits: By appointment only
Contact: Amélie Jabiol at Château Cadet-Piola

VINEYARDS (red)
Surface area: 7.5 acres
Average age of vines: 35 years
Blend: 80% Merlot, 10% Cabernet Franc, 10% Cabernet Sauvignon
Density of plantation: 5,500 vines per hectare
Average yields (over the last 5 years): 35 hectoliters per hectare
Total average annual production: 14,000 bottles

GRAND VIN (red)
Brand name: Château de Pasquette
Appellation: St.-Emilion Grand Cru
Mean annual production: 14,000 bottles
Upbringing: Fermentations and macerations last 18 days in stainless-steel vats. Wines are aged in oak barrels and vats for 22 months. They are fined and filtered.

SECOND WINE
Very rarely produced.

PATRIS

Classification: St.-Emilion Grand Cru
Location of vineyards: St.-Emilion
Owner: Michel Querre
Address: Patris, 33330 St.-Emilion
Mailing address: c/o Les Hospices de la Madeleine, B.P. 51, 33330 St.-Emilion
Telephone: 33 5 57 55 51 60; telefax: 33 5 57 55 51 61
Visits: By appointment only
Contact: Thierry Delon or Laurent Simon

VINEYARDS (red)
Surface area: 29.6 acres
Average age of vines: 40 years
Blend: 78% Merlot, 15% Cabernet Franc, 7% Cabernet Sauvignon
Density of plantation: 5,400 vines per hectare
Average yields (over the last 5 years): 45 hectoliters per hectare
Total average annual production: 60,000 bottles

GRAND VIN (red)
Brand name: Château Patris
Appellation: St.-Emilion Grand Cru
Mean annual production: 24,000 bottles
Upbringing: Fermentations and macerations take place in temperature-controlled tanks. Fifty percent of the yield undergoes malolactics in new oak barrels, the rest in vats. Wines are aged 12–15 months in 50% new oak barrels. They are fined but not systematically filtered.

SECOND WINE
Brand name: Filius du Château Patris
Average annual production: 30,000 bottles

PAVILLON-CADET

Classification: St.-Emilion Grand Cru
Production: 1,300 cases
Blend: 60% Merlot, 40% Cabernet Franc
Secondary label: None
Vineyard size: 6.2 acres
Proprietor: Morvan-Leamas
Time spent in barrels: 14–22 months
Average age of vines: 25 years

Evaluation of present classification: The quality equivalent of a good Médoc Cru Bourgeois
Plateau of maturity: 5–14 years following the vintage

PETIT-FAURIE-DE-SOUTARD

Classification: St.-Emilion Grand Cru Classé
Location of vineyards: St.-Emilion
Owner: Françoise Capdemourlin
Address: 33330 St.-Emilion

Mailing address: Château Roudier, 33570 Montagne
Telephone: 33 5 57 74 62 06; telefax: 33 5 57 74 59 34
Visits: By appointment only
Contact: Françoise Capdemourlin

VINEYARDS (red)
Surface area: 19.8 acres
Average age of vines: 31 years
Blend: 60% Merlot, 30% Cabernet Franc, 10% Cabernet Sauvignon
Density of plantation: 5,400 vines per hectare
Average yields (over the last 5 years): 46 hectoliters per hectare
Total average annual production: 3,500 cases

GRAND VIN (red)
Brand name: Château Petit-Faurie-de-Soutard
Appellation: St.-Emilion Grand Cru
Mean annual production: 320 hectoliters
Upbringing: Fermentations last approximately 3–4 weeks in concrete vats
lined with enamel, and equipped with a temperature-control system (with
Fréon). After malolactics, wines are aged for 14–16 months in oak
barrels, 35% of which are new. They are both fined and filtered.

SECOND WINE
Brand name: Petit-Faurie-de-Soutard deuxième
Average annual production: Rarely produced

Evaluation of present classification: The quality equivalent of a good
Médoc Cru Bourgeois
Plateau of maturity: 5–12 years following the vintage

This is an under-rated St.-Emilion property with a relatively small production.
The administrator, the Capdemourlin family, often promotes the wines from
Balestard-La-Tonnelle more than those from Petit-Faurie-de-Soutard. Nevertheless, this vineyard, once part of the famous Soutard domain, is well situated on the limestone plateau. The wines tend to have a great deal of fat and
richness of fruit, much like Balestard, but also perhaps more structure and
grip because of higher tannin levels. The best recent vintages have been
1982, 1983, 1985, 1989, and 1990. Unlike Balestard-La-Tonnelle, this is a
wine that needs 3–4 years in the bottle to shed the tannins; it can last for
more than a decade.

PETIT FIGEAC

Classification: None
Owner: AXA Millésimes
Address: 33330 St.-Emilion
Telephone: 33 5 57 24 62 61; telefax: 33 5 57 24 68 25
Visits: By appointment only
Contact: AXA Millésimes

VINEYARDS (red)
Surface area: 7.5 acres
Blend: 60% Merlot, 30% Cabernet Franc, 10% Cabernet Sauvignon
Density of plantation: 5,500 vines per hectare
Average yields (over the last 5 years): 45 hectoliters per hectare
Total average annual production: 1,500 cases

GRAND VIN (red)
Brand name: Château Petit Figeac
Appellation: St.-Emilion
Mean annual production: 1,500 cases
Upbringing: 14–16 months in oak casks.

SECOND WINE
None produced.

Evaluation of present classification: The quality equivalent of a Médoc
Cru Bourgeois
Plateau of maturity: 3–10 years

DOMAINE DE PEYRELONGUE

Classification: St.-Emilion Grand Cru
Location of vineyards: St.-Emilion
Owner: Pierre Cassat
Address: 33330 St.-Emilion
Mailing address: B.P. 44, 33330 St.-Emilion
Telephone: 33 5 57 24 72 36; telefax: 33 5 57 74 48 54
Visits: By appointment, Monday through Friday
Contact: Olivier Cassat

VINEYARDS (red)
Surface area: 14.8 acres
Average age of vines: 35–40 years

Blend: 65% Merlot, 25% Cabernet Franc, 10% Cabernet Sauvignon
Density of plantation: 5,400 vines per hectare
Average yields (over the last 5 years): 45 hectoliters per hectare
Total average annual production: 32,000 bottles

GRAND VIN (red)
Brand name: Domaine de Peyrelongue
Appellation: St.-Emilion Grand Cru
Mean annual production: 270 hectoliters
Upbringing: Alcoholic fermentations last 10 days and macerations
15 days in temperature-controlled tanks. Wines are aged for 12 months
in oak barrels, 10%–15% of which are new, the rest of which are 2 and
3 vintages old. They are fined and filtered.

SECOND WINE
None produced.

PINDEFLEURS

Classification: St.-Emilion Grand Cru
Address: 33330 St.-Emilion
Telephone: 33 5 57 24 72 04
Production: 3,500 cases
Blend: 55% Merlot, 45% Cabernet Franc
Secondary label: Clos Lescure
Vineyard size: 21.2 acres
Proprietor: Micheline Dior
Time spent in barrels: 18–22 months
Average age of vines: 22 years

Evaluation of present classification: Should be elevated to a St.-Emilion
Grand Cru Classé; the quality equivalent of a very good Médoc Cru
Bourgeois
Plateau of maturity: 3–14 years following the vintage

PIPEAU

Classification: St.-Emilion Grand Cru
Location of vineyards: St.-Laurent des Combes
Owner: Dominique Lauret and Richard Mestreguilhem
Address: 33330 St.-Laurent des Combes

Mailing address: Same as above
Telephone: 33 5 57 24 72 95; telefax: 33 5 57 24 71 25
Visits: On open days, between 9 A.M. and noon, and 2 P.M. and 6 P.M.
Contact: Dominique Lauret and Richard Mestreguilhem

VINEYARDS (red)
Surface area: 86.5 acres
Average age of vines: 35 years
Blend: 80% Merlot, 10% Cabernet Franc, 10% Cabernet Sauvignon
Density of plantation: 6,600 vines per hectare
Average yields (over the last 5 years): 45 hectoliters per hectare
Total average annual production: 150,000 bottles

GRAND VIN (red)
Brand name: Château Pipeau
Appellation: St.-Emilion Grand Cru
Mean annual production: 150,000 bottles
Upbringing: Fermentations and macerations last 4–5 weeks. Wines are
aged 18 months in oak barrels that are renewed by a third at each
vintage. They are fined but remain unfiltered.

SECOND WINE
None produced.

PONTET-FUMET

Classification: St.-Emilion Grand Cru
Location of vineyards: Vignonet
Owner: S.C.E.A. Vignobles Bardet
Address: 17, La Cale, 33330 Vignonet
Mailing address: Same as above
Telephone: 33 5 57 84 53 16; telefax: 33 5 57 74 93 47
Visits: By appointment only

VINEYARDS (red)
Surface area: 32 acres
Average age of vines: 25 years
Blend: 80% Merlot, 20% Cabernet Franc
Density of plantation: 6,000 vines per hectare
Average yields (over the last 5 years): 50 hectoliters per hectare
Total average annual production: 80,000 bottles

GRAND VIN (red)
Brand name: Château Pontet-Fumet
Appellation: St.-Emilion Grand Cru
Mean annual production: 80,000 bottles
Upbringing: Fermentations and macerations last 5–8 weeks in
stainless-steel and concrete tanks depending upon the vintage. Wines are
aged 18–24 months in oak barrels that are renewed by a third each
vintage. They are fined and filtered.

SECOND WINE
None produced.

LE PRIEURÉ

Classification: St.-Emilion Grand Cru Classé
Location of vineyards: St.-Emilion, near Trotte Vieille, Troplong-Mondot,
and Lasserre, opposite Ausone
Owner: Olivier Guichard
Address: Château Le Prieuré, 33330 St.-Emilion
Mailing address: S.C.E. Baronne Guichard, Château Siaurac, 33500 Néac
Telephone: 33 5 57 51 64 58; telefax: 33 5 57 51 41 56
Visits: By appointment only
Contact: Gino Bortoletto

VINEYARDS (red)
Surface area: 14.8 acres
Average age of vines: 30 years
Blend: 60% Merlot, 30% Cabernet Franc, 10% Cabernet Sauvignon
Density of plantation: 5,500 vines per hectare
Average yields (over the last 5 years): 43 hectoliters per hectare
Total average annual production: 260 hectoliters

GRAND VIN (red)
Brand name: Château Le Prieuré
Appellation: St.-Emilion Grand Cru Classé
Mean annual production: 260 hectoliters
Upbringing: Fermentations and macerations last 3–4 weeks in
temperature-controlled concrete vats. Thirty percent of the yield
completes its malolactics in new oak barrels; the rest remains in vats
until the end of this process. Wines are transferred to oak barrels after
malolactics (30% new oak and 70% 1-year-old barrels) for
20 months of aging. They are fined with albumin and remain unfiltered.

SECOND WINE
None produced.

Evaluation of present classification: The quality equivalent of a Médoc
Cru Bourgeois
Plateau of maturity: 3–8 years following the vintage

PRIEURÉ-LESCOURS

Classification: St.-Emilion Grand Cru
Address: 33330 St.-Emilion
Telephone: 33 5 57 51 64 58; telefax: 33 5 57 51 41 56
Production: 2,500 cases
Blend: 60% Merlot, 30% Cabernet Franc, 10% Malbec
Secondary label: L'Olivier
Vineyard size: 13.8 acres
Proprietor: S.C.E. Baronne Guichard
Time spent in barrels: 12–14 months
Average age of vines: 30 years

Evaluation of present classification: The quality equivalent of a Médoc
Cru Bourgeois
Plateau of maturity: 3–8 years following the vintage

PUY-BLANQUET

Classification: St.-Emilion Grand Cru
Location of vineyards: St.-Etienne de Lisse
Owner: Roger Jacquet
Address: 33330 St.-Etienne de Lisse
Mailing address: Same as above
Telephone: 33 5 57 40 18 18; telefax: 33 5 57 40 29 14
Visits: By appointment, Monday through Friday, between 8 A.M. and
noon, and 2 P.M. and 6 P.M.
Contact: Pierre Meunier

VINEYARDS (red)
Surface area: 56.8 acres
Average age of vines: 25 years
Blend: 80% Merlot, 15% Cabernet Franc, 5% Cabernet Sauvignon

Density of plantation: 5,300 vines per hectare
Average yields (over the last 5 years): 50 hectoliters
Total average annual production: 1,150 hectoliters

GRAND VIN (red)
Brand name: Château Puy-Blanquet
Appellation: St.-Emilion Grand Cru
Mean annual production: 900 hectoliters
Upbringing: Fermentations and macerations last 3 weeks in concrete vats.
Malolactics occur in vats. Twenty percent of the yield is aged 12 months
in oak barrels, one-third of which are new, the remaining 80% of the
wines are aged in concrete vats. The wines are fined and filtered.

SECOND WINE
Brand name: Château Laberne
Average annual production: 250 hectoliters

Evaluation of present classification: The quality equivalent of a Médoc
Cru Bourgeois
Plateau of maturity: 3–8 years following the vintage

PUY-RAZAC

Classification: St.-Emilion and St.-Emilion Grand Cru
Location of vineyards: St.-Emilion
Owner: Guy Thoilliez
Address: 33330 St.-Emilion
Mailing address: Same as above
Telephone: 33 5 57 24 73 32; telefax: 33 5 57 24 73 32
Visits: By appointment only
Contact: Guy Thoilliez

VINEYARDS (red)
Surface area: 14.8 acres
Average age of vines: 20 years
Blend: 50% Merlot, 50% Cabernet Franc
Density of plantation: 5,200 vines per hectare
Average yields (over the last 5 years): 52 hectoliters per hectare
Total average annual production: 300 hectoliters

GRAND VIN (red)
Brand name: Château Puy-Razac
Appellation: St.-Emilion Grand Cru

Mean annual production: 300 hectoliters
Upbringing: Fermentations and macerations last 21 days in cement vats (temperatures are controlled manually). Wines are aged 22 months in vats, racked every 2 months, fined, and filtered.

SECOND WINE
None produced.

QUERCY

Classification: St.-Emilion Grand Cru
Location of vineyards: Vignonnet
Owner: Apelbaum-Pidoux family
Address: 3, Grave, 33330 Vignonnet
Mailing address: Same as above
Telephone: 33 5 57 84 56 07; telefax: 33 5 57 84 54 82
Visits: By appointment only, every day
Contact: Stéphane Apelbaum

VINEYARDS (red)
Surface area: 14.8 acres
Average age of vines: 45 years
Blend: 70% Merlot, 30% Cabernet Franc
Density of plantation: 6,500 vines per hectare
Average yields (over the last 5 years): 40 hectoliters
Total average annual production: 240 hectoliters

GRAND VIN (red)
Brand name: Château Quercy
Appellation: St.-Emilion Grand Cru
Mean annual production: 15,000 bottles
Upbringing: Fermentations and macerations last 20–40 days in concrete vats. Malolactics occur partly in vats and partly in barrels. Wines are aged 18 months in oak barrels, 50% of which are new. They are racked every 3 months, fined with egg whites, and filtered.

SECOND WINE
Brand name: Graves de Peyroutas
Average annual production: Variable

RIPEAU

Classification: St.-Emilion Grand Cru Classé
Location of vineyards: St.-Emilion, near Cheval Blanc and Figeac
Owner: G.F.A. du Château Ripeau—Françoise de Wilde
Address: 33330 St.-Emilion
Mailing address: Same as above
Telephone: 33 5 57 74 41 41; telefax: 33 5 57 74 41 57
Visits: Preferably by appointment
Contact: Françoise de Wilde

VINEYARDS (red)
Surface area: 37.5 acres
Average age of vines: 35 years
Blend: 60% Merlot, 30% Cabernet Franc, 10% Cabernet Sauvignon
Density of plantation: 5,500 vines per hectare
Average yields (over the last 5 years): 44 hectoliters per hectare
Total average annual production: 700 hectoliters

GRAND VIN (red)
Brand name: Château Ripeau
Appellation: St.-Emilion Grand Cru Classé
Mean annual production: 700 hectoliters
Upbringing: Fermentations and macerations last 4–5 weeks in
temperature-controlled vats. Wines are aged in oak barrels, which are
renewed by half in each vintage, for 10–18 months. They are fined and
lightly filtered.

SECOND WINE
Brand name: Roc de Pipeau (young vines planted in 1997)

Evaluation of present classification: The quality equivalent of a Médoc
Cru Bourgeois
Plateau of maturity: 3–12 years following the vintage

Ripeau is one of the older estates of St.-Emilion, taking its name from the parcel of land on which the vineyard and château are situated. The soil is primarily sand intermixed with some gravel. Ripeau's vineyard sits near Cheval Blanc and La Dominique but is less well placed than either. The new owners acquired the property in 1976, and major renovations have taken place. This has always been a relatively chunky, fruity wine that lacked consistency, but when it was good it could be counted on to drink well for at least a decade.

ROCHER

Classification: St.-Emilion Grand Cru
Location of vineyards: St.-Etienne de Lisse
Owner: G.F.A. Château du Rocher
Address: 33330 St.-Etienne de Lisse
Mailing address: Same as above
Telephone: 33 5 57 40 18 20; telefax: 33 5 57 40 37 26
Visits: By appointment only
Contact: Baron de Montfort

VINEYARDS (red)
Surface area: 37 acres
Average age of vines: 30 years
Blend: 70% Merlot, 15% Cabernet Franc, 15% Cabernet Sauvignon
Density of plantation: 5,500 vines per hectare
Average yields (over the last 5 years): 45 hectoliters per hectare
Total average annual production: 675 hectoliters

GRAND VIN (red)
Brand name: Château du Rocher
Appellation: St.-Emilion Grand Cru
Mean annual production: 675 hectoliters
Upbringing: Fermentations take place in stainless-steel vats and in concrete vats. Half the yield is aged in stainless-steel vats, and the other half in oak barrels (35% of the yield is in new oak). The wines are fined and filtered.

SECOND WINE
None produced.

ROCHER-BELLEVUE-FIGEAC

Classification: St.-Emilion Grand Cru
Location of vineyards: On the plateau of Bellevue
Owner: Mr. and Mrs. Dutruilh
Address: 33330 St.-Emilion
Mailing address: 14, rue d'Aviau, 33000 Bordeaux
Telephone: 33 5 56 81 19 69; telefax: 33 5 56 81 19 69
Visits: By appointment only
Contact: Mr. and Mrs. Dutruilh

VINEYARDS (red)
Surface area: 17.3 acres
Average age of vines: 29 years
Blend: 80% Merlot, 20% Cabernet Franc
Density of plantation: 5,500–6,000 vines per hectare
Average yields (over the last 5 years): 47.5 hectoliters per hectare
Total average annual production: 330 hectoliters

GRAND VIN (red)
Brand name: Château Rocher-Bellevue-Figeac
Appellation: St.-Emilion Grand Cru
Mean annual production: 270 hectoliters
Upbringing: Fermentations and macerations last 4–5 weeks in
stainless-steel vats. Forty percent of the yield undergoes malolactics in
new oak; the rest remains in vats. Wines are aged 15–18 months in oak
barrels (40% of which are new, 40% are 1 vintage old, and 20% are 2
vintages old). They are fined but remain unfiltered.

SECOND WINE
Brand name: Pavillon La Croix Figeac
Average annual production: 8,500 bottles

Evaluation of present classification: The quality equivalent of a good
Médoc Cru Bourgeois
Plateau of maturity: 3–8 years following the vintage

The Domaines Cordier has been overseeing the vinification and commercialization of this wine since the mid-1980s. The wines have definitely benefited
from the attention of Cordier's brilliant oenologist, Georges Pauli. However,
this is not one of St.-Emilion's long-lived wines. Why? No doubt because the
vineyard, situated on the plateau near both Figeac and the border of Pomerol,
is planted with an extremely high percentage of Merlot. The result is a juicy,
almost succulently fruity, round wine that makes for delicious drinking early
and is best consumed by 7–8 years of age. I would be cautious about buying
anything older.

ROLLAND-MAILLET

Classification: St.-Emilion Grand Cru
Telephone: 33 5 57 51 10 94; telefax: 33 5 57 25 05 54
Production: 2,000 cases
Blend: 75% Merlot, 25% Cabernet Franc
Secondary label: None

Vineyard size: 10 acres
Proprietor: Michel Rolland
Time spent in barrels: 18 months
Average age of vines: 25 years

Evaluation of present classification: A solidly made St.-Emilion that is
consistently good to very good
Plateau of maturity: 3–9 years following the vintage

Bordeaux insiders often look for this well-made St.-Emilion owned and vinified by the famous Libourne oenologist Michel Rolland. It tends to be a
chunky, robust, deeply concentrated, opaquely colored St.-Emilion that can
age for up to a decade. What it lacks in finesse and elegance, it often makes
up for with pure power and robustness.

LA ROSE POURRET

Classification: St.-Emilion Grand Cru
Location of vineyards: St.-Emilion
Owner: Mr. and Mrs. Philippe Warion
Address: 33330 St.-Emilion
Mailing address: Same as above
Telephone: 33 5 57 27 71 13; telefax: 33 5 57 74 43 93
Visits: Every day, between 8 A.M. and noon, and 2 P.M. to 6 P.M.; by
appointment during weekends
Contact: Philippe Warion

VINEYARDS (red)
Surface area: 19.7 acres
Average age of vines: 35 years
Blend: 70% Merlot, 30% Cabernet Franc
Density of plantation: 6,000 vines per hectare
Average yields (over the last 5 years): 46 hectoliters per hectare
Total average annual production: 50,000 bottles

GRAND VIN (red)
Brand name: Château La Rose Pourret
Appellation: St.-Emilion Grand Cru
Mean annual production: 50,000 bottles
Upbringing: Fermentations are long and traditional and take place in
temperature-controlled vats. Wines are aged 15–18 months in oak

barrels, 30%–40% of which are new. They are fined and very lightly filtered.

SECOND WINE
None produced.

ROYLLAND

Classification: St.-Emilion Grand Cru
Location of vineyards: St.-Emilion
Owner: Bernard Oddo
Address: 33330 St.-Emilion
Mailing address: Same as above
Telephone: 33 5 57 24 68 27; telefax: 33 5 57 24 65 25
Visits: By appointment, on weekdays, between 2 P.M. and 6 P.M.
Contact: Anne Masset

VINEYARDS (red)
Surface area: 25 acres
Average age of vines: 25–30 years
Blend: 85% Merlot, 15% Cabernet Franc
Density of plantation: 6,000 vines per hectare
Average yields (over the last 5 years): 45 hectoliters per hectare
Total average annual production: 50,000 bottles

GRAND VIN (red)
Brand name: Château Roylland
Appellation: St.-Emilion
Mean annual production: 50,000 bottles
Upbringing: Fermentations and macerations last 4–8 weeks in concrete and stainless-steel tanks equipped with a temperature control. After malolactics, 60% of yield is transferred to oak barrels (renewed by half in each vintage), while the remaining 40% is aged in vats. Wines are aged 18 months, racked every 2 months, fined with fresh egg whites, and remain unfiltered.

SECOND WINE
None produced.

ST.-GEORGES-CÔTE PAVIE

Classification: St.-Emilion Grand Cru Classé
Location of vineyards: On the hillside of Pavie, between Château Pavie
and La Gaffelière
Owner: Jacques and Marie-Gabrielle Masson
Address: 33330 St.-Emilion
Mailing address: Same as above
Telephone: 33 5 57 74 44 23
Visits: By appointment only
Contact: Jacques Masson

VINEYARDS (red)
Surface area: 13.5 acres
Average age of vines: 25–30 years
Blend: 80% Merlot, 20% Cabernet Franc
Density of plantation: 5,500 vines per hectare
Average yields (over the last 5 years): 46 hectoliters per hectare
Total average annual production: 30,000 bottles

GRAND VIN (red)
Brand name: Château St.-Georges-Côte Pavie
Appellation: St.-Emilion Grand Cru
Mean annual production: 30,000 bottles
Upbringing: Fermentations and macerations last approximately 20 days
in temperature-controlled vats. Wines are aged in oak barrels, 25% of
which are new. They are fined with albumin.

SECOND WINE
Brand name: Côte Madeleine
Average annual production: Not produced since 1992

Evaluation of present classification: The quality equivalent of a Médoc
Cru Bourgeois
Plateau of maturity: 3–12 years following the vintage

This is another tiny St.-Emilion vineyard that is extremely well placed on the hillside known as the Côte de Pavie. In fact, the vineyards of Pavie sit on one side of this property, with those of La Gaffelière on the other.

The only vintages I have tasted, 1988, 1989, and 1990, were round, generously endowed, easy to like St.-Emilions that lacked complexity but offered copious amounts of straightforward, chunky black fruit married nicely with the scent of new oak and herbaceous aromas. My best guess is that they will last for 8–12 or more years. This could be a property to take seriously.

ST.-LÔ

Classification: St.-Emilion Grand Cru
Location of vineyards: St.-Pey d'Armens, St.-Hippolyte, and St.-Laurent
des Combes
Owner: Vatana and Sons
Address: 33330 St.-Pey d'Armens
Mailing address: c/o Consulate of Thailand, 26, avenue Carnot,
33000 Bordeaux
Telephone: 33 06 09 72 11 24; telefax: 33 5 57 22 11 70
Visits: Monday through Friday, between 9 A.M. and noon, and 2 P.M. and
4:30 P.M.
Contact: Jean-François Vergne, telephone 33 5 57 47 15 22

VINEYARDS (red)
Surface area: 32 acres
Average age of vines: 17 years
Blend: 85% Merlot, 15% Cabernet Franc
Density of plantation: 5,500 vines per hectare
Average yields (over the last 5 years): 48 hectoliters per hectare
Total average annual production: 60,000 bottles

GRAND VIN (red)
Brand name: Château St.-Lô
Appellation: St.-Emilion Grand Cru
Mean annual production: 10,000 bottles
Upbringing: Fermentations and macerations last approximately 2 weeks.
Wines are aged 18 months in oak barrels, 50% of which are new. They
are fined and filtered.

SANSONNET

Classification: St.-Emilion Grand Cru
Location of vineyards: St.-Emilion
Owner: G.F.A. du Château Sansonnet
Address: 33330 St.-Emilion
Mailing address: Same as above
Telephone: 33 5 57 51 03 65; telefax: 33 5 57 25 00 20
Visits: By appointment only
Contact: Francis Robin

VINEYARDS (red)
Surface area: 17.3 acres
Average age of vines: 35 years
Blend: 65% Merlot, 20% Cabernet Franc, 15% Cabernet Sauvignon
Density of plantation: 5,500 vines per hectare
Average yields (over the last 5 years): 45 hectoliters per hectare
Total average annual production: 40,000 bottles

GRAND VIN (red)
Brand name: Château Sansonnet
Appellation: St.-Emilion Grand Cru
Mean annual production: 30,000 bottles
Upbringing: Fermentations and macerations last 15–20 days. Wines are transferred to oak barrels, which are renewed by a third at each vintage, for 15–18 months aging. They are fined with egg whites and slightly filtered.

SECOND WINE
Brand name: Domaine de la Salle
Average annual production: 10,000–15,000 bottles

Evaluation of present classification: The quality equivalent of a Médoc Cru Bourgeois
Plateau of maturity: 4–14 years following the vintage

TAUZINAT L'HERMITAGE

Classification: St.-Emilion Grand Cru
Location of vineyards: St.-Christophe des Bardes and St.-Hippolyte
Owner: S.C.E. Vignobles Bernard Moueix
Address: 33330 St.-Emilion
Mailing address: c/o Château Taillefer, 33330 St.-Emilion
Telephone: 33 5 57 25 50 45; telefax: 33 5 57 25 50 45
Visits: By appointment only

VINEYARDS (red)
Surface area: 23.5 acres
Average age of vines: 35 years
Blends: 90% Merlot, 10% Cabernet Franc
Density of plantation: 6,500 vines per hectare
Average yields (over the last 5 years): 50 hectoliters per hectare
Total average annual production: 60,000 bottles

GRAND VIN (red)
Brand name: Château Tauzinat L'Hermitage
Appellation: St.-Emilion Grand Cru
Mean annual production: 4,000 cases
Upbringing: Fermentations and macerations last 4–5 weeks in
temperature-controlled vats. Wines are aged 12 months in oak barrels,
15% of which are new. They are fined but remain unfiltered upon bottling.

SECOND WINE
Brand name: Grand Treuil
Average annual production: 1,000 cases

Evaluation of present classification: The quality equivalent of a Médoc
Cru Bourgeois
Plateau of maturity: 3–8 years following the vintage

TOUR BALADOZ

Classification: St.-Emilion Grand Cru
Location of vineyards: St.-Laurent des Combes
Owner: S.C.E.A. Château Tour Baladoz
Manager: Jacques de Schepper
Address: 33330 St.-Laurent des Combes
Mailing address: Same as above
Telephone: 33 5 57 88 94 17; telefax: 33 5 57 88 39 14
Visits: By appointment only
Contact: Jean-Michel Garcion

VINEYARDS (red)
Surface area: 22 acres
Average age of vines: 28 years
Blend: 80% Merlot, 15% Cabernet Franc, 5% Cabernet Sauvignon
Density of plantation: 6,000 vines per hectare
Average yields (over the last 5 years): 45 hectoliters per hectare
Total average annual production: 400 hectoliters

GRAND VIN (red)
Brand name: Château Tour Baladoz
Appellation: St.-Emilion Grand Cru
Mean annual production: 300 hectoliters
Upbringing: Fermentations and macerations last 3–5 weeks in
stainless-steel tanks equipped with a trickle cooling system. Wines

remain 4–8 months in vats and are transferred for 10–18 months aging to oak barrels, 60%–85% of which are new. They are fined and filtered.

SECOND WINE

Brand name: Château Tour St.-Laurent
Average annual production: 100 hectoliters

LA TOUR-FIGEAC

Classification: St.-Emilion Grand Cru Classé
Location of vineyards: Bordering Pomerol, between Figeac and Cheval Blanc
Owner: Rettenmaier family
Address: S.C. La Tour-Figeac, B.P. 07, 33330 St.-Emilion
Mailing address: Same as above
Telephone: 33 5 57 51 77 62; telefax: 33 5 57 25 36 92
Visits: By appointment only
Contact: Otto Max Rettenmaier

VINEYARDS (red)

Surface area: 35.8 acres
Average age of vines: 35 years
Blend: 60% Merlot, 40% Cabernet Franc
Density of plantation: 7,000 vines per hectare
Average yields (over the last 5 years): 45 hectoliters per hectare

GRAND VIN (red)

Brand name: Château La Tour-Figeac
Appellation: St.-Emilion Grand Cru
Upbringing: Fermentations and macerations last 3–5 weeks in temperature-controlled stainless-steel vats, with maximum temperatures going up to 32–34 degrees centigrade. Malolactics occur in casks for part of the yield; the rest remains in vats. Wines are aged 12–18 months in oak barrels, 30%–50% of which are new. They are rarely fined and/or filtered.

SECOND WINE

Brand Name: Sold as St.-Emilion
Average annual production: 7 hectoliters

Evaluation of present classification: The quality equivalent of a good Médoc Cru Bourgeois
Plateau of maturity: 3–10 years following the vintage

This property, like so many St.-Emilion estates with the name Figeac, was once part of the huge domain of Figeac until it was partitioned in 1879. The vineyard, which is easy to spot because of the tower that sits in the middle of the vineyards, and from which the château takes part of its name, is bordered on one side by Cheval Blanc and on the south by Figeac. To the west is the appellation of Pomerol.

The winemaking has been very good at La Tour-Figeac, although vintages in the mid- and late eighties were off form. Since the property was acquired by the Rettenmaier family in 1994, quality has increased dramatically, as evidenced by the 1996.

LA TOUR-DU-PIN-FIGEAC-GIRAUD-BÉLIVIER

Classification: St.-Emilion Grand Cru Classé
Location of vineyards: In the northwestern part of the appellation, next to Cheval Blanc, near the road going from Pomerol to St.-Emilion
Owner: G.F.A. Giraud Bélivier—Mr. André Giraud (manager)
Address: 33330 St.-Emilion
Mailing address: c/o André Giraud, Château Le Caillou, 33500 Pomerol
Telephone: 33 5 57 51 63 93; telefax: 33 5 57 51 74 95
Visits: By appointment, Monday through Friday, between 9 A.M. and noon, and 2 P.M. and 6 P.M.
Contact: Sylvie Giraud

VINEYARDS (red)
Surface area: 27 acres
Average age of vines: 30 years
Blend: 75% Merlot, 25% Cabernet Franc
Density of plantation: 5,800 vines per hectare
Average yields (over the last 5 years): 45 hectoliters per hectare
Total average annual production: 64,000 bottles

GRAND VIN (red)
Brand name: Château La-Tour-du-Pin-Figeac-Giraud-Bélivier
Appellation: St.-Emilion Grand Cru
Mean annual production: 46 hectoliters per hectare
Upbringing: Fermentations and macerations last 3–4 weeks in concrete vats. Two-thirds of the yield then go into oak barrels, and one-third remains in vats for 12 months aging. There is a rotation every 3 months at the time of racking. Wines are assembled, kept for 4 months in vats, then fined with egg whites before bottling. They are not filtered.

SECOND WINE
None produced.

Evaluation of present classification: The quality equivalent of a Médoc
Cru Bourgeois
Plateau of maturity: 3–9 years following the vintage

TRIMOULET

Classification: St.-Emilion Grand Cru
Location of vineyards: St.-Emilion
Address: 33330 St.-Emilion
Mailing address: B.P. 60, 33330 St.-Emilion
Telephone: 33 5 57 24 70 56; telefax: 33 5 57 74 41 69
Visits: By appointment only
Contact: Michel Jean

VINEYARDS (red)
Surface area: 39.5 acres
Average age of vines: 30 years
Blend: 60% Merlot, 35% Cabernet Franc, 5% Cabernet Sauvignon
Density of plantation: 6,000 vines per hectare
Average yields (over the last 5 years): 50 hectoliters per hectare
Total average annual production: 100,000 bottles

GRAND VIN (red)
Brand name: Château Trimoulet
Appellation: St.-Emilion Grand Cru
Mean annual production: 50,000 bottles
Upbringing: Fermentations last 8–10 days and macerations
approximately 3 weeks in temperature-controlled concrete vats.
Wines are transferred after malolactics to oak barrels, 30%–40% of
which are new, for 12 months aging. They are fined but remain
unfiltered.

SECOND WINE
Brand name: Emilius
Average annual production: 55,000 bottles

Evaluation of present classification: The quality equivalent of a Médoc
Cru Bourgeois
Plateau of maturity: 3–7 years following the vintage

VAL D'OR

Classification: St.-Emilion Grand Cru
Location of vineyards: Vignonnet
Owner: S.C.E.A. Vignobles Bardet
Address: 17, La Cale, 33330 Vignonnet
Mailing address: Same as above
Telephone: 33 5 57 84 53 16; telefax: 33 5 57 74 93 47
Visits: By appointment only

VINEYARDS (red)
Surface area: 27 acres
Average age of vines: 30 years
Blend: 80% Merlot, 15% Cabernet Franc, 5% Cabernet Sauvignon
Density of plantation: 6,000 vines per hectare
Average yields (over the last 5 years): 50 hectoliters per hectare
Total average annual production: 75,000 bottles

GRAND VIN (red)
Brand name: Château du Val d'Or
Appellation: St.-Emilion Grand Cru
Mean annual production: 75,000 bottles
Upbringing: Fermentations and macerations last 5–8 weeks in stainless-steel and concrete tanks. Wines are aged 18–24 months in oak barrels that are renewed by a third at each vintage. They are fined and filtered.

SECOND WINE
None produced.

VIEUX-CHÂTEAU-CARRÉ

Classification: St.-Emilion Grand Cru
Production: 1,500 cases
Blend: 60% Merlot, 20% Cabernet Franc, 20% Cabernet Sauvignon
Secondary label: None
Vineyard size: 7.5 acres
Proprietor: Yvon Dubost
Time spent in barrels: 14–20 months
Average age of vines: 20 years

Evaluation of present classification: The quality equivalent of a Médoc Cru Bourgeois
Plateau of maturity: 3–7 years following the vintage

VIEUX SARPE

Classification: St.-Emilion Grand Cru
Location of vineyards: East of St.-Emilion, on a calcareous plateau
between Trottevieille and Haut-Sarpe
Owner: Jean and Françoise Janoueix
Address: 33330 St.-Emilion
Mailing address: c/o Maison Janoueix, 37, rue Pline Parmentier, B.P. 192,
33506 Libourne
Telephone: 33 5 57 51 41 86; telefax: 33 5 57 51 53 16
Visits: By appointment only
Contact: Maison J. Janoueix at above telephone and fax numbers

NOTE: The following information applies to Château Vieux Sarpe *before
1996*. Following the latest St.-Emilion classification, 24.7 acres of
Château Vieux Sarpe that historically were part of Haut Sarpe (Grand Cru
Classé) were reintegrated into this latter estate, bringing its new surface
area to nearly 52 acres. The Château Haut-Sarpe was bought by Joseph
Janoueix in 1930, and the Château Vieux Sarpe (detached from it in the
early 19th century) was bought by Jean-François Janoueix in 1950.

Since the 1996 vintage, Château Haut Sarpe's second wine will be called
Château Vieux Sarpe (and no longer Le Second de Haut-Sarpe), and the
remaining almost 5 acres that constitute the Château Vieux Sarpe will be
labeled Château Haut-Badette (name of the second wine prior to 1996).

VINEYARDS (red)
Surface area: 27 acres under vines
Average age of vines: 40 years
Blend: 70% Merlot, 20% Cabernet Franc, 10% Cabernet Sauvignon
Density of plantation: 6,000 vines per hectare
Average yields (over the last 5 years): 45 hectoliters per hectare
Total average annual production: 500 hectoliters

GRAND VIN (red)
Brand name: Château Vieux Sarpe
Appellation: St.-Emilion Grand Cru
Mean annual production: 280 hectoliters
Upbringing: Fermentations and macerations last 3–4 weeks in
temperature-controlled concrete and stainless-steel vats. After
malolactics, wines are aged 2 years in oak barrels, 30% of which are new.
They are racked 8 times, are fined with egg whites, and remain unfiltered.

SECOND WINE
Brand name: Château Haut-Badette
Average annual production: 200 hectoliters

JEAN VOISIN

Classification: St.-Emilion Grand Cru
Location of vineyards: St.-Emilion
Owner: S.C.E.A. du Château Jean-Voisin—Chassagnoux
Address: 33330 St.-Emilion
Mailing address: Same as above
Telephone: 33 5 57 24 70 40; telefax: 33 5 57 24 79 57
Visits: By appointment Monday through Saturday, from 8 A.M. to noon, and 2 P.M. to 7 P.M.
Contact: Pierre Chassagnoux

VINEYARDS (red)
Surface area: 35.8 acres
Average age of vines: 20 years
Blend: 75% Merlot, 20% Cabernet Franc, 5% Cabernet Sauvignon
Density of plantation: 5,200 vines per hectare
Average yields (over the last 5 years): 450 hectoliters per hectare
Total average annual production: 650 hectoliters

GRAND VIN (red)
Brand name: Château Jean Voisin "Cuvée Amédée"
Appellation: St.-Emilion Grand Cru
Mean annual production: 350 hectoliters
Upbringing: Fermentations and macerations last 20–30 days in concrete and stainless-steel temperature-controlled tanks. Twenty percent of the yield undergoes malolactics in new oak barrels. Wines are aged 12 months in oak casks that are renewed by a third each vintage. They are fined with fresh egg whites and filtered.

SECOND WINE
Brand name: Château Jean Voisin
Average annual production: 300 hectoliters

YON-FIGEAC

Classification: St.-Emilion Grand Cru Classé
Location of vineyards: On sandy soils (St.-Emilion)
Owner: Denis Londeix
Address: Château Yon-Figeac, 3 and 5 Yon, 33330 St.-Emilion
Mailing address: Same as above
Telephone: 33 5 57 42 66 66; telefax: 33 5 57 64 36 20
Visits: By appointment only
Contact: Marie Fabre

VINEYARDS (red)
Surface area: 61.75 acres
Average age of vines: 25 years
Blend: 80% Merlot, 20% Cabernet Franc
Density of plantation: 5,500 vines per hectare
Average yields (over the last 5 years): 45 hectoliters per hectare
Total average annual production: 1,125 hectoliters

GRAND VIN (red)
Brand name: Château Yon-Figeac
Appellation: St.-Emilion
Mean annual production: 800 hectoliters
Upbringing: Cold maceration (*préfermentaire à froid*) lasts 4–5 days.
Fermentations and macerations last about 3–4 weeks in
temperature-controlled stainless-steel tanks. Malolactics occur partially
in oak barrels. Wines are transferred to oak casks for 12–15 months
aging (30%–40% new oak is utilized). They are racked twice during the
aging process, fined with fresh egg whites, but remain unfiltered.

SECOND WINE
Brand name: Château Yon Saint-Martin
Production: 200 hectoliters

Evaluation of present classification: The quality equivalent of a Médoc
Cru Bourgeois
Plateau of maturity: 3–10 years following the vintage

Yon-Figeac is a beautifully turreted château, with vineyards located northwest
of the town of St.-Emilion on shallow, sandy soil. The style of wine produced
tends to be round and silky, with a great deal of red and black fruit character.
It is not a wine that would seemingly last long, although I have had no
experience with vintages older than 7 years.

THE WINES OF
BARSAC AND
SAUTERNES

The Barsac and Sauternes wine-producing regions are located a short 40-minute drive south from downtown Bordeaux. Labor intensive and expensive to produce, the sweet wines of Barsac and Sauternes have long had huge climatic and manpower problems to overcome almost every year. Additionally, for most of this century the producers have had to confront a dwindling demand for these luscious, sweet, sometimes decadently rich and exotic wines because of the consumer's growing demand for drier wines. Given the fact that it is rare for a particular decade to produce more than three excellent vintages for these wines, the producers in this charming and rural viticultural region have become increasingly pessimistic that their time has passed. Château owners have changed at a number of properties, and more and more vineyards are also producing a dry white wine to help ease cash flow problems.

Yet surprisingly, many growers continue. They know they make one of the most remarkable wines in the world, and they hope that Mother Nature, good luck, and an increasing consumer awareness of their products will result in accelerated demand and appreciation of these white wines, which until recently were France's most undervalued and underappreciated great wines.

Perhaps their persistence has finally paid off. The second half of the eighties may well be viewed by future historians as the beginning of the renaissance for Barsac and Sauternes. There are many reasons for this turnaround in fortune. The fact that Mother Nature produced three superb, perhaps even legendary, vintages—1986, 1988, and 1989—helped focus attention on the regions' producers and their wines. Moreover, the 1990s started auspiciously, with 1990 producing sumptuous and powerful wines.

Second, a number of estates that had been in the doldrums for a while began to turn out wine that merited significant interest. In particular, the resurrection of the French Ministry of Agriculture's famed Château La Tour Blanche, with profound wines in 1988, 1989, and 1990, served as a sign that even the French government was interested in vindicating the great reputation of this famous estate.

Another Premier Grand Cru Classé, Rabaud-Promis, also began to make topflight wines, culminating in sensational efforts in 1988, 1989, and 1990.

SAUTERNES & BARSAC

CHÂTEAU
ROAD

GARONNE

PREIGNAC

D10

N113

D114

D118

D109

D8

A62

Nairac
BARSAC
Suau
Broustet
Coutet
Doisy-Daëne
Doisy-Védrines
Caillou
Climens
Gilette

Libourne
DORDOGNE
Bordeaux
GARONNE
Barsac
Sauternes

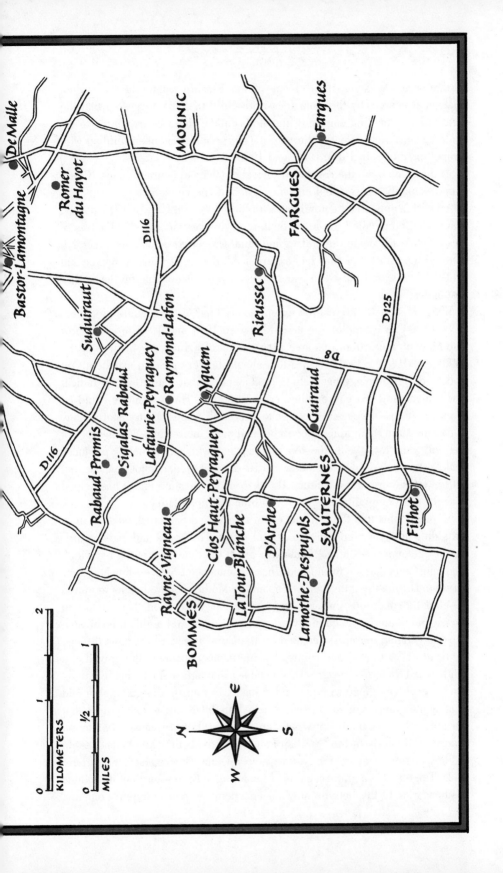

Furthermore, the acquisition of one of the flagship estates of the region, Château Rieussec, by the Domaines Rothschild in 1984 suggested that the great red winemaking empire of the Rothschilds would be expanded to include lavishly rich, sweet white wines. That promise has been fulfilled with compelling efforts in 1988, 1989, and 1990.

At the same time, the continued revival of Château Guiraud, under Canadian ownership, has resulted in a succession of fine vintages.

All of this appeared to culminate with the 1988, 1989, and 1990 vintages, which are being called the finest Sauternes vintages since 1937. Futures of these vintages became difficult to find, and a renewed confidence emerged. After all the difficulties they had experienced, the sweet wines of Barsac and Sauternes appeared poised to become once again fashionable on the world's best tables.

While Mother Nature can be exceptionally kind to the region's producers (1986–1990 for example), the period between 1991 and 1995 produced few inspirational wines from this area. At the time of writing, my tastings of the 1996s and 1997s revealed wines that should be very good to excellent. Yet modern-day technology has helped producers combat nature with a radical new winemaking procedure called cryo-extraction. This technique could be employed in less successful vintages to freeze the grapes and transform many so-so wines into something much richer and more interesting. Whether or not this will gain favor with the top estates, and whether or not it produces weaknesses in the wines when they are 10–25 years old, cannot be measured until after the turn of the century. But there is no question that it has helped raise the current quality of many wines from this appellation.

No one doubts that the winemakers of Barsac and Sauternes face the most forbidding odds for producing successful wines. The hopes and fears regarding the outcome of a vintage normally begin at the time most of the red wine–producing appellations to the north have commenced or even finished their harvests. During the latter half of September Mother Nature begins to unfold the climatic conditions that will be important for this region. The climate in Barsac and Sauternes is normally misty, mild, and humid at this time of year. The foggy, damp mornings (created by the Ciron River, which runs through the heart of Sauternes) and sunny, dry afternoons encourage the growth of a mold called *Botrytis cinerea*. This mold—commonly called "noble rot"—attacks each ripe, mature grape individually, devouring the grape skin and causing the grape to die and become dehydrated. Of course, only grapes that are attacked by the noble botrytis rot are selected. Botrytis causes a profound change particularly in the Semillon grape. It shrivels the skin, consumes up to 50% of the sugar content, forms glycerol, and decomposes the tartaric acids. The result is a grape capable of rendering only one-fourth of its volume of juice prior to the botrytis attack—an unctuous, concentrated, aromatic, sweet nectar. Curiously, the reaction causes a super-concentration of the grape's juice, which becomes considerably higher in sugar than normal. This happens without any loss of acidity.

This process is erratic and time-consuming. It can often take as long as 1 or 2 months for a significant portion of the white grapes to become infected by the botrytis mold. In some years very little botrytis develops and the wines lack flavor dimension and complexity. When the noble rot does form, its growth is painfully slow and uneven. Therefore, the great wines of this region can be made only by an arduous, time-consuming, labor-intensive process of sending teams of pickers into the vineyard to pick the afflicted grapes one at a time rather than bunch by bunch. The best estates have their pickers descend on the vineyard up to half a dozen times over this period, which usually occurs throughout October and November. The famous Château d'Yquem often sends pickers through the vineyard ten separate times. As expensive and time-consuming as picking is, the most hazardous risk of all is the weather. Heavy rains, hailstorms, or frost, all common meteorological developments for Bordeaux in late fall, can instantly transform a promising vintage into a disaster.

Since the conditions for making great wine are so different for Barsac and Sauternes, it is not surprising that what can be a great vintage for the red wines of Bordeaux can be mediocre for the sweet white wines from this area. The years 1982 and 1961 are two vintages in point. Both are undeniably great years for the red wines, but for the sweet wines of Barsac and Sauternes, the vintages are at best average. In contrast, 1988, 1980, 1967, and 1962 are four vintages for Barsac and Sauternes that most observers would consider very fine to superb. With the exception of 1988 and 1962, these vintages were less successful for most of the red wines of Bordeaux. Like the red wines of the Médoc, the wines of Barsac and Sauternes were considered important enough to be classified into quality groupings in 1855. The hierarchy (see page 1344) established Yquem as the best of the region, and it was called a "Premier Grand Cru Classé." Following Yquem were "Premiers Crus Classés" (now eleven as a result of several vineyards' being partitioned), and fourteen "Deuxièmes Crus Classés" (now twelve because one has ceased to exist and two others have merged).

From a consumer's perspective, three unclassified Cru Bourgeois estates, Raymond-Lafon, de Fargues, and Gilette, are making exquisite wines that rival all of the best estates' wines except for Yquem. However, they were not included in the 1855 classification. Additionally, there are a number of first-growths and second-growths that simply cannot afford to make wine the traditional way—using numerous crews of pickers working sporadically over a 4- to 8-week period. Several do not merit their current status and have been downgraded in my evaluations of the châteaux of these regions.

As for Château d'Yquem, it towers (both literally and figuratively) above the other estates here, producing a splendidly rich, distinctive, unique wine.

In my opinion, it is Bordeaux's single greatest wine. The official first-growths of the Médoc have worthy challengers every year, often producing wine equally impressive, and the right bank trio of Cheval Blanc, Ausone, and Pétrus can in some vintages not only be matched, but be surpassed by the brilliance of other estates in their respective appellations. Yquem, however, rarely has a challenger (except perhaps the elusive microscopic luxury cuvées of Coutet and Suduiraut called Cuvée Madame). This is not because top Barsac and Sauternes properties such as Climens, Rieussec, or Suduiraut cannot produce superlative wine, but rather that Yquem produces a wine at such an extravagantly expensive level of quality that it is commercial madness for any other property even to attempt to emulate it.

When I wrote the first edition of *Bordeaux* in 1984, I was skeptical about the potential of all but a handful of the Barsac/Sauternes estates. Today the entire region has been transformed by the great success of the vintages of 1986, 1988, 1989, and 1990, and for the most part, are enjoying a degree of financial prosperity (perhaps even security) that they had only dreamed of in the early eighties. These wines, even with such revolutionary techniques as cryo-extraction, will always be among the most difficult in the world to produce, and a few bad vintages in a row or over-reliance on new technology would no doubt dampen much of the appellation's enthusiasm. But for now, optimism reigns supreme in what once was one of the most distressingly sad regions of Bordeaux.

BARSAC and SAUTERNES
(An Insider's View)

Overall Appellation Potential: Good to Superb

The Most Potential for Aging: Climens, Coutet-Cuvée Madame, Gilette, Rieussec, Suduiraut, Yquem

The Most Elegant: Climens, Coutet, Doisy-Védrines, Rieussec, La Tour Blanche

The Most Concentrated: D'Arche-Pugneau, Coutet-Cuvée Madame, Lafaurie-Peyraguey, Raymond-Lafon, Suduiraut, Yquem

The Best Value: D'Arche-Pugneau, Bastor-Lamontagne, Haut-Claverie, Les Justices, Rabaud-Promis, La Tour Blanche

The Most Exotic: D'Arche-Pugneau, Raymond-Lafon

The Most Difficult to Understand (when young): Until these wines are 4–6 years old, they rarely reveal much delineation or true personalities.

The Most Underrated: Rabaud-Promis, La Tour Blanche

The Most Difficult to Appreciate Young: All of them, at least until they are 4–6 years old.

Up-and-Coming Estates: D'Arche-Pugneau, Rabaud-Promis, La Tour Blanche

Greatest Recent Vintages: 1990, 1989, 1988, 1986, 1983, 1976, 1975, 1967, 1962, 1959

NOTE: Both 1996 and 1997 have promising potential, but neither year is likely to be as compelling as 1988, 1989, and 1990.

BARSAC and SAUTERNES—AN OVERVIEW

Location: Southeast of Bordeaux, about 26 miles from the center of the city

Acres under Vine: 4,940; Sauternes—3,952; Barsac—998

Communes: Barsac, Bommes, Fargus, Preignac, and Sauternes

Average annual production: Sauternes—325,000 cases; Barsac—145,000 cases

Classified growths: 26 classified growths and 1 Premier Cru Supérieur—Château d'Yquem; 11 first-growths and 14 second-growths

Principal grape varieties: Semillon and Sauvignon Blanc, with tiny quantities of Muscadelle

Principal Soil Type: Deep gravel beds over thick layers of limestone. In less desirable parts of the appellation, some sand and clay can be found. ·

A CONSUMER'S CLASSIFICATION OF THE CHÂTEAUX OF BARSAC AND SAUTERNES

OUTSTANDING

Climens, Coutet-Cuvée Madame, Gilette, Rieussec, Suduiraut-Cuvée Madame, Yquem*

EXCELLENT

D'Arche-Pugneau, Coutet, de Fargues, Guiraud, Lafaurie-Peyraguey, Raymond-Lafon, Suduiraut, La Tour Blanche

VERY GOOD

Doisy-Dubroca, Doisy-Védrines, Haut-Claverie, Rabaud-Promis, Sigalas Rabaud

GOOD

D'Arche, Bastor-Lamontagne, Broustet, Clos Haut-Peyraguey, Doisy-Daëne, Filhot, Les Justices, Lamothe, Lamothe-Guignard, Liot, de Malle, Nairac, Piada, Rayne-Vigneau, Romer du Hayot, Roumieu-Lacoste

OTHER NOTABLE PROPERTIES OF SAUTERNES AND BARSAC

Caillou, Lamourette, de Rolland, Saint-Marc, Suau

---

* Yquem, despite the existence of other outstanding estates, rarely has any competition and must be considered the only Bordeaux wine in a class by itself.

ARCHE　　　　　　　　　　　　　　　　　　　　　　　　　GOOD

Classification: Second growth in 1855
Location of vineyards: Sauternes
Owner: S.A. Château d'Arche
Address: 33210 Sauternes
Mailing address: S.C.E.A. Vignobles Pierre Perromat, 33540 Gornac
Telephone: 33 5 56 61 97 64; telefax: 33 5 56 61 95 67
Visits: By appointment, on weekdays
Contact: Jérôme Cosson

VINEYARDS (white)
Surface area: 69 acres
Average age of vines: 35 years
Blend: 90% Semillon, 10% Sauvignon
Density of plantation: 6,000 and 6,500 vines per hectare
Average yields (over the last 5 years): 15 hectoliters per hectare
Total average annual production: 55,000 bottles

GRAND VIN (white)
Brand name: Château d'Arche
Appellation: Sauternes
Mean annual production: 45,000 bottles
Upbringing: Fermentations last 15 days in temperature-controlled
stainless-steel tanks of small capacity, and wines are then aged
4 months minimum in oak barrels, one-third of which is new. Fining
depends upon the vintage, and wines are generally filtered.

SECOND WINE
Brand name: Cru de Braneyre
Average annual production: 10,000 bottles

Evaluation of present classification: Should be maintained
Plateau of maturity: 5–15 or more years following the vintage

Château d'Arche is a Sauternes that began producing better and better wine
during the eighties. Given the quality of the wines, their prices are among the
most reasonable of the appellation. The style of wine produced at d'Arche
offers very unctuous, rich fruit, no doubt because of the high percentage of
Semillon, but also because of the late harvesting and the proprietor's serious
commitment (there are normally 7 to 10 passes through the vineyard to pick
only those grapes affected by the *Botrytis cinerea*).

VINTAGES

1990—The 1990 d'Arche may be over-ripe and too alcoholic. It is quite powerful,
•   but its lack of acidity may prove to be its undoing. If the wine pulls itself
87?   together, it will turn out to be a good to very good, muscular Sauternes that
        will offer big, thick, chewy fruit in a high alcohol, fiery format. Hopefully it
        will evolve for another decade. Last tasted, 11/94.

1989—The 1989, which seemed heavy-handed and out of focus in both barrel and
•   bottle, appears to have come together (a hopeful sign for the 1990), displaying
86   straightforward, ripe, chewy, muscular fruit in a low-acid, moderately sweet
        style. It should drink well for 7–8 years. Last tasted, 11/94.

1988—This is a beautifully made, intense wine with a gorgeous nose of honeyed
•   pineapple fruit. In the mouth, it is unctuous and full bodied, with great
88   sweetness and presence and a long, rich, nearly viscous finish. It is very
        forward for the vintage. Anticipated maturity: Now–2005. Last tasted, 4/91.

1986—This is another highly successful vintage for d'Arche. Not so rich or thick as
•   the 1988, but more classy from an aromatic point of view, this full-bodied,
88   concentrated wine exhibits telltale flavors of honeyed oranges and pineapples
        and even the smell of coconut. The finish is long and crisp, with a great deal
        of botrytis in evidence. Anticipated maturity: Now–2006. Last tasted, 3/90.

OLDER VINTAGES

D'Arche made a very good 1983 and a less interesting 1982 and 1981. I also
have notes on a surprisingly good 1969. I think it can be safely said that the
efforts of proprietor Pierre Perromat, who took over the running of the property
in 1981, have resulted in far greater wines in the eighties than in previous
decades.

BASTOR-LAMONTAGNE   GOOD

Classification: None
Location of vineyards: Preignac
Owner: Foncier-Vignobles
Address: 33210 Preignac
Mailing address: Same as above
Telephone: 33 5 56 63 27 66; telefax: 33 5 56 76 87 03
Visits: Monday through Friday, between 8:30 A.M. and 12:30 P.M., and
2 P.M. and 6 P.M.
Contact: Michel Garat

VINEYARDS (white)
Surface area: 143 acres
Average age of vines: 35 years
Blend: 80% Semillon, 20% Sauvignon

Density of plantation: 7,000 vines per hectare
Average yields (over the last 5 years): 20 hectoliters per hectare
Total average annual production: 1,150 hectoliters

GRAND VIN (white)
Brand name: Château Bastor-Lamontagne
Appellation: Sauternes
Mean annual production: 100,000 bottles
Upbringing: 25% of the yield undergoes fermentations in oak barrels and
the rest in temperature-controlled stainless-steel vats for 3 weeks. Wines
are aged in oak barrels (25% new) for 15 months and are fined and
filtered.

SECOND WINE
Brand name: Les Remparts de Bastor
Average annual production: 30,000 bottles

Evaluation of present classification: Should be upgraded to a Deuxième
Cru Classé
Plateau of maturity: 3–15 years following the vintage

Bastor-Lamontagne has always been a personal favorite of mine, particularly
when I am looking for a reasonably priced Sauternes to buy as an alternative
to some of the more glamorous (as well as more expensive) names. The
property, located in Preignac, near the great estate of Suduiraut, has, to my
knowledge, never made bad wines. Everything I have tasted from the mid-
1970s onward has been made in an intelligent, ripe, rich, velvety style filled
with opulent, pure fruit. These are not woody Sauternes since very little new
oak (only 20%) is used. Rather, they are luscious, amply endowed, sweet
wines for drinking in their first 10–15 years of life.

As the following tasting notes attest, Bastor-Lamontagne, while never outstanding, is consistently very fine. In fact, the great value is the realistic price
and steady quality from vintage to vintage.

VINTAGES

1989—Very typical of the vintage, the 1989 Bastor-Lamontagne is extremely low in
•　　acidity and ripe, with surprisingly evolved medium gold color and a great
85　　deal of fruit and coarseness that I have rarely seen in other vintages of this
　　　wine. It will no doubt have to be drunk quite early. Anticipated maturity:
　　　Now. Last tasted, 4/91.
1988—This is an excellent wine, with abundant quantities of botrytis, as evidenced
•　　by its honeyed pineapple-and-orange-scented nose. In the mouth, it is full,
87　　wonderfully pure, focused, and long, with moderate sweetness. This Sauternes

could actually serve as a good apéritif as well as a dessert wine. Anticipated maturity: Now. Last tasted, 4/91.

1986—Another excellent example of Bastor-Lamontagne, the 1986 offers an enthrall-
•   ing nose of caramel, oranges, and spices intermixed with scents of flowers.
86   Full bodied and luscious, with a lot of alcohol and glycerin, as well as evidence of botrytis, this honeyed wine is already drinking beautifully. Antici-pated maturity: Now. Last tasted, 3/89.

1983—A voluptuous, luscious wine with oodles of ripe, botrytised pineapple fruit,
•   medium- to full-bodied texture, and a long, rich, silky finish all combine
87   to titillate the palate. This Bastor-Lamontagne is precocious, but so tasty. Anticipated maturity: Now. Last tasted, 3/88.

1982—Bastor-Lamontagne has made a shockingly good wine in 1982. It is a lovely,
•   richly fruity, moderately sweet, well-balanced Sauternes with plenty of char-
85   acter. The wine is forward and ready. Anticipated maturity: Now. Last tasted, 1/85.

1980—The aromas of ripe pineapples and fresh melons are quite apparent in this
•   medium-weight wine with a lush, nicely concentrated personality. Not as good
82   as the 1982 or 1983, this is still a notable effort from what is Sauternes's best-priced estate-bottled wine. Anticipated maturity: Now. Last tasted, 1/84.

1976—Bastor-Lamontagne is a success in this very fine vintage for the wines of
•   Barsac and Sauternes. Fully mature, but capable of holding, this unctuous,
85   ripe, orange-and-apricot-scented and -flavored wine has plenty of body to go along with its excellent flavor. Anticipated maturity: Now. Last tasted, 3/86.

1975—A lemony, buttery, tropical fruit–scented bouquet, ripe, medium- to full-
•   bodied flavors, and good crisp acidity all complement each other in this
85   moderately sweet, well-structured wine. Anticipated maturity: Now. Last tasted, 2/83.

BROUSTET   GOOD

Classification: Second-growth in 1855
Location of vineyards: Barsac
Owner: Didier Laulan
Address: 33720 Barsac
Mailing address: Same as above
Telephone: 33 5 56 27 16 87; telefax: 33 5 56 27 05 93
Visits: By appointment only, except on Sundays
Contact: Didier Laulan

VINEYARDS (white)
Surface area: 39.5 acres
Average age of vines: 35 years
Blend: 75% Semillon, 15% Sauvignon, 10% Muscadelle
Density of plantation: 6,600 vines per hectare

Average yields (over the last 5 years): 15 hectoliters
Total average annual production: 210 hectoliters

GRAND VIN (white)
Brand name: Château Broustet
Appellation: Barsac/Sauternes
Mean annual production: 20,000 bottles
Upbringing: Fermentations take place in small temperature-controlled
stainless-steel tanks of 27–50-hectoliter capacity. Wines are aged in oak
barrels for the first year and in stainless-steel vats for the second. They
are fined and filtered.

SECOND WINE
Brand name: Château de Ségur

Evaluation of present classification: Should be maintained
Plateau of maturity: 5–20 or more years following the vintage

Broustet is one of the rarely encountered and least-known Barsacs, largely
because the production is so small. The property was in the Fournier family
between 1885 and 1992, when it was sold to Didier Laulan.

Many improvements have been made at Broustet since the mid-1980s.
While the wine is still fermented in stainless-steel tanks, the percentage of
new oak barrels has been increased to 50%, and the château has introduced
a second wine for weaker vats. They have also added a dry white wine to their
portfolio.

VINTAGES

1989—The 1989 should be consumed in its first decade of life because it already
  •   offers a big, fat, plump, juicy mouthful of wine. Surprisingly elegant for a
  86   1989, but still extremely alcoholic and not that complex, it is a sweeter wine
        than the 1988 but lacks the flavor dimension and character of the previous
        vintage. Anticipated maturity: Now–2002. Last tasted, 4/91.

1988—The 1988 has the advantage of having more acidity, additional complexity,
  •   and an uplifting bouquet of honeyed apricot/peach fruit, which, along with its
  88   vibrancy, gives its powerful, rich, intense flavors a sense of balance and focus.
        It is the best Broustet I have ever tasted. Anticipated maturity: Now–2008.
        Last tasted, 4/91.

1980—A successful vintage for Broustet, the 1980 is chunky and displays good
  •   botrytis, creamy pineapple fruitiness, and a soft, ripe, generous finish. Antici-
  82   pated maturity: Now. Last tasted, 1/85.

1978—Quite aggressively oaky, the 1978 Broustet has clean, crisp, ripe fruity flavors
  •   behind a wall of oak. On the palate, the wine is relatively full bodied but
  80   seems a little hollow and less succulent and sweet than it should be. It's big

and oaky, but a little more fleshy ripe fruit would have made a big difference. Anticipated maturity: Now. Last tasted, 2/84.

1975—One of the better Broustets I have tasted, the 1975 is a rather powerful wine
• with a luscious pineapple, peachy, appley sweet fruitiness, medium to full
85 body, and a medium-bodied feel on the palate. The long, lively finish is surprisingly crisp. Anticipated maturity: Now. Last tasted, 4/82.

1971—Beginning to fade and lose its freshness and vigor, the 1971 Broustet is spicy,
• a touch too oaky, but medium to full bodied with good concentration and
78 slightly sweet flavors. Anticipated maturity: Now—may be in decline. Last tasted, 4/78.

CAILLOU

Classification: Deuxième Cru Classé
Production: 4,500 cases
Telephone: 33 5 56 27 16 38; telefax: 33 5 56 27 09 60
Blend: 90% Semillon, 10% Sauvignon Blanc
Secondary label: Haut-Mayne
Vineyard size: 32.1 acres
Proprietor: Jean-Bernard Bravo
Dry white wine: Vin Sec de Château Caillou
Time spent in barrels: 20–24 months
Average age of vines: 25 years

Evaluation of present classification: Should be maintained, although readers should take note of the fact that the quality has increased since the mid-1980s
Plateau of maturity: 5–10 years following the vintage

This is a relatively obscure Barsac property located on route D118 to the east of Barsac. The vineyard's soil is limestone and clay. The château's twin towers dominate the modest two-and-a-half-story building and are easily seen from the road.

The reputation of Caillou's wines has been mixed, although many critics have claimed Caillou has been largely ignored as a competent producer of lighter-styled Barsacs. Fermentation takes place in temperature-controlled, stainless-steel tanks, after which the wine is filtered before it goes into small barrels, of which 20% are new each year. I have never been that impressed with the wines of Caillou, although a 1947 I tasted in 1987 was in good shape. Recently there does appear to have been significant improvement, as the 1988, 1989, and 1990 all tasted more serious and complex than their predecessors.

VINTAGES

1990—Caillou tends to produce compact, richly fruity, moderately sweet wines that
•   rarely have the complexity found in the better Barsac/Sauternes estates. The
88   1990 displays a honeyed, ripe cherry/apricot/orange–scented nose, surprisingly good acidity, and a medium- to full-bodied, thick, chewy finish. About
as impressive as Caillou can be, it will last for 10–15 years. Last tasted,
11/94.

1989—The 1989 is a fat, sweet, chunky wine without much complexity or delinea-
•   tion. I liked previous examples more, but the wine's low acidity is causing it
84   to taste more diffuse as it ages. Last tasted, 11/94.

1988—The 1988 is thick, ripe, and rich, with attractive honeyed pineapple–like
•   fruitiness, medium to full body, and a more elegant personality than its two
86   siblings. It should drink well for another decade. Last tasted, 11/94.

1986—This is an unexciting, even insipid wine that lacks depth and finishes with a
•   short, attenuated feel. It is hard to understand what went wrong in this
77   excellent vintage. Anticipated maturity: Now. Last tasted, 3/90.

1985—Light-intensity flavors of pineapples and oranges are attractive in a low-key
•   way. In the mouth, the wine is off dry, medium bodied, and relatively light,
82   with no evidence of botrytis. Anticipated maturity: Now. Last tasted, 3/90.

CLIMENS   OUTSTANDING

Classification: First-growth in 1855
Location of vineyards: On the highest part of Barsac
Owner: Lurton family
Address: 33720 Barsac
Mailing address: Same as above
Telephone: 33 5 56 27 15 33; telefax: 33 5 56 27 21 04
Visits: By appointment only
Contact: Christian Broustaut or Bérénice Lurton

VINEYARDS (white)
Surface area: 71.6 acres
Average age of vines: 35 years
Blend: 100% Semillon
Density of plantation: 6,600 vines per hectare
Average yields (over the last 5 years): 16 hectoliters per hectare

GRAND VIN (white)
Brand name: Château Climens
Appellation: Barsac Sauternes
Mean annual production: 40,000 bottles (variable)
Upbringing: Fermentations take place in oak barrels in which wines are
aged for 12–18 months. One-third new oak is utilized. Wines are not
fined, but they may be filtered.

SECOND WINE
Brand name: Les Cyprès de Climens
Average annual production: Variable

Evaluation of present classification: One of the greatest sweet wines
produced in the world
Plateau of maturity: 7–25 or more years following the vintage

The most famous estate of the Barsac/Sauternes region is, without question, Château d'Yquem, which makes the most concentrated and expensive sweet white wine in France. But the wine I find most companionable with food, and most complex and compelling to drink, is that of Château Climens in Barsac. Climens has been owned since 1971 by the Lurton family, who presides over a considerable empire of Bordeaux estates, including the famous Margaux properties of Châteaux Brane-Cantenac, Durfort-Vivens, and Desmirail. All of these properties produce good wine, but none of them has quite the standing in its respective commune that Château Climens has in Barsac.

For much of the last 2 centuries, Climens has been considered one of the two leading estates in the commune of Barsac. The 72-acre vineyard and modest 1-story château (the only physical distinctions are two slate-roofed towers at each end) is located just north of the tiny village of La Pinesse, sitting on the highest plateau of the Barsac region, a full 70 feet above sea level. Most observers claim that this elevation has contributed to the vineyard's excellent drainage, giving Climens a distinct advantage over lower-lying properties in wet years.

While the names of most châteaux here can be traced back to former owners, no one is quite sure how Climens acquired its name. For most of the nineteenth century the château was owned by the Lacoste family, who produced a wine they called Château Climenz-Lacoste. At that time the vineyard's 70 acres achieved an annual production of 6,000 cases, but the devastating effects of phylloxera in the late nineteenth century destroyed most of the vineyards in Bordeaux, including those of Climens. In 1871 Climens was sold to Alfred Ribet, the owner of another estate called Château Pexoto, which was subsequently absorbed into what is today known as Château Sigalas Rabaud.

In 1885 Ribet sold the property to Henri Gounouilhou, whose family managed Climens until the current proprietor, the dynamic Lucien Lurton, purchased it in 1971. It was Henri Gounouilhou, director of Bordeaux's most famous daily newspaper, *Sud-Ouest*, and his successors who raised not only the level of quality at Climens, but also the public's awareness of this great estate. The legendary vintages of 1929, 1937, and 1947 enabled Climens to surpass the reputation of its larger neighbor, Château Coutet, and rival even that of the great Château d'Yquem.

The Lurtons, Brigitte and Bérénice, have merely enhanced the extraordinary reputation of this outstanding property. Their only change has been the removal of the small quantities of Muscadelle planted in the gravel, red sand, and claylike soil of the vineyard. The current plantings, which they believe produce the best wine from the *terroir* of Château Climens, are 100% Semillon. The Lurtons eschew Sauvignon in the wine because it has a tendency to lose its aroma after several years. The average age of the vines is maintained at an impressive 35 years, as the Lurtons believe in replanting only 3%–4% of the vineyard per year. In addition, their yield of 16 hectoliters per hectare remains one of the smallest of all the estates in the Sauternes/Barsac region. (Today, when most major wine-producing estates are doubling the yields from their vineyards, Climens commendably maintains an average annual production of only 3,333 cases, from a vineyard area 1.6 acres larger than it was in the mid–nineteenth century.) No doubt this statistic alone accounts for the exceptional concentration and quality of the wine produced.

The wine is fermented in cask and aged for 12–18 months in 55-gallon barrels before being bottled. In most vintages 33% new oak is used; this is believed to develop the proper marriage of honeyed pineapple-and-apricot-flavored fruit with the vanillin toastiness of new oak barrels.

What makes Climens so precious is that it produces the region's most compellingly elegant wine. There is no doubt that for sheer power, viscosity, and opulence Climens will never rival Château d'Yquem, nor even Château Rieussec, Château Suduiraut, and the luxurious, rare "Cuvée Madame" of Château Coutet. However, if one measures the greatness of a wine by its extraordinary balance and finesse, Climens not only has no peers, it deserves the reputation as the most quintessentially graceful wine of the region. Many Sauternes can border on the cloying, but in the top vintages Climens seems to combine a rich, luscious, exotic character of honeyed pineapple fruit with a remarkable inner core of lemony acidity—giving the wine zestiness, precision to its flavors, and a profound, hauntingly pleasurable bouquet.

VINTAGES

1990—The 1990 continues to develop exceptionally well (better than I thought) and
  •   now looks to be a worthy rival of the dazzling 1988. The superb aromatics
  95   (pineapple, acacia, vanilla, and honey) are followed by a rich, full-bodied,
       atypically powerful Climens that possesses adequate acidity, high alcohol,
       and even higher levels of extract and fruit. Anticipated maturity: 2000–2030.
       Last tasted, 11/94.

1989—For whatever reason, the 1989 is merely outstanding rather than dazzling.
  •   Although it lacks the complexity of the 1988, it is a plump, muscular, rich,
  90   intense, full-bodied, and sweeter than usual Climens. For a 1989, it possesses
       good acidity. If more complexity and grip develop, my rating may look stingy.
       Anticipated maturity: Now–2010. Last tasted, 11/94.

1988 — The 1988 reveals layer upon layer of honeyed pineapple-and-orange-scented
•   and -flavored fruit, vibrant acidity, high levels of botrytis, and a fabulously
96   long, yet well-focused finish. It is a great wine. Anticipated maturity: Now–
         2015. Last tasted, 11/94.

1986 — A totally compelling Climens and every bit as good as the 1988. It is probably
•   the best Climens made since their spectacular 1971. Still light gold in color,
96   it has an expansive bouquet of new oak, oranges, pineapples, and other
         tropical fruits. In the mouth, there is great richness that seems all the more
         impressive because of the wine's remarkable clarity and definition. There is
         as much botrytis in the 1986 as in the 1988. Despite the intensity and extract
         levels, this sweet wine comes across as crisp and relatively light. The 1986 is
         a stunning example of Climens at its very best. Anticipated maturity: Now–
         2010. Last tasted, 1/91.

1985 — The problem with virtually all the wines from the 1985 vintage in the Barsac/
•   Sauternes region is that there was very little botrytis. Nevertheless, Climens
85   has made an attractive, fruity, floral, honey-styled wine without a great deal
         of complexity. It does offer rich, forward, tasty flavors in a medium- to full-
         bodied format. Anticipated maturity: Now–2003. Last tasted, 11/90.

1983 — The 1983 has consistently improved since bottling and is a far greater wine
•   than I ever imagined after tasting it from cask. It exhibits the classic honeyed
92   pineapple and spicy oakiness that makes Climens so profound. In the mouth,
         this wine is opulent and extremely rich, with gobs of glycerin yet enough
         acidity to give it plenty of definition and crispness. It is a beautifully made,
         stunning Barsac that is eclipsed by the great 1986 and 1988. Anticipated
         maturity: Now–2009. Last tasted, 11/90.

1982 — Only tasted twice, but on each occasion Climens did not display the crisp
•   acidity and structure that one has come to expect from this property. Some-
80   what diffuse, sweet, and flabby, without enough counterbalancing acidity, this
         is a wine that will no doubt mature quite quickly. Anticipated maturity: Now–
         1993. Last tasted, 3/86.

1980 — The 1980 is a wonderful vintage of Climens, which has produced an outstand-
•   ing Barsac. An exotic bouquet of tropical fruit, pineapples, and melons is
90   really top class. On the palate, the wine is rich, yet never heavy or cloyingly
         sweet, with crisp, medium-bodied, lush, velvety, ripe fruity flavors. This is a
         superb effort from Climens and one of the best sweet wines of the vintage.
         Anticipated maturity: Now–2000. Last tasted, 12/90.

1979 — A success for Climens, this pale golden–colored wine with a greenish tint is
•   less concentrated and affected by botrytis than the 1980. Lighter and drier,
85   but still relatively rich, this stylish and graceful wine has great flexibility as
         a Barsac in that it can be matched with a dessert or served to open a meal.
         Anticipated maturity: Now–2000. Last tasted, 3/88.

1978 — The 1978 Climens is slightly more concentrated than the 1979, but like the
•   1979, it lacks the extra dimension that botrytis gives these wines. Because of
86   the weather conditions, little botrytis formed in this vintage. The 1978 is a
         plump wine, with a fat, fruity concentration, moderate sweetness, full body,

and a top-class bouquet of grilled nuts, flowers, and candied apples. This is an elegant wine. Anticipated maturity: Now. Last tasted, 2/85.

1977— Climens produced a very respectable wine from this poor vintage. Light
• golden with a green tint, the wine lacks richness and depth but offers surpris-
80 ingly crisp, fresh tropical fruit flavors, good elegance, and a style not unlike a good dry Graves. Anticipated maturity: Now—may be in decline. Last tasted, 3/84.

1976— Quite fat and advanced in evolution for Climens, the 1976 is drinking gor-
• geously now. Charmingly fruity, with an expansive bouquet of ripe fruit, fresh
87 honey, a vanillin oakiness, and some subtle herbal notes, this medium-bodied wine has average acidity and a plump, soft texture. Anticipated maturity: Now. Last tasted, 3/88.

1975— Still remarkably youthful and closed, the 1975 Climens has a light golden
• color and a tight bouquet of coconut, flowers, and ripe fruit. On the palate,
89 it is impeccably balanced, displaying crisp acidity, excellent richness, and an alcoholic, rich, very, very long finish. Full bodied and powerful for Climens, as well as still remarkably backward and unevolved, this will surely be a long-distance runner. Anticipated maturity: Now—2020. Last tasted, 3/90.

1973— One of the top successes in this vintage that produced such lightweight wines,
• the 1973 Climens should be drunk now before its freshness and crisp, lively,
84 fruity intensity disappear. Rather dry for a Barsac, and medium bodied, this wine has good acidity and enough flavor to merit interest. Anticipated maturity: Now. Last tasted, 3/84.

1972— I was shocked at how good this wine was when I first tasted it. The year 1972
• was dreadful, but Climens managed to produce a wine with good ripeness,
80 some hints of botrytis, a fleshy texture, and sound balance. Anticipated maturity: Now—may be in decline. Last tasted, 3/84.

1971— I have had some of the fabled mature vintages of Climens (the 1947 and 1949
• come to mind immediately), but the 1971 remains my favorite mature vintage
94 of this wine. It is a classic Climens, powerful yet restrained, rich and opulent, yet also delicate. This wine has superb balance, a long, lively, crisp finish, and moderate sweetness kept light and delightful by excellent acidity. It is one of the finest Barsacs I have ever tasted. The honeyed pineapple character, so much a personality trait of this wine, is abundantly displayed. Anticipated maturity: Now—2001. Last tasted, 12/97.

1970— The 1970 is only an adequate Climens, as it is dull, a little clumsy, and
• heavy. Its pale gold color is nice enough, but this lighter-styled Climens lacks
70 grip and, as the English say, "attack." It seems to be an uninspired winemak-ing effort. Last tasted, 5/82.

1967— Perhaps I have been unlucky and never seen a topflight bottle of the 1967,
• but I have generally found this wine to be powerful and richly concentrated,
83 yet not the best-balanced example of Climens. Nevertheless, it is full and mouth-filling, and if the finish is a little coarse and unpolished, the wine is still quite satisfying. Anticipated maturity: Now. Last tasted, 12/79.

1962—Beginning to deepen in color and take on an amber/golden color, the 1962
•   Climens must certainly be the best Climens of the sixties. A fragrant, roasted
89   bouquet of melted caramel and brown sugar sautéed in butter is captivating.
On the palate, the wine has rich, luscious, unctuous flavors that have remained crisp and lively because of good acidity. It is a worthy challenger to
the Yquem in 1962. Anticipated maturity: Now. Last tasted, 1/85.

OLDER VINTAGES

Notwithstanding the legendary vintages of 1929 and 1937 (rated 92 and 90,
respectively, when tasted alongside each other in 11/88), the 1947 (I have
experienced several disappointing bottles of that wine—the result of poor
storage; however, one bottle justified its phenomenal reputation, rated 94 in
11/90), and the 1949 (rated 94 in 4/91), it seems to me that Climens has
never been stronger in terms of both greatness and consistency than it is now,
some 2 decades after Lucien Lurton assumed control. Of the fifties vintages,
only the 1959 (rated 90 in 1/89) stands out as memorable. Climens did not
begin to produce its greatest wines until the seventies.

CLOS HAUT-PEYRAGUEY   GOOD

Classification: First-growth in 1855
Location of vineyards: Bommes
Owner: G.F.A. du Château Clos Haut-Peyraguey (Jacqueline and Jacques
Pauly)
Address: 33210 Bommes
Mailing address: Château Haut-Bommes, 33210 Bommes
Telephone: 33 5 56 76 61 53; telefax: 33 5 56 76 69 65
Visits: By appointment for groups, open every day
Contact: Jacques or Jacqueline Pauly

VINEYARDS (white)
Surface area: 42 acres
Average age of vines: 35 years
Blend: 90% Semillon, 10% Sauvignon
Density of plantation: 6,600 vines per hectare
Average yields (over the last 5 years): 14 hectoliters per hectare
Total average annual production: 225 hectoliters

GRAND VIN (white)
Brand name: Château Clos Haut-Peyraguey
Appellation: Sauternes
Mean annual production: 180 hectoliters
Upbringing: Fermentations take place in oak barrels, 25% of which

are new, and wines are aged 24 months. They are fined but remain unfiltered.

SECOND WINE
Brand name: Château Haut-Bommes
Average annual production: 80 hectoliters

Evaluation of present classification: Should be downgraded to a Cru Bourgeois
Plateau of maturity: 5–12 years following the vintage

In the 1855 classification there was only one Premier Cru Classé, Château Peyraguey, but in 1879 the property was divided. The smaller parcel became known as Clos Haut-Peyraguey. For much of the sixties, seventies, and early eighties, the quality of the wines was indifferent. However, improvements have been made in the late eighties and nineties.

VINTAGES

1990—The 1990 is a rich, full-bodied, unctuously textured, and powerful wine. This
  •   dramatic, ostentatious, alcoholic Sauternes has 20 years of evolution ahead.
  90   Last tasted, 11/94.

1989—The 1989 suffers in comparison with the 1990 and 1988 vintages, largely
  •   because it is drier, with a waxy, Tokay–Pinot Gris-like personality. Although
  86   it shows well, it appears smaller-scaled than the fragrant 1988 and super-rich
        1990. It will last for 2 decades, but it does not have the same level of fruit
        extraction, so once it begins to dry out, it will be less interesting. Last tasted,
        11/94.

1988—The finest bouquet and aromatics are found in the 1988, which exhibits a strik-
  •   ing nose of honeysuckle and sweet peaches, apricots, and pineapples. This me-
  89   dium- to full-bodied, elegant wine will last for 15 years. Last tasted, 11/94.

1986—While much lighter than most 1986s, this is still an attractive and fruity, me-
  •   dium-bodied wine with good length and balance and some evidence of botrytis
  85   in its peach/apricot flavors. Anticipated maturity: Now. Last tasted, 3/89.

1985—One-dimensional, straightforward, simple honeyed flavors offer little com-
  •   plexity or grip. I could not detect any evidence of botrytis. Anticipated
  75   maturity: Now–1993. Last tasted, 6/87.

COUTET   EXCELLENT/OUTSTANDING

Classification: First-growth in 1855
Location of vineyards: Barsac
Owner: Philippe and Dominique Baly
Address: 33720 Barsac

Mailing address: Same as above
Telephone: 33 5 56 27 15 46; telefax: 33 5 56 27 02 20
Visits: By appointment, Monday through Saturday
Contact: Mrs. Bertrand Constantin

VINEYARDS (white)
Surface area: 88.4 acres
Average age of vines: 35 years
Blend: 75% Semillon, 23% Sauvignon, 2% Muscadelle
Density of plantation: 5,600 vines per hectare
Average yields (over the last 5 years): 12 hectoliters per hectare
Total average annual production: 45,000 bottles

GRAND VIN (white)
Brand name: Château Coutet
Appellation: Sauternes/Barsac
Mean annual production: 35,000 bottles
Upbringing: Fermentations last 3–6 weeks in oak barrels, 35% of which
are new. They stop naturally. Wines are then aged 16–18 months in oak
barrels. They are fined and filtered.

SECOND WINE
Brand name: Chartreuse du Château Coutet
Average annual production: 10,000 bottles

COUTET CUVÉE MADAME
This special cuvée is produced only in great vintages, the last one being
1990 (although a 1996 may also be declared). The grapes usually come
from a special parcel of 5–6 acres (35 years of age) and are picked
one by one, when they are considered extremely mature with a
homogeneous concentration. They are usually picked in one passage.
Fermentations last 3–6 weeks in 100% new oak barrels, and the wines
are aged 24 months. Wines are fined and filtered. Quantities produced
are very small (the blend is the same as for Château Coutet).

Evaluation of present classification: Should be maintained, but the Cuvée
Madame is the only wine of the Barsac/Sauternes region that is the
quality equivalent of Château d'Yquem
Plateau of maturity: 5–25 years following the vintage

Coutet has always been one of the leading as well as one of the largest estates
of Barsac. Famous for an elegant, less sweet, and less powerful wine, Coutet
is usually well made, stylish, and probably a more flexible choice to serve
with a variety of food dishes than many of the intense, super-concentrated,
lavishly oaked wines that this region produces in abundance.

Coutet does produce a tiny amount of incredibly rich, unctuous wine that is rarely ever seen commercially but is worth mentioning because it is one of this region's two finest wines (the other, of course, being Yquem). In certain vintages Coutet produces a special cuvée called Cuvée Madame. Between 1943 and 1997 it was produced only in 1943, 1949, 1950, 1959, 1971, 1975, 1981, 1986, 1988, and 1989. Approximately 1,200 bottles—or just 4 barrels—of this wine are made, and should you ever see any, do not hesitate to try it, because the Cuvée Madame of Coutet is pure nectar. The 1971, 1981, 1986, 1988, and 1989 vintages of Cuvée Madame, along with the 1921 Yquem, represent the greatest sweet wines from this region that I have ever tasted.

As for the regular cuvée of Coutet, the vintages produced immediately after Marcel Baly purchased the property in 1977 appeared light and indifferent; but since 1983 Coutet has been making top-notch wines nearly every vintage. In fact, this appears to be a property that is deadly serious about challenging Climens's historical role as the top estate in the Barsac region.

Coutet also produces a dry wine that is very fresh, attractively priced, and best drunk when it is 4–5 years old.

VINTAGES

1990—The full-bodied 1990 is sweet, rich, and honeyed, but it lacks the clarity and
•   complexity of the 1989. Last tasted, 11/94.
88

1990—Cuvée Madame: The 1990 is the richest and most powerful. All three vintages
•   (1990, 1989, and 1988) offer a profound bouquet of smoky, toasty new oak
98   combined with honeyed peaches and apricots, as well as coconuts and a touch
of crème brûlée. With extraordinarily rich, full-bodied, marvelously extracted personalities, as well as wonderful underlying acidity, these are spectacular wines. Anticipated maturity: 2002–2030. Last tasted, 11/94.

1989—This was one of the few wines where the 1989 was the superior offering. The
•   richest, sweetest, and fattest, it offers a pure nose of pineapples, full body,
90   and excellent concentration. Anticipated maturity: 2000–2015. Last tasted, 3/96.

1989—Cuvée Madame: Deep, bright gold in color, this blockbuster sweet wine offers
•   up aromas of coffee, custard, *pain grillé*, honeyed tropical fruits, and a note
95   of coconut. Unctuously textured, and oozing glycerin, extract, and richness, this full-bodied yet extraordinarily well-delineated wine offers the rare combination of power and complexity. It is an amazingly thick Cuvée Madame that suffers only in comparison with its surrounding siblings. Anticipated maturity: Now–2030. Last tasted, 11/94.

1988—The lighter-bodied, drier 1988 is less weighty than the 1989 and 1990, with
•   attractive, spicy, vanillin, citrus scents, medium body, and an earthy note that
89+   kept my score from going higher. Anticipated maturity: 2001–2018. Last tasted, 11/94.

1988 — Cuvée Madame: Cut from the same mold as other Cuvée Madames, but
• perhaps the ultimate example because the intense botrytis and unctuosness
99 the wine possesses is buttressed by slightly more acidity, giving the wine all
the weight and massiveness of its two younger siblings, the 1989 and 1990,
but with more focus and vibrancy. It is difficult for readers who have never
tasted Cuvée Madame to imagine a wine of such honeyed richness, power,
and flavor dimension not tasting heavy. The 1988 is still young, even more
youthful than the 1989 and 1990, with good underlying acidity and luxuriantly rich layers of viscous, full-bodied flavors of crème brûlée, peaches,
apricots, and pears. The finish lasts for over 40 seconds. This may turn out to
be the most compelling of all the profound Cuvée Madames that have been
made to date. Anticipated maturity: 2000–2035. Last tasted, 11/94.

1986 — This is a fine example of Coutet, quite precocious, with an evolved bouquet
• of tropical fruit, honey, and spring flowers. It is full bodied and rich, with
87 crisp acidity and plenty of evidence of botrytis in its apricot/peach–like
flavors. The finish is heady and long, with just enough acidity for balance.
Anticipated maturity: Now–2005. Last tasted, 11/91.

1986 — Cuvée Madame: This unbelievably decadent, unctuous wine has the type of
• extract (but without the overlay of heavy, toasty oak) that one normally finds
96 only in a great vintage of Yquem. The wine is much less evolved than the
regular cuvée of Coutet. At the moment, it is crammed with honeyed tropical
fruit that comes across in a powerful format. This is an enormously rich,
almost overwhelmingly intense Barsac that needs another decade to begin to
reveal its subtleties and complexities. It is mind-blowing! Anticipated maturity: Now–2020. Last tasted, 3/97.

1985 — The problem with so many 1985 Barsac/Sauternes is that they come across
• as monolithic and one-dimensional, particularly when compared with years
84 where there is a great deal more botrytis, such as 1986 and 1988. Nevertheless, for those readers who like to drink these wines as an apéritif, 1985
is the type of vintage where the wines can be drunk early in the meal. The
1985 is fresh, with plenty of fruit, but lacking the complexity one normally
associates with this château. Anticipated maturity: Now–2000. Last tasted,
3/90.

1983 — Not the biggest, most concentrated, or most luscious Coutet, this wine gets
• high marks because of undeniable elegance, breed, class, and a fresh, lively
87 feel on the palate. The flavors reveal excellent ripeness, and the wine's
refreshing crispness makes this an exceptionally enjoyable, non-cloying Barsac. Anticipated maturity: Now–2005. Last tasted, 3/89.

1981 — Surprisingly mature and ready to drink, the 1981 Coutet is an agreeable wine
• but lacks richness and complexity. What it does offer is straightforward,
78 fruity, lemony, melon aromas and moderately sweet, somewhat short flavors.
Drink up. Anticipated maturity: Now. Last tasted, 6/84.

1981 — Cuvée Madame: This is a medium-golden wine with a huge honeyed aroma
• filled with the scents of oranges, toast, coconuts, and other tropical fruits.
96 Thick, unctuous flavors coat the palate. There is just enough acidity to provide

lift and focus. This is a colossal wine. Anticipated maturity: Now–2008. Last tasted, 12/90.

1980—A good but rather uninspired effort from Coutet, the 1980 lacks richness and
•   depth, even for the lighter-scaled wines of Coutet. Nevertheless, the wine is
80   perfect as an apéritif Barsac and can do double duty with lighter, not too sweet desserts. Anticipated maturity: Now. Last tasted, 3/86.

1979—The 1979 is one of the better efforts from Coutet in this period when the
•   property may have been slightly off its normally top form. Light golden, with
83   a spicy, lemony, floral, fruity bouquet, this wine is elegant, has medium weight, and is clean and crisp in the mouth. Anticipated maturity: Now. Last tasted, 7/82.

1978—Quite light and a little insubstantial, this medium-bodied, moderately sweet
•   Coutet is fruity and pleasant but reveals little evidence of botrytis and seems
75   to tail off in the mouth. Anticipated maturity: Now. Last tasted, 5/82.

1976—One of the best Coutets of the seventies, the 1976 is a relatively big wine,
•   with a surprising amount of alcohol (15%), a ripe apricot, spicy, floral, lemon-
86   scented bouquet, full body, fat, succulent flavors, and Coutet's trademark— crisp, fresh acidity. Anticipated maturity: Now. Last tasted, 3/86.

1975—Every bit as good as the more open-knit and expressive 1976, the 1975 is
•   lighter and more typically Coutet in its proportions, with a graceful, fresh
86   taste, very good concentration, and years of evolution ahead. Anticipated maturity: Now–2002. Last tasted, 3/86.

1971—The 1971 is a gorgeous example of a Barsac that is not that powerful but has
•   an authoritative presence in the mouth and wonderful, fresh, crisp acidity
87   that admirably balances the apricot, honeyed flavors. Anticipated maturity: Now. Last tasted, 3/86.

1971—Cuvée Madame: Wines such as this are almost impossible to describe effec-
•   tively. It was spectacular the first time I tasted it in the mid-1970s, and I
98   have been fortunate enough to have had this wine three more times. Each bottle has been better than the last, suggesting that perhaps more magical things may emerge. There is an extraordinary fragrance of spring flowers, honeyed fruits, herbs, and vanillin and a strong scent of crème brûlée. In the mouth, there is remarkable richness and super-acidity that give the wines clarity and lift. Gobs of botrytis are obvious, and the richness and extract levels are amazing. The color has changed little since I first tasted it. I would predict at least another 10–20 years of longevity. This is one wine to go out of your way to taste. Anticipated maturity: Now–2005. Last tasted, 3/88.

1970—Rather undistinguished, the 1970 Coutet seems diluted, with a bizarre, tarry,
•   vegetal aroma, and little depth. Last tasted, 2/79.
72

1967—In this very fine vintage for the wines of Barsac and Sauternes, Coutet is a
•   disappointment. Extremely light and a little herbaceous, this is more akin to
70   a dry Graves than a sweet wine. Last tasted, 12/80.

DOISY-DAËNE GOOD

Classification: Second-growth in 1855
Location of vineyards: Barsac
Owner: Pierre and Denis Dubourdieu
Address: 33720 Barsac
Mailing address: Same as above
Telephone: 33 5 56 27 15 84; telefax: 33 5 56 27 18 99
Visits: By appointment only

VINEYARDS (white)
Surface area: 37 acres
Average age of vines: 35 years
Blend: 70% Semillon, 20% Sauvignon, 10% Muscadelle
Total average annual production: 90,000 bottles

GRAND VIN (white)
Brand name: Château Doisy-Daëne (100% Semillon)
Appellation: Barsac
Mean annual production: 50,000–60,000 bottles
Upbringing: Fermentations (with addition of yeasts, no temperature control) take place in oak barrels that are renewed by a third in each vintage. Wines are aged 24 months, with regular rackings every 3 months. They are fined with bentonite and filtered.

SECOND WINE
Brand name: Château Doisy-Daëne (dry white Bordeaux)
Average annual production: 30,000 bottles (70% Sauvignon, 20% Semillon, 10% Muscadelle)

NOTE: On rare occasions, a very rich, sweet wine is made called L'Extravagance de Doisy Daëne.

Evaluation of present classification: Should be maintained
Plateau of maturity: 3–12 years following the vintage

One of the most ambitiously and innovatively run estates in Bordeaux, Doisy-Daëne produces a very fine Barsac that seems to be undervalued in the scheme of Barsac/Sauternes realities. While I would not rate it a Premier Cru Classé, it is certainly one of the leaders among the Deuxièmes Crus Classés. The proprietors of Doisy-Daëne, Pierre and Denis Dubourdieu, also produce one of the finest dry wines of the region, Doisy-Daëne Sec, a full and refreshing, vibrant, fruity, and—best of all—very inexpensive white wine. Pierre's son, Denis, a professor at the Institute of Oenology in Bordeaux, more than anyone else has totally revolutionized white winemaking in the Bordeaux region with his classic *macération pelliculaire* (skin contact and very cool fermentation temperatures). The objective is to produce wines that retain their remarkable fruit and freshness and to reduce the amount of sulfur used in the winemaking process to negligible quantities.

Doisy-Daëne's sweet wine is surprisingly enjoyable when young, causing many tasters to think that it will not last. Although the style today is certainly different from when the 1924 and 1959 were made, I remember drinking both of those wines in 1984 when they were still fresh, lively, and full of fruit. Doisy-Daëne remains one of the more fairly priced sweet wines of the Barsac/Sauternes region. For those who want to drink their sweet wines on the younger side, this is a property of which to take note.

VINTAGES

1990—The 1990 regular cuvée is revealing far more complexity and richness than it
•   did in the past. It is a bold, opulent, exquisite example of Barsac, with
91   more richness and intensity than I have encountered in previous vintages of
         Doisy-Daëne. Light to medium gold colored, with a honeyed, botrysized nose,
         huge amounts of alcohol and power, and a heady finish, the wine possesses
         just enough acidity to balance out its bold flavors and forcefulness. Drink it
         over the next 15+ years. Last tasted, 11/94.

1990—L'Extravagance: In 1990 Doisy-Daëne produced 100 cases of a sensational
•   luxury cuvée called L'Extravagance. It possesses considerable botrytis, awe-
95   some extract levels and intensity, and, despite massive power, remarkable
         balance. Readers are unlikely to find any of this wine (bottled in a heavy
         375-milliliter bottle) outside Bordeaux. Its medium gold color and extraordi-
         nary richness and power suggest it will age effortlessly for another 20+ years.
         Last tasted, 11/94.

1989—The 1989 exhibits plenty of honeyed ripe fruit, a more elegant personality,
•   fine richness, chunkiness, and depth, full body, and low acidity. It does not
89   reveal the botrytis found in the 1990 or 1988. Last tasted, 11/94.

1988—The 1988 is the lightest of these wines, with medium body and a fragrant
•   pineapple-, peach-, and apple-scented nose, with a honeysuckle component
89   that adds complexity. The wine is crisp, dry, and ideal for drinking now and
         over the next 10 years. Last tasted, 11/94.

1986—While less viscous and chewy than the 1983, this is still an admirably rich,
•   husky, intense Barsac, with vividly pure, well-focused fruit, full body, and a
88   long, honeyed finish. Anticipated maturity: Now–2005. Last tasted, 3/90.

1985—I could find no evidence of botrytis in this wine, which comes across as
•   relatively fat, uncomplex, and straightforward. Anticipated maturity: Now.
82   Last tasted, 3/90.

1983—Doisy-Daëne finished its harvest 1 month after Yquem and has possibly
•   produced this property's finest wine in over 2 decades. A big, ripe bouquet of
90   pineapples, peaches, and spring flowers is very attractive. On the palate, the

wine is concentrated, full bodied, and unctuous, without being too heavy or alcoholic. Excellent acidity suggests a long, eventful evolution. Anticipated maturity: Now–2005. Last tasted, 3/90.

1982— One of the better 1982s, ripe and fruity, with the taste of fresh oranges,
•   this medium-bodied Doisy-Daëne has good length, a fresh, lemony acidity,
82   moderate sweetness, and a solid finish. Anticipated maturity: Now. Last tasted, 3/87.

1981— Somewhat light, and perhaps dominated by oak to an extreme, this fruity, soft,
•   moderately concentrated wine has little botrytis and a short finish. Antici-
78   pated maturity: Now. Last tasted, 1/85.

1980— Surprisingly advanced on the nose, the 1980 Doisy-Daëne has a light golden
•   color, an aromatic floral-and-pineapple-scented bouquet, soft, moderately
82   sweet, fat, plump flavors, and just enough acidity to keep the wine from feeling heavy. Anticipated maturity: Now. Last tasted, 6/84.

1979— A tightly knit, restrained rendition of Doisy-Daëne, the 1979 exhibits very
•   good ripeness, a rich, full-bodied texture, plenty of vanillin, oaky aromas, and
84   good acidity. Anticipated maturity: Now–2000. Last tasted, 11/85.

1978— Not a terribly impressive vintage, this wine made from grapes picked very
•   late in November displays less intensity than the 1979 but has an elegant,
83   fruity, spicy nose, firm, sweet flavors, and good, firm acidity. Anticipated maturity: Now. Last tasted, 6/84.

1975— Some disturbing sulfur aromas in the bouquet seem to constantly appear in
•   bottles of this wine. On the palate, the wine is rich and creamy, with a honeyed,
78   pineapple fruitiness and a succulent, sweet finish. The taste is considerably better than the bouquet. Anticipated maturity: Now. Last tasted, 11/82.

DOISY-DUBROCA   VERY GOOD

Classification: Second-growth in 1855
Location of vineyards: Barsac
Owner: Louis Lurton
Address: 33720 Barsac
Mailing address: c/o Château Haut-Nouchet, 33650 Martillac
Telephone: 33 5 56 72 69 74
Visits: By appointment only
Contact: Louis Lurton

VINEYARDS (white)
Surface area: 8.1 acres
Average age of vines: 20 years
Blend: 100% Semillon
Density of plantation: 6,600 vines per hectare
Average yields (over the last 5 years): 19 hectoliters per hectare
Total average annual production: 65 hectoliters

GRAND VIN (white)
Brand name: Château Doisy-Dubroca
Appellation: Barsac
Mean annual production: 500 cases
Upbringing: The whole yield is fermented in oak barrels. Wines are aged
1 year in oak barrels that are renewed by a third in each vintage. They
are fined and filtered upon bottling.

SECOND WINE
Brand name: Demoiselle de Doisy
Average annual production: 150 cases

Evaluation of present classification: I have too little experience with this
wine to be certain, but this could well justify elevation to Premier Cru
Classé status
Plateau of maturity: 7–20 years following the vintage

While I have tasted only a handful of recent vintages of Doisy-Dubroca, this
wine bears an uncanny resemblance to the Barsac estate of Climens. In fact,
for years the vinification and aging of the wines has been controlled by the
same team that makes the wine at Climens.

As great as this wine has tasted in vintages such as 1986, 1988, and 1989,
it has remained a fabulous value, largely because so little of it is made and
most consumers know little about this château. It remains very much an
insider's wine to buy.

VINTAGES

1989—A gorgeous lemony, pineapple, waxy nose is followed by unctuous, rich flavors
•　　　that exhibit more acidity and definition than I found in many 1989s. Full
89　　bodied, round, and generous, with excellent concentration, this beauty should
　　　continue to drink well for another 15–20 years. Anticipated maturity: Now–
　　　2008. Last tasted, 4/91.

1988—This could easily be confused with the great 1988 Climens. The stylish yet
•　　　authoritative bouquet of pineapples, spring flowers, and underlying citrusy,
92　　mineral scents is provocative. In the mouth, the wine exhibits great concentra-
　　　tion, remarkable delineation and focus (because of good acidity), and a
　　　smashingly long, zesty, crisp finish. This is a brilliant marriage of power and
　　　finesse. Anticipated maturity: Now–2010. Last tasted, 4/91.

1986—Gorgeously opulent, roasted pineapple fruit and new oak are followed by a
•　　　rich, full-bodied wine exhibiting a great deal of the apricot, peachy, botrytis
90　　flavors. Full, rich, and long, this wine is just now reaching full maturity.
　　　Anticipated maturity: Now–2005. Last tasted, 4/91.

DOISY-VÉDRINES VERY GOOD

Classification: Second-growth in 1855
Location of vineyards: Haut-Barsac
Owner: Pierre Castéja
Address: Route de Budos, 33720 Barsac
Mailing address: Same as above
Telephone: 33 5 56 27 15 13; telefax: 33 5 56 27 26 76
Visits: By appointment only
Contact: Pierre Castéja

VINEYARDS (white)
Surface area: 66.7 acres
Average age of vines: 30 years
Blend: 80% Semillon, 17% Sauvignon, 3% Muscadelle
Density of plantation: 6,600 vines per hectare
Average yields (over the last 5 years): 16 hectoliters per hectare
Total average annual production: 480 hectoliters

GRAND VIN (white)
Brand name: Château Doisy-Védrines
Appellation: Sauternes
Mean annual production: 24,000 bottles
Upbringing: Fermentations last 3 weeks in barrels, 70% of which are
new. Wines are aged 18 months in cask. They are fined and filtered.

SECOND WINE
None produced.

Evaluation of present classification: Should be maintained
Plateau of maturity: 4–16 years following the vintage

This Barsac estate is well placed just to the southeast of the two most famous Barsacs, Climens and Coutet. Unfortunately, the tiny production of sweet Doisy-Védrines prevents many wine enthusiasts from ever discovering how good this wine can be. Most wine drinkers are probably better acquainted with the dry white and red table wine produced at this estate. It is called Chevalier de Védrines and is a delightful commercial wine that is equally good in either white or red. As for the sweet wine, Doisy-Védrines is much fatter, richer, and more intense than the wine of next-door neighbor Doisy-Daëne. Doisy-Védrines is a wine that is usually at its best 5–7 years after the vintage but will age considerably longer, particularly in the top vintages.

The estate is run by the well-known Pierre Castéja, whose family controls the *négociant* firm Roger Joanne. Doisy-Védrines has been in the Castéja family since 1840. Castéja is one of the few Barsac producers who is quick to declassify any vintage he deems to be of unsatisfactory quality. For example, no wine was produced under the Doisy-Védrines label in 1974, 1968, 1965, 1964, or 1963.

VINTAGES

1990—Although somewhat monolithically styled, there is no doubting the 1990's
• unctuously textured, thick, sweet style. The color is light medium gold. The
87 wine offers plenty of honeyed citrus fruit in addition to smoke and vanillin. Medium to full bodied, with good acidity, some evidence of botrytis, and a plump, low-acid finish, this heavyweight, chunky wine should age nicely for 15–20 years. Anticipated maturity: Now–2015. Last tasted, 3/97.

1989—Medium gold colored, with botrytis, crème brûlée, and honeyed tropical fruits
• in the nose, this full-bodied, sweet wine possesses good acidity, layers of
88 glycerin-embued, plump, chewy, honeyed fruit, and plenty of spice and alcohol in the lusty finish. It is a luxuriously made, in-your-face style of sweet wine. Anticipated maturity: Now–2012. Last tasted, 3/97.

1988—A youthful-tasting (the youngest when compared with the bigger, thicker 1989
• and 1990) wine, the 1988 is made in a more elegant style, with smoky, crème
86 brûlée, and honeyed citrus and pineapple notes in the aromatics and flavors, medium to full body, moderate sweetness, zesty acidity, and a fine finish. This promising, youthful wine possesses 20 more years of longevity. Anticipated maturity: Now–2018. Last tasted, 3/97.

1986—Doisy-Védrines made a superb wine in 1986. It is powerful, complex, and
• nearly as mouth-filling as their great 1989. It does have crisper acidity and,
90 for the moment, a more complex, floral, honeyed bouquet. There is no denying the unctuous, huge, tropical fruit flavors. Anticipated maturity: Now–2005. Last tasted, 11/90.

1985—This wine strikes me as surprisingly mediocre, even in a vintage where there
• was too little botrytis to give the wines that honeyed, unctuous quality. It is
75 straightforward and crisp and comes across as uncomplicated, short, and compact. Anticipated maturity: Now. Last tasted, 11/90.

1983—The 1983 has reached its apogee. It comes across on the palate as a plump,
• round, tasty wine with a great deal of fruit, sweetness, and surprising unctu-
87 ousness. However, it lacks acidity for grip and focus. Nevertheless, there is a great deal to admire about this chunky, lush, very sweet Barsac. Anticipated maturity: Now. Last tasted, 11/90.

1980—A fat, spicy, apricot-and-coconut-scented bouquet is quite captivating. On
• the palate, the wine is ripe, very sweet, almost jammy and marmalade-like,
84 with a good, sweet, alcoholic finish. It lacks a little finesse, but the 1980 Doisy-Védrines exhibits plenty of fruit and a chewy texture. Anticipated maturity: Now. Last tasted, 2/85.

1978—Charming but considerably lighter in style than normal, the 1978 lacks botry-
• tis but has a fresh, clean, lemony, pineapple fruitiness and a decent finish. It
80 may now be tiring. Anticipated maturity: Now. Last tasted, 2/82.

1976—In many respects a typically chunky, fat, corpulent Doisy-Védrines, the 1976
* reveals plenty of ripe, viscous, honeyed fruit, good botrytis, full body, and
84 enough acidity to keep the wine from tasting cloyingly sweet or heavy. Anticipated maturity: Now. Last tasted, 9/82.

1975—A tight, reticent bouquet needs coaxing from the glass. In the mouth, there is
* no doubt this is an intense, full-bodied, ripe, very fruity Doisy-Védrines.
86 Unctuous, luscious flavors of apricots and melons are admirably balanced by
spicy oak and good acidity. Anticipated maturity: Now–2003. Last tasted,
3/89.

FARGUES　　　　　　　　　　　　　　　　　　　　EXCELLENT

Classification: None
Location of vineyards: Fargues de Langon
Owner: Lur Saluces family
Address: 33210 Fargues de Langon
Mailing address: Same as above
Telephone: 33 5 57 98 04 20; telefax: 33 5 57 98 04 21
Visits: Monday through Friday, between 9 A.M. and noon, and 2 P.M. and
6 P.M.
Contact: François Amirault

VINEYARDS (white)
Surface area: 32.1 acres
Average age of vines: 35 years
Blend: 80% Semillon, 20% Sauvignon
Density of plantation: 6,600 vines per hectare
Average yields (over the last 5 years): 9 hectoliters per hectare
Total average annual production: 12,000–15,000 bottles

GRAND VIN (white)
Brand name: Château de Fargues
Appellation: Sauternes
Mean annual production: 12,000–15,000 bottles
Upbringing: Fermentations and aging in oak barrels for 3½ years. Wines
are fined if necessary and remain unfiltered.

SECOND WINE
Brand name: Guilhem de Fargues (dry white Bordeaux)
Average annual production: 3,000 bottles

Evaluation of present classification: Should be elevated to a Premier Cru
Classé
Plateau of maturity: 8–25 or more years following the vintage

In 1472, 300 years before the Lur Saluces family acquired the famous Châ-teau d'Yquem, they owned Château de Fargues. While de Fargues has never been classified, the quality of the wine produced is brilliant. Still owned by the Lur Saluces family, it receives virtually the identical winemaking care that Yquem does. In some vintages de Fargues has often been the second-best wine produced in the Sauternes region, and when it is tasted blind, many tasters, including most experts, usually judge it to be Yquem. In all fairness, the wine lacks the aging potential of Yquem, but when young, the resemblance can be extraordinary.

Interestingly, the vineyard of de Fargues is located well to the east of Yquem's, and the harvest occurs on an average of 10 days later. Additionally, the yield is less than at Yquem, causing some to say that if Yquem's tiny yield per vine equals only 1 glass of wine, the yield of a vine at de Fargues must equal only two-thirds of a glass of wine.

De Fargues's similarity to Yquem is uncanny, and given the price charged for de Fargues—approximately one-third that paid for a bottle of Yquem—it is irrefutably a bargain. Unfortunately, the production of de Fargues is tiny, thereby reducing the opportunity for many wine enthusiasts to taste this wine (which some, by the way, jokingly call Yquem Jr.).

VINTAGES

1986—This is the finest young vintage of de Fargues I have had the privilege of
•　　tasting. That should not come as a surprise given how extraordinary Yquem
93　　turned out in this vintage. The toasty, honeyed, rich bouquet is redolent of pineapples, coconut, crème brûlée and coffee. In the mouth, this fabulously rich, full-bodied wine offers plenty of the botrytised, pineapple and other tropical fruit flavors, a lavish, unctuous texture, enough acidity to provide freshness and focus, and a heady, spicy, truly intoxicating finish. Anticipated maturity: Now–2010. Last tasted, 3/90.

1985—This is a big, corpulent, chunky wine without much botrytis but with plenty
•　　of flesh and a muscular, heady alcohol content. The wine drinks beautifully
87　　now because of the forward, lush fruit married with copious amounts of smoky, toasty new oak. The good acidity gives the wine freshness. While I am sure this wine will evolve nicely, I do not expect to ever encounter a great deal of complexity. Anticipated maturity: Now–2002. Last tasted, 3/90.

1983—While no match for the extraordinary wine produced at Yquem in this vintage,
•　　the 1983 de Fargues (aged 3 years in 100% new oak casks) is, nevertheless,
92　　a sensational example of a Sauternes with an amazing resemblance to Yquem. A big, buttery, caramel, smoky, crème brûlée, and honeyed pineapple nose is enthralling. In the mouth, the wine is powerful, very sweet, rich, extremely full, and framed beautifully by toasty new oak. Quite full bodied and intense, this large-scaled wine should have a great future. Anticipated maturity: Now–2008. Last tasted, 3/90.

1981—This wine has improved significantly and actually tastes better than the 1981
• Yquem—as hard as that may be to believe. Spectacularly rich, very sweet,
90 and alcoholic, it has taken on a medium gold color. There is plenty of
evidence of botrytis, but the low acidity and unctuous, thick, viscous feel on
the palate suggest this is a wine probably best drunk over the next decade.
Anticipated maturity: Now–2000. Last tasted, 3/90.

1980—A great vintage for de Fargues, the 1980 from this estate is very powerful,
• opulent, and exotic. The bouquet of coconuts, apricots, grilled almonds, and
91 spicy oak is sensational. In the mouth, the wine is decadently rich, full
bodied, and remarkably similar in taste, texture, and viscosity to Yquem.
Retasted twice in 1989 with equally enthusiastic notes. Anticipated maturity:
Now–2000. Last tasted, 3/89.

1979—Less powerful and rich than normal, the 1979 de Fargues is light golden, with
• a toasty, lemony, fruity, oaky bouquet, medium to full body, some botrytis,
85 good acidity, and a clean, spicy, rich, alcoholic finish. Anticipated maturity:
Now. Last tasted, 3/86.

1976—A full-blown crème brûlée aroma intermingled with scents of caramel and
• apricots is penetrating. Full bodied, with viscous, sweet, ripe flavors of tropi-
90 cal fruit and smoked nuts, this big, robust, yet surprisingly mature wine
remains fully mature but displays no signs of declining. Anticipated maturity:
Now–2005. Last tasted, 2/91.

1975—The 1975 is one of the finest de Fargues ever produced. It has the Yquem-like
• bouquet of coconuts, grilled nuts, ripe exotic fruit, and spicy oak. On the
91 palate, the 1975 is much tighter structured and less evolved than the 1976.
It has a lighter golden color and more acidity, but every bit as much concentration and richness. Anticipated maturity: Now–2010. Last tasted, 2/91.

1971—Incredibly rich, unctuous, fat, spicy, and chewy, this huge wine offers oodles
• of coconut, apricot, and almond flavors, yet viscous fruitiness, huge body, and
90 a head-spinning alcohol content. Fully mature, this is a big, old-style, intense
Sauternes. Anticipated maturity: Now. Last tasted, 12/80.

FILHOT
GOOD

Classification: Second-growth in 1855
Location of vineyards: Sauternes
Owner: G.F.A. Château Filhot—de Vaucelles family
Address: 33210 Sauternes
Mailing address: Same as above
Telephone: 33 5 56 76 61 09; telefax: 33 5 56 76 67 91
Visits: By appointment only
Contact: Henri de Vaucelles

VINEYARDS (white)
Surface area: 149.2 acres
Average age of vines: 26 years

Blend: 55% Semillon, 40% Sauvignon, 5% Muscadelle
Density of plantation: 6,000 vines per hectare
Average yields (over the last 5 years): 13–14 hectoliters per hectare
Total average annual production: 900 hectoliters

GRAND VIN (white)
Brand name: Château Filhot
Appellation: Sauternes
Mean annual production: Approximately 120,000 bottles
Upbringing: Fermentations take place in temperature-controlled
stainless-steel vats and last approximately 2 weeks at 21–22 degrees
centigrade. Wines are aged both in stainless-steel vats and in oak barrels
(more than 5 years old) for 24–36 months. They are fined with bentonite
and lightly filtered.

SECOND WINE
Will be produced as from 1999.

Evaluation of present classification: Should be maintained
Plateau of maturity: 4–12 years following the vintage

Filhot, one of the most magnificent estates in the entire Sauternes region, possesses an eighteenth-century manor home beautifully situated among ancient trees that has the look of an Ivy League college campus. This property has the potential to produce extraordinary wines, particularly given this superb location just to the north of the village of Sauternes on gravelly hillside beds with a southwest orientation. However, it has only been since the mid-1980s that Filhot has begun to produce wines that merit its Deuxième Cru Classé status.

Because of the relatively high percentage of Sauvignon and the refusal to use any new oak, Filhot tastes fruitier, more aromatic, and lighter than some of the larger-scaled Sauternes wines. That fact does not, however, account for the lack of consistency and the numerous indifferent and mediocre efforts that were turned out by Filhot during the sixties, seventies, and early eighties. Yet quality clearly appeared to rebound in the late eighties.

VINTAGES

1990—Filhot, which prefers to tank rather than barrel ferment its wines, produced a
· 　　1990 that is clearly the best wine I have tasted from this estate. It exhibits
90　　gorgeously ripe, honeyed tropical fruit, an intense, medium- to full-bodied
　　　personality, wonderful purity, fine acidity, plenty of botrytis, and a long, zesty

finish. What makes this wine so appealing is its combination of richness, crisp acidity, liveliness, and zestiness. Last tasted, 11/94.

1989—The thick, very sweet, slightly heavy 1989 appears to be maturing at a fast
•   pace. If drunk over the next 5–8 years, it will provide an uncomplicated
86   mouthful of sweet, candied fruit. Last tasted, 11/94.

1988—The 1988 displayed a wonderfully pure, honeyed pineapple–scented nose,
•   rich, medium- to full-bodied flavors, fine underlying acidity, an earthiness that
88   added to the wine's complexity, and a clean, rich, crisp finish. Drinkable now, it
    should continue to evolve gracefully for 10–15 years. Last tasted, 11/94.

1986—The 1986 is the best Filhot in my memory. The light golden color is followed
•   by a wine with a floral, pineapple, and tropical fruit bouquet, medium body,
87   and lovely, elegant, and brilliantly pure, botrytised, lively flavors. Just me-
    dium sweet, this wine could be served as an apéritif. Anticipated maturity:
    Now. Last tasted, 3/90.

1985—Extremely sweet to the point of being cloying, with unstructured, flabby, fat
•   flavors, this is a straightforward, indifferent style of Sauternes that lacks a
78   centerpoint and focus. Anticipated maturity: Now. Last tasted, 3/90.

1983—This is an attractive, lighter-weight Sauternes without any evidence of serious
•   botrytis. The wine possesses straightforward, flowery, ripe quasi-viscous fla-
83   vors presented in a medium-bodied format. There is an overall lack of focus
    and complexity. Anticipated maturity: Now. Last tasted, 4/86.

GILETTE   OUTSTANDING

Classification: Cru Bourgeois
Location of vineyards: Preignac
Owner: Christian Médeville
Address: 33210 Preignac
Mailing address: Same as above
Telephone: 33 5 56 76 28 44; telefax: 33 5 56 76 28 43
Visits: By appointment, Monday through Thursday, between 9 A.M. and
1 P.M., and 2 P.M. and 6 P.M.; on Fridays, till 5 P.M. only
Contact: Andrée Médeville

VINEYARDS (white)
Surface area: 11.1 acres
Average age of vines: 45 years
Blend: 90% Semillon, 8% Sauvignon, 2% Muscadelle
Density of plantation: 6,600 vines per hectare
Average yields (over the last 5 years): 10 hectoliters
Total average annual production: 45 hectoliters

GRAND VIN (white)
Brand name: Château Gilette
Appellation: Sauternes

Mean annual production: 6,000 bottles
Upbringing: Fermentations take place in stainless-steel vats. Wines
remain in vats for about 15 months and are released many years after
bottling. They are fined and filtered.

SECOND WINE
None produced.

Evaluation of present classification: Should be upgraded to a Premier Cru
Classé
Plateau of maturity: 20–40 years following the vintage

Gilette is one of the most unusually run properties in the Sauternes region. It
is one of the finest-made wines in Sauternes despite the fact that Gilette was
not classified. The vineyard, situated several miles north of Yquem, adjacent
to route D109, is planted on sandy soil with a subsoil of rock and clay.
However, what is bizarre and unbelievable in today's harsh world of commercial realities is that Gilette's proprietor, Christian Médeville, holds his sweet
wines for over 20 years in concrete vats prior to bottling them. For example,
he bottled the 1955 in 1984, 29 years after the vintage. The fact that his
wines are excellent and have a honeyed maturity has caused some of France's
leading restaurateurs (like Pierre Troisgros) to beat a path to his door to
purchase his old vintages of Sauternes.

Gilette's late-released wines, called "Crème de Tête," are extremely well
balanced, remarkably well-preserved wines, with plenty of viscous, fruity
flavors and deep amber/golden colors. After being held in vats for decades,
the wines often taste much younger when they are released than their vintage
date would suggest. If my instincts are correct, most vintages of Gilette can
benefit from another 15–25 years of cellaring after being released. The following are some of the vintages of Gilette that have been released for sale by
M. Médeville over the last decade.

VINTAGES

1975—Crème de Tête: A stunning example of this vintage, Gilette's 1975, released
•　　in 1997, exhibits a deep gold color, followed by a spicy, vanillin-scented nose
93　　with loads of fresh, lively, honeyed citrus, buttery pineapple/pear–like fruit.
　　　The wine is probably sweeter than it tastes, but because of the good acidity,
　　　it comes across as an off-dry, dazzlingly rich, full-bodied, exceptionally fresh
　　　Sauternes with razor-sharp definition and a finish that lasts for more than 30
　　　seconds. It is stunningly youthful, as well as complex and marvelous. Antici-
　　　pated maturity: Now–2010. Last tasted, 3/97.

1971—Crème de Tête: This is a more reserved, austere, restrained wine, with a
•　　tight but attractive nose of loamy earth, roasted coffee, herbs, and sweet,
88　　honeyed fruit. Medium to full bodied, with tightly wound flavors, good

acidity, and moderate levels of botrytis, this is a less generous yet stylish, polite Gilette that should continue to age well for 15 or more years. Last tasted, 3/97.

1970—Crème de Tête: The 1970 has a deep, rich golden color and a big, spicy
   •   bouquet of buttery, apricot-scented fruit, is full bodied and amazingly fresh
  88   and youthful for its age, and will probably keep another 15–25 years. It
lacks the complexity of the great vintages of Gilette but, nevertheless, is an impressively full, complex wine. Anticipated maturity: Now–2005. Last tasted, 3/90.

1967—Crème de Tête: Everyone agrees that no greater wine was made in 1967 than
   •   Château d'Yquem, but I would love to have the opportunity to taste Gilette's
  96   1967 Crème de Tête alongside Yquem. This fabulously rich wine has an
awesomely intense bouquet of caramel and buttery hazelnuts, combined with intense aromas of honeyed fruit such as pineapples, oranges, and apricots. Decadently rich, with an unctuous, chewy texture, yet with enough acidity to provide great delineation and balance, this is a magnificent wine that has miraculously retained an amazing freshness for its 23 years of age. It should continue to evolve and improve for another 30, perhaps even 40, years. This is an outrageous thrill-a-sip Sauternes! Anticipated maturity: Now–2025. Last tasted, 3/90.

1962—Crème de Tête: The 1962 offers a very complex, honeyed nose filled with
   •   decadent apricot and peach scents that can come from heavily botrytised
  90   fruit. Very full bodied, with good acidity and opulent, rich crème brûlée
flavors, this luscious, full-throttle Sauternes should continue to drink well for at least another 15–20 years. Anticipated maturity: Now–2015. Last tasted, 3/90.

1961—Crème de Tête: I have never tasted a great 1961 Sauternes, although I am
   •   sure this region's wines benefited immensely from the great reputation of the
  87   reds in this vintage. However, the white wines were nowhere near the quality
of either the 1962s or 1959s. Most have turned out to be very good, relatively dry, old white wines with a great deal of alcohol but not much charm or fat. Gilette's 1961 is very fine, although significantly less rich and opulent than the 1962. It is almost dry. It could be the perfect partner with a rich dish that contained foie gras as one of the primary ingredients. Anticipated maturity: Now–2001. Last tasted, 3/90.

1959—Crème de Tête: This is a decadent, honey-pot of a wine. It is medium deep
   •   golden, with a huge bouquet of smoked nuts, coffee, mocha, coconut, and
  94   decadently jammy apricot-and-peach-like fruit. In the mouth, the wine has
astonishing richness, super glycerin content, a great deal of body, and a long, alcoholic, smashingly intense, heady finish. Seemingly fully mature, yet still remarkably fresh and young, this wine can easily last for another 20 or more years. Anticipated maturity: Now–2010. Last tasted, 3/90.

1955—Crème de Tête: Fully mature, but still astonishingly fresh and alive, the 1955
   •   Gilette is deep golden in color, with a rich, honeyed bouquet, full body, and
  87   a ripe, long finish. It can probably last another 10–15 years. Anticipated
maturity: Now–2005. Last tasted, 11/90.

1953 — Crème de Tête: Slightly less rich and fat than the 1955, the 1953 is spicy and
 • oaky, with a bouquet suggesting melted caramel and ripe pineapples. Full
 86 bodied, still fresh and lively, this unctuous, rich wine is quite impressive.
 Anticipated maturity: Now–2001. Last tasted, 11/90.

1950 — Quite fat and sweet, with excellent ripeness, full body, and a long, deep,
 • velvety finish, this wine is a revelation given its age. This is a big, heavy-
 89 weight Sauternes that will last for 15–20 more years. Anticipated maturity:
 Now–2005. Last tasted, 1/85.

GUIRAUD   EXCELLENT

Classification: First-growth in 1855
Location of vineyards: Sauternes
Owner: S.A. du Château Guiraud
Manager: Xavier Planty
Address: 33210 Sauternes
Mailing address: Same as above
Telephone: 33 5 56 76 61 01; telefax: 33 5 56 76 67 52
Visits: By appointment, every day, between 8 A.M. and noon, and 2 P.M.
and 6 P.M.
Contact: Mrs. Eymery

VINEYARDS (white)
Surface area: 234.6 acres
Average age of vines: 30 years
Blend: 65% Semillon, 35% Sauvignon Blanc
Density of plantation: 6,660 vines per hectare
Average yields (over the last 5 years): 10 hectoliters per hectare
Total average annual production: 9,500 cases

GRAND VIN (white)
Brand name: Château Guiraud
Appellation: Sauternes
Mean annual production: 8,000 cases
Upbringing: Fermentations take place in oak barrels, 50% of which are
new. Wines remain in barrels for 18–36 months aging. They are fined
and filtered.

SECOND WINE
Brand name: Le Dauphin du Château Guiraud
Average annual production: 1,500 cases

Evaluation of present classification: Should be maintained
Plateau of maturity: 5–20 or more years following the vintage

Guiraud is one of the largest estates of the Sauternes district, covering almost 300 acres, of which 234 are planted with vines. Curiously, the estate produces a red wine with the Bordeaux Supérieur appellation and a dry white wine called "G."

The sweet wine of Guiraud has undergone a metamorphosis. In 1981 an ambitious Canadian, Hamilton Narby, purchased the estate and made bold promises that Yquem-like techniques of individual grape picking, barrel fermentation, and long aging in new oak barrels would be employed at Guiraud. Consequently, Bordeaux wine enthusiasts, particularly the nectar lovers, have taken great interest in the goings-on at Guiraud in the hopes that his administrator, Xavier Planty, has the talent to bring Narby's dreams to fruition.

The most surprising thing about Guiraud is that the wine is so rich given the high percentage of Sauvignon Blanc (35%) used in the blend. No doubt the use of new oak, late picking, and numerous passes through the vineyard ensure that only the ripest Sauvignon Blanc is harvested. But I am still perplexed as to why this wine is so intense despite that Sauvignon Blanc. Vintages since 1983 have been especially strong, and Guiraud is often one of the top half dozen wines now being made in the Barsac/Sauternes region.

VINTAGES

1990—In the past, I preferred the 1988 Guiraud, followed by the 1989, and, last,
•   the 1990. In recent tastings the 1990 has taken first prize with its showy
91   display of power, highly extracted, smoky, buttery, pineapple-and-orange-scented fruit, lavish quantities of toasty new oak, and unctuously thick, massive flavors and texture. This huge wine avoids being overbearing because of its adequate acidity. It should evolve well for 15–20 more years. Last tasted, 11/94.

1989—The 1989 is extremely disjointed. Although big and rich, it tastes like a glob
•   of sugar, alcohol, and wood. This was a disappointing showing for the 1989.
86   It should gain focus and return to the form predicted for it when it was in barrel. Last tasted, 11/94.

1988—More tight and backward than I remembered it, the 1988 exhibits a stylish,
•   spicy nose of ripe fruit, some botrytis, medium- to full-bodied flavors with
89+   well-integrated oak, an attractive, smoky, honeyed fruit character, and a lively finish. It is more shy and reticent than usual. It should last for 20–30 years. Last tasted, 5/98.

1986—Wealthy collectors will have a great deal of fun comparing the 1986, 1988,
•   and 1989 as they evolve over the years. The 1986 was the finest Guiraud
92   made up to that point, athough I suspect the 1988 will last longer and have higher acidity and better overall balance. However, the 1986 is a super-concentrated, aromatic wine with gobs of botrytis and creamy, unctuous, peach, pineapple, and apricot flavors. There is plenty of new oak to frame the wine, although the overall acidity is less than in the 1988. The finish is exceptionally long and well balanced. This is a massive, concentrated wine

that should easily develop over several decades. Anticipated maturity: Now–2009. Last tasted, 3/90.

1985—Guiraud has turned out a well-made 1985, with a great deal of sweetness,
• plenty of ripeness, and obvious aromas of toasty, smoky new oak. There is no
85 botrytis in evidence, and the wine exhibits less finesse and complexity than vintages such as 1983 and 1986. Nevertheless, this straightforward style of Sauternes will have its admirers, particularly among those who like to drink these wines as an apéritif. Anticipated maturity: Now. Last tasted, 3/90.

1983—Light golden, with a ripe, intense bouquet of apricots and pineapples, as well
• as the vanillin scents from having been aged in cask, this full-bodied, lush,
88 rich wine has excellent concentration, superb balance, and a zesty, long, alcoholic finish. Anticipated maturity: Now–2005. Last tasted, 3/90.

1982—Big and ponderous on the palate, with a sticky, viscous fruitiness that comes
• too close to being ponderous and heavy, and lacking finesse and sufficient
78 acidity to give the wine crispness, this effort from Guiraud has plenty of richness but is tiring to drink. Anticipated maturity: Now. Last tasted, 6/84.

1981—An attractively fruity bouquet displays aromas of new oak, some spice, an
• herbal element, and some pineapple fruit. On the palate, the wine is fruity
80 and medium to full bodied but lacks complexity and dimension. Anticipated maturity: Now. Last tasted, 6/84.

1980—Surprisingly dull, and too aggressively oaky, the 1980 Guiraud tastes fruity
• but flat. Anticipated maturity: Now. Last tasted, 6/84.
75

1979—Firm, with a reticent bouquet of fresh oranges and vanillin spices, this
• medium- to full-bodied wine has good acidity and good concentration and
84 length. Anticipated maturity: Now. Last tasted, 3/84.

1976—Dark amber/gold in color, this wine has a roasted, ripe fruity bouquet sugges-
• tive of sautéed oranges and almonds. On the palate, the wine is full bodied,
87 sweet, and rich, with a heady alcoholic finish. The wine has reached its plateau of maturity. Anticipated maturity: Now–2009. Last tasted, 3/84.

1975—Significantly lighter in color than the 1976, the 1975 Guiraud has a honeyed
• bouquet of peach-and-orange-like scents intermingled with the scent of new
86 oak. On the palate, the wine is fat and full bodied, with hints of almonds, butter, and caramel. This is a rich, impressive Guiraud. Anticipated maturity: Now. Last tasted, 3/87.

LAFAURIE-PEYRAGUEY   EXCELLENT

Classification: Sauternes Premier Grand Cru Classé
Location of vineyards: Bommes
Owner: Domaines Cordier
Address: Bommes, 33210 Langon
Mailing address: c/o Domaines Cordier, 53, rue du Dehez, 33290 Blanquefort
Telephone: 33 5 56 95 53 00; telefax: 33 5 56 95 53 01

Visits: By appointment only
Contact: Domaines Cordier at above telephone and fax numbers

VINEYARDS (white)
Surface area: 101.3 acres
Average age of vines: 35 years
Blend: 90% Semillon, 5% Sauvignon, 5% Muscadelle
Density of plantation: 6,666 vines per hectare
Average yields (over the last 5 years): 13 hectoliters per hectare
Total average annual production: 70,000–75,000 bottles

GRAND VIN (white)
Brand name: Château Lafaurie-Peyraguey
Appellation: Sauternes Premier Grand Cru Classé
Upbringing: Fermentations take place in barrels at low temperatures
(less than 18 degrees centigrade). Wines are aged in oak barrels that are
renewed by a third in each vintage. They are racked every 3 months,
fined with egg whites, and bottled after 24–30 months aging.

SECOND WINE
Brand name: La Chapelle de Lafaurie

NOTE: A third wine is also produced: Le Brut de Lafaurie (dry white
Bordeaux).

Evaluation of present classification: Should be maintained
Plateau of maturity: 5–25 years following the vintage

Long in the doldrums, Lafaurie-Peyraguey has emerged in the eighties as one
of the great producers of decadently rich, complex, and compelling Sauternes.
The Cordiers' decisions to reduce the percentage of Sauvignon in the wine,
to increase the amount of new oak, and to institute a stricter selection began to result in a string of highly successful Sauternes, starting with 1981
and culminating with the great wines produced in 1983, 1986, 1988, and
1989.

The château, one of the most extraordinary in the Sauternes region, was
built in the thirteenth century as a fortification overlooking the surrounding
countryside. The property was acquired by the Cordiers in 1913. At present,
based on the performance of Lafaurie-Peyraguey during the last decade, this
is one of the top half dozen Sauternes, combining an unctuous richness with
great finesse and a profound fragrance of honeyed fruit.

In the late eighties a dry white wine called Le Brut de Lafaurie was
introduced. While I am not a great admirer of many of the relatively heavy,
dry white wines made in the Sauternes region, this is the best I have tasted

from the appellation. It is produced from 40% Sauvignon Blanc, 40% Semillon, and 20% Muscadelle and can be wonderfully delicious, perfumed, and surprisingly rich, yet totally dry and crisp.

VINTAGES

1990—I remember how one-dimensional, diffuse, thick, and alcoholic this wine
• tasted from cask and immediately after bottling, but it has progressed enor-
92 mously. The 1990 exhibits a deep golden corn–like color, followed by sensational aromatics (honeyed citrus, pineapple, and pear intertwined with smoke
and crème brûlée–like notes). In the mouth, the wine is massive and full
bodied, with an unctuous texture and powerful, juicy flavors that possess
mouth-staining extract, glycerin, and viscosity. This is a blockbuster-style,
sweet Sauternes with at least 30 years of longevity. Anticipated maturity:
2004–2030. Last tasted, 12/97.

1989—Sandwiched between two extraordinary vintages for Lafaurie-Peyraguey, the
• 1989 may turn out to be an outstanding wine with more aging potential. The
89 problem is that I have always tasted it in a minivertical with two glorious
examples of this château. The 1989 is an excellent, possibly outstanding,
wine made in a more restrained and less viscous style than the 1990 and
1988. The 1989 possesses a lively aromatic profile consisting of honeyed
tropical fruits with a touch of a fresh Amontillado sherry added for complexity.
Full bodied, with good acidity, less evidence of botrytis than I would have
expected, and excellent, possibly outstanding, extract, the 1989 reveals a
more monolithic, oaky personality, but these wines often take 8–10 years to
reveal their true characters. There is good depth and richness in the finish,
and the wine is long. Anticipated maturity: 2002–2025. Last tasted, 12/97.

1988—The massively rich, yet fresh, lively 1988 offers a compelling, flowery, hon-
• eyed bouquet of vanilla custard, buttery orange/apricot scents, and smoky
95 crème brûlée. The wine's zesty acidity brings everything into extraordinary
clarity. With plenty of botrytis evident, this is a full-bodied, super-
concentrated, fascinating, powerful, yet elegant Sauternes that will age beautifully for 25–30 years. Anticipated maturity: 2001–2030. Last tasted, 12/97.

1986—A wonderful bouquet of pineapples, smoky nuts, honeysuckle, and other
• flowers soars from the glass. In the mouth, the wine is rich, with the essence
92 of apricots, pineapples, and other tropical fruits. The acidity is crisp, giving
the wine great definition and clarity. The finish is sweet, honeyed, and long.
This beautifully made Sauternes is one of my favorites from the 1986 vintage.
Anticipated maturity: Now–2010. Last tasted, 11/96.

1985—Because of the lack of botrytis, the 1985 is a relatively straightforward, fruity,
• fat, yet fresh-tasting Sauternes that would be ideal as an apéritif rather than
86 a dessert wine. It will last for 10–15 years but is best drunk within the next
decade. Anticipated maturity: Now–2000. Last tasted, 3/91.

1983—The staff at Cordier have every right to be happy with this splendidly concen-
• trated, complex, fully mature wine. Tremendous intensity, viscous, ripe, and
92 layered with honeyed, apricot-flavored fruit, this unctuous wine is not tiring

or heavy to drink, but lively and effusively fruity. Anticipated maturity: Now–2000. Last tasted, 3/91.

1982—Much lighter than the 1983, with little botrytis evident, the 1982 is quite
• fresh and fruity, with aromas of melons and flowers present. On the palate,
84 the wine is medium bodied, moderately sweet, spicy, and cleanly made. Anticipated maturity: Now. Last tasted, 3/87.

1981—Quite exceptional, the 1981 Lafaurie-Peyraguey exhibits ripe apricot aromas,
• a rich, chewy, viscous texture, good acidity, and a long, sweet, fat finish. This
88 wine displays considerable botrytis and is clearly one of the top efforts in this vintage. Anticipated maturity: Now. Last tasted, 6/84.

1980—Not quite up to the top-quality wines produced in 1983 and 1981, the
• Lafaurie-Peyraguey is competent. Medium in weight for a Sauternes, with a
84 good, ripe pineapple, spicy fruitiness, this wine has average acidity. Anticipated maturity: Now. Last tasted, 3/83.

1979—The 1979 is first in a line of successful Lafaurie-Peyraguey wines that seem
• to have taken on greater richness as the Cordier firm has moved to upgrade
85 the quality. A lovely spicy-scented pineapple bouquet is attractive. The wine displays good botrytis, good acidity, moderate sweetness, and a crisp, clean finish. Anticipated maturity: Now. Last tasted, 3/82.

1976—There is really nothing wrong with this wine, but it seems one-dimensional
• and innocuous and clearly lacks character and depth. It is a minor Sauternes.
75 Anticipated maturity: Now. Last tasted, 11/82.

1975—A very atypical Sauternes, the 1975 has an olive-like, earthy aroma that
• seems slightly unclean and unripe. On the palate, the wine is light and
67 surprisingly thin and finishes poorly. Something clearly went wrong in 1975 for Lafaurie-Peyraguey. Last tasted, 12/80.

1970—The 1970 is pleasant and agreeable, but very short on the palate and not very
• sweet or concentrated. It is disappointing for a Sauternes of this class. Last
74 tasted, 12/80.

LAMOTHE   GOOD

Classification: Second-growth in 1855
Location of vineyards: Sauternes
Owner: Guy Despujols
Address: 33210 Sauternes
Mailing address: Same as above
Telephone: 33 5 56 76 67 89; telefax: 33 5 56 76 63 77
Visits: Preferably by appointment, between 10 A.M. and 12:30 P.M., and 2:30 P.M. and 6 P.M.
Contact: Mr. or Mrs. Guy Despujols

VINEYARDS (white)
Surface area: 18.6 acres
Average age of vines: 40 years

Blend: 85% Semillon, 10% Sauvignon, 5% Muscadelle
Density of plantation: 7,400 vines per hectare
Average yields (over the last 5 years): 22.5 hectoliters per hectare
Total average annual production: 155 hectoliters

GRAND VIN (white)
Brand name: Château Lamothe
Appellation: Sauternes
Mean annual production: 14,000 bottles
Upbringing: Fermentations last 15–30 days depending upon the lots and
the vintage, in vats of small capacity (45 hectoliters). Approximately
50%–75% of the yield remains in vats, and the rest is transferred to oak
barrels, 30%–60% of which are new, for 20–30 months aging. The wines
are fined and filtered.

SECOND WINE
Brand name: Les Tourelles de Lamothe
Average annual production: 3,000 bottles

Evaluation of present classification: Too inconsistent to merit its rank;
should be downgraded to a Cru Bourgeois
Plateau of maturity: 3–12 years following the vintage

Known in the nineteenth century as Lamothe-d'Assault, this property was
partitioned and there are now two Lamothe estates, both carrying the suffix of
the current owner's family name. Lamothe (Despujols) tends to make relatively light wines, but they are worth tasting since there have been some
surprises (as in 1986). With the high percentage of Muscadelle in the blend,
the style is one of fragrance and soft, forward fruit. I thought there was a
noticeable increase in quality in the late eighties.

VINTAGES

1990 — The 1990 reveals an oily personality, big, ripe, honeyed fruit flavors, low
•   acidity, plenty of intensity, and a full-bodied, chewy style that suggests it
88   should be drunk over the next 10 years. Last tasted, 11/94.

1989 — The 1989 is displaying far greater richness, intensity, and cleanliness than
•   previous examples revealed. It exhibited good fatness, an unctuous texture,
87   low acidity, and lovely rich, intense, tropical fruit. It should drink well for
     7–8 years. Last tasted, 11/94.

1988 — It is hard to understand what could have happened at Lamothe-Despujols in
•   such a superb vintage as 1988. This wine is dull, muted, and lacking fruit,
72   freshness, and character. It performed this way in three separate tastings.
     Anticipated maturity: Now. Last tasted, 4/91.

1986—For as inconsistent and indifferent as Lamothe-Despujols can be, the 1986 is
• irrefutably a sleeper of the vintage. A wonderful honeyed nose with a whiff of
88 toasty oak is followed by an opulent, intense, rich, glycerin-filled, full-bodied,
beautifully balanced Sauternes that should drink well for another 10–15
years. It is undoubtedly the best example I have ever tasted from this property.
Anticipated maturity: Now–2005. Last tasted, 3/90.

1985—This big, fat, surprisingly rich and intense wine exhibits a great deal more
• weight and character than many other properties in this vintage. There is
85 very little evidence of botrytis, but there are gobs of fruit in a relatively straightforward, chunky style. Anticipated maturity: Now. Last tasted,
3/90.

LAMOTHE-GUIGNARD   GOOD

Classification: Second-growth in 1855
Location of vineyards: Sauternes
Owner: Philippe and Jacques Guignard
Address: 33210 Sauternes
Mailing address: Same as above
Telephone: 33 5 56 76 60 28; telefax: 33 5 56 76 69 05
Visits: Monday through Friday, from 8 A.M. to noon, and 2 P.M. to 6 P.M.
Contact: Philippe and Jacques Guignard

VINEYARDS (white)
Surface area: 42 acres
Average age of vines: 35 years
Blend: 90% Semillon, 5% Muscadelle, 5% Sauvignon
Density of plantation: 6,600 vines per hectare
Average yields (over the last 5 years): 17 hectoliters per hectare
Total average annual production: 20,000–40,000 bottles

GRAND VIN (white)
Brand name: Château Lamothe-Guignard
Appellation: Sauternes
Mean annual production: 20,000–40,000 bottles
Upbringing: Fermentations take place in vats of small capacity. Wines are
aged in oak barrels, 25% of which are new, for 12–15 months. They are
fined and filtered.

SECOND WINE
None produced.

Evaluation of present classification: Should be maintained
Plateau of maturity: 5–15 years following the vintage

The proprietors of Lamothe-Guignard, Philippe and Jacques Guignard, purchased this property in 1981 and have set about in an aggressive manner to resurrect the image of Lamothe-Guignard. This could be a property to keep a close eye on in the nineties, as the quality of the wines has been promising.

The vineyard is well located several miles to the south of Yquem, just off route D125. Among the Premiers Crus Classés, it is closest to Guiraud, La Tour Blanche, and Lafaurie-Peyraguey. The proprietors have increased the percentage of new oak and have begun making more passes through the vineyard to harvest only fully botrytised grapes. The results have been impressive and somewhat undervalued wines.

VINTAGES

1990—The 1990 is a forceful, unctuous, thick, chewy Sauternes with plenty of
•   heady alcohol, gobs of fruit, and an exuberant personality. It reveals greater
91   aromatics, complexity, dimension, and delineation than it did several years ago. It should age well and evolve for 15–20 more years. Last tasted, 11/94.

1989—The 1989 also displays more personality and complexity. Although it pos-
•   sesses very high alcohol (nearly 15%), it is a massive, highly extracted,
91   extremely rich, impressively endowed wine that is oozing with honeyed, buttery, apricot, orange, pineapple, and lemony fruit. Noticeable acidity gives uplift and vibrance to this huge wine. Lamothe-Guignard's 1989 has turned out to be a sleeper of the vintage and should be available at a reasonable price. It should last for 20+ years. Last tasted, 11/94.

1988—The backward, streamlined 1988 possesses a waxy, honeyed, Tokay–Pinot
•   Gris-like fragrance and rich, full-bodied flavors that appear reticent and
89+   restrained because of the wine's good acidity. A shy example of this estate's wine, it is not nearly as ostentatious or muscular as the 1989 or 1990. It should last for 20–25 years. Last tasted, 11/94.

1986—The 1986 Lamothe-Guignard has a lovely moderately intense, pineapple
•   fruitiness, rich, velvety flavors, plenty of botrytis, and a long, silky finish.
87   While it will not be one of the longest-lived 1986s, it certainly is capable of providing immense satisfaction for another 5–7 years. Anticipated maturity: Now–1999. Last tasted, 3/90.

1985—Once again, the shortcomings of the 1985 Barsac/Sauternes vintage are obvi-
•   ous in this straightforward, relatively fat, but uninteresting and monolithically
84   styled Sauternes. It is sweet, rich, full, and heavy, but there is a lack of grip as well as complexity. Anticipated maturity: Now. Last tasted, 3/90.

MALLE   GOOD

Classification: Deuxième Cru Classé
Address: 33210 Preignac
Telephone: 33 5 56 65 36 86; telefax: 33 5 56 76 82 40
Production: 1,300 cases

Blend: 75% Semillon, 25% Sauvignon Blanc
Secondary label: Château de Sainte-Hélène
Vineyard size: 123 acres
Proprietor: Comtesse de Bournazel
Dry white wine: Chevalier de Malle
Time spent in barrels: 24 months
Average age of vines: 25 years

Evaluation of present classification: Should be maintained
Plateau of maturity: 5–15 years following the vintage

This magnificent estate, with its extraordinary seventeenth-century château, was at one time owned by a member of the Lur Saluces family (the proprietors of Yquem and de Fargues). However, that ownership ended in 1785. Since then the property has been in the Bournazel family. De Malle is a vast estate, with over half its acreage in Graves. Those readers who have tasted the excellent white Graves made by Château de Malle, the M. de Malle, or their red wine, Château Cardaillan, know how serious those wines can be. I also recommend that visitors to the Barsac/Sauternes region go out of their way to get an appointment to visit Château de Malle, which was classified as a historic monument by the French government in 1949.

Even if you have no interest in architecture, the wines are worth tasting, as they are among the most elegant of the appellation. At times they can have a tendency to turn out light, but most vintages (from the more restrained and refined school of Sauternes) have been extremely well made. I should note that the 1990 de Malle is the finest young wine I have tasted from the property, a sentiment shared by many of the region's cognoscenti.

VINTAGES

1990—Château de Malle's 1990 is the finest sweet wine the estate had made in
•   decades. Certainly it is an outstanding effort, and given the reasonable price,
90   it is a noteworthy purchase. The 1990 is full bodied, with excellent sweetness,
       fine purity, and plenty of rich, honeyed fruit buttressed by noticeable new
       oak. It has not yet developed the complexity and aromatics displayed by the
       1988, but the 1990 is clearly an outstanding effort for the vintage. It should
       evolve gracefully for 10–15 years. Last tasted, 11/94.

1989—The 1989 appeared to be somewhat simple. It is medium to full bodied, with
•   ripe, rich fruit, enough acidity to provide uplift, and a fleshy finish. It should
87   drink well for another decade. Last tasted, 11/94.

1988—The 1988 was "singing" at the top of its lungs in a recent tasting. Closer to
•   maturity than the 1990, the 1988 offers a heavenly bouquet of cherries and
91   coconuts as well as an ostentatious display of honeyed pineapples and toasty

oak. Medium to full bodied, with excellent purity, freshness, and ripeness, it is an ideal candidate for drinking or cellaring over the next 10–12 years. Last tasted, 11/94.

1986—The 1986 is a medium-bodied, deliciously fruity wine that is relatively light
•   but offers a considerable display of fruit salad–like flavors. There is plenty of
84   freshness, but not as much botrytis as I would have expected given the vintage. Anticipated maturity: Now. Last tasted, 3/90.

1985—I have always found this wine to be one-dimensional and innocuous, with
•   straightforward, slightly sweet, monochromatic flavors. Anticipated maturity:
79   Now. Last tasted, 3/90.

NAIRAC   GOOD

Classification: Second-growth in 1855
Location of vineyards: Barsac
Owner: Nicole Tari-Heeter
Address: 33720 Barsac
Mailing address: Same as above
Telephone: 33 5 56 27 16 16; telefax: 33 5 56 27 26 50
Visits: By appointment only
Contact: Nicolas Heeter

VINEYARDS (white)
Surface area: 42 acres
Average age of vines: 40 years
Blend: 90% Semillon, 6% Sauvignon, 4% Muscadelle
Density of plantation: 8,000 vines per hectare

GRAND VIN (white)
Brand name: Château Nairac
Appellation: Barsac
Mean annual production: 10,000 bottles
Upbringing: Fermentations last 1–3 months in oak barrels, and wines are aged 2½ years before bottling. They are fined and filtered.

SECOND WINE
None produced.

Evaluation of present classification: Should be maintained
Plateau of maturity: 5–15 years following the vintage

Nairac is one of the most meticulously and passionately operated Barsac estates. In 1971 the property was purchased by American-born Tom Heeter and Nicole Tari. Heeter apprenticed at the red wine–producing property Giscours, in the Margaux appellation, where he met his wife (they are now divorced), a member of the Tari winemaking family. During the eighties the celebrated Emile Peynaud was brought in to provide oenological advice, and Nairac began to produce some of the best wines of Barsac.

Nairac is a relatively big-styled, oaky, ripe, concentrated wine for a Barsac. To say that it is impeccably made is an understatement. No compromises are made, and this is clearly demonstrated by the fact that no Nairac was made in 1977 and 1978.

Nairac represents a good value and should be sought out by consumers looking for a very good Barsac at a reasonable price.

VINTAGES

1989—When I first tasted the 1989 Nairac from cask, it appeared to be excessively
 • oaky as well as a bit too fat and alcoholic. However, it has evolved gracefully
 87 in the cask and now exhibits plenty of toasty vanillin—scented new oak, an opulently rich nose and texture, long, heady, unctuous flavors, and enough acidity for grip and focus. It will evolve quickly, as the color is already a deep medium golden. Anticipated maturity: Now–2003. Last tasted, 4/91.

1988—This wine has consistently tasted dull and muted, with its fruit suppressed. It
 • was like that from cask and has repeatedly performed in a similar manner
 ? from bottle. It is hard to understand why this wine tastes so backward and unexpressive. Judgment reserved. Last tasted, 4/91.

1986—This is one of the finest Nairacs I have ever tasted. It is an especially
 • rich, powerful, concentrated wine with gobs of glycerin-injected pineapple
 89 fruit, full body, and a long, luscious, smooth finish. There is plenty of acidity and evidence of botrytis, so I would expect a relatively long evolution for this top-class wine. Anticipated maturity: Now–2010. Last tasted, 3/90.

1985—The 1985 lacks botrytis, a problem that is typical of most wines of the 1985
 • vintage. Other than that, there is straightforward orange and pineapple fruit,
 81 heavily dosed with generous quantities of toasty new oak. Anticipated maturity: Now. Last tasted, 3/89.

1983—Extremely aromatic, the 1983 Nairac has a flowery, tropical fruit—scented
 • bouquet, big, rich, fruit salad—like flavors, full body, and a luscious, honeyed
 86 finish. Anticipated maturity: Now–2002. Last tasted, 3/90.

1982—Probably the most successful Barsac of the vintage, Nairac's 1982 exhibits a
 • light golden color, a spicy pineapple and vanillin oaky bouquet, medium
 85 to full body, and surprisingly good concentration and length. It is a nice, medium-weight Barsac. Anticipated maturity: Now. Last tasted, 3/89.

1981—Certainly good, but like many 1981s, Nairac's wine lacks the botrytis that
 • gives the great vintages of this region so much character. Perhaps a little too
 83 plump, and with a tendency toward dullness, this medium- to full-bodied wine has average acidity. Anticipated maturity: Now. Last tasted, 11/84.

1980—Nairac's 1980 is a well-balanced, light golden—colored wine that displays a
 • good level of botrytis, a spicy, tropical fruit, oaky bouquet, medium body, soft
 84 acidity, and a fat, tasty finish. It is fully mature. Anticipated maturity: Now. Last tasted, 11/84.

1979—A good Barsac, rather light for Nairac, but elegant, adequately concentrated,
 •   with a crisp, clean, moderately sweet finish. Anticipated maturity: Now. Last
83   tasted, 11/84.
1976—One of the best Nairacs, the 1976 has a powerful, oaky, ripe fruity bouquet
 •   and strong vanillin, spicy, oaky notes. On the palate, the wine is full bodied,
86   long, lush, and quite concentrated, and has a high level of botrytis. Antici-
      pated maturity: Now. Last tasted, 11/84.
1975—Lighter in style than the 1976, with less power and obvious appeal, the 1975
 •   Nairac has a quiet, introverted charm, with a fresh, lively fruitiness, good
84   acidity and presence on the palate, and a long, moderately sweet finish. It is
      quite well made. Anticipated maturity: Now. Last tasted, 11/84.

RABAUD-PROMIS   VERY GOOD

Classification: Premier Cru Classé
Address: 33210 Bommes
Telephone: 33 5 56 76 67 38; telefax: 33 5 56 76 63 10
Production: 5,000 cases
Blend: 80% Semillon, 18% Sauvignon Blanc, 2% Muscadelle
Secondary label: Domaine de l'Estremade
Vineyard size: 82 acres
Proprietor: G.F.A. du Château Rabaud-Promis
Administrator: Philippe Dejean
Dry white wine: None
Time spent in barrels: 24–30 months
Average age of vines: 35–40 years

Evaluation of present classification: Since 1986 the wines have merited
their classification; previously the wines ranged from mediocre to
disappointing
Plateau of maturity: 5–20 or more years following the vintage

Rabaud-Promis was once part of a huge ancient domain called Rabaud. In
1903 Rabaud was divided into Rabaud-Promis and the more well-known
Sigalas Rabaud. Curiously, the properties were reunited 26 years later, then
partitioned again in 1952.

Until 1986 Rabaud-Promis may have been the most disappointing wine
among the Premiers Crus Classés. However, no estate has made more progress
in such a short period of time. Not only has a second wine been introduced,
but the top wine now goes into small oak barrels, of which a healthy percentage is new each year. In the past, there was no selection and the entire crop
was matured in cement vats.

Shrewd connoisseurs of the sweet wines of Barsac/Sauternes should put such information to use, as it will probably take several years before the price catches up to the quality level now being exhibited. If the excellent examples of Rabaud-Promis that have emerged from the 1986, 1988, 1989, and 1990 vintages are typical of the new direction of this property, it will be one of the fuller-bodied, more luscious and intense Sauternes on the market.

VINTAGES

1990—The 1990 reveals plenty of honeyed richness, a full-blown, heavyweight style,
 •   and considerable spice. While there is a slight lack of acidity, it is a huge,
 90   full-bodied wine for drinking over the next 15 or so years. Last tasted, 11/94.

1989—The 1989 is rich and complex aromatically, as well as huge and massive. It
 •   exhibits great delineation, with enough freshness and vibrancy to make a
 92   strong case for this estate's 1989. It should age well for 20–25 years. Last
      tasted, 11/94.

1988—The 1988 remains the most classic of these three vintages. It possesses great
 •   richness, sweetness, and unctuous texture, as well as higher acidity, plenty of
 93   botrytis, a wonderful, rich, honeyed pineapple-, coconut-, and orange-scented
      nose, gobs of rich fruit, and excellent delineation. Approachable now, it
      promises to age effortlessly for 25–30 years. Last tasted, 11/94.

1986—The 1986 marked the first in a succession of vintages manifesting the return
 •   of Rabaud-Promis to its status as a Premier Cru Classé. Full bodied, with an
 89   intense bouquet of caramel, pineapples, and apricots, this wine has gobs of
      glycerin, adequate acidity for balance, and an oaky, rich finish. Its evolution
      should continue to be graceful and long. Anticipated maturity: Now–2010.
      Last tasted, 3/90.

1985—An attractive nose of flowers, pineapples, and coffee is followed by a straight-
 •   forward, relatively powerful wine with a great deal of fruit, but it is lacking
 83   the complexity and focus that is essential for these large-scaled sweet wines.
      Anticipated maturity: Now. Last tasted, 3/90.

1983—This wine has turned out slightly better than I initially believed it would. It
 •   is fat, round, and full bodied, with gobs of fruit, but it comes across as a bit
 84   cloying and heavy-handed, without sufficient botrytis or acidity. It was made
      at a time when Rabaud-Promis was aging its wine in vats rather than small
      oak casks, which probably explains the wine's lack of delineation. Anticipated
      maturity: Now. Last tasted, 3/90.

RAYMOND-LAFON   EXCELLENT

Classification: None
Location of vineyards: Sauternes, bordering Yquem
Owner: Meslier family
Address: 33210 Sauternes
Mailing address: Same as above

Telephone: 33 5 56 63 21 02; telefax: 33 5 56 63 19 58
Visits: By appointment only, every day
Contact: Marie-Françoise Meslier

VINEYARDS (white)
Surface area: 44.5 acres, but only 39.5 are under vine
Average age of vines: 35 years
Blend: 80% Semillon, 20% Sauvignon
Density of plantation: 6,666 vines per hectare
Average yields (over the last 5 years): 9 hectoliters per hectare
Total average annual production: 20,000 bottles

GRAND VIN (white)
Brand name: Château Raymond-Lafon
Appellation: Sauternes
Mean annual production: 20,000 bottles
Upbringing: Wines are aged 36 months in new oak barrels. They are
fined but remain unfiltered.

SECOND WINE
Brand name: Château Lafon-Laroze
Average annual production: Not produced every year

Evaluation of present classification: Should be upgraded to a Premier Cru
Classé
Plateau of maturity: 8–25 or more years following the vintage

Raymond-Lafon is a name to watch in the Sauternes district, particularly if
one is looking for a wine that is close to the brilliance and majestic richness
of Yquem for less than one-third the price.

This small estate abuts Yquem's vineyard and has had an excellent reputation. The 1921 Raymond-Lafon was considered even better than Yquem's
wine in that great vintage. I have never tasted the 1921 Raymond-Lafon, but
the single greatest Sauternes I have ever drunk was the Yquem of that vintage.
However, the estate of Raymond-Lafon fell into neglect, and it was not until
1972 that Pierre Meslier, the manager of Yquem, purchased this vineyard and
began to rebuild this wine's once fabulous reputation.

With a tiny yield of 9 hectoliters per hectare (even less than Yquem's),
with the same grape blend and winemaking techniques employed as Yquem,
and with the same ruthless selection procedure (normally 20%–100% of a
harvest is declassified), Raymond-Lafon has already produced a succession
of splendid Sauternes, beginning with a great 1975 and just recently concluding with a monumental 1990.

Raymond-Lafon looks to be well on the road to becoming one of the great classic wines of Sauternes. Unfortunately, the wine is extremely difficult to find because of the tiny production and the fact that proprietor Pierre Meslier sells much of it to private clients in Europe. One must wonder why this vineyard, situated next to Yquem and surrounded by all the Premiers Crus Classés of Sauternes, was overlooked in the 1855 classification.

VINTAGES

1990—The 1990 may be the most complete and richest of recent Raymond-Lafons.
•   It possesses a light to medium gold color, with massive, full-bodied, honeyed
95   flavors. Anticipated maturity: 2002–2025. Last tasted 3/96.

1989—The 1989 exhibits aromas of honeyed pineapple/tropical fruit and toasty new
•   oak, as well as an exotic, flashy perfume that is not as pronounced in either
91+   the 1990 or 1988. The 1989 exhibits less botrytis than the other two vintages. All three wines share opulent, full-bodied, exotic, lavishly rich personalities, moderate sweetness (the 1990 is the sweetest), and huge quantities of extract, glycerin, and alcohol in their finishes. The 1990 appears to be the richest. Anticipated maturity: 2000–2025. Last tasted, 3/96.

1988—The 1988 offers the most refined aromatic profile and the tightest structure,
•   and the 1989 tastes the most restrained. All of these wines can be drunk now,
92+   but purchasers are advised to wait until the turn of the century and enjoy them over the following 2 decades. Last tasted, 11/94.

1987—Very light, with straightforward, fruity, slightly sweet flavors, this would make
•   an attractive but lowbrow apéritif wine. It does not have the requisite weight,
84   sweetness, or complexity to stand by itself as a dessert wine. Anticipated maturity: Now. Last tasted, 4/91.

1986—It is hard to believe this wine will eclipse the great 1983, but the differences
•   in the two wines are negligible. I do not believe the 1986 makes quite the
92   impact on the palate that the huge, massive 1983 does, but there is a great deal of botrytis and a profound, penetrating fragrance of sautéed pineapple, vanillin, toast, and honeyed peaches. In the mouth, the wine is more stream-lined than the 1983, but lusciously rich and full bodied, with very good acidity and a creamy, intense finish. It will be interesting to compare the 1983 and 1986 as they evolve. My guess is that the 1986 will age faster. Anticipated maturity: Now–2012. Last tasted, 3/90.

1985—This is one of the best 1985s I have tasted from Sauternes. It is rich and full,
•   and although there is a general absence of any botrytis, the quality of the fruit
87   is impeccably high. There is plenty of citrusy, pear-, peach-, and apricot-scented fruit backed up by some vague notes of roasted almonds. This is a delicious 1985 that should evolve gracefully. Anticipated maturity: Now–2002. Last tasted, 3/90.

1983—This is a magnificent wine. Light golden, with a wonderfully pure tropical
•   fruit aroma of ripe pineapples and melons, this decadently rich, full-bodied
93   wine has layers of viscous, sweet fruit, an astonishing finish, and excellent

balancing acidity. The wine remains stubbornly slow to evolve. Anticipated maturity: Now–2020. Last tasted, 11/90.

1982—In this rain-plagued harvest, Raymond-Lafon bottled only 33% of its produc-
• tion, and all of that from grapes picked prior to the rain. The wine is fat, very
86 fruity, sweet, and rich, with good botrytis, a full-bodied, rich, velvety texture, and low to moderate acidity. This vintage of Raymond-Lafon should develop fairly quickly. Anticipated maturity: Now. Last tasted, 3/87.

1981—Because of low acidity, I predict a rapid evolution for the 1981 Raymond-
• Lafon. A glorious bouquet of spicy, vanillin oak, lemony, honeyed, pineapple
87 fruit, and floral scents is intense and expansive. On the palate, the wine is quite fat, succulent, rich, and sweet, with high alcohol and a soft, supple, long, clean finish. Anticipated maturity: Now. Last tasted, 3/87.

1980—The 1980 was a great vintage for Raymond-Lafon, as it also was for Yquem
• and de Fargues, two other properties that proprietor Pierre Meslier looks
90 after. A full-intensity bouquet of ripe tropical fruit and spicy oak is followed by an unctuous, powerful, very rich, full-bodied wine, with layers of fruit, refreshingly high, crisp acidity, and a decade of evolution ahead. Anticipated maturity: Now–2005. Last tasted, 3/87.

1978—This was a good, but hardly special, vintage for the wines of Sauternes.
• However, the 1978 Raymond-Lafon gets my nod as the best sweet wine of
89 this vintage. It lacks the high level of botrytis found in vintages such as 1975 and 1980, but the wine exhibits beautifully textured, viscous, velvety flavors, full body, a refreshing lemony acidity, and a clean, crisp finish. This is not the biggest Raymond-Lafon, but it is certainly one of the most graceful. Anticipated maturity: Now–2000. Last tasted, 1/85.

1975—Like many Sauternes from this vintage, Raymond-Lafon has been slow to
• develop. Light golden with a green tint, this luscious, rich, creamy wine has
90 a tight yet expansive bouquet of very ripe fruit. Full bodied, rich, and sweet, yet tightly knit because of good acidity, this big, rich wine has enormous potential. Anticipated maturity: Now–2005. Last tasted, 3/86.

RAYNE-VIGNEAU   GOOD

Classification: Sauternes Premier Grand Cru Classé
Location of vineyards: Bommes
Owner: S.C. du Château Rayne-Vigneau
Address: 33210 Bommes
Mailing address: 17, cours de la Martinique, B.P. 90, 33027 Bordeaux Cedex
Telephone: 33 5 56 01 30 10; telefax: 33 5 56 79 23 57
Visits: For professionals of the wine trade only, by appointment
Contact: Brigitte Cruse

VINEYARDS (white)
Surface area: 193.4 acres
Average age of vines: 29 years

Blend: 71% Semillon, 27% Sauvignon, 2% Muscadelle
Density of plantation: 6,000 vines per hectare
Average yields (over the last 5 years): 18.5 hectoliters
Total average annual production: 1,413 hectoliters

GRAND VIN (white)
Brand name: Château de Rayne-Vigneau
Appellation: Sauternes Premier Grand Cru Classé
Mean annual production: 850 hectoliters
Upbringing: Fermentations last 3 weeks in temperature-controlled
stainless-steel vats, and part of the yield is fermented in new oak barrels.
Wines are aged 18–24 months in barrels that are renewed by half in each
vintage. They are fined and filtered.

SECOND WINE
Brand name: Madame de Rayne
Average annual production: 300 hectoliters (depending upon the vintage)

Evaluation of present classification: Until the mid-1980s a strong
argument could have been made that this property should have been
downgraded; since 1986, however, the quality has improved immensely
Plateau of maturity: 5–20 years following the vintage

During the nineteenth century Rayne-Vigneau had a reputation second only
to that of Yquem. Few estates in the region are as superbly located as
Rayne-Vigneau. However, because of neglect and indifferent winemaking, the
twentieth century has not been kind to the reputation of Rayne-Vigneau.
Since 1971 the estate has been managed and the wines commercialized by
Mestrezat, a well-run *négociant* firm. They are also the proprietors of the
classified-growth Pauillac Grand-Puy-Ducasse. They appear to have become
deadly serious about the quality of their wines since the early eighties.
Rayne-Vigneau has improved immensely since 1985, with the 1986, 1988,
and 1990 being the best wines I have tasted from this estate. The wine now
spends nearly 24 months in oak barrels, of which 50% are new each year. In
the past, the percentage of new oak utilized was minimal, and one always
suspected there was a lack of strict selection.

VINTAGES

1990—This sweet, thick, juicy Sauternes does not possess as much complexity as
•   the top wines of the vintage. Perhaps more will emerge with aging, as the
87   wine is more sugary, cloying, and plump than previous examples from this
      estate. The color is light golden. This honeyed, buttery Rayne-Vigneau does
      not reveal as much precision, definition, or evidence of botrytis as exists in
      the vintage's finest offerings. Nevertheless, there is plenty to enjoy in this

straightforward, monolithic 1990. Anticipated maturity: 2000–2012. Last tasted, 3/97.

1989 — The 1989's flowery, peach, and honey nose and medium- to full-bodied,
• complex, finesse style is refreshing, yet has sweet, low acid. Drink this
89 commercially styled Sauternes over the next decade. Last tasted, 11/94.

1988 — The 1988 is the best example I have tasted from this property. An intense,
• honeyed, pear, flower, and apricot fragrance is reminiscent of Muscat de
91 Beaumes de Venise. In the mouth, there is exceptional richness, super focus because of fine acidity, a wonderful touch of toasty new oak, and an elegant, very positive, crisp finish. This is a beautifully made, authoritative tasting, and impeccably well-balanced Sauternes. Anticipated maturity: Now–2006. Last tasted, 3/90.

1987 — This straightforward, soft, fat, richly fruity wine comes across as sweet and
• disjointed, but pleasant in a low-key way. It lacks focus, botrytis, and acidity,
82 but for drinking as an apéritif it has a place. Anticipated maturity: Now. Last tasted, 11/90.

1986 — This is the first reassuring example of Rayne-Vigneau in years, exhibiting a
• deft touch of new oak, an elegant yet concentrated, flavorful style, and a great
90 deal of finesse. The overwhelming impression is one of pears, pineapples, and great balance and character. Anticipated maturity: Now–2001. Last tasted, 11/90.

1985 — This is a ripe pineapple-scented and -flavored wine with just enough new oak
• and relatively thick, monolithic flavors, but it lacks acidity and comes across
85 as monochromatic. It is tasty and juicy, but a bit simple. Anticipated maturity: Now. Last tasted, 11/90.

1983 — Light aromas of pineapples and some faint botrytis emerge with breathing
• from this simply proportioned Sauternes. In the mouth, the wine reveals good
82 ripeness, a pleasant, velvety, creamy texture, medium sweetness, and crisp acidity. In the context of the vintage, this is an uninspiring wine, but for Rayne-Vigneau, it is a good effort. Anticipated maturity: Now. Last tasted, 11/90.

1982 — One-dimensional, fruity, sweet flavors offer little complexity but do exhibit
• pleasing ripeness and adequate balancing acidity. Anticipated maturity:
75 Now–may be in decline. Last tasted, 1/85.

1981 — Soft, fruity, moderately sweet flavors exhibit average concentration and some
• alluring scents of grilled almonds and pineapples, but this wine has a diluted
75 finish and just not enough stuffing and concentration to warrant much interest. Anticipated maturity: Now–may be in decline. Last tasted, 2/85.

1979 — A straightforward, fruity, rather sweet wine, without much botrytis but dis-
• playing solid, underripe flavors of peaches and mint. Typically light, and
74 lacking muscle and concentration, the 1979 Rayne-Vigneau should be drunk up. Anticipated maturity: Now. Last tasted, 6/83.

1976 — For a 1976 this is a lightweight wine, but it does have a good, ripe apricot
• fruitiness, medium body, and a decent, moderately sweet finish. I am tempted
78 to say that this is a nice picnic Sauternes. Anticipated maturity: Now. Last tasted, 2/84.

1975—A disappointing effort, the 1975 has excessively high acidity, a lean, austere,
 •   ungenerous texture, and light, vegetal, washed-out flavors. One wonders what
 65   could have gone afoul in this excellent vintage. Last tasted, 6/84.
1971—Hot alcohol tends to intrude on this wine's soft, delicate pineapple fruitiness
 •   and medium-bodied texture. It will only become more imbalanced. Antici-
 75   pated maturity: Now. Last tasted, 2/80.

RIEUSSEC   OUTSTANDING

Classification: First-growth in 1855
Location of vineyards: Fargues de Langon
Owner: Château Rieussec S.A.—Domaines Barons de Rothschild
Address: 33210 Fargues de Langon
Mailing address: c/o Domaines Barons de Rothschild, 33250 Pauillac
Telephone: 33 1 53 89 78 00; telefax: 33 1 53 89 78 01
Visits: By appointment only

VINEYARDS (white)
Surface area: 185.3 acres
Average age of vines: 33 years
Blend: 90% Semillon, 7% Sauvignon, 3% Muscadelle
Density of plantation: 7,000 vines per hectare
Average yields (over the last 5 years): 20 hectoliters per hectare
Total average annual production: 160,000 bottles

GRAND VIN (white)
Brand name: Château Rieussec
Appellation: Sauternes
Mean annual production: 80,000 bottles
Upbringing: Wines are fermented and aged in 70% new oak barrels and
bottled after 24 months. They are fined with egg whites and filtered.

SECOND WINE
Brand name: Clos Labère
Average annual production: 80,000 bottles

Evaluation of present classification: Since the acquisition by the
Domaines Rothschild in 1984, the quality of Rieussec has soared to even
greater heights; it is now one of the six best wines of the region
Plateau of maturity: 6–25 or more years following the vintage

As one approaches the heart of the Sauternes appellation, Château Rieussec
and its prominent lookout tower can be spotted on one of the highest hillsides.
The Rieussec vineyard, spread across the hillsides of Fargues and Sauternes
overlooking the left bank of the Garonne, has the highest altitude after that of

Yquem. Quite surprising for a Bordeaux property, the entire vineyard is one single unit.

Rieussec has always had an outstanding reputation, but after its acquisition by Albert Vuillier in 1971, the quality improved even more, largely because of the increase in new oak and more frequent passes through the vineyard to harvest only heavily botrytised grapes. In fact, some critics of Rieussec claimed that Vuillier's wines took on too deep a color as they aged (like the 1976, for example). Vuillier sold a majority interest in 1984 to the Domaines Barons de Rothschild, who have spared no expense or permitted any compromising in the making of Rieussec. The results since 1986 have been truly profound wines that are now routinely among the top half dozen of the appellation. Wealthy collectors will no doubt argue for decades whether the 1988, 1989, or 1990 produced the most profound Rieussec.

Under the Rothschild ownership, it is unlikely that Rieussec's style—one of power and almost roasted richness—will change. The wine is usually deeply colored and generally alcoholic, with excellent viscosity. Rieussec, like several other estates in Barsac and Sauternes, produces a tiny amount of decadently rich, intensely concentrated wine under a "Crème de Tête" label. Should you ever come across this rare, unctuous nectar, don't hesitate to give it a try. Rieussec also produces a dry white wine called "R." Such wines help ease cash flow problems considerably, and "R" is one of the most popular and best of the dry Sauternes.

VINTAGES

1990—The 1990 is precocious and flattering, with a tropical fruit–scented nose, big,
•   spicy, rich, high-alcohol flavors, and a fine underpinning of acidity giving
90   everything clarity and crispness. The 1990 will be drinkable at an earlier age
    than the 1989, but it will last just as long. Anticipated maturity: Now–2020.
    Last tasted, 11/94.

1989—After a period of prolonged disjointedness, this wine has pulled itself together.
•   The color is deep straw, and the wine displays an intense perfume of crème
92   brûlée custard, baked apple pie, and sweet, ripe pineapples and pears. Full
    bodied, rich, alcoholic, and fat, with low acidity and considerable sweetness,
    this is a luxuriously rich, unctuously textured, heavyweight Sauternes that
    should become more civilized with age. Anticipated maturity: 2000–2025.
    Last tasted, 11/97.

1988—The 1988 remains a very backward wine. Full bodied and powerful, extremely
•   rich and dense, it may be the least evolved 1988. The nose offers enticing
93+   coconut, orange, vanilla, and honeyed scents. The flavors are highly extracted.
    The wine's acidity and youthfulness suggest this wine needs another 5–10
    years of cellaring. It should keep for 30 years. Last tasted, 5/98.

1986—This is a stunningly complex and elegant wine, but it is less muscular as well
•   as less fat than either the 1983 or 1989. There are plenty of smoky almonds,
91   peaches, and honeyed apricot fruit in the nose and flavors. In the mouth, the

wine has a certain elegance and perhaps not quite the punch one normally expects from Rieussec. Nevertheless, it is still a compelling Sauternes that should age magnificently. Anticipated maturity: Now–2010. Last tasted, 11/90.

1985—This is a very good Sauternes for the vintage—rich, round, open knit, with a
• great deal of juicy, sweet, candied fruit—but the absence of botrytis results
86 in a wine lacking in complexity, which comes across as plump and succulent, but not terribly interesting. Anticipated maturity: Now. Last tasted, 11/90.

1983—Light golden with just the slightest tint of green, the 1983 Rieussec, from an
• excellent year for Sauternes, is certainly one of this property's greatest wines.
92 Well structured, with excellent acidity and a deep, long, rich, full-bodied, viscous texture, this wine, despite the richness and power, is neither heavy nor cloying. It has gorgeous balance and a very long, lingering, spectacular finish. One of the great successes of the vintage. Anticipated maturity: Now–2005. Last tasted, 3/88.

1982—In this maligned vintage for the sweet white wines of Bordeaux, Rieussec has,
• through a very strict selection process, turned out a lovely, fruity, spicy,
82 lighter-styled wine with medium body and delicate tropical fruit flavors. Anticipated maturity: Now. Last tasted, 3/86.

1981—One of the top 1981s, Rieussec must certainly be among the best Sauternes
• of this vintage. A very fragrant, spicy, richly fruity bouquet intermingled with
86 scents of apricots and melted butter is top class. On the palate, the wine is well balanced, fairly big and rich, and already showing well. Anticipated maturity: Now. Last tasted, 3/86.

1980—Somewhat dull and a trifle heavy, Rieussec's 1980 is a good, relatively rich,
• spicy, full-bodied wine revealing high acidity, some botrytis, and adequate
80 flavor intensity. However, it is not one of the leaders in this vintage. Anticipated maturity: Now–may be in decline. Last tasted, 3/84.

1979—A lightweight Rieussec that does not have the intensity and richness of
• vintages such as 1981 or 1983, it does offer an elegant, well-made, less
84 powerful wine that is light enough to be served as an apéritif. Anticipated maturity: Now. Last tasted, 3/84.

1978—The 1978 Rieussec just missed the mark. While quite good, it is not special.
• Too alcoholic, and a trifle too heavy and overblown, this wine has a nice
82 honeyed character and rich, unctuous flavors, but it evidences little botrytis. Anticipated maturity: Now. Last tasted, 6/84.

1976—This is one of the most controversial vintages of Rieussec. It is very dark gold
• in color, and some observers have said it is oxidized and falling apart. Despite
90 the dark color, the remarkable taste seems to suggest that this wine has a way to go. The huge nose of toasted almonds, caramel, chocolate, and brown sugar does exhibit a trace of volatile acidity, so technocrats are likely to be turned off. Incredibly rich and full bodied, with a honeyed, luscious texture and extremely intense flavors, this exotic, hugely proportioned wine (15% alcohol) can be served *only* as a dessert. The yield at Rieussec in 1976 was 2.5 hectoliters per hectare, which is approximately one-third of a glass of wine per vine. This is a bold, rather overblown style of Sauternes, but I love it. Anticipated maturity: Now–2005. Last tasted, 12/90.

1975—Still remarkably youthful looking and slow to evolve, this is a powerful,
- concentrated, and rich Sauternes, with decades of life ahead of it. Lemon,
90 tropical fruit, and vanillin oaky aromas titillate the olfactory glands. Tight,
yet rich, full-bodied flavors reveal marvelous balance and richness. It is aging
at a snail's pace. Anticipated maturity: Now–2025. Last tasted, 12/90.

1971—Now fully mature, the 1971 Rieussec has a light-intensity, honeyed, ripe
- apricot, oaky nose, a ripe, sweet, full-bodied feel on the palate, and a crisp,
85 spicy finish. Anticipated maturity: Now. Last tasted, 10/80.

1970—A little heavier to taste and a bit less elegant than the 1971, the 1970 is a
- corpulent, rich, sweet mouthful of viscous, chewy Sauternes. The moderately
82 amber/gold color is a sign of approaching maturity, but this wine has the
acidity and overall balance to drink nicely for at least another decade. Anticipated maturity: Now. Last tasted, 6/83.

1967—Rieussec made a very fine 1967. Not having tasted it for some time, I suspect
- this wine has been fully mature since the mid-1970s. It is lighter in style and
84 body than some of the more recent vintages of Rieussec, but richly fruity and
spicy, with a roasted, grilled nut aroma. Anticipated maturity: Now. Last
tasted, 9/79.

## ROMER DU HAYOT	GOOD

Classification: Second-growth in 1855
Location of vineyards: Preignac and Fargues de Langon
Owner: S.C.E. Vignobles du Hayot
Address: 33720 Barsac
Mailing address: Same as above
Telephone: 33 5 56 27 15 37; telefax: 33 5 56 27 04 24
Visits: Monday through Friday, between 8 A.M. and noon, and 2 P.M. and
6 P.M.

VINEYARDS (white)
Surface area: 39.5 acres
Average age of vines: 35 years
Blend: 70% Semillon, 25% Sauvignon, 5% Muscadelle
Density of plantation: 6,500 vines per hectare
Average yields (over the last 5 years): 25 hectoliters per hectare
Total average annual production: 50,000 bottles

GRAND VIN (white)
Brand name: Château Romer du Hayot
Appellation: Sauternes
Mean annual production: 50,000 bottles
Upbringing: Fermentations take place in temperature-controlled
stainless-steel vats. Wines are aged partly in vats and partly in oak

barrels that are renewed by a third in each vintage, for 18 months. They are fined and filtered.

SECOND WINE
None produced.

Evaluation of present classification: Should be maintained
Plateau of maturity: 3–15 years following the vintage

I have generally enjoyed the wines of Romer du Hayot, a small Sauternes estate located near the beautiful Château de Malle. The style of wine produced emphasizes a fresh fruity character, medium body, and moderate sweetness. The wine sees limited aging in barrels, so its exuberant fruitiness is not masked by spicy, oaky aromas and flavors.

While Romer du Hayot is a lighter-styled Sauternes, it has plenty of interest and generally ages well for 4–7 years. The 1983, 1979, 1976, and 1975 were all successful vintages for Romer du Hayot. Fortunately, the price asked for the wines from this little-known property is reasonable.

VINTAGES

1990—The 1990 Romer du Hayot exhibits a moderately intense, pineapple-scented
• nose, medium-bodied, ripe, sweet flavors, and a clean, fresh finish. It is an
86 uncomplicated, easygoing wine for drinking over the next 7–8 years. Last tasted, 11/94.

1989—The 1989 revealed excessive sulfur in the nose, combined with a pronounced
• pungent, dirty earthiness in the mouth. Behind the annoying off components
85? is a simple, medium-bodied, moderately sweet wine. Last tasted, 11/94.

1988—The 1988, a wine I have noted as possessing off aromas in the past, has gotten
• worse rather than better. Although there is good ripeness and concentration,
? the wine's skunky aromas are unpleasant. Last tasted, 11/94.

1986—Fully mature, this tasty, complex wine exhibits fine richness and length as
• well as evidence of botrytis in its honeyed peach, pear, and apricot flavors.
86 Anticipated maturity: Now. Last tasted, 3/90.

1985—Sweet, round, and aromatic, but one-dimensional, with monochromatic fla-
• vors, this medium-bodied, chunky Sauternes provides unexciting drinking.
78 Anticipated maturity: Now. Last tasted, 3/89.

SIGALAS RABAUD   VERY GOOD

Classification: First-growth in 1855
Location of vineyards: Bommes
Owner: Lambert des Granges family
Address: Bommes, 33210 Langon

Mailing address: c/o Domaines Cordier, 53, rue du Dehez, 33290
Blanquefort
Telephone: 33 5 56 95 53 00; telefax: 33 5 56 95 53 01
Visits: By appointment, Monday through Friday, from 9 A.M. to noon, and
2 P.M. to 5 P.M.
Contact: Bruno Laporte

VINEYARDS (white)
Surface area: 35 acres
Average age of vines: 45 years
Blend: 85% Semillon, 15% Sauvignon
Density of plantation: 6,666 vines per hectare
Average yields (over the last 5 years): 18 hectoliters per hectare
Total average annual production: 26,000 bottles

GRAND VIN (white)
Brand name: Château Sigalas Rabaud
Appellation: Sauternes
Mean annual production: 18,000 bottles
Upbringing: Fermentations take place in barrels at low temperatures (18
degrees centigrade). Wines are aged 20 months minimum in oak barrels
that are renewed by a third in each vintage, with regular racking every 3
months. They are fined and filtered.

SECOND WINE
Brand name: Cadet de Sigalas
Average annual production: 8,000 bottles

Evaluation of present classification: Since the early eighties it has
merited its Premier Cru Classé status
Plateau of maturity: 5–15 years following the vintage

This has always been a perplexing wine to evaluate. There is no question
that the ideal positioning of the south-facing vineyard on the hillsides of
Haut-Bommes, with gravelly clay soil, should produce exceptionally ripe
grapes. However, when tasting the wines of Sigalas Rabaud, I have always
sensed a certain laissez-faire attitude. Since the mid-1980s the wines have
improved significantly.

The style of wine produced at Sigalas Rabaud is much lighter and, at its
best, more elegant and graceful than several of its overblown, rich, and
alcoholic peers. Interestingly, the proprietors at this estate prefer to age their
wines in cement and stainless-steel vats rather than oak barrels. For that
reason, I always find Sigalas Rabaud to have one of the most exuberantly

fruity bouquets and tastes, no doubt pleasing to more wine enthusiasts than some of the aggressively alcoholic, thick, viscous, oaky giants found elsewhere in Sauternes.

VINTAGES

1990—Moderate gold colored, this is one of the finest wines produced at this château
•   in a number of years. Sweet *pain grillé*, toffee, and crème brûlée aromas are
91   dominated by an explosion of honeyed citrus and tropical fruit. Full bodied, sweet, unctuously textured, pure, and thick, with a Viognier-like over-ripe peach fruitiness in the flavors, this is a hefty, chewy, alcoholic Sauternes that should become more refined and subtle with extended cellaring. Anticipated maturity: 2002–2020. Last tasted, 3/97.

1989—This is an evolved wine, with an advanced medium gold color, a loosely knit
•   personality, medium body, some bitterness in the finish, but ripe toffee/apricot
88   fruit, low acidity, and earth and oak nuances. It is a muscular, forceful wine that is still slightly disjointed, although impressively large. The 1989 is not as rich or complete as either the 1988 or 1990. Anticipated maturity: Now–2015. Last tasted, 3/97.

1988—Typical of the vintage, the 1988 Sigalas Rabaud is a stylish, finesse-styled
•   Sauternes, with a lovely roasted/sweet honeyed character with melon, trop-
89   ical fruit, and vanillin scents. More restrained, and not as large, muscular, or sweet as either the 1989 or 1990, the 1988 is an elegant, complex, medium-weight wine that should drink well for 15 more years. Last tasted. 3/97.

1986—Sigalas Rabaud made a complex, elegant, botrytis-filled 1986. The honeyed,
•   flowery, spicy aromas leap from the glass in this beautifully proportioned
90   wine. In the mouth, there is fine acidity, some rich, honeyed, pear- and pineapple-like fruit, and a soft, yet adequately delineated, long, alcoholic finish. Anticipated maturity: Now–2002. Last tasted, 11/90.

1985—Elegant, stylish, and medium bodied, but essentially one-dimensional given
•   the lack of botrytis, this wine is already offering pleasant, satisfying drinking.
84   Anticipated maturity: Now. Last tasted, 11/90.

1983—The 1983 has an intensely fruity bouquet suggestive of pineapples, fine depth
•   and concentration, an unctuous quality, and crisp, fresh acidity. It is a very
86   fruity, moderately sweet, well-knit Sauternes. Anticipated maturity: Now. Last tasted, 1/85.

1982—The 1982 is a middle-of-the-road Sauternes, with good fruit, medium body,
•   and a pleasant finish; but like so many 1982s, it has no complexity. Antici-
75   pated maturity: Now. Last tasted, 1/85.

1981—Light but charming, with a fragrant, fruity, herbaceous, almost flowery bou-
•   quet, the 1981 seems to be a typically proportioned, medium-weight wine
80   from Sigalas Rabaud. Anticipated maturity: Now. Last tasted, 6/84.

1980—Rather one-dimensional and dull, the 1980 is light, not very concentrated,
•   and missing the usual fruity intensity and charm that this wine frequently
75   offers. Anticipated maturity: Now–may be in decline. Last tasted, 2/84.

1979—Quite appealing in a lighter, more refreshing manner, the 1979 Sigalas Ra-
  •　　baud has a moderately intense, fruity, minty, spicy bouquet, medium body,
  78　　not much botrytis, but crisp acidity and some sweetness. It is a charming
  　　　Sauternes. Anticipated maturity: Now. Last tasted, 9/83.

1976—Light, fruity, and typically Sigalas Rabaud, this medium-bodied wine has a
  •　　subtle perfume of pineapple fruit, good acidity, and moderately sweet, nicely
  80　　balanced flavors. It is fully mature. Anticipated maturity: Now—may be in
  　　　decline. Last tasted, 7/80.

1975—Highly touted by the château, this wine has more in common with a German
  •　　Auslese from the Mosel than a Sauternes. Flowery, rather simple and com-
  ?　　pact, this lean, atypical Sigalas Rabaud is also suffering from an intrusive
  　　　amount of sulfur dioxide. Last tasted, 3/86.

1971—This is another lightweight effort from Sigalas Rabaud, but it is graceful and
  •　　fruity, with a honeyed, fruity bouquet that is clean and fresh. Medium body,
  82　　moderately sweet flavors, and crisp acidity are admirably balanced. Antici-
  　　　pated maturity: Now. Last tasted, 3/81.

1967—Just beginning to lose its fruit and freshness, this has always been one of my
  •　　favorite vintages of Sigalas Rabaud. The antithesis of a powerhouse, oaky,
  85　　viscous Sauternes, the 1967 is moderately sweet and has a honeyed bouquet
  　　　of pineapples. Medium bodied and concentrated, but surprisingly light, this is
  　　　a textbook example of Sigalas Rabaud that requires consumption. Anticipated
  　　　maturity: Now. Last tasted, 3/87.

SUAU

Classification: Second-growth in 1855
Location of vineyards: Barsac
Owner: Roger Biarnès
Address: 33720 Barsac
Mailing address: c/o Château de Navarro, 33720 Illats
Telephone: 33 5 56 27 20 27; telefax: 33 5 56 27 26 53
Visits: Monday through Friday, between 9 A.M. and 6 P.M.
Contact: Nicole Biarnès

VINEYARDS (white)
Surface area: 19.8 acres
Average age of vines: 29 years
Blend: 80% Semillon, 10% Sauvignon, 10% Muscadelle
Density of plantation: 6,000 vines per hectare
Average yields (over the last 5 years): 20 hectoliters per hectare
Total average annual production: 19,000 bottles

GRAND VIN (white)
Brand name: Château Suau
Appellation: Barsac Sauternes

Mean annual production: 19,000 bottles
Upbringing: Fermentations take place at 20 degrees centigrade in
stainless-steel vats and last 2–3 weeks. Wines are aged 24 months, half
in stainless-steel tanks and half in oak barrels, one-third of which are
new. They are fined and filtered.

SECOND WINE
None produced.

Evaluation of present classification: Should be downgraded to a Cru
Bourgeois
Plateau of maturity: 3–10 years following the vintage

The tiny estate of Suau tucked away on a back road of Barsac is largely unknown. Much of the production is sold directly to consumers. The quality is
uninspiring. In general, this is a wine to consume within its first decade of life.

VINTAGES

1990—The 1990 is the most opulent, concentrated, and powerful Suau I have ever
• tasted. Big and full bodied, the wine now offers greater precision and com-
89 plexity in its nose, an improvement over its original monolithic personality. A
fine example of Suau, it should age well for 7–8 years. Last tasted, 11/94.

1989—The 1989 exhibits elegance combined with medium body, which is atypical
• for this fat, heavyweight vintage. The wine possesses considerable finesse, a
87 lovely apricot/pineapple–like fruitiness, and a crisp, fresh personality. It is
not a wine for aging, but, rather, one for drinking over the next 5–7 years.
Last tasted, 11/94.

1988—Given the fact that I never have had a high opinion of the 1988, I was not
• surprised by its mediocre showing. Last tasted, 11/94.
78

1986—Among the recent vintages, this is the best example of this Barsac I have
• tasted. An interesting bouquet of oranges and pineapples makes for a fine
85 initial impression. In the mouth, the wine is soft, unctuous, and very precocious. Anticipated maturity: Now. Last tasted, 11/90.

1985—This one-dimensional, chunky, muscular, relatively fat-styled wine with little
• complexity or character should be drunk over the next 2–3 years. Anticipated
79 maturity: Now. Last tasted, 11/90.

SUDUIRAUT   EXCELLENT

Classification: First-growth in 1855
Location of vineyards: Preignac, bordering Yquem
Owner: AXA Millésimes
Address: 33210 Preignac

Mailing address: Same as above
Telephone: 33 5 56 63 27 29; telefax: 33 5 56 63 07 00
Visits: By appointment only
Contact: Alain Pascaud

VINEYARDS (white)
Surface area: 217.4 acres
Average age of vines: 25 years
Blend: 90% Semillon, 10% Sauvignon
Density of plantation: 7,000 vines per hectare
Average yields (over the last 5 years): 15 hectoliters
Total average annual production: Variable

GRAND VIN (white)
Brand name: Château Suduiraut
Appellation: Sauternes Premier Grand Cru Classé
Mean annual production: Variable between 70,000 and 140,000 bottles
Upbringing: Fermentations take place in oak barrels (since 1992) and
last between 10 and 30 days. Wines are aged in oak barrels, 20%–30%
of which are new, for 18–24 months. Fining is done with bentonite, and
wines are filtered.

SECOND WINE
Brand name: Castelnau de Suduiraut
Average annual production: 24,000 bottles

Evaluation of present classification: Should be maintained
Plateau of maturity: 5–25 or more years following the vintage

Just down the road from Yquem, abutting Yquem's vineyards on the north, is the large, beautiful estate of Suduiraut. Suduiraut can be one of the great wines of Sauternes. For example, the 1959, 1967, 1976, 1982, 1988, 1989, and 1990 are staggering examples of Suduiraut's potential. At its best, Suduiraut turns out very rich, luscious wines that in blind tastings can be confused with Yquem. However, I have always been perplexed by the shocking inconsistency in quality of the wines from this estate. In the first half of the seventies, Suduiraut produced several wines well below acceptable standards.

When Suduiraut is good, it is very, very good. In great vintages, the wine needs a decade to be at its best but will keep easily for 25 years. Richly colored, quite perfumed, and decadently rich, even massive in the top years, Suduiraut, while less consistent than properties like Climens and Rieussec, appears to now be back on track.

In 1982 and 1989 the château produced a sumptuous, super quality, rare, and expensive Crème de Tête—Cuvée Madame. This cuvée, much like the limited edition Cuvée Madame of Château Coutet, is capable of rivaling Yquem, but the production is minuscule—fewer than 1,000 cases.

VINTAGES

1990—The evolved, medium gold color of the 1990 is prematurely advanced, raising
•   questions about future longevity. The 1990 possesses plenty of intensity and
88   an unctuous, thick, juicy style, but high alcohol and coarseness kept my
       rating down. Last tasted, 11/94.

1989—The 1989 is well balanced, but its fruit does not appear to be sufficient to
•   stand up to the wine's high alcohol and aggressive style. It offers little delinea-
89   tion, so cellaring should prove beneficial, as it has admirable levels of extract.
       Last tasted, 11/94.

1989—Cuvée Madame: This is an extraordinary Sauternes. Fabulously concentrated,
•   with an unctuous texture and what must be nearly 14%–15% natural alcohol,
96   this mammoth-size Sauternes should prove to be one of the monumental
       efforts of the vintage. For those who prefer power and finesse, the 1988 may
       take preference; for those who want pure brute strength and unbelievable
       size, the 1989 Cuvée Madame is without equal. Anticipated maturity: 2000–
       2025. Last tasted, 4/91.

1988—The 1988 reveals a textbook, light gold color with a slight greenish hue.
•   Although it does not display the weight of the 1990 or 1989, it has better
88?   acidity, high alcohol, and considerable sweetness. It is somewhat disjointed,
       needing time to knit together. It is impressive if its components are evaluated
       separately, but it is less noteworthy when reviewed from an overall perspec-
       tive. Last tasted, 11/94.

1986—I would have expected Suduiraut to be outstanding in 1986, but it is not. It is
•   very good, but this wine should have been a classic. Plump, rich, honeyed,
87   pineapple, coconut, and buttery fruit flavors abound in this full-bodied, rich
       wine that falls just short of being profound. It is muscular and rich, but it is
       missing an element of complexity that I found in many other 1986s. Also, is it
       possible that the 1986 Suduiraut has less botrytis than the other top examples
       from this vintage? Anticipated maturity: Now–2008. Last tasted, 3/90.

1985—Shockingly light, with straightforward, bland, even innocuous flavors, this
•   fruity yet one-dimensional Suduiraut is disappointing given the reputation of
79   the château. Anticipated maturity: Now. Last tasted, 3/90.

1983—This looks to be a good Suduiraut. A medium golden color, with a very
•   honeyed, rich, floral bouquet, this full-bodied wine is not as profound as the
87   other 1983s. Sweet, with fine honeyed flavors, this is an elegant, graceful
       Suduiraut with plenty of character. However, given the vintage, I had expected
       even more. Anticipated maturity: Now–2005. Last tasted, 3/90.

1982—Cuvée Madame: The 1982 vintage, while great for Bordeaux's red wines, is
•   not special for the sweet wines. However, the 1982 Suduiraut Cuvée Madame
90   is a smashing success. The *régisseur* thought this was the best wine made at

the property since the great 1967 and 1959. Only the grapes harvested before the rains fell were used, and the result is a very concentrated, deep, luscious, honeyed wine, with great length, the buttery, viscous richness that Suduiraut is famous for, and superb balance. If it had just a trifle more botrytis character, it would be perfect. Anticipated maturity: Now–2010. Last tasted, 3/90.

1981—A very attractive, elegant Suduiraut, the 1981 does not have the richness of
• the 1982 or 1983 but is agreeably forward, spicy, and ripe, with less power
84 and concentration than normal. It is clearly well made and moderately sweet. Anticipated maturity: Now. Last tasted, 3/84.

1979—One of the top 1979s, Suduiraut has produced an uncommonly rich, deep,
• powerful wine for this vintage. The wine is medium golden, with a ripe, toasty,
86 caramel-and-apricot-scented bouquet, full body, plenty of viscous fruit, and a long finish. Anticipated maturity: Now. Last tasted, 3/84.

1978—A down-scaled version of the 1979, the 1978 is elegant, less sweet, and
• significantly less rich, with medium body, fairly light texture for a Suduiraut,
83 and good acidity. Anticipated maturity: Now. Last tasted, 3/86.

1976—For me, the 1976 is the greatest Suduiraut of the seventies and the only
• wine other than the 1989 that resembles the magnificent 1959 this property
92 produced. Medium to dark amber/gold, this full-bodied, massive wine has a very intense bouquet of vanillin oak, ripe pineapples, and melted caramel. Very deep and viscous, this is a decadently opulent Suduiraut with enormous presence in the mouth. Anticipated maturity: Now–2010. Last tasted, 3/90.

1975—Produced when Suduiraut was in a slump, this wine, from an excellent vin-
• tage, has good ripeness but is shockingly light and a little too simple and
78 one-dimensional for a top-rated estate. The finish also leaves a lot to be desired. Anticipated maturity: Now. Last tasted, 6/82.

1971—Pleasant, but light and rather meagerly endowed, the 1971 Suduiraut, while
• agreeable and quite palatable, is a disappointment for a wine from this estate.
75 I have not tasted it recently, but this wine is probably in decline. Last tasted, 2/78.

1970—A good Suduiraut, but despite the concentration and depth, it tastes flabby,
• overly alcoholic, and just too one-dimensional. Anticipated maturity: Now–
80 may be in decline. Last tasted, 8/81.

1969—Surprisingly rich, fruity, and mouth-filling, the 1969 Suduiraut is one of a
• number of 1969 Sauternes that turned out considerably better than their red
78 wine siblings. Anticipated maturity: Now–may be in decline. Last tasted, 6/77.

1967—A classic vintage for Suduiraut, this rich, full-bodied, expansive, viscous,
• fully mature wine has a wonderful honeyed, almond, caramel-scented bou-
89 quet, rich, sweet, deep, succulent flavors, full body, and a muscular, aggressive finish. The 1967 is perhaps not a match for the 1959 or 1976, but it is certainly the best wine produced at this château between these two vintages. Anticipated maturity: Now–2000. Last tasted, 3/88.

OLDER VINTAGES

In the tasting notes I alluded to the great 1959 Suduiraut produced. I have consistently rated this wine between 92 and 94 on the occasions I have tasted it (most recently 12/89). Among the other vintages for which I have notes, I have given excellent ratings to the 1945 (rated 90 in 11/86) and the 1947 (rated 93 in 7/87). I have never seen a pre–World War II vintage, but the 1928 and 1899 are considered legendary years for this estate. The other years I have tasted, 1949 and 1955, left me unmoved.

LA TOUR BLANCHE   EXCELLENT

Classification: First-growth in 1855
Location of vineyards: Bommes
Owner: Ministry of Agriculture (France)
Address: 33210 Bommes
Mailing address: Same as above
Telephone: 33 5 57 98 02 73; telefax: 33 5 57 98 02 78
Visits: Monday through Friday

VINEYARDS (white)
Surface area: 89 acres
Average age of vines: 24 years
Blend: 77% Semillon, 17% Sauvignon, 6% Muscadelle
Density of plantation: 6,000 vines per hectare
Average yields (over the last 5 years): 11 hectoliters per hectare
Total average annual production: 50,000 bottles

GRAND VIN (white)
Brand name: Château La Tour Blanche
Appellation: Sauternes
Mean annual production: 40,000 bottles
Upbringing: Fermentations are carried out in new oak barrels for the Semillon and in vats for Sauvignon and Muscadelle. Wines are aged 20 months in new oak barrels, fined and filtered.

SECOND WINE
Brand name: Les Charmilles de la Tour Blanche
Average annual production: 6,000 bottles

Evaluation of present classification: Since 1986 the quality of La Tour Blanche has increased dramatically, with truly compelling wines being made in 1988, 1989, and 1990; the château now merits its classification
Plateau of maturity: 5–30 years following the vintage

La Tour Blanche was ranked in the top of its class right behind Yquem in the 1855 classification of the wines of the Sauternes region. Since 1910 the Ministry of Agriculture has run La Tour Blanche and until the mid-1980s seemed content to produce wines that at best could be called mediocre. That has changed significantly with the employment of 100% new oak beginning in 1988, followed by a complete fermentation of the 1989 in new oak barrels. The cellars are completely air-conditioned, and the yields have been reduced to a meager 11 hectoliters per hectare. All things considered, La Tour Blanche looks to be one of the up-and-coming superstars of the appellation of Sauternes during the nineties. Fortunately, prices have not yet caught up with La Tour Blanche's new quality.

There are also small quantities of a second wine made from weaker vats, as well as two different dry Bordeaux blancs.

VINTAGES

1990—The 1990 is less aromatic, but richer and fuller bodied than the 1988 La Tour
 • 　Blanche. It has not lost any of its elegant, honeyed, botrytised style. The 1990
 92 　comes across as fat and rich, a classic Sauternes that remains under-priced
 　　given the resurgence of this well-known estate. It will keep for 3 decades or
 　　more. Last tasted, 11/94.

1989—Although loosely structured, the 1989 reveals plenty of intense, honeyed fruit
 • 　in a rich, authoritative, full-bodied format. A big, powerhouse, sweet, heavy
 90 　wine with a penetrating fragrance of honey and flowers, this generously en-
 　　dowed wine already drinks well but can easily last for 15–20 years. Last
 　　tasted, 11/94.

1988—The 1988 exhibits superb richness, plenty of botrytis, creamy, honeyed, tropi-
 • 　cal fruit (pineapples galore), wonderfully integrated, toasty oak, crisp acidity,
 92 　and a rich, full-bodied, long finish. The wine is just beginning to evolve, and
 　　it is clearly capable of lasting for 25–35 years. Last tasted, 11/94.

1986—When I tasted this wine from cask I thought it would be better. But it
 • 　has turned out to be a relatively straightforward, compact, monolithic-styled
 82 　Sauternes, with good fruit but without the great underlying depth and evi-
 　　dence of botrytis one normally sees in this vintage. It should provide good
 　　but uninspired drinking for another decade or more. Anticipated maturity:
 　　Now–2003. Last tasted, 3/90.

1985—Normally the 1985 Sauternes are less impressive than the 1986s, but La Tour
 • 　Blanche's 1985 comes across as more concentrated, with greater intensity
 84 　and length than the 1986. Nevertheless, there is still a glaring lack of com-
 　　plexity and botrytis. Anticipated maturity: Now–2001. Last tasted, 3/90.

OLDER VINTAGES

The finest older vintage of La Tour Blanche I have had the privilege of tasting was a very fine example of the 1975 (rated 87 in 1990). It was still youthful when tasted at age 15.

YQUEM

OUTSTANDING *

Classification: Premier Cru Supérieur in 1855
Location of vineyards: Sauternes
Owner: Lur Saluces family
Address: 33210 Sauternes
Mailing address: Same as above
Telephone: 33 5 57 98 07 07; telefax: 33 5 57 98 07 08
Visits: By appointment, Monday through Friday, between 2:30 P.M. and
4 P.M.
Contact: Valérie Lailheugue

VINEYARDS (white)
Surface area: 259 acres (in production)
Average age of vines: 27 years
Blend: 80% Semillon, 20% Sauvignon
Density of plantation: 6,600 vines per hectare
Average yields (over the last 5 years): 10 hectoliters per hectare
Total average annual production: 100,000 bottles

GRAND VIN (white)
Brand name: Château d'Yquem
Appellation: Sauternes
Mean annual production: 100,000 bottles
Upbringing: Wines are fermented and aged 3½ years in new oak barrels.
They are fined and lightly filtered.

SECOND WINE
None produced.

NOTE: This estate also produces a dry white Bordeaux wine called
"Y d'Yquem."
* Evaluation of present classification: Probably the only Bordeaux wine
that truly can be said to be in a class by itself
Plateau of maturity: 10–70 years or more following the vintage; top
vintages can actually last for over 100 years

Yquem, located in the heart of the Sauternes region, sits magnificently atop a small hill overlooking the surrounding vineyards of many of the Premiers Crus Classés. Between 1785 and 1997 this estate was in the hands of just one family. Comte Alexandre de Lur Saluces is the most recent member of this family to have responsibility for managing this vast estate, having taken over for his uncle in 1968. In 1997 the estate was sold to the giant Moët-Hennessy conglomerate, but the sale was contested by Comte de Lur Saluces.

At the time of writing, no legal decision about the legitimacy of the sale had been rendered by France's judicial system.

Yquem's greatness and uniqueness are certainly a result of a number of factors. First, it has a perfect location with its own microclimate. Second, the Lur Saluces family installed an elaborate drainage system with over 60 miles of pipes. Third, there is a fanatical obsession at Yquem to produce only the finest wines regardless of financial loss or trouble. It is this last factor that is the biggest reason Yquem is so superior to its neighbors.

At Yquem they proudly boast that only 1 glass of wine per vine is produced. The grapes are picked at perfect maturity one by one by a group of 150 pickers who frequently spend 6–8 weeks at Yquem and go through the vineyard a minimum of four separate times. In 1964 they canvased the vineyard thirteen separate times, only to have harvested grapes that were deemed unsuitable, leaving Yquem with no production whatsoever in that vintage. Few winemaking estates are willing or financially able to declassify the entire crop. However, no wine has been produced at Yquem in 1964, 1972, or 1974.

Yquem has unbelievable aging possibilities. Because it is so rich, opulent, and sweet, much is drunk before it ever reaches its tenth birthday. However, Yquem almost always needs 15–20 years to show best, and the great vintages will be fresh and decadently rich for as long as 50 or more years. The greatest Yquem I ever drank was the 1921. It was remarkably fresh and alive, with a luxuriousness and richness I shall never forget.

This passionate commitment to quality does not stop in the vineyard. The wine is aged for over 3 years in new oak casks, at a loss of 20% of the total crop volume due to evaporation. Even when the Comte de Lur Saluces deems the wine ready for bottling, a severe selection of only the best casks is made. In excellent years, such as 1975, 1976, and 1980, 20% of the barrels were eliminated. In difficult years, such as 1979, 60% of the wine was declassified, and in the troublesome vintage of 1978, 85% of the wine was declared unworthy of being sold as Yquem. To my knowledge, no other property has such a ruthless selection process. Yquem is never filtered for fear of removing some of the richness.

Yquem also produces a dry wine called "Y." It is a distinctive wine, with a bouquet not unlike that of Yquem, but oaky and dry to taste and usually very full bodied and noticeably alcoholic. It is a powerful wine and, to my palate, best served with a rich food such as foie gras. Yquem, unlike other famous Bordeaux wines, is not sold *en primeur* or as a wine future. The wine is usually released 4 years after the vintage at a very high price, but given the labor involved, the risk, and the brutal selection process, it is one of the few luxury-priced wines that merits a stratospheric price tag.

VINTAGES

1990—An extraordinary effort in this powerful, blockbuster vintage, Yquem's 1990
•   is the richest of the fabulous trilogy of superb sweet wine vintages in Bordeaux
99   —1988, 1989, 1990. This wine also possesses more elegance and finesse
than many 1990s, at least at this stage of their development. The wine's
medium gold color is accompanied by an exceptionally sweet nose of honeyed
tropical fruits, peaches, and apricots. High-quality, subtle toasty oak is well
integrated. The wine is massive on the palate, with layers of intensely ripe
botrytis-tinged fruit. Surprisingly good acidity and a seamless, full-bodied
power and richness are remarkably harmonious and pure. It is tempting to
compare this wine with such behemoths as the 1989 and 1983. Certainly it is
one of the richest Yquems I have ever tasted, with 50–75 years potential
longevity. It should mature at a quicker pace than either the 1989 or 1986,
but all of these wines can easily last 50+ years. Anticipated maturity: 2003–
2050+. Last tasted, 11/97.

1989—The favorite sweet wine of millionaires, Château d'Yquem has, not unexpect-
•   edly, turned in a brilliant effort with their 1989. It is a large-scale, massively
97+   rich, unctuously textured wine that should evolve effortlessly for a half century or more. It does not reveal the compelling finesse and complexity of the
1988 or 1986, but it is a far heavier, richer wine than either of those vintages.
It is reminiscent of the 1976, with additional fat and glycerin. The wine is
extremely alcoholic and rich, with a huge nose of smoky, honey-covered
coconuts and over-ripe pineapples and apricots. As with most young vintages
of Yquem, the wine's structure is barely noticeable. These wines are so highly
extracted and rich, yet approachable young, it is difficult to believe they will
last for 50 or more years. The 1989 is the richest Yquem made in the eighties,
and it has an edge in complexity over the powerhouse 1983. It remains to be
seen whether this wine will develop the extraordinary aromatic complexity
possessed by the promising 1988 and 1986 Yquems. Last tasted, 11/97.

1988—The 1988 is a more backward-styled Yquem, built along the lines of the
•   extraordinary 1975. With a honeyed, smoky, orange/coconut/pineapple-
99   scented nose, this powerful wine possesses full body, layers of highly concentrated, extracted flavors, considerable botrytis, and a sensational finish. Last
tasted, 12/97.

1986—This is another fascinating effort. With greater evidence of botrytis than the
•   colossal 1983, but less power and alcohol, the 1986 Yquem tastes reminiscent
98   of the 1975, only more precocious, as well as more concentrated. Several
highly respected Bordeaux *négociants* who are Yquem enthusiasts claim the
1986 Yquem is the greatest wine produced at the property since the legendary
1937. Its enthralling bouquet of pineapples, sautéed hazelnuts, vanillin, and
ripe apricots is breathtaking. Compellingly concentrated, this wine, in
breadth as well as depth of flavor, seemingly knows no limits. This full-
bodied, powerful, yet impeccably balanced Yquem should provide memorable
drinking for 40–55 more years. Like the 1983, this is another winemaking
tour de force. Anticipated maturity: 2000–2040. Last tasted, 4/91.

1985—The 1985 Yquem is a very powerful, rich, exceptionally concentrated wine.
•   Yet because of the lack of botrytis in the vineyards during this hot, dry
89   vintage, the wine does not have the complexity so frequently encountered.
Nevertheless, this massive, unctuous, light golden–colored Yquem makes
quite a mouthful of wine given the honeyed flavors. It is hard to know when a
wine such as this will be fully mature, but I have no hesitation saying that it
will certainly last for 25–30 or more years. But I do not see it ever being
among the great Yquems. Anticipated maturity: Now–2025. Last tasted, 3/90.

1984—This is a surprisingly good wine made under very trying conditions. Yquem
•   began to harvest on October 15 and made the last pass through the vineyards
87   on November 13. Seventy-five percent of the crop was retained for Yquem.
The wine at present exhibits a great deal of toasty oak in the bouquet, which
is also filled with scents of smoked almonds, glazed pineapples, and honey
and caramel. In the mouth, the wine is less flamboyant, with less glycerin and
power than usual, but it is still a rich, full-bodied Yquem with a great deal of
personality and character. It will not have the great aging potential of the top
vintages, but I fully expect it to last at least another 20 years. Anticipated
maturity: Now–2008. Last tasted, 3/90.

1983—The 1983 is among the most concentrated wines from this property over the
•   last 20 years, with a staggering display of extract and a mind-boggling amount
96   of glycerin. The vintage commenced early for Yquem, beginning on September
29 and finishing on November 18. Most observers feel the 1983 will mature
more slowly than the 1986 and will last for almost 100 years. Given Yquem's
unbelievable aging potential, such comments do not seem farfetched. At
present, the 1983 is enormous, with huge, honeyed, pineapple, coconut, and
caramel flavors, massive extract, and an unctuous quality barely framed by
acidity and new oak. I do not feel the wine has changed since bottling, and I
would not want to start drinking it for at least another 10–15 years. Anticipated maturity: 2005–2050. Last tasted, 12/90.

1982—This vintage, seriously maligned because of the rains that plagued the harvest
•   in Sauternes, was actually outstanding for both Yquem and its nearby neigh-
92   bor, Château Suduiraut, which brought in much of their crops before the rains
did any damage. Yquem then waited until the vineyards dried out, bringing
in their last grapes on November 7. The 1982 is a very forward style of
Yquem, plump, succulent, with honeyed pineapple, peach, and apricot flavors, exhibiting some, but not a great deal of, botrytis. In the mouth, it is
massive, thick, and almost as impressive as the 1983, but one does not sense
the same degree of length or potential complexity. Nevertheless, this is still a
great Yquem that has been somewhat overlooked because of the attention
lavished on the 1983 and 1986. Anticipated maturity: Now–2020. Last tasted,
12/90.

1981—The 1981 is certainly an outstanding Yquem, but it will not be considered
•   one of this property's greatest efforts. Light golden, with a moderately intense
90   bouquet of spicy, vanillin oak, fresh melons, and tropical fruit, this full-bodied
Yquem has average acidity and a plump, viscous, somewhat precocious feel

on the palate. Remarkably long and clean in the finish, it will develop relatively rapidly. Anticipated maturity: Now–2015. Last tasted, 3/87.

1980—This year is a perfect example of a vintage that was much better for the sweet
•   wines of Barsac and Sauternes than it was for the red wines. Yquem produced
93   its greatest wine since the twin titans of 1975 and 1976. Medium golden, with
       a big, opulent, honeyed, oaky, flowery, tropical fruit bouquet, this wine is rich
       and concentrated, has very good acidity, a lot of botrytis, and a stunning
       finish. It is a great success, and it continues to evolve at a snail's pace.
       Anticipated maturity: Now–2035. Last tasted, 12/90.

1979—This is an immensely attractive Yquem, yet it seems to be missing something.
•   Light golden, with Yquem's typically oaky, spicy, buttery, ripe bouquet, it is
88   only slightly more reserved than usual. On the palate, this full-bodied wine
       is intense and well balanced but falls just a trifle short in the finish. The 1979
       Yquem is not as powerful or as rich as this wine can be in the top vintages.
       Only 40% of the crop was retained. Anticipated maturity: Now–2020. Last
       tasted, 12/90.

1978—The 1978 vintage was extremely difficult for the wine producers in Barsac
•   and Sauternes. Unlike the red wines, which benefited from a late yet excellent
87   harvest, the whites suffered from weather that was not humid enough for the
       formation of the noble rot. While the wines are rich, full bodied, and viscous,
       they lack character and often taste dull. Yquem's 1978 is the best wine
       produced in the appellation. It is rich and honeyed, with excellent concentra-
       tion and plenty of alcohol and body. Unfortunately, it does not have the
       majestic bouquet and complex flavors and aromas that can result only from
       rampant botrytis-infected grapes. Only 15% of the crop went into Yquem.
       Anticipated maturity: Now–2008. Last tasted, 12/90.

1977—In what was a miserable vintage, Yquem managed to produce a toasty, ripe,
•   pineapple-and-buttery-scented wine with a predominate oaky character. Sev-
85   enty percent of the crop was eliminated in 1977, and the result is a wine that
       may well turn out to be almost as good as the underrated 1973. Anticipated
       maturity: Now–2000. Last tasted, 2/84.

1976—The 1976 Yquem continues to go from strength to strength. Who can ignore
•   the awesome bouquet of spices, honeyed fruit, pineapples, bananas, coconuts,
96   and overripe melons? This full-bodied, viscous, luscious wine has been abso-
       lutely delicious since bottling, given its relatively low acidity and precocious
       personality. It is one of the few true great vintages of Yquem that can actually
       be drunk with tremendous pleasure at such a young age. Eighty percent of
       the harvest made it into the final wine. Anticipated maturity: Now–2025. Last
       tasted, 5/97.

1975—The 1975 may turn out to be the greatest of the modern-day Yquems. When
•   fully mature in another 25–30 years, it may rival the extraordinary 1937 and
99   1921. This wine continues to evolve at a stubbornly slow pace. It is far more
       backward than recent vintages such as 1983 and 1986. Nevertheless, it is
       awesomely concentrated, has perfect balance, and displays the telltale Yquem
       aromas of vanillin oak, tropical fruit, pineapples, honeyed peaches, and

grilled almonds. There is exceptionally crisp acidity that pulls all of the massive extract into precise focus. This is a wine of astonishing power and finesse, with a finish that must be tasted to be believed. It is a monumental effort that may well justify a perfect score in another decade. Anticipated maturity: 2005–2060. Last tasted, 5/97.

1973—Surprisingly successful in what was a mediocre vintage for the wines of this
  •   region, the 1973 Yquem is overtly oaky and too spicy but has very good
  86   concentration and less sweetness and botrytis than in vintages like 1975 and 1976 and is well balanced, fat, and long on the palate (only 12% of the crop was used for Yquem). Anticipated maturity: Now. Last tasted, 3/84.

1971—This is an outstanding Yquem, but I have been plagued by bad bottles in
  •   tastings, which I hope is attributable only to poor storage and handling. The
  91   top bottles exhibit plenty of ripe, concentrated tropical fruit and botrytis. Full bodied, deep golden in color, with a spicy, caramel, toasted *rôti*, fat flavor, this big, rich wine is developing quickly for an Yquem. Although irrefutably outstanding, this may be a slightly overrated vintage for Yquem. Anticipated maturity: Now–2010. Last tasted, 6/98.

1970—Somewhat less evolved than the 1971, and for me always a shade less interest-
  •   ing and complex, the 1970 Yquem is a large-scaled, rich, full-bodied, fairly
  90   alcoholic Yquem with significant flavor interest as well as crisp acidity. Unlike the 1971, which is close to peak maturity, this wine has a long way to go and is impressive but not yet revealing all its potential. Anticipated maturity: Now–2025. Last tasted, 11/84.

1967—Based solely on the strength of what is unquestionably a great Yquem, many
  •   have concluded that 1967 was a superb vintage for Sauternes. The truth is
  96   that 1967 was a very good but irregular vintage. As for Yquem, it is close to perfection. Medium amber/golden, with a full-intensity bouquet of vanillin spice, honey, ripe pineapples, and coconut, this intense, very ripe, unctuous Yquem has layers of sweet, opulent fruit, excellent balance, and a hefty, powerful finish. Almost too big and rich to be served with food, this wine should be drunk alone as a dessert. Anticipated maturity: Now–2035. Last tasted, 6/98.

1966—The 1966 is a very good wine, but for Yquem it is mediocre. Not nearly as
  •   rich and intense as one would expect, this wine is still big, a trifle clumsy,
  85   and too oaky, but enjoyable. Anticipated maturity: Now–2000. Last tasted, 1/82.

1962—This is an excellent, even outstanding, Yquem, but I must admit to being less
  •   impressed with it than others who have ecstatically called it one of the
  90   greatest Yquems produced. It is rich and honeyed, with a spicy, oaky, tropical fruit aroma, rich butterscotch, toasted fruit, and caramel flavors, and an astringent, dry, slightly coarse finish that, for me, keeps it from getting higher marks. Anticipated maturity: Now–2025. Last tasted, 11/82.

1961—The year 1961 was only a mediocre vintage for Barsac and Sauternes; how-
  •   ever, the sales of these wines have long been helped by the greatness of this
  84   vintage for the red wines of Bordeaux. I have consistently found Yquem's

1961 to be a muscular, out-of-balance wine, with a burnt character to the bouquet and overly oaky, aggressive flavors that lack this estate's ripeness and great richness. The wine is now beginning to dry out and become more awkward. Drink it up. Anticipated maturity: Now. Last tasted, 4/82.

OLDER VINTAGES

There is no doubt that the two most profound and mature Yquems made in the twentieth century were the 1921 (rated 100 on two separate occasions, most recently 9/96) and the 1937 (rated between 96 and 99 on three separate occasions in the late 1980s). After those two vintages, there are a number of superb Yquems that I have had the good fortune to taste, but frankly, none have matched the 1921 and 1937. My favorites in order of preference are 1928 (rated 97 in 4/91), 1929 (rated 97 in 3/90), 1959 (rated between 94 and 96 on three occasions in the late 1980s), and 1945 (rated 91 in 10/95). The 1945 is, by all responsible accounts, a magnificent wine. However, the bottle I tasted in October 1995 was brown and slightly maderized, although well perfumed, but drying out. With any tasting of a wine over 20 years of age, it should be remembered that "there are no great wines, only great bottles." Although I have tasted the 1947 only once (that is my birth year), I was surprised by how dry the wine tasted, without the fat and sweetness one finds in the great vintages of Yquem.

With respect to vintages from the nineteenth century, I had the good fortune to taste four nineteenth-century vintages at a tasting in October 1995. The 1825 Yquem (89 points) displayed a dark gold color and tasted nearly dry after having lost its fruit. It revealed high acidity in its crème brûlée–like flavors and finish. The very dry, earthy 1814 Yquem (67 points) possessed a dark gold color and an unattractive mustiness that obliterated any fruit that may have remained intact. However, the 1811 Yquem (100 points), with its dark gold color, awesomely intense, sweet nose, unctuous, thick, fabulous flavor extraction, pinpoint precision, and a finish that lasted a minute or more, is the kind of wine on which Yquem's reputation is based. It was liquefied crème brûlée—an astonishing wine. Remember, this was the famous "year of the comet" vintage. (Incidentally, readers looking for a few good chuckles should rent the movie video Year of the Comet, a wine-dominated comedy that I highly recommend.) The 1847 Yquem (100 points) would have received more than 100 points if possible. The wine is massive, with a surprisingly youthful color, remarkable honeyed and botrytised flavors, staggering richness, and a finish that lasted 40+ seconds. The question that must be asked is whether the great modern-day Yquem vintages will last as long. I say, yes, though I doubt any of my readers will live long enough to find out what the 1975, 1976, 1983, 1986, 1988, 1989, or 1990 will taste like at age 148!

OTHER BARSAC/SAUTERNES ESTATES

ANDOYSE DU HAYOT

Classification: None
Location of vineyards: Barsac
Owner: S.C.E. Vignobles du Hayot
Address: 33720 Barsac
Mailing address: Same as above
Telephone: 33 5 56 27 15 37; telefax: 33 5 56 27 04 24
Visits: Monday through Friday, between 8 A.M. and noon, and 2 P.M. and 6 P.M.

VINEYARDS (white)
Surface area: 49.4 acres
Average age of vines: 35 years
Blend: 70% Semillon, 25% Sauvignon, 5% Muscadelle
Density of plantation: 6,500 vines per hectare
Average yields (over the last 5 years): 25 hectoliters per hectare
Total average annual production: 65,000 bottles

GRAND VIN (white)
Brand name: Château Andoyse du Hayot
Appellation: Sauternes
Mean annual production: 65,000 bottles
Upbringing: Fermentations take place in temperature-controlled stainless-steel tanks. Wines are aged partly in tanks and partly in oak barrels (renewed by one-third at each vintage) for 18 months. They are fined and filtered.

SECOND WINE
None produced.

ARCHE PUGNEAU   EXCELLENT

Classification: None
Location of vineyards: Bommes, Preignac, Sauternes, and Barsac
Owner: Jean-Francis Daney
Address: 24, Le Biton, Boutoc, 33210 Preignac
Mailing address: Same as above
Telephone: 33 5 56 63 50 55; telefax: 33 5 56 63 39 69

Visits: Preferably by appointment, especially during weekends; on weekdays, between 9 A.M. and 8 P.M.
Contact: Jean-Pierre or Jean-Francis Daney, telephone 33 5 56 63 24 84

VINEYARDS (white)
Surface area: Approximately 32 acres
Average age of vines: 40 years
Blend: 75% Semillon, 20% Sauvignon, 5% Muscadelle
Density of plantation: 7,000 vines per hectare
Average yields (over the last 5 years): 16 hectoliters per hectare
Total average annual production: 192 hectoliters

GRAND VIN (Special Cuvée)
Brand name: Cru d'Arche Pugneau Trie Exceptionnelle
Appellation: Sauternes
Mean annual production: 0–85 hectoliters
Upbringing: Fermentations may last between 15 and 40 days in oak barrels (relatively new). Wines are aged 36 months, and are fined and filtered.

GRAND VIN
Brand name: Cru d'Arche Pugneau
Average annual production: 0–192 hectoliters (aged 24–38 months)

This property is well worth searching out, as the wines are exceptionally well made and clearly compete with the top classified growths of Barsac/Sauternes. I have had remarkable wines from Cru d'Arche Pugneau, which I rated in the mid-90s, particularly vintages from the late eighties. Even the 1991 was an amazing wine. Readers should look for the limited cuvée called Cru d'Arche Pugneau Trie Exceptionnelle, a wine that can approach Yquem– and Coutet Cuvée Madame–like richness and intensity. This is a virtually unknown estate that makes terrific wines.

BARREJATS

Classification: None
Location of vineyards: Barsac, between Châteaux Climens and Caillou
Owner: Mireille Daret and Philippe Andurand
Address: Clos de Gensac, Mareuil, 33210 Pujols sur Ciron
Mailing address: Same as above
Telephone: 33 5 56 76 69 06; telefax: 33 5 56 76 69 06
Visits: By appointment only
Contact: Mireille Daret

VINEYARDS (white)
Surface area: 6.6 acres
Average age of vines: 40 years
Blend: 85% Semillon, 10% Sauvignon, 5% Muscadelle
Density of plantation: 6,600 vines per hectare
Average yields (over the last 5 years): 16 hectoliters per hectare
Total average annual production: 5,600 bottles

GRAND VIN (white)
Brand name: Cru Barrejats
Appellation: Sauternes
Mean annual production: 2,400–3,600 bottles
Upbringing: Fermentations take place in new oak barrels in which wines
are aged for 18–36 months. They are fined and filtered.

SECOND WINE
Brand name: Accabailles de Barrejats
Average annual production: 1,200–3,000 bottles

CANTEGRIL

Classification: None
Location of vineyards: Barsac
Owner: Pierre and Denis Dubourdieu
Address: 33720 Barsac
Mailing address: Same as above
Telephone: 33 5 56 27 15 84; telefax: 33 5 56 27 18 99
Visits: By appointment only

VINEYARDS (white)
Surface area: 49.4 acres
Average age of vines: 35 years
Blend: 70% Semillon, 20% Sauvignon, 10% Muscadelle
Total average annual production: 50,000–60,000 bottles

GRAND VIN (white)
Brand name: Château Cantegril
Appellation: Barsac-Sauternes
Mean annual production: 50,000–60,000 bottles
Upbringing: Fermentations (with addition of yeasts, no temperature
control) take place in oak barrels that are renewed by one-third in each

vintage. Wines are aged 24 months, with regular rackings every 3 months. They are fined with bentonite and filtered.

SECOND WINE
None produced.

GRAVAS

Classification: Cru Bourgeois
Location of vineyards: Barsac
Owner: Bernard family
Address: Domaines Bernard, 33210 Barsac
Mailing address: Same as above
Telephone: 33 5 56 27 06 91; telefax: 33 5 56 27 29 83
Visits: Every day
Contact: P. Bernard

VINEYARDS (white)
Surface area: 27.2 acres
Average age of vines: 40 years
Blend: 90% Semillon, 10% Muscadelle
Density of plantation: 6,600 vines per hectare
Average yields (over the last 5 years): 25 hectoliters per hectare
Total average annual production: 240 hectoliters

GRAND VIN (white)
Brand name: Château Gravas
Appellation: Sauternes
Mean annual production: 30,000 bottles
Upbringing: Fermentations take place in vats, and wines are aged in vats (50%) and oak barrels (50%). They are fined and filtered.

SECOND WINE
None produced.

GUITERONDE DU HAYOT

Classification: None
Location of vineyards: Barsac
Owner: S.C.E. Vignobles du Hayot
Address: 33720 Barsac
Mailing address: Same as above

Telephone: 33 5 56 27 15 37; telefax: 33 5 56 27 04 24
Visits: Monday through Friday, between 8 A.M. and noon, and 2 P.M. and
6 P.M.

VINEYARDS (white)
Surface area: 86.5 acres
Average age of vines: 35 years
Blend: 70% Semillon, 25% Sauvignon, 5% Muscadelle
Density of plantation: 6,500 vines per hectare
Average yields (over the last 5 years): 25 hectoliters per hectare
Total average annual production: 100,000 bottles

GRAND VIN (white)
Brand name: Château Guiteronde du Hayot
Appellation: Sauternes
Mean annual production: 100,000 bottles
Upbringing: Fermentations take place in temperature-controlled
stainless-steel vats, and wines are aged partly in stainless-steel vats and
partly in oak barrels (renewed by a third in each vintage) for 18 months.
They are fined and filtered.

SECOND WINE
None produced.

HAUT-BERGERON

Classification: None
Location of vineyards: Sauternes, Preignac, Bommes, and Barsac
Owner: Robert Lamothe and Sons
Address: 33210 Preignac
Mailing address: Same as above
Telephone: 33 5 56 63 24 76; telefax: 33 5 56 62 23 31
Visits: Monday through Saturday, from 8 A.M. to noon, and 2 P.M. to
7 P.M.
Contact: Patrick and Hervé Lamothe

VINEYARDS (white)
Surface area: 58.5 acres
Average age of vines: 60 years
Blend: 90% Semillon, 5% Sauvignon, 5% Muscadelle
Density of plantation: 8,000 vines per hectare
Average yields (over the last 5 years): 19 hectoliters per hectare
Total average annual production: 50,000 bottles

GRAND VIN (white)
Brand name: Château Haut-Bergeron
Appellation: Sauternes
Mean annual production: 28,000 bottles (last 5 years)
Upbringing: Fermentations take place at low temperatures and are
stimulated only with indigenous yeasts. Wines are aged 18–24 months in
oak barrels, 50% of which are new. They are fined and filtered.

SECOND WINE
Brand name: Château Fontebride
Average annual production: 20,000 bottles (last 5 years)

NOTE: The estate also produces a special cuvée (debut vintage 1996)
Surface area: 0.98 acres
Average age of vines: 100 years
Blend: 100% Semillon
Density of plantation: 9,000 vines per hectare
Average yields (over the last 5 years): 12 hectoliters per hectare
Total average annual production: 50–75 cases
Brand Name: Cuvée 100
Appellation: Sauternes
Mean annual production: 600 bottles in 1996
Upbringing: Fermentations take place in new oak barrels and last
approximately 60 days. Wines will be aged 30 months in new oak and
will be bottled in 1999. They will be fined, but shall remain unfiltered.

HAUT-CLAVERIE   VERY GOOD

Classification: Cru Bourgeois
Owner: SCEA Sendrey Frères
Address: 33210 Preignac
Telephone: 33 5 56 63 24 76; telefax: 33 5 56 63 23 31
Production: 3,000 cases
Blend: 85% Semillon, 10% Sauvignon Blanc, 5% Muscadelle
Secondary label: None
Vineyard size: 35 acres
Proprietor: Sendrey family
Dry white wine: None
Time spent in barrels: 15–20 months
Average age of vines: 30 years
Plateau of maturity: 5–15 years following the vintage

This obscure yet excellent property is located just south of the village of Fargues. In a number of blind tastings held in France, Haut-Claverie consistently has come out near the top. The wine continues to sell at bargain basement prices. The secret here is not only an excellent micro-climate, but late harvesting, several passes through the vineyard, and one of the most conscientious owners in the entire appellation. This could well be one of the up-and-coming stars from the Barsac/Sauternes region.

HAUT-PICK

Classification: None
Location of vineyards: Preignac
Owner: Foncier Vignobles
Address: Domaine de Lamontagne, 33210 Preignac
Mailing address: Same as above
Telephone: 33 5 56 63 27 66; telefax: 33 5 56 76 87 03
Visits: By appointment only
Contact: Michel Garat

VINEYARDS (white)
Surface area: 22 acres
Average age of vines: 35 years
Blend: 100% Semillon
Density of plantation: 7,000 vines per hectare
Average yields (over the last 5 years): 23 hectoliters per hectare
Total average annual production: 200 hectoliters

GRAND VIN (white)
Brand name: Château du Haut-Pick
Appellation: Sauternes
Mean annual production: 200 hectoliters
Upbringing: Fermentations take place in temperature-controlled stainless-steel vats. Seventy-five percent of the yield is aged in stainless-steel vats and the rest in oak barrels. Wines are fined and filtered.

SECOND WINE
None produced.

LES JUSTICES   GOOD

Classification: Cru Bourgeois
Location of vineyards: Preignac
Owner: Christian Médeville
Address: 33210 Preignac
Mailing address: c/o Château Gilette, 33210 Preignac
Telephone: 33 5 56 76 28 44; telefax: 33 5 56 76 28 43
Visits: By appointment, Monday through Thursday, between 9 A.M. and
1 P.M., and 2 P.M. and 6 P.M.; on Fridays, to 5 P.M. only
Contact: Andrée Médeville

VINEYARDS (white)
Surface area: 19.8 acres
Average age of vines: 35 years
Blend: 88% Semillon, 10% Sauvignon, 2% Muscadelle
Density of plantation: 6,600 vines per hectare
Average yields (over the last 5 years): 21 hectoliters
Total average annual production: 160 hectoliters

GRAND VIN (white)
Brand name: Château Les Justices
Appellation: Sauternes
Mean annual production: 21,000 bottles
Upbringing: Fermentations take place in stainless-steel vats. Wines are
aged 6 months in vats and 10–12 months in oak barrels, 20% of which
are new. They are fined and filtered.

SECOND WINE
None produced.

LAFON

Classification: None
Location of vineyards: Sauternes, Bommes, Preignac, and Fargues
Owner: Mrs. Fauthoux
Address: 33210 Sauternes
Mailing address: Same as above
Telephone: 33 5 56 63 30 82; telefax: 33 5 56 63 30 82
Visits: By appointment only
Contact: Mrs. Fauthoux

VINEYARDS (white)
Surface area: 24.7 acres
Average age of vines: 35 years
Blend: 95% Semillon, 5% Sauvignon
Density of plantation: 6,500 vines per hectare
Average yields (over the last 5 years): 22 hectoliters per hectare
Total average annual production: 240 hectoliters

GRAND VIN (white)
Brand name: Château Lafon
Appellation: Sauternes
Mean annual production: 240 hectoliters
Upbringing: Fermentations take place in temperature-controlled
stainless-steel tanks. Wines are aged 18 months in oak. They are fined
but remain unfiltered.

SECOND WINE
None produced.

Evaluation of present classification: Should be elevated to a Deuxième
Cru Classé
Plateau of maturity: 3–15 years following the vintage

LAMOURETTE

Classification: Cru Bourgeois
Production: 2,000 cases
Blend: 90% Semillon, 5% Sauvignon Blanc, 5% Muscadelle
Secondary label: None
Vineyard size: 18.5 acres
Proprietor: Ann-Marie Leglise
Dry white wine: None
Time spent in barrels: None; aging takes place in vats
Average age of vines: 25 years

Evaluation of present classification: Should be maintained
Plateau of maturity: 3–8 years following the vintage
This is a straightforward, fruity, soft style of Sauternes that is meant to be
consumed upon release. The best vintage I have tasted was a stylish
1986.

LIOT

Classification: None
Location of vineyards: Barsac
Owner: Jean-Gérard David
Address: 33720 Barsac
Mailing address: Same as above
Telephone: 33 5 56 27 15 31; telefax: 33 5 56 27 14 42
Visits: By appointment, Monday through Friday, between 9 A.M. and noon, and 2 P.M. and 5 P.M.
Contact: Mr. or Mrs. David

VINEYARDS (white)
Surface area: 49.4 acres
Average age of vines: 30–40 years
Blend: 80% Semillon, 10% Muscadelle, 10% Sauvignon
Density of plantation: 7,500 vines per hectare
Average yields (over the last 5 years): 23 hectoliters per hectare
Total average annual production: 460 hectoliters

GRAND VIN (white)
Brand name: Château Liot
Appellation: Sauternes/Barsac
Mean annual production: 3,300 cases
Upbringing: Fermentations last approximately 3 weeks in vats. Wines are transferred after fermentation to oak barrels, renewed by 15% in each vintage, for 15–18 months aging. They are fined and filtered.

SECOND WINE
Brand name: Château du Levant
Average annual production: 20,000 bottles

Evaluation of present classification: Should be maintained
Plateau of maturity: 3–10 years following the vintage

This relatively obscure yet competently run vineyard sits on the limestone/clay plateau of the Haut-Barsac hills. The wines I have tasted—1983, 1985, and 1986—were rich, fruity, round, straightforward examples that were cleanly made and pure, if not terribly sweet. This is a vineyard area with plenty of potential because it adjoins the great estate of Château Climens. Based on the handful of vintages I have tasted, this is a wine that must be consumed when young.

MAURAS

Classification: Cru Bourgeois
Location of vineyards: At the northern extremity of the appellation, north of Rabaud-Promis
Owner: Société Viticole de France
Address: 33210 Sauternes
Mailing address: Château du Grava, 33550 Haux
Telephone: 33 5 56 67 23 89; telefax: 33 5 56 67 08 38
Visits: By appointment only
Contact: Patrick Duale

VINEYARDS (white)
Surface area: 37 acres
Average age of vines: 25–30 years
Blend: 67% Semillon, 30% Sauvignon, 3% Muscadelle
Density of plantation: 6,000 vines per hectare
Average yields (over the last 5 years): 20–25 hectoliters per hectare
Total average annual production: 350 hectoliters

GRAND VIN (white)
Brand name: Château Mauras
Appellation: Sauternes

SECOND WINE
Brand name: Clos du Ciron

MAYNE

Classification: None
Location of vineyards: Barsac, east of the railway road and next to Château Suau
Owner: Sanders family
Address: 33720 Barsac
Mailing address: Same as above
Telephone: 33 5 56 27 17 07; telefax: 33 5 56 27 16 02
Visits: On weekdays and during office hours
Contact: Jean Sanders, telephone 33 5 56 63 19 54

VINEYARDS (white)
Surface area: 19.7 acres
Average age of vines: Over 30 years
Blend: 60% Semillon, 40% Sauvignon

Density of plantation: 7,800 vines per hectare
Average yields (over the last 5 years): 17 hectoliters per hectare
Total average annual production: 140 hectoliters

GRAND VIN (white)
Brand name: Château du Mayne
Appellation: Barsac-Sauternes
Mean annual production: 140 hectoliters
Upbringing: Fermentations take place in vats, and wines are transferred
to oak barrels, 20% of which are new, for 12 months aging. They are
fined but remain unfiltered.

SECOND WINE
None produced.

MONT-JOYE

Classification: This estate did not exist at the time of the classification
Location of vineyards: Barsac
Owner: Franck and Marguerite Glaunès
Address: Quartier Miaille, 33720 Barsac
Mailing address: c/o Domaine du Pas-St.-Georges, 33190 Casseuil
Telephone: 33 5 56 71 12 73; telefax: 33 5 56 71 12 41
Visits: By appointment only
Contact: Franck and Marguerite Glaunès

VINEYARDS (white)
Surface area: 49.4 acres in all (part of this surface area is dedicated to
the production of dry white Bordeaux and dry white Graves)
Average age of vines: 35 years
Blend: 75% Semillon, 15% Sauvignon, 10% Muscadelle
Density of plantation: 6,600 vines per hectare
Average yields (over the last 5 years): 20 hectoliters
Total average annual production: 2,800 cases

GRAND VIN (white)
Brand name: Château Mont-Joye
Appellation: Barsac/Sauternes
Mean annual production: 1,000 cases
Upbringing: Fermentations take place partly in oak barrels and partly in
lined vats. They are aged 24 months by rotation in vats and new oak
barrels. They are fined and filtered upon bottling.

SECOND WINE
Brand name: Château Jacques le Haut
Average annual production: 5,000–10,000 bottles
Upbringing: Fermentations last approximately 18 days in barrels, 30% of
which are new, and wines are aged 20–24 months. They are fined and
filtered upon bottling.

MONTEILS

Classification: Cru Bourgeois
Location of vineyards: Preignac
Owner: Le Diascorn family
Address: 33210 Preignac
Mailing address: Same as above
Telephone: 33 5 56 76 12 12; telefax: 33 5 56 76 28 63
Visits: Preferably by appointment
Contact: Hervé Le Diascorn

VINEYARDS (white)
Surface area: 27.2 acres in production
Average age of vines: 25 years
Blend: 75% Semillon, 20% Sauvignon, 5% Muscadelle
Density of plantation: 5,500 vines per hectare
Average yields (over the last 5 years): 21 hectoliters per hectare
Total average annual production: 30,000 bottles

GRAND VIN (white)
Brand name: Château Monteils
Appellation: Sauternes
Mean annual production: 30,000 bottles
Upbringing: Fermentations take place in small stainless-steel vats
and are stopped by addition of alcohol. Wines are aged 18 months
in concrete vats and in new oak barrels. They are fined and
filtered.

SECOND WINE
None produced.

PERNAUD

Classification: Cru Bourgeois
Location of vineyards: Sauternes-Barsac
Owner: G.F.A. du Château Pernaud (managed by the Regelsperger family)
Address: 33720 Barsac
Mailing address: Same as above
Telephone: 33 5 56 27 26 52; telefax: 33 5 56 27 32 08
Visits: By appointment
Contact: Jean-Gabriel Jacolin

VINEYARDS (white)
Surface area: 38.7 acres
Average age of vines: 30–35 years
Blend: 80% Semillon, 15% Sauvignon, 5% Muscadelle
Density of plantation: 7,000 vines per hectare
Average yields (over the last 5 years): 21.5 hectoliters per hectare
Total average annual production: 300–375 hectoliters

GRAND VIN (white)
Brand name: Château Pernaud
Appellation: Sauternes
Mean annual production: 70–100 hectoliters
Upbringing: Fermentations take place at 20 degrees centigrade in temperature-controlled stainless-steel tanks. Wines are aged 18 months in oak barrels (5%–10% are new). They are fined if necessary and filtered.

SECOND WINE
Brand name: Château Pey-Arnaud
Average annual production: 5,000–15,000 bottles

PEYRAGUEY

Classification: None
Location of vineyards: Preignac, Bommes, and Sauternes
Owner: Mussotte family
Address: 33210 Preignac
Mailing address: Same as above
Telephone: 33 5 56 44 43 48; telefax: 33 5 56 01 71 89
Visits: By appointment only
Contact: Hubert Mussotte

VINEYARDS (white)
Surface area: 17.3 acres
Average age of vines: 25 years
Blend: 80% Semillon, 20% Sauvignon
Density of plantation: 7,000 vines per hectare
Average yields (over the last 5 years): 22 hectoliters per hectare
Total average annual production: 130 hectoliters

GRAND VIN (white)
Brand name: Cru Peyraguey
Appellation: Sauternes
Mean annual production: 130 hectoliters
Upbringing: Fermentations take place partly in vats and partly in barrels.
Wines are aged 24 months in oak barrels, the percentage of new oak
varying with each vintage. They are sometimes fined and filtered.

SECOND WINE
None produced.

PIADA   GOOD

Classification: Cru Bourgeois
Location of vineyards: Barsac
Owner: Jean Lalande
Address: 33720 Barsac
Mailing address: Same as above
Telephone: 33 5 56 27 16 13; telefax: 33 5 56 27 26 30
Visits: Every day, between 8 A.M. and 7:30 P.M.
Contact: Jean Lalande

VINEYARDS (white)
Surface area: 24.7 acres
Average age of vines: 40 years
Blend: 95% Semillon, 3% Sauvignon, 2% Muscadelle
Density of plantation: 7,900 vines per hectare
Average yields (over the last 5 years): 25 hectoliters per hectare
Total average annual production: 250 hectoliters

GRAND VIN (white)
Brand name: Château Piada
Appellation: Barsac
Mean annual production: 130 hectoliters

Upbringing: After fermentations in barrels, wines are aged with 25% new oak for a period of 12 months. They are racked every 3 months and bottled unfined but filtered after 18 months.

SECOND WINE
Brand name: Clos du Roy
Average annual production: 120 hectoliters

Evaluation of present classification: One of the best of the Cru Bourgeois, this property would get serious consideration for elevation to a Deuxième Cru Classé
Plateau of maturity: 3–12 years following the vintage

This is one of the oldest estates of the Barsac region. Amazingly, it can trace its history as a wine-producing estate to the late thirteenth century. The wines tend to be richly fruity, round, and honeyed, which is not surprising given the fact that half the crop is aged in stainless-steel cuvées and the other half in oak casks.

While the aging potential of Piada is suspect, it can be a delicious wine to drink in its first 5–10 years. The best recent vintages include 1988 and 1986.

ROLLAND

Classification: Cru Bourgeois
Production: 4,000 cases
Blend: 60% Semillon, 20% Sauvignon Blanc, 20% Muscadelle
Secondary label: None
Vineyard size: 50 acres
Proprietor: Jean Guignard
Dry white wine: None
Time spent in barrels: 18 months
Average age of vines: 25 years

Evaluation of present classification: Should be maintained
Plateau of maturity: 3–10 years following the vintage

ROUMIEU-LACOSTE   GOOD

Classification: Cru Bourgeois
Location of vineyards: Haut-Barsac, the highest part of Barsac
Owner: Hervé Dubourdieu
Address: 33720 Barsac

Mailing address: Same as above
Telephone: 33 5 56 27 16 29; telefax: 33 5 56 27 02 65
Visits: By appointment only
Contact: Hervé Dubourdieu

VINEYARDS (white)
Surface area: 29.6 acres
Average age of vines: 55 years
Blend: 100% Semillon
Density of plantation: 6,800 vines per hectare
Average yields (over the last 5 years): 15 hectoliters per hectare
Total average annual production: 20,000 bottles

GRAND VIN (white)
Brand name: Château Roumieu-Lacoste
Appellation: Sauternes
Mean annual production: 10,000 bottles
Upbringing: Half the yield undergoes fermentation in oak barrels and half
in vats. Wines are then aged 10–16 months in oak barrels, 30% of which
are new (in 1990 100% new oak was utilized). They are fined but remain
unfiltered.

SECOND WINE
Brand name: Château Ducasse
Average annual production: 10,000 bottles

Evaluation of present classification: Should be elevated to a Deuxième
Cru Classé
Plateau of maturity: 5–12 years following the vintage

The quality of the wines at Roumieu-Lacoste should not be surprising given
the fact that this vineyard is adjacent to the famed Climens in Barsac. The
old vines and impeccable winemaking practices of the Dubourdieu family
result in consistently high-quality wines. The style, as befitting a Barsac, is
relatively light, but there is plenty of complexity, rich pineapple fruit, and
just a touch of toasty new oak. This would appear to be a wine that is best
consumed within 10–12 years of the vintage.

SAINT-AMAND

Classification: None
Location of vineyards: Preignac
Owner: Anne-Mary Fachetti Ricard
Address: 33210 Preignac

Mailing address: Same as above
Telephone: 33 5 56 76 84 89; telefax: 33 5 56 76 24 87
Visits: Preferably by appointment, Monday through Thursday, between
2 P.M. and 6 P.M.

VINEYARDS (white)
Surface area: 49.4 acres
Average age of vines: 30–50 years
Blend: 85% Semillon, 14% Sauvignon, 1% Muscadelle
Density of plantation: 5,000 vines per hectare
Average yields (over the last 5 years): 15 hectoliters per hectare
Total average annual production: 40,000–50,000 bottles

GRAND VIN (white)
Brand name: Château Saint-Amand
Appellation: Sauternes
Mean annual production: 15–20 hectoliters per hectare depending upon
the vintage
Upbringing: 2 years in concrete vats. Wines are fined and filtered.

SECOND WINE
Brand name: Château La Chartreuse

SAINT-MARC

Classification: None
Location of vineyards: Barsac
Owner: Didier Laulan
Address: 33720 Barsac
Mailing address: Same as above
Telephone: 33 5 56 27 16 87; telefax: 33 5 56 27 05 93
Visits: By appointment only, except on Sundays
Contact: Didier Laulan

VINEYARDS (white)
Surface area: 37 acres
Average age of vines: 35 years
Blend: 80% Semillon, 10% Sauvignon, 10% Muscadelle
Density of plantation: 6,600 vines per hectare
Average yields (over the last 5 years): 23 hectoliters
Total average annual production: 350 hectoliters

GRAND VIN (white)
Brand name: Château Saint-Marc
Appellation: Barsac/Sauternes
Mean annual production: 30,000 bottles
Upbringing: Fermentations take place in small temperature-controlled
stainless-steel tanks of 27–50-hectoliter capacity. Wines are then aged
18 months in stainless-steel vats. They are fined and filtered upon
bottling.

SECOND WINE
None produced.

Evaluation of present classification: Should be maintained
Plateau of maturity: 3–10 years following the vintage

SIMON

Classification: None
Location of vineyards: Barsac, Preignac
Owner: G.F.A. du Château Simon
Address: 33720 Barsac
Mailing address: Same as above
Telephone: 33 5 56 27 15 35; telefax: 33 5 56 27 24 79
Visits: Preferably by appointment, normally from 8 A.M. to noon, and
2 P.M. to 4 P.M.
Contact: J. Dufour

VINEYARDS (white)
Surface area: 42 acres
Average age of vines: 30 years
Blend: 90% Semillon, 8% Sauvignon, 2% Muscadelle
Density of plantation: 7,000 vines per hectare
Average yields (over the last 5 years): 21 hectoliters per hectare
Total average annual production: 45,000 bottles

GRAND VIN (white)
Brand name: Château Simon
Appellation: Barsac or Sauternes
Mean annual production: 25,000 bottles
Upbringing: Fermentations take place in stainless-steel vats
(only indigenous yeast is used). Wines are then aged 1 year in

oak barrels (10%–30% are new). Wines remain unfined but are filtered.

SECOND WINE
Brand name: Château Piaut
Average annual production: 20,000 bottles

THE SATELLITE APPELLATIONS OF BORDEAUX

There are very large quantities of wine produced in a bevy of other lesser-known appellations of Bordeaux. Most of these wines are widely commercialized in France but have met with little success in America because of this country's obsession with luxury names and prestigious appellations. For the true connoisseur, the wines of Bordeaux's satellite appellations can in fact represent outstanding bargains, particularly in top vintages such as 1982, 1985, 1989, and 1990, where excellent climatic conditions and the improved use of modern technology by many of these estates resulted in a vast selection of fine wines at modest prices.

On my two trips to Bordeaux each year I have spent considerable time tasting the wines from the satellite communes in an all-out effort to try to discover who's who in these obscure appellations. In this section I have listed the top estates from the major satellite appellations of Bordeaux, and I unhesitatingly recommend those wines rated as very good or excellent to Bordeaux wine enthusiasts looking for sensational values from this area.

The satellite appellations are listed in order of my opinion of their overall ability to produce high-quality wine. In short, this is the frugal consumer's guide to fine Bordeaux.

FRONSAC AND CANON-FRONSAC

In the eighteenth and nineteenth centuries the vineyards sprinkled over the hillsides and hollows of Fronsac and Canon-Fronsac—only several miles

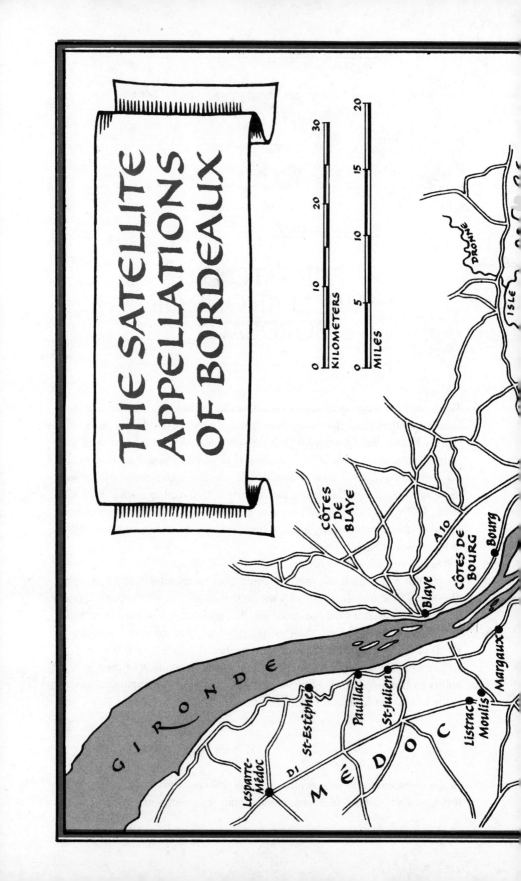

THE SATELLITE
APPELLATIONS
OF BORDEAUX

KILOMETERS
0   10   20   30
MILES
0   5   10   15   20

GIRONDE

ISLE

DRONNE

CÔTES
DE
BLAYE

Blaye

A10

CÔTES DE
BOURG

Bourg

MÉDOC

Lesparre-
Médoc

D1   St-Estèphe

Pauillac

St-Julien

Listrac
Moulis

Margaux

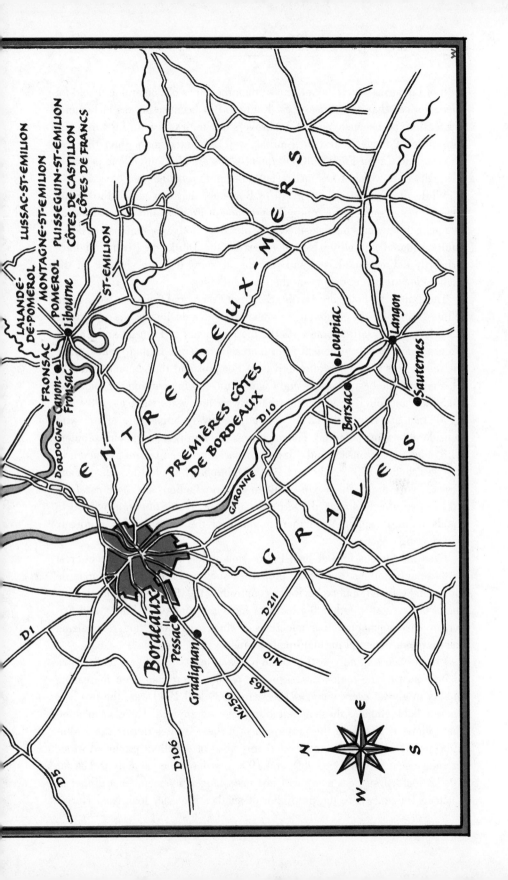

LUSSAC-ST-EMILION
MONTAGNE-ST-EMILION
PUISSEGUIN-ST-EMILION
CÔTES DE CASTILLON
CÔTES DE FRANCS

LALANDE-
DE-POMEROL
FRONSAC
POMEROL
Libourne

ST-EMILION

E N T R E - D E U X - M E R S

Dordogne Canon-
Fronsac

PREMIÈRES CÔTES
DE BORDEAUX

D10

Loupiac

Langon

Barsac

Sauternes

GARONNE

G R A V E S

Bordeaux
Pessac

Gradignan

D211

N10

A63

N250

D106

D1

D5

N
W   E
S

west of Libourne—were better known than the wines of Pomerol and sold for higher prices than the wines of St.-Emilion. But because access to Pomerol was easier and because most of the brokers had their offices in Libourne, the vineyards of Pomerol and St.-Emilion were exploited more than those of Fronsac and Canon-Fronsac. Consequently this area fell into a long period of obscurity from which it has just recently begun to rebound.

While there is no village in all of Bordeaux that can match the scenic beauty of St.-Emilion, the tranquil landscape of Fronsac and Canon-Fronsac is among the region's most aesthetically pleasing. Both appellations are beautifully situated on rolling hills overlooking the Dordogne River and have primarily a limestone-based soil running in veins that are shallow on the higher elevations and deeper on the lower hillsides.

The grapes of choice are Merlot, Cabernet Franc, and Cabernet Sauvignon. While Malbec is still planted in a number of vineyards, its use has decreased. Largely ignored until the mid-1980s, the producers of Fronsac and Canon-Fronsac have begun to benefit from increasing interest in their wines. Once viewed as less expensive alternatives to Pomerol and the glamour wines of St.-Emilion, the best Fronsacs and Canon-Fronsacs are carving out their own identities and offering wines (particularly in top years such as 1989 and 1990) that are rich, full darkly colored, relatively large-scale efforts with considerable aging potential. The toughness and hardness, so much a problem with older-style Fronsacs and Canon-Fronsacs, has been less of a concern in vintages such as 1985, 1989, and 1990. Additionally, the fertile soils of many Fronsac vineyards, which can result in over-production, are more carefully and conservatively managed. Oddly enough, far greater attention is paid to yields in these appellations than in many of the more famous Bordeaux winemaking regions.

Even the famous firm of Jean-Pierre Moueix has taken an active interest in these appellations, buying up properties such as La Dauphine, Canon de Brem, and Canon (Moueix), as well as controlling the distribution and marketing of other estates. Other Bordeaux *négociants,* principally Vintex and Europvin, have augmented their selections of wines from this region, recognizing the excellent potential for high-quality wines.

I have been routinely tasting these wines at least once a year, and I have visited most of the major estates in the region. There has been increasing quality in almost every vintage. The years 1989 and 1990 were the two best back-to-back vintages these appellations have yet enjoyed. The classification that follows is based on the performance of these estates during the 1985–1996 period. All of the estates rated very good or excellent produced wines in vintages such as 1985, 1989, and 1990 that have the capacity to last for 10–12 years. I suspect many will last even longer. I remember a dinner at Château Dalem, where the proprietor of another Fronsac, Jean-Noël Hervé, brought a bottle of 1928 Moulin-Haut-Laroque. It was quite stunning at age 60. I am not suggesting these wines will routinely have that kind of aging potential, but they are wines with a great deal of firmness and richness that tend to possess a Médoc-like austerity and structure to them. Even though the vineyards are in close proximity to Pomerol, the wines seem, for the most part, very un-Pomerol-like.

FRONSAC—AN OVERVIEW

Location: On the right bank of Bordeaux's Dordogne River, 15 miles from Bordeaux's city center

Acres under Vine: 2,050

Communes: Fronsac, La Rivière, Saillans, St.-Aignan, St.-Germain-La-Rivière

Average Annual Production: 550,000 cases

Classified Growths: No classification exists for the châteaux of Fronsac

Principal Grape Varieties: Merlot dominates, followed by Cabernet Franc, Cabernet Sauvignon, and decreasing quantities of Malbec

Principal Soil Type: Clay and limestone, with some sandstone; most of the Fronsac vineyards are on the lower ground

A CONSUMER'S CLASSIFICATION OF THE CHÂTEAUX OF FRONSAC

EXCELLENT

Fontenil, Moulin-Haut-Laroque, La Vieille-Cure, Villars

VERY GOOD

Dalem, La Dauphine, Rouet

GOOD

Cardeneau, de Carles, Clos du Roy, La Croix, La Grave, Jeandeman, Meyney, La Rivière, Trois-Croix

CANON-FRONSAC—AN OVERVIEW

Location: On the right bank of Bordeaux's Dordogne River, 15 miles from Bordeaux's city center

Acres under Vine: 741

Communes: All of the châteaux are located within the communes of St.-Michel-de-Fronsac and Fronsac

Average Annual Production: 195,000 cases

Classified Growths: None

Principal Grape Varieties: Merlot, followed by Cabernet Franc, Cabernet Sauvignon, and small quantities of Malbec

Principal Soil Type: Clay and limestone; most of the châteaux are on the upper slopes of this area's hills

A CONSUMER'S CLASSIFICATION OF THE CHÂTEAUX OF CANON-FRONSAC

EXCELLENT

Canon (Moueix), Canon de Brem, Cassagne-Haut-Canon-La-Truffière, La Croix-Canon, Moulin-Pey-Labrie, Pavillon

VERY GOOD

Barrabaque, Canon, La Fleur-Cailleau, Grand-Renouil, Mazeris, Pez-Labrie

GOOD

Bodet, Mazeris-Bellevue, Vrai-Canon-Bouché, Vray-Canon-Boyer

PROFILES—THE TOP CHÂTEAUX

Canon (Canon-Fronsac)

Proprietor: Mademoiselle Henriette Horeau

Vineyard size: 25 acres

Production: 4,000 cases

Plateau of maturity: 5–15 years

Grape varieties:
Merlot—95%
Cabernet Franc—5%

Canon de Brem (Canon-Fronsac)

Proprietor: Firm of Jean-Pierre Moueix

Vineyard size: 50 acres

Production: 8,000 cases

Plateau of maturity: 5–15 years

Grape varieties:
Merlot—66%
Cabernet Franc—34%

Canon (Moueix) (Canon-Fronsac)

Proprietor: Christian Moueix

Vineyard size: 2.7 acres

Production: 500 cases

Plateau of maturity: 5–15 years

Grape varieties:
Merlot—80%
Cabernet Franc—20%

Cassagne-Haut-Canon-La-Truffière (Canon-Fronsac)

Proprietor: Dubois family
Vineyard size: 29.6 acres
Production: 4,500 cases, of which
2,000 cases of the luxury cuvée La
Truffière are produced
Plateau of maturity: 3–10 years

Grape varieties:
Merlot—70%
Cabernet Franc—20%
Cabernet Sauvignon—10%

Dalem (Fronsac)

Proprietor: Michel Rullier
Vineyard size: 29.6 acres
Production: 6,500 cases
Plateau of maturity: 4–12 years

Grape varieties:
Merlot—70%
Cabernet Franc—20%
Cabernet Sauvignon—10%

La Croix-Canon (Canon-Fronsac)

Proprietor: Christian Moueix
Vineyard size: 35 acres
Production: 4,800 cases
Plateau of maturity: 4–15 years

Grape Varieties:
Merlot—75%
Cabernet Sauvignon—25%

La Dauphine (Fronsac)

Proprietor: Firm of Jean-Pierre
Moueix
Vineyard size: 25 acres
Production: 4,500 cases
Plateau of maturity: 4–10 years

Grape varieties:
Merlot—60%
Cabernet Franc—40%

Fontenil (Fronsac)

Proprietor: Michel Rolland
Vineyard size: 17.3 acres
Production: 3,500 cases
Plateau of maturity: 4–14 years

Grape varieties:
Merlot—85%
Cabernet Sauvignon—15%

Mazeris (Canon-Fronsac)

Proprietor: Christian de Cournuaud
Vineyard size: 35 acres
Production: 4,500 cases
Plateau of maturity: 5–15 years

Grape varieties:
Merlot—75%
Malbec—25%

Moulin-Haut-Laroque (Fronsac)

Proprietor: Jean-Noël Hervé
Vineyard size: 34.6 acres
Production: 6,000 cases
Plateau of maturity: 5–20 years

Grape varieties:
Merlot—65%
Cabernet Franc—20%
Cabernet Sauvignon—10%
Malbec—5%

Moulin-Pey-Labrie (Canon-Fronsac)

Proprietor: B. & G. Hubau
Vineyard size: 20 acres

Grape varieties:
Merlot—75%

Production: 4,000 cases

Cabernet Sauvignon—15%

Plateau of maturity: 5–15 years

Cabernet Franc—5%

Malbec—5%

Pez-Labrie (Canon-Fronsac)

Proprietor: Société Civile—Eric
 Vareille

Grape varieties:

Merlot—70%

Vineyard size: 14 acres

Cabernet Sauvignon—20%

Production: 2,000 cases

Cabernet Franc—10%

Plateau of maturity: 4–12 years

La Vieille-Cure (Fronsac)

Proprietor: S.N.C., an American
 syndicate; contact—Colin C.
 Ferenbach

Grape varieties:

Merlot—80%

Cabernet Franc—15%

Vineyard size: 47 acres

Cabernet Sauvignon—5%

Production: 8,000 cases

Plateau of maturity: 4–12 years

LALANDE-DE-POMEROL

Lalande-de-Pomerol is a satellite commune of nearly 2,500 acres of vineyards located just to the north of Pomerol. It includes the two communes of Lalande-de-Pomerol and Néac. The vineyards, which produce only red wine, are planted on relatively light, gravelly, sandy soils with the meandering river, Barbanne, as the appellation's northern boundary. The very top level of good Lalande-de-Pomerol is easily the equivalent of a mid-level Pomerol, with certain wines, such as Belles-Graves, Château Grand Ormeau, Bertineau-St.-Vincent, La Croix-St.-André, and du Chapelain, very good, even by Pomerol's standards.

Prices for these wines have risen, but the top efforts still represent reasonably good values for wines that are essentially dominated by their Merlot content.

A CONSUMER'S CLASSIFICATION
OF THE CHÂTEAUX OF LALANDE-DE-POMEROL

EXCELLENT

Belles-Graves, du Chapelain, La Croix-St.-André, Grand-Ormeau

VERY GOOD

Bel-Air, Bertineau-St.-Vincent, Chambran, Jean du Gué Cuvée Prestige, La Fleur-St.-Georges, Siaurac, Tournefeuille

GOOD

Des Annereaux, Clos des Templiers, Garraud, Haut-Chatain, Haut-Surget,
Les Hauts-Conseillants, Laborde, Moncets

PROFILES—THE TOP CHÂTEAUX

Bel-Air

Proprietor: Musset family   Grape varieties:
Vineyard size: 30 acres   Merlot—60%
Production: 5,000 cases   Cabernet Franc—15%
Plateau of maturity: 3–12 years   Pressac—15%
     Cabernet Sauvignon—10%

Belles-Graves

Proprietor: Madame Theallet   Grape varieties:
Vineyard size: 28.4 acres   Merlot—60%
Production: 5,500 cases   Cabernet Franc—40%
Plateau of maturity: 3–10 years

Bertineau-St.-Vincent

Proprietor: Michel Rolland   Grape varieties:
Vineyard size: 10 acres   Merlot—80%
Production: 2,000 cases   Cabernet Franc—20%
Plateau of maturity: 3–10 years

Du Chapelain

Proprietor: Madame Xann Marc   Grape varieties:
Vineyard size: 2.5 acres   Merlot—90%
Production: 350 cases   Cabernet Franc—10%
Plateau of maturity: 5–10 years

Chambrun

Proprietor: Jean-Philippe Janoueix   Grape varieties:
Vineyard size: 3.7 acres   Merlot—90%
Production: 800 cases   Cabernet Franc—10%
Plateau of maturity: 3–10 years

La Croix-St.-André

Proprietor: Francis Carayon   Grape varieties:
Vineyard size: 37 acres   Merlot—70%
Production: 6,500 cases   Cabernet Franc—30%
Plateau of maturity: 4–12 years

La Fleur-St.-Georges

Proprietor: A.G.F.   Grape varieties:
Vineyard size: 42 acres   Merlot—70%
Production: 10,000 cases   Cabernet Franc—30%
Plateau of maturity: 3–8 years

Grand-Ormeau

Proprietor: Jean-Claude Beton
Vineyard size: 28.4 acres
Production: 4,800 cases
Plateau of maturity: 4–10 years

Grape varieties:
Merlot—65%
Cabernet Franc—25%
Cabernet Sauvignon—10%

Siaurac

Proprietor: Baronne Guichard
Vineyard size: 62 acres
Production: 7,500 cases
Plateau of maturity: 3–10 years

Grape varieties:
Merlot—75%
Cabernet Franc—25%

Tournefeuille

Proprietor: G.F.A. Sautarel
Vineyard size: 45 acres
Production: 6,500 cases
Plateau of maturity: 5–12 years

Grape varieties:
Merlot—70%
Cabernet Franc—15%
Cabernet Sauvignon—15%

CÔTES DE BOURG

The Côtes de Bourg, a surprisingly vast appellation of over 9,200 acres (in vine), is located on the right bank of the Gironde River, just a 5-minute boat ride from the more famous appellation of Margaux. The vineyards here are actually older than those in the Médoc, as this attractively hilly area was once the center of the strategic forts built during the Plantagenet period of France's history. The views from those hillside vineyards adjacent to the river are magnificent. The local chamber of commerce has attempted to draw the public's attention to this area by calling Bourg "the Switzerland of the Gironde." They should instead stress the appeal of the best wines from the Côtes de Bourg, which are made in an uncomplicated but fruity, round, appealing style, and the lovely port village of the area, the ancient hillside town of Bourg-Sur-Gironde.

The Bourg appellation, located north of Fronsac and south of the Côtes de Blaye, has variable soils. They are primarily limestone based, with different proportions of clay, gravel, and sand. The soils exhibit a far greater degree of fertility than in the Médoc, and consequently the problem facing many producers is to keep their yields reasonable in order to obtain a degree of concentration in their wines. The dominant grape is Merlot, followed by Cabernet Franc, Cabernet Sauvignon, Malbec, and, to a very small extent, Petit Verdot.

Most of the wines of the Côtes de Bourg are average to below average in quality, lack concentration (because of excessive yields), and often have tannins that are too green and high (because of the tendency to harvest too early). However, there are at least a dozen or so estates that consistently make good wines and several whose wines can easily age for 10 or more years. This could be an increasingly important appellation in the future because the enhanced demand for wines from the prestigious appellations of Bordeaux has caused prices to soar. Most Côtes de Bourg wines are reasonably priced.

CÔTES DE BOURG—AN OVERVIEW

Location: 18 miles north of Bordeaux, on the right bank of the Dordogne River

Acres under Vine: 9,206

Communes: Bayon, Bourg, Comps, Gauriac, Lansac, Mombrier, Prignac-et-Marcamps, St.-Ciers-de-Canesse, St.-Seurin-de-Bourg, St.-Trojan, Samonac, Tauriac, Teuillac, Villeneuve

Average Annual Production: 350,000 cases (of which approximately 1% is white wine)

Classified Growths: There is no classification, but there are just over 300 estates and 4 cooperatives in the region

Principal Grape Varieties: red wine—Merlot, followed by Cabernet Franc and Cabernet Sauvignon, with some Malbec; white wine—Semillon, Sauvignon Blanc, and Muscadelle

Principal Soil Type: Everything from clay, limestone, sandstone, and pure gravel can be found in the Côtes de Bourg

A CONSUMER'S CLASSIFICATION
OF THE CHÂTEAUX OF THE CÔTES DE BOURG

EXCELLENT
Roc de Cambes, Tayac—Cuvée Prestige

VERY GOOD
De Barbe, Brûlesécaille, Guerry, Haut-Maco, Mercier, Tayac—Cuvée Réservée

GOOD
Clos La Barette, Croûte-Courpon, Falfas, La Grolet, Gros Moulin, Les Heaumes, Moulin des Graves, Moulin Vieux, Nodoz, Rousselle, Rousset, Soulignac de Robert, Tayac, La Tour-Séguy

PROFILES—THE TOP CHÂTEAUX

De Barbe

Proprietor: Savary de Beauregard   Grape varieties:
Vineyard size: 138 acres   Merlot—70%

Production: 35,000 cases
Plateau of maturity: 3–8 years

Cabernet Sauvignon—25%
Malbec—5%

Brûlesécaille

Proprietor: Jacques Rodet
Vineyard size: 50 acres
Production: 6,500 cases
Plateau of maturity: 3–8 years

Grape varieties:
Merlot—50%
Cabernet Franc—50%

Guerry

Proprietor: Bertrand de Rivoyre
Vineyard size: 54 acres
Production: 8,500 cases
Plateau of maturity: 4–12 years

Grape varieties:
Malbec—34%
Cabernet Sauvignon—33%
Merlot—33%

Haut-Maco

Proprietors: Mallet brothers
Vineyard size: 86 acres
Production: 12,000 cases
Plateau of maturity: 3–7 years

Grape varieties:
Cabernet Franc—70%
Merlot—30%

Mercier

Proprietor: Philippe Chéty
Vineyard size: 74 acres
Production: 6,000 cases
Plateau of maturity: 3–10 years

Grape varieties:
Merlot—55%
Cabernet Sauvignon—25%
Cabernet Franc—15%
Malbec—5%

Roc de Cambes

Proprietor: François Mitjavile
Vineyard size: 23 acres
Production: 3,000 cases
Plateau of maturity: 3–10 years

Grape varieties:
Merlot—65%
Cabernet Sauvignon—20%
Cabernet Franc—10%
Malbec—5%

VINTAGES

1996—The deep ruby/purple–colored 1996 Roc de Cambes is a strong effort from
•   this property, owned by François Mitjavile. The wine offers a decadent,
88–   smoky, sweet, jammy berry-scented nose that is both obvious and appealing.
90   Medium to full bodied and round, with low acidity and a plump, forward
       personality, this is a delicious offering from the finest estate in the Côtes de
       Bourg. Drink it over the next 5–8 years. Last tasted, 11/97.

1995—An opaque purple color and a stunning nose of black cherries, earth, leather,
•   and sweet berry and mocha-tinged fruit are outstanding. The wine is medium
88   bodied, with excellent concentration, a firm underpinning of tannin, and
       decent acidity. It should be drinkable when released and last for a decade.
       Remarkably, this wine achieved 13.7% alcohol—naturally! Anticipated ma-
       turity: Now–2007. Last tasted, 11/97.

1994— Less impressive in the bottle than cask tastings suggested, this wine displays
• a soft ruby color, a soft, spicy, earthy, truffle-like nose, tasty, round, ripe,
86 medium-bodied flavors, and an easygoing finish. It tastes noticeably less fat
and concentrated since bottling. Anticipated maturity: Now–2003. Last
tasted, 1/97.

1993— This delicious, value-packed wine from Tertre-Roteboeuf's proprietor, Fran-
• çois Mitjavile, offers an impressive dark ruby/purple color, a big, smoky,
86 chocolatey, berry-scented nose, dense, opulent flavors, medium body, and a
supple finish. Drink it over the next 5–7 years. It is a terrific restaurant
selection. Last tasted, 11/94.

1992— The 1992 is round and velvety textured, with more fruit and ripeness evident
• in both the bouquet and flavors. There is even some spicy oak to be found.
84 Its soft, medium-bodied personality will offer uncritical but pleasant drinking
for 2–4 years. Last tasted, 3/98.

1991— The 1991 exhibits a medium ruby color, ripe, berry aromas, light to medium
• body, soft tannin, and a smooth finish. Drink it over the next 3–4 years.
82

1990— I have been a big believer in this Côte de Bourg made by the obsessive-
• compulsive François Mitjavile, who is better known for his outstanding small
90 St.-Emilion estate, Le Tertre-Roteboeuf. I initially rated these wines 89 for the
1990 and 88 for the 1989. In this recent tasting I was thrilled to see how well
the wines showed. Both are fully mature yet capable of lasting another 7–8
years. With the price escalation for wines such as Le Tertre-Roteboeuf, I suppose Roc de Cambes will now be known as the "poor person's Roteboeuf." The
1990 barely edged out the 1989. The deep ruby/garnet–colored 1990 offers a
creamy, smoky, roasted nut, jammy black cherry–scented nose, followed by
soft, round, supple flavors, outstanding concentration, and a low-acid, plush
finish. This delicious offering is proof that wines from lowly regarded appellations can be just as delicious as those that possess higher pedigrees and cost
5–6 times as much. Anticipated maturity: Now–2003. Last tasted, 11/96.

1989— The 1989 revealed the high pH color (plenty of amber at the edges), a
• tobacco, spicy, Graves-like nose, beefy, animal-like flavors, gobs of chocolatey
89 fruit, and a soft, round finish. Both the 1989 and 1990 are at their peak of
maturity, but with its greater length and riper fruit, the 1990 will outlive the
1989 by 3–5 years. Readers who bought these wines early should be pleased
that their $16–$18 investments now taste like wines costing $50–$100.
Anticipated maturity: Now–2004. Last tasted, 6/98.

Tayac—Cuvée Prestige

Proprietor: Pierre Saturny
Vineyard size: 50 acres
Production: 1,000–2,000 cases
Plateau of maturity: 5–15 years

Grape varieties: Approximately
75% Cabernet Sauvignon, 20%
Merlot, and 5% Cabernet Franc.
This luxury curvée is made only in
great years such as 1982, 1985,
1986, 1988, 1989, and 1990.

BLAYE

There are just over 9,880 acres of vines in the Blaye region, located directly north of Bourg. The best vineyard areas are entitled to the appellation Premières Côtes de Blaye. While quantities of white wine are produced in the Blaye region, most of the Premières Côtes de Blaye are dedicated to the production of red wine, which is very similar to the red wine of Bourg. At its best, it is forward, round, richly fruity, soft, and immensely satisfying in a low-key manner.

Blaye, like Bourg, is a much older wine-producing region than the more renowned Médoc. Its origins date back to Roman times, when the area served as a defensive front line against invaders intent on attacking the city of Bordeaux. Today the tourist route from Bourg to Blaye is one of the more charming in the Bordeaux region. In Blaye itself is a perfectly preserved seventeenth-century military fortress (the citadel) that is classified as a historical monument by the French government. Additionally, gourmets may be surprised to note that if the French government ever permits extensive sturgeon fishing and caviar preparation, Blaye would probably be the center for this industry because of the growing population of sturgeon that make the nearby Gironde River their habitat.

Most of the Blaye vineyards sit on steeply sloping hills with a southerly exposure overlooking the Gironde. The soil tends to be dominated by limestone, with outbreaks of clay and, from time to time, gravel. It is a very fertile soil that must be cultivated conservatively if the yields are to be kept under control. The grape varieties are essentially the same as in Bourg, with Merlot dominating the blend, followed by Cabernet Franc, Cabernet Sauvignon, and Malbec. The best red wines from the Côtes de Blaye are extremely well made and richly fruity and are best drunk within their first 5–6 years of life. An interesting group of white varietals is planted in the appellation, including Semillon, Sauvignon Blanc, Muscadelle, Merlot Blanc, Folle Blanche, Colombard, Chenin Blanc, and Ugni Blanc.

BLAYE—AN OVERVIEW

Location: On the right bank of the Gironde River, approximately 30 miles from Bordeaux's city center; the Côtes de Bourg lies to the south

Acres under Vine: 9,880 acres

Communes: There are over 40 communes in this large appellation

Average Annual Production: 2,250,000 cases, of which 90% is red wine and 10% white

Classified Growths: None, but there are 520 estates and 6 cooperatives boasting over 500 members

Principal Grape Varieties: Red—Merlot dominates; white—Sauvignon and
Semillon, along with smaller quantities of Muscadelle and Colombard
Principal Soil Type: Clay intermixed with limestone, sand, and gravel

A CONSUMER'S CLASSIFICATION
OF THE CHÂTEAUX OF BLAYE

EXCELLENT
Bel Air La Royère, Haut-Bertinerie, La Tonnelle

VERY GOOD
Haut-Sociando, Les Jonqueyres, Pérenne, Peyraud, Segonzac

GOOD
Bellevue, La Bretonnière, Graulet, Peraud, Petits-Arnauds

AVERAGE
Barbé, Chante-Alouette-la-Roseraie, Clairac, Le
Cone-Taillasson-de-Lagarcie, L'Escarde, La Grange, Loumede,
Magdeleine-Bouhou, Mayne-Boyer-Chaumet, Les Moines, Pardaillan,
Peybonhomme, Peymelon, Ricaud, Sociando, Les Videaux

PROFILES—THE TOP CHÂTEAUX

Bel Air La Royère
Proprietor: Corinne and Xavier
 Loriaud
Vineyard size: 12 acres
Production: 950–1,000 cases
Plateau of maturity: 2–8 years

Grape varieties:
80%—Merlot
20%—Malbec

Haut-Bertinerie
Proprietor: Daniel Bantegnies
Vineyard size: 111 acres
Production: red—26,000 cases;
 white—6,000 cases
Plateau of maturity: red, 3–10
 years; white, 1–2 years

Grape varieties:
Cabernet Sauvignon—45%
Merlot—45%
Cabernet Franc—10%

NOTE: This is the only estate in the Blaye appellation producing an excellent
white wine made from 95% Sauvignon Blanc. 2% Semillon, 2% Colombard,
and 1% Muscadelle.

Haut-Sociando

Proprietor: Louis Martinaud
Vineyard size: 35 acres
Production: 6,000 cases
Plateau of maturity: 2–3 years

Grape varieties:
Merlot—65%
Cabernet Franc—35%

Les Jonqueyres

Proprietor: Pascal Montaut
Vineyard size: 35 acres
Production: 5,000 cases
Plateau of maturity: 2–7 years

Grape varieties:
Merlot—75%
Cabernet Franc—25%

Pérenne

Proprietor: A syndicate of Danish
  bankers
Vineyard size: 227 acres
Production: 32,000 cases
Plateau of maturity: 2–5 years

Grape varieties:
Merlot—54%
Cabernet Franc—44%
Cabernet Sauvignon—1%
Malbec—1%

Peyraud

Proprietor: Rey family
Vineyard size: 25 acres
Production: 4,500 cases
Plateau of maturity: 3–6 years

Grape varieties:
Merlot—50%
Cabernet Sauvignon—30%
Cabernet Franc—15%
Malbec—5%

Segonzac

Proprietor: Jacob Marmet
Vineyard size: 75 acres
Production: 19,000 cases
Plateau of maturity: 3–6 years

Grape varieties:
Merlot—60%
Cabernet Sauvignon—20%
Cabernet Franc—10%
Malbec—10%

NOTE: There is also a very fine Cuvée Vieilles Vignes produced.

La Tonnelle

Proprietor: Eve Rouchi
Vineyard size: 25 acres
Production: 5,000 cases
Plateau of maturity: 2–5 years

Grape varieties:
Merlot—75%
Cabernet Franc—25%

PUISSEGUIN-ST.-EMILION

Puisseguin-St.-Emilion, the eastern-most of the satellite appellations, has been growing in size. The name is of Celtic origin, meaning "the hill with the powerful wine." Over one-half of the appellation's production is dominated by the local cooperative under the label "Roc de Puisseguin," but most of the estates that bottle their wines produce noteworthy wines that require drinking within 5–6 years of the vintage. They are considerably less expensive than most St.-Emilions.

Vintages in Puisseguin tend to follow those of the Libournais, with top years, such as 1982, 1989, 1990, and 1995, the best for bargain hunters in this appellation.

PUISSEGUIN-ST.-EMILION—AN OVERVIEW

Location: On the right bank of the Dordogne River, approximately 25 miles northeast of Bordeaux and 6 miles east of Libourne
Acres under Vine: 1,803
Communes: Puisseguin
Average Annual Production: 520,000 cases
Classified Growths: None; but there are 73 separate estates and 1 large cooperative
Principal Grape Varieties: Merlot dominates, followed by Cabernet Franc and small quantities of Cabernet Sauvignon
Principal Soil Type: Limestone and clay, with small amounts of sandstone

A CONSUMER'S CLASSIFICATION
OF THE CHÂTEAUX OF PUISSEGUIN-ST.-EMILION

GOOD

Durand Laplagne, de Roques, Vieux-Château-Guibeau

AVERAGE

Beauséjour, Cassat, La Croix-de-Mouchet, Fayan, Gontet-Robin, de Mole, Moulin, Rigaud, Roc de Boissac, Soleil, Teyssier, La Tour Guillotin

PROFILES—THE TOP CHÂTEAUX

Durand Laplagne

Proprietor: Consorts Bessou
Vineyard size: 32 acres
Production: 6,000 cases
Plateau of maturity: 3–7 years

Grape varieties:
Merlot—70%
Cabernet Franc—15%
Cabernet Sauvignon—15%

De Roques

Proprietor: Société Civile
Vineyard size: 62 acres

Grape varieties:
Merlot—60%

Production: 12,000 cases

Plateau of maturity: 3–10 years

Vieux-Château-Guibeau

Proprietor: Société Civile

Vineyard size: 100 acres

Production: 25,000 cases

Plateau of maturity: 2–7 years

Cabernet Franc—40%

Grape varieties:

Merlot—66%

Cabernet Franc—17%

Cabernet Sauvignon—17%

LUSSAC-ST.-EMILION

Lussac, located in the northeastern portion of the viticultural region of St.-Emilion, encompasses more than 3,458 acres. Over one-half of the vineyard area is controlled by the local cooperative, but there are a number of fine estates making smooth, delicious, round, fruity wine that must be consumed in the first 5–6 years of life.

The vineyards generally consist of limestone-dominated *terroirs,* with a handful on more sandy soils. As with the other satellite appellations in St.-Emilion, Lussac is a veritable treasure trove for bargains.

LUSSAC-ST.-EMILION—AN OVERVIEW

Location: 25 miles northeast of Bordeaux and 6 miles northeast of Libourne on the right bank of the Dordogne River

Acres under Vine: 3,458

Communes: Lussac

Average Annual Production: 775,000 cases

Classified Growths: None, although there are 215 estates and 1 cooperative with 90 members

Principal Grape Varieties: Merlot and Cabernet Franc

Principal Soil Type: Sand, clay, gravel, and clay/limestone dominate the diverse soil types of this appellation

A CONSUMER'S CLASSIFICATION
OF THE CHÂTEAUX OF LUSSAC-ST.-EMILION

VERY GOOD

Bel-Air, Bellevue, Cap de Merle, Carteyron, Courlat, Lyonnat, Mayne-Blanc, Villadière

GOOD

De Barbe-Blanche, Croix-de-Rambeau, Lucas, de Tabuteau, La Tour de Grenet, La Tour de Ségur, des Vieux Chênes

PROFILES—THE TOP CHÂTEAUX

Bel-Air

Proprietor: Jean-Noël Roi	Grape varieties:
Vineyard size: 50 acres	Merlot—70%
Production: 10,000 cases	Cabernet Franc—20%
Plateau of maturity: 3–7 years	Cabernet Sauvignon—10%

Bellevue

Proprietor: Charles Chatenoud	Grape varieties:
Vineyard size: 26 acres	Merlot—70%
Production: 4,000 cases	Cabernet Franc—30%
Plateau of maturity: 3–10 years	

Cap de Merle

Proprietor: Jacques Bessou	Grape varieties:
Vineyard size: 20 acres	Merlot—75%
Production: 3,000 cases	Cabernet Franc—25%
Plateau of maturity: 2–7 years	

Courlat

Proprietor: Pierre Bourotte	Grape varieties:
Vineyard size: 42 acres	Merlot—70%
Production: 8,000 cases	Cabernet Franc—20%
Plateau of maturity: 2–6 years	Cabernet Sauvignon—10%

Du Lyonnat

Proprietor: Jean Milhade	Grape varieties:
Vineyard size: 111 acres	Merlot—75%
Production: 25,000 cases	Cabernet Franc—12.5%
Plateau of maturity: 5–12 years	Cabernet Sauvignon—12.5%

Mayne-Blanc

Proprietor: Jean Boncheau	Grape varieties:
Vineyard size: 37 acres	Merlot—60%
Production: 7,500 cases	Cabernet Sauvignon—30%
Plateau of maturity: 2–6 years	Cabernet Franc—10%

MONTAGNE-ST.-EMILION

Not far from the graves sector of northern St.-Emilion and Pomerol is the satellite commune of Montagne-St.-Emilion. The hillside soils of this area consist of a clay/limestone blend, and the plateaus are primarily limestone-based soils intermixed with hard outbreaks of rock.

The best wines of Montagne almost always emerge from the hilly terrain along the southern border, with a splendid view of the Barbanne River that runs through Lalande-de-Pomerol and Pomerol. Among all the satellite communes, some of the deepest, richest wines consistently come from Montagne. The top wines can represent excellent bargains since they are the qualitative equivalent of a good Grand Cru St.-Emilion.

MONTAGNE-ST.-EMILION—AN OVERVIEW

Location: 23 miles northeast of Bordeaux on the right bank of the Dordogne River

Acres under Vine: 3,829

Communes: Montagne

Average Annual Production: 950,000 cases

Classified Growths: None, but there are 220 estates and 1 cooperative with 30 members

Principal Grape Varieties: Merlot

Principal Soil Type: Limestone/clay

A CONSUMER'S CLASSIFICATION OF THE CHÂTEAUX OF MONTAGNE-ST.-EMILION

EXCELLENT
Roudier

VERY GOOD
Calon, Croix-Beauséjour, Faizeau, Maison Blanche, Tour-Musset, des Tours, Vieux-Château-St.-André

AVERAGE
Barraud, Beauséjour, Bonneau, Chevalier St.-Georges, Corbin, Coucy, La Croix-de-Mouchet, Gachon, Gilet, Grand-Baril, Guadet-Plaisance, de Maison Neuve, Montaiguillon, Négrit, La Papeterie, Petit-Clos-du-Roy, Rouchet-Gardet

PROFILES—THE TOP CHÂTEAUX

Calon

Proprietor: Jean-Noël Boidron

Vineyard size: 100 acres

Production: 14,000 cases

Plateau of maturity: 5–15 years

Grape varieties:

Merlot—70%

Cabernet Franc—15%

Cabernet Sauvignon—15%

Croix-Beauséjour

Proprietor: Olivier Laporte

Vineyard size: 19 acres

Grape varieties:

Merlot—70%

Production: 3,500 cases   Cabernet Franc—15%

Plateau of maturity: 5–12 years   Malbec—15%

Faizeau

Proprietors: Chantel Lebreton and   Grape varieties:

  Alain Raynaud   Merlot—85%

Vineyard size: 25 acres   Cabernet Sauvignon—10%

Production: 5,000 cases   Cabernet Franc—5%

Plateau of maturity: 2–8 years

Maison Blanche

Proprietors: Françoise and Gérard   Grape varieties:

  Despagne-Rapin   Merlot—70%

Vineyard size: 80 acres   Cabernet Franc—20%

Production: 15,000 cases   Cabernet Sauvignon—10%

Plateau of maturity: 4–12 years

Roudier

Proprietor: Jacques Capdemourlin   Grape varieties:

Vineyard size: 75 acres   Merlot—60%

Production: 15,000 cases   Cabernet Franc—25%

Plateau of maturity: 5–12 years   Cabernet Sauvignon—15%

Tour-Musset

Proprietor: Henri Guiter   Grape varieties:

Vineyard size: 62 acres   Merlot—50%

Production: 12,000 cases   Cabernet Sauvignon—50%

Plateau of maturity: 2–7 years

Des Tours

Proprietor: G.F.A. Louis Yerles   Grape varieties:

Vineyard size: 175 acres   Merlot—34%

Production: 55,000 cases   Cabernet Franc—34%

Plateau of maturity: 2–5 years   Malbec—32%

Vieux-Château-St.-André

Proprietor: Jean-Claude Berrouet   Grape varieties:

Vineyard size: 15.8 acres   Merlot—75%

Production: 3,200 cases   Cabernet Franc—25%

Plateau of maturity: 3–12 years

ST.-GEORGES ST.-EMILION

Beginning in 1972, the proprietors in the tiny commune of St.-Georges St.-Emilion were permitted to label their wines with the Montagne-St.-Emilion appellation. However, a number of them continued to seek their own identity with their appellation listed as St.-Georges St.-Emilion.

There are several serious estates in St.-Georges, including Château St.-Georges and the much smaller Château St.-André Corbin.

ST.-GEORGES ST.-EMILION—AN OVERVIEW

Location: 23 miles northeast of Bordeaux on the right bank of the Dordogne
    River
Acres under Vine: 445
Communes: St.-Georges St.-Emilion is part of the Montagne commune
Average Annual Production: 95,000 cases
Classified Growths: None, but there are 19 estates
Principal Grape Varieties: Merlot
Principal Soil Type: Clay/limestone

A CONSUMER'S CLASSIFICATION
OF THE CHÂTEAUX OF ST.-GEORGES ST.-EMILION

VERY GOOD

St.-André Corbin, St.-Georges

AVERAGE

Macquin-St. Georges, Belair-Montaiguillon, Tour-du-Pas-St. Georges

PROFILES—THE TOP CHÂTEAUX

St.-André Corbin

Proprietors: Jean-Claude Berrouet
  and Robert Carré
Vineyard size: 42 acres
Production: 8,000 cases
Plateau of maturity: 4–12 years

Grape varieties:
Merlot—70%
Cabernet Franc—30%

St.-Georges

Proprietor: Georges Desbois
Vineyard size: 125 acres
Production: 25,000 cases
Plateau of maturity: 4–15 years

Grape varieties:
Merlot—60%
Cabernet Sauvignon—20%
Cabernet Franc—20%

THE CÔTES DE CASTILLON

The Côtes de Castillon is located east of Puisseguin-St.-Emilion, approximately 25 miles from Bordeaux. The appellation is named after the commune Castillon-la-Bataille, which commemorates the Battle of Castillon. This 1453 battle marked the conclusion of the Hundred Years' War when the English commander, Talbot, died during the defeat of his army.

The Côtes de Castillon is one of the older winemaking regions in the area, with viticultural practices that can be traced to Roman times. The soils, at times extremely fertile, gravelly, or sandy, mix with more gravel and clay moving up the hillsides. On the highest areas, the soils are limestone mixed with clay, marl, and sandstone. According to the syndicate, 65% of the area's production is controlled by the large Cooperative de Castillon. Appellation status was awarded in 1955, and there has been significantly more interest expressed in the wines as a lower-priced alternative to the wines of St.-Emilion.

If the Côtes de Castillon is never a source of superb wines, several properties make round, supple, deliciously fruity, occasionally complex wines that can be found at bargain prices.

CÔTES DE CASTILLON—AN OVERVIEW

Location: On the right bank of the Dordogne River, 24 miles east of Bordeaux, bordered on the north by the appellation of Côtes de Francs, on the south by the Dordogne River, and on the west by St.-Emilion

Acres under Vine: 7,410

Communes: There are a total of 8 communes, a bevy of which include the word "Castillon" as an appendage to the commune name; principal communes include Belvès-de-Castillon, Castillon-la-Bataille, Ste.-Colombe, St.-Genès-de-Castillon, St.-Magne-de-Castillon, Les Salles-de-Castillon, and St.-Philippe-d'Aiguille

Average Annual Production: 1,650,000 cases

Classified Growths: None, but there are 250 estates and 1 cooperative with over 150 members

Principal Grape Varieties: Merlot, followed by Cabernet Franc

Principal Soil Type: Clay/limestone on the hillsides and more gravelly, sandy soil on the lower slopes

A CONSUMER'S CLASSIFICATION
OF THE CHÂTEAUX OF THE CÔTES DE CASTILLON

VERY GOOD

Cap de Faugères, Dubois-Grimon, Pitray, Vieux-Champs de Mars

GOOD

de Belcier, Côte Montpezat, Puycarpin, La Terrasse, Veyry

AVERAGE

D'Aiguilhe, Beynat, Blanzac, du Bois, Les Desmoiselles, Faugères, Fontbaude, La Fourquerie, Haut-Tuquet, Lartigue, Maisières-Aubert,

Moulin-Neuf, Moulin Rouge, Palanquey, Robin, Rocher-Bellevue, Roquevieille, Terrasson

PROFILES—THE TOP CHÂTEAUX

Cap de Faugères

Proprietor: Corinne Guisez
Vineyard size: 64 acres
Production: 13,000 cases
Plateau of maturity: 2–8 years

Grape varieties:
Merlot—50%
Cabernet Franc—38%
Cabernet Sauvignon—12%

Dubois-Grimon

Proprietor: Gilbert Grimon
Vineyard size: 12.5 acres
Production: 3,000 cases
Plateau of maturity: 2–5 years

Grape varieties:
Merlot—60%
Cabernet Franc—35%
Malbec—5%

Pitray

Proprietor: Madame de Boigne
Vineyard size: 75 acres
Production: 16,000 cases
Plateau of maturity: 2–8 years

Grape varieties:
Merlot—70%
Cabernet Franc—28%
Malbec—2%

Vieux-Champs de Mars

Proprietor: Régis Moro
Vineyard size: 42 acres
Production: 9,500 cases
Plateau of maturity: 2–8 years

Grape varieties:
Merlot—80%
Cabernet Franc—15%
Cabernet Sauvignon—5%

THE CÔTES DE FRANCS

The Côtes de Francs is one of the newer appellations in the environs of St.-Emilion. Although the area traces wine-producing origins to the eleventh century, it received appellation status only in 1976. There are 2,211 acres of vines, of which 20% is planted in white wine varietals, such as Semillon, Sauvignon Blanc, and Muscadelle.

The highest potential would appear to be for red wines, as the Côtes de Francs is a natural extension to the east of Puisseguin-St.-Emilion and Lussac-St.-Emilion. The soils are ideal, with the lower slopes and valley floors containing a lot of clay and the hillsides clay and limestone mixtures with outbreaks of marl and chalk. The grapes of choice are Cabernet Sauvignon, Cabernet Franc, Malbec, and Merlot. The Côtes de Francs does bear the distinction of having one of Bordeaux's only east-facing vineyard areas.

CÔTES DE FRANCS—AN OVERVIEW

Location: Nearly 30 miles from Bordeaux's city center, on the right bank of the Dordogne River, Côtes de Francs is west of Puisseguin and Lussac

Acres under Vine: 2,211

Average Annual Production: 240,000 cases, of which 90% is red and 10% white

Classified Growths: None, but there are 30 estates and 1 cooperative with 30 members

Principal Grape Varieties: Merlot

Principal Soil Type: Clay/limestone

A CONSUMER'S CLASSIFICATION OF THE CHÂTEAUX OF THE CÔTES DE FRANCS

VERY GOOD

Château de Francs, Marsau, La Prade, Puygueraud

GOOD

Les Charmes-Godard

PROFILES—THE TOP CHÂTEAUX

Chateau de Francs

Proprietor: Hébrard and Böuard
Vineyard size: 67 acres
Production: 10,000 cases
Plateau of maturity: 3–8 years

Grape varieties:
Merlot—60%
Cabernet Franc—40%

Marsau

Proprietors: Jean-Marie and Sylvie
  Chadronnier
Vineyard size: 24 acres
Production: 4,500 cases
Plateau of maturity: 2–8 years

Grape varieties:
Merlot—85%
Cabernet Franc—15%

La Prade

Proprietor: Patrick Valette
Vineyard size: 11 acres
Production: 2,200 cases
Plateau of maturity: 2–6 years

Grape varieties:
Merlot—80%
Cabernet Sauvignon—10%
Cabernet Franc—10%

Puygueraud

Proprietor: Thienpont family
Vineyard size: 75 acres
Production: 15,000 cases
Plateau of maturity: 3–8 years

Grape varieties:
Merlot—55%
Cabernet Franc—30%
Cabernet Sauvignon—15%

LOUPIAC AND STE.-CROIX-DU-MONT

With the wine prices of Barsac and Sauternes soaring, I predict a more important role for the producers of the sweet white wines of Loupiac and Ste.-Croix-du-Mont. These two appellations, 24 miles south of Bordeaux on the right bank of the Garonne, facing Barsac and Sauternes across the river, have an ideal southern exposure. These areas received appellation status in 1930, and many observers believe the excellent exposition of the top vineyards and the clay/limestone soil base is favorable for producing sweet wines, particularly in view of the fact that the morning mists—so essential for the formation of the noble rot, *Botrytis cinerea*—are a common occurrence in this area. Although the sweet wines are receiving increasing attention from wine lovers, dry white wines, as well as a moderate quantity of dry red wines, are also produced.

LOUPIAC—AN OVERVIEW

Location: On the right bank of the Garonne River, approximately 24 miles southeast of Bordeaux and only 6 miles from Langon
Acres under Vine: 865
Communes: Loupiac
Average Annual Production: 115,000 cases
Classified Growths: None, but there are 70 estates
Principal Grape Varieties: Semillon, Sauvignon Blanc, and Muscadelle
Principal Soil Type: Clay/limestone and gravelly clay with sandstone

STE.-CROIX-DU-MONT—AN OVERVIEW

Location: 24 miles southeast of Bordeaux, and 5 miles from Langon
Acres under Vine: 1,087
Communes: Ste.-Croix-du-Mont
Average Annual Production: 175,000 cases
Classified Growths: None, but there are 90 estates
Principal Grape Varieties: Semillon, Sauvignon Blanc, and Muscadelle
Principal Soil Type: Limestone/clay dominates the region

A CONSUMER'S CLASSIFICATION
OF THE CHÂTEAUX OF LOUPIAC AND STE.-CROIX-DU-MONT

Sweet Wines

VERY GOOD

Bourdon-Loupiac, Clos Jean, Crabitan-Bellevue (Cuvée Speciale), du Cros,
Loubens, Loupiac-Gaudiet, Domaine du Noble, La Rame

PROFILES—THE TOP CHÂTEAUX

Clos Jean

Proprietor: Lionel Bord
Vineyard size: 40 acres
Production: 10,800 cases
Plateau of maturity: 4–15 years for
the sweet wine; 1–3 years for the
dry wine

Grape varieties:
Semillon—80%
Sauvignon Blanc—20%

NOTE: This property also makes an excellent Graves-like dry white wine.

Crabitan-Bellevue (Cuvée Speciale)

Proprietor: G.F.A. B. Solan et Fils
Vineyard size: 81 acres
Production: 15,000 cases
Plateau of maturity: 5–12 years

Grape varieties:
Semillon—85%
Sauvignon—8%
Muscadelle—7%

NOTE: The production of the Cuvée Speciale is extremely limited.

Du Cros

Proprietor: Michel Boyer
Vineyard size: 106 acres
Production: 17,000 cases
Plateau of maturity: 3–10 years for
the sweet wine; 1–3 years for the
dry wine

Grape varieties:
Semillon—70%
Sauvignon Blanc—30%

NOTE: This property also makes one of the finest dry white wines of the region.

Loubens

Proprietor: Arnaud de Sèce
Vineyard size: 50 acres

Grape varieties:
Semillon—97%

Production: 8,500 cases   Sauvignon—3%
Plateau of maturity: 5–10 years

Loupiac-Gaudiet

Proprietor: Marc Ducau   Grape varieties:
Vineyard size: 67 acres   Semillon—80%
Production: 7,500 cases   Sauvignon Blanc—20%
Plateau of maturity: 3–12 years

Domaine du Noble

Proprietor: Patrick Dejean   Grape varieties:
Vineyard size: 35 acres   Semillon—85%
Production: 4,400 cases   Sauvignon—15%
Plateau of maturity: 3–10 years

La Rame

Proprietor: Yves Armand   Grape varieties:
Vineyard size: 50 acres   Semillon—75%
Production: 4,000 cases   Sauvignon Blanc—25%
Plateau of maturity: 5–15 years

NOTE: A special cuvée, Réserve de Château, is even richer.

OTHER APPELLATIONS

While so much of the world of wine connoisseurship focuses on the great names and renowned appellations, there are a number of perennial over-achievers operating in lowly regarded appellations.

I make it a habit to taste through the so-called *petits vins* of Bordeaux each time I visit. The following dry white and red wines represent the *crème de la crème* of my tastings from such appellations as Entre-Deux-Mers, Premières Côtes de Bordeaux, and generic Bordeaux. These wines are very fine, are, for the most part, humbly priced, and are made by highly motivated, sometimes compulsive-obsessive proprietors. I enthusiastically recommend that readers search them out. Even allowing for wide fluctuations in the value of the dollar, these wines rarely retail for more than $15 a bottle, yet frequently compete with wines selling for twice as much.

RECOMMENDED PRODUCERS FROM THE APPELLATIONS OF ENTRE-DEUX-MERS, BORDEAUX, BORDEAUX SUPÉRIEUR, AND PREMIÈRES CÔTES DE BORDEAUX

White Wines

Bauduc-Les Trois-Hectares (Bordeaux)
Bonnet (Entre-Deux-Mers)
Bonnet-Cuvée Reservée (Entre-Deux-Mers)

Bourdicotte (Entre-Deux-Mers)
Carpia (Bordeaux)
Cayla (Bordeaux)
Cayla-Le Grand-Vent (Bordeaux)
La Closière (Bordeaux)
Fondarzac (Entre-Deux-Mers)
Fongrave (Entre-Deux-Mers)
Launay (Entre-Deux-Mers)
Moulin-de-Launay (Entre-Deux-Mers)
Numero 1-Dourthe (Bordeaux)
Reynon-Vieilles Vignes (Bordeaux)
Château de Racaud (Cadillac)
Roquefort (Entre-Deux-Mers)

Thieuley (Bordeaux)
Thieuley-Cuvée Francis Courselle (Bordeaux)
Toulet (Bordeaux)
La Tour Mirambeau (Entre-Deux-Mers)
Turcaud (Entre-Deux-Mers)

Red Wines

Balestard (Bordeaux)
Bon Jouan (Bordeaux Supérieur)
Bouilh (Bordeaux Supérieur)
de Bru (Bordeaux)
Cablanc (Bordeaux)
Carsin (Premières Côtes de Bordeaux)
Cazalis (Bordeaux)
de Chastelet (Premières Côtes de Bordeaux)
Clos Chaumont (Premières Côtes de Bordeaux)
La Cour d'Argent (Bordeaux Supérieur)
Courteillac (Bordeaux)
La Croix de Roche (Bordeaux Supérieur)
Le Doyenne (Premières Côtes de Bordeaux)
Fontenille (Bordeaux Supérieur)
Fussignac (Bordeaux Supérieur)
Le Grand-Verdus (Bordeaux Supérieur)
La Grande-Chapelle (Bordeaux Supérieur)
Hostens-Picant (Ste.-Foy de Bordeaux)
Jonqueyres (Bordeaux Supérieur)
La Joye (Bordeaux Supérieur)
La Maréchale (Bordeaux Supérieur)
Parenchère (Bordeaux Supérieur)

Paranchère Cuvée Raphael Gazaniol (Premières Côtes de Bordeaux)
Peyrat Cuvée La Fontaine (Premières Côtes de Bordeaux)
Pintey (Bordeaux Supérieur)
Piras (Premières Côtes de Bordeaux)
Plaisance-Cuvée Tradition (Bordeaux)
de Plassan (Bordeaux)
Prieuré-Ste.-Anne (Premières Côtes de Bordeaux)
Recougne (Bordeaux Supérieur)
Reignac Cuvée Speciale (Bordeaux Supérieur)
Reynon (Premières Côtes de Bordeaux)
La Terasse (Bordeaux Supérieur)
Terres d'Agnès (Bordeaux Supérieur)
Thieuley (Bordeaux)
Château de la Tour (Bordeaux Supérieur)
Tour de l'Espérance (Bordeaux Supérieur)
La Tuilerie de Puy (Bordeaux Supérieur)

4: THE BORDEAUX WINE CLASSIFICATIONS

Bordeaux wines, in the minds of the wine trade and the wine consumer, are only as good as their official placement in one of the many classifications of wine quality. These classifications of wine quality have operated both for and against the consumer. Those few châteaux fortunate enough to "make the grade" have had guaranteed to them various degrees of celebrity status and respect. They have been able to set their price according to what their peers charged and have largely been the only châteaux to be written about by wine writers. As this book demonstrates, these top châteaux have not always produced wine becoming of their status in the official French wine hierarchy. As for the other châteaux, many have produced excellent wine for years, but because they were not considered of classified-growth quality in 1855, or 1955, or 1959 (the dates at which the major classifications of wine quality occurred), they have received significantly less money for their wines and significantly less attention, particularly from writers. Yet it is the excellent wine produced from some of these lesser-known châteaux that represents potential gustatory windfalls for the wine consumer.

THE 1855 CLASSIFICATION OF THE WINES OF THE GIRONDE

Of all the classifications of wine quality in Bordeaux, it is the 1855 Classification of the Wines of the Gironde that is by far the most important of these historical categorizations of Bordeaux wine quality. Among the thousands of châteaux in the Bordeaux region, 61 châteaux and winemaking estates in the Médoc and 1 in the Graves region were selected on the basis of their selling price and vineyard condition. Since 1855 only one change has occurred to the classification. In 1973 Château Mouton-Rothschild was elevated to first-growth status. The 1855 classification,* which established a five-tiered pyramid with originally 4 (now 5 as the result of the elevation of Mouton-Rothschild) first-growths, 15 second-growths, 14 third-growths, 10 fourth-growths, and 18 fifth-growths, while being a good general guide to the quality of some of the best Bordeaux wines, it has numerous deficiencies that are chronicled in detail throughout this book.

While the classification of the wines of the Gironde dealt with red wine–producing estates, there was also a classification in 1855 of the estates in the Sauternes/Barsac region south of the city of Bordeaux, which produce sweet white wines.† One estate, Château d'Yquem, was rated first, followed by 23 other châteaux divided equally into two groupings, "Premiers Crus" and "Deuxièmes Crus."

The other classifications of Bordeaux wine quality are much more modern-day creations yet are no more accurate or reliable than the 1855 classification. In 1959, the wines of the Graves region immediately south of the city of

---

* See page 1343: *Bordeaux Wine: The Official Classification of 1855.*
† See page 1344: *Sauternes-Barsac: The Official Classification of 1855.*

Bordeaux were classified.* Thirteen châteaux that produced red wine were given classified, or "Cru Classé," status. Eight châteaux that produced white wine were classified. In 1955 the wines of St.-Emilion were classified into two categories, "Premiers Grands Crus Classés," or first great growths, and "Grands Crus Classés." This was followed by some corrections to the 1955 classification in 1959 and a revised classification in 1969. The 1996 revision appears on page 1346.

Pomerol, the smallest of the major Bordeaux wine districts, just northwest of St.-Emilion, has never had a classification of the wine quality of its châteaux. The lack of any categorization of Pomerol's wines has certainly not deterred quality. The most expensive and sought-after wine of all Bordeaux is Pétrus, and it is a Pomerol. In addition to Pétrus, there are at least another dozen châteaux in this district that fetch prices for their wines that are equivalent to any one of the Médoc's famous second-growths.

There is still another classification of Bordeaux wines that merits significant attention. It is the classification of the so-called Crus Bourgeois of the Médoc. Pejoratively called "petits châteaux" by many, these numerous, small, moderate, and large properties have never had the prestige or glory of the famous classified growths. Regardless of how high the quality of winemaking was, or how carefully the vineyards were managed and cared for, the Crus Bourgeois have for years been considered minor wines. In fact, many of them are, but increasing numbers of these châteaux are making wine on a very high level of excellence, comparable to at least a Médoc classified growth. Furthermore, they represent outstanding value and quality to knowledgeable wine consumers.

There were several unsuccessful attempts in the early half of the century to get an effective organization to promote the virtues of the Médoc's hundreds of lesser-known châteaux. A classification was accomplished in 1932 that listed 444 Cru Bourgeois châteaux, broken down into three categories. There are 6 "Crus Bourgeois Supérieurs Exceptionnels," 99 "Crus Bourgeois Supérieurs," and 339 "Crus Bourgeois."

Over the following decades many of these vineyards were absorbed by adjacent properties or went out of the winemaking business. In an effort to update this classification, new rankings were issued in 1966 by an organization of the Bourgeois châteaux called the Syndicat des Crus Bourgeois. The most recent result has been an updated list of 128 châteaux issued in 1978.† Eighteen châteaux were given "Cru Grand Bourgeois Exceptionnel" status, 41 are entitled to the title "Cru Grand Bourgeois," and 68 are designated "Cru Bourgeois."

The selection process utilized by the Syndicat left open a number of

* See page 1345: *Graves: 1959 Official Classification.*
† See page 1347: *The Crus Bourgeois of the Médoc: The 1978 Syndicat's Classification.*

questions regarding the overall validity of the 1978 classification. First, only members of the Syndicat were entitled to be recognized in the classification. For example, highly respected Cru Bourgeois châteaux such as de Pez in St.-Estèphe and Gloria in St.-Julien refused to join the Syndicat and are therefore excluded from its official rankings. In short, there is no question that while the current classification of the Crus Bourgeois is of some benefit, the exclusion of at least 10 well-known Crus Bourgeois producing top-quality wine, merely on the grounds that they refused to become members of the Syndicat, leaves a lot to be desired.

While Bordeaux has an elaborate "ranking" system for its multitude of wine-producing châteaux, it is true that many of the châteaux clearly merit their placement, but many don't. In addition, quite a few châteaux have not been officially recognized at all but make very fine wine year in and year out.

These historic classifications of wine quality were employed both to promote Bordeaux wines and to establish well-delineated quality benchmarks. The classification system was based on the vineyard's soil base and reputation. However, owners and winemakers change, and whereas some famous Bordeaux estates consistently make the best wine possible given the year's climatic conditions, others, because of negligence, incompetence, or just greed, produce mediocre and poor wine that hardly reflects its official pedigree.

The Bordeaux classifications are looked at in this book only from a consumer's or buyer's perspective. The quality of wine produced by a vineyard over the period 1961–1996 has been examined thoroughly. A qualitative analysis rather than historical analysis of each major and many serious lesser-known estates has been conducted, focusing on 1) the style and overall quality of the wine, 2) the wine's relative quality and record of quality over the period 1961–1997, and 3) the wine's relative value.

The judgments, commentaries, and evaluations of the wines in this book are mine. They have been made on the basis of my extensive comparative tastings and numerous trips to Bordeaux since 1970. While no one will argue with the premise that the enjoyment of wine is strictly a personal and subjective matter, it is important to note that critical wine tasting at either the amateur or professional level without prejudice usually results in general agreement as to the greatest and worst wines. There are indeed quality benchmarks for Bordeaux wines, as there are for all the world's finest wines, and this book is intended to be a guide to those Bordeaux vineyards that establish the benchmarks not only for quality, but also for value.

BORDEAUX WINE: THE OFFICIAL CLASSIFICATION OF 1855

FIRST-GROWTHS (Premiers Crus)

Château Lafite-Rothschild	Pauillac
Château Latour	Pauillac
Château Margaux	Margaux
Château Haut-Brion*	Pessac, Graves

SECOND-GROWTHS (Deuxièmes Crus)

Château Mouton-Rothschild †	Pauillac
Château Rauzan-Ségla	Margaux
Château Rauzan-Gassies	Margaux
Château Léoville-Las Cases	St.-Julien
Château Léoville-Poyferré	St.-Julien
Château Léoville-Barton	St.-Julien
Château Durfort-Vivens	Margaux
Château Lascombes	Margaux
Château Gruaud-Larose	St.-Julien
Château Brane-Cantenac	Cantenac-Margaux
Château Pichon-Longueville Baron	Pauillac
Château Pichon Lalande	Pauillac
Château Ducru-Beaucaillou	St.-Julien
Château Cos d'Estournel	St.-Estèphe
Château Montrose	St.-Estèphe

THIRD-GROWTHS (Troisièmes Crus)

Château Giscours	Labarde-Margaux
Château Kirwan	Cantenac-Margaux
Château d'Issan	Cantenac-Margaux
Château Lagrange	St.-Julien
Château Langoa-Barton	St.-Julien
Château Malescot St.-Exupéry	Margaux
Château Cantenac-Brown	Cantenac-Margaux
Château Palmer	Cantenac-Margaux
Château La Lagune	Ludon-Haut-Médoc
Château Desmirail	Margaux
Château Calon-Ségur	St.-Estèphe
Château Ferrière	Margaux

* This wine, although a Graves, was universally recognized and classified as one of the 4 first-growths.
† This wine was decreed a first-growth in 1973.

Château Marquis d'Alesme-Becker	Margaux
Château Boyd-Cantenac	Cantenac-Margaux

FOURTH-GROWTHS *(Quatrièmes Crus)*

Château St.-Pierre	St.-Julien
Château Branaire	St.-Julien
Château Talbot	St.-Julien
Château Duhart-Milon	Pauillac
Château Pouget	Cantenac-Margaux
Château La Tour-Carnet	St.-Laurent-Haut-Médoc
Château Lafon-Rochet	St.-Estèphe
Château Beychevelle	St.-Julien
Château Prieuré-Lichine	Cantenac-Margaux
Château Marquis-de-Terme	Margaux

FIFTH-GROWTHS *(Cinquièmes Crus)*

Château Pontet-Canet	Pauillac
Château Batailley	Pauillac
Château Grand-Puy-Lacoste	Pauillac
Château Grand-Puy-Ducasse	Pauillac
Château Haut-Batailley	Pauillac
Château Lynch-Bages	Pauillac
Château Lynch-Moussas	Pauillac
Château Dauzac	Labarde-Margaux
Château Mouton-Baronne-Philippe (now d'Armhailac)	Pauillac
Château du Tertre	Arsac-Margaux
Château Haut-Bages-Libéral	Pauillac
Château Pédesclaux	Pauillac
Château Belgrave	St.-Laurent-Haut-Médoc
Château de Camensac	St.-Laurent-Haut-Médoc
Château Cos Labory	St.-Estèphe
Château Clerc-Milon-Rothschild	Pauillac
Château Croizet-Bages	Pauillac
Château Cantemerle	Macau-Haut-Médoc

SAUTERNES-BARSAC: THE OFFICIAL CLASSIFICATION OF 1855

FIRST GREAT GROWTH

Château d'Yquem

FIRST-GROWTHS

Château Guiraud

Château La Tour Blanche

Château Lafaurie-Peyraguey

Château de Rayne-Vigneau

Château Sigalas Rabaud

Château Rabaud-Promis

Clos Haut-Peyraguey

Château Coutet

Château Climens

Château Suduiraut

Château Rieussec

SECOND-GROWTHS

Château d'Arche

Château Filhot

Château Lamothe

Château de Myrat

Château Doisy-Védrines

Château Doisy-Daëne

Château Suau

Château Broustet

Château Caillou

Château Nairac

Château de Malle

Château Romer

GRAVES: 1959 OFFICIAL CLASSIFICATION

CLASSIFIED RED WINES OF GRAVES

Château Haut-Brion	Pessac
Château Bouscaut	Cadaujac
Château Carbonnieux	Léognan
Domaine de Chevalier	Léognan
Château de Fieuzal	Léognan
Château Haut-Bailly	Léognan
Château La Mission-Haut-Brion	Pessac
Château La Tour-Haut-Brion	Talence
Château La Tour-Martillac	Martillac
Château Malartic-Lagravière	Léognan
Château Olivier	Léognan
Château Pape-Clément	Pessac
Château Smith-Haut-Lafitte	Martillac

CLASSIFIED WHITE WINES OF GRAVES

Château Bouscaut	Cadaujac
Château Carbonnieux	Léognan
Domaine de Chevalier	Léognan
Château Couhins	Villenave-d'Ornon
Château Laville-Haut-Brion	Talence
Château Malartic-Lagravière	Léognan
Château Olivier	Léognan
Château La Tour-Martillac	Martillac

ST.-EMILION: 1996 OFFICIAL CLASSIFICATION

FIRST GREAT GROWTHS (St.-Emilion—Premiers Grands Crus Classés)

(A) Château Ausone
Château Cheval Blanc
(B) Château Angélus
Château Beau-Séjour Bécot
Château Beauséjour
   (Duffau-Lagarrosse)
Château Belair

Château Canon
Château Clos Fourtet
Château Figeac
Château La Gaffelière
Château Magdelaine
Château Pavie
Château Trotte Vieille

GREAT GROWTHS (St.-Emilion—Grands Crus Classès)

Château L'Arrosée
Château Balestard-La-Tonnelle
Château Bellevue
Château Bergat
Château Berliquet
Château Cadet-Bon
Château Cadet-Piola
Château Canon-La-Gaffelière
Château Cap de Mourlin
Château Chauvin
Château Clos des Jacobins
Château Clos de l'Oratoire
Château Clos St.-Martin
Château La Clotte
Château La Clusière
Château Corbin
Château Corbin-Michotte
Château La Couspaude
Château Couvent-des-Jacobins
Château Curé-Bon
Château Dassault
Château La Dominique
Château Faurie-de-Souchard
Château Fonplégade
Château Fonroque
Château Franc-Mayne
Château Grand-Mayne
Château Grand-Pontet
Château Les Grandes-Murailles

Château Guadet St.-Julien
Château Haut-Corbin
Château Haut-Sarpe
Château Lamarzelle
Château Laniote
Château Larcis-Ducasse
Château Larmande
Château Laroque
Château Laroze
Château Matras
Château Moulin du Cadet
Château Pavie-Decesse
Château Pavie-Macquin
Château Petit-Faurie-de-Soutard
Château Le Prieuré
Château Ripeau
Château St.-Georges-Côte Pavie
Château La Serre
Château Soutard
Château Tertre-Daugay
Château La Tour-Figeac
Château La Tour-du-Pin-Figeac
   (Giraud-Bélivier)
Château La Tour-du-Pin-Figeac
   (Moueix)
Château Troplong-Mondot
Château Villemaurine
Château Yon-Figeac

THE CRUS BOURGEOIS OF THE MÉDOC: THE 1978 SYNDICAT'S CLASSIFICATION

CRUS GRANDS BOURGEOIS EXCEPTIONNELS

D'Agassac (Ludon)
Andron-Blanquet (St.-Estèphe)
Beau-Site (St.-Estèphe)
Capbern-Gasqueton (St.-Estèphe)
Caronne-St.-Gemme (St.-Laurent)
Chasse-Spleen (Moulis)
Cissac (Cissac)
Citran (Avensan)
Le Crock (St.-Estèphe)
Dutruch Grand-Poujeaux (Moulis)
Fourcas-Dupré (Listrac)
Fourcas-Hosten (Listrac)
Du Glana (St.-Julien)
Haut-Marbuzet (St.-Estèphe)
De Marbuzet (St.-Estèphe)
Meyney (St.-Estèphe)
Phélan-Ségur (St.-Estèphe)
Poujeaux (Moulis)

CRUS GRANDS BOURGEOIS

Beaumont (Cussac)
Bel-Orme (St.-Seurin-de-Cadourne)
Brillette (Moulis)
La Cardonne (Blaignan)
Colombier-Monpelou (Pauillac)
Coufran (St.-Seurin-de-Cadourne)
Coutelin-Merville (St.-Estèphe)
Duplessis-Hauchecorne (Moulis)
La Fleur Milon (Pauillac)
Fontesteau (St.-Sauveur)
Greysac (Bégadan)
Hanteillan (Cissac)
Lafon (Listrac)
De Lamarque (Lamarque)
Lamothe-Cissac (Cissac)
Larose-Trintaudon (St.-Laurent)
Laujac (Bégadan)
Liversan (St.-Sauveur)
Loudenne (St.-Yzans-de-Médoc)
De Malleret (Le Pian)
Martinens (Margaux)
Morin (St.-Estèphe)
Moulin à Vent (Moulis)
Le Meynieu (Vertheuil)
Les-Ormes-de-Pez (St.-Estèphe)
Les Ormes-Sorbet (Couquèques)
Patache d'Aux (Bégadan)
Paveil-de-Luze (Soussans)
Peyrabon (St.-Sauveur)
Pontoise-Cabarrus
    (St.-Seurin-de-Cadourne)
Potensac (Potensac)
Reysson (Vertheuil)
Ségur (Parempuyre)
Sigognac (St.-Yzans de Médoc)
Sociando-Mallet
    (St.-Seurin-de-Cadourne)
Du Taillan (Le Taillan)
La Tour de By (Bégadan)
La Tour du Haut-Moulin (Cussac)
Tronquoy-Lalande (St.-Estèphe)
Verdignan (St.-Seurin-de-Cadourne)

CRUS BOURGEOIS

Aney (Cussac)
Balac (St.-Laurent)
La Bécade (Listrac)
Bellerive (Valeyrac)
Bellerose (Pauillac)
Les Bertins (Valeyrac)
Bonneau (St.-Seurin-de-Cadourne)
Le Boscq (St.-Christoly)

Du Breuilh (Cissac)
La Bridane (St.-Julien)
De By (Bégadan)
Cailloux de By (Bégadan)
Cap Léon Veyrin (Listrac)
Carcanieux (Queyrac)
Castera (Cissac)
Chambert (St.-Estèphe)
La Clare (St.-Estèphe)
Clarke (Listrac)
La Closerie (Moulis)
De Conques (St.-Christoly)
Duplessis-Fabre (Moulis)
Fonpiqueyre (St.-Sauveur)
Fonréaud (Listrac)
Fort Vauban (Cussac)
La France (Blaignan)
Gallais-Bellevue (Potensac)
Grand-Duroc-Milon (Pauillac)
Grand-Moulin
    (St.-Seurin-de-Cadourne)
Haut-Bages-Monpelou (Pauillac)
Haut-Canteloup (Couquèques)
Haut-Garin (Bégadan)
Haut-Padargnac (Pauillac)
Houbanon (Prignac)
Hourton-Ducasse (St.-Sauveur)
De Labat (St.-Laurent)
Lamothe-Bergeron (Cussac)
Le Landat (Cissac)
Landon (Bégadan)
Larivière (Blaignan)

Lartigue-de-Brochon
    (St.-Seurin-de-Cadourne)
Lassalle (Potensac)
Lavalière (St.-Christoly)
Lestage (Listrac)
MacCarthy (St.-Estèphe)
Monthil (Bégadan)
Moulin de la Roque (Bégadan)
Moulin-Rouge (Cussac)
Panigon (Civrac)
Pibran (Pauillac)
Plantey de la Croix
    (St.-Seurin-de-Cadourne)
Pontet (Blaignan)
Ramage La Batisse (St.-Sauveur)
Romefort (Cussac)
La Roque de By (Bégadan)
De la Rose Maréchale
    (St.-Seurin-de-Cadourne)
St.-Bonnet (St.-Christoly)
St.-Roch (St.-Estèphe)
Saransot (Listrac)
Soudars (Avensac)
Tayac (Soussans)
La Tour Blanche (St.-Christoly)
La Tour du Haut-Caussan (Blaignan)
La Tour du Mirail (Cissac)
La Tour St.-Bonnet (St.-Christoly)
La Tour St.-Joseph (Cissac)
Des Tourelles (Blaignan)
Vernous (Lesparre)
Vieux-Robin (Bégadan)

WHO'S ON FIRST?

The 1855 Classification of the Wines of the Gironde and the subsequent classifications of the wines of Graves and St.-Emilion created a rigid hierarchy that, to this day, dictates how much a consumer must spend for a bottle of classified-growth Bordeaux. Ironically, these historic classifications, which were created in an attempt to classify the quality of Bordeaux wine, are of little relevance with respect to determining the quality of wine produced by a specific château. At most, these classifications should be regarded by both the wine connoisseur and the novice as informational items of historical significance only.

The following is my classification of the top 160 wines of Bordeaux divided into the same five-tiered hierarchy that was used in 1855. It is based on the performance of these châteaux from 1961 to 1997. More weight has been given to the direction the property is heading and the quality of wine produced from 1982 to 1997 than to what the property may have done in the 1961–1981 period. This is done simply because today is the golden age of Bordeaux. Bordeaux is prosperous, and more properties are making better wine with better facilities and advice than ever before.

There are 160 properties in my classification. Since I have included the wines of all the major appellations of Bordeaux, particularly St.-Emilion, Pomerol, Graves, Fronsac, and Canon-Fronsac, that were excluded (except for Haut-Brion), the number of top classified growths is larger than the 61 that made the grade in 1855.

This classification is, of course, my own, but I can say that I have tasted all of these producers' wines from all of the significant vintages, not once but numerous times. In addition, I have visited the great majority of these properties and have studied their placement in this classification intensely. Nothing I have stated is arbitrary, but it is a personal judgment based on years of tasting and years of visiting Bordeaux. Furthermore, I think I can say it was done with no bias. Some of the proprietors with whom I have had some very difficult times over the years are included as first-growths. Some of the owners whom I personally like and respect have not done well. That is the risk, but in the end I hope this consumer's look at the top estates in Bordeaux serves a constructive purpose for those properties that feel unfairly demoted, while I hope those that have won acclaim and recognition here will continue to do what it takes to make the best wine.

MY CLASSIFICATION OF THE TOP CHÂTEAUX OF BORDEAUX (as of 1998)

FIRST-GROWTH QUALITY (21)

Angélus (St.-Emilion)

Ausone (St.-Emilion)

Cheval Blanc (St.-Emilion)

Clinet (Pomerol)

Cos d'Estournel (St.-Estèphe)

Ducru-Beaucaillou (St.-Julien)

L'Evangile (Pomerol)

Haut-Brion (Graves)

Lafite-Rothschild (Pauillac)

Lafleur (Pomerol)

Latour (Pauillac)

Léoville-Las Cases (St.-Julien)

Margaux (Margaux)
La Mission-Haut-Brion (Graves)
La Mondotte (St.-Emilion)
Mouton-Rothschild (Pauillac)
Palmer (Margaux)

Pétrus (Pomerol)
Pichon Lalande (Pauillac)
Le Pin (Pomerol)
Valandraud (St.-Emilion)

SECOND-GROWTHS (22)

Beauséjour-Duffau (St.-Emilion)
Canon-la-Gaffelière (St.-Emilion)
Certan de May (Pomerol)
La Conseillante (Pomerol)
Eglise-Clinet (Pomerol)
Figeac (St.-Emilion)
La Fleur de Gay (Pomerol)
La Gomerie (St.-Emilion)
Gruaud-Larose (St.-Julien)
La Lagune (Ludon)
Léoville-Barton (St.-Julien)

Léoville-Poyferré (St.-Julien)
Lynch-Bages (Pauillac)
Montrose (St.-Estèphe)
Pape-Clément (Graves)
Pichon-Longueville Baron (Pauillac)
Rauzan-Ségla (Margaux)
Smith-Haut-Lafitte (Pessac-Léognan)
Le Tertre-Roteboeuf (St.-Emilion)
Troplong-Mondot (St.-Emilion)
Trotanoy (Pomerol)
Vieux-Château-Certan (Pomerol)

THIRD-GROWTHS (26)

L'Arrosée (St.-Emilion)
Beau-Séjour Bécot (St.-Emilion)
Branaire-Ducru (St.-Julien)
Calon-Ségur (St.-Estèphe)
Cantemerle (Macau)
Clos de l'Oratoire (St.-Emilion)
Domaine de Chevalier (Graves)
La Dominique (St.-Emilion)
Duhart-Milon (Pauillac)
La Gaffelière (St.-Emilion)
Giscours (Margaux)
Grand-Mayne (St.-Emilion)
Grand-Puy Lacoste (Pauillac)

Haut-Bailly (Graves)
Haut-Marbuzet (St.-Estèphe)
La Fleur Pétrus (Pomerol)
Lagrange (St.-Julien)
Larmande (St.-Emilion)
Latour à Pomerol (Pomerol)
Magdelaine (St.-Emilion)
Malescot St.-Exupéry (Margaux)
Monbousquet (St.-Emilion)
Pontet-Canet (Pauillac)
Rol Valentin (St.-Emilion)
Sociando-Mallet (Médoc)
Talbot (St.-Julien)

FOURTH-GROWTHS (18)

Beychevelle (St.-Julien)
Bon Pasteur (Pomerol)
Les Carmes Haut-Brion (Graves)
Chasse-Spleen (Moulis)
Clerc-Milon (Pauillac)

La Couspaude (St.-Emilion)
Ferrand-Lartigue (St.-Emilion)
De Fieuzal (Graves)
Les Forts de Latour (Pauillac)
Le Gay (Pomerol)

Gloria (St.-Julien)
Lafon-Rochet (St.-Estèphe)
La Louvière (Graves)
Moulin St.-Georges (St.-Emilion)

Pavie-Macquin (St.-Emilión)
Quinault-l'Enclos (St.-Emilion)
St.-Pierre (St.-Julien)
Soutard (St.-Emilion)

FIFTH-GROWTHS (73)

Angludet (Margaux)
D'Armailhac (Pauillac)
Bahans-Haut-Brion (Graves)
Balestard-La-Tonnelle (St.-Emilion)
Barde-Haut (St.-Emilion)
Batailley (Pauillac)
Belair (St.-Emilion)
Bourgneuf (Pomerol)
Brane-Cantenac (Margaux)
Cadet-Piola (St.-Emilion)
Canon (St.-Emilion)
Canon de Brem (Canon-Fronsac)
Canon (Moueix) (Canon-Fronsac)
Cantenac-Brown (Margaux)
Cassagne-Haut-Canon-La Truffière
   (Canon-Fronsac)
Certan-Giraud (Pomerol)
Charmail (Médoc)
Citran (Médoc)
Clos des Jacobins (St.-Emilion)
Clos René (Pomerol)
Couvent-des-Jacobins
   (St.-Emilion)
La Croix du Casse (Pomerol)
La Croix de Gay (Pomerol)
Croque-Michotte (St.-Emilion)
Dalem (Fronsac)
La Dauphine (Fronsac)
Dauzac (Margaux)
Durfort-Vivens (Margaux)
Domaine L'Eglise (Pomerol)
L'Enclos (Pomerol)
Faugères (St.-Emilion)
La Fleur-de-Jaugue (St.-Emilion)
Fontenil (Fronsac)

Fourcas-Loubaney (Listrac)
Gazin (Pomerol)
Gombaude-Guillot (Pomerol)
Grand-Pontet (St.-Emilion)
Grand-Puy-Ducasse (Pauillac)
La Grave à Pomerol (Pomerol)
Haut-Bages-Libéral (Pauillac)
Haut-Batailley (Pauillac)
L'Hermitage (St.-Emilion)
D'Issan (Margaux)
Kirwan (Margaux)
Labégorce-Zédé (Margaux)
Lanessan (Haut-Médoc)
Langoa-Barton (St.-Julien)
Larcis-Ducasse (St.-Emilion)
Lascombes (Margaux)
Marquis-de-Terme (Margaux)
Maucaillou (Moulis)
Meyney (St.-Estèphe)
Moulin-Haut-Laroque (Fronsac)
Moulin-Pey-Labrie (Canon-Fronsac)
Les-Ormes-de-Pez (St.-Estèphe)
Nenin (Pomerol)
Pavie (St.-Emilion)
Pavie-Decesse (St.-Emilion)
Pavillon Rouge du Château
   Margaux (Margaux)
Petit-Village (Pomerol)
Potensac (Médoc)
Poujeaux (Moulis)
Prieuré-Lichine (Margaux)
Roc de Cambes (Côtes de Bourg)
Siran (Margaux)
Tayac-Cuvée Prestige (Côtes de
   Bourg)

Du Tertre (Margaux)

La Tour-Haut-Brion (Graves)

Tour Haut-Caussan (Médoc)

Tour du Haut-Moulin (Haut-Médoc)

La Tour-du-Pin-Figeac-Moueix (St.-Emilion)

Trotte Vieille (St.-Emilion)

La Vieille-Cure (Fronsac)

5: THE ELEMENTS FOR MAKING GREAT BORDEAUX WINE

Traditionalists often wax poetic about "the good ol' days," insisting that "they just don't make Bordeaux the way they used to." In fact, for Bordeaux wines, times have never been better, both climatically and financially. Moreover, the quality of winemaking in Bordeaux has never been higher. The greatest wines ever made in Bordeaux are those that are produced today. The most prominent factor about the best red and white wines of Bordeaux is their remarkable longevity. In great years, the aging potential of these wines is unequaled by any other table wines produced in the world. Even in lesser vintages, the wines often need a good 5–8 years to develop fully. The reasons? In order of importance: the grape varieties, the soil, the climate, and the methods of winemaking that are discussed in the sections that follow.

BORDEAUX GRAPES FOR RED WINES

For red wines there are three major grape varieties planted and two minor varieties that have largely now fallen out of favor. The choice of grape varieties used for making Bordeaux has a profound influence on the style of wine that is ultimately produced. Hundreds of years of practice have allowed specific winemaking châteaux to select only the grape varieties that perform best in their soil.

For red wines in the Médoc, if one were to give an average formula for a percentage of grapes planted at a majority of the Médoc châteaux, it would be 60%–65% Cabernet Sauvignon, 10%–15% Cabernet Franc, 20%–35% Merlot, and 3%–8% Petit Verdot. Each château has its own best formula for planting its vineyards; some prefer to use more Merlot, some prefer more Cabernet Sauvignon or Cabernet Franc, and some, more Petit Verdot. As a general rule, the very light, highly drained, gravel soils tend to support Cabernet Sauvignon better than Merlot. For that reason, one finds very high percentages of Cabernet Sauvignon in the appellation of Margaux. In contrast, in the heavier, more clay-dominated soils of St.-Estèphe, Merlot tends to fare better. Consequently, a higher percentage of Merlot is found in St.-Estèphe. Of course, there are exceptions. In the Margaux appellation, Château Palmer uses a significant portion of Merlot in their final blend, as does Château Pichon-Longueville–Comtesse de Lalande in Pauillac. However, the two most important grapes for a highly successful vintage in the Médoc are Cabernet Sauvignon and Merlot. The Cabernet is more widely planted in the Médoc simply because it ripens well and flourishes in the gravelly, well-drained soil that exists in the top vineyards there. The Merlot is popular because, when blended with the tannic, tough, deeply colored Cabernet Sauvignon, it offers softness, flesh, and suppleness to balance out the sterner texture of the Cabernet Sauvignon.

If a château uses a high percentage of Cabernet Sauvignon in its blend, in all likelihood the wine will be densely colored, big, full bodied, tannic, and very ageworthy. On the other hand, if a high percentage of Merlot is used in the blend, then in most cases suppleness and precocious charm are the preferred personality traits.

In the Médoc, Cabernet Franc is also used in small percentages. Cabernet

Franc lacks the color of Cabernet Sauvignon and Merlot but does offer complex aromatic components (particularly aromas of mint, herbs, and spices) that the Bordelais call finesse. The Petit Verdot is planted in very small percentages despite the fact that it ripens very late and in most vintages rarely achieves full maturity. It is often used by those châteaux that employ a high percentage of Merlot because the Petit Verdot provides the hard tannic backbone that is otherwise absent as a result of a high concentration of Merlot.

Each of these four major red grape varieties ripens at a different time. The Merlot is always the first grape to blossom and to become fully mature. Cabernet Franc is second, followed by Cabernet Sauvignon and then Petit Verdot. Few wine consumers realize that spring frost and varying weather patterns at different times during the growing season can seriously affect some of these grape varieties, while sparing others. The production from the Merlot grape, because of its early flowering characteristic, is frequently curtailed by spring frost. In addition, Merlot is the grape most susceptible to rot from moist or damp weather conditions because its skin is less tough and less resistant to disease than that of the Cabernet Sauvignon or Petit Verdot.

This fact alone can be critical for the success of châteaux with extensive Merlot plantations. Late-season rains have on more than one occasion washed out the late-picking properties with vineyards dominated by Cabernet Sauvignon, while the vineyards of Merlot plantings have already been harvested under optimum conditions. When one asks why the Merlot-based wines, such as Pétrus and Trotanoy, were so successful in 1964 as compared to the disappointing Cabernet Sauvignon–based wines, such as Mouton-Rothschild and Lafite-Rothschild, the answer is that the Merlot crop was harvested in perfect weather conditions long before the Cabernet crop, which was drenched and diluted by late-occurring torrential rains.

On the right bank of the Gironde River are the two principal appellations of St.-Emilion and Pomerol. Here, significantly higher percentages of the Merlot and Cabernet Franc grapes are planted. Much of the soil of these two appellations is less well drained and frequently heavier because of a significant clay content. The Cabernet Sauvignon is not fond of such soils, and accordingly smaller amounts of it are planted, unless the vineyard is situated on a particularly well-drained, gravelly soil base, as a few are in these appellations. The Merlot, however, takes well to this type of heavier soil, and surprisingly, so does the Cabernet Franc. There are many exceptions, but in St.-Emilion the standard formula for grape varieties is close to 50% Merlot and 50% Cabernet Franc, with Cabernet Sauvignon mixed in various percentages. In Pomerol, Merlot is clearly the key. Except for a handful of estates, such as Clos l'Eglise and Vieux-Château-Certan, little Cabernet Sauvignon is planted. The average vineyard's composition in Pomerol would be 70%–80%

Merlot and 20%–30% Cabernet Franc. Consequently, it is not surprising to find wines from these two regions maturing faster and being generally fruitier, more supple, and lusher than wines from the Médoc.

In the Graves region, the soil is extremely gravelly as the name implies, thereby affording excellent drainage. As in the Médoc, the Cabernet Sauvignon is favored, but there is more Cabernet Franc and Merlot in Graves, with wines that are usually lighter as a result. However, in rainy years the Graves wines frequently turn out better than others simply because of the outstanding drainage the vineyards enjoy in this region. The 1987 vintage is a classic case in point.

The advantage of knowing the percentage of grape varieties planted at a particular château is that one can predict with some degree of certainty which areas may have performed better than others even before the critics begin issuing their tasting judgments. This can be done by knowing the climatic conditions leading up to and during the harvest and matching those conditions against how the different grape varieties perform under such conditions.

Rarely does Bordeaux have a perfect vintage for all four red wine grape varieties. In 1995, 1990, 1989, 1985, and 1982, all the grape varieties ripened superbly, and everyone agrees that Merlot and Petit Verdot were virtually perfect. These years were profoundly influenced by the opulence and ripeness of the Merlot grape, and consequently, the wines are higher in alcohol, fleshier, and softer than in years that favor the Cabernet Sauvignon. Two classic examples of top Cabernet Sauvignon years are 1996 and 1986. The Merlot overproduced, and many wines that contain a large percentage of Merlot were fluid and lacking structure. Those Médocs with a high percentage of Cabernet Sauvignon produced superb wines that were very much influenced by their fully ripe Cabernet Sauvignon grapes.

CABERNET SAUVIGNON—A grape that is highly pigmented, very astringent, and tannic that provides the framework, strength, dark color, character, and longevity for the wines in a majority of the vineyards in the Médoc. It ripens late, is resistant to rot because of its thick skin, and has a pronounced black currant aroma that is sometimes intermingled with subtle herbaceous scents that take on the smell of cedar wood with aging. Virtually all Bordeaux châteaux blend Cabernet Sauvignon with other red grape varieties. In the Médoc, the percentage of Cabernet Sauvignon in the blend averages 40%–85%; in Graves, 40%–60%; in St.-Emilion, 10%–50%; and in Pomerol, 0%–20%.

MERLOT—Utilized by virtually every château in Bordeaux because of its ability to provide a round, generous, fleshy, supple, alcoholic wine, Merlot ripens, on an average, 1–2 weeks earlier than Cabernet Sauvignon. In the Médoc, this grape reaches its zenith in several châteaux that use high percentages of it (Palmer and Pichon-Lalande), but its fame is in the wines it renders in Pomerol, where it is used profusely. In the Médoc, the percentage of Merlot in the blend averages 5%–45%. In Graves, it averages 20%–40%; in St.-Emilion, 25%–80%; and in Pomerol, 35%–100%. Merlot produces wines lower in acidity and tannin than Cabernet Sauvignon, and as a general rule, wines with a higher percentage of Merlot mature faster than wines with a higher percentage of Cabernet Sauvignon.

CABERNET FRANC—A relative of Cabernet Sauvignon that ripens slightly earlier, Cabernet Franc (called Bouchet in St.-Emilion and Pomerol) is used in small to modest proportions to add complexity and bouquet to a wine. Cabernet Franc has a pungent, often very spicy, minty, sometimes weedy, olive-like aroma. It does not have the fleshy, supple character of Merlot, or the astringency, power, and color of Cabernet Sauvignon. In the Médoc, an average percentage of Cabernet Franc used in the blend is 0%–30%; in Graves, 5%–35%; in St.-Emilion, 25%–66%; in Pomerol, 5%–50%.

PETIT VERDOT—A useful but generally difficult red grape because of its very late ripening characteristics, Petit Verdot provides intense color, mouth-gripping tannins, and high sugar (and thus high alcohol) when it ripens fully, as it did in 1982, 1989, 1990, and 1996 in Bordeaux. When unripe, it provides a nasty, sharp, acidic character. In the Médoc, few châteaux use more than 5% in the blend. In Graves, St.-Emilion, and Pomerol, very little Petit Verdot now exists.

MALBEC—The least-utilized red grape (also called Pressac in St.-Emilion and Pomerol) of the major varietals, Malbec has fallen into disfavor and in most vineyards has now been replanted with one of the more favored grapes. Its future in Bordeaux's best vineyards seems doubtful.

BORDEAUX GRAPES FOR WHITE WINES

Bordeaux produces both dry and sweet white wine. Usually only three grape varieties are used, Sauvignon Blanc and Semillon for both dry and sweet wine, and Muscadelle, which is used sparingly for the sweet wines.

SAUVIGNON BLANC—Used for making both the dry white wines of Graves and the sweet white wines of the Barsac/Sauternes region, Sauvignon Blanc renders a very distinctive wine with a pungent, somewhat herbaceous aroma and crisp, austere flavors. Among the dry white Graves, a few châteaux employ 100% Sauvignon Blanc, but most blend it with Semillon. Less Sauvignon Blanc is used in the winemaking blends in the Sauternes region than in Graves.

SEMILLON—Very susceptible to the famous noble rot called botrytis, which is essential to the production of excellent, sweet wines, Semillon is used to provide a rich, creamy, intense texture to both the dry wines of Graves and the rich, sweet wines of Sauternes. Semillon is quite fruity when young, and wines with a high percentage of Semillon seem to take on weight and viscosity as they age. For these reasons, higher percentages of Semillon are used in making the sweet wines of the Sauternes/Barsac region than in producing the white wines of Graves.

MUSCADELLE—The least planted of the white wine grapes in Bordeaux, Muscadelle is a very fragile grape that is quite susceptible to disease, but when healthy and mature, it produces a wine with an intense flowery, perfumed character. It is used only in tiny proportions by châteaux in the Sauternes/Barsac region. It is used sparingly by the white wine producers of Graves.

SOIL

It is not unusual to hear Bordeaux's best winemakers say that the "wine is made in the vineyard," not the winery. It is interesting to compare the traditional attitude in California, where the primary considerations for making quality wine have been the region's climatic profile, the expertise of the winemaker, and the availability of high technology to sculpture the wine. While a growing number of California wineries are beginning to pay greater attention to soil, few Bordelais will argue with the premise that the greatness of their wine is a result of the soil, or *terroir*, and not the winemaker or vinification equipment.

The famous Médoc area of Bordeaux is a triangular landmass, bordered on the west by the Atlantic Ocean, on the east by the wide Gironde River, and on the south by the city of Bordeaux. The top vineyards of the Médoc stretch out on the eastern half of this generally flat land on slightly elevated slopes facing the Gironde River. The soil is largely unfit for any type of agriculture other than grape growing. It is extremely gravelly and sandy, and the subsoil of the Médoc ranges from heavy clay soil (producing heavier, less fine wines) to lighter chalk and gravels (producing finer, lighter wines).

The very gravelly soil that is the predominant geological characteristic of the Bordeaux vineyards operates as an excellent drainage system, as well as being permeable enough for the vines' roots to penetrate deep into the sub-soil for nutrients, water, and minerals.

The Graves region, south of the city of Bordeaux, derives its name from the very rocky soil, which is even more deeply embedded with gravel than in the Médoc. This contributes to the unique flavor that some commentators have suggested is a mineral-like, earthy taste in the wines of this region. The regions of St.-Emilion and Pomerol are situated 20 miles to the east of the city of Bordeaux. St.-Emilion has various soil bases. Around the charming medieval city of St.-Emilion are the châteaux that are said to sit on the *côtes,* or hillsides. These hillsides were once the sides of a river valley, and the soil is primarily chalk, clay, and limestone. Some of the famous châteaux that sit on the *côtes* of St.-Emilion include Ausone, Canon, Pavie, and Belair.

Several miles to the northwest of St.-Emilion is the *graves* section of St.-Emilion, a gravelly, sandy outcropping bordering the Pomerol appellation. The St.-Emilion châteaux located in this *graves* area produce a different style of wine—more fleshy, more fruity, and more accessible than the austere, tannic, and reserved wines produced from vineyards on the limestone, chalk, and clay hillsides of the town of St.-Emilion. Two of the best-known châteaux in this area of St.-Emilion are Cheval Blanc and Figeac. Of course, exceptions in style within each sub-region exist, but in broad terms, there are two major types of St.-Emilion wines, a *graves* style and a *côtes* style, and the style is a direct result of the soil base in which the vines are planted.

In Pomerol, which borders the *graves* section of St.-Emilion, the soil composition is quite similar, yet variations exist. Pomerol's most famous estate—Pétrus—sits on an elevated plateau that has a unique, rather heavy clay soil unlike that of any other vineyard in Pomerol.

The subtle differences in soil composition and their effect on the style and personality of the wine are best exemplified by three examples of adjoining vineyards. On the border of the Médoc communes of Pauillac and St.-Julien, three highly respected properties—the first-growth Pauillac Latour, the second-growth St.-Julien Léoville-Las Cases, and the second-growth Pauillac Pichon-Longueville Baron—sit together, with each one's vineyard contiguous to the other. The yield from the vineyards, the percentage of each vine planted, the method of making the wine, the average age of the vines, the types of grape varieties, and finally, the time the wine spends aging in the cask are not dramatically different for all three châteaux. However, all three wines differ substantially in taste, style, texture, and evolution. All three have totally different soil bases.

In Pomerol, one has only to compare the soil of that appellation's most famous wine, Pétrus—which has heavy clay rich in iron—with the soil of its immediate neighbor, La Fleur-Pétrus—which has little clay, but much more sand and gravel. Both wines could not, despite almost exactly the same vinifications by the same people, be more different.

Soil is undoubtedly a very important factor in the character and diverse style of Bordeaux wines. It is not, as the Bordelais would have one believe, the only element necessary to make a great wine. The importance of a hospitable climate, conservative viticultural practices whereby the use of fertilizers is kept to a minimum, aggressive pruning procedures, and of course, careful vinification and handling are all significant factors in the making of great wine. Even with the finest technology, a great winemaking team, and the best, well-drained, gravelly soil, great wine can not be made without optimal climatic conditions that produce fully mature ripe grapes.

CLIMATE

The great vintages of Bordeaux have always been characterized by growing seasons that have been abnormally hot, dry, and sunny. The excellent to great vintages of Bordeaux such as 1900, 1921, 1929, 1945, 1947, 1949, 1959, 1961, 1982, 1989, 1990, and 1995 have all shared several distinctive climatic characteristics—heat, sunshine, and droughtlike conditions. Several prominent Bordeaux château proprietors, who have recently claimed that disastrous vintages such as 1968, 1965, and 1963 will never occur again because of the technological winemaking advances, seem to forget that good wine cannot be made from unripe, vegetal-tasting grapes. Bordeaux, like any major viticultural area, must have plenty of sunshine, dry weather, and heat in order to produce excellent wine.

When the Bordeaux châteaux have to wait until October to harvest their grapes (rather than harvesting in September), it is usually a sign that the growing season has been abnormally cool and, even worse, wet. A review of the finest vintages in Bordeaux reveals that the commencement date of the harvest almost always occurs in September.

1870—September 10	1961—September 22
1893—August 18	1970—September 27
1899—September 24	1975—September 22
1900—September 24	1978—October 7
1921—September 15	1982—September 13
1929—September 23	1985—September 29
1945—September 13	1986—September 23
1947—September 15	1989—August 31
1949—September 27	1990—September 12
1953—September 28	1995—September 20
1959—September 20	1996—September 16

In comparison, here are the commencement dates of the harvests for some of Bordeaux's notoriously bad vintages.

1951—October 9	1969—October 6
1954—October 10	1972—October 7
1956—October 14	1977—October 3
1957—October 4	1984—October 5
1963—October 7	1991—September 30
1965—October 2	1992—September 29
1968—September 20	1993—September 26

The pattern would appear to be obvious. Great years are characterized by plentiful amounts of sunshine, heat, and dry weather. Under such conditions the grapes ripen steadily and quickly, and the harvests begin early. Poor years result from inadequate supplies of these precious natural commodities. The grapes never ripen fully and are picked in either an unripe or a rain-diluted condition.

There are few exceptions to the climatic patterns for excellent and poor vintages. For example, 1979 (picked October 3) was a late October harvest year that produced very good wines. In recent years there has been a growing tendency by producers to attempt to obtain what they call *sur-maturité*. The old rule that governed the harvest in Bordeaux was the so-called 100-day rule, which dictated harvesting the grapes 100 days after the flowering. Now, in an effort to make wines full bodied, richer, and lower in acidity, the 100-day custom has grown to 110 or even 120 days. This new trend in Bordeaux may well result in many more excellent October harvests, such as 1979, than in the past, when an October harvest often meant poorer quality.

The climatic patterns leading to excellent vintages for red wines in Bordeaux do not apply to the production of the sweet white wines made in the Sauternes/Barsac region. Great vintages in this region require a combination of misty, humid mornings and dry, sunny afternoons. This daily pattern of climatic events enable the noble rot (botrytis) to begin to develop on the grapes. It is interesting that each grape succumbs to the botrytis infection on a different timetable. Some grapes become totally infected quickly, others not until weeks later. The key to forming the great, luscious, sweet wines in this area is an extended period of alternating humidity and dry heat that permits the botrytis infection to take place. During this period, the château must harvest the infected grapes by hand numerous times if the highest quality is to be achieved, for it is the botrytis infection that causes the remaining grape juice to be intensely concentrated and imparts to it the distinctive smell and flavor of a late harvest, decadently rich, sweet wine. Of course, the harvest for the sweet wines of Barsac/Sauternes almost always takes place long after the red wine grapes have been picked and made into wine in the Médoc, Graves, St.-Emilion, and Pomerol. It also occurs when Bordeaux's weather becomes the most risky—late October and November.

A week or more of a deluge can destroy the chances for a successful crop in Sauternes and Barsac. More often than not, the grape crop is damaged by late season rains that wash the noble rot from the grapes and also cause other grapes to swell, thus diminishing their intensity. In the last 20 years, only 1971, 1975, 1976, 1983, 1986, 1988, 1989, 1990, and 1996 have been uniformly excellent growing seasons for the sweet wine producers of this region.

THE VINIFICATION AND *ÉLEVAGE* OF BORDEAUX WINES

The production of red wine begins when the freshly harvested grapes are crushed. The steps are as follows: 1) picking, 2) destemming and crushing, 3) pumping into fermentation tanks, 4) fermenting of grape sugar into alcohol, 5) macerating, or keeping the grape skins and pips in contact with the grape juice for additional extract and color, 6) racking, or transferring the wine to small 55-gallon barrels or large tanks for the secondary or malolactic fermentation to be completed, 7) putting the wine in oak barrels for aging, and 8) bottling the wine.

In Bordeaux, the average harvest takes 3 weeks or more to complete for the dry white and red wines. For the sweet wines, the harvest can take as long as 2 months to complete. The white wine grapes used for making the dry wines ripen earliest and are picked first. This is followed by the red grape Merlot and then the other red grape varieties, Cabernet Franc, Cabernet Sauvignon, and, last, Petit Verdot. The fact that the Merlot ripens earliest makes it an interesting sequence to monitor. In 1964, 1967, 1987, and 1994, the châteaux that had extensive plantings of Merlot, primarily those in St.-Emilion and Pomerol, harvested early, and their vineyards produced much better wines than the châteaux in the Médoc that had to wait for their Cabernet to ripen and were caught by fall rains. In such a year when significant rains damage the overall crop quality, the early pickers, normally the right bank communes of St.-Emilion and Pomerol, will have completed most of their harvest. As vintages such as 1964, 1967, 1987, and 1994 attest, they may have succeeded brilliantly, whereas their counterparts in the Médoc have had to deal with bloated, rain-swollen Cabernet Sauvignon grapes.

MAKING
THE RED WINE

The most critical decision when it comes to making quality wine is the date of harvest. An error made at harvesting cannot be reversed, and a previous year's work can be largely undone. Grapes must be picked at the peak of maturity or the flavors will be marred by either too much acidity or too much herbaceousness. Assuming the grapes are harvested properly at full physiological ripeness, when the grapes arrive from the vineyards the top châteaux will go through a traditional and laborious method of hand-sorting them before they go to the destemmer-crusher machine. This process of sorting grapes and discarding those that are damaged, rotten, or under-ripe is essential to produce high-quality wine. One château, Valandraud, not only hand-sorts but hand-destems the grapes, something that is almost unimaginable at other Bordeaux châteaux.

Most châteaux claim to get the best results by instructing their pickers to remove and discard damaged or unhealthy grape bunches in the vineyard. Certainly the need for careful picking of grapes exists every year, but in vintages where there has been extensive rot in the vineyards, the most reputable châteaux have the pickers make a very severe selection—called a *triage* —in which the damaged berries are removed from each bunch at the time of picking.

The first decision the winemaker must make is whether the grapes are to be partially or totally destemmed. Today the great majority of the châteaux destem completely. This policy is in keeping with Bordeaux's current passion to make rich, supple wines that can be drunk young but will age well. Several notable châteaux continue to throw a percentage of stems into the fermentation tank with the crushed grapes.

The opponents of adding the stems argue that they add a vegetal coarseness to a wine, soak up some of the color-giving material, and can add too much tannin to the wine.

Once the grapes have been destemmed by an apparatus the French call a *égrappoir,* the partially crushed berries are pumped into tanks for the commencement of the fermentation.

For the last thirty years the trend in Bordeaux has been to replace the large, old, oak and cement fermentation vats with stainless-steel, temperature-controlled tanks. They are easy to clean and make it simple to control the temperature, an element that is especially important when the grapes are harvested in torridly hot conditions, as in 1982. Despite the increasing numbers of properties that have converted to stainless-steel tanks, the traditional large oak *cuves* and concrete *cuves* can still be found.

While stainless steel may be easier to use, great vineyards managed by meticulous winemakers have proven that great wine can be made in oak, cement, or steel fermentation tanks. Once the grapes have been put into the vat, the wild yeasts that inhabit the vineyard, and in many cases additional cultured yeasts, begin the process called fermentation—the conversion of the grape sugars into alcohol. At this critical point, the temperature of the fermenting juice must be monitored with extreme care, and how hot or how cold the fermentation is affects the resulting style of the wine.

Some of the breakthrough technology being utilized in Bordeaux today comes into play with grape must. Very expensive machines (costing up to $200,000) that perform procedures to remove water from swollen grapes via two primary methods—1) reverse osmosis, and 2) evaporation under a vacuum—are increasingly applied by wealthy estates, particularly in years where Bordeaux has had too much rain. These techniques, which have been employed largely since the late eighties, do indeed concentrate the wines by removing water while leaving the extract of flavor and solids of the wine undisturbed. I have discussed at length with leading Bordeaux oenologists the long-term effect reverse osmosis and evaporation by vacuum might have on the resulting wines. Opinion is largely unanimous that the results to date have been impressive (particularly with reverse osmosis), although wines made with these methods will need 10–20 years of cellaring before they can be judged effectively. Nevertheless, the early promise shown by such methods as removing water from the diluted must in rainy years has been a technological breakthrough.

Most Bordeaux winemakers ferment a red wine at 25–30 degrees centigrade. Few châteaux allow the temperature to exceed 30 degrees centigrade. These properties allow the fermentation to go up to 32–33 degrees centigrade. The higher temperatures are aimed at extracting as much color and tannins as possible from the grape skins. The risk of a temperature in excess of 35 degrees centigrade is that acetic bacteria will grow and flourish. It is these acetic bacteria that cause a wine to take on a flawed, vinegary smell. An additional danger of fermentation temperatures in excess of 35 degrees centigrade is that the natural yeasts will be destroyed by the heat and the fermentation will stop completely, causing what is referred to as a "stuck fermentation." As a general rule, the châteaux that ferment at high temperatures are aiming for high-extract, rich, tannic wines. Those châteaux that ferment at cooler temperatures of 25 degrees centigrade or less usually are trying to achieve a lighter, fruitier, less tannic style of wine. However, for châteaux that ferment at high temperatures, constant vigilance is mandatory.

Fermentation tanks must be watched 24 hours a day, and if a dangerously high temperature is reached, the grape juice must be cooled immediately. With stainless-steel tanks, this can be done rather simply by running cool water over the outside of the tanks. With concrete and wooden tanks, the wine must be siphoned off and run through cooling tubes.

During the vinification, a cap, or *chapeau,* is formed as a result of the solid materials, grape skins, stems, and pips rising to the top of the fermentation tank. Winemakers must be careful to keep the cap moist, even submerged in some cases, to encourage additional extractive material to be removed from the color- and tannin-giving skins. Additionally, the cap must be kept wet so as to prevent bacterial growth. The pumping of the fermented wine juice over the cap is called the *remontage* in French and "pumping over the cap" in English.

When the fermentation begins, the winemaker must make another critical decision that will influence the style of the wine: to chaptalize or not. Chaptalization is the addition of sugar to increase the alcohol content. It is employed widely in Bordeaux because this region only occasionally has a vintage where perfect grape ripeness and maturity are obtained. In most years the grapes do not have sufficient natural sugar content to produce wines with 12% alcohol. Therefore, the Bordeaux châteaux aim to increase the alcohol content by 1–2 degrees. Only in years such as 1961, 1982, 1989, 1990, and 1996 (for Cabernet Sauvignon) has little chaptalization been necessary because of the superb ripeness achieved by these grapes.

After the total grape sugar (and added sugar, if necessary) has been converted to alcohol, the primary or alcoholic fermentation is completed. It is at this stage that another important winemaking decision must be made: how long to macerate the grape skins with the wine. The length of the maceration period has a direct bearing on whether the wine will be rich, well colored, tannic, and long-lived, or supple, precocious, and ready to drink earlier. At most major Bordeaux châteaux the maceration period is 7–14 days, making the average total time the wine spends in contact with the skins about 21 days. This period is called the *cuvaison.*

Following the *cuvaison,* the infant wine is transferred off its lees, which are composed of the grape skins and pips—called the *marc*—into clean tanks or wood barrels. This free-run juice is called the *vin de goutte.* The skins are then pressed, and the resulting press wine, or *vin de presse,* is a heavily pigmented, tannic, chewy, and coarse wine that will, in many instances, be eventually blended back into the free-run wine juice. Some winemakers, not wanting a firm, tannic wine, refuse to use any press wine in the blend. Others, who want to add a little muscle and firmness to their wines, will add 10%–20%. Some winemakers desirous of a robustly styled, intense wine will blend it all back in with the free-run *vin de goutte.* In most cases, the decision to utilize the press wine is predicated on the type of wine the vintage produced. In a year such as 1975 or 1986, the addition of press wine would, in most cases, make the wine too tannic and robust. In light vintages, where the quality of the free-run juice lacks strength, firmness, and color (for example, 1973 and 1980), more of the highly pigmented, tannic press wine will be used.

The secondary fermentation, or malolactic fermentation, in which the tart malic acidity is converted into softer, creamier, lactic acidity, is a gentle step in the evolution of the young red wine. In some châteaux, the malolactic fermentation occurs simultaneously with the alcoholic fermentation, but at most properties the malolactic fermentation takes place over a period of months, usually October following the harvest through the end of January. In certain years, the malolactic fermentation may continue through spring and summer following the vintage, but this is quite unusual. Malolactic fermentation is especially critical for red wines because it adds roundness and character. One movement that began in the late eighties and is supported in the nineties by more and more top-quality châteaux is the application of malolactic fermentation in barrels as opposed to vats. This procedure, commonly employed in Burgundy, is relatively revolutionary in Bordeaux because the estates are so large, and fermentations, both primary and malolactic, have traditionally occurred in vat. However, malolactic fermentation in barrels is believed to give the wines a creamier texture, as well as better integration of oak. Certainly those estates that have employed this procedure have produced very successful wines.

The use of new versus old oak barrels for wine aging has been hotly debated in winemaking circles. In Bordeaux, the famous first-growths— Lafite-Rothschild, Mouton-Rothschild, Latour, Margaux, Haut-Brion, and the famous trio from the right bank communes of St.-Emilion and Pomerol, Cheval Blanc, Ausone, and Pétrus—use 100% new oak barrels for virtually every vintage. For the other well-run châteaux, 33%–60% new oak barrels per vintage seems to produce a comfortable marriage of fruit, tannin, and oak. Unquestionably, the higher the percentage of new oak barrels used, the richer the wine must be so as not to be overwhelmed by the oaky, vanillin aromas and flavors. For example, many of the wines from the 1973 and 1980 vintages, which produced light yet fruity wines, were simply not big enough or rich enough to handle aging in the new oak barrels they received. New barrels impart a significant tannin content, as well as vanillin oakiness, to a wine, and therefore they must be used judiciously.

One of the side effects of Bordeaux's modern-day prosperity from the success of recent vintages is the tremendous investment in new winery equipment and, in particular, new barrels. Abuse of new oak can obliterate the fruit of a wine, and while the huge massive fruit and concentration of wines from a vintage like 1982 can easily handle exposure to ample amounts of new oak, my tastings of the more delicate, less intense and concentrated 1981s, and even some 1989s, has frequently left me wondering whether too much new oak cooperage was doing more harm than good. It seems that with many of the estates below the first-growth level now routinely using 50%–75% new oak, there is a danger that too many Bordeaux wines are becoming excessively woody. While the use of new oak is recommended and avoids the potential sanitation problems posed by the usage of older barrels, the extremely high yields witnessed in Bordeaux since the mid-1980s and lack of extract in many wines is not fully masked by the gobs of new oak aromas often found in recent Bordeaux vintages.

One of the remarkable aspects of a red Bordeaux wine is its long sojourn in small oak barrels. In most vintages, this period of aging will take from 12 months to as long as 24–30 months. This period of barrel aging has been shortened noticeably over the last several decades. Is the rush to get the wine in the bottle and to the marketplace becoming an obsession? Bordeaux winemakers have tried to capture more fruit and freshness in their wines and to reduce the risk of oxidation or overly woody, dry, tannic wines from too much exposure to wood. The great majority of Bordeaux châteaux now bottle their wine in late spring and early summer of the second year after the harvest. For example, the 1995 and 1996 Bordeaux wines were bottled from May through July in 1996 and 1997, respectively. It is rare for a château to bottle in late fall or the following winter, as was the practice 20 years ago. Several prominent châteaux that do bottle later than the others include Margaux, Haut-Brion, Clinet, and Calon-Ségur, all of which rarely bottle unless the wine has had at least 24 months in small oak casks.

The period of cask aging will be shorter in vintages like 1997, 1993, 1992, 1981, 1979, or 1976, where the wines lack great concentration and depth of character, and will be longer in years such as 1975, 1982, 1983, 1986, 1990, 1995, and 1996, where the wines are very full, rich, highly pigmented, and concentrated. The principle is simple: Lighter, frailer wines can easily be overwhelmed by oak aging, whereas robust, virile, rich wines need and can take significantly more exposure to oak casks. However, there is no question that the practical and commercial realities of the Bordeaux wine business now dictate bottling the wine within 2 years of the harvest in all but the most unusual circumstances.

During the aging period in oak barrels, the new wine is often racked four times the first year. Racking is an essential step necessary for clarifying the wine. This process involves transferring the clear wine off the deposit, or lees, that have precipitated to the bottom of the barrel. If racking is not done promptly or carefully, the wine will take on a smell of rotten eggs as a result of hydrogen sulfide emissions that come off the lees. The rackings are an intensely laborious process, but the French theory is that it is these lees, which float in the wines and eventually fall to the bottom of the barrel, that are the substance and material that give Bordeaux wines their remarkable aromatic and flavor complexity.

One of the most significant new technological developments in this area is the filtration of the new wine prior to its placement in barrels. This process, employed widely in California, removes the solids from the wine and results in a clearer wine that needs to be racked significantly less—only one time the first year. The proponents of this process get a cleaner, purer wine that does not have to be handled as much and therefore is less prone to oxidation. They also can get their wine into new oak barrels by the end of October, giving it a 3- to 4-month head start on its neighbors when the critics arrive in April to do their tastings. Opponents of such a procedure argue that the process strips the wine of its solids and therefore deprives it of the important elements necessary for it to achieve complex aromas and flavors. The critics claim that it is only a labor-saving, cunning procedure designed to make the wine show well at an early stage.

While the red wine rests in barrels, most châteaux carry out another procedure designed to ensure that the wine is brilliant, clean, and free of hazy, suspended colloidal matter when bottled. It is called fining. Fining has traditionally been done with egg whites that function to attract and trap suspended solids in the barrel of wine. They are then dropped to the bottom of the barrel with the other solids that have been precipitated. Wines that are overly fined lose body, length, concentration, and character. Today, fining is often done immediately prior to bottling, in large tanks. Additionally, many châteaux have abandoned the traditional egg whites in favor of more efficacious substances like bentonite and gelatin. In Bordeaux, a wine is rarely fined more than twice for fear of removing too much flavor at the expense of absolute clarity. There is no doubt that too many wines in Bordeaux are excessively fined and stripped of flavor and body.

In addition to the careful vinification and handling of the young red wine, one of the common characteristics at the best-run châteaux in Bordeaux is an extremely rigid selection process for determining which wine will be bottled under the château's name and which wine will be bottled under a secondary label or sold in bulk to a cooperative or broker in Bordeaux. The best châteaux make their first selection in the vineyard. For example, the wine from young vines (normally those under 7–8 years old) is vinified separately from the wine from older vines. The difference even to a neophyte taster between wine produced from 25-year-old vines and wine produced from 5-year-old vines is remarkable. Young vines may produce a well-colored wine, but it rarely has the depth or rich, concentrated character of a wine from older vines. For that reason, the top châteaux never blend wine from the younger section of the vineyard with wine from the older vines.

There are a number of châteaux that refuse to discriminate between old and new vines, and the quality of their wines frequently suffers as a result.

In addition to the selection process in the vineyard, the best châteaux also make a strict selection of the finished wine, normally in January or February following the vintage. At this time, the winemaking staff, together with the consulting oenologist and in many cases the owner, will taste all the different lots of wine produced in the vintage and then decide which lots, or cuvées, will go into the château's wine and which lots will be bottled under a secondary label or sold off in bulk. This procedure is also accompanied by the *assemblage,* wherein the best lots of wine are blended together, including the blending of the different red grape varieties, Merlot, Cabernet Sauvignon, Cabernet Franc, and Petit Verdot. It is no coincidence that the châteaux that make the most severe selections frequently produce the best wines of Bordeaux. Virtually all châteaux make their *assemblage* in December or January following the vintage.

Unless something unusual occurs in the barrel (a dirty barrel that causes bacterial spoilage is the most common problem) during the aging process, called *élevage,* the wine will be transferred from the barrel to the fermentation tanks, given its last fining, and then bottled at the château.

The idea of bottling the wine exclusively at the château (it is designated on the label as *mise en bouteille au château*) is a rather recent development. Until the late sixties many of the Bordeaux châteaux routinely sent barrels of their wine to brokers in Bordeaux and merchants in Belgium or England, where the wine would be bottled. Such a practice was fraught with the potential not only for fraud, but for sloppy handling of the wine as a result of poor, and unsanitary bottling facilities.

Now the châteaux all have modern bottling facilities, and all the classified growths, as well as the great majority of Crus Bourgeois, bottle their own wine. The bottling of the château's entire production in a given vintage can take from 1 month to almost 3 months at the largest properties. Yet one of the distinctive characteristics of Bordeaux wine is that each château's production for a given year is bottled within this time frame. This guarantees to the consumer that, given the same treatment and cellar storage, the wine should be relatively consistent from bottle to bottle.

At the time of the bottling operation, the winemaker has one last decision to make that will influence the style (and perhaps the quality) of the wine. More and more châteaux have purchased German-made, sophisticated micropore filter machines to remove any solids or other colloidal particles that may have escaped the various racking procedures and finings. Fortunately, most châteaux continue to filter only by passing the wine through a coarse cellulose filter pad. I know of no serious property that sterile filters their wines. Some châteaux believe that filtration is essential for a healthy, clean bottle of wine, whereas others claim that it is totally unnecessary and robs and strips the wine of body, flavor, and potential life.

Who is right? There are supporters on both sides in the filtration versus nonfiltration argument. Certainly the current fear on the part of retailers, restaurateurs, wholesalers, importers, and the wine producers themselves that wine consumers think sediment is a sign of a flawed wine has tragically caused many châteaux to overreact and run their wines through very fine, tight filters that undoubtedly eviscerate the wine. Fortunately the major châteaux have been content to do just a slight, coarse polishing filtration, aimed at removing large colloidal suspensions, or have simply refused to filter the wine at all, hoping the fickle consumer will learn one day that a sediment, or *dépôt* as the French say, is in reality one of the healthiest signs in an older bottle of Bordeaux.

Since filtration of wine is a relatively recent trend (it became popular beginning in the mid-1970s) in oenology, only time in the bottle will tell whether filtration robs a wine of richness, complexity, and life, as its opponents argue. For the record, if the wine is biologically stable and clear, as are most Bordeaux wines, excessive fining and filtration seems unnecessary. I have done enough blind tastings of filtered versus unfiltered cuvées to remain adamantly against the entire process. Anyone who says that filtration removes nothing from an otherwise stable wine is either a fool or a liar.

Once the wine is bottled, the châteaux usually refuse to release the wine for shipment until it has rested for 2–4 months. The theory is that the bottling operation churns up the wine so much that it is shocked and requires at least several months to recover. My tastings of immediately bottled Bordeaux have often corroborated this fact.

MAKING THE WHITE WINE

The most important consideration when producing the dry white wines of Bordeaux is to retain an element of crispness and freshness in the wines. Otherwise they would taste stale or heavy. No one in Bordeaux has made more progress with white wine vinification than Denis Dubourdieu. It was Dubourdieu, the great white wine–making guru of Bordeaux, who pioneered the use of cold fermentation temperatures (15–17 degrees centigrade) and extended skin contact called *macération pelliculaire.* Because the skins impart the wine's aroma and flavor, this process extracts considerably more fragrance and flavor intensity. These techniques have resulted in a plethora of interesting, tasty, character-filled, dry white wines not only from the prestigious Graves region of Bordeaux, but also from such appellations as Premières Côtes de Bordeaux and Entre-Deux-Mers.

The style of the wine is also affected by whether it is either vinified and/or aged in stainless-steel tanks or oak barrels. In either case, the winemaker must be careful to guard against oxidation. This is easily done by treating the wine with sulfur dioxide, an antioxidant. Most of the high-class white wines, such as Domaine de Chevalier, Haut-Brion-Blanc, Laville-Haut-Brion, and de Fieuzal, clarify the young, grapy white wine by a process known as *débourbage* (decanting off the gross lees). More commercially oriented producers use a centrifuge, or intensely filter the wine after the vinification to clarify it. The more traditional *débourbage,* in my opinion, produces a more complex and interesting wine.

Another of the most crucial decisions made regarding the ultimate style of white Bordeaux is whether or not the wine is allowed to go through a malolactic fermentation. Malolactic fermentation can be encouraged by heating the vats. This secondary fermentation converts higher, sharper malic acids into the softer, creamier malolactic acids. While most Burgundies are put through a malolactic fermentation, Bordeaux wines usually have their malolactic blocked by the addition of sulfur. The numerous low-acid vintages of the eighties dictated that malolactic fermentation be eschewed.

Most dry white wines of Bordeaux tend to be bottled within 3–6 months of the vintage in order to emphasize their freshness and crispness. Those white wines that are meant to be longer lived and more ageworthy are often kept in new oak casks from 1 month to as long as 16–18 months (as in the case of the great white wine made at Domaine de Chevalier). All dry white Bordeaux wine is routinely fined and filtered at bottling. Yet producers of wines such as de Fieuzal, Laville-Haut-Brion, Haut-Brion-Blanc, and Domaine de Chevalier process them as minimally as possible for fear of stripping the wines of their aromatic complexity and flavor dimension.

The production of the sweet white wines of Barsac and Sauternes is an even more labor-intensive and risky procedure. The best wines are almost always the result of numerous passes through the vineyard to select only those grapes that have been attacked by the noble rot, *botrytis cinerea* (see page 1216). The yields from such selective harvesting (done grape by grape rather than bunch by bunch) are not permitted to exceed 25 hectoliters per hectare, which is well below 2 tons per acre. Compared with the 50–65 hectoliters per hectare that many of the neighboring red wine producers routinely obtain, the difficult economics of producing a Barsac/Sauternes wine are obvious. Once the botryos grapes are harvested, the grapes are crushed. The fermentation is allowed to continue until the sugar is converted into a 14%–15% alcohol level in the wines. This still leaves unfermented sugar in the wine. The combination of the heady alcohol character with the sweetness of the wine, as well as the distinctive aromas and lavishly rich texture created in part by the botrytis, results in sweet wines that are among the most riveting in the world.

One of the interesting techniques developed in Barsac/Sauternes was the introduction in the late eighties of a procedure called cryo-extraction. This controversial process involves freezing the incoming grapes (at temperatures of 21 degrees Fahrenheit) in order to turn their water into ice particles before pressing, leaving the water behind and increasing the concentration of richness in the grape must. It has been practiced at such celebrated châteaux as Rayne-Vigneau, Rieussec, and Rabaud-Promis. A cryo-extraction machine even exists at Château Yquem. This procedure, while still experimental, has yielded impressive early results. Critics who claim that it is simply a labor-saving gimmick may be proven wrong. With cryo-extraction, the botrytis-affected grapes are processed without any potential for dilution because the frozen water is left behind, concentrating the extracted juice to just the essence of the grapes.

After the fermentation, the sweet white wines of the top estates are usually aged in cask, of which a significant percentage is new. At Yquem the wine is always aged in 100% new oak for at least 3 years. At other top estates, such as Climens and Suduiraut, the percentage of new oak varies from 50%–100%. There remain a handful of estates, most notably Gilette, that abhor new oak yet also produce great wine.

At bottling, most of the sweet wines are fined and lightly filtered.

6: A USER'S GUIDE TO BORDEAUX

CELLARING

Bordeaux, like any fine wine, has to be stored properly if it is to be served in a healthy condition when mature. All wine enthusiasts know that subterranean wine cellars that are vibration free, dark, damp, and kept at a constant 55 degrees Fahrenheit are considered perfect for wine. However, few of us have our own castle with such accommodations for our beloved wines. While such conditions are the ideal, Bordeaux wines will thrive and develop well in other environments as well. I have tasted many old Bordeaux wines from closet and basement cellars that reach 65 degrees Fahrenheit in the summer, and the wines have been perfect. When cellaring Bordeaux, keep the follow-

ing rules in mind and you are not likely to be disappointed by a wine that has gone prematurely over the hill.

RULE 1

Do try to guarantee that the wine is kept as cool as possible. The upper safe limit for long-term cellaring of 10 years or more is 65 degrees Fahrenheit, but no higher. Wines kept at such temperatures will age a bit faster, but they will not age badly. If you can somehow get the temperature down to 65 degrees or below, you will never have to worry about the condition of your wines. At 55 degrees Fahrenheit—the ideal temperature—the wines actually evolve so slowly that your grandchildren will probably benefit from them more than you do. As for temperature, constancy is highly prized and any changes in temperature should occur slowly. White wines are much more sensitive to less than ideal cellar temperatures. Therefore, while the dry white wines of Bordeaux should be kept at temperatures as close to 55 degrees as possible, the bigger, more alcoholic, sweet white wines of Barsac and Sauternes can age quite well at cellar temperatures up to 65 degrees Fahrenheit.

RULE 2

Be sure the storage area is odor free, vibration free, and dark. A humidity level of 50%–80% is ideal. Above 80% is fine for the wine, but the labels will become moldy and deteriorate. A humidity level below 50% can cause the corks to become drier than desired.

RULE 3

Bordeaux wines from vintages that produced powerful, rich, concentrated, full-bodied wines travel and age significantly better than wines from vintages that produced lightweight wines. For example, the oceanic voyage for Bordeaux can be traumatic for wines from vintages such as 1971, 1976, 1977, and 1980. The wines from these vintages—less concentrated, less tannic, and more fragile—often suffer considerably more from travel to this country than big, rich, tannic, full-bodied wines such as 1970, 1975, 1978, 1982, 1983, 1985, 1986, 1988, 1989, 1990, 1995, and 1996. When you decide which Bordeaux wines to cellar, keep in mind that the fragile wines will develop much faster—even under ideal storage conditions.

RULE 4

When buying new vintages of Bordeaux to cellar, I personally recommend buying the wine as soon as it appears on the market, assuming, of course, you have tasted the wine and like it. The reason for this is that few wine merchants, importers, wholesalers, or distributors care about how wine is stored. This attitude—that wine is just another spirit that like whiskey or beer can be left standing upright and exposed to dramatic extremes of temperature, as well as damaging light—is fortunately changing as more knowledgeable wine people assume positions of control in major wine shops. However, far too many fine wines are damaged early in their life by terrible storage conditions, so the only way a wine enthusiast can prevent such tragedies from happening is to assume custody and control over the wine as early in its life as possible. This means acting promptly to secure your wines.

SERVING

There are no secrets concerning the formalities of serving Bordeaux. All one needs is a good corkscrew, a clean, odor-free decanter and glasses, as well as a sense of order as to how Bordeaux wines should be served and whether the wine should breathe.

Bordeaux wines do throw a sediment, particularly after they have attained 6 or 7 years of age. This mandates decanting—the procedure where the wine is poured into a clean decanter to separate the brilliant wine from the dusty particles that have precipitated to the bottom of the bottle. First, older bottles of Bordeaux should be removed carefully from storage so as not to disturb them and make the wine cloudy. Decanting can be an elaborate procedure, but all one needs is a clean, soap- and odor-free decanter and a steady hand. If you lack a steady hand, consider buying a decanting machine, which is a wonderful, albeit expensive, invention for making decanting fun and easier. Most important of all, be sure to rinse the decanter with unchlorinated well or mineral water regardless of how clean you think it is. A decanter or a wine glass left sitting in a china closet or cupboard acts as a wonderful trap for room and kitchen odors that are invisible but rear their off-putting smell when the wine is poured into the decanter or glass. In addition, many glasses have an invisible soapy residue left in them from less than perfect dishwasher rinses. I can't begin to tell you how many dinner parties I have attended where the wonderful cedary, black currant bouquet of a 15- or 20-year-old Pauillac was flawed by the smell of dishwasher detergents or some stale kitchen odor that accumulated in the glass between uses.

Assuming that you have poured the wine into a clean decanter, you should also consider the optimal temperature at which the wine should be served, whether you should allow the wine to breathe, and, if you are serving several Bordeaux wines, the order of presentation.

The breathing or airing of a Bordeaux wine is rather controversial. Some connoisseurs adamantly claim that breathing is essential, while others claim it is simply all nonsense. Who is right? I have done numerous comparisons with wines to see if breathing works or doesn't. I still don't know the answers, if in fact they exist, but here are my observations. The act of decanting a Bordeaux wine is probably all the breathing most wines need. I have found that when serving young, muscular, rich, tannic vintages of Bordeaux, 20–90 minutes of breathing can sometimes result in a softer wine. However, the immediate gush of intense fruitiness that often spills forth when the wine is opened and decanted does subside a bit. So for the big, rich wines of Bordeaux, breathing is often a trade-off—you get some softening of the wine, but you also lose some of the wine's fruity aroma.

With lighter-weight, less tannic Bordeaux wines, I have found extended breathing to be detrimental. Such wines are more fragile and often less endowed, and prolonged breathing tends to cause them to fade. With respect to older vintages of Bordeaux, 15–20 minutes of decanting is usually all that is necessary. With lightweight, older vintages and very old vintages, I recommend opening the wine, decanting it, and serving it immediately. Once an old wine begins to fade, it can never be resuscitated.

There are always exceptions to such rules, and I can easily think of 1945s and even a few 1961s that seemed at their peak 4–5 hours after decanting rather than the 20–25 minutes that I have suggested here. However, it is always better to err on the side of needing more time to breathe and let the guest swirl and aerate the wine in the glass than to wait too long and then serve a wine that, while magnificently scented when opened and decanted, has lapsed into a dumb comatose state by the time it is served. I have noticed that the more massive 1982s have benefited from 12–14 hours of airing, but that is probably because of their size and density.

The serving temperature of wine is another critical aspect of presenting Bordeaux. I am always surprised at how many times I am given a great Bordeaux wine that is too warm. Every wine book talks about serving fine red wines at room temperature. In America's overly warm and generously heated dining rooms, room temperature is often 70–75 degrees Fahrenheit, a temperature that no fine red Bordeaux cares for. A Bordeaux served at such a temperature will often taste flat and flabby, and its bouquet will be diffuse and unfocused. The alcohol content will also seem higher than it should. The ideal temperature for red Bordeaux is 65–67 degrees Fahrenheit; for a white Bordeaux, 55–60 degrees. If your best wines cannot be served at this temperature, then you are doing them a great injustice. If a red Bordeaux must be put in an ice bucket for 10 minutes to lower its temperature, then do it. I have often requested on a hot summer day in Bordeaux or the Rhône Valley to have my Pomerol or Châteauneuf du Pape "iced" for 10 minutes rather than drink it at a temperature of 80 degrees Fahrenheit.

Last, the effective presentation of Bordeaux wines at a dinner party will necessitate a sense of order. The rules here are easy to follow. Lighter-weight Bordeaux wines or wines from light vintages should always precede richer, fuller wines from great vintages. If such an order is not followed, the lighter, more delicate wines will taste pale after a rich, full-bodied wine has been served. For example, to serve a delicate 1979 Margaux like d'Issan after a 1975 Lafleur would be patently unfair to the d'Issan. Another guideline is to sequence the wines from youngest to oldest. This should not be applied blindly, but younger, more astringent wines should precede older, more mellow, mature wines.

BORDEAUX
WITH FOOD

The art of serving the right bottle of Bordeaux with a specific course or type of food has become one of the most overly legislated areas, all to the detriment of the enjoyment of both wine and food. Newspaper and magazine articles, and even books, are filled with precise rules that practically make it a sin not to choose the perfect wine for a particular meal. Thus, instead of enjoying their dinner party, most hosts and hostesses fret, usually needlessly, over choosing the wine. They would be better off to remember the wise advice from a noted French restaurateur, Henri Berau, who stated it best: "The first conditions of a pleasant meal depend, essentially, upon the proper choice of guests."

The basics of the Bordeaux/food match-up game are not difficult to master. These are the tried-and-true, allegedly cardinal principles, such as young wines before old, dry before sweet, white before red, red with meat, and white with fish. However, times have changed, and many of the old shibboleths have disappeared. Today one would not be surprised to hear that a certain variety of edible flower—nasturtiums, for example—should be served with a flowery white Graves.

The question one should pose is, Does the food offer simple or complex flavors? Two of the favorite grapes of American wine drinkers are Merlot and Cabernet Sauvignon, both of which are able to produce majestic wines of exceptional complexity and depth of flavor. However, as food wines, they are remarkably one-dimensional. As complex and rewarding as they can be, they work well only with dishes that contain relatively simple flavors. Both marry beautifully with basic meat and potato dishes: filet mignon, lamb filets, steaks that are sautéed or grilled. Furthermore, as Cabernet Sauvignon and Merlot-based wines get older and more complex, they require increasingly simpler dishes to complement yet not overwhelm their complex flavors. This principle is applied almost across the board in restaurants and dining rooms in Bordeaux. The main courses chosen to show off red wines are usually a simple lamb or beef dish. Thus the principle is: Simple wines with complex dishes, complex wines with simple dishes. Richard Olney made this same observation in his classic treatise on food, *The French Menu Cookbook.*

Another question to be posed is, What is the style of wine produced in the vintage that you have chosen? Several of France's greatest chefs have told me they prefer off-years of Bordeaux to great years and have instructed their sommeliers to buy the wines for the restaurant accordingly. Can this be true? From the chef's perspective, the food, not the wine, should be the focal point of the meal. Many chefs feel that a great vintage of Bordeaux, with wines that are exceptionally rich, powerful, alcoholic, and concentrated, not only takes attention away from their cuisine, but makes matching a wine with the food much more troublesome. Thus chefs prefer a 1992, 1987, or 1980 Bordeaux rather than a super-concentrated 1990, 1989, 1986, or 1982. Curiously, the richest vintages, while being marvelous wines, are not always the best years to choose when considering a food match-up. Lighter-weight yet tasty wines from unexceptional years can complement delicate and understated cuisine considerably better than the great vintages, which should be reserved for very simple food.

BUYING BORDEAUX WINE FUTURES: THE PITFALLS AND PLEASURES

The purchase of wine, already fraught with pitfalls for consumers, becomes immensely more complex and risky when one enters the wine futures sweepstakes.

On the surface, buying wine futures is nothing more than investing money in a case or cases of wine at a predetermined "future price" long before the wine is bottled and shipped to this country. You invest your money in wine futures on the assumption that the wine will appreciate significantly in price between the time you purchase the future and the time the wine has been bottled and imported to America. Purchasing the right wine, from the right vintage, in the right international financial climate, can represent significant savings. On the other hand, it can be quite disappointing to invest heavily in a wine future only to witness the wine's arrival 12–18 months later at a price equal to or below the future price and to discover the wine to be inferior in quality as well.

For years, future offerings have been largely limited to Bordeaux wines, although they are seen occasionally from other regions. In Bordeaux, during the spring following the harvest, the estates or châteaux offer for sale a portion of their crops. The first offering, or *première tranche*, usually provides a good indication of the trade's enthusiasm for the new wine, the prevailing market conditions, and the ultimate price the public will have to pay.

Those brokers and *négociants* who take an early position on a vintage frequently offer portions of their purchases to importers/wholesalers/retailers to make available publicly as a "wine future." These offerings are usually made to the retail shopper during the first spring after the vintage. For example, the charming yet hardly profound 1997 Bordeaux vintage was being offered for sale as a "wine future" in April 1998. Purchasing wine at this time is not without numerous risks. While 90% of the quality of the wine and the style of the vintage can be ascertained by professionals tasting the wine in its infancy, the increased interest in buying Bordeaux wine futures has led to a soaring number of journalists—some qualified, some not—to judge young Bordeaux wines. The results have been predictable. Many writers serve no purpose other than to hype the vintage as great and have written more glowing accounts of a vintage than the publicity firms doing promotion for the Bordeaux wine industry.

Consumers should read numerous points of view from trusted professionals and ask the following questions: 1) Is the professional taster experienced in tasting young as well as old Bordeaux vintages? 2) How much time does the taster actually spend tasting Bordeaux during the year, visiting the properties, and studying the vintage? 3) Does the professional taster express his viewpoint in an independent, unbiased form, free of trade advertising? 4) Has the professional looked deeply at the weather conditions, harvesting conditions, grape variety ripening profiles, and soil types that respond differently depending on the weather scenario?

When wine futures are offered for sale, there is generally a great deal of enthusiasm for the newest vintage from both the proprietors and the wine trade. The saying in France that "the greatest wines ever made are the ones that are available for sale" are the words many wine producers and merchants live by. The business of the wine trade is to sell wine, and consumers should be aware that they will no doubt be inundated with claims of "great wines from a great vintage at great prices." This has been used time and time again for good vintages and, in essence, has undermined the credibility of many otherwise responsible retailers, as well as a number of journalists. In contrast, those writers who fail to admit or recognize greatness where warranted are no less inept and irresponsible.

In short, there are only four valid reasons to buy Bordeaux wine futures.

1. Are you buying top-quality, preferably superb wine, from an excellent—or better yet, great—vintage?

No vintage can be reviewed in black-and-white terms. Even in the greatest vintages there are disappointing appellations, as well as mediocre wines. At the same time, vintages that are merely good to very good can produce some superb wines. Knowing the underachievers and overachievers is paramount to making an intelligent buying decision. Look at the last 25 years. The only truly great vintages to emerge from Bordeaux, and only for the specific appellations listed, have been the following:

1996—Margaux, St.-Julien, Pauillac, St.-Estèphe
1995—St.-Julien, Pauillac, St.-Estèphe, Graves, Pomerol, St.-Emilion
1990—St.-Julien, Pauillac, St.-Estèphe, Pomerol, St.-Emilion, Barsac/Sauternes
1989—Pomerol, Barsac/Sauternes
1988—Barsac/Sauternes
1986—St.-Julien, Pauillac, St.-Estèphe, Barsac/Sauternes
1982—St.-Julien, Pauillac, St.-Estèphe, Graves, Pomerol, St.-Emilion

There is no reason to buy wines as futures except for the top performers in a given vintage, because prices generally will not appreciate in the period between the release of the future prices and when the wines are bottled. The exceptions are always the same—top wines and great vintages. If the financial climate is such that the wine will not be at least 25–30% more expensive when it arrives in the marketplace, then most purchasers are better off investing their money elsewhere. Keep in mind that even in 1990, a vintage that has soared in price over the last 8 years, the wines came out at a lower price than the 1989s. The 1990s did not begin to move up in price until the wines had been in the bottle for 12 months. The marketplace was saturated at the time the 1990s came out. The 1989s had received far too much hype as another "vintage of the century," and the big buyers had already spent their money on the 1989s and could not purchase the 1990s with any force. Once the wines were in the bottle and were tasted, prices for the 1990s began to soar in 1994 and 1995. That has continued, as 1990 is unquestionably a great vintage.

Recent history of the 1975 and 1978 Bordeaux future offerings provides a revealing prospectus to "futures" buyers. Purchasers of 1975 futures did extremely well. When offered in 1977, the 1975 future prices included $140–$160 per case for such illustrious wines as Lafite-Rothschild and Latour, and $64–$80 for second-growths, including such proven thoroughbreds as Léoville-Las Cases, La Lagune, and Ducru-Beaucaillou. By the time these wines had arrived on the market in 1978, the vintage's outstanding and potentially classic quality was an accepted fact, and the first-growths were retailing for $325–$375 per case; the lesser growths, $112–$150 per case. Buyers of 1975 futures have continued to prosper, as this vintage is now very scarce and its prices have continued to escalate to $900–$1,200 a case for first-growths and $350–$550 for second- through fifth-growths. In 1998 the 1975 prices have come to a standstill because of doubts about how gracefully many of the wines are evolving. I would not be surprised to see some prices even drop—another pitfall that must always be considered.

The 1978 Bordeaux futures, offered in 1980, present a different picture: 1978 was another good year, with wines similar in style but less intense than the excellent 1970 vintage. Opening prices for the 1978 Bordeaux were very high and were inflated because of a weak dollar abroad and an excessive demand for the finest French wines. Prices for first-growths were offered at $430–$500, prices for second- through fifth-growths at $165–$230. Consumers who invested heavily in Bordeaux have purchased good wine, but when the wines arrived on the market in spring 1981, the retail prices for these wines were virtually the same as future price offerings. Thus consumers who purchased 1978 futures and invested their money to the tune of 100% of the case price could have easily obtained a better return simply by investing in any interest-bearing account.

With respect to the vintages 1979, 1980, 1981, 1982, 1983, and 1985, the only year that has represented a great buy from a "futures" perspective was 1982. The 1980 was not offered to the consumer as a wine future because it was of mediocre quality. As for the 1979 and 1981, the enthusiast who purchased these wines on a future basis no doubt was able, 2 years after putting his or her money up, to buy the wines when they arrived in America at approximately the same price. While this was not true for some of the highly rated 1981s, it was true for the 1979s. As for the 1982s, they have jumped in price at an unbelievable pace, outdistancing any vintage in the last 20 years. The first-growths of 1982 were offered to consumers in late spring 1983 at prices of $350–$450 for wines like Lafite-Rothschild, Latour,

Mouton-Rothschild, Haut-Brion, and Cheval Blanc. By March 1985 the Cheval Blanc had jumped to $650–$800, the Mouton to $800–$1,000, and the rest to $700. Today, prices for first-growths range from a low of $2,500 a case for Haut-Brion, to $5,000 or more a case for any of the three Pauillac first-growths. This is a significant price increase for wines so young, but it reflects the insatiable worldwide demand for a great vintage. Rare, limited-production wines—for instance, the Pomerols—have also skyrocketed in price. Pétrus has clearly been the top performer in terms of escalating prices; it jumped from an April 1983 future price of $600 to a spring 1998 price of $20,000. This seems absurd given the fact that the wines will not be close to maturity for a decade. Other top 1982 Pomerols such as Trotanoy, Certan de May, and l'Evangile have quadrupled and quintupled in price. Trotanoy, originally available for $280, now sells (when you can find it) for at least $3,000. Certan de May has jumped from $180 to $3,500, as has l'Evangile.

The huge demand for 1982 Bordeaux futures and tremendous publicity surrounding this vintage have led many to assume that subsequent years would similarly escalate in price. That has not happened, largely because Bordeaux has had too many high-quality, abundant vintages in the decade of the eighties. The only exceptions have been the 1986 first-growths, which continue to accelerate because they are great, long-lived, so-called classic vintage wines.

2. Do the prices you must pay look good enough that you will ultimately save money by paying less for the wine as a future than for the wine when it is released in 2–3 years?

Many factors must be taken into consideration to make this determination. In certain years, Bordeaux may release wines at lower prices than it did the previous year (the most recent examples are 1986 and 1990). There is also the question of the international marketplace. In 1991, when the 1990s were first priced, the American dollar was beginning to rebound but was still weak, not to mention the fact that our country was still mired in a recession. Other significant Bordeaux buying countries, such as England and France, had unsettled and troublesome financial problems as well. The Far East was not a principal player, and even Germany, which has always bought a lot of Bordeaux, was experiencing an economic downspin because of the financial ramifications of trying to revitalize the moribund economy of East Germany. In addition, two vintages of relatively high quality, 1989 and 1988, were backed up in the marketplace. Hence the 1990s, as great as they were, did not increase in price until they had been in the bottle for almost a year. Those who purchased the 1990s as futures could have picked them up at the same price 3 years after the vintage. However, these cycles are short-lived. Look, for example, at the overheated buying frenzy for Bordeaux wine futures in the 1995 and 1996 vintages. In both cases the wines came out at the highest future prices ever demanded, with some 1996s 100% more expensive than their 1995 counterparts. Except for a few glitches in Asia, the international economic climate was buoyant, and the demand for luxury products (fine cars, wine, watches, and so on) was insatiable. Consequently, Bordeaux had no problem selling everything of quality produced in 1995 and 1996 long before either vintage had been bottled. Prices for 1995s and 1996s soared, despite the fact that they came out at record high levels.

3. Do you want to be guaranteed of getting top, hard-to-find wine from a producer with a great reputation who makes only small quantities of wine?

Even if the vintage is not irrefutably great, or you cannot be assured that prices will increase, there are always a handful of small estates, particularly in Pomerol and St.-Emilion, that produce such limited quantities of wine and have worldwide followers, such that their wines warrant buying as futures, if only to reserve a case from an estate whose wines have pleased you in the past. In Pomerol, limited-production wines such as Le Pin, Clinet, La Conseillante, l'Evangile, La Fleur de Gay, Lafleur, and Bon Pasteur have produced many popular wines during the decade of the eighties yet are very hard to find in the marketplace. In St.-Emilion, some of the less-renowned yet modestly sized estates such as Angélus, L'Arrosée, La Gomerie, Grand-Mayne, Pavie-Macquin, La Dominique, Le Tertre-Roteboeuf, Troplong-Mondot, and Valandraud produce wines that are not easy to find after bottling. Consequently, their admirers throughout the world frequently reserve and pay for these wines as futures. Limited-production wines from high-quality estates merit buying futures even in good to very good years.

4. Do you want to buy wine in half bottles, magnums, double magnums, jeroboams, or imperials?

Frequently overlooked as one of the advantages of buying wine futures is that you can request that your merchant have the wines bottled to your specifications. There is always a surcharge for such bottlings, but if you have children born in a certain year, or you want the luxury of buying half bottles (a size that makes sense for daily drinking), the only time to do this is when buying the wine as a future.

Last, should you decide to enter the futures market, be sure you know the other risks involved. The merchant you deal with could go bankrupt, and your unsecured sales slip would make you one of probably hundreds of unsecured creditors of the bankrupt wine merchant hoping for a few cents on your investment. Another risk is that the supplier the merchant deals with could go bankrupt or be fraudulent. You may get a refund from the wine merchant, but you will not get your wine. Therefore be sure to deal only with a wine merchant who has sold wine futures before and one who is financially solvent. Finally, buy wine futures only from a wine merchant who has received confirmed commitments as to the quantities of wine he or she will receive. Some merchants sell Bordeaux futures to consumers before they have received commitments from suppliers. Be sure to ask for proof of the merchant's allocations. If you do not, then the words *caveat emptor* could have special significance for you.

For many Bordeaux wine enthusiasts, buying wine futures of the right wine, in the right vintage, at the right time, guarantees that they have liquid gems worth four or five times the price they paid for the wine. However, as history has proven, only a handful of vintages over the last 25 years have appreciated that significantly in their first 2 or 3 years.

7: A VISITOR'S GUIDE TO BORDEAUX

HOTELS AND RESTAURANTS

MÉDOC

Pauillac—**L'Hôtel France et Angleterre** (30 miles from downtown Bordeaux), 3, quai Albert Pichon; tel.—33.5.56.59.01.20; fax—33.5.56.59.02.31

Twenty-nine rooms for about $60 a person. Ask for a room in the annex, which is quieter. The restaurant is surprisingly good, with a competent wine list.

Pauillac—**Château Cordeillan Bages** (adjacent to Lynch-Bages on the south side of Pauillac next to D2)
Tel.—33.5.56.59.24.24; fax—33.5.56.59.01.89
The deluxe restaurant, hotel, and wine school of Jean Michel Cazes, the proprietor of Lynch-Bages. The excellent restaurant boasts a stupendous wine list, and the hotel is quiet and spacious. This is the place to stay and eat when visiting châteaux in St.-Julien, Pauillac, and St.-Estèphe. Expect to pay $125–$200 per night for lodging and approximately the same for dinner for two.

Margaux—**Relais de Margaux** (14 miles from downtown Bordeaux)
Tel.—33.5.57.88.38.30; fax—33.5.57.88.31.73
A luxury hotel with 28 rooms for $150–$175 that has had ups and downs since opening in the mid-eighties. Rooms are splendid, the cooking over-priced, contrived, and inconsistent. The wine selection is good, but the mark-ups of 200%–400% are appalling.

Arcins—**Lion d'Or** (in the village next to D2)
Tel.—33.5.56.58.96.79 (closed Sunday and Monday)
Jean-Paul Barbier's roadside restaurant in Arcins (several miles north of the village of Margaux) has become one of the hottest eating spots in the Médoc. Barbier, an enthusiastic chef of some talent, encourages clients to bring their own bottles to complement his rustic country cooking. Portions are generous, the restaurant noisy, and if you bring a good bottle, or you are with a well-known proprietor, chances are Barbier will be at your side most of the time. This is a fun place with surprisingly good food, but if you are looking for a quiet, relaxing evening, Lion d'Or is not the place. Who can resist the idea of doing your own comparative tasting with such local specialties as shad in cream sauce and the famous lamb from Pauillac? Prices are moderate.

Gaillan-en-Médoc—**Château Layauga** (2 miles from Lesparre)
Tel.—33.5.56.41.26.83; fax—33.5.56.41.19.52
This charming restaurant (there are also 7 attached rooms), which has been coming on strong, earned its first star from the *Guide Michelin* in 1991. The cooking is excellent, featuring many wonderful fish courses as well as local specialties such as the lamb of Pauillac and the famed *lamproie Bordelaise* (eels cooked in their own blood). As reprehensible as that may sound, I find this dish superb and one of the few fish courses that works sensationally well with a big, rich bottle of red Bordeaux.

BORDEAUX

Hôtel Burdigala, 115, rue Georges Bonnac; tel.—33.5.56.90.16.16; fax—33.5.56.93.15.06

This is one of Bordeaux's newest hotels and the "in" spot for many business travelers. There are 68 rooms, 15 suites, and an excellent restaurant, and the location in the center of the city, not far from the Place Gambetta, is ideal. Prices are $140–$260 a night.

Hôtel Normandie, 7, cours 30 Juillet; tel.—33.5.56.52.16.80; fax—33.5.56.51.68.91

Located several blocks from the opera and Maison du Vin in the center of the city, the Hôtel Normandie has always been the top spot for visiting wine writers because of its ideal location just off the Allées de Tourny. The three leading Bordeaux wine shops are within a 3-minute walk. The rooms are spacious but clearly not as modernly equipped as the newer hotels. There is a certain charm about the Hôtel Normandie, but if you have a car, parking in this area is often troublesome. Rates ($50–$120 a night) for one of the 100 rooms at the Normandie make it one of the best values in Bordeaux.

Hôtel Sainte-Catherine, 27, rue Parlement Ste.-Catherine; tel.—33.5.56.81.95.12; fax—33.5.56.44.50.51

Not as well-known as many others, this lovely, moderately sized hotel with rooms that cost about $80–$200 a night is located in the middle of the city. For those looking for privacy and anonymity, this discreet hotel is a good choice.

Mercure Château Chartrons, 81, cours St.-Louis; tel.—33.5.56.43.15.00; fax—33.5.56.69.15.21

This large, modern hotel, situated just north of the city center, has easily accessible parking facilities as well as 144 rooms priced between $95 and $100.

Claret, 18, Parvis des Chartrons (located in the Cité Mondiale du Vin); tel.—33.5.56.01.79.79; fax—33.5.56.01.79.00

This hotel is exceptionally well located in downtown Bordeaux in the Cité Mondiale du Vin, which is a failed international showcase for wine producers. Rates are $85–$100.

Le Chapon Fin, 5, rue Montesqieu; tel.—33.5.56.79.10.10; fax—33.5.56.79.09.10 (Chef Garcia)

Given that this is one of the finest restaurants in France, it has always puzzled me as to why Chef Garcia has not received a second star in *Guide Michelin*. Admittedly, I am unable to eat here anonymously and perhaps see better service than a stranger off the street. I have enjoyed extraordinary food from Garcia everywhere he has been. He was the force that resurrected the reputation of the Pessac restaurant/hotel La

Réserve before he moved across from Bordeaux's train station and opened Clavel. He is in the famous turn-of-the-century grotto-like restaurant, Le Chapon Fin, just off the Place des Grands Hommes. The ambience is superb, the wine list excellent, and the cooking outstanding. Garcia is a generous chef, and I have never left his restaurant without a feeling of total satisfaction. Prices are high but not unreasonable. Le Chapon Fin is closed on Sunday and Monday.

La Chamade, 20, rue Piliers de Tutelle; tel.—33.5.56.48.13.74; fax—33.5.56.79.29.67 (Chef Carrère)

This basement restaurant in the old section of Bordeaux, just a few minutes walk from the Place de la Bourse, consistently turns out fine cooking. It is one of my favorite places to eat on Sunday evening, when just about every other restaurant in the city has shut down. If you visit La Chamade, do not miss the superb first course called "Salade de Chamade." La Chamade's prices are moderately expensive.

Jean Ramet, 7, place J. Jaurès; tel.—33.5.56.44.12.51; fax—33.5.56.52.19.80 (Chef Ramet)

Jean Ramet's tiny restaurant located just down the street from the Grand Theater, near the Gironde, just past the Place J. Jaurès, should not be missed. The cooking merits two, perhaps even three, stars, but Ramet will never receive them because of the minuscule size of the restaurant, which seats only twenty-seven people. Ramet, who apprenticed under such great chefs as Pierre Troisgros and Michel Guérard, is a wizard. I cannot recommend this moderately expensive restaurant enough. The Jean Ramet restaurant serves only dinner on Saturday and is closed Sunday.

La Tupina, 6, rue Porte de la Monnaie; tel.—33.5.56.91.56.37; fax—33.5.56.31.92.11 (Chef Xiradakis)

This moderately priced restaurant in the old city is run by one of Bordeaux's great characters, Jean-Pierre Xiradakis. He is unquestionably a wine enthusiast, but his first love is his restaurant, which features the cooking of southwestern France. Consequently, expect to eat rich, heavy, abundant quantities of food such as duck and foie gras. The wine list focuses on high-quality, little-known producers, and there is also a selection of rare Armagnacs. The restaurant, which is difficult to find, is located near the Cathedral of Ste.-Croix, between the rue Sauvageau and the riverside Quai de la Monnaie. Closed on Sunday.

Le Pavillon des Boulevards, 120, rue Croix de Seguey; tel.—33.5.56.81.51.02; fax—33.5.56.51.14.58 (Chef Franc)

This relative newcomer burst on the scene in the late eighties and has become one of Bordeaux's hottest restaurants. The cooking tends to reflect an Asian influence, and those who have tired of nouvelle cuisine will find Pavillon des Boulevards a bit too precious. But the undeniable talent of Chef Franc is evident in every dish. Prices are moderately expensive. Closed on Sunday.

Le Père Ouvrard, 12, rue du Maréchal Joffre; tel.—33.5.56.44.11.58

About as straightforward a bistro as I have ever been in: imagine approaching a restaurant with a plaque on the outside stating *"Menu de Canard"* and finding live ducks (clients can choose their victim) caged on the sidewalk outside the restaurant's entrance! This young couple (the Ouvrards) is turning out marvelous renditions of traditional classics at this unassuming bistro.

THE SUBURBS OF BORDEAUX

Bordeaux Le Lac—10 minutes from the city center

Hôtel Sofitel Aquitania

Tel.—33.5.56.69.66.60; fax—33.5.56.69.66.00

Hôtel Nôvotel,

Tel.—33.5.56.50.99.70; fax—33.5.56.43.00.66

I have spent a considerable amount of my lifetime at the Hôtel Sofitel Aquitania and Hôtel Nôvotel. Bordeaux Le Lac, an ambience-free commercial center just north of Bordeaux, is an ideal lodging spot, particularly if you have a car. The hotels offer antiseptic rooms with hot running water, telephones, and fax machines that work. Sofitel Aquitania is more expensive, costing $100–$125 a night, whereas the Nôvotel is about $90–$100 a night. Both have similar rooms, although the Sofitel does offer minibars. Both have hassle-free parking, which I consider to be of considerable importance. They also are good choices because the Médoc, Pomerol, and St.-Emilion are only 20 minutes away.

Bouliac—a 20-minute drive from Bordeaux

Le St.-James, Place C. Holstein; tel.—33.5.57.97.06.00; fax—33.5.56.20.92.58 (Chef Amat)

For the last decade, Le St.-James, run by the idiosyncratic Chef Amat, has been considered the best restaurant in the Bordeaux region. The inspired, eccentric cooking of Amat wins rave reviews also from the *Gault-Millau Guide.* I have had some remarkable courses, but having eaten there over a dozen times in the last decade, I have also had disappointing courses as well as listless, unenthusiastic service. Frankly, I find the restaurant over-rated and too expensive, and I am still not used to the sommelier drinking at least 3 or 4 ounces of one's bottle of wine to "test it." Nevertheless, there is immense talent in the kitchen. If Amat's attitude is correct, then one can be tantalized by some of his courses. A luxury hotel has recently been opened nearby. Prices are extremely high. For infrequent visitors to Bordeaux, the best way to get to Bouliac is to take one of the bridges across the Garonne, immediately picking up D113 south. Within 4 or 5 miles, signs for Bouliac and Le St.-James restaurant should be visible on your left.

Pessac—a 10-minute drive from the city center

Hôtel La Réserve, Bourgailh; tel.—33.5.56.07.13.28; fax—33.5.56.07.13.28

When Chef Garcia was at La Réserve it was the finest restaurant in the region. However, he left and its reputation fell because of inattention to detail, and for much of the 1980s La Reserve has been trying to regain its standing. The tranquil setting in the woods makes it an ideal place to stay if you are visiting the nearby Château Haut-Brion or La Mission-Haut-Brion. It is also a good location if you want to be close to the city of Bordeaux and have immediate access to the region of Barsac/Sauternes or the other Graves estates. Rooms average $125–$150 per night. Although there are signs that the restaurant is coming back, it is still far behind the other top Bordeaux restaurants. La Réserve is reached by taking exit 13 off the beltway that encircles the northern, western, and southern sides of Bordeaux. The hotel is well marked once you leave the beltway.

Langon—30 miles south of Bordeaux

Claude Darroze, 95, cours General Leclerc; tel.—33.5.56.63.00.48; fax—33.5.56.63.41.15 (Chef Darroze)

Some of the finest meals I have eaten in France have been at the superb restaurant Claude Darroze, located in the center of Langon. Langon is a good place to stop if you are visiting the châteaux of Barsac/Sauternes. Of primary importance is the superb quality of Darroze's cooking, and there are also 16 rooms, reasonably priced at about $60–$75 a night. Darroze's cooking emphasizes foie gras, truffles in season, and excellent lamb and fish. It is a rich, highly imaginative style of cooking that clearly merits the one star it has earned from the *Guide Michelin.* The wine list is also super, as well as reasonably priced. Should you be an Armagnac lover, the finest Bas-Armagnacs from Darroze's brother, Francis Darroze, are available, going back to the beginning of this century. Prices are a steal given the quality of these rare items. If you are driving from Bordeaux, the best way to get to Claude Darroze is to take the autoroute (A62), exit at Langon, and follow the signs for "Centre Ville." You cannot miss Darroze's restaurant/hotel once you are in the center of the city.

Langoiran—25 minutes from downtown Bordeaux

Restaurant Saint-Martin (located directly on the Garonne River)
Tel.—33.5.56.67.02.67

If you are looking for a tiny, charming restaurant/hotel in a historic village that few people other than the locals know about, consider eating and staying at the Restaurant Saint-Martin. Located on the Garonne, the restaurant offers country French food that is imaginative, well prepared, and moderately priced. The wine list is excellent. To reach the village of Langoiran, take autoroute A62, exit at Labrede, and follow the signs and Route 113 to Portets and then turn left, following the signs for Langoiran. This charming, quiet village is reached by a frightfully ancient bridge over the Garonne. Rooms are bargain priced at $45–$60 a night.

St.-Emilion—24 miles east of Bordeaux

Hôtel Plaisance, Place Clocher; tel.—33.5.57.24.72.32; fax— 33.5.57.74.41.11

This is the leading hotel in the fascinating walled town of St.-Emilion, which gets my vote as the most interesting and charming area in the entire Bordeaux region. The hotel is situated on the Place Clocher, overlooking the hilly town. The dozen comfortable rooms are priced between $100 and $150. The restaurant serves fine food, and of course the wine list is chock full of St.-Emilions.

St.-Emilion—**Logis des Remparts,** rue Guadet; tel.—33.5.57.24.70.43

There is no restaurant, but this is a fine hotel if you cannot get into Plaisance. There are 17 rooms that range in price from $50 to $80.

St.-Emilion—**Logis de la Cadène,** Place Marché au Bois; tel.— 33.5.57.24.71.40

Run with great enthusiasm by the Chailleau family, this is my favorite restaurant in the city of St.-Emilion. Situated just down the hill from the Hotel Plaisance, Logis de la Cadène serves up copious quantities of robust bistro food. The wine list is interesting, but the real gems here are the numerous vintages of Château La Clotte, the Grand Cru Classé St.-Emilion that is owned by the restaurant owners. One of the better St.-Emilions, it is rarely seen in the export market because so much of the production is consumed on the premises of this eating establishment. Prices are moderate.

St.-Emilion—**Château Grand Barrail,** 33330 St.-Emilion; tel.— 33.5.57.55.37.00; fax—33.5.57.55.37.49

This former wine-producing château is situated in the middle of St.-Emilion's vineyards, just on the outskirts of Libourne, on Route D243. It is a luxury establishment, with 28 rooms priced between $200 and $275. For those with lots of discretionary income, who want to sleep in a château in the middle of a vineyard, this venue is hard to beat.

Bourg-Blaye—**Hôtel La Citadelle,** tel.—33.5.57.42.17.10; fax— 33.5.57.42.10.34

Monsieur Chaboz runs this superbly situated hotel with an unsurpassed view of the Gironde. The hotel is in the historic citadel of Blaye. The restaurant serves up well-prepared, reasonably priced local specialties. The 21 rooms are a bargain (how many foreigners pass through Blaye?) at $50–$60 a night. There is also a tennis court and a swimming pool.

ROMANTIC AND HEDONISTIC EXCURSIONS

Brantôme—about 60 miles northeast of Bordeaux

Moulin de L'Abbaye

Tel.—33.5.53.05.80.22; fax—33.5.53.05.75.27

Take plenty of money to this splendidly situated old mill located along the side of an easy-flowing river in the beautiful town of Brantôme in the heart of the Dordogne. Brantôme is a good 2 hours from Bordeaux, but it is a beautiful scenic drive when you cross over the Garonne and take N89 through Libourne, past the vineyards of Pomerol and Lalande-de-Pomerol in the direction of Perigeux. Once in Perigèux, Brantôme is only 15 minutes away. There are only 9 rooms (costing about $175 a night) and 3 apartments in the gorgeous Moulin de L'Abbaye. The food is excellent, occasionally superb. My main objection is that the wine list is absurdly expensive.

Champagnac de Belair—2 hours from Bordeaux

Moulin du Roc

Tel.—33.5.53.02.86.00; fax—33.5.53.54.21.31

Three miles northeast of Brantôme, off of D78, is the quaint village of Champagnac de Belair and another ancient mill that is built over a meandering river. This is the most romantic hotel and restaurant in the region. For those special occasions, or just a sublime night away, ask for one of the 4 apartments in the Moulin du Roc. It will cost you close to $200 a night, but it is a magnificent setting and the charm and tranquillity of this establishment, run with perfection by Madame Gardillou, is unsurpassed. The food is superb, though expensive. Only the wine list leaves me less than excited because of its outrageously high prices. Nevertheless, even that can be overlooked when eating and sleeping in paradise.

Eugénie-Les-Bains—a 2-hour drive south of Bordeaux

Les Prés d'Eugénie

Tel.—33.5.58.05.06.07; fax—33.5.58.51.10.10 (Chef Guérard)

If I had one last meal to eat, I would be hard-pressed not to have it at this magnificent establishment located several hours south of Bordeaux. The nearest town is Mont-de-Marsan, which is approximately 18 miles to the north. Michel Guérard is an internationally famous chef, and his restaurant has long been one of the renowned three-star eating establishments in France. There are many three-star restaurants that I would downgrade to two stars, and there are others that are so superb one wonders why the *Guide Michelin* does not create a four-star category. The latter is the case at Les Prés d'Eugénie, where innovation, originality, and quality all come together with the formidable talents of Michel Guérard to create what are some of the most remarkable dishes my wife and I have ever eaten. Huge quantities of money are necessary to enjoy the food, but the 17-room hotel has surprisingly fair prices, averaging $210–$275 a night. Should you want to splurge, there are 12 apartments that cost $350–$400 a night. If you have the time, money, and appetite, try to have at least two meals from this genius.

Arcachon—36 miles west of Bordeaux

Arc Hôtel sur Mer, 39 Blvd. de la Plage

Tel.—33.5.56.83.06.85; fax—33.5.56.83.53.72

Le Nautic, 20, Blvd. de la Plage; tel.—33.5.56.83.01.48; fax—33.5.56.83.04.67

Thirty-six miles west of Bordeaux is the seaside resort town of Arcachon. The easiest way to get there is by taking the autoroute A63 south from Bordeaux and then picking up A66 directly into Arcachon. Another route is RN250, which runs directly from Bordeaux to Arcachon. The two hotels above have excellent locations on the beach, modern accommodations, and reasonable prices of $70–$90 a night. I do not know the restaurants in Arcachon to the extent that I do those in the vineyard areas and Bordeaux itself, but I have enjoyed fine meals at **Chez Yvette,** 59, Général Leclerc, tel.—33.5.56.83.05.11. This is a place to order fish and the superb oysters that come from the nearby oyster beds.

OTHER DIVERSIONS

WINE SHOPS

Bordeaux—**L'Intendant,** 2, allées de Tourny; tel.—33.5.56.43.26.39; fax—33.5.56.43.26.45

Buying Bordeaux either from the châteaux or in the city itself is usually far more expensive than buying the same wines in the United States. However, it is always interesting to see the wine selection in shops in another country. Bordeaux boasts L'Intendant, the most architecturally stunning wine shop I have ever seen. Furthermore, its selection of Bordeaux wines is exceptional. Located on the luxury shopping street Allées de Tourny (just across from the Grand Théâtre), it offers an extraordinary number of wines as well as many old vintages. Just visiting the shop is a must because of its fabulous design and spiral staircase. Within this four-floor tower are 15,000 bottles of Bordeaux. Bordeaux wine enthusiasts will require at least an hour to view the incredible selection. It is one of the greatest wine shops, not only in France, but in the world—exclusively for Bordeaux.

Bordeaux—**Badie,** 62, allées de Tourny; tel.—33.5.56.52.23.72; fax—33.5.56.81.31.16

Badie, situated several blocks away from L'Intendant, has the same owners, but the selection is not so comprehensive. Still, it is a fine shop renowned for its values and knowledgeable staff. Since 1880 it has been the *magasin des Bordelais.*

Bordeaux—**Badie Champagne**

Tel.—33.5.56.52.15.66; fax—33.5.56.81.31.16

This shop has the largest selection of champagne in the world. An astonishing shop that has to be seen to be believed. *450 références.*

Bordeaux—**La Vinothèque,** 8, cours du 30 Juillet; tel.—33.5.56.52.32.05

La Vinothèque offers relatively high prices for decent wines, as well as a plethora of wine accessories, but it is overshadowed by L'Intendant, Badie, and Bordeaux Magnum.

Bordeaux—**Bordeaux Magnum,** 3, rue Godineau; tel.—33.5.56.48.00.06

Bordeaux Magnum does not specialize so much in larger-format bottlings such as magnums, but it does concentrate on high-class Bordeaux wines.

BOOKSHOPS, ETC.

Bordeaux—**Librairie Mollat,** 15, rue Vital-Carles; tel.—33.5.56.56.40.40
One of the greatest bookshops in France, the Librairie Mollat is located in the old city on one of the walking streets. Its collection of wine books is extraordinary. Just about anything you could ever want in terms of literature is available at Mollat. The collection of English books is limited.

Bordeaux—**Virgin Megastore,** Place Gambetta; tel.—33.5.56.56.05.70
This high-tech, state-of-the-art shop is a must for those looking for that rare compact disc or wine book. The Bordelais, who are proud to have the second Virgin shop (the first is on the Champs-Élysées in Paris), make this one of the most heavily trafficked spots in all of Bordeaux. The shop includes a small cafeteria that serves surprisingly good food and great coffee.

VISITING BORDEAUX CHÂTEAUX

When visiting Bordeaux, I recommend that someone in your party be able to speak a little French. Most of the big-name Bordeaux châteaux now have someone working there who speaks English, but do not count on many châteaux other than first-growths or super-seconds having anyone fluent in English.

For getting the maximum out of your visit, you should write directly for an appointment or ask your local wine merchant to have an importer set up an appointment for you.

If planning a program for visiting the Bordeaux châteaux, you should remember that four full visits a day are probably the maximum. Unless you and your travel mates are true aficionados, four a day is probably too many. In deciding which châteaux to visit, you should always arrange visits at châteaux that are close to each other. For example, if you want to visit Château Margaux at 9:30 A.M., you should allow 45–60 minutes for a visit, as well as a 30- to 35-minute car drive from downtown Bordeaux. It is also advisable to schedule only one other visit that morning, preferably in the commune of Margaux. If you schedule an appointment in Pauillac or St.-Estèphe for 11:00 A.M., the 30- to 40-minute drive north from Margaux to either of these two appellations would probably make you late for your appointment. Remember, the French are far more respectful of appointment hours than most Americans tend to be, and it is an insult not to arrive on time.

The following are several recommended itineraries that include visits to the most interesting properties and allow sufficient time to do so. You can expect to taste the two youngest vintages on your visit, but do not hesitate to ask to sample a recent vintage that has been bottled. Unless you are a Hollywood superstar, it is unlikely that anything older than 4–5 years will be opened. A visit generally involves a tour of the château, a tour of the cellars, and then a short tasting. Spitting out the wine is not only permissible, it is expected. Normally you spit into small buckets filled with sawdust. In some of the up-to-date tasting rooms that have been constructed at the châteaux, huge, state-of-the-art spittoons are available.

Must visits in the Médoc are Mouton-Rothschild, with its splendid museum; Prieuré-Lichine, home of the late Alexis Lichine and the only château open 7 days a week; and of course, any property of which you have numerous vintages squirreled away in your cellar.

Some important things to remember are that Bordeaux, as elsewhere in France, takes a 2-hour lunch between 12:00 and 2:00 P.M., which means you will not be able to see any properties during that time. Second, very few châteaux receive visitors during the harvest. During the decade of the eighties the harvests have tended to be relatively early because of the hot summers. In general harvests can be expected to occur between mid-September and mid-October.

RECOMMENDED ITINERARIES

Itinerary I (Margaux)

8:45 A.M.—Leave Bordeaux
9:30 A.M.—Château Giscours
10:30 A.M.—Château Margaux
2:00 P.M.—Château Palmer
3:30 P.M.—Château Prieuré-Lichine

NOTE: Have lunch at the Lion d'Or in Arcins, a tiny village several miles north of Margaux.

Itinerary II (Pauillac)

8:15 A.M.—Leave Bordeaux
9:30 A.M.—Château Latour
11:00 A.M.—Château Pichon-Longueville–Comtesse de Lalande
2:00 P.M.—Château Lynch-Bages
3:30 P.M.—Château Pichon-Longueville Baron
5:00 P.M.—Château Mouton-Rothschild

NOTE: Have lunch at the restaurant Cordeillan-Bages, just south of the town of Pauillac and only 5 minutes from any of these châteaux.

Itinerary III (St.-Julien)

8:30 A.M.—Leave Bordeaux
9:30 A.M.—Château Beychevelle
11:00 A.M.—Château Ducru-Beaucaillou
2:00 P.M.—Château Talbot
3:30 P.M.—Château Léoville-Las Cases

NOTE: Lunch at Cordeillan-Bages.

Itinerary IV (St.-Estèphe and Pauillac)

8:15 A.M.—Leave Bordeaux
9:30 A.M.—Château Lafite-Rothschild
11:00 A.M.—Château Cos d'Estournel
2:00 P.M.—Château Montrose
3:30 P.M.—Château Calon-Ségur

NOTE: It is preferable to stay at Cordeillan-Bages in Pauillac when visiting St.-Estèphe, St.-Julien, and Pauillac.

Itinerary V (Graves)

8:30 A.M.—Leave Bordeaux
9:30 A.M.—Châteaux Haut-Brion and La Mission-Haut-Brion
11:00 A.M.—Château Pape-Clément
2:30 P.M.—Domaine de Chevalier
4:00 P.M.—Haut-Bailly

NOTE: Have lunch at La Réserve in Pessac, which can also be utilized as your hotel if you want to save 15–20 minutes of travel time from Bordeaux.

Itinerary VI (Barsac/Sauternes)

8:30 A.M.—Leave Bordeaux
9:30 A.M.—Château Yquem
11:00 A.M.—Château Suduiraut
2:00 P.M.—Château Rieussec
3:00 P.M.—Château Climens

NOTE: Have lunch at the great restaurant Claude Darroze in Langon. If you decide to lodge at Darroze's restaurant/hotel, travel time to any of the Sauternes properties is less than 15 minutes.

Itinerary VII (St.-Emilion)

8:30 A.M.—Leave Bordeaux

9:30 A.M.—Château Cheval Blanc

11:00 A.M.—Château Couvent-des-Jacobins

2:00 P.M.—Château Ausone and Belair

3:00 P.M.—Château Pavie

NOTE: Have lunch at either Plaisance or Logis de la Cadène. If you stay at a hotel in St.-Emilion, the time to reach any St.-Emilion or Pomerol estate is less than 10 minutes.

Itinerary VIII (Pomerol)

8:30 A.M.—Leave Bordeaux

9:30 A.M.—Château Pétrus

11:00 A.M.—Vieux-Château-Certan

2:00 P.M.—Château de Sales

3:30 P.M.—Château La Conseillante

NOTE: Lunch in St.-Emilion at La Plaisance or Logis de la Cadène. If you stay in St.-Emilion, travel time to Pétrus, or any of the Pomerol estates, is less than 10 minutes.

When arriving in Bordeaux, the Maison du Vin, 1, cours 30 Juillet, tel.—33.5.56.52.82.82, in downtown central Bordeaux is a good place to pick up information on Bordeaux wine regions in addition to some decent maps.

If you want to write directly to the châteaux to make an appointment, you can use a format similar to those in the following letters, one in French and one in English. To address the letter, just put the name of the château, its commune, and zip code. The major châteaux zip codes are as follows:

for châteaux in St.-Estèphe	—33250 St.-Estèphe, France
for châteaux in Pauillac	—33250 Pauillac, France
for châteaux in St.-Julien	—St.-Julien-Beychevelle, France
for châteaux in Margaux	—33460 Margaux, France
for châteaux in Graves (Pessac)	—33602 Pessac, France
for châteaux in Graves (Léognan)	—33850 Léognan, France
for châteaux in Sauternes	—33210 Langon, France
for châteaux in Barsac	—Barsac 33720 Podensac, France
for châteaux in St.-Emilion	—33330 St.-Emilion, France
for châteaux in Pomerol	—33500 Pomerol, France

These zip codes will cover a great majority of the châteaux, but some of the major properties are controlled by *négociants*, or brokers, and it is better to write directly to the *négociant* to request an appointment at one of their châteaux. The following are the addresses for the top *négociants* that own some of the major Bordeaux châteaux.

The Cordier firm—for visiting Talbot, Meyney, Cantemerle, Lafaurie-Peyraguey, and Clos des Jacobins, send a letter to La Maison Cordier, 10, quai de Paludate, 33800 Bordeaux, France.

The Moueix firm—for visiting Pétrus, Trotanoy, Magdelaine, La Fleur

Pétrus, Latour à Pomerol, and La Grave à Pomerol, send a letter to La Maison Jean-Pierre Moueix, 34, quai du Priourat, 33500 Libourne, France.

RECOMMENDED FORM LETTER

(English Version)

> To: Château Margaux 33460 Margaux, France
> re: Visit

To Whom It May Concern:

I would like to visit Château Margaux on Monday, March 14, 1999, to see the winemaking facilities and receive a tour of the château. If possible, I would like to be able to taste several recent vintages of Château Margaux. If this is agreeable, I will arrive at the château at 9:30 A.M. on Monday, March 14.

I realize that you are busy, but I am an admirer of your wine and it would be a great pleasure to visit the property. I look forward to hearing from you.

> Sincerely,

(French Version)

> Messieurs,

Amateur de longue date des vins de votre château, il me serait agréable de pouvoir le visiter lors de mon prochain passage dans la région. J'aimerais également déguster les deux derniers millésimes, si cela était possible. Pourriez-vous m'indiquer si un rendez-vous le

lundi (date)	janvier à (time)
mardi (date)	février à (time)
mercredi (date)	mars à (time)
jeudi (date)	avril à (time)
vendredi (date)	mai à (time)
samedi (date)	juin à (time)
dimanche (date)	juillet à (time)
	août
	septembre
	octobre
	novembre
	décembre

vous conviendrait?

Vous remerciant vivement d'une prompte réponse, je vous prie d'agréer, Messieurs, l'expression de mes sentiments distingués.

> (Signature)

8: A GLOSSARY OF WINE TERMS

acetic—Wines, no matter how well made, contain quantities of acetic acid. If there is an excessive amount of acetic acid, the wine will have a vinegary smell.

acidic—Wines need natural acidity to taste fresh and lively, but an excess of acidity results in an acidic wine that is tart and sour.

acidity—The acidity level in a wine is critical to its enjoyment and livelihood. The natural acids that appear in wine are citric, tartaric, malic, and lactic. Wines from hot years tend to be lower in acidity, whereas wines from cool years tend to be high in acidity. Acidity in a wine preserves the wine's freshness and keeps the wine lively.

aftertaste—As the term suggests, the taste left in the mouth after one swallows is the aftertaste. This word is a synonym for length or finish. The longer the aftertaste lingers in the mouth (assuming it is a pleasant taste), the finer the quality of the wine.

aggressive—Aggressive is usually applied to wines that are high in either acidity or harsh tannins or both.

angular—Angular wines lack roundness, generosity, and depth. Wine from poor vintages or wines that are too acidic are often described as being angular.

aroma—Aroma is the smell of a young wine before it has had sufficient time to develop nuances of smell that are then called its bouquet. The word *aroma* is commonly used to mean the smell of a relatively young, unevolved wine.

astringent—Wines that are astringent are not necessarily bad or good wines. Astringent wines are harsh and coarse to taste, either because they are too young and tannic and just need time to develop or because they are not well made. The level of tannin in a wine contributes to its degree of astringency.

austere—Wines that are austere are generally not terribly pleasant to drink. An austere wine is hard and rather dry, lacking richness and generosity. However, young, promising Bordeaux can often express itself as austere, and aging will reveal a wine with considerably more generosity than its youthful austerity suggested.

balance—One of the most desired traits in a wine is good balance, where the concentration of fruit, level of tannin, and acidity are in total harmony. Well-balanced wines are symmetrical and tend to age gracefully.

barnyard—An unclean, farmyard, fecal aroma that is imparted to a wine because of unclean barrels or generally unsanitary winemaking facilities.

berry-like—As this descriptive term implies, wines, particularly Bordeaux wines that are young and not overly oaked, have an intense berry fruit character that can suggest blackberries, raspberries, black cherries, mulberries, or even strawberries and cranberries.

big—A big wine is large framed and full bodied, with an intense, concentrated feel on the palate. Bordeaux wines in general are not big wines in the same sense that Rhône wines are, but the top vintages of Bordeaux produce very rich, concentrated, deep wines.

black currant—A pronounced smell of the black currant fruit is commonly associated with red Bordeaux wines. It can vary in intensity from faint to very deep and rich.

body—Body is the weight and fullness of a wine that can be sensed as it crosses the palate. Full-bodied wines tend to have a lot of alcohol, concentration, and glycerin.

Botrytis cinerea—The fungus that attacks the grape skins under specific climatic conditions (usually interchanging periods of moisture and sunny weather). It causes the grape to become superconcentrated because it facilitates a natural dehydration. *Botrytis cinerea* is essential for the great sweet white wines of Barsac and Sauternes.

bouquet—As a wine's aroma becomes more developed from bottle aging, the aroma is transformed into a bouquet, which is ideally more than just the smell of the grape.

brawny—A hefty, muscular, full-bodied wine with plenty of weight and flavor, although not always the most elegant or refined sort of wine.

briary—I usually think of California Zinfandel rather than Bordeaux when the term *briary* comes into play. Briary denotes that the wine is aggressive and rather spicy.

brilliant—Brilliant relates to the color of the wine. A brilliant wine is one that is clear and shiny, with no haze or cloudiness.

browning—As red wines age, their color changes from ruby/purple, to dark ruby, to medium ruby, to ruby with an amber edge, to ruby with a brown edge. When a wine is browning it is usually fully mature and is not likely to get better.

cedar—Bordeaux reds often have a bouquet that suggests either faintly or overtly the smell of cedar wood. It is a complex aspect of the bouquet.

chewy—If a wine has a rather dense, viscous texture from a high glycerin content, it is often referred to as being chewy. High-extract wines from great vintages can often be chewy.

closed—The term *closed* is used to denote that the wine is not showing its potential, which remains locked in because it is too young. Young Bordeaux wines often close up about 12–18 months after bottling and, depending on the vintage and storage conditions, remain in such a state for several years to more than a decade.

complex—One of the most subjective descriptive terms used, a complex wine is one that the taster never gets bored with and finds interesting to drink. Complex wines tend to have a variety of subtle scents and flavors that hold one's interest in the wine.

concentrated—Fine wines, whether they are light, medium, or full bodied, should have concentrated flavors. Concentrated denotes that the wine has a depth and richness of fruit that gives it appeal and interest. Deep is a synonym of concentrated.

corked—A "corked" wine is a flawed wine that has taken on the smell of cork as a result of an unclean or faulty cork. It is perceptible in a bouquet that shows no fruit, only the smell of a musty cork or damp cardboard.

decadent—If you are an ice cream and chocolate lover, you know the feeling of eating a huge sundae lavished with hot fudge, real whipped cream, and rich vanilla ice cream. If you are a wine enthusiast, a wine loaded with opulent, even unctuous, layers of fruit, with a huge bouquet and a plump, luxurious texture, can be said to be decadent.

deep—Essentially the same as concentrated, the word *deep* expresses the fact that the wine is rich, full of extract, and mouth filling.

delicate—As this word implies, delicate wines are light, subtle, and understated, prized for their shyness rather than extroverted robust character. White wines are usually more delicate than red wines.

diffuse—Wines that smell and taste unstructured and unfocused are said to be diffuse. Often when red wines are served at too warm a temperature, they become diffuse.

dumb—A dumb wine is also a closed wine, but the term *dumb* is used in a more pejorative sense. Closed wines may need only time to reveal their richness and intensity. Dumb wines may never become any better.

earthy—This term may be used in both a negative and a positive sense; however, I prefer to use "earthy" to denote a positive aroma of fresh, rich, clean soil. Earthy is a more intense smell than woodsy or truffle scents.

elegant—Although more white wines than red are described as being elegant, lighter-styled, graceful, well-balanced Bordeaux wines can be elegant.

exuberant—Like extroverted, somewhat hyper people, wines too can be gushing with fruit and seem nervous and intensely vigorous.

fat—When Bordeaux gets a very hot year for its crop, and the wines attain a great level of maturity, they are often quite rich and concentrated, with low to average acidity. Often such wines are said to be fat, which is a prized commodity. If they become too fat, that is a flaw, and they are then called flabby.

flabby—A wine that is too fat or obese is a flabby wine. Flabby wines lack structure and are heavy to taste.

fleshy—Fleshy is a synonym for chewy, meaty, or beefy. It denotes that the wine has a lot of body, alcohol, and extract and usually a high glycerin content. Pomerols and St.-Emilions tend to be fleshier wines than Médocs.

floral—With the exception of some Sauternes, I rarely think of Bordeaux wines as having a floral or flowery aspect to their bouquets or aromas. However, wines like Riesling or Muscat do have a flowery component.

focused—With a fine wine, both bouquet and flavor should be focused. Focused simply means that the scents, aromas, and flavors are precise and clearly delineated. If they are not, the wine is like an out-of-focus picture: diffuse, hazy, and problematic.

forward—A wine is said to be forward when its charm and character are fully revealed.

While it may not be fully mature yet, a forward wine is generally quite enjoyable and drinkable. Forward is the opposite of backward.

fresh—Freshness in both young and old wines is a welcome and pleasing component. A wine is said to be fresh when it is lively and cleanly made. The opposite of fresh is stale.

fruity—A very good wine should have enough concentration of fruit so that it can be said to be fruity. Fortunately, the best Bordeaux wines will have more than just a fruity personality.

full-bodied—Wines rich in extract, alcohol, and glycerin are full-bodied wines.

green—Green wines are made from under-ripe grapes, lack richness and generosity, and have a vegetal character. Green wines were often made in Bordeaux in poor vintages, such as 1972 and 1977.

hard—Wines with abrasive, astringent tannins or high acidity are said to be hard. Young vintages of Bordeaux can be hard, but they should never be harsh.

harsh—If a wine is too hard, it is said to be harsh. Harshness in a wine, young or old, is a flaw.

hedonistic—Certain styles of wine are meant to be inspected and are more introspective and intellectual. Others are designed to provide sheer delight, joy, and euphoria. Hedonistic wines can be criticized because in one sense they provide so much ecstasy that they can be called obvious, but in essence they are totally gratifying wines meant to fascinate and enthrall—pleasure at its best.

herbaceous—Many wines have a distinctive herbal smell that is generally said to be herbaceous. Specific herbal smells can be of thyme, lavender, rosemary, oregano, fennel, or basil.

hollow—A synonym for shallow; hollow wines are diluted and lack depth and concentration.

honeyed—A common personality trait of sweet Barsacs and Sauternes; a honeyed wine is one that has the smell and taste of bees' honey.

hot—Rather than mean that the temperature of the wine is too warm to drink, hot denotes that the wine is too high in alcohol and therefore leaves a burning sensation in the back of the throat when swallowed. Wines with alcohol levels in excess of 14.5% are often hot.

jammy—When Bordeaux wines have a great intensity of fruit from excellent ripeness, such as in great vintages like 1961 and 1982, they are referred to as jammy; a jammy wine is a very concentrated, flavorful wine with superb extract.

leafy—A leafy character in a wine is similar to an herbaceous character only in that it refers to the smell of leaves rather than herbs. A wine that is too leafy is a vegetal or green wine.

lean—Lean wines are slim and rather streamlined, lacking generosity and fatness but still enjoyable and pleasant.

lively—A synonym for fresh or exuberant, a lively wine is usually a young wine with good acidity and a thirst-quenching personality.

long—A very desirable trait in a fine Bordeaux is that it be long in the mouth. Long (or length) relates to a wine's finish, meaning that after you swallow the wine, you sense its presence for a long time. (Thirty seconds to several minutes is great length.)

lush—Lush wines are velvety, soft, richly fruity wines that are both concentrated and fat. A lush wine can never be astringent or hard.

massive—In great vintages where there is a high degree of ripeness and superb concentration, some wines can turn out to be so big, full bodied, and rich that they are called massive. Great wines, such as the 1961 Latour and Pétrus and the 1982 Pétrus, are textbook examples of massive wines.

meaty—A chewy, fleshy wine is also said to be meaty.

mouth-filling—Big, rich, concentrated wines that are filled with fruit extract and are high in alcohol and glycerin are wines that tend to texturally fill the mouth. A mouth-filling wine is also a chewy, fleshy, fat wine.

nose—The general smell and aroma of a wine as sensed through one's nose and olfactory senses is often called the wine's nose.

oaky—Most top Bordeaux wines are aged from 12 months to 30 months in small oak barrels. At the very best properties, a percentage of the oak barrels are new, and these barrels impart a toasty, vanillin flavor and smell to the wine. If the wine is not rich and concentrated, the barrels can overwhelm the wine, making it taste overly oaky. However, when the wine is rich and concentrated and the winemaker has made a judicious use of new oak barrels, the results are a wonderful marriage of fruit and oak.

off—If a wine is not showing its true character, or is flawed or spoiled in some way, it is said to be "off."

over-ripe—An undesirable characteristic; grapes left too long on the vine become too ripe, lose their acidity, and produce wines that are heavy and unbalanced. This happens much more frequently in hot viticultural areas than in Bordeaux.

oxidized—If a wine has been excessively exposed to air during either its making or its aging, the wine loses freshness and takes on a stale, old smell and taste. Such a wine is said to be oxidized.

peppery—Usually noticeable in many Rhône wines, which have an aroma of black pepper and a pungent flavor. A peppery quality occasionally appears in some Bordeaux wines.

perfumed—This term usually is more applicable to fragrant, aromatic white wines than to red Bordeaux wines. However, some of the dry white wines and sweet white wines can have a strong perfumed smell.

plummy—Rich, concentrated wines can often have the smell and taste of ripe plums. When they do, the term *plummy* is applicable.

ponderous—Ponderous is often used as a synonym for massive, but in my usage a massive wine is simply a big, rich, very concentrated wine with balance, whereas a ponderous wine is one that has become heavy and tiring to drink.

precocious—Wines that mature quickly—as well as those that may last and evolve gracefully over a long period of time but taste as if they are aging quickly because of their tastiness and soft, early charms—are said to be precocious.

pruney—Wines produced from over-ripe grapes take on the character of prunes. Pruney wines are flawed.

raisiny—Late harvest wines that are meant to be drunk at the end of a meal can often be slightly raisiny, which in some ports and sherries is desirable. However, in dry Bordeaux wines a raisiny quality is a major flaw.

rich—Wines high in extract, flavor, and intensity of fruit are described as rich.

ripe—A wine is ripe when its grapes have reached the optimum level of maturity. Less than fully mature grapes produce wines that are under-ripe, and overly mature grapes produce wines that are over-ripe.

round—A very desirable character of wines, roundness occurs in fully mature Bordeaux that have lost their youthful, astringent tannins and also in young Bordeaux that are low in tannin and acidity and meant to be consumed young.

savory—A general descriptive term that denotes that the wine is round, flavorful, and interesting to drink.

shallow—A weak, feeble, watery, or diluted wine lacking concentration is said to be shallow.

sharp—An undesirable trait; sharp wines are bitter and unpleasant, with hard, pointed edges.

silky—A synonym for velvety or lush; silky wines are soft, sometimes fat, but never hard or angular.

smoky—Some wines, either because of the soil or because of the barrels used to age the wine, have a distinctive smoky character. In Bordeaux, some Graves wines occasionally are smoky.

soft—A soft wine is round, fruity, and low in acidity and has an absence of aggressive, hard tannins.

spicy—Wines often smell quite spicy, with aromas of pepper, cinnamon, and other well-known spices. These pungent aromas are usually lumped together and called spicy. Scents and flavors of Asian spices refer to wines that have aromas and/or flavors of soy sauce, ginger, hoisin sauce, and sesame oil.

stale—Dull, heavy wines that are oxidized or lack balancing acidity for freshness are called stale.

stalky—A synonym for vegetal but used more frequently to denote that the wine has probably had too much contact with the stems and the result is a green, vegetal, or stalky character to the wine.

supple—A supple wine is one that is soft, lush, velvety, and very attractively round and tasty. It is a highly desirable characteristic, as it suggests that the wine is harmonious.

tannic—The tannins of a wine, which are extracted from the grape skins and stems, are, along with a wine's acidity and alcohol, its lifeline. Tannins give a wine firmness and some roughness when young but gradually fall away and dissipate. A tannic wine is one that is young and unready to drink.

tart—Sharp, acidic, lean, unripe wines are called tart. In general, a red Bordeaux that is tart is not pleasurable.

thick—Rich, ripe, concentrated wines that are low in acidity are often said to be thick.

thin—A synonym for shallow, thinness is an undesirable characteristic meaning that the wine is watery, lacking in body, and just diluted.

tightly knit—Young wines that have good acidity levels and good tannin levels and are well made are called tightly knit, meaning they have yet to open up and develop.

toasty—A smell of grilled toast can often be found in wines because the barrels the wines are aged in are charred or toasted on the inside.

tobacco—Many red Graves wines have the scent of fresh burning tobacco. It is a distinctive and wonderful smell in wine.

unctuous—Rich, lush, intense wines with layers of concentrated, soft, velvety fruit are said to be unctuous. In particular, the sweet wines of Barsac and Sauternes are unctuous.

vegetal—An undesirable characteristic; wines that smell and taste vegetal are usually made from unripe grapes. In some wines a subtle vegetable garden smell is pleasant and adds complexity, but if it is the predominant characteristic, it is a major flaw.

velvety—A textural description and synonym for lush or silky, a velvety wine is rich, soft, and smooth to taste. It is a very desirable characteristic.

viscous—Viscous wines tend to be relatively concentrated, fat, almost thick wines with a great density of fruit extract, plenty of glycerin, and high alcohol content. If they have balancing acidity, they can be tremendously flavorful and exciting wines. If they lack acidity, they are often flabby and heavy.

volatile—A volatile wine is one that smells of vinegar as a result of an excessive amount of acetic bacteria. It is a seriously flawed wine.

woody—When a wine is overly oaky it is often said to be woody. Oakiness in a wine's bouquet and taste is good up to a point. Once past that point the wine is woody and its fruity qualities are masked by excessive oak aging.

INDEX

(Page references in **boldface** refer to producer profiles.)